Two Powerful Student Software Tools on One CD-ROM

Houghton Mifflin General Ledger Software for Windows provid journals, ledgers, and reporting features students need to complete a problems in the text (identified in the text by an icon). It also includes eight open problems for individual use.

The Accounting Transaction Tutor (ATT) reinforces understanding of financial accounting transactions in the first four chapters of the text* by helping students review important terms and accounting procedures. Specifically, students will be able to:

- Study more efficiently. Built-in diagnostic tests identify strengths and weaknesses and allow students to select exercises where they need the most help.
- Learn interactively. Interactive exercises prompt students to discover the correct answers on their own while working at their own study speed.
- Seek glossary help when needed. The Tutor provides access to key accounting terms and concepts.
- Get more out of this accounting text. The Accounting Transaction Tutor is linked to the text's learning objectives.

Also Available on the Student CD-ROM:

Selected Video Cases from the in-class video series can be viewed at home. The videos include Intel Corporation, Office Depot, Inc., Fermi National Accelerator Laboratory, Lotus Development Corporation, and UPS.

Web link to the Needles Accounting Resource Center Web Site.

*A full version of the software, including tutorials for all chapters of the text, is also available online.

Principles of Accounting

Principles of Accounting

2002©

INSTRUCTOR'S ANNOTATED EDITION

Belverd E. Needles, Jr., Ph.D., C.P.A., C.M.A.
DePaul University

Marian Powers, Ph.D.
Northwestern University

Susan V. Crosson, M.S. Accounting, C.P.A.
Santa Fe Community College, Florida

Houghton Mifflin Company   Boston   New York

To Jennifer, Jeffrey, Annabelle, and Abigail

To Bruce Crosson, and to J. Brent Crosson, Courtney Crosson, and Helen and Bryce Van Valkenburgh

Senior Sponsoring Editor: Bonnie Binkert
Senior Development Editor: Margaret M. Kearney
Associate Project Editor: Claudine Bellanton
Senior Production/Design Coordinator: Sarah L. Ambrose
Senior Manufacturing Coordinator: Priscilla J. Bailey
Marketing Manager: Steven Mikels
Associate Editor: Damaris Curran

Cover Image: © Theo Rudnak

PHOTO CREDITS: page 3, © PhotoDisc, Inc.; page 4, Courtesy of Intel Corporation; page 47, © 2000 Corbis; page 91, © Vesey/Vanderburgh/International Stock; page 133, Courtesy of Dell Computer Corporation; page 173, © PhotoDisc, Inc.; page 174, Courtesy of Office Depot, Inc.; page 221, © 2000 Corbis; page 305, © PhotoDisc, Inc.; page 347, © PhotoDisc, Inc.; page 387, © PhotoDisc, Inc.; page 427, © PhotoDisc, Inc.; page 467, © PhotoDisc, Inc.; page 468, Courtesy of Fermi National Accelerator Laboratory; page 515, © Peter Christopher/Wonderfile; page 549, © Stockbyte/PictureQuest; page 587, © Andrew Sacks/ Tony Stone Images; page 588, Courtesy of Lotus Development Corporation; page 627, © Danny Lehman/Corbis; page 667, © PhotoDisc, Inc.; page 711, © PhotoDisc, Inc.; page 713, Courtesy of Goodyear Tire & Rubber Company; page 765, © 2000 Corbis; page 807, Courtesy of American Honda Motor Co.; page 808, Courtesy of United Parcel Service; page 847, Permission granted by Caterpillar, Inc.; page 897, © G. Bliss/Wonderfile; page 939, © PhotoDisc, Inc.; page 983, © Mike Dobel/Wonderfile; page 1023, © PhotoDisc, Inc.; page 1024, Courtesy of Enterprise Rent-A-Car; page 1071, © PhotoDisc, Inc.; page 1111, © PhotoDisc, Inc.; page 1112, Courtesy of Harley-Davidson, Inc.; page 1151, © 2000 Corbis.

The Toys "R" Us Annual Report for the year ended January 29, 2000, which appears at the end of Chapter 6 (pages 277–303) and in excerpts throughout the book, is reprinted by permission.

Printed in the U.S.A.
Library of Congress Control Number: 2001089367
Student Text ISBN: 0-618-12422-5
Instructor's Annotated Edition ISBN: 0-618-12424-1

23456789-VH-05 04 03 02

Brief Contents

Contents

Part Nine
Information Analysis for Planning

Part Ten
Performance Measurement and Evaluation

Preface

Principles of Accounting, 2002©, is intended for the first course in accounting and as such is designed for students—both business and accounting majors—with no previous training in accounting or business. It is part of a well-integrated text and technology program that includes an array of print and electronic support materials for students and instructors. The text consists of 27 chapters; the first 18 are devoted to financial accounting topics, and the remaining 9 focus on managerial accounting topics.

We recognize that the majority of students taking the first accounting course are business and management majors rather than accounting majors; our goal therefore is to provide information for decision making throughout a student's career. We want our text to enable students to

- Recognize the value of accounting to their future careers regardless of their majors.
- Read and interpret internal and external financial reports and gain an understanding of their underlying concepts and techniques.
- Make intelligent decisions using internal and external accounting information.
- Analyze the effects of these decisions on the performance of a company.

A course that achieves these objectives will give students a valuable and realistic portrayal of accounting practices.

An Integrated Text and Technology Program

The business environment has changed, driven mostly by the trend toward globalization and the growing use of technology. We have therefore developed an integrated text and technology program dedicated to helping instructors stay on top of the change curve and take advantage of the opportunities created by new instructional technologies. Whether an instructor wants to present a user or procedural orientation, incorporate new instructional strategies, develop students' core skills and competencies, or integrate technology into the classroom, the new 2002© text provides a total solution, making it the leading choice among instructors of first-year accounting courses.

Applying and Using Technology

The 2002© text incorporates a number of electronic teaching and learning solutions. Each student and instructor copy of the textbook comes with a CD containing a variety of resources. The HMClassPrep CD for instructors provides valuable support material, including the popular Course Manual of instructor resources and teaching strategies, PowerPoint slides, and other electronic tools. The Student CD, packaged with every text, includes the Accounting Transaction Tutor software for Chapters 1–4, the Houghton Mifflin General Ledger Software for Windows, and selected video cases. Both CDs include a web link to other valuable materials at the Needles Accounting Resource Center web site at http://college.hmco.com. In addition, the text includes a variety of Internet exercises with links to real company financial statements. ACE icons in the end-of-chapter review sections of the text provide a visual link between the text and ACE, an interactive self-quizzing program available at our web site. Additional online tutoring help is available through the HM Web Tutor, powered by SmarThinking.

Given the common usage of workplace computers, students need practice in spreadsheet analysis. Numerous assignments that can be worked with Excel templates provide this opportunity. A spreadsheet icon indicates that an assignment can be solved using the Excel Templates CD.

For faculty who want an online component to their accounting courses, we provide a rich array of resources, including text-specific content that is available either in Blackboard Course Cartridges or WebCT e-Packs. These customized course materials may be used to enhance a traditional classroom setting or as a complete distance learning solution.

Houghton Mifflin's Teaching Accounting Online course provides online support to faculty who want to thoughtfully integrate web-based technology into their classes. The course was designed by a group of accounting faculty led by Susan Crosson, the new co-author of this edition. She has also developed courses for WebCT and Blackboard learning platforms.

A Balanced Approach to Beginning Accounting

Because of changes in the business environment, the needs of today's students have changed. This change is reflected in the analysis by Robert Elliott, KPMG partner and recent chairman of the IACPA, who has identified the five stages of the "value chain" in accounting as shown below:*

I.	II.	III.	IV.	V.
Business Events >	Data >	Information >	Knowledge >	Decisions

Elliott argues that too much time is spent on low-value activities represented by the first three stages (I, II, III) as opposed to the high-value activities represented in stages IV and V. The first three stages focus on transactions and information processing, which in today's business environment are likely to be achieved through the use of technology. We agree that the focus of accounting education today should be on the higher-level activities (stages IV and V) that provide a foundation for decision making. We also believe that business majors, who make up the vast majority of beginning accounting students, will benefit from this approach in subsequent business courses and throughout their business careers. Although our text provides a basic knowledge of the more procedural activities associated with stages I to III, our primary focus is on high-value learning activities, providing a balance between the procedural or preparer side of accounting and a more user-oriented approach.

Our overall objective is to provide a flexible learning system. To achieve balance and flexibility, the 2002© text includes far less procedural detail and fewer "pencil pushing" assignments. Because our focus is on the application of concepts, we have substantially revised many chapters to reduce procedural detail. We have accomplished this by placing procedures that are not essential to conceptual understanding in supplemental objectives at the ends of the chapters. In the end-of-chapter assignments, we have scrutinized all exercises and problems with a view toward

*W. Steve Albrecht and Robert J. Sack, *Accounting Education: Charting the Course Through a Perilous Future* (Sarasota, Fla.: American Accounting Association, 2000), p.36.

reducing the number of journal entries and the amount of posting required. In addition, we now employ T accounts more frequently as a form of analysis. Consistent with the emphasis on management decision making and performance evaluation, we have eliminated all journal entries from the managerial accounting chapters.

A Strong Emphasis on Decision Making and Critical Thinking

The AICPA, IMA, and other business organizations have emphasized the importance of developing students' core competencies and basic skills in such areas as communication, critical thinking, analysis and decision making, ethics, the use of technology, and teamwork. The pedagogical system underlying *Principles of Accounting*, 2002©, is based on a model that encompasses a growing group of instructional strategies designed to develop and strengthen a broad skill set in students. This model, which includes learning objectives, the teaching-learning cycle, cognitive levels of learning, and output skills, is described in the Course Manual, which is now available to instructors on the HMClassPrep CD. The Course Manual contains a Chapter Planning Matrix for each chapter to assist instructors in planning assignments to achieve learning objectives.

Just as accounting education has changed, today's students have changed also. Our new text edition is designed to accommodate a variety of learning styles to ensure student success. A few examples of the text's pedagogical features follow:

Learning Objectives Learning objectives are clearly stated at the beginning of each chapter. They are keyed to the chapter discussion and assignment material and are used throughout the text and ancillary package. They provide a valuable "road map" for students.

Chapter 1 "User's Manual" New, annotated Chapter 1 provides a built-in "user's manual" to help students understand the purpose and value of the pedagogical framework and how to use it to their advantage.

Color Scheme A consistent color scheme throughout the text presents inputs to the accounting system (source documents) in gold, the processing of accounting data (working papers and accounting forms) in green, and outputs of the system (financial and management reports) in purple.

Key Ratios Key ratios are integrated throughout the text at appropriate points to emphasize the use of accounting information in decision making and the importance this information plays in performance evaluation. These ratios (identified by the Key Ratio icon %) are usually introduced in the "management issues" section at the beginning of most chapters. We bring all the ratios together in a comprehensive financial analysis of Sun Microsystems, Inc., in Chapter 18. In the managerial accounting chapters, we examine how managers use various measurement tools to enhance performance evaluation and decision making.

Cash Flows We emphasize the effect of business activities on cash flow throughout the text. After introducing the statement of cash flows in Chapter 1, we point out in various subsequent chapters the difference between income measurement and cash flow, and we reinforce understanding through a variety of end-of-chapter assignments. A Cash Flow icon highlights these discussions in the text.

Revised Managerial Accounting Chapters with a Focus on What Managers Need to Know

With this edition, we welcome our new co-author, Susan Crosson. With Professor Crosson's help, we have achieved a major revision of the managerial accounting chapters of *Principles of Accounting* in terms of both structure and content. In writing and revising the managerial chapters, we have systematically questioned every paragraph, illustration, and assignment from a manager's viewpoint. Even the most traditional accounting topics have been scrutinized and revised on the basis of what today's managers need to know.

Future managers need to be able to read, understand, and use accounting information for making decisions. Our book is designed specifically to meet the needs of first-year students, the vast majority of whom are future managers, *not* accounting majors. Therefore, rather than focusing on the technical details of cost accounting, as is done in other textbooks, the managerial chapters emphasize topics critical to operating a successful business. For example, the chapter on standard costing now emphasizes standard costs used in performance management; the chapter on capital investment analysis emphasizes the net present value method. Also, we emphasize the approaches of the most progressive companies, such as the balanced scorecard, just-in-time operating environment, activity-based management, theory of constraints, and target costing.

Management use of information today goes far beyond product and service costing. This book explores the full range of innovative managerial systems in a value-centered economy in which managers must make critical decisions concerning product quality, customer service, and long-term relationships. The text discusses the latest in management models and technology, plus it emphasizes that performance measurement, evaluation, and compensation are essential to a manager's success in today's competitive environment. Service businesses, where many students will ultimately work, receive expanded emphasis within the text discussion and the chapter assignments. The following contemporary topics are included in the revised managerial accounting chapters:

- Total quality management
- Continuous improvement
- Balanced scorecard
- Theory of constraints
- Just-in-time operating environment
- Activity-based management
- Target costing
- Back-flush costing
- Costs of quality
- Performance measurement
- Impact of e-commerce
- Integrated management information systems
- Management performance incentives and compensation

Relevant Real-World Coverage

We have taken many steps to increase the real-world emphasis of the text in order to reflect current business practice in a way that is relevant and exciting for students.

Real Companies We use information from the annual reports of real companies and from business publications, such as *Business Week*, *Forbes*, and *The Wall Street Journal*, to enhance students' appreciation of the usefulness and relevance of accounting information. In addition, we use more than 100 publicly held companies as examples, and we have substantially increased the number of real companies appearing in the assignment materials. A Hot Links to Real Companies icon or a CD-ROM icon identifies these companies. Our Needles Accounting Resource Center Student web site provides direct links to the web pages of most of these companies.

Actual Financial Statements We have incorporated examples from the annual reports of real companies in both the text and assignment material. Chapter 6 presents the financial statements of Dell Computer in graphic form using the Fingraph® Financial Analyst™ CD that accompanies this book. A supplement to Chapter 6 contains a section entitled "How to Read an Annual Report," as well as the actual annual report of Toys "R" Us. As noted earlier, the comprehensive financial analysis in Chapter 18 features the financial statements of Sun Microsystems, Inc. These are only a few examples of the scores of other well-known companies featured in the text.

Decision Points Every chapter begins with a Decision Point. Based on excerpts from real companies' annual reports or from articles in the business press, Decision Points present a situation requiring a decision by managers or other accounting information users; they also demonstrate how the decision can be made using accounting information. Decision Points in the financial chapters present "A User's Focus," and those in the managerial chapters provide "A Manager's Focus."

Focus on Business These boxes appear throughout each chapter and emphasize business strategy as it relates to four key themes:

- Focus on Business Ethics
- Focus on Business Practice
- Focus on Business Technology
- Focus on International Business

International Accounting Among the many foreign companies mentioned in the text and assignments are Yamaha Motor Company, Ltd. (Japanese), Glaxo-Wellcome (British), Philips Electronics, N.V. and Heineken N.V. (Dutch), Roche Group (Swiss), Nokia (Finnish), and Goslar Corporation (German).

Real-World Graphic Illustrations Graphs, tables, and exhibits illustrating the relationship of actual business practices to chapter topics are a regular feature of the book. Many of these illustrations are based on data from studies of 600 annual reports published in *Accounting Trends and Techniques*. Beginning with Chapter 6, most chapters include a graph that shows various ratios for selected industries based on Dun & Bradstreet data. Service industry examples include advertising and interstate trucking companies. Manufacturing industry examples include pharmaceutical and tableware companies.

GOVERNMENTAL AND NOT-FOR-PROFIT ORGANIZATIONS Acknowledging the importance of governmental and not-for-profit organizations in our society, we include discussions and examples of these organizations at appropriate points in the text.

Expanded Assignment Materials Geared to Flexibility

In answer to the demand for a more sophisticated skill set for students and greater pedagogical choice for faculty members, we have expanded the variety of assignments and accompanying materials as described in the following sections.

Video Cases

Two new 5-minute video vignettes featuring Goodyear Tire & Rubber Company and Harley-Davidson, Inc., have been added to the series of four financial video cases and two managerial video cases. The videos, each accompanied by an in-text case, work equally well as individual or group assignments, and all eight include a written critical thinking component. Each video case, indicated by a video icon, serves as an introduction to the chapter in which it is found.

- *Intel Corporation* (Chapter 1) examines the business goals of liquidity and profitability and the business activities of financing, investing, and operating.
- *Office Depot, Inc.* (Chapter 5), discusses the merchandising company, the merchandising income statement, and the concept of the operating cycle.
- *Fermi National Accelerator Laboratory* (Chapter 11) demonstrates the importance of long-term assets to a unique scientific laboratory.
- *Lotus Development Corporation* (Chapter 14) tells the history of Lotus from its beginning as a small start-up company through its growth to one of America's most successful companies and finally to its sale to IBM. The case emphasizes Lotus's equity financing needs along the way.
- *Goodyear Tire & Rubber Company* (Chapter 17) describes the vision and objectives of the world's largest tire and rubber company and how Goodyear will need strong cash flows to carry out its objectives.
- *UPS* (Chapter 19) introduces management accounting within the context of the management cycle and examines the concept of performance measures.
- *Enterprise Rent-A-Car* (Chapter 24) presents the budgeting process in the management cycle and describes the master budget process for a service company.
- *Harley-Davidson, Inc.* (Chapter 26), demonstrates how a company uses the concepts of responsibility accounting and the balanced scorecard in its performance management and evaluation system.

The Annual Report Project

Because real companies' annual reports are rapidly becoming the most popular topic of term projects in the introductory accounting course, the Supplement to Chapter 6 provides a suggested annual report project that we have used in our classes for several years. To allow for projects of varied comprehensiveness, we have developed four assignment options, including the use of Fingraph® Financial Analyst™ data-base software.

Building Your Knowledge Foundation

This end-of-chapter section consists of a variety of questions, exercises, and problems designed to develop basic knowledge, comprehension, and application of the concepts and techniques presented in the chapter.

Questions (Q) Fifteen to 24 review questions that cover the essential topics of the chapter.

Short Exercises (SE) Approximately ten very brief exercises suitable for classroom use.

Exercises (E) An average of 15 single-topic exercises that stress application.

Problems (P) At least five extensive applications of chapter topics, often covering more than one learning objective and often containing writing components. All problems can be worked on our Excel Templates CD; some can be solved using our General Ledger Software for Windows.

Alternate Problems (P) An alternative set of the most popular problems, based on our study of users' syllabi.

The assignments most suitable for computer applications are marked with the following icons:

Ledger icons indicate problems that can be solved using our General Ledger Software for Windows.

Spreadsheet icons indicate problems that can be solved using our Excel Templates CD.

Expanding Your Critical Thinking, Communication, and Interpersonal Skills

Recognizing that students need to be better prepared to communicate clearly, both in written and oral formats, we have included ten or more cases that deal with skills development (SD), financial reporting and analysis (FRA), or managerial reporting and analysis (MRA). These cases are usually based on real companies. All require critical thinking and communication skills in the form of writing. At least one assignment in each chapter requires students to practice good business communication skills by writing a memorandum reporting results and offering recommendations. In addition, all cases are suitable for development of interpersonal skills through group activities. We have designated selected cases as being especially appropriate for group activities and for these have provided specific instructions for applying a group methodology. We use icons to identify these cases, as well as to provide guidance in the best use of other assignments. A list of these icons follows.

Cash Flow icons indicate assignments dealing with cash flow; they also indicate text discussions of cash flow.

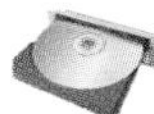
CD-ROM icons indicate assignments designed to be worked with the Fingraph® Financial Analyst™ CD.

Communication icons identify assignments designed to help students develop their ability to understand and communicate accounting information successfully.

Critical Thinking icons indicate assignments intended to strengthen students' critical thinking skills.

Ethics icons identify assignments that address ethical issues.

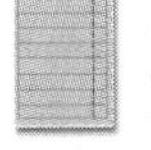
General Ledger icons indicate problems that can be solved using Houghton Mifflin General Ledger Software for Windows.

Group Activity icons identify assignments appropriate for groups or teamwork.

Hot Links to Real Companies icons indicate companies whose annual reports can be accessed by direct link from the Needles Accounting Resource Center web site. These icons are used in text discussions as well as in assignments.

International icons indicate international company cases.

Internet icons designate assignments featuring use of the Internet.

Key Ratio icons indicate the presence of financial analysis ratios in both the text and assignments.

Memorandum icons point to problems and cases that require students to write short business memorandums.

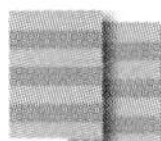
Spreadsheet icons indicate problems that can be solved using the Excel Templates CD.

Each Skills Development (SD) assignment has a specific purpose:

CONCEPTUAL ANALYSIS These short cases address conceptual accounting issues and are based on real companies and situations. They are designed so that a written solution is appropriate, but they may also be used in other communication modes.

ETHICAL DILEMMA Recognizing the need for accounting and business students to be exposed in all their courses to ethical considerations, we have included in every chapter a short case, often based on a real company, in which students must address an ethical dilemma directly related to the chapter content.

RESEARCH ACTIVITY These exercises enhance student learning and participation in the classroom by acquainting students with business periodicals, annual reports and business references, and resources in the library and on the Internet. Some exercises are designed to improve students' interviewing and observation skills through field activities at actual businesses. An icon in the margin indicates activities that can be researched on the Internet.

DECISION-MAKING PRACTICE Acting as decision makers—managers, investors, analysts, or creditors—students are asked to extract relevant data from a case, make computations as necessary, and arrive at a decision.

Cases in financial or managerial reporting and analysis (FRA/MRA) sharpen students' ability to comprehend and analyze financial and nonfinancial data:

INTERPRETING FINANCIAL (MANAGERIAL) REPORTS These short cases are abstracted from business articles and the annual reports of well-known corporations and organizations, such as Netscape Communications Corporation, Sun Microsystems, Cisco Systems, RJR Nabisco, Mellon Bank, Charles Schwab, and Amazon.com. They require students to extract relevant data, make computations, and interpret the results.

Formulating Management Reports Students strengthen analytical, critical thinking, and written communication skills with these assignments in the managerial chapters. Students are asked to examine, synthesize, and organize information with the object of preparing reports, such as a memo to a company president identifying sources of waste and estimating the current costs associated with the waste.

International Company These exercises include companies from around the world. The focus is on companies that have an accounting experience compatible with chapter content.

Toys "R" Us Annual Report The actual Toys "R" Us Annual Report, reproduced in the Supplement to Chapter 6, forms the basis of these analytical cases, which appear in the financial accounting chapters.

Fingraph® Financial Analyst™ These cases, which appear in the financial accounting chapters, may be worked in conjunction with the Fingraph® Financial Analyst™ data-base software. This CD includes web links to the annual reports of more than 20 well-known companies. Students utilize the software to analyze the financial statements of the companies.

Internet Case Each chapter of the text now features an Internet case, which asks students to research a topic on the Internet, answer critical and analytical thinking questions, and then prepare either a written or oral report of their findings.

Excel Spreadsheet Analysis These assignments in the managerial accounting chapters may be worked using our Excel Templates CD. They provide opportunities for written communication, interpretation, and analysis.

Financial Analysis Cases Also accompanying the text are a series of comprehensive financial analysis cases that may be integrated throughout the course after Chapter 5, or they may be used as capstone cases for the entire course. The first, "General Mills, Inc., Annual Report: A Decision Case in Financial Analysis," uses the actual financial statements of General Mills Corporation. The other cases, "Heartland Airways, Inc.," and "Richard Home Centers, Inc.," present complete annual reports for an airline company and a home improvement retailing chain. They will guide students through a complete financial analysis. Although these cases may be assigned individually, they also make excellent group assignments.

Readable, Accessible Text

Growing numbers of students who take the financial accounting course are from foreign countries, and English is a second language for them. To meet their needs fully, we as instructors must be aware of how the complexities and nuances of English, particularly business English, may hinder these students' understanding.

Each chapter of *Principles of Accounting*, 2002©, has been reviewed by business instructors who teach English as a Second Language (ESL) courses and English for Special Purposes courses, as well as by students taking these classes. With their assistance and advice, we have taken the following measures to ensure that the text is accessible.

- *Word Choice:* We replaced words and phrases that were unfamiliar to ESL students with ones they more readily recognize and understand. For instance, we substituted *raise* for *bolster*, *require* for *call for*, and *available* for *on hand*.
- *Length:* Because short, direct sentences are more easily comprehended than sentences containing multiple clauses, we paid strict attention to the length and grammatical complexity of our sentences.
- *Examples:* Examples reinforce concepts discussed and help make the abstract concrete. We have therefore added many simple, straightforward examples.

Supplementary Support Materials

Supplementary Learning Aids

Our goal is to provide a complete supplemental learning system, including manual and technology applications for computer, CD-ROM, videotape, and the Internet. Supplementary learning aids include the following:

NEW! Student CD
NEW! Needles Accounting Resource Center Student Web Site
Fingraph® Financial Analyst™ CD
NEW! HM Web Tutor, powered by SmarThinking
NEW! Peachtree 8.0 Educational Version
Working Papers for Exercises and Problems
NEW! Excel Templates CD
Study Guide
Houghton Mifflin Brief Accounting Dictionary

Financial Practice Cases

Collegiate Ts
College Words and Sounds Store, Fifth Edition
Micro-Tec, Fifth Edition

Managerial Decision Cases

Aspen Food Products Company
McHenry Hotels, Inc., Second Edition

Instructor's Support Materials

Instructor's Annotated Edition
Instructor's Solutions Manual
NEW! HMClassPrep Instructor CD
NEW! Needles Accounting Resource Center Instructor Web Site
Test Bank with Achievement Test Masters and Answers
HMTesting
Solutions Transparencies
NEW! Video Cases
NEW! Blackboard Course Cartridges
NEW! WebCT e-Packs
NEW! Teaching Accounting Online

Acknowledgments

Preparing an accounting text is a long and demanding project that cannot really succeed without the help of one's colleagues. We are grateful to numerous professional colleagues and students for their many constructive comments on the text. Unfortunately, any attempt to list all who have helped means that some who have contributed might inadvertently be slighted by omission. Some attempt, however, must be made to mention those who have been closely involved.

We wish to thank Dr. Sherry Mills and Hank Anderson for their contribution to the prior editions of this text.

We wish to express our deep appreciation to our colleagues at DePaul University who have been extremely supportive and encouraging. We also wish to thank our colleagues at Lake Forest Graduate School of Management and Santa Fe Community College for their input and support.

The thoughtful and meticulous work of Edward H. Julius (California Lutheran University) is reflected not only in the Study Guide and Test Bank but in many other ways as well. We also want to thank Debbie Luna (El Paso Community College) for her work on the Study Guide, and Marion Taube (University of Pittsburgh) and Mark Dawson (La Roche College) for their work on the Test Bank.

Also important to the quality of the book is the work of Mary Cavanagh and J. Sophie Buchanan, who helped prepare the manuscript, and Cynthia Fostle and Jacquie Commanday, who developed the manuscript. We greatly appreciate the supportive collaboration of our senior sponsoring editor, Bonnie Binkert. We benefited from the ideas and guidance of senior development editor Margaret Kearney, associate editor Damaris Curran, associate project editor Claudine Bellanton, and editorial assistant James Dimock. We also extend thanks to Sarah Evans for her careful oversight of the production of this text.

Others who have been supportive and have had an impact on this book through their reviews and class testing are:

Kym Anderson	
Gregory D. Barnes	Clarion University
Charles M. Betts	Delaware Technical & Community College
Michael C. Blue	Bloomsburg University
Cynthia Bolt-Lee	The Citadel
Gary R. Bower	Community College of Rhode Island
Lee Cannell	El Paso Community College
Lloyd Carroll	The Borough of Manhattan Community College
Naranjan Chipalkatti	Ohio Northern University
Stanley Chu	The Borough of Manhattan Community College
John D. Cunha	University of California—Berkeley
Mark W. Dawson	La Roche College
Patricia A. Doherty	Boston University
Lizabeth England	American Language Academy
David Fetyko	Kent State University
Roxanne Gooch	Cameron University
Christine Uber Grosse	The American Graduate School of International Management
Dennis A. Gutting	Orange County Community College
Edward H. Julius	California Lutheran University
Howard A. Kanter	DePaul University
Debbie Luna	El Paso Community College
Kevin McClure	ESL Language Center
George McGowan	
Anita R. McKie	University of South Carolina—Aiken

Gail A. Mestas	
Michael F. Monahan	
Janette Moody	The Citadel
Jenine Moscove	
Glenn Owen	Alan Hancock College
Debra Parker-Fleming	Ohio Dominican College
Beth Brooks Patel	University of California—Berkeley
Yvonne Phangi-Hatami	The Borough of Manhattan Community College
LaVonda Ramey	Schoolcraft College
Roberta Rettner	American Ways
Donald Shannon	DePaul University
S. Murray Simons	Northeastern University
Ellen L. Sweatt	DeKalb College—Dunwoody
Marion Taube	University of Pittsburgh
Rita Taylor	University of Cincinnati
Robert G. Unterman	Glendale Community College
Stan Weikert	College of the Canyons
Kay Westerfield	University of Oregon
Carol Yacht	
Glenn Allen Young	Tulsa Junior College

To the Student

How to Study Accounting Successfully

The introductory accounting course is fundamental to the business curriculum and to success in the business world beyond college. Whether you are majoring in accounting or in another business discipline, it is one of the most important classes you will take. The course has multiple purposes because its students have diverse interests, backgrounds, and purposes for taking it. What are your goals in studying accounting? Being clear about your goals can contribute to your success in this course.

Success in this class also depends on your desire to learn and your willingness to work hard. And it depends on your understanding of how the text complements the way your instructor teaches and the way you learn. A familiarity with how this text is structured will help you to study more efficiently, make better use of classroom time, and improve your performance on examinations and other assignments.

To be successful in the business world after you graduate, you will need a broad set of skills, which may be summarized as follows:

Technical/Analytical Skills A major objective of your accounting course is to give you a firm grasp of the essential business and accounting terminology and techniques that you will need to succeed in a business environment. With this foundation, you then can begin to develop the higher-level perception skills that will help you acquire further knowledge on your own.

An even more crucial objective of this course is to help you develop analytical skills that will allow you to evaluate data. An important aspect of analytical skills is the ability to use technology effectively in making analyses. Well-developed analytical and decision-making skills are among the professional skills most highly valued by employers and will serve you well throughout your academic and professional careers.

Communication Skills Another skill highly prized by employers is the ability to express oneself in a manner that others correctly understand. This can include writing skills, speaking skills, and presentation skills. Communication skills are developed through particular tasks and assignments and are improved through constructive criticism. Reading skills and listening skills support the direct communication skills.

Interpersonal Skills Effective interaction between two people requires a solid foundation of interpersonal skills. The success of such interaction depends on empathy, or the ability to identify with and understand the problems, concerns, and motives of others. Leadership, supervision, and interviewing skills also facilitate a professional's interaction with others.

Personal/Self Skills Personal/self skills form the foundation for growth in the use of all other skills. To succeed, a professional must take initiative, possess self-confidence, show independence, and be ethical in all areas of life. Personal/self skills can be enhanced significantly by the formal learning process and by peers and mentors who provide models upon which one can build. Accounting is just one course in your entire curriculum, but it can play an important role in your skill development. Your instructor is interested in helping you gain both a knowledge of accounting and the more general skills you will need to succeed in the business world. The following sections describe how you can get the most out of this course.

The Teaching/Learning Cycle™

Both teaching and learning have natural, parallel, and mutually compatible cycles. This teaching/learning cycle, as shown in Figure 1, interacts with the basic structure of learning objectives in this text.

The Teaching Cycle The inner (tan) circle in Figure 1 shows the steps an instructor takes in teaching a chapter. Your teacher *assigns* material, *presents* the subject in lecture, *explains* by going over assignments and answering questions, *reviews* the subject prior to an exam, and *assesses* your knowledge and understanding using examinations and other means of evaluation.

The Learning Cycle Moving outward, the next circle (green) in Figure 1 shows the steps you should take in studying a chapter. You should *preview* the material, *read* the chapter, *apply* your understanding by working the assignments, *review* the chapter, and *recall* and *demonstrate* your knowledge and understanding of the material in examinations and other assessments.

Integrated Learning Objectives Your textbook supports the teaching/learning cycle through the use of integrated learning objectives. Learning objectives are simply statements of what you should be able to do after you have completed a chapter. In Figure 1, the outside (blue) circle shows how learning objectives are integrated into your text and other study aids and how they interact with the teaching/learning cycle.

1. Learning objectives listed at the beginning of each chapter aid your teacher in making assignments and help you preview the chapter.
2. Each learning objective is referenced in the margin of the text at the point where that subject is covered to assist your teacher in presenting the material and to help you organize your thoughts as you read the material.
3. Every exercise, problem, and case in the end-of-chapter assignments shows the applicable learning objective(s) so you can refer to the text if you need help.
4. A summary of the key points for each learning objective, a list of new concepts and terms referenced by learning objectives, and a review problem covering key learning objectives assist you in reviewing each chapter. The Study Guide, also organized by learning objectives, provides additional review.

Why Students Succeed Students succeed in their accounting course when they coordinate their personal learning cycle with their instructor's cycle. Students who do a good job of previewing their assignments, reading the chapters before the instructor is ready to present them, preparing homework assignments before they are discussed in class, and reviewing carefully will ultimately achieve their potential on exams. Those who get out of phase with their instructor, for whatever reason, will do poorly or fail. To ensure that your learning cycle is synchronized with your instructor's teaching cycle, check your study habits against the following suggestions.

Previewing the Chapter

1. Read the learning objectives at the beginning of the chapter. These learning objectives specifically describe what you should be able to do after completing the chapter.

Figure 1
The Teaching/Learning Cycle™ with Integrated Learning Objectives

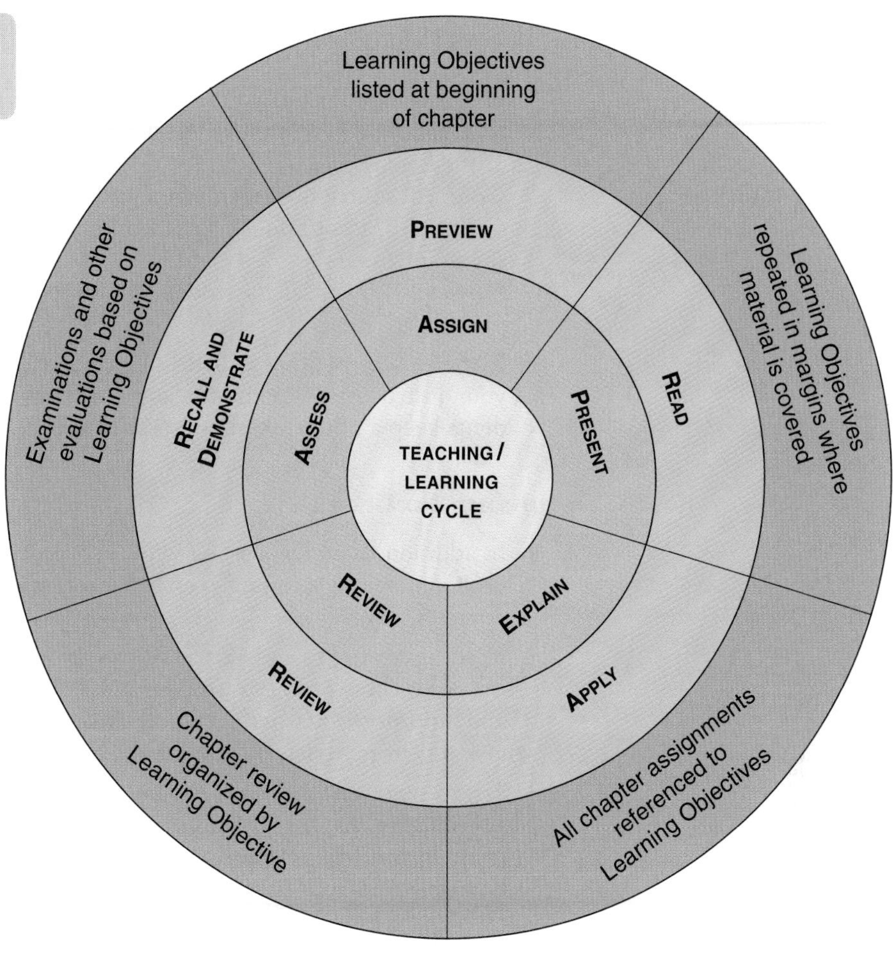

2. Study your syllabus. Know where you are in the course and where you are going. Know the rules of the course.
3. Realize that in an accounting course, each assignment builds on previous ones. If you do poorly in Chapter 1, you may have difficulty in Chapter 2 and be lost in Chapter 3.

Reading the Chapter

1. As you read each chapter, be aware of the learning objectives in the margins. They will tell you why the material is relevant.
2. Allow yourself plenty of time to read the text. Accounting is a technical subject. Accounting books are so full of information that almost every sentence is important.
3. Strive to understand not only how each procedure is done, but also why it is done. Accounting is logical and requires reasoning. If you understand why something is done in accounting, there is little need to memorize.

4. Relate each new topic to its learning objective and be able to explain it in your own words.
5. Be aware of colors as you read. They are designed to help you understand the text. (For handy reference, the use of color is also explained on the back cover of the book.)
   Gold: All source documents and inputs are in gold.
   Green: All accounting forms, working papers, and accounting processes are shown in green.
   Purple: All financial statements, the output or final product of the accounting process, are shown in purple.
6. If there is something you do not understand, prepare specific questions for your instructor. Pinpoint the topic or concept that confuses you. Some students keep a notebook of points with which they have difficulty.

Applying the Chapter

1. In addition to understanding why each procedure is done, you must be able to do it yourself by working exercises, problems, and cases. Accounting is a "do-it-yourself" course.
2. Read assignments and instructions carefully. Each assignment has a specific purpose. The wording is precise, and a clear understanding of it will save time and improve your performance. Acquaint yourself with the end-of-chapter assignment materials by reading the description of them in the Preface.
3. Try to work exercises, problems, and cases without referring to their discussions in the chapter. If you cannot work an assignment without looking in the chapter, you will not be able to work a similar problem on an exam. After you have tried on your own, refer to the chapter (based on the learning objective reference) and check your answer. Try to understand any mistakes you may have made.
4. Be neat and orderly. Sloppy calculations, messy papers, and general carelessness cause most errors on accounting assignments.
5. Allow plenty of time to work the chapter assignments. You will find that assignments seem harder and that you make more errors when you are feeling pressed for time.
6. Keep up with your class. Check your work against the solutions presented in class. Find your mistakes. Be sure you understand the correct solutions.
7. Note the part of each exercise, problem, or case that causes you difficulty so you can ask for help.
8. Attend class. Most instructors design classes to help you and to answer your questions. Absence from even one class can hurt your performance.

Reviewing the Chapter

1. Read the summary of learning objectives in the chapter review. Be sure you know the definitions of all the words in the review of concepts and terminology.
2. Review all assigned exercises, problems, and cases. Know them cold. Be sure you can work the assignments without the aid of the book.
3. Determine the learning objectives for which most of the problems were assigned. They refer to topics that your instructor is most likely to emphasize on an exam. Scan the text for such learning objectives and pay particular attention to the examples and illustrations.

Check Figures

These check figures provide a key number in the solutions to the problems at the end of each chapter.

Chapter 1 Problems

P 1. Total Assets: $8,750
P 2. Total Assets: $11,530
P 3. Total Assets: $8,060
P 4. Total Assets: $57,500
P 5. Total Assets: $4,620
P 6. Total Assets: $10,420
P 7. Total Assets: $70,600
P 8. Total Assets: $48,750

Chapter 2 Problems

P 1. No check figure
P 2. Trial Balance: $21,100
P 3. Trial Balance: $22,780
P 4. Trial Balance: $10,540
P 5. Trial Balance: $56,960
P 6. No check figure
P 7. Trial Balance: $23,100
P 8. Trial Balance: $10,880

Chapter 3 Problems

P 1. No check figure
P 2. No check figure
P 3. Adjusted Trial Balance: $121,792
P 4. Adjusted Trial Balance: $16,436
P 5. Adjusted Trial Balance: $26,040
P 6. No check figure
P 7. No check figure
P 8. Adjusted Trial Balance: $106,167

Chapter 4 Problems

P 1. Total Assets: $96,929
P 2. Total Assets: $113,616
P 3. May Adjusted Trial Balance: $9,366; Total Assets: $8,151; Post-Closing Trial Balance: $8,186; June Adjusted Trial Balance: $9,580; Total Assets: $8,087; Post-Closing Trial Balance: $8,157
P 4. Total Assets: $9,897
P 5. Total Assets: $350,868
P 6. Total Assets: $1,255,600
P 7. Total Assets: $6,943
P 8. Total Assets: $247,148
Comprehensive Problem: Adjusted Trial Balance Totals: $30,990; Total Assets: $25,810; Net Income: $3,960

Chapter 5 Problems

P 1. Net Income: $15,435
P 2. No check figure
P 3. Net Income: $3,435
P 4. No check figure
P 5. Net Income: $30,105; Total Assets: $199,008
P 6. Net Income: $2,440; Total Assets: $533,590
P 7. No check figure
P 8. Net Income: $10,522
P 9. No check figure
P 10. Net Income: $23,941
P 11. No check figure

Chapter 6 Problems

P 1. No check figure
P 2. Net Income: $127,252
P 3. Total Assets: $794,286
P 4. Current Ratio: 20x4, 2.0; 20x3, 2.6; Return on Assets: 20x4, 14.8%; 20x3, 13.2%
P 5. Net Income: $29,130; Total Assets: $367,740
P 6. No check figure
P 7. Net Income (Loss): ($860)
P 8. Current Ratio: 20x4, 2.3; 20x3, 3.5; Return on Assets: 20x4, 12.5%; 20x3, 11.0%

Chapter 7 Problems

P 1. Lamb Company's Total Accounts Receivable: $3,020; Lamb Company's Total Accounts Payable: $2,600
P 2. Cash total in cash receipts journal: $66,968; Cash total in cash payments journal: $28,644
P 3. Accounts Payable total: $16,464
P 4. Trial Balance: $42,292
P 5. Trial Balance: $30,558
P 6. Dune Company's Total Accounts Receivable: $870; Dune Company's Total Accounts Payable: $2,100
P 7. Cash total in cash receipts journal: $23,340; Cash total in cash payments journal: $17,012
P 8. Trial Balance: $45,808

Chapter 8 Problems

P 1. Adjusted book balance: $27,242.80
P 2. Adjusted book balance: $21,608
P 3. No check figure
P 4. No check figure
P 5. Total Unpaid Vouchers: $3,159
P 6. No check figure
P 7. Adjusted book balance: $74,736.64
P 8. No check figure

Chapter 9 Problems

P 1. Short-Term Investments (at market): $903,875
P 2. No check figure
P 3. Amount of adjustment: $9,533

P 4. No check figure
P 5. Short-Term Investments (at market): $354,000
P 6. No check figure
P 7. Amount of adjustment: $73,413
P 8. No check figure

Chapter 10 Problems
P 1. 1. Cost of goods available for sale: $10,560,000
P 2. 1. Cost of goods sold: June, $19,320; July, $44,237
P 3. 1. Cost of goods sold: June, $19,160; July, $43,982
P 4. Estimated inventory shortage: at cost, $42,431; at retail, $56,200
P 5. Estimated destroyed inventory: $730,000
P 6. Cost of goods available for sale: $315,960
P 7. 1. Cost of goods sold: March, $4,578; April, $15,457
P 8. 1. Cost of goods sold: March, $4,560; April, $15,424

Chapter 11 Problems
P 1. Totals: Land: $426,212; Land Improvements: $166,560; Buildings: $833,940; Machinery: $1,262,640; Expense: $18,120
P 2. 1. Depreciation, Year 3: a. $54,250; b. $81,375; c. $53,407
P 3. Total Depreciation Expense: 20x1: $71,820; 20x2: $103,092; 20x3: $84,072
P 4. a. Gain on Sale of Computer: $6,000; b. Loss on Sale of Computer: $3,000; c. Gain on Exchange of Computer: $4,500; d. Loss on Exchange of Computer: $2,000; e. no gain recognized; f. Loss on Exchange of Computer: $2,000; g. Computer (new): $31,500; h. Computer (new): $38,000
P 5. Part A: d. Leasehold Amortization Expense: $6,000; e. Leasehold Improvements Amortization Expense: $13,500; Part B: c. Patent Amortization Expense: $148,000; d. Loss on Write-off of Patent: $1,184,000
P 6. Totals: Land: $723,900; Land Improvements: $142,000; Building: $1,383,600; Equipment: $210,800
P 7. 1. Depreciation, Year 3: a. $330,000; b. $264,000; c. $180,000
P 8. Total Depreciation Expense: 20x2: $26,560; 20x3: $37,520; 20x4: $31,456

Chapter 12 Problems
P 1. Total Current Liabilities: $36,988.20
P 2. No check figure
P 3. 1.b. Estimated Product Warranty Liability: $10,800
P 4. 3. Payroll Taxes Expense: $31,938.70
P 5. Net Pay, total: $8,176.32
P 6. No check figure
P 7. 1.b. Estimated Product Warranty Liability: $10,080
P 8. 3. Payroll Taxes Expense: $44,221.38

Chapter 13 Problems
P 1. 2.f. Chan's share of loss, 20x1: $11,000
P 2. 1. Gregory's share of income: $112,500
P 3. d. Luke, Capital: $94,000
P 4. 1. Cash distribution to Dawn: $208,800
P 5. Cash distribution to Stanford: $108,000
P 6. 3. Gloria's share of income: $16,080
P 7. d. Maureen, Capital: $96,000
P 8. Cash distribution to Nguyen: ($168,000)

Chapter 14 Problems
P 1. 2. Total Stockholders' Equity: $1,488,000
P 2. 1. 20x3 Total dividends: Preferred, $420,000; Common, $380,000
P 3. No check figure
P 4. 2. Total Stockholders' Equity: $1,446,900
P 5. 2. Total Stockholders' Equity: $330,375
P 6. 2. Total Stockholders' Equity: $351,400
P 7. 1. 20x3 Total dividends: Preferred, $120,000; Common, $68,000
P 8. 2. Total Stockholders' Equity: $475,040

Chapter 15 Problems
P 1. 2. Difference in net income: $97,600
P 2. Income Before Extraordinary Items and Cumulative Effect of Accounting Change: $410,000
P 3. Income from Continuing Operations, December 31, 20x3: $157,500
P 4. 2. Total Stockholders' Equity, December 31, 20x5: $2,964,000
P 5. 2. Retained Earnings: $250,000; Total Stockholders' Equity: $2,350,000
P 6. 2. Total Stockholders' Equity: $2,802,800
P 7. Income Before Extraordinary Items and Cumulative Effect of Accounting Change: $216,000
P 8. 2. Total Stockholders' Equity, December 31, 20x3: $518,500
P 9. 2. Retained Earnings: $397,000; Total Stockholders' Equity: $2,577,000

Chapter 16 Problems
P 1. 1. Bond Interest Expense: Nov. 30, $517,500
P 2. 1. Bond Interest Expense: Sept. 1, $377,200
P 3. Bond Interest Expense: June 30, 20x2, $289,332; Sept. 1, 20x2, $186,580
P 4. 2. Loss on early retirement: $2,261,504
P 5. Loss on Retirement of Bonds: Feb. 28, 20x5, $1,600,000

P 6. 1. Bond Interest Expense: Sept. 1, $374,400
P 7. 1. Bond Interest Expense: Nov. 30, $1,040,300
P 8. 1. Bond Interest Expense: June 30, 20x1, $93,195; Sept. 30, 20x1, $193,800

Chapter 17 Problems
P 1. No check figure
P 2. 1. Net Cash Flows from: Operating Activities, $46,800; Investing Activities, ($14,400); Financing Activities, $102,000
P 3. 1. Net Cash Flows from: Operating Activities, ($106,000); Investing Activities, $34,000; Financing Activities, $44,000
P 4. 2. Net Cash Flows from: Operating Activities, ($106,000); Investing Activities, $34,000; Financing Activities, $44,000
P 5. Net Cash Flows from Operating Activities: $47,600
P 6. 1. Net Cash Flows from: Operating Activities, $63,300; Investing Activities, ($12,900); Financing Activities, $7,000
P 7. No check figure
P 8. 1. Net Cash Flows from: Operating Activities, $548,000; Investing Activities: $6,000; Financing Activities, ($260,000)
P 9. 2. Net Cash Flows from: Operating Activities, $63,300; Investing Activities, ($12,900); Financing Activities, $7,000

Chapter 18 Problems
P 1. No check figure
P 2. Increase: a, b, e, f, l, m
P 3. 1.c. Receivable turnover, 20x2: 14.1 times; 20x1: 14.4 times
P 4. 1.b. Quick ratio, Lewis: 1.5 times; Ramsey: 1.2 times; 2.d. Return on equity, Lewis: 8.8%; Ramsey, 4.9%
P 5. Increase: d, h, i
P 6. 1.a. Current ratio, 20x2: 1.5 times; 20x1: 1.5 times; 2.c. Return on assets, 20x2: 5.0%; 20x1: 10.7%

Chapter 19 Problems
P 1. No check figure
P 2. Using the attachment, machine BD sorts 42,871 more checks than average in Week 8
P 3. No check figure
P 4. 2.a. Gross Margin: $191,800; 2.d. Cost of Goods Manufactured: $312,100
P 5. 1.a. $4; 1.e. $10; 1.n. $10
P 6. Molding, Week 1, First Shift, hours per board: 3.50
P 7. No check figure
P 8. 2.a. Gross Margin: $181,200; 2.d. Cost of Goods Manufactured: $253,500

Chapter 20 Problems
P 1. 2. Total unit cost: $13.72
P 2. Cost of goods manufactured: $10,163,200
P 3. a. $2; f. $4
P 4. 1. Predetermined overhead rate for 20x3: $5.014 per machine hour
P 5. 2. Total costs assigned to Altun order, activity-based costing method: $41,805.60
P 6. 2. Overhead applied to Job 2214: $29,717
P 7. 2. Total costs assigned to Winkowsky order, activity-based costing method: $69,280.40
P 8. 1.c. Rigger II: $11,665; BioScout: $14,940

Chapter 21 Problems
P 1. Cost of units sold: $218,160
P 2. 1. Job A product unit cost: $5.00
P 3. 2. Cost of units completed and transferred: $76,470
P 4. 1.c. Cost of ending work in process inventory: $37,200
P 5. 1.b. Total cost per equivalent unit: $3.78
P 6. 2. Under-applied overhead: $260
P 7. 2. Cost of units completed and transferred: $185,073
P 8. 1.b. Total cost per equivalent unit: $.59

Chapter 22 Problems
P 1. No check figure
P 2. 1. Product unit cost: $270.00; 4. Product unit cost: $279.53
P 3. 1.a. Total materials handling cost rate: 30% per dollar of materials
P 4. 3. Total direct cost, Toy Bridge work cell: $17,000
P 5. 3. Cost of goods sold: $564,400
P 6. 1. Product unit cost: $878.25
P 7. 3. Product unit cost: $10.433
P 8. 3. Cost of goods sold: $391,520

Chapter 23 Problems
P 1. 4. Cost per Job: $81.65
P 2. 1. 740 Systems
P 3. 1.a. 7,900 Units
P 4. 2. 190,000 Units
P 5. 2. 418 Loans
P 6. 1. 7,500 Billable Hours
P 7. 1.a. 3,500 Units
P 8. 3. $806.60 per Job

Chapter 24 Problems
P 1. 1. Total Manufacturing Costs Budgeted, November: $1,157,000
P 2. 8. Income from Operations: $3,086
P 3. 1. Ending Cash Balance, February: ($2,900)
P 4. 1. Net Income: $52,404

P 5. Ending Cash Balance, February: $19,555
P 6. 1. Net Income: $1,860,830
P 7. 1. Ending Cash Balance, August: $1,800
P 8. 1. Projected Net Income: $101,812

Chapter 25 Problems

P 1. Total standard unit cost of front entrance, Year 20x1: $8,510
P 2. 1. Direct materials price variance—Liquid Plastic: $386 (F); 2. Direct labor rate variance—Trimming/Packing: $56 (U)
P 3. 2. Flexible budget formula: Total Budgeted Costs = ($.35 x units produced) + $10,500
P 4. 1.b. Direct materials quantity variance: $3,720 (U); 1.f. Manufacturing overhead volume variance: $320 (F)
P 5. c. $11.50
P 6. 1. Total standard direct materials cost per unit: $167.52
P 7. 1. Direct materials price variance—Metal: $832 (F) 2. Direct labor rate variance—Molding: $510 (F)
P 8. 1.a. Direct materials price variance—Chemicals: $12,200 (F); 1.e. Controllable manufacturing overhead variance: $3,100 (U)

Chapter 26 Problems

P 1. Flexible Budget, Total Cost: $7,248,000
P 2. 2. Center Income: $194,782
P 3. 1. Flexible Budget, Contribution Margin: $88,200
P 4. 3. Economic value added for 20x4: $21,850
P 5. 1. Residual income: ($2,500)
P 6. 2. Center Income: $418,555
P 7. 3.a. Actual Return on Investment: 6.3%
P 8. 3. Economic value added: $126,000

Chapter 27 Problems

P 1. 1. Total cost to buy: $1,350,000
P 2. Contribution margin: $7,725
P 3. 3. Operating income from further processing, bagel sandwiches: $.50
P 4. 2. Net present value: ($5,430)
P 5. 1. Average annual net income, Cal Machine: $34,965; Average annual net income, Hawk Machine: $40,670
P 6. 1. Total cost to make: $3,084,000
P 7. 1. Net present value: $16,573
P 8. 1. Exalt Machine: ($32,379); 2. Exalt Machine: 20.7%; 3. Exalt Machine: 5.4 years

Principles of Accounting

1 Uses of Accounting Information and the Financial Statements

LEARNING OBJECTIVES

Look to the learning objectives (LOs) as a guide to help you master the material. You will see many references to LOs throughout each chapter.

1 Define *accounting*, identify business goals and activities, and describe the role of accounting in making informed decisions.
2 Identify the many users of accounting information in society.
3 Explain the importance of business transactions, money measure, and separate entity to accounting measurement.
4 Identify the three basic forms of business organization.
5 Define *financial position*, state the accounting equation, and show how they are affected by simple transactions.
6 Identify the four financial statements.
7 State the relationship of generally accepted accounting principles (GAAP) to financial statements and the independent CPA's report, and identify the organizations that influence GAAP.
8 Define *ethics* and describe the ethical responsibilities of accountants.

DECISION POINT: A USER'S FOCUS

Microsoft Corporation Microsoft Corporation, the giant software company, is considered one of the world's most successful companies. Why is Microsoft considered successful? An ordinary person sees the quality of the company's enormously successful products, such as Microsoft Windows, Microsoft Word, and Microsoft Excel; an investment company and others with a financial stake in the company evaluate Microsoft and its management in financial terms. Many Microsoft employees have become millionaires by owning a part of the company through stock ownership. This success is reflected in the Financial Highlights from the company's 2000 annual report, shown here.[1]

A Decision Point introduces each chapter to show how leading businesses use accounting information reported in annual reports to make business decisions.

These Financial Highlights contain a number of terms for common financial measures of all companies, large or small. These measures are used to evaluate a company's management and to evaluate a company in comparison to other companies. It is easy to see the large increases at Microsoft over the years in such measures as revenue, net income, total assets, and stockholders' equity, but what do these terms mean? What financial knowledge do Microsoft's managers need in order to measure progress toward their financial goals? What financial knowledge does anyone who is evaluating Microsoft in relation to other companies need in order to understand these measures?

Microsoft's managers must have a thorough knowledge of accounting to understand how the operations for which they are responsible contribute to the firm's overall financial health.

Financial Highlights

(In millions, except earnings per share)

	Year Ended June 30				
	1996	1997	1998	1999	**2000**
Revenue	$ 8,671	$11,358	$14,484	$19,747	**$22,956**
Net income	2,195	3,454	4,490	7,785	**9,421**
Earnings per share	0.86	1.32	1.67	1.42	**1.70**
Cash and short-term investments	6,940	8,966	13,927	17,236	**23,798**
Total assets	10,093	14,387	22,357	37,156	**52,150**
Stockholders' equity	6,908	10,777	16,627	28,438	**41,368**

Point to Emphasize: Management must have a good understanding of accounting to set financial goals and to make financial decisions. Management not only must understand how accounting information is compiled and processed but also must realize that accounting information is imperfect and should be interpreted with caution.

Critical Thinking Question: Why would a business have more than one financial goal? **Answer:** Multiple financial goals signal that there is not just one measure of performance that is of interest to all users. For example, lenders are concerned primarily with cash flow, and owners are concerned with earnings and dividends.

People with a financial stake in the company, such as owners, investors, creditors, employees, attorneys, and governmental regulators, must also know accounting to evaluate the financial performance of a business. Anyone who aspires to any of these roles in a business requires mastery of accounting terminology and concepts, the process of producing financial information, and how that information is interpreted and analyzed. The purpose of this course and this textbook is to assist you in acquiring that mastery.

Video cases introduce key concepts and techniques presented in the chapter in the context of a real company.

VIDEO CASE

Intel Corporation

Objectives

- To examine the principal activities of a business enterprise: financing, investing, and operating.
- To explore the principal performance goals of a business enterprise: liquidity and profitability.
- To relate these activities and goals to the financial statements.

Background for the Case

You are probably familiar with the slogan "Intel Inside," from a marketing campaign for Intel Corporation, one of the most successful companies in the world. In 1971, Intel introduced the world's first microprocessor. The microprocessor made possible the personal computer (PC), which has changed the world. Today, Intel supplies the computing industry with chips, boards, systems, and software. Its principal products include:

- **Microprocessors.** Also called central processing units (CPUs), these are frequently described as the "brains" of a computer because they act as the central control for the processing of data in PCs. This category includes the famous Pentium® processor.
- **Networking and Communications Products.** These products enhance the capabilities and ease of use of PC systems by allowing users to talk to each other and to share information.
- **Semiconductor Products.** Semiconductors facilitate flash memory, making possible easily reprogrammable memory for computers, mobile phones, and many other products. Included in this category are embedded control chips that are programmed to regulate specific functions in products such as automobile engines, laser printers, disk drives, and home appliances.

In addition to PC users, Intel's customers include manufacturers of computers and computer systems, automobiles, and a wide range of other industrial and telecommunications equipment.

For more information about Intel Corporation, visit the company's web site through the Needles Accounting Resource Center at:

http://college.hmco.com

Required

View the video on Intel Corporation that accompanies this book. As you are watching the video, take notes related to the following:

1. All businesses engage in three basic activities—financing, investing, and operating—but how they engage in them differs from company to company. Describe in your own words the nature of each of these activities and give as many examples as you can of how Intel engages in each activity.
2. To be successful, all businesses must achieve two performance objectives—liquidity and profitability. Describe in your own words the nature of each of these goals and describe how each applies to Intel.
3. There are four financial statements that apply to business enterprises. Which statements are most closely associated with the goal of liquidity? Which statement is most closely associated with the goal of profitability? Which statement shows the financial position of the company?

Accounting as an Information System

OBJECTIVE

1 Define *accounting*, identify business goals and activities, and describe the role of accounting in making informed decisions

Each LO is stated in the margin to introduce the related text material.

Related Text Assignments:
Q: 1, 2, 3, 4
E: 1
SD: 1, 4
FRA: 2, 4, 5

Today's accountant focuses on the ultimate needs of decision makers who use accounting information, whether those decision makers are inside or outside the business. **Accounting** "is not an end in itself,"[2] but is *an information system that measures, processes, and communicates financial information about an identifiable economic entity*. An economic entity is a unit that exists independently—for example, a business, a hospital, or a governmental body. The central focus of this book is on business entities and business activities, although other economic units, such as hospitals and governmental units, will be mentioned at appropriate points in the text and assignment material.

Accounting provides a vital service by supplying the information that decision makers need in order to make "reasoned choices among alternative uses of scarce resources in the conduct of business and economic activities."[3] As shown in Figure 1, accounting is a link between business activities and decision makers. First, accounting measures business activities by recording data about them for future use. Second, the data are stored until needed and then processed to become useful information. Third, the information is communicated, through reports, to decision makers. We might say that data about business activities are the input to the accounting system and that useful information for decision makers is the output.

Business Goals, Activities, and Performance Measures

Key terms are highlighted in blue and followed by their definition.

A **business** is an economic unit that aims to sell goods and services to customers at prices that will provide an adequate return to its owners. For example, listed

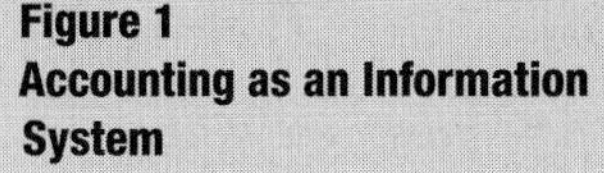

Figure 1
Accounting as an Information System

Figures visually show relationships between concepts and/or processes.

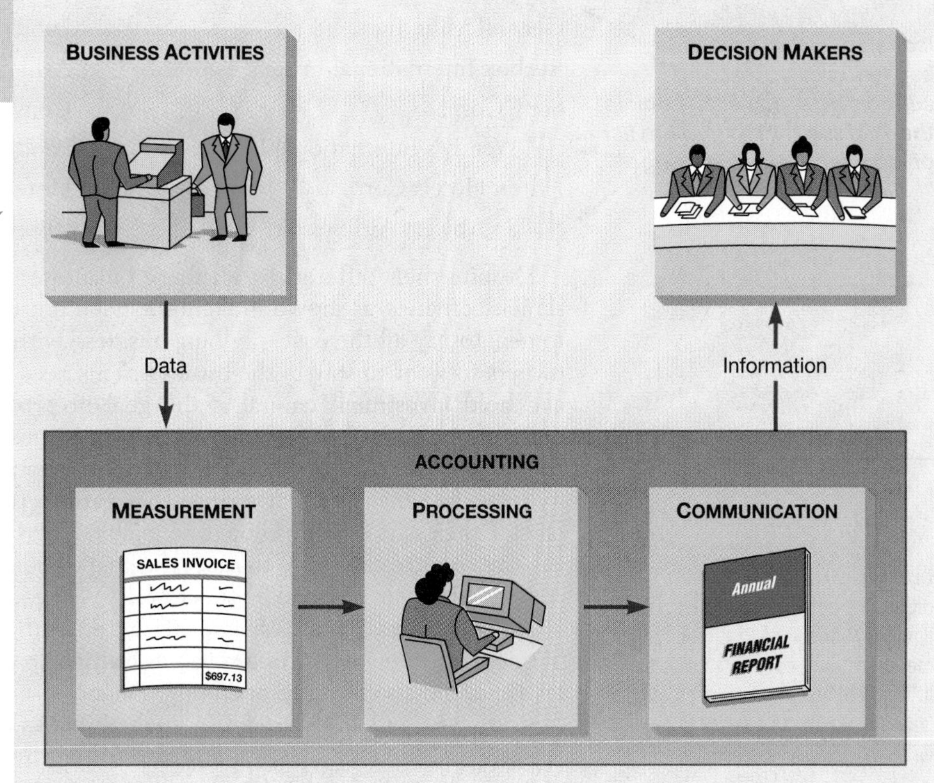

Point to Emphasize: It is the usefulness of the information generated by accounting that makes accounting a valuable discipline. That is, the primary purpose of accounting is to provide decision makers with financial information that can be used to make intelligent decisions.

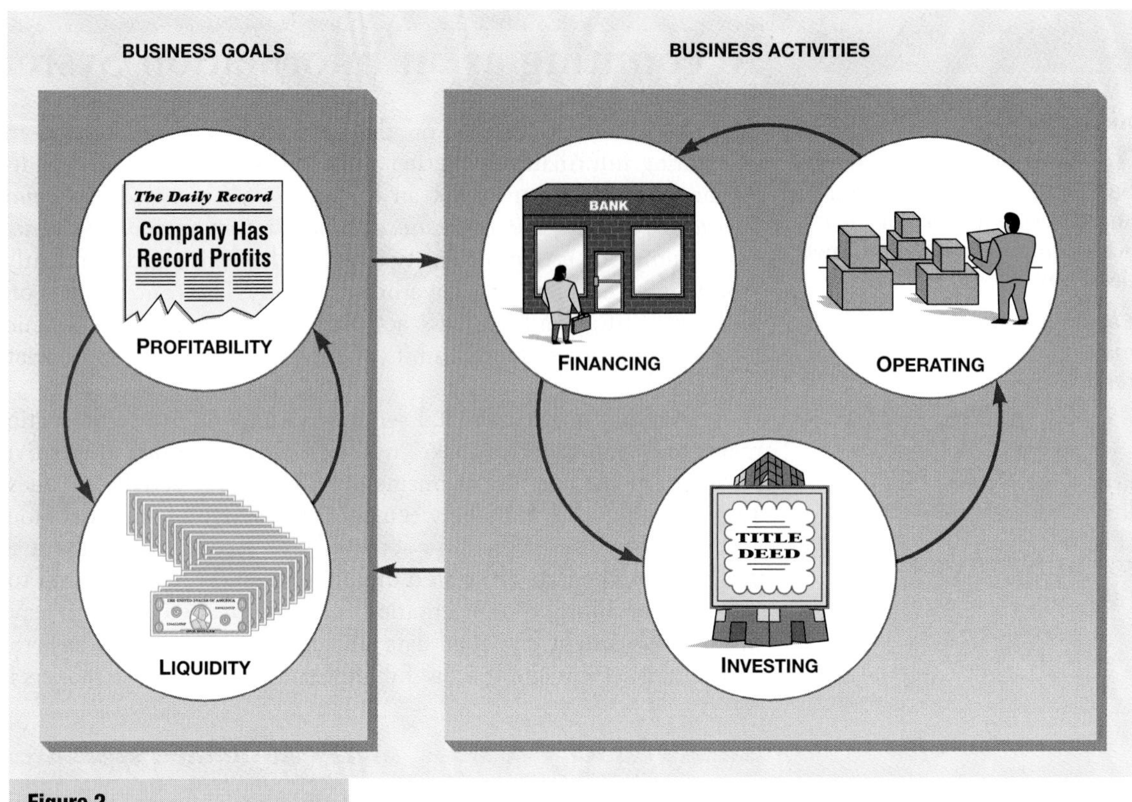

Figure 2
Business Goals and Activities

below are some well-known companies and the principal goods or services that they sell:

Icons are visual guides to key features of text and supporting study aids. Look in the Preface for a complete list of icons and their meanings.

General Mills, Inc.	Food products
Reebok International Ltd.	Athletic footwear and clothing
Sony Corp.	Consumer electronics
Wendy's International Inc.	Food service
Hilton Hotels Corp.	Hotels and resorts service
Southwest Airlines Co.	Passenger airline service

Despite their differences, all these businesses have similar goals and engage in similar activities, as shown in Figure 2. Each must take in enough money from customers to pay all the costs of doing business, with enough left over as profit for the owners to want to stay in the business. This need to earn enough income to attract and hold investment capital is the goal of **profitability**. In addition, businesses must meet the goal of liquidity. **Liquidity** means having enough cash available to pay debts when they are due. For example, Toyota may meet the goal of profitability by selling many cars at a price that earns a profit. But if its customers do not pay for their cars quickly enough to enable Toyota to pay its suppliers and employees, the company may fail to meet the goal of liquidity. Both goals must be met if a company is to survive and be successful.

Discussion Question: What is the difference between profitability and liquidity? **Answer:** Profitability means earning enough income to attract and hold investment capital; liquidity means being able to pay debts when they fall due.

All businesses pursue their goals by engaging in similar activities. First, each business must engage in **financing activities** to obtain adequate funds, or capital, to begin and to continue operating. Financing activities include obtaining capital from owners and from creditors, such as banks and suppliers. They also include repaying creditors and paying a return to the owners. Second, each business must engage in **investing activities** to spend the capital it receives in ways that are productive and will help the business achieve its objectives. Investing activities include buying land, buildings, equipment, and other resources that are needed in the operation of the business, and selling these resources when they are no longer needed. Third, each business must engage in **operating activities**. In addition to the selling of goods and services to customers, operating activities include such actions as employing managers and workers, buying and producing goods and services, and paying taxes to the government.

The cash flow icon highlights discussion in the text of cash as a measure of liquidity.

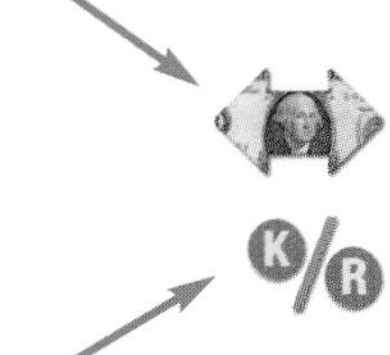

The key ratio icon highlights discussion of a measure used to evaluate the performance of a company.

An important function of accounting is to provide **performance measures**, which indicate whether managers are achieving their business goals and whether the business activities are well managed. It is important that these performance measures align with the goals of the business. For example, earned income is a measure of profitability and cash flow is a measure of liquidity. Ratios of accounting measures are also used as performance measures. For instance, one performance measure for operating activities might be the ratio of expenses to the revenue of the business. A performance measure for financing activities might be the ratio of money owed by the business to total resources controlled by the company. Because managers are usually evaluated on whether targeted levels of specific performance measures are achieved, they must have a knowledge of accounting to understand how they are evaluated and how they can improve their performance. Further, because managers will act to achieve the targeted performance measures, these measures must be crafted in such a way as to motivate managers to take actions that are in the best interests of the owners of the business.

Financial and Management Accounting

The hot links to real companies icon highlights hot links to the Internet through the Needles Accounting Resource Center at http://college.hmco.com.

Accounting's role of assisting decision makers by measuring, processing, and communicating information is usually divided into the categories of management accounting and financial accounting. Although there is considerable overlap in the functions of management accounting and financial accounting, the two can be distinguished by who the principal users of their information will be. **Management accounting** provides internal decision makers, who are charged with achieving the goals of profitability and liquidity, with information about financing, investing, and operating activities. Managers and employees, who conduct the activities of the business, need information that tells them how they have done in the past and what they can expect in the future. For example, The Gap, a retail clothing business, needs an operating report on each mall outlet that tells how much was sold at that outlet and what costs were incurred. It needs a budget for each outlet that projects the sales and costs for the next year. **Financial accounting** generates reports and communicates them to external decision makers so that they can evaluate how well the business has achieved its goals. These reports to external users are called **financial statements**. The Gap, for instance, will send its financial statements to its owners (called *stockholders*), its banks and other creditors, and government regulators. Financial statements report directly on the goals of profitability and liquidity and

Focus on Business Practice

A study of chief executive officer bonus contracts shows that almost all companies use financial measures for determining annual bonuses. The most frequent measures are earnings per share, net income, operating income, return on equity, and cash flow. About one-third of the companies studied also use nonfinancial measures to determine bonuses. Examples of nonfinancial measures are customer satisfaction, product or service quality, nonfinancial strategic objectives, efficiency or productivity, and employee safety.[4]

Focus on Business boxes highlight the relevance of accounting in four different areas: practice, technology, ethics, and international.

FOCUS ON BUSINESS PRACTICE

Microsoft Corporation projects its performance in meeting the major business objectives in its annual report.[5]

Liquidity: "Management believes existing cash and short-term investments together with funds generated from operations will be sufficient to meet operating requirements ."

Profitability: "Because of the fixed nature of a significant portion of operating expenses, coupled with the possibility of slower revenue growth, operating margins [profitability] in 2001 may decrease from those in 2000."

Microsoft's main business activities are shown at the right.

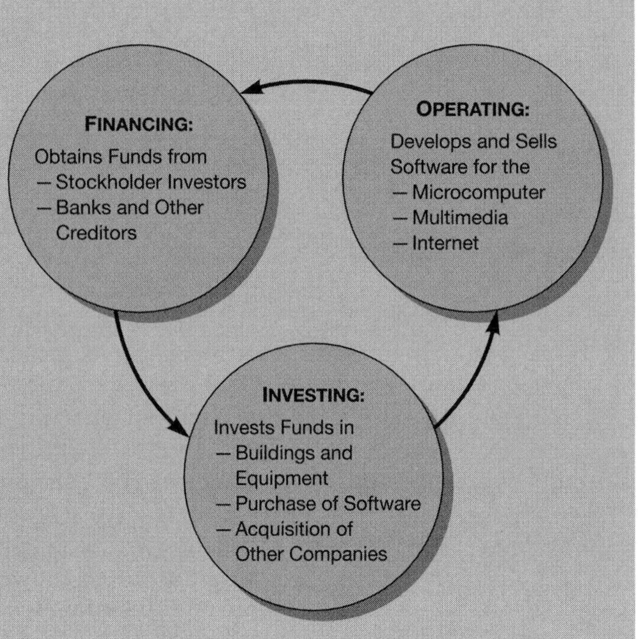

are used extensively both inside and outside a business to evaluate the business's success. It is important for every person involved with a business to understand financial statements. They are a central feature of accounting and are the primary focus of this book.

Processing Accounting Information

Teaching Note: Students often have difficulty distinguishing between accounting and bookkeeping. Perhaps a Venn diagram showing bookkeeping as a small circle within a much larger circle identified as accounting can help make the distinction.

To avoid misunderstandings, it is important to distinguish accounting itself from the ways in which accounting information is processed by bookkeeping, the computer, and management information systems.

People often fail to understand the difference between accounting and bookkeeping. **Bookkeeping** is the process of recording financial transactions and keeping financial records. Mechanical and repetitive, bookkeeping is only a small—but important—part of accounting. Accounting, on the other hand, includes the design of an information system that meets the user's needs. The major goals of accounting are the analysis, interpretation, and use of information.

Point to Emphasize: Computerized accounting information is only as reliable and useful as the data input into the system. The accountant must have a thorough understanding of the concepts that underlie accounting to ensure the data's reliability and usefulness.

The **computer** is an electronic tool that is used to collect, organize, and communicate vast amounts of information with great speed. Accountants were among the earliest and most enthusiastic users of computers, and today they use microcomputers in all aspects of their work. It may appear that the computer is doing the accountant's job; in fact, it is only a tool that is instructed to do routine bookkeeping and to perform complex calculations.

With the widespread use of the computer today, a business's many information needs are organized into what is called a **management information system (MIS)**. A management information system consists of the interconnected subsystems that provide the information needed to run a business. The accounting information system is the most important subsystem because it plays the key role of managing the flow of economic data to all departments within a business and to interested parties outside the business.

Decision Makers: The Users of Accounting Information

OBJECTIVE

2 Identify the many users of accounting information in society

Related Text Assignments:
Q: 5, 6, 7, 8, 9
E: 1
SD: 1, 4

The people who use accounting information to make decisions fall into three categories: (1) those who manage a business; (2) those outside a business enterprise who have a direct financial interest in the business; and (3) those people, organizations, and agencies that have an indirect financial interest in the business, as shown in Figure 3. These categories apply to government and not-for-profit organizations as well as to profit-oriented ventures.

Management

Instructional Strategy: Assign SD 4 for homework. Change to require a half-page written answer. Discuss in class.

Enrichment Note: Management is an *internal* user that requires its own set of accounting information.

Management, collectively, is the people who have overall responsibility for operating a business and for meeting its profitability and liquidity goals. In a small business, management may include the owners. In a large business, management more often consists of people who have been hired. Managers must decide what to do, how to do it, and whether the results match their original plans. Successful managers consistently make the right decisions based on timely and relevant information. To make good decisions, managers need answers to such questions as: What was the company's net income during the past quarter? Is the rate of return to the owners adequate? Does the company have enough cash? Which products are most profitable? What is the cost of manufacturing each product? Because so many key decisions are based on accounting data, management is one of the most important users of accounting information.

In carrying out its decision-making process, management performs a set of functions that are essential to the operation of the business. Although larger businesses will have more elaborate operations, the same basic functions must be accomplished in businesses of all sizes. Each requires accounting information for decision making. The basic management functions are:

Financing the business Financial management obtains financial resources so that the company can begin and continue operating.

Investing the resources of the business Asset management invests the financial resources of the business in productive assets that support the company's goals.

Figure 3
The Users of Accounting Information

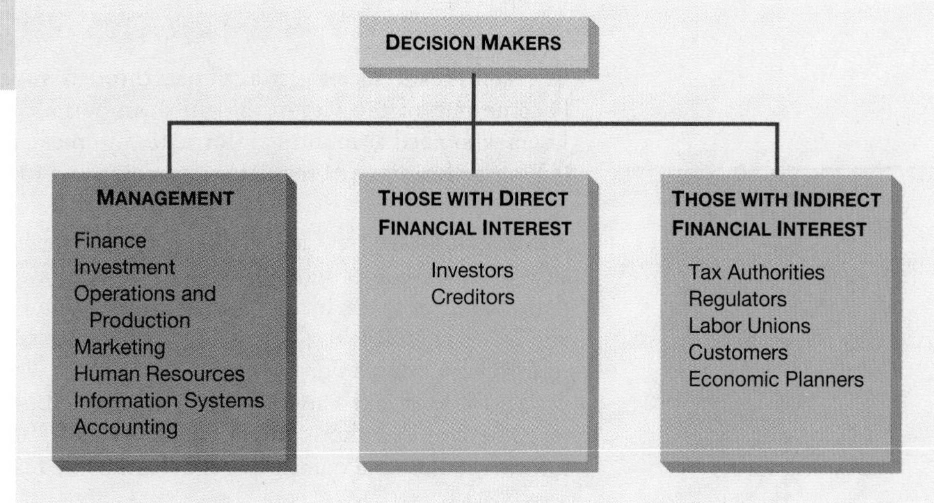

Teaching Note: An interesting way to present this learning objective is to ask your students to name the many users of financial information while you list them on the board or on an overhead transparency. Students should understand that the list in Figure 3 is not meant to be exhaustive.

Producing goods and services Operations and production management develops and produces products and services.

Marketing goods and services Marketing management sells, advertises, and distributes goods and services.

Managing employees Human resource management encompasses the hiring, evaluation, and compensation of employees.

Providing information to decision makers Information systems management captures data about all aspects of the company's operations, organizes the data into usable information, and provides reports to internal managers and appropriate outside parties. Accounting plays a key role in this function.

Users with a Direct Financial Interest

Point to Emphasize: The primary external users of accounting information are investors and creditors.

Another group of decision makers who need accounting information are those with a direct financial interest in a business. They depend on accounting to measure and report information about how a business has performed. Most businesses periodically publish a set of general-purpose financial statements that report their success in meeting the goals of profitability and liquidity. These statements show what has happened in the past, and they are important indicators of what will happen in the future. Many people outside the company carefully study these financial reports. The two most important outside groups are investors and creditors.

INVESTORS Those who invest or may invest in a business are interested in its past performance and its potential earnings. A thorough study of a company's financial statements helps potential investors judge the prospects for a profitable investment. After investing in a company, investors must continually review their commitment. To accomplish this, they again examine the company's financial statements.

CREDITORS Most companies borrow money for both long- and short-term operating needs. Creditors, those who lend money or deliver goods and services before being paid, are interested mainly in whether a company will have the cash to pay interest charges and repay debt at the appropriate time. They study a company's liquidity and cash flow as well as its profitability. Banks, finance companies, mortgage companies, securities firms, insurance firms, suppliers, and other lenders must analyze a company's financial position before they make a loan.

Users with an Indirect Financial Interest

In recent years, society as a whole, through government and public groups, has become one of the largest and most important users of accounting information. Users who need accounting information to make decisions on public issues include (1) tax authorities, (2) regulatory agencies, and (3) other groups.

TAX AUTHORITIES Government at every level is financed through the collection of taxes. Under federal, state, and local laws, companies and individuals pay many kinds of taxes, including federal, state, and city income taxes; social security and other payroll taxes; excise taxes; and sales taxes. Each tax requires special tax returns, and often a complex set of records as well. Proper reporting is generally a matter of law and can be very complicated. The Internal Revenue Code, for instance, contains thousands of rules governing the preparation of the accounting information used in computing federal income taxes.

Focus on Business Practice

John Connors, corporate controller of Microsoft, emphasizes that providing information to decision makers is an important accounting function, as follows:

The way I look at it, the controller's principal job is providing information that the business needs to make good decisions. . . . The real purpose is getting the information that managers need to do their jobs better, whether it is in sales and marketing, research and development, in the support groups, or operations.[6]

Regulatory Agencies Most companies must report periodically to one or more regulatory agencies at the federal, state, and local levels. For example, all public corporations must report periodically to the **Securities and Exchange Commission (SEC)**. This body, which was set up by Congress to protect the public, regulates the issuing, buying, and selling of stocks in the United States. Companies that are listed on a stock exchange also must meet the special reporting requirements of their exchange.

Other Groups Labor unions study the financial statements of corporations as part of preparing for contract negotiations. A company's income and costs often play an important role in these negotiations. Those who advise investors and creditors—financial analysts and advisers, brokers, underwriters, lawyers, economists, and the financial press—also have an indirect interest in the financial performance and prospects of a business. Consumer groups, customers, and the general public have become more concerned about the financing and earnings of corporations as well as the effects that corporations have on inflation, the environment, social problems, and the quality of life. Economic planners, among them members of the President's Council of Economic Advisers and the Federal Reserve Board, use aggregated accounting information to set economic policies and to evaluate economic programs.

Government and Not-for-Profit Organizations

More than 30 percent of the U.S. economy is generated by government and not-for-profit organizations (hospitals, universities, professional organizations, and charities). The managers of these diverse entities need to understand and to use accounting information to perform the same functions as managers in businesses. They need to raise funds from investors, creditors, taxpayers, and donors, and to deploy scarce resources. They need to plan to pay for operations and repay creditors on a timely basis. Moreover, they have an obligation to report their financial performance to legislators, boards, and donors, as well as to deal with tax authorities, regulators, and labor unions. Although most of the examples throughout this text focus on business enterprises, the same basic principles apply to government and not-for-profit organizations.

Accounting Measurement

OBJECTIVE

3 Explain the importance of business transactions, money measure, and separate entity to accounting measurement

Accounting is an information system that measures, processes, and communicates financial information. In this section, you begin the study of the measurement aspects of accounting. Here you learn what accounting actually measures and study the effects of certain transactions on a company's financial position.

To make an accounting measurement, the accountant must answer four basic questions:

1. What is measured?
2. When should the measurement be made?

Related Text Assignments:
Q: 10
SE: 1
E: 2, 3, 4
SD: 2

Terminology Note: *Measurement* means the analysis of transactions in terms of recognition, valuation, and classification. That is, it answers the question: How is this transaction best represented in the accounting records?

3. What value should be placed on what is measured?
4. How should what is measured be classified?

All these questions deal with basic assumptions and generally accepted accounting principles, and their answers establish what accounting is and what it is not. Accountants in industry, professional associations, public accounting, government, and academic circles debate the answers to these questions constantly, and the answers change as new knowledge and practice require. But the basis of today's accounting practice rests on a number of widely accepted concepts and conventions, which are described in this book. We begin by focusing on the first question: What is measured?

What Is Measured?

The world contains an unlimited number of things to measure and ways to measure them. For example, consider a machine that makes bottle caps. How many measurements of this machine could you make? You might start with size and then go on to location, weight, cost, or many other units of measurement. Some of these measurements are relevant to accounting; some are not. Every system must define what it measures, and accounting is no exception. Basically, financial accounting uses money measures to gauge the impact of business transactions on separate business entities. The concepts of business transactions, money measure, and separate entity are discussed in the next sections.

Business Transactions as the Object of Measurement

Business transactions are economic events that affect the financial position of a business entity. Business entities can have hundreds or even thousands of transactions every day. These business transactions are the raw material of accounting reports.

Common Student Confusion: Students already have a feel for what a business transaction is, but they probably do not know the difference between an exchange transaction and a nonexchange transaction.

A transaction can be an exchange of value (a purchase, sale, payment, collection, or loan) between two or more independent parties. A transaction also can be an economic event that has the same effect as an exchange transaction but does not involve an exchange. Some examples of "nonexchange" transactions are losses from fire, flood, explosion, and theft; physical wear and tear on machinery and equipment; and the day-by-day accumulation of interest.

To be recorded, a transaction must relate directly to a business entity. For example, suppose a customer buys a shovel from Ace Hardware but has to buy a hoe from a competing store because Ace is out of hoes. The transaction in which the shovel was sold is entered in Ace's records. However, the purchase of the hoe from the competitor is not entered in Ace's records because even though it indirectly affects Ace economically, it does not involve a direct exchange of value between Ace and the customer.

Money Measure

All business transactions are recorded in terms of money. This concept is termed **money measure**. Of course, information of a nonfinancial nature may be recorded, but it is through the recording of monetary amounts that the diverse transactions and activities of a business are measured. Money is the only factor that is common to all business transactions, and thus it is the only practical unit of measure that can produce financial data that are alike and can be compared.

The monetary unit a business uses depends on the country in which the business resides. For example, in the United States, the basic unit of money is the dol-

A table gives factual information referred to in the text.

Table 1. Partial Listing of Foreign Exchange Rates

Country	Price in $ U.S.	Country	Price in $ U.S.
Australia (dollar)	0.559	Hong Kong (dollar)	0.128
Brazil (real)	0.55	Japan (yen)	0.009
Britain (pound)	1.438	Mexico (peso)	0.10
Canada (dollar)	0.677	Russia (ruble)	0.359
Europe (euro)	0.871	Singapore (dollar)	0.577

Source: Data from *The Wall Street Journal,* September 7, 2000.

Point to Emphasize: The common unit of measurement in the United States for financial reporting purposes is the dollar.

lar. In Japan, it is the yen; in Europe, the euro; and in the United Kingdom, the pound. If there are transactions between countries, exchange rates must be used to translate from one currency to another. An **exchange rate** is the value of one currency in terms of another. For example, a British person purchasing goods from a U.S. company and paying in U.S. dollars must exchange British pounds for U.S. dollars before making payment. In effect, the currencies are goods that can be bought and sold. Table 1 illustrates the exchange rates for several currencies in dollars. It shows the exchange rate for British pounds as $1.438 per pound on a particular date. Like the prices of most goods or services, these prices change daily according to supply and demand for the currencies. For example, a few years earlier the exchange rate for British pounds was $1.64. Although our discussion in this book focuses on dollars, selected examples and certain assignments will be in foreign currencies.

The Concept of Separate Entity

Teaching Note: At this point, most students do not realize that there is a difference between separate *legal* entity and separate *economic* entity. Make the distinction, and emphasize that for accounting purposes a business is *always* separate and distinct from its owners, creditors, and customers.

For accounting purposes, a business is a **separate entity**, distinct not only from its creditors and customers but also from its owner or owners. It should have a completely separate set of records, and its financial records and reports should refer only to its own financial affairs.

For example, the Jones Florist Company should have a bank account that is separate from the account of Kay Jones, the owner. Kay Jones may own a home, a car, and other property, and she may have personal debts, but these are not the Jones Florist Company's resources or debts. Kay Jones also may own another business, say a stationery shop. If she does, she should have a completely separate set of records for each business.

Forms of Business Organization

OBJECTIVE

4 Identify the three basic forms of business organization

Related Text Assignments:
Q: 11
E: 3

There are three basic forms of business organization: sole proprietorships, partnerships, and corporations. Accountants recognize each form as an economic unit separate from its owners, although legally only the corporation is considered separate from its owners. Other legal differences among the three forms are summarized in Table 2 and discussed briefly in the following sections. In this book, we begin with accounting for the sole proprietorship because it is the simplest form of accounting. At critical points, however, we call attention to its essential differences from accounting for partnerships and corporations.

Table 2. Comparative Features of the Forms of Business Organization

	Sole Proprietorship	Partnership	Corporation
1. Legal status	Not a separate legal entity	Not a separate legal entity	Separate legal entity
2. Risk of ownership	Owner's personal resources at stake	Partners' personal resources at stake	Limited to investment in corporation
3. Duration or life	Limited by choice or death of owner	Limited by choice or death of any partner	Indefinite, possibly unlimited
4. Transferability of ownership	Sale by owner establishes new company	Changes in any partner's percentage of interest requires new partnership	Transferable by sale of stock
5. Accounting treatment	Separate economic unit	Separate economic unit	Separate economic unit

Sole Proprietorships

Point to Emphasize: In many ways, a sole proprietorship and a partnership are alike. A corporation, however, is very different from the other two forms of business organization.

A **sole proprietorship** is a business that is owned by one person and is not incorporated. This form of organization gives the individual a means of controlling the business apart from his or her personal interests. Legally, however, the proprietorship is the same economic unit as the individual. The individual receives all profits or losses and is liable for all obligations of the business. Proprietorships represent the largest number of businesses in the United States, but they transact far less business in dollar terms than do corporations. In addition, they are typically the smallest in size. The life of a sole proprietorship ends when the owner wants it to or when the owner dies or becomes incapacitated.

Partnerships

Point to Emphasize: A key disadvantage of the partnership is the unlimited liability of its owners. Unlimited liability can be avoided by organizing the business as a corporation.

A **partnership** is like a proprietorship in most ways except that it has more than one owner. A partnership is not a legal entity separate from the owner; it is an unincorporated association that brings together the talents and resources of two or more people. The partners share the profits and losses of the partnership according to an agreed-upon formula. Generally, any partner can bind the partnership to another party, and, if necessary, the personal resources of each partner can be called on to pay the obligations of the partnership. In some cases, one or more partners limit their liability, but at least one partner must have unlimited liability. A partnership must be dissolved when ownership changes—for example, when a partner leaves or dies. For the business to continue as a partnership, a new partnership must be formed.

Point to Emphasize: In a sole proprietorship or partnership, the owners generally manage the business. In a corporation, however, there is a separation between ownership and management. The owners (stockholders) elect a board of directors, which appoints managers to run the daily operations of the business.

Corporations

A **corporation** is a business unit that is granted a state charter and is recognized as legally separate from its owners (the stockholders). The owners, whose ownership

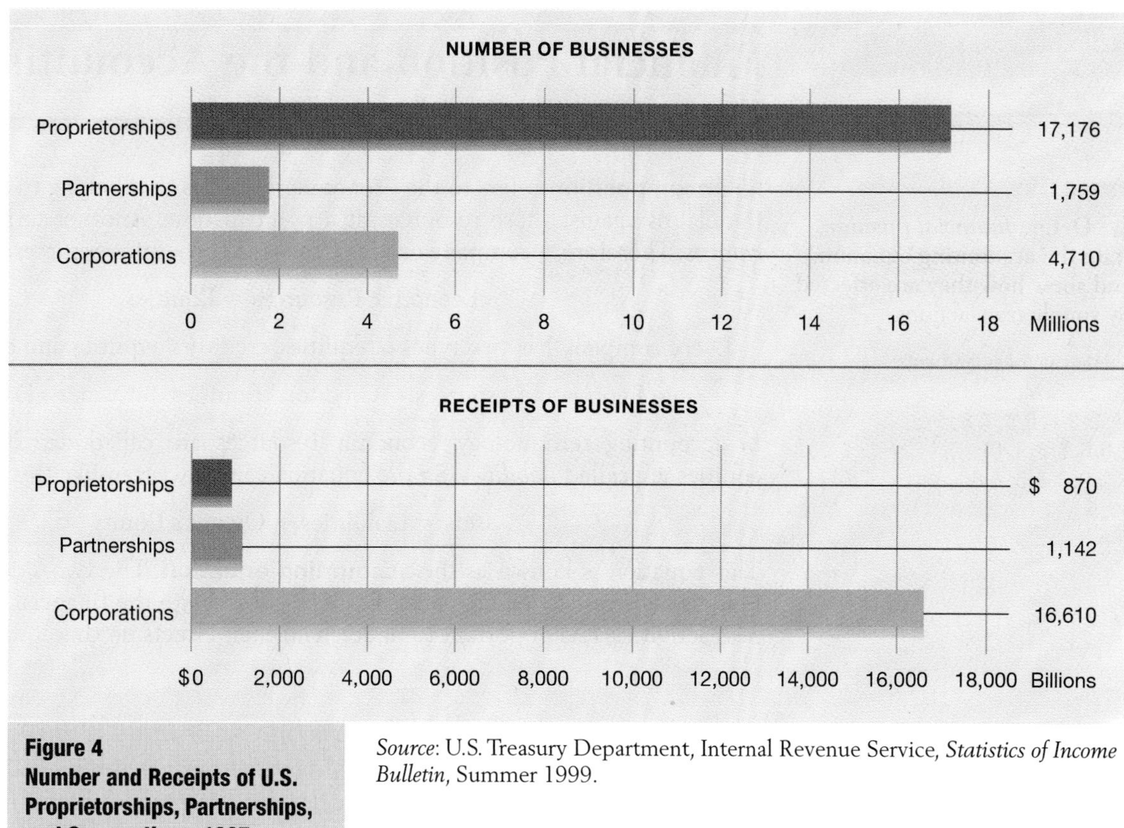

Figure 4
Number and Receipts of U.S. Proprietorships, Partnerships, and Corporations, 1997

Source: U.S. Treasury Department, Internal Revenue Service, *Statistics of Income Bulletin*, Summer 1999.

is represented by shares of stock in the corporation, do not control the operations of the corporation directly. Instead, they elect a board of directors, which appoints managers to run the corporation for the benefit of the stockholders. In exchange for limited involvement in the corporation's actual operations, stockholders enjoy limited liability. That is, their risk of loss is limited to the amount they paid for their shares. If they want, stockholders can sell their shares to other people, without affecting corporate operations. Because of this limited liability, stockholders often are willing to invest in riskier, but potentially more profitable, activities. Also, because ownership can be transferred without dissolving the corporation, the life of a corporation is unlimited; it is not subject to the whims or health of a proprietor or partner.

Corporations have several important advantages over proprietorships and partnerships that make them very efficient in amassing capital for the formation and growth of very large companies. Even though corporations are fewer in number than sole proprietorships and partnerships, they contribute much more to the U.S. economy in monetary terms (see Figure 4). For example, in 1999, General Motors generated more revenue than all but 30 of the world's countries.

Focus on Business Practice

Most people think of corporations as large national or global companies whose shares of stock are held by thousands of people and institutions. Indeed, corporations can be huge and have many stockholders. However, of the approximately 4.7 million corporations in the United States, only about 15,000 have stock that is publicly bought and sold. The vast majority of corporations are small businesses that are privately held by a few stockholders. In Illinois alone there are more than 250,000 corporations. For this reason, the study of corporations is just as relevant to small businesses as it is to large ones.

Financial Position and the Accounting Equation

OBJECTIVE

5 Define *financial position*, state the accounting equation, and show how they are affected by simple transactions

Related Text Assignments:
Q: 12, 13, 14, 15
SE: 2, 3, 4, 5, 6, 7, 8
E: 5, 6, 7, 8, 9, 10
P: 1, 2, 3, 5, 6, 7, 8
SD: 5
FRA: 5

Financial position refers to the economic resources that belong to a company and the claims against those resources at a point in time. Another term for claims is *equities*. Therefore, a company can be viewed as economic resources and equities:

Economic Resources = Equities

Every company has two types of equities, creditors' equities and owner's equity:

Economic Resources = Creditors' Equities + Owner's Equity

In accounting terminology, economic resources are called *assets* and creditors' equities are called *liabilities*. So the equation can be written like this:

Assets = Liabilities + Owner's Equity

This equation is known as the **accounting equation**. The two sides of the equation always must be equal, or "in balance." To evaluate the financial effects of business activities, it is important to understand their effects on this equation.

Assets

Teaching Note: An effective way to introduce assets, liabilities, and owner's equity is to set up a skeleton balance sheet and ask your students to provide examples of each. Explain that assets are the resources of a business, the essence of which is expected future benefits.

Assets are economic resources owned by a business that are expected to benefit future operations. Certain kinds of assets—for example, cash and money owed to the company by customers (called *accounts receivable*)—are monetary items. Other assets—inventories (goods held for sale), land, buildings, and equipment—are nonmonetary physical things. Still other assets—the rights granted by patents, trademarks, or copyrights—are nonphysical.

Liabilities

Point to Emphasize: A liability is a debt or obligation that is satisfied with the payment of cash or the performance of a service.

Liabilities are present obligations of a business to pay cash, transfer assets, or provide services to other entities in the future. Among these obligations are debts of the business, amounts owed to suppliers for goods or services bought on credit (called *accounts payable*), borrowed money (for example, money owed on loans payable to banks), salaries and wages owed to employees, taxes owed to the government, and services to be performed.

As debts, liabilities are claims recognized by law. That is, the law gives creditors the right to force the sale of a company's assets if the company fails to pay its debts. Creditors have rights over owners and must be paid in full before the owners receive anything, even if payment of a debt uses up all the assets of a business.

Owner's Equity

Owner's equity represents the claims by the owner to the assets of the business. It equals the residual interest, or *residual equity*, in the assets of an entity that remains after deducting the entity's liabilities. Theoretically, it is what would be left if all the liabilities were paid, and it is sometimes referred to as **net assets**. By rearranging the accounting equation, we can define owner's equity this way:

Owner's Equity = Assets − Liabilities

The four types of transactions that affect owner's equity are shown in Figure 5. Two of these transactions, **owner's investments** and **owner's withdrawals**, are

Figure 5
Four Types of Transactions That Affect Owner's Equity

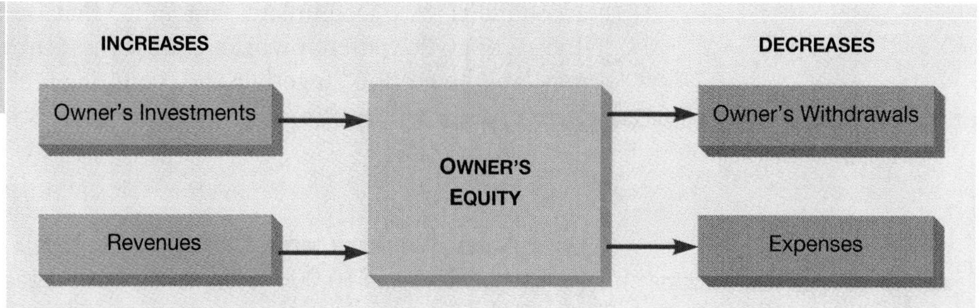

Teaching Note: A mnemonic for remembering which types of accounts affect owner's equity is *WIRE*: Withdrawals, Investments, Revenues, and Expenses.

assets that the owner either puts into the business or takes out of the business. For instance, if the owner of Shannon Realty, John Shannon, takes cash out of his personal bank account and deposits it in the business bank account, he has made an owner's investment. The assets (cash) of the business increase, and John Shannon's equity in those assets also increases. Conversely, if John Shannon takes cash out of the business bank account and deposits it in his personal bank account, he has made a withdrawal from the business. The assets of the business decrease, and John Shannon's equity in the business also decreases.

The other two types of transactions that affect owner's equity are revenues and expenses. Simply stated, **revenues** and **expenses** are the increases and decreases in owner's equity that result from operating a business. For example, the amount a customer pays (or agrees to pay in the future) to Shannon Realty in return for a service provided by the company is a revenue. The assets (cash or accounts receivable) of Shannon Realty increase, and the owner's equity in those assets also increases. On the other hand, the amount Shannon Realty pays out (or agrees to pay in the future) in the process of providing a service is an expense. Now the assets (cash) decrease or the liabilities (accounts payable) increase, and the owner's equity in the assets decreases.

Generally speaking, a company is successful if its revenues exceed its expenses. When revenues exceed expenses, the difference is called **net income**; when expenses exceed revenues, the difference is called **net loss**.

Some Illustrative Transactions

Let us now examine the effects of some of the most common business transactions on the accounting equation. Suppose that John Shannon opens a real estate agency called Shannon Realty on December 1. During December, his business engages in the transactions described in the following paragraphs.

Owner's Investments John starts his business by depositing $50,000 in a bank account in the name of Shannon Realty. The transfer of cash from his personal account to the business account is an owner's investment. The first balance sheet of the new company would show the asset Cash and the owner's equity (John Shannon, Capital):

Point to Emphasize: The account name is "John Shannon, Capital," not "Owner's Equity" because capital accounts show the equity attributed to the specific owner.

	Assets	=	Owner's Equity (OE)	
	Cash		John Shannon, Capital	Type of OE Transaction
1.	$50,000		$50,000	Owner's Investments

At this point, the company has no liabilities, and assets equal the owner's equity. The labels Cash and John Shannon, Capital are called **accounts** and are used by accountants to accumulate amounts that result from similar transactions. Transactions that affect owner's equity are identified by type so that similar types may later be grouped together on accounting reports.

Point to Emphasize: The purchase of an asset does not affect owner's equity.

PURCHASE OF ASSETS WITH CASH John finds a good location and pays cash to purchase a lot for $10,000 and a small building on the lot for $25,000. This transaction does not change the total assets, liabilities, or owner's equity of Shannon Realty, but it does change the composition of the assets—it decreases Cash and increases Land and Building:

	Assets			=	Owner's Equity	
	Cash	Land	Building		John Shannon, Capital	Type of OE Transaction
bal.	$50,000				$50,000	
2.	−35,000	+$10,000	+$25,000			
bal.	$15,000	$10,000	$25,000		$50,000	
		$50,000				

Point to Emphasize: Assets purchased on credit are recorded for the full amount at the time of the purchase.

PURCHASE OF ASSETS BY INCURRING A LIABILITY Assets do not always have to be purchased with cash. They may also be purchased on credit, that is, on the basis of an agreement to pay for them later. Suppose Shannon Realty buys some office supplies for $500 on credit. This transaction increases the assets (Supplies) and increases the liabilities of Shannon Realty. This liability is designated by an account called Accounts Payable:

	Assets				=	Liabilities	+	Owner's Equity	
	Cash	Supplies	Land	Building		Accounts Payable		John Shannon, Capital	Type of OE Transaction
bal.	$15,000		$10,000	$25,000				$50,000	
3.		+$500				+$500			
bal.	$15,000	$500	$10,000	$25,000		$500		$50,000	
		$50,500					$50,500		

Notice that this transaction increases both sides of the accounting equation to $50,500.

Point to Emphasize: Payment of a liability does not affect owner's equity or the asset purchased on credit.

PAYMENT OF A LIABILITY If Shannon Realty later pays $200 of the $500 owed for the supplies, both assets (Cash) and liabilities (Accounts Payable) decrease, but Supplies is unaffected:

Exhibit 2
Income Statement, Statement of Owner's Equity, Balance Sheet, and Statement of Cash Flows for Shannon Realty

Shannon Realty
Income Statement
For the Month Ended December 31, 20xx

Revenues		
Commissions Earned		$3,500
Expenses		
Equipment Rental Expense	$1,000	
Wages Expense	400	
Utilities Expense	300	
Total Expenses		1,700
Net Income		$1,800

Shannon Realty
Statement of Owner's Equity
For the Month Ended December 31, 20xx

John Shannon, Capital, December 1, 20xx		$ 0
Add: Investments by John Shannon	$50,000	
Net Income for the Month	1,800	51,800
Subtotal		$51,800
Less Withdrawals by John Shannon		600
John Shannon, Capital, December 31, 20xx		$51,200

Shannon Realty
Statement of Cash Flows
For the Month Ended December 31, 20xx

Cash Flows from Operating Activities		
Net Income		$ 1,800
Noncash Expenses and Revenues Included in Income		
Increase in Accounts Receivable	($ 1,000)*	
Increase in Supplies	(500)	
Increase in Accounts Payable	600	(900)
Net Cash Flows from Operating Activities		$ 900
Cash Flows from Investing Activities		
Purchase of Land	($10,000)	
Purchase of Building	(25,000)	
Net Cash Flows from Investing Activities		(35,000)
Cash Flows from Financing Activities		
Investments by John Shannon	$50,000	
Withdrawals by John Shannon	(600)	
Net Cash Flows from Financing Activities		49,400
Net Increase (Decrease) in Cash		$15,300
Cash at Beginning of Month		0
Cash at End of Month		$15,300

*Parentheses indicate a negative impact or cash outflow.

Shannon Realty
Balance Sheet
December 31, 20xx

Assets		**Liabilities**	
Cash	$15,300	Accounts Payable	$ 600
Accounts Receivable	1,000		
Supplies	500	**Owner's Equity**	
Land	10,000	John Shannon, Capital	51,200
Building	25,000		
Total Assets	$51,800	Total Liabilities and Owner's Equity	$51,800

Point to Emphasize: Notice the sequence in which these financial statements must be prepared. Stress that the statement of owner's equity is a link between the income statement and the balance sheet and that the statement of cash flows is prepared last.

Instructional Strategy: Create a game with rewards. Divide the class into small groups and assign P 4 or E 13. The first group to complete the problem correctly wins. Prizes may include 1 or 2 extra points added to a quiz or test score, chocolate bars, novelty erasers, and such. If E 13 was done for homework, use of P 4 in this activity will reinforce learning. Another idea: Use FRA 1 for this activity.

shown in Exhibit 1. It is assumed that the time period covered is the month of December 20xx. Notice that each statement is headed in a similar way. Each heading identifies the company and the kind of statement. The income statement, the statement of owner's equity, and the statement of cash flows give the time period to which they apply; the balance sheet gives the specific date to which it applies. Much of this book deals with developing, using, and interpreting more complete versions of these basic statements.

Point to Emphasize: Businesses communicate financial information to decision makers in the form of four major financial statements.

The Income Statement

Terminology Note: The income statement is also called the *statement of earnings*, the *statement of operations*, or the *profit and loss statement*. Its purpose is to measure a company's performance over an accounting period.

The **income statement** summarizes the revenues earned and expenses incurred by a business over a period of time. Many people consider it the most important financial report because it shows whether or not a business achieved its profitability goal of earning an acceptable income. In Exhibit 2, Shannon Realty had revenues in the form of commissions earned of $3,500 ($2,000 of revenue earned on credit and $1,500 of cash). From this amount, total expenses of $1,700 were deducted (equipment rental expense of $1,000, wages expense of $400, and utilities expense of $300), to arrive at a net income of $1,800. To show that it applies to a period of time, the statement is dated "For the Month Ended December 31, 20xx."

The Statement of Owner's Equity

Terminology Note: The statement of owner's equity is also called the *capital statement*. It indicates changes in owner's capital over an accounting period.

The **statement of owner's equity** shows the change in the owner's capital over a period of time. In Exhibit 2, the beginning capital is zero because the company was started in this accounting period. During the month, John Shannon made an investment in the business of $50,000, and the company earned income (as shown on the income statement) of $1,800, for a total increase of $51,800. Deducted from this amount are the withdrawals for the month of $600, leaving an ending balance of $51,200 in the capital account.

The Balance Sheet

Terminology Note: The balance sheet is also called the *statement of financial position*. It represents two different views of a business: The left side shows the resources of the business; the right side shows who provided those resources (the creditors and the owner).

The purpose of a **balance sheet** is to show the financial position of a business on a certain date, usually the end of the month or year. For this reason, it often is called the *statement of financial position* and is dated as of a certain date. The balance sheet presents a view of the business as the holder of resources, or assets, that are equal to the claims against those assets. The claims consist of the company's liabilities and the owner's equity in the company. In Exhibit 2, Shannon Realty has several categories of assets, which total $51,800. These assets equal the total liabilities of $600 (Accounts Payable) plus the ending balance of owner's capital of $51,200. Notice that the owner's capital amount on the balance sheet comes from the ending balance on the statement of owner's equity.

The Statement of Cash Flows

Point to Emphasize: The purpose of the statement of cash flows is to explain the change in cash in terms of operating, investing, and financing activities over an accounting period. It provides valuable information that cannot be determined in an examination of the other three financial statements.

Whereas the income statement focuses on a company's profitability goal, the **statement of cash flows** is directed toward the company's liquidity goal. **Cash flows** are the inflows and outflows of cash into and out of a business. Net cash flows are the difference between the inflows and outflows. The statement of cash flows shows the cash produced by operating a business as well as important investing and financing transactions that take place during an accounting period. Exhibit 2 shows the statement of cash flows for Shannon Realty. Notice that the statement explains how the Cash account changed during the period. Cash increased by $15,300. Operating activities produced net cash flows of $900, and financing

Parenthetical Note: An entire chapter of this text is devoted to the statement of cash flows.

activities produced net cash flows of $49,400. Investing activities used cash flows of $35,000.

This statement is related directly to the other three statements. Notice that net income comes from the income statement and that investments by owners and withdrawals come from the statement of owner's equity. The other items in the statement represent changes in the balance sheet accounts: Accounts Receivable, Supplies, Accounts Payable, Land, and Building.

Generally Accepted Accounting Principles

OBJECTIVE

7 State the relationship of generally accepted accounting principles (GAAP) to financial statements and the independent CPA's report, and identify the organizations that influence GAAP

Related Text Assignments:
Q: 21, 22, 23
E: 1, 15

Point to Emphasize: Explain that GAAP are constantly evolving, that they are not like laws of science. They are designed to measure the performance of businesses accurately. They can be abused to make a company look better on paper than it really is.

To ensure that financial statements will be understandable to their users, a set of practices, called **generally accepted accounting principles (GAAP)**, has been developed to provide guidelines for financial accounting. Although the term has several meanings in the literature of accounting, perhaps this is the best definition: "Generally accepted accounting principles encompass the conventions, rules, and procedures necessary to define accepted accounting practice at a particular time."[7] In other words, GAAP arise from wide agreement on the theory and practice of accounting at a particular time. These "principles" are not like the unchangeable laws of nature found in chemistry or physics. They are developed by accountants and businesses to serve the needs of decision makers, and they can be altered as better methods evolve or as circumstances change.

In this book, we present accounting practice, or GAAP, as it is today. We also try to explain the reasons or theory on which the practice is based. Both theory and practice are important to the study of accounting. However, you should realize that accounting is a discipline that is always growing, changing, and improving. Just as years of research are necessary before a new surgical method or lifesaving drug can be introduced, it may take years for research and new discoveries in accounting to be commonly implemented. As a result, you may encounter practices that seem contradictory. In some cases, we point out new directions in accounting. Your instructor also may mention certain weaknesses in current theory or practice.

Financial Statements, GAAP, and the Independent CPA's Report

Enrichment Note: According to *Public Accounting Report*, the top-grossing U.S. accounting firm in 1999 was PricewaterhouseCoopers, but the firm with the most partners was Ernst & Young.

Financial statements are prepared by the management of a company and could be falsified for personal gain. All companies that sell ownership to the public and many companies that apply for sizable loans must have their financial statements audited by an independent certified public accountant. **Certified public accountants (CPAs)** are licensed by all states for the same reason that lawyers and doctors are—to protect the public by ensuring the quality of professional service. One important attribute of CPAs is independence: They have no financial or other compromising ties with the companies they audit. This gives the public confidence in their work. The firms listed in Table 3 employ about 25 percent of all CPAs.

Table 3. Large International Certified Public Accounting Firms

Firm	Home Office	Some Major Clients
Arthur Andersen	Chicago	ITT, Texaco, United Airlines
Deloitte & Touche	New York	General Motors, Procter & Gamble, Sears
Ernst & Young	New York	Coca-Cola, McDonald's, Amgen
KPMG	New York	General Electric, Xerox, BMW
PricewaterhouseCoopers	New York	Du Pont, IBM, Ford

The CD-ROM icon indicates that data for the company in the text is available on the Fingraph® CD-ROM.

Point to Emphasize: The purpose of an audit is to lend credibility to a set of financial statements. The auditor does *not* attest to the absolute accuracy of the published information or to the value of the company as an investment. All he or she renders is an opinion, based on appropriate testing, about the fairness of the presentation of the financial information.

Ethical Consideration: To lend credibility to the work of the independent auditor, the profession has developed a set of guidelines that dictate appropriate professional behavior. Known as the AICPA Code of Professional Ethics, the current guidelines were adopted in 1988 and are based on earlier standards. Learning Objective 8 covers the topic of ethics in detail.

An independent CPA performs an **audit**, which is an examination of a company's financial statements and the accounting systems, controls, and records that produced them. The purpose of the audit is to ascertain that the financial statements have been prepared in accordance with generally accepted accounting principles. If the independent accountant is satisfied that this standard has been met, his or her report contains the following language:

> In our opinion, the financial statements . . . present fairly, in all material respects . . . in conformity with generally accepted accounting principles.

This wording emphasizes the fact that accounting and auditing are not exact sciences. The framework of GAAP provides room for interpretation, and the application of GAAP necessitates the making of estimates. As a result, the auditor can render an opinion or judgment only that the financial statements *present fairly* or conform *in all material respects* to GAAP. The accountant's report does not preclude minor or immaterial errors that might exist in the financial statements. However, it does imply that on the whole, investors and creditors can rely on those statements.

Historically, auditors have enjoyed a strong reputation for competence and independence. As a result, banks, investors, and creditors are willing to rely on an auditor's opinion when deciding to invest in a company or to make loans to a firm that has been audited. The independent audit is an important factor in the worldwide growth of financial markets.

Organizations That Influence Current Practice

Common Student Confusion: Regarding the organizations that influence GAAP, most students are familiar with the IRS and perhaps the SEC but have difficulty distinguishing among the others and learning their acronyms. The more you can "bring these organizations to life," the more understanding students will have.

Point to Emphasize: The FASB is the primary source of GAAP.

Point to Emphasize: The AICPA is considered the primary organization of certified public accountants.

Enrichment Note: The SEC imposes its own strict set of regulations on the companies it regulates, based in part on the standards set by the FASB.

Clarification Note: The GASB is responsible for issuing standards for state and local governments, whereas the FASB is responsible for issuing financial accounting standards for all other entities.

Enrichment Note: The primary purpose of the tax law is to generate revenue for the operation of the government, not to measure business income.

Many organizations directly or indirectly influence GAAP and so influence much of what is in this book. The **Financial Accounting Standards Board (FASB)** is the most important body for developing and issuing rules on accounting practice. This independent body issues *Statements of Financial Accounting Standards*. The **American Institute of Certified Public Accountants (AICPA)** is the professional association of certified public accountants and influences accounting practice through the activities of its senior technical committees. The Securities and Exchange Commission (SEC) is an agency of the federal government that has the legal power to set and enforce accounting practices for companies whose securities are offered for sale to the general public. As such, it has enormous influence on accounting practice. The **Governmental Accounting Standards Board (GASB)**, which was established in 1984 under the same governing body as the Financial Accounting Standards Board, is responsible for issuing accounting standards for state and local governments.

With the growth of financial markets throughout the world, worldwide cooperation in the development of accounting principles has become a priority. The **International Accounting Standards Committee (IASC)** has approved more than 30 international standards, which have been translated into six languages.

U.S. tax laws that govern the assessment and collection of revenue for operating the federal government also influence accounting practice. Because a major source of the government's revenue is the income tax, these laws specify the rules for determining taxable income. These rules are interpreted and enforced by the **Internal Revenue Service (IRS)**. In some cases, these rules conflict with good accounting practice, but they still are an important influence on that practice. Businesses use certain accounting practices simply because they are required by the tax laws. Sometimes companies follow an accounting practice specified in the tax laws to take advantage of rules that can help them financially. Cases in which the tax laws affect accounting practice are noted throughout this book.

Professional Ethics and the Accounting Profession

OBJECTIVE

8 Define *ethics* and describe the ethical responsibilities of accountants

Related Text Assignments:
Q: 24
SD: 3

Instructional Strategy: Divide the class into small groups and assign each a different ethical dilemma from SD 3 to discuss. Each group will report the results of its discussion to the class and take questions from other students.

Ethical issues are discussed in each chapter; they relate to real business situations that require ethical judgments.

Enrichment Note: When a professional accountant is in willful violation of the code of professional ethics, he or she runs the risk of criminal penalties.

Enrichment Note: Professional accountants must avoid situations in which there is even the *appearance* of an impropriety.

Ethics is a code of conduct that applies to everyday life. It addresses the question of whether actions are right or wrong. Ethical actions are the product of individual decisions. You are faced with many situations involving ethical issues every day. Some may be potentially illegal—the temptation to take office supplies from your employer to use when you do homework, for example. Others are not illegal but are equally unethical—for example, deciding not to tell a fellow student who missed class that a test has been announced for the next class meeting.

When an organization is said to act ethically or unethically, it means that individuals within the organization have made a decision to act ethically or unethically. When a company uses false advertising, cheats customers, pollutes the environment, treats its employees poorly, or misleads investors by presenting false information in the financial statements, members of management and other employees have made a conscious decision to act unethically. In the same way, ethical behavior within a company is a direct result of the actions and decisions of the company's employees.

Professional ethics is a code of conduct that applies to the practice of a profession. Like the ethical conduct of a company, the ethical actions of a profession are a collection of individual actions. As members of a profession, accountants have a responsibility, not only to their employers and clients but to society as a whole, to uphold the highest ethical standards. Historically, accountants have been held in high regard. For example, a survey of over one thousand prominent people in business, education, and government ranked the accounting profession second only to the clergy as having the highest ethical standards.[8] It is the responsibility of every person who becomes an accountant to uphold the high standards of the profession, regardless of the field of accounting the individual enters.

To ensure that its members understand the responsibilities of being professional accountants, the AICPA and each state have adopted codes of professional conduct that must be followed by certified public accountants. Fundamental to these codes is responsibility to the public, including clients, creditors, investors, and anyone else who relies on the work of the certified public accountant. In resolving conflicts among these groups, the accountant must act with integrity, even to the sacrifice of personal benefit. **Integrity** means that the accountant is honest and candid, and subordinates personal gain to service and the public trust. The accountant must also be objective. **Objectivity** means that he or she is impartial and intellectually honest. Furthermore, the accountant must be independent. **Independence** means avoiding all relationships that impair or even appear to impair the accountant's objectivity.

One way in which the auditor of a company maintains independence is by having no direct financial interest in the company and by not being an employee of the company. The accountant must exercise **due care** in all activities, carrying out professional responsibilities with competence and diligence. For example, an accountant must not accept a job for which he or she is not qualified, even at the risk of losing a client to another firm, and careless work is not acceptable. These broad principles are supported by more specific rules that public accountants must follow. (For instance, with certain exceptions, client information must be kept strictly confidential.) Accountants who violate the rules can be disciplined or even suspended from practice.

A professional association, the **Institute of Management Accountants (IMA)**, has adopted the Code of Professional Conduct for Management Accountants. This ethical code emphasizes that management accountants have a responsibility to be competent in their jobs, to keep information confidential except when authorized or legally required to disclose it, to maintain integrity and avoid conflicts of interest, and to communicate information objectively and without bias.[9]

The Chapter Review restates each learning objective and its main ideas.

Chapter Review

REVIEW OF LEARNING OBJECTIVES

Check out ACE, a self-quizzing program on chapter content, at http://college.hmco.com.

1. **Define *accounting*, identify business goals and activities, and describe the role of accounting in making informed decisions.** Accounting is an information system that measures, processes, and communicates information, primarily financial in nature, about an identifiable entity for the purpose of making economic decisions. Management accounting focuses on the preparation of information primarily for internal decision making by management. Financial accounting is concerned with the development and use of accounting reports that are communicated to those external to the business organization as well as to management. Accounting is not an end in itself but a tool that provides the information that is necessary to make reasoned choices among alternative uses of scarce resources in the conduct of business and economic activities.

2. **Identify the many users of accounting information in society.** Accounting plays a significant role in society by providing information to managers of all institutions and to individuals with a direct financial interest in those institutions, including present or potential investors or creditors. Accounting information is also important to those with an indirect financial interest in the business—for example, tax authorities, regulatory agencies, and economic planners.

3. **Explain the importance of business transactions, money measure, and separate entity to accounting measurement.** To make an accounting measurement, the accountant must determine what is measured, when the measurement should be made, what value should be placed on what is measured, and how what is measured should be classified. Generally accepted accounting principles define the object of accounting measurement as business transactions that are measured in terms of money and are for separate entities. Relating these concepts, financial accounting uses money measure to gauge the impact of business transactions on a separate business entity.

4. **Identify the three basic forms of business organization.** The three basic forms of business organization are sole proprietorships, partnerships, and corporations. Legally, sole proprietorships, which are formed by one individual, and partnerships, which are formed by more than one individual, are not separate from their owners. In accounting, however, they are treated as separate. Corporations, whose ownership is represented by shares of stock, are separate entities for both legal and accounting purposes.

Want more review? The student study guide is a very thorough review of each learning objective, providing a detailed outline, true/false and multiple choice questions, and exercises. Answers are included. Ask for it at your bookstore.

5. **Define *financial position*, state the accounting equation, and show how they are affected by simple transactions.** Financial position is the economic resources that belong to a company and the claims against those

return unused supplies to Suburban Landscaping Company for a full credit of $25. When she brought back the rented lawn equipment, Suburban Landscaping also would return a deposit of $100 she had made in June. She owed Suburban Landscaping $260 for equipment rentals and supplies. In addition, she owed the students who had worked for her $50, and she still owed her father $350. Although Henderson feels she did quite well, she is not sure just how successful she was.

1. Prepare a balance sheet dated June 1 and one dated August 31 for Henderson Lawn Care Company.
2. Comment on the performance of Henderson Lawn Care Company by comparing the two balance sheets. Did the company have a profit or a loss? (Assume that Henderson used none of the company's assets for personal purposes.)
3. If Henderson wants to continue her business next summer, what kind of information from her recordkeeping system would help make it easier to tell whether or not she is earning a profit?

Financial Reporting and Analysis

Interpreting Financial Reports

FRA 1
LO 6 Nature of Cash, Assets, and Net Income

Using excerpts from business articles or annual reports of well-known companies, you are asked to extract relevant data, make computations, and interpret your results.

Charles Schwab Corporation is a rapidly growing financial services firm. Information for 1999 and 1998 adapted from the company's annual report is presented below.[12] (All numbers are in thousands.) Three students who were looking at Charles Schwab's annual report were overhead to make the following comments:

Student A: What a great year Charles Schwab had in 1999! The company earned net income of $7,034,671,000 because its total assets increased from $22,264,390,000 to $29,299,061,000.

Student B: But the change in total assets isn't the same as net income! The company had a net income of only $923,200,000 because cash increased from $1,155,928,000 to $2,079,128,000.

Charles Schwab
Condensed Balance Sheets
December 31, 1999 and 1998
(in thousands)

	1999	1998
Assets		
Cash	$ 2,079,128	$ 1,155,928
Other Assets	27,219,933	21,108,462
Total Assets	$29,299,061	$22,264,390
Liabilities		
Total Liabilities	$27,025,126	$20,835,768
Owner's Equity		
Owner's Capital	2,273,935	1,428,622
Total Liabilities and Owner's Equity	$29,299,061	$22,264,390

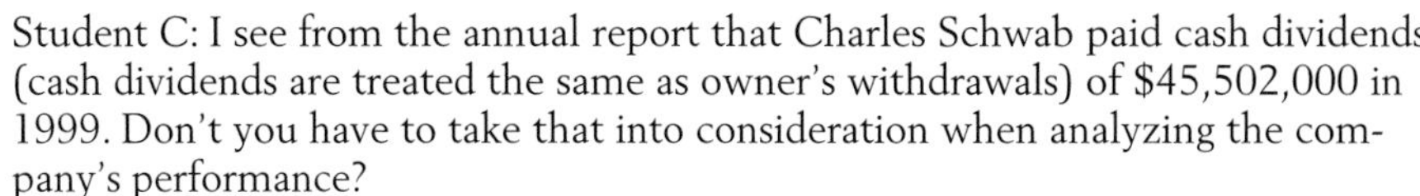

Student C: I see from the annual report that Charles Schwab paid cash dividends (cash dividends are treated the same as owner's withdrawals) of $45,502,000 in 1999. Don't you have to take that into consideration when analyzing the company's performance?

REQUIRED

1. Comment on the interpretations of Students A and B, and then answer Student C's question.
2. Calculate Charles Schwab's net income for 1999. (**Hint:** Reconstruct the statement of owner's equity.)

Group Activity: After discussing **1**, let groups compete to see which one can come up with the answer to **2** first.

International Company

FRA 2.
LO 1 The Goal of Profitability

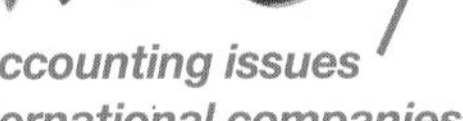

Explore accounting issues facing international companies.

The celebrated Danish toy company ***Lego Group*** reported its first loss since the 1930s in 1998. While its bright plastic bricks are famous around the globe, Lego is rapidly losing market share to computer and video games. The company's president said, "The Lego Group is not in critical condition, but action is needed. . . . We have to acknowledge that growth and innovation are not enough. We also have to be a profitable business."[13] Discuss the meaning of *profitability*. What other goal must a business achieve? Why is the goal of profitability important to Lego's president? What is the accounting measure of profitability, and on which statement is it determined?

Toys "R" Us Annual Report

FRA 3.
LO 6 The Four Financial Statements

Every financial chapter has a case on Toys "R" Us; the complete Toys "R" Us Annual Report for a recent year follows Chapter 6.

Refer to the Toys "R" Us annual report to answer the questions below. Keep in mind that every company, while following basic principles, adapts financial statements and terminology to its own special needs. Therefore, the complexity of the financial statements and the terminology in the Toys "R" Us statements will sometimes differ from those in the text. (Note that 2000 refers to the year ended January 29, 2000, and 1999 refers to the year ended January 30, 1999.)

1. What names does Toys "R" Us give its four basic financial statements? (Note that the use of the word "Consolidated" in the names of the financial statements means that these statements combine those of several companies owned by Toys "R" Us.)
2. Prove that the accounting equation works for Toys "R" Us on January 29, 2000, by finding the amounts for the following equation: Assets = Liabilities + Stockholders' Equity.
3. What were the total revenues of Toys "R" Us for the year ended January 29, 2000?
4. Was Toys "R" Us profitable in the year ended January 29, 2000? How much was net income (loss) in that year, and did it increase or decrease from the year ended January 30, 1999?
5. Did the company's cash and cash equivalents increase from January 30, 1999, to January 29, 2000? By how much? In what two places in the statements can this number be found or computed?
6. Did cash flows from operating activities, cash flows from investing activities, and cash flows from financing activities increase or decrease from 1999 to 2000?

Group Activity: Assign the above to in-class groups of three or four students. Set a time limit. The first group to answer all questions correctly wins.

Use the professional software Fingraph® to investigate annual reports and analyze financial data.

Fingraph® Financial Analyst™

FRA 4.
LO 1 Financial Statements,
LO 6 Business Activities, and Goals

Choose any company in the Fingraph® Financial Analyst™ CD-ROM software.

1. In the company's annual report, find a description of the business. What is the nature of the company's business? How would you describe its operating activities?

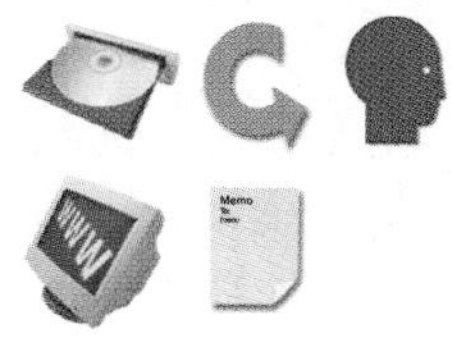

2. Find and identify the company's four basic financial statements. Which statement shows the resources of the business and the various claims to those resources? From the balance sheet, prove the balance sheet equation by showing that the company's assets equal its liabilities plus stockholders' equity. What is the company's largest category of assets? Which statement shows changes in all or part of the company's stockholders' equity during the year? Did the company pay any dividends in the last year?
3. Which statement is most closely associated with the company's profitability goal? How much net income did the company earn in the last year? Which statement is most closely associated with the company's liquidity goal? Did cash (and cash equivalents) increase in the last year? Which provided the most positive cash flows in the last year: operating, investing, or financing activities?
4. Prepare a one-page executive summary that highlights what you have learned from parts **1, 2,** and **3.** An executive summary is a short, easy-to-read report that emphasizes important information and conclusions by listing them by numbered paragraphs or bullet points.

Internet cases are accounting cases tailored to the Internet, based on concepts and applications from the chapter.

Internet Case

FRA 5.
LO 1 Financial Performance
LO 5 Comparison of Two High-Tech Companies

Microsoft Corporation and ***Intel, Inc.,*** are two of the most successful high-tech companies. Compare the two companies financial performance first by going to the Needles Accounting Resource Center web site at http://college.hmco.com and clicking on Intel under Chapter 1 companies. Utilizing the consolidated balance sheet and consolidated statement of income from the annual report, find the amount of total assets, revenues, and net income for the most recent year shown. Then compare these amounts to the same amounts for Microsoft shown in the first decision point of this chapter. Also compute net income to revenues and net income to total assets for both companies. Which company is larger? Which is more profitable?

Endnotes

1. Microsoft Corporation, *Annual Report*, 2000.
2. *Statement of Financial Accounting Concepts No. 1*, "Objectives of Financial Reporting by Business Enterprises" (Norwalk, Conn.: Financial Accounting Standards Board, 1978), par. 9.
3. Ibid.
4. Christopher D. Ittner, David F. Larcker, and Madhav V. Rajan, "The Choice of Performance Measures in Annual Bonus Contracts," *The Accounting Review*, April 1997.
5. Microsoft Corporation, *Annual Report*, 2000.
6. Kathy Williams and James Hart, "Microsoft: Tooling the Information Age," *Management Accounting*, May 1996, p. 42.
7. *Statement of the Accounting Principles Board No. 4*, "Basic Concepts and Accounting Principles Underlying Financial Statements of Business Enterprises" (New York: American Institute of Certified Public Accountants, 1970), par. 138.
8. Touche Ross & Co., "Ethics in American Business" (New York: Touche Ross & Co., 1988), p. 7.
9. *Statement Number IC*, "Standards of Ethical Conduct for Management Accountants" (Montvale, N.J.: Institute of Management Accountants, 1983, revised 1997).
10. J.C. Penney Company, Inc., *Annual Report*, 1995.
11. Southwest Airlines Co., *Annual Report*, 1996.
12. The Charles Schwab Corporation, *Annual Report*, 1999.
13. Robert Frank, "Facing a Loss, Lego Narrates a Sad Toy Story," *The Wall Street Journal*, January 22, 1999.

2 Measuring Business Transactions

LEARNING OBJECTIVES

1. Explain, in simple terms, the generally accepted ways of solving the measurement issues of recognition, valuation, and classification.
2. Describe the chart of accounts and recognize commonly used accounts.
3. Define *double-entry system* and state the rules for double entry.
4. Apply the steps for transaction analysis and processing to simple transactions.
5. Prepare a trial balance and describe its value and limitations.
6. Record transactions in the general journal.
7. Post transactions from the general journal to the ledger.

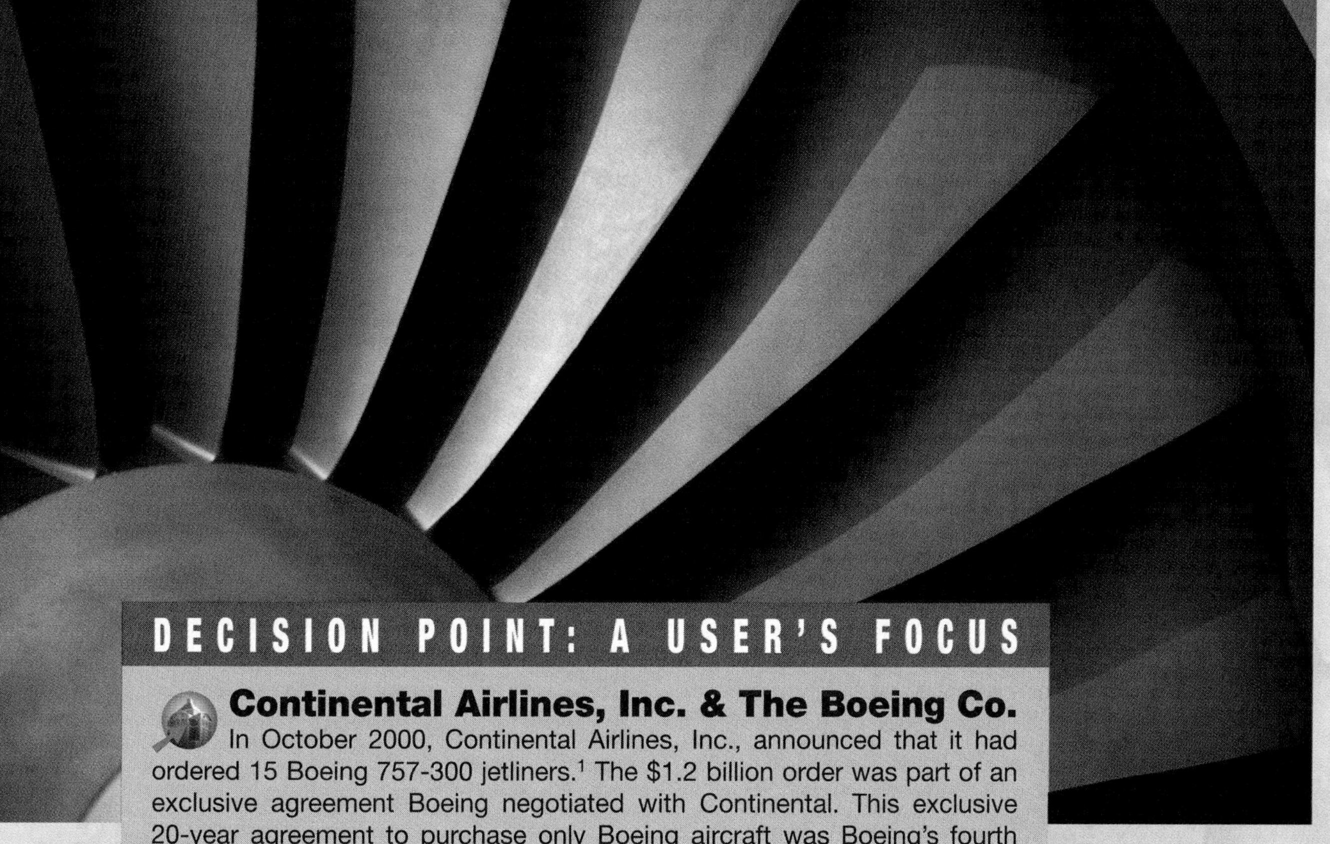

DECISION POINT: A USER'S FOCUS

Continental Airlines, Inc. & The Boeing Co.

In October 2000, Continental Airlines, Inc., announced that it had ordered 15 Boeing 757-300 jetliners.[1] The $1.2 billion order was part of an exclusive agreement Boeing negotiated with Continental. This exclusive 20-year agreement to purchase only Boeing aircraft was Boeing's fourth such agreement with a major airline and positioned the company favorably against Airbus, its European competitor. How should this important order have been recorded, if at all, in the records of Continental and Boeing? When should the purchase and sale that result from this order be recorded in the companies' records?

The order obviously was an important event, one with long-term consequences for both companies. But, as you will see in this chapter, it was not recorded in the accounting records of either company. At the time the order was placed, the aircraft were yet to be manufactured and would not begin to be delivered for several years. Even for "firm" orders, Boeing has cautioned that "an economic downturn could result in airline equipment requirements less than currently anticipated resulting in requests to negotiate the rescheduling or possible cancellation of firm orders."[2] The aircraft were not assets of Continental, and the company had not incurred a liability. No aircraft had been delivered or even built, so Continental was not obligated to pay at that point. And Boeing could not record any revenue until the aircraft were manufactured and delivered to Continental, and title to the aircraft shifted from Boeing to Continental. In fact, Boeing later experienced cancellation or extension of large previously firm orders from China because of the economic slowdown in Asia.[3]

To understand and use financial statements, it is important to know how to analyze events in order to determine the extent of their impact on those statements.

Point to Emphasize: Many students approach the topic of measurement (as well as accounting itself) as though it were fairly cut-and-dried. But they should realize that there are several ways to approach the recognition, valuation, and classification issues, only one of which, typically, follows GAAP. As shown in this Decision Point, the recognition issue is not always resolved easily.

Critical Thinking Question: How might other businesses use purchase orders? **Answer:** Purchase orders are common in business. Examples include a supermarket ordering inventory or an appliance repair shop ordering parts and supplies.

Measurement Issues

OBJECTIVE

1 Explain, in simple terms, the generally accepted ways of solving the measurement issues of recognition, valuation, and classification

Related Text Assignments:
Q: 1, 2, 3, 4, 5
SE: 1
E: 1, 2
P: 4, 7
SD: 1, 2, 3
FRA: 4

Business transactions are economic events that affect the financial position of a business entity. To measure a business transaction, the accountant must decide when the transaction occurred (the recognition issue), what value to place on the transaction (the valuation issue), and how the components of the transaction should be categorized (the classification issue).

These three issues—recognition, valuation, and classification—underlie almost every major decision in financial accounting today. They lie at the heart of accounting for pension plans, for mergers of giant companies, and for international transactions. In discussing the three basic issues, we follow generally accepted accounting principles and use an approach that promotes an understanding of the basic ideas of accounting. Keep in mind, however, that controversy does exist, and that solutions to some problems are not as cut-and-dried as they appear.

The Recognition Issue

Terminology Note: *Recognize* here means to record a transaction or event.

Point to Emphasize: A purchase should not be recognized (recorded) before title is transferred because, until that point, the vendor has not fulfilled its contractual obligation and the buyer has no liability.

Business-World Example: Recognition is also a problem for franchisers, such as McDonald's, which cannot record initial franchise fees until they have performed the agreed-on services.

The **recognition** issue refers to the difficulty of deciding when a business transaction should be recorded. Often the facts of a situation are known, but there is disagreement about *when* the event should be recorded. Suppose, for instance, that a company orders, receives, and pays for an office desk. Which of the following actions constitutes a recordable event?

1. An employee sends a purchase requisition to the purchasing department.
2. The purchasing department sends a purchase order to the supplier.
3. The supplier ships the desk.
4. The company receives the desk.
5. The company receives the bill from the supplier.
6. The company pays the bill.

The answer to this question is important because amounts in the financial statements are affected by the date on which a purchase is recorded. According to accounting tradition, the transaction is recorded when title to the desk passes from the supplier to the purchaser, creating an obligation to pay. Thus, depending on the details of the shipping agreement, the transaction is recognized (recorded) at the time of either action **3** or action **4.** This is the guideline that we generally use in this book. However, in many small businesses that have simple accounting systems, the transaction is not recorded until the bill is received (action **5**) or paid (action **6**) because these are the implied points of title transfer. The predetermined time at which a transaction should be recorded is the **recognition point**.

The recognition issue is not always easy to solve. Consider the case of an advertising agency that is asked by a client to prepare a major advertising campaign. People may work on the campaign several hours a day for a number of weeks. Value is added to the plan as the employees develop it. Should this added value be

FOCUS ON BUSINESS PRACTICE

Many companies include information on the recognition rules followed by the company in the "Summary of Significant Accounting Policies" section of their annual reports. For instance, Sun Microsystems Inc., the large supplier of networked workstations, servers, and other computer software and hardware, describes its revenue recognition rules as follows:

> *Sun generally recognizes revenues from hardware and software sales at the time of shipment. Service revenues are recognized ratably over the contractual period or as the services are provided.*[4]

recognized as the campaign is being produced or at the time it is completed? Normally, the increase in value is recorded at the time the plan is finished and the client is billed for it. However, if a plan is going to take a long period to develop, the agency and the client may agree that the client will be billed at key points during its development. A transaction is recorded at each billing.

The Valuation Issue

Enrichment Note: The value of a transaction usually is based on a business document—a canceled check or an invoice. In general, appraisals or other subjective amounts are not recorded.

Valuation is perhaps the most controversial issue in accounting. The **valuation** issue focuses on assigning a monetary value to a business transaction. Generally accepted accounting principles state that the appropriate value to assign to all business transactions—and therefore to all assets, liabilities, and components of owner's equity, including revenues and expenses, recorded by a business—is the original cost (often called *historical cost*).

Cost is defined here as the exchange price associated with a business transaction at the point of recognition. According to this guideline, the purpose of accounting is not to account for value in terms of worth, which can change after a transaction occurs, but to account for value in terms of cost at the time of the transaction. For example, the cost of an asset is recorded when the asset is acquired, and the value is held at that level until the asset is sold, expires, or is consumed. In this context, *value* means the cost at the time of the transaction. The practice of recording transactions at cost is referred to as the **cost principle**.

Suppose that a person offers a building for sale at $120,000. It may be valued for real estate taxes at $75,000, and it may be insured for $90,000. One prospective buyer may offer $100,000 for the building, and another may offer $105,000. At this point, several different, unverifiable opinions of value have been expressed. Finally, suppose the seller and a buyer settle on a price and complete the sale for $110,000. All of these figures are values of one kind or another, but only the selling price of $110,000 is sufficiently reliable to be used in the records. The market value of the building may vary over the years, but the building will remain on the new buyer's records at $110,000 until it is sold again. At that point, the accountant will record the new transaction at the new exchange price, and a profit or loss will be recognized. The cost principle is used because the cost is verifiable. It results from the actions of independent buyers and sellers who come to an agreement on price. An exchange price is an objective price that can be verified by evidence created at the time of the transaction. It is this final price, verified by agreement of the two parties, at which the transaction is recorded.

Focus on Business Practice

With many aspects of accounting, there are sometimes exceptions to the general rules. For instance, the cost principle is not followed in all parts of the financial statements. Investments, for example, are often accounted for at fair or market value because these investments are available for sale. The fair or market value is the best measure of the potential benefit to the company. Intel Corp., the large microprocessor company, states in its annual report:

A substantial majority of the company's marketable investments are classified as available-for-sale as of the balance sheet date and are reported at fair value.[5]

The Classification Issue

The **classification** issue has to do with assigning all the transactions in which a business engages to appropriate categories, or accounts. For example, a company's ability to borrow money can be affected by the way in which its debts are categorized. Or a company's income can be affected by whether purchases of small items such as tools are considered repair expenses (a component of owner's equity) or equipment (assets).

Not only are the accounting solutions related to recognition (when a transaction occurred), valuation (what value to place on the transaction), and classification (how the components of the transaction should be categorized) important for good financial reporting, but they are also designed to help a company's management fulfill its responsibilities to the owners and the public. Informix Corporation was one of the most successful software companies and was a serious challenger in the market for large corporate databases. However, when the public discovered that Informix Corporation was using a questionable application of the recognition principle, its stock price plummeted, the NASDAQ stock market began actions to delist the company, and some questioned whether it would ultimately survive. Its problems occurred when management disclosed that a substantial portion of the company's revenue came from shipments to resellers that had not been sold to the final user, bringing into question whether sales had actually occurred.[6]

Point to Emphasize: Assets, liabilities, and the components of owner's equity are not accounts, but account *classifications*. For example, Cash is a type of asset account, and Accounts Payable is a type of liability account.

Proper classification depends not only on correctly analyzing the effect of each transaction on the business but also on maintaining a system of accounts that reflects that effect. The rest of this chapter explains the classification of accounts and the analysis and recording of transactions.

Accounts and the Chart of Accounts

OBJECTIVE

2 Describe the chart of accounts and recognize commonly used accounts

Related Text Assignments:
Q: 6, 7, 8, 23
SE: 2
E: 3
FRA: 1, 5

In the measurement of business transactions, large amounts of data are gathered. These data require a method of storage. Businesspeople should be able to retrieve transaction data quickly and in usable form. In other words, there should be a filing system to sort out or classify all the transactions that occur in a business. This filing system consists of accounts. Recall that accounts are the basic storage units for accounting data and are used to accumulate amounts from similar transactions. An accounting system has a separate account for each asset, each liability, and each component of owner's equity, including revenues and expenses. Whether a company keeps records by hand or by computer, management must be able to refer to accounts so that it can study the company's financial history and plan for the future. A very small company may need only a few dozen accounts; a multinational corporation may need thousands.

In a manual accounting system, each account is kept on a separate page or card. These pages or cards are placed together in a book or file called the **general ledger**. In the computerized systems that most companies have today, accounts are maintained on magnetic tapes or disks. However, as a matter of convenience, accountants still refer to the group of company accounts as the *general ledger*, or simply the *ledger*.

Point to Emphasize: A chart of accounts is a table of contents for the ledger. The accounts typically are listed in the same order as they appear in the ledger, and the numbering scheme should allow for some flexibility.

To help identify accounts in the ledger and to make them easy to find, the accountant often numbers them. A list of these numbers with the corresponding account names is called a **chart of accounts**. A very simple chart of accounts appears in Exhibit 1. Notice that the first digit refers to the major financial statement classifications. An account number that begins with the digit 1 represents an asset, an account number that begins with a 2 represents a liability, and so forth.

Teaching Note: Explain that account names must be both concise and descriptive. Although some account names, such as Cash and Land, are commonly used, alternative account names may be encountered.

Teaching Note: Also explain that accounts are usually listed in the order in which they appear on the financial statements.

Common Student Confusion: Students frequently confuse the account Notes Receivable with the piece of paper called a *promissory note.* Also, they might not understand how notes receivable are assets for those who hold a note (it is a payment, not the note, that is a receivable). A visual demonstration should clear up any confusion.

Discussion Question: Why are prepaid expenses classified as an asset? **Answer:** Because they represent future benefits for which payment has already been made.

Common Student Confusion: At this point, many students do not know the difference between office supplies and office equipment. Explain that office supplies are consumed gradually, whereas office equipment remains intact.

Point to Emphasize: A liability is essentially a debt or obligation that is discharged with the disbursement of cash or with the performance of a service.

Discussion Question: In what way are unearned revenues the opposite of prepaid expenses? **Answer:** With unearned revenues (a liability), cash is *received* in advance of performance. With prepaid expenses (an asset), cash is *paid* in advance of receiving a service.

Exhibit 1
Chart of Accounts for a Small Business

Account Number	Account Name	Description
		Assets
111	Cash	Money and any medium of exchange, including coins, currency, checks, postal and express money orders, and money on deposit in a bank
112	Notes Receivable	Amounts due from others in the form of promissory notes (written promises to pay definite sums of money at fixed future dates)
113	Accounts Receivable	Amounts due from others for revenues or sales on credit (sales on account)
114	Fees Receivable	Amounts arising from services performed but not yet billed to customers
115	Art Supplies	Prepaid expense; art supplies purchased and not used
116	Office Supplies	Prepaid expense; office supplies purchased and not used
117	Prepaid Rent	Prepaid expense; rent paid in advance and not used
118	Prepaid Insurance	Prepaid expense; insurance purchased and not expired; unexpired insurance
141	Land	Property owned for use in the business
142	Buildings	Structures owned for use in the business
143	Accumulated Depreciation, Buildings	Sum of the periodic allocation of the cost of buildings to expense
144	Art Equipment	Art equipment owned for use in the business
145	Accumulated Depreciation, Art Equipment	Sum of the periodic allocation of the cost of art equipment to expense
146	Office Equipment	Office equipment owned for use in the business
147	Accumulated Depreciation, Office Equipment	Sum of the periodic allocation of the cost of office equipment to expense
		Liabilities
211	Notes Payable	Amounts due to others in the form of promissory notes
212	Accounts Payable	Amounts due to others for purchases on credit (purchases on account)
213	Unearned Art Fees	Unearned revenue; customer advances for artwork to be provided in future
214	Wages Payable	Amounts due to employees for wages earned and not paid
221	Mortgage Payable	Amounts due on loans that are backed by the company's property and buildings

(continued)

Exhibit 1
Chart of Accounts for a Small Business *(continued)*

Account Number	Account Name	Description
		Owner's Equity
311	Capital	Owner's investment in the company
312	Withdrawals	Assets withdrawn from the business by the owner for personal use
313	Income Summary	Temporary account used at the end of the accounting period to summarize revenues and expenses for the period
		Revenues
411	Advertising Fees Earned	Revenues derived from performing advertising services
412	Art Fees Earned	Revenues derived from performing art services
		Expenses
511	Wages Expense	Amounts earned by employees
512	Utilities Expense	Amounts for utilities, such as water, electricity, and gas, used
513	Telephone Expense	Amounts for telephone services used
514	Rent Expense	Amounts for rent on property and buildings used
515	Insurance Expense	Amounts for insurance expired
516	Art Supplies Expense	Amounts for art supplies used
517	Office Supplies Expense	Amounts for office supplies used
518	Depreciation Expense, Buildings	Amount of buildings' cost allocated to expense
519	Depreciation Expense, Art Equipment	Amount of art equipment costs allocated to expense
520	Depreciation Expense, Office Equipment	Amount of office equipment costs allocated to expense
521	Interest Expense	Amount of interest on debts

Point to Emphasize: Although withdrawals are a component of owner's equity, they normally appear only in the statement of owner's equity, not in the owner's equity section of the balance sheet. In addition, they do not appear as an expense on the income statement.

Point to Emphasize: Although revenues and expenses are components of owner's equity, they appear on the income statement, not in the owner's equity section of the balance sheet. Figure 1 illustrates this point.

The second and third digits refer to individual accounts. Notice the gaps in the sequence of numbers. These gaps allow the accountant to expand the number of accounts. The accounts shown in Exhibit 1 will be used in this chapter, as well as in the next two chapters, through the sample case of the Joan Miller Advertising Agency.

Owner's Equity Accounts

In the chart of accounts that appears in Exhibit 1, the revenue and expense accounts are separated from the other owner's equity accounts. The relationships of these accounts to each other and to the basic financial statements are illustrated

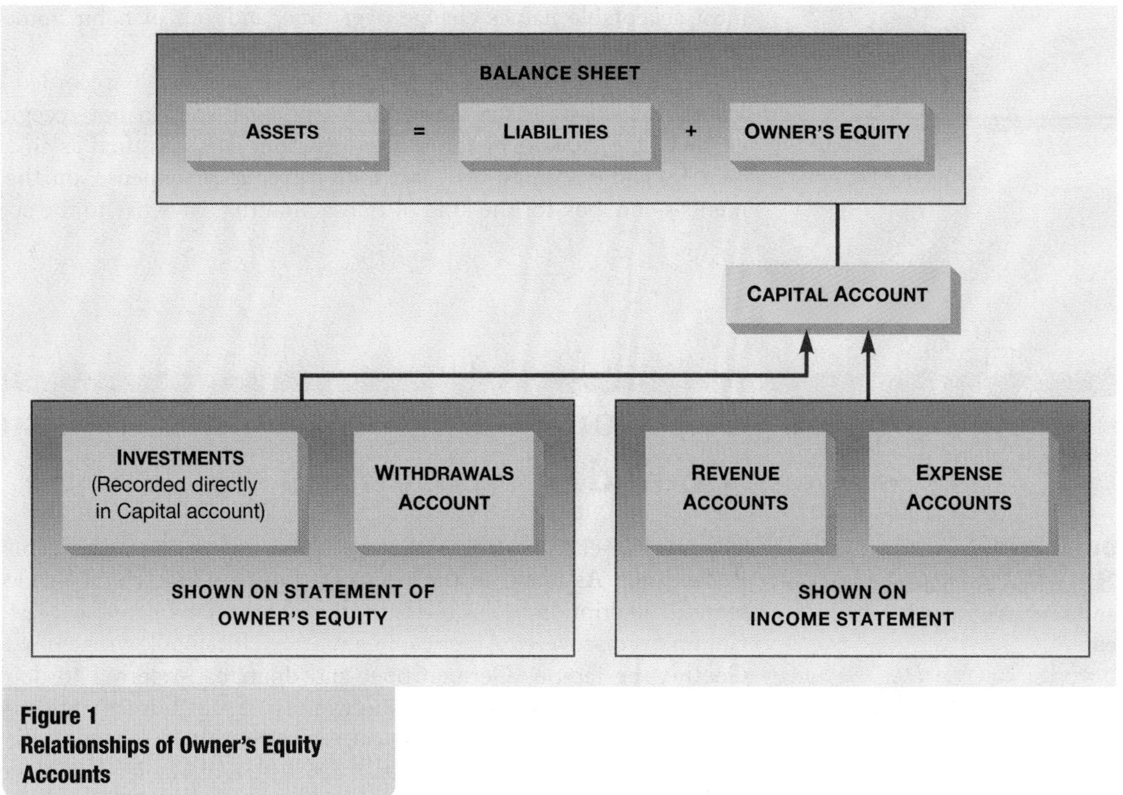

Figure 1
Relationships of Owner's Equity Accounts

Teaching Note: A mnemonic for the types of accounts that affect owner's equity is WIRE—Withdrawals, Investments, Revenues, and Expenses.

in Figure 1. The distinctions among them are important for legal and financial reporting purposes.

First, for income tax reporting, financial reporting, and other purposes, the law requires that Capital and Withdrawals accounts be separated from revenues and expenses. The Capital account represents the owner's interest in the assets of the company. The Withdrawals account is used to record assets taken out of the business by the owner for personal use. These withdrawals are not described as salary or wages, although the owner may think of them as such, because there is no change in the ownership of the money withdrawn. In practice, the Withdrawals account often goes by other names, among them *Personal* and *Drawing*. Corporations do not use a Withdrawals account.

Second, management needs a detailed breakdown of revenues and expenses for budgeting and operating purposes. From these accounts, which are listed on the income statement, management can identify the sources of all revenues and the nature of all expenses. In this way, accounting gives management information about how it has achieved its primary goal of earning a net income.

Account Titles

The names of accounts often confuse beginning accounting students because some of the words are new or have technical meanings. Also, the same asset, liability, or owner's equity account can have different names in different companies. (Actually, this is not so strange. People, too, often are called different names by their friends, families, and associates.) For example, Fixed Assets, Plant and Equipment, Capital Assets, and Long-Lived Assets are all names for long-term asset accounts. Even the most acceptable names change over time, and, out of habit, some companies use names that are out of date.

In general, an account title should describe what is recorded in the account. When you come across an account title that you do not recognize, you should examine the context of the name—whether it is classified as an asset, liability, or owner's equity component, including revenue or expense, on the financial statements—and look for the kind of transaction that gave rise to the account.

The Double-Entry System: The Basic Method of Accounting

OBJECTIVE

3 **Define *double-entry system* and state the rules for double entry**

Related Text Assignments:
Q: 9, 10, 11, 12, 13
FRA: 4

Point to Emphasize: Each transaction must include at least one debit and one credit, and the debit totals must equal the credit totals.

The double-entry system, the backbone of accounting, evolved during the Renaissance. As noted in the Focus on Business Practice box below, the first systematic description of double-entry bookkeeping appeared in 1494, two years after Columbus discovered America, in a mathematics book written by Fra Luca Pacioli. Goethe, the famous German poet and dramatist, referred to double-entry bookkeeping as "one of the finest discoveries of the human intellect." And Werner Sombart, an eminent economist and sociologist, believed that "double-entry bookkeeping is born of the same spirit as the system of Galileo and Newton."

What is the significance of the double-entry system? The system is based on the *principle of duality*, which means that every economic event has two aspects—effort and reward, sacrifice and benefit, source and use—that offset or balance each other. In the **double-entry system**, each transaction must be recorded with at least one debit and one credit, so that the total dollar amount of debits and the total dollar amount of credits equal each other. Because of the way it is designed, the whole system is always in balance. All accounting systems, no matter how sophisticated, are based on the principle of duality.

The T Account

The T account is a good place to begin the study of the double-entry system. In its simplest form, an account has three parts: (1) a title, which describes the asset, the liability, or the owner's equity account; (2) a left side, which is called the **debit**

FOCUS ON BUSINESS PRACTICE

Accounting is a very old discipline. Forms of it have been essential to commerce for more than five thousand years. Accounting, in a version close to what we know today, gained widespread use in the 1400s, especially in Italy, where it was instrumental in the development of shipping, trade, construction, and other forms of commerce. This system of double-entry bookkeeping was documented by the famous Italian mathematician, scholar, and philosopher Fra Luca Pacioli. In 1494, Pacioli published his most important work, *Summa de Arithmetica, Geometrica, Proportioni et Proportionalita*, which contained a detailed description of accounting as practiced in that age. This book became the most widely read book on mathematics in Italy and firmly established Pacioli as the "Father of Accounting."

Point to Emphasize: A T account is simply an abbreviated version of a ledger account. T accounts are used by accountants, instructors, students, and textbooks to quickly analyze a set of transactions; ledger accounts are used in the accounting records.

Common Student Error: Many students have preconceived ideas about what *debit* and *credit* mean. They think that *debit* means "decrease" (or implies something bad) and that *credit* means "increase" (or implies something good). It is important that they realize that *debit* simply means "left side" and *credit* simply means "right side."

side; and (3) a right side, which is called the **credit** side. This form of an account, called a **T account** because it resembles the letter *T*, is used to analyze transactions. It looks like this:

Title of Account	
Debit (left) side	Credit (right) side

Any entry made on the left side of the account is a debit, or debit entry; and any entry made on the right side of the account is a credit, or credit entry. The terms *debit* (abbreviated Dr., from the Latin *debere*) and *credit* (abbreviated Cr., from the Latin *credere*) are simply the accountant's words for "left" and "right" (not for "increase" or "decrease"). We present a more formal version of the T account later in this chapter, where we examine the ledger account form.

The T Account Illustrated

In the chapter on uses of accounting information and the basic financial statements, Shannon Realty had several transactions that involved the receipt or payment of cash. These transactions can be summarized in the Cash account by recording receipts on the left (debit) side of the account and payments on the right (credit) side:

Point to Emphasize: Notice that the debits and credits do not act independently. That is, one is netted out against the other to produce the account balance.

Cash			
(1)	50,000	(2)	35,000
(5)	1,500	(4)	200
(7)	1,000	(8)	1,000
		(9)	400
		(11)	600
	52,500		37,200
Bal.	15,300		

The cash receipts on the left total $52,500. (The total is written in small figures so that it cannot be confused with an actual debit entry). The cash payments on the right total $37,200. These totals are simply working totals, or **footings**. Footings, which are calculated at the end of each month, are an easy way to determine cash on hand. The difference in dollars between the total debit footing and the total credit footing is called the **balance**, or *account balance.* If the balance is a debit, it is written on the left side. If it is a credit, it is written on the right side. Notice that Shannon Realty's Cash account has a debit balance of $15,300 ($52,500 − $37,200). This is the amount of cash the business has on hand at the end of the month.

Analyzing and Processing Transactions

The two rules of double-entry bookkeeping are that every transaction affects at least two accounts and that the total of the debits must equal the total of the credits. In other words, for every transaction, one or more accounts must be debited and one or more accounts must be credited, and the total dollar amount of the debits must equal the total dollar amount of the credits.

Look again at the accounting equation:

$$\text{Assets} = \text{Liabilities} + \text{Owner's Equity}$$

You can see that if a debit increases assets, then a credit must be used to decrease assets on the same side of the equal sign or increase liabilities or owner's equity on opposite sides of the equal sign. Likewise, if a credit decreases assets, then a debit must be used to increase assets or decrease liabilities or owner's equity. These rules can be shown as follows:

Teaching Note: Students often ask why the rules of debit and credit are what they are. Simply state that they are an *arbitrary* set of rules whose interrelationships make them work.

Assets		=	Liabilities		+	Owner's Equity	
Debit for increases (+)	Credit for decreases (−)		Debit for decreases (−)	Credit for increases (+)		Debit for decreases (−)	Credit for increases (+)

1. Increases in assets are debited to asset accounts. Decreases in assets are credited to asset accounts.
2. Increases in liabilities and owner's equity are credited to liability and owner's equity accounts. Decreases in liabilities and owner's equity are debited to liability and owner's equity accounts.

One of the more difficult points to understand is the application of double-entry rules to the owner's equity components. The key is to remember that withdrawals and expenses are deductions from owner's equity. Thus, transactions that *increase* withdrawals or expenses *decrease* owner's equity. Consider this expanded version of the accounting equation:

Reinforcement Exercise: To emphasize the importance of knowing the rules of debit and credit, have your students identify as a debit or a credit an increase in assets, a decrease in assets, an increase in liabilities, and so on.

$$\text{Assets} = \text{Liabilities} + \overbrace{\text{Capital} - \text{Withdrawals} + \text{Revenues} - \text{Expenses}}^{\text{Owner's Equity}}$$

This equation may be rearranged by shifting withdrawals and expenses to the left side, as follows:

Assets		+	Withdrawals		+	Expenses		=	Liabilities		+	Capital		+	Revenues	
+ (debits)	− (credits)		+ (debits)	− (credits)		+ (debits)	− (credits)		− (debits)	+ (credits)		− (debits)	+ (credits)		− (debits)	+ (credits)

Note that the rules for double entry for all the accounts on the left of the equal sign are just the opposite of the rules for all the accounts on the right of the equal sign. Assets, withdrawals, and expenses are increased by debits and decreased by credits. Liabilities, capital, and revenues are increased by credits and decreased by debits.

With this basic information about double entry, it is possible to analyze and process transactions by following the five steps illustrated in Figure 2. To show how the steps are applied, assume that on June 1, Koenig Art Supplies borrows $100,000 from its bank on a promissory note. The transaction is analyzed and processed as follows:

Point to Emphasize: Identifying the accounts involved in a transaction takes practice. Often, account names are not used in the description of a transaction.

1. *Analyze the transaction in order to determine its effect on assets, liabilities, and owner's equity.* In this case, both an asset (Cash) and a liability (Notes Payable) increase. A transaction is usually supported by some kind of **source**

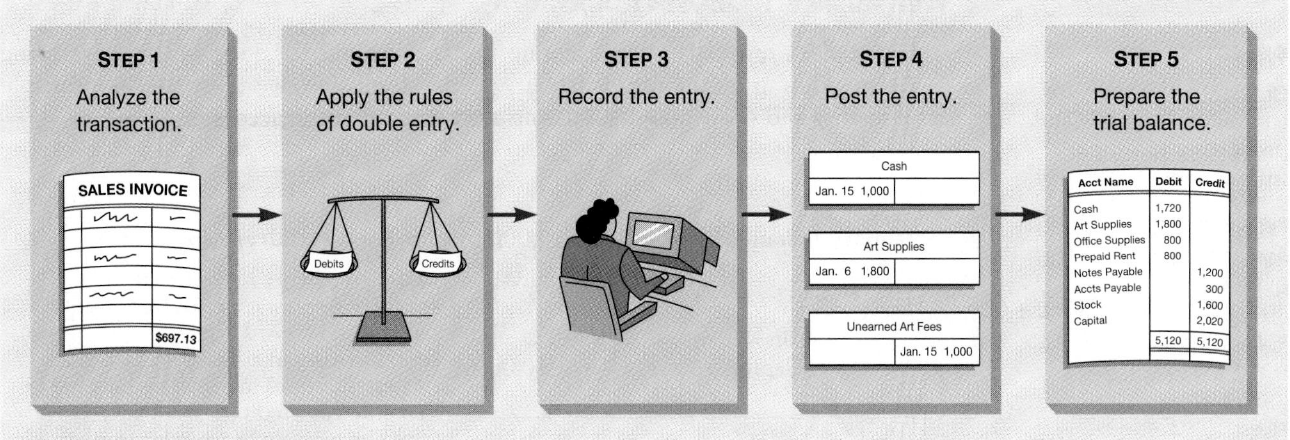

Figure 2
Analyzing and Processing Transactions

document—an invoice, a receipt, a check, or a contract. Here, a copy of the signed note would be the source document.

2. *Apply the rules of double entry.* Increases in assets are recorded by debits. Increases in liabilities are recorded by credits.
3. *Record the entry.* Transactions are recorded in chronological order in a journal. In one form of journal, which is explained in greater detail later on in this chapter, the date, the debit account, and the debit amount are recorded on one line, and the credit account and the credit amount are indented and recorded on the next line, as is shown below:

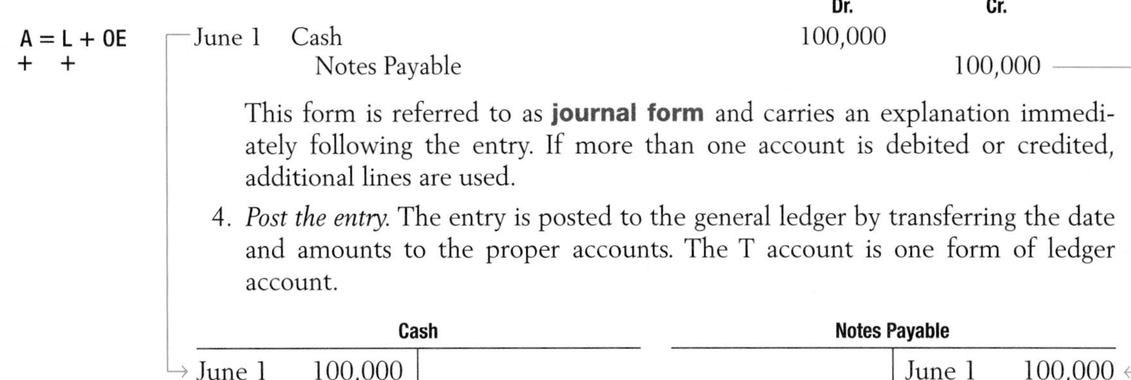

A = L + OE
\+ \+

		Dr.	Cr.
June 1	Cash	100,000	
	Notes Payable		100,000

This form is referred to as **journal form** and carries an explanation immediately following the entry. If more than one account is debited or credited, additional lines are used.

4. *Post the entry.* The entry is posted to the general ledger by transferring the date and amounts to the proper accounts. The T account is one form of ledger account.

Cash

June 1 100,000	

Notes Payable

	June 1 100,000

In formal records, step 3 is never omitted. However, for purposes of analysis, accountants often bypass step 3 and record entries directly in T accounts because doing so clearly and quickly shows the effects of transactions on the accounts. Some of the assignments in this chapter use the same approach to emphasize the analytical aspects of double entry.

5. *Prepare the trial balance to confirm the balance of the accounts.* Periodically, accountants prepare a trial balance to confirm that the accounts are still in balance after the recording and posting of transactions. Preparation of the trial balance is explained later in this chapter.

Transaction Analysis Illustrated

OBJECTIVE

4 Apply the steps for transaction analysis and processing to simple transactions

Related Text Assignments:
Q: 14, 15, 16, 20
SE: 4, 5
E: 4, 5, 7, 12
P: 1, 2, 3, 4, 5, 6, 7, 8
SD: 2, 4, 5
FRA: 1, 2, 3, 4, 5

Common Student Error: For this transaction, many students incorrectly credit "Owner's Equity" rather than Joan Miller, Capital. Owner's equity is an account *classification,* not an account title.

In the next few pages, we examine the transactions for Joan Miller Advertising Agency during the month of January. In the discussion, we illustrate the principle of duality and show how transactions are recorded in the accounts.

January 1: Joan Miller invests $10,000 to start her own advertising agency.

A = L + OE
\+   +

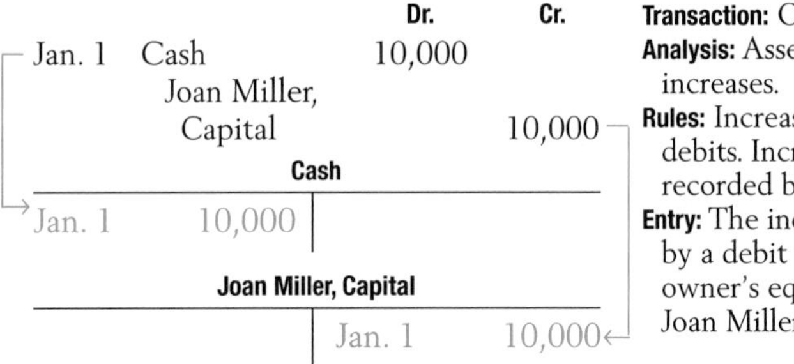

Transaction: Owner's investment.
Analysis: Assets increase. Owner's equity increases.
Rules: Increases in assets are recorded by debits. Increases in owner's equity are recorded by credits.
Entry: The increase in assets is recorded by a debit to Cash. The increase in owner's equity is recorded by a credit to Joan Miller, Capital.

Analysis: If Joan Miller had invested assets other than cash in the business, the appropriate asset accounts would be debited.

Point to Emphasize: Notice the exchange of one asset for another asset.

A = L + OE
\+
−

Teaching Note: For this learning objective, it is extremely beneficial to discuss as many related end-of-chapter exercises and problems as time permits.

January 2: Rents an office, paying two months' rent, $800, in advance.

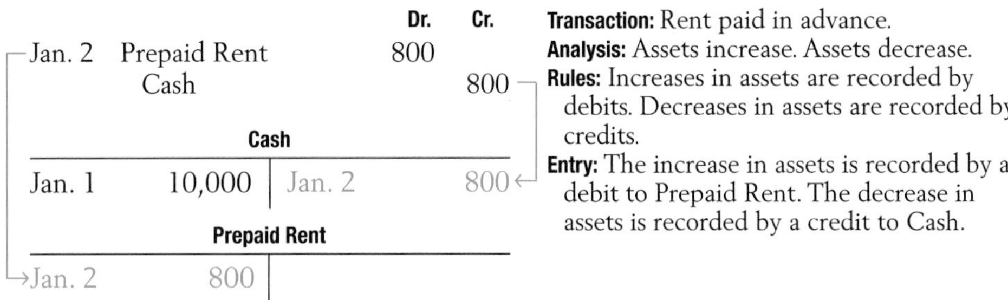

Transaction: Rent paid in advance.
Analysis: Assets increase. Assets decrease.
Rules: Increases in assets are recorded by debits. Decreases in assets are recorded by credits.
Entry: The increase in assets is recorded by a debit to Prepaid Rent. The decrease in assets is recorded by a credit to Cash.

January 3: Orders art supplies, $1,800, and office supplies, $800.

Analysis: No entry is made because no transaction has occurred. According to the recognition issue, there is no liability until the supplies are shipped or received and there is an obligation to pay for them.

January 4: Purchases art equipment, $4,200, with cash.

A = L + OE
\+
−

Common Student Error: Students often attach unnecessary verbs to account names. Point out that terms such as *Cash Paid* and *Art Equipment Purchased* are not acceptable account names. *Cash* and *Art Equipment* are the correct account names.

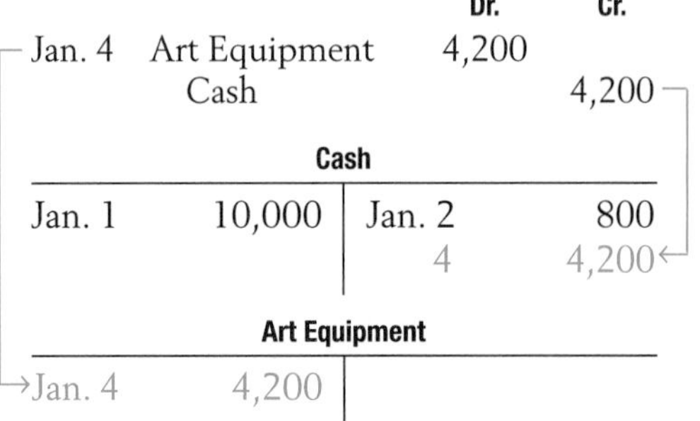

Transaction: Purchase of equipment.
Analysis: Assets increase. Assets decrease.
Rules: Increases in assets are recorded by debits. Decreases in assets are recorded by credits.
Entry: The increase in assets is recorded by a debit to Art Equipment. The decrease in assets is recorded by a credit to Cash.

January 5: Purchases office equipment, $3,000, from Morgan Equipment; pays $1,500 in cash and agrees to pay the rest next month.

A = L + OE
\+ \+
−

Point to Emphasize: Notice that the office equipment is recorded at the full $3,000, even though only half of it has been paid for.

		Dr.	Cr.
Jan. 5	Office Equipment	3,000	
	Cash		1,500
	Accounts Payable		1,500

Cash

Jan. 1	10,000	Jan. 2	800
		4	4,200
		5	1,500

Office Equipment

Jan. 5	3,000		

Accounts Payable

		Jan. 5	1,500

Transaction: Purchase of equipment and partial payment.
Analysis: Assets increase. Assets decrease. Liabilities increase.
Rules: Increases in assets are recorded by debits. Decreases in assets are recorded by credits. Increases in liabilities are recorded by credits.
Entry: The increase in assets is recorded by a debit to Office Equipment. The decrease in assets is recorded by a credit to Cash. The increase in liabilities is recorded by a credit to Accounts Payable.

January 6: Purchases art supplies, $1,800, and office supplies, $800, from Taylor Supply Company, on credit.

A = L + OE
\+ \+
\+

Point to Emphasize: Notice that Accounts Payable is used when there is a delay between purchase and payment.

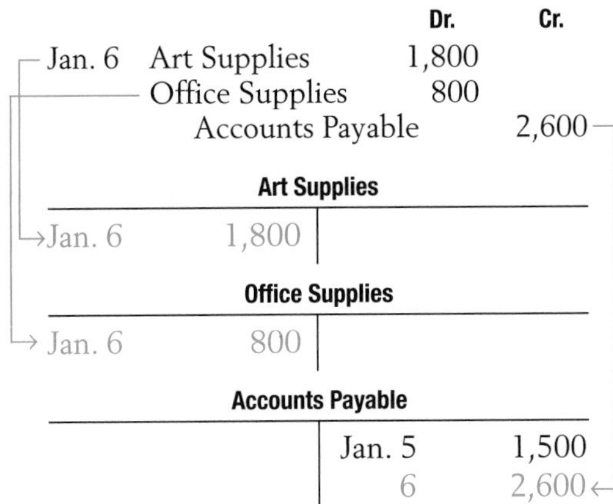

		Dr.	Cr.
Jan. 6	Art Supplies	1,800	
	Office Supplies	800	
	Accounts Payable		2,600

Art Supplies

Jan. 6	1,800		

Office Supplies

Jan. 6	800		

Accounts Payable

		Jan. 5	1,500
		6	2,600

Transaction: Purchase of supplies on credit.
Analysis: Assets increase. Liabilities increase.
Rules: Increases in assets are recorded by debits. Increases in liabilities are recorded by credits.
Entry: The increase in assets is recorded by debits to Art Supplies and Office Supplies. The increase in liabilities is recorded by a credit to Accounts Payable.

January 8: Pays for a one-year life insurance policy, $480, with coverage effective January 1.

A = L + OE
\+
−

		Dr.	Cr.
Jan. 8	Prepaid Insurance	480	
	Cash		480

Cash

Jan. 1	10,000	Jan. 2	800
		4	4,200
		5	1,500
		8	480

Prepaid Insurance

Jan. 8	480		

Transaction: Insurance purchased in advance.
Analysis: Assets increase. Assets decrease.
Rules: Increases in assets are recorded by debits. Decreases in assets are recorded by credits.
Entry: The increase in assets is recorded by a debit to Prepaid Insurance. The decrease in assets is recorded by a credit to Cash.

January 9: Pays Taylor Supply Company $1,000 of the amount owed.

A = L + OE
− −

Point to Emphasize: Notice that Accounts Payable, not Art Supplies or Office Supplies, is debited. Also explain that a liability usually is credited before it can be debited.

		Dr.	Cr.
Jan. 9	Accounts Payable	1,000	
	Cash		1,000

Cash

Jan. 1	10,000	Jan. 2	800
		4	4,200
		5	1,500
		8	480
		9	1,000

Accounts Payable

Jan. 9	1,000	Jan. 5	1,500
		6	2,600

Transaction: Partial payment on a liability.
Analysis: Assets decrease. Liabilities decrease.
Rules: Decreases in liabilities are recorded by debits. Decreases in assets are recorded by credits.
Entry: The decrease in liabilities is recorded by a debit to Accounts Payable. The decrease in assets is recorded by a credit to Cash.

January 10: Performs a service for an automobile dealer by placing advertisements in the newspaper and collects a fee, $1,400.

A = L + OE
\+ +

Common Student Error: Often, students credit the owner's Capital account and not the revenue account (such as Advertising Fees Earned). Although this is theoretically correct, they should know that, in practice, the owner's Capital account is not updated for revenues (or for expenses or withdrawals) until the end of the accounting period.

		Dr.	Cr.
Jan. 10	Cash	1,400	
	Advertising Fees Earned		1,400

Cash

Jan. 1	10,000	Jan. 2	800
10	1,400	4	4,200
		5	1,500
		8	480
		9	1,000

Advertising Fees Earned

		Jan. 10	1,400

Transaction: Revenue earned and cash collected.
Analysis: Assets increase. Owner's equity increases.
Rules: Increases in assets are recorded by debits. Increases in owner's equity are recorded by credits.
Entry: The increase in assets is recorded by a debit to Cash. The increase in owner's equity is recorded by a credit to Advertising Fees Earned.

January 12: Pays the secretary two weeks' wages, $600.

A = L + OE
− −

		Dr.	Cr.
Jan. 12	Wages Expense	600	
	Cash		600

Cash

Jan. 1	10,000	Jan. 2	800
10	1,400	4	4,200
		5	1,500
		8	480
		9	1,000
		12	600

Wages Expense

Jan. 12	600		

Transaction: Payment of wages expense.
Analysis: Assets decrease. Owner's equity decreases.
Rules: Decreases in owner's equity are recorded by debits. Decreases in assets are recorded by credits.
Entry: The decrease in owner's equity is recorded by a debit to Wages Expense. The decrease in assets is recorded by a credit to Cash.

January 15: Accepts an advance fee, $1,000, for artwork to be done for another agency.

A = L + OE
\+ +

Common Student Error: Here, many students credit Art Fees Earned, forgetting that a liability account is what must be credited.

		Dr.	Cr.
Jan. 15	Cash	1,000	
	Unearned Art Fees		1,000

Cash

Jan. 1	10,000	Jan. 2	800
10	1,400	4	4,200
15	1,000	5	1,500
		8	480
		9	1,000
		12	600

Unearned Art Fees

		Jan. 15	1,000

Transaction: Payment received for future services.
Analysis: Assets increase. Liabilities increase.
Rules: Increases in assets are recorded by debits. Increases in liabilities are recorded by credits.
Entry: The increase in assets is recorded by a debit to Cash. The increase in liabilities is recorded by a credit to Unearned Art Fees.

January 19: Performs a service by placing several major advertisements for Ward Department Stores. The fee, $2,800, is billed now but will be collected next month.

A = L + OE
\+ +

Point to Emphasize: Revenue is recognized even though payment has not been received yet. Also, point out that Accounts Receivable is used when there is a delay between the sale of services or merchandise and payment.

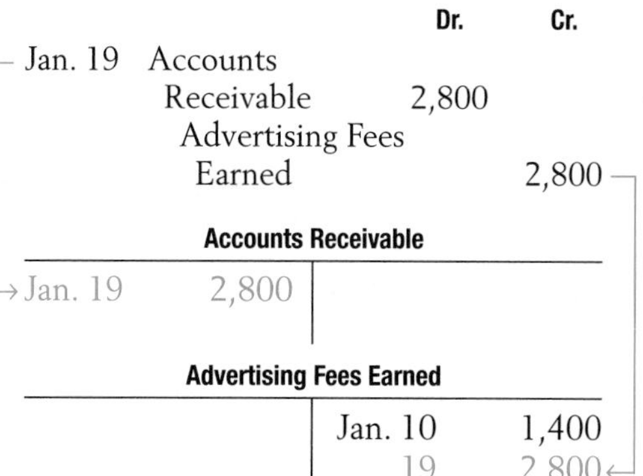

		Dr.	Cr.
Jan. 19	Accounts Receivable	2,800	
	Advertising Fees Earned		2,800

Accounts Receivable

Jan. 19	2,800		

Advertising Fees Earned

		Jan. 10	1,400
		19	2,800

Transaction: Revenue earned, to be received later.
Analysis: Assets increase. Owner's equity increases.
Rules: Increases in assets are recorded by debits. Increases in owner's equity are recorded by credits.
Entry: The increase in assets is recorded by a debit to Accounts Receivable. The increase in owner's equity is recorded by a credit to Advertising Fees Earned.

January 26: Pays the secretary two more weeks' wages, $600.

A = L + OE
− −

		Dr.	Cr.
Jan. 26	Wages Expense	600	
	Cash		600

Cash

Jan. 1	10,000	Jan. 2	800
10	1,400	4	4,200
15	1,000	5	1,500
		8	480
		9	1,000
		12	600
		26	600

Wages Expense

Jan. 12	600		
26	600		

Transaction: Payment of wages expense.
Analysis: Assets decrease. Owner's equity decreases.
Rules: Decreases in owner's equity are recorded by debits. Decreases in assets are recorded by credits.
Entry: The decrease in owner's equity is recorded by a debit to Wages Expense. The decrease in assets is recorded by a credit to Cash.

January 29: Receives and pays the utility bill, $100.

A = L + OE
− −

		Dr.	Cr.
Jan. 29	Utilities Expense	100	
	Cash		100

Cash

Jan. 1	10,000	Jan. 2	800
10	1,400	4	4,200
15	1,000	5	1,500
		8	480
		9	1,000
		12	600
		26	600
		29	100

Utilities Expense

Jan. 29	100		

Transaction: Payment of utilities expense.
Analysis: Assets decrease. Owner's equity decreases.
Rules: Decreases in owner's equity are recorded by debits. Decreases in assets are recorded by credits.
Entry: The decrease in owner's equity is recorded by a debit to Utilities Expense. The decrease in assets is recorded by a credit to Cash.

January 30: Receives (but does not pay) the telephone bill, $70.

A = L + OE
+ −

		Dr.	Cr.
Jan. 30	Telephone Expense	70	
	Accounts Payable		70

Accounts Payable

Jan. 9	1,000	Jan. 5	1,500
		6	2,600
		30	70

Telephone Expense

Jan. 30	70		

Transaction: Expense incurred, to be paid later.
Analysis: Liabilities increase. Owner's equity decreases.
Rules: Decreases in owner's equity are recorded by debits. Increases in liabilities are recorded by credits.
Entry: The decrease in owner's equity is recorded by a debit to Telephone Expense. The increase in liabilities is recorded by a credit to Accounts Payable.

Discussion Question: Why are the expense and liability recognized at this point? After all, payment has not yet been made. **Answer:** An expense has been incurred because telephone services have been used. The obligation to pay exists.

January 31: Joan Miller withdraws $1,400 from the business for personal living expenses.

A = L + OE
− −

		Dr.	Cr.
Jan. 31	Joan Miller, Withdrawals	1,400	
	Cash		1,400

Cash

Jan. 1	10,000	Jan. 2	800
10	1,400	4	4,200
15	1,000	5	1,500
		8	480
		9	1,000
		12	600
		26	600
		29	100
		31	1,400

Joan Miller, Withdrawals

Jan. 31	1,400		

Transaction: Owner's withdrawal for personal use.
Analysis: Assets decrease. Owner's equity decreases.
Rules: Decreases in assets are recorded by credits. Decreases in owner's equity are recorded by debits.
Entry: The decrease in owner's equity is recorded by a debit to Joan Miller, Withdrawals. The decrease in assets is recorded by a credit to Cash.

Discussion Question: Why are withdrawals not considered an expense? **Answer:** Expenses are costs of operating a business, but withdrawals are assets that the owner takes out of the business.

Summary of Transactions

In Exhibit 2 the transactions for January are shown in their accounts and in relation to the accounting equation. Note that all transactions have been recorded on the date they are recognized. Most of these transactions involve either the receipt or payment of cash as may be seen in the Cash account. There are important exceptions, however. For instance, on January 19 Advertising Fees were earned, but receipt of cash for these fees will come later. Also, on January 5, 6, and 30 there were transactions recognized that totaled $4,170 in Accounts Payable. This means the company can wait to pay. At the end of the month, only the $1,000 recorded on January 9 had been paid. These lags between recognition of transactions and the subsequent cash inflows or outflows impact achieving the goal of liquidity.

Exhibit 2
Summary of Sample Accounts and Transactions for Joan Miller Advertising Agency

Assets = Liabilities + Owner's Equity

Assets

Cash

Jan. 1	10,000	Jan. 2	800
10	1,400	4	4,200
15	1,000	5	1,500
		8	480
		9	1,000
		12	600
		26	600
		29	100
		31	1,400
	12,400		10,680
Bal.	1,720		

This account links to the statement of cash flows.

Accounts Receivable

Jan. 19	2,800		

Art Supplies

Jan. 6	1,800		

Office Supplies

Jan. 6	800		

Prepaid Rent

Jan. 2	800		

Prepaid Insurance

Jan. 8	480		

Art Equipment

Jan. 4	4,200		

Office Equipment

Jan. 5	3,000		

Liabilities

Accounts Payable

Jan. 9	1,000	Jan. 5	1,500
		6	2,600
		30	70
	1,000		4,170
		Bal.	3,170

Unearned Art Fees

		Jan. 15	1,000

Owner's Equity

Joan Miller, Capital

		Jan. 1	10,000

Joan Miller, Withdrawals

Jan. 31	1,400		

Advertising Fees Earned

		Jan. 10	1,400
		19	2,800
		Bal.	4,200

Wages Expense

Jan. 12	600		
26	600		
Bal.	1,200		

Utilities Expense

Jan. 29	100		

Telephone Expense

Jan. 30	70		

These accounts link to the income statement.

The Trial Balance

OBJECTIVE

5 Prepare a trial balance and describe its value and limitations

Related Text Assignments:
Q: 17, 18, 19, 24
SE: 3, 6, 7
E: 3, 6, 8, 9, 10, 11
P: 2, 3, 4, 5, 7, 8
SD: 5

For every amount debited, an equal amount must be credited. This means that the total of debits and credits in the T accounts must be equal. To test this, the accountant periodically prepares a **trial balance**. Exhibit 3 shows a trial balance for Joan Miller Advertising Agency. It was prepared from the accounts in Exhibit 2.

The trial balance may be prepared at any time but is usually prepared on the last day of the month. Here are the steps in preparing a trial balance:

1. List each T account that has a balance, with debit balances in the left column and credit balances in the right column. Accounts are listed in the order in which they appear in the ledger.
2. Add each column.
3. Compare the totals of the columns.

Point to Emphasize: The trial balance is prepared at the end of the accounting period. It is an initial check that the ledger is in balance.

Instructional Strategy: Play a *Jeopardy*-type game using E 3 to reinforce account classifications and normal balance. All students participate by writing their own answers on a piece of paper, with headings as shown in the text. Consider performance-based rewards.

In accounts in which increases are recorded by debits, the **normal balance** (the usual balance) is a debit balance; where increases are recorded by credits, the normal balance is a credit balance. Table 1 summarizes the normal account balances of the major account categories. According to the table, the T account Accounts Payable (a liability) typically has a credit balance and is copied into the trial balance as a credit balance.

Once in a while, a transaction leaves an account with a balance that is not "normal." For example, when a company overdraws its account at the bank, its Cash account (an asset) will show a credit balance instead of a debit balance. The "abnormal" balance should be copied into the trial balance columns as it stands, as a debit or a credit.

The trial balance proves whether or not the ledger is in balance. *In balance* means that the total of all debits recorded equals the total of all credits recorded.

Exhibit 3
Trial Balance

Point to Emphasize: Notice that the accounts are listed in the same order as in the ledger. At this point, the Capital account does not reflect any revenues, expenses, or withdrawals for the period.

Joan Miller Advertising Agency
Trial Balance
January 31, 20xx

Cash	$ 1,720	
Accounts Receivable	2,800	
Art Supplies	1,800	
Office Supplies	800	
Prepaid Rent	800	
Prepaid Insurance	480	
Art Equipment	4,200	
Office Equipment	3,000	
Accounts Payable		$ 3,170
Unearned Art Fees		1,000
Joan Miller, Capital		10,000
Joan Miller, Withdrawals	1,400	
Advertising Fees Earned		4,200
Wages Expense	1,200	
Utilities Expense	100	
Telephone Expense	70	
	$18,370	$18,370

Teaching Note: A mnemonic for accounts with normal debit balances is AWE—Assets, Withdrawals, and Expenses.

Table 1. Normal Account Balances of Major Account Categories

	Increases Recorded by		Normal Balance	
Account Category	Debit	Credit	Debit	Credit
Assets	x		x	
Liabilities		x		x
Owner's Equity:				
Capital		x		x
Withdrawals	x		x	
Revenues		x		x
Expenses	x		x	

Teaching Note: Give your students several examples of errors made in the journal, ledger, and trial balance, and ask them to state whether or not each error produces an imbalance in the trial balance.

But the trial balance does not prove that the transactions were analyzed correctly or recorded in the proper accounts. For example, there is no way of determining from the trial balance that a debit should have been made in the Art Equipment account rather than the Office Equipment account. And the trial balance does not detect whether transactions have been omitted, because equal debits and credits will have been omitted. Also, if an error of the same amount is made in both a debit and a credit, it will not be discovered by the trial balance. The trial balance proves only that the debits and credits in the accounts are in balance.

If the debit and credit columns of the trial balance are not equal, look for one or more of the following errors: (1) a debit was entered in an account as a credit, or vice versa; (2) the balance of an account was computed incorrectly; (3) an error was made in carrying the account balance to the trial balance; or (4) the trial balance was summed incorrectly.

Other than simply incorrectly adding the columns, the two most common mistakes in preparing a trial balance are (1) recording an account with a debit balance as a credit, or vice versa, and (2) transposing two numbers when transferring an amount to the trial balance (for example, entering $23,459 as $23,549). The first of these mistakes causes the trial balance to be out of balance by an amount divisible by 2. The second causes the trial balance to be out of balance by a number divisible by 9. Thus, if a trial balance is out of balance and the addition has been verified, determine the amount by which the trial balance is out of balance and divide it first by 2 and then by 9. If the amount is divisible by 2, look in the trial balance for an amount equal to the quotient. If you find the amount, it is probably in the wrong column. If the amount is divisible by 9, trace each amount to the ledger account balance, checking carefully for a transposition error. If neither of these techniques identifies the error, first recompute the balance of each account in the ledger, then, if the error still has not been found, retrace each posting from the journal to the ledger.

Some Notes on Presentation

A ruled line appears in financial reports before each subtotal or total to indicate that the amounts above are added or subtracted. It is common practice to use a double line under a final total to show that it has been checked, or verified.

Dollar signs ($) are required in all financial statements, including the balance sheet and income statement, and in the trial balance and other schedules. On these

Focus on International Business

Determining the dollar amount or valuation of a sale or purchase transaction is often not difficult because it equals the amount of cash that changes hands. However, in some areas of the world it is not so easy to determine. In a country where the currency is declining in value and there is high inflation, companies often are forced to resort to barter transactions, in which one good or service is traded for another. In Russia, for example, perhaps as many as two-thirds of all transactions are barter-type transactions. It is not uncommon for companies often to end up with piles of goods stacked around their offices and warehouses. In one case, an electric utility company provided a textile-machinery plant with electricity in exchange for wool blankets, which the plant had received in exchange for equipment sold to another company. Determining the value can be difficult in this case because it becomes a matter of determining the fair value of the goods being traded.[7]

statements, a dollar sign should be placed before the first amount in each column and before the first amount in a column following a ruled line. Dollar signs in the same column are aligned. Dollar signs are not used in journals and ledgers.

Point to Emphasize: Placing a dash in the cents column is preferable to leaving it blank. (It's possible to infer from a blank cents column that the bookkeeper simply forgot to enter the figure for cents.)

On unruled paper, commas and decimal points are used in dollar amounts. On paper with ruled columns—like the paper in journals and ledgers—commas and decimal points are not needed. In this book, because most problems and illustrations are in whole dollar amounts, the cents column usually is omitted. When accountants deal with whole dollars, they often use a dash in the cents column to indicate whole dollars rather than take the time to write zeros.

Recording and Posting Transactions

OBJECTIVE

6 Record transactions in the general journal

Related Text Assignments:
Q: 20, 21, 23, 24
SE: 8
E: 12, 13
P: 3, 5, 8

Let us now take a look at the formal process of recording transactions in the general journal and posting them to the ledger.

The General Journal

Point to Emphasize: The journal is a chronological record of events. Only the general journal is discussed in this chapter.

As you have seen, transactions can be entered directly into the accounts. But this method makes identifying individual transactions or finding errors very difficult because the debit is recorded in one account and the credit in another. The solution is to record all transactions chronologically in a **journal**. The journal is sometimes called the *book of original entry* because it is where transactions first enter the accounting records. Later, the debit and credit portions of each transaction can be transferred to the appropriate accounts in the ledger. A separate **journal entry** is used to record each transaction, and the process of recording transactions is called **journalizing**.

Teaching Note: Refer students to Exhibit 4 as you describe the general journal.

Most businesses have more than one kind of journal. The simplest and most flexible type is the **general journal**, the one we focus on in this chapter. Entries in the general journal include the following information about each transaction:

1. The date
2. The names of the accounts debited and the dollar amounts on the same lines in the debit column
3. The names of the accounts credited and the dollar amounts on the same lines in the credit column

4. An explanation of the transaction
5. The account identification numbers, if appropriate

Exhibit 4 displays two of the earlier transactions for Joan Miller Advertising Agency. The procedure for recording transactions in the general journal is as follows:

1. Record the date by writing the year in small figures on the first line at the top of the first column, and the month on the next line of the first column. Then record the day in the second column opposite the month. For subsequent entries on the same page for the same month and year, the month and year can be omitted.
2. Write the exact names of the accounts debited and credited in the Description column. Starting on the same line as the date, write the name(s) of the account(s) debited next to the left margin and indent the name(s) of the account(s) credited. The explanation is placed on the next line and further indented. The explanation should be brief but sufficient to explain and identify the transaction. A transaction can have more than one debit or credit entry; this is called a **compound entry**. In a compound entry, all debit accounts are listed before any credit accounts. (The January 6 transaction of Joan Miller Advertising Agency in Exhibit 4 is an example of a compound entry.)
3. Write the debit amounts in the Debit column opposite the accounts to be debited, and write the credit amounts in the Credit column opposite the accounts to be credited.
4. At the time the transactions are recorded, nothing is placed in the Post. Ref. (posting reference) column. (This column is sometimes called *LP* or *Folio*.) Later, if the company uses account numbers to identify accounts in the ledger, fill in the account numbers to provide a convenient cross-reference from the general journal to the ledger and to indicate that the entry has been posted to the ledger. If the accounts are not numbered, use a checkmark (√).
5. It is customary to skip a line after each journal entry.

Common Student Error: Check your students' journals for proper form. Frequent errors are forgetting to skip a space between entries, not indenting the credits, using the Post. Ref. column before posting is done, journalizing amounts that do not balance, entering a credit before a debit, and forgetting to enter the explanation.

Common Student Confusion: Invariably, a student asks if it matters *which* debit is listed first or *which* credit is listed before the others. The order does not matter, as long as all the debits in the entry are listed before any of the credits.

Instructional Strategy: Have students work SD 2 in small groups. This exercise requires a journal entry and comprehension of Objective 1.

Exhibit 4
The General Journal

General Journal — Page 1

Date		Description	Post. Ref.	Debit	Credit
20xx					
Jan.	6	Art Supplies		1,800	
		Office Supplies		800	
		Accounts Payable			2,600
		Purchased art and office supplies on credit			
	8	Prepaid Insurance		480	
		Cash			480
		Paid one-year life insurance premium			

A = L + OE
\+ \+
\+

A = L + OE
\+
−

The General Ledger

OBJECTIVE

7 Post transactions from the general journal to the ledger

Related Text Assignments:
Q: 22, 23, 24
SE: 9
E: 13
P: 3, 5, 8

The general journal is used to record the details of each transaction. The general ledger is used to update each account.

THE LEDGER ACCOUNT FORM The T account is a simple, direct means of recording transactions. In practice, a somewhat more complicated form of the account is needed in order to record more information. The **ledger account form**, which contains four columns for dollar amounts, is illustrated in Exhibit 5.

The account title and number appear at the top of the account form. The date of the transaction appears in the first two columns as it does in the journal. The Item column is used only rarely to identify transactions, because explanations already appear in the journal. The Post. Ref. column is used to note the journal page where the original entry for the transaction can be found. The dollar amount of the entry is entered in the appropriate Debit or Credit column, and a new account balance is computed in the final two columns after each entry. The advantage of this form of account over the T account is that the current balance of the account is readily available.

Teaching Note: Explain that posting is much like sorting mail. It is a tedious, but necessary, procedure, conveniently accomplished by a computer.

POSTING TO THE LEDGER After transactions have been entered in the journal, they must be transferred to the ledger. The process of transferring journal entry information from the journal to the ledger is called **posting**. Posting is usually done after several entries have been made—for example, at the end of each day or less frequently, depending on the number of transactions. As shown in Exhibit 6, through posting, each amount in the Debit column of the journal is transferred into the Debit column of the appropriate account in the ledger, and each amount in the Credit column of the journal is transferred into the Credit column of the appropriate account in the ledger. The steps in the posting process are as follows:

1. In the ledger, locate the debit account named in the journal entry.
2. Enter the date of the transaction and, in the Post. Ref. column of the ledger, the journal page number from which the entry comes.
3. Enter in the Debit column of the ledger account the amount of the debit as it appears in the journal.
4. Calculate the account balance and enter it in the appropriate Balance column.

Teaching Note: Compare and contrast the structure of the general ledger (Exhibit 5) with that of the general journal (Exhibit 4). It is especially important at this point that students be able to compute account balances.

Exhibit 5
Accounts Payable in the General Ledger

General Ledger

Accounts Payable — Account No. 212

Date		Item	Post. Ref.	Debit	Credit	Balance Debit	Balance Credit
20xx							
Jan.	5		J1		1,500		1,500
	6		J1		2,600		4,100
	9		J1	1,000			3,100
	30		J2		70		3,170

2. Post the transactions to the ledger accounts.

General Ledger

Cash — Account No. 111

Date		Item	Post. Ref.	Debit	Credit	Balance Debit	Balance Credit
20xx							
May	1		J1	2,000		2,000	
	3		J1		300	1,700	
	9		J1		200	1,500	
	12		J1		100	1,400	
	18		J1		50	1,350	
	27		J1		40	1,310	

Accounts Receivable — Account No. 112

Date		Item	Post. Ref.	Debit	Credit	Balance Debit	Balance Credit
20xx							
May	15		J1	35		35	

Medical Supplies — Account No. 115

Date		Item	Post. Ref.	Debit	Credit	Balance Debit	Balance Credit
20xx							
May	9		J1	200		200	

Prepaid Rent — Account No. 117

Date		Item	Post. Ref.	Debit	Credit	Balance Debit	Balance Credit
20xx							
May	3		J1	300		300	

Equipment — Account No. 144

Date		Item	Post. Ref.	Debit	Credit	Balance Debit	Balance Credit
20xx							
May	12		J1	400		400	

(continued)

Accounts Payable						Account No. 212	
						Balance	
Date		Item	Post. Ref.	Debit	Credit	Debit	Credit
20xx May	12		J1		300		300
	18		J1	50			250

Laura Stors, Capital						Account No. 311	
						Balance	
Date		Item	Post. Ref.	Debit	Credit	Debit	Credit
20xx May	1		J1		2,000		2,000

Veterinary Fees Earned						Account No. 411	
						Balance	
Date		Item	Post. Ref.	Debit	Credit	Debit	Credit
20xx May	15		J1		35		35

Utilities Expense						Account No. 512	
						Balance	
Date		Item	Post. Ref.	Debit	Credit	Debit	Credit
20xx May	27		J1	40		40	

3. Complete the trial balance.

Laura Stors, Veterinarian Trial Balance May 31, 20xx		
Cash	$1,310	
Accounts Receivable	35	
Medical Supplies	200	
Prepaid Rent	300	
Equipment	400	
Accounts Payable		$ 250
Laura Stors, Capital		2,000
Veterinary Fees Earned		35
Utilities Expense	40	
	$2,285	$2,285

4. The transaction is recorded, or recognized, on May 15, even though no cash is received. The revenue is earned because the service was provided to and accepted by the buyer. The customer now has an obligation to pay the seller. It is recorded as an accounts receivable because the customer has been allowed to pay later. The transaction on May 9 is classified as an asset, Medical Supplies, because these supplies will benefit the company in the future. The transaction on May 27 is classified as an expense, Utilities Expense, because the utilities have already been used and will not benefit the company in the future.

Chapter Assignments

Building Your Knowledge Foundation

Questions

1. What three issues underlie most accounting measurement decisions?
2. Why is recognition an issue for accountants?
3. A customer asks the owner of a store to save an item for him and says that he will pick it up and pay for it next week. The owner agrees to hold it. Should this transaction be recorded as a sale? Explain your answer.
4. Why is it practical for accountants to rely on original cost for valuation purposes?
5. Under the cost principle, changes in value after a transaction is recorded are not usually recognized in the accounts. Comment on this possible limitation of using original cost in accounting measurements.
6. What is an account, and how is it related to the ledger?
7. Tell whether each of the following accounts is an asset account, a liability account, or an owner's equity account:
   a. Notes Receivable
   b. Land
   c. Withdrawals
   d. Mortgage Payable
   e. Prepaid Rent
   f. Insurance Expense
   g. Service Revenue
8. In the owner's equity accounts, why do accountants maintain separate accounts for revenues and expenses rather than using the Capital account?
9. Why is the system of recording entries called the double-entry system? What is significant about this system?
10. "Double-entry accounting refers to entering a transaction in both the journal and the ledger." Comment on this statement.
11. "Debits are bad; credits are good." Comment on this statement.
12. What are the rules of double entry for (a) assets, (b) liabilities, and (c) owner's equity?
13. Why are the rules of double entry the same for liabilities and owner's equity?
14. What is the meaning of the statement "The Cash account has a debit balance of $500"?
15. Explain why debits, which decrease owner's equity, also increase expenses, which are a component of owner's equity.
16. What are the five steps in analyzing and processing a transaction?
17. What does a trial balance prove?
18. What is the normal balance of Accounts Payable? Under what conditions could Accounts Payable have a debit balance?
19. Can errors be present even though a trial balance balances? Explain your answer.
20. Is it a good idea to forgo the journal and enter a transaction directly into the ledger? Explain your answer.

21. In recording entries in a journal, which is written first, the debit or the credit? How is indentation used in the journal?
22. What is the relationship between the journal and the ledger?
23. Describe each of the following:
    a. Account
    b. Journal
    c. Ledger
    d. Book of original entry
    e. Post. Ref. column
    f. Journalizing
    g. Posting
    h. Footings
    i. Compound entry
24. List the following six items in sequence to illustrate the flow of events through the accounting system:
    a. Analysis of the transaction
    b. Debits and credits posted from the journal to the ledger
    c. Occurrence of the business transaction
    d. Preparation of the financial statements
    e. Entry made in the journal
    f. Preparation of the trial balance

SHORT EXERCISES

SE 1. **LO 1 Recognition**

Which of the following events would be recognized and entered in the accounting records of Hawthorne Company? Why?

Jan. 10 Hawthorne Company places an order for office supplies.
Feb. 15 Hawthorne Company receives the office supplies and a bill for them.
Mar. 1 Hawthorne Company pays for the office supplies.

SE 2. **LO 2 Classification of Accounts**

Tell whether each of the following accounts is an asset, a liability, a revenue, an expense, or none of these.

a. Accounts Payable
b. Supplies
c. Withdrawals
d. Fees Earned
e. Supplies Expense
f. Accounts Receivable
g. Unearned Revenue
h. Equipment

SE 3. **LO 5 Normal Balances**

Tell whether the normal balance of each account in **SE 2** is a debit or a credit.

SE 4. **LO 4 Transaction Analysis**

For each of the following transactions, tell which account is debited and which account is credited.

May 2 Joe Hurley started a computer programming business, Hurley's Programming Service, by investing $5,000.
5 Purchased a computer for $2,500 in cash.
7 Purchased supplies on credit for $300.
19 Received cash for programming services performed, $500.
22 Received cash for programming services to be performed, $600.
25 Paid the rent for May, $650.
31 Billed a customer for programming services performed, $250.

SE 5. **LO 4 Recording Transactions in T Accounts**

Set up T accounts and record each transaction in **SE 4**. Determine the balance of each account.

SE 6. **LO 5 Preparing a Trial Balance**

From the T accounts created in **SE 5**, prepare a trial balance dated May 31, 20x1.

SE 7. **LO 5 Correcting Errors in a Trial Balance**

The trial balance at the top of the next page is out of balance. Assuming that all balances are normal, place the accounts in proper order and correct the trial balance so that debits equal credits.

Sanders Boating Service Trial Balance January 31, 20x1		
Cash	$2,000	
Accounts Payable	400	
Fuel Expense		$ 800
Unearned Service Revenue	250	
Accounts Receivable		1,300
Prepaid Rent		150
Sara Sanders, Capital		2,800
Service Revenue	1,750	
Wages Expense		300
Sara Sanders, Withdrawals		650
	$4,400	$6,000

SE 8. **LO 6 Recording Transactions in the General Journal**

Prepare a general journal form like the one in Exhibit 4 and label it Page 4. Record the following transactions in the journal.

Sept. 6 Billed a customer for services performed, $1,900.
16 Received partial payment from the customer billed on Sept. 6, $900.

SE 9. **LO 7 Posting to the Ledger Accounts**

Prepare ledger account forms like the ones in Exhibit 5 for the following accounts: Cash (111), Accounts Receivable (113), and Service Revenue (411). Post the transactions that are recorded in **SE 8** to the ledger accounts, at the same time making proper posting references.

Exercises

E 1. **LO 1 Recognition**

Which of the following events would be recognized and recorded in the accounting records of the Rockwell Company on the date indicated?

Feb. 17 Rockwell Company offers to purchase a tract of land for $280,000. There is a high likelihood that the offer will be accepted.
Mar. 7 Rockwell Company receives notice that its rent will be increased from $1,000 per month to $1,200 per month effective April 1.
Apr. 28 Rockwell Company receives its utility bill for the month of April. The bill is not due until May 10.
May 19 Rockwell Company places a firm order for new office equipment costing $42,000.
June 27 The office equipment ordered on May 19 arrives. Payment is not due until September 1.

E 2. **LO 1 Application of Recognition Point**

Yoshima's Body Shop uses a large amount of supplies in its business. The following table summarizes selected transaction data for orders of supplies purchased:

Order	Date Shipped	Date Received	Amount
a	April 28	May 7	$300
b	May 8	13	750
c	10	16	400
d	15	21	600
e	25	June 1	750
f	June 3	9	500

Determine the total purchases of supplies for May alone if:

1. Yoshima's Body Shop recognizes purchases when orders are shipped.
2. Yoshima's Body Shop recognizes purchases when orders are received.

E 3. **LO 2 LO 5 Classification of Accounts**

Listed below are the ledger accounts of the Blatz Service Company:

a. Cash
b. Accounts Receivable
c. Vonette Blatz, Capital
d. Vonette Blatz, Withdrawals
e. Service Revenue
f. Prepaid Rent
g. Accounts Payable
h. Investments in Securities
i. Wages Payable
j. Land
k. Supplies Expense
l. Prepaid Insurance
m. Utilities Expense
n. Fees Earned
o. Unearned Revenue
p. Office Equipment
q. Rent Payable
r. Notes Receivable
s. Interest Expense
t. Notes Payable
u. Supplies
v. Interest Receivable

Complete the following table, indicating with two Xs for each account its classification and its normal balance (whether a debit or credit increases the account):

	Type of Account						Normal Balance (increases balance)	
			Owner's Equity					
Item	Asset	Liability	Owner's Capital	Owner's Withdrawals	Revenue	Expense	Debit	Credit
a.	X						X	

E 4. **LO 4 Transaction Analysis**

Analyze transactions **a–g**, following the example below.

a. Horace Orcutt established Orcutt's Barber Shop by placing $2,400 in a bank account.
b. Paid two months' rent in advance, $840.
c. Purchased supplies on credit, $120.
d. Received cash for barbering services, $100.
e. Paid for supplies purchased in **c**.
f. Paid utility bill, $72.
g. Took cash out of the business for personal expenses, $100.

Example

a. The asset Cash was increased. Increases in assets are recorded by debits. Debit Cash, $2,400. A component of owner's equity, Horace Orcutt, Capital, was increased. Increases in owner's equity are recorded by credits. Credit Horace Orcutt, Capital, $2,400.

E 5. **LO 4 Recording Transactions in T Accounts**

Open the following T accounts: Cash; Repair Supplies; Repair Equipment; Accounts Payable; Sally Felipe, Capital; Sally Felipe, Withdrawals; Repair Fees Earned; Salaries Expense; and Rent Expense. Record the following transactions for the month of June directly in the T accounts; use the letters to identify the transactions in your T accounts. Determine the balance in each account.

a. Sally Felipe opened the Flagship Repair Service by investing $4,300 in cash and $1,600 in repair equipment.
b. Paid $400 for current month's rent.
c. Purchased repair supplies on credit, $500.
d. Purchased additional repair equipment for cash, $300.
e. Paid salary to a helper, $450.
f. Paid $200 of amount purchased on credit in **c**.
g. Withdrew $600 from business for living expenses.
h. Accepted cash for repairs completed, $1,860.

E 6. **LO 5 Trial Balance**

After recording the transactions in **E 5**, prepare a trial balance in proper sequence for Flagship Repair Service as of June 30, 20xx.

E 7. **LO 4 Analysis of Transactions**

Explain each transaction (**a** through **h**) entered in the following T accounts.

Cash

	Debit		Credit
a.	60,000	b.	15,000
g.	1,500	e.	3,000
h.	900	f.	4,500

Accounts Receivable

	Debit		Credit
c.	6,000	g.	1,500

Equipment

	Debit		Credit
b.	15,000	h.	900
d.	9,000		

Accounts Payable

	Debit		Credit
f.	4,500	d.	9,000

J. Seymour, Capital

	Debit		Credit
		a.	60,000

Service Revenue

	Debit		Credit
		c.	6,000

Wages Expense

	Debit		Credit
e.	3,000		

E 8. **LO 5 Preparing a Trial Balance**

The following accounts of the Collie Service Company as of October 31, 20xx, are listed in alphabetical order. The amount of Accounts Payable is omitted.

Accounts Payable	?	Equipment	$24,000
Accounts Receivable	$ 6,000	Land	10,400
Wanda Collie, Capital	62,900	Notes Payable	40,000
Building	68,000	Prepaid Insurance	2,200
Cash	18,000		

Prepare a trial balance with the proper heading (see Exhibit 3) and with the accounts listed in the chart of accounts sequence (see Exhibit 1). Compute the balance of Accounts Payable.

E 9. **LO 5 Effect of Errors on a Trial Balance**

Which of the following errors would cause a trial balance to have unequal totals? Explain your answers.

a. A payment to a creditor was recorded as a debit to Accounts Payable for $172 and a credit to Cash for $127.
b. A payment of $200 to a creditor for an account payable was debited to Accounts Receivable and credited to Cash.
c. A purchase of office supplies of $560 was recorded as a debit to Office Supplies for $56 and a credit to Cash for $56.
d. A purchase of equipment for $600 was recorded as a debit to Supplies for $600 and a credit to Cash for $600.

E 10. **LO 5 Correcting Errors in a Trial Balance**

This was the trial balance for LaPietro Services at the end of September:

LaPietro Services
Trial Balance
September 30, 20xx

Cash	$ 3,840	
Accounts Receivable	5,660	
Supplies	120	
Prepaid Insurance	180	
Equipment	8,400	
Accounts Payable		$ 4,540
M. LaPietro, Capital		11,560
M. LaPietro, Withdrawals		700
Revenues		5,920
Salaries Expense	2,600	
Rent Expense	600	
Advertising Expense	340	
Utilities Expense	26	
	$21,766	$22,720

The trial balance does not balance because of a number of errors. LaPietro's accountant compared the amounts in the trial balance with the ledger, recomputed the account balances, and compared the postings. He found the following errors:

a. The balance of Cash was understated by $400.
b. A cash payment of $420 was credited to Cash for $240.
c. A debit of $120 to Accounts Receivable was not posted.
d. Supplies purchased for $60 were posted as a credit to Supplies.
e. A debit of $180 to Prepaid Insurance was not posted.
f. The Accounts Payable account had debits of $5,320 and credits of $9,180.
g. The Notes Payable account, with a credit balance of $2,400, was not included in the trial balance.
h. The debit balance of M. LaPietro, Withdrawals was listed in the trial balance as a credit.
i. A $200 debit to M. LaPietro, Withdrawals was posted as a credit.
j. The actual balance of Utilities Expense, $260, was listed as $26 in the trial balance.

Prepare a correct trial balance.

E 11.
LO 5 Preparing a Trial Balance

The Zigler Construction Company builds foundations for buildings and parking lots. The following alphabetical list shows the company's account balances as of November 30, 20xx.

Accounts Payable	$ 11,700	Notes Payable	$60,000
Accounts Receivable	30,360	Office Trailer	6,600
Cash	?	Prepaid Insurance	13,800
Construction Supplies	5,700	Revenue Earned	52,200
Equipment	73,500	Supplies Expense	21,600
Dan Zigler, Capital	120,000	Utilities Expense	1,260
Dan Zigler, Withdrawals	23,400	Wages Expense	26,400

Prepare a trial balance for the company with the proper heading and with the accounts in balance sheet sequence. Determine the correct balance for the Cash account on November 30, 20xx.

E 12.
LO 4 Analysis of Unfamiliar
LO 6 Transactions

Managers and accountants often encounter transactions with which they are unfamiliar. Use your analytical skills to analyze and record in journal form the transactions below, which have not yet been discussed in the text.

a. Purchased merchandise inventory on account, $1,600.
b. Purchased marketable securities for cash, $4,800.
c. Returned part of merchandise inventory purchased in **a** for full credit, $500.
d. Sold merchandise inventory on account, $1,600 (record sale only).
e. Purchased land and a building for $600,000. Payment is $120,000 cash and a thirty-year mortgage for the remainder. The purchase price is allocated $200,000 to the land and $400,000 to the building.
f. Received an order for $24,000 in services to be provided. With the order was a deposit of $8,000.

E 13.
LO 6 Recording Transactions
LO 7 in the General Journal and Posting to the Ledger Accounts

Open a general journal form like the one in Exhibit 4, and label it Page 10. After opening the form, record the following transactions in the journal.

Dec. 14 Purchased an item of equipment for $6,000, paying $2,000 as a cash down payment.
28 Paid $3,000 of the amount owed on the equipment.

Prepare three ledger account forms like the one shown in Exhibit 5. Use the following account numbers: Cash, 111; Equipment, 144; and Accounts Payable, 212. Then post the two transactions from the general journal to the ledger accounts, being sure to make proper posting references.

Assume that the Cash account has a debit balance of $8,000 on the day prior to the first transaction.

PROBLEMS

LO 4 Transaction Analysis

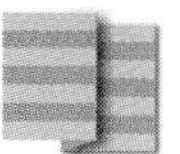

P 1. The following accounts are applicable to Omega Pool Service, a company that maintains swimming pools.

1. Cash	7. Capital
2. Accounts Receivable	8. Withdrawals
3. Supplies	9. Pool Services Revenue
4. Prepaid Insurance	10. Wages Expense
5. Equipment	11. Rent Expense
6. Accounts Payable	12. Utilities Expense

Omega Pool Service completed the following transactions.

	Debit	Credit
a. Received cash from customers billed last month.	1	2
b. Made a payment on accounts payable.		
c. Purchased a new one-year insurance policy in advance.		
d. Purchased supplies on credit.		
e. Billed a client for pool services.		
f. Made a rent payment for the current month.		
g. Received cash from customers for pool services.		
h. Paid wages for the staff.		
i. Ordered equipment.		
j. Paid the current month's utility bill.		
k. Received and paid for the equipment ordered in **i.**		
l. Returned for full credit some of the supplies purchased in **d** because they were defective.		
m. Paid for supplies purchased in **d,** less the return in **l.**		
n. Withdrew cash for personal expenses.		

REQUIRED

Analyze each transaction and show the accounts affected by entering the corresponding numbers in the appropriate debit or credit columns as shown in transaction **a.** Indicate no entry, if appropriate.

LO 4 Transaction Analysis,
LO 5 T Accounts, and Trial Balance

P 2. Diane Pastore established a small business, Pastore Training Center, to teach spreadsheet analysis, word processing, and other techniques on microcomputers.

a. Pastore began by transferring the following assets to the business.

Cash	$9,200
Furniture	3,100
Microcomputers	7,300

b. Paid the first month's rent on a small storefront, $580.
c. Purchased computer software on credit, $750.
d. Paid for an advertisement in the school newspaper, $100.
e. Received enrollment applications from five students for a five-day course to start next week. Each student will pay $200 if he or she actually begins the course.
f. Paid wages to a part-time helper, $150.
g. Received cash payment from three of the students enrolled in **e,** $600.
h. Billed the two other students in **e,** who attended but did not pay in cash, $400.
i. Paid the utility bill for the current month, $110.
j. Made a payment on the software purchased in **c,** $250.
k. Received payment from one student billed in **h,** $200.
l. Purchased a second microcomputer for cash, $4,700.
m. Transferred cash to personal checking account, $300.

REQUIRED

1. Set up the following T accounts: Cash; Accounts Receivable; Software; Furniture; Microcomputers; Accounts Payable; Diane Pastore, Capital; Diane Pastore, Withdrawals; Tuition Revenue; Wages Expense; Utilities Expense; Rent Expense; and Advertising Expense.
2. Record the transactions by entering debits and credits directly in the T accounts, using the transaction letter to identify each debit and credit.

3. Prepare a trial balance using the current date.
4. Contrast the effects on cash flows of transactions **c** and **j** with **d** and of transactions **h** and **k** with transaction **g.**

LO 4 Transaction Analysis,
LO 5 General Journal,
LO 6 Ledger Accounts,
LO 7 and Trial Balance

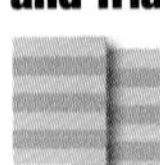

P 3. Vic Kostro opened a photography and portrait studio on March 1 and completed the following transactions during the month.

Mar. 1 Opened the business checking account, $17,000.
2 Paid two months' rent in advance for a studio, $900.
3 Transferred to the business personal photography equipment valued at $4,300.
4 Ordered additional photography equipment, $2,500.
5 Purchased office equipment for cash, $1,800.
8 Received and paid for the photography equipment ordered on March 4, $2,500.
10 Purchased photography supplies on credit, $700.
15 Received cash for portraits, $380.
16 Billed customers for portraits, $750.
21 Paid for half the supplies purchased on March 10, $350.
24 Paid the utility bill for March, $120.
25 Paid the telephone bill for March, $70.
29 Received payment from the customers billed on March 16, $250.
30 Paid wages to an assistant, $400.
31 Withdrew cash for personal expenses, $1,200.

REQUIRED

1. Prepare journal entries to record the above transactions in the general journal (Pages 1 and 2).
2. Set up the following ledger accounts and post the journal entries: Cash (111); Accounts Receivable (113); Photography Supplies (115); Prepaid Rent (116); Photography Equipment (141); Office Equipment (143); Accounts Payable (211); Vic Kostro, Capital (311); Vic Kostro, Withdrawals (312); Portrait Revenue (411); Wages Expense (511); Utilities Expense (512); and Telephone Expense (513).
3. Prepare a trial balance for Kostro Portrait Studio as of March 31, 20xx.

LO 1 Transaction Analysis,
LO 4 Journal Form,
LO 5 T Accounts, and Trial Balance

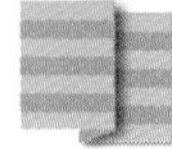 

P 4. Hassan Rahim won a concession to rent bicycles in the local park during the summer. In the month of June, Rahim completed the following transactions for his bicycle rental business:

June 2 Began business by placing $7,200 in a business checking account.
3 Purchased supplies on credit for $150.
4 Purchased ten bicycles for $2,500, paying $1,200 down and agreeing to pay the rest in thirty days.
5 Received $470 in cash for rentals during the first week of operation.
6 Purchased a small shed to hold the bicycles and to use for other operations for $2,900 in cash.
8 Paid $400 in cash for shipping and installation costs (considered an addition to the cost of the shed) to place the shed at the park entrance.
9 Received $500 in cash for rentals during the second week of operation.
10 Hired a part-time assistant to help out on weekends at $8 per hour.
13 Paid a maintenance person $75 to clean the grounds.
16 Paid the assistant $80 for a weekend's work.
17 Paid $150 for the supplies purchased on June 3.
18 Paid a $55 repair bill on bicycles.
20 Received $550 in cash for rentals during the third week of operation.
22 Paid the assistant $80 for a weekend's work.
23 Billed a company $110 for bicycle rentals for an employees' outing.
25 Paid the $100 fee for June to the Park District for the right to the bicycle concession.
27 Received $410 in cash for rentals during the week.
29 Paid the assistant $80 for a weekend's work.
30 Transferred $500 to a personal checking account.

REQUIRED

1. Prepare entries to record these transactions in journal form using the account titles in Part **2**.
2. Set up the following T accounts and post all the journal entries: Cash; Accounts Receivable; Supplies; Shed; Bicycles; Accounts Payable; Hassan Rahim, Capital; Hassan Rahim, Withdrawals; Rental Revenue; Wages Expense; Maintenance Expense; Repair Expense; and Concession Fee Expense.
3. Prepare a trial balance for Rahim Rentals as of June 30, 20xx.
4. Compare how recognition applies to the transactions of June 23 and 27 and their effects on cash flows and how classification applies to the transactions of June 8 and 13.

LO 4 Transaction Analysis,
LO 5 General Journal,
LO 6 Ledger Accounts,
LO 7 and Trial Balance

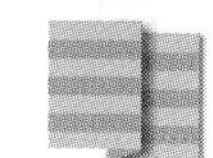

P 5. Delta Security Service provides ushers and security personnel for athletic events and other functions. Delta's trial balance at the end of April was as shown below.

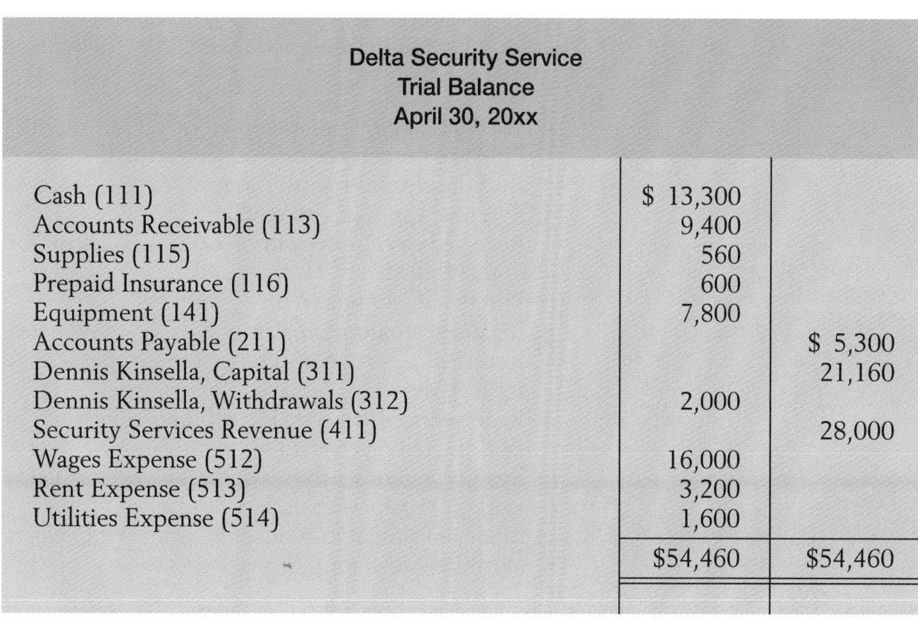

Delta Security Service
Trial Balance
April 30, 20xx

Cash (111)	$ 13,300	
Accounts Receivable (113)	9,400	
Supplies (115)	560	
Prepaid Insurance (116)	600	
Equipment (141)	7,800	
Accounts Payable (211)		$ 5,300
Dennis Kinsella, Capital (311)		21,160
Dennis Kinsella, Withdrawals (312)	2,000	
Security Services Revenue (411)		28,000
Wages Expense (512)	16,000	
Rent Expense (513)	3,200	
Utilities Expense (514)	1,600	
	$54,460	$54,460

During May, Delta engaged in the following transactions.

May 1 Received cash from customers billed last month, $4,200.
2 Made a payment on accounts payable, $3,100.
3 Purchased a new one-year insurance policy in advance, $3,600.
5 Purchased supplies on credit, $430.
6 Billed a client for security services, $2,200.
7 Made a rent payment for May, $800.
9 Received cash from customers for security services, $1,600.
14 Paid wages for the security staff, $1,400.
16 Ordered equipment, $800.
17 Paid the current month's utility bill, $400.
18 Received and paid for the equipment ordered on May 16, $800.
19 Returned for full credit some of the supplies purchased on May 5 because they were defective, $120.
24 Withdrew cash for personal expenses, $1,000.
28 Paid for supplies purchased on May 5, less the return on May 19, $310.
30 Billed a customer for security services performed, $1,800.
31 Paid wages to the security staff, $1,050.

REQUIRED

1. Enter these transactions in the general journal (Pages 26 and 27).
2. Open ledger accounts for the accounts shown in the trial balance.
3. Enter the April 30, 20xx account balances from the trial balance in the appropriate ledger account.

4. Post the entries to the ledger accounts. Be sure to make the appropriate posting references in the journal and ledger as you post.
5. Prepare a trial balance as of May 31, 20xx.

ALTERNATE PROBLEMS

LO 4 Transaction Analysis

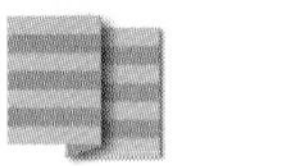

P 6. The following accounts are applicable to Jackson Communications:

1. Cash
2. Accounts Receivable
3. Supplies
4. Prepaid Insurance
5. Equipment
6. Notes Payable
7. Accounts Payable
8. Capital
9. Withdrawals
10. Service Revenue
11. Rent Expense
12. Repair Expense

Jackson Communications completed the following transactions:

	Debit	Credit
a. Paid for supplies purchased on credit last month.	7	1
b. Billed customers for services performed.		
c. Paid the current month's rent.		
d. Purchased supplies on credit.		
e. Received cash from customers for services performed but not yet billed.		
f. Purchased equipment on account.		
g. Received a bill for repairs.		
h. Returned a portion of the equipment that was purchased in **f** for a credit.		
i. Received payments from customers previously billed.		
j. Paid the bill received in **g.**		
k. Received an order for services to be performed.		
l. Paid for repairs with cash.		
m. Made a payment to reduce the principal of the note payable.		
n. Withdrew cash for personal expenses.		

REQUIRED

Analyze each transaction and show the accounts affected by entering the corresponding numbers in the appropriate debit or credit column as shown in transaction **a.** Indicate no entry, if appropriate.

LO 1 Transaction Analysis,
LO 4 Journal Form,
LO 5 T Accounts, and Trial Balance

P 7. Tim Sauk is a house painter. During the month of June, he completed the following transactions:

June 3 Began his business with equipment valued at $2,460 and placed $14,200 in a business checking account.
5 Purchased a used truck costing $3,800. Paid $1,000 in cash and signed a note for the balance.
7 Purchased supplies on account for $640.
8 Completed a painting job and billed the customer $960.
10 Received $300 in cash for painting two rooms.
11 Hired an assistant at $12 per hour.
12 Purchased supplies for $320 in cash.
13 Received a $960 check from the customer billed on June 8.
14 Paid $800 for an insurance policy for eighteen months' coverage.
16 Billed a customer $1,240 for a painting job.
18 Paid the assistant $300 for twenty-five hours' work.
19 Paid $80 for a tune-up for the truck.
20 Paid for the supplies purchased on June 7.
21 Purchased a new ladder (equipment) for $120 and supplies for $580, on account.
23 Received a telephone bill for $120, due next month.
24 Received $660 in cash from the customer billed on June 16.
25 Transferred $600 to a personal checking account.

June 26 Received $720 in cash for painting a five-room apartment.
28 Paid $400 on the note signed for the truck.
29 Paid the assistant $360 for thirty hours' work.

REQUIRED

1. Prepare journal entries to record these transactions in journal form. Use the accounts listed below.
2. Set up the following T accounts and post all the journal entries: Cash; Accounts Receivable; Supplies; Prepaid Insurance; Equipment; Truck; Notes Payable; Accounts Payable; Tim Sauk, Capital; Tim Sauk, Withdrawals; Painting Fees Earned; Wages Expense; Telephone Expense; and Truck Expense.
3. Prepare a trial balance for Sank Painting Service as of June 30, 20xx.
4. Compare how recognition applies to the transactions of June 8 and 10 and their effects on cash flows and how classification applies to the transactions of June 14 and 18.

LO 4 Transaction Analysis,
LO 5 General Journal,
LO 6 Ledger Accounts,
LO 7 and Trial Balance

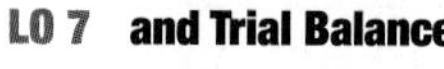

P 8. The account balances for Lou's Landscaping Service at the end of July are shown in the trial balance below. During August, Mr. Jacobson completed these transactions:

Aug. 1 Paid for supplies purchased on credit last month, $140.
2 Billed customers for services, $410.
3 Paid the lease on a truck, $290.
5 Purchased supplies on credit, $150.
7 Received cash from customers not previously billed, $290.
8 Purchased new equipment from Pendleton Manufacturing Company on account, $1,300.
9 Received a bill for an oil change on the truck, $40.
12 Returned a portion of the equipment that was purchased on August 8 for a credit, $320.
13 Received payments from customers previously billed, $190.
14 Paid the bill received on August 9.
16 Took cash from the business for personal use, $110.
19 Paid for the supplies purchased on August 5.
20 Billed customers for services, $270.
23 Purchased equipment from a friend who is retiring, $280. Payment was made from Lou's personal checking account, but the equipment will be used in the business. (**Hint:** Treat this as an owner's investment.)
25 Received payments from customers previously billed, $390.
27 Purchased gasoline for the truck with cash, $30.
29 Made a payment to reduce the principal of the note payable, $600.

Lou's Landscaping Service
Trial Balance
July 31, 20xx

Cash (111)	$3,100	
Accounts Receivable (113)	220	
Supplies (115)	460	
Prepaid Insurance (116)	400	
Equipment (141)	4,400	
Notes Payable (211)		$3,000
Accounts Payable (212)		700
Lou Jacobson, Capital (311)		4,200
Lou Jacobson, Withdrawals (312)	420	
Service Revenue (411)		1,490
Lease Expense (511)	290	
Truck Expense (512)	100	
	$9,390	$9,390

REQUIRED

1. Enter these transactions in the general journal (Pages 11 and 12).
2. Open accounts in the ledger for the accounts in the trial balance.
3. Enter the July 31, 20xx account balances from the trial balance.
4. Post the entries to the ledger accounts. Be sure to make the appropriate posting references in the journal and ledger as you post.
5. Prepare a trial balance as of August 31, 20xx.

EXPANDING YOUR CRITICAL THINKING, COMMUNICATION, AND INTERPERSONAL SKILLS

SKILLS DEVELOPMENT

Conceptual Analysis

LO 1 Valuation Issue

SD 1. *Nike, Inc.,* manufactures athletic shoes and related products. In one of its annual reports, Nike made this statement: "Property, plant, and equipment are recorded at cost."[8] Given that the property, plant, and equipment undoubtedly were purchased over several years and that the current value of those assets was likely to be very different from their original cost, tell what authoritative basis there is for carrying the assets at cost. Does accounting generally recognize changes in value subsequent to the purchase of property, plant, and equipment? Assume you are a Nike accountant. Write a memo to management explaining the rationale underlying Nike's approach.

LO 1 Recognition, Valuation,
LO 4 and Classification Issues

SD 2. *Chambers Development,* a landfill development company, announced a change in its accounting practices. The company said the change would result in a restatement of its prior year's earnings. News of the accounting change caused the stock price to drop from $30½ to $11⅛ in one day, and it continued to decline to a low of $1⅞ two years later. According to one account,

> At the core of the problem was how Chambers accounted for millions of dollars it was spending to develop landfills. The company's choice: charge the costs in the year in which they were incurred or over the life of the landfill. The first method would increase operating costs, thereby depressing current earnings. On the other hand, writing off the costs gradually—"capitalizing" them in accounting parlance—would boost current earnings.[9]

Chambers initially chose to capitalize these costs (as an asset) and expense them gradually over future years. The change to immediate expensing led to a reduction of prior years' earnings of $362 million. The SEC required the restatement of Chambers' financial statements back to the year the company went public. The SEC determined that the amounts capitalized exceeded the reported pretax earnings. Instead of earning profits, the company had actually incurred losses.

The SEC discovered that management would set a target earnings level and back into the amount of costs to be capitalized to achieve the earnings target. The SEC investigation concluded "that the accounting practices that created millions of dollars in false profits were well outside the general bounds of generally accepted accounting practices. They were based on queered mathematics and an overzealous desire to please Wall Street, not an uncommon cause of corporate accounting scandals."[10]

1. Prepare the journal entry that Chambers made to record landfill costs as an asset (prepaid landfill costs). Prepare the journal entry to reduce its prepaid landfill costs by $362 million.

Cash Flow
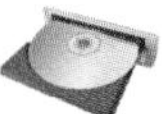
CD-ROM

Communication

Critical Thinking

Ethics

General Ledger

Group Activity

Hot Links to Real Companies

International

Internet

Key Ratio

Memo

Spreadsheet

2. Three issues that must be addressed when recording a transaction are recognition, valuation, and classification. Which of these issues were of most concern to the SEC in the Chambers case? Explain how each applies to the transactions in part **1**.

Group Activity: Students work in groups to complete part **1**. Discuss part **2** as a class.

Ethical Dilemma

SD 3.
LO 1 Recognition Point and Ethical Considerations

One of ***Penn Office Supplies Corporation***'s sales representatives, Jerry Hasbrow, is compensated on a commission basis and receives a substantial bonus for meeting his annual sales goal. The company's recognition point for sales is the day of shipment. On December 31, Hasbrow realizes that he needs sales of $2,000 to reach his sales goal and receive the bonus. He calls a purchasing agent for a local insurance company, whom he knows well, and asks him to buy $2,000 worth of copier paper today. The purchasing agent says, "But Jerry, that's more than a year's supply for us." Hasbrow says, "Buy it today. If you decide it's too much, you can return however much you want for full credit next month." The purchasing agent says, "Okay, ship it." The paper is shipped on December 31 and recorded as a sale. On January 15, the purchasing agent returns $1,750 worth of paper for full credit (okayed by Hasbrow) against the bill. Should the shipment on December 31 be recorded as a sale? Discuss the ethics of Hasbrow's action.

Group Activity: Divide the class into informal groups to discuss and report on the ethical issues of this case.

Research Activity

SD 4.
LO 4 Transactions in a Business Article

Locate an article on a company you recognize or on a company in a business that interests you in one of the following sources: a recent issue of a business journal (such as *Barron's, Fortune, The Wall Street Journal, Business Week,* or *Forbes*), or the Needles Accounting Resource Center web site at http://college.hmco.com. Read the article carefully, noting any references to transactions in which the company engages. These may be normal transactions (sales, purchases) or unusual transactions (a merger, the purchase of another company). Bring a copy of the article to class and be prepared to describe how you would analyze and record the transactions you have noted.

Decision-Making Practice

SD 5.
LO 4 Transaction Analysis and
LO 5 Evaluation of a Trial Balance

Ben Obi hired an attorney to help him start ***Obi Repairs Company.*** On June 1, Obi invested $23,000 in cash in the business. When he paid the attorney's bill of $1,400, the attorney advised him to hire an accountant to keep his records. However, Obi was so busy that it was June 30 before he asked you to straighten out his records. Your first task is to develop a trial balance based on the June transactions.

After making the investment and paying the attorney, Obi borrowed $10,000 from the bank. He later paid $520, which included interest of $120, on this loan. He also purchased a pickup truck in the company's name, paying $5,000 down and financing $14,800. The first payment on the truck is due July 15. Obi then rented an office and paid three months' rent, $1,800, in advance. Credit purchases of office equipment for $1,400 and repair tools for $1,000 must be paid for by July 13.

In June, Obi Repairs completed repairs of $2,600, of which $800 were cash transactions. Of the credit transactions, $600 were collected during June, and $1,200 remained to be collected at the end of June. Wages of $800 were paid to employees. On June 30, the company received a $150 bill for June utilities and a $100 check from a customer for work to be completed in July.

1. Record the June transactions in journal form.
2. Set up T accounts, post the general journal entries to the T accounts, and determine the balance of each account.
3. Prepare a June 30 trial balance for Obi Repairs Company.

4. Ben Obi is unsure how to evaluate the trial balance. His Cash account balance is $24,980, which exceeds his original investment of $23,000 by $1,980. Did he make a profit of $1,980? Explain why the Cash account is not an indicator of business earnings. Cite specific examples to show why it is difficult to determine net income by looking solely at figures in the trial balance.

FINANCIAL REPORTING AND ANALYSIS

Interpreting Financial Reports

LO 2 Interpreting a Bank's
LO 4 Financial Statements

FRA 1. *Mellon Bank* is a large eastern bank holding company. Selected accounts from the company's 1999 annual report are as follows (in millions):[11]

Cash and Due from Banks	$ 3,410	Investment Securities	$ 1,193
Loans to Customers	30,248	Deposits by Customers	33,421

REQUIRED

1. Indicate whether each of the accounts just listed is an asset, a liability, or a component of owner's equity on Mellon's balance sheet.
2. Assume that you are in a position to do business with Mellon. Prepare the entry on the bank's books in journal form to record each of the following transactions:
   a. You sell securities in the amount of $2,000 to the bank.
   b. You deposit the $2,000 received in step **a** in the bank.
   c. You borrow $5,000 from the bank.

International Company

LO 4 Transaction Analysis

FRA 2. *Ajinomoto Company,* a Japanese company with operations in 22 countries, is primarily engaged in the manufacture and sale of food products. The following selected aggregate cash transactions were reported in the statement of cash flows in Ajinomoto's annual report (amounts in millions of yen):[12]

Dividends paid	¥ 7,793
Purchase of property, plant, and equipment	46,381
Proceeds from long-term debt	10,357
Repayment of long-term debt	11,485

REQUIRED

Prepare entries in journal form to record the above transactions.

Toys "R" Us Annual Report

LO 4 Transaction Analysis

FRA 3. Refer to the balance sheet in the Toys "R" Us annual report. Prepare T accounts for the accounts Cash and Cash Equivalents, Accounts and Other Receivables, Prepaid Expenses and Other Current Assets, Accounts Payable, and Income Taxes Payable. Properly place the balance of the account at January 29, 2000, in the T accounts. Below are some typical transactions in which Toys "R" Us would engage. Analyze each transaction, enter it in the T accounts, and determine the balance of each account. Assume all entries are in millions.

a. Paid cash in advance for certain expenses, $20.
b. Received cash from customers billed previously, $35.
c. Paid cash for income taxes previously owed, $70.
d. Paid cash to suppliers for amounts owed, $120.

Fingraph® Financial Analyst™

LO 1 Transaction
LO 3 Identification
LO 4

FRA 4. Choose any company in the Fingraph® Financial Analyst™ CD-ROM software.

1. From the company's annual report, determine the industry(ies) in which the company operates.
2. Find the summary of significant accounting policies that appears following the financial statements. In these policies, find examples of the application of recognition, valuation, and classification.

3. Identify six types of transactions that your company would commonly engage in. Are any of these transactions more common in the industry in which your company operates than in other industries? For each transaction, tell what account would typically be debited and what account would be credited.
4. Prepare a one-page executive summary that highlights what you have learned from parts **1, 2,** and **3.**

Internet Case

FRA 5.
LO 2 Comparison of Contrasting
LO 4 Companies

Sun Microsystems and ***Oracle Corporation*** are leading computer and software companies. Compare and contrast the balance sheets of the two companies by first going to the Needles Accounting Resource Center web site at http://college.hmco.com. After choosing your textbook, click on "Chapter Resources" for Chapter 2. Then click on "Links to Companies in Text." Both companies are here. For each company, find its balance sheet. First, what differences and similarities do you find in the account titles used by Sun Microsystems and those used by Oracle? What differences and similarities do you find in the account titles used by the two companies and those used in your text? Second, although the companies are in the same general industry, their businesses differ. How are these differences reflected on the balance sheets? What types of transactions resulted in the differences?

Endnotes

1. "Boeing Scores a Deal to Sell 10 Planes to Air France for Long-Haul Routes," *The Wall Street Journal*, October 5, 2000.
2. The Boeing Co., *Annual Report*, 1994.
3. Craig S. Smith, "China Halts New Purchases of Jets," *The Wall Street Journal*, February 9, 1999.
4. Sun Microsystems Inc., *Annual Report*, 1999.
5. Intel Corp., *Annual Report*, 2000.
6. David Bank, "Informix Says Accounting Problems Were More Serious Than First Disclosed," *The Wall Street Journal*, September 23, 1997.
7. Patricia Kranz, "Rubles? Who Needs Rubles?" *Business Week*, April 13, 1998; Andrew Higgins, "Lacking Money to Pay, Russian Firms Survive on Deft Barter System," *The Wall Street Journal*, August 27, 1998.
8. Nike, Inc., *Annual Report*, 2000.
9. Len Boselovic, "A Look at How the SEC Disposed of Chambers' Claims," *Pittsburgh Post-Gazette*, May 14, 1995.
10. Ibid.
11. Mellon Bank, *Annual Report*, 1999.
12. Ajinomoto Company, *Annual Report*, 2000.

3 Measuring Business Income

LEARNING OBJECTIVES

1. Define *net income* and its two major components, *revenues* and *expenses*.
2. Explain the difficulties of income measurement caused by the accounting period issue, the continuity issue, and the matching issue.
3. Define *accrual accounting* and explain two broad ways of accomplishing it.
4. State four principal situations that require adjusting entries.
5. Prepare typical adjusting entries.
6. Prepare financial statements from an adjusted trial balance.

SUPPLEMENTAL OBJECTIVE

7. Analyze cash flows from accrual-based information.

DECISION POINT: A USER'S FOCUS

Southwest Airlines Co. Southwest Airlines Co. has become one of the most successful airlines by providing low-fare service between city pairs that are relatively close together. During any given year, Southwest incurs various operating expenses that are recorded as expenses when they are paid. However, at the end of the year, some expenses—including, for example, the wages of employees during the last days before the end of the year—will have been incurred but will not be paid until the next year. If these expenses are not accounted for correctly, they will appear in the wrong year—the year in which they are paid instead of the year in which Southwest benefited from them. The result is a misstatement of the company's income, a key profitability performance measure. How is this problem avoided?

According to the concepts of accrual accounting and the matching rule, which you will learn about in this chapter, the amount of expenses that have been incurred but not paid must be determined. Then they are recorded as expenses of the current year with corresponding liabilities to be paid the next year. The accompanying Financial Highlights shows the liabilities, called *accrued liabilities*, that resulted from this process at Southwest Airlines.[1] Accrued liabilities for aircraft rentals, employee profit sharing and savings plans, vacation pay, and other were $477,448,000 in 1998 and $535,024,000 in 1999. If these items had not been recorded in their respective years, income would have been misstated by a significant amount and the readers would have been misled.

Critical Thinking Question: Why should all companies record identical business activities in the same way? **Answer:** In general, recording activities in a like manner increases the comparability of income among companies. If, for example, all companies record a payroll adjusting entry in the same way, then users know that all payroll costs associated with revenues recorded are included in total expenses and resulting net income.

Financial Highlights: Notes to the Financial Statements

3. ACCRUED LIABILITIES

(In thousands)	1999	1998
Aircraft rentals	$131,219	$121,868
Employee profitsharing and savings plans	138,566	123,195
Vacation pay	62,937	54,781
Other	202,302	177,604
Total accrued liabilities	$535,024	$477,448

Profitability Measurement: The Role of Business Income

Point to Emphasize: An important purpose of accounting is to measure and report a business's profitability. The extent of the reported profit or loss communicates the company's success or failure with regard to this business goal.

Profitability is one of the two major goals of a business (the other being liquidity). For a business to succeed, or even to survive, it must earn a profit. The word **profit**, though, has many meanings. One is the increase in owner's equity that results from business operations. However, even this definition can be interpreted differently by economists, lawyers, businesspeople, and the public. Because the word *profit* has more than one meaning, accountants prefer to use the term *net income*, which can be precisely defined from an accounting point of view. Net income is reported on the income statement and is a performance measure used by management, owners, and others to monitor a business's progress in meeting the goal of profitability. Readers of income statements need to understand how the accountant defines net income and to be aware of its strengths and weaknesses as a measure of company performance.

Net Income

OBJECTIVE

1 Define *net income* and its two major components, *revenues* and *expenses*

Related Text Assignments:
Q: 1, 2
SD: 5
FRA: 5

Net income is the net increase in owner's equity that results from the operations of a company and is accumulated in the owner's Capital account. Net income, in its simplest form, is measured by the difference between revenues and expenses when revenues exceed expenses:

$$\text{Net Income} = \text{Revenues} - \text{Expenses}$$

When expenses exceed revenues, a **net loss** occurs.

Common Student Confusion: At this point, students do not understand the difference between cash and revenue. Point out the difference in terms of both their placement in the financial statements and the intangible nature of revenue.

Point to Emphasize: The essence of revenue is that something has been *earned* through the sale of goods or services. That is why cash received through a loan does not constitute revenue.

REVENUES **Revenues** are increases in owner's equity resulting from selling goods, rendering services, or performing other business activities. Revenues are inflows, usually of cash or receivables, received in exchange for products or services. In the simplest case, revenues equal the price of goods sold and services rendered over a specific period of time. When a business delivers a product or provides a service to a customer, it usually receives either cash or a promise to pay cash in the near future. The promise to pay is recorded in either Accounts Receivable or Notes Receivable. The revenue for a given period equals the total of cash and receivables generated from goods and services provided to customers during that period.

Liabilities generally are not affected by revenues, and some transactions that increase cash and other assets do not produce revenues. For example a bank loan increases liabilities and cash but does not produce revenue. The collection of accounts receivable, which increases cash and decreases accounts receivable, does not produce revenue either. Remember that when a sale on credit takes place, the asset account Accounts Receivable increases; at the same time, an owner's equity revenue account increases. So counting the collection of the receivable as revenue later would be counting the same sale twice.

Not all increases in owner's equity arise from revenues. Owner investments increase owner's equity but are not revenue.

Point to Emphasize: The primary purpose of an expense is to generate revenue.

EXPENSES **Expenses** are decreases in owner's equity resulting from the costs of selling goods, rendering services, or performing other business activities. In other words, expenses are the costs of the goods and services used up in the course of earning revenues. Often called the *cost of doing business*, expenses include the cost of goods sold, the costs of activities necessary to carry on a business, and the costs of attracting and serving customers. Other examples are salaries, rent, advertising, telephone service, expired or used assets, and depreciation (allocation of cost) of a building or office equipment.

Business-World Example: Income measurement is difficult in many industries because of the uncertainties associated with their revenues and expenses. For example, in the period of the sale, cereal companies must recognize the expense associated with boxtops and coupons expected to be redeemed ultimately. And construction companies must estimate their revenues based upon a project's percentage of completion.

Just as not all cash receipts are revenues, not all cash payments are expenses. A cash payment to reduce a liability does not result in an expense because no good or service was used in the exchange. The liability, however, may have come from incurring a previous expense, such as advertising, that is to be paid later. There may also be two steps before an expenditure of cash becomes an expense. For example, prepaid expenses and plant assets (such as machinery and equipment) are recorded as assets when they are acquired. Later, as their usefulness expires in the operation of the business, their cost is allocated to expenses. In fact, expenses sometimes are called *expired costs*.

Not all decreases in owner's equity arise from expenses. Owner withdrawals decrease owner's equity, but they are not expenses.

The Accounting Period Issue

OBJECTIVE

2 Explain the difficulties of income measurement caused by the accounting period issue, the continuity issue, and the matching issue

Related Text Assignments:
Q: 3, 4, 5
SE: 1
E: 1
SD: 1, 3
FRA: 1, 3

The **accounting period issue** addresses the difficulty of assigning revenues and expenses to a short period of time, such as a month or a year. Not all transactions can be easily assigned to specific time periods. Purchases of buildings and equipment, for example, have effects that extend over many years. Accountants solve this problem by estimating the number of years the buildings or equipment will be in use and the cost that should be assigned to each year. In the process, they make an assumption about **periodicity**: that the net income for any period of time less than the life of the business, although tentative, is still a useful estimate of the entity's profitability for the period.

Point to Emphasize: Accounting periods must be of equal length so that one period can be compared to the next.

Generally, to make comparisons easier, the time periods are of equal length. Financial statements may be prepared for any time period. Accounting periods of less than one year—for example, a month or a quarter—are called *interim periods*. The 12-month accounting period used by a company is called its **fiscal year**. Many companies use the calendar year, January 1 to December 31, for their fiscal year. Others find it convenient to choose a fiscal year that ends during a slack season rather than a peak season. In this case, the fiscal year corresponds to the company's yearly cycle of business activity. The time period should always be noted in the financial statements.

The Continuity Issue

The process of measuring business income requires that certain expense and revenue transactions be allocated over several accounting periods. The number of accounting periods raises the **continuity issue**. How long will the business entity

Focus on Business Practice

The table on the right shows the diverse fiscal years used by some well-known companies. Many governmental and educational units use fiscal years that end June 30 or September 30.

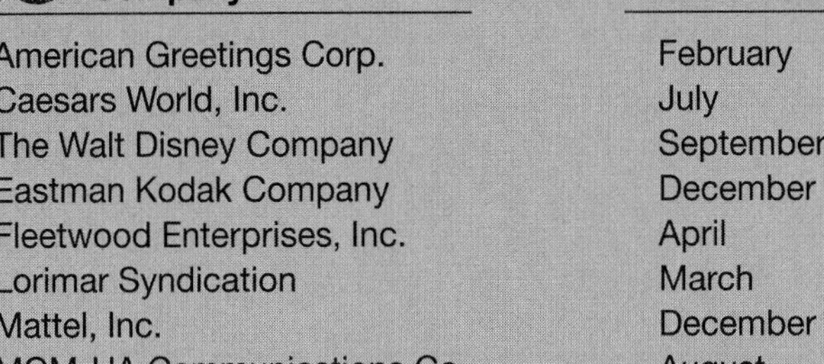

Company	Last Month of Fiscal Year
American Greetings Corp.	February
Caesars World, Inc.	July
The Walt Disney Company	September
Eastman Kodak Company	December
Fleetwood Enterprises, Inc.	April
Lorimar Syndication	March
Mattel, Inc.	December
MGM-UA Communications Co.	August
Polaroid Corp.	December

Business-World Example: The continuity assumption is set aside when an organization is formed for a limited venture, such as a World's Fair or an Olympics.

last? Many businesses last less than five years; in any given year, thousands of businesses go bankrupt. To prepare financial statements for an accounting period, the accountant must make an assumption about the ability of the business to survive. Specifically, unless there is evidence to the contrary, the accountant assumes that the business will continue to operate indefinitely, that the business is a **going concern**. Justification for all the techniques of income measurement rests on the assumption of continuity. For example, this assumption allows the cost of certain assets to be held on the balance sheet until a future year, when it will become an expense on the income statement.

Another example has to do with the value of assets on the balance sheet. The accountant records assets at cost and does not record subsequent changes in their value. But the value of assets to a going concern is much higher than the value of assets to a firm facing bankruptcy. In the latter case, the accountant may be asked to set aside the assumption of continuity and to prepare financial statements based on the assumption that the firm will go out of business and sell all of its assets at liquidation value—that is, for what they will bring in cash.

The Matching Issue

Point to Emphasize: Although the cash basis often is used for tax purposes, it seldom produces an accurate measurement of a business's performance for financial reporting purposes.

Discussion Question: Suppose a company buys a building and expenses its cost in the year of the purchase. What financial reporting problem does this create, and what is the correct way to account for the building? **Answer:** Expensing the building immediately understates income (and total assets) in the year of the purchase and overstates income in the remaining years of the building's life. The cost of the building should be expensed over the years during which the building will benefit the business.

Revenues and expenses can be accounted for on a cash received and cash paid basis. This practice is known as the **cash basis of accounting**. Individuals and some businesses may use the cash basis of accounting for income tax purposes. Under this method, revenues are reported in the period in which cash is received, and expenses are reported in the period in which cash is paid. Taxable income, therefore, is calculated as the difference between cash receipts from revenues and cash payments for expenses.

Although the cash basis of accounting works well for some small businesses and many individuals, it does not meet the needs of most businesses. As explained above, revenues can be earned in a period other than the one in which cash is received, and expenses can be incurred in a period other than the one in which cash is paid. To measure net income adequately, revenues and expenses must be assigned to the appropriate accounting period. The accountant solves this problem by applying the **matching rule**:

> Revenues must be assigned to the accounting period in which the goods are sold or the services performed, and expenses must be assigned to the accounting period in which they are used to produce revenue.

Accounting practices are meant to inform the readers of financial statements, not to deceive them. Accounting assumptions and rules, such as the periodicity assumption and the matching rule, should not be applied in a way that will distort or obscure financial results. In recent years, Securities and Exchange Commission Chairman Arthur Levitt has waged a public campaign against corporate accounting practices that arise when companies manage or manipulate their earnings to meet Wall Street analysts' expectations. Management in these cases is fearful that a shortfall will trigger a big decline in its company's stock price. Companies, for instance, may increase expenses, inappropriately applying the matching rule and periodicity assumption by reducing earnings in a year of unusually high income and boosting income in subsequent years by reducing expenses. The SEC has challenged the accounting of many companies, including Sunbeam-Oster Company, Inc., and Cisco Systems.[2]

Discussion Question: Why must a company recognize warranty expense in the year of the sale rather than in the year of the repair or replacement? **Answer:** To measure a company's performance accurately, each expense must be matched with the related revenue. Otherwise, net income will be overstated and the liability will be understated.

Direct cause-and-effect relationships seldom can be demonstrated for certain, but many costs appear to be related to particular revenues. The accountant recognizes these expenses and the related revenues in the same accounting period. Examples are the costs of goods sold and sales commissions. When there is no direct means of connecting expenses and revenues, the accountant tries to allocate costs in a systematic way among the accounting periods that benefit from the costs. For example, a building is converted from an asset to an expense by allocating its cost over the years during which the company benefits from its use.

Accrual Accounting

OBJECTIVE

3 Define *accrual accounting* and explain two broad ways of accomplishing it

Related Text Assignments:
Q: 6, 7, 8
SE: 1
E: 1
SD: 1, 2, 3
FRA: 3

To apply the matching rule, accountants have developed accrual accounting. **Accrual accounting** "attempts to record the financial effects on an enterprise of transactions and other events and circumstances . . . in the periods in which those transactions, events, and circumstances occur rather than only in the periods in which cash is received or paid by the enterprise."[3] That is, accrual accounting consists of all the techniques developed by accountants to apply the matching rule. It is done in two general ways: (1) by recording revenues when earned and expenses when incurred and (2) by adjusting the accounts.

Recognizing Revenues When Earned and Expenses When Incurred

Common Student Error: Students have difficulty understanding the relationship between accrual accounting and the matching rule. Explain that accrual accounting is a set of *procedures* (such as journal entries) devised to follow the *guideline* known as the matching rule.

The first application of accrual accounting is the recognition of revenues when earned and expenses when incurred. For example, when Joan Miller Advertising Agency makes a sale on credit by placing advertisements for a client, revenue is recorded at the time of the sale by debiting Accounts Receivable and crediting Advertising Fees Earned. This is how the accountant recognizes the revenue from a credit sale before the cash is collected. Accounts Receivable serves as a holding account until payment is received. The process of determining when revenue is earned, and consequently when it should be recorded, is referred to as **revenue recognition**.

When Joan Miller Advertising Agency receives its telephone bill, the expense is recognized both as having been incurred and as helping to produce revenue. The transaction is recorded by debiting Telephone Expense and crediting Accounts Payable. Until the bill is paid, Accounts Payable serves as a holding account. Notice that recognition of the expense does not depend on the payment of cash.

Adjusting the Accounts

The second application of accrual accounting is adjusting the accounts. Adjustments are necessary because the accounting period, by definition, ends on a particular day. The balance sheet must list all assets and liabilities as of the end of that day, and the income statement must contain all revenues and expenses applicable to the period ending on that day. Although operating a business is a continuous process, there must be a cutoff point for the periodic reports. Some transactions invariably span the cutoff point; thus, some accounts need adjustment.

For example, some of the accounts in the end-of-the-period trial balance for Joan Miller Advertising Agency (Exhibit 1) do not show the correct balances for preparing the financial statements. The January 31 trial balance lists prepaid rent

Exhibit 1
Trial Balance for Joan Miller Advertising Agency

Joan Miller Advertising Agency Trial Balance January 31, 20xx		
Cash	$ 1,720	
Accounts Receivable	2,800	
Art Supplies	1,800	
Office Supplies	800	
Prepaid Rent	800	
Prepaid Insurance	480	
Art Equipment	4,200	
Office Equipment	3,000	
Accounts Payable		$ 3,170
Unearned Art Fees		1,000
Joan Miller, Capital		10,000
Joan Miller, Withdrawals	1,400	
Advertising Fees Earned		4,200
Wages Expense	1,200	
Utilities Expense	100	
Telephone Expense	70	
	$18,370	$18,370

Teaching Note: Students may ask why the accountant waits until the end of an accounting period to update certain revenues and expenses. Explain that even though the revenues and expenses theoretically have changed during the period, many as a result of time passing, there usually is no need to adjust them until the end of the period, when the financial statements are prepared. In fact, it would be impractical, even impossible, to adjust the accounts each time they are affected.

of $800. At $400 per month, this represents rent for the months of January and February. So on January 31, one-half of the $800, or $400, represents rent expense for January; the remaining $400 represents an asset that will be used in February. An adjustment is needed to reflect the $400 balance in the Prepaid Rent account on the balance sheet and the $400 rent expense on the income statement. As you will see on the following pages, several other accounts in the Joan Miller Advertising Agency trial balance do not reflect their correct balances. Like the Prepaid Rent account, they need to be adjusted.

Accrual Accounting and Performance Measures

Accrual accounting can be difficult to understand. The related adjustments take time to calculate and enter in the records. Also, adjusting entries do not affect cash flows in the current period because they never involve the Cash account. You might ask, "Why go to all the trouble of making them? Why worry about them?" The Securities and Exchange Commission, in fact, has identified issues related to accrual accounting and adjustments to be an area of utmost importance because of the potential for abuse and misrepresentation.[4]

Critical Thinking Question: If adjustments are not made, what type of operating performance measure would you have? Answer: Cash receipts from operations minus cash disbursements from operations yields net cash either from or used by operations. Remind students that adjusting entries never affect cash but are necessary to measure net income.

All adjustments are important because they are necessary to calculate key profitability performance measures. Adjusting entries affect net income on the income statement, and they affect profitability comparisons from one accounting period to the next. Adjusting entries also affect assets and liabilities on the balance sheet and thus provide information about a company's *future* cash inflows and outflows. This information is needed to assess management's short-term goal of achieving sufficient liquidity to meet its needs for cash to pay ongoing obligations. The potential for abuse arises from the fact that considerable judgment underlies the application of adjusting entries. Misuse of this judgment can result in misleading measures of performance.

the months pass, the amount of accumulated depreciation grows, and the net amount shown as an asset declines. In six months, Accumulated Depreciation, Art Equipment will show a balance of $420; when this amount is subtracted from Art Equipment, a net amount of $3,780 will remain. The net amount is called the **carrying value**, or *book value*, of the asset.

Type 2: Recognizing Unrecorded Expenses (Accrued Expenses)

At the end of an accounting period, there usually are expenses that have been incurred but not recorded in the accounts. These expenses require adjusting entries. One such case is interest on borrowed money. Each day, interest accumulates on the debt. As shown in Figure 4, at the end of the accounting period, an adjusting entry is made to record this accumulated interest, which is an expense of the period, and the corresponding liability to pay the interest. Other common unrecorded expenses are wages and utilities. As the expense and the corresponding liability accumulate, they are said to *accrue*—hence the term **accrued expenses**.

Accrued Wages Suppose the calendar for January looks like this:

Common Student Error: Some students may not understand why the adjustment in this example is for Monday through Wednesday, not for Thursday and Friday. Point out that Thursday and Friday are not covered in this accounting period.

January

Su	M	T	W	Th	F	Sa
	1	2	3	4	5	6
7	8	9	10	11	12	13
14	15	16	17	18	19	20
21	22	23	24	25	26	27
28	29	30	31			

By the end of business on January 31, the secretary at Joan Miller Advertising Agency will have worked three days (Monday, Tuesday, and Wednesday) beyond

Figure 4
Adjustment for Unrecorded (Accrued) Expenses

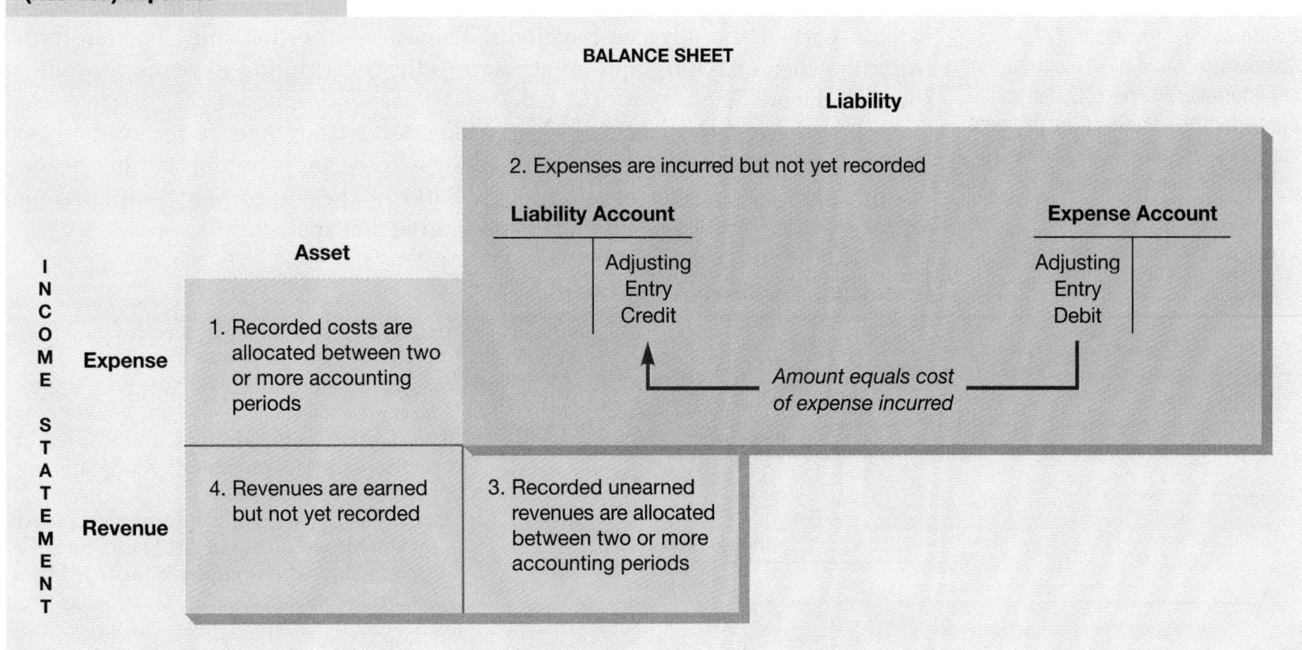

Instructional Strategy: To reinforce the idea that every adjusting entry affects one balance sheet account and one income statement account, use FRA 4 or the Joan Miller Advertising Agency balance sheet in Exhibit 4. Ask students which balance sheet accounts are most likely to have had adjusting entries and what the corresponding income statement accounts would be.

the last biweekly pay period, which ended on January 26. The employee has earned the wages for these days, but she will not be paid until the regular payday in February. The wages for these three days are rightfully an expense for January, and the liabilities should reflect the fact that the company owes the secretary for those days. Because the secretary's wage rate is $600 every two weeks, or $60 per day ($600 ÷ 10 working days), the expense is $180 ($60 × 3 days).

Accrued Wages (Adjustment g)

A = L + OE
    + −

		Dr.	Cr.
Jan. 31	Wages Expense	180	
	Wages Payable		180

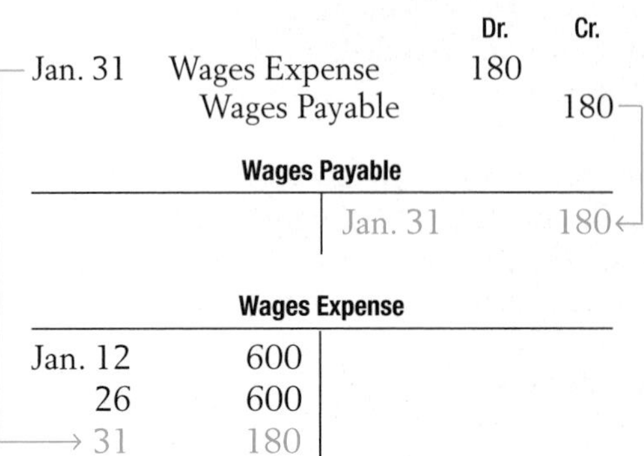

Wages Payable

		Jan. 31	180

Wages Expense

Jan. 12	600		
26	600		
31	180		

Transaction: Accrual of unrecorded expense.
Analysis: Liabilities increase. Owner's equity decreases.
Rules: Decreases in owner's equity are recorded by debits. Increases in liabilities are recorded by credits.
Entries: The decrease in owner's equity is recorded by a debit to Wages Expense. The increase in liabilities is recorded by a credit to Wages Payable.

Reinforcement Exercise: XYZ Company pays wages of $1,500 every Friday (for a five-day work week). Assuming that the period ends on a Tuesday, prepare XYZ's adjusting entry. Solution:

Wages Expense	600	
Wages Payable		600

Point to Emphasize: Remember that an expense must be recorded in the period in which it is incurred, regardless of when payment is made.

The liability of $180 is now reflected correctly in the Wages Payable account. The actual expense incurred for wages during January, $1,380, is also correct.

Type 3: Allocating Recorded Unearned Revenues Between Two or More Accounting Periods (Deferred Revenues)

Point to Emphasize: Unearned Revenue is a liability because there is an obligation either to deliver goods or perform a service, or to return the payment. Once the goods have been delivered or the service performed, the liability is converted into revenue.

Just as expenses can be paid before they are used, revenues can be received before they are earned. When revenues are received in advance, the company has an obligation to deliver goods or perform services. Therefore, **unearned revenues** are shown in a liability account. For example, publishing companies usually receive payment in advance for magazine subscriptions. These receipts are recorded in a liability account. If the company fails to deliver the magazines, subscribers are entitled to their money back. As the company delivers each issue of the magazine, it earns a part of the advance payments. This earned portion must be transferred from the Unearned Subscriptions account to the Subscription Revenue account, as shown in Figure 5.

During the month of January, Joan Miller Advertising Agency received $1,000 as an advance payment for advertising designs to be prepared for another agency. Assume that by the end of the month, $400 of the design was completed and accepted by the other agency. Here is the transaction analysis:

Reinforcement Exercise: XYZ Company received $500 in advance of performing a service. By the end of the period, one-fourth of the payment had been earned. Prepare the end-of-period adjustment. Solution:

Unearned Revenues	125	
Revenue from Services		125

Unearned Art Fees (Adjustment h)

A = L + OE
    − +

		Dr.	Cr.
Jan. 31	Unearned Art Fees	400	
	Art Fees Earned		400

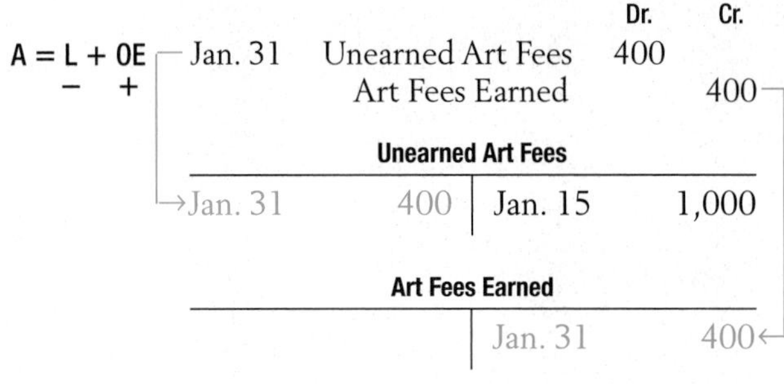

Unearned Art Fees

Jan. 31	400	Jan. 15	1,000

Art Fees Earned

		Jan. 31	400

Transaction: Performance of services paid for in advance.
Analysis: Liabilities decrease. Owner's equity increases.
Rules: Decreases in liabilities are recorded by debits. Increases in owner's equity are recorded by credits.
Entries: The decrease in liabilities is recorded by a debit to Unearned Art Fees. The increase in owner's equity is recorded by a credit to Art Fees Earned.

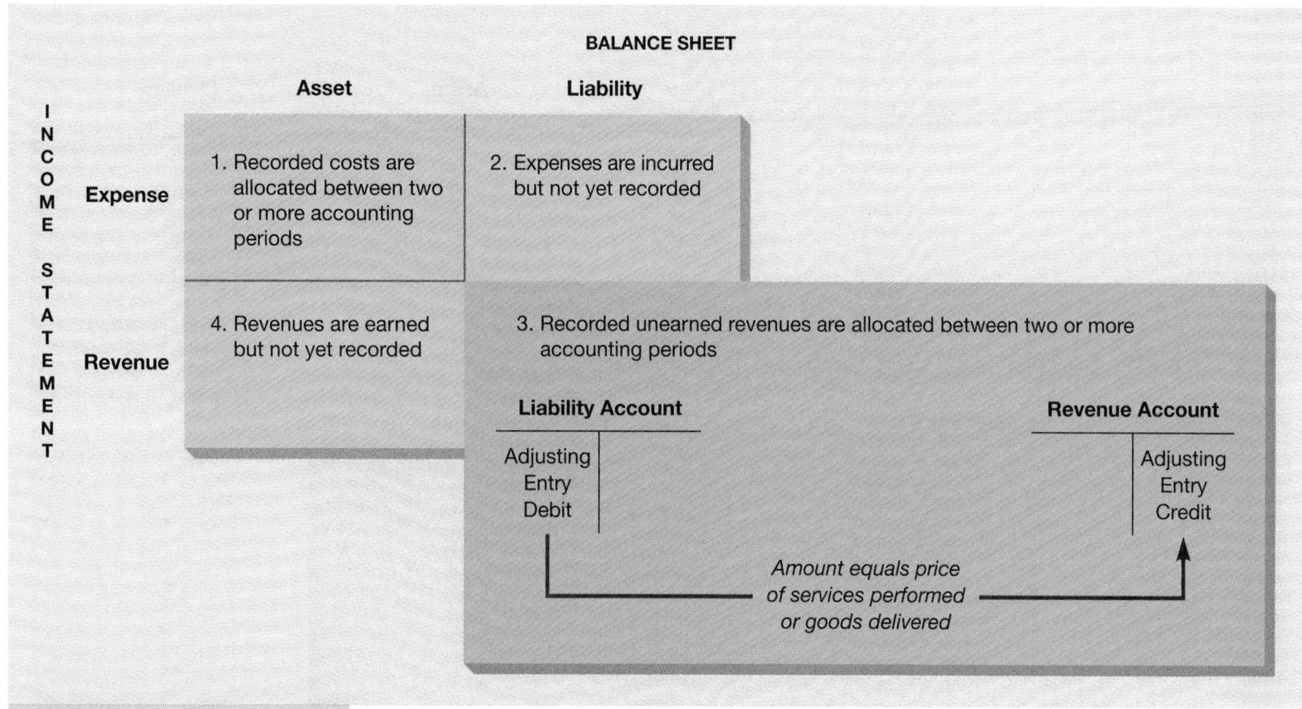

Figure 5
Adjustment for Unearned (Deferred) Revenues

The liability account Unearned Art Fees now reflects the amount of work still to be performed, $600. The revenue account Art Fees Earned reflects the services performed and the revenue earned for them during January, $400.

Type 4: Recognizing Unrecorded Revenues (Accrued Revenues)

Teaching Note: Distinguish between unearned revenues and accrued revenues by pointing out that with accrued revenues, cash is not received in advance or by the end of the period.

Accrued revenues are revenues for which a service has been performed or goods delivered but for which no entry has been recorded. Any revenues earned but not recorded during the accounting period require an adjusting entry that debits an asset account and credits a revenue account, as shown in Figure 6. For example, the interest on a note receivable is earned day by day but may not be received until another accounting period. Interest Receivable should be debited and Interest Income should be credited for the interest accrued at the end of the current period.

Focus on Business Technology

New businesses engaged in electronic commerce over the Internet have been receiving much attention in recent years. Electronic sales and purchases involving Web-based companies like Amazon.com, Webvan™, and BlueLight.com have been growing steadily. The total value of goods and services traded on the Web will be $433 billion in 2002, of which $94 billion will be retail sales.[5]

It is important to realize that electronic transactions are analyzed and recorded in exactly the same way as transactions that take place in a physical store. In addition, companies operating on the Web require insurance, employee payrolls, buildings, and other assets and liabilities, and they must make the adjusting entries in the same way any other business does.

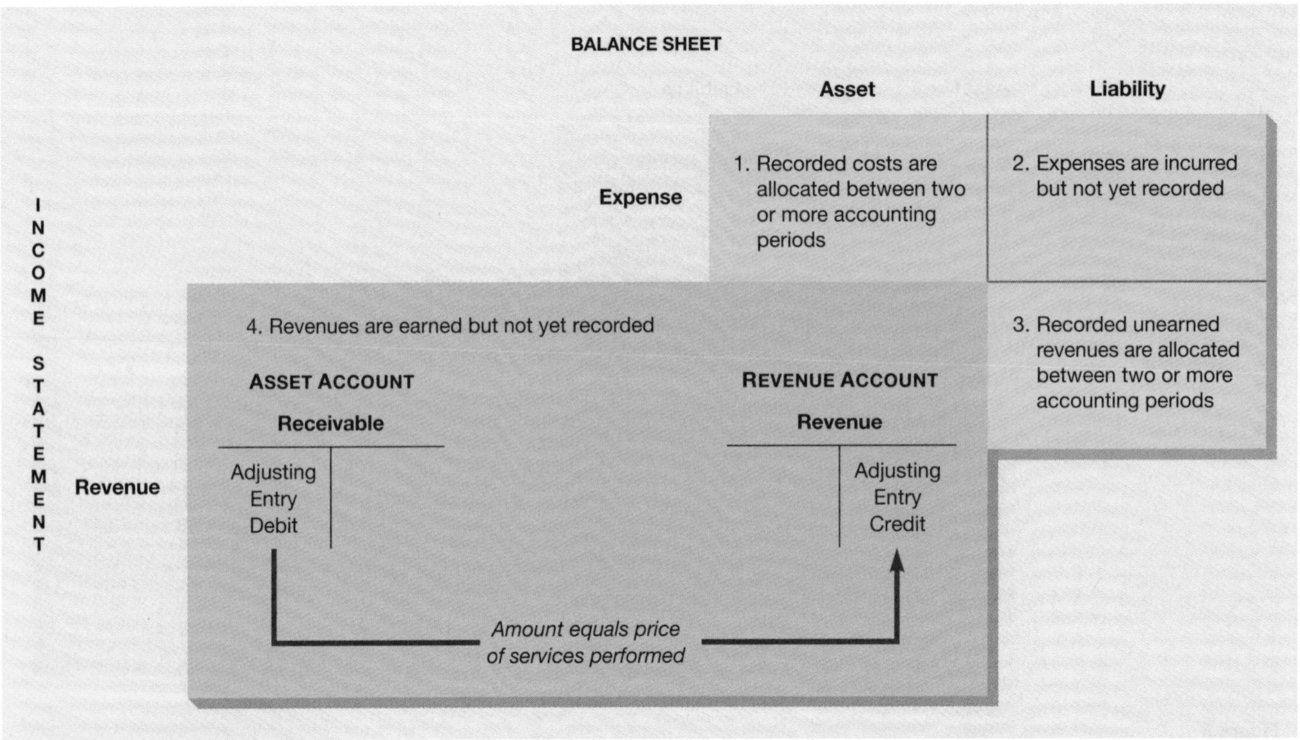

BALANCE SHEET

INCOME STATEMENT

		Asset	Liability
Expense		1. Recorded costs are allocated between two or more accounting periods	2. Expenses are incurred but not yet recorded
Revenue	4. Revenues are earned but not yet recorded		3. Recorded unearned revenues are allocated between two or more accounting periods

ASSET ACCOUNT

Receivable

Adjusting Entry Debit

REVENUE ACCOUNT

Revenue

Adjusting Entry Credit

Amount equals price of services performed

Figure 6
Adjustment for Unrecorded (Accrued) Revenues

Suppose that Joan Miller Advertising Agency has agreed to place a series of advertisements for Marsh Tire Company and that the first advertisement appears on January 31, the last day of the month. The fee of $200 for this advertisement, which has been earned but not recorded, should be recorded this way:

Accrued Advertising Fees (Adjustment i)

A = L + OE
\+ \+

		Dr.	Cr.
Jan. 31	Fees Receivable	200	
	Advertising Fees Earned		200

Fees Receivable

Jan. 31	200		

Advertising Fees Earned

		Jan. 10	1,400
		19	2,800
		31	200

Transaction: Accrual of unrecorded revenue.
Analysis: Assets increase. Owner's equity increases.
Rules: Increases in assets are recorded by debits. Increases in owner's equity are recorded by credits.
Entries: The increase in assets is recorded by a debit to Fees Receivable. The increase in owner's equity is recorded by a credit to Advertising Fees Earned.

Reinforcement Exercise: By the end of the accounting period, a law firm has rendered $800 in legal services for which payment has not been received. Prepare the firm's end-of-period adjustment. **Solution:**

Fees Receivable	800	
Legal Fees Earned		800

Now both the asset and the revenue accounts show the correct balance: The $200 in Fees Receivable is owed to the company, and the $4,400 in Advertising Fees Earned has been earned by the company during January. Marsh Tire Company will be billed for the series of advertisements when they are completed.

A Note About Journal Entries

Thus far we have presented a full analysis of each journal entry. The analyses showed you the thought process behind each entry. By now, you should be fully

Focus on Business Technology

In a computerized accounting system, adjusting entries can be entered just like any other transactions. Some adjusting entries, such as those for insurance expense and depreciation expense, may be similar for each accounting period, and others, such as those for accrued wages, may always involve the same accounts. In such cases, the computer can be programmed to display the adjusting entries automatically so that all the accountant has to do is verify the amounts or enter the correct amounts. Then the adjusting entries are entered and posted, and the adjusted trial balance is prepared with the touch of a button.

aware of the effects of transactions on the accounting equation and the rules of debit and credit. For this reason, in the rest of the book, journal entries are presented without full analysis.

Using the Adjusted Trial Balance to Prepare Financial Statements

OBJECTIVE

6 Prepare financial statements from an adjusted trial balance

Related Text Assignments:
Q: 20, 21
SE: 7, 8
E: 9
P: 4, 5

Point to Emphasize: The adjusted trial balance is a second check that the ledger is still in balance. Because it reflects updated information from the adjusting entries, it may be used to prepare the formal financial statements.

After adjusting entries have been recorded and posted, an **adjusted trial balance** is prepared by listing all accounts and their balances. If the adjusting entries have been posted to the accounts correctly, the adjusted trial balance should have equal debit and credit totals.

The adjusted trial balance for Joan Miller Advertising Agency is shown on the left side of Exhibit 3. Notice that some accounts, such as Cash and Accounts Receivable, have the same balances they have in the trial balance (see Exhibit 1) because no adjusting entries affected them. Some new accounts, such as Fees Receivable, depreciation accounts, and Wages Payable, appear in the adjusted trial balance, and other accounts, such as Art Supplies, Office Supplies, Prepaid Rent, and Prepaid Insurance, have balances different from those in the trial balance because adjusting entries did affect them.

From the adjusted trial balance, the financial statements can be easily prepared. The income statement is prepared from the revenue and expense accounts, as shown in Exhibit 3. Then, as shown in Exhibit 4, the statement of owner's equity and the balance sheet are prepared. Notice that the net income from the income statement is combined with withdrawals on the statement of owner's equity to give the net change in the Joan Miller, Capital account. The resulting balance of Joan Miller, Capital on January 31 is used on the balance sheet, as are the asset and liability accounts.

Cash Flows from Accrual-Based Information

SUPPLEMENTAL OBJECTIVE

7 Analyze cash flows from accrual-based information

Management has the short-range goal of achieving sufficient liquidity to meet its needs for cash to pay its ongoing obligations. It is important for managers to be able to use accrual-based financial information to analyze cash flows in order to plan payments to creditors and assess the need for short-term borrowing.

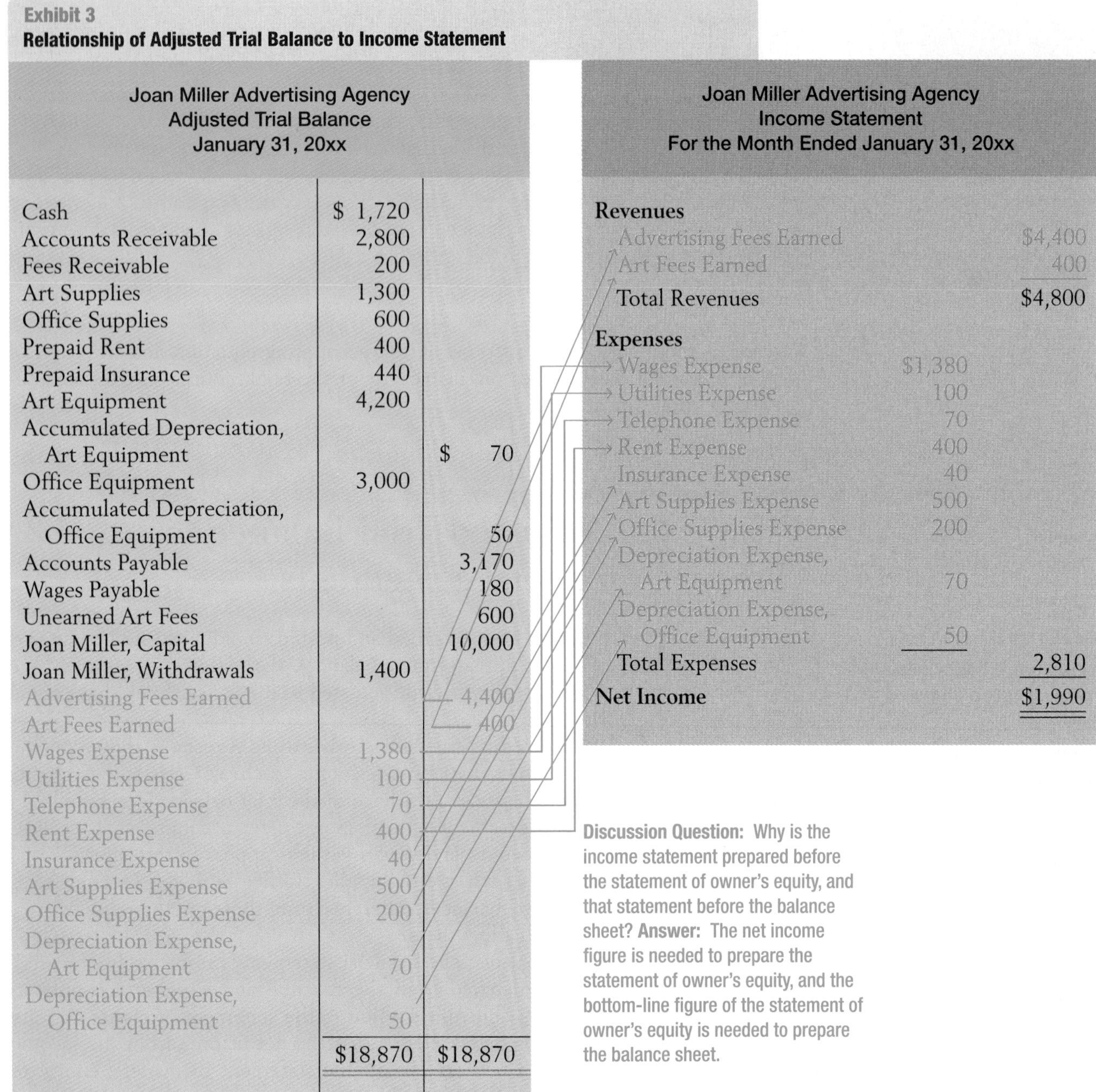

Exhibit 3
Relationship of Adjusted Trial Balance to Income Statement

Joan Miller Advertising Agency
Adjusted Trial Balance
January 31, 20xx

Account	Debit	Credit
Cash	$ 1,720	
Accounts Receivable	2,800	
Fees Receivable	200	
Art Supplies	1,300	
Office Supplies	600	
Prepaid Rent	400	
Prepaid Insurance	440	
Art Equipment	4,200	
Accumulated Depreciation, Art Equipment		$ 70
Office Equipment	3,000	
Accumulated Depreciation, Office Equipment		50
Accounts Payable		3,170
Wages Payable		180
Unearned Art Fees		600
Joan Miller, Capital		10,000
Joan Miller, Withdrawals	1,400	
Advertising Fees Earned		4,400
Art Fees Earned		400
Wages Expense	1,380	
Utilities Expense	100	
Telephone Expense	70	
Rent Expense	400	
Insurance Expense	40	
Art Supplies Expense	500	
Office Supplies Expense	200	
Depreciation Expense, Art Equipment	70	
Depreciation Expense, Office Equipment	50	
	$18,870	$18,870

Joan Miller Advertising Agency
Income Statement
For the Month Ended January 31, 20xx

Revenues		
Advertising Fees Earned		$4,400
Art Fees Earned		400
Total Revenues		$4,800
Expenses		
Wages Expense	$1,380	
Utilities Expense	100	
Telephone Expense	70	
Rent Expense	400	
Insurance Expense	40	
Art Supplies Expense	500	
Office Supplies Expense	200	
Depreciation Expense, Art Equipment	70	
Depreciation Expense, Office Equipment	50	
Total Expenses		2,810
Net Income		$1,990

Discussion Question: Why is the income statement prepared before the statement of owner's equity, and that statement before the balance sheet? **Answer:** The net income figure is needed to prepare the statement of owner's equity, and the bottom-line figure of the statement of owner's equity is needed to prepare the balance sheet.

Related Text Assignments:
Q: 22
SE: 9, 10
E: 10, 11, 12
FRA: 5

Every revenue or expense account on the income statement has one or more related accounts on the balance sheet. For instance, Supplies Expense is related to Supplies, Wages Expense to Wages Payable, and Art Fees Earned to Unearned Art Fees. As shown in this chapter, these accounts are related to one another through adjusting entries whose purpose is to apply the matching rule in the measurement of net income.

The cash flows generated or paid by company operations may also be determined by analyzing these relationships. For example, suppose that after receiving the financial statements in Exhibits 3 and 4, management wants to know how much cash was expended for art supplies. On the income statement, Art Supplies Expense is $500, and on the balance sheet, Art Supplies is $1,300. Because January

Exhibit 4
Relationship of Adjusted Trial Balance to Balance Sheet and Statement of Owner's Equity

Joan Miller Advertising Agency
Adjusted Trial Balance
January 31, 20xx

Cash	$ 1,720	
Accounts Receivable	2,800	
Fees Receivable	200	
Art Supplies	1,300	
Office Supplies	600	
Prepaid Rent	400	
Prepaid Insurance	440	
Art Equipment	4,200	
Accumulated Depreciation, Art Equipment		$ 70
Office Equipment	3,000	
Accumulated Depreciation, Office Equipment		50
Accounts Payable		3,170
Wages Payable		180
Unearned Art Fees		600
Joan Miller, Capital		10,000
Joan Miller, Withdrawals	1,400	
Advertising Fees Earned		4,400
Art Fees Earned		400
Wages Expense	1,380	
Utilities Expense	100	
Telephone Expense	70	
Rent Expense	400	
Insurance Expense	40	
Art Supplies Expense	500	
Office Supplies Expense	200	
Depreciation Expense, Art Equipment	70	
Depreciation Expense, Office Equipment	50	
	$18,870	$18,870

Joan Miller Advertising Agency
Balance Sheet
January 31, 20xx

Assets		
Cash		$ 1,720
Accounts Receivable		2,800
Fees Receivable		200
Art Supplies		1,300
Office Supplies		600
Prepaid Rent		400
Prepaid Insurance		440
Art Equipment	$4,200	
Less Accumulated Depreciation	70	4,130
Office Equipment	$3,000	
Less Accumulated Depreciation	50	2,950
Total Assets		$14,540
Liabilities		
Accounts Payable	$3,170	
Wages Payable	180	
Unearned Art Fees	600	
Total Liabilities		$ 3,950
Owner's Equity		
Joan Miller, Capital		10,590
Total Liabilities and Owner's Equity		$14,540

Joan Miller Advertising Agency
Statement of Owner's Equity
For the Month Ended January 31, 20xx

Joan Miller, Capital, January 1, 20xx		—
Add: Investment by Joan Miller	$10,000	
Net Income	1,990	$11,990
Subtotal		$11,990
Less Withdrawals		1,400
Joan Miller, Capital, January 31, 20xx		$10,590

From Income Statement in Exhibit 3.

Point to Emphasize: Notice that the adjusted trial balance figure for Joan Miller, Capital does not reflect net income or withdrawals during the period. The balance is updated when the closing entries are prepared.

was the first month of operation for the company, there was no prior balance of art supplies, and so the amount of cash expended for art supplies during the month was $1,800. The cash flow used to purchase art supplies ($1,800) was much greater than the amount expensed in determining income ($500). In planning for February, management can anticipate that the cash needed may be less than the amount expensed because, given the large inventory of art supplies, it will probably not be necessary to buy art supplies for more than a month. Understanding these cash flow effects enables management to better predict the business's need for cash during February.

The general rule for determining the cash flow received from any revenue or paid for any expense (except depreciation, which is a special case not covered here) is to determine the potential cash payments or cash receipts and deduct the amount not paid or received. The application of the general rule varies with the type of asset or liability account, which is shown as follows:

Type of Account	Potential Payment or Receipt	Not Paid or Received	Result
Prepaid Expense	Ending Balance + Expense for the Period	− Beginning Balance	= Cash Payments for Expenses
Unearned Revenue	Ending Balance + Revenue for the Period	− Beginning Balance	= Cash Receipts from Revenues
Accrued Expense	Beginning Balance + Expense for the Period	− Ending Balance	= Cash Payments for Expenses
Accrued Revenue	Beginning Balance + Revenue for the Period	− Ending Balance	= Cash Receipts from Revenues

Teaching Note: Balance sheet T accounts also work well to illustrate calculation of cash receipts and cash payments. Students have three pieces of information about the balance sheet account and must solve for one unknown. This approach reinforces the concept of normal balances. After the accrual number is entered, solve for the unknown cash effect.

For instance, assume that on May 31 a company had a balance of $480 in Prepaid Insurance and that on June 30 the balance was $670. If the insurance expense during June was $120, the amount of cash expended on insurance during June can be computed as follows:

Prepaid Insurance at June 30	$670
Insurance Expense during June	120
Potential cash payments for insurance	$790
Less Prepaid Insurance at May 31	480
Cash payments for insurance during June	$310

The beginning balance is deducted because it was paid in a prior accounting period. Note that the cash payments equal the expense plus the increase in the balance of the Prepaid Insurance account [$120 + ($670 − $480) = $310]. In this case, the cash paid was almost three times the amount of insurance expense. In future months, cash payments are likely to be less than the expense.

Chapter Review

REVIEW OF LEARNING OBJECTIVES

1. **Define *net income* and its two major components, *revenues* and *expenses*.** Net income is the net increase in owner's equity that results from the operations of a company. Net income equals revenues minus expenses, unless expenses exceed revenues, in which case a net loss results. Revenues equal the price of goods sold and services rendered during a specific period. Expenses are the costs of goods and services used up in the process of producing revenues.

2. **Explain the difficulties of income measurement caused by the accounting period issue, the continuity issue, and the matching**

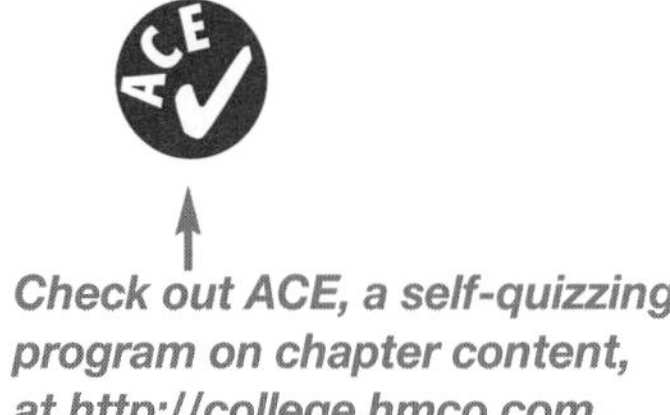

Check out ACE, a self-quizzing program on chapter content, at http://college.hmco.com.

issue. The accounting period issue recognizes that net income measurements for short periods of time are necessarily tentative. The continuity issue recognizes that even though businesses face an uncertain future, without evidence to the contrary, accountants must assume that a business will continue indefinitely. The matching issue involves the difficulty of assigning revenues and expenses to a period of time. It is addressed by applying the matching rule: Revenues must be assigned to the accounting period in which the goods are delivered or the services performed, and expenses must be assigned to the accounting period in which they are used to produce revenue.

3. **Define *accrual accounting* and explain two broad ways of accomplishing it.** Accrual accounting consists of all the techniques developed by accountants to apply the matching rule. The two general ways of accomplishing accrual accounting are (1) by recognizing revenues when earned and expenses when incurred and (2) by adjusting the accounts.

4. **State four principal situations that require adjusting entries.** Adjusting entries are required (1) when recorded costs have to be allocated between two or more accounting periods, (2) when unrecorded expenses exist, (3) when recorded unearned revenues must be allocated between two or more accounting periods, and (4) when unrecorded revenues exist.

5. **Prepare typical adjusting entries.** The preparation of adjusting entries is summarized in the following table:

Type of Adjusting Entry	Type of Account: Debited	Type of Account: Credited	Balance Sheet Account Examples
1. Allocating recorded costs (previously paid, now expired)	Expense	Asset (or contra-asset)	Prepaid Rent Prepaid Insurance Supplies Accumulated Depreciation, Buildings Accumulated Depreciation, Equipment
2. Accrued expenses (previously incurred, now unpaid)	Expense	Liability	Wages Payable Interest Payable
3. Allocating recorded unearned revenues (previously received, now earned)	Liability	Revenue	Unearned Fees
4. Accrued revenues (previously earned, now not received)	Asset	Revenue	Fees Receivable Interest Receivable

6. **Prepare financial statements from an adjusted trial balance.** An adjusted trial balance is prepared after adjusting entries have been posted to the accounts. Its purpose is to test whether the adjusting entries are posted correctly before the financial statements are prepared. The income statement is prepared from the revenue and expense accounts in the adjusted trial balance.

The balance sheet is prepared from the asset and liability accounts in the adjusted trial balance and from the statement of owner's equity.

SUPPLEMENTAL OBJECTIVE

7. **Analyze cash flows from accrual-based information.** Cash flow information bears on management's liquidity goal. The general rule for determining the cash flow effect of any revenue or expense (except depreciation, which is a special case not covered here) is to determine the potential cash payments or cash receipts and deduct the amount not paid or received.

REVIEW OF CONCEPTS AND TERMINOLOGY

The following concepts and terms were introduced in this chapter:

LO 2 **Accounting period issue:** The difficulty of assigning revenues and expenses to a short period of time.

LO 4 **Accrual:** The recognition of an expense or revenue that has arisen but has not yet been recorded.

LO 3 **Accrual accounting:** The attempt to record the financial effects of transactions and other events in the periods in which those transactions or events occur, rather than only in the periods in which cash is received or paid by the business; all the techniques developed by accountants to apply the matching rule.

LO 5 **Accrued expenses:** Expenses that have been incurred but are not recognized in the accounts; unrecorded expenses.

LO 5 **Accrued revenues:** Revenues for which a service has been performed or goods delivered but for which no entry has been made; unrecorded revenues.

LO 5 **Accumulated depreciation accounts:** Contra-asset accounts used to accumulate the depreciation expense of specific long-lived assets.

LO 6 **Adjusted trial balance:** A trial balance prepared after all adjusting entries have been recorded and posted to the accounts.

LO 4 **Adjusting entries:** Entries made to apply accrual accounting to transactions that span more than one accounting period.

LO 5 **Carrying value:** The unexpired portion of the cost of an asset. Also called *book value*.

LO 2 **Cash basis of accounting:** Accounting for revenues and expenses on a cash received and cash paid basis.

LO 2 **Continuity issue:** The difficulty associated with not knowing how long a business entity will survive.

LO 5 **Contra account:** An account whose balance is subtracted from an associated account in the financial statements.

LO 4 **Deferral:** The postponement of the recognition of an expense that already has been paid or of a revenue that already has been received.

LO 5 **Depreciation:** The portion of the cost of a tangible long-term asset allocated to any one accounting period. Also called *depreciation expense*.

LO 1 **Expenses:** Decreases in owner's equity resulting from the costs of goods and services used up in the course of earning revenues. Also called *cost of doing business* or *expired costs*.

LO 2 **Fiscal year:** Any 12-month accounting period used by an economic entity.

LO 2 **Going concern:** The assumption, unless there is evidence to the contrary, that a business entity will continue to operate indefinitely.

LO 2 **Matching rule:** Revenues must be assigned to the accounting period in which the goods are sold or the services performed, and expenses must be assigned to the accounting period in which they are used to produce revenue.

LO 1 **Net income:** The net increase in owner's equity that results from business operations and is accumulated in the owner's Capital account; revenues less expenses when revenues exceed expenses.

LO 1 **Net loss:** The net decrease in owner's equity that results from business operations when expenses exceed revenues. It is accumulated in the owner's Capital account.

LO 2 **Periodicity:** The recognition that net income for any period less than the life of the business, although tentative, is still a useful measure.

LO 5 **Prepaid expenses:** Expenses paid in advance that have not yet expired; an asset account.

LO 1 **Profit:** The increase in owner's equity that results from business operations.

LO 3 **Revenue recognition:** In accrual accounting, the process of determining when revenue is earned.

LO 1 **Revenues:** Increases in owner's equity resulting from selling goods, rendering services, or performing other business activities.

LO 5 **Unearned revenues:** Revenues received in advance for which the goods have not yet been delivered or the services performed; a liability account.

Review Problem

Determining Adjusting Entries, Posting to T Accounts, Preparing Adjusted Trial Balance, and Preparing Financial Statements

LO 5
LO 6 The following is the unadjusted trial balance for Certified Answering Service on December 31, 20x2.

Certified Answering Service Trial Balance December 31, 20x2		
Cash	$2,160	
Accounts Receivable	1,250	
Office Supplies	180	
Prepaid Insurance	240	
Office Equipment	3,400	
Accumulated Depreciation, Office Equipment		$ 600
Accounts Payable		700
Unearned Revenue		460
James Neal, Capital		4,870
James Neal, Withdrawals	400	
Answering Service Revenue		2,900
Wages Expense	1,500	
Rent Expense	400	
	$9,530	$9,530

The following information is also available:

a. Insurance that expired during December amounted to $40.
b. Office supplies on hand at the end of December totaled $75.
c. Depreciation for the month of December totaled $100.
d. Accrued wages at the end of December totaled $120.

e. Revenues earned for services performed in December but not yet billed on December 31 totaled $300.
f. Revenues earned in December for services performed that were paid in advance totaled $160.

REQUIRED

1. Prepare T accounts for the accounts in the trial balance and enter the balances.
2. Determine the required adjusting entries and record them directly to the T accounts. Open new T accounts as needed.
3. Prepare an adjusted trial balance.
4. Prepare an income statement, a statement of owner's equity, and a balance sheet for the month ended December 31, 20x2. The owner made no new investments during the month.

ANSWER TO REVIEW PROBLEM

1. T accounts set up and amounts from trial balance entered
2. Adjusting entries recorded

Cash

Bal.	2,160		

Accounts Receivable

Bal.	1,250		

Service Revenue Receivable

(e)	300		

Office Supplies

Bal.	180	(b)	105
Bal.	75		

Prepaid Insurance

Bal.	240	(a)	40
Bal.	200		

Office Equipment

Bal.	3,400		

Accumulated Depreciation, Office Equipment

		Bal.	600
		(c)	100
		Bal.	700

Accounts Payable

		Bal.	700

Unearned Revenue

(f)	160	Bal.	460
		Bal.	300

Wages Payable

		(d)	120

James Neal, Capital

		Bal.	4,870

James Neal, Withdrawals

Bal.	400		

Answering Service Revenue

		Bal.	2,900
		(e)	300
		(f)	160
		Bal.	3,360

Wages Expense

Bal.	1,500		
(d)	120		
Bal.	1,620		

Rent Expense

Bal.	400		

Insurance Expense

(a)	40		

Office Supplies Expense

(b)	105		

Depreciation Expense, Office Equipment

(c)	100		

3. Adjusted trial balance prepared

Certified Answering Service Adjusted Trial Balance December 31, 20x2		
Cash	$ 2,160	
Accounts Receivable	1,250	
Service Revenue Receivable	300	
Office Supplies	75	
Prepaid Insurance	200	
Office Equipment	3,400	
Accumulated Depreciation, Office Equipment		$ 700
Accounts Payable		700
Unearned Revenue		300
Wages Payable		120
James Neal, Capital		4,870
James Neal, Withdrawals	400	
Answering Service Revenue		3,360
Wages Expense	1,620	
Rent Expense	400	
Insurance Expense	40	
Office Supplies Expense	105	
Depreciation Expense, Office Equipment	100	
	$10,050	$10,050

4. Financial statements prepared

Certified Answering Service Income Statement For the Month Ended December 31, 20x2		
Revenues		
Answering Service Revenue		$3,360
Expenses		
Wages Expense	$1,620	
Rent Expense	400	
Insurance Expense	40	
Office Supplies Expense	105	
Depreciation Expense, Office Equipment	100	
Total Expenses		2,265
Net Income		$1,095

Certified Answering Service Statement of Owner's Equity For the Month Ended December 31, 20x2	
James Neal, Capital, November 30, 20x2	$4,870
Net Income	1,095
Subtotal	$5,965
Less Withdrawals	400
James Neal, Capital, December 31, 20x2	$5,565

Certified Answering Service Balance Sheet December 31, 20x2		
Assets		
Cash		$2,160
Accounts Receivable		1,250
Service Revenue Receivable		300
Office Supplies		75
Prepaid Insurance		200
Office Equipment	$3,400	
Less Accumulated Depreciation	700	2,700
Total Assets		$6,685
Liabilities		
Accounts Payable		$ 700
Unearned Revenue		300
Wages Payable		120
Total Liabilities		$1,120
Owner's Equity		
James Neal, Capital		5,565
Total Liabilities and Owner's Equity		$6,685

Chapter Assignments

BUILDING YOUR KNOWLEDGE FOUNDATION

QUESTIONS

1. Why does the accountant use the term *net income* instead of *profit*?
2. Define the terms *revenues* and *expenses*.
3. Why does the need for an accounting period cause problems?
4. What is the significance of the continuity assumption?
5. "The matching rule is the most significant concept in accounting." Do you agree with this statement? Explain your answer.

The income statement shows subscriptions revenue for October of $44,800. Determine the amount of cash received from customers for subscriptions during October. Why is this calculation important to management?

E 12.
SO 7 Relationship of Expenses to Cash Paid

The income statement for Griffon Company included the following expenses for 20xx:

Rent Expense	$ 5,200
Interest Expense	7,800
Salaries Expense	83,000

Listed below are the related balance sheet account balances at year end for last year and this year:

	Last Year	This Year
Prepaid Rent	—	$ 900
Interest Payable	$1,200	—
Salaries Payable	5,000	9,600

1. Compute the cash paid for rent during the year.
2. Compute the cash paid for interest during the year.
3. Compute the cash paid for salaries during the year.

Problems

P 1.
LO 5 Determining Adjustments

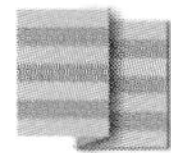

At the end of the first three months of operation, the trial balance of Thomas Answering Service appears as shown below. Lily Thomas, the owner, has hired an accountant to prepare financial statements to determine how well the company is doing after three months. Upon examining the accounting records, the accountant finds the following items of interest:

a. An inventory of office supplies reveals supplies on hand of $266.
b. The Prepaid Rent account includes the rent for the first three months plus a deposit for April's rent.
c. Depreciation on the equipment for the first three months is $416.
d. The balance of the Unearned Answering Service Revenue account represents a 12-month service contract paid in advance on February 1.
e. On March 31, accrued wages total $160.

The balance of the Capital account represents investments by Lily Thomas.

Thomas Answering Service
Trial Balance
March 31, 20x2

Cash	$ 6,964	
Accounts Receivable	8,472	
Office Supplies	1,806	
Prepaid Rent	1,600	
Equipment	9,400	
Accounts Payable		$ 5,346
Unearned Answering Service Revenue		1,776
Lily Thomas, Capital		11,866
Lily Thomas, Withdrawals	4,260	
Answering Service Revenue		18,004
Wages Expense	3,800	
Office Cleaning Expense	690	
	$36,992	$36,992

REQUIRED

All adjustments affect one balance sheet account and one income statement account. For each of the above situations, show the accounts affected, the amount of the adjustment (using a + or − to indicate an increase or decrease), and the balance of the account after the adjustment in the following format.

Balance Sheet Account	Amount of Adjustment (+ or −)	Balance After Adjustment	Income Statement Account	Amount of Adjustment (+ or −)	Balance After Adjustment

P 2.
LO 5 Preparing Adjusting Entries

On May 31, the end of the current fiscal year, the following information was available to help Viera Company's accountants make adjusting entries:

a. The Supplies account showed a beginning balance of $2,174. Purchases during the year were $4,526. The end-of-year inventory revealed supplies on hand that cost $1,397.

b. The Prepaid Insurance account showed the following on May 31:

Beginning Balance	$3,580
February 1	4,200
April 1	7,272

The beginning balance represents the portion of a one-year policy that remained unexpired at the beginning of the current fiscal year. The February 1 entry represents a new one-year policy, and the April 1 entry represents additional coverage in the form of a three-year policy.

c. The following table contains the cost and annual depreciation for buildings and equipment, all of which were purchased before the current year:

Account	Cost	Annual Depreciation
Buildings	$286,000	$14,500
Equipment	374,000	35,400

d. On March 1, the company completed negotiations with a client and accepted payment of $16,800, which represented one year's services paid in advance. The $16,800 was credited to Unearned Service Revenue.

e. The company calculated that as of May 31, it had earned $4,000 on an $11,000 contract that would be completed and billed in September.

f. Among the liabilities of the company is a note payable in the amount of $300,000. On May 31, the accrued interest on this note amounted to $15,000.

g. On Saturday, June 2, the company, which is on a six-day work week, will pay its regular salaried employees $12,300.

h. On May 29, the company completed negotiations and signed a contract to provide services to a new client at an annual rate of $17,500.

REQUIRED

Prepare adjusting entries for each item listed above.

P 3.
LO 5 Determining Adjusting Entries, Posting to T Accounts, and Preparing an Adjusted Trial Balance

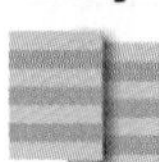

The trial balance for Fleet Relay Services on December 31, 20xx, is at the top of the next page.

The following information is also available:

a. Ending inventory of office supplies, $264.
b. Prepaid rent expired, $440.
c. Depreciation of office equipment for the period, $660.
d. Accrued interest expense at the end of the period, $550.
e. Accrued salaries at the end of the month, $330.
f. Fees still unearned at the end of the period, $1,166.
g. Fees earned but unrecorded, $2,200.

REQUIRED

1. Open T accounts for the accounts in the trial balance plus the following: Fees Receivable; Interest Payable; Salaries Payable; Office Supplies Expense; Depreciation Expense, Office Equipment; and Interest Expense. Enter the balances.
2. Determine the adjusting entries and post them directly to the T accounts.
3. Prepare an adjusted trial balance.

Fleet Relay Services Trial Balance December 31, 20xx		
Cash	$ 16,500	
Accounts Receivable	8,250	
Office Supplies	2,662	
Prepaid Rent	1,320	
Office Equipment	9,240	
Accumulated Depreciation, Office Equipment		$ 1,540
Accounts Payable		5,940
Notes Payable		11,000
Unearned Fees		2,970
Sandy Chee, Capital		24,002
Sandy Chee, Withdrawals	22,000	
Fees Revenue		72,600
Salaries Expense	49,400	
Rent Expense	4,400	
Utilities Expense	4,280	
	$118,052	$118,052

P 4. **LO 5 LO 6 Determining Adjusting Entries and Tracing Their Effects to Financial Statements**

The Crescent Custodial Service is owned by Mike Podgorney. After six months of operation, the June 30, 20xx, trial balance for the company, presented below, was prepared. The balance of the Capital account reflects investments made by Mike Podgorney.

Crescent Custodial Service Trial Balance June 30, 20xx		
Cash	$ 762	
Accounts Receivable	914	
Prepaid Insurance	380	
Prepaid Rent	700	
Cleaning Supplies	1,396	
Cleaning Equipment	1,740	
Truck	3,600	
Accounts Payable		$ 170
Unearned Janitorial Fees		480
Mike Podgorney, Capital		7,095
Mike Podgorney, Withdrawals	3,000	
Janitorial Fees		7,487
Wages Expense	2,400	
Gas, Oil, and Other Truck Expenses	340	
	$15,232	$15,232

The following information is also available.

a. Cleaning supplies of $117 are on hand.
b. Prepaid insurance represents the cost of a one-year policy purchased on January 1.
c. Prepaid rent represents a $100 payment made on January 1 toward the last month's rent of a three-year lease plus $100 rent per month for each of the six past months.

d. The cleaning equipment and the truck are depreciated at the rate of 20 percent per year (10 percent for each six-month period).
e. The unearned revenue represents a six-month payment in advance made by a customer on May 1.
f. During the last week of June, Podgorney completed the first stage of work on a contract that will not be billed until the contract is completed. The amount that has been earned at this stage is $400.
g. On Saturday, July 3, Podgorney will owe his employees $540 for one week's work (six-day work week).

REQUIRED

1. Open T accounts for the accounts in the trial balance plus the following: Fees Receivable; Accumulated Depreciation, Cleaning Equipment; Accumulated Depreciation, Truck; Wages Payable; Rent Expense; Insurance Expense; Cleaning Supplies Expense; Depreciation Expense, Cleaning Equipment; and Depreciation Expense, Truck. Record the balances shown on the trial balance.
2. Determine the adjusting entries and post them directly to the T accounts.
3. Prepare an adjusted trial balance, an income statement, a statement of owner's equity, and a balance sheet.

P 5. Here is the trial balance for New Wave Dance Studio at the end of its current fiscal year.

LO 5 LO 6 Determining Adjusting Entries and Tracing Their Effects to Financial Statements

New Wave Dance Studio
Trial Balance
October 31, 20x2

Cash (111)	$ 1,028	
Accounts Receivable (112)	517	
Supplies (115)	170	
Prepaid Rent (116)	400	
Prepaid Insurance (117)	360	
Equipment (141)	4,100	
Accumulated Depreciation, Equipment (142)		$ 400
Accounts Payable (211)		380
Unearned Dance Fees (213)		900
Midge Bronson, Capital (311)		2,500
Midge Bronson, Withdrawals (312)	12,000	
Dance Fees (411)		20,995
Wages Expense (511)	3,200	
Rent Expense (512)	2,200	
Utilities Expense (515)	1,200	
	$25,175	$25,175

Midge Bronson made no investments in the business during the year. The following information is available to assist in the preparation of adjusting entries.

a. An inventory of supplies reveals $92 still on hand.
b. The prepaid rent reflects the rent for October plus the rent for the last month of the lease.
c. Prepaid insurance consists of a two-year policy purchased on May 1, 20x2.
d. Depreciation on equipment is estimated at $800.
e. Accrued wages are $65 on October 31.
f. Two-thirds of the unearned dance fees have been earned by October 31.

Given these figures, Jamison is planning to withdraw $50,000 for personal expenses. However, Jamison's accountant has found that the following items were overlooked:

a. Although the balance of the Printing Supplies account is $32,000, only $14,000 in supplies is on hand at the end of the year.
b. Depreciation of $20,000 on equipment has not been recorded.
c. Wages of $9,400 have been earned by employees but not recognized in the accounts.
d. A liability account called Unearned Subscriptions has a balance of $16,200, although it is determined that one-third of these subscriptions have been mailed to subscribers.

1. Prepare the necessary adjusting entries.
2. Recast the condensed financial statement figures after making the adjustments.
3. Discuss the performance of Jamison's business after the adjustments have been made. (**Hint:** Compare net income to revenues and total assets before and after the adjustments.) Do you think that making the withdrawal is advisable?

Financial Reporting and Analysis

Interpreting Financial Reports

FRA 1.

LO 2 Analysis of an Asset
LO 5 Account

The Walt Disney Company is engaged in the financing, production, and distribution of motion pictures and television programming. In The Walt Disney Company's 1999 annual report, the balance sheet contains an asset called Film and Television Costs. Film and television costs, which consist of the cost associated with producing films and television programs less the amount expensed, were $4,071,000,000.

The statement of cash flows in the annual report reveals that the amount of film and television costs expensed (amortized) during 1999 was $2,472,000,000. The amount spent for new film productions was $3,020,000,000.[7]

REQUIRED

1. What are film and television costs and why would they be classified as an asset?
2. Prepare an entry to record the amount spent on new film and television production during 1999 (assume all expenditures are paid for in cash).
3. Prepare the adjusting entry that would be made to record the expense for film and television productions in 1999.
4. Can you suggest a method by which The Walt Disney Company might have determined the amount of the expense in **3** in accordance with the matching rule?

FRA 2.

LO 5 Identification of Accruals

H.J. Heinz Company, a major food company, had a net income of $474,341,000 in 1999 and had the following current liabilities at the end of 1999.[8]

Current Liabilities (In thousands)	1999
Short-term debt	$ 290,841
Portion of long-term debt due within one year	613,366
Accounts payable	945,488
Salaries and wages	74,098
Accrued marketing	182,024
Accrued restructuring costs	147,786
Other accrued liabilities	372,623
Income taxes	160,096
Total current liabilities	$2,786,322

REQUIRED

1. Which of the current liabilities definitely arose as the result of an adjusting entry at the end of the year? Which ones may partially have arisen from an adjusting entry? Which ones probably did not arise from an adjusting entry?
2. What effect do adjustments that create new liabilities have on net income or loss? Based on your answer in **1**, what percentage of current liabilities was definitely the result of an adjusting entry? Assuming the adjusting entries for these items had not been performed, what would have been Heinz's net income or loss?

International Company

FRA 3.
LO 2 Account Identification
LO 3 and Accrual Accounting

Takashimaya Company, Limited, is Japan's largest department store chain. An account on Takashimaya's balance sheet called Gift Certificates contains ¥41,657 million ($404 million).[9] Is this account an asset or a liability? What transaction gives rise to the account? How is this account an example of the application of accrual accounting? Explain the conceptual issues that must be resolved for an adjusting entry to be valid.

Toys "R" Us Annual Report

FRA 4.
LO 4 Analysis of Balance Sheet and Adjusting Entries

Refer to the balance sheet in the Toys "R" Us annual report. Examine the accounts listed in the current assets, property and equipment, and current liabilities sections. Which accounts are most likely to have had year-end adjusting entries? Tell the nature of the adjusting entries. For more information about the property and equipment section, refer to the notes to the consolidated financial statements.

Fingraph® Financial Analyst™

FRA 5.
LO 1 Income Measurement
LO 4 and Adjustments
SO 7

Choose any company in the Fingraph® Financial Analyst™ CD-ROM software.

1. Does the company have a calendar year end or use some other fiscal year? Do you think the year end corresponds to the company's natural business year?
2. Find the company's balance sheet. From the asset accounts and liability accounts, find four examples of accounts that might have been related to an adjusting entry at the end of the year. For each example, tell whether the adjustment is a deferral or an accrual and suggest an income statement account that might be associated with it.
3. Find the summary of significant accounting policies, which appears following the financial statements. In these policies, find examples of the application of going concern and accrual accounting. Explain your choices of examples.
4. Prepare a one-page executive summary that highlights what you have learned from parts **1, 2,** and **3.**

Internet Case

FRA 6.
LO 4 Comparison of Accrued Expenses

How important are accrued expenses? Randomly choose the annual reports of four companies from the Needles Accounting Resource Center web site at http://college.hmco.com. For each company, find the section of the balance sheet labeled "Current Liabilities" and identify the current liabilities that are accrued expenses (sometimes called *accrued liabilities*). More than one account may be involved. On a pad, write the information you find in four columns: name of company, total current liabilities, total accrued liabilities, and total accrued liabilities as a percentage of total current liabilities. Write a memorandum to your instructor listing the companies you chose, telling how you obtained their reports, reporting the data you have gathered in the form of a table, and stating a conclusion, with reasons, as to the importance of accrued expenses to the companies you studied. (**Hint:** Compute the average percentage of total accrued expenses for the four companies you chose).

Endnotes

1. Southwest Airlines Co., Inc., *Annual Report*, 1999.
2. Elizabeth MacDonald, "SEC Says Earnings Scrutiny Goes Too Far," *The Wall Street Journal*, February 1, 1999.
3. *Statement of Financial Accounting Concepts No. 1*, "Objectives of Financial Reporting by Business Enterprises" (Norwalk, Conn.: Financial Accounting Standards Board, 1978), par. 44.
4. Michael Schroeder and Elizabeth MacDonald, "SEC Expects More Big Cases on Accounting," *The Wall Street Journal*, December 24, 1998.
5. PricewaterhouseCoopers presentation, 1999.
6. Lyric Opera of Chicago, *Annual Report*, 2000.
7. The Walt Disney Company, *Annual Report*, 1999.
8. H.J. Heinz Company, *Annual Report*, 1999.
9. Takashimaya Company, Limited, *Annual Report*, 2000.

4 Completing the Accounting Cycle

LEARNING OBJECTIVES

1. State all the steps in the accounting cycle.
2. Explain the purposes of closing entries.
3. Prepare the required closing entries.
4. Prepare the post-closing trial balance.
5. Prepare reversing entries as appropriate.
6. Prepare a work sheet.
7. Use a work sheet for three different purposes.

DECISION POINT: A USER'S FOCUS

Dell Computer Corporation Dell Computer Corporation is the world's largest computer company. As a company whose shares are traded on the New York Stock Exchange, Dell is required to prepare both annual and quarterly financial statements for its stockholders. Note the interim income statement from Dell's quarterly report, filed with the Securities and Exchange Commission, that appears here.[1] It shows that Dell's net revenue (sales) for the three months ended October 29, 1999, was greater than that for the same period of the preceding year by almost $2 billion, but that net income declined approximately 25 percent from $384,000,000 to $289,000,000 for the same period.

Whether required by law or not, the preparation of *interim financial statements* every quarter, or even every month, is a good idea for all businesses because such reports give stockholders an ongoing view of financial performance. What costs and time are involved in preparing interim financial statements?

The preparation of interim financial statements throughout the year requires more effort than the preparation of a single set of financial statements for the entire year. Each time the financial statements are prepared, adjusting entries must be determined, prepared, and recorded. Also, the ledger accounts must be prepared to begin the next accounting period. These procedures are time-

Financial Highlights: Interim Income Statement

(Unaudited—in millions)

	Three Months Ended	
	October 29, 1999	**November 1, 1998**
Net revenue	$6,784	$4,818
Cost of revenue	5,414	3,732
Gross margin	1,370	1,086
Operating expenses:		
Selling, general and administrative	622	471
Research, development and engineering	98	76
Purchased research & development	194	
Total operating expenses	914	547
Operating income	456	539
Financing and other	40	9
Income before income taxes	496	548
Provision for income taxes	207	164
Net income	$ 289	$ 384

Critical Thinking Question: What economic conditions give interim financial statements greater importance for decision making? **Answer:** When prices or costs are changing rapidly, interim financial statements enable a business to respond quickly to ensure its profitability.

Clarification Note: The same set of accounting principles applies regardless of the accounting period chosen (month, quarter, or year). Preparing interim financial statements can be difficult and time-consuming because of the need to allocate certain costs and revenues to several different accounting periods.

consuming and costly. The advantages of preparing interim financial statements, even when they are not required, usually outweigh the costs, however, because such statements give management timely information for making decisions that will improve operations. This chapter explains the procedures used to prepare financial statements at the end of an accounting period, whether that period is a month, a quarter, or a year.

Overview of the Accounting Cycle

OBJECTIVE

1 State all the steps in the accounting cycle

Related Text Assignments:
Q: 1
SE: 1
P: 3
SD: 1, 3, 4, 5
FRA: 2, 3, 4

Common Student Confusion: Even though most of the accounting cycle has been introduced by this point, students have difficulty both remembering the steps and understanding the rationale for their order. Remind them that steps 1 through 3 are carried out throughout the period, whereas steps 4 through 6 are carried out at the end of the period only.

The **accounting cycle** is a series of steps in the accounting system whose purpose is to measure business activities in the form of transactions and to transform these transactions into financial statements that will communicate useful information to decision makers. The steps in the accounting cycle, shown in Figure 1, are as follows:

1. *Analyze* business transactions from source documents.
2. *Record* the entries in the journal.
3. *Post* the entries to the ledger and prepare a trial balance.
4. *Adjust* the accounts and prepare an adjusted trial balance.
5. *Close* the accounts and prepare a post-closing trial balance.
6. *Prepare* financial statements.

You are already familiar with steps 1 through 4 and 6. Step 5 is covered in this chapter. The order of these steps can vary to some extent depending on the system in place. For instance, the financial statements (step 6) may be completed before the closing entries are prepared (step 5). In fact, in a computerized system, step 6 usually must be performed before step 5. The point is that all these steps must be accomplished to complete the accounting cycle. At key points in the accounting cycle, trial balances are prepared to ensure that the ledger remains in balance.

Closing Entries

OBJECTIVE

2 Explain the purposes of closing entries

Related Text Assignments:
Q: 2, 3, 4
SD: 4
FRA: 1

Teaching Note: Many students confuse adjusting and closing entries at this point. A quick review of the purpose of adjusting entries can help eliminate the confusion.

Balance sheet accounts are considered to be **permanent accounts**, or *real accounts*, because they carry their end-of-period balances into the next accounting period. On the other hand, revenue and expense accounts are **temporary accounts**, or *nominal accounts*, because they begin each accounting period with a zero balance, accumulate a balance during the period, and are then cleared by means of closing entries.

Closing entries are journal entries made at the end of an accounting period. They have two purposes. First, closing entries set the stage for the next accounting period by clearing revenue, expense, and withdrawal accounts of their balances. Remember that the income statement reports net income (or loss) for a single accounting period and shows revenues and expenses for that period only. For the income statement to present the activity of a single accounting period, the revenue and expense accounts must begin each new period with zero balances. The zero balances are obtained by using closing entries to clear the balances in the revenue and expense accounts at the end of each accounting period. The Withdrawals account is closed in a similar manner.

Exhibit 3

Posting the Closing Entry of the Debit Balances from the Income Statement Accounts to the Income Summary Account

Discussion Question: The credit balance of the Income Summary account at this point ($1,990) represents what key measure? **Answer:** Net income.

Wages Expense — Account No. 511

Date	Item	Post. Ref.	Debit	Credit	Balance Debit	Balance Credit
Jan. 12		J2	600		600	
26		J2	600		1,200	
31	Adj. (g)	J3	180		1,380	
31	Closing	J4		1,380	—	

Income Summary — Account No. 313

Date	Item	Post. Ref.	Debit	Credit	Balance Debit	Balance Credit
Jan. 31	Closing	J4		4,800		4,800
31	Closing	J4	2,810			1,990

Utilities Expense — Account No. 512

Date	Item	Post. Ref.	Debit	Credit	Balance Debit	Balance Credit
Jan. 29		J2	100		100	
31	Closing	J4		100	—	

Telephone Expense — Account No. 513

Date	Item	Post. Ref.	Debit	Credit	Balance Debit	Balance Credit
Jan. 30		J2	70		70	
31	Closing	J4		70	—	

1,380
100
70
400
40
500
50
70
200
2,810

Rent Expense — Account No. 514

Date	Item	Post. Ref.	Debit	Credit	Balance Debit	Balance Credit
Jan. 31	Adj. (a)	J3	400		400	
31	Closing	J4		400	—	

Office Supplies Expense — Account No. 517

Date	Item	Post. Ref.	Debit	Credit	Balance Debit	Balance Credit
Jan. 31	Adj. (d)	J3	200		200	
31	Closing	J4		200	—	

Insurance Expense — Account No. 515

Date	Item	Post. Ref.	Debit	Credit	Balance Debit	Balance Credit
Jan. 31	Adj. (b)	J3	40		40	
31	Closing	J4		40	—	

Depreciation Expense, Art Equipment — Account No. 519

Date	Item	Post. Ref.	Debit	Credit	Balance Debit	Balance Credit
Jan. 31	Adj. (e)	J3	70		70	
31	Closing	J4		70	—	

Art Supplies Expense — Account No. 516

Date	Item	Post. Ref.	Debit	Credit	Balance Debit	Balance Credit
Jan. 31	Adj. (c)	J3	500		500	
31	Closing	J4		500	—	

Depreciation Expense, Office Equipment — Account No. 520

Date	Item	Post. Ref.	Debit	Credit	Balance Debit	Balance Credit
Jan. 31	Adj. (f)	J3	50		50	
31	Closing	J4		50	—	

Discussion Question: Could the Income Summary account contain a debit balance when the income statement accounts are closed to it? **Answer:** Yes, if a net loss had been incurred.

of posting the closing entry when the company has a net income is shown in Exhibit 4. Notice the dual effect of (1) closing the Income Summary account and (2) transferring the balance, net income in this case, to Joan Miller's Capital account.

STEP 4: CLOSING THE WITHDRAWALS ACCOUNT TO THE CAPITAL ACCOUNT The Withdrawals account shows the amount by which capital is reduced during the period by withdrawals of cash or other assets from the business for the owner's personal use. The debit balance of

Exhibit 4
Posting the Closing Entry of the Income Summary Account to the Capital Account

Income Summary					Account No. 313	
					Balance	
Date	Item	Post. Ref.	Debit	Credit	Debit	Credit
Jan. 31	Closing	J4		4,800		4,800
31	Closing	J4	2,810			1,990
31	Closing	J4	1,990			—

Joan Miller, Capital					Account No. 311	
					Balance	
Date	Item	Post. Ref.	Debit	Credit	Debit	Credit
Jan. 1		J1		10,000		10,000
31	Closing	J4		1,990		11,990

Exhibit 5
Posting the Closing Entry of the Withdrawals Account to the Capital Account

Point to Emphasize: Notice that the Withdrawals account is closed to the Capital account, not to the Income Summary account.

Joan Miller, Withdrawals					Account No. 312	
					Balance	
Date	Item	Post. Ref.	Debit	Credit	Debit	Credit
Jan. 31		J2	1,400		1,400	
31	Closing	J4		1,400	—	

Joan Miller, Capital					Account No. 311	
					Balance	
Date	Item	Post. Ref.	Debit	Credit	Debit	Credit
Jan. 1		J1		10,000		10,000
31	Closing	J4		1,990		11,990
31	Closing	J4	1,400			10,590

the Withdrawals account is closed to the Capital account, as shown in Exhibit 1. The effect of this closing entry, as shown in Exhibit 5, is to (1) close the Withdrawals account and (2) transfer the balance to the Capital account.

The Accounts After Closing

After all steps in the closing process have been completed and all closing entries have been posted to the accounts, everything is ready for the next accounting period. The ledger accounts of Joan Miller Advertising Agency, as they appear at this point, are shown in Exhibit 6. The revenue, expense, and Withdrawals accounts (temporary accounts) have zero balances. The Capital account has been increased to reflect the agency's net income and decreased for the owner's withdrawals. The balance sheet accounts (permanent accounts) show the correct balances, which are carried forward to the next period.

FOCUS ON BUSINESS TECHNOLOGY

When General Mills needed to speed up its year-end closing procedures, it selected a team from its Financial Reporting and Information Services Division to design an automated fiscal year-end accounting package. The team put together a system using software spreadsheets like Lotus and Microsoft Excel to record and consolidate annual results. Their effort accelerated the process, increased accuracy, reduced outside help and overtime, and provided flexibility. In addition, its cost was very low because it used PCs and software that the company already owned. The whole process was reduced from nine weeks to just six work days.[2]

Exhibit 6
The Accounts After Closing Entries Are Posted

Teaching Note: A good way to review is to examine each ledger account and discuss where it fits (if at all) into the adjusting and closing procedures. The Cash account, for example, is never a part of adjusting or closing entries.

Cash — Account No. 111

Date	Item	Post. Ref.	Debit	Credit	Balance Debit	Balance Credit
Jan. 1		J1	10,000		10,000	
2		J1		800	9,200	
4		J1		4,200	5,000	
5		J1		1,500	3,500	
8		J1		480	3,020	
9		J1		1,000	2,020	
10		J2	1,400		3,420	
12		J2		600	2,820	
15		J2	1,000		3,820	
26		J2		600	3,220	
29		J2		100	3,120	
31		J2		1,400	1,720	

Accounts Receivable — Account No. 113

Date	Item	Post. Ref.	Debit	Credit	Balance Debit	Balance Credit
Jan. 19		J2	2,800		2,800	

Fees Receivable — Account No. 114

Date	Item	Post. Ref.	Debit	Credit	Balance Debit	Balance Credit
Jan. 31	Adj. (i)	J3	200		200	

Art Supplies — Account No. 115

Date	Item	Post. Ref.	Debit	Credit	Balance Debit	Balance Credit
Jan. 6		J1	1,800		1,800	
31	Adj. (c)	J3		500	1,300	

Office Supplies — Account No. 116

Date	Item	Post. Ref.	Debit	Credit	Balance Debit	Balance Credit
Jan. 6		J1	800		800	
31	Adj. (d)	J3		200	600	

Prepaid Rent — Account No. 117

Date	Item	Post. Ref.	Debit	Credit	Balance Debit	Balance Credit
Jan. 2		J1	800		800	
31	Adj. (a)	J3		400	400	

Prepaid Insurance — Account No. 118

Date	Item	Post. Ref.	Debit	Credit	Balance Debit	Balance Credit
Jan. 8		J1	480		480	
31	Adj. (b)	J3		40	440	

Art Equipment — Account No. 144

Date	Item	Post. Ref.	Debit	Credit	Balance Debit	Balance Credit
Jan. 4		J1	4,200		4,200	

Accumulated Depreciation, Art Equipment — Account No. 145

Date	Item	Post. Ref.	Debit	Credit	Balance Debit	Balance Credit
Jan. 31	Adj. (e)	J3		70		70

Office Equipment — Account No. 146

Date	Item	Post. Ref.	Debit	Credit	Balance Debit	Balance Credit
Jan. 5		J1	3,000		3,000	

Accumulated Depreciation, Office Equipment — Account No. 147

Date	Item	Post. Ref.	Debit	Credit	Balance Debit	Balance Credit
Jan. 31	Adj. (f)	J3		50		50

Accounts Payable — Account No. 212

Date	Item	Post. Ref.	Debit	Credit	Balance Debit	Balance Credit
Jan. 5		J1		1,500		1,500
6		J1		2,600		4,100
9		J1	1,000			3,100
30		J2		70		3,170

Unearned Art Fees — Account No. 213

Date	Item	Post. Ref.	Debit	Credit	Balance Debit	Balance Credit
Jan. 15		J2		1,000		1,000
31	Adj. (h)	J3	400			600

Wages Payable — Account No. 214

Date	Item	Post. Ref.	Debit	Credit	Balance Debit	Balance Credit
Jan. 31	Adj. (g)	J3		180		180

(continued)

Exhibit 6
The Accounts After Closing Entries Are Posted *(continued)*

Joan Miller, Capital					Account No. 311	
					Balance	
Date	Item	Post. Ref.	Debit	Credit	Debit	Credit
Jan. 1		J1		10,000		10,000
Jan. 31	Closing	J4		1,990		11,990
31	Closing	J4	1,400			10,590

Joan Miller, Withdrawals					Account No. 312	
					Balance	
Date	Item	Post. Ref.	Debit	Credit	Debit	Credit
Jan. 31		J2	1,400		1,400	
31	Closing	J4		1,400	—	

Income Summary					Account No. 313	
					Balance	
Date	Item	Post. Ref.	Debit	Credit	Debit	Credit
Jan. 31	Closing	J4		4,800		4,800
31	Closing	J4	2,810			1,990
31	Closing	J4	1,990			—

Advertising Fees Earned					Account No. 411	
					Balance	
Date	Item	Post. Ref.	Debit	Credit	Debit	Credit
Jan. 10		J2		1,400		1,400
19		J2		2,800		4,200
31	Adj. (i)	J3		200		4,400
31	Closing	J4	4,400			—

Art Fees Earned					Account No. 412	
					Balance	
Date	Item	Post. Ref.	Debit	Credit	Debit	Credit
Jan. 31	Adj. (h)	J3		400		400
31	Closing	J4	400			—

Wages Expense					Account No. 511	
					Balance	
Date	Item	Post. Ref.	Debit	Credit	Debit	Credit
Jan. 12		J2	600		600	
26		J2	600		1,200	
31	Adj. (g)	J3	180		1,380	
31	Closing	J4		1,380	—	

Utilities Expense					Account No. 512	
					Balance	
Date	Item	Post. Ref.	Debit	Credit	Debit	Credit
Jan. 29		J2	100		100	
31	Closing	J4		100	—	

Telephone Expense					Account No. 513	
					Balance	
Date	Item	Post. Ref.	Debit	Credit	Debit	Credit
Jan. 30		J2	70		70	
31	Closing	J4		70	—	

Rent Expense					Account No. 514	
					Balance	
Date	Item	Post. Ref.	Debit	Credit	Debit	Credit
Jan. 31	Adj. (a)	J3	400		400	
31	Closing	J4		400	—	

Insurance Expense					Account No. 515	
					Balance	
Date	Item	Post. Ref.	Debit	Credit	Debit	Credit
Jan. 31	Adj. (b)	J3	40		40	
31	Closing	J4		40	—	

Art Supplies Expense					Account No. 516	
					Balance	
Date	Item	Post. Ref.	Debit	Credit	Debit	Credit
Jan. 31	Adj. (c)	J3	500		500	
31	Closing	J4		500	—	

Office Supplies Expense					Account No. 517	
					Balance	
Date	Item	Post. Ref.	Debit	Credit	Debit	Credit
Jan. 31	Adj. (d)	J3	200		200	
31	Closing	J4		200	—	

Depreciation Expense, Art Equipment					Account No. 519	
					Balance	
Date	Item	Post. Ref.	Debit	Credit	Debit	Credit
Jan. 31	Adj. (e)	J3	70		70	
31	Closing	J4		70	—	

Depreciation Expense, Office Equipment					Account No. 520	
					Balance	
Date	Item	Post. Ref.	Debit	Credit	Debit	Credit
Jan. 31	Adj. (f)	J3	50		50	
31	Closing	J4		50	—	

Discussion Question: If Joan Miller, Capital is a permanent account, why is it a part of the closing procedure? **Answer:** Because Joan Miller, Capital is closed *into*, not closed *out*.

Focus on International Business

For companies with extensive international operations, like Caterpillar Inc., The Dow Chemical Co., Phillips Petroleum Co., Gillette Co., and Bristol-Myers Squibb Co., closing the records and preparing financial statements on a timely basis used to be a problem. It was common practice for foreign divisions of companies like these to end their fiscal year one month before the end of the fiscal year of their counterparts in the United States. This gave them the extra time they needed to perform closing procedures and mail the results back to U.S. headquarters to be used in preparation of the company's overall financial statements. This procedure is usually unnecessary today because high-speed computers and electronic communications enable companies to close records and prepare financial statements for both foreign and domestic operations in less than a week.

The Post-Closing Trial Balance

OBJECTIVE

4 Prepare the post-closing trial balance

Related Text Assignments:
Q: 6, 7
P: 3
SD: 4

Because errors may occur in posting the closing entries to the ledger accounts, a **post-closing trial balance** is prepared at the end of the accounting period after all adjusting and closing entries have been posted. This is necessary to determine that all temporary accounts have zero balances and to double-check that total debits equal total credits by preparing a new trial balance. The post-closing trial balance is shown in Exhibit 7 for Joan Miller Advertising Agency. Notice that only the balance sheet accounts show balances because the income statement accounts and the Withdrawals account have all been closed.

Discussion Question: Which three types of accounts are absent from the post-closing trial balance? **Answer:** Revenue and expense accounts and the Withdrawals account.

Point to Emphasize: Notice that Joan Miller, Capital now reflects the correct month-end balance, $10,590.

Exhibit 7
Post-Closing Trial Balance

Joan Miller Advertising Agency
Post-Closing Trial Balance
January 31, 20xx

Cash	$ 1,720	
Accounts Receivable	2,800	
Fees Receivable	200	
Art Supplies	1,300	
Office Supplies	600	
Prepaid Rent	400	
Prepaid Insurance	440	
Art Equipment	4,200	
Accumulated Depreciation, Art Equipment		$ 70
Office Equipment	3,000	
Accumulated Depreciation, Office Equipment		50
Accounts Payable		3,170
Unearned Art Fees		600
Wages Payable		180
Joan Miller, Capital		10,590
	$14,660	$14,660

Reversing Entries: The Optional First Step in the Next Accounting Period

OBJECTIVE

5 Prepare reversing entries as appropriate

Related Text Assignments:
Q: 8, 9
SE: 7, 8
E: 2, 7
P: 4, 5, 8
SD: 2, 4

Point to Emphasize: Reversing entries are the opposite of adjusting entries and are dated the first day of the new period. They apply to only certain adjusting entries and are never required.

At the end of each accounting period, adjusting entries are made to bring revenues and expenses into conformity with the matching rule. A **reversing entry** is a general journal entry made on the first day of a new accounting period that is the exact reverse of an adjusting entry made at the end of the previous period. Reversing entries are optional and, when made, simplify the bookkeeping process for transactions involving certain types of adjustments. Not all adjusting entries should be reversed. For the recording system used in this book, only adjustments for accruals (accrued revenues and accrued expenses) are reversed. Deferrals should not be reversed because such reversals would not simplify the bookkeeping process in future accounting periods.

To see how reversing entries can be helpful, consider the adjusting entry made in the records of Joan Miller Advertising Agency to accrue wages expense:

A = L + OE
　　＋　−

Jan. 31	Wages Expense	180	
	Wages Payable		180
	Accrued unrecorded wages		

When the secretary is paid on the next regular payday, the accountant would make this entry:

A = L + OE
−　−　−

Feb. 9	Wages Payable	180	
	Wages Expense	420	
	Cash		600
	Paid two weeks' wages to secretary, $180 of which accrued in the previous period		

Discussion Question: What is the purpose of reversing entries? **Answer:** Reversing entries enable the bookkeeper to continue preparing routine journal entries early in the new period. (More complex entries are needed when reversing entries are not used.)

Notice that when the payment is made, if there is no reversing entry, the accountant must look in the records to find out how much of the $600 applies to the current accounting period and how much is applicable to the previous period. This may seem easy in our example, but think how difficult and time-consuming it would be if a company had hundreds of employees, all working on different schedules.

Point to Emphasize: Adjustments that eventually are followed by the receipt or payment of cash (that is, accruals) can be reversed. Adjustments that do not involve a cash follow-up (deferrals) cannot be reversed.

A reversing entry helps solve the problem of applying revenues and expenses to the correct accounting period. It is exactly what its name implies: a reversal made by debiting the credits and crediting the debits of a previously made adjusting entry.

For example, notice the following sequence of entries and their effects on the ledger account Wages Expense:

1. **Adjusting Entry**
   Jan. 31 Wages Expense 180
   Wages Payable 180
2. **Closing Entry**
   Jan. 31 Income Summary 1,380
   Wages Expense 1,380
3. **Reversing Entry**
   Feb. 1 Wages Payable 180
   Wages Expense 180
4. **Payment Entry**
   Feb. 9 Wages Expense 600
   Cash 600

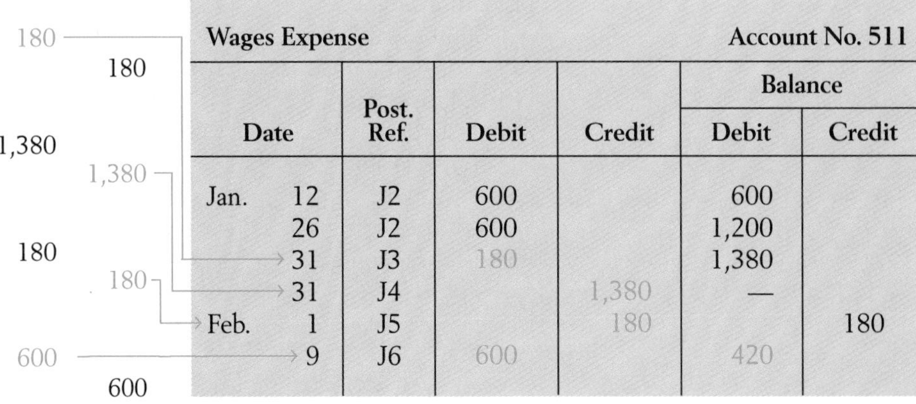

Wages Expense						Account No. 511
					Balance	
Date		Post. Ref.	Debit	Credit	Debit	Credit
Jan.	12	J2	600		600	
	26	J2	600		1,200	
	31	J3	180		1,380	
	31	J4		1,380	—	
Feb.	1	J5		180		180
	9	J6	600		420	

Entry 1 adjusted Wages Expense to accrue $180 in the January accounting period.

Entry 2 closed the $1,380 in Wages Expense for January to Income Summary, leaving a zero balance.

Point to Emphasize: Notice the abnormal credit balance as of February 1. This situation is "corrected" with the February 9 entry, an entry the bookkeeper can make easily.

Entry 3, the reversing entry, set up a credit balance of $180 on February 1 in Wages Expense, which is the expense recognized through the adjusting entry in January (and also reduced the liability account Wages Payable to a zero balance). The reversing entry always sets up an abnormal balance in the income statement account and produces a zero balance in the balance sheet account.

Entry 4 recorded the $600 payment of two weeks' wages as a debit to Wages Expense, automatically leaving a balance of $420, which represents the correct wages expense to date in February. The reversing entry simplified the process of making the payment entry on February 9.

Discussion Question: Is it "more accurate" to prepare reversing entries than not? **Answer:** No, because the same results are obtained whether or not reversing entries have been prepared.

Reversing entries apply to any accrued expenses or revenues. In the case of Joan Miller Advertising Agency, wages expense was the only accrued expense. However, the asset Fees Receivable was created as a result of the adjusting entry made to accrue fees earned but not yet billed. The adjusting entry for this accrued revenue would require the following reversing entry:

A = L + OE
− −

Feb. 1	Advertising Fees Earned	200	
	Fees Receivable		200
	Reversed the adjusting entry for accrued fees receivable		

Instructional Strategy: After reviewing the reversing entry for accrued revenue, check students' comprehension by dividing the class into pairs and assigning E 2. Use students' answers to summarize reversing entries for the entire class.

When the series of advertisements is finished, the company can credit all the proceeds to Advertising Fees Earned without regard to the amount accrued in the previous period. The credit will automatically be reduced to the amount earned during February by the $200 debit in the account.

As noted earlier, under the system of recording used in this book, reversing entries apply only to accruals. Reversing entries do not apply to deferrals, such as the entries that involve supplies, prepaid rent, prepaid insurance, depreciation, and unearned art fees.

The Work Sheet: An Accountant's Tool

OBJECTIVE

6 Prepare a work sheet

Related Text Assignments:
Q: 10, 11, 12, 13, 14, 15, 16, 17
E: 3, 4
P: 4, 5, 8

As seen earlier, the flow of information that affects a business does not stop arbitrarily at the end of an accounting period. In preparing financial reports, accountants must collect relevant data to determine what should be included. For example, they need to examine insurance policies to see how much prepaid insurance has expired, examine plant and equipment records to determine depreciation, take an inventory of supplies on hand, and calculate the amount of accrued wages. These calculations, together with other computations, analyses, and preliminary drafts of statements, make up the accountants' **working papers**. Working papers are important for two reasons. First, they help accountants organize their work and thus avoid omitting important data or steps that affect the financial statements. Second, they provide evidence of past work so that accountants or auditors can retrace their steps and support the information in the financial statements.

Point to Emphasize: The work sheet is extremely useful when an accountant must prepare numerous adjustments. It is not a financial statement, it is not required, and it is not made public.

A special kind of working paper is the **work sheet**. The work sheet is often used as a preliminary step in recording adjusting and closing entries and the preparation of financial statements. Using a work sheet reduces the possibility of omitting an adjustment, helps the accountant check the arithmetical accuracy of the accounts, and facilitates the preparation of financial statements. The work sheet is never published and is rarely seen by management. It is a tool for the accountant. Because preparing a work sheet is a very mechanical process, many accountants use a microcomputer. In some cases, accountants use a spreadsheet program to prepare the work sheet. In other cases, they use general ledger software to prepare financial statements from the adjusted trial balance.

Preparing the Work Sheet

Point to Emphasize: For complicated end-of-period situations, the work sheet is ideal because incorrect information can be erased along the way. As a result, the correctly completed work sheet can be used to facilitate the preparation of formal adjusting and closing entries, which can be corrected only with additional formal entries.

So far, adjusting entries have been entered directly in the journal and posted to the ledger, and the financial statements have been prepared from the adjusted trial balance. The process has been relatively simple because Joan Miller Advertising Agency is a small company. For larger companies, which may require many adjusting entries, a work sheet is essential. To illustrate the preparation of the work sheet, we continue with the Joan Miller Advertising Agency example.

A common form of work sheet has one column for account names and/or numbers and ten more columns with the headings shown in Exhibit 8. Notice that the work sheet is identified by a heading that consists of (1) the name of the company, (2) the title "Work Sheet," and (3) the period of time covered (as on the income statement).

There are five steps in the preparation of a work sheet:

1. Enter and total the account balances in the Trial Balance columns.
2. Enter and total the adjustments in the Adjustments columns.
3. Enter and total the adjusted account balances in the Adjusted Trial Balance columns.
4. Extend the account balances from the Adjusted Trial Balance columns to the Income Statement columns or the Balance Sheet columns.
5. Total the Income Statement columns and the Balance Sheet columns. Enter the net income or net loss in both pairs of columns as a balancing figure, and recompute the column totals.

Point to Emphasize: The work sheet Trial Balance columns take the place of the "traditional" trial balance.

Common Student Confusion: Now that students are comfortable with the general ledger format, they are being asked to enter amounts into a new form, a working paper. Assure them that they will get used to the work sheet and that exactly the same rules of debit and credit apply.

1. **Enter and total the account balances in the Trial Balance columns.** The titles and balances of the accounts as of January 31 are copied directly from the ledger into the Trial Balance columns, as shown in Exhibit 8. When a work sheet is used, the accountant does not have to prepare a separate trial balance.
2. **Enter and total the adjustments in the Adjustments columns.** The required adjustments for Joan Miller Advertising Agency are entered in the Adjustments columns of the work sheet as shown in Exhibit 9. As each adjustment is entered, a letter is used to identify its debit and credit parts. The first adjustment, which is identified by the letter **a,** is to recognize rent expense, which results in a debit to Rent Expense and a credit to Prepaid Rent. In practice, this letter may be used to reference supporting computations or documentation underlying the adjusting entry, and it may simplify the recording of adjusting entries in the general journal.

   If an adjustment calls for an account that has not been used in the trial balance, the new account is added below the accounts listed in the trial balance. The trial balance includes only those accounts that have balances. For example, Rent Expense has been added in Exhibit 9. The only exception to this rule is the Accumulated Depreciation accounts, which have a zero balance only in the initial period of operation. Accumulated Depreciation accounts are listed immediately after their associated asset accounts.

   When all the adjustments have been made, the two Adjustments columns must be totaled. This step proves that the debits and credits of the adjustments are equal and generally reduces errors in the preparation of the work sheet.

Common Student Confusion: Crossfooting is far more difficult than adding and subtracting vertically, especially when one must pay particular attention to debits versus credits. Assure students that it is normal to be uncomfortable with crossfooting at first, but that they will quickly become accustomed to it.

3. **Enter and total the adjusted account balances in the Adjusted Trial Balance columns.** Exhibit 10 shows the adjusted trial balance. It is prepared by combining the amount of each account in the original Trial Balance columns with the corresponding amount in the Adjustments columns and entering each result in the Adjusted Trial Balance columns.

   Some examples from Exhibit 10 illustrate **crossfooting**, or adding and subtracting a group of numbers horizontally. The first line shows Cash with a debit balance of $1,720. Because there are no adjustments to the Cash account, $1,720 is entered in the debit column of the Adjusted Trial Balance columns. The second line is Accounts Receivable, which shows a debit of $2,800 in the Trial Balance columns. Because there are no adjustments to Accounts Receivable, the $2,800 balance is carried over to the debit column of the Adjusted Trial Balance columns. The next line is Art Supplies, which shows a debit of $1,800 in the Trial Balance columns and a credit of $500 from adjustment c in the Adjustments columns. Subtracting $500 from $1,800 results in a $1,300 debit balance in the Adjusted Trial Balance columns. This process is followed for all the accounts, including those added below the trial balance totals. The Adjusted Trial Balance columns are then footed (totaled) to check the accuracy of the crossfooting.

4. **Extend the account balances from the Adjusted Trial Balance columns to the Income Statement columns or the Balance Sheet columns.** Every account in the adjusted trial balance is either a balance sheet account or an income statement account. Each account is extended to its proper place as a debit or credit in either the Income Statement columns or the Balance Sheet columns. The result of extending the accounts is shown in Exhibit 11. Revenue and expense accounts are copied to the Income Statement columns. Assets, liabilities, and the Capital and Withdrawals accounts are extended to the Balance Sheet columns. To avoid overlooking an account, extend the accounts line by line, beginning with the first line (which is Cash) and not omitting any subsequent lines. For instance, the Cash debit balance of $1,720 is extended to the debit column of the Balance Sheet columns, the Accounts Receivable debit balance of $2,800 is extended to the same debit column, and so forth. Each amount is carried across to only one column.

Discussion Question: Under what circumstances would the Income Statement and Balance Sheet columns balance when initially totaled? **Answer:** When net income equals exactly $0.

5. **Total the Income Statement columns and the Balance Sheet columns. Enter the net income or net loss in both pairs of columns as a balancing figure, and recompute the column totals.** This last step, as shown in Exhibit 12, is necessary to compute net income or net loss and to prove the arithmetical accuracy of the work sheet.

   Net income (or net loss) is equal to the difference between the total debits and credits of the Income Statement columns. It also equals the difference between the total debits and credits of the Balance Sheet columns.

Revenue (Income Statement credit column total)	$4,800
Expenses (Income Statement debit column total)	(2,810)
Net Income	$1,990

   In this case, revenues (credit column) exceed expenses (debit column). Consequently, the company has a net income of $1,990. The same difference is shown between the total debits and credits of the Balance Sheet columns.

   The $1,990 is entered in the debit side of the Income Statement columns to balance the columns, and it is entered in the credit side of the Balance Sheet columns to balance the columns. Remember that the excess of revenues over expenses (net income) increases owner's equity and that increases in owner's equity are recorded by credits.

When a net loss occurs, the opposite rule applies. The excess of expenses over revenues—net loss—is placed in the credit side of the Income Statement columns as a balancing figure. It is then placed in the debit side of the Balance Sheet columns because a net loss decreases owner's equity, and decreases in owner's equity are recorded by debits.

As a final check, the four columns are totaled again. If the Income Statement columns and the Balance Sheet columns do not balance, an account may have been extended or sorted to the wrong column, or an error may have been made in adding the columns. Of course, equal totals in the two pairs of columns are not absolute proof of accuracy. If an asset has been carried to the Income Statement debit column and a similar error involving revenues or liabilities has been made, the work sheet will still balance, but the net income figure will be wrong.

Using the Work Sheet

OBJECTIVE

7 Use a work sheet for three different purposes

Related Text Assignments:
Q: 18, 19
SE: 9
E: 5, 6, 7, 8
P: 4, 5, 8
SD: 4

The completed work sheet assists the accountant in three principal tasks: (1) recording the adjusting entries, (2) recording the closing entries in the general journal to prepare the records for the beginning of the next period, and (3) preparing the financial statements.

RECORDING THE ADJUSTING ENTRIES For Joan Miller Advertising Agency, the adjustments were determined while completing the work sheet because they are essential to the preparation of the financial statements. The adjusting entries may be recorded in the general journal at that point.

Recording the adjusting entries with appropriate explanations in the general journal, as shown in Exhibit 13, is an easy step. The information can be copied from the work sheet. Adjusting entries are then posted to the general ledger.

RECORDING THE CLOSING ENTRIES The four closing entries for Joan Miller Advertising Agency are entered in the journal and posted to the ledger as shown in Exhibits 1 through 5. All accounts that need to be closed, except for Withdrawals, may be found in the Income Statement columns of the work sheet.

PREPARING THE FINANCIAL STATEMENTS Once the work sheet has been completed, preparing the financial statements is simple because the account balances have been sorted into Income Statement and Balance Sheet columns. The income statement shown in Exhibit 14 was prepared from the account balances in the Income Statement columns of Exhibit 12. The statement of owner's equity and the

FOCUS ON BUSINESS TECHNOLOGY

The work sheet is a good application for electronic spreadsheet software programs like Lotus and Microsoft Excel. Constructing a work sheet using spreadsheet software takes time, but once it is done, the work sheet can be used over and over. The principal advantage of electronic preparation over manual preparation is that each time a number is entered or revised, the entire electronic work sheet is updated automatically, without the possibility of addition or extension mistakes. For example, if an error in an adjusting entry is corrected, the proper extensions to the other columns are made, all columns are re-added, and net income is recomputed. Of course, the software is purely mechanical. People are still responsible for inputting the correct numbers and equations initially.

FINANCIAL REPORTING AND ANALYSIS

Interpreting Financial Reports

LO 2 Closing Entries
LO 3

FRA 1. *H&R Block, Inc.,* is the world's largest tax preparation service firm. Information adapted from the statement of earnings (in thousands) from its annual report for the year ended April 30, 1999, is as follows:[3]

Revenues	
Service Revenues	$1,324,494
Product Sales	174,124
Royalties	123,201
Other Revenues	22,846
Total Revenues	$1,644,665
Expenses	
Employee Compensation and Benefits	$ 610,866
Occupancy and Equipment Expense	232,003
Marketing and Advertising Expense	90,056
Bad Debt Expense	71,662
Interest Expense	69,038
Supplies, Freight, and Postage Expense	57,457
Other Operating Expenses	158,509
Total Expenses	$1,289,591
Earnings Before Income Taxes	$ 355,074
Income Taxes	145,746
Net Earnings	$ 209,328

The company reported distributing cash in the amount of $95,004,000 to the owners in 1999.

REQUIRED

1. Prepare, in journal form, the closing entries that would have been made by H&R Block on April 30, 1999. Treat income taxes as an expense, and treat cash distributions as withdrawals.
2. Based on the way you handled expenses and cash distributions in 1 and their ultimate effect on the owner's capital, what theoretical reason can you give for not including expenses and cash distributions in the same closing entry?

International Company

LO 1 Accounting Cycle and
LO 3 Closing Entries

FRA 2. *Nestlé S.A.,* maker of such well-known products as Nescafé, Lean Cuisine, and Perrier, is one of the largest and most internationally diverse companies in the world. Only 2 percent of its $52.2 billion in revenues comes from its home country of Switzerland, with the rest coming from sales in almost every other country of the world. Nestlé has over 220,000 employees in 70 countries[4] and is highly decentralized; that is, many of its divisions operate as separate companies in their countries. Managing the accounting operations of such a vast empire is a tremendous challenge. In what ways do you think the accounting cycle, including the closing process, would be the same for Nestlé as it is for Joan Miller Advertising Agency, and in what ways would it be different?

Toys "R" Us Annual Report

LO 1 Fiscal Year, Closing Process, and Interim Reports

FRA 3. Refer to the Notes to Consolidated Financial Statements in the Toys "R" Us annual report. When does Toys "R" Us end its fiscal year? What reasons can you give for the company's having chosen this date? From the standpoint of completing the accounting cycle, what advantages does this date have? Does Toys "R" Us prepare interim financial statements? What are the implications of interim financial statements for the accounting cycle?

Fingraph® Financial Analyst™

This activity is not applicable to the chapter.

Internet Case

LO 1 Interim Financial Statements

FRA 4. Go to the Needles Accounting Resource Center web site at http://college.hmco.com and access the web site for ***Dell Computer Corporation.*** Find the latest quarterly financial report. Compare the results of the latest quarter available to you with the one in the Decision Point at the beginning of this chapter. Are Dell's net revenue (sales) and net income greater or less in the more recent quarter? What other information do you find in the quarterly report?

ENDNOTES

1. Dell Computer Corporation, *Annual Report*, 1999.
2. Earl E. Robertson, and Dean Lockwood, "Tapping the Power of the PC at General Mills," *Management Accounting*, August 1994.
3. Adapted from H&R Block, Inc., *Annual Report*, 1999.
4. Nestlé S.A., *Annual Report*, 1998.

Comprehensive Problem: Joan Miller Advertising Agency

This problem continues with the Joan Miller Advertising Agency, the company used to illustrate the accounting cycle in the chapters on measuring business transactions, measuring business income, and completing the accounting cycle. It is necessary in some instances to refer to those chapters in completing this problem.

The January 31, 20xx, post-closing trial balance for the Joan Miller Advertising Agency is as follows:

Joan Miller Advertising Agency
Post-Closing Trial Balance
January 31, 20xx

Cash	$ 1,720	
Accounts Receivable	2,800	
Fees Receivable	200	
Art Supplies	1,300	
Office Supplies	600	
Prepaid Rent	400	
Prepaid Insurance	440	
Art Equipment	4,200	
Accumulated Depreciation, Art Equipment		$ 70
Office Equipment	3,000	
Accumulated Depreciation, Office Equipment		50
Accounts Payable		3,170
Unearned Art Fees		600
Wages Payable		180
Joan Miller, Capital		10,590
	$14,660	$14,660

During February, the agency engaged in the following transactions.

Feb. 1 Received an additional investment of cash from Joan Miller, $6,300.
2 Purchased additional office equipment with cash, $1,200.

Feb. 5 Received art equipment transferred to the business from Joan Miller, $1,400.
6 Purchased additional office supplies with cash, $90.
7 Purchased additional art supplies on credit from Taylor Supply Company, $450.
8 Completed the series of advertisements for Marsh Tire Company that began on January 31 (see page 106) and billed Marsh Tire Company for the total services performed, including the accrued revenues (fees receivable) that had been recognized in an adjusting entry in January, $800.
9 Paid the secretary for two weeks' wages, $600.
12 Paid the amount due to Morgan Equipment for the office equipment purchased last month, $1,500.
13 Accepted an advance fee in cash for artwork to be done for another agency, $1,600.
14 Purchased a copier (office equipment) from Morgan Equipment for $2,100, paying $350 in cash and agreeing to pay the rest in equal payments over the next five months.
15 Performed advertising services and received a cash fee, $1,450.
16 Received payment on account from Ward Department Stores for services performed last month, $2,800.
19 Paid amount due for the telephone bill that was received and recorded at the end of January, $70.
20 Performed advertising services for Ward Department Stores and agreed to accept payment next month, $3,200.
21 Performed art services for a cash fee, $580.
22 Received and paid the utility bill for February, $110.
23 Paid the secretary for two weeks' wages, $600.
26 Paid the rent for March in advance, $400.
27 Received the telephone bill for February, which is to be paid next month, $80.
28 Paid out cash to Joan Miller as a withdrawal for personal living expenses, $1,400.

REQUIRED

1. Record in the general journal and post to the general ledger the optional reversing entries on February 1 for Wages Payable and Fees Receivable (see Adjustment **g** on page 104 and Adjustment **i** on page 106). (Begin the general journal on Page 5.)
2. Record the transactions for February in the general journal.
3. Post the February transactions to the general ledger accounts.
4. Prepare a trial balance in the Trial Balance columns of a work sheet.
5. Prepare adjusting entries and complete the work sheet using the information below.
   a. One month's prepaid rent has expired, $400.
   b. One month's prepaid insurance has expired, $40.
   c. An inventory of art supplies reveals $600 still on hand on February 28.
   d. An inventory of office supplies reveals $410 still on hand on February 28.
   e. Depreciation on art equipment for February is calculated to be $100.
   f. Depreciation on office equipment for February is calculated to be $100.
   g. Art services performed for which payment has been received in advance total $1,300.
   h. Advertising services performed that will not be billed until March total $290.
   i. Three days' wages had accrued by the end of February (assume a five-day week).
6. From the work sheet prepare an income statement, a statement of owner's equity, and a balance sheet.
7. Record the adjusting entries in the general journal, and post them to the general ledger.
8. Record the closing entries in the general journal, and post them to the general ledger.
9. Prepare a post-closing trial balance.

This Comprehensive Problem covers all of the Learning Objectives in the chapters on measuring business transactions, measuring business income, and completing the accounting cycle.

5 Merchandising Operations

LEARNING OBJECTIVES

1. Identify the management issues related to merchandising businesses.
2. Compare the income statements for service and merchandising concerns, and define the components of the merchandising income statement.
3. Define and distinguish the terms of sale for merchandising transactions.
4. Prepare an income statement and record merchandising transactions under the perpetual inventory system.

SUPPLEMENTAL OBJECTIVES

5. Prepare an income statement and record merchandising transactions under the periodic inventory system.
6. Prepare a work sheet and closing entries for a merchandising concern using the perpetual inventory system.
7. Prepare a work sheet and closing entries for a merchandising concern using the periodic inventory system.
8. Apply sales and purchases discounts to merchandising transactions.

DECISION POINT: A USER'S FOCUS

Target Stores The management of merchandising businesses has two key decisions to make: the price at which merchandise is sold and the level of service the company provides. For example, a department store can set the price of its merchandise at a relatively high level and provide a great deal of service. A discount store, on the other hand, may price its merchandise at a relatively low level and provide limited service. The figures in the table below show that Target Stores, a division of Target Corp., is successful.[1] What decisions did Target Stores' management make about pricing and service to achieve this success?

Target distinguishes itself from other discounters by providing its guests with quality, trend-right merchandise, superior service, a convenient shopping experience, and competitive prices. In other words, Target emphasizes high-quality, name-brand merchandise that might be sold at full price in specialty stores, but sells it at discount prices that are competitive with the prices of other discount stores that sell less well-known merchandise. Target's chief executive officer says, "Our performance in 1999 was driven by superior results at our Target division. . . . At the core of Target's future growth and financial success is our differentiated merchandise strategy."[2]

Critical Thinking Question: What types of costs can a merchandiser reduce to sell goods at a lower price while maintaining profitability? **Answer:** Labor costs, display costs, and retail store (rental) cost per square foot.

Financial Highlights

(Millions of dollars, except stores and square feet)

	1999	1998	1997
Revenues	**$26,080**	$23,014	$20,368
Operating profit	**$ 2,022**	$ 1,578	$ 1,287
Stores	**912**	851	796
Retail square feet*	**102,945**	94,553	87,158

*In thousands, reflects total square feet, less office, warehouse, and vacant space.

Business-World Example: In terms of sales dollars, the largest retailers in 1999 were Wal-Mart, Sears, and Kmart.

Management Issues in Merchandising Businesses

OBJECTIVE

1 Identify the management issues related to merchandising businesses

Related Text Assignments:
Q: 1, 2, 3, 4, 5, 6, 7
SE: 1
E: 1, 2
P: 1, 3, 8, 10
SD: 1, 2, 4
FRA: 2, 4, 5, 6

Up to this point you have studied business and accounting issues related to the simplest type of business—the service business. **Service businesses**, such as advertising agencies and law firms, perform services for fees or commissions. **Merchandising businesses**, on the other hand, earn income by buying and selling products or merchandise. These companies, whether wholesale or retail, use the same basic accounting methods as do service companies, but the buying and selling of merchandise adds to the complexity of the process. As a foundation for discussing the accounting issues of merchandising businesses, we must first identify the management issues involved in running such a business.

VIDEO CASE

Office Depot, Inc.

Objectives

- To become familiar with the nature of merchandising operations.
- To identify the management issues associated with a merchandising business.
- To show how gross margin and operating expenses affect the business goal of profitability.

Background for the Case

All retailing companies are merchandising companies. Office Depot, Inc., is the world's largest office products retailer and one of the fastest-growing retailing companies in the world. Through its chain of office products superstores and delivery warehouses, the company serves the growing market of small and medium-size businesses, home offices, and individual consumers. A typical Office Depot store is 25,000 to 30,000 square feet in size and features over 6,000 name-brand products at prices that are generally 60 percent below manufacturers' suggested retail or catalogue prices. Office Depot's merchandise assortment includes office supplies, business electronics, state-of-the-art computer hardware and software, office furniture, and a complete business service center. The company operates a national network of Customer Service Centers where customers can pick up purchases or have them delivered. The delivery business represents more than 30 percent of the company's total sales. Office Depot is expanding by opening megastores of approximately 50,000 square feet, free-standing furniture stores, and copying and publishing services outlets. The company is faced with intense competition from companies such as OfficeMax, Inc., and Staples, Inc.

For more information about Office Depot, Inc., visit the company's web site through the Needles Accounting Resource Center web site at:

http://college.hmco.com

Required

View the video on Office Depot, Inc., that accompanies this book. As you are watching the video, take notes related to the following questions:

1. All merchandising companies have inventories and need to control these inventories. In your own words, what is inventory, and why is it important to implement controls over it? Identify the types of products that Office Depot typically has in inventory and some ways in which the company might control its inventory.
2. All merchandising companies have an operating cycle. Describe the operating cycle and explain how it applies to Office Depot.
3. All merchandising companies try to achieve the goal of profitability by producing a satisfactory gross margin and maintaining acceptable levels of operating expenses. What is gross margin, and how does it relate to operating expenses? Describe how Office Depot's operations affect gross margin and operating expenses in a way that enables the company to achieve superior profitability.

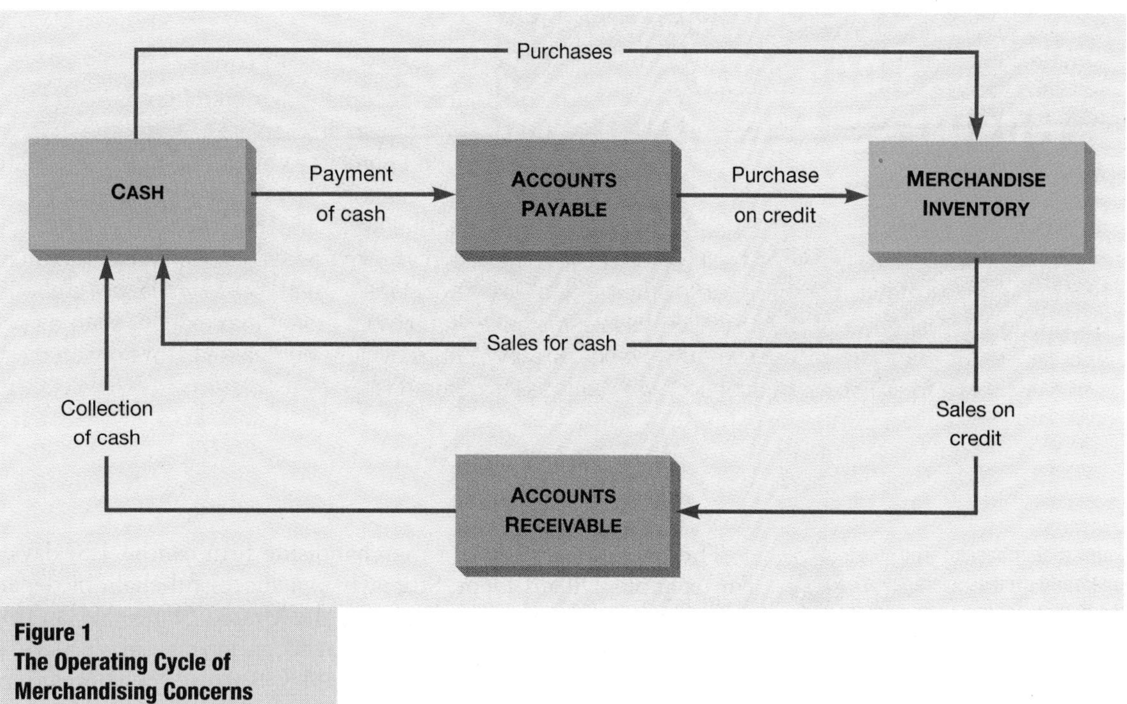

Figure 1
The Operating Cycle of Merchandising Concerns

Cash Flow Management

Merchandising businesses differ from service businesses in that they have goods on hand for sale to customers, called **merchandise inventory**, and they engage in a series of transactions called the **operating cycle**, as shown in Figure 1.

The transactions in the operating cycle of a merchandising business consist of (1) purchase of merchandise inventory for cash or on credit, (2) payment for purchases made on credit, (3) sales of merchandise inventory for cash or on credit, and (4) collection of cash from credit sales. Purchases of merchandise are usually made on credit, so the merchandiser has a period of time before payment is due, but this period is generally less than the time it takes to sell the merchandise. Therefore, management will have to plan for cash flows from within the company or from borrowing to finance the inventory until it is sold and the resulting revenue has been collected.

Point to Emphasize: A sale takes place when title to the goods transfers to the buyer.

In the case of cash sales, the cash is collected immediately. Sales on bank credit cards, such as Visa or MasterCard, are considered cash sales because funds from these sales are available to the merchandiser immediately. In the case of credit sales, the merchandising concern must wait a period of time before receiving the cash. Some very small retail stores may have mostly cash or credit card sales and very few credit sales, whereas large wholesale concerns may have almost all credit sales. Most merchandising concerns, however, have a combination of cash sales and credit sales.

Regardless of the relationships of purchases, payments, cash and credit sales, and collections, the operators of a merchandising business must carefully manage cash flow, or liquidity. Such **cash flow management** involves planning the company's receipts and payments of cash. If a company is not able to pay its bills when they are due, it may be forced out of business. As mentioned above, merchandise that is purchased must often be paid for before it is sold and the cash from its sale collected. For example, if a retail business must pay for its purchases in 30 days, it must have cash available or arrange for borrowing if it cannot sell and collect payment for the merchandise in 30 days.

FOCUS ON BUSINESS TECHNOLOGY

An increasing percentage of merchandising transactions are conducted electronically. Credit cards have long been in use, but debit, purchase, and Smart cards are becoming integral parts of the so-called cashless society. The debit card allows consumers to access their bank accounts for ATM transactions or with any seller that accepts major credit cards. The price of the sale is withdrawn immediately from the customer's account when purchases are made at grocery stores, drugstores, gas stations, dry cleaners, or hardware stores. The purchase card, the business equivalent of a debit card, allows employees to purchase merchandise for their business. Smart cards have an embedded integrated circuit that stores information, such as prepaid amounts from which purchases are deducted at the point of purchase.

Point to Emphasize: The operating cycle is average day's inventory on hand plus the average number of days to collect credit sales.

The operating cycle for a merchandising firm can be 120 days, or even longer. For example, Dillard Dept. Stores, Inc., a successful chain of department stores in the South and Southwest regions of the United States, has an operating cycle of about 218 days. Its inventory is on hand an average of 78 days, and it takes, on average, 140 days to collect its receivables. Because the company pays for its merchandise in an average of 66 days, a much shorter time, management must carefully plan its cash flow.

Profitability Management

In addition to managing cash flow, management must achieve a satisfactory level of profitability in terms of performance measures. It must sell its merchandise at a price that exceeds its cost by a sufficient margin to pay operating expenses and have enough left to provide sufficient income, or profitability. **Profitability management** is a complex activity that includes, first, achieving a satisfactory gross margin and, second, maintaining acceptable levels of operating expenses. Achieving a satisfactory gross margin depends on setting appropriate prices for merchandise and purchasing merchandise at favorable prices and terms. Maintaining acceptable levels of operating expenses depends on controlling expenses and operating efficiently.

Point to Emphasize: An operating budget is a financial plan for achieving the goal of profitability.

One of the more effective ways of controlling expenses is to use operating budgets. An **operating budget** reflects management's operating plans. It consists of detailed listings of projected selling expenses and general and administrative expenses for a company. At key times during the year and at the end of the year, management should compare the budget with actual expenses and make adjustments to operations as appropriate. An example of an operating budget for Fenwick Fashions Company is shown in Exhibit 1. Total selling expenses exceeded the budget by only $80, but four of the expense categories exceeded the budget by a total of $2,080. Management should investigate the possibility that underspending in advertising of $2,000 hid inefficiencies and waste in other areas. Also, sales may have been penalized by not spending the budgeted amount on advertising. Total general and administrative expenses exceeded the budget by $6,904. Management should determine why large differences occurred for office salaries expense, insurance expense, and office supplies expense. The amount of insurance expense is usually set by the insurance company; thus an error in the initial budgeting of insurance expense may have caused the unfavorable result. The operating budget helps management focus on the specific areas that need attention.

Exhibit 1
An Example of an Operating Budget

Fenwick Fashions Company
Operating Budget
For the Year Ended December 31, 20x2

Operating Expenses	Budget	Actual	Difference Under (Over) Budget
Selling Expenses			
Sales Salaries Expense	$22,000	$22,500	($ 500)
Freight Out Expense	5,500	5,740	(240)
Advertising Expense	12,000	10,000	2,000
Insurance Expense, Selling	800	1,600	(800)
Store Supplies Expense	1,000	1,540	(540)
Total Selling Expenses	$41,300	$41,380	($ 80)
General and Administrative Expenses			
Office Salaries Expense	$23,000	$26,900	($3,900)
Insurance Expense, General	2,100	4,200	(2,100)
Office Supplies Expense	500	1,204	(704)
Depreciation Expense, Building	2,600	2,600	—
Depreciation Expense, Office Equipment	2,000	2,200	(200)
Total General and Administrative Expenses	$30,200	$37,104	($6,904)
Total Operating Expenses	$71,500	$78,484	($6,984)

Choice of Inventory System

Another issue the management of a merchandising business must address is the choice of inventory system. Management must choose the system or combination of systems that is best for achieving the company's goals. There are two basic systems of accounting for the many items in the merchandise inventory: the perpetual inventory system and the periodic inventory system.

Point to Emphasize: Under the perpetual inventory system, the Merchandise Inventory account and the Cost of Goods Sold account are updated with every sale.

Under the **perpetual inventory system** continuous records are kept of the quantity and, usually, the cost of individual items as they are bought and sold. The detailed data available under the perpetual inventory system enable management to respond to customers' inquiries about product availability, to order inventory more effectively and thus avoid running out of stock, and to control the financial costs associated with investments in inventory. Under this system, the cost of each item is recorded in the Merchandise Inventory account when it is purchased. As merchandise is sold, its cost is transferred from the Merchandise Inventory account to the Cost of Goods Sold account. Thus, at all times the balance of the Merchandise Inventory account equals the cost of goods on hand, and the balance in Cost of Goods Sold equals the cost of merchandise sold to customers.

Point to Emphasize: The valuation of ending inventory on the balance sheet is determined by multiplying the quantity of each inventory item by its unit cost.

Under the **periodic inventory system**, the inventory not yet sold, or on hand, is counted periodically, usually at the end of the accounting period. No detailed records of the actual inventory on hand are maintained during the accounting period. The figure for inventory on hand is accurate only on the balance sheet date. As

FOCUS ON BUSINESS TECHNOLOGY

Many grocery stores, which traditionally used the periodic inventory system, now employ bar coding to update the physical inventory as items are sold. At the checkout counter, the cashier scans the electronic marking on each product, called a *bar code* or *universal product code* (UPC), into the cash register, which is linked to a computer. The price of the item appears on the cash register, and its sale is recorded by the computer. Bar coding has become common in all types of retail companies, and in manufacturing firms and hospitals as well. Some retail businesses now use the perpetual system for keeping track of the physical flow of inventory and the periodic system for preparing the financial statements.

soon as any purchases or sales are made, the figure becomes a historical amount, and it remains so until the new ending inventory amount is entered at the end of the next accounting period.

Enrichment Note: Although computerization has made the perpetual inventory system more popular in recent years, a physical count still should be made periodically to ensure that the actual number of goods on hand matches the quantity indicated by the computer records.

Some retail and wholesale businesses use periodic inventory systems to reduce the amount of clerical work. If a business is fairly small, management can maintain control over its inventory simply through observation or by the use of an off-line system of cards or computer records. On the other hand, for larger businesses, the lack of detailed records could lead to either lost sales or high operating costs.

Traditionally, the periodic inventory system has been used by companies that sell items of low value in high volume because of the difficulty and expense of accounting for the purchase and sale of each item. Examples of such companies are drugstores, automobile parts stores, department stores, discount stores, and grain companies. In contrast, companies that sell items of high unit value, such as appliances or automobiles, tend to use the perpetual inventory system. This distinction between high and low unit value for inventory systems has blurred considerably in recent years because of the widespread use of computers. Although use of the periodic inventory system is still widespread, use of the perpetual inventory system has increased greatly.

Control of Merchandising Operations

The principal transactions of merchandising businesses, such as buying and selling, involve assets—cash, accounts receivable, and merchandise inventory—that are vulnerable to theft and embezzlement. One reason for this vulnerability is that cash and inventory are fairly easy to steal. Another is that these assets are usually involved in a large number of transactions, such as cash receipts, receipts on account, payments for purchases, plus receipts and shipments of inventory, which can become difficult to monitor. If a merchandising company does not take steps to protect its assets, it can have high losses of cash and inventory. Management's responsibility is to establish an environment, accounting systems, and control procedures that will protect the company's assets. These systems and procedures are called **internal controls**.

Maintaining control over merchandise inventory is facilitated by taking a **physical inventory.** This process involves an actual count of all merchandise on hand. It can be a difficult task because it is easy to accidentally omit items or to count them twice. A physical inventory must be taken under both the periodic and the perpetual inventory systems.

Merchandise inventory includes all goods intended for sale that are owned by a concern, regardless of where they are located—on shelves, in storerooms, in warehouses, or in trucks between warehouses and stores. It also includes goods in transit from suppliers if title to the goods has passed to the merchant. Ending inventory does not include merchandise that has been sold but has not yet been delivered to customers or goods that cannot be sold because they are damaged or obsolete. If the damaged or obsolete goods can be sold at a reduced price, however, they should be included in ending inventory at their reduced value.

The actual count is usually taken after the close of business on the last day of the fiscal year. To facilitate taking the physical inventory, many companies end their fiscal year in a slow season, when inventories are at relatively low levels. Retail department stores often end their fiscal year in January or February, for example. After hours, at night, or on the weekend, employees count all items and record the results on numbered inventory tickets or sheets, following procedures to make sure that no items are missed. Sometimes a store closes for all or part of a day for inventory taking. The use of bar coding to take inventory electronically has greatly facilitated the taking of a physical inventory in many companies.

Income Statement for a Merchandising Concern

OBJECTIVE

2 Compare the income statements for service and merchandising concerns, and define the components of the merchandising income statement

Many service companies require only a simple income statement. For those companies, as shown in Figure 2, net income represents the difference between revenues and expenses. But merchandising companies, because they buy and sell merchandise inventory, require a more complex income statement. As shown in Figure 2, the income statement for a merchandiser consists of three major parts: (1) net

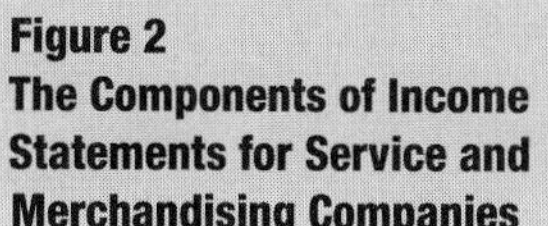

Figure 2
The Components of Income Statements for Service and Merchandising Companies

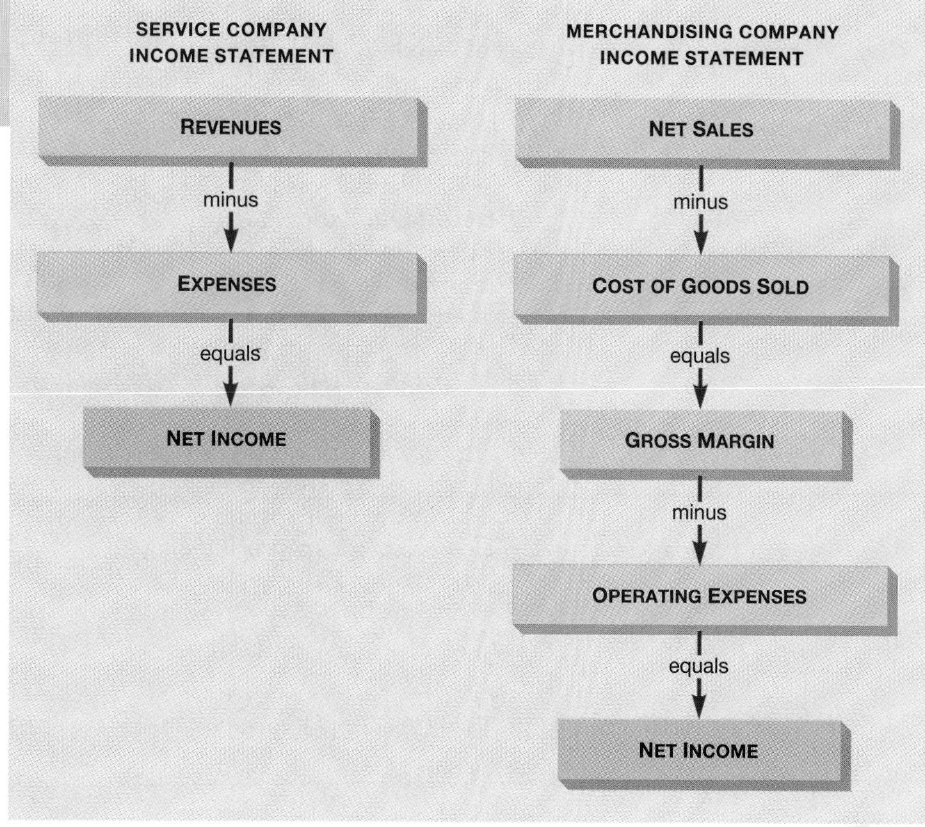

Related Text Assignments:
Q: 8, 9, 10
SE: 2
E: 3
SD: 1, 4, 5
FRA: 1, 2, 5

sales, (2) cost of goods sold, and (3) operating expenses. There is also a subtotal for gross margin.

The main difference between a merchandiser's income statement and that of a service business is that the merchandiser must compute gross margin before operating expenses are deducted. In the following discussion, the income statement for Fenwick Fashions Company, presented in Exhibit 2, will serve as an example of a merchandising income statement.

Net Sales

Point to Emphasize: A sale takes place when title to the goods transfers to the buyer.

The first major part of the merchandising income statement is **net sales**, or often simply *sales*. Net sales consist of the gross proceeds from sales of merchandise, or gross sales, less sales returns and allowances. **Gross sales** consist of total cash sales and total credit sales occurring during an accounting period. Even though the cash may not be collected until the following accounting period, revenue is recognized, under the revenue recognition rule, as being earned when title for merchandise passes from seller to buyer at the time of sale. **Sales Returns and Allowances** is a contra-revenue account used to accumulate cash refunds, credits on account, and

Exhibit 2
Income Statement Under the Perpetual Inventory System

Fenwick Fashions Company
Income Statement
For the Year Ended December 31, 20x2

Net Sales			
Gross Sales			$246,350
Less Sales Returns and Allowances			7,025
Net Sales			$239,325
Cost of Goods Sold*			131,360
Gross Margin			$107,965
Operating Expenses			
Selling Expenses			
Sales Salaries Expense	$22,500		
Freight Out Expense	5,740		
Advertising Expense	10,000		
Insurance Expense, Selling	1,600		
Store Supplies Expense	1,540		
Total Selling Expenses		$41,380	
General and Administrative Expenses			
Office Salaries Expense	$26,900		
Insurance Expense, General	4,200		
Office Supplies Expense	1,204		
Depreciation Expense, Building	2,600		
Depreciation Expense, Office Equipment	2,200		
Total General and Administrative Expenses		37,104	
Total Operating Expenses			$ 78,484
Net Income			$ 29,481

*Freight In has been included in Cost of Goods Sold.

allowances off selling prices made to customers who have received defective or otherwise unsatisfactory products. If other discounts or allowances are given to customers (see supplemental objective 8, for instance), they also should be deducted from gross sales.

Management, investors, and others often use the amount of sales and trends suggested by sales as indicators of a firm's progress. Increasing sales suggest growth; decreasing sales indicate the possibility of decreased future earnings and other financial problems. To detect trends, comparisons are frequently made between the net sales of different accounting periods.

Cost of Goods Sold

Terminology Note: The cost of goods sold (also called the *cost of sales*) is an expense.

Enrichment Note: The matching rule precludes the cost of inventory from being expensed until the inventory has been sold.

Cost of goods sold, or simply *cost of sales*, is the amount a merchandiser paid for the merchandise sold during an accounting period or the cost to a manufacturer of manufacturing the products sold during an accounting period. It is the second part of the income statement for a merchandiser or manufacturer.

Gross Margin

Discussion Question: If a company sold all its goods to the public "at cost," would the company realize a profit of exactly $0? **Answer:** No. Its gross margin would equal $0, but the company would suffer a net loss equal to its operating expenses.

Parenthetical Note: When gross margin is insufficient to cover operating expenses, the company has suffered a net loss.

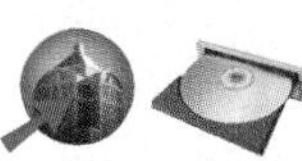

The difference between net sales and cost of goods sold on the merchandising income statement is **gross margin**, or *gross profit*. To be successful, merchants must sell goods for an amount greater than cost—that is, gross margin must be great enough to pay operating expenses and provide an adequate income. Management is interested in both the amount and the percentage of gross margin. The percentage of gross margin is computed by dividing the dollar amount of gross margin by net sales. In the case of Fenwick Fashions, the dollar amount of gross margin is $107,965 and the percentage of gross margin is 45.1 percent ($107,965 ÷ $239,325). This information is helpful in planning business operations. For instance, management may try to increase total sales dollars by reducing the selling price. This strategy reduces the percentage of gross margin, but it will work if the total items sold increase enough to raise the absolute amount of gross margin. This is the strategy followed by a discount warehouse store like Sam's Clubs. On the other hand, management may keep a high gross margin and attempt to increase sales and the amount of gross margin by increasing operating expenses such as advertising. This is the strategy followed by upscale specialty stores like Neiman Marcus. Other strategies to increase gross margin, such as improving purchasing methods to reduce cost of goods sold, can also be explored.

Operating Expenses

Point to Emphasize: The most common types of operating expenses are selling expenses and general and administrative expenses. They are deducted from gross margin on the income statement.

The third major area of the merchandising income statement consists of **operating expenses**, which are the expenses other than cost of goods sold that are incurred in running a business. They are similar to the expenses of a service company. It is customary to group operating expenses into categories, such as selling expenses and general and administrative expenses. Selling expenses include the costs of storing goods and preparing them for sale, displaying, advertising, and otherwise promoting sales; making sales; and delivering goods to the buyer, if the seller bears the cost of delivery. The latter cost is often accumulated in an account called **Freight Out Expense** or *Delivery Expense*. Among the general and administrative expenses are general office expense, which includes expenses for accounting, personnel, credit and collections, and any other expenses that apply to overall operation. General occupancy expenses, such as rent expense, insurance expense, and utilities expense, are often classified as general and administrative expenses. However, they may also be allocated between the selling and the general and administrative categories. Careful planning and control of operating expenses can improve a company's profitability.

Net Income

Net income, the final figure or "bottom line" of the income statement, is what remains after operating expenses are deducted from gross margin. It is an important performance measure because it represents the amount of business earnings that accrue to the owners. It is the amount that is transferred to owner's equity from all the income-generating activities during the period. Both management and owners often use net income to measure whether a business has been operating successfully during the past accounting period.

Terms of Sale

OBJECTIVE

3 Define and distinguish the terms of sale for merchandising transactions

Related Text Assignments:
Q: 11, 12
SE: 3
E: 4
FRA: 3, 6

When goods are sold on credit, both parties should understand the amount and timing of payment as well as other terms of the purchase, such as who pays delivery or freight charges and what warranties or rights of return apply. Sellers quote prices in different ways. Many merchants quote the price at which they expect to sell their goods. Others, particularly manufacturers and wholesalers, provide a price list or catalogue and quote prices as a percentage (usually 30 percent or more) off the list or catalogue prices. Such a reduction of the list price is called a **trade discount.** For example, if an article was listed at $1,000 with a trade discount of 40 percent, or $400, the seller would record the sale at $600 and the buyer would record the purchase at $600. If the seller wishes to change the selling price, the trade discount can be raised or lowered. At times the trade discount may vary depending on the quantity purchased. The list price and trade discount are used only to reach agreement on price; they do not appear in the accounting records.

Teaching Note: Students would benefit from looking at a comprehensive income statement for Fenwick Fashions Company before studying the individual sections. See Exhibit 2.

The terms of sale are usually printed on the sales invoice and thus constitute part of the sales agreement. Customary terms differ from industry to industry. In some industries, payment is expected in a short period of time, such as 10 or 30 days. In these cases, the invoice is marked "n/10" or "n/30" (read as "net 10" or "net 30"), meaning that the amount of the invoice is due either 10 days or 30 days after the invoice date. If the invoice is due 10 days after the end of the month, it is marked "n/10 eom."

Common Student Confusion: Students frequently confuse the terms *trade discount* and *sales discount*. A trade discount applies to the list or catalogue price. A sales discount encourages early payment by buyer.

Enrichment Note: Early collection also has the advantage of reducing to zero the probability of a customer's defaulting.

In some industries it is customary to give a discount for early payment. This discount, called a **sales discount**, is intended to increase the seller's liquidity by reducing the amount of money tied up in accounts receivable. An invoice that offers a sales discount might be labeled "2/10, n/30," which means that the buyer either can pay the invoice within 10 days of the invoice date and take a 2 percent discount or can wait 30 days and then pay the full amount of the invoice. It is almost always advantageous for a buyer to take the discount because the saving of 2 percent over a period of 20 days (from the eleventh day to the thirtieth day) represents an effective annual rate of 36.5 percent (365 days ÷ 20 days × 2% = 36.5%). Most companies would be better off borrowing money to take the discount. The practice of giving sales discounts has been declining because it is costly to the seller and because, from the buyer's viewpoint, the amount of the discount is usually very small in relation to the price of the purchase. Accounting for sales discounts is covered in supplemental objective 8.

In some industries, it is customary for the seller to pay transportation costs and to charge a price that includes those costs. In other industries, it is customary for the purchaser to pay transportation charges on merchandise. Special terms designate whether the seller or the purchaser pays the freight charges. **FOB shipping point** means that the seller places the merchandise "free on board" at the point of origin, and the buyer bears the shipping costs. The title to the merchandise passes to the buyer at that point. For example, when the sales agreement for the purchase of a car says "FOB factory," the buyer must pay the freight from where the car was made to wherever he or she is located, and the buyer owns the car from the time it leaves the factory.

On the other hand, **FOB destination** means that the seller bears the transportation costs to the place where the merchandise is delivered. The seller retains title until the merchandise reaches its destination and usually prepays the shipping costs, in which case the buyer makes no accounting entry for freight. The effects of these special shipping terms are summarized as follows:

Shipping Term	Where Title Passes	Who Pays the Cost of Transportation
FOB shipping point	At origin	Buyer
FOB destination	At destination	Seller

Applying the Perpetual Inventory System

OBJECTIVE

4 Prepare an income statement and record merchandising transactions under the perpetual inventory system

Related Text Assignments:
Q: 13, 14, 16, 17
SE: 4, 5, 6
E: 5, 6, 7
P: 1, 2, 8, 9
SD: 2
FRA: 3, 6

The income statement for Fenwick Fashions Company under the perpetual inventory system is shown previously in Exhibit 2. The focal point of this income statement is cost of goods sold, which is deducted from net sales to arrive at gross margin. Under the perpetual inventory system, this account is continually updated during the accounting period as purchases, sales, and other inventory transactions take place. The Merchandise Inventory account on the balance sheet is updated at the same time. In Exhibit 2, freight in is included in cost of goods sold. Theoretically, freight in should be allocated between ending inventory and cost of goods sold, but most companies choose to include the cost of freight in with the cost of goods sold on the income statement because it is a relatively small amount.

Transactions Related to Purchases of Merchandise

The recording of typical transactions related to purchases of merchandise under the perpetual inventory system is illustrated in the following sections.

Purchases of Merchandise on Credit

Point to Emphasize: The Merchandise Inventory account is increased when a purchase is made.

Oct. 3 Received merchandise purchased on credit from Neebok Company, invoice dated October 1, terms n/10, FOB shipping point, $4,890.

A = L + OE
\+ \+

Oct. 3	Merchandise Inventory	4,890	
	Accounts Payable		4,890
	Purchased merchandise from Neebok Company, terms n/10, FOB shipping point, invoice dated Oct. 1		

Under the perpetual inventory system, the cost of merchandise purchased is placed in the Merchandise Inventory account at the time of purchase.

Transportation Costs on Purchases

Oct. 4 Received bill from Transfer Freight Company for transportation costs on October 3 shipment, invoice dated October 1, terms n/10, $160.

A = L + OE
\+ −

Oct. 4	Freight In	160	
	Accounts Payable		160
	Received transportation charges on Oct. 3 purchase, Transfer Freight Company, terms n/10, invoice dated Oct. 1		

Common Student Confusion: Students often confuse freight in and freight out expense. Explain that Freight In appears within the cost of goods sold section of the income statement and that Freight Out Expense appears as an operating expense.

Freight in, also called *transportation in*, is the transportation cost of receiving merchandise. Transportation costs are accumulated in a Freight In account because most shipments contain multiple items. It is usually not practical to identify the specific cost of shipping each item of inventory.

In some cases, the seller pays the freight charges and bills them to the buyer as a separate item on the invoice. When this occurs, the entries are the same as in the October 3 example, except that a debit is made to Freight In for the amount of the freight charges and Accounts Payable is increased by a like amount.

Purchases Returns and Allowances

Oct. 6 Returned merchandise received from Neebok Company on October 3 for credit, $480.

A = L + OE				
– –	Oct. 6	Accounts Payable	480	
		Merchandise Inventory		480
		Returned merchandise from purchase of Oct. 3 to Neebok Company for full credit		

If a seller sends the wrong product or one that is otherwise unsatisfactory, the buyer may be allowed to return the item for a cash refund or credit on account, or the buyer may be given an allowance off the sales price. Under the perpetual inventory system, the returned merchandise is removed from the Merchandise Inventory account.

Payments on Account

Oct. 10 Paid in full the amount due to Neebok Company for the purchase of October 3, part of which was returned on October 6.

A = L + OE				
– –	Oct. 10	Accounts Payable	4,410	
		Cash		4,410
		Made payment on account to Neebok Company $4,890 – $480 = $4,410		

Transactions Related to Sales of Merchandise

Under the perpetual inventory system, at the time of a sale, the cost of the merchandise is transferred from the Merchandise Inventory account to the Cost of Goods Sold account. In the case of a return of sold merchandise, the cost of the merchandise is transferred from Cost of Goods Sold back to Merchandise Inventory. Transactions related to sales made by Fenwick Fashions Company follow.

Sales of Merchandise on Credit

Oct. 7 Sold merchandise on credit to Gonzales Distributors, terms n/30, FOB destination, $1,200; the cost of the merchandise was $720.

A = L + OE				
+ +	Oct. 7	Accounts Receivable	1,200	
		Sales		1,200
		Sold merchandise to Gonzales Distributors, terms n/30, FOB destination		

A = L + OE				
– –		Cost of Goods Sold	720	
		Merchandise Inventory		720
		Transferred cost of merchandise inventory sold to Cost of Goods Sold account		

Point to Emphasize: Point out that there are more entries associated with a perpetual inventory system than with a periodic inventory system.

Under the perpetual inventory system, two entries are necessary. First, the sale is recorded. Second, Cost of Goods Sold is updated by a transfer from Merchandise Inventory. In the case of cash sales, Cash rather than Accounts Receivable is debited for the amount of the sale.

Payment of Delivery Costs

Oct. 8 Paid transportation costs for the sale on October 7, $78.

A = L + OE
− −

Oct. 8	Freight Out Expense	78	
	Cash		78
	Paid delivery costs on Oct. 7 sale		

A seller will often absorb delivery or freight out costs in the belief that doing so will facilitate the sale of its products. These costs are accumulated in an account called Freight Out Expense, or *Delivery Expense,* which is shown as a selling expense on the income statement.

Returns of Merchandise Sold

Oct. 9 Merchandise sold on October 7 accepted back from Gonzales Distributors for full credit and returned to merchandise inventory, $300; the cost of the merchandise was $180.

A = L + OE
− −

Oct. 9	Sales Returns and Allowances	300	
	Accounts Receivable		300
	Accepted returned merchandise from Gonzales Distributors		

A = L + OE
+ +

	Merchandise Inventory	180	
	Cost of Goods Sold		180
	Transferred cost of merchandise returned to the Merchandise Inventory account		

Point to Emphasize: Because the Sales account is established with a credit, its contra accounts, Sales Returns and Allowances and Sales Discounts, are each established with a debit.

Because returns and allowances to customers for wrong or unsatisfactory merchandise are often an indicator of customer dissatisfaction, such amounts are accumulated in a Sales Returns and Allowances account. This account is a contra-revenue account with a normal debit balance and is deducted from Sales on the income statement. Under the perpetual inventory system, the cost of the merchandise must also be transferred from the Cost of Goods Sold account back into the Merchandise Inventory account. If an allowance is made instead of accepting a return, or if the merchandise cannot be returned to inventory and resold, this transfer is not made.

Focus on Business Practice

In some industries a high percentage of sales returns is an accepted business practice. A book publisher like Simon & Schuster will produce and ship more copies of a best-seller than it expects to sell because, to gain the attention of potential buyers, copies must be distributed to a wide variety of outlets, such as bookstores, department stores, and discount stores. As a result, returns of unsold books may run as high as 30 to 50 percent of the books shipped. The same sales principles apply to magazines, such as *People*, that are sold on newsstands and to popular recordings produced by companies like Motown Records. In all these businesses, management scrutinizes the Sales Returns and Allowances account for ways to reduce returns and increase profitability.

Receipts on Account

Nov. 5 Received payment in full from Gonzales Distributors for sale of merchandise on October 7, less the return on October 9.

A = L + OE				
+	Nov. 5	Cash	900	
−		Accounts Receivable		900
		Received on account from Gonzales Distributors $1,200 − $300 = $900		

Credit Card Sales

Many retailers allow customers to charge their purchases to a third-party company that the customer will pay later. These transactions are normally handled with credit cards. Five of the most widely used credit cards are American Express, Discover Card, Diners Club, MasterCard, and Visa. The customer establishes credit with the lender (the credit card issuer) and receives a plastic card to use in making charge purchases. If the seller accepts the card, an invoice is prepared and signed by the customer at the time of the sale. The seller then deposits the invoice in the bank and receives cash.

Because the seller does not have to establish the customer's credit, collect from the customer, or tie money up in accounts receivable, the seller receives an economic benefit provided by the lender. As payment, the lender takes a discount of 2 to 6 percent on the credit card sales invoices rather than paying 100 percent of their total amount. The discount is a selling expense for the merchandiser. For example, assume that a restaurant made sales of $1,000 on Visa credit cards and that Visa takes a 4 percent discount on the sales. Assume also that the sales invoices are deposited in a special Visa bank account in the name of the company, in much the same way that checks from cash sales are deposited. The sales are recorded as follows:

A = L + OE			
+	Cash	960	
−	Credit Card Discount Expense	40	
+	Sales		1,000
	Made sales on Visa cards		

Inventory Losses

Enrichment Note: Inventory shortages could result from honest mistakes. That is, inventory could have been tagged with the wrong number.

Most companies experience losses of merchandise inventory from spoilage, shoplifting, and theft by employees. When such losses occur, the periodic inventory system provides no means of identifying them because the costs are automatically included in the cost of goods sold. For example, assume that a company has lost $1,250 in stolen merchandise during an accounting period. When the physical inventory is taken, the missing items are not in stock, so they cannot be counted. Because the ending inventory does not contain these items, the amount subtracted from goods available for sale is less than it would be if the goods were in stock. The cost of goods sold, then, is overstated by $1,250. In a sense, the cost of goods sold is inflated by the amount of merchandise that has been lost.

Clarification Note: An adjustment to the Merchandise Inventory account will be needed if the physical inventory reveals a difference between the actual inventory and the amount in the records.

The perpetual inventory system makes it easier to identify such losses. Because the Merchandise Inventory account is continuously updated for sales, purchases, and returns, the loss will show up as the difference between the inventory records and the physical inventory taken at the end of the accounting period. Once the amount of the loss has been identified, the ending inventory is updated by crediting the Merchandise Inventory account. The offsetting debit is usually an increase in Cost of Goods Sold because the loss is considered a cost that reduces the company's gross margin.

Applying the Periodic Inventory System

SUPPLEMENTAL OBJECTIVE

5 Prepare an income statement and record merchandising transactions under the periodic inventory system

Related Text Assignments:
Q: 13, 14, 15, 16, 17, 18
SE: 7, 8, 9
E: 8, 9, 10, 11
P: 3, 4, 7, 10, 11
SD: 2
FRA: 3

The income statement for Fenwick Fashions Company under the periodic inventory system is shown in Exhibit 3 and illustrated in Figure 3. A major feature of this income statement is the computation of cost of goods sold. Cost of goods sold

Enrichment Note: Most published financial statements are condensed, eliminating much of the detail shown here.

Fenwick Fashions Company
Income Statement
For the Year Ended December 31, 20x2

Net Sales			
Gross Sales			$246,350
Less Sales Returns and Allowances			7,025
Net Sales			$239,325
Cost of Goods Sold			
Merchandise Inventory, December 31, 20x1		$ 52,800	
Purchases	$126,400		
Less Purchases Returns and Allowances	7,776		
Net Purchases	$118,624		
Freight In	8,236		
Net Cost of Purchases		126,860	
Goods Available for Sale		$179,660	
Less Merchandise Inventory, December 31, 20x2		48,300	
Cost of Goods Sold			131,360
Gross Margin			$107,965
Operating Expenses			
Selling Expenses			
Sales Salaries Expense	$ 22,500		
Freight Out Expense	5,740		
Advertising Expense	10,000		
Insurance Expense, Selling	1,600		
Store Supplies Expense	1,540		
Total Selling Expenses		$ 41,380	
General and Administrative Expenses			
Office Salaries Expense	$ 26,900		
Insurance Expense, General	4,200		
Office Supplies Expense	1,204		
Depreciation Expense, Building	2,600		
Depreciation Expense, Office Equipment	2,200		
Total General and Administrative Expenses		37,104	
Total Operating Expenses			78,484
Net Income			$ 29,481

Exhibit 3
Income Statement Under the Periodic Inventory System

Figure 3
The Components of Cost of Goods Sold

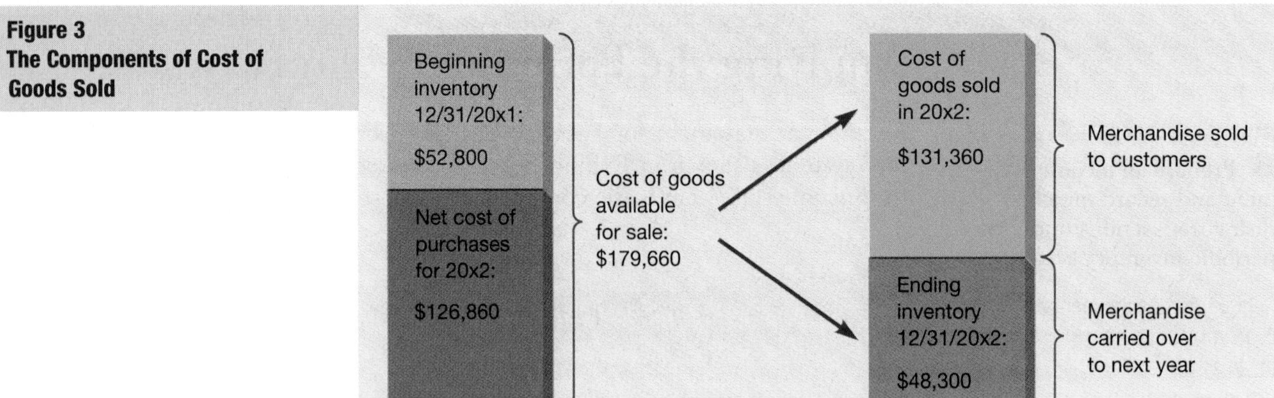

must be computed because it is not updated for purchases, sales, and other transactions during the accounting period as it is under the perpetual inventory system.

Cost of Goods Sold

The method of computing cost of goods sold when using the periodic inventory method is sometimes confusing because it must take into account both merchandise inventory on hand at the beginning of the accounting period, called the **beginning inventory**, and merchandise inventory on hand at the end of the accounting period, called the **ending inventory.** The ending inventory appears on the balance sheet at the end of the accounting period and becomes the beginning inventory for the next accounting period.

To calculate cost of goods sold, the **goods available for sale** must first be determined. The goods available for sale during the year is the sum of two factors, beginning inventory and the net cost of purchases during the year. In this case, the goods available for sale is $179,660 ($52,800 + $126,860).

If a company sold all the goods available for sale during an accounting period, the cost of goods sold would equal the goods available for sale. In most businesses, however, some merchandise will remain unsold and on hand at the end of the period. This merchandise, or ending inventory, must be deducted from the goods available for sale to determine the cost of goods sold. In the case of Fenwick Fashions Company, the ending inventory on December 31, 20x2, is $48,300. Thus, the cost of goods sold is $131,360 ($179,660 − $48,300).

An important component of the cost of goods sold section is **net cost of purchases**, which consists of net purchases plus any freight charges on the purchases. **Net purchases** equals total purchases less any deductions, such as purchases returns and allowances and any discounts allowed by suppliers for early payment (see supplemental objective 8). Because transportation charges, or freight in, are a necessary cost of receiving merchandise for sale, they are added to net purchases to arrive at the net cost of purchases, as shown in Exhibit 3.

Transactions Related to Purchases of Merchandise

The primary difference in accounting between the perpetual and the periodic inventory systems is that under the perpetual inventory system, the Merchandise Inventory account is continuously adjusted because purchases, sales, and other inventory transactions are entered in the account as they occur. Under the periodic

and move sequentially down the work sheet, one account at a time, entering each account balance in the correct Income Statement or Balance Sheet column.

Adjusting Entries The adjusting entries from the work sheet are now entered into the general journal and posted to the ledger, as they would be in a service company. There is no difference in this procedure between a service company and a merchandising company.

Closing Entries The closing entries for Fenwick Fashions Company are shown in Exhibit 5. The Cost of Goods Sold account is closed to Income Summary along with the expense accounts because the Cost of Goods Sold account has a debit balance. No closing entries affect the Merchandise Inventory account.

Exhibit 5
Closing Entries for Fenwick Fashions Company: Perpetual Inventory System

General Journal — Page 10

Date		Description	Post. Ref.	Debit	Credit
20x2		*Closing entries:*			
Dec.	31	Income Summary		216,869	
		Sales Returns and Allowances			7,025
		Cost of Goods Sold			123,124
		Freight In			8,236
		Sales Salaries Expense			22,500
		Freight Out Expense			5,740
		Advertising Expense			10,000
		Office Salaries Expense			26,900
		Insurance Expense, Selling			1,600
		Insurance Expense, General			4,200
		Store Supplies Expense			1,540
		Office Supplies Expense			1,204
		Depreciation Expense, Building			2,600
		Depreciation Expense, Office Equipment			2,200
		To close the temporary expense and revenue accounts having debit balances			
	31	Sales		246,350	
		Income Summary			246,350
		To close the temporary revenue account having a credit balance			
	31	Income Summary		29,481	
		Gloria Fenwick, Capital			29,481
		To close the Income Summary account			
	31	Gloria Fenwick, Capital		20,000	
		Gloria Fenwick, Withdrawals			20,000
		To close the Withdrawals account			

The Periodic Inventory System

SUPPLEMENTAL OBJECTIVE

7 Prepare a work sheet and closing entries for a merchandising concern using the periodic inventory system

Related Text Assignments:
Q: 18, 19, 20
SE: 10
E: 13
P: 6

Teaching Note: The mnemonic BEE refects the treatment of inventory in the Income Statement and Balance Sheet columns: Beginning, Ending, and Ending amounts, starting with the debit side of the Income Statement columns.

The accounts for a merchandising company using the periodic inventory system generally include Sales, Sales Returns and Allowances, Sales Discounts, Purchases, Purchases Returns and Allowances, Purchases Discounts, Freight In, and Merchandise Inventory. Except for Merchandise Inventory, these accounts are treated in much the same way as revenue and expense accounts for a service company. On the work sheet, they are extended to the Income Statement columns. In the closing process, they are transferred to the Income Summary account.

The Merchandise Inventory account requires special treatment because, under the periodic inventory system, purchases of merchandise are accumulated in the Purchases account, and no entries are made to Merchandise Inventory during the accounting period. As a result, at the end of the period, the balance in Merchandise Inventory is the same as it was at the beginning of the period: the beginning inventory amount. To calculate net income, the closing entries must (1) remove the beginning inventory from the Merchandise Inventory account, (2) enter the ending inventory in the Merchandise Inventory account, and (3) transfer both inventory amounts to the Income Summary account. The following T accounts illustrate the flow of the inventory amounts at Fenwick Fashions.

Merchandise Inventory

Dec. 31, 20x1	Beg. Bal.	52,800	Dec. 31, 20x2	52,800
Dec. 31, 20x2	End. Bal.	48,300		

Income Summary

Dec. 31, 20x2	52,800	Dec. 31, 20x2	48,300

Teaching Note: Remind your students that asset accounts are increased with debits and decreased with credits. Ending inventory must be established with a debit, and beginning inventory eliminated with a credit.

The beginning merchandise inventory was $52,800. This amount is removed from the Merchandise Inventory account by a credit, which leaves a zero balance, and transferred to the Income Summary account by a debit. The ending inventory was $48,300. This amount is entered in the Merchandise Inventory account by a debit and recorded in the Income Summary account by a credit. The results of the two closing entries mirror the calculation of cost of goods sold, in which beginning inventory is added to net cost of purchases and ending inventory is then subtracted. When beginning inventory is debited to the Income Summary account, it is, in effect, added to net purchases because the balance in the Purchases account is also debited to Income Summary through a closing entry. And when ending inventory is credited to Income Summary, it is, in effect, deducted from the sum of beginning inventory and net cost of purchases. Keep these effects in mind while studying the work sheet for Fenwick Fashions Company shown in Exhibit 6.

Point to Emphasize: The Income Summary account does not appear on this work sheet.

INCOME STATEMENT AND BALANCE SHEET COLUMNS As explained earlier, the Merchandise Inventory row requires special treatment. The beginning inventory balance of $52,800 (which is already in the trial balance) is extended to the debit column of the Income Statement columns, as shown in Exhibit 6. This procedure has the effect of adding beginning inventory to net purchases because the Purchases account is also in the debit column of the Income Statement columns. The ending inventory balance of $48,300 (determined by the physical inventory and not in the trial balance) is then inserted in the credit column of the Income Statement columns. This procedure has the effect of subtracting the ending inventory from goods available for sale in order to calculate the cost of goods sold. Finally, the ending merchandise inventory ($48,300) is inserted in the debit side of the Balance Sheet columns because it will appear on the balance sheet.

After all the items have been extended into the correct columns, the four columns are totaled. The net income or net loss is the difference between the debit

Exhibit 6
Work Sheet for Fenwick Fashions Company: Periodic Inventory System

Fenwick Fashions Company
Work Sheet
For the Year Ended December 31, 20x2

	Trial Balance		Adjustments		Income Statement		Balance Sheet	
Account Name	Debit	Credit	Debit	Credit	Debit	Credit	Debit	Credit
Cash	29,410						29,410	
Accounts Receivable	42,400						42,400	
Merchandise Inventory	52,800				52,800	48,300	48,300	
Prepaid Insurance	17,400			(a) 5,800			11,600	
Store Supplies	2,600			(b) 1,540			1,060	
Office Supplies	1,840			(c) 1,204			636	
Land	4,500						4,500	
Building	20,260						20,260	
Accumulated Depreciation, Building		5,650		(d) 2,600				8,250
Office Equipment	8,600						8,600	
Accumulated Depreciation, Office Equipment		2,800		(e) 2,200				5,000
Accounts Payable		25,683						25,683
Gloria Fenwick, Capital		118,352						118,352
Gloria Fenwick, Withdrawals	20,000						20,000	
Sales		246,350				246,350		
Sales Returns and Allowances	7,025				7,025			
Purchases	126,400				126,400			
Purchases Returns and Allowances		7,776				7,776		
Freight In	8,236				8,236			
Sales Salaries Expense	22,500				22,500			
Freight Out Expense	5,740				5,740			
Advertising Expense	10,000				10,000			
Office Salaries Expense	26,900				26,900			
	406,611	406,611						
Insurance Expense, Selling			(a) 1,600		1,600			
Insurance Expense, General			(a) 4,200		4,200			
Store Supplies Expense			(b) 1,540		1,540			
Office Supplies Expense			(c) 1,204		1,204			
Depreciation Expense, Building			(d) 2,600		2,600			
Depreciation Expense, Office Equipment			(e) 2,200		2,200			
			13,344	13,344	272,945	302,426	186,766	157,285
Net Income					29,481			29,481
					302,426	302,426	186,766	186,766

and credit Income Statement columns. In this case, Fenwick Fashions Company has earned a net income of $29,481, which is extended to the credit side of the Balance Sheet columns. The four columns are then added to prove that total debits equal total credits.

CLOSING ENTRIES The closing entries for Fenwick Fashions Company appear in Exhibit 7. Notice that Merchandise Inventory is credited for the amount of the beginning inventory ($52,800) in the first entry and debited for the amount of the ending inventory ($48,300) in the second entry. Otherwise, these closing entries

Exhibit 7
Closing Entries for Fenwick Fashions Company: Periodic Inventory System

General Journal					Page 10
Date		Description	Post. Ref.	Debit	Credit
20x2		*Closing entries:*			
Dec.	31	Income Summary		272,945	
		Merchandise Inventory			52,800
		Sales Returns and Allowances			7,025
		Purchases			126,400
		Freight In			8,236
		Sales Salaries Expense			22,500
		Freight Out Expense			5,740
		Advertising Expense			10,000
		Office Salaries Expense			26,900
		Insurance Expense, Selling			1,600
		Insurance Expense, General			4,200
		Store Supplies Expense			1,540
		Office Supplies Expense			1,204
		Depreciation Expense, Building			2,600
		Depreciation Expense, Office Equipment			2,200
		To close the temporary expense and revenue accounts having debit balances and to remove the beginning inventory			
	31	Merchandise Inventory		48,300	
		Sales		246,350	
		Purchases Returns and Allowances		7,776	
		Income Summary			302,426
		To close the temporary expense and revenue accounts having credit balances and to establish the ending inventory			
	31	Income Summary		29,481	
		Gloria Fenwick, Capital			29,481
		To close the Income Summary account			
	31	Gloria Fenwick, Capital		20,000	
		Gloria Fenwick, Withdrawals			20,000
		To close the Withdrawals account			

are very similar to those for a service company except that the merchandising accounts also must be closed to Income Summary. All income statement accounts with debit balances, including the merchandising accounts of Sales Returns and Allowances, Purchases, and Freight In, are credited in the first entry. The total of these accounts ($272,945) equals the total of the debit column in the Income Statement columns of the work sheet. All income statement accounts with credit balances—Sales and Purchases Returns and Allowances—are debited in the second entry. The total of these accounts ($302,426) equals the total of the Income Statement credit column in the work sheet. The third and fourth entries are used to close the Income Summary account and transfer net income to the Capital account, and to close the Withdrawals account to the Capital account.

Accounting for Discounts

Sales Discounts

SUPPLEMENTAL OBJECTIVE

8 **Apply sales and purchases discounts to merchandising transactions**

Related Text Assignments:
Q: 21
SE: 11
E: 14, 15, 16
P: 7
SD: 3

As mentioned earlier, some industries give sales discounts for early payment. Because it usually is not possible to know at the time of the sale whether the customer will pay in time to take advantage of them, sales discounts are recorded only at the time the customer pays. For example, assume that Fenwick Fashions Company sells merchandise to a customer on September 20 for $300, on terms of 2/10, n/60. This is the entry at the time of the sale:

A = L + OE
\+   +

Sept. 20	Accounts Receivable	300	
	Sales		300
	Sold merchandise on credit, terms 2/10, n/60		

The customer can take advantage of the sales discount any time on or before September 30, ten days after the date of the invoice. If the customer pays on September 29, the entry in Fenwick's records would look like this:

A = L + OE
\+   −
−

Sept. 29	Cash	294	
	Sales Discounts	6	
	Accounts Receivable		300
	Received payment for Sept. 20 sale; discount taken		

Point to Emphasize: Notice that Accounts Receivable must be credited for the full $300 even though only $294 has been received.

If the customer does not take advantage of the sales discount but waits until November 19 to pay for the merchandise, the entry would be as follows:

A = L + OE
\+
−

Nov. 19	Cash	300	
	Accounts Receivable		300
	Received payment for Sept. 20 sale; no discount taken		

Instructional Strategy: Divide the class into small groups and assign SD 3. Allow 8–10 minutes for group analysis, debrief the groups, and summarize.

At the end of the accounting period, the Sales Discounts account has accumulated all the sales discounts taken during the period. Because sales discounts reduce revenues from sales, Sales Discounts is a contra-revenue account with a normal debit balance that is deducted from gross sales in the income statement. Sales Discounts is treated the same as Sales Returns and Allowances on the work sheet and in the closing entries.

Purchases Discounts

Merchandise purchases are usually made on credit and sometimes involve **purchases discounts** for early payment. Purchases discounts are discounts taken for early payment for merchandise purchased for resale. They are to the buyer what sales discounts are to the seller. The amount of discounts taken is recorded in a separate account. Assume that Fenwick made a credit purchase of merchandise on November 12 for $1,500 with terms of 2/10, n/30 and returned $200 in merchandise on November 14. When payment is made, the journal entry looks like this:

A = L + OE
− − +

Nov. 22	Accounts Payable		1,300	
	Purchases Discounts			26
	Cash			1,274
	Paid the invoice of Nov. 12			
	Purchase Nov. 12	$1,500		
	Less return Nov. 14	200		
	Net purchase	$1,300		
	Discount: 2%	26		
	Cash paid	$1,274		

Point to Emphasize: Notice that Accounts Payable must be debited for the full $1,300 even though only $1,274 has been paid.

If the purchase is not paid for within the discount period, this is the entry:

A = L + OE
− −

Dec. 12	Accounts Payable	1,300	
	Cash		1,300
	Paid the invoice of Nov. 12, less the return, on due date; no discount taken		

Discussion Question: Can you think of a drawback to recording the December 12 payment in this way? Answer: No record was made of the discount that was lost.

Like Purchases Returns and Allowances, Purchases Discounts is a contra-purchases account with a normal credit balance that is deducted from Purchases on the income statement. If a company makes only a partial payment on an invoice, most creditors allow the company to take the discount applicable to the partial payment. The discount usually does not apply to freight, postage, taxes, or other charges that might appear on the invoice. Purchases Discounts is treated the same as Purchases Returns and Allowances on the work sheet and in the closing entries.

Chapter Review

REVIEW OF LEARNING OBJECTIVES

Check out ACE, a self-quizzing program on chapter content, at http://college.hmco.com.

1. **Identify the management issues related to merchandising businesses.** Merchandising companies differ from service companies in that they earn income by buying and selling products or merchandise. The buying and selling of merchandise adds to the complexity of the business and raises four issues that management must address. First, the series of transactions that merchandising companies engage in (the operating cycle) requires careful cash flow management. Second, profitability management requires the company to price goods and control costs and expenses in ways that ensure the earning of an adequate income after operating expenses have been paid. Third, the company must choose whether to use the perpetual or the periodic inventory system. Fourth, management must establish an internal control structure that protects the assets of cash, merchandise inventory, and accounts receivable.

2. **Compare the income statements for service and merchandising concerns, and define the components of the merchandising income statement.** In the simplest case, the income statement for a service company consists only of revenues and expenses. The income statement for a merchandising company has three major parts: (1) net sales, (2) cost of goods sold, and (3) operating expenses. Gross margin is the difference between revenues from net sales and the cost of goods sold. Net income is the "bottom line" after operating expenses are deducted from the gross margin.

3. **Define and distinguish the terms of sale for merchandising transactions.** Trade discounts are a reduction from the catalogue or list price of a product. A sales discount is a discount given for early payment of a sale on credit. FOB shipping point means the buyer bears the cost of transportation, and title to the goods passes to the buyer at the shipping origin. FOB destination means that the seller bears the cost of transportation, and title does not pass to the buyer until the goods reach their destination.

4. **Prepare an income statement and record merchandising transactions under the perpetual inventory system.** Under the perpetual inventory system, records of the quantity and, usually, the cost of individual items of inventory are kept throughout the year. The cost of goods sold is recorded as goods are transferred to customers, and the inventory balance is kept current throughout the year as items are bought and sold. The main advantage of the perpetual inventory system is that it provides management with timely information about the status of the inventory. The main disadvantages are that it is more difficult to maintain and more costly than a periodic inventory system. A physical inventory, or physical count, is taken at the end of the accounting period to establish a basis for accuracy and detect possible inventory losses under the perpetual inventory system. The Merchandise Inventory account is continuously adjusted by entering purchases, sales, and other inventory transactions as they occur. Purchases increase the Merchandise Inventory account, and purchases returns decrease it. As goods are sold, their cost is transferred from the Merchandise Inventory account to the Cost of Goods Sold account.

Supplemental Objectives

5. **Prepare an income statement and record merchandising transactions under the periodic inventory system.** Under the periodic inventory system, no detailed records of the actual inventory on hand are maintained during the accounting period. A physical count of inventory is made at the end of the accounting period to update the Inventory account and to determine cost of goods sold. The main advantages of the periodic inventory system are that it is simpler and less costly than the perpetual inventory system. The main disadvantage of the periodic inventory system is that the lack of detailed records may lead to inefficiencies, lost sales, and higher operating costs. When the periodic inventory system is used, the income statement must include a cost of goods sold section that includes the following elements:

Gross Purchases	−	Purchases Returns and Allowances	+	Freight In	=	Net Cost of Purchases

Beginning Merchandise Inventory	+	Net Cost of Purchases	=	Goods Available for Sale

Goods Available for Sale	−	Ending Merchandise Inventory	=	Cost of Goods Sold

Under the periodic inventory system, the Merchandise Inventory account stays at the beginning level until the physical inventory is recorded at the end of the period. A Purchases account is used to accumulate purchases of merchandise during the accounting period, and a Purchases Returns and Allowances account is used to accumulate returns of and allowances on purchases.

6. **Prepare a work sheet and closing entries for a merchandising concern using the perpetual inventory system.** Preparing a work sheet for a merchandising concern is much like preparing one for a service concern, except that there are additional accounts relating to merchandising transactions, such as Sales, Sales Returns and Allowances, Cost of Goods Sold, and Freight In. These accounts must be extended to the appropriate Income Statement columns. Also, since the Merchandise Inventory account is kept up to date, its

ending balance is extended directly to the debit column of the Balance Sheet columns. There is no need to place it in the Income Statement columns. Further, the Cost of Goods Sold account replaces the Purchases and Purchases Returns and Allowances accounts and is extended to the debit column of the Income Statement columns. The closing entries for a merchandising concern under the perpetual inventory system are the same as those for a service business. There is no need to include the Merchandise Inventory account.

7. **Prepare a work sheet and closing entries for a merchandising concern using the periodic inventory system.** The work sheet under the periodic inventory system is the same as under the perpetual inventory system with the exception that the beginning merchandise inventory from the trial balance is extended to the debit column of the Income Statement columns, and the ending balance of Merchandise Inventory is inserted in both the credit column of the Income Statement columns and the debit column of the Balance Sheet columns. The closing entries for a merchandising concern under the periodic inventory system are similar to those for a service business, with one exception. The exception is that the closing entries include a credit to Merchandise Inventory for the amount of the beginning inventory and a debit to Merchandise Inventory for the amount of the ending inventory.

8. **Apply sales and purchases discounts to merchandising transactions.** Sales discounts are discounts for early payment. Terms of 2/10, n/30 mean that the buyer can take a 2 percent discount if the invoice is paid within ten days of the invoice date. Otherwise, the buyer is obligated to pay the full amount in thirty days. Discounts on sales are recorded in the Sales Discounts account, and discounts on purchases are recorded in the Purchases Discounts account.

REVIEW OF CONCEPTS AND TERMINOLOGY

The following concepts and terms were introduced in this chapter:

SO 5 **Beginning inventory:** Merchandise on hand at the start of an accounting period.

LO 1 **Cash flow management:** The planning of a company's receipts and payments of cash.

LO 2 **Cost of goods sold:** The amount a merchant paid for the merchandise sold during an accounting period. Also called *cost of sales*.

SO 5 **Ending inventory:** Merchandise on hand at the end of an accounting period.

LO 3 **FOB destination:** A shipping term that means that the seller bears transportation costs to the place of delivery.

LO 3 **FOB shipping point:** A shipping term that means that the buyer bears transportation costs from the point of origin.

LO 4 **Freight in:** Transportation charges on merchandise purchased for resale. Also called *transportation in*.

LO 2 **Freight Out Expense:** The account that accumulates transportation charges on merchandise sold, which are shown as an operating expense. Also called *Delivery Expense*.

SO 5 **Goods available for sale:** The sum of beginning inventory and the net cost of purchases during the period; the total goods available for sale to customers during an accounting period.

LO 2 **Gross margin:** The difference between net sales and cost of goods sold. Also called *gross profit*.

LO 2 **Gross sales:** Total sales for cash and on credit occurring during an accounting period.

LO 1 **Internal controls:** The environment, accounting systems, and control procedures established by management and designed to safeguard the assets of a business and provide reliable accounting records.

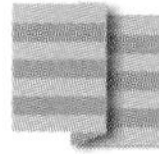

inventory for Carol's Kitchen Shop was $38,200 at the beginning of the year and $29,400 at the end of the year.

Carol's Kitchen Shop Partial Adjusted Trial Balance March 31, 20x4		
Sales		$165,000
Sales Returns and Allowances	$ 2,000	
Purchases	70,200	
Purchases Returns and Allowances		2,600
Freight In	2,300	
Store Salaries Expense	32,625	
Office Salaries Expense	12,875	
Advertising Expense	24,300	
Rent Expense	2,400	
Insurance Expense	1,200	
Utilities Expense	1,560	
Store Supplies Expense	2,880	
Office Supplies Expense	1,175	
Depreciation Expense, Store Equipment	1,050	
Depreciation Expense, Office Equipment	800	

REQUIRED

1. Using the information given, prepare an income statement for Carol's Kitchen Shop. Store Salaries Expense; Advertising Expense; Store Supplies Expense; and Depreciation Expense, Store Equipment are selling expenses. The other expenses are general and administrative expenses. The company uses the periodic inventory system. Show detail of net sales and operating expenses.
2. Based on your knowledge at this point in the course, how would you use the income statement for Carol's Kitchen Shop to evaluate the company's profitability? What other financial statements should be considered and why?

P 4.
SO 5 Merchandising Transactions: Periodic Inventory System

Use the data in **P 2** for this problem.

REQUIRED

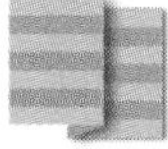

Prepare entries in journal form to record the transactions, assuming the periodic inventory system is used.

P 5.
SO 6 Work Sheet, Financial Statements, and Closing Entries for a Merchandising Company: Perpetual Inventory System

The trial balance at the top of the next page was taken from the ledger of Metzler Music Store at the end of its annual accounting period.

REQUIRED

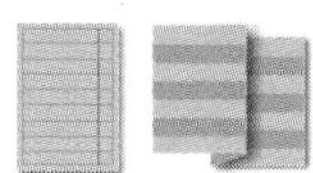

1. Assuming the company uses the perpetual inventory system, enter the trial balance on a work sheet, and complete the work sheet using the following information: ending store supplies inventory, $912; unexpired prepaid insurance, $600; estimated depreciation on store equipment, $12,900; sales salaries payable, $240; and accrued utilities expense, $450.
2. Prepare an income statement, a statement of owner's equity, and a balance sheet. Sales Salaries Expense; Other Selling Expenses; Store Supplies Expense; and Depreciation Expense, Store Equipment are all selling expenses.
3. From the work sheet, prepare the closing entries.

Metzler Music Store Trial Balance November 30, 20x4		
Cash	$ 18,075	
Accounts Receivable	27,840	
Merchandise Inventory	99,681	
Store Supplies	5,733	
Prepaid Insurance	4,800	
Store Equipment	111,600	
Accumulated Depreciation, Store Equipment		$ 46,800
Accounts Payable		36,900
Susan Metzler, Capital		167,313
Susan Metzler, Withdrawals	36,000	
Sales		306,750
Sales Returns and Allowances	2,961	
Cost of Goods Sold	156,567	
Freight In	6,783	
Sales Salaries Expense	64,050	
Rent Expense	10,800	
Other Selling Expenses	7,842	
Utilities Expense	5,031	
	$557,763	$557,763

P 6.

SO 7 Work Sheet, Financial Statements, and Closing Entries for a Merchandising Company: Periodic Inventory System

The year-end trial balance below was taken from the ledger of Le Bere Office Supplies Company at the end of its annual accounting period, on September 30, 20x4.

Le Bere Office Supplies Company Trial Balance September 30, 20x4		
Cash	$ 21,150	
Accounts Receivable	74,490	
Merchandise Inventory	214,200	
Store Supplies	11,400	
Prepaid Insurance	14,400	
Store Equipment	253,900	
Accumulated Depreciation, Store Equipment		$ 76,500
Accounts Payable		116,850
Grace Le Bere, Capital		484,050
Grace Le Bere, Withdrawals	72,000	
Sales		1,225,750
Sales Returns and Allowances	25,440	
Purchases	754,800	
Purchases Returns and Allowances		18,150
Freight In	31,200	
Sales Salaries Expense	193,800	
Rent Expense	144,000	
Other Selling Expenses	98,730	
Utilities Expense	11,790	
	$1,921,300	$1,921,300

REQUIRED

1. Assuming the company uses the periodic inventory system, enter the trial balance on a work sheet, and complete the work sheet using the following information: end-

ing merchandise inventory, $266,700; ending store supplies inventory, $1,650; expired insurance, $7,200; estimated depreciation on store equipment, $15,000; sales salaries payable, $1,950; and accrued utilities expense, $300.

2. Prepare an income statement, a statement of owner's equity, and a balance sheet. Sales Salaries Expense; Other Selling Expenses; Store Supplies Expense; and Depreciation Expense, Store Equipment are selling expenses.
3. From the work sheet, prepare the closing entries.

P 7. **SO 5, SO 8 Merchandising Transactions, Including Discounts: Periodic Inventory System**

The following is a list of transactions for Attention Promotions Company for the month of March 20xx:

Mar. 1 Sold merchandise on credit to M. Gaberman, terms 2/10, n/60, FOB shipping point, $2,200.
3 Purchased merchandise on credit from King Company, terms 2/10, n/30, FOB shipping point, $12,800.
4 Received freight bill for shipment received on March 3, $900.
6 Sold merchandise for cash, $1,100.
7 Sold merchandise on credit to B. Gomez, terms 2/10, n/60, $2,400.
9 Purchased merchandise from Armstrong Company, terms 1/10, n/30, FOB shipping point, $6,180, which includes freight charges of $400.
10 Sold merchandise on credit to G. Horn, terms 2/10, n/20, $4,400.
10 Received check from M. Gaberman for payment in full for sale of March 1.
11 Purchased merchandise from King Company, terms 2/10, n/30, FOB shipping point, $16,400.
12 Received freight bill for shipment of March 11, $1,460.
13 Paid King Company for purchase of March 3.
14 Returned merchandise from the March 9 shipment that was the wrong size and color, for credit, $580.
16 G. Horn returned some of the merchandise sold to him on March 10 for credit, $400.
17 Received payment from B. Gomez for half of his purchase on March 7. A discount is allowed on partial payment.
18 Paid Armstrong Company balance due on account from transactions on March 9 and 14.
20 In checking the purchase of March 11 from King Company, the accounting department found an overcharge of $800. King agreed to issue a credit.
21 Paid freight company for freight charges of March 4 and 12.
23 Purchased cleaning supplies on credit from Moon Company, terms n/5, $500.
24 Discovered that some of the cleaning supplies purchased on March 23 had not been ordered. Returned them to Moon Company for credit, $100.
25 Sold merchandise for cash, $1,600.
27 Paid Moon Company for the March 23 purchase less the March 24 return.
28 Received payment in full from G. Horn for transactions on March 10 and 16.
29 Paid King Company for purchase of March 11 less allowance of March 20.
31 Received payment for balance of amount owed from B. Gomez from transactions of March 7 and 17.

REQUIRED

Prepare entries in journal form to record the transactions, assuming that the periodic inventory system is used.

Alternate Problems

P 8. **LO 1, LO 4 Merchandising Income Statement: Perpetual Inventory System**

At the end of the fiscal year, June 30, 20x3, selected accounts from the adjusted trial balance for Hans' Video Store appeared as shown on the next page.

REQUIRED

1. Prepare a multistep income statement for Hans' Video Store. Freight In should be combined with Cost of Goods Sold. Store Salaries Expense; Advertising Expense; Store Supplies Expense; and Depreciation Expense, Store Equipment are selling expenses. The other expenses are general and administrative expenses. Hans' Video

Hans' Video Store Partial Adjusted Trial Balance June 30, 20x3		
Sales		$867,824
Sales Returns and Allowances	$ 22,500	
Cost of Goods Sold	442,370	
Freight In	20,156	
Store Salaries Expense	215,100	
Office Salaries Expense	53,000	
Advertising Expense	36,400	
Rent Expense	28,800	
Insurance Expense	5,600	
Utilities Expense	17,520	
Store Supplies Expense	4,928	
Office Supplies Expense	3,628	
Depreciation Expense, Store Equipment	3,600	
Depreciation Expense, Office Equipment	3,700	

Store uses the perpetual inventory system. Show detail of net sales and operating expenses.

2. Based on your knowledge to this point in the course, how would you use the income statement for Hans' Video Store to evaluate the company's profitability? What other financial statement should be considered and why?

P 9.

LO 4 Merchandising Transactions: Perpetual Inventory System

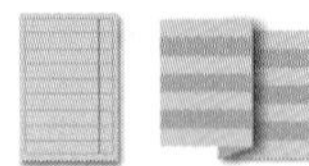

Tonia Company engaged in the following transactions in July 20xx:

July 1 Sold merchandise to Su Long on credit, terms n/30, FOB shipping point, $4,200 (cost, $2,520).
3 Purchased merchandise on credit from Angier Company, terms n/30, FOB shipping point, $7,600.
5 Paid Mix Freight for freight charges on merchandise received, $580.
6 Purchased store supplies on credit from Exto Supply Company, terms n/20, $1,272.
8 Purchased merchandise on credit from Ginn Company, terms n/30, FOB shipping point, $7,200, which includes $400 freight costs paid by Ginn Company.
12 Returned some of the merchandise received on July 3 for credit, $1,200.
15 Sold merchandise on credit to Pete Smith, terms n/30, FOB shipping point, $2,400 (cost, $1,440).
16 Returned some of the store supplies purchased on July 6 for credit, $400.
17 Sold merchandise for cash, $2,000 (cost, $1,200).
18 Accepted for full credit a return from Su Long and returned merchandise to inventory, $400 (cost, $240).
24 Paid Angier Company for purchase of July 3 less return of July 12.
25 Received full payment from Su Long for her July 1 purchase less the return on July 18.

REQUIRED

Prepare entries in journal form to record the transactions, assuming use of the perpetual inventory system.

P 10.

LO 1 Merchandising Income
SO 5 Statement: Periodic Inventory System

The data on the next page come from Dan's Sports Equipment's adjusted trial balance as of September 30, 20x5, the fiscal year end. The company's beginning merchandise inventory was $81,222, and ending merchandise inventory is $76,664 for the period.

REQUIRED

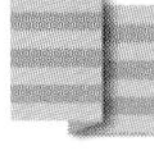

1. Prepare a multistep income statement for Dan's Sports Equipment. Store Salaries Expense; Advertising Expense; Store Supplies Expense; and Depreciation Expense, Store Equipment are selling expenses. The other expenses are general and adminis-

Dan's Sports Equipment Partial Adjusted Trial Balance September 30, 20x5		
Sales		$433,912
Sales Returns and Allowances	$ 11,250	
Purchases	221,185	
Purchases Returns and Allowances		30,238
Freight In	10,078	
Store Salaries Expense	107,550	
Office Salaries Expense	26,500	
Advertising Expense	18,200	
Rent Expense	14,400	
Insurance Expense	2,800	
Utilities Expense	18,760	
Store Supplies Expense	464	
Office Supplies Expense	814	
Depreciation Expense, Store Equipment	1,800	
Depreciation Expense, Office Equipment	1,850	

trative expenses. The company uses the periodic inventory system. Show detail of net sales and operating expenses.

2. Based on your knowledge at this point in the course, how would you use the income statement for Dan's Sports Equipment to evaluate the company's profitability? What other financial statements should be considered and why?

P 11. Use the data in P 9 for this problem.

SO 5 Merchandising Transactions: Periodic Inventory System

REQUIRED

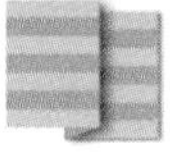

Prepare entries in journal form to record the transactions, assuming the periodic inventory system is used.

Expanding Your Critical Thinking, Communication, and Interpersonal Skills

Skills Development

Conceptual Analysis

SD 1.

LO 1 LO 2 Merchandising Income Statement

Village TV and *TV Warehouse* sell television sets and other video equipment in the Phoenix area. Village TV gives each customer individual attention, with employees explaining the features, advantages, and disadvantages of each video component. When a customer buys a television set or video system, Village provides free delivery, installs and adjusts the equipment, and teaches the family how to use it. TV Warehouse sells the same video components through showroom display. If a customer wants to buy a

Cash Flow

CD-ROM

Communication

Critical Thinking

Ethics

General Ledger

Group Activity

Hot Links to Real Companies

International

Internet

Key Ratio

Memo
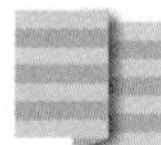
Spreadsheet

video component or a system, he or she fills out a form and takes it to the cashier for payment. After paying, the customer drives to the back of the warehouse to pick up the component, which he or she then takes home and installs. Village TV charges higher prices than TV Warehouse for the same components. Discuss how you would expect the income statements of Village TV and TV Warehouse to differ. Is it possible to tell which approach is more profitable?

Group Activity: Divide the class into informal groups. In addition to answering the above questions, ask each group to decide which store they would prefer to shop in and why. Allow 15 minutes and debrief immediately.

SD 2.
LO 1 Periodic Versus Perpetual
LO 4 Inventory Systems
SO 5

The Book Nook is a well-established chain of 20 bookstores in eastern Michigan. In recent years the company has grown rapidly, adding five new stores in regional malls. Management has relied on the manager of each store to place orders keyed to the market in his or her neighborhood, selected from a master list of available titles provided by the central office. Every six months, a physical inventory is taken, and financial statements are prepared using the periodic inventory system. At that time, books that have not sold well are placed on sale or, whenever possible, returned to the publisher. As a result of the company's fast growth, there are many new store managers, who management has found do not have the same ability to judge the market as do managers of the older, established stores. Thus, management is considering a recommendation to implement a perpetual inventory system and carefully monitor sales from the central office. Do you think The Book Nook should switch to the perpetual inventory system or stay with the periodic inventory system? Discuss the advantages and disadvantages of each system.

Ethical Dilemma

SD 3.
SO 8 Ethics and Purchases Discounts

The purchasing power of some customers is such that they can exert pressure on suppliers to go beyond the suppliers' customary allowances. For example, ***Wal-Mart*** represents more than 10 percent of annual sales for many suppliers, such as Fruit of the Loom, Rubbermaid, Sunbeam, and Coleman. *Forbes* magazine reports that while many of these suppliers allow a 2 percent discount if bills are paid within 15 days, "Wal-Mart routinely pays its bills closer to 30 days and takes the 2 percent discount anyway on the gross amount of the invoice, not the net amount, which deducts for [trade] discounts and things like freight costs."[3] Identify three ways in which Wal-Mart's practice benefits Wal-Mart. Do you think this practice is unethical, or is it just good cash management on the part of Wal-Mart? Are the suppliers harmed by it?

Research Activity

SD 4.
LO 1 Merchandising Companies
LO 2

Conduct an individual field trip by visiting any retail or wholesale business. It may be a business where you buy a product, a company where you work, or a family business. It is not necessary for you to talk to anyone at the business, but it may be helpful to do so. Determine why the business is a merchandising business. List the products or groups of products that the company sells. Does the company offer any services? How do services differ from merchandise? Make a list of the types of transactions the business engages in. Also identify and list all the operating expenses you can think of that would be relevant to this business. Organize your findings in the form of a memo to your instructor.

Decision-Making Practice

SD 5.
LO 2 Analysis of Merchandising Income Statement

In 20x5 Les Solty opened a small retail store in a suburban mall. Called ***Solty Denim Company,*** the shop sold designer jeans. Solty worked 14 hours a day and controlled all aspects of the operation. All sales were for cash or bank credit card. The business was such a success that in 20x6 Solty decided to open a second store in another mall. Because the new shop needed his attention, he hired a manager to work in the original store with two sales clerks. During 20x6 the new store was successful, but the operations of the original store did not match the first year's performance.

Concerned about this turn of events, Solty compared the two years' results for the original store. The figures are as follows:

	20x6	20x5
Net Sales	$325,000	$350,000
Cost of Goods Sold	225,000	225,000
Gross Margin	$100,000	$125,000
Operating Expenses	75,000	50,000
Net Income	$ 25,000	$ 75,000

In addition, Solty's analysis revealed that the cost and selling price of jeans were about the same in both years and that the level of operating expenses was roughly the same in both years, except for the new manager's $25,000 salary. Sales returns and allowances were insignificant amounts in both years.

Studying the situation further, Solty discovered the following facts about the cost of goods sold:

	20x6	20x5
Gross purchases	$200,000	$271,000
Total purchases allowances	15,000	20,000
Freight in	19,000	27,000
Physical inventory, end of year	32,000	53,000

Still not satisfied, Solty went through all the individual sales and purchases records for the year. Both sales and purchases were verified. However, the 20x6 ending inventory should have been $57,000, given the unit purchases and sales during the year. After puzzling over all this information, Solty comes to you for accounting help.

1. Using Solty's new information, recompute the cost of goods sold for 20x5 and 20x6, and account for the difference in net income between 20x5 and 20x6.
2. Suggest at least two reasons for the discrepancy in the 20x6 ending inventory. How might Solty improve the management of the original store?

Financial Reporting and Analysis

Interpreting Financial Reports

FRA 1.
LO 2 Comparison of Operating Performance

Wal-Mart Stores, Inc., and *Kmart Corp.,* two of the largest retailers in the United States, have different approaches to retailing. Their success has been different also. At one time, Kmart was larger than Wal-Mart. Today, Wal-Mart is almost three times as large. You can see the difference by analyzing their respective income statements and merchandise inventories. Selected information from their annual reports for the year ended January 31, 2000, is presented below. (All amounts are in millions.)[4]

Wal-Mart: Net Sales, $165,013; Cost of Goods Sold, $129,664; Operating Expenses, $27,040; Ending Inventory, $19,793

Kmart: Net Sales, $35,925; Cost of Goods Sold, $28,102; Operating Expenses, $6,523; Ending Inventory, $7,101

REQUIRED

1. Prepare a schedule computing the gross margin and income from operations for both companies as dollar amounts and as percentages of net sales. Also, compute inventory as a percentage of the cost of goods sold.
2. From what you know about the different retailing approaches of these two companies, do the gross margins and incomes from operations you computed in **1** seem compatible with these approaches? What is it about the nature of Wal-Mart's operations that produces lower gross margin and lower operating expenses in percentages in comparison to Kmart? Which company's approach was more successful in the fiscal year ending January 31, 2000? Explain your answer.

3. Both companies have chosen a fiscal year that ends on January 31. Why do you suppose they made this choice? How realistic do you think the inventory figures are as indicators of inventory levels during the rest of the year? Which company appears to make most efficient use of its inventory?

FRA 2.
LO 1 Business Objectives and
LO 2 Income Statements

Superior Products, Inc., is one of the nation's largest discount retailers, operating 216 stores in 30 states. In a letter to stockholders in the 1999 annual report (fiscal year ended January 31, 2000), the chairman and chief executive officer of the company stated, "Our operating plan for fiscal 2000 (year ended January 31, 2001) calls for moderate sales increases, continued improvement in gross margins, and a continuation of aggressive expense reduction programs." The following data are taken from the income statements presented in the 2000 annual report (dated January 30, 2001) (in millions):

	Year Ended		
	January 30, 2001	January 31, 2000	February 1, 1999
Net Sales	$2,067	$2,142	$2,235
Cost of Goods Sold	1,500	1,593	1,685
Operating Expenses	466	486	502

REQUIRED

Did Superior Products, Inc., achieve the objective stated by its chairman? (**Hint:** Prepare an income statement for each year and compute gross margin and operating expenses as percentages of net sales.)

International Company

FRA 3.
LO 3 Terminology for
LO 4 Merchandising
SO 5 Transactions in England

Harrods is a large English retailer with department stores throughout England and in other European countries. Merchandising terms in England differ from those in the United States. For instance, in England, the income statement is called the profit and loss account, sales is called turnover, merchandise inventory is called stocks, accounts receivable is called debtors, and accounts payable is called creditors. Of course, the amounts are stated in terms of the pound (£). In today's business world, it is important to understand and use terminology employed by professionals from other countries. Explain in your own words why the English may use the terms *profit and loss account*, *turnover*, *stocks*, *debtors*, and *creditors* in place of the American terms.

Toys "R" Us Annual Report

FRA 4.
LO 1 Operating Cycle

Refer to the Toys "R" Us annual report at the end of Chapter 6 and to Figure 1 in this chapter. Write a memorandum to your instructor on the subject of the Toys "R" Us operating cycle. This memorandum should identify the most common transactions in the operating cycle as it applies to Toys "R" Us and should support the answer by referring to the importance of accounts receivable, accounts payable, and merchandise inventory in the Toys "R" Us financial statements. Complete the memorandum by explaining why this operating cycle is favorable to Toys "R" Us.

Fingraph® Financial Analyst™

FRA 5.
LO 1 Income Statement Analysis
LO 2

Choose any retail company from the Fingraph® Financial Analyst™ CD-ROM software and display the Income Statements Analysis: Income from Operations in tabular and graphical form for the company. Write an executive summary that analyzes the change in the company's income from operations from the first to the second year. In preparing your response, focus on the reasons the change occurred by answering the following questions: Did the company's income from operations improve or decline from the first to the second year? What was the relationship of the change to the change in net sales? Was the change in income from operations primarily due to a change in gross margin or a change in operating expenses? Suggest some possible reasons for the change in gross margin or operating expenses. Use percentages to support your answer.

Internet Case

FRA 6.
LO 1 LO 3 LO 4 Comparison of Traditional Merchandising to E-commerce

E-commerce is a word coined to describe merchandising companies that attempt to establish retail business over the Internet. This type of business is similar in some ways to traditional retailing, but it also presents new challenges. Choose a company with traditional retail outlets that is also selling over the Internet and go to its web site. Some examples to choose from are ***Wal-Mart Stores, Inc., Kmart Corp., Toys "R" Us, Barnes & Noble***, and ***Lands End.*** Investigate and list the steps a customer makes to purchase a good on the site. How do these steps differ from those in a traditional retail store? What are some of the accounting challenges in recording the transaction? Be prepared to discuss your results in class.

ENDNOTES

1. Target Corp., *Annual Report*, 1999.
2. Ibid.
3. Matthew Schifrin, "The Big Squeeze," *Forbes*, March 11, 1996.
4. Wal-Mart Stores, Inc., *Annual Report*, 1999; and Kmart Corp., *Annual Report*, 1999.

6 Financial Reporting and Analysis

LEARNING OBJECTIVES

1. State the objectives of financial reporting.
2. State the qualitative characteristics of accounting information and describe their interrelationships.
3. Define and describe the use of the conventions of *comparability* and *consistency, materiality, conservatism, full disclosure*, and *cost-benefit*.
4. Explain management's responsibility for ethical financial reporting and define *fraudulent financial reporting.*
5. Identify and describe the basic components of a classified balance sheet.
6. Prepare multistep and single-step classified income statements.
7. Evaluate liquidity and profitability using classified financial statements.

DECISION POINT: A USER'S FOCUS

General Mills, Inc. The management of a corporation is judged by the company's financial performance. This financial performance is reported to stockholders and others outside the business in the company's published annual report, which includes the company's financial statements and other relevant information. Performance measures are usually based on the relationships of key data in the financial statements and are communicated by management to the reader. For large companies, this often means condensing a tremendous amount of information to a few numbers considered important by management. For example, what key measures does the management of General Mills, Inc., a successful food products company with brands such as Cheerios, Wheaties, Hamburger Helper, and Fruit Roll-ups, choose to focus on as its goals?

After restoring double-digit earnings per share growth over the last two years (see chart), General Mills' management, in a recent press release, presented the company's growth model for 2000–2010, which included the following goals:

- *To generate 7 to 8 percent compound annual sales growth over the next decade.*
- *To generate continued double-digit earnings per share growth over the next decade.*

The General Mills' chief executive stated, "We believe that if we meet these growth goals, our performance will result in superior returns to our shareholders."[1]

Of course, investors and creditors will want to conduct their own analysis of General Mills as well. This will require reading and interpretation of the financial statements and the calculation of other ratios. However, this analysis will be meaningless unless the reader understands financial statements and generally accepted accounting principles, on

Critical Thinking Question: What financial statement information is most useful to investors? **Answer:** The most common response is net earnings. This response, however, is too narrow. Management compensation contracts focus not only on earnings but also on cash flows and asset utilization, which affect management behavior in achieving financial performance.

General Mills Earnings Per Share (EPS) Growth

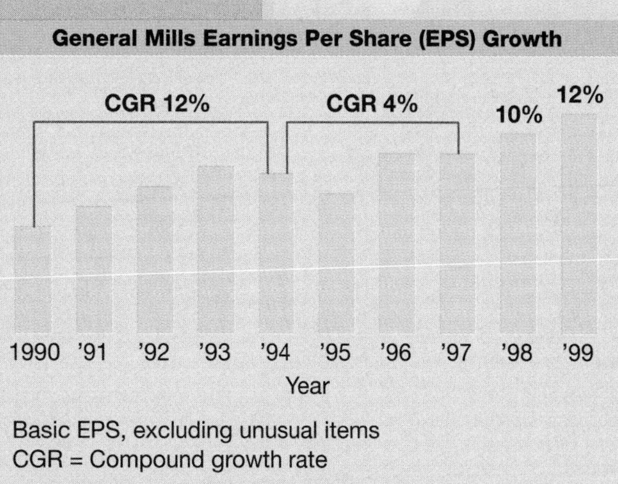

Basic EPS, excluding unusual items
CGR = Compound growth rate

which the statements are based. Also important to learning how to read and interpret financial statements is a comprehension of the categories and classifications used in balance sheets and income statements. Key financial ratios used in financial statement analysis are based on those categories. The chapter begins by describing the objectives, characteristics, and conventions that underlie the preparation of financial statements.

Objectives of Financial Information

OBJECTIVE

1 State the objectives of financial reporting

Related Text Assignments:
Q: 1
E: 2

Discussion Question: What is the difference between stocks and bonds? **Answer:** One difference is that stocks are a form of ownership interest, whereas bonds are a form of creditor interest.

The United States has a highly developed exchange economy. In this kind of economy, most goods and services are exchanged for money or claims to money instead of being used or bartered by their producers. Most business is carried on through corporations, including many extremely large firms that buy, sell, and obtain financing in U.S. and world markets.

By issuing stocks and bonds that are traded in financial markets, businesses can raise capital for production and marketing activities. Investors are interested mainly in returns from dividends and increases in the market price of their investments. Creditors want to know if the business can repay a loan plus interest in accordance with required terms. Thus, investors and creditors both need to know if a company can generate adequate cash flows. Financial statements are important to both groups in making that judgment. They offer valuable information that helps investors and creditors judge a company's ability to pay dividends and repay debts with interest. In this way, the market puts scarce resources to work in the companies that can use them most efficiently.

The information needs of users and the general business environment are the basis for the Financial Accounting Standards Board's (FASB) three objectives of financial reporting:[2]

Point to Emphasize: Although people reading reports need some understanding of business, they do not need the skills required of a CPA.

1. *To furnish information that is useful in making investment and credit decisions.* Financial reporting should offer information that can help present and potential investors and creditors make rational investment and credit decisions. The reports should be in a form that makes sense to those who have some understanding of business and are willing to study the information carefully.
2. *To provide information useful in assessing cash flow prospects.* Financial reporting should supply information to help present and potential investors and creditors judge the amounts, timing, and risk of expected cash receipts from dividends or interest and the proceeds from the sale, redemption, or maturity of stocks or loans.
3. *To provide information about business resources, claims to those resources, and changes in them.* Financial reporting should give information about the company's assets, liabilities, and stockholders' equity, and the effects of transactions on the company's assets, liabilities, and stockholders' equity.

Enrichment Note: The Securities and Exchange Commission (SEC) requires audited financial statements for publicly traded companies.

Financial statements are the most important way of periodically presenting to parties outside the business the information that has been gathered and processed in the accounting system. For this reason, the financial statements—the balance sheet, the income statement, the statement of owner's equity, and the statement of cash flows—are the most important output of the accounting system. These financial statements are "general purpose" because of their wide audience. They are "external" because their users are outside the business. Because of a potential conflict of interest between managers, who must prepare the statements, and investors or creditors, who invest in or lend money to the business, these statements often are audited by outside accountants to increase confidence in their reliability.

Qualitative Characteristics of Accounting Information

OBJECTIVE

2 **State the qualitative characteristics of accounting information and describe their interrelationships**

Related Text Assignments:
Q: 2
E: 2

Clarification Note: Financial statements are not perfect, but they should be free of material misstatements.

It is easy for students in their first accounting course to get the idea that accounting is 100 percent accurate. This idea is reinforced by the fact that all the problems in this and other introductory books can be solved. The numbers all add up; what is supposed to equal something else does. Accounting seems very much like mathematics in its precision. In this course, the basics of accounting are presented in a simple form to help you understand them. In practice, however, accounting information is neither simple nor precise, and it rarely satisfies all criteria. The FASB emphasizes this fact in the following statement:

> The information provided by financial reporting often results from approximate, rather than exact, measures. The measures commonly involve numerous estimates, classifications, summarizations, judgments and allocations. The outcome of economic activity in a dynamic economy is uncertain and results from combinations of many factors. Thus, despite the aura of precision that may seem to surround financial reporting in general and financial statements in particular, with few exceptions the measures are approximations, which may be based on rules and conventions, rather than exact amounts.[3]

The goal of accounting information—to provide the basic data that different users need to make informed decisions—is an ideal. The gap between the ideal and the actual provides much of the interest and controversy in accounting. To facilitate interpretation, the FASB has described the **qualitative characteristics** of accounting information, which are standards for judging that information. In addition, there are generally accepted conventions for recording and reporting that simplify interpretation. The relationships among these concepts are shown in Figure 1.

The most important qualitative characteristics are understandability and usefulness. **Understandability** depends on both the accountant and the decision maker. The accountant prepares the financial statements in accordance with accepted practices, generating important information that is believed to be understandable. But the decision maker must interpret the information and decide how to use it in making decisions.

Reinforcement Exercise: Provide an example in which relevance would apply to a department of a company. For instance, a company prepares separate income schedules for each department. When management observes that a certain department (such as housewares) is not contributing on target to the company's profit, it uses that feedback to make other decisions. For example, management might take action to increase revenue in housewares or to abandon a housewares section and contribute that space and its resources to more profitable items.

For accounting information to meet the standard of **usefulness**, it must have two major qualitative characteristics: relevance and reliability. **Relevance** means that the information can affect the outcome of a decision. In other words, a different decision would be made if the relevant information were not available. To be relevant, information must provide feedback, help predict future conditions, and be timely. For example, the income statement provides information about how a company performed over the past year (feedback), and it helps in planning for the next year (prediction). In order to be useful, however, it also must be communicated soon enough after the end of the accounting period to enable the reader to make decisions (timeliness).

In addition to being relevant, accounting information must have **reliability**. In other words, the user must be able to depend on the information. It must represent what it is meant to represent. It must be verifiable by independent parties using the same methods of measuring. It also must be neutral. Accounting should

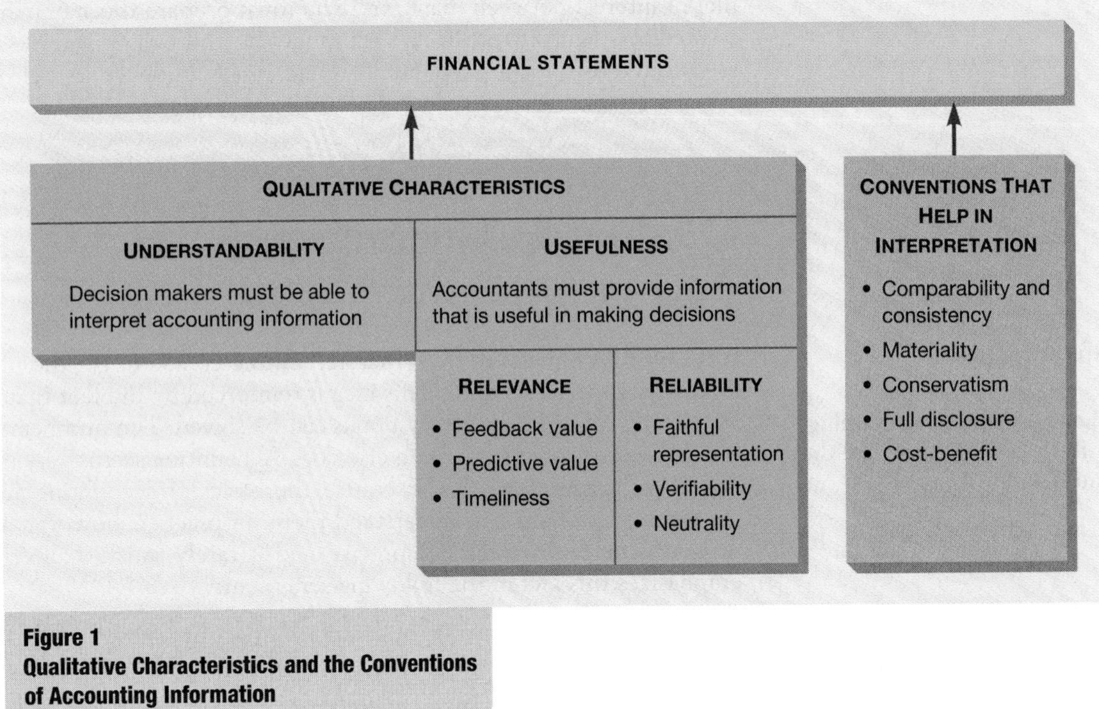

Figure 1
Qualitative Characteristics and the Conventions of Accounting Information

convey information about business activity as faithfully as possible without influencing anyone in a specific direction. For example, the balance sheet should represent the economic resources, obligations, and owner's equity of a business as faithfully as possible in accordance with generally accepted accounting principles, and this balance sheet should be verifiable by an auditor.

Conventions That Help in the Interpretation of Financial Information

OBJECTIVE

3 Define and describe the use of the conventions of *comparability* and *consistency, materiality, conservatism, full disclosure,* and *cost-benefit*

Related Text Assignments:
Q: 3
SE: 1
E: 1, 2
P: 1, 6
SD: 1, 2

To a large extent, financial statements are based on estimates and application of accounting rules for recognition and allocation. In this book, we point out a number of difficulties with financial statements. One is failing to recognize the changing value of the dollar caused by inflation. Another is treating intangibles, such as research and development costs, as assets if they are purchased outside the company and as expenses if they are developed within the company. Such problems do not mean that financial statements are useless; they are essential. However, users must know how to interpret them. To help in this interpretation, accountants depend on five **conventions**, or rules of thumb, in recording transactions and preparing financial statements: (1) comparability and consistency, (2) materiality, (3) conservatism, (4) full disclosure, and (5) cost-benefit.

Comparability and Consistency

A characteristic that increases the usefulness of accounting information is comparability. Information about a company is more useful if it can be compared with similar facts about the same company over several time periods or about another company for the same time period. **Comparability** means that the information is presented in such a way that a decision maker can recognize similarities, differences, and trends over different time periods or between different companies.

Consistent use of accounting measures and procedures is important in achieving comparability. The **consistency** convention requires that an accounting procedure, once adopted by a company, remain in use from one period to the next unless users are informed of the change. Thus, without a note to the contrary, users of financial statements can assume that there has been no arbitrary change in the treatment of a particular transaction, account, or item that would affect the interpretation of the statements.

If management decides that a certain procedure is no longer appropriate and should be changed or if reporting requirements change, generally accepted accounting principles require that the change and its dollar effect be described in the notes to the financial statements:

> The nature of and justification for a change in accounting principle and its effect on income should be disclosed in the financial statements of the period in which the change is made. The justification for the change should explain clearly why the newly adopted accounting principle is preferable.[4]

For example, in a recent year, Reynolds Metals Company changed its method of accounting for business start-up costs because the AICPA changed the requirements for accounting for this type of cost.[5]

Materiality

Business-World Example: By definition, a $10 stapler is a long-term asset that, theoretically, should be capitalized and depreciated over its useful life. However, the convention of materiality allows the stapler to be expensed entirely in the year of purchase because its cost is small and writing it off in one year has no effect on anyone's decision making.

The term **materiality** refers to the relative importance of an item or event. If an item or event is material, it is probably relevant to the user of financial statements. In other words, an item is material if users would have done something differently if they had not known about the item. The accountant is often faced with decisions about small items or events that make little difference to users no matter how they are handled. For example, a large company may decide that expenditures for durable items of less than $500 should be charged as expenses rather than recorded as long-term assets and depreciated.

In general, an item is material if there is a reasonable expectation that knowing about it would influence the decisions of users of financial statements. The materiality of an item normally is determined by relating its dollar value to an element of the financial statements, such as net income or total assets. Some accountants feel that when an item is 5 percent or more of net income, it is material. However, materiality also depends on the nature of the item, not just its value. For example, in a multimillion-dollar company, a mistake of $5,000 in recording an item may not be important, but the discovery of a $5,000 bribe or theft can be very important. Also, many small errors can combine into a material amount. Accountants judge the materiality of many things, and the users of financial statements depend on their judgments being fair and accurate. The SEC has recently questioned companies' judgment in using the materiality convention to avoid showing certain items in the financial statements.

Point to Emphasize: Illegal acts involving small dollar amounts should still be investigated.

Conservatism

Common Student Error: Students sometimes think that the purpose of conservatism is to produce the lowest net income and lowest asset value. Stress that it is a guideline for choosing among GAAP alternatives and that it should be used with care.

Accountants try to base their decisions on logic and evidence that lead to the fairest report of what happened. In judging and estimating, however, accountants often are faced with uncertainties. In these cases, they look to the convention of **conservatism**. This convention means that when accountants face major uncertainties about which accounting procedure to use, they generally choose the one that is least likely to overstate assets and income.

One of the most common applications of the conservatism convention is the use of the lower-of-cost-or-market method in accounting for inventories. Under this method, if an item's market value is greater than its cost, the more conservative cost figure is used. If the market value falls below the cost, the more conservative market value is used. The latter situation often occurs in the computer industry.

Point to Emphasize: Stress that expensing a long-term asset in the period of purchase is not a GAAP alternative.

Conservatism can be a useful tool in doubtful cases, but its abuse leads to incorrect and misleading financial statements. Suppose that someone incorrectly applies the conservatism convention by expensing a long-term asset of material cost in the period of purchase. In this case, there is no uncertainty. Income and assets for the current period would be understated, and income in future periods would be overstated. For this reason, accountants depend on the conservatism convention only when there is uncertainty about which accounting procedure to use.

Full Disclosure

Enrichment Note: Significant events arising after the balance sheet date must be disclosed in the statements. Suppose a firm purchased a piece of land for a future subdivision. Shortly after the end of its fiscal year, the firm is served papers to halt construction because the Environmental Protection Agency asserts that the land was once a toxic waste dump. This information, which obviously affects the users of the financial statements, must be disclosed in the statements for the just-ended fiscal year.

The convention of **full disclosure** requires that financial statements and their notes present all information that is relevant to the users' understanding of the statements. That is, the statements should offer any explanation that is needed to keep them from being misleading. Explanatory notes are considered an integral part of the financial statements. For instance, a change from one accounting procedure to another should be reported. In general, the form of the financial statements can affect their usefulness in making certain decisions. In addition, certain items, such as the amount of depreciation expense on the income statement and the accumulated depreciation on the balance sheet, are essential to the readers of financial statements.

Other examples of disclosures required by the Financial Accounting Standards Board and other official bodies are the accounting procedures used in preparing the statements, important terms of the company's debt, commitments and contingencies, and important events taking place after the date of the statements. However, there is a point at which the statements become so cluttered that notes impede rather than help understanding. Beyond required disclosures, the application of the full-disclosure convention is based on the judgment of management and of the accountants who prepare the financial statements. In recent years, the principle of full disclosure also has been influenced by users of accounting information.

FOCUS ON BUSINESS PRACTICE

When is "full disclosure" too much? When does the cost exceed the benefits? The big-five accounting firm of Ernst & Young reports that over a 20-year period the total number of pages in the annual reports of 25 large, well-known companies increased an average of 84 percent and the number of pages of notes increased 325 percent—from 4 pages to 17 pages. Management's discussion and analysis increased 300 percent, from 3 pages to 12.[6] Because some people feel that "these documents are so daunting that people don't read them at all," the Securities and Exchange Commission (SEC) allows companies to issue "summary reports" to the public that would eliminate many of the current notes. These reports would be more accessible and less costly. This is a controversial action because many analysts feel that it is in the notes that one gets the detailed information necessary to understand complex business operations. One analyst remarked, "To banish the notes for fear they will turn off readers would be like eliminating fractions from math books on the theory that the average student prefers to work with whole numbers."[7] Where this controversy will end, nobody knows. Detailed reports still must be filed with the SEC, but more and more companies are providing summary reports to the public.

To protect investors and creditors, independent auditors, the stock exchanges, and the SEC have made more demands for disclosure by publicly owned companies. The SEC has been pushing especially hard for the enforcement of full disclosure. As a result, more and better information about corporations is available to the public today than ever before.

Business-World Example: Firms use the convention of cost-benefit for nonaccounting decisions as well. Department stores could almost completely stop shoplifting if they were to hire five times as many clerks to watch customers. The benefit would be reduced shoplifting. The cost would be reduced sales (customers do not like being watched closely) and increased wages expense for clerks. Although shoplifting is a serious problem for department stores, the benefit of reducing shoplifting in this way does not outweigh the cost.

Instructional Strategy: To check students' comprehension of accounting conventions, break the class into small groups to discuss SD 1. Randomly select groups to present their results. Each group could discuss a different convention as it applies to the case. Encourage class members to ask the presenters questions, and be prepared to ask questions yourself. Reward performance with class participation points.

Cost-Benefit

The **cost-benefit** convention underlies all the qualitative characteristics and conventions. It holds that the benefits to be gained from providing accounting information should be greater than the costs of providing it. Of course, minimum levels of relevance and reliability must be reached if accounting information is to be useful. Beyond the minimum levels, however, it is up to the FASB and the SEC, which require the information, and the accountant, who provides the information, to judge the costs and benefits in each case. Most of the costs of providing information fall at first on the preparers; the benefits are reaped by both preparers and users. Finally, both the costs and the benefits are passed on to society in the form of prices and social benefits from more efficient allocation of resources.

The costs and benefits of a particular requirement for accounting disclosure are both direct and indirect, immediate and deferred. For example, it is hard to judge the final costs and benefits of a far-reaching and costly regulation. The FASB, for instance, allows certain large companies to make a supplemental disclosure in their financial statements of the effects of changes in current costs. Most companies choose not to present this information because they believe the costs of producing and providing it exceed its benefits to the readers of their financial statements. Cost-benefit is a question faced by all regulators, including the FASB and the SEC. Even though there are no definitive ways of measuring costs and benefits, much of an accountant's work deals with these concepts.

Management's Responsibility for Ethical Reporting

OBJECTIVE

4 Explain management's responsibility for ethical financial reporting and define *fraudulent financial reporting*

Related Text Assignments:
Q: 4
SD: 3, 4, 5

The users of financial statements depend on the good faith of those who prepare these statements. This dependence places a duty on a company's management and its accountants to act ethically in the reporting process. That duty is often expressed in the report of management that accompanies financial statements. For example, the report of the management of Quaker Oats Co., a company known for strong financial reporting and controls, states:

> Management is responsible for the preparation and integrity of the Company's financial statements. The financial statements have been prepared in accordance with generally accepted accounting principles and necessarily include some amounts that are based on management's estimates and judgment.[8]

Quaker Oats' management also tells how it meets this responsibility:

> To fulfill its responsibility, management's goal is to maintain strong systems of internal controls, supported by formal policies and procedures that are communicated throughout the Company. Management regularly evaluates its systems of internal control with an eye toward improvement. Management also

There is a difference between management's choosing to follow accounting principles that are favorable to its actions and fraudulent financial reporting. For example, a company may choose to recognize revenue as soon as possible after a sale takes place; however, when Cendant Corp., a franchising and marketing company, inflated its revenues and earnings by recording fictitious revenue of over $300 million during a three-year period, it engaged in fraudulent financial reporting. Management had looked at the actual numbers, compared them to the analysts' expectations, and, if there was a gap, recorded phony revenue and increased accounts receivable. The company is undergoing both an extensive internal investigation as well as an investigation by the Securities and Exchange Commission.[9]

maintains a staff of internal auditors who evaluate the adequacy of and investigate the adherence to these controls, policies, and procedures.[10]

The intentional preparation of misleading financial statements is called **fraudulent financial reporting**.[11] It can result from the distortion of records (the manipulation of inventory records), falsified transactions (fictitious sales or orders), or the misapplication of accounting principles (treating as an asset an item that should be expensed). There are a number of possible motives for fraudulent reporting—for instance, to obtain a higher price when a company is sold, to meet the expectations of stockholders, or to obtain a loan. Other times, the incentive is personal gain, such as additional compensation, promotion, or avoidance of penalties for poor performance. The personal costs of such actions can be high—individuals who authorize or prepare fraudulent financial statements may face criminal penalties and financial loss. Others, including investors and lenders to the company, employees, and customers, suffer from fraudulent financial reporting as well.

Incentives for fraudulent financial reporting exist to some extent in every company. It is management's responsibility to insist on honest financial reporting, but it is also the company accountants' responsibility to maintain high ethical standards. Ethical reporting demands that accountants apply financial accounting concepts to present a fair view of the company's operations and financial position and to avoid misleading readers of the financial statements.

Classified Balance Sheet

OBJECTIVE

5 Identify and describe the basic components of a classified balance sheet

Related Text Assignments:
Q: 5, 6, 7, 8, 9, 10, 11, 12, 13
SE: 2, 3
E: 3, 4
P: 3, 5
FRA: 4, 5

The balance sheets you have seen in the chapters thus far categorize accounts as assets, liabilities, and owner's equity. Because even a fairly small company can have hundreds of accounts, simply listing accounts in such broad categories is not particularly helpful to a statement user. Setting up subcategories within the major categories often makes financial statements much more useful. Investors and creditors study and evaluate the relationships among the subcategories. General-purpose external financial statements that are divided into useful subcategories are called **classified financial statements**.

The balance sheet presents the financial position of a company at a particular time. The subdivisions of the classified balance sheet shown in Exhibit 1 are typical of most companies in the United States. The subdivisions under owner's equity, of course, depend on the form of business.

Exhibit 1
Classified Balance Sheet for Shafer Auto Parts Company

Parenthetical Note: With some accounts—for example, Notes Receivable and Accounts Receivable—it is a toss-up which to list first.

Instructional Strategy: Play "Classification *Jeopardy*" using Exhibit 1 and E 3. Students could write their responses individually or play in 2 to 4 teams. Don't forget to have a Double *Jeopardy* question. Reward the winning team or individuals with bonus points on the next quiz or test.

Shafer Auto Parts Company
Balance Sheet
December 31, 20xx

Assets			
Current Assets			
Cash		$10,360	
Short-Term Investments		2,000	
Notes Receivable		8,000	
Accounts Receivable		35,300	
Merchandise Inventory		60,400	
Prepaid Insurance		6,600	
Store Supplies		1,060	
Office Supplies		636	
Total Current Assets			$124,356
Investments			
Land Held for Future Use			5,000
Property, Plant, and Equipment			
Land		$ 4,500	
Building	$20,650		
Less Accumulated Depreciation	8,640	12,010	
Delivery Equipment	$18,400		
Less Accumulated Depreciation	9,450	8,950	
Office Equipment	$ 8,600		
Less Accumulated Depreciation	5,000	3,600	
Total Property, Plant, and Equipment			29,060
Intangible Assets			
Trademark			500
Total Assets			$158,916
Liabilities			
Current Liabilities			
Notes Payable		$15,000	
Accounts Payable		23,883	
Salaries Payable		2,000	
Current Portion of Mortgage Payable		1,800	
Total Current Liabilities			$ 42,683
Long-Term Liabilities			
Mortgage Payable			17,800
Total Liabilities			$ 60,483
Owner's Equity			
Fred Shafer, Capital			98,433
Total Liabilities and Owner's Equity			$158,916

Assets

Parenthetical Note: Examples of accounts that would be classified as "other assets" are long-term receivables and bond issue costs.

A company's assets are often divided into four categories: (1) current assets; (2) investments; (3) property, plant, and equipment; and (4) intangible assets. For simplicity, some companies group investments, intangible assets, and other miscellaneous assets into a category called "other assets." The categories are listed in the order of their presumed ease of conversion into cash. For example, current assets are usually more easily converted to cash than are property, plant, and equipment.

CURRENT ASSETS **Current assets** are cash or other assets that are reasonably expected to be converted to cash, sold, or consumed within the next year or within the normal operating cycle of the business, whichever is longer. The normal operating cycle of a company is the average time needed to go from cash to cash. For example, cash is used to buy merchandise inventory, which is sold for cash or for a promise of cash if the sale is made on account. If a sale is made on account, the resulting receivable must be collected before the cycle is completed.

Point to Emphasize: Use one year as the current period unless the normal operating cycle happens to be longer.

The normal operating cycle for most companies is less than one year, but there are exceptions. Boeing Company, for example, can take more than one year to make commercial aircraft. The cost of those aircraft are considered current assets while they are being made because they will be sold in the current operating cycle. Another example is a company that sells on the installment basis. The payments for a television set or stove can be extended over 24 or 36 months, but such receivables are still considered current assets.

Cash is obviously a current asset. Temporary investments, notes and accounts receivable, and inventory are also current assets because they are expected to be converted to cash within the next year or during the normal operating cycle. On the balance sheet, they are listed in the order of their ease of conversion into cash.

Point to Emphasize: The firm does not consume prepaid expenses, but it does enjoy the benefit of the space rented, the insurance protection provided and so forth.

Prepaid expenses, such as rent and insurance paid for in advance, and inventories of supplies bought for use rather than for sale should also be classified as current assets. Such assets are current in the sense that if they had not been bought earlier, a current outlay of cash would be needed to obtain them.[12]

Point to Emphasize: For an investment to be classified as current, management must intend to sell it within the next year or the current operating cycle, and it must be readily marketable.

In deciding whether an asset is current or noncurrent, the idea of "reasonable expectation" is important. For example, Short-Term Investments is an account used for temporary investments of idle cash or cash that is not immediately required for operating purposes. Management can reasonably expect to sell those securities as cash needs arise over the next year or operating cycle. Investments in securities that management does not expect to sell within the next year and that do not involve the temporary use of idle cash should be shown in the investments category of a classified balance sheet.

INVESTMENTS The **investments** category includes assets, usually long term, that are not used in the normal operation of the business and that management does not plan to convert to cash within the next year. Items in that category are securities held for long-term investment, long-term notes receivable, land held for future use, plant or equipment not used in the business, and special funds established to pay off a debt or buy a building. Also included are large permanent investments in another company for the purpose of controlling that company.

PROPERTY, PLANT, AND EQUIPMENT The **property, plant, and equipment** category includes long-term assets used in the continuing operation of the business. They represent a place to operate (land and buildings) and equipment to produce, sell, deliver, and service the company's goods. Consequently, they may also be called *operating assets* or, sometimes, *fixed assets, tangible assets, long-lived assets,* or *plant assets*. Through depreciation, the costs of such assets (except land) are spread over the periods they benefit. Past depreciation is recorded in the Accumulated

its components, together with total stockholders' equity, are on the right side. The composition of the assets and liabilities, their relation to stockholders' equity, and the changes in them from 1999 to 2000 are clearly seen. These graphs show that overall there was significant growth in both totals and most components for Dell from 1999 to 2000. Also note that showing the balance sheet visually reduces the detailed clutter of the statement. For instance, all current assets are combined and represented by a single component line.

Forms of the Income Statement

OBJECTIVE

6 Prepare multistep and single-step classified income statements

Related Text Assignments:
Q: 14, 15
SE: 4, 5, 6
E: 5, 6, 7
P: 2, 5, 7
FRA: 5

For internal management, a detailed income statement is helpful in analyzing the company's performance. But for external reporting purposes, the income statement is usually presented in condensed form. **Condensed financial statements** present only the major categories of the detailed financial statements. There are two common forms of the condensed income statement, the multistep form and the single-step form. The **multistep form**, illustrated in Exhibit 3, derives net income in the same step-by-step fashion as a detailed income statement would, except that only the totals of significant categories are given. Usually, some breakdown is shown for operating expenses, such as the totals for selling expenses and for general and administrative expenses. In the Shafer statement, gross margin less operating expenses is called **income from operations** and a new section, **other revenues and expenses**, has been added to include nonoperating revenues and expenses. The latter section includes revenues from investments (such as dividends and interest from stocks, bonds, and savings accounts) and interest earned on credit or notes extended to customers. It also includes interest expense and other expenses

Exhibit 3
Condensed Multistep Income Statement for Shafer Auto Parts Company

Point to Emphasize: Financial analysts often focus on income from operations as a key profitability measure.

Shafer Auto Parts Company
Income Statement
For the Year Ended December 31, 20xx

Net Sales		$289,656
Cost of Goods Sold		181,260
Gross Margin		$108,396
Operating Expenses		
Selling Expenses	$54,780	
General and Administrative Expenses	34,504	
Total Operating Expenses		89,284
Income from Operations		$ 19,112
Other Revenues and Expenses		
Interest Income	$ 1,400	
Less Interest Expense	2,631	
Excess of Other Expenses over Other Revenues		1,231
Net Income		$ 17,881

Exhibit 4
Condensed Single-Step Income Statement for Shafer Auto Parts Company

Shafer Auto Parts Company Income Statement For the Year Ended December 31, 20xx		
Revenues		
Net Sales		$289,656
Interest Income		1,400
Total Revenues		$291,056
Costs and Expenses		
Cost of Goods Sold	$181,260	
Selling Expenses	54,780	
General and Administrative Expenses	34,504	
Interest Expense	2,631	
Total Costs and Expenses		273,175
Net Income		$ 17,881

Teaching Note: The multistep income statement is a valuable analytical tool that is often overlooked. Analysts will frequently convert a single-step statement into a multistep one because the latter separates operating from nonoperating sources of net income. Investors want net income to result primarily from operations, not from one-time gains on sales of assets.

that result from borrowing money or from credit extended to the company. If the company has other revenues and expenses that are not related to normal business operations, they too are included in this part of the income statement. Thus an analyst who wants to compare two companies independent of their financing methods—that is, before considering other revenues and expenses—would focus on income from operations.

The **single-step form** of income statement, illustrated in Exhibit 4, derives net income in a single step by putting the major categories of revenues in the first part of the statement and the major categories of costs and expenses in the second part. The multistep form and the single-step form each have advantages. The multistep form shows the components that are used in deriving net income; the single-step form has the advantage of simplicity. Approximately an equal number of large U.S. companies use each form in their public reports.

Net income from the income statement becomes an element of the statement of owner's equity.

Reading and Graphing Real Company Income Statements

As with the presentation of balance sheets, you will rarely find income statements that are exactly like the one for Shafer Auto Parts Company. You will encounter terms and structure that differ, such as those on the multistep income statement for Dell Computer Corp. in Exhibit 5, where management provides three years of data for comparison purposes. Sometimes there may be components in the income statement that are not covered in this chapter. If this occurs, refer to the index at the end of the book to find the topic and read about it.

Using the Fingraph® Financial Analyst™ CD-ROM software that accompanies this text to graphically present Dell's income from operations, as shown in Figure 3, helps to show the company's progress in meeting its profitability objectives. On the left side of the graph are the components of income from operations, beginning with net revenues at the top and ending with income from operations at the bottom. On the right side, the changes in the components are graphed. Increases are shown on the right of the vertical column, and decreases are shown on the left. Income from operations increased by only $217 million (10.6 percent), even

Exhibit 5
Income Statement for Dell Computer Corp.

Dell Computer Corp.
Consolidated Statements of Income

(In millions)

	Fiscal Year Ended		
	Jan. 28, 2000	Jan. 29, 1999	Feb. 1, 1998
Net revenues	**$25,265**	$18,243	$12,327
Cost of revenue	**20,047**	14,137	9,605
Gross margin	**5,218**	4,106	2,722
Operating expenses:			
Selling, general and administrative	**2,387**	1,788	1,202
Research and development	**374**	272	204
Purchased in-process research and development	**194**	—	—
Total operating expenses	**2,955**	2,060	1,406
Operating income	**2,263**	2,046	1,316
Financing and other income	**188**	38	52
Income before income taxes	**2,451**	2,084	1,368
Provision for income taxes	**785**	624	424
Net income	**$ 1,666**	$ 1,460	$ 944

Source: Dell Computer Corp., *Annual Report,* 2000.

Figure 3
Graphical Presentation of Dell Computer Corp.'s Income Statement

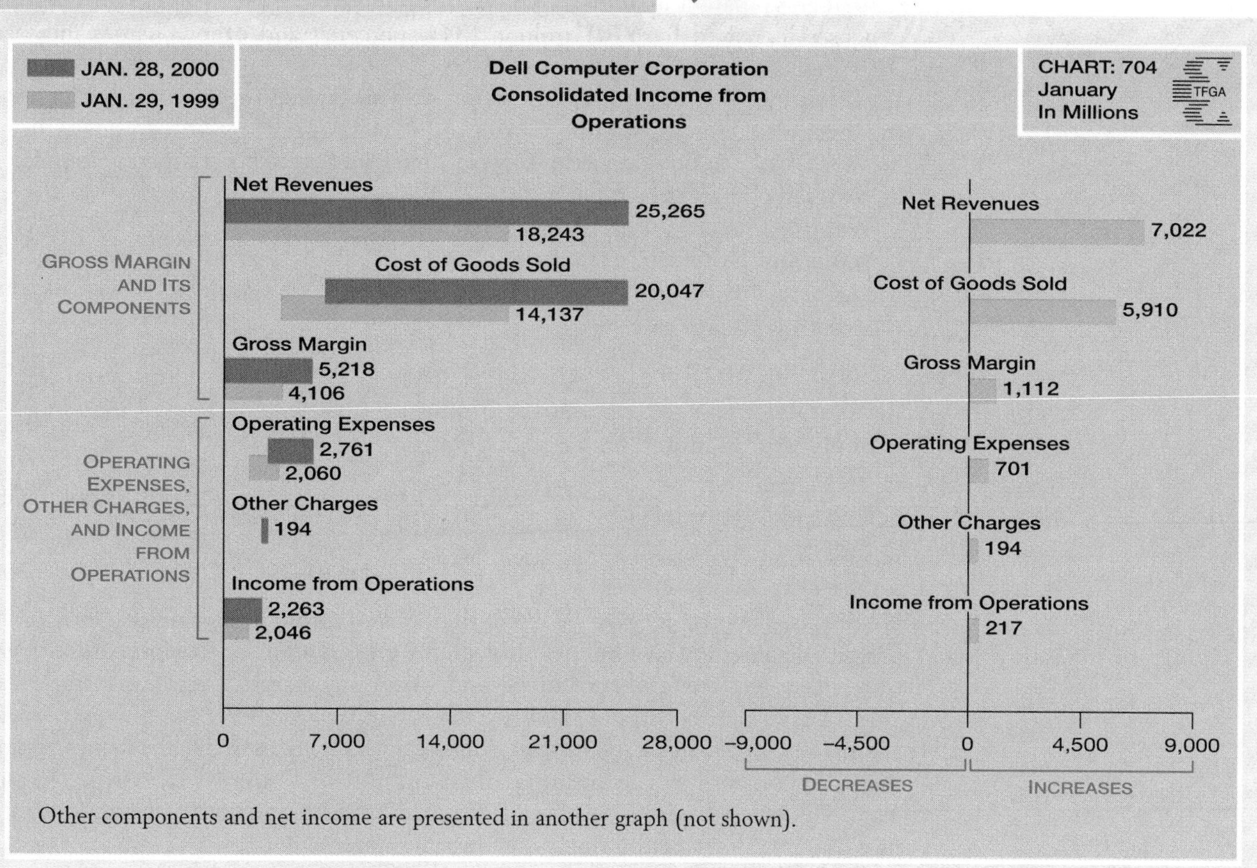

Other components and net income are presented in another graph (not shown).

Exhibit 6
Single-Step Income Statement for Nike, Inc.

Nike, Inc.
Consolidated Statements of Income

(In millions, except per share data)

	Year Ended May 31		
	1999	1998	1997
Revenues	**$8,776.9**	$9,553.1	$9,186.5
Costs and expenses:			
Costs of sales	**$5,493.5**	$6,065.5	$5,503.0
Selling and administrative	**2,426.6**	2,623.8	2,303.7
Interest expense	**44.1**	60.0	52.3
Other income/expense, net	**21.5**	20.9	32.2
Restructuring charge	**45.1**	129.9	—
	$8,030.8	$8,900.1	$7,891.3
Income before income taxes	**$ 746.1**	$ 653.0	$1,295.2
Income taxes	**294.7**	253.4	499.4
Net income	**$ 451.4**	$ 399.6	$ 795.8
Basic income per common share	**$ 1.59**	$ 1.38	$ 2.76

The accompanying notes to consolidated financial statements are an integral part of this statement.

Source: Nike, Inc., *Annual Report*, 1999.

though gross margin increased by $1,112 million (27.1 percent) because operating expenses increased by $701 million (34.0 percent) and other charges increased $194 million from zero the prior year.

A separate graphical presentation (not shown) is used to show the remainder of the income statement, starting with income from operations and ending with net income. The income statement shows annual increases in net income similar to increases in operating income.

When a company uses the single-step form, as Nike, Inc., the footwear company, does in Exhibit 6, most analysts will still calculate gross margin and income from operations and each component's percentages of revenues, as shown below for Nike, Inc.:

	1999	Percent	1998	Percent
Revenues	$8,776.9	100.0	$9,553.1	100.0
Cost of Sales	5,493.5	62.6	6,065.5	63.5
Gross Margin	3,283.4	37.4	$3,487.6	36.5
Selling and Administrative	2,426.6	27.6	2,623.8	27.5
Income from Operations	$ 856.8	9.8	$ 863.8	9.0

From this analysis, it may be seen that Nike's profitability results are mixed. Despite declines in the amounts of revenues, gross margin, and income from operations, the gross margin percentage and operating margin percentage improved. Cost of sales declined faster than revenue, creating a higher gross margin percentage in 1999. However, selling and administrative expenses declined only slightly slower than revenues, giving up a small amount of the gross margin percentage gain. This type of analysis is often performed because a majority of public companies use some form of the single-step income statement.

Using Classified Financial Statements

OBJECTIVE

7 **Evaluate liquidity and profitability using classified financial statements**

Related Text Assignments:
Q: 16, 17, 18, 19, 20
SE: 7, 8
E: 8, 9, 10
P: 4, 5, 8
SD: 6
FRA: 1, 2, 3, 4, 5, 6, 7

Discussion Question: How can a company be earning a profit but be forced out of business? **Answer:** A firm that sells on credit but does not collect its accounts receivable would not have enough cash to pay its obligations. (There are, of course, other valid answers to this question.)

Earlier in this chapter, you learned that financial reporting, according to the Financial Accounting Standards Board, seeks to provide information that is useful in making investment and credit decisions, in judging cash flow prospects, and in understanding business resources, claims to those resources, and changes in them. These objectives are related to two of the more important goals of management—maintaining adequate liquidity and achieving satisfactory profitability—because investors and creditors base their decisions largely on their assessment of a company's potential liquidity and profitability. The following analysis focuses on those two important goals.

In this section a series of charts shows average ratios for six industries based on data obtained from *Industry Norms and Key Business Ratios*, a publication of Dun and Bradstreet. There are two examples from service industries, advertising agencies and interstate trucking; two examples from merchandising industries, auto and home supply and grocery stores; and two examples from manufacturing industries, pharmaceuticals and computers. Shafer Auto Parts Company, the example used in this chapter, falls into the auto and home supply industry.

Evaluation of Liquidity

Liquidity means having enough money on hand to pay bills when they are due and to take care of unexpected needs for cash. Two measures of liquidity are working capital and the current ratio.

Point to Emphasize: It is imperative that accounts be classified correctly before the ratios are computed. If accounts are not classified correctly, the ratios will not be correct.

WORKING CAPITAL The first measure, **working capital**, is the amount by which total current assets exceed total current liabilities. This is an important measure of liquidity because current liabilities are debts that must be paid or obligations that must be performed within one year, and current assets are assets that will be realized in cash or that will be used up within one year or one operating cycle, whichever is longer. By definition, current liabilities are paid out of current assets. So the excess of current assets over current liabilities is the net current assets on hand to continue business operations. It is the working capital that can be used to buy inventory, obtain credit, and finance expanded sales. Lack of working capital can lead to a company's failure.

For Shafer Auto Parts Company, working capital is computed as shown on the next page.

FOCUS ON BUSINESS PRACTICE

Caldor, a discounter that was based in Connecticut, had plans for a major expansion and remodeling. To finance this growth, the company could have issued stock, borrowed using long-term debt, or used working capital. Caldor's management chose to use working capital to fund the expansion. In less than a year the company was forced to declare bankruptcy because it could not pay its short-term debt, even though it was still earning a profit. Caldor had violated a fundamental rule of financial management. Working capital should be used to maintain liquidity, and long-term sources, such as debt and stock, should be used to finance long-term expansion. Because its working capital dropped from $80 million to zero and its stock price dropped from $32 to $5, Caldor's creditors no longer saw the company as credit-worthy and would not extend any further credit. As one creditor summed it up, "They were expanding using working capital—which, of course, is supposed to be used for short-term liquidity."[13]

Figure 4
Average Current Ratio for Selected Industries

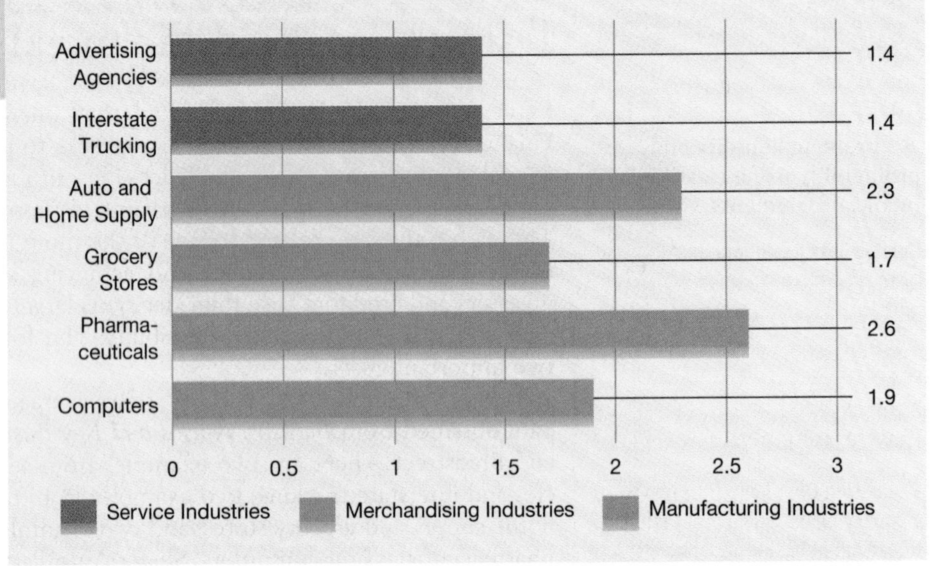

Source: Data from Dun and Bradstreet, *Industry Norms and Key Business Ratios*, 1999–2000.

Current assets	$124,356
Less current liabilities	42,683
Working capital	$ 81,673

CURRENT RATIO The second measure of liquidity, the current ratio, is closely related to working capital and is believed by many bankers and other creditors to be a good indicator of a company's ability to pay its bills and to repay outstanding loans. The **current ratio** is the ratio of current assets to current liabilities. For Shafer Auto Parts Company, it would be computed like this:

$$\text{Current Ratio} = \frac{\text{Current Assets}}{\text{Current Liabilities}} = \frac{\$124{,}356}{\$42{,}683} = 2.9$$

Thus Shafer has $2.90 of current assets for each $1.00 of current liabilities. Is that good or bad? The answer requires the comparison of this year's ratio with ratios of earlier years and with similar measures for successful companies in the same industry. The average current ratio varies widely from industry to industry, as shown in Figure 4. For advertising agencies, which have no merchandise inventory, the current ratio is 1.4. In contrast, auto and home supply companies, which carry large merchandise inventories, have an average current ratio of 2.3. Shafer Auto Parts Company, with a ratio of 2.9, exceeds the average for its industry. A very low current ratio, of course, can be unfavorable, but so can a very high one. The latter may indicate that the company is not using its assets effectively.

Discussion Question: Why may a low current ratio be a sign of trouble? **Answer:** The business may have difficulty paying its obligations.

Business-World Example: Some successful companies, such as McDonald's, manage to have very low current ratios by carefully planning their cash flows.

Discussion Question: Why is it inadvisable to have too high a current ratio? **Answer:** The firm could probably use the excess funds more effectively to increase its overall profit.

Evaluation of Profitability

Just as important as paying bills on time is **profitability**—the ability to earn a satisfactory income. As a goal, profitability competes with liquidity for managerial attention because liquid assets, although important, are not the best profit-producing resources. Cash, for example, means purchasing power, but a satisfactory profit can be made only if purchasing power is used to buy profit-producing (and less liquid) assets, such as inventory and long-term assets.

Among the common measures of a company's ability to earn income are (1) profit margin, (2) asset turnover, (3) return on assets, (4) debt to equity, and (5) return on equity. To evaluate a company meaningfully, one must relate its profit performance to its past performance and prospects for the future as well as to the averages for other companies in the same industry.

PROFIT MARGIN The **profit margin** shows the percentage of each sales dollar that results in net income. It is figured by dividing net income by net sales. It should not be confused with gross margin, which is not a ratio but rather the amount by which revenues exceed the cost of goods sold.

Shafer Auto Parts Company has a profit margin of 6.2 percent:

$$\text{Profit Margin} = \frac{\text{Net Income}}{\text{Net Sales}} = \frac{\$17{,}881}{\$289{,}656} = .062\ (6.2\%)$$

On each dollar of net sales, Shafer Auto Parts Company made 6.2 cents. A difference of 1 or 2 percent in a company's profit margin can mean the difference between a fair year and a very profitable one.

Discussion Question: How could a company increase its asset turnover ratio? **Answer:** By managing assets better—by carrying minimum quantities of inventory and having efficient ordering procedures to avoid running out of merchandise.

ASSET TURNOVER **Asset turnover** measures how efficiently assets are used to produce sales. Computed by dividing net sales by average total assets, it shows how many dollars of sales were generated by each dollar of assets. A company with a higher asset turnover uses its assets more productively than one with a lower asset turnover. Average total assets is computed by adding total assets at the beginning of the year to total assets at the end of the year and dividing by 2.

Assuming that total assets for Shafer Auto Parts Company were $148,620 at the beginning of the year, its asset turnover is computed as follows:

Point to Emphasize: Average total assets equal assets at the beginning of the year plus assets at the end of the year, divided by 2.

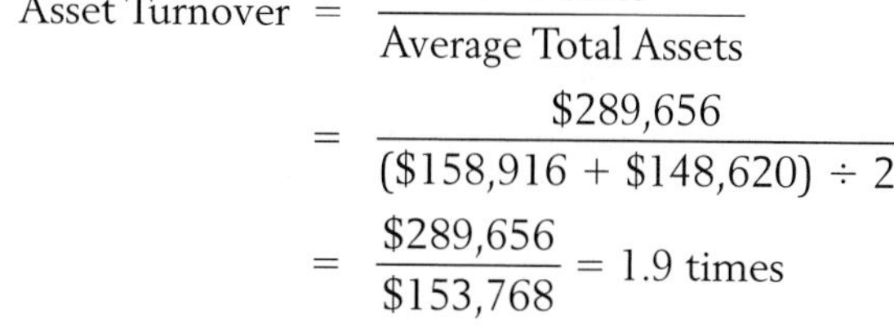

$$\text{Asset Turnover} = \frac{\text{Net Sales}}{\text{Average Total Assets}}$$
$$= \frac{\$289{,}656}{(\$158{,}916 + \$148{,}620) \div 2}$$
$$= \frac{\$289{,}656}{\$153{,}768} = 1.9 \text{ times}$$

Shafer Auto Parts Company produces $1.90 in sales for each $1.00 invested in average total assets. This ratio shows a meaningful relationship between an income statement figure and a balance sheet figure.

Point to Emphasize: Return on assets is one of the most widely used measures of profitability because it reflects both the profit margin and asset turnover.

RETURN ON ASSETS Both the profit margin and the asset turnover ratios have some limitations. The profit margin ratio does not take into consideration the assets necessary to produce income, and the asset turnover ratio does not take into account the amount of income produced. The **return on assets** ratio overcomes these deficiencies by relating net income to average total assets. It is computed like this:

$$\text{Return on Assets} = \frac{\text{Net Income}}{\text{Average Total Assets}}$$
$$= \frac{\$17{,}881}{(\$158{,}916 + \$148{,}620) \div 2}$$
$$= \frac{\$17{,}881}{\$153{,}768} = .116\ (11.6\%)$$

For each dollar invested, Shafer Auto Parts Company's assets generated 11.6 cents of net income. This ratio indicates the income-generating strength (profit margin) of the company's resources and how efficiently the company is using all its assets (asset turnover).

Return on assets, then, combines profit margin and asset turnover, as follows:

Figure 5
Average Profit Margin for Selected Industries

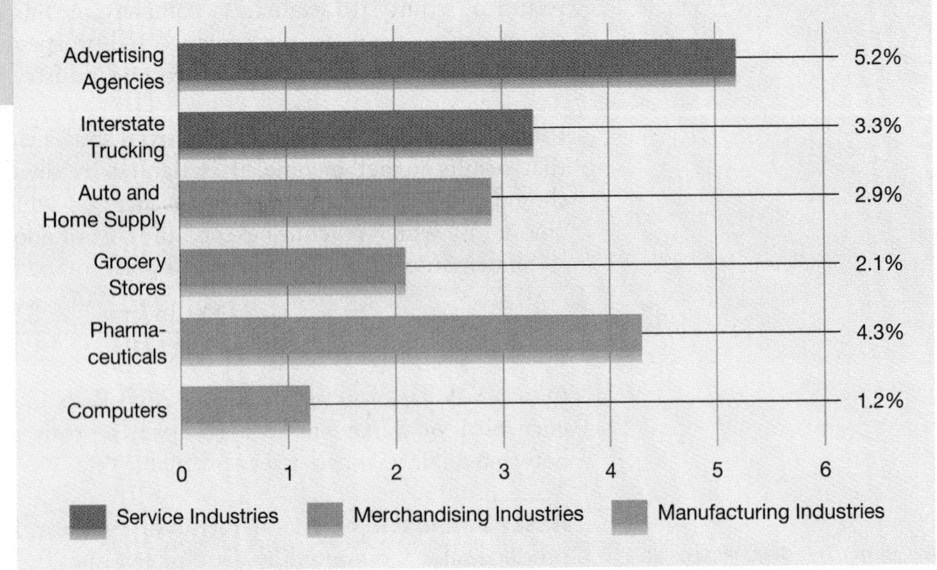

Source: Data from Dun and Bradstreet, *Industry Norms and Key Business Ratios*, 1999–2000.

$$\frac{\text{Net Income}}{\text{Net Sales}} \times \frac{\text{Net Sales}}{\text{Average Total Assets}} = \frac{\text{Net Income}}{\text{Average Total Assets}}$$

$$\text{Profit Margin} \times \text{Asset Turnover} = \text{Return on Assets}$$

$$6.2\% \times 1.9 \text{ times} = 11.8\%^*$$

* The slight difference between 11.6 and 11.8 is due to rounding.

Thus a company's management can improve overall profitability by increasing the profit margin, the asset turnover, or both. Similarly, in evaluating a company's overall profitability, the financial statement user must consider the interaction of both ratios to produce return on assets.

Careful study of Figures 5, 6, and 7 shows the different ways in which the selected industries combine profit margin and asset turnover to produce return on

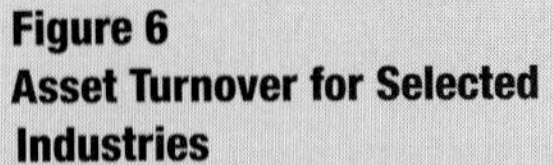

Figure 6
Asset Turnover for Selected Industries

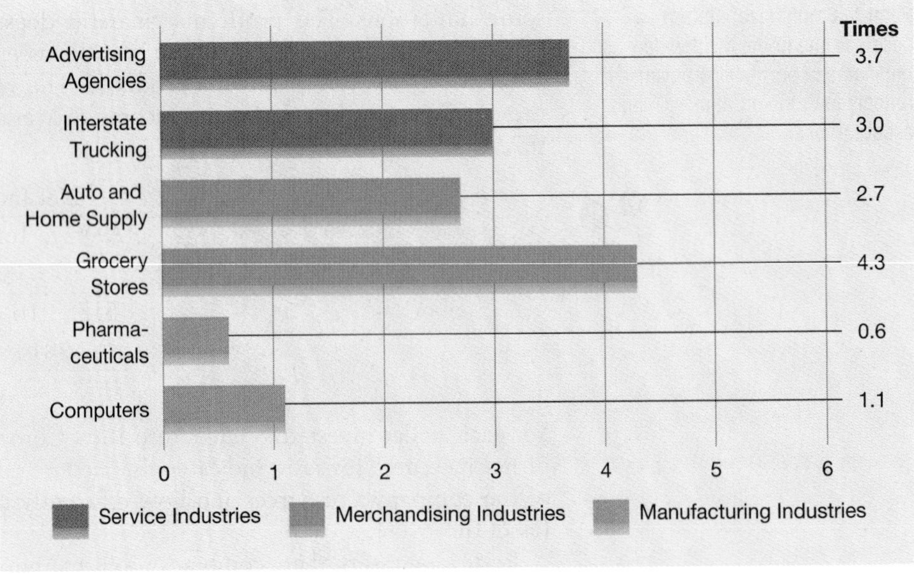

Source: Data from Dun and Bradstreet, *Industry Norms and Key Business Ratios*, 1999–2000.

Figure 7
Return on Assets for Selected Industries

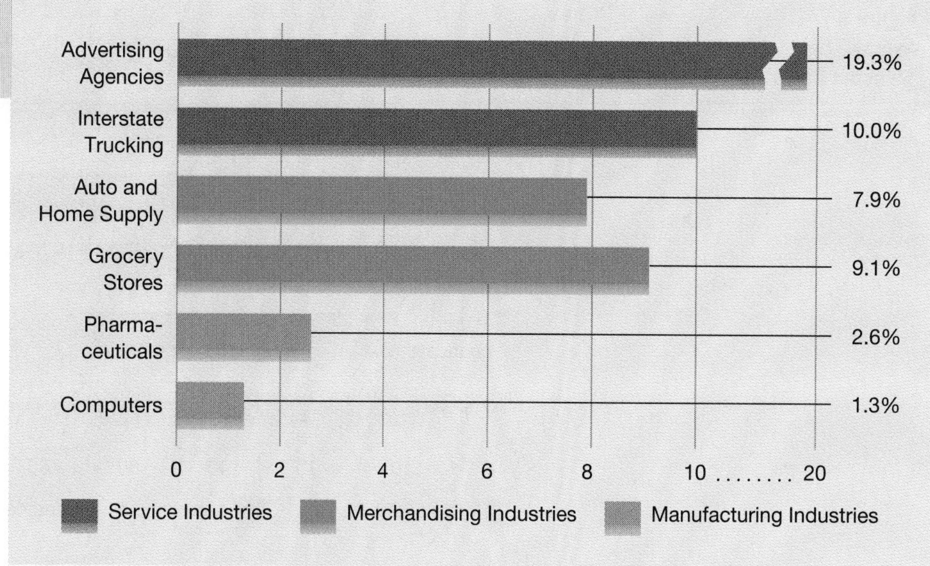

Source: Data from Dun and Bradstreet, *Industry Norms and Key Business Ratios*, 1999–2000.

assets. For instance, compare the return on assets for grocery stores and auto and home supply, and see how they achieve it in very different ways. Grocery stores have a smaller profit margin, 2.1 percent, which when multiplied by a higher asset turnover, 4.3 times, gives a return on assets of 9.1 percent. Auto and home supply stores, on the other hand, have a higher profit margin, 2.9 percent, and a lower asset turnover, 2.7 times, which produces a return on assets of 7.9 percent.

Shafer Auto Parts Company's profit margin of 6.2 percent is well above the auto and home supply industry average of 2.9 percent, but its turnover of 1.9 times lags behind the industry average of 2.7 times. Shafer is sacrificing asset turnover to achieve a high profit margin. It is clear that the strategy is working, because Shafer's return on assets of 11.6 percent exceeds the industry average of 7.9 percent.

Point to Emphasize: A company with a low debt to equity ratio has a better chance of surviving in rough times. Debt requires additional expenses (interest) that must be paid.

DEBT TO EQUITY Another useful measure is the **debt to equity** ratio, which shows the proportion of the company financed by creditors in comparison to that financed by the owners. This ratio is computed by dividing total liabilities by owner's equity. Since the balance sheets of many companies do not show total liabilities, a short way of determining total liabilities is to deduct owner's equity from total assets. A debt to equity ratio of 1.0 means that total liabilities equal owner's equity—that half of the company's assets are financed by creditors. A ratio of .5 would mean that one-third of the assets are financed by creditors. A company with a high debt to equity ratio is more vulnerable in poor economic times because it must continue to repay creditors. Owner's investments, on the other hand, do not have to be repaid, and withdrawals can be deferred if the company is suffering because of a poor economy.

Shafer Auto Parts Company's debt to equity ratio is computed as follows:

K/R

$$\text{Debt to Equity} = \frac{\text{Total Liabilities}}{\text{Owner's Equity}} = \frac{\$60{,}483}{\$98{,}433} = .614\ (61.4\%)$$

A debt to equity ratio of 61.4 percent, which is less than 100 percent, means that Shafer Auto Parts Company receives less than half its financing from creditors and more than half from its owner, Fred Shafer.

The debt to equity ratio does not fit neatly into either the liquidity or the profitability category. It is clearly very important to liquidity analysis because it relates to debt and its repayment. However, the debt to equity ratio is also relevant to

Figure 8
Average Debt to Equity for Selected Industries

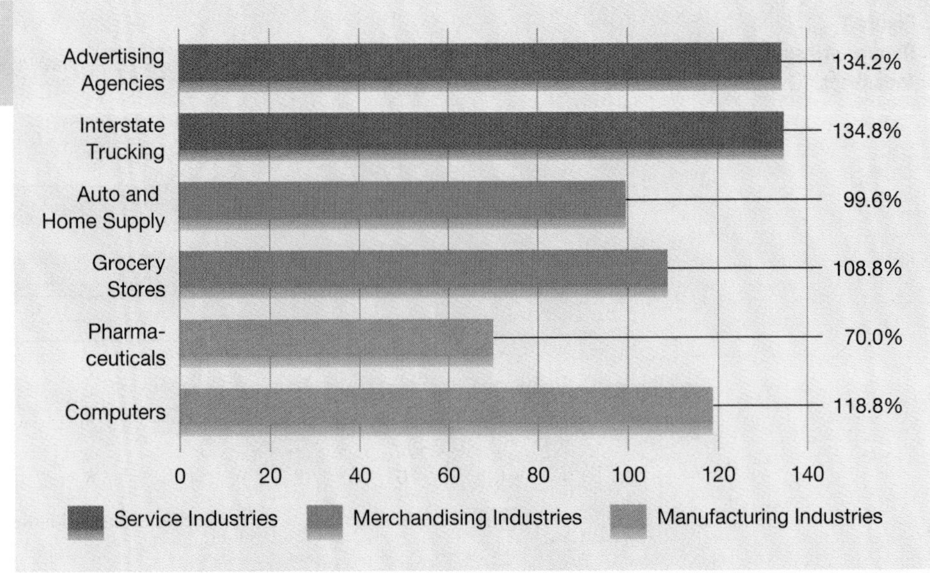

Source: Data from Dun and Bradstreet, *Industry Norms and Key Business Ratios*, 1999–2000.

profitability for two reasons. First, creditors are interested in the proportion of the business that is debt financed because the more debt a company has, the more profit it must earn to protect the payment of interest to its creditors. Second, an owner is interested in the proportion of the business that is debt financed, because the amount of interest that must be paid on the debt affects the amount of profit that is left to provide a return on the owner's investment. The debt to equity ratio also shows how much expansion is possible by borrowing additional long-term funds. Figure 8 shows that the debt to equity ratio in our selected industries varies from a low of 70.0 percent in the pharmaceutical industry to a high of 134.8 percent in interstate trucking and 134.2 percent in the advertising agency industry.

RETURN ON EQUITY Of course, Fred Shafer is interested in how much he has earned on his investment in the business. His **return on equity** is measured by the ratio of net income to average owner's equity. Taking the ending owner's equity

FOCUS ON BUSINESS PRACTICE

To what level of profitability should a company aspire? At one time, a company earning a 20 percent return on equity was considered among the elite. Walt Disney, Wal-Mart, Coca-Cola, and a few other companies were able to achieve this level of profitability. However, *The Wall Street Journal* reported that in the first quarter of 1995, for the first time, the average company of the Standard & Poor's 500 companies made a return on equity of 20.12 percent. It said that this performance was "akin to the average ball player hitting .350."[14] This means that stockholders' equity will double every four years.

Why did this happen? First, a good business environment and cost cutting led to more profitable operations. Second, special charges and other accounting transactions reduced the amount of stockholders' equity for many companies.

The number of companies with a return on equity of 20 percent or more has also continued to increase as profits have grown.

Figure 9
Average Return on Equity for Selected Industries

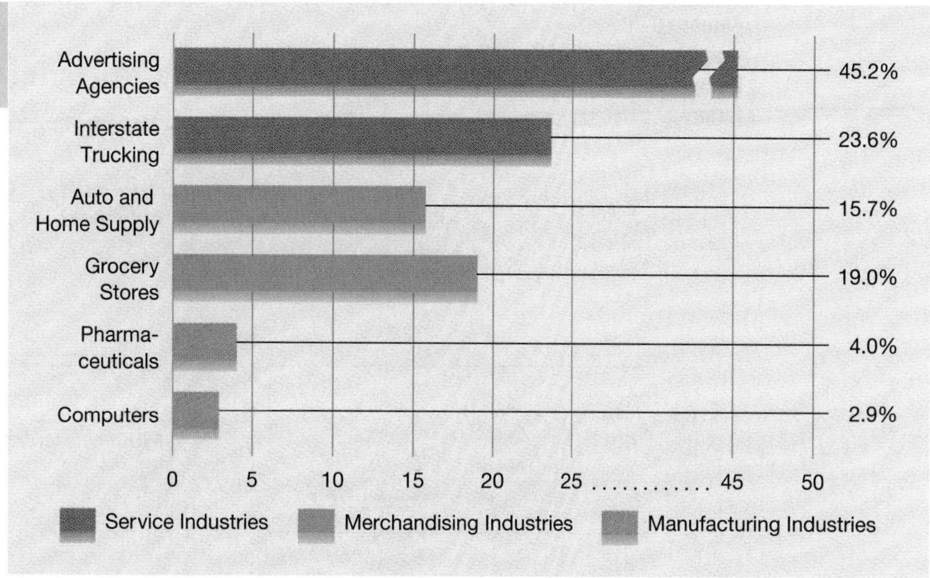

Source: Data from Dun and Bradstreet, *Industry Norms and Key Business Ratios*, 1999–2000.

from the balance sheet and assuming that beginning owner's equity is $100,553, Shafer's return on equity is computed as follows:

$$\text{Return on Equity} = \frac{\text{Net Income}}{\text{Average Owner's Equity}}$$
$$= \frac{\$17{,}881}{(\$98{,}433 + \$100{,}553) \div 2}$$
$$= \frac{\$17{,}881}{\$99{,}493} = .180\ (18.0\%)$$

In 20xx, Shafer Auto Parts Company earned 18.0 cents for every dollar invested by the owner, Fred Shafer.

Whether or not this is an acceptable return depends on several factors, such as how much the company earned in prior years and how much other companies in the same industry earned. As measured by return on equity (Figure 9), advertising agencies are the most profitable of our sample industries, with a return on equity of 45.2 percent. Shafer Auto Parts Company's average return on equity of 18.0 percent exceeds the average of 15.7 percent for the auto and home supply industry.

GRAPHING RATIO ANALYSIS Using the Fingraph® Financial Analyst™ CD-ROM software that accompanies this text to graphically present Dell Computer Corp.'s profitability ratios involving net income, shown in Figure 10, helps us visualize the progress of the company in meeting its profitability objectives. On the left of the figure are the components of the ratios. On the right of the figure are the ratios for the past two years. It may be seen that the changes in Dell Computer Corp.'s return on equity and return on assets are linked to changes in profit margin or asset turnover.

The Fingraph® Financial Analyst™ CD-ROM software graphs all the ratios used in this book and provides narrative analysis. The asset turnover ratio is shown graphically with the balance sheet analysis.

Figure 10
Graphical Presentation of Dell Computer Corp.'s Profitability Ratios

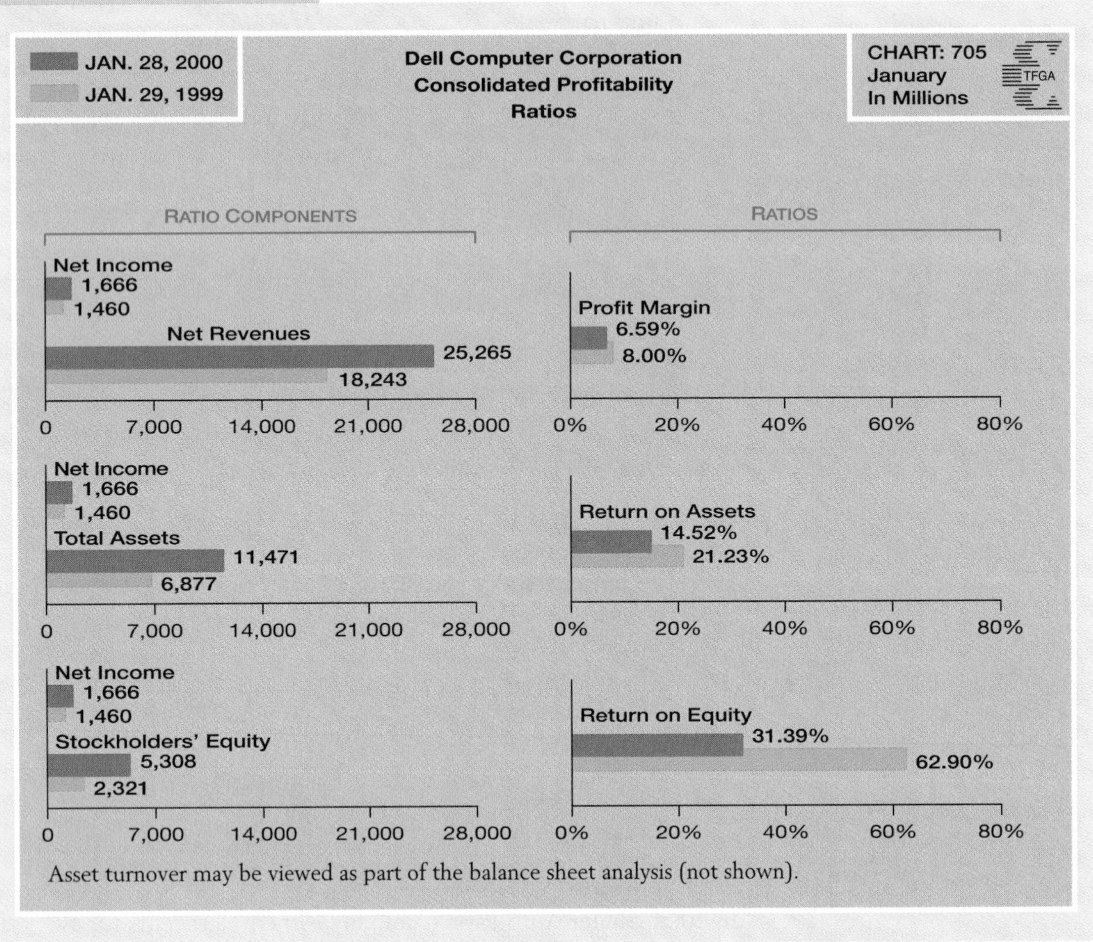

Asset turnover may be viewed as part of the balance sheet analysis (not shown).

Chapter Review

Review of Learning Objectives

Check out ACE, a self-quizzing program on chapter content, at http://college.hmco.com.

1. **State the objectives of financial reporting.** The objectives of financial reporting are (1) to furnish information that is useful in making investment and credit decisions; (2) to provide information that can be used to assess cash flow prospects; and (3) to provide information about business resources, claims to those resources, and changes in them.

2. **State the qualitative characteristics of accounting information and describe their interrelationships.** Understandability depends on the knowledge of the user and the ability of the accountant to provide useful information. Usefulness is a function of two primary characteristics, relevance and reliability. Information is relevant when it affects the outcome of a decision. Information that is relevant has feedback value and predictive value, and is

timely. To be reliable, information must represent what it is supposed to represent, must be verifiable, and must be neutral.

3. **Define and describe the use of the conventions of *comparability* and *consistency, materiality, conservatism, full disclosure*, and *cost-benefit.*** Because accountants' measurements are not exact, certain conventions have come to be applied in current practice to help users interpret financial statements. One of these conventions is consistency, which requires the use of the same accounting procedures from period to period and enhances the comparability of financial statements. The second is materiality, which has to do with the relative importance of an item. The third is conservatism, which entails using the procedure that is least likely to overstate assets and income. The fourth is full disclosure, which means including all relevant information in the financial statements. The fifth is cost-benefit, which suggests that above a minimum level of information, additional information should be provided only if the benefits derived from the information exceed the costs of providing it.

4. **Explain management's responsibility for ethical financial reporting and define *fraudulent financial reporting.*** Management is responsible for the preparation of financial statements in accordance with generally accepted accounting principles and for the internal controls that provide assurance that this objective is achieved. Fraudulent financial reporting is the intentional preparation of misleading financial statements.

5. **Identify and describe the basic components of a classified balance sheet.** The classified balance sheet is subdivided as follows:

Assets	Liabilities
Current Assets	Current Liabilities
Investments	Long-Term Liabilities
Property, Plant, and Equipment	**Owner's Equity**
Intangible Assets	
(Other Assets)	(Content depends on the form of business)

A current asset is an asset that can reasonably be expected to be realized in cash or consumed during the next year or the normal operating cycle, whichever is longer. Investments are long-term assets that are not usually used in the normal operation of a business. Property, plant, and equipment are long-term assets that are used in day-to-day operations. Intangible assets are long-term assets whose value stems from the rights or privileges they extend to the owner. A current liability is a liability that can reasonably be expected to be paid or performed during the next year or the normal operating cycle, whichever is longer. Long-term liabilities are debts that fall due more than one year in the future or beyond the normal operating cycle. The equity section of the balance sheet for a corporation differs from that for a proprietorship in that it has subdivisions of contributed capital (the value of assets invested by stockholders) and retained earnings (stockholders' claim to assets earned from operations and reinvested in operations).

6. **Prepare multistep and single-step classified income statements.** Condensed income statements for external reporting can be in multistep or single-step form. The multistep form arrives at net income through a series of steps; the single-step form arrives at net income in a single step. There is usually a separate section in the multi-step form for other revenues and expenses.

7. **Evaluate liquidity and profitability using classified financial statements.** One important use of classified financial statements is to evaluate a company's liquidity and profitability. Two simple measures of liquidity are

working capital and the current ratio. Five simple measures of profitability are profit margin, asset turnover, return on assets, debt to equity, and return on equity.

REVIEW OF CONCEPTS AND TERMINOLOGY

The following concepts and terms were introduced in this chapter:

LO 7 **Asset turnover:** A measure of profitability that shows how efficiently assets are used to produce sales; net sales divided by average total assets.

LO 5 **Classified financial statements:** General-purpose external financial statements divided into useful subcategories.

LO 3 **Comparability:** The convention of presenting information in a way that enables decision makers to recognize similarities, differences, and trends over different time periods or between different companies.

LO 6 **Condensed financial statements:** Financial statements for external reporting that present only the major categories of information.

LO 3 **Conservatism:** The convention that requires that, when faced with equally acceptable alternatives, accountants must choose the one least likely to overstate assets and income.

LO 3 **Consistency:** The convention that requires that an accounting procedure, once adopted, not be changed from one period to another unless users are informed of the change.

LO 5 **Contributed capital:** The accounts that reflect the stockholders' investment in a corporation. Also called *paid-in capital.*

LO 3 **Conventions:** Rules of thumb or customary ways of recording transactions or preparing financial statements.

LO 3 **Cost-benefit:** The convention that holds that benefits gained from providing accounting information should be greater than the costs of providing that information.

LO 5 **Current assets:** Cash or other assets that are reasonably expected to be converted to cash, sold, or consumed within one year or within the normal operating cycle, whichever is longer.

LO 5 **Current liabilities:** Obligations due to be paid or performed within one year or within the normal operating cycle, whichever is longer.

LO 7 **Current ratio:** A measure of liquidity; current assets divided by current liabilities.

LO 7 **Debt to equity:** A ratio that measures the relationship of assets financed by creditors to those financed by owners; total liabilities divided by owner's equity.

LO 4 **Fraudulent financial reporting:** The intentional preparation of misleading financial statements.

LO 3 **Full disclosure:** The convention that requires that financial statements and their notes present all information relevant to the users' understanding of the company's financial condition.

LO 6 **Income from operations:** Gross margin less operating expenses.

LO 5 **Intangible assets:** Long-term assets that have no physical substance but that have a value based on rights or privileges that belong to their owner.

LO 5 **Investments:** Assets, usually long term, that are not used in the normal operation of a business and that management does not intend to convert to cash within the next year.

LO 7 **Liquidity:** Having enough money on hand to pay bills when they are due and to take care of unexpected needs for cash.

LO 5 **Long-term liabilities:** Debts that fall due more than one year in the future or beyond the normal operating cycle, or that are to be paid out of noncurrent assets.

LO 3 **Materiality:** The convention that refers to the relative importance of an item or event in a financial statement and its influence on the decisions of the users of financial statements.

LO 6 **Multistep form:** A form of condensed income statement that arrives at net income in the same steps as a detailed income statement but that presents only the totals of significant categories.

LO 5 **Other assets:** The balance sheet category that may include various types of assets other than current assets and property, plant, and equipment.

LO 6 **Other revenues and expenses:** The section of a multistep income statement that includes nonoperating revenues and expenses.

LO 7 **Profitability:** The ability of a business to earn a satisfactory income.

LO 7 **Profit margin:** A measure of profitability that shows the percentage of each sales dollar that results in net income; net income divided by net sales.

LO 5 **Property, plant, and equipment:** Tangible long-term assets used in the continuing operation of a business. Also called *operating assets, fixed assets, tangible assets, long-lived assets*, or *plant assets*.

LO 2 **Qualitative characteristics:** Standards for judging the information that accountants give to decision makers.

LO 2 **Relevance:** The qualitative characteristic of information bearing directly on the outcome of a decision.

LO 2 **Reliability:** The qualitative characteristic of information being representationally faithful, verifiable, and neutral.

LO 5 **Retained Earnings:** The account that reflects the stockholders' claim to the assets earned from operations and reinvested in corporate operations. Also called *Earned Capital.*

LO 7 **Return on assets:** A measure of profitability that shows how efficiently a company uses its assets to produce income; net income divided by average total assets.

LO 7 **Return on equity:** A measure of profitability that relates the amount earned by a business to the owner's investment in the business; net income divided by average owner's equity.

LO 6 **Single-step form:** A form of condensed income statement that arrives at net income in a single step.

LO 2 **Understandability:** The qualitative characteristic of communicating an intended meaning.

LO 2 **Usefulness:** The qualitative characteristic of accounting information being relevant and reliable.

LO 7 **Working capital:** A measure of liquidity equal to the net current assets on hand to continue business operations; total current assets minus total current liabilities.

Review Problem

Analyzing Liquidity and Profitability Using Ratios

LO 7 Flavin Shirt Company has faced increased competition from overseas shirtmakers in recent years. Key information for the last two years is as follows:

	20x2	20x1
Current Assets	$ 200,000	$ 170,000
Total Assets	880,000	710,000
Current Liabilities	90,000	50,000
Long-Term Liabilities	150,000	50,000
Owner's Equity	640,000	610,000
Sales	1,200,000	1,050,000
Net Income	60,000	80,000

Total assets and owner's equity at the beginning of 20x1 were $690,000 and $590,000, respectively.

REQUIRED

Use (1) liquidity analysis and (2) profitability analysis to document the declining financial position of Flavin Shirt Company.

ANSWER TO REVIEW PROBLEM

1. Liquidity analysis

	Current Assets	Current Liabilities	Working Capital	Current Ratio
20x1	$170,000	$50,000	$120,000	3.4
20x2	200,000	90,000	110,000	2.2
Decrease in working capital			($ 10,000)	
Decrease in current ratio				1.2

Both working capital and the current ratio declined because, although current assets increased by $30,000 ($200,000 − $170,000), current liabilities increased by a greater amount, $40,000 ($90,000 − $50,000), from 20x1 to 20x2.

2. Profitability analysis

	Net Income	Sales	Profit Margin	Average Total Assets	Asset Turnover	Return on Assets	Average Owners' Equity	Return on Equity
20x1	$80,000	$1,050,000	7.6%	$700,000[1]	1.50	11.4%	$600,000[3]	13.3%
20x2	60,000	1,200,000	5.0	795,000[2]	1.51	7.5	625,000[4]	9.6
Increase (decrease)	($20,000)	$ 150,000	(2.6)%	$ 95,000	0.01	(3.9)%	$ 25,000	(3.7)%

[1]($710,000 + $690,000) ÷ 2
[2]($880,000 + $710,000) ÷ 2
[3]($610,000 + $590,000) ÷ 2
[4]($640,000 + $610,000) ÷ 2

Net income decreased by $20,000 despite an increase in sales of $150,000 and an increase in average total assets of $95,000. The results were decreases in profit margin from 7.6 percent to 5.0 percent and in return on assets from 11.4 percent to 7.5 percent. Asset turnover showed almost no change and so did not contribute to the decline in profitability. The decrease in return on equity from 13.3 percent to 9.6 percent was not as great as the decrease in return on assets because the growth in total assets was financed by debt instead of owner's equity, as shown by the following capital structure analysis.

	Total Liabilities	Owner's Equity	Debt to Equity Ratio
20x1	$100,000	$610,000	16.4%
20x2	240,000	640,000	37.5
Increase	$140,000	$ 30,000	21.1%

Total liabilities increased by $140,000 while owner's equity increased by $30,000. As a result, the amount of the business financed by debt in relation to the amount of the business financed by owner's equity increased from 20x1 to 20x2.

Chapter Assignments

Building Your Knowledge Foundation

Questions

1. What are the three objectives of financial reporting?
2. What are the qualitative characteristics of accounting information, and what is their significance?
3. What are the accounting conventions? How does each help in the interpretation of financial information?
4. Who is responsible for preparing reliable financial statements, and what is a principal way of fulfilling the responsibility?
5. What is the purpose of classified financial statements?
6. What are four common categories of assets?
7. What criteria must an asset meet to be classified as current? Under what condition is an asset considered current even though it will not be realized as cash within a year? What are two examples of assets that fall into this category?
8. In what order should current assets be listed?
9. What is the difference between a short-term investment in the current assets section and a security in the investments section of the balance sheet?
10. What is an intangible asset? Give at least three examples.
11. Name the two major categories of liabilities.
12. What are the primary differences between the equity section of the balance sheet for a sole proprietorship or partnership and the corresponding section for a corporation?
13. Explain the difference between contributed capital and retained earnings.
14. Explain how the multistep form of income statement differs from the single-step form. What are the relative merits of each?
15. Why are other revenues and expenses separated from operating revenues and expenses in the multistep income statement?
16. Define *liquidity* and name two measures of liquidity.
17. How is the current ratio computed and why is it important?
18. Which is the more important goal—liquidity or profitability? Explain your answer.
19. Name five measures of profitability.
20. Evaluate the following statement: "Return on assets is a better measure of profitability than profit margin."

Short Exercises

SE 1.
LO 3 Accounting Conventions

State which of the accounting conventions—comparability and consistency, materiality, conservatism, full disclosure, or cost-benefit—is being followed in each of these cases:

1. Management provides detailed information about the company's long-term debt in the notes to the financial statements.
2. A company does not account separately for discounts received for prompt payment of accounts payable because few such transactions occur and the total amount of the discounts is small.
3. Management eliminates a weekly report on property, plant, and equipment acquisitions and disposals because no one finds it useful.

4. A company follows the policy of recognizing a loss on inventory when the market value of an item falls below its cost but does nothing if the market value rises.
5. When several accounting methods are acceptable, management chooses a single method and follows that method from year to year.

SE 2. **LO 5 Classification of Accounts: Balance Sheet**

Tell whether each of the following accounts is a current asset; an investment; property, plant, and equipment; an intangible asset; a current liability; a long-term liability; owner's equity; or not on the balance sheet.

1. Delivery Trucks
2. Accounts Payable
3. Note Payable (due in 90 days)
4. Delivery Expense
5. Y. San, Capital
6. Prepaid Insurance
7. Trademark
8. Investment to Be Held Six Months
9. Interest Payable
10. Factory Not Used in Business

SE 3. **LO 5 Classified Balance Sheet**

Using the following accounts, prepare a classified balance sheet at year end, May 31, 20xx: Accounts Payable, $400; Accounts Receivable, $550; Accumulated Depreciation, Equipment, $350; Cash, $100; Equipment, $2,000; Franchise, $100; Investments (long-term), $250; Merchandise Inventory, $300; Notes Payable (long-term), $200; B. Pamp, Capital, ?; and Wages Payable, $50.

SE 4. **LO 6 Classification of Accounts: Income Statement**

Tell whether each of the following accounts is part of net sales, cost of goods sold, operating expenses, other revenues and expenses, or not on the income statement.

1. Delivery Expense
2. Interest Expense
3. Unearned Revenue
4. Sales Returns and Allowances
5. Purchases
6. Depreciation Expense
7. Investment Income
8. Withdrawals

SE 5. **LO 6 Single-Step Income Statement**

Using the following accounts, prepare a single-step income statement at year end, May 31, 20xx: Cost of Goods Sold, $280; General Expenses, $150; Interest Expense, $70; Interest Income, $30; Net Sales, $800; and Selling Expenses, $185.

SE 6. **LO 6 Multistep Income Statement**

Using the accounts presented in **SE 5**, prepare a multistep income statement.

SE 7. **LO 7 Liquidity Ratios**

Using the following information from a year-end balance sheet, compute working capital and the current ratio.

Accounts Payable	$ 7,000
Accounts Receivable	10,000
Cash	4,000
V. Smyth, Capital	20,000
Marketable Securities	2,000
Merchandise Inventory	12,000
Notes Payable in Three Years	13,000
Property, Plant, and Equipment	40,000

SE 8. **LO 7 Profitability Ratios**

Using the following information from a balance sheet and an income statement, compute the (1) profit margin, (2) asset turnover, (3) return on assets, (4) debt to equity, and (5) return on equity. (The previous year's total assets were $100,000 and owner's equity was $70,000.)

Total Assets	$120,000	Net Sales	$130,000
Total Liabilities	30,000	Cost of Goods Sold	70,000
Total Owner's Equity	90,000	Operating Expenses	45,000

EXERCISES

E 1. **LO 3 Accounting Concepts and Conventions**

Each of the following statements violates a convention in accounting. State which of the following accounting conventions is violated: comparability and consistency, materiality, conservatism, full disclosure, or cost-benefit.

1. A series of reports that are time-consuming and expensive to prepare is presented to the board of directors each month even though the reports are never used.

2. A company changes its method of accounting for depreciation.
3. The company in **2** does not indicate in the financial statements that the method of depreciation was changed, nor does it specify the effect of the change on net income.
4. A new office building next to the factory is debited to the Factory account because it represents a fairly small dollar amount in relation to the factory.
5. The asset account for a pickup truck still used in the business is written down to what the truck could be sold for even though the carrying value under conventional depreciation methods is higher.

E 2. **LO 1 LO 2 LO 3 Financial Accounting Concepts**

The lettered items below represent a classification scheme for the concepts of financial accounting. Match each numbered term with the letter of the category in which it belongs.

a. Decision makers (users of accounting information)
b. Business activities or entities relevant to accounting measurement
c. Objectives of accounting information
d. Accounting measurement considerations
e. Accounting processing considerations
f. Qualitative characteristics
g. Accounting conventions
h. Financial statements

1. Conservatism
2. Verifiability
3. Statement of cash flows
4. Materiality
5. Reliability
6. Recognition
7. Cost-benefit
8. Understandability
9. Business transactions
10. Consistency
11. Full disclosure
12. Furnishing information useful to investors and creditors
13. Specific business entities
14. Classification
15. Management
16. Neutrality
17. Internal accounting control
18. Valuation
19. Investors
20. Timeliness
21. Relevance
22. Furnishing information useful in assessing cash flow prospects

E 3. **LO 5 Classification of Accounts: Balance Sheet**

The lettered items below represent a classification scheme for a balance sheet, and the numbered items are account titles. Match each account with the letter of the category in which it belongs.

a. Current assets
b. Investments
c. Property, plant, and equipment
d. Intangible assets
e. Current liabilities
f. Long-term liabilities
g. Owner's equity
h. Not on balance sheet

1. Patent
2. Building Held for Sale
3. Prepaid Rent
4. Wages Payable
5. Note Payable in Five Years
6. Building Used in Operations
7. Fund Held to Pay Off Long-Term Debt
8. Inventory
9. Prepaid Insurance
10. Depreciation Expense
11. Accounts Receivable
12. Interest Expense
13. Unearned Revenue
14. Short-Term Investments
15. Accumulated Depreciation
16. B. Dobecki, Capital

E 4. **LO 5 Classified Balance Sheet Preparation**

The following data pertain to a corporation: Cash, $31,200; Investment in Six-Month Government Securities, $16,400; Accounts Receivable, $38,000; Inventory, $40,000; Prepaid Rent, $1,200; Investment in Corporate Securities (long-term), $20,000; Land, $8,000; Building, $70,000; Accumulated Depreciation, Building, $14,000; Equipment, $152,000; Accumulated Depreciation, Equipment, $17,000; Copyright, $6,200;

Accounts Payable, $51,000; Revenue Received in Advance, $2,800; Bonds Payable, $60,000; Common Stock, $10 par, 10,000 shares authorized, issued, and outstanding, $100,000; Paid-in Capital in Excess of Par Value, $50,000; and Retained Earnings, $88,200.

Prepare a classified balance sheet; omit the heading.

E 5. **LO 6 Classification of Accounts: Income Statement**

Using the classification scheme below for a multistep income statement, match each account with the letter of the category in which it belongs.

a. Net sales
b. Cost of goods sold
c. Selling expenses
d. General and administrative expenses
e. Other revenues and expenses
f. Not on income statement

1. Purchases
2. Sales Discounts
3. Merchandise Inventory (beginning)
4. Interest Income
5. Advertising Expense
6. Office Salaries Expense
7. Freight Out Expense
8. Prepaid Insurance
9. Utilities Expense
10. Sales Salaries Expense
11. Rent Expense
12. Purchases Returns and Allowances
13. Freight In
14. Depreciation Expense, Delivery Equipment
15. Taxes Payable
16. Interest Expense

E 6. **LO 6 Preparation of Income Statements**

The following data pertain to a sole proprietorship: Sales, $405,000; Cost of Goods Sold, $220,000; Selling Expenses, $90,000; General and Administrative Expenses, $60,000; Interest Expense, $4,000; and Interest Income, $3,000.

1. Prepare a condensed single-step income statement.
2. Prepare a condensed multistep income statement.

E 7. **LO 6 Condensed Multistep Income Statement**

A condensed single-step income statement appears below. Present this information in a condensed multistep income statement, and tell what insights can be obtained from the multistep form as opposed to the single-step form.

Rosala Housewares Company
Income Statement
For the Year Ended June 30, 20xx

Revenues		
Net Sales	$1,197,132	
Interest Income	5,720	
Total Revenues		$1,202,852
Costs and Expenses		
Cost of Goods Sold	$ 777,080	
Selling Expenses	203,740	
General and Administrative Expenses	100,688	
Interest Expense	13,560	
Total Costs and Expenses		1,095,068
Net Income		$ 107,784

LO 7 Liquidity Ratios

E 8. The following accounts and balances are taken from the general ledger of Quan Company.

Accounts Payable	$ 49,800
Accounts Receivable	30,600
Cash	4,500
Current Portion of Long-Term Debt	30,000
Long-Term Investments	31,200
Marketable Securities	37,800
Merchandise Inventory	76,200
Notes Payable, 90 days	45,000
Notes Payable, 2 years	60,000
Notes Receivable, 90 days	78,000
Notes Receivable, 2 years	30,000
Prepaid Insurance	1,200
Property, Plant, and Equipment	180,000
F. Abruzzi, Capital	84,900
Salaries Payable	2,550
Supplies	1,050
Property Taxes Payable	3,750
Unearned Revenue	2,250

Compute the (1) working capital and (2) current ratio.

LO 7 Profitability Ratios

E 9. The following end-of-year amounts are taken from the financial statements of Van Guyse Company: Total Assets, $852,000; Total Liabilities, $344,000; Owner's Equity, $508,000; Net Sales, $1,564,000; Cost of Goods Sold, $972,000; Operating Expenses, $404,000; and Withdrawals, $80,000.

During the past year, total assets increased by $150,000. Total owner's equity was affected only by net income and withdrawals.

Compute (1) profit margin, (2) asset turnover, (3) return on assets, (4) debt to equity, and (5) return on equity.

LO 7 Computation of Ratios

E 10. The simplified balance sheet and income statement for a sole proprietorship appear below and on the following page.

Total assets and owner's equity at the beginning of 20xx were $360,000 and $280,000, respectively.

Balance Sheet
December 31, 20xx

Assets		**Liabilities**	
Current Assets	$100,000	Current Liabilities	$ 40,000
Investments	20,000	Long-Term Liabilities	60,000
Property, Plant, and Equipment	293,000	Total Liabilities	$100,000
Intangible Assets	27,000	**Owner's Equity**	
		P. Cavafy, Capital	340,000
Total Assets	$440,000	Total Liabilities and Owner's Equity	$440,000

Income Statement For the Year Ended December 31, 20xx	
Net Sales	$820,000
Cost of Goods Sold	500,000
Gross Margin	$320,000
Operating Expenses	270,000
Net Income	$ 50,000

1. Compute the following liquidity measures: (a) working capital and (b) current ratio.
2. Compute the following profitability measures: (a) profit margin, (b) asset turnover, (c) return on assets, (d) debt to equity, and (e) return on equity.

PROBLEMS

P 1. **LO 3 Accounting Conventions**

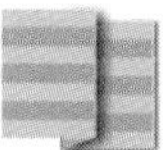

In each case below, accounting conventions may have been violated.

1. Figuero Manufacturing Company uses the cost method for computing the balance sheet amount of inventory unless the market value of the inventory is less than the cost, in which case the market value is used. At the end of the current year, the market value is $77,000 and the cost is $80,000. Figuero uses the $77,000 figure to compute net income because management feels it is the more cautious approach.
2. Margolis Company has annual sales of $5,000,000. It follows the practice of charging any items costing less than $100 to expenses in the year purchased. During the current year, it purchased several chairs for the executive conference rooms at $97 each, including freight. Although the chairs were expected to last for at least ten years, they were charged as an expense in accordance with company policy.
3. Choi Company closed its books on December 31, 20x3, before preparing its annual report. On December 30, 20x3, a fire destroyed one of the company's two factories. Although the company had fire insurance and would not suffer a loss on the building, a significant decrease in sales in 20x4 was expected because of the fire. The fire damage was not reported in the 20x3 financial statements because the operations for that year were not affected by the fire.
4. Shumate Drug Company spends a substantial portion of its profits on research and development. The company has been reporting its $2,500,000 expenditure for research and development as a lump sum, but management recently decided to begin classifying the expenditures by project even though the recordkeeping costs will increase.
5. During the current year, McMillan Company changed from one generally accepted method of accounting for inventories to another method.

REQUIRED

In each case, state the convention that applies, tell whether or not the treatment is in accord with the convention and generally accepted accounting principles, and briefly explain why.

P 2. **LO 6 Forms of the Income Statement**

The income statement accounts from the September 30, 20x2, year-end adjusted trial balance of Muramoto Hardware Company appear at the top of the next page. Beginning merchandise inventory was $350,400 and ending merchandise inventory is $315,300. The company is a sole proprietorship.

REQUIRED

From the information provided, prepare the following:

1. A detailed income statement.

Account Name	Debit	Credit
Sales		$1,082,460
Sales Returns and Allowances	$ 30,596	
Purchases	424,672	
Purchases Returns and Allowances		12,318
Freight In	22,442	
Sales Salaries Expense	204,060	
Sales Supplies Expense	3,284	
Rent Expense, Selling Space	36,000	
Utilities Expense, Selling Space	22,512	
Advertising Expense	43,972	
Depreciation Expense, Selling Fixtures	13,556	
Office Salaries Expense	95,824	
Office Supplies Expense	1,564	
Rent Expense, Office Space	8,000	
Depreciation Expense, Office Equipment	6,502	
Utilities Expense, Office Space	6,228	
Postage Expense	1,252	
Insurance Expense	5,400	
Miscellaneous Expense	962	
Interest Expense	7,200	
Interest Income		1,600

2. A condensed income statement in multistep form.
3. A condensed income statement in single-step form.

P 3. **LO 5 Classified Balance Sheet**

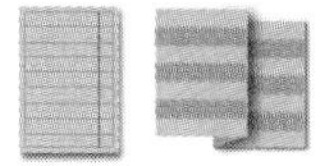

The following information was taken from the September 30, 20x2, post-closing trial balance of Tasheki Hardware Company.

Account Name	Debit	Credit
Cash	$ 48,000	
Short-Term Investments	26,300	
Notes Receivable	90,000	
Accounts Receivable	153,140	
Merchandise Inventory	313,500	
Prepaid Rent	4,000	
Prepaid Insurance	2,400	
Sales Supplies	852	
Office Supplies	194	
Land Held for Future Expansion	23,000	
Selling Fixtures	144,800	
Accumulated Depreciation, Selling Fixtures		$ 44,000
Office Equipment	48,200	
Accumulated Depreciation, Office Equipment		24,100
Trademark	8,000	
Accounts Payable		219,490
Salaries Payable		1,574
Interest Payable		1,200
Notes Payable (due in three years)		72,000
Thomas Tasheki, Capital		500,022

REQUIRED

From the information provided, prepare a classified balance sheet.

P 4.

LO 7 Ratio Analysis: Liquidity and Profitability

Below is a summary of data taken from the income statements and balance sheets of Heard Construction Supply for the past two years.

	20x4	20x3
Current Assets	$ 183,000	$ 155,000
Total Assets	1,160,000	870,000
Current Liabilities	90,000	60,000
Long-Term Liabilities	300,000	290,000
Owner's Equity	670,000	520,000
Net Sales	2,300,000	1,740,000
Net Income	150,000	102,000

Total assets and owner's equity at the beginning of 20x3 were $680,000 and $420,000, respectively.

REQUIRED

1. Compute the following liquidity measures for 20x3 and 20x4: (a) working capital and (b) current ratio. Comment on the differences between the years.
2. Compute the following measures of profitability for 20x3 and 20x4: (a) profit margin, (b) asset turnover, (c) return on assets, (d) debt to equity, and (e) return on equity. Comment on the change in performance from 20x3 to 20x4.

P 5.

LO 5 Classified Financial
LO 6 Statement Preparation
LO 7 and Evaluation

The following accounts (in alphabetical order) and amounts were taken or calculated from the December 31, 20x4 year-end adjusted trial balance of Blossom Lawn Equipment Center: Accounts Payable, $36,300; Accounts Receivable, $84,700; Accumulated Depreciation, Building, $26,200; Accumulated Depreciation, Equipment $17,400; Building, $110,000; Cash, $10,640; Cost of Goods Sold, $246,000; Dividend Income, $1,280; Equipment, $75,600; General and Administrative Expenses, $60,600; Nancy Gregorio, Capital, $211,210; Nancy Gregorio, Withdrawals, $23,900; Interest Expense, $12,200; Inventory, $56,150; Land (used in operations), $29,000; Land Held for Future Use, $20,000; Mortgage Payable, $90,000; Notes Payable (short term), $25,000; Notes Receivable, $12,000; Sales (net), $448,000; Selling Expenses, $101,350; Short-Term Investment (100 shares of General Motors), $6,500; and Trademark, $6,750. Total assets on December 31, 20x3 were $343,950.

REQUIRED

1. From the information above, prepare (a) an income statement in condensed multi-step form, (b) a statement of owner's equity, and (c) a classified balance sheet.
2. Calculate the following measures of liquidity: (a) working capital and (b) current ratio.
3. Calculate the following measures of profitability: (a) profit margin, (b) asset turnover, (c) return on assets, (d) debt to equity, and (e) return on equity.

ALTERNATE PROBLEMS

P 6.

LO 3 Accounting Conventions

In each case that follows, accounting conventions *may* have been violated.

1. After careful study, Hawthorne Company, which has offices in 40 states, has determined that in the future its method of depreciating office furniture should be changed. The new method is adopted for the current year, and the change is noted in the financial statements.
2. In the past, Regalado Corporation has recorded operating expenses in general accounts for each classification (for example, Salaries Expense, Depreciation Expense, and Utilities Expense). Management has determined that despite the additional recordkeeping costs, the company's income statement should break down each operating expense into its components of selling expense and administrative expense.
3. Callie Watts, the auditor of Burleson Corporation, discovered that an official of the company may have authorized the payment of a $1,000 bribe to a local official. Management argued that because the item was so small in relation to the size of the company ($1,000,000 in sales), the illegal payment should not be disclosed.

4. Kuberski's Bookstore built a small addition to its main building to house a new computer games section. Because no one could be sure that the computer games section would succeed, the accountant took a conservative approach and recorded the addition as an expense.
5. Since its origin ten years ago, Hsu Company has used the same generally accepted inventory method. Because there has been no change in the inventory method, the company does not declare in its financial statements what inventory method it uses.

REQUIRED

In each case, state the convention that applies, tell whether or not the treatment is in accord with the convention and generally accepted accounting principles, and briefly explain why.

P 7. **LO 6 Forms of the Income Statement**

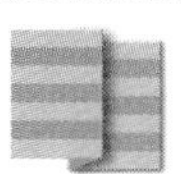

The March 31, 20x3, year-end income statement accounts that follow are for O'Dell Hardware Company. Beginning merchandise inventory was $86,400 and ending merchandise inventory is $72,500. O'Dell Hardware Company is a sole proprietorship.

Account Name	Debit	Credit
Sales		$461,100
Sales Returns and Allowances	$ 26,900	
Purchases	224,500	
Purchases Returns and Allowances		11,920
Freight In	17,400	
Sales Salaries Expense	62,160	
Sales Supplies Expense	1,640	
Rent Expense, Selling Space	7,200	
Utilities Expense, Selling Space	2,960	
Advertising Expense	16,800	
Depreciation Expense, Delivery Equipment	4,400	
Office Salaries Expense	29,240	
Office Supplies Expense	9,760	
Rent Expense, Office Space	2,400	
Utilities Expense, Office Space	1,000	
Postage Expense	2,320	
Insurance Expense	2,680	
Miscellaneous Expense	1,440	
General Management Salaries Expense	42,000	
Interest Expense	5,600	
Interest Income		420

REQUIRED

From the information provided, prepare the following:

1. A detailed income statement.
2. A condensed income statement in multistep form.
3. A condensed income statement in single-step form.

P 8. **LO 7 Ratio Analysis: Liquidity and Profitability**

Sambito Products Company has been disappointed with its operating results for the past two years. As the accountant for the company, you have the following information available to you:

	20x4	20x3
Current Assets	$ 90,000	$ 70,000
Total Assets	290,000	220,000
Current Liabilities	40,000	20,000
Long-Term Liabilities	40,000	—
Owner's Equity	210,000	200,000
Net Sales	524,000	400,000
Net Income	32,000	22,000

Total assets and owner's equity at the beginning of 20x3 were $180,000 and $160,000, respectively.

REQUIRED

1. Compute the following measures of liquidity for 20x3 and 20x4: (a) working capital and (b) current ratio. Comment on the differences between the years.
2. Compute the following measures of profitability for 20x3 and 20x4: (a) profit margin, (b) asset turnover, (c) return on assets, (d) debt to equity, and (e) return on equity. Comment on the change in performance from 20x3 to 20x4.

EXPANDING YOUR CRITICAL THINKING, COMMUNICATION, AND INTERPERSONAL SKILLS

SKILLS DEVELOPMENT

Conceptual Analysis

SD 1. **LO 3 Accounting Conventions**

Sulu Parking, which operates a seven-story parking building in downtown Chicago, has a calendar year end. It serves daily and hourly parkers, as well as monthly parkers who pay a fixed monthly rate in advance. The company traditionally has recorded all cash receipts as revenues when received. Most monthly parkers pay in full during the month prior to that in which they have the right to park. The company's auditors have said that beginning in 2001, the company should consider recording the cash receipts from monthly parking on an accrual basis, crediting Unearned Revenues. Total cash receipts for 2001 were $2,500,000, and the cash receipts received in 2001 and applicable to January 2002 were $125,000. Discuss the relevance of the accounting conventions of consistency, materiality, and full disclosure to the decision to record the monthly parking revenues on an accrual basis.

SD 2. **LO 3 Materiality**

Brown Electronics, Inc., operates a chain of consumer electronics stores in the Atlanta area. This year the company achieved annual sales of $50 million, on which it earned a net income of $2 million. At the beginning of the year, management implemented a new inventory system that enabled it to track all purchases and sales. At the end of the year, a physical inventory revealed that the actual inventory was $80,000 below what the new system indicated it should be. The inventory loss, which probably resulted from shoplifting, is reflected in a higher cost of goods sold. The problem concerns management but seems to be less important to the company's auditors. What is materiality? Why might the inventory loss concern management more than it does the auditors? Do you think the amount is material?

Ethical Dilemma

SD 3. **LO 4 Ethics and Financial Reporting**

Dawes Software, located outside Boston, develops computer software and licenses it to financial institutions. The firm uses an aggressive accounting method that records revenues from the software it has developed on a percentage of completion basis. Consequently, revenue for partially completed projects is recognized based on the proportion of the project that is completed. If a project is 50 percent completed, then 50 percent of the contracted revenue is recognized. In 20x2, preliminary estimates for a $5 million project are that the project is 75 percent complete. Because the estimate of completion is a matter of judgment, management asks for a new report showing the

Cash Flow

CD-ROM

Communication

Critical Thinking

Ethics

General Ledger

Group Activity

Hot Links to Real Companies

International

Internet

Key Ratio

Memo

Spreadsheet

project to be 90 percent complete. The change will enable senior managers to meet their financial goals for the year and thus receive substantial year-end bonuses. Do you think management's action is ethical? If you were the company controller and were asked to prepare the new report, would you do it? What action would you take?

Group Activity: Use in-class groups to debate the ethics of the action.

SD 4.
LO 4 Ethics and Financial Reporting

Orion Microsystems, Inc., a Silicon Valley manufacturer of microchips for personal computers, has just completed its year-end physical inventory in advance of preparing financial statements. To celebrate, the entire accounting department goes out for a New Year's Eve party at a local establishment. As senior accountant, you join the fun. At the party, you fall into conversation with an employee of one of your main competitors. After a while, the employee reveals that the competitor plans to introduce a new product in 60 days that will make Orion's principal product obsolete.

On Monday morning, you go to the financial vice president with this information, stating that the inventory may have to be written down and net income reduced. To your surprise, the financial vice president says that you were right to come to her, but urges you to say nothing about the problem. She says, "It is probably a rumor, and even if it is true, there will be plenty of time to write down the inventory in sixty days." You wonder if this is the appropriate thing to do. You feel confident that your source knew what he was talking about. You know that the salaries of all top managers, including the financial vice president, are tied to net income. What is fraudulent financial reporting? Is this an example of fraudulent financial reporting? What action would you take?

Research Activity

SD 5.
LO 4 Accounting and Fraud

Most university and public libraries have access to indexes of leading newspapers such as *The Wall Street Journal* and *The New York Times* on CD-ROM. Go to a library and do a search for a recent year using the key words "accounting and fraud," "accounting and restatement," or "accounting and irregularities." Choose one of the articles you find and read it. What company is involved and how is accounting connected with the fraud, restatement, or irregularity? Describe the situation. Does it involve an apparently legal or illegal activity? Does it involve fraudulent financial reporting? Explain your answer and be prepared to discuss it in class.

Decision-Making Practice

SD 6.
LO 7 Financial Analysis for Loan Decision

Rosa Corona was recently promoted to loan officer at the ***First National Bank***. She has authority to issue loans up to $50,000 without approval from a higher bank official. This week two small companies, Handy Harvey, Inc., and Sheila's Fashions, Inc., have each submitted a proposal for a six-month $50,000 loan. To prepare financial analyses of the two companies, Rosa has obtained the information summarized below.

Handy Harvey, Inc., is a local lumber and home improvement company. Because sales have increased so much during the past two years, Handy Harvey has had to raise additional working capital, especially as represented by receivables and inventory. The $50,000 loan is needed to assure the company of enough working capital for the next year. Handy Harvey began the year with total assets of $740,000 and stockholders' equity of $260,000. During the past year the company had a net income of $40,000 on net sales of $760,000. The company's current unclassified balance sheet appears as follows:

Assets		Liabilities and Stockholders' Equity	
Cash	$ 30,000	Accounts Payable	$200,000
Accounts Receivable (net)	150,000	Notes Payable (short term)	100,000
Inventory	250,000	Notes Payable (long term)	200,000
Land	50,000	Common Stock	250,000
Buildings (net)	250,000	Retained Earnings	50,000
Equipment (net)	70,000		
Total Assets	$800,000	Total Liabilities and Stockholders' Equity	$800,000

Sheila's Fashions, Inc., has for three years been a successful clothing store for young professional women. The leased store is located in the downtown financial district. Sheila's loan proposal asks for $50,000 to pay for stocking a new line of women's suits during the coming season. At the beginning of the year, the company had total assets of $200,000 and total stockholders' equity of $114,000. Over the past year, the company earned a net income of $36,000 on net sales of $480,000. The firm's unclassified balance sheet at the current date appears as follows:

Assets		Liabilities and Stockholders' Equity	
Cash	$ 10,000	Accounts Payable	$ 80,000
Accounts Receivable (net)	50,000	Accrued Liabilities	10,000
Inventory	135,000	Common Stock	50,000
Prepaid Expenses	5,000	Retained Earnings	100,000
Equipment (net)	40,000		
Total Assets	$240,000	Total Liabilities and Stockholders' Equity	$240,000

1. Prepare a financial analysis of each company's liquidity before and after receiving the proposed loan. Also compute profitability ratios before and after, as appropriate. Write a brief summary of the effect of the proposed loan on each company's financial position.
2. Assume you are Rosa Corona and you can make a loan to only one of these companies. Write a memorandum to the bank's vice president naming the company to which you would recommend loaning $50,000. Be sure to state what positive and negative factors could affect each company's ability to pay back the loan in the next year. Also indicate what other information of a financial or nonfinancial nature would be helpful in making a final decision.

FINANCIAL REPORTING AND ANALYSIS

Interpreting Financial Reports

FRA 1.
LO 7 Comparison of Profitability

Two of the largest chains of grocery/drugstores in the United States are ***Albertson's Inc.*** and ***Safeway, Inc.*** In its fiscal year ended February 3, 2000, Albertson's had a net income of $955 million, and in its fiscal year ended December 28, 1999, Safeway had a net income of $971 million. It is difficult to judge which company is more profitable from those figures alone because they do not take into account the relative sales, sizes, and investments of the companies. Data (in millions) to complete a financial analysis of the two companies follow:[15]

	Albertson's	Safeway
Net Sales	$37,478	$28,860
Beginning Total Assets	15,131	11,390
Ending Total Assets	15,701	14,900
Beginning Total Liabilities	9,609	8,308
Ending Total Liabilities	10,000	10,814
Beginning Stockholders' Equity	5,522	3,082
Ending Stockholders' Equity	5,701	4,086

REQUIRED

1. Determine which company was more profitable by computing profit margin, asset turnover, return on assets, debt to equity, and return on equity for the two companies. Comment on the relative profitability of the two companies.
2. What do the ratios tell you about the factors that go into achieving an adequate return on assets in the grocery industry? For industry data, refer to Figures 5 through 9.

3. How would you characterize the use of debt financing in the grocery industry and the use of debt by the two companies?

Group Activity: Assign each ratio or company to a group and hold a class discussion.

FRA 2.
LO 7 Evaluation of Profitability

Walt Half-Moon is the principal stockholder and president of ***Half-Moon Tapestries, Inc.,*** which wholesales fine tapestries to retail stores. Because Half-Moon was not satisfied with the company earnings in 20x3, he raised prices in 20x4, increasing gross margin from sales from 30 percent in 20x3 to 35 percent in 20x4. Half-Moon is pleased that net income did go up from 20x3 to 20x4, as shown in the following comparative income statements.

	20x4	20x3
Revenues		
Net Sales	$611,300	$693,200
Costs and Expenses		
Cost of Goods Sold	$397,345	$485,240
Selling and Administrative Expenses	154,199	152,504
Total Costs and Expenses	$551,544	$637,744
Income Before Income Taxes	$ 59,756	$ 55,456
Income Taxes	15,000	14,000
Net Income	$ 44,756	$ 41,456

Total assets for Half-Moon Tapestries, Inc., at year end for 20x2, 20x3, and 20x4 were $623,390, $693,405, and $768,455, respectively. Has Half-Moon Tapestries' profitability really improved? (**Hint:** Compute profit margin and return on assets, and comment.) What factors has Half-Moon overlooked in evaluating the profitability of the company? (**Hint:** Compute asset turnover and comment on the role it plays in profitability.)

FRA 3.
LO 7 Financial Analysis with Industry Comparison

Exhibits 2 and 5 in this chapter contain the comparative balance sheet and income statement for ***Dell Computer Corp.*** Assume you are the chief financial officer.

REQUIRED

1. Compute liquidity ratios (working capital and current ratio) and profitability ratios (profit margin, asset turnover, return on assets, debt to equity, and return on equity) for 1999 and 2000 and show the industry ratios (except working capital) from Figures 4 to 9 in the chapter. In 1998, total assets were $4,268 million and stockholders' equity was $1, 293 million.
2. Write a short memorandum to the board of directors in executive summary form summarizing changes in Dell's liquidity and profitability performance from 1999 to 2000 compared with the industry averages.

International Company

FRA 4.
LO 5 Interpretation and
LO 7 Analysis of British Financial Statements

At the top of the next page are the classified balance sheets for the British company ***Glaxo Wellcome plc,*** a pharmaceutical firm with marketing and manufacturing operations in 57 countries.[16]

In the United Kingdom, the format used for classified financial statements is usually different from that used in the United States. To compare the financial statements of companies in different countries, it is important to develop the ability to interpret a variety of formats.

REQUIRED

1. For each line on Glaxo Wellcome plc's balance sheet, indicate the corresponding term that would be found on a U.S. balance sheet. (For this exercise, consider Provisions for Liabilities and Charges to be long-term liabilities.) What is the focus or rationale behind the format of the U.K. balance sheet?

Glaxo Wellcome plc and Subsidiaries Consolidated Balance Sheets	1999 £m	1998 £m
Fixed assets		
Goodwill	144	106
Tangible assets	3,720	3,633
Investments	483	98
	4,347	3,837
Current assets		
Stocks	1,537	1,154
Debtors	2,577	2,470
Equity investments	52	28
Liquid investments	1,697	1,617
Cash at bank	217	240
	6,080	5,509
Creditors: amounts due within one year		
Loans and overdrafts	2,250	1,317
Other creditors	3,013	2,828
	5,263	4,145
Net current (liabilities)/assets	817	1,364
Total assets less current liabilities	5,164	5,201
Creditors: amounts due after one year		
Loans	1,260	1,804
Other creditors	116	161
	1,376	1,965
Provisions for liabilities and charges	595	468
Net assets	3,193	2,768
Capital and reserves		
Called up share capital	910	906
Share premium account	1,249	1,149
Other reserves	983	647
Equity shareholders' funds	3,142	2,702
Equity minority interests	51	66
Capital employed	3,193	2,768

2. Assuming that Glaxo Wellcome plc earned a net income of £1,951 million and £1,836 million in 1999 and 1998, respectively, compute the current ratio, debt to equity, return on assets, and return on equity for 1999 and 1998. (Use year-end amounts to compute ratios.)

Toys "R" Us Annual Report

FRA 5. **LO 5 LO 6 LO 7 Reading and Analyzing an Annual Report**

Refer to the Toys "R" Us annual report to answer the following questions. (Note that 2000 refers to the year ended January 29, 2000, and 1999 refers to the year ended January 30, 1999.)

1. Consolidated balance sheets: (a) Did the amount of working capital increase or decrease from 1999 to 2000? By how much? (b) Did the current ratio improve from 1999 to 2000? (c) Does the company have long-term investments or intangible

assets? (d) Did the debt to equity ratio of Toys "R" Us change from 1999 to 2000? (e) What is the contributed capital for 2000? How does it compare with retained earnings?

2. Consolidated statements of earnings: (a) Does Toys "R" Us use a multistep or a single-step form of income statement? (b) Is it a comparative statement? (c) What is the trend of net earnings? (d) How significant are income taxes for Toys "R" Us? (e) Did the profit margin increase from 1999 to 2000? (f) Did asset turnover improve from 1999 to 2000? (g) Did the return on assets increase from 1999 to 2000? (h) Did the return on equity increase from 1999 to 2000? Total assets and total stockholders' equity for 1998 may be obtained from the financial highlights.
3. Multistep income statement: In Toys "R" Us's 1987 annual report, management stated that the company's "[operating] expense levels were among the best controlled in retailing [at] 18.8 percent. . . . We were able to operate with lower merchandise margins and still increase our earnings and return on sales."[17] Prepare a multistep income statement for Toys "R" Us down to income from operations for 1999 and 2000, excluding the restructuring, and compute the ratios of gross margin, operating expenses, and income from operations to net sales. Comment on whether the company continued, as of 2000, to maintain the level of performance indicated by management in 1987. In 1987, gross margin was 31.2 percent and income from operations was 12.4 percent of net sales.

Fingraph® Financial Analyst™

FRA 6.
LO 7 Analysis of Dell Computer Corp. or Toys "R" Us

Choose one or both of the following analyses:

1. *Alternative to FRA 3:* Analyze Dell Computer Corp.'s balance sheet and income statement using Fingraph® Financial Analyst™ CD-ROM software. To do this assignment, you will need to enter the data from Dell's financial statements shown in this chapter. Complete part 1 of **FRA 3.** Prepare the memorandum required in part 2 of **FRA 3** separately.
2. *Alternative to FRA 5:* Analyze the Toys "R" Us balance sheet and income statement using Fingraph® Financial Analyst™ CD-ROM software. The CD-ROM contains the 2000 Toys "R" Us data entry spreadsheet for the annual report that appears in this textbook. Complete requirements 1, 2, and 3 of **FRA 5.**

Internet Case

FRA 7.
LO 7 Annual Reports and Financial Analysis

Obtain the annual report for a large, well-known company from either your college's library or the Needles Accounting Resource Center web site at http://college.hmco.com. Companies in this chapter include General Mills, Dell Computer, Nike, and Quaker Oats. In the annual report, identify the four basic financial statements and the notes to the financial statements. Perform a liquidity analysis, including the calculation of working capital and the current ratio. Perform a profitability analysis, calculating profit margin, asset turnover, return on assets, debt to equity, and return on equity. Be prepared to present your findings in class.

ENDNOTES

1. General Mills, Inc., "General Mills Outlines Year 2010 Growth Goals," press release, February 22, 2000.
2. *Statement of Financial Accounting Concepts No. 1,* "Objectives of Financial Reporting by Business Enterprises" (Norwalk, Conn.: Financial Accounting Standards Board, 1978), pars. 32–54.
3. *Statement of Financial Accounting Concepts No. 1,* "Qualitative Characteristics of Accounting Information" (Norwalk, Conn.: Financial Accounting Standards Board, 1980), par. 20.

4. Accounting Principles Board, "Accounting Changes," *Opinion No. 20* (New York: American Institute of Certified Public Accountants, 1971), par. 17.
5. Reynolds Metals Company, *Annual Report*, 1998.
6. Ray J. Groves, "Here's the Annual Report. Got a Few Hours?" *The Wall Street Journal Europe*, August 26–27, 1994.
7. Roger Lowenstein, "Investors Will Fish for Footnotes in 'Abbreviated' Annual Reports," *The Wall Street Journal*, September 14, 1995.
8. Quaker Oats Co., *Annual Report*, 1998.
9. Emily Nelson and Joann J. Lublin, "How Whistle-Blowers Set Off a Fraud Probe that Crushed Cendant," *The Wall Street Journal*, August 13, 1998.
10. Quaker Oats Co., *Annual Report*, 1998.
11. National Commission on Fraudulent Financial Reporting, *Report of the National Commission on Fraudulent Financial Reporting* (Washington, D.C., 1987), p. 2.
12. *Accounting Research and Terminology Bulletin*, final ed. (New York: American Institute of Certified Public Accountants, 1961), p. 20.
13. Roger Lowenstein, "Lenders' Stampede Tramples Caldor," *The Wall Street Journal*, October 26, 1995.
14. Roger Lowenstein, "The '20% Club' No Longer Is Exclusive," *The Wall Street Journal*, May 4, 1995.
15. Albertson's Inc. and Safeway, Inc., *Annual Reports*, February 3, 2000, and December 28, 1999, respectively.
16. Glaxo Wellcome plc, *Annual Report*, 1999.
17. Toys "R" Us, *Annual Report*, 1987.

- Name of the company's independent accountants (auditors). In your own words, what did the accountants say about the company's financial statements?
- The most recent price of the company's stock and its dividend per share. Be sure to provide the date for this information.

B. Industry Situation and Company Plans

Describe the industry and its outlook; then summarize the company's future plans based on your library research and on reading the annual report. Be sure to read the letter to the stockholders. Include relevant information about the company's plans from that discussion.

C. Financial Statements

Income Statement: Is the format most like a single-step or multistep format? Determine gross profit, income from operations, and net income for the last two years; comment on the increases or decreases in these amounts.

Balance Sheet: Show that Assets = Liabilities + Stockholders' Equity for the past two years.

Statement of Cash Flows: Are cash flows from operations more or less than net income for the past two years? Is the company expanding through investing activities? What is the company's most important source of financing? Overall, has cash increased or decreased over the past two years?

D. Accounting Policies

What are the significant accounting policies, if any, relating to revenue recognition, cash, short-term investments, merchandise inventories, property and equipment, and preopening costs?

What are the topics of the notes to the financial statements?

E. Financial Analysis

For the past two years, calculate and discuss the significance of the following ratios:

Option (a): Basic (After Completing Chapters 1–6)

Liquidity Ratios
- Working capital
- Current ratio

Profitability Ratios
- Profit margin
- Asset turnover
- Return on assets
- Debt to equity
- Return on equity

Option (b): Basic with Enhanced Liquidity Analysis (After Completing Chapters 1–10)

Liquidity Ratios
- Working capital
- Current ratio
- Receivable turnover
- Average days' sales uncollected
- Inventory turnover
- Average days' inventory on hand

Profitability Ratios
- Profit margin
- Asset turnover
- Return on assets
- Debt to equity
- Return on equity

Option (c): Comprehensive (After Completing Chapters 1–18)

Liquidity Ratios
- Working capital
- Current ratio
- Receivable turnover
- Average days' sales uncollected
- Inventory turnover
- Average days' inventory on hand

Profitability Ratios
- Profit margin
- Asset turnover
- Return on assets
- Return on equity

Long-Term Solvency Ratios
- Debt to equity
- Interest coverage

Cash Flow Adequacy
- Cash flow yield
- Cash flows to sales
- Cash flows to assets
- Free cash flow

Market Strength Ratios
- Price/earnings per share
- Dividends yield

Option (d): Comprehensive Using Fingraph® Financial Analyst™ Software on the CD-ROM That Accompanies This Text

2000 **&** *Beyond:*
"R" **Winning** *Strategies*

1999 **Annual** Report

This annual report is for the year ended January 29, 2000. Pages 1–7 and 20–39 reprinted courtesy of Toys "R" Us, Inc.

Table Of Contents

Financial Highlights

TOYS"R"US, INC. AND SUBSIDIARIES

(Dollars in millions except per share data) Fiscal Year Ended

	Jan. 29, 2000*	Jan. 30, 1999**	Jan. 31, 1998	Feb.1, 1997**	Feb. 3, 1996**	Jan. 28, 1995	Jan. 29, 1994	Jan. 30, 1993	Feb. 1, 1992	Feb. 2, 1991
OPERATIONS:										
Net Sales	**$11,862**	$11,170	$11,038	$ 9,932	$ 9,427	$ 8,746	$ 7,946	$ 7,169	$ 6,124	$ 5,510
Net Earnings/(Loss)	**279**	(132)	490	427	148	532	483	438	340	326
Basic Earnings/(Loss) Per Share	**1.14**	(0.50)	1.72	1.56	0.54	1.88	1.66	1.51	1.18	1.12
Diluted Earnings/(Loss) Per Share	**1.14**	(0.50)	1.70	1.54	0.53	1.85	1.63	1.47	1.15	1.11
FINANCIAL POSITION AT YEAR END:										
Working Capital	**$ 35**	$ 106	$ 579	$ 619	$ 326	$ 484	$ 633	$ 797	$ 328	$ 177
Real Estate-Net	**2,342**	2,354	2,435	2,411	2,336	2,271	2,036	1,877	1,751	1,433
Total Assets	**8,353**	7,899	7,963	8,023	6,738	6,571	6,150	5,323	4,583	3,582
Long-Term Debt	**1,230**	1,222	851	909	827	785	724	671	391	195
Stockholders' Equity	**3,680**	3,624	4,428	4,191	3,432	3,429	3,148	2,889	2,426	2,046
NUMBER OF STORES AT YEAR END:										
Toys"R"Us - United States	**710**	704	700	682	653	618	581	540	497	451
Toys"R"Us - International	**462**	452	441	396	337	293	234	167	126	97
Kids"R"Us - United States	**205**	212	215	212	213	204	217	211	189	164
Babies"R"Us - United States	**131**	113	98	82	–	–	–	–	–	–
Imaginarium	**40**	–	–	–	–	–	–	–	–	–
Total Stores	**1,548**	1,481	1,454	1,372	1,203	1,115	1,032	918	812	712

*Includes the company's Internet subsidiary, toysrus.com.

**After restructuring and other charges.

4

To Our Shareholders

This is my first formal opportunity to communicate with many of you, and I'm pleased to share with you my enthusiasm for the future of Toys"R"Us.

As a relative newcomer, I have a different perspective of the company, and I'd like you to take a moment to see it through my eyes. When I look at Toys"R"Us, I see a great family of brands and a financially healthy company with a solid cash flow. I also see lots of opportunity.

It comes as no surprise to anyone that Toys"R"Us needs to improve its performance. No doubt many of you have been frustrated by the performance of the company over the last few years, including the holiday season of 1999 which yielded disappointing results. Those financials are thoroughly examined in this report. While we can't change the past, we can learn from it. I believe we have, and I want to tell you why I'm optimistic about the future of Toys"R"Us, and what our priorities are for the next 24 months.

We've got a strong organization of talented and dedicated people, a brand that is second to none in the toy industry, and a solid financial foundation. Let me share with you the strategies that we are focused on executing in 2000 and 2001.

Differentiation.

We're going to focus on four key priorities, beginning with our merchandise offering. It is essential that we differentiate our content from that of our competitors. We will still be the headquarters for the toy brands known and loved by our customers, but we'll be more. We are committed to offering new and exciting products first, and to that end we will be focusing a significant amount of time and attention on developing exclusive new concepts and technologies to offer more unique, fun and interesting products.

We made important strides in that effort here in the U.S. recently. In February, we announced a new line of exclusive branded products with Animal Planet. Animal Planet is the fastest growing cable station in the U.S., and this unique, interactive product line will be unlike anything else on the market. The Animal Planet line will be introduced in our stores this fall, and it is only the beginning of new, exclusive products to come.

The company has also entered into an exclusive partnership with Home Depot. Together with Home Depot, we'll be the store where kids and their parents can buy "real" tools for kids — actual working tools that are scaled appropriately to a kid's size and capability. These will come complete with accessories like tool belts, safety goggles and work aprons. We'll also offer construction kits for kids that will enable them to build things such as a birdhouse or a bookshelf on their own or under the guidance of an adult. And the Home Depot line of toys will also include role-play items like workbenches or drills that actually simulate the motion of a real drill. We will begin introducing these products in our stores in May with a full assortment rolled out by the end of the summer. We are very excited about this partnership and this line of creative and interactive toys available only at Toys"R"Us.

We've signed a unique licensing agreement with OshKosh B'Gosh, Inc., for a line of baby products under the well-known OshKosh brand. These products, which will be available in our stores in August, bring additional equity to our juvenile line and will include items such as basic juvenile toys, dolls, plush, soft toys and other items.

Toys"R"Us will also develop exclusive products with our most important resources that support their principal brands. This will further strengthen our relationships with key manufacturers while providing interesting and unique products available only at Toys"R"Us.

The Animal Planet Line is only the beginning of new, exclusive products to come.

Our focus is on better category segmentation

Refining our Store Format.

There is no question that we have made significant financial investment in remodeling stores over the last few years, both in the C-3 and the Concept 2000 formats. The good news is that the new store formats are out performing the old ones — and the gap continues to widen with this more customer-friendly format. The new format is a major step forward, and provides a solid foundation on which to build. We also think it provides us with further opportunity to unlock additional performance gains.

The best news, though, is that even with the progress we've made, we're not yet close to maximizing the potential of our new format. That's why we've developed 16 test stores across the country to provide us with laboratories for experimenting with new concepts and refinements.

This test store effort focuses on the reconfiguration of fixturing, better category segmentation and clear projection of merchandising concepts — all designed to make the shopping experience more pleasant and productive for our guests, the customers who shop at Toys"R"Us. It also includes the addition of many new business categories, the addition of Imaginarium as a child development center, demonstration areas where we can delight our guests with the newest products, and a redefinition of our service level. These test stores include selling specialists and a truly service-focused management commitment. We believe the opportunities for sales growth and guest satisfaction are material. As these concepts are validated, we expect to execute significant rollout by holiday season 2000.

Redeployment of Inventory Investment.

We are redeploying inventory investment to ensure major intensification supporting the most important volume-producing toys in our assortment. We missed many selling opportunities during the holiday season in 1999 by not having enough investment behind the top 1,000 items. We will dramatically improve this process in 2000, and have already begun substantial order placements to ensure key item availability.

Our objective this year is to fund a doubling of the investment in our top 1,000 items by reducing our current levels of non-key inventory and by working with our resources to more tightly focus our investment behind their most important properties. We will still offer the broadest selection of any bricks and mortar store in the world, but this redeployment of inventory depth behind the most important items will help to energize our sales this coming holiday season by ensuring that we have the most wanted items.

Redeployment of Expense Dollars.

We have challenged each operating and support division worldwide to analyze every expense dollar and to eliminate spending that does not productively serve our guests, generate sales or improve productivity.

Those expense dollars are being redeployed to fund guest service, pricing and marketing initiatives designed to drive sales growth in our stores.

Unlocking the Value of our Assets.

There are many assets within this company that offer tremendous value to our shareholders. This was evident in our recent announcement regarding an initial public offering (IPO) plan for Toys"R"Us - Japan. Under the IPO plan, Toys"R"Us - Japan and the company will offer primary and secondary shares, respectively, to the public in Japan. Such shares should begin trading on the

Demonstration areas delight our customers

Babies"R"Us is a clear winner

Japanese OTC market on April 25, 2000. Following that offering, the company will retain a 48% ownership stake of Toys"R"Us - Japan.

This action is beneficial to our shareholders in several ways: we will continue to derive benefits from our 48% share of Toys"R"Us - Japan's future earnings, as well as through royalty income. In addition, the IPO will enable Toys"R"Us - Japan to fund its future growth without support from the company, therefore greatly enhancing our financial flexibility. Furthermore, we expect that the sale of shares, which reduces our ownership position from 80% to 48%, will result in a significant gain for the company.

We will continue to explore other opportunities and alternatives as appropriate to further unlock the value of our assets.

Other Aspects of the Business.

We have begun many initiatives in our U.S. toy stores already, and more are planned in the months ahead. But we're making strides in other areas of our business as well.

Babies"R"Us is a clear winner in the juvenile products market. This division marked the new millenium by reaching the billion-dollar sales mark in January. Babies"R"Us has excelled in all areas of the business, including outstanding guest service, terrific juvenile assortment and strong merchandising and operational capabilities. In addition, the success we have had with our Baby Registry is second to none — Babies"R"Us registers more expectant parents than any other retailer in the U.S. We're pleased with the strong growth of Babies"R"Us and expect to open 20 new stores this year.

Performance of Kids"R"Us has reached a plateau, but we are making substantial progress in rethinking how to rekindle growth in sales and profits for this division. We have seen significant success with leveraging our Kids"R"Us buying expertise and infrastructure up to our combo stores — essentially placing Kids"R"Us stores within Toys"R"Us stores — and we expect to roll out many more of these in 2000.

I mentioned the addition of Imaginarium child development centers within our Toys"R"Us stores earlier in this letter. Based on the tremendous success of the 19 initial tests of this concept, we plan to have upwards of 100 Imaginarium worlds within our Toys"R"Us stores by year-end. In addition, we expect to open five or more free-standing Imaginarium "neighborhood stores" this year as well.

Our International business had a terrific year with a much-improved performance, as the financials indicate. Our International stores have been the vanguard of the redeployment of expense and inventory dollars to maximize their opportunities for this past holiday. We think the future has never been brighter for that segment of our business. A major milestone for the year 2000 will include the opening of our 100th store in Japan, our largest International market.

Finally, our toysrus.com business has proven the power of our brand on the Internet, and we are confident that our "clicks and mortar" strategy will be a long-term winner.

During the last few months of 1999, toysrus.com became one of the fastest growing Web sites on the Internet. With its new management, the advantage of an unbeatable brand name, and brick and mortar assets, we are confident that toysrus.com will become the undisputed one-stop shop for kids, parents and grandparents anywhere in the world.

We took a giant step forward in achieving that goal in February when we announced an exciting strategic partnership between Toys"R"Us, toysrus.com and SOFTBANK, the world's leading Internet venture capital firm. SOFTBANK's $57 million investment is a strong endorsement of our Internet business. SOFTBANK's investment capital will be used to accelerate the development of toysrus.com's infrastructure to support further growth. Their track record, international savvy and unbeatable industry experience will help us in building a world-class e-commerce platform.

Conclusion.

As we look at the months ahead and as we begin to write a new chapter in Toys"R"Us history, it's important to remember that we're building on a strong foundation. Ours is a profitable business that can and will do much better.

We're moving ahead aggressively with our store refinements, adding new products and pockets of excitement as we go. Our stores are going to be more fun and interactive, and more guest-friendly. Our merchandise assortments will be more interesting and captivating with greater guest appeal than competitors can offer. These are realistic, achievable goals, and my commitment to you is that our company will put every resource we have against these goals. We're going to get better, we're going to perform better, and we're going to maintain that momentum.

Many people have asked me over the past few months about my decision to join Toys"R"Us. I can say in all honesty that after working with this organization and looking at what needs to be done, I am even more optimistic and enthusiastic than I was when I first joined. We know what we need to do. Some of you may be skeptical and say that you've heard this before. My request to you, as a shareholder, is to have the patience and the faith in Toys"R"Us to let this strategy unfold. We are moving forward with the greatest possible energy, emotion and commitment. When I look ahead to the future of Toys"R"Us, I see a bright future, and I know that the best days of this company are still in front of us.

John H. Eyler Jr.
President and
Chief Executive Officer
March 27, 2000

Financial Section

Management's Discussion and Analysis

OF RESULTS OF OPERATIONS AND FINANCIAL CONDITION

RESULTS OF OPERATIONS*

Comparison of Fiscal Year 1999 to 1998

The company's total sales increased 6% to $11.9 billion from $11.2 billion. The total sales growth was primarily driven by a 3% increase in comparable store sales, as well as continued new store expansion, partially offset by the closing of 46 under-performing stores in 1999 and 1998 (see "Restructuring and Other Charges" below). Comparable store sales for the USA toy store division increased 3%. The USA comparable toy store sales increases were driven primarily by improved merchandising trends and strong sales of Pokémon and electronic and video products. These gains were partially offset by the deflationary impact of video hardware sales, and were limited by industry-wide shortages of electronic and other products during the holiday season. The International toy store division results of operations discussed below include the results of Toys"R"Us - Japan. Total sales for the International toy store division increased 7% and comparable international toy store sales, on a local currency basis, increased 2%. The comparable international toy store sales increases reflect improved performances in several merchandise categories, in particular, the juvenile, toy and electronics categories. Total sales for the Babies"R"Us division exceeded the $1 billion milestone in 1999 and increased 28%. Comparable store sales for Babies"R"Us increased 9%. The Kids"R"Us division reported a 3% comparable store sales decrease. The company's toysrus.com Internet subsidiary reported total sales of $49 million from its inception in May 1999.

International sales were favorably impacted by the translation of local currency into U.S. dollars by approximately $59 million in 1999 and unfavorably impacted by approximately $30 million in 1998. Neither the translation of currency into U.S. dollars nor inflation had a material effect on the company's operating results for 1999.

In 1998, the company recorded restructuring and other non-recurring charges of $698 million to reposition its world-wide business, as set forth below. For comparability purposes, the following discussion regarding results of operations excludes the impact of these charges.

On a consolidated basis, 1999's cost of sales as a percentage of sales was 70.1% versus 70.2%. The USA toy store division reported cost of sales as a percentage of sales of 71.6% as compared to 71.0%. This increase was a result of increased markdowns to keep inventory fresh. The International toy store division reported cost of sales as a percentage of sales of 69.2% versus 69.1%. The Babies"R"Us division reported cost of sales as a percentage of sales of 67.2% versus 69.0%, reflecting a favorable change in the sales mix.

On a consolidated basis, selling, general and administrative expenses (SG&A) as a percentage of sales increased to 23.1% from 21.3%. This increase was due in part to establishing and operating toysrus.com, the company's Internet subsidiary, the implementation of strategic initiatives targeted to improve the company's long-term performance, and costs related to the reformatting of the company's toy stores to the C-3 format. The USA toy store division reported SG&A as a percentage of sales of 19.8% versus 18.6%, while the International toy store division reported SG&A as a percentage of sales of 23.4% versus 23.6%. The Babies"R"Us division reported SG&A as a percentage of sales of 24.0% versus 25.0%.

Depreciation and amortization increased to $278 million from $255 million. This increase was due in part to additional new stores and renovations to the C-3 format, as well as strategic investments to improve management information systems.

Interest expense decreased by $11 million. This decrease was due primarily to lower average interest rates in 1999. Also included in 1998 interest expense is $6 million relating to the early extinguishment of long-term debt.

Included in the company's 1999 results are net costs to establish and operate the company's Internet subsidiary, toysrus.com. Excluding the impact of these net costs, 1999 earnings before income taxes, net earnings and diluted earnings per share would have been $526 million, $334 million and $1.36, respectively.

The company's effective tax rate was unchanged at 36.5%, excluding the restructuring and other charges.

Comparison of Fiscal Year 1998 to 1997

The company's total sales increased to $11.2 billion from $11.0 billion. In 1998, sales were negatively impacted by the overall weakness in the worldwide toy industry which was cycling against strong sales of virtual pets, action figures and plush from the prior year. In addition, sales were negatively impacted by sales of video hardware and software at lower price points as well as the deflationary effect from sales of clearance merchandise related to the company's inventory reduction program. Comparable store sales for the USA toy store division declined 4%, while the International toy store division had a 2% comparable store sales decline, in local currency. The Babies"R"Us division reported a 19% comparable store sales increase and the Kids"R"Us division reported a 2% comparable store sales decrease.

International sales were unfavorably impacted by the translation of local currency into U.S. dollars by approximately $30 million in 1998 and $250 million in 1997. Neither the translation of currency into U.S. dollars nor inflation had a material effect on the company's operating results for 1998 and 1997.

* References to 1999, 1998 and 1997, are for the 52 weeks ended January 29, 2000, January 30, 1999 and January 31, 1998, respectively.

Management's Discussion and Analysis

OF RESULTS OF OPERATIONS AND FINANCIAL CONDITION

On a consolidated basis, cost of sales as a percentage of sales was 70.2% versus 69.8%. The USA toy store division reported cost of sales as a percentage of sales of 71.0% versus 70.5%. The International toy store division reported cost of sales as a percentage of sales of 69.1% versus 68.8%. These increases were due to a shift in the sales mix to lower margin video software merchandise from higher margin action figures and virtual pet products. The Babies"R"Us division reported cost of sales as a percentage of sales of 69.0% versus 70.7%.

On a consolidated basis, SG&A as a percentage of sales was 21.3% versus 20.2%. The USA toy store division reported SG&A as a percentage of sales of 18.6% versus 17.5%, the International toy store division reported SG&A as a percentage of sales of 23.6% versus 23.1%. These increases were primarily a result of the implementation of strategic initiatives, as well as store expansion. The Babies"R"Us division reported SG&A as a percentage of sales of 25.0% versus 27.1%.

Depreciation, amortization and write-offs were $255 million as compared to $253 million.

Interest expense increased by $17 million primarily due to higher average borrowings outstanding throughout the year as a result of the company's share repurchase programs. Also included in 1998 interest expense is $6 million relating to the early extinguishment of long-term debt.

The company's effective tax rate for 1998 was unfavorably affected by the restructuring and other charges recorded in 1998. Excluding the impact of these charges, the company's effective tax rate was unchanged at 36.5%.

Restructuring and Other Charges

During 1998, the company announced strategic initiatives to reposition its worldwide business and other charges including the customer-focused reformatting of its toy stores into the new C-3 format, as well as the restructuring of its international operations, all of which resulted in a charge of $353 million ($279 million net of tax benefits, or $1.05 per share). The strategic initiatives resulted in a restructuring charge of $294 million. The other charges of $59 million primarily consisted of changes in accounting estimates and provisions for legal settlements. The company has closed 46 under-performing stores and 7 administrative offices, as well as 4 distribution centers. The company is continuing to aggressively negotiate the closing/downsizing of the remaining stores and distribution centers included in its repositioning program and intends to execute the remainder of the initiatives included in the program. Details on the components of the charges are described in the notes to the consolidated financial statements and are as follows:

Description	Charge	Utilized in 1998	Reserve Balance 1/30/99	Utilized in 1999	Reserve Balance 1/29/00
Closings/downsizings:					
Lease commitments	$ 81	$ -	$ 81	$ 19	$ 62
Severance and other closing costs	29	4	25	11	14
Write-down of property, plant and equipment	155	155	-	-	-
Other	29	5	24	13	11
Total restructuring	$ 294	$ 164	$ 130	$ 43	$ 87
Changes in accounting estimates and provisions for legal settlements	$ 59	$ 20	$ 39	$ 9	$ 30

In 1998, the company also announced markdowns and other charges of $345 million ($229 million net of tax benefits, or $0.86 per share). Of this charge, $253 million related to markdowns required to clear excess inventory from stores, primarily to enable the company to proceed with the C-3 conversions on an accelerated basis. The company's objective with its new C-3 concept is to provide customers with a better shopping experience leading to increased sales and higher inventory turns. In addition, the company recorded $29 million in markdowns related to the store closings discussed previously. The company also recorded charges to cost of sales of $63 million related to inventory system refinements and changes in accounting estimates. Unused reserves at January 29, 2000 are expected to be utilized in the company's upcoming business cycle. Details of the markdowns and other charges are as follows:

Description	Charge	Utilized in 1998	Reserve Balance 1/30/99	Utilized in 1999	Reserve Balance 1/29/00
Markdowns					
Clear excess inventory	$ 253	$ 179	$ 74	$ 72	$ 2
Store closings	29	2	27	15	12
Change in accounting estimates and other	63	57	6	6	–
Total cost of sales	$ 345	$ 238	$ 107	$ 93	$ 14

The company has substantially completed its restructuring program that was announced in 1995, with the exception of long-term lease commitment reserves that will be utilized throughout 2000 and thereafter.

The company believes all reserves are adequate to complete its restructuring programs.

Liquidity and Capital Resources

The company's cash flow from operations were $865 million in 1999 and $964 million in 1998. The difference relates primarily to the non-cash portion of the 1998 restructuring charge as well as a significant decrease in inventories in 1998, partially offset by higher net earnings in 1999. Cash flows from operations increased to $964 million in 1998 from $509 million in 1997 primarily due to a significant reduction in inventories during 1998 as well as higher accounts payable, accrued expenses and other liabilities.

Corporate Data and Citizenship

TOYS"R"US, INC. AND SUBSIDIARIES

Annual Meeting

The Annual Meeting of the Stockholders of Toys"R"Us will be held at The 200 Fifth Club, 200 Fifth Avenue, New York, New York, on June 7, 2000 at 10:00 A.M.

The Offices of The Company are Located at

461 From Road
Paramus, New Jersey 07652
Telephone: 201-262-7800

225 Summit Avenue
Montvale, New Jersey 07645
Telephone: 201-802-5000

General Counsel

Cadwalader, Wickersham & Taft
100 Maiden Lane
New York, New York 10036

Independent Auditors

Ernst & Young LLP
787 Seventh Avenue
New York, New York 10019

Registrar and Transfer Agent

American Stock Transfer and Trust Company
40 Wall Street
New York, New York 10005
Telephone: 718-921-8200

Common Stock Listed

New York Stock Exchange, Symbol: TOY

Stockholder Information

The company will supply to any owner of its common stock, upon written request to Mr. Louis Lipschitz of the company at the above address and without charge, a copy of the annual report on Form 10-K for the year ended January 29, 2000, which has been filed with the Securities and Exchange Commission.

Stockholder information, including quarterly earnings and other corporate news releases, can be obtained by calling 800-785-TOYS, or at our web site on the Internet at www.toysrus.com

Significant news releases are anticipated to be available as follows:

Call after...	For the following...
May 15, 2000	1st Quarter Results
Aug. 14, 2000	2nd Quarter Results
Nov. 13, 2000	3rd Quarter Results
Jan. 4, 2001	Holiday Sales Results
Mar. 14, 2001	2000 Results

Corporate Citizenship

Toys"R"Us maintains a company-wide giving program focused on improving the health care needs of children by supporting many national and regional children's health care organizations. The Counsel on Economic Priority awarded Toys"R"Us the Pioneer Award in Global Ethics. This award was the direct result of the implementation of our Code of Conduct for suppliers which outlines the company's position against child labor and unsafe working conditions. In order for a vendor's product to be sold in any of our stores, they must comply with our Code of Conduct. If you would like to receive more information on Toys"R"Us' corporate citizenship please write to Mr. Roger Gaston of the company at the above address.

Visit us on the Internet at www.toysrus.com and www.imaginarium.com.

7 Accounting Information Systems

LEARNING OBJECTIVES

1. Identify the principles of accounting systems design.
2. Describe how general ledger software and spreadsheet software are used in accounting.
3. Describe the use of microcomputer systems in small businesses.
4. Explain how accountants use the Internet.
5. Explain the objectives and uses of special-purpose journals.
6. Explain the purposes and relationships of controlling accounts and subsidiary ledgers.
7. Construct and use a sales journal, purchases journal, cash receipts journal, cash payments journal, and other special-purpose journals.

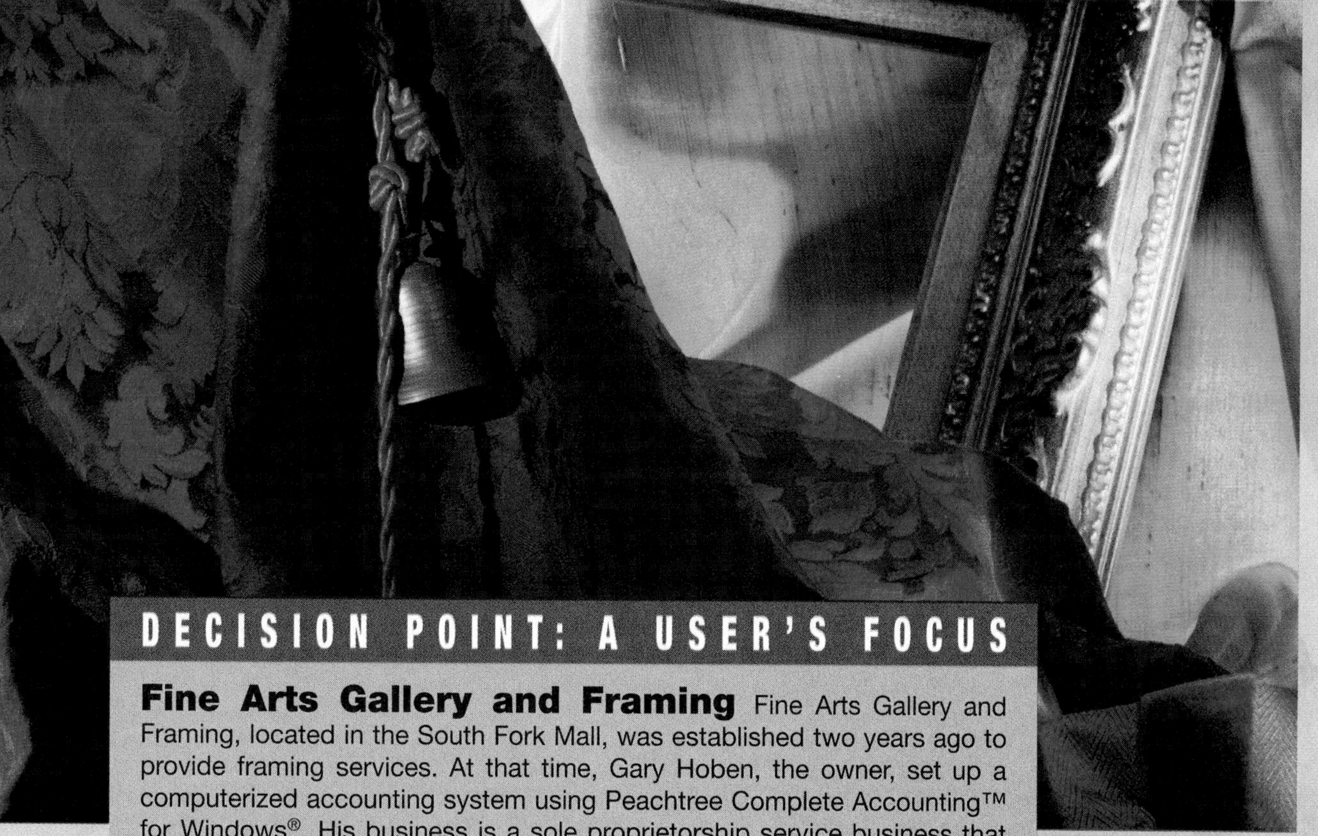

DECISION POINT: A USER'S FOCUS

Fine Arts Gallery and Framing Fine Arts Gallery and Framing, located in the South Fork Mall, was established two years ago to provide framing services. At that time, Gary Hoben, the owner, set up a computerized accounting system using Peachtree Complete Accounting™ for Windows®. His business is a sole proprietorship service business that uses Peachtree Complete's general journal and general ledger features. Because all sales were for cash or by credit card and because Hoben made a practice of paying all bills by the end of the month, the gallery had few receivables or payables. Over the past year, however, Hoben has added an inventory of color prints and posters, which carry a high profit margin. In addition, the new suppliers offer generous terms for payment. As a result, Hoben has allowed customers who buy framed prints or posters to pay over a period of three months. With the increased number of transactions involving inventory, accounts receivable, and accounts payable, Hoben's general journal/general ledger accounting system is now outdated. What kind of accounting system could Hoben use to handle the increased number and complexity of the store's transactions?

After analyzing the transactions in which his business engages, Hoben divided these transactions into five categories: credit sales, credit purchases, cash receipts, cash payments, and miscellaneous. Because more than 95 percent of the store's transactions fall into the first four categories, he decided to use Peachtree Complete's accounts payable and accounts receivable system. The accounts payable and accounts receivable system includes a separate or special-purpose journal for each of the categories that he defined. Hoben will use the general journal for his adjusting entries and some miscellaneous transactions. Because Hoben has been using Peachtree Complete's general journal/general ledger features for two years, he is eager to learn how to use the software's special journals and subsidiary ledgers. This chapter identifies the principles to consider when designing or buying a computerized accounting system and describes the basic features of computer hardware and software.

Critical Thinking Question: Will the use of a computerized accounting system for recording business transactions add more steps to the accounting cycle? Why or why not? **Answer:** No additional steps are added to the accounting cycle. However, the posting of transactions to the ledger and the preparation of a trial balance will be accomplished automatically, saving much time.

Point to Emphasize: The five kinds of transactions—credit sales, credit purchases, cash receipts, cash payments, and miscellaneous—are common in the typical business. In a manual system, a separate journal should be used for each type of transaction, with a general journal used for all other transactions. In a computer system, a separate function is chosen for each type.

Principles of Accounting Systems Design

OBJECTIVE

1 Identify the principles of accounting systems design

Related Text Assignments:
Q: 1, 2
SE: 1
SD: 1
FRA: 1, 2, 3

Clarification Note: To work effectively with a computerized accounting system, students must understand how a manual accounting system works. A computerized system functions exactly like a manual system, except that it processes information at lightning speed.

Accounting systems summarize financial data about a business and organize the data into useful forms. Accountants communicate the results to management. The means by which an accounting system accomplishes these objectives is called **data processing**. Management uses the resulting information to make a variety of business decisions. As businesses have grown larger and more complex, the role of accounting systems has also grown. Today, the need for a total information system with accounting as its base is more pressing. For this reason, accountants must understand all phases of their company's operations as well as the latest developments in systems design and technology.

Most businesses use computerized accounting systems that can be set up, monitored, and operated by accountants. However, their primary role is to provide timely accounting information to decision makers. Computer use does not eliminate the need to understand the accounting process. In fact, it is impossible to use accounting software without a basic knowledge of accounting. The opposite is also true: An accountant must have a basic knowledge of computer systems.

Analysis of computer system choices begins with the four general principles of accounting systems design: (1) cost-benefit principle, (2) control principle, (3) compatibility principle, and (4) flexibility principle.

Cost-Benefit Principle

Point to Emphasize: The cost of making a wrong decision is an intangible cost that can easily be overlooked in designing an accounting system. It is the systems analyst's job to strike the optimal balance between expected benefits and costs.

The most important systems principle, the **cost-benefit principle**, holds that the benefits derived from an accounting system and the information it generates must be equal to or greater than the system's cost. In addition to certain routine tasks—preparing payroll and tax reports and financial statements, and maintaining internal control—management may want or need other information. The benefits from that information must be weighed against both the tangible and the intangible costs of gathering it. Among the tangible costs are those for personnel, forms, and equipment. One of the intangible costs is the cost of wrong decisions stemming from the lack of good information. For instance, wrong decisions can lead to loss of sales, production stoppages, or inventory losses. Some companies have spent thousands of dollars on computer systems that do not offer enough benefits. On the other hand, some managers have failed to realize the important benefits that could be gained from investing in more advanced systems. It is the job of the accountant and the systems designer or analyst to weigh the costs and benefits.

Control Principle

Point to Emphasize: An accounting system should help protect the company's assets and provide reliable data.

The **control principle** requires that an accounting system provide all the features of internal control needed to protect the firm's assets and ensure that data are reliable. For example, before expenditures are made, they should be approved by a responsible member of management.

Compatibility Principle

Point to Emphasize: A systems analyst must carefully consider a business's activities and objectives, as well as the behavioral characteristics of its employees.

The **compatibility principle** holds that the design of an accounting system must be in harmony with the organizational and human factors of the business. The organizational factors have to do with the nature of a company's business and the formal roles its units play in meeting business objectives. For example, a company can organize its marketing efforts by region or by product. If a company is organized by region, its accounting system should report revenues and expenses by region. If a company is organized by product, its system should report revenues and expenses first by product and then by region.

The human factors of business have to do with the people within the organization and their abilities, behaviors, and personalities. The interest, support, and competence of a company's employees are very important to the success or failure of the system. In changing systems or installing new ones, the accountant must deal with the people who are presently carrying out or supervising existing procedures. Such people must understand, accept, and, in many cases, be trained in the new procedures.

Flexibility Principle

The **flexibility principle** holds that an accounting system must be flexible enough to allow the volume of transactions to grow and organizational changes to be made. Businesses do not stay the same. They grow, offer new products, add new branch offices, sell existing divisions, or make other changes that require adjustments in the accounting system. A carefully designed system allows a business to grow and change without making major alterations in the accounting system. For example, the chart of accounts should be designed to allow the addition of new asset, liability, owner's equity, revenue, and expense accounts.

Computer Software for Accounting

OBJECTIVE

2 Describe how general ledger software and spreadsheet software are used in accounting

Related Text Assignments:
Q: 3,4
SD: 2

Accountants use a variety of software programs to assist them in performing their jobs. Two of the most important types of these are general ledger software and spreadsheet software.

General Ledger Software

General ledger software is the term commonly used to identify the group of integrated software programs that an accountant uses to perform major functions such as accounting for sales and accounts receivable, purchases and accounts payable, and payroll. Today, most general ledger software is written using the Windows® operating system. Windows® has a **graphical user interface (GUI)**. A graphical user interface employs symbols called **icons** to represent common operations. Examples of icons include a file folder, eraser, hourglass, and magnifying glass. When programs use Windows® as their graphical user interface, the program is termed *Windows®-compatible*. The keyboard can be used in the traditional way, or a *mouse* or *trackball* may be used. The visual format and the ability to use a mouse or trackball make Windows®-compatible software easy to use.

Figure 1 shows how Peachtree Complete Accounting™ for Windows® uses a combination of text and icons. It is an example of what a graphical user interface looks like on your computer.

One of the benefits of Windows®-compatible software is the use of standardized terms and operations within software programs. Once you know how to use Peachtree Complete, you can use other Windows®-compatible applications, as they are similar.

Two software programs available for this book are General Ledger Software and Peachtree Complete Accounting™ for Windows®. General Ledger Software is used to supplement end-of-chapter problems. It is designed for educational use and cannot be purchased commercially. Peachtree Complete can be purchased through retail stores. It can also be used with selected end-of-chapter problems.

Figure 1
Graphical User Interface

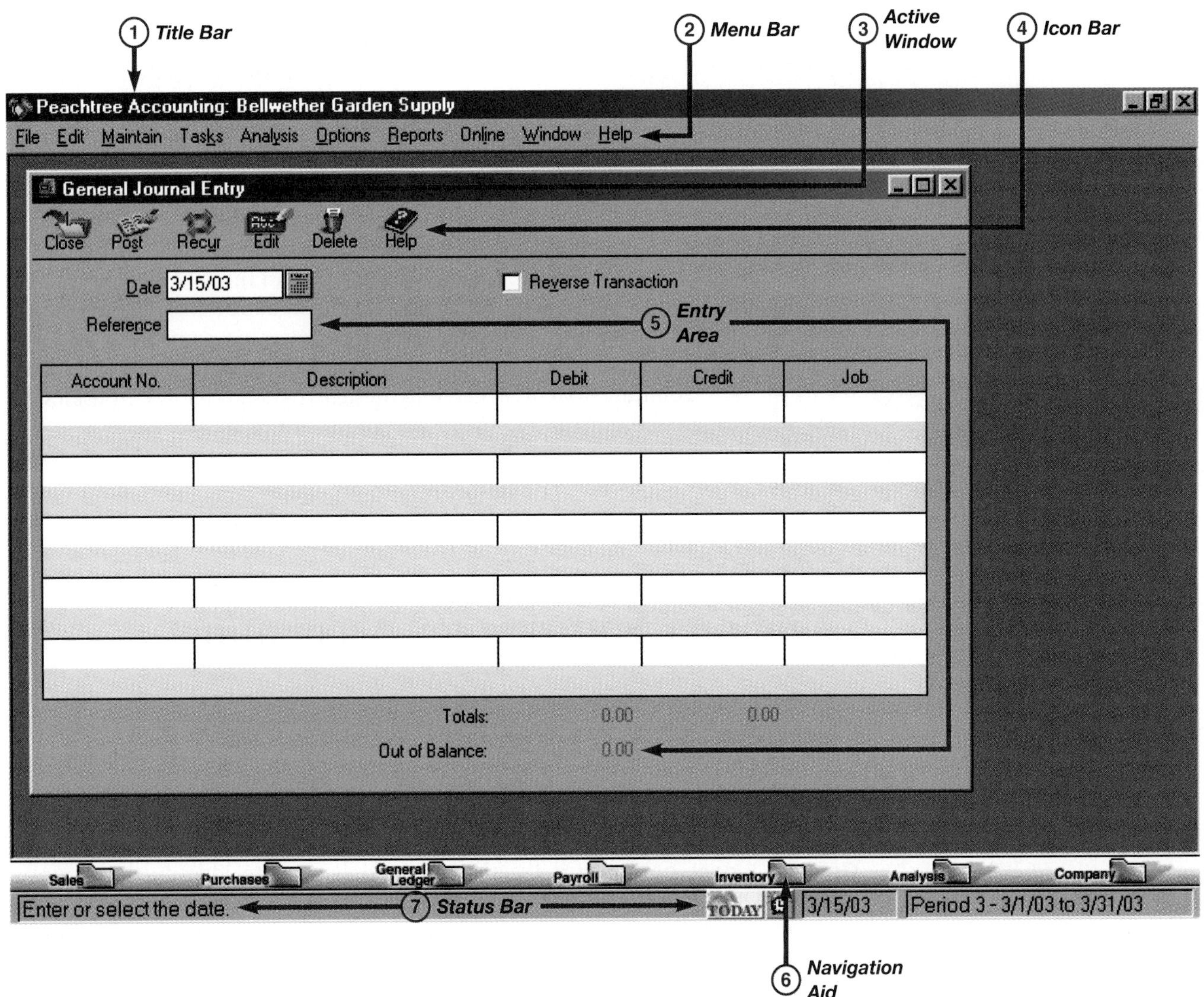

(1) ***Title Bar:*** The title bar is the bar at the top of your screen. When you enter the program, the name of the company is displayed on the title bar with Peachtree Accounting.

(2) ***Menu Bar:*** When you click on one of the menu bar headings, a submenu of options is pulled down or opened. These options are selected with a mouse or by holding down the <Alt> key and pressing the letter that is underlined in the desired menu bar option.

(3) ***Active Window:*** The "General Journal Entry" window has been chosen here in order to record an entry. This bar shows what window is open or "active."

(4) ***Icon Bar:*** The icon bar shows visual images that pertain to the window. Some icons are common to all windows, whereas other icons are specific to a particular window. You click on an icon to perform that function.

(5) ***Entry Area:*** This part of the screen is where information is entered for the journal entry.

(6) ***Navigation Aid:*** The navigation aid offers a graphical supplement to the menu bar. The major functions of the program are represented as icons or pictures that show you how tasks flow through the system.

(7) ***Status Bar:*** The gray bar (screen colors may vary) at the bottom of the window shows "help" information about the window, the current date, and the current accounting period.

Source: From Peachtree Complete Accounting™ for Windows®. Reprinted by permission.

Spreadsheet Software

Accountants use spreadsheet software in addition to general ledger software. General ledger software is effective for transactions that require double-entry accounting. Spreadsheets are used to analyze data. A **spreadsheet** is a grid made up of columns and rows into which are placed data or formulas used for financial planning, cost estimating, and other accounting tasks. Windows® Excel and Lotus are popular commercial spreadsheet programs used for financial analysis and other spreadsheet applications.

Computerized Accounting Systems

OBJECTIVE

3 Describe the use of microcomputer systems in small businesses

Related Text Assignments:
Q: 5, 6, 7
SE: 2
SD: 1, 2

Most businesses use computerized accounting systems. The parts of such systems may be put together in many ways, and companies use their computers for many different purposes. A company's overall goal is to meet all its computing needs at the lowest possible cost. The computer system is the nerve center of the company. Large, multinational companies have vast computer resources and increasingly make use of **enterprise resource management (ERM)** systems. An ERM system is a very complex software system developed by companies like SAP AG from Germany and PeopleSoft from the United States. These systems use very powerful computers that are linked together to provide communication and data transfer around the world. Their objective is to integrate not just the financial operations but all functions of the business in a vast information network. However, even in these large companies and in most small companies, the microcomputer system has become a critical element in the processing of information. This will be more critical as the Internet develops and companies expand the use of the Internet to communicate and transact business.

Reinforcement Exercise: A good way to test your students' understanding of a typical accounting system is to ask them to match the source documents shown in Figure 2 with the related processing function.

Most small businesses purchase commercial accounting software that is already programmed to perform accounting functions. Most of these programs are organized so that each module performs a major task of the accounting system. A typical configuration of general ledger software is shown in Figure 2. Note that there is a software module, or function, for each major accounting function—sales/accounts receivable, purchases/accounts payable, cash receipts, cash disbursements, payroll, and general journal. When these features interact with one another, the software is called an *integrated program*.

Point to Emphasize: At least one source document should support each business transaction entered in the records. The accounting system should provide easy reference to the source documents to facilitate subsequent examination (by an auditor, for example). Checks should be filed by check number after they have been returned by the bank, for instance.

Each transaction entered into the accounting system should be supported by **source documents**, or written evidence. Source documents verify that a transaction occurred and provide the details of the transaction. For example, a customer's invoice should support each sale on account, and a vendor's invoice should support each purchase. Even though the transactions are recorded by the computer in a file (on floppy disks or hard disks), the documents should be kept so that they can be examined at a later date if a question arises about the accuracy of the accounting records. After transactions are processed, a procedure is followed to post them to and update the ledgers and to prepare the trial balance. Finally, the financial statements and other accounting reports are printed.

Peachtree Complete Accounting™ for Windows'® general ledger program allows either batch posting or real-time posting. In a batch posting system, source documents are recorded in the appropriate journal and saved. Posting is done at the end of the day, week, or month. In a real-time posting system, documents are posted as they are recorded in the journal. The basic goal of general ledger software is to computerize existing accounting tasks to make them less time-consuming and more accurate and dependable. However, it is important to understand, in principle, just what the computer is accomplishing. Knowledge of the underlying

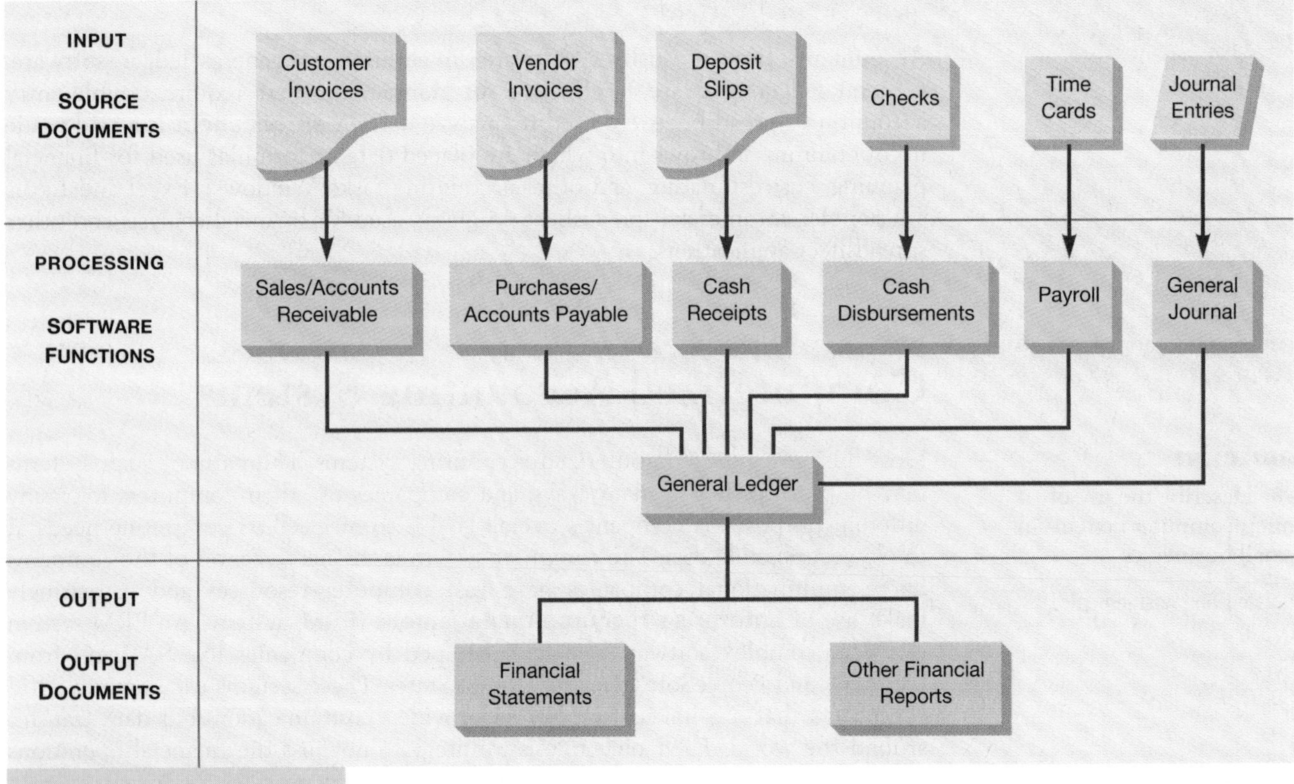

Figure 2
Microcomputer Accounting System Using General Ledger Software

accounting process helps ensure that the accounting records are accurate, helps protect the assets of the business, and aids in the analysis of financial statements.

Accountants and the Internet

OBJECTIVE

4 Explain how accountants use the Internet

Related Text Assignments:
Q: 8
SD: 4
FRA: 1

The **Internet** is the world's largest computer network. The Internet allows any computer on the network to communicate with any other computer on the network. Internet usage is the fastest-growing part of the computer revolution. To access the Internet, a computer needs a modem that connects it to a phone line. A subscription to an Internet service provider (ISP) is usually necessary. Some ISPs are America Online (AOL), MCI World Com, and AT&T. Local Internet service providers are also available.

The Internet has many capabilities:

- Electronic mail **Electronic mail (E-mail)** is the sending and receiving of communications over a computer network. *Electronic mailing lists* are subscriptions to organizations that share a common interest.
- World Wide Web The **World Wide Web** is a repository that provides access to enormous amounts of information over the Internet. It can be compared to the biggest library in the world. When people type in a World Wide Web address, they may not only get access to the material at that location, but be in a position to do what is commonly called "surfing the Web." The software used to navigate the Web is known as a *browser*. The most popular browsers today are Netscape Navigator and Microsoft Internet Explorer.
- Information retrieval **Information retrieval** is the downloading of files from the Internet to an individual's computer. Companies sometimes offer upgrades

Focus on Business Technology

Every year the American Institute of CPAs identifies the ten most important technological challenges facing businesses. In 2000, the list emphasized the growing role of the Internet in business activities and related issues of security, controls, training, reliability, and privacy. The latest list of the top ten technology priorities is as follows:[1]

1. E-business
2. Information security and controls
3. Training and technology competency
4. Disaster recovery
5. High availability and resiliency of systems
6. Technology management and budgeting
7. Electronic financial reporting
8. Other Internet issues
9. The virtual office
10. Privacy

of their software this way. Sometimes the information is free and sometimes there is a charge.

- **Bulletin boards** **Bulletin boards** allow people who have common interests to share information with one another over the Internet. Many hardware and software companies offer bulletin boards for technical support and troubleshooting.
- **E-business** **E-business** is a term used to describe the broadest use of the Internet by business. It involves the use of the Internet to perform a wide array of business functions including, but not limited to, electronic commerce. Examples of other uses include human resource planning, business planning, and collaborating with strategic partners.
- **Electronic commerce** Businesses and consumers increasingly are using the Internet for transacting business with vendors, suppliers, and customers. Such activities as selling books, buying stocks, and paying bills are examples. These practices and others using computers to conduct business transactions are called **electronic commerce** and provide new challenges for accountants in terms of keeping records of transactions and maintaining good internal controls.

- **Search engines** **Search engines** such as Yahoo!, Lycos, and Excite are Internet sites that enable the user to research or search for information on any topic of interest.

Manual Data Processing: Journals and Procedures

OBJECTIVE

5 Explain the objectives and uses of special-purpose journals

Related Text Assignments:
Q: 9
SE: 3
E: 1, 2
SD: 1, 5

The method of accounting described in prior chapters, and presented in Figure 3, is a form of **manual data processing**. It has been a useful way to present basic accounting theory and practice in small businesses. Data are fed into the system manually by entering each transaction from a source document into the general journal. Then each debit and credit is posted to the correct ledger account. A work sheet is used as a tool to prepare the financial statements that are distributed to users. This system, although useful for explaining the basic concepts of accounting, is actually used in only the smallest of companies.

Companies involved in more transactions, perhaps hundreds or thousands every week or every day, must have a more efficient and economical way of recording transactions in the journal and posting entries to the ledger. The easiest approach is to group typical transactions into common categories and use an input device

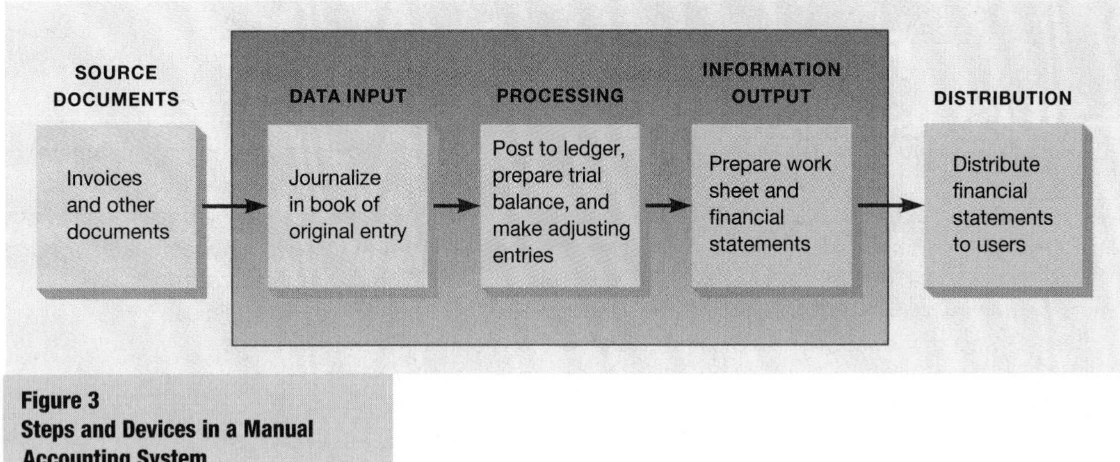

Figure 3
Steps and Devices in a Manual Accounting System

Instructional Strategy: Ask students to test their understanding of special-purpose journals by completing E 1 in class. Review the answers. Then check performance by asking how many missed 0–1, 2–3, 4–5, etc. Recommend SE 3 for those who want additional practice.

Point to Emphasize: Although a transaction could fall outside the four categories listed to the right, a transaction cannot fall into more than one category.

Common Student Confusion: Students know that all transactions can be entered into the general journal, but they do not realize that special-purpose journals save considerable amounts of time and effort. Furthermore, students sometimes mistakenly enter all transactions initially into the general journal and then transcribe them into special-purpose journals. Students also enter detail in the special-purpose journal and then enter detail instead of totals in the ledgers.

called a **special-purpose journal** for each category. The objectives of special-purpose journals are efficiency, economy, and control. Although manual special-purpose journals are used by companies that have not yet computerized their systems, the concepts underlying special-purpose journals also underlie the software programs that drive computerized accounting systems.

Most business transactions—90 to 95 percent—fall into one of the following four categories. Each kind of transaction can be recorded in a special-purpose journal.

Transaction	Special-Purpose Journal	Posting Abbreviation
Sale of merchandise on credit	Sales journal	S
Purchase on credit	Purchases journal	P
Receipt of cash	Cash receipts journal	CR
Disbursement of cash	Cash payments journal	CP

Notice that these special-purpose journals correspond to the accounting functions shown in the microcomputer system in Figure 2, except for payroll.

The general journal is used to record transactions that do not fall into any of the special categories. For example, purchase returns, sales returns, and adjusting and closing entries are recorded in the general journal. (When transactions are posted from the general journal to the ledger accounts, the posting abbreviation is J.)

Using special-purpose journals greatly reduces the work involved in entering and posting transactions. For example, instead of posting every debit and credit for each transaction, in most cases only column totals—the sum of many transactions—are posted. In addition, labor can be divided, with each journal assigned to a different employee. This division of labor is important in establishing good internal control.

Controlling Accounts and Subsidiary Ledgers

OBJECTIVE

6 **Explain the purposes and relationships of controlling accounts and subsidiary ledgers**

Controlling accounts and subsidiary ledgers contain important details about the figures in special-purpose journals and other books of original entry. A **controlling account**, also called a *control account,* is an account in the general ledger that maintains the total balance of all related accounts in a subsidiary ledger. A **subsidiary ledger** is a ledger separate from the general ledger that contains a group of related accounts; the total of the balances in the subsidiary ledger accounts equals or ties in with the balance in the corresponding controlling account. For example, up to this point a single Accounts Receivable account has been used. But the balance in the single Accounts Receivable account does not tell how much each cus-

Focus on Business Practice

Accounting information systems are obviously important for financial reporting, but they are increasingly becoming a means of providing good customer service as well. For instance, Walgreens, the world's largest prescription pharmacy company, has established direct communications with the insurance companies, employers, and government agencies that pay the bills of Walgreens' customers. From an accounting perspective, such links enhance Walgreens' profitability by eliminating rejected prescriptions, facilitating billing, and speeding collections. From the customers' point of view, instant communication with payers means faster service and immediate confirmation of payments—no forms, no paperwork, and no-hassle service.[2]

Related Text Assignments:
Q: 10, 13
SE: 5, 7, 8, 9
E: 2, 5, 6, 7, 8
P: 1, 3, 4, 5, 6, 8
SD: 3, 5

tomer bought and paid for and how much each customer owes. Consequently, in practice, all companies that sell on credit keep an individual accounts receivable record for each customer. If a company has 6,000 credit customers, it has 6,000 accounts receivable. Including all those accounts with the other assets, liabilities, and owner's equity accounts would make the ledger very bulky. Therefore, companies take the individual customers' accounts out of the general ledger and place them in a separate, subsidiary ledger. In the accounts receivable subsidiary ledger, customers' accounts are filed either alphabetically or numerically (if account numbers are used).

Discussion Question: What other general ledger accounts would be good candidates for controlling accounts? **Answer:** Any account, such as Notes Payable or Buildings, that requires a detailed listing of individual balances.

When individual customers' accounts are put in an accounts receivable subsidiary ledger, the total balance is maintained in one Accounts Receivable account in the general ledger. The Accounts Receivable account in the general ledger is the controlling account in that its balance should equal the total of the individual account balances in the subsidiary ledger, as shown in Figure 4. Entries that involve accounts receivable, such as credit sales, must be posted to the individual customers' accounts every day. Postings to the controlling account in the general ledger are made at least once a month. When the amounts in the subsidiary ledger and the controlling account do not match, the accountant knows there is an error that must be found and corrected.

Figure 4
Relationship of Subsidiary Accounts to the Controlling Account

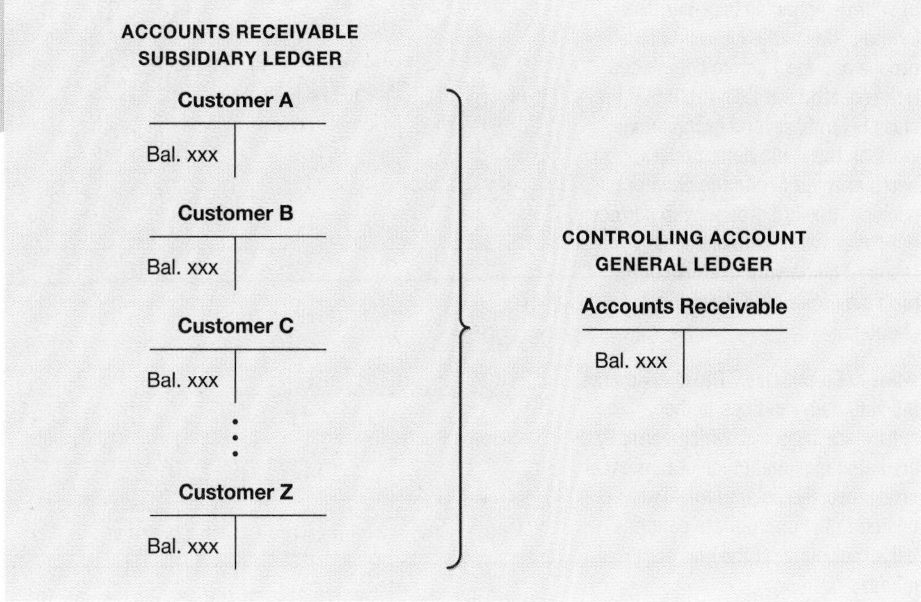

Most companies use an accounts payable subsidiary ledger as well. It is possible to use a subsidiary ledger for almost any account in the general ledger, such as Notes Receivable, Short-Term Investments, and Equipment, when management wants specific information on individual items.

Sales Journal

OBJECTIVE

7 Construct and use a sales journal, purchases journal, cash receipts journal, cash payments journal, and other special-purpose journals

Related Text Assignments:
Q: 11, 12, 13
SE: 4, 5, 6, 7, 8, 9
E: 2, 3, 4, 5, 6, 7, 8
P: 1, 2, 3, 4, 5, 6, 7, 8
SD: 5

The **sales journal** is designed to contain all credit sales, and only credit sales. Cash sales are recorded in the cash receipts journal. Exhibit 1 illustrates a page from a typical sales journal. It shows the recording of six sales transactions involving five customers.

Notice how the sales journal saves time:

1. Only one line is needed to record each transaction. Each entry consists of a debit to a customer in Accounts Receivable and a corresponding credit to Sales.
2. The account names do not have to be written out because each entry automatically is debited to Accounts Receivable and credited to Sales.
3. No explanations are necessary because the function of the special-purpose journal is to record just one type of transaction. Only credit sales are recorded in the sales journal. Sales for cash are recorded in the cash receipts journal.
4. Only one amount—the total credit sales for the month—has to be posted to the general ledger accounts. It is posted twice: once as a debit to Accounts Receivable and once as a credit to Sales. You can see the time this saves in Exhibit 1, with just six transactions. Imagine the time saved when there are hundreds of sales transactions.

Exhibit 1
Sales Journal and Related Ledger Accounts

Sales Journal — Page 1

Date		Account Debited	Invoice Number	Terms	Post. Ref.	Amount (Debit/ Credit Accounts Receivable/Sales)
July	1	Peter Clark	721	2/10, n/30	√	750
	5	Georgetta Jones	722	2/10, n/30	√	500
	8	Eugene Cumberland	723	2/10, n/30	√	335
	12	Maxwell Gertz	724	2/10, n/30	√	1,165
	18	Peter Clark	725	1/10, n/30	√	1,225
	25	Michael Powers	726	2/10, n/30	√	975
						4,950
						(114/411)

Post total at end of month.

Accounts Receivable — 114

Date		Post. Ref.	Debit	Credit	Balance Debit	Balance Credit
July	31	S1	4,950		4,950	

Sales — 411

Date		Post. Ref.	Debit	Credit	Balance Debit	Balance Credit
July	31	S1		4,950		4,950

Instructional Strategy: To underscore the advantages and form of well-designed special-purpose journals, divide the class into small groups and ask each to complete a different required item in SD 5. If the class is large, several groups may work on the same item. State whether reference to the chapter is allowed. Reward groups with correct or best answers with one less required homework exercise or problem (preferable) from this chapter.

Point to Emphasize: The checkmarks indicate daily postings to the subsidiary accounts, which normally are listed in alphabetical or numerical order. Also, the column totals are posted to the appropriate general ledger accounts at the end of the month.

Point to Emphasize: Accounts in the subsidiary ledger are maintained in alphabetical order. If account numbers are used to identify customers, the accounts would be listed in account number order.

Parenthetical Note: The daily posting to the individual accounts keeps the subsidiary ledger accounts up-to-date. The general ledger accounts, however, are normally totaled and reconciled with the subsidiary ledger once a month.

Discussion Question: Why are subsidiary accounts posted daily? Answer: (1) For control—to prevent customers from exceeding their credit limits. (2) To have up-to-date balances for customers wishing to pay their accounts.

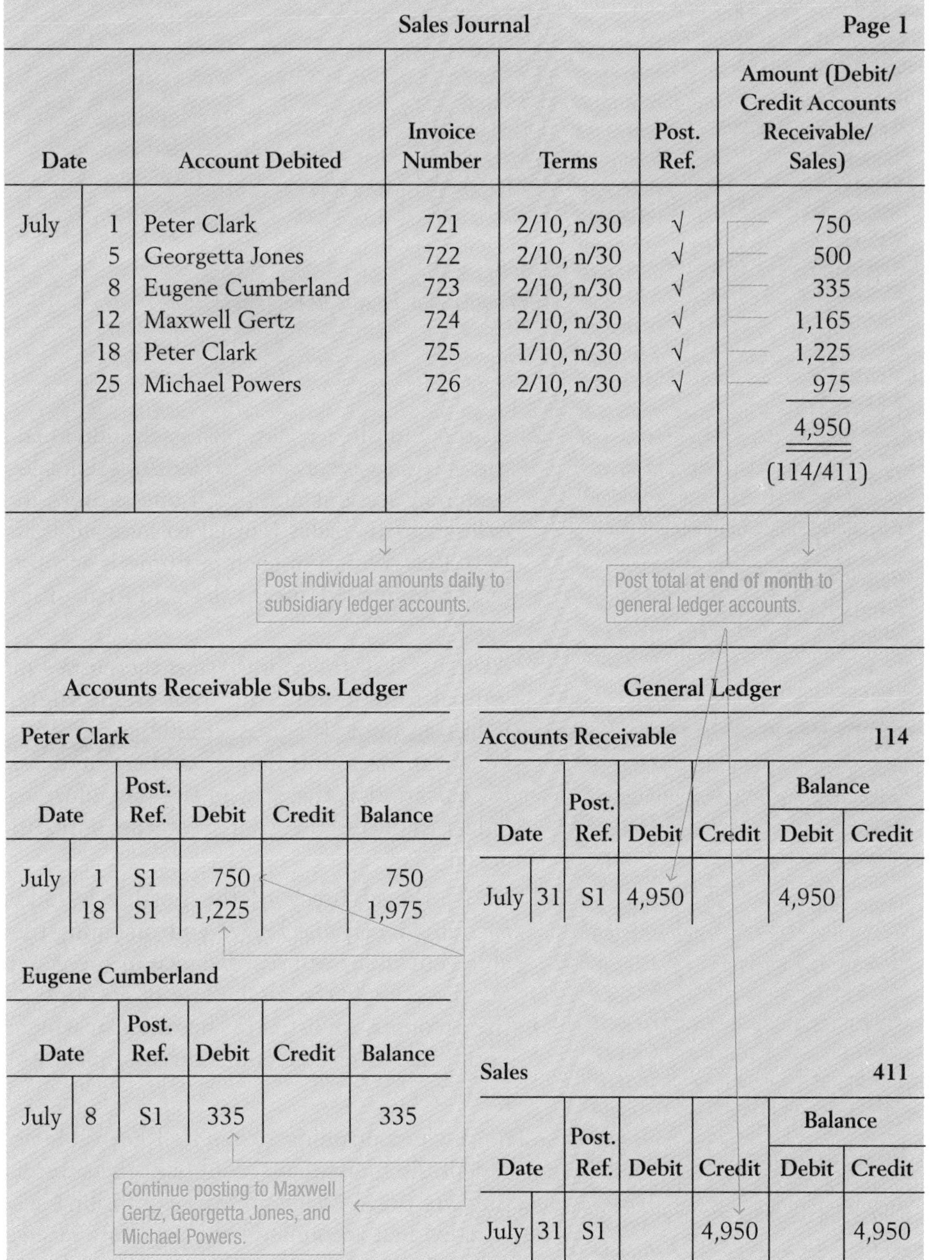

Exhibit 2
Relationship of Sales Journal, General Ledger, and Accounts Receivable Subsidiary Ledger and the Posting Procedure

Sales Journal — Page 1

Date		Account Debited	Invoice Number	Terms	Post. Ref.	Amount (Debit/ Credit Accounts Receivable/ Sales)
July	1	Peter Clark	721	2/10, n/30	√	750
	5	Georgetta Jones	722	2/10, n/30	√	500
	8	Eugene Cumberland	723	2/10, n/30	√	335
	12	Maxwell Gertz	724	2/10, n/30	√	1,165
	18	Peter Clark	725	1/10, n/30	√	1,225
	25	Michael Powers	726	2/10, n/30	√	975
						4,950
						(114/411)

Accounts Receivable Subs. Ledger

Peter Clark

Date		Post. Ref.	Debit	Credit	Balance
July	1	S1	750		750
	18	S1	1,225		1,975

Eugene Cumberland

Date		Post. Ref.	Debit	Credit	Balance
July	8	S1	335		335

General Ledger

Accounts Receivable — 114

Date		Post. Ref.	Debit	Credit	Balance Debit	Balance Credit
July	31	S1	4,950		4,950	

Sales — 411

Date		Post. Ref.	Debit	Credit	Balance Debit	Balance Credit
July	31	S1		4,950		4,950

Teaching Note: Working with special-purpose journals and subsidiary ledgers is a mechanical, not a mathematical, task. Accordingly, expect your students to be confused at first about where, when, and how transactions should be entered and posted. With practice, they will grasp the basic concepts.

Summary of the Sales Journal Procedure Exhibit 2 shows the relationships among the sales journal, the accounts receivable subsidiary ledger, and the general ledger accounts. It also illustrates the procedure for using a sales journal, the steps of which are outlined in the list that follows.

1. Enter each sales invoice in the sales journal on a single line. Record the date, the customer's name, the invoice number, and the amount. No column is needed for the terms if the terms on all sales are the same.

Discussion Question: In a schedule of accounts payable, what should the total accounts payable equal?
Answer: It should equal the total in the Accounts Payable controlling account in the general ledger.

Mitchell's Used Car Sales Schedule of Accounts Receivable July 31, 20xx	
Peter Clark	$1,975
Eugene Cumberland	335
Maxwell Gertz	1,165
Georgetta Jones	500
Michael Powers	975
Total Accounts Receivable	$4,950

Exhibit 3
Schedule of Accounts Receivable

Teaching Note: If terms of sale, including discounts, have not been previously covered, it is recommended that they be treated at this point.

Common Student Error: Students often forget to use the Post. Ref. columns of the ledger accounts, or they forget to reference the appropriate journal.

Parenthetical Note: The account number on the left is the account that was debited. The account number on the right is the account that was credited.

Point to Emphasize: In theory, the sum of the account balances from the subsidiary accounts must equal the balance in the related general ledger controlling account. In practice, however, the equality is verified only at the end of the month, when the general ledger is posted.

Point to Emphasize: Only the general ledger accounts are listed in the trial balance and financial statements.

2. At the end of each day, post each individual sale to the customer's account in the accounts receivable ledger. As each sale is posted, place a checkmark (or customer account number, if one is used) in the Post. Ref. (posting reference) column of the sales journal to indicate that the sale has been posted. In the Post. Ref. column of each customer's account, place an **S** and the sales journal page number (**S1** means Sales Journal—Page 1) to indicate the source of the entry.
3. At the end of the month, sum the entries in the Amount column in the sales journal to determine the total credit sales and post the total to the general ledger accounts (debit Accounts Receivable and credit Sales). Place the numbers of the accounts debited and credited beneath the total in the sales journal to indicate that this step in the procedure has been completed. In the general ledger, indicate the source of the entry in the Post. Ref. column of each account.
4. Verify the accuracy of the posting by adding the account balances of the accounts receivable ledger and matching the total with the Accounts Receivable controlling account balance in the general ledger. You can do this by listing the accounts in a schedule of accounts receivable. As shown in Exhibit 3, the accounts are listed in the order in which they are maintained. This step is performed after collections on account in the cash receipts journal have been posted.

The single controlling Accounts Receivable account in the general ledger summarizes all the individual accounts in the subsidiary ledger. Because the individual accounts are posted daily and the controlling account is posted monthly, the total of the individual accounts in the accounts receivable ledger equals the controlling account only after the monthly posting. The monthly trial balance is prepared using only the general ledger accounts.

SALES TAXES Many retailers are required to collect a sales tax from their customers and periodically remit the total collected to the city or state. In such cases, an additional column is needed in the sales journal to record the credit to Sales Tax Payable on credit sales. The form of the entry is shown in Exhibit 4. The procedure for posting to the ledger is exactly the same as described above, except that the total of the Sales Tax Payable column must be posted as a credit to the Sales Tax Payable account at the end of the month.

Sales Journal								Page 7
						Debit	Credits	
Date		Account Debited	Invoice Number	Terms	Post. Ref.	Accounts Receivable	Sales Tax Payable	Sales
Sept.	1	Ralph P. Hake	727	2/10, n/30	√	206	6	200

Exhibit 4
Section of a Sales Journal with a Column for Sales Tax

Point to Emphasize: Columns can be added to a special-purpose journal for accounts that are commonly used.

Purchases Journal

Common Student Error: It is easy to forget that a cash purchase is entered into the cash payments journal, not into the purchases journal.

The **purchases journal** is used to record purchases on credit. It can take the form of either a single-column journal or a multicolumn journal. In a single-column journal, shown in Exhibit 5, only credit purchases of merchandise for resale to customers are recorded. This kind of transaction is recorded with a debit to Purchases and a credit to Accounts Payable. When a single-column purchases journal is used, credit purchases of things other than merchandise are recorded in the general journal. Cash purchases are never recorded in the purchases journal; they are recorded in the cash payments journal, which we explain later.

Like Accounts Receivable, the Accounts Payable account in the general ledger is commonly used as a controlling account. The company keeps a separate account for each supplier in an accounts payable subsidiary ledger in order to know how much it owes each supplier. The process described above for using the accounts receivable subsidiary ledger and the general ledger controlling account also applies to the accounts payable subsidiary ledger and the general ledger controlling account. Thus, the total of the separate accounts in the accounts payable subsidiary ledger should equal the balance of the Accounts Payable controlling account in the general ledger. Here, too, the monthly total of the credit purchases posted to the individual accounts each day must equal the total credit purchases posted to the controlling account each month.

The procedure for using the purchases journal is much like that for using the sales journal.

1. Enter each purchase invoice in the purchases journal on a single line. Record the date, the supplier's name, the invoice date, the terms (if given), and the amount. It is not necessary to record the shipping terms in the Terms column because they do not affect the payment date.
2. At the end of each day, post each individual purchase to the supplier's account in the accounts payable subsidiary ledger. As each purchase is posted, place a checkmark in the Post. Ref. column of the purchases journal to show that it has been posted. Also place a **P** and the page number in the purchases journal (**P1** stands for Purchases Journal—Page 1) in the Post. Ref. column of each supplier's account to show the source of the entry.
3. At the end of the month, sum the Amount column and post the total to the general ledger accounts (a debit to Purchases and a credit to Accounts Payable). Place the numbers of the accounts debited and accounts credited beneath the total in the purchases journal to show that this step has been carried out.
4. Check the accuracy of the posting by adding the balances of the accounts payable ledger accounts and matching the total with the balance of the

Teaching Note: Explain that the single-column purchases journal works exactly the same way as a sales journal, except that different ledger accounts are used.

Point to Emphasize: Accounts in the subsidiary ledger are generally maintained in alphabetical order. If account numbers are used to identify suppliers, the accounts would be listed in account number order.

Exhibit 5
Relationship of Single-Column Purchases Journal to the General Ledger and the Accounts Payable Subsidiary Ledger

Purchases Journal — Page 1

Date		Account Credited	Date of Invoice	Terms	Post. Ref.	Amount (Debit/Credit Purchases/ Accounts Payable)
July	1	Jones Chevrolet	7/1	2/10, n/30	√	2,500
	2	Marshall Ford	7/2	2/15, n/30	√	300
	3	Dealer Sales	7/3	n/30	√	700
	12	Thomas Auto	7/11	n/30	√	1,400
	17	Dealer Sales	7/17	2/10, n/30	√	3,200
	19	Thomas Auto	7/17	n/30	√	1,100
						9,200
						(511/212)

Post individual amounts **daily**.

Post total at **end of month**.

Accounts Payable Subs. Ledger

Dealer Sales

Date		Post. Ref.	Debit	Credit	Balance
July	3	P1		700	700
	17	P1		3,200	3,900

Jones Chevrolet

Date		Post. Ref.	Debit	Credit	Balance
July	1	P1		2,500	2,500

Continue posting to Marshall Ford and Thomas Auto.

General Ledger

Accounts Payable — 212

Date		Post. Ref.	Debit	Credit	Balance Debit	Balance Credit
July	31	P1		9,200		9,200

Purchases — 511

Date		Post. Ref.	Debit	Credit	Balance Debit	Balance Credit
July	31	P1	9,200		9,200	

Accounts Payable controlling account in the general ledger. This step can be carried out by preparing a schedule of accounts payable.

The single-column purchases journal can be expanded to record credit purchases of things other than merchandise by adding separate debit columns for other accounts that are used often. For example, the multicolumn purchases journal in Exhibit 6 has columns for Freight In, Store Supplies, Office Supplies, and Other Accounts. Here, the total credits to Accounts Payable ($9,637) equal the

Exhibit 6
A Multicolumn Purchases Journal

Purchases Journal													Page 1
						Credit	Debits						
											Other Accounts		
Date		Account Credited	Date of Invoice	Terms	Post. Ref.	Accounts Payable	Purchases	Freight In	Store Supplies	Office Supplies	Account	Post. Ref.	Amount
July	1	Jones Chevrolet	7/1	2/10, n/30	√	2,500	2,500						
	2	Marshall Ford	7/2	2/15, n/30	√	300	300						
	2	Shelby Car Delivery	7/2	n/30	√	50		50					
	3	Dealer Sales	7/3	n/30	√	700	700						
	12	Thomas Auto	7/11	n/30	√	1,400	1,400						
	17	Dealer Sales	7/17	2/10, n/30	√	3,200	3,200						
	19	Thomas Auto	7/17	n/30	√	1,100	1,100						
	25	Osborne Supply	7/21	n/10	√	187			145	42			
	28	Auto Supply	7/28	n/10	√	200					Parts	120	200
						9,637	9,200	50	145	42			200
						(212)	(511)	(514)	(132)	(133)			(√)

Point to Emphasize: The multicolumn purchases journal can accommodate the purchase of *anything* on credit. Each column total (except the total of Other Accounts) must be posted at the end of the month.

total debits to Purchases, Freight In, Store Supplies, Office Supplies, and Other Accounts ($9,200 + $50 + $145 + $42 + $200). Again, the individual transactions in the Accounts Payable column are posted regularly to the accounts payable subsidiary ledger, and the totals of each named account column in the journal are posted monthly to the correct general ledger accounts. Entries in the Other Accounts column are posted individually to the named accounts, and the column total is not posted.

Cash Receipts Journal

All transactions involving receipts of cash are recorded in the **cash receipts journal**. Examples of such transactions are cash from cash sales, cash from credit customers in payment of their accounts, and cash from other sources. The cash receipts journal must have several columns because, although all cash receipts require a debit to Cash, they require a variety of credit entries. Note the use of an

Focus on Business Technology

In manual accounting systems, subsidiary ledgers are often maintained in alphabetical order because that is a convenient way for people to organize information. With computers, however, numbers are much faster and easier to process than letters. For this reason, numbers are essential for all types of computer data processing. There are customer numbers, order numbers, social security numbers, product numbers, credit card numbers, and many more. When numbers are used, every account can be given a unique identification number. Then the potential confusion of having more than one Janet Smith or Juan Sanchez as customers can be avoided because each customer is assigned a different number.

Other Accounts column, the use of account numbers in the Post. Ref. column, and the daily posting of the credits to other accounts.

The cash receipts journal shown in Exhibit 7 has three debit columns and three credit columns. The three debit columns are as follows:

1. *Cash* Each entry must have an amount in this column because each transaction must be a receipt of cash.
2. *Sales Discounts* This company allows a 2 percent discount for prompt payment. Therefore, it is useful to have a column for sales discounts. Notice that in the transactions of July 8 and 28, the total of debits to Cash and Sales Discounts equals the credit to Accounts Receivable.
3. *Other Accounts* The Other Accounts column (sometimes called *Sundry Accounts*) is used for transactions that involve both a debit to Cash and a debit to some other account besides Sales Discounts.

These are the credit columns:

1. *Accounts Receivable* This column is used to record collections on account from customers. The customer's name is written in the Account Debited/Credited column so that the payment can be entered in the corresponding account in the accounts receivable subsidiary ledger. Postings to the individual accounts receivable accounts are usually done daily so that each customer's account balance is up-to-date.
2. *Sales* This column is used to record all cash sales during the month. Retail firms that use cash registers would make an entry at the end of each day for the total sales from each cash register for that day. The debit, of course, is in the Cash debit column.
3. *Other Accounts* This column is used for the credit portion of any entry that is neither a cash collection from accounts receivable nor a cash sale. The name of the account to be credited is indicated in the Account Debited/Credited column. For example, the transactions of July 1, 20, and 24 involve credits to accounts other than Accounts Receivable or Sales. These individual postings should be done daily (or weekly if there are just a few of them). If a company finds that it is consistently crediting a certain account in the Other Accounts column, it can add another credit column to the cash receipts journal for that particular account.

Point to Emphasize: The cash receipts journal can accommodate *all* receipts of cash. Daily postings are made, not only to the subsidiary accounts, but also to the "other accounts." The Other Accounts column totals, therefore, are not posted at the end of the month. Only at the end of the month are the control account balances meaningful or correct.

The procedure for posting the cash receipts journal, which is shown in Exhibit 7, is as follows:

1. Post the Accounts Receivable column daily to each individual account in the accounts receivable subsidiary ledger. The amount credited to the customer's account is the same as that credited to Accounts Receivable. A checkmark in the Post. Ref. column of the cash receipts journal indicates that the amount has been posted, and a **CR** plus the cash receipts journal page number (**CR1** means Cash Receipts Journal—Page 1) in the Post. Ref. column of each ledger account indicates the source of the entry.
2. Post the debits/credits in the Other Accounts columns daily, or at convenient short intervals during the month, to the general ledger accounts. As the individual items are posted, write the account number in the Post. Ref. column of the cash receipts journal to indicate that the posting has been done. Write **CR** and the page number of the cash receipts journal in the Post. Ref. column of each ledger account to indicate the source of the entry.
3. At the end of the month, total the columns in the cash receipts journal. The sum of the Debits column totals must equal the sum of the Credits column totals (see page 322). This step is called *crossfooting*.

Exhibit 7
Relationship of the Cash Receipts Journal to the General Ledger and the Accounts Receivable Subsidiary Ledger

Cash Receipts Journal — Page 1

Date		Account Debited/Credited	Post. Ref.	Debits			Credits		
				Cash	Sales Discounts	Other Accounts	Accounts Receivable	Sales	Other Accounts
July	1	Henry Mitchell, Capital	311	20,000					20,000
	5	Sales		1,200				1,200	
	8	Georgetta Jones	√	490	10		500		
	13	Sales		1,400				1,400	
	16	Peter Clark	√	750			750		
	19	Sales		1,000				1,000	
	20	Store Supplies	132	500					500
	24	Notes Payable	213	5,000					5,000
	26	Sales		1,600				1,600	
	28	Peter Clark	√	588	12		600		
				32,528	22		1,850	5,200	25,500
				(111)	(412)		(114)	(411)	(√)

General Ledger

Cash — 111

Date		Post Ref.	Debit	Credit	Balance Debit	Balance Credit
July	31	CR1	32,528		32,528	

Accounts Receivable — 114

Date		Post. Ref.	Debit	Credit	Balance Debit	Balance Credit
July	31	S1	4,950		4,950	
	31	CR1		1,850	3,100	

Store Supplies — 132

Date		Post. Ref.	Debit	Credit	Balance Debit	Balance Credit
Bal.					500	
July	20	CR1		500	—	

Accounts Receivable Subsidiary Ledger

Peter Clark

Date		Post. Ref.	Debit	Credit	Balance
July	1	S1	750		750
	16	CR1		750	—
	18	S1	1,225		1,225
	28	CR1		600	625

Georgetta Jones

Date		Post. Ref.	Debit	Credit	Balance
July	5	S1	500		500
	8	CR1		500	—

Debits Column Totals		Credits Column Totals	
Cash	$32,528	Accounts Receivable	$ 1,850
Sales Discounts	22	Sales	5,200
Other Accounts	—	Other Accounts	25,500
Total Debits	$32,550	Total Credits	$32,550

4. Post the Debits column totals as follows:
   a. Post the total of the Cash column as a debit to the Cash account.
   b. Post the total of the Sales Discounts column as a debit to the Sales Discounts account.
5. Post the Credits column totals as follows:
   a. Post the total of the Accounts Receivable column as a credit to the Accounts Receivable controlling account.
   b. Post the total of the Sales column as a credit to the Sales account.
6. Write the account numbers below each column in the cash receipts journal as the totals are posted to indicate that this step has been completed. A **CR** and the page number of the cash receipts journal are written in the Post. Ref. column of each account to indicate the source of the entry.
7. Notice that the total of the Other Accounts column is not posted to a general ledger account, because each entry is posted separately when the transaction occurs. The individual accounts are posted in step **2.** Place a checkmark (√) at the bottom of each Other Accounts column to show that postings in that column have been made and that the total is not posted.

Cash Payments Journal

Point to Emphasize: The cash payments journal can accommodate *all* cash payments. It functions like the cash receipts journal, although it uses some different general ledger accounts.

All transactions involving payments of cash are recorded in the **cash payments journal** (also called the *cash disbursements journal*). The cash payments journal shown in Exhibit 8 has three credit columns and two debit columns. The credit columns for the cash payments journal are as follows:

1. *Cash* Each entry must have an amount in this column because each transaction must involve a payment of cash.
2. *Purchases Discounts* When purchases discounts are taken, they are recorded in this column.
3. *Other Accounts* This column is used to record credits to accounts other than Cash or Purchases Discounts. Notice that the July 31 transaction shows a purchase of land for $15,000, with a check for $5,000 and a note payable for $10,000.

The debit columns are as follows:

1. *Accounts Payable* This column is used to record payments to suppliers that have extended credit to the company. Each supplier's name is written in the Payee column so that the payment can be entered in his or her account in the accounts payable subsidiary ledger.
2. *Other Accounts* Cash can be expended for many reasons. Thus, an Other Accounts or Sundry Accounts column is needed in the cash payments journal. The title of the account to be debited is written in the Account Credited/Debited column, and the amount is entered in the Other Accounts debit column. If a company finds that a particular account appears often in the Other Accounts column, it can add another debit column to the cash payments journal.

Exhibit 8
Relationship of the Cash Payments Journal to the General Ledger and the Accounts Payable Subsidiary Ledger

Cash Payments Journal — Page 1

Date		Ck. No.	Payee	Account Credited/Debited	Post. Ref.	Credits: Cash	Credits: Purchases Discounts	Credits: Other Accounts	Debits: Accounts Payable	Debits: Other Accounts
July	2	101	Sondra Tidmore	Purchases	511	400				400
	6	102	Daily Journal	Advertising Expense	612	200				200
	8	103	Siviglia Agency	Rent Expense	631	250				250
	11	104	Jones Chevrolet		√	2,450	50		2,500	
	16	105	Charles Kuntz	Salary Expense	611	600				600
	17	106	Marshall Ford		√	294	6		300	
	24	107	Grabow & Company	Prepaid Insurance	119	480				480
	27	108	Dealer Sales		√	3,136	64		3,200	
	30	109	A&B Equipment Company	Office Equipment	144	900				400
				Service Equipment	146					500
	31	110	Burns Real Estate	Notes Payable	213	5,000		10,000		
				Land	141					15,000
						13,710	120	10,000	6,000	17,830
						(111)	(512)	(√)	(212)	(√)

Post individual amounts in Other Accounts column daily.

Post individual amounts in Accounts Payable column daily.

Post totals at end of month.

Totals not posted.

General Ledger

Cash — 111

Date		Post. Ref.	Debit	Credit	Balance Debit	Balance Credit
July	31	CR1	32,528		32,528	
	31	CP1		13,710	18,818	

Prepaid Insurance — 119

Date		Post. Ref.	Debit	Credit	Balance Debit	Balance Credit
July	24	CP1	480		480	

Continue posting to Land, Office Equipment, Service Equipment, Notes Payable, Purchases, Salary Expense, Advertising Expense, and Rent Expense.

Continue posting to Purchases Discounts and Accounts Payable.

Accounts Payable Subsidiary Ledger

Dealer Sales

Date		Post. Ref.	Debit	Credit	Balance
July	3	P1		700	700
	17	P1		3,200	3,900
	27	CP1	3,200		700

Jones Chevrolet

Date		Post. Ref.	Debit	Credit	Balance
July	1	P1		2,500	2,500
	11	CP1	2,500		—

Marshall Ford

Date		Post. Ref.	Debit	Credit	Balance
July	2	P1		300	300
	17	CP1	300		—

The procedure for posting the cash payments journal, shown in Exhibit 8, is as follows:

1. Post the Accounts Payable column daily to the individual accounts in the accounts payable subsidiary ledger. Place a checkmark in the Post. Ref. column of the cash payments journal to indicate that the posting has been made.
2. Post the debits/credits in the Other Accounts debit/credit columns to the general ledger daily or at convenient short intervals during the month. As the individual items are posted, write the account number in the Post. Ref. column of the cash payments journal to indicate that the posting has been completed and **CP** plus the cash payments journal page number (**CP1** means Cash Payments Journal—Page 1) in the Post. Ref. column of each ledger account.
3. At the end of the month, the columns are footed and crossfooted. That is, the sum of the Credits column totals must equal the sum of the Debits column totals, as follows:

Credits Column Totals		Debits Column Totals	
Cash	$ 13,710	Accounts Payable	$ 6,000
Purchases Discounts	120	Other Accounts	17,830
Other Accounts	10,000	Total Debits	$23,830
Total Credits	$23,830		

4. Post the column totals for Cash, Purchases Discounts, and Accounts Payable at the end of the month to their respective accounts in the general ledger. Write the account number below each column in the cash payments journal as the total is posted to indicate that this step has been completed and **CP** plus the cash payments journal page number in the Post. Ref. column of each ledger account. Place a checkmark under the total of each Other Accounts column in the cash payments journal to indicate that the postings in the column have been made and that the total is not posted.

General Journal

Transactions that do not involve sales, purchases, cash receipts, or cash payments should be recorded in the general journal. Usually, there are only a few such transactions. The two examples in Exhibit 9 require entries that do not fit in a special-purpose journal. They are a return of merchandise and an allowance from a supplier for credit. Adjusting and closing entries are also recorded in the general journal.

Exhibit 9
Transactions Recorded in the General Journal

General Journal — Page 1

Date		Description	Post. Ref.	Debit	Credit
July	25	Accounts Payable, Thomas Auto	212/√	700	
		Purchases Returns and Allowances	513		700
		Returned used car for credit; invoice date 7/11			
	26	Sales Returns and Allowances	413	35	
		Accounts Receivable, Maxwell Gertz	114/√		35
		Allowance for faulty tire			

Point to Emphasize: The general journal is used only to record transactions that cannot be accommodated by the special-purpose journals. Whenever a controlling account is recorded, it must be "double posted" to the general ledger and the subsidiary accounts. All general journal entries are posted daily; column totals are neither obtained nor posted.

North America that instantaneously links stores with headquarters' computer data bases to make ordering, inventory control, and customer transaction authorization more cost-efficient. Explain how this computer technology and centralized data bases comply with the principles of cost-benefit, control, compatibility, and flexibility.

Fingraph® Financial Analyst™

This category is not applicable to this chapter.

Internet Case

FRA 3.
LO 1 Accounting and Systems Careers

Many accountants are involved in systems careers. Go to the Needles Accounting Resource Center at http://college.hmco.com. Under Companies Web Links, go to the annual reports on the web sites for ***PeopleSoft***, ***Accenture*** (formerly ***Andersen Consulting***), and ***PricewaterhouseCoopers***. Find information describing these firms' businesses and look for the sections on career opportunities that relate to accounting and systems. For each firm, summarize its business and the career opportunities and be prepared to discuss what you find in class.

Endnotes

1. "E-Business Tops Tech Priorities for CPAs," *Journal of Accountancy*, March 2000.
2. Walgreen, *Annual Report*, 1993.
3. Anthony Bianco, "Virtual Bookstores to Get Real," *Business Week*, October 27, 1997.

8 Internal Control

LEARNING OBJECTIVES

1 Define *internal control,* identify the five components of internal control, and explain seven examples of control activities.

2 Describe the inherent limitations of internal control.

3 Apply internal control activities to common merchandising transactions.

4 Demonstrate the control of cash by preparing a bank reconciliation.

SUPPLEMENTAL OBJECTIVES

5 Demonstrate the use of a simple imprest system.

6 Define *voucher system* and describe the components of a voucher system.

7 Describe and carry out the five steps in operating a voucher system.

Business Document	Prepared by	Sent to	Verification and Related Procedures
① Purchase requisition	Requesting department	Purchasing department	Purchasing verifies authorization.
② Purchase order	Purchasing department	Supplier	Supplier sends goods or services in accordance with purchase order.
③ Invoice	Supplier	Accounting department	Accounting receives invoice from supplier.
④ Receiving report	Receiving department	Accounting department	Accounting compares invoice, purchase order, and receiving report. Accounting verifies prices.
⑤ Check authorization	Accounting department	Treasurer	Accounting attaches check authorization to invoice, purchase order, and receiving report.
⑥ Check	Treasurer	Supplier	Treasurer verifies all documents before preparing check.
⑦ Bank statement	Buyer's bank	Accounting department	Accounting compares amount and payee's name on returned check with check authorization.

⑦

Statement of Account with
THE LAKE PARK NATIONAL BANK
Chicago, Illinois

Martin Maintenance Company
8428 Rocky Island Avenue
Chicago, Illinois 60643

Checking Acct No
8030-647-4
Period covered
Sept.30-Oct.31,20xx

Previous Balance	Checks/Debits—No.	Deposits/Credits—No.	S.C.	Current Balance
$2,645.78	$4,319.33 --16	$5,157.12 --7	$12.50	$3,471.07

CHECKS/DEBITS			DEPOSITS/CREDITS		DAILY BALANCES	
Posting Date	Check No.	Amount	Posting Date	Amount	Date	Amount
					09/30	2,645.78
10/01	2564	100.00	10/01	586.00	10/01	2,881.78
10/01	2565	250.00	10/05	1,500.00	10/04	2,825.60
10/04	2567	56.18	10/06	300.00	10/05	3,900.46
10/05	2566	425.14	10/16	1,845.50	10/06	4,183.34
10/06	2568	17.12	10/21	600.00	10/12	2,242.34
10/12	2569	1,705.80	10/24	300.00CM	10/16	3,687.84
10/12	2570	235.20	10/31	25.62IN	10/17	3,589.09
10/16	2571	400.00			10/21	4,189.09
10/17	2572	29.75			10/24	3,745.59
10/17	2573	69.00			10/25	3,586.09
10/24	2574	738.50			10/28	3,457.95
10/24		5.00DM			10/31	3,471.07
10/25	2575	7.50				
10/25	2577	152.00				
10/28		118.14NSF				
10/28		10.00DM				
10/31		12.50SC				

Explanation of Symbols:

CM – Credit Memo
DM – Debit Memo
NSF – Non-Sufficient Funds

SC – Service Charge
EC – Error Correction
OD – Overdraft
IN – Interest on Average Balance

The last amount in this column is your balance.

Please examine; if no errors are reported within ten (10) days, the account will be considered to be correct.

FOCUS ON BUSINESS TECHNOLOGY

One of the more difficult challenges facing computer programmers is to build good internal controls into computerized accounting programs. Such computer programs must include controls that prevent unintentional errors as well as unauthorized access and tampering. The programs prevent errors through reasonableness checks that, for example, may allow no transactions over a specified amount, mathematical checks that verify the arithmetic of transactions, and sequence checks that require documents and transactions to be in their proper order. They typically use passwords and questions about randomly selected personal data to prevent unauthorized access to computer records. With unauthorized Internet access easily available in many systems, data encryption and firewalls are important. Data encryption is a way of coding data so that if they are stolen, they are useless to the thief. A firewall is a strong electronic barrier to access from outside a computer system.

Reinforcement Exercise: A good way to review the material in Figure 2 is to construct a quiz that asks students to match each business document with the preparer, recipient, and procedure. Students with little business experience often find this topic difficult to understand.

Common Student Confusion: Students often think that a purchase requisition is the same as a purchase order. Emphasize that a purchase requisition is sent to the purchasing department and that a purchase order is sent to the vendor.

Point to Emphasize: *Invoice* is the business term for *bill*. Notice that every business document must have a number, for purposes of reference.

scheme to make illegal payments to the supplier because the receiving department independently records receipts and the accounting department verifies prices. The receiving department cannot steal goods because the receiving report must equal the invoice. For the same reason, the supplier cannot bill for more goods than it ships. The accounting department's work is verified by the treasurer, and the treasurer ultimately is checked by the accounting department.

Using the forms shown with Figure 2, follow the typical sequence of documents used in this internal control plan for the purchase of 20 boxes of fax paper rolls. To begin, the credit office (requesting department) of Martin Maintenance Company fills out a formal request for a purchase, or **purchase requisition**, for 20 boxes of fax paper rolls (item 1). The department head approves it and forwards it to the purchasing department. The people in the purchasing department prepare a **purchase order**, as shown in item 2. The purchase order is addressed to the vendor (seller) and contains a description of the items ordered; the expected price, terms, and shipping date; and other shipping instructions. Martin Maintenance Company does not pay any bill that is not accompanied by a purchase order number.

After receiving the purchase order, the vendor, Henderson Supply Company, ships the goods and sends an **invoice** or bill (item 3) to Martin Maintenance Company. The invoice gives the quantity and description of the goods delivered and the terms of payment. If goods cannot all be shipped immediately, the estimated date for shipment of the remainder is indicated.

When the goods reach the receiving department of Martin Maintenance Company, an employee writes the description, quantity, and condition of the goods on a form called a **receiving report** (item 4). The receiving department does not receive a copy of the purchase order or the invoice, so its employees do not know what should be received or its value. Thus, they are not tempted to steal any excess that may be delivered.

The receiving report is sent to the accounting department, where it is compared with the purchase order and the invoice. If everything is correct, the accounting department completes a **check authorization** and attaches it to the three supporting documents. The check authorization form shown in item 5 has a space for each item to be checked off as it is examined. Notice that the accounting department has all the documentary evidence for the transaction but does not have access to the assets purchased. Nor does it write the check for payment. This means that the people performing the accounting function cannot gain by falsifying documents in an effort to conceal fraud.

Finally, the treasurer examines all the documents and issues an order to the bank for payment, called a **check** (item 6), for the amount of the invoice less any

What happens to all the paper—records and documents of all sorts—generated by a company's accounting system? Some of it, of course, must be saved for tax and legal purposes, but much of it is discarded after a time. Because accounting records and documents contain much information that companies want to keep confidential, management is reluctant to simply throw the paper in the trash. As a result, a nationwide industry of information-destruction firms has grown up and produces annual revenues of more than $250 million. Companies such as DocuShred, Inc., of Pennsylvania specialize in picking up paper and shredding it in a confidential way. Some shredding machines can make confetti of up to ten tons of paper per hour at seven to fifteen cents per pound. This is cheaper, faster, and more secret than the companies could do it themselves. Data destruction companies recycle about 95 percent of the shredded paper.[6]

appropriate discount. In some systems, the accounting department fills out the check so that all the treasurer has to do is inspect and sign it. The check is then sent to the supplier, with a remittance advice that shows the reason the check was issued. A supplier who is not paid the proper amount will complain, of course, thus providing a form of outside control over the payment. Using a deposit ticket, the supplier deposits the check in the bank, which returns the canceled check with Martin Maintenance Company's next bank statement (item 7). If the treasurer has made the check out for the wrong amount (or altered a pre-filled-in check), the problem will show up in the bank reconciliation.

There are many variations of the system just described. This example is offered as a simple system that provides adequate internal control.

Preparing a Bank Reconciliation

OBJECTIVE

4 Demonstrate the control of cash by preparing a bank reconciliation

Related Text Assignments:
Q: 9, 10
SE: 6, 7
E: 6, 7, 8
P: 1, 2, 7
SD: 2

Rarely will the balance of a company's Cash account exactly equal the cash balance shown on the bank statement. Certain transactions shown in the company's records may not have been recorded by the bank, and certain bank transactions may not appear in the company's records. Therefore, a necessary step in internal control is to prove both the balance shown on the bank statement and the balance of Cash in the accounting records. A **bank reconciliation** is the process of accounting for the differences between the balance appearing on the bank statement and the balance of Cash according to the company's records. This process involves making additions to and subtractions from both balances to arrive at the adjusted cash balance.

The most common examples of transactions shown in the company's records but not entered in the bank's records are the following:

Enrichment Note: Periodically, banks detect individuals who are *kiting*. Kiting is the illegal issuing of checks when there is not enough money to cover them. Before one kited check clears the bank, a kited check from another account is deposited to cover it, making an endless circle.

1. *Outstanding checks* These are checks that have been issued and recorded by the company but that do not yet appear on the bank statement.

2. *Deposits in transit* These are deposits that were mailed or taken to the bank but that were not received in time to be recorded on the bank statement.

Transactions that may appear on the bank statement but that have not been recorded by the company include the following:

Instructional Strategy: Students often assume that bank reconciliations do not present ethical dilemmas. Assign SD 2 to small groups for in-class discussion. Each group should appoint one member to take careful notes so that he or she can report results to the class. Challenge students to suggest at least five ways for Jean McGuire to respond. From a show of hands, determine which alternative is favored and discuss why.

1. *Service charges (SC)* Banks often charge a fee, or service charge, for the use of a checking account. Many banks base the service charge on a number of factors, such as the average balance of the account during the month or the number of checks drawn.

2. *NSF (nonsufficient funds) checks* An NSF check is a check deposited by the company that is not paid when the company's bank presents it to the maker's bank. The bank charges the company's account and returns the check so that the company can try to collect the amount due. If the bank has deducted the NSF check from the bank statement but the company has not deducted it from its book balance, an adjustment must be made in the bank reconciliation. The depositor usually reclassifies the NSF check from Cash to Accounts Receivable because the company must now collect from the person or company that wrote the check.

Critical Thinking Question: How could a small business use information from bank statements and technology to reduce its cash management costs? **Answer:** Using computer software to reconcile the cash balance with the bank statement will save time monthly. A detailed listing by category of all bank charges for previous periods may highlight areas where costs are controllable and could be reduced. Even small companies can save money by evaluating how they conduct business.

3. *Interest income* It is very common for banks to pay interest on a company's average balance. These accounts are sometimes called NOW or money market accounts, but they can take other forms. Such interest is reported on the bank statement.

4. *Miscellaneous charges and credits* Banks also charge for other services, such as collection and payment of promissory notes, stopping payment on checks, and printing checks. The bank notifies the depositor of each deduction by including a debit memorandum with the monthly statement. A bank will sometimes serve as an agent in collecting on promissory notes for the depositor. In such a case, a credit memorandum will be included.

An error by either the bank or the depositor will, of course, require immediate correction.

Illustration of a Bank Reconciliation

Point to Emphasize: The ending bank statement balance does not represent the amount that should appear on the balance sheet for cash. There are events and items, such as deposits in transit and outstanding checks, that the bank is unaware of at the cutoff date. This is why a bank reconciliation must be prepared.

Assume that the October bank statement for Martin Maintenance Company indicates a balance on October 31 of $3,471.07 and that, in its records, Martin Maintenance Company has a cash balance on October 31 of $2,415.91. The purpose of a bank reconciliation is to identify the items that make up the difference between these amounts and to determine the correct cash balance. The bank reconciliation for Martin Maintenance Company is given in Exhibit 1. The numbered items in the exhibit refer to the following:

1. A deposit in the amount of $276.00 was mailed to the bank on October 31 and has not been recorded by the bank.

2. Five checks issued in October or prior months have not yet been paid by the bank, as follows:

Check No.	Date	Amount
551	Sept. 14	$150.00
576	Oct. 30	40.68
578	Oct. 31	500.00
579	Oct. 31	370.00
580	Oct. 31	130.50

3. The deposit for cash sales of October 6 was incorrectly recorded in Martin Maintenance Company's records as $330.00. The bank correctly recorded the deposit as $300.00.

Exhibit 1
Bank Reconciliation

Martin Maintenance Company Bank Reconciliation October 31, 20xx		
Balance per bank, October 31		$3,471.07
① Add deposit of October 31 in transit		276.00
		$3,747.07
② Less outstanding checks:		
No. 551	$150.00	
No. 576	40.68	
No. 578	500.00	
No. 579	370.00	
No. 580	130.50	1,191.18
Adjusted bank balance, October 31		**$2,555.89**
Balance per books, October 31		$2,415.91
Add:		
④ Note receivable collected by bank	$280.00	
④ Interest income on note	20.00	
⑦ Interest income	15.62	315.62
		$2,731.53
Less:		
③ Overstatement of deposit of October 6	$ 30.00	
④ Collection fee	5.00	
⑤ NSF check of Arthur Clubb	128.14	
⑥ Service charge	12.50	175.64
Adjusted book balance, October 31		**$2,555.89**

Note: The circled numbers refer to the items listed in the text on the previous page and below.

Parenthetical Note: Even though the September 14 check was deducted on the September 30 reconciliation, it must be deducted again in each subsequent month in which it remains outstanding.

Clarification Note: It is possible to place an item in the wrong section of a bank reconciliation and still have it balance. The *correct* adjusted bank balance must be obtained.

Discussion Question: Some companies stipulate that checks they issue must be cashed within a certain period of time, such as 60 days, or the bank is instructed not to accept them. In a bank reconciliation, how should a company handle a check that was not deposited by the payee by the end of the stipulated time period? **Answer:** Add the amount to the balance per books.

Clarification Note: A credit memorandum means that an amount was *added* to the bank balance; a debit memorandum means that an amount was *deducted*.

4. Among the returned checks was a credit memorandum showing that the bank had collected a promissory note from A. Jacobs in the amount of $280.00, plus $20.00 in interest on the note. A debit memorandum was also enclosed for the $5.00 collection fee. No entry had been made on Martin Maintenance Company's records.

5. Also returned with the bank statement was an NSF check for $128.14. This check had been received from a customer named Arthur Clubb. The NSF check from Clubb was not reflected in the company's accounting records.

6. A debit memorandum was enclosed for the regular monthly service charge of $12.50. This charge had not yet been recorded by Martin Maintenance Company.

7. Interest earned by Martin Maintenance Company on the average balance was reported as $15.62.

Reinforcement Exercise: On May 31, a company's balance per bank is $750. Deposits in transit total $900, outstanding checks total $400, and the bank balance includes a $300 note receivable collected by the bank. What should the May 31 adjusted bank balance be? **Answer:** $1,250.

Note in Exhibit 1 that, starting from their separate balances, both the bank and book amounts are adjusted to the amount of $2,555.89. This adjusted balance is the amount of cash owned by the company on October 31 and thus is the amount that should appear on its October 31 balance sheet.

Recording Transactions After Reconciliation

Parenthetical Note: Notice that only those transactions the company was not aware of before receiving the bank statement are recorded.

The adjusted balance of cash differs from both the bank statement and Martin Maintenance Company's records. The bank balance will automatically become correct when outstanding checks are presented for payment and the deposit in transit is received and recorded by the bank. Entries must be made by the depositor (company) only for the transactions necessary to update the book balance. Only the items reported by the bank but not yet recorded by the company are recorded in the general journal by means of the following entries:

A = L + OE	Date	Account / Explanation	Debit	Credit
+ / + (A), − (A) / + (OE)	Oct. 31	Cash	300.00	
		Notes Receivable		280.00
		Interest Income		20.00
		Note receivable of $280.00 and interest of $20.00 collected by bank from A. Jacobs		
+ / +	31	Cash	15.62	
		Interest Income		15.62
		Interest on average bank account balance		
− / −	31	Sales	30.00	
		Cash		30.00
		Correction of error in recording a $300.00 deposit as $330.00		
+ / −	31	Accounts Receivable	128.14	
		Cash		128.14
		NSF check of Arthur Clubb returned by bank		
− / −	31	Bank Service Charges Expense	17.50	
		Cash		17.50
		Bank service charge ($12.50) and collection fee ($5.00) for October		

Point to Emphasize: Every entry involves either a debit or a credit to Cash.

Instructional Strategy: To assess comprehension of check-writing procedures, ask students to complete SE 3 in class.

It is acceptable to record these entries in one or two compound entries to save time and space.

Petty Cash Procedures

SUPPLEMENTAL OBJECTIVE

5 Demonstrate the use of a simple imprest system

Related Text Assignments:
Q: 11, 12, 13, 14, 15, 16
SE: 8
E: 9, 10
P: 3, 8

It is not always practical to make every disbursement by check. For example, it is sometimes necessary to make small payments of cash for such things as postage stamps, incoming postage, shipping charges due, or minor purchases of pens, paper, and the like.

For situations in which it is inconvenient to pay by check, most companies set up a **petty cash fund**. One of the best methods of maintaining control over the fund is to use an **imprest system**. Under this system, a petty cash fund is established for a fixed amount. Each cash payment from the fund is documented by a voucher. Then the fund is periodically reimbursed, based on the vouchers, for the exact amount necessary to restore the original cash balance.

Establishing the Petty Cash Fund

Some companies have a regular cashier or other employee who administers the petty cash fund. To establish the fund, the company issues a check for an amount that is intended to cover two to four weeks of small expenditures. The check is cashed, and the money is placed in the petty cash box, drawer, or envelope.

The only entry required when the fund is established is to record the check.

A = L + OE
+
−

Oct. 14	Petty Cash	100.00	
	Cash		100.00
	To establish the petty cash fund		

Making Disbursements from the Petty Cash Fund

Point to Emphasize: Even though withdrawals from petty cash are generally small, the cumulative total over time can represent a substantial amount. Accordingly, an effective system of internal control must be established for the management of the fund.

The custodian of the petty cash fund should prepare a **petty cash voucher**, or written authorization, for each expenditure, as shown in Figure 3. On each petty cash voucher, the custodian enters the date, amount, and purpose of the expenditure. The voucher is signed by the person who receives the payment.

The custodian should be informed that unannounced audits of the fund will be made occasionally. The cash in the fund plus the sum of the petty cash vouchers should at all times equal the amount shown in the Petty Cash account.

Reimbursing the Petty Cash Fund

Point to Emphasize: When the petty cash fund is replenished, the Petty Cash account is neither debited nor credited. But if the size of the fund is changed, there should be an entry to Petty Cash.

At specified intervals, when the fund becomes low, and at the end of an accounting period, the petty cash fund is replenished by a check issued to the custodian for the exact amount of the expenditures. From time to time, there may be minor discrepancies in the amount of cash left in the fund at the time of reimbursement. In those cases, the amount of the discrepancy is recorded in a Cash Short or Over account, as a debit if short or as a credit if over.

Assume that after two weeks the petty cash fund established earlier has a cash balance of $14.27 and petty cash vouchers as follows: postage, $25.00; supplies, $30.55; and freight in, $30.00. The entry to replenish, or replace, the fund would be:

A = L + OE
+ −
− −

Oct. 28	Postage Expense	25.00	
	Supplies	30.55	
	Freight In	30.00	
	Cash Short or Over	.18	
	Cash		85.73
	To replenish the petty cash fund		

Notice that the Petty Cash account was not affected by the entry to replenish the fund. The Petty Cash account is debited when the fund is established or the fund level is changed. Expense or asset accounts are debited each time the fund is replenished, including in this case $.18 to Cash Short or Over for a small cash shortage. In most cases, no further entries to the Petty Cash account are needed unless the firm wants to change the fixed amount of the fund.

Figure 3
Petty Cash Voucher

PETTY CASH VOUCHER

No. X 744

Date Oct. 23, 20xx

For Postage due

Charge to Postage Expense

Amount $2.86

W.S. — Approved by

Tom L. — Received by

The petty cash fund should be replenished at the end of an accounting period to bring it up to its fixed amount and ensure that changes in the other accounts involved are reflected in the current period's financial statements. If, through an oversight, the petty cash fund is not replenished at the end of the period, expenditures for the period still must appear on the income statement. They are shown through an adjusting entry debiting the expense accounts and crediting Petty Cash. The result is a reduction in the petty cash fund and the Petty Cash account by the amount of the adjusting entry. On the financial statements, the balance of the Petty Cash account is usually combined with other cash accounts.

Voucher Systems

SUPPLEMENTAL OBJECTIVE

6 Define *voucher system* and describe the components of a voucher system

Related Text Assignments:
Q: 17, 18, 19
SE: 9

Point to Emphasize: The purpose of a voucher system is to control expenditures through mandatory documentation and written authorization.

A **voucher system** is any system that gives documentary proof of and written authorization for business transactions. In this section, we present a voucher system designed to keep the tightest possible control over a company's expenditures. It consists of records and procedures for systematically gathering, recording, and paying expenditures. The system provides strong internal control by separating duties and responsibilities in the following functions:

1. Authorization of expenditures
2. Receipt of goods and services
3. Validation of liability by examination of invoices from suppliers for correctness of prices, extensions (quantity times price), shipping costs, and credit terms
4. Payment of expenditure by check, taking discounts when possible

Under a voucher system, every liability must be recorded as soon as it is incurred. A written authorization, called a **voucher**, is prepared for each expenditure when it becomes an obligation to pay, and checks are written only for approved vouchers. No one person has the authority both to incur expenses and to issue checks. In large companies, the duties of authorizing expenditures, verifying receipt of goods and services, checking invoices, recording liabilities, and issuing checks are divided among different people. So, for both accounting and management control, every expenditure must be carefully and routinely reviewed and verified before payment. For each transaction, the written approval leaves a trail of documentary evidence, or what is called an **audit trail**.

Although there is more than one way to set up a voucher system, most systems use (1) vouchers, (2) voucher checks, (3) a voucher register, and (4) a check register.

FOCUS ON BUSINESS PRACTICE

E-tailing, the selling of business (goods) to consumers (B-to-C), gets the most publicity, but the most rapidly growing segment of business use of the Internet is business to business (B-to-B) transactions. It is projected that B-to-B transactions will exceed $14 trillion, compared with $7 trillion for B-to-C transactions. Industries leading in B-to-B transactions are automotive, chemicals, paper and office products, computers and electronics, and utilities. Manual voucher systems are obviously not sufficient for this volume of activity. B-to-B voucher systems will require strong internal controls that ensure proper delivery, precise product specifications, high levels of customer service, and timely, accurate bill payment.[7]

Figure 4
Front and Back of a Typical Voucher Form

Thomas Appliance Company

Payee	Belmont Products	Voucher No.	704
Address	Gary, Indiana	Date Due	7/13
		Date Paid	7/13
Terms	2/10, n/30	Check No.	205

Date	Invoice No.	Description	Amount
7/3	XL1066	10 cases Model 70X14	1,200--

Approved M.N. (Controller) Approved A. Thomas (Treasurer)

BACK OF VOUCHER

Account Debited	Acct. No.	Amount		
Purchases	511	1,200.00	Voucher No.	704
Freight In	512		Payee	Belmont Products
Rent Expense	631		Address	Gary, Indiana
Salary Expense	611		Invoice Amount	1,200.00
Utilities Expense	635		Less Discount	24.00
			Net	1,176.00
			Date Due	7/13
			Date Paid	7/13
			Check No.	205
Total		$1,200.00		

Parenthetical Note: A voucher not only provides for the necessary signatures but also includes information and document numbers that are important in creating an audit trail.

Vouchers

Point to Emphasize: A voucher serves the same purpose as a check authorization form.

Any business can use vouchers to control expenditures. A voucher serves as the basis of an accounting entry. To facilitate tracking, all vouchers are sequentially numbered, and a separate voucher is attached to each bill as it comes in. In the cash disbursement system introduced earlier in this chapter, a voucher would replace the check authorization form. On the face of a typical voucher (Figure 4) is important information about the expenditure and the authorizing signatures required for payment. On the reverse side of the voucher is information about the accounts and amounts to be debited and credited. The voucher identifies the transaction by both voucher number and check number and is recorded in both the voucher register and the check register, as described in the following sections.

Voucher Checks

Point to Emphasize: Payment is made with a voucher check.

Although regular checks can be used effectively with a voucher system, many businesses use a form of **voucher check**, which tells the payee the reason the check was issued. The information is written either on the check itself or on a detachable stub.

Exhibit 2
Voucher Register

Point to Emphasize: The voucher register contains a Vouchers Payable column that functions exactly like the Accounts Payable column in a purchases journal.

Voucher Register

Date		Voucher No.	Payee	Payment Date	Payment Check No.	Credit Vouchers Payable	Debits Purchases	Debits Freight In	Debits Store Supplies
20xx									
July	1	701	Common Utility	7/6	203	75			
	2	702	Ade Realty	7/2	201	400			
	2	703	Buy Rite Supplies	7/6	202	25			
	3	704	Belmont Products	7/13	205	1,200	1,200		
	6	705	M&M Freight			60		60	
	7	706	J. Jay, Petty Cash	7/7	204	50			
	8	707	Belmont Products	7/18	208	600	600		
	11	708	M&M Freight			30		30	
	11	709	Mack Truck			5,600			
	12	710	Livingstone Wholesale	7/22	209	785	750	35	
	14	711	Payroll	7/14	206	2,200			
	17	712	First National Bank	7/17	207	4,250			
	20	713	Livingstone Wholesale			525	500	25	
	21	714	Belmont Products			400	400		
	24	715	M&M Freight			18		18	
	30	716	Payroll	7/30	210	2,200			
	31	717	J. Jay, Petty Cash	7/31	211	47		17	
	31	718	Maintenance Company			175			
	31	719	Store Supply Company			350			350
						18,990	3,450	185	350
						(211)	(511)	(512)	(116)

Voucher Register

Point to Emphasize: All approved vouchers are recorded in the voucher register.

The **voucher register** is the book of original entry in which vouchers are recorded after they have been approved. The voucher register takes the place of the purchases journal in companies that use special-purpose journals. There is one important difference between the two journals: All expenditures—expenses, payroll, plant, and equipment, as well as purchases of merchandise—are recorded in a voucher register; only purchases of merchandise on credit are recorded in a single-column purchases journal.

A voucher register appears in Exhibit 2. Notice that a column called Vouchers Payable replaces the Accounts Payable column. As you can see, the first entry in

International Company

FRA 2.

LO 1 Internal Control and Accounting Education in a Developing Country

Zambia, a country in southern Africa, has 8.5 million inhabitants. It has an elected government and is moving toward capital markets through privatization of government-owned business. For example, the government-owned beer company was recently sold to private interests for $13 million. One national priority calls for the training of competent professional accountants, and the ***Zambian Centre for Accountancy Studies*** has been established with the assistance of the World Bank. There are only about 250 native-born certified accountants in all of Zambia. A state with a comparable population in the United States would have more than 20,000 certified public accountants. One reason for placing a priority on the training of accountants is the importance of good internal controls to the development of a country like Zambia. What are the purposes of internal control, and what are some ways in which such controls would aid the development of a country like Zambia? What are some other reasons for making accounting education a high national priority?

Toys "R" Us Annual Report

FRA 3.

LO 1 Internal Control
LO 3 Considerations

Refer to the annual report for Toys "R" Us in the supplement to Chapter 6. How many stores did Toys "R" Us operate in the United States and abroad in the most recent year? The typical store contains a showroom where customers wheel grocery carts down aisles to select toys and other products for purchase, a warehouse where larger items may be picked up after purchase, a bank of cash registers, and a service desk where returns and other unusual transactions can be authorized. Identify the main activities or transactions for which Toys "R" Us management would need to establish internal controls in each new store. Discuss the objectives of internal controls in each case.

Fingraph® Financial Analyst™

This activity is not appropriate for this chapter.

Internet Case

FRA 4.

LO 1 Comparison of Reports of Management on Internal Control

Through the Needles Accounting Resource Center at http://college.hmco.com, go to the annual reports in the web sites for ***Tandy Corporation*** and ***Circuit City Stores, Inc.*** Find the "Report of Management on Internal Accounting Controls" in the case of Tandy and "Management's Report" in the case of Circuit City in the companies' respective annual reports. A portion of the Circuit City's report is quoted in the text. Compare management statements. What similarities do you find in the content? What is a difference in the reports? Which, in your opinion, does a better job of explaining what management has done to fulfill its responsibility of internal control?

ENDNOTES

1. Kyle Pope, "Dell Refocuses on Groundwork to Cope with Rocketing Sales," *The Wall Street Journal*, June 18, 1993.
2. Circuit City Stores, *Annual Report*, 1998.
3. *Professional Standards*, Vol. 1 (New York: American Institute of Certified Public Accountants, June 1, 1999), Sec. AU 322.07.
4. Ibid., Sec. AU 325.16.
5. "1998 Fraud Survey," KPMG Peat Marwick, 1998.
6. Lynnette Khalfani, "Information-Destruction Finds Lucrative Business in Going to Waste," *The Wall Street Journal*, December 6, 1996.
7. "B-to-B Communities," *Business 2.0*, December 1999.

9 Short-Term Liquid Assets

LEARNING OBJECTIVES

1. Identify and explain the management issues related to short-term liquid assets.
2. Explain *cash, cash equivalents,* and the importance of electronic funds transfer.
3. Account for short-term investments.
4. Define *accounts receivable* and apply the allowance method of accounting for uncollectible accounts, using both the percentage of net sales method and the accounts receivable aging method.
5. Define and describe a *promissory note,* and make calculations and journal entries involving promissory notes.

DECISION POINT: A USER'S FOCUS

Pioneer Electronic Corporation A company must use its assets to maximize income earned while maintaining liquidity. Pioneer Electronic Corporation, a leading provider of electronics for home, commerce, and industry, manages about $2.4 billion in short-term liquid assets. **Short-term liquid assets** are financial assets that arise from cash transactions, the investment of cash, and the extension of credit. What is the composition of these assets? Why are they important to Pioneer's management?

Pioneer's short-term liquid assets (in millions), as reported on the balance sheet in this Japanese company's annual report, are shown here.[1] These assets make up almost 43 percent of Pioneer's total assets, and they are very important to the company's strategy for meeting its goals. Effective asset management techniques ensure that these assets remain liquid and usable for the company's operations.

A commonly used ratio for measuring the adequacy of short-term liquid assets is the quick ratio. The **quick ratio** is the ratio of short-term liquid assets to current liabilities. Because Pioneer's current liabilities are (in millions) ¥202,735 ($1,912.6), its quick ratio is 1.26, which is computed as follows:

$$\text{Quick Ratio} = \frac{\text{Short-Term Liquid Assets}}{\text{Current Liabilities}} = \frac{\$2{,}409{,}400{,}000}{\$1{,}912{,}600{,}000} = 1.26$$

A quick ratio of about 1.0 is a common benchmark. However, it is more important to look at industry characteristics and at the trends for a particular company to see if the ratio is improving or not. A lower ratio may mean that a company is a very good manager of its short-term liquid assets. Pioneer has maintained a quick ratio of over 1.0 for several years. Through

Financial Highlights

(In millions)

	Yen	Dollars
Cash and Cash Equivalents	¥151,805	$1,432.1
Short-Term Investments	1,606	15.1
Accounts Receivable, Net of Allowances of ¥5,077 ($47.9)	94,813	894.5
Notes Receivable	7,174	67.7
Total Short-Term Liquid Assets	¥255,398	$2,409.4

Critical Thinking Question: For what types of businesses would you expect short-term liquid assets to be a large percentage of total assets? **Answer:** Financial institutions, credit card companies, and service businesses.

good cash management, the company has not tied up excess funds in quick assets relative to current liabilities. This chapter emphasizes management of, and accounting for, short-term liquid assets to achieve liquidity.

Management Issues Related to Short-Term Liquid Assets

OBJECTIVE

1 Identify and explain the management issues related to short-term liquid assets

Related Text Assignments:
Q: 1, 2
SE: 1, 2
E: 1, 2
P: 2, 6
SD: 1, 2, 3, 4, 5
FRA: 2, 3, 4

The management of short-term liquid assets is critical to the goal of providing adequate liquidity. In dealing with short-term liquid assets, management must address three key issues: managing cash needs during seasonal cycles, setting credit policies, and financing receivables.

Managing Cash Needs During Seasonal Cycles

Most companies experience seasonal cycles of business activity during the year. These cycles involve some periods when sales are weak and other periods when sales are strong. There are also periods when expenditures are greater and periods when expenditures are smaller. In some companies, such as toy companies, college publishers, amusement parks, construction companies, and sports equipment companies, the cycles are dramatic, but all companies experience them to some degree.

Seasonal cycles require careful planning of cash inflows, cash outflows, borrowing, and investing. For example, Figure 1 might represent the seasonal cycles for a home improvement company like The Home Depot, Inc. As you can see, cash receipts from sales are highest in the late spring, summer, and fall because that is when most people make home improvements. Sales are relatively low in the winter months. On the other hand, cash expenditures are highest in late winter and spring as the company builds up inventory for spring and summer selling. During the late summer, fall, and winter, the company has excess cash on hand that it needs to invest in a way that will earn a return, but still permit access as needed. During the late spring and early summer, the company needs to plan for short-term borrowing to tide it over until cash receipts pick up later in the year. The discussion in this

FOCUS ON BUSINESS PRACTICE

Big buyers often have significant power over small suppliers, and their cash management decisions can cause severe cash flow problems for the little companies that depend on them. For instance, in an effort to control costs and optimize cash flow, Ameritech Corp. told 70,000 suppliers that it would begin paying its bills in 45 days instead of 30 days. Other large companies routinely take 90 days or more to pay. Small suppliers are so anxious to get the big companies' business that they fail to realize the implications of the deals they make until it is too late. When Earthly Elements, Inc., accepted a $10,000 order for dried floral gifts from a national home shopping network, management was ecstatic because the deal increased sales by 25 percent. But in four months, the resulting cash crunch forced the company to close down. When the shopping network finally paid for the big order six months later, it was too late to revive Earthly Elements.[2]

cates of deposit at banks and other financial institutions, in government securities such as U.S. Treasury notes, or in other securities. Such actions are rightfully called investments. However, if the investments have a term of 90 days or less when they are purchased, they are called **cash equivalents** because the funds revert to cash so quickly that they are regarded as cash on the balance sheet. For example, Verizon (formerly Bell Atlantic Corp.) follows this practice. Its policy is stated as follows: "The Company considers all highly liquid investments with a maturity of 90 days or less when purchased to be cash equivalents. Cash equivalents are stated at cost, which approximates market value."[6] A survey of 600 large U.S. corporations found that 57 of them, or 9 percent, used the term *cash* as the balance sheet caption and 502, or 84 percent, used the phrase *cash and cash equivalents* or *cash and equivalents.* Thirty-one companies, or 5 percent, combined cash with marketable securities.[7] The average amount of cash held can also vary by industry.

Most companies need to keep some currency and coins on hand. Currency and coins are needed for cash registers and for paying expenses that are impractical to pay by check. A company may need to advance cash to sales representatives for travel expenses, to divisions to cover their payrolls, and to individual employees to cash their paychecks.

One way to control a cash fund or cash advances is through the use of an **imprest system**. A common form of imprest system is a petty cash fund, which is established at a fixed amount. Each cash payment from the fund is documented by a receipt. Then the fund is periodically reimbursed, based on the documented expenditures, by the exact amount necessary to restore its original cash balance. The person responsible for the petty cash fund must always be able to account for its contents by having cash and receipts whose total equals the originally fixed amount.

Banking and Electronic Funds Transfer

Enrichment Note: Periodically, banks detect individuals who are *kiting.* Kiting is the illegal issuing of checks when there is not enough money to cover them. Before one kited check clears the bank, a kited check from another account is deposited to cover it, making an endless circle.

Banks greatly help businesses to control both cash receipts and cash disbursements. Banks serve as safe depositories for cash, negotiable instruments, and other valuable business documents, such as stocks and bonds. The checking accounts that banks provide improve control by minimizing the amount of currency a company needs to keep on hand and by supplying permanent records of all cash payments. Banks can also serve as agents in a variety of transactions, such as the collection and payment of certain kinds of debts and the exchange of foreign currencies.

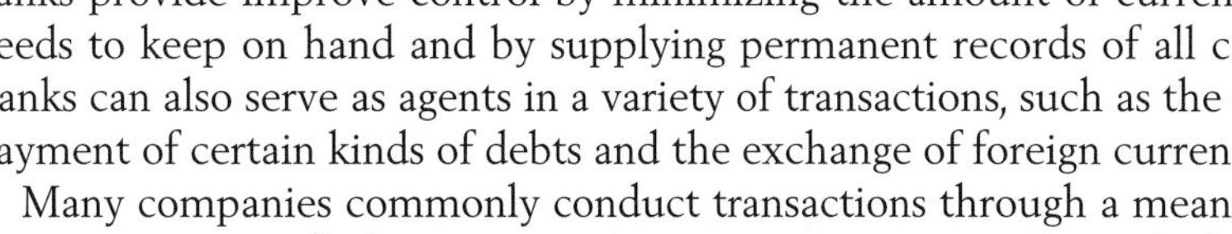

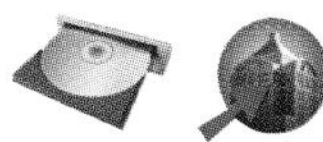

Many companies commonly conduct transactions through a means of electronic communication called **electronic funds transfer (EFT)**. Instead of writing checks to pay for purchases or to repay loans, the company arranges to have cash transferred electronically from its bank to another company's bank. Wal-Mart Stores,

To combat the laundering of money by drug dealers, U.S. law requires banks to report cash transactions in excess of $10,000. Not to be deterred, money launderers began to sidestep the regulation by electronically transferring funds from overseas to banks, money exchanges, and brokerage firms. In response, the Treasury Department set up rules that require those institutions to keep records about the sources and recipients of all electronic transfers. Given the widespread use of electronic transfers in today's business world, it is questionable how much effect this action will have in the ongoing battle against drugs. Looking for drug money by combing the millions of transfers that occur every day is "like looking for a needle in a haystack."[8]

Inc., for example, operates the largest electronic funds network in the retail industry and makes 75 percent of its payments to suppliers by this method. The actual cash, of course, is not transferred. For the banks, an electronic transfer is simply a bookkeeping entry.

In serving customers, banks may also offer automated teller machines (ATMs) for making deposits, withdrawing cash, transferring funds among accounts, and paying bills. Large consumer banks like Citibank, BankOne, and Bank of America will process hundreds of thousands of ATM transactions each week. Many banks also give customers the option of paying bills over the telephone and with *debit cards.* When a customer makes a retail purchase using a debit card, the amount of the purchase is deducted directly from the buyer's bank account. The bank usually documents debit card transactions for the retailer, but the retailer must develop new internal controls to ensure that the transactions are recorded properly and that unauthorized transfers are not permitted. It is expected that within a few years 25 percent of all retail activity will be handled electronically.

Short-Term Investments

OBJECTIVE

3 Account for short-term investments

Related Text Assignments:
Q: 5, 6
SE: 4, 5
E: 4, 5
P: 1, 5
SD: 1, 5, 6

When investments have a maturity of more than 90 days but are intended to be held only until cash is needed for current operations, they are called **short-term investments** or **marketable securities**.

Investments that are intended to be held for more than one year are called *long-term investments.* Long-term investments are reported in an investments section of the balance sheet, not in the current assets section. Although long-term investments may be just as marketable as short-term assets, management intends to hold them for an indefinite period of time.

Securities that may be held as short-term or long-term investments fall into three categories, as specified by the Financial Accounting Standards Board: held-to-maturity securities, trading securities, and available-for-sale securities.[9] Trading securities are classified as short-term investments. Held-to-maturity securities and available-for-sale securities, depending on their length to maturity or management's intent to hold them, may be classified as either short-term or long-term investments. The three categories of securities when held as short-term investments are discussed here.

Held-to-Maturity Securities

Point to Emphasize: Any broker costs or taxes paid to acquire securities are part of the cost of the securities.

Held-to-maturity securities are debt securities that management intends to hold to their maturity date and whose cash value is not needed until that date. Such securities are recorded at cost and valued on the balance sheet at cost adjusted for the effects of interest. For example, suppose that on December 1, 20x1, Lowes Company pays $97,000 for U.S. Treasury bills, which are short-term debt of the federal government. The bills will mature in 120 days at $100,000. The following entry would be made by Lowes:

A = L + OE	20x1			
+	Dec. 1	Short-Term Investments	97,000	
−		Cash		97,000
		Purchase of U.S. Treasury bills that mature in 120 days		

At Lowes' year end on December 31, the entry to accrue the interest income earned to date would be as follows:

	Date	Account	Debit	Credit
A = L + OE	20x1			
+ +	Dec. 31	Short-Term Investments	750	
		Interest Income		750
		Accrual of interest on U.S. Treasury bills		
		$3,000 × 30/120 = $750		

On December 31, the U.S. Treasury bills would be shown on the balance sheet as a short-term investment at their amortized cost of $97,750 ($97,000 + $750). When Lowes receives the maturity value on March 31, 20x2, the entry is as follows:

	Date	Account	Debit	Credit
A = L + OE	20x2			
+ +	Mar. 31	Cash	100,000	
−		Short-Term Investments		97,750
		Interest Income		2,250
		Receipt of cash at maturity of U.S. Treasury bills and recognition of related income		

Trading Securities

Discussion Question: What is the difference between investments in debt securities and investments in equity securities? **Answer:** Debt securities are to be redeemed at a specified time and pay a return in the form of interest. Equity securities are an ownership interest in an entity and are subject to market fluctuations. Return takes the form of dividends and changes in the price of the securities.

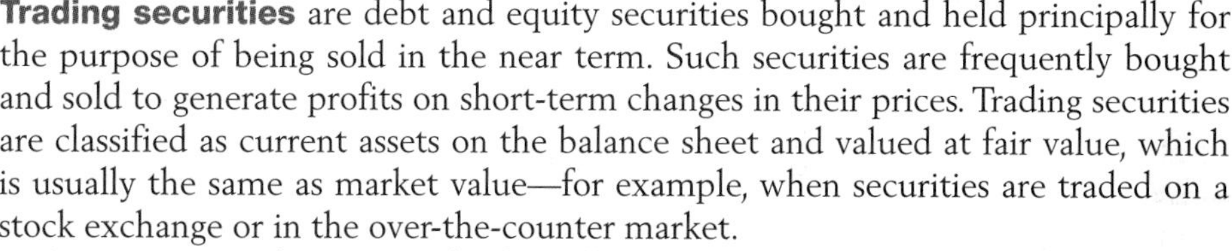

Trading securities are debt and equity securities bought and held principally for the purpose of being sold in the near term. Such securities are frequently bought and sold to generate profits on short-term changes in their prices. Trading securities are classified as current assets on the balance sheet and valued at fair value, which is usually the same as market value—for example, when securities are traded on a stock exchange or in the over-the-counter market.

An increase or decrease in the fair value of the total trading portfolio (the group of securities held for trading purposes) is included in net income in the accounting period in which the increase or decrease occurs. For example, assume that Franklin Company purchases 10,000 shares of Exxon Mobil Corporation for $900,000 ($90 per share) and 5,000 shares of Texaco Inc. for $300,000 ($60 per share) on October 25, 20x1. The purchase is made for trading purposes; that is, management intends to realize a gain by holding the shares for only a short period. The entry to record the investment at cost follows:

	Date	Account	Debit	Credit
A = L + OE	20x1			
+	Oct. 25	Short-Term Investments	1,200,000	
−		Cash		1,200,000
		Investment in stocks for trading ($900,000 + $300,000 = $1,200,000)		

Assume that at year end Exxon Mobil's stock price has decreased to $80 per share and Texaco's has risen to $64 per share. The trading portfolio is now valued at $1,120,000:

Security	Market Value	Cost	Gain (Loss)
Exxon Mobil (10,000 shares)	$ 800,000	$ 900,000	
Texaco (5,000 shares)	320,000	300,000	
Totals	$1,120,000	$1,200,000	($80,000)

Because the current fair value of the portfolio is $80,000 less than the original cost of $1,200,000, an adjusting entry is needed, as follows:

	Date	Account	Debit	Credit
A = L + OE	20x1			
− −	Dec. 31	Unrealized Loss on Investments	80,000	
		Allowance to Adjust Short-Term Investments to Market		80,000
		Recognition of unrealized loss on trading portfolio		

The unrealized loss will appear on the income statement as a reduction in income. (The loss is unrealized because the securities have not been sold.) The Allowance to Adjust Short-Term Investments to Market account appears on the balance sheet as a contra-asset, as follows:

Short-Term Investments (at cost)	$1,200,000
Less Allowance to Adjust Short-Term Investments to Market	80,000
Short-Term Investments (at market)	$1,120,000

Point to Emphasize: The Allowance to Adjust Short-Term Investments to Market account is never changed when securities are sold. It changes only with an adjusting entry at year end.

or more simply,

Short-Term Investments (at market value, cost is $1,200,000)	$1,120,000

If Franklin sells its 5,000 shares of Texaco for $70 per share on March 2, 20x2, a realized gain on trading securities is recorded as follows:

A = L + OE
\+ +
−

20x2			
Mar. 2	Cash	350,000	
	Short-Term Investments		300,000
	Realized Gain on Investments		50,000
	Sale of 5,000 shares of Texaco for $70 per share; cost was $60 per share		

The realized gain will appear on the income statement. Note that the realized gain is unaffected by the adjustment for the unrealized loss at the end of 20x1. The two transactions are treated independently. If the stock had been sold for less than cost, a realized loss on investments would have been recorded. Realized losses also appear on the income statement.

Let's assume that during 20x2 Franklin buys 2,000 shares of BP Amoco Corporation at $64 per share and has no transactions involving Exxon Mobil. Also assume that by December 31, 20x2, the price of Exxon Mobil's stock has risen to $95 per share, or $5 per share more than the original cost, and that BP Amoco's stock price has fallen to $58, or $6 less than the original cost. The trading portfolio now can be analyzed as follows:

Security	Market Value	Cost	Gain (Loss)
Exxon Mobil (10,000 shares)	$ 950,000	$ 900,000	
BP Amoco (2,000 shares)	116,000	128,000	
Totals	$1,066,000	$1,028,000	$38,000

Point to Emphasize: The entry to Allowance to Adjust Short-Term Investments to Market is equal to the change in the market value. Compute the new allowance and then compute the amount needed to change the account. The unrealized loss or gain is the other half of the entry.

The market value of the portfolio now exceeds the cost by $38,000 ($1,066,000 − $1,028,000). This amount represents the targeted ending balance for the Allowance to Adjust Short-Term Investments to Market account. Recall that at the end of 20x1, that account had a credit balance of $80,000, meaning that the market value of the trading portfolio was less than the cost. The account has no entries during 20x2 and thus retains its balance until adjusting entries are made at the end of the year. The adjustment for 20x2 must be $118,000—enough to result in a debit balance of $38,000 in the allowance account.

A = L + OE
\+ +

20x2			
Dec. 31	Allowance to Adjust Short-Term Investments to Market	118,000	
	Unrealized Gain on Investments		118,000
	Recognition of unrealized gain on trading portfolio ($80,000 + $38,000 = $118,000)		

The 20x2 ending balance of the allowance account may be determined as follows:

FOCUS ON INTERNATIONAL BUSINESS

Companies in emerging economies do not always follow the accounting practices accepted in the United States. The Shanghai Stock Exchange is one of the fastest-growing stock markets in the world. Few Chinese companies acknowledge that uncollected receivables are not worth full value even though many receivables have been outstanding for a year or more. It is common practice in the United States to write off receivables more than six months old. Now that Chinese companies like Shanghai Steel Tube and Shanghai Industrial Sewing Machine are making their shares of stock available to outsiders, they must estimate uncollectible accounts in accordance with international accounting standards. Recognition of this expense could easily wipe out annual earnings.[11]

The entry to record this estimate is as follows:

A = L + OE
− −

20x9			
Dec. 31	Uncollectible Accounts Expense	12,000	
	Allowance for Uncollectible Accounts		12,000
	To record uncollectible accounts expense at 2 percent of $600,000 net sales		

After the above entry is posted, Allowance for Uncollectible Accounts will have a balance of $15,600.

Allowance for Uncollectible Accounts

	Dec. 31	3,600
	Dec. 31 adj.	12,000
	Dec. 31 bal.	**15,600**

Parenthetical Note: The percentage of net sales method, unlike the direct charge-off method, matches revenues with expenses.

The balance consists of the $12,000 estimated uncollectible accounts receivable from 20x9 sales and the $3,600 estimated uncollectible accounts receivable from previous years.

Enrichment Note: The aging method is often superior to the percentage of net sales method during changing economic times. For example, during a recession, more bad debts occur. The aging method automatically reflects the economic change as accounts receivable age because customers are unable to pay. A company using the percentage of net sales method must anticipate the change and modify the percentage it uses.

ACCOUNTS RECEIVABLE AGING METHOD The **accounts receivable aging method** asks the question, How much of the year-end balance of accounts receivable will not be collected? Under this method, the year-end balance of Allowance for Uncollectible Accounts is determined directly by an analysis of accounts receivable. The difference between the amount determined to be uncollectible and the actual balance of Allowance for Uncollectible Accounts is the expense for the year. In theory, this method should produce the same result as the percentage of net sales method, but in practice it rarely does.

The **aging of accounts receivable** is the process of listing each customer's receivable account according to the due date of the account. If the customer's account is past due, there is a possibility that the account will not be paid. And the further past due an account is, the greater that possibility. The aging of accounts receivable helps management evaluate its credit and collection policies and alerts it to possible problems.

The aging of accounts receivable for Myer Company is illustrated in Exhibit 1. Each account receivable is classified as being not yet due or as 1–30 days, 31–60 days, 61–90 days, or over 90 days past due. The estimated percentage uncollectible in each category is multiplied by the amount in each category in order to determine the estimated, or target, balance of Allowance for Uncollectible Accounts. In total, it is estimated that $2,459 of the $44,400 accounts receivable will not be collected.

Myer Company Analysis of Accounts Receivable by Age December 31, 20xx						
Customer	Total	Not Yet Due	1–30 Days Past Due	31–60 Days Past Due	61–90 Days Past Due	Over 90 Days Past Due
A. Arnold	$ 150		$ 150			
M. Benoit	400			$ 400		
J. Connolly	1,000	$ 900	100			
R. Deering	250				$ 250	
Others	42,600	21,000	14,000	3,800	2,200	$1,600
Totals	$44,400	$21,900	$14,250	$4,200	$2,450	$1,600
Estimated percentage uncollectible		1.0	2.0	10.0	30.0	50.0
Allowance for Uncollectible Accounts	$ 2,459	$ 219	$ 285	$ 420	$ 735	$ 800

Exhibit 1
Analysis of Accounts Receivable by Age

Once the target balance for Allowance for Uncollectible Accounts has been found, it is necessary to determine how much the adjustment is. The amount of the adjustment depends on the current balance of the allowance account. Let us assume two cases for the December 31 balance of Myer Company's Allowance for Uncollectible Accounts: (1) a credit balance of $800 and (2) a debit balance of $800.

Point to Emphasize: When the write-offs in an accounting period exceed the amount of the allowance, a debit balance in the Allowance for Uncollectible Accounts account results.

In the first case, an adjustment of $1,659 is needed to bring the balance of the allowance account to $2,459, calculated as follows:

Targeted Balance for Allowance for Uncollectible Accounts	$2,459
Less Current Credit Balance of Allowance for Uncollectible Accounts	800
Uncollectible Accounts Expense	$1,659

The uncollectible accounts expense is recorded as follows:

A = L + OE
−   −

20x2			
Dec. 31	Uncollectible Accounts Expense	1,659	
	Allowance for Uncollectible Accounts		1,659
	To bring the allowance for uncollectible accounts to the level of estimated losses		

Discussion Question: What is the balance before adjustment in Allowance for Uncollectible Accounts in the trial balance: debit, credit, or zero? **Answer:** There is no way to determine this, except in the first year of operations. The balance depends, in part, upon how quickly the entity writes off uncollectible accounts.

The resulting balance of Allowance for Uncollectible Accounts is $2,459, as follows:

Allowance for Uncollectible Accounts

Debit	Credit	
	Dec. 31	800
	Dec. 31 adj.	1,659
	Dec. 31 bal.	**2,459**

In the second case, because Allowance for Uncollectible Accounts has a debit balance of $800, the estimated uncollectible accounts expense for the year will have to be $3,259 to reach the targeted balance of $2,459. This calculation is as follows:

Targeted Balance for Allowance for Uncollectible Accounts	$2,459
Plus Current Debit Balance of Allowance for Uncollectible Accounts	800
Uncollectible Accounts Expense	$3,259

The uncollectible accounts expense is recorded as follows:

A = L + OE	20x2			
− −	Dec. 31	Uncollectible Accounts Expense	3,259	
		Allowance for Uncollectible Accounts		3,259
		To bring the allowance for uncollectible accounts to the level of estimated losses		

Point to Emphasize: Describing the aging method as the balance sheet method emphasizes that the computation is based on ending accounts receivable, rather than on net sales for the period.

After this entry, Allowance for Uncollectible Accounts has a credit balance of $2,459, as shown below:

Allowance for Uncollectible Accounts

Dec. 31	800	Dec. 31 adj.	3,259
		Dec. 31 bal.	**2,459**

COMPARISON OF THE TWO METHODS Both the percentage of net sales method and the accounts receivable aging method estimate the uncollectible accounts expense in accordance with the matching rule, but as shown in Figure 4, they do so in different ways. The percentage of net sales method is an income statement approach. It assumes that a certain proportion of sales will not be collected, and this proportion is the *amount of Uncollectible Accounts Expense* for the accounting period. The accounts receivable aging method is a balance sheet approach. It assumes that a certain proportion of accounts receivable outstanding will not be collected. This proportion is the *targeted balance of the Allowance for Uncollectible*

Figure 4
Two Methods of Estimating Uncollectible Accounts

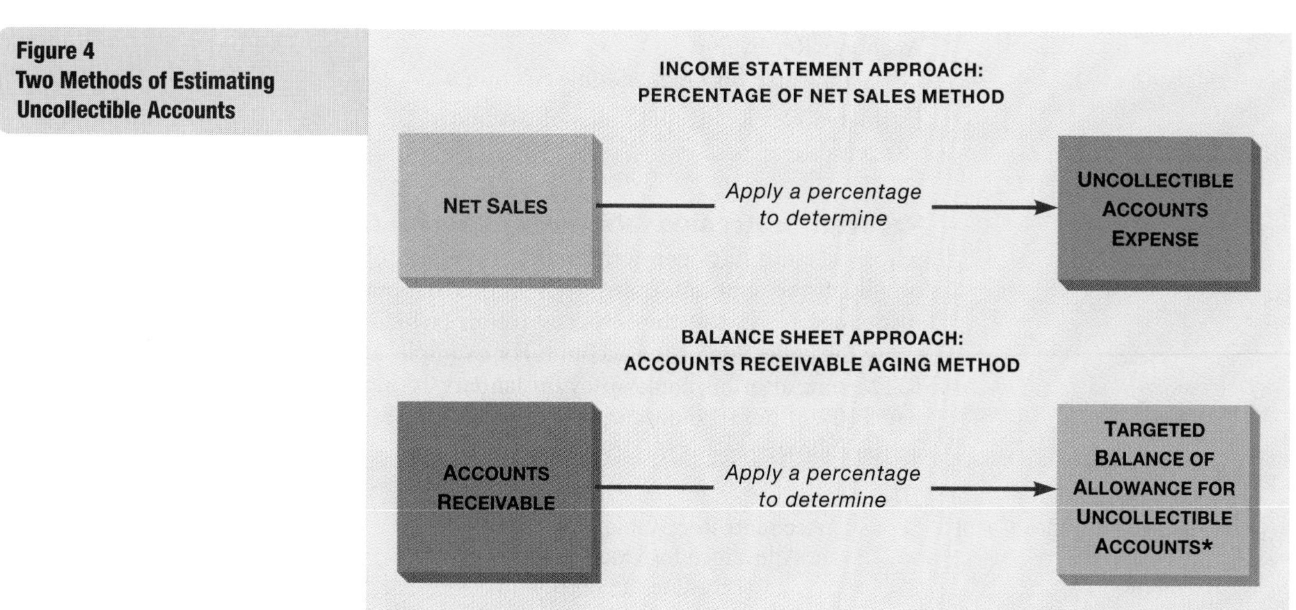

*Add current debit balance or subtract current credit balance to determine uncollectible accounts expense.

Accounts account. The expense for the accounting period is the difference between the targeted balance and the current balance of the allowance account.

WHY ACCOUNTS WRITTEN OFF WILL DIFFER FROM ESTIMATES Regardless of the method used to estimate uncollectible accounts, the total of accounts receivable written off in any given year will rarely equal the estimated uncollectible amount. The allowance account will show a credit balance when the total of accounts written off is less than the estimated uncollectible amount. The allowance account will show a debit balance when the total of accounts written off is greater than the estimated uncollectible amount.

Writing Off an Uncollectible Account

Teaching Note: Bankruptcy as the point for writing off an account makes great sense to students. However, ask them what other events would justify writing off an account.

When it becomes clear that a specific account receivable will not be collected, the amount should be written off to Allowance for Uncollectible Accounts. Remember that the uncollectible amount was already accounted for as an expense when the allowance was established. For example, assume that on January 15, 20x3, R. Deering, who owes Myer Company $250, is declared bankrupt by a federal court. The entry to *write off* this account is as follows:

A = L + OE	20x3			
+	Jan. 15	Allowance for Uncollectible Accounts	250	
−		Accounts Receivable		250
		To write off receivable from R. Deering as uncollectible; Deering declared bankrupt on January 15		

Common Student Error: When writing off an individual account, students frequently debit Uncollectible Accounts Expense rather than Allowance for Uncollectible Accounts.

Although the write-off removes the uncollectible amount from Accounts Receivable, it does not affect the estimated net realizable value of accounts receivable. The write-off simply reduces R. Deering's account to zero and reduces Allowance for Uncollectible Accounts by a similar amount, as shown below:

	Balances Before Write-off	Balances After Write-off
Accounts Receivable	$44,400	$44,150
Less Allowance for Uncollectible Accounts	2,459	2,209
Estimated Net Realizable Value of Accounts Receivable	$41,941	$41,941

RECOVERY OF ACCOUNTS RECEIVABLE WRITTEN OFF Occasionally, a customer whose account has been written off as uncollectible will later be able to pay some or all of the amount owed. When this happens, two journal entries must be made: one to reverse the earlier write-off (which is now incorrect) and another to show the collection of the account. For example, assume that on September 1, 20x3, R. Deering, after his bankruptcy on January 15, notified the company that he could pay $100 of his account and sent a check for $50. The entries to record this transaction follow:

A = L + OE	20x3			
+	Sept. 1	Accounts Receivable	100	
−		Allowance for Uncollectible Accounts		100
		To reinstate the portion of the account of R. Deering now considered collectible; originally written off January 15		

A = L + OE	Sept. 1	Cash	50	
+		Accounts Receivable		50
−		Collection from R. Deering		

Discussion Question: What would have been the entry to record the collection if there had been no write-off? **Answer:** Only the second entry on September 1 would have been journalized.

The collectible portion of R. Deering's account must be restored to his account and credited to Allowance for Uncollectible Accounts for two reasons. First, it turned out to be wrong to write off the full $250 on January 15 because only $150 was actually uncollectible. Second, the accounts receivable subsidiary account for R. Deering should reflect his ability to pay a portion of the money he owed despite his declaration of bankruptcy. Documentation of this action will give a clear picture of R. Deering's credit record for future credit action.

Notes Receivable

OBJECTIVE

5 **Define and describe a *promissory note,* and make calculations and journal entries involving promissory notes**

Related Text Assignments:
Q: 18, 19
SE: 9
E: 12, 13, 14, 15
P: 4, 8

A **promissory note** is an unconditional promise to pay a definite sum of money on demand or at a future date. The entity who signs the note and thereby promises to pay is called the *maker* of the note. The entity to whom payment is to be made is called the *payee.*

The promissory note illustrated in Figure 5 is dated May 20, 20x1, and is an unconditional promise by the maker, Samuel Mason, to pay a definite sum, or principal ($1,000), to the payee, Cook County Bank & Trust Company, at the future date of August 18, 20x1. The promissory note bears an interest rate of 8 percent. The payee regards all promissory notes it holds that are due in less than one year as **notes receivable** in the current assets section of the balance sheet. The maker regards them as **notes payable** in the current liabilities section of the balance sheet.

This portion of the chapter is concerned primarily with notes received from customers. The nature of a business generally determines how frequently promissory notes are received from customers. Firms selling durable goods of high value,

Figure 5
A Promissory Note

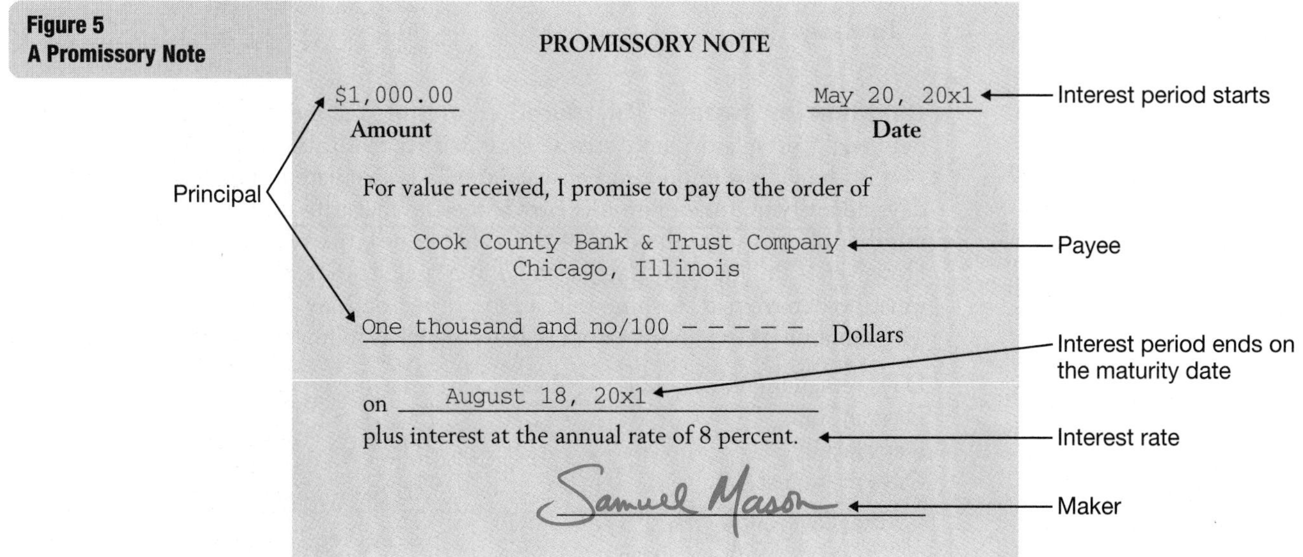

such as farm machinery and automobiles, will often accept promissory notes. Among the advantages of promissory notes are that they produce interest income and represent a stronger legal claim against a debtor than do accounts receivable. In addition, selling or discounting promissory notes to banks is a common financing method. Almost all companies will occasionally receive a note, and many companies obtain notes receivable in settlement of past-due accounts.

Computations for Promissory Notes

In accounting for promissory notes, the following terms are important to remember: (1) maturity date, (2) duration of note, (3) interest and interest rate, and (4) maturity value.

MATURITY DATE The **maturity date** is the date on which the note must be paid. This date must either be stated on the promissory note or be determinable from the facts stated on the note. Among the most common statements of maturity date are the following:

1. A specific date, such as "November 14, 20xx"
2. A specific number of months after the date of the note, for example, "three months after date"
3. A specific number of days after the date of the note, for example, "60 days after date"

The maturity date is obvious when a specific date is stated. And when the maturity date is a number of months from the date of the note, one simply uses the same day in the appropriate future month. For example, a note that is dated January 20 and that is due in two months would be due on March 20.

When the maturity date is a specific number of days from the date of the note, however, the exact maturity date must be determined. In computing the maturity date, it is important to exclude the date of the note. For example, a note dated May 20 and due in 90 days would be due on August 18, computed as follows:

Days remaining in May (31 − 20)	11
Days in June	30
Days in July	31
Days in August	18
Total days	90

Teaching Note: Another way to compute the duration of notes is to begin with the interest period, as follows:

90	Interest period
−11	days remaining in May (31 − 20)
79	
−30	days in June
49	
−31	days in July
18	due date in August

DURATION OF NOTE The **duration of note** is the length of time in days between a promissory note's issue date and its maturity date. Knowing the duration of the note is important because interest is calculated for the exact number of days. Identifying the duration is easy when the maturity date is stated as a specific number of days from the date of the note because the two numbers are the same. However, if the maturity date is stated as a specific date, the exact number of days must be determined. Assume that a note issued on May 10 matures on August 10. The duration of the note is 92 days, determined as follows:

Days remaining in May (31 − 10)	21
Days in June	30
Days in July	31
Days in August	10
Total days	92

Focus on Business Practice

Practice as to the computation of interest varies. Most banks use a 365-day year for all loans, but some use a 360-day year for commercial loans. The brokerage firm of May Financial Corporation of Dallas, Texas, states in its customer loan agreement, "Interest is calculated on a 360-day basis." In Europe, use of a 360-day year is common. Financial institutions that use the 360-day basis earn slightly more interest than those that use the 365-day basis. In this book, we use a 360-day year to keep the computations simple.

Interest and Interest Rate The **interest** is the cost of borrowing money or the return for lending money, depending on whether one is the borrower or the lender. The amount of interest is based on three factors: the principal (the amount of money borrowed or lent), the rate of interest, and the loan's length of time. The formula used in computing interest is as follows:

$$\text{Principal} \times \text{Rate of Interest} \times \text{Time} = \text{Interest}$$

Interest rates are usually stated on an annual basis. For example, the interest on a one-year, 8 percent, $1,000 note would be $80 ($1,000 × 8/100 × 1 = $80). If the term, or time period, of the note were three months instead of a year, the interest charge would be $20 ($1,000 × 8/100 × 3/12 = $20).

When the term of a note is expressed in days, the exact number of days must be used in computing the interest. To keep the computation simple, let us compute interest on the basis of 360 days per year. Therefore, if the term of the above note were 45 days, the interest would be $10, computed as follows: $1,000 × 8/100 × 45/360 = $10.

Maturity Value The **maturity value** is the total proceeds of a note at the maturity date. The maturity value is the face value of the note plus interest. The maturity value of a 90-day, 8 percent, $1,000 note is computed as follows:

$$\begin{aligned}\text{Maturity Value} &= \text{Principal} + \text{Interest}\\ &= \$1{,}000 + (\$1{,}000 \times 8/100 \times 90/360)\\ &= \$1{,}000 + \$20\\ &= \$1{,}020\end{aligned}$$

There are also so-called non-interest-bearing notes. The maturity value is the face value, or principal amount. In this case, the principal includes an implied interest cost.

Illustrative Accounting Entries

Parenthetical Note: The entry to record receipt of a note does not include interest because no interest has yet been earned.

The accounting entries for promissory notes receivable fall into these four groups: (1) recording receipt of a note, (2) recording collection on a note, (3) recording a dishonored note, and (4) recording adjusting entries.

Recording Receipt of a Note Assume that on June 1 a 30-day, 12 percent note is received from a customer, J. Halsted, in settlement of an existing account receivable of $4,000. The entry for this transaction is as follows:

A = L + OE				
+	June 1	Notes Receivable	4,000	
−		Accounts Receivable		4,000
		Received 30-day, 12 percent note in payment of account of J. Halsted		

RECORDING COLLECTION ON A NOTE When the note plus interest is collected 30 days later, the entry is as follows:

A = L + OE				
+ +	July 1	Cash	4,040	
−		Notes Receivable		4,000
		Interest Income		40
		Collected 30-day, 12 percent note from J. Halsted		

RECORDING A DISHONORED NOTE When the maker of a note does not pay the note at maturity, the note is said to be dishonored. The holder, or payee, of a **dishonored note** should make an entry to transfer the total amount due from Notes Receivable to an account receivable from the debtor. If J. Halsted dishonors her note on July 1, the following entry would be made:

Clarification Note: Dishonored notes are, in effect, not written off. The amounts are merely transferred to accounts receivable, which can be written off later.

A = L + OE				
+ +	July 1	Accounts Receivable	4,040	
−		Notes Receivable		4,000
		Interest Income		40
		30-day, 12 percent note dishonored by J. Halsted		

The interest earned is recorded because, although J. Halsted did not pay the note, she is still obligated to pay both the principal and the interest.

Two things are accomplished by transferring a dishonored note receivable into an Accounts Receivable account. First, this leaves the Notes Receivable account with only notes that have not matured and are presumably negotiable and collectible. Second, it establishes a record in the borrower's accounts receivable account that he or she has dishonored a note receivable. Such information may be helpful in deciding whether to extend future credit to the customer.

Enrichment Note: The interest rate on the account receivable is usually not the same as the rate on the note. It is usually higher than the rate on the note.

RECORDING ADJUSTING ENTRIES A promissory note received in one period may not be due until a following accounting period. Because the interest on a note accrues by a small amount each day of the note's duration, it is necessary, according to the matching rule, to apportion the interest earned to the periods in which it belongs. For example, assume that on August 31 a 60-day, 8 percent, $2,000 note was received and that the company prepares financial statements monthly. The following adjusting entry is necessary on September 30 to show how the interest earned for September has accrued.

A = L + OE				
+ +	Sept. 30	Interest Receivable	13.33	
		Interest Income		13.33
		To accrue 30 days' interest earned on a note receivable $2,000 × 8/100 × 30/360 = $13.33		

Reinforcement Exercise: What adjusting entry would the maker of the note have made on September 30? **Answer:** Debit Interest Expense, 13.33; credit Interest Payable, 13.33.

The account Interest Receivable is a current asset on the balance sheet. When payment of the note plus interest is received on October 30, the following entry is made:*

*Some firms may follow the practice of reversing the September 30 adjusting entry. Here we assume that a reversing entry is not made.

A = L + OE	Oct. 30	Cash	2,026.67	
+ +		Notes Receivable		2,000.00
−		Interest Receivable		13.33
−		Interest Income		13.34
		Receipt of note receivable plus interest		

Reinforcement Exercise: What journal entry would the maker of the note have made on October 30? **Answer:** Debit Notes Payable for 2,000.00, Interest Payable for 13.33, and Interest Expense for 13.34; credit Cash for 2,026.67.

As seen from these transactions, both September and October receive the benefit of one-half the interest earned.

Chapter Review

Review of Learning Objectives

Check out ACE, a self-quizzing program on chapter content, at http://college.hmco.com.

1. **Identify and explain the management issues related to short-term liquid assets.** In managing short-term liquid assets, management must (1) consider the effects of seasonal cycles on the need for short-term investing and borrowing as the business's balance of cash fluctuates, (2) establish credit policies that balance the need for sales with the ability to collect, and (3) assess the need for additional cash flows through the financing of receivables.

2. **Explain *cash, cash equivalents,* and the importance of electronic funds transfer.** Cash consists of coins and currency on hand, checks and money orders received from customers, and deposits in bank accounts. Cash equivalents are investments that have a term of 90 days or less. Conducting transactions through electronic communication or electronic funds transfer is important because of its efficiency: Much of the paperwork associated with traditional recordkeeping is eliminated.

3. **Account for short-term investments.** Short-term investments may be classified as held-to-maturity securities, trading securities, or available-for-sale securities. Held-to-maturity securities are debt securities that management intends to hold to the maturity date; they are valued on the balance sheet at cost adjusted for the effects of interest. Trading securities are debt and equity securities bought and held principally for the purpose of being sold in the near term; they are valued at fair value or at market value. Unrealized gains or losses on trading securities appear on the income statement. Available-for-sale securities are debt and equity securities that do not meet the criteria for either held-to-maturity or trading securities. They are accounted for in the same way as trading securities, except that an unrealized gain or loss is reported as a special item in the stockholders' equity section of the balance sheet.

4. **Define *accounts receivable* and apply the allowance method of accounting for uncollectible accounts, using both the percentage of net sales method and the accounts receivable aging method.** Accounts receivable are amounts still to be collected from credit sales to customers. Because credit is offered to increase sales, uncollectible accounts associated with credit sales should be charged as expenses in the period in which the sales are made. However, because of the time lag between the sales and the time the accounts are judged uncollectible, the accountant must estimate the amount of bad debts in any given period.

   Uncollectible accounts expense is estimated by either the percentage of net sales method or the accounts receivable aging method. When the first method is used, bad debts are judged to be a certain percentage of sales during the period. When the second method is used, percentages are applied to groups of accounts receivable that have been arranged by due dates.

Allowance for Uncollectible Accounts is a contra-asset account to Accounts Receivable. The estimate of uncollectible accounts is debited to Uncollectible Accounts Expense and credited to the allowance account. When an individual account is determined to be uncollectible, it is removed from Accounts Receivable by debiting the allowance account and crediting Accounts Receivable. If the written-off account should later be collected, the earlier entry should be reversed and the collection recorded in the normal way.

5. **Define and describe a *promissory note,* and make calculations and journal entries involving promissory notes.** A promissory note is an unconditional promise to pay a definite sum of money on demand or at a future date. Companies selling durable goods of high value, such as farm machinery and automobiles, often accept promissory notes, which can be sold to banks as a financing method.

   In accounting for promissory notes, it is important to know how to calculate the maturity date, duration of note, interest and interest rate, and maturity value. The accounting entries for promissory notes receivable fall into four groups: recording receipt of a note, recording collection on a note, recording a dishonored note, and recording adjusting entries.

REVIEW OF CONCEPTS AND TERMINOLOGY

The following concepts and terms were introduced in this chapter:

LO 4 **Accounts receivable:** Short-term liquid assets that arise from sales on credit at the wholesale or retail level.

LO 4 **Accounts receivable aging method:** A method of estimating uncollectible accounts based on the assumption that a predictable proportion of each dollar of accounts receivable outstanding will not be collected.

LO 4 **Aging of accounts receivable:** The process of listing each customer's receivable account according to the due date of the account.

LO 4 **Allowance for Uncollectible Accounts:** A contra-asset account that reduces accounts receivable to the amount that is expected to be collected in cash; also called *Allowance for Bad Debts.*

LO 4 **Allowance method:** A method of accounting for uncollectible accounts by expensing estimated uncollectible accounts in the period in which the related sales take place.

LO 3 **Available-for-sale securities:** Debt and equity securities that do not meet the criteria for either held-to-maturity or trading securities.

LO 1 **Average days' sales uncollected:** A ratio that shows on average how long it takes to collect accounts receivable; 365 days divided by receivable turnover.

LO 2 **Cash:** Coins and currency on hand, checks and money orders from customers, and deposits in bank checking accounts.

LO 2 **Cash equivalents:** Short-term investments that will revert to cash in 90 days or less from when they are purchased.

LO 2 **Compensating balance:** A minimum amount that a bank requires a company to keep in its account as part of a credit-granting arrangement.

LO 1 **Contingent liability:** A potential liability that can develop into a real liability if a possible subsequent event occurs.

LO 4 **Direct charge-off method:** A method of accounting for uncollectible accounts by directly debiting an expense account when bad debts are discovered instead of using the allowance method; this method violates the matching rule but is required for federal income tax computations.

LO 1 **Discounting:** A method of selling notes receivable in which the bank deducts the interest from the maturity value of the note to determine the proceeds.

LO 5 **Dishonored note:** A promissory note that the maker cannot or will not pay at the maturity date.

LO 5 **Duration of note:** The length of time in days between a promissory note's issue date and its maturity date.

LO 2 **Electronic funds transfer (EFT):** The transfer of funds from one bank to another through electronic communication.

LO 1 **Factor:** An entity that buys accounts receivable.

LO 1 **Factoring:** The selling or transferring of accounts receivable.

LO 3 **Held-to-maturity securities:** Debt securities that management intends to hold to their maturity or their payment date and whose cash value is not needed until that date.

LO 2 **Imprest system:** A system for controlling small cash disbursements by establishing a fund at a fixed amount and periodically reimbursing the fund by the amount necessary to restore its original cash balance.

LO 4 **Installment accounts receivable:** Accounts receivable that are payable in a series of time payments.

LO 5 **Interest:** The cost of borrowing money or the return for lending money, depending on whether one is the borrower or the lender.

LO 3 **Marketable securities:** Short-term investments intended to be held until needed to pay current obligations; also called *short-term investments.*

LO 5 **Maturity date:** The date on which a promissory note must be paid.

LO 5 **Maturity value:** The total proceeds of a promissory note, including principal and interest, at the maturity date.

LO 5 **Notes payable:** Collective term for promissory notes owed by the entity (maker) who promises payment to other entities.

LO 5 **Notes receivable:** Collective term for promissory notes held by the entity to whom payment is promised (payee).

LO 4 **Percentage of net sales method:** A method of estimating uncollectible accounts based on the assumption that a predictable proportion of each dollar of sales will not be collected.

LO 5 **Promissory note:** An unconditional promise to pay a definite sum of money on demand or at a future date.

LO 1 **Quick ratio:** A ratio for measuring the adequacy of short-term liquid assets; short-term liquid assets divided by current liabilities.

LO 1 **Receivable turnover:** A ratio for measuring the average number of times receivables were turned into cash during an accounting period; net sales divided by average net accounts receivable.

LO 3 **Short-term investments:** Temporary investments of excess cash, intended to be held until needed to pay current obligations; also called *marketable securities.*

LO 1 **Short-term liquid assets:** Financial assets that arise from cash transactions, the investment of cash, and the extension of credit.

LO 4 **Trade credit:** Credit granted to customers by wholesalers or retailers.

LO 3 **Trading securities:** Debt and equity securities bought and held principally for the purpose of being sold in the near term.

LO 4 **Uncollectible accounts:** Accounts receivable owed by customers who cannot or will not pay; also called *bad debts.*

REVIEW PROBLEM

Estimating Uncollectible Accounts, Receivables Analysis, and Notes Receivable Transactions

LO 1
LO 4
LO 5

The Farm Implement Company sells merchandise on credit and also accepts notes for payment. During the year ended June 30, the company had net sales of $1,200,000, and at the end of the year it had Accounts Receivable of $400,000 and a debit balance in Allowance for Uncollectible Accounts of $2,100. In the past, approximately 1.5 percent of net sales have proved uncollectible. Also, an aging analysis of accounts receivable reveals that $17,000 in accounts receivable appears to be uncollectible.

The Farm Implement Company sold a tractor to R. C. Sims. Payment was received in the form of a 90-day, 9 percent, $15,000 note dated March 16. On June 14, Sims dishonored the note. On June 29, the company received payment in full from Sims plus additional interest from the date of the dishonored note.

REQUIRED

1. Compute Uncollectible Accounts Expense and determine the ending balance of Allowance for Uncollectible Accounts and Accounts Receivable, Net under (a) the percentage of net sales method and (b) the accounts receivable aging method.
2. Compute the receivable turnover and average days' sales uncollected using the data from the accounts receivable aging method in **1** and assuming that the prior year's net accounts receivable were $353,000.
3. Prepare entries in journal form relating to the note received from R. C. Sims.

ANSWER TO REVIEW PROBLEM

1. Uncollectible Accounts Expense computed and balances determined
   a. Percentage of net sales method:

      Uncollectible Accounts Expense = 1.5 percent × $1,200,000 = $18,000

      Allowance for Uncollectible Accounts = $18,000 − $2,100 = $15,900

      Accounts Receivable, Net = $400,000 − $15,900 = $384,100

   b. Accounts receivable aging method:

      Uncollectible Accounts Expense = $2,100 + $17,000 = $19,100

      Allowance for Uncollectible Accounts = $17,000

      Accounts Receivable, Net = $400,000 − $17,000 = $383,000

2. Receivable turnover and average days' sales uncollected computed

$$\text{Receivable Turnover} = \frac{\$1{,}200{,}000}{(\$383{,}000 + \$353{,}000) \div 2} = 3.3 \text{ times}$$

$$\text{Average Days' Sales Uncollected} = \frac{365 \text{ days}}{3.3} = 110.6 \text{ days}$$

3. Journal entries related to the note prepared

	Date	Account	Debit	Credit
A = L + OE + +	Mar. 16	Notes Receivable	15,000.00	
		Sales		15,000.00
		Tractor sold to R. C. Sims; terms of note: 90 days, 9 percent		
A = L + OE + + −	June 14	Accounts Receivable	15,337.50	
		Notes Receivable		15,000.00
		Interest Income		337.50
		The note was dishonored by R. C. Sims Maturity value: $15,000 + ($15,000 × 9/100 × 90/360) = $15,337.50		

Time	Percentage Considered Uncollectible
Not yet due	2
1–30 days past due	5
31–60 days past due	15
61–90 days past due	25
Over 90 days past due	50

REQUIRED

1. Complete the aging analysis of accounts receivable.
2. Determine the end-of-year balances (before adjustments) of Accounts Receivable and Allowance for Uncollectible Accounts.
3. Prepare an analysis computing the estimated uncollectible accounts.
4. Prepare the entry in journal form to record the estimated uncollectible accounts expense for the year (round the adjustment to the nearest whole dollar).

LO 5 Notes Receivable Transactions

P 8. Ault Importing Company engaged in the following transactions involving promissory notes:

Jan.	14	Sold merchandise to Riordan Company for $37,000, terms n/30.
Feb.	13	Received $8,400 in cash from Riordan Company and received a 90-day, 8 percent promissory note for the balance of the account.
May	14	Received payment in full from Riordan Company.
	15	Received a 60-day, 12 percent note from Calvin Eng Company in payment of a past-due account, $12,000.
July	14	When asked to pay, Calvin Eng Company dishonored the note.
	20	Received a check from Calvin Eng Company for payment of the maturity value of the note and interest at 12 percent for the six days beyond maturity.
	25	Sold merchandise to Leona Fancy Company for $36,000, with payment of $6,000 cash down and the remainder on account.
	31	Received a 45-day, 10 percent, $30,000 promissory note from Leona Fancy Company for the outstanding account receivable.
Sept.	14	When asked to pay, Leona Fancy Company dishonored the note.
	25	Wrote off the Leona Fancy Company account as uncollectible following news that the company had declared bankruptcy.

REQUIRED

Prepare entries in journal form to record the preceding transactions.

Expanding Your Critical Thinking, Communication, and Interpersonal Skills

Skills Development

Conceptual Analysis

LO 1 LO 2 LO 3 Management of Cash

SD 1. *Academia Publishing Company* publishes college textbooks in the sciences and humanities. More than 50 percent of the company's sales occur in July, August, and December. Its cash balances are largest in August, September, and January. During the rest of the year, its cash receipts are low. The corporate treasurer keeps the cash in a bank checking account earning little or no interest and pays bills from this account as they come due. To survive, the company has borrowed money during some slow sales

Cash Flow

CD-ROM

Communication

Critical Thinking

Ethics

General Ledger

Group Activity

Hot Links to Real Companies
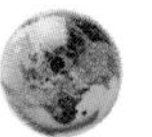
International

Internet

Key Ratio

Memo
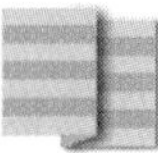
Spreadsheet

months. The loans were repaid in the months when cash receipts were largest. A management consultant has suggested that the company institute a new cash management plan under which cash would be invested in marketable securities as it is received and securities would be sold when the funds are needed. In this way, the company will earn income on the cash and may realize a gain through an increase in the value of the securities, thus reducing the need for borrowing. The president of the company has asked you to assess the plan. Write a memorandum to the president that lays out the accounting implications of this cash management plan for cash and cash equivalents and for the three types of marketable securities. Include an assessment of the plan and any disadvantages to it.

LO 1 Role of Credit Sales
LO 4

SD 2. ***Mitsubishi Corp.,***[12] a broadly diversified Japanese corporation, instituted a credit plan called Three Diamonds for customers who buy its major electronic products, such as large-screen televisions and videotape recorders, from specified retail dealers. Under the plan, approved customers who make purchases in July of one year do not have to make any payments until September of the next year and pay no interest for the intervening months. Mitsubishi pays the dealer the full amount less a small fee, sends the customer a Mitsubishi credit card, and collects from the customer at the specified time. What was Mitsubishi's motivation for establishing such generous credit terms? What costs are involved? What are the accounting implications?

LO 1 Receivables Financing

SD 3. ***Siegel Appliances, Inc.,*** is a small manufacturer of washing machines and dryers located in central Michigan. Siegel sells most of its appliances to large, established discount retail companies that market the appliances under their own names. Siegel sells the appliances on trade credit terms of n/60. If a customer wants a longer term, however, Siegel will accept a note with a term of up to nine months. At present, the company is having cash flow troubles and needs $5 million immediately. Its cash balance is $200,000, its accounts receivable balance is $2.3 million, and its notes receivable balance is $3.7 million. How might Siegel's management use its accounts receivable and notes receivable to raise the cash it needs? What are the company's prospects for raising the needed cash?

Group Activity: Assign to in-class groups and debrief.

Ethical Dilemma

LO 1 Ethics, Uncollectible
LO 4 Accounts, and Short-Term Objectives

SD 4. ***Fitzsimmons Designs,*** a successful retail furniture company, is located in an affluent suburb where a major insurance company has just announced a restructuring that will lay off 4,000 employees. Fitzsimmons sells quality furniture, usually on credit. Accounts Receivable represents one of the major assets of the company and, although the company's annual uncollectible accounts losses are not out of line, they represent a sizable amount. The company depends on bank loans for its financing. Sales and net income have declined in the past year, and some customers are falling behind in paying their accounts. George Fitzsimmons, owner of the business, knows that the bank's loan officer likes to see a steady performance. Therefore, he has instructed the controller to underestimate the uncollectible accounts this year to show a small growth in earnings. Fitzsimmons believes the short-term action is justified because future successful years will average out the losses, and since the company has a history of success, the adjustments are meaningless accounting measures anyway. Are Fitzsimmons's actions ethical? Would any parties be harmed by his actions? How important is it to try to be accurate in estimating losses from uncollectible accounts?

Group Activity: Assign to in-class groups and debate the ethical issues.

Research Activity

LO 1 Stock and Treasury
LO 3 Investments

SD 5. Find a recent issue of *The Wall Street Journal* in your school library. Turn to the third, or C, section, entitled "Money & Investing." From the index at the top of the page, locate the listing of New York Stock Exchange (NYSE) stocks and turn to that page. From the

listing of stocks, find five companies you have heard of, such as IBM, Deere, McDonald's, or Ford. Copy down the range of each company's stock price for the last year and the current closing price. Also copy down the dividend, if any, per share. How much did the market values of the common stocks you picked vary in the last year? Do these data demonstrate the need to value short-term investments of this type at market? How does accounting for short-term investments in these common stocks differ from accounting for short-term investments in U.S. Treasury bills? How are dividends received on investments in these common stocks accounted for?

Be prepared to hand in your notes and to discuss the results of your investigation during class.

Decision-Making Practice

SD 6.

LO 3 Accounting for Short-Term Investments

Norman Christmas Tree Company's business—the growing and selling of Christmas trees—is seasonal. By January 1, after its heavy selling season, the company has cash on hand that will not be needed for several months. The company has minimal expenses from January to October and heavy expenses during the harvest and shipping months of November and December. The company's management follows the practice of investing the idle cash in marketable securities, which can be sold as the funds are needed for operations. The company's fiscal year ends on June 30. On January 10 of the current year, the company has cash of $597,300 on hand. It keeps $20,000 on hand for operating expenses and invests the rest as follows:

$100,000 three-month Treasury bills	$ 97,800
1,000 shares of Ford Motor Co. ($50 per share)	50,000
2,500 shares of McDonald's ($50 per share)	125,000
2,100 shares of IBM ($145 per share)	304,500
Total short-term investments	$577,300

During the next few months, Norman Christmas Tree Company receives two quarterly cash dividends from each company (assume February 10 and May 10): $.50 per share from Ford, $.05 per share from McDonald's, and $.25 per share from IBM. The Treasury bills are redeemed at face value on April 10. On June 1 management sells 500 shares of McDonald's at $55 per share. On June 30 the market values of the investments are:

Ford Motor Co.	$61 per share
McDonald's	$46 per share
IBM	$140 per share

Another quarterly dividend is received from each company (assume August 10). All the remaining shares are sold on November 1 at the following prices:

Ford Motor Co.	$55 per share
McDonald's	$44 per share
IBM	$160 per share

1. Record the investment transactions that occurred on January 10, February 10, April 10, May 10, and June 1. The Treasury bills are accounted for as held-to-maturity securities, and the stocks are trading securities. Prepare the required adjusting entry on June 30, and record the investment transactions on August 10 and November 1.
2. Explain how the short-term investments would be shown on the balance sheet on June 30.
3. After November 1, what is the balance of Allowance to Adjust Short-Term Investments to Market, and what will happen to this account next June?
4. What is your assessment of Norman Christmas Tree Company's strategy with regard to idle cash?

FINANCIAL REPORTING AND ANALYSIS

Interpreting Financial Reports

FRA 1.
LO 4 Accounting for Accounts Receivable

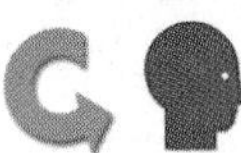

Bex Co. is a major consumer goods company that sells over 3,000 products in 135 countries. The company's annual report to the Securities and Exchange Commission presented the following data (in thousands) pertaining to net sales and accounts related to accounts receivable for 1999, 2000, and 2001.

	2001	2000	1999
Net Sales	$4,910,000	$4,865,000	$4,888,000
Accounts Receivable	523,000	524,000	504,000
Allowance for Uncollectible Accounts	18,600	21,200	24,500
Uncollectible Accounts Expense	15,000	16,700	15,800
Uncollectible Accounts Written Off	19,300	20,100	17,700
Recoveries of Accounts Previously Written Off	1,700	100	1,000

REQUIRED

1. Compute the ratios of Uncollectible Accounts Expense to Net Sales and to Gross Accounts Receivable and of Allowance for Uncollectible Accounts to Gross Accounts Receivable for 1999, 2000, and 2001.
2. Compute the receivable turnover and average days' sales uncollected for each year, assuming 1998 net accounts receivable are $465,000,000.
3. What is your interpretation of the ratios? What appears to be management's attitude with respect to the collectibility of accounts receivable over the three-year period?

International Company

FRA 2.
LO 1 Comparison and Interpretation of Ratios

Philips Electronics, N.V., and ***Heineken N.V.*** are two of the most famous Dutch companies. Philips is a large, diversified electronics, music, and media company, and Heineken makes a popular beer. Philips is about four times bigger than Heineken, with 1999 revenues of 31.5 billion euros versus 7.1 billion euros for Heineken. Ratios can help in comparing and understanding the companies. For example, the receivable turnovers for the companies for two past years are as follows:[13]

	1999	1998
Philips	6.6 times	7.2 times
Heineken	7.8 times	8.1 times

What do the ratios tell you about the credit policies of the two companies? How long does it take each on average to collect a receivable? What do the ratios tell about the companies' relative needs for capital to finance receivables? Can you tell which company has a better credit policy? Explain your answers.

Toys "R" Us Annual Report

FRA 3.
LO 1 Analysis of Short-Term
LO 2 Liquid Assets
LO 4

Refer to the Toys "R" Us annual report to answer the following questions.

1. How much cash and cash equivalents did Toys "R" Us have in 2000? Do you suppose most of that amount is cash in the bank or cash equivalents?
2. Toys "R" Us does not disclose an allowance for uncollectible accounts. How do you explain the lack of disclosure?
3. Compute the quick ratios for 1999 and 2000 and comment on them.
4. Compute receivable turnover and average days' sales uncollected for 1999 and 2000 and comment on Toys "R" Us credit policies. Accounts Receivable in 1998 were $175,000,000.

Fingraph® Financial Analyst™

FRA 4.
LO 1 Comparison and Analysis of Short-Term Liquid Assets

Choose any two companies from the same industry in the Fingraph® Financial Analyst™ CD-ROM software. The industry chosen should be one in which accounts receivable is likely to be an important current asset. Suggested industries from which to choose are manufacturing, consumer products, consumer food and beverage, and computers.

1. Find and read in the annual reports for the companies you have selected any reference to cash and cash equivalents, short-term or marketable securities, and accounts receivable in the summary of significant accounting policies or notes to the financial statements.
2. Display and print for the companies you have selected (a) the Current Assets and Current Liabilities Analysis page and (b) the Liquidity and Asset Utilization Analysis page in tabular and graphical form. Prepare a table that compares the quick ratio, receivable turnover, and average days' sales uncollected for both companies for two years.
3. Find and read the liquidity analysis section of management's discussion and analysis in each annual report.
4. Write a one-page executive summary that highlights the accounting policies for short-term liquid assets and compares the short-term liquidity position of the two companies. Include your assessment of the companies' relative liquidity and make reference to management's assessment. Include the Fingraph® pages and your table as an attachment to your report.

Internet Case

FRA 5.
LO 4 Comparison of J.C. Penney and Sears

Go to the Needles Accounting Resource Center at http://college.hmco.com. Under web links, go to the annual reports on the web sites for ***J.C. Penney Company, Inc.,*** and ***Sears, Roebuck and Co.*** Find the accounts receivable and marketable securities (if any) on each company's balance sheet and the notes related to these accounts in the notes to the financial statements. If either company has marketable securities, what is the cost and what is the market value of the securities? Does the company currently have a gain or loss on the securities? Which company has the most accounts receivable as a percentage of total assets? What is the percentage of the allowance account to gross accounts receivable for each company? Which company experienced the highest loss rate on its receivables? Why do you think there is a difference? Do the companies finance their receivables? Be prepared to discuss your findings in class.

ENDNOTES

1. Pioneer Electronic Corporation, *Annual Report*, 2000.
2. Michael Selz, "Big Customers' Late Bills Choke Small Suppliers," *The Wall Street Journal*, June 22, 1994.
3. Linda Sandler, "Bally Total Fitness's Accounting Procedures Are Getting Some Skeptical Investors Exercised," *The Wall Street Journal*, August 28, 1998.
4. American Greetings Corp., *Annual Report*, 2000.
5. Adapted from Circuit City Stores, Inc., *Annual Report*, 2000.
6. Bell Atlantic Corp., *Annual Report*, 2000.
7. *Accounting Trends & Techniques* (New York: American Institute of CPAs, 1999), p. 140.
8. Jeffrey Taylor, "Rules on Electronic Transfers of Money Are Being Tightened by U.S. Treasury," *The Wall Street Journal*, September 26, 1994.
9. *Statement of Financial Accounting Standards No. 115*, "Accounting for Certain Investments in Debt and Equity Securities" (Norwalk, Conn.: Financial Accounting Standards Board, 1993).
10. Pioneer Electronic Corporation, *Annual Report*, 1999.
11. Craig S. Smith, "Chinese Companies Writing off Old Debt," *The Wall Street Journal*, December 28, 1995.
12. Information based on promotional brochures received from Mitsubishi Electric Corp.
13. Philips Electronics, N.V., *Annual Report*, 1999; and Heineken N.V., *Annual Report*, 1999.

10 Inventories

LEARNING OBJECTIVES

1 Identify and explain the management issues associated with accounting for inventories.

2 Define *inventory cost* and relate it to goods flow and cost flow.

3 Calculate the pricing of inventory, using the cost basis under the periodic inventory system, according to the specific identification method; average-cost method; first-in, first-out (FIFO) method; and last-in, first-out (LIFO) method.

4 Apply the perpetual inventory system to the pricing of inventories at cost.

5 State the effects of inventory methods and misstatements of inventory on income determination, income taxes, and cash flows.

6 Apply the lower-of-cost-or-market (LCM) rule to inventory valuation.

SUPPLEMENTAL OBJECTIVE

7 Estimate the cost of ending inventory using the retail inventory method and gross profit method.

DECISION POINT: A USER'S FOCUS

J.C. Penney Company, Inc. The management of inventory for profit is one of management's most complex and challenging tasks. In terms of dollars, the inventory of goods held for sale is one of the largest assets of a merchandising business. As a major retailer, with department stores in all 50 states and Puerto Rico, J.C. Penney Company, Inc., devotes 25 percent, or $6.0 billion, of its $23.6 billion in assets to inventories. What challenges does J.C. Penney's management face in managing its inventory?

Not only must J.C. Penney's management purchase fashions and other merchandise that customers will want to buy, but it must also have the merchandise available in the right locations at the times when customers want to buy it. Management also must try to minimize the cost of inventory while maintaining quality. To these ends, J.C. Penney maintains purchasing offices throughout the world, including Hong Kong, Taipei, Osaka, Seoul, Bangkok, Singapore, Bombay, and Florence. Quality assurance experts operate out of 22 domestic and 14 international offices. Further, the amount of money tied up in inventory must be controlled because of the high cost of borrowing funds and storing inventory. Important accounting decisions include what assumptions to make about the flow of inventory costs, what prices to put on inventory, what inventory systems to use, and how to protect inventory against loss. Proper management of inventory helped J.C. Penney earn net income of $594 million in 1998, but small variations in any inventory decision can mean the difference between a net profit and a net loss.

After three years of steady or increasing profits, J.C. Penney's 1999 net income was down 43 percent to $336 million. Gross margin percentage was lower on higher net sales. J.C. Penney's chairman said, "Improving the profitability of our core department store and drug store business is our top priority." The company announced its plans to close underperforming stores and liquidate certain inventories in the coming year.[1]

Critical Thinking Question: How does competition influence inventory management issues? **Answer:** Profit making in a competitive environment requires management to control costs. For example, many businesses have reduced the level of excess inventory carried and place orders so that goods are received "just in time." This approach reduces financing and storage costs and requires suppliers to meet orders quickly.

Management Issues Associated with Accounting for Inventories

OBJECTIVE

1 Identify and explain the management issues associated with accounting for inventories

Related Text Assignments:
Q: 1, 2, 3
SE: 1, 2
E: 1, 2
P: 1, 6
SD: 1, 3
FRA: 3, 4, 5

Inventory is considered a current asset because it will normally be sold within a year's time or within a company's operating cycle. For a merchandising business like J.C. Penney or Toys "R" Us, **merchandise inventory** consists of all goods owned and held for sale in the regular course of business.

Inventories are also important for manufacturing companies. Because manufacturers are engaged in the actual making of products, they have three kinds of inventory: raw materials to be used in the production of goods, partially completed products (often called *work in process*), and finished goods ready for sale. For example, in its 1999 annual report, Illinois Tool Works, Inc., disclosed the following inventories (in thousands):

Financial Highlights	1999	1998
Inventories		
Raw materials	$ 409,532	$ 376,892
Work in process	94,815	89,073
Finished goods	579,865	570,852
Total inventories	$1,084,212	$1,036,817

Common Student Confusion: Even though merchandise inventory is one of a business's largest assets (in terms of dollars), students have difficulty envisioning it as a major asset because it often comprises thousands of items. A $2 million building is easier to visualize than $2 million in inventory.

In manufacturing operations, the costs of the work in process and the finished goods inventories include not only the cost of the raw materials that go into the product, but also the cost of the labor used to convert the raw materials to finished goods and the overhead costs that support the production process. Included in this latter category are such costs as indirect materials (for example, paint, glue, and nails), indirect labor (such as the salaries of supervisors), factory rent, depreciation of plant assets, utilities costs, and insurance costs. The methods for maintaining and pricing inventory explained in this chapter are applicable to manufactured goods, but because the details of accounting for manufacturing companies are usually covered as a management accounting topic, this chapter focuses on accounting for merchandising firms.

Applying the Matching Rule to Inventories

Point to Emphasize: Merchandise inventory affects both the income statement and the balance sheet.

The American Institute of Certified Public Accountants states, "A major objective of accounting for inventories is the proper determination of income through the process of matching appropriate costs against revenues."[2] Note that the objective is the proper determination of income through the matching of costs and revenues, not the determination of the most realistic inventory value. These two objectives are sometimes incompatible, in which case the objective of income determination takes precedence.

The reason inventory accounting is so important to income measurement is linked to the way income is measured on the merchandising income statement. Recall that gross margin is computed as the difference between net sales and cost of goods sold and that cost of goods sold is dependent on the cost assigned to inventory or goods not sold. Because of those relationships, the higher the cost of ending inventory, the lower the cost of goods sold and the higher the resulting gross margin. Conversely, the lower the value assigned to ending inventory, the higher the cost of goods sold and the lower the gross margin. Because the amount of gross margin has a direct effect on the amount of net income, the amount assigned to ending inventory directly affects the amount of net income. *In effect, the value assigned to the ending inventory determines what portion of the cost of goods available for sale is assigned to cost of goods sold and what portion is assigned to the balance sheet as inventory to be carried over into the next accounting period.*

Assessing the Impact of Inventory Decisions

Figure 1 summarizes the management choices with regard to inventory systems and methods. The decisions usually result in different amounts of reported net income. As a result, the choices affect both the external evaluation of the company by investors and creditors and such internal evaluations as performance reviews, bonuses, and executive compensation. Because income is affected, the valuation of inventory may also have a considerable effect on the amount of income taxes paid. Federal income tax authorities have specific regulations about the acceptability of different methods. As a result, management is sometimes faced with balancing the goal of proper income determination with that of minimizing income taxes. Another consideration is that since the choice of inventory valuation method affects the amount of income taxes paid, it also affects a company's cash flows.

Evaluating the Level of Inventory

The level of inventory has important economic consequences for a company. Ideally, management wants to have a great variety and quantity on hand so that

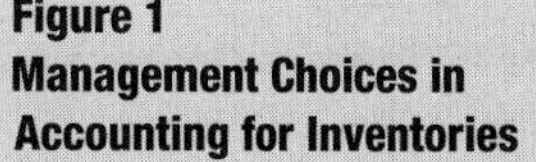

Figure 1
Management Choices in Accounting for Inventories

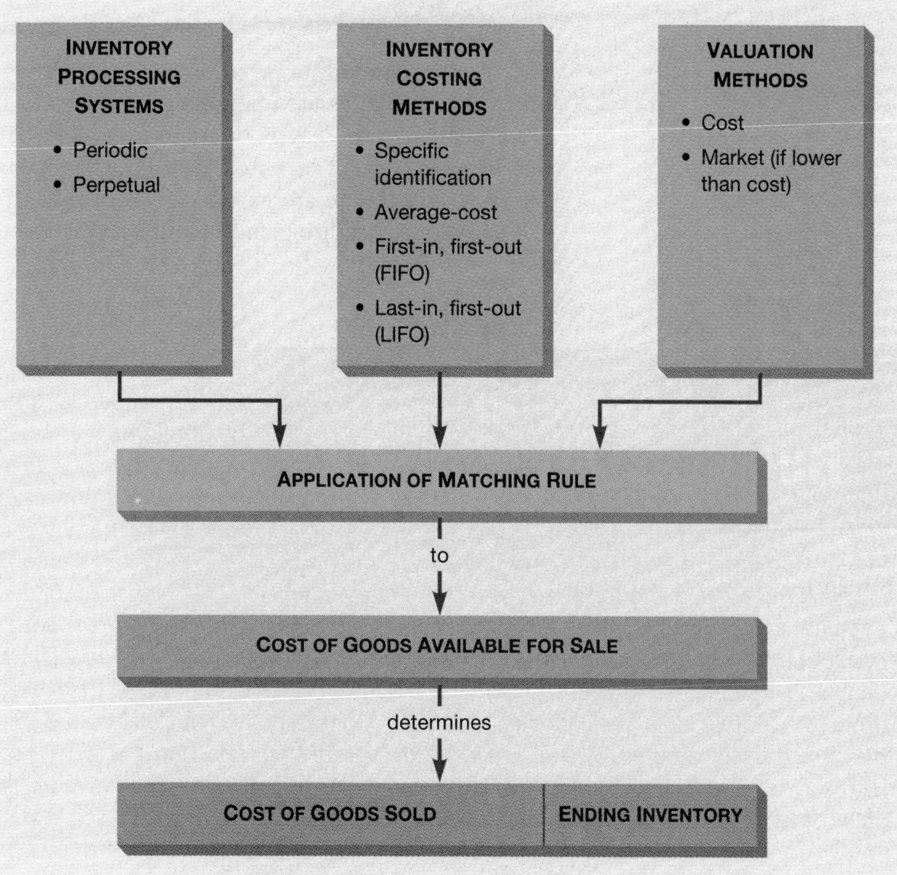

Enrichment Note: Management considers the behavior of inventory prices over time when selecting inventory costing methods.

Discussion Question: What are some of the costs associated with carrying inventory? **Answer:** Insurance, property tax, and storage costs. There is also the possibility of additional spoilage and employee theft.

Instructional Strategy: Instead of lecturing on evaluating the level of inventory, assign SD 1 to small groups. Debrief the case by capturing results on the chalkboard or other media. Ask for a student volunteer to summarize the main points and close the exercise.

customers have a large choice and do not have to wait. Such an inventory policy is not costless, however. The cost of handling and storage and the interest cost of the funds necessary to maintain high inventory levels are usually substantial. On the other hand, the maintenance of low inventory levels may result in lost sales and disgruntled customers. Common measures used in the evaluation of inventory levels are inventory turnover and its related measure, average days' inventory on hand. **Inventory turnover** is a measure similar to receivable turnover. It indicates the number of times a company's average inventory is sold during an accounting period. Inventory turnover is computed by dividing cost of goods sold by average inventory. For example, J.C. Penney's cost of goods sold was \$23,374 million in 1999, and its merchandise inventory was \$5,947 million at the end of 1999 and \$6,031 million at the end of 1998. Its inventory turnover is computed as follows:

$$\text{Inventory Turnover} = \frac{\text{Cost of Goods Sold}}{\text{Average Inventory}}$$

$$= \frac{\$23{,}374{,}000{,}000}{(\$5{,}947{,}000{,}000 + \$6{,}031{,}000{,}000) \div 2}$$

$$= \frac{\$23{,}374{,}000{,}000}{\$5{,}989{,}000{,}000} = 3.9 \text{ times}$$

The **average days' inventory on hand** indicates the average number of days required to sell the inventory on hand. It is found by dividing the number of days in a year by the inventory turnover, as follows:

$$\text{Average Days' Inventory on Hand} = \frac{\text{Number of Days in a Year}}{\text{Inventory Turnover}}$$

$$= \frac{365 \text{ days}}{3.9 \text{ times}} = 93.6 \text{ days}$$

J.C. Penney turned its inventory over 3.9 times in 1999, or on average every 93.6 days. These figures are reasonable because J.C. Penney is in a business where fashions change every season, or about every 100 days. Management would want to sell all of each season's inventory within 90 days, even while making purchases for the next season. There are natural levels of inventory in every industry, as shown for selected merchandising and manufacturing industries in Figures 2 and 3. However,

FOCUS ON BUSINESS TECHNOLOGY

Computer maker Dell Computer Corporation has long been a model of excellent inventory management with high inventory turnover ratios and keen cost controls. The use of computer technology has been critical to its success in these areas. Dell's speed from order to delivery sets the industry standard. Consider that a computer ordered by 9 A.M. can be delivered the next day by 9 P.M. How can Dell do this when it doesn't start ordering components and assembling computers until an order is booked? First, Dell's suppliers keep components warehoused just minutes from Dell's factories, making possible efficient, just-in-time operations. Another time and money saver is the handling of monitors. Dell sends an e-mail message to a shipper such as United Parcel Service. The shipper pulls a computer monitor from supplier stocks and schedules it to arrive with the PC. Monitors are no longer shipped first to Dell and then on to buyers. In addition to contributing to a high inventory turnover, this practice saves Dell about \$30 per monitor in freight costs. Dell is showing the world how to run a business in the cyber age by selling more than \$1 million worth of computers a day on its web site.[3]

Figure 2
Inventory Turnover for Selected Industries

Enrichment Note: Inventory turnover will be systematically higher if year-end inventory levels are low. For example, Toys "R" Us inventory levels on January 30 are at their lowest point of the year.

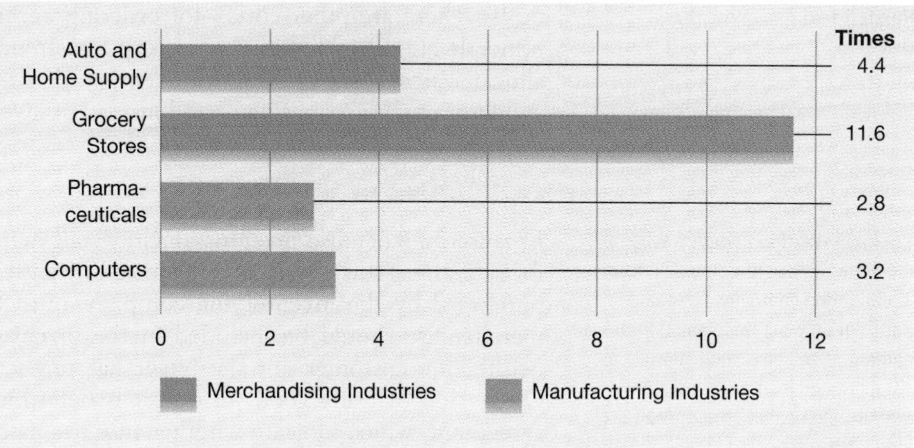

Source: Data from Dun & Bradstreet, *Industry Norms and Key Business Ratios,* 1999–2000.

Figure 3
Average Days' Inventory on Hand for Selected Industries

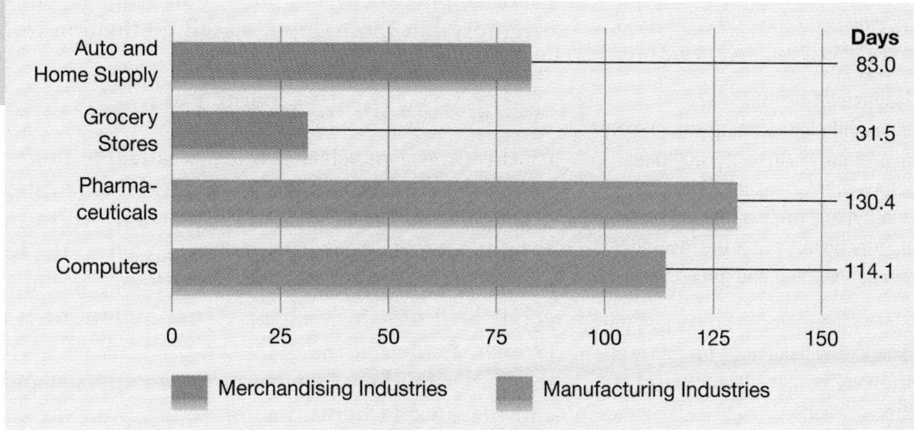

Source: Data from Dun & Bradstreet, *Industry Norms and Key Business Ratios,* 1999–2000.

companies that are able to maintain their inventories at lower levels and still satisfy customer needs are the most successful.

Merchandising and manufacturing companies are attempting to reduce their levels of inventory by changing to a **just-in-time operating environment**. In such an environment, rather than stockpiling inventories for later use, companies work closely with suppliers to coordinate and schedule shipments so that goods arrive just at the time they are needed. Less money is tied up in inventories, and the costs associated with carrying inventories are reduced. For example, Pacific Bell was able to close six warehouses by implementing just-in-time inventory management.

Pricing Inventory Under the Periodic Inventory System

OBJECTIVE

2 Define *inventory cost* and relate it to goods flow and cost flow

According to the AICPA, "The primary basis of accounting for inventories is cost, which has been defined generally as the price paid or consideration given to acquire an asset."[4] This definition of **inventory cost** has generally been interpreted to include the following costs: (1) invoice price less purchases discounts; (2) freight or transportation in, including insurance in transit; and (3) applicable taxes and

Related Text Assignments:
Q: 4, 5, 6
SD: 4

tariffs. There are other costs—for ordering, receiving, and storing—that should in principle also be included in inventory cost. In practice, however, it is so difficult to allocate such costs to specific inventory items that they are usually considered expenses of the accounting period instead of inventory costs.

Merchandise in Transit

Business-World Example: When a customer orders merchandise from a catalogue company, he or she pays not only the price listed in the catalogue, but also such charges as shipping and insurance. Consequently, the cost is greater than the catalogue price.

Common Student Error: It would be helpful to review the terms *FOB shipping point* and *FOB destination*, as students often confuse the two.

Because merchandise inventory includes all items owned by a company and held for sale, the status of any merchandise in transit, whether it is being sold or being purchased by the inventorying company, must be examined to determine if the merchandise should be included in the inventory count. As Figure 4 illustrates, neither the customer nor the buyer has physical possession of the merchandise. Ownership of these goods in transit is determined by the terms of the shipping agreement, which indicate whether title has passed. Outgoing goods shipped FOB (free on board) destination would be included in the seller's merchandise inventory, whereas those shipped FOB shipping point would not. Conversely, incoming goods shipped FOB shipping point would be included in the buyer's merchandise inventory, but those shipped FOB destination would not.

Merchandise on Hand Not Included in Inventory

Discussion Question: Who is responsible for counting and pricing the inventory? **Answer:** Company management is responsible for counting and pricing the inventory. Auditors observe that the inventory is properly counted and priced.

Point to Emphasize: Stress that the consignor will count as inventory all merchandise placed (consigned) at other locations.

At the time a physical inventory is taken, there may be merchandise on hand to which the company does not hold title. One category of such goods is merchandise that has been sold and is awaiting delivery to the buyer. Since the sale has been completed, title to the goods has passed to the buyer, and the merchandise should be included in the inventory of the buyer and not of the seller. A second category is goods held on consignment. A **consignment** is merchandise placed by its owner (known as the *consignor*) on the premises of another company (the *consignee*) with the understanding that payment is expected only when the merchandise is sold and that unsold items may be returned to the consignor. Title to consigned goods remains with the consignor until the consignee sells the goods. Consigned goods should not be included in the physical inventory of the consignee because they still belong to the consignor.

Methods of Pricing Inventory at Cost

The prices of most kinds of merchandise vary during the year. Identical lots of merchandise may have been purchased at different prices. Also, when identical items

Figure 4
Merchandise in Transit

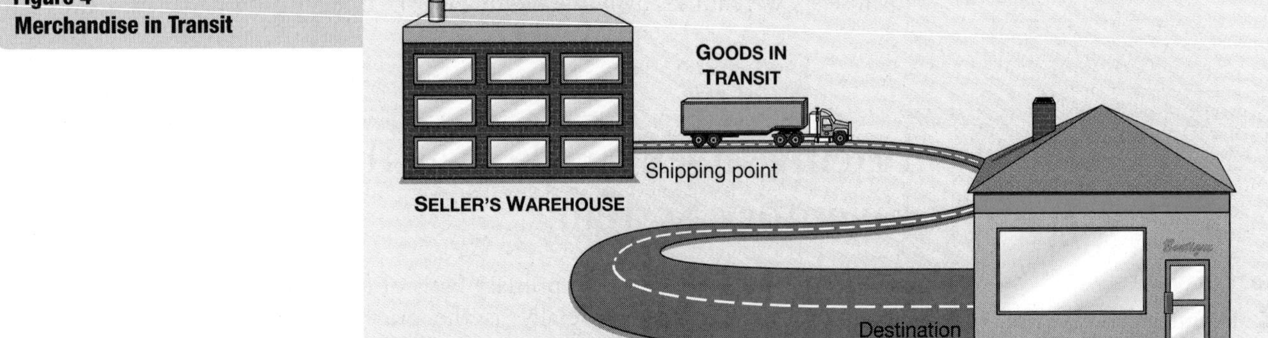

Enrichment Note: Businesses usually try to have the actual flow of inventory proceed in a FIFO manner. This means that the oldest merchandise would be sold first, leaving the freshest merchandise in inventory.

Point to Emphasize: The assumed flow of costs for inventory pricing does not have to correspond to the natural flow of goods.

are bought and sold, it is often impossible to tell which have been sold and which are still in inventory. For this reason, it is necessary to make an assumption about the order in which items have been sold. Because the assumed order of sale may or may not be the same as the actual order of sale, the assumption is really about the *flow of costs* rather than the *flow of physical inventory.*

The term **goods flow** refers to the actual physical movement of goods in the operations of a company, and the term **cost flow** refers to the association of costs with their *assumed* flow in the operations of a company. The assumed cost flow may or may not be the same as the actual goods flow. The possibility of a difference between cost flow and goods flow may seem strange at first, but it arises because several choices of assumed cost flow are available under generally accepted accounting principles. In fact, it is sometimes preferable to use an assumed cost flow that bears no relationship to goods flow because it gives a better estimate of income, which is the main goal of inventory valuation.

Accountants usually price inventory by using one of the following generally accepted methods, each based on a different assumption of cost flow: (1) specific identification method; (2) average-cost method; (3) first-in, first-out (FIFO) method; and (4) last-in, first-out (LIFO) method. The choice of method depends on the nature of the business, the financial effects of the methods, and the costs of implementing the methods.

To illustrate the four methods under the periodic inventory system, the following data for the month of June will be used:

Inventory Data—June 30

June 1	Inventory	50 units @ $1.00	$ 50
6	Purchase	50 units @ $1.10	55
13	Purchase	150 units @ $1.20	180
20	Purchase	100 units @ $1.30	130
25	Purchase	150 units @ $1.40	210
Goods available for sale		500 units	$625
Sales		280 units	
On hand June 30		220 units	

Notice that there is a total of 500 units available for sale at a total cost of $625. Stated simply, the problem of inventory pricing is to divide the $625 between the 280 units sold and the 220 units on hand. Recall that under the periodic inventory system, the inventory is not updated after each purchase and sale. Thus it is not necessary to know when the individual sales take place.

OBJECTIVE

3 Calculate the pricing of inventory, using the cost basis under the periodic inventory system, according to the specific identification method; average-cost method; first-in, first-out (FIFO) method; and last-in, first-out (LIFO) method

Related Text Assignments:
Q: 7, 8, 9
SE: 3, 4, 5, 6
E: 3, 4, 5, 7, 9
P: 1, 2, 6, 7

SPECIFIC IDENTIFICATION METHOD If the units in the ending inventory can be identified as coming from specific purchases, the **specific identification method** may be used to price the inventory by identifying the cost of each item in ending inventory. For instance, assume that the June 30 inventory consisted of 50 units from the June 1 inventory, 100 units from the purchase of June 13, and 70 units from the purchase of June 25. The cost assigned to the inventory under the specific identification method would be $268, determined as follows:

Periodic Inventory System—Specific Identification Method

50 units @ $1.00	$ 50	Cost of goods available for sale	$625
100 units @ $1.20	120		
70 units @ $1.40	98	Less June 30 inventory	268
220 units at a cost of	$268	Cost of goods sold	$357

Discussion Question: Even if it were possible to track each individual inventory item, why would a company not do so? **Answer:** It would be excessively expensive to track which items were left in inventory. The cost would clearly exceed the benefit.

The specific identification method might be used in the purchase and sale of high-priced articles, such as automobiles, heavy equipment, and works of art. Although this method may appear logical, it is not used by many companies because it has two definite disadvantages. First, in many cases, it is difficult and impractical to keep track of the purchase and sale of individual items. Second, when a company deals in items that are identical but were purchased at different costs, deciding which items are sold becomes arbitrary; thus the company can raise or lower income by choosing to sell the lower- or higher-cost items.

Business-World Example: The physical flow of goods sometimes may seem to dictate a particular method, such as in a milk producer's operations in which the perishable nature of the product requires a *physical flow* of FIFO. However, the milk producer's management can choose an inventory method based on an assumed *cost flow* that differs from FIFO, such as average-cost or LIFO.

AVERAGE-COST METHOD Under the **average-cost method**, inventory is priced at the average cost of the goods available for sale during the period. Average cost is computed by dividing the total cost of goods available for sale by the total units available for sale. This gives an average unit cost that is applied to the units in ending inventory. In our illustration, the ending inventory would be $275, or $1.25 per unit, determined as follows:

Periodic Inventory System—Average-Cost Method

Cost of Goods Available for Sale ÷ Units Available for Sale = Average Unit Cost
$625 ÷ 500 units = $1.25

Ending inventory: 220 units @ $1.25 =	$275
Cost of goods available for sale	$625
Less June 30 inventory	275
Cost of goods sold	$350

The average-cost method tends to level out the effects of cost increases and decreases because the cost for the ending inventory calculated under this method is influenced by all the prices paid during the year and by the beginning inventory price. Some, however, criticize the average-cost method because they believe that recent costs are more relevant for income measurement and decision making.

Enrichment Note: When you make a FIFO cost flow assumption, you use it even if you can prove that one of the first-purchased items is still in inventory. Let's say that for the first week of January, perfume was packaged in blue boxes, and then the company changed to red packaging. When you price inventory using the FIFO method, you assume the blue boxes (the older merchandise) were sold, even if you have some of them left in inventory.

FIRST-IN, FIRST-OUT (FIFO) METHOD The **first-in, first-out (FIFO) method** is based on the assumption that the costs of the first items acquired should be assigned to the first items sold. The costs of the goods on hand at the end of a period are assumed to be from the most recent purchases, and the costs assigned to goods that have been sold are assumed to be from beginning inventory and the earliest purchases. The FIFO method of determining inventory cost may be adopted by any business, regardless of the actual physical flow of goods, because the assumption is made regarding the flow of costs and not the flow of goods.

In our illustration, the June 30 inventory would be $301 when the FIFO method is used. It is computed as follows:

Periodic Inventory System—First-In, First-Out Method

150 units @ $1.40 from purchase of June 25	$210
70 units @ $1.30 from purchase of June 20	91
220 units at a cost of	$301
Cost of goods available for sale	$625
Less June 30 inventory	301
Cost of goods sold	$324

The effect of the FIFO method is to value the ending inventory at the most recent costs and include earlier costs in cost of goods sold. During periods of consistently rising prices, the FIFO method yields the highest possible amount of net income because cost of goods sold will show the earliest costs incurred, which are lower during periods of inflation. Another reason for this result is that businesses tend to increase selling prices as costs rise, even when inventories were purchased before the price rise. The reverse effect occurs in periods of price decreases. Consequently, a major criticism of FIFO is that it magnifies the effects of the business cycle on income.

Business-World Example: An example of physical flow under LIFO would be a gravel pile. As gravel on top is sold, more is purchased and added on top. The gravel on the bottom may never be sold. Despite this LIFO physical flow, any acceptable cost flow assumption may be made.

LAST-IN, FIRST-OUT (LIFO) METHOD The **last-in, first-out (LIFO) method** of costing inventories is based on the assumption that the costs of the last items purchased should be assigned to the first items sold and that the cost of ending inventory reflects the cost of the merchandise purchased earliest.

Under this method, the June 30 inventory would be $249, computed as follows:

Common Student Confusion: Students often reverse FIFO and LIFO. Remind them that under FIFO we assume that the first goods purchased are the first ones sold. Thus, we assume that we still have the ones purchased most recently.

Periodic Inventory System—Last-In, First-Out Method

50 units @ $1.00 from June 1 inventory	$ 50
50 units @ $1.10 from purchase of June 6	55
120 units @ $1.20 from purchase of June 13	144
220 units at a cost of	$249
Cost of goods available for sale	$625
Less June 30 inventory	249
Cost of goods sold	$376

Discussion Question: If your company uses LIFO and the inventory shown on your balance sheet is excessively low by replacement standards, how would you disclose this to the readers of your financial statements? **Answer:** By note.

The effect of LIFO is to value inventory at the earliest prices and to include in cost of goods sold the cost of the most recently purchased goods. This assumption, of course, does not agree with the actual physical movement of goods in most businesses.

There is, however, a strong logical argument to support LIFO, based on the fact that a certain size inventory is necessary in a going concern. When inventory is sold, it must be replaced with more goods. The supporters of LIFO reason that the fairest determination of income occurs if the current costs of merchandise are matched against current sales prices, regardless of which physical units of merchandise are sold. When prices are moving either upward or downward, the cost of goods sold will, under LIFO, show costs closer to the price level at the time the goods were sold. As a result, the LIFO method tends to show a smaller net income during inflationary times and a larger net income during deflationary times than other methods of inventory valuation. The peaks and valleys of the business cycle tend to be smoothed out. In inventory valuation, the flow of costs, and hence income determination, is more important than the physical movement of goods and balance sheet valuation.

An argument may also be made against the LIFO method. Because the inventory valuation on the balance sheet reflects earlier prices, it often gives an unrealistic picture of the current value of the inventory. Such balance sheet measures as working capital and current ratio may be distorted and must be interpreted carefully.

FOCUS ON BUSINESS PRACTICE

A new type of retail business called the "category killer" seems to ignore the tenets of good inventory management. These retailers, such as The Home Depot, Inc., in home improvements; Barnes & Noble Inc. in bookstores; Wal-Mart Stores, Inc., in groceries and dry goods; Toys "R" Us, Inc., in toys; and Blockbuster Entertainment Corporation in videos, maintain huge inventories at such low prices that smaller competitors find it hard to compete. Although these companies have a large amount of money tied up in inventories, they maintain very sophisticated just-in-time operating environments that require suppliers to meet demanding standards for delivery of products and reduction of inventory costs. Some suppliers are required to stock the shelves and keep track of inventory levels. By minimizing handling and overhead costs and buying at favorably low prices, the category killers achieve great success.

Figure 5
Summary of Cost Flow Assumptions' Impact on Income Statement and Balance Sheet Using Periodic Inventory System

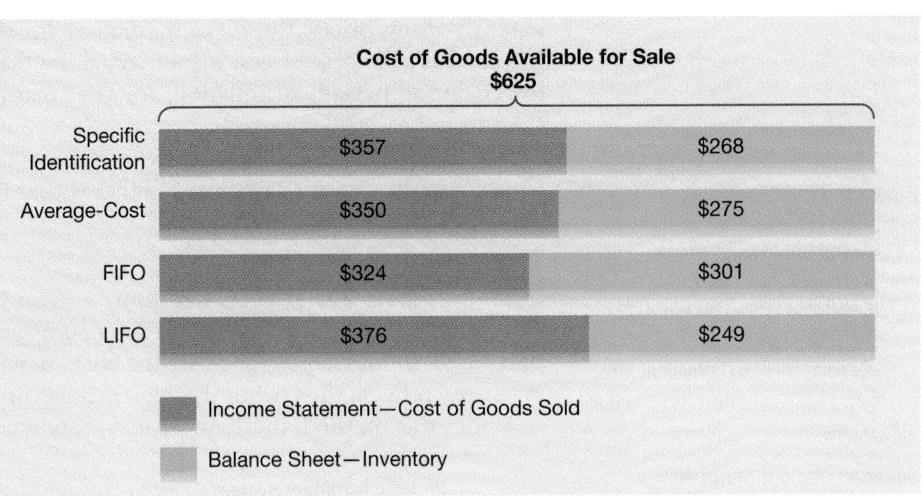

Figure 5 summarizes the impact of the four inventory cost allocation methods on the cost of goods sold as reported on the income statement and on inventory as reported on the balance sheet when a company uses the periodic inventory system. In periods of rising prices, the FIFO method yields the highest inventory valuation, the lowest cost of goods sold, and hence a higher net income. The LIFO method yields the lowest inventory valuation, the highest cost of goods sold, and thus a lower net income.

Pricing Inventory Under the Perpetual Inventory System

OBJECTIVE

4 Apply the perpetual inventory system to the pricing of inventories at cost

Related Text Assignments:
Q: 10
SE: 7, 8, 9
E: 6, 7
P: 3, 8
SD: 4

The pricing of inventories under the perpetual inventory system differs from pricing under the periodic inventory system. The difference occurs because under the perpetual inventory system, a continuous record of quantities and costs of merchandise is maintained as purchases and sales are made. Under the periodic inventory system, only the ending inventory is counted and priced. Cost of goods sold is determined by deducting the cost of the ending inventory from the cost of goods available for sale. Under the perpetual inventory system, cost of goods sold is accumulated as sales are made and costs are transferred from the Inventory account to Cost of Goods Sold. The cost of the ending inventory is the balance of the Inventory account. To illustrate pricing methods under the perpetual inventory system, the same data will be used as before, but specific sales dates and amounts will be added, as follows:

Inventory Data—June 30

June	1	Inventory	50 units @ $1.00
	6	Purchase	50 units @ $1.10
	10	Sale	70 units
	13	Purchase	150 units @ $1.20
	20	Purchase	100 units @ $1.30
	25	Purchase	150 units @ $1.40
	30	Sale	210 units
	30	Inventory	220 units

and finished goods, and compares the inventory utilization of the two companies, including reference to management's assessment. Comment specifically on the financing implications of the companies' relative operating cycles. Include the Fingraph® page and your table as an attachment to your report.

Internet Case

FRA 6.
LO 5 Effect of LIFO on Income and Cash Flows

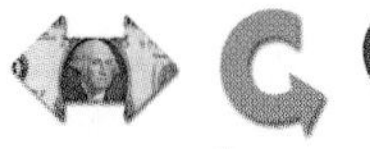

Maytag Corporation, an appliance manufacturer, uses the LIFO inventory method. Go to www.maytagcorp.com and select "About Maytag." Then select "Financial Center." After finding the income statement and inventory note, calculate what net income would have been had the company used FIFO. Calculate how much cash the company saved for the year and cumulatively by using LIFO. What is the difference between the LIFO and FIFO gross margin and profit margin results? Which reporting alternative is better for the company?

ENDNOTES

1. J.C. Penney Company, Inc., *Annual Report,* 1999.
2. American Institute of Certified Public Accountants, *Accounting Research Bulletin No. 43* (New York: AICPA, 1953), ch. 4.
3. Gary McWilliams, "Whirlwind on the Web," *Business Week,* April 7, 1997.
4. American Institute of Certified Public Accountants, *Accounting Research Bulletin No. 43* (New York: AICPA, 1953), ch. 4.
5. Micah Frankel and Robert Trezevant, "The Year-End LIFO Inventory Purchasing Decision: An Empirical Test," *The Accounting Review,* April 1994.
6. American Institute of Certified Public Accountants, *Accounting Trends & Techniques* (New York: AICPA, 1999).
7. Teri Agins, "Report Is Said to Show Pervasive Fraud at Leslie" and "Leslie Fay Co.'s Profits Restated for Past 3 Years," *The Wall Street Journal,* September 27 and 30, 1993.
8. International Paper Company, *Annual Report,* 1999.
9. American Institute of Certified Public Accountants, *Accounting Trends & Techniques* (New York: AICPA, 1999).
10. "Everybody's Falling into The Gap," *Business Week,* September 23, 1991, p. 36; and The Gap Inc., *Annual Report,* 1999.
11. American Institute of Certified Public Accountants, *Accounting Trends & Techniques* (New York: AICPA,1999).
12. Based on Ann Hagedorn, "Crazy Eddie Says About $45 Million of Goods Missing," *The Wall Street Journal,* November 20, 1987, p. 47.
13. RJR Nabisco, Inc., *Annual Report,* 1997.
14. Pioneer Electronic Corporation, *Annual Report,* 1999; and Yamaha Motor Co. Ltd., *Annual Report,* 1999.

11 Long-Term Assets

LEARNING OBJECTIVES

1 Identify the types of long-term assets and explain the management issues related to accounting for them.

2 Distinguish between capital and revenue expenditures, and account for the cost of property, plant, and equipment.

3 Define *depreciation,* state the factors that affect its computation, and show how to record it.

4 Compute periodic depreciation under the straight-line method, production method, and declining-balance method.

5 Account for the disposal of depreciable assets not involving exchanges.

6 Account for the disposal of depreciable assets involving exchanges.

7 Identify the issues related to accounting for natural resources and compute depletion.

8 Apply the matching rule to intangible assets, including research and development costs and goodwill.

SUPPLEMENTAL OBJECTIVE

9 Apply depreciation methods to problems of partial years, revised rates, groups of similar items, special types of capital expenditures, and cost recovery.

DECISION POINT: A USER'S FOCUS

H. J. Heinz Company The effects of management's decisions regarding long-term assets are most apparent in the areas of reported total assets and net income. How does one learn about the significance of those items to a company? An idea of the extent of a company's long-term assets and their importance can be gained from the financial statements. For example, this list of assets (in thousands of dollars) is taken from the annual report of H. J. Heinz Company, one of the world's largest food companies.

Of the company's approximately $8.9 billion in total assets, about 27 percent consists of property, plant, and equipment, and another 37.5 percent is goodwill and other noncurrent assets. On the income statement, depreciation and amortization expenses associated with those assets are more than $306 million, or about 34 percent of net income. On the statement of cash flows, more than $452 million was spent on new long-term assets.[1] This chapter deals with long-term assets: property, plant, and equipment and intangible assets.

Financial Highlights

(In thousands)

	2000	1999
Property, Plant, and Equipment:		
Land	**$ 45,959**	$ 48,649
Buildings and leasehold improvements	**860,873**	798,307
Equipment, furniture, and other	**3,440,915**	3,227,019
	$4,347,747	$4,073,975
Less accumulated depreciation	**1,988,994**	1,902,951
Total property, plant, and equipment, net	**$2,358,753**	$2,171,024
Other Noncurrent Assets:		
Goodwill (net of amortization: 2000—$312,433 and 1999—$352,209)	**$1,609,672**	$1,781,466
Trademarks (net of amortization: 2000—$104,125 and 1999—$84,672)	**674,279**	511,608
Other intangibles (net of amortization: 2000—$147,343 and 1999—$117,038)	**127,779**	177,290
Other noncurrent assets	**910,225**	525,468
Total other noncurrent assets	**$3,321,955**	$2,995,832

Critical Thinking Question: Heinz has invested $4.3 billion in gross property, plant, and equipment and has expensed, as of 2000, slightly less than $2 billion. What does the nearly $2.4 billion in total property, plant, and equipment, net represent? **Answer:** It is the undepreciated acquisition cost of these assets. It will be allocated as depreciation expense to future accounting periods. It does not represent the value of the assets.

Management Issues Related to Accounting for Long-Term Assets

OBJECTIVE

1 Identify the types of long-term assets and explain the management issues related to accounting for them

Long-term assets are assets that (1) have a useful life of more than one year, (2) are acquired for use in the operation of a business, and (3) are not intended for resale to customers. For many years, it was common to refer to long-term assets as *fixed assets*, but use of this term is declining because the word *fixed* implies that they last forever. The relative importance of long-term assets to various industries is shown in Figure 1. Long-term assets range from 17.1 percent of total assets in computers to 53.5 percent in interstate trucking.

VIDEO CASE

Fermi National Accelerator Laboratory

Objectives

- To describe the characteristics of long-term assets.
- To identify the four issues that must be addressed in applying the matching rule to long-term assets.
- To define depreciation and state the principal causes of depreciation.
- To identify the issues related to intangible assets, including research and development.

Background for the Case

The Fermi National Accelerator Laboratory (Fermilab), located 30 miles west of Chicago, is a U.S. Department of Energy national laboratory. Its primary mission is to advance the understanding of the fundamental nature of matter and energy.

Fermilab operates the world's highest-energy particle accelerator, the Trevatron, or "atom-smasher." Circling through rings of magnets four miles in circumference, particle beams generate experimental conditions equivalent to those that existed in the first quadrillionth of a second after the birth of the universe. This capability to re-create such high energy levels places Fermilab at the frontier of global physics research. It provides leadership and resources for qualified experimenters to conduct basic research at the leading edge of high-energy physics and related disciplines. In the year 2000, with Collider Run II, Fermilab began probing the smallest dimensions that humans have ever examined. These scientists have the best opportunity to make important discoveries that could answer some of today's questions in particle physics.

Although a unit of the U.S. government, Fermilab is a financially independent nonprofit corporation with a governing body consisting of the presidents of 87 member research universities. With annual revenues of about $300 million, consisting mostly of government contracts, and annual expenses of about $260 million, Fermilab faces the same management challenges that a for-profit corporation faces. It must make huge investments in long-term assets. Other than salaries, depreciation is the lab's largest expense. In addition, Fermilab creates intellectual capital through basic research that it shares cooperatively with U.S. industry to encourage economic development.

For more information about Fermi National Accelerator Laboratory, visit the laboratory's web site through the Needles Accounting Resource Center at:

http://college.hmco.com

Required

View the video on Fermi National Accelerator Laboratory that accompanies this book. As you are watching the video, take notes related to the following questions:

1. What are the characteristics that distinguish long-term assets? What are some examples of long-term assets at Fermilab?
2. What four issues must be addressed in applying the matching rule to long-term assets?
3. What is depreciation and what are the two major causes of depreciation?
4. What are research and development costs and how does Fermilab account for them? How might this method understate the assets of Fermilab?

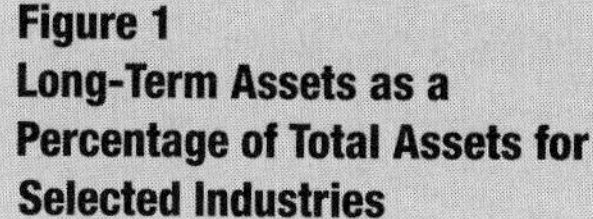
Figure 1
Long-Term Assets as a Percentage of Total Assets for Selected Industries

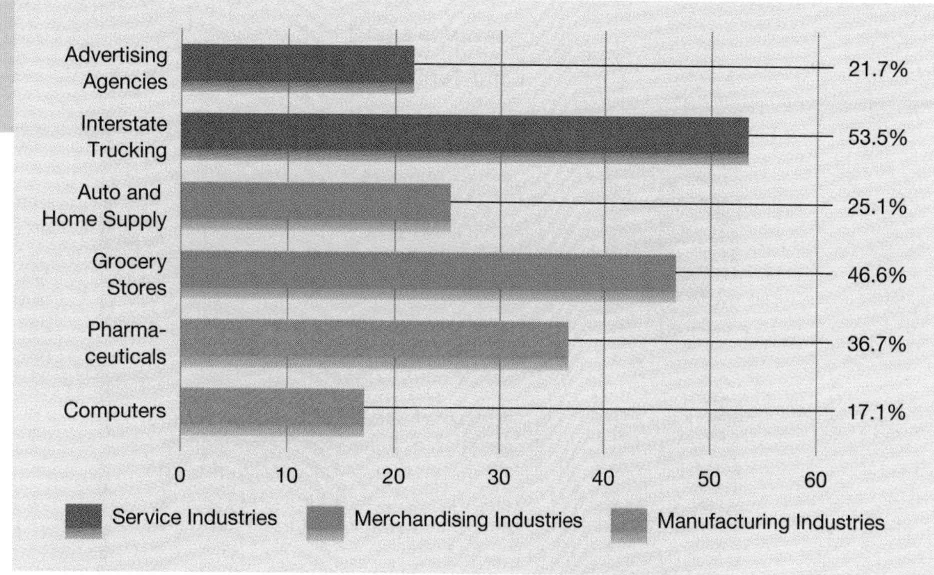

Source: Data from Dun & Bradstreet, *Industry Norms and Key Business Ratios,* 1999–2000.

Related Text Assignments:
Q: 1, 2, 3, 4, 5, 6, 7
SE: 1
E: 1, 2
SD: 5, 6
FRA: 3, 4

Clarification Note: For an asset to be classified as property, plant, and equipment, it must be "put in use." This means that it is available for its intended purpose. An emergency generator is "put in use" when it is available for emergencies, even if it is never used.

Point to Emphasize: A computer used in the office would be considered plant and equipment, whereas an identical computer held for sale to customers would be considered inventory.

Point to Emphasize: The purchase of a long-term asset is in reality a prepayment for some form of future benefit.

Although there is no strict minimum useful life an asset must have to be classified as long term, the most common criterion is that the asset must be capable of repeated use for a period of at least a year. Included in this category is equipment used only in peak or emergency periods, such as generators.

Assets that are not used in the normal course of business should not be included in this category. Thus, land held for speculative reasons or buildings no longer used in ordinary business operations should not be included in the property, plant, and equipment category. Instead, they should be classified as long-term investments.

Finally, if an item is held for resale to customers, it should be classified as inventory—not plant and equipment—no matter how durable it is. For example, a printing press that is held for sale by a printing press manufacturer would be considered inventory, whereas the same printing press would be considered plant and equipment for a printing company that buys it for use in operations.

Long-term assets differ from current assets in that they support the operating cycle instead of being a part of it. They are also expected to benefit the business for a longer period than do current assets. Current assets are expected to be used up or converted to cash within one year or during the operating cycle, whichever is longer. Long-term assets are expected to last beyond that period. Long-term assets and their related expenses are summarized in Figure 2.

Generally, long-lived assets are reported at carrying value, as presented in Figure 3. **Carrying value** is the unexpired part of the cost of an asset, not its market value; it is also called *book value.* If a long-lived asset loses some or all of its revenue-generating potential prior to the end of its useful life, the asset may be deemed impaired and its carrying value reduced. **Asset impairment** occurs when the sum of the expected cash flows from the asset is less than the carrying value of the asset.[2] Reducing carrying value to fair value, as measured by the present value of future cash flows, is an application of conservatism. All long-term assets are subject to an asset impairment evaluation. A reduction in carrying value as a result of impairment is recorded as a loss.

Facing deregulation and competition for the first time, six of the seven Baby Bell regional telephone companies, including Pacific Telesis, Bell South, and NYNEX, took writedowns in the billions of dollars. In the past, the cost of old equipment

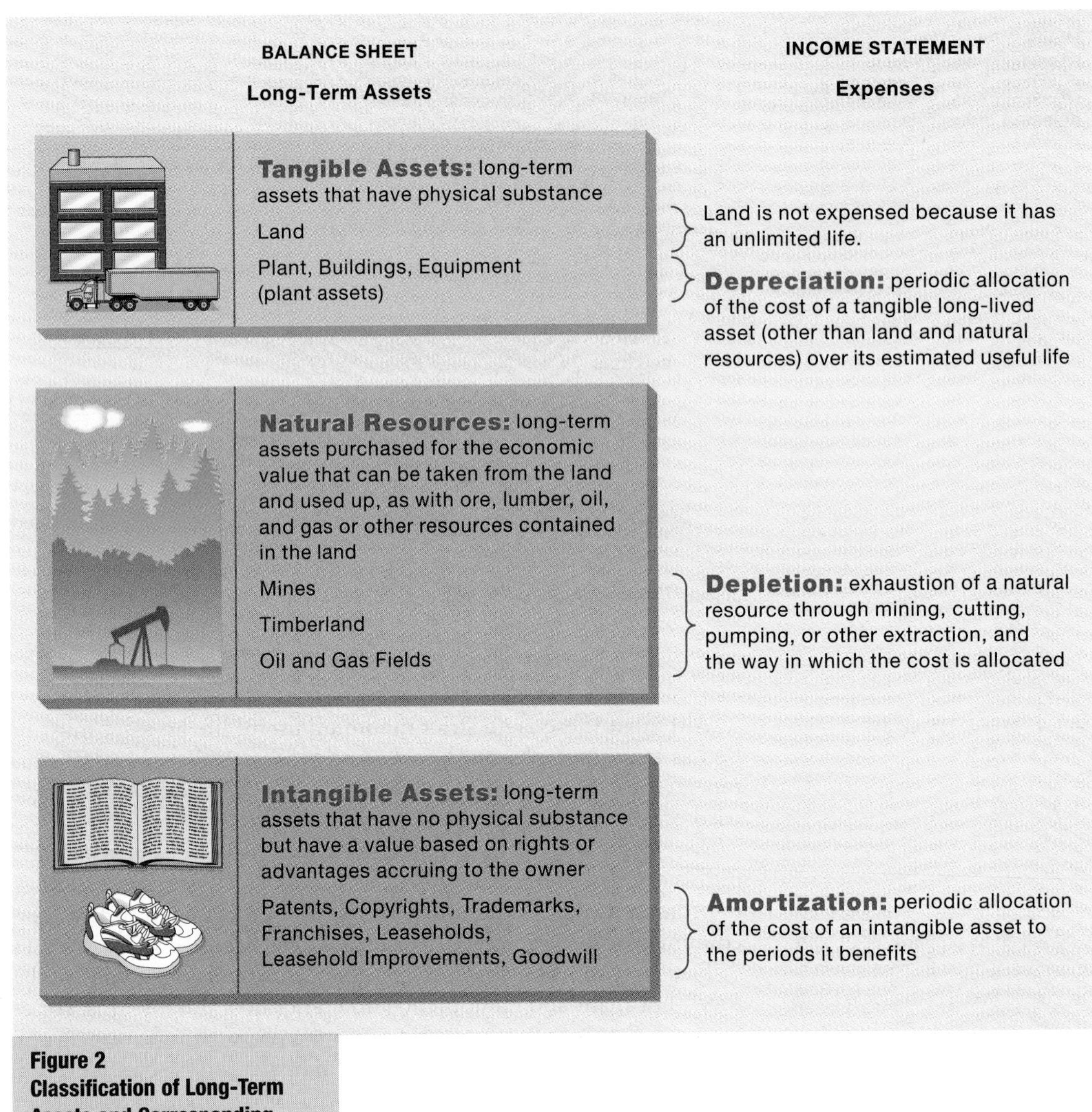

Figure 2
Classification of Long-Term Assets and Corresponding Expenses

Point to Emphasize: For an asset to be classified as intangible, it must lack physical substance, be long term, and (normally) represent a legal right or advantage.

could be passed on to consumers through regulated rate increases, but with competition, rates are decreasing, not increasing. As a result, the future cash flows cannot justify the recorded asset carrying values of aging copper telephone lines, switching gear, and other equipment. Estimated useful lives for these assets have been reduced by 50 percent or more. The writedowns have caused the companies to report operating losses.[3]

Deciding to Acquire Long-Term Assets

The decision to acquire a long-term asset involves a complex process. Methods of evaluating data to make rational decisions in this area are grouped under a topic called *capital budgeting*, which is usually covered as a management accounting topic. However, an awareness of the general nature of the problem is helpful in understanding the accounting issues related to long-term assets. To illustrate the

Plant Assets	Natural Resources	Intangible Assets
Less Accumulated Depreciation	Less Accumulated Depletion	Less Accumulated Amortization
Carrying Value	Carrying Value	Carrying Value

Figure 3
Carrying Value of Long-Term Assets on Balance Sheet

acquisition decision, let us assume that Irena Markova, M.D., is considering the purchase of a $5,000 computer for her office. Dr. Markova estimates that if she purchases the computer, she can reduce the hours of a part-time employee sufficiently to save net cash flows of $2,000 per year for four years and that the computer will be worth about $1,000 at the end of that period. These data are summarized as follows:

	20x1	20x2	20x3	20x4
Acquisition cost	($5,000)			
Net annual savings in cash flows	$2,000	$2,000	$2,000	$2,000
Disposal price				1,000
Net cash flows	($3,000)	$2,000	$2,000	$3,000

To place the cash flows on a comparable basis, it is helpful to use present value tables such as Tables 3 and 4 in the appendix on future value and present value tables. Assuming that the appropriate interest rate is 10 percent compounded annually, the purchase may be evaluated as follows:

		Present Value
Acquisition cost	Present value factor = 1.000 1.000 × $5,000	($5,000)
Net annual savings in cash flows	Present value factor = 3.170 (Table 4: 4 periods, 10%) 3.170 × $2,000	6,340
Disposal price	Present value factor = .683 (Table 3: 4 periods, 10%) .683 × $1,000	683
Net present value		$2,023

As long as the net present value is positive, Dr. Markova will earn at least 10 percent on the investment. In this case, the return is greater than 10 percent because the net present value is a positive $2,023. Based on this analysis, Dr. Markova makes the decision to purchase. However, there are other important considerations that have to be taken into account, such as the costs of training and maintenance, and the possibility that, because of unforeseen circumstances, the savings may not be as great as expected. In Dr. Markova's case, the decision to purchase is likely to be a good one because the net present value is both positive and large relative to the investment.

Information about a company's acquisitions of long-term assets may be found under investing activities in the statement of cash flows. For example, in referring

to this section of its annual report, the management of Ford Motor Company, a manufacturer of automobiles, makes the following statement: "We spent $7.9 billion for capital goods, such as machinery, equipment, tooling, and facilities."[4]

Financing Long-Term Assets

In addition to deciding whether or not to acquire a long-term asset, management must decide how to finance the asset if it is acquired. Some companies are profitable enough to pay for long-term assets out of cash flows from operations, but when financing is needed, some form of long-term arrangement related to the life of the asset is usually most appropriate. For example, an automobile loan generally spans four or five years, whereas a mortgage loan on a house may span as many as 30 years.

For a major long-term acquisition, a company may issue capital stock, long-term notes, or bonds. A good place to study a company's long-term financing is in the financing activities section of the statement of cash flows. For instance, in discussing this section, Ford Motor Company's management states, "Our automotive debt totaled $7.9 billion, which was 31 percent of total capitalization (stockholders' equity and Automotive debt), compared with 30 percent of total capitalization a year ago."[5]

Applying the Matching Rule to Long-Term Assets

Accounting for long-term assets requires the proper application of the matching rule through the resolution of two important issues. The first is how much of the total cost to allocate to expense in the current accounting period. The second is how much to retain on the balance sheet as an asset to benefit future periods. To resolve these issues, four important questions about the acquisition, use, and disposal of each long-term asset, as illustrated in Figure 4, must be answered:

1. How is the cost of the long-term asset determined?
2. How should the expired portion of the cost of the long-term asset be allocated against revenues over time?
3. How should subsequent expenditures, such as repairs and additions, be treated?
4. How should disposal of the long-term asset be recorded?

Clarification Note: Useful life is measured by the service units a business expects to receive from an asset. It should not be confused with physical life, which is often much longer. If the management of a new business is having difficulty determining an asset's estimated useful life, it may obtain help from trade magazines. Nearly every industry has at least one.

Because of the long life of long-term assets and the complexity of the transactions involving them, management has many choices and estimates to make. For example, acquisition cost may be complicated by group purchases, trade-ins, or construction costs. In addition, to allocate the cost of the asset to future periods effectively, management must estimate how long the asset will last and what it will be worth at the end of its use.

When making such estimates, it is helpful to think of a long-term asset as a bundle of services to be used in the operation of the business over a period of years. A delivery truck may provide 100,000 miles of service over its life. A piece of equipment may have the potential to produce 500,000 parts. A building may provide shelter for 50 years. As each of those assets is purchased, the company is paying in advance for 100,000 miles, the capacity to produce 500,000 parts, or 50 years of service. In essence, each asset is a type of long-term prepaid expense. The accounting problem is to spread the cost of the services over the useful life of the asset. As the services benefit the company over the years, the cost becomes an expense rather than an asset.

Point to Emphasize: Depreciation is the allocation of the acquisition cost of an asset, and any similarity between undepreciated cost and current market value is pure coincidence.

It is possible that, because of an advantageous purchase and specific market conditions, the market value of a building may rise. Nevertheless, depreciation must continue to be recorded because it is the result of an allocation, not a valuation, process. Eventually the building will wear out or become obsolete regardless of interim fluctuations in market value.

Factors That Affect the Computation of Depreciation

Four factors affect the computation of depreciation: (1) cost, (2) residual value, (3) depreciable cost, and (4) estimated useful life.

COST As explained earlier in the chapter, cost is the net purchase price plus all reasonable and necessary expenditures to get the asset in place and ready for use.

RESIDUAL VALUE The **residual value** of an asset is its estimated net scrap, salvage, or trade-in value as of the estimated date of disposal. Other terms often used to describe residual value are *salvage value* and *disposal value.*

Point to Emphasize: Residual value is the portion of an asset's acquisition cost expected to be recovered at the asset's disposal date.

Point to Emphasize: It is depreciable cost, not acquisition cost, that is allocated over the useful life of a plant asset.

DEPRECIABLE COST The **depreciable cost** of an asset is its cost less its residual value. For example, a truck that costs $12,000 and has a residual value of $3,000 would have a depreciable cost of $9,000. Depreciable cost must be allocated over the useful life of the asset.

ESTIMATED USEFUL LIFE **Estimated useful life** is the total number of service units expected from a long-term asset. Service units may be measured in terms of years the asset is expected to be used, units expected to be produced, miles expected to be driven, or similar measures. In computing the estimated useful life of an asset, an accountant should consider all relevant information, including (1) past experience with similar assets, (2) the asset's present condition, (3) the company's repair and maintenance policy, (4) current technological and industry trends, and (5) local conditions such as weather.

Depreciation is recorded at the end of the accounting period by an adjusting entry that takes the following form:

A = L + OE			
− −	Depreciation Expense, Asset Name	XXX	
	Accumulated Depreciation, Asset Name		XXX
	To record depreciation for the period		

FOCUS ON BUSINESS PRACTICE

Most airlines depreciate airplanes over an estimated useful life of 10 to 20 years. But how long will a properly maintained airplane really last? In July 1968 Western Airlines paid $3.3 million for a new Boeing 737. More than 78,000 flights and 30 years later this aircraft was still flying for a no-frills airline named Vanguard Airlines. During the course of its life, the owners of this aircraft have included Piedmont, Delta, US Airways, and other airlines. Virtually every part of the plane has been replaced over the years. Boeing believes the plane could theoretically make double the number of flights before it is retired.

The useful lives of many types of assets can be extended indefinitely if the assets are correctly maintained, but proper accounting in accordance with the matching rule requires depreciation over a "reasonable" useful life. Each airline that owned the plane would have accounted for the plane in this way.

Methods of Computing Depreciation

OBJECTIVE

4 Compute periodic depreciation under the straight-line method, the production method, and the declining-balance method

Related Text Assignments:
Q: 15, 16
SE: 4, 5, 6
E: 5, 6, 7
P: 2, 3, 7, 8
SD: 1
FRA: 1, 3, 4, 5

Many methods are used to allocate the cost of plant assets to accounting periods through depreciation. Each is proper for certain circumstances. The most common methods are (1) the straight-line method, (2) the production method, and (3) an accelerated method known as the declining-balance method.

Clarification Note: The straight-line depreciation method should be used when approximately equal asset benefit is obtained each year.

Point to Emphasize: Residual value and useful life are, at best, educated guesses.

STRAIGHT-LINE METHOD When the **straight-line method** is used to calculate depreciation, the depreciable cost of the asset is spread evenly over the estimated useful life of the asset. The straight-line method is based on the assumption that depreciation depends only on the passage of time. The depreciation expense for each period is computed by dividing the depreciable cost (cost of the depreciating asset less its estimated residual value) by the number of accounting periods in the asset's estimated useful life. Under this method, the rate of depreciation is the same in each year.

Suppose, for example, that a delivery truck costs $10,000 and has an estimated residual value of $1,000 at the end of its estimated useful life of five years. The annual depreciation would be $1,800 under the straight-line method, calculated as follows:

$$\frac{\text{Cost} - \text{Residual Value}}{\text{Estimated Useful Life}} = \frac{\$10{,}000 - \$1{,}000}{5 \text{ years}} = \$1{,}800 \text{ per year}$$

The depreciation for the five years would be as follows:

Depreciation Schedule, Straight-Line Method

	Cost	Yearly Depreciation	Accumulated Depreciation	Carrying Value
Date of purchase	$10,000	—	—	$10,000
End of first year	10,000	$1,800	$1,800	8,200
End of second year	10,000	1,800	3,600	6,400
End of third year	10,000	1,800	5,400	4,600
End of fourth year	10,000	1,800	7,200	2,800
End of fifth year	10,000	1,800	9,000	1,000

Instructional Strategy: In lieu of lecture and illustration, assign P 2 to small groups to prepare either in class or outside class. A member of each group will present part of P 2 and answer questions from the class. Encourage students to use good presentation skills. Review these, as necessary. Presenters may be randomly selected, so all should come prepared.

There are three important points to note from the depreciation schedule for the straight-line depreciation method. First, the depreciation is the same each year. Second, the accumulated depreciation increases uniformly. Third, the carrying value decreases uniformly until it reaches the estimated residual value.

PRODUCTION METHOD The **production method** of depreciation is based on the assumption that depreciation is solely the result of use and that the passage of time plays no role in the depreciation process. If we assume that the delivery truck from the previous example has an estimated useful life of 90,000 miles, the depreciation cost per mile would be determined as follows:

$$\frac{\text{Cost} - \text{Residual Value}}{\text{Estimated Units of Useful Life}} = \frac{\$10{,}000 - \$1{,}000}{90{,}000 \text{ miles}} = \$.10 \text{ per mile}$$

If we assume that the use of the truck was 20,000 miles for the first year, 30,000 miles for the second, 10,000 miles for the third, 20,000 miles for the fourth, and 10,000 miles for the fifth, the depreciation schedule for the delivery truck would appear as follows:

Parenthetical Note: The production method is appropriate when a company has widely fluctuating rates of production. For example, carpet mills often close during the first two weeks in July. Charging a full month's depreciation would not achieve the goal of matching cost with revenue. Conversely, the same mills may run double shifts in September. At that time, twice the usual amount of depreciation should be charged.

Depreciation Schedule, Production Method

	Cost	Miles	Yearly Depreciation	Accumulated Depreciation	Carrying Value
Date of purchase	$10,000	—	—	—	$10,000
End of first year	10,000	20,000	$2,000	$2,000	8,000
End of second year	10,000	30,000	3,000	5,000	5,000
End of third year	10,000	10,000	1,000	6,000	4,000
End of fourth year	10,000	20,000	2,000	8,000	2,000
End of fifth year	10,000	10,000	1,000	9,000	1,000

There is a direct relation between the amount of depreciation each year and the units of output or use. Also, the accumulated depreciation increases each year in direct relation to units of output or use. Finally, the carrying value decreases each year in direct relation to units of output or use until it reaches the estimated residual value.

Under the production method, the unit of output or use employed to measure the estimated useful life of each asset should be appropriate for that asset. For example, the number of items produced may be an appropriate measure for one machine, but the number of hours of use may be a better measure for another. The production method should be used only when the output of an asset over its useful life can be estimated with reasonable accuracy.

DECLINING-BALANCE METHOD An **accelerated method** of depreciation results in relatively large amounts of depreciation in the early years of an asset's life and smaller amounts in later years. Such a method, which is based on the passage of time, assumes that many kinds of plant assets are most efficient when new, and so provide more and better service in the early years of their useful life. It is consistent with the matching rule to allocate more depreciation to earlier years than to later years if the benefits or services received in the earlier years are greater.

Parenthetical Note: Accelerated depreciation is appropriate for assets that provide the greatest benefits in their early years. Under such a method, depreciation charges will be high in years when revenue generation from the asset is high.

An accelerated method also recognizes that changing technologies make some equipment lose service value rapidly. Thus, it is realistic to allocate more to depreciation in earlier years than in later years. New inventions and products result in obsolescence of equipment bought earlier, making it necessary to replace equipment sooner than if technology changed more slowly.

Another argument in favor of an accelerated method is that repair expense is likely to be greater in later years than in earlier years. Thus, the total of repair and depreciation expense remains fairly constant over a period of years. This result naturally assumes that the services received from the asset are roughly equal from year to year.

Point to Emphasize: The double-declining-balance method is the only method presented in which the residual value is not deducted before beginning the depreciation calculation.

Point to Emphasize: Under the double-declining-balance method, depreciation in the last year rarely equals the exact amount needed to reduce carrying value to residual value. Emphasize that depreciation in the last year is limited to the amount necessary to reduce carrying value to residual value.

The **declining-balance method** is the most common accelerated method of depreciation. Under this method, depreciation is computed by applying a fixed rate to the carrying value (the declining balance) of a tangible long-lived asset, resulting in higher depreciation charges during the early years of the asset's life. Though any fixed rate can be used, the most common rate is a percentage equal to twice the straight-line percentage. When twice the straight-line rate is used, the method is usually called the **double-declining-balance method**.

In our earlier example, the delivery truck had an estimated useful life of five years. Consequently, under the straight-line method, the depreciation rate for each year was 20 percent (100 percent ÷ 5 years).

Under the double-declining-balance method, the fixed rate is 40 percent (2 × 20 percent). This fixed rate is applied to the *remaining carrying value* at the end of each year. Estimated residual value is not taken into account in figuring depreciation except in a year when calculated depreciation exceeds the amount necessary to bring the carrying value down to the estimated residual value. The depreciation schedule for this method is as follows:

Depreciation Schedule, Double-Declining-Balance Method

	Cost	Yearly Depreciation		Accumulated Depreciation	Carrying Value
Date of purchase	$10,000		—	—	$10,000
End of first year	10,000	(40% × $10,000)	$4,000	$4,000	6,000
End of second year	10,000	(40% × $6,000)	2,400	6,400	3,600
End of third year	10,000	(40% × $3,600)	1,440	7,840	2,160
End of fourth year	10,000	(40% × $2,160)	864	8,704	1,296
End of fifth year	10,000		296*	9,000	1,000

*Depreciation limited to amount necessary to reduce carrying value to residual value: $296 = $1,296 (previous carrying value) − $1,000 (residual value).

Parenthetical Note: An asset remains on the books as long as it is in use. Even if the asset is fully depreciated, the company should not remove it from the books until it is taken out of service.

Note that the fixed rate is always applied to the carrying value at the end of the previous year. The depreciation is greatest in the first year and declines each year after that. Finally, the depreciation in the fifth year is limited to the amount necessary to reduce carrying value to residual value.

COMPARING THE THREE METHODS A visual comparison may provide a better understanding of the three depreciation methods described above. Figure 5 compares yearly depreciation and carrying value under the three methods. In the left-hand graph, which shows yearly depreciation, straight-line depreciation is uniform at $1,800 per year over the five-year period. However, the double-declining-balance method begins at an amount greater than straight-line ($4,000) and decreases each year to amounts that are less than straight-line (ultimately, $296). The production method does not generate a regular pattern because of the random fluctuation of the depreciation from year to year. The three yearly depreciation patterns are reflected in the graph of carrying value. In that graph, each method starts in the same place (cost of $10,000) and ends at the same place (residual value of $1,000). It is the patterns during the useful life of the asset that differ for each method. For instance, the carrying value under the straight-line method is always greater than that under the double-declining-balance method, except at the beginning and end of useful life.

Figure 5
Graphical Comparison of Three Methods of Determining Depreciation

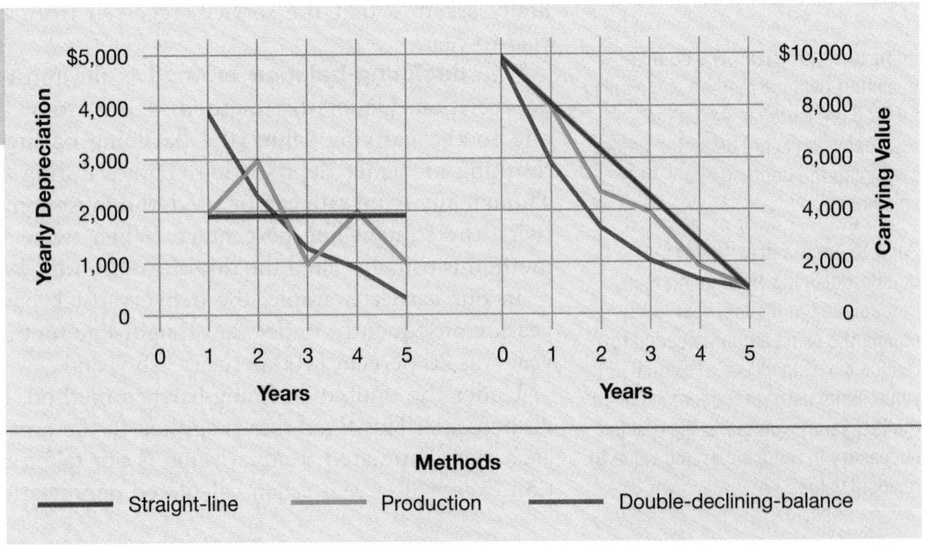

Focus on Business Practice

Most companies choose the straight-line method of depreciation for financial reporting purposes, as shown in Figure 6. Only about 13 percent use some type of accelerated method and 6 percent use the production method. These figures tend to be misleading about the importance of accelerated depreciation methods, however, especially when it comes to income taxes. Federal income tax laws allow either the straight-line method or an accelerated method. For tax purposes, according to *Accounting Trends & Techniques,* about 75 percent of the 600 large companies studied preferred an accelerated method. Companies use different methods of depreciation for good reason. The straight-line method can be advantageous for financial reporting because it can produce the highest net income, and an accelerated method can be beneficial for tax purposes because it can result in lower income taxes.

Figure 6
Depreciation Methods Used by 600 Large Companies

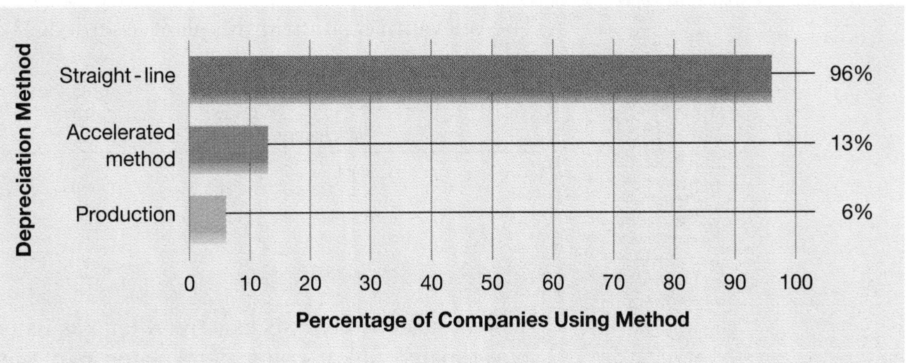

Total percentage exceeds 100 because some companies used different methods for different types of depreciable assets.

Source: Reprinted with permission from *Accounting Trends & Techniques,* Copyright © 1999 by the American Institute of Certified Public Accountants, Inc.

Clarification Note: There are conflicting objectives here. For financial reporting purposes, the objective is to accurately measure performance. For tax purposes, the objective is to minimize tax liability.

Disposal of Depreciable Assets

OBJECTIVE

5 Account for the disposal of depreciable assets not involving exchanges

Related Text Assignments:
Q: 17, 18
SE: 7
E: 8, 9
P: 4
FRA: 5

When plant assets are no longer useful because they are worn out or obsolete, they may be discarded, sold, or traded in on the purchase of new plant and equipment. For accounting purposes, a plant asset may be disposed of in three different ways: It may be (1) discarded, (2) sold for cash, or (3) exchanged for another asset. To illustrate how each of these cases is recorded, assume that MGC Company purchased a machine on January 1, 20x0, for $6,500 and planned to depreciate it on a straight-line basis over an estimated useful life of ten years. The residual value at the end of ten years was estimated to be $500. On January 1, 20x7, the balances of the relevant accounts in the plant asset ledger appear as follows:

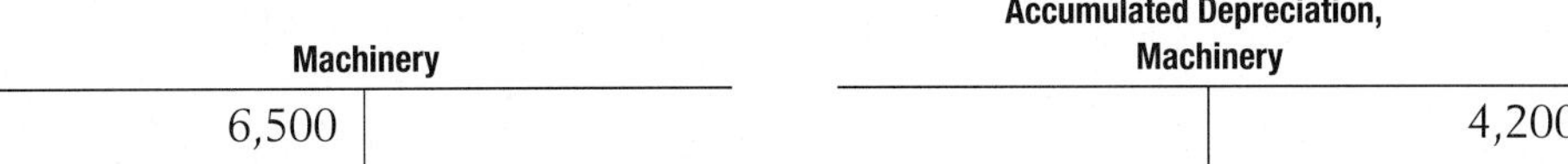

Machinery		Accumulated Depreciation, Machinery	
6,500			4,200

Enrichment Note: Plant assets may also be disposed of by involuntary conversion (e.g., fire, theft, flood) or governmental condemnation. For reporting purposes, involuntary conversions are treated as if the assets were discarded or sold.

On September 30, 20x7, management disposes of the asset. The next few sections illustrate the accounting treatment to record depreciation for the partial year and the disposal under several assumptions.

Depreciation for Partial Year

Teaching Note: Explain that when an asset is disposed of, a company must do two things. First, it must bring the depreciation up to date. Second, it must remove all evidence of ownership of the asset, including the contra account Accumulated Depreciation.

When a plant asset is discarded or disposed of in some other way, it is first necessary to record depreciation expense for the partial year up to the date of disposal. This step is required because the asset was used until that date and, under the matching rule, the accounting period should receive the proper allocation of depreciation expense.

In this illustration, MGC Company disposes of the machinery on September 30. The entry to record the depreciation for the first nine months of 20x7 (nine-twelfths of a year) is as follows:

A = L + OE
− −

Sept. 30	Depreciation Expense, Machinery	450	
	Accumulated Depreciation, Machinery		450
	To record depreciation up to date of disposal		

$$\frac{\$6{,}500 - \$500}{10} \times \frac{9}{12} = \$450$$

The relevant accounts in the plant asset ledger appear as follows after the entry is posted:

Machinery	
6,500	

Accumulated Depreciation, Machinery	
	4,650

Discarded Plant Assets

Point to Emphasize: A fully depreciated asset is kept on the books as long as it is still being used in the business. When a physical count of plant assets is made and reconciled with the general ledger control account and the subsidiary ledger, all assets must be accounted for.

A plant asset rarely lasts exactly as long as its estimated life. If it lasts longer than its estimated life, it is not depreciated past the point at which its carrying value equals its residual value. The purpose of depreciation is to spread the depreciable cost of an asset over the estimated life of the asset. Thus, the total accumulated depreciation should never exceed the total depreciable cost. If an asset remains in use beyond the end of its estimated life, its cost and accumulated depreciation remain in the ledger accounts. Proper records will thus be available for maintaining control over plant assets. If the residual value is zero, the carrying value of a fully depreciated asset is zero until the asset is disposed of. If such an asset is discarded, no gain or loss results.

In the illustration, however, the discarded equipment has a carrying value of $1,850 at the time of its disposal. The carrying value is computed from the ledger accounts above as machinery of $6,500 less accumulated depreciation of $4,650. A loss equal to the carrying value should be recorded when the machine is discarded.

A = L + OE
+ −
−

Sept. 30	Accumulated Depreciation, Machinery	4,650	
	Loss on Disposal of Machinery	1,850	
	Machinery		6,500
	Discarded machine no longer used in the business		

Gains and losses on disposals of plant assets are classified as other revenues and expenses on the income statement.

Plant Assets Sold for Cash

The entry to record a plant asset sold for cash is similar to the one just illustrated except that the receipt of cash should also be recorded. The following entries show how to record the sale of a machine under three assumptions about the selling price. In the first case, the $1,850 cash received is exactly equal to the $1,850 carrying value of the machine; therefore, no gain or loss results.

A = L + OE				
+ + −	Sept. 30	Cash Accumulated Depreciation, Machinery Machinery Sale of machine for carrying value; no gain or loss	1,850 4,650	 6,500

In the second case, the $1,000 cash received is less than the carrying value of $1,850, so a loss of $850 is recorded.

A = L + OE				
+ − + −	Sept. 30	Cash Accumulated Depreciation, Machinery Loss on Sale of Machinery Machinery Sale of machine at less than carrying value; loss of $850 ($1,850 − $1,000) recorded	1,000 4,650 850	 6,500

In the third case, the $2,000 cash received exceeds the carrying value of $1,850, so a gain of $150 is recorded.

A = L + OE				
+ + + −	Sept. 30	Cash Accumulated Depreciation, Machinery Gain on Sale of Machinery Machinery Sale of machine at more than the carrying value; gain of $150 ($2,000 − $1,850) recorded	2,000 4,650	 150 6,500

Exchanges of Plant Assets

OBJECTIVE

6 Account for the disposal of depreciable assets involving exchanges

Related Text Assignments:
Q: 19, 20
SE: 8
E: 8, 9
P: 4

Teaching Note: It is important for students to understand the difference between similar and dissimilar assets. For assets to be similar, they must be used for similar purposes. A typewriter, for example, is similar to a word processor. Dissimilar assets, such as a pickup truck and a cement mixer, are not used for similar purposes.

Discussion Question: Are gains on similar assets completely unrecognized? **Answer:** No. Since the basis of the new asset is reduced by the unrecognized gain, there will be less depreciation expense over the life of the new asset.

Businesses also dispose of plant assets by trading them in on the purchase of other plant assets. Exchanges may involve similar assets, such as an old machine traded in on a newer model, or dissimilar assets, such as a machine traded in on a truck. In either case, the purchase price is reduced by the amount of the trade-in allowance.

The basic accounting for exchanges of plant assets is similar to accounting for sales of plant assets for cash. If the trade-in allowance received is greater than the carrying value of the asset surrendered, there has been a gain. If the allowance is less, there has been a loss. There are special rules for recognizing these gains and losses, depending on the nature of the assets exchanged.

Exchange	Losses Recognized	Gains Recognized
For financial accounting purposes		
Of dissimilar assets	Yes	Yes
Of similar assets	Yes	No
For income tax purposes		
Of dissimilar assets	Yes	Yes
Of similar assets	No	No

Both gains and losses are recognized when a company exchanges dissimilar assets. Assets are dissimilar when they perform different functions or do not meet specific monetary and type of business criteria for being considered similar assets. For financial accounting purposes, most exchanges are considered to be exchanges of dissimilar assets. In rare cases, when exchanges meet the specific criteria for them to be considered exchanges of similar assets, the gains are not recognized. In these cases, you could think of the trade-in as an extension of the life and usefulness of the original machine. Instead of recognizing a gain at the time of the exchange, the company records the new machine at the sum of the carrying value of the older machine plus any cash paid.[10]

Parenthetical Note: Recognizing losses but not gains on similar assets follows the convention of conservatism.

For income tax purposes, similar assets are defined as those performing the same function. Neither gains nor losses on exchanges of these assets are recognized in computing a company's income tax liability. Thus, in practice, accountants face cases where both gains and losses are recognized (exchanges of dissimilar assets), cases where losses are recognized and gains are not recognized (exchanges of similar assets), and cases where neither gains nor losses are recognized (exchanges of similar assets for income tax purposes). Since all these options are used in practice, they are all illustrated in the following paragraphs.

LOSS RECOGNIZED ON THE EXCHANGE A loss is recognized for financial accounting purposes on all exchanges in which a material loss occurs. A loss occurs when the trade-in allowance is less than the carrying value of the old asset. To illustrate the recognition of a loss, let us assume that the firm in our example exchanges the machine for a newer, more modern machine on the following terms:

Discussion Question: What is the relationship, if any, between carrying value and trade-in value? **Answer:** There is none. Carrying value is original cost minus accumulated depreciation to date, whereas trade-in value is fair market value on the date of the exchange.

List price of new machine	$12,000
Trade-in allowance for old machine	(1,000)
Cash payment required	$11,000

In this case the trade-in allowance ($1,000) is less than the carrying value ($1,850) of the old machine. The loss on the exchange is $850 ($1,850 − $1,000). The following journal entry records this transaction under the assumption that the loss is to be recognized.

A = L + OE	Date	Account	Debit	Credit
+ −	Sept. 30	Machinery (new)	12,000	
+		Accumulated Depreciation, Machinery	4,650	
−		Loss on Exchange of Machinery	850	
−		Machinery (old)		6,500
		Cash		11,000
		Exchange of machines		

LOSS NOT RECOGNIZED ON THE EXCHANGE In the previous example, in which a loss was recognized, the new asset was recorded at the purchase price of $12,000 and a loss of $850 was recorded. If the transaction involves similar assets and is to be recorded for income tax purposes, the loss should not be recognized. In this case, the cost basis of the new asset will reflect the effect of the unrecorded loss. The cost basis is computed by adding the cash payment to the carrying value of the old asset:

Point to Emphasize: For income tax purposes, gains and losses on the exchange of similar assets are not recognized.

Carrying value of old machine	$ 1,850
Cash paid	11,000
Cost basis of new machine	$12,850

Note that no loss is recognized in the entry to record this transaction.

A = L + OE	Date	Account	Debit	Credit
+	Sept. 30	Machinery (new)	12,850	
+		Accumulated Depreciation, Machinery	4,650	
−		Machinery (old)		6,500
−		Cash		11,000
		Exchange of machines		

Note that the new machinery is reported at the purchase price of $12,000 plus the unrecognized loss of $850. The nonrecognition of the loss on the exchange is, in effect, a postponement of the loss. Since depreciation of the new machine will be computed based on a cost of $12,850 instead of $12,000, the "unrecognized" loss results in more depreciation each year on the new machine than if the loss had been recognized.

GAIN RECOGNIZED ON THE EXCHANGE Gains on exchanges are recognized for accounting purposes when dissimilar assets are involved. To illustrate the recognition of a gain, we continue with our example, assuming the following terms and assuming the machines being exchanged serve different functions:

List price of new machine	$12,000
Trade-in allowance for old machine	(3,000)
Cash payment required	$ 9,000

Here the trade-in allowance ($3,000) exceeds the carrying value ($1,850) of the old machine by $1,150. Thus, there is a gain on the exchange, assuming that the price of the new machine has not been inflated to allow for an excessive trade-in value. In other words, a gain exists if the trade-in allowance represents the fair market value of the old machine. Assuming that this condition is true, the entry to record the transaction is as follows:

A = L + OE				
+ +	Sept. 30	Machinery (new)	12,000	
+		Accumulated Depreciation, Machinery	4,650	
−		Gain on Exchange of Machinery		1,150
−		Machinery (old)		6,500
		Cash		9,000
		Exchange of machines		

GAIN NOT RECOGNIZED ON THE EXCHANGE When assets meeting the criteria for similar assets are exchanged, gains are not recognized for accounting or income tax purposes. The cost basis of the new machine must reflect the effect of the unrecorded gain. This cost basis is computed by adding the cash payment to the carrying value of the old asset.

Carrying value of old machine	$ 1,850
Cash paid	9,000
Cost basis of new machine	$10,850

The entry to record the transaction is as follows:

A = L + OE				
+	Sept. 30	Machinery (new)	10,850	
+		Accumulated Depreciation, Machinery	4,650	
−		Machinery (old)		6,500
−		Cash		9,000
		Exchange of machines		

As with the nonrecognition of losses, the nonrecognition of the gain on an exchange is, in effect, a postponement of the gain. In this illustration, when the new machine is eventually discarded or sold, its cost basis will be $10,850 instead of its original price of $12,000. Since depreciation will be computed on the cost basis of $10,850, the "unrecognized" gain is reflected in lower depreciation each year on the new machine than if the gain had been recognized.

Accounting for Natural Resources

OBJECTIVE

7 Identify the issues related to accounting for natural resources and compute depletion

Natural resources are shown on the balance sheet as long-term assets with such descriptive titles as Timberlands, Oil and Gas Reserves, and Mineral Deposits. The distinguishing characteristic of these assets is that they are converted into inventory by cutting, pumping, or mining. In terms of two of our examples, an oil field is a reservoir of unpumped oil, and a coal mine is a deposit of unmined coal. When

Related Text Assignments:
Q: 21, 22
SE: 9
E: 10
FRA: 4

the timber is cut, the oil is pumped, or the coal is mined, it becomes an inventory of the product to be sold. Natural resources are recorded at acquisition cost, which may also include some costs of development. As the resource is converted through the process of cutting, pumping, or mining, the asset account must be proportionally reduced. The carrying value of oil reserves on the balance sheet, for example, is reduced by a small amount for each barrel of oil pumped. As a result, the original cost of the oil reserves is gradually reduced, and depletion is recognized in the amount of the decrease.

Depletion

Clarification Note: Students often erroneously classify natural resources as intangible assets. They are correctly classified as components of property, plant, and equipment.

Enrichment Note: When determining the total units available for depletion, management uses only the total units that are economically feasible to extract. This follows the cost-benefit principle. That is, when the cost of extracting a mineral is greater than the expected revenue from the sale of the mineral, the company stops extracting it.

The term *depletion* is used to describe not only the exhaustion of a natural resource but also the proportional allocation of the cost of a natural resource to the units extracted. The costs are allocated in a way that is much like the production method used to calculate depreciation. When a natural resource is purchased or developed, there must be an estimate of the total units that will be available, such as barrels of oil, tons of coal, or board-feet of lumber. The depletion cost per unit is determined by dividing the cost of the natural resource (less residual value, if any) by the estimated number of units available. The amount of the depletion cost for each accounting period is then computed by multiplying the depletion cost per unit by the number of units pumped, mined, or cut and sold. For example, for a mine having an estimated 1,500,000 tons of coal, a cost of $1,800,000, and an estimated residual value of $300,000, the depletion charge per ton of coal is $1. Thus, if 115,000 tons of coal are mined and sold during the first year, the depletion charge for the year is $115,000. This charge is recorded as follows:

A = L + OE
− −

Dec. 31	Depletion Expense, Coal Deposits	115,000	
	Accumulated Depletion, Coal Deposits		115,000
	To record depletion of coal mine: $1 per ton for 115,000 tons mined and sold		

Discussion Question: Why would an extracted natural resource be recorded as inventory until it is sold? **Answer:** The matching rule dictates that the extracted resource be treated as an asset until it is sold. At that point, the asset cost is converted into an expense.

On the balance sheet, the mine would be presented as follows:

Coal Deposits	$1,800,000	
Less Accumulated Depletion	115,000	$1,685,000

Sometimes a natural resource that is extracted in one year is not sold until a later year. It is important to note that it would then be recorded as a depletion *expense* in the year it is *sold*. The part not sold is considered inventory.

Depreciation of Closely Related Plant Assets

Discussion Question: Why would a company abandon equipment that is still in good working condition? **Answer:** One reason is that it might cost the company more to dismantle the equipment and move it to another site than to abandon it.

Discussion Question: Using the production method to depreciate long-term assets located at excavation sites is justified by which accounting convention? **Answer:** The matching rule.

Natural resources often require special on-site buildings and equipment, such as conveyors, roads, tracks, and drilling and pumping devices that are necessary to extract the resource. If the useful life of those assets is longer than the estimated time it will take to deplete the resource, a special problem arises. Because such long-term assets are often abandoned and have no useful purpose once all the resources have been extracted, they should be depreciated on the same basis as the depletion is computed. For example, if machinery with a useful life of ten years is installed on an oil field that is expected to be depleted in eight years, the machinery should be depreciated over the eight-year period, using the production method. That way, each year's depreciation will be proportional to the year's depletion. If one-sixth of the oil field's total reserves is pumped in one year, then the depreciation should be one-sixth of the machinery's cost minus the residual value. If the useful life of a long-term asset is less than the expected life of the depleting asset, the shorter life should be used to compute depreciation. In such cases, or when an asset will not be abandoned once the reserves have been fully depleted, other depreciation methods, such as straight-line or declining-balance, are appropriate.

Development and Exploration Costs in the Oil and Gas Industry

The costs of exploration and development of oil and gas resources can be accounted for under either of two methods. Under the **successful efforts method**, successful exploration—for example, the cost of a producing oil well—is a cost of the resource. This cost should be recorded as an asset and depleted over the estimated life of the resource. An unsuccessful exploration—such as the cost of a dry well—is written off immediately as a loss. Because of these immediate write-offs, successful efforts accounting is considered the more conservative method and is used by most large oil companies.

Exploration-minded independent oil companies, on the other hand, argue that the cost of dry wells is part of the overall cost of the systematic development of an oil field and thus a part of the cost of producing wells. Under this **full-costing method**, all costs, including the cost of dry wells, are recorded as assets and depleted over the estimated life of the producing resources. This method tends to improve earnings performance in the early years for companies using it. Either method is permitted by the Financial Accounting Standards Board.[11]

Accounting for Intangible Assets

OBJECTIVE

8 Apply the matching rule to intangible assets, including research and development costs and goodwill

Related Text Assignments:
Q: 23, 24, 25, 26, 27, 28, 29
SE: 10
E: 11
P: 5
SD: 2, 4, 5
FRA: 2, 3, 4, 5

The purchase of an intangible asset is a special kind of capital expenditure. An intangible asset is long term, but it has no physical substance. Its value comes from the long-term rights or advantages it offers to its owner. The most common examples—patents, copyrights, leaseholds, leasehold improvements, trademarks and brand names, franchises, licenses, and goodwill—are described in Table 1. Some current assets, such as accounts receivable and certain prepaid expenses, have no physical substance, but they are not classified as intangible assets because they are short term. Intangible assets are both long term and nonphysical.

Intangible assets are accounted for at acquisition cost—that is, the amount that was paid for them. Some intangible assets, such as goodwill and trademarks, may be acquired at little or no cost. Even though they may have great value and be needed for profitable operations, they should not appear on the balance sheet unless they have been purchased from another party at a price established in the marketplace.

Point to Emphasize: Generally, intangible assets, including goodwill, are recorded only when purchased. An exception is the cost of internally developed computer software after a working prototype has been developed.

The accounting issues connected with intangible assets are the same as those connected with other long-lived assets. The Accounting Principles Board, in its *Opinion No. 17*, lists them as follows:

1. Determining an initial carrying amount
2. Accounting for that amount after acquisition under normal business conditions —that is, through periodic write-off or amortization—in a manner similar to depreciation
3. Accounting for that amount if the value declines substantially and permanently[12]

Terminology: Useful life refers to how long an intangible asset will be contributing income to a firm.

Besides these three problems, an intangible asset has no physical substance and, in some cases, may be impossible to identify. For these reasons, its value and its useful life may be quite hard to estimate.

Table 1. Accounting for Intangible Assets

Type	Description	Accounting Treatment
Patent	An exclusive right granted by the federal government for a period of 20 years to make a particular product or use a specific process. A design may be granted a patent for 14 years.	The cost of successfully defending a patent in a patent infringement suit is added to the acquisition cost of the patent. Amortize over the useful life, which may be less than the legal life.
Copyright	An exclusive right granted by the federal government to the possessor to publish and sell literary, musical, or other artistic materials for a period of the author's life plus 70 years; includes computer programs.	Record at acquisition cost and amortize over the useful life, which is often much shorter than the legal life, but not to exceed 40 years. For example, the cost of paperback rights to a popular novel would typically be amortized over a useful life of two to four years.
Leasehold	A right to occupy land or buildings under a long-term rental contract. For example, Company A, which owns but does not want to use a prime retail location, sells or subleases Company B the right to use it for ten years in return for one or more rental payments. Company B has purchased a leasehold.	Debit Leasehold for the amount of the rental payment, and amortize it over the remaining life of the lease. Payments to the lessor during the life of the lease should be debited to Lease Expense.
Leasehold improvements	Improvements to leased property that become the property of the lessor (the person who owns the property) at the end of the lease.	Debit Leasehold Improvements for the cost of improvements, and amortize the cost of the improvements over the remaining life of the lease.
Trademark, brand name	A registered symbol or name that can be used only by its owner to identify a product or service.	Debit Trademark or Brand Name for the acquisition cost, and amortize it over a reasonable life, not to exceed 40 years.
Franchise, license	A right to an exclusive territory or market, or the right to use a formula, technique, process, or design.	Debit Franchise or License for the acquisition cost, and amortize it over a reasonable life, not to exceed 40 years.
Goodwill	The excess of the cost of a group of assets (usually a business) over the fair market value of the net assets if purchased individually.	Debit Goodwill for the acquisition cost. Goodwill is not subject to amortization after 2001, but its value is evaluated annually for impairment.

The Accounting Principles Board has decided that a company should record as assets the costs of intangible assets acquired from others. However, the company should record as expenses the costs of developing intangible assets. Also, intangible assets that have a determinable useful life, such as patents, copyrights, and leaseholds, should be written off through periodic amortization over that useful life in much the same way that plant assets are depreciated. Even though some intangible assets, such as brand names and trademarks, have no measurable limit on their lives, they should still be amortized over a reasonable length of time (not to exceed 40

Point to Emphasize: Intangible assets should never be amortized over more than 40 years.

survey of large businesses indicated that 65 percent used group depreciation for all or part of their plant assets.[19]

Special Types of Capital Expenditures

Point to Emphasize: Other examples of betterments would include replacing stairs with an escalator in a department store and paving a gravel parking lot.

In addition to the acquisition of plant assets, natural resources, and intangible assets, capital expenditures also include additions and betterments. An **addition** is an enlargement to the physical layout of a plant asset. As an example, if a new wing is added to a building, the benefits from the expenditure will be received over several years, and the amount paid for it should be debited to the asset account. A **betterment** is an improvement that does not add to the physical layout of a plant asset but rather increases the quality of the asset or its output. Installation of an air-conditioning system is an example of a betterment that will offer benefits over a period of years; thus its cost should be charged to an asset account.

Among the more usual kinds of revenue expenditures for plant equipment are the repairs, maintenance, lubrication, cleaning, and inspection necessary to keep an asset in good working condition. Repairs fall into two categories: ordinary repairs and extraordinary repairs. **Ordinary repairs** are expenditures that are necessary to maintain an asset in good operating condition in order to achieve its original intended useful life. Trucks must have periodic tune-ups, their tires and batteries must be regularly replaced, and other routine repairs must be made. Offices and halls must be painted regularly, and broken tiles or woodwork must be replaced. Such repairs are a current expense.

Point to Emphasize: More examples of extraordinary repairs would be putting a new motor in a cement mixer and replacing the roof on a building, thereby extending its life.

Extraordinary repairs are repairs of a more significant nature—they affect the estimated residual value or estimated useful life of an asset. For example, a boiler for heating a building may be given a complete overhaul, at a cost of several thousand dollars, that will extend its useful life by five years. Typically, extraordinary repairs are recorded by debiting the Accumulated Depreciation account, under the assumption that some of the depreciation previously recorded has now been eliminated. The effect of this reduction in the Accumulated Depreciation account is to increase the carrying value of the asset by the cost of the extraordinary repair. Consequently, the new carrying value of the asset should be depreciated over the new estimated useful life.

Let us assume that a machine that cost $10,000 had no estimated residual value and an original estimated useful life of ten years. After eight years, the accumulated depreciation under the straight-line method was $8,000, and the carrying value was $2,000 ($10,000 − $8,000). At that point, the machine was given a major overhaul costing $1,500. This expenditure extended the machine's useful life three years beyond the original ten years. The entry for the extraordinary repair would be as follows:

A = L + OE				
+	Jan. 4	Accumulated Depreciation, Machinery	1,500	
−		Cash		1,500
		Extraordinary repair to machinery		

The annual periodic depreciation for each of the five years remaining in the machine's useful life would be calculated as follows:

Carrying value before extraordinary repairs	$2,000
Extraordinary repairs	1,500
Total	$3,500

$$\text{Annual periodic depreciation} = \frac{\$3{,}500}{5 \text{ years}} = \$700$$

If the machine remains in use for the five years expected after the major overhaul, the total of the five annual depreciation charges of $700 will exactly equal the new carrying value, including the cost of the extraordinary repair.

Cost Recovery for Federal Income Tax Purposes

In 1986, Congress passed the Tax Reform Act of 1986, arguably the most sweeping revision of federal tax laws since the original enactment of the Internal Revenue Code in 1913. First, a company may elect to expense the first $17,500 (which increases to $25,000 by tax year 2003) of equipment expenditures rather than recording them as an asset. Second, a new method for writing off expenditures recorded as assets, the **Modified Accelerated Cost Recovery System (MACRS)**, may be elected. MACRS discards the concepts of estimated useful life and residual value. Instead, it requires that a cost recovery allowance be computed (1) on the unadjusted cost of property being recovered and (2) over a period of years prescribed by the law for all property of similar types. The accelerated method prescribed under MACRS for most property other than real estate is 200 percent declining balance with a half-year convention (only one half-year's depreciation is allowed in the year of purchase, and one half-year's depreciation is taken in the last year). In addition, the period over which the cost may be recovered is specified. Recovery of the cost of property placed in service after December 31, 1986, is calculated as prescribed in the 1986 law.

Congress hoped that MACRS would encourage businesses to invest in new plant and equipment by allowing them to write off such assets rapidly. MACRS accelerates the write-off of these investments in two ways. First, the prescribed recovery periods are often shorter than the estimated useful lives used for calculating depreciation for the financial statements. Second, the accelerated method allowed under the new law enables businesses to recover most of the cost of their investments early in the depreciation process.

Clarification Note: MACRS depreciation is used for tax purposes only. It cannot be used for financial reporting.

Tax methods of depreciation are not usually acceptable for financial reporting under generally accepted accounting principles because the recovery periods are shorter than the depreciable assets' estimated useful lives.

Chapter Review

REVIEW OF LEARNING OBJECTIVES

Check out ACE, a self-quizzing program on chapter content, at http://college.hmco.com.

1. **Identify the types of long-term assets and explain the management issues related to accounting for them.** Long-term assets are assets that are used in the operation of a business, are not intended for resale, and have a useful life of more than one year. Long-term assets are either tangible or intangible. In the former category are land, plant assets, and natural resources. In the latter are trademarks, patents, franchises, goodwill, and other rights. The accounting issues associated with long-term assets relate to the decision to acquire the assets, the means of financing the assets, and the methods of accounting for the assets.

2. **Distinguish between capital and revenue expenditures, and account for the cost of property, plant, and equipment.** It is important to distinguish between capital expenditures, which are recorded as assets, and revenue expenditures, which are recorded as expenses of the current period. The error of classifying one as the other will have an important effect on net income. The acquisition cost of property, plant, and equipment includes all expenditures

that are reasonable and necessary to get such an asset in place and ready for use. Among these expenditures are purchase price, installation cost, freight charges, and insurance during transit.

3. **Define *depreciation,* state the factors that affect its computation, and show how to record it.** Depreciation is the periodic allocation of the cost of a plant asset over its estimated useful life. It is recorded by debiting Depreciation Expense and crediting a related contra-asset account called Accumulated Depreciation. Factors that affect the computation of depreciation are cost, residual value, depreciable cost, and estimated useful life.

4. **Compute periodic depreciation under the straight-line method, production method, and declining-balance method.** Depreciation is commonly computed by the straight-line method, the production method, or an accelerated method. The straight-line method is related directly to the passage of time, whereas the production method is related directly to use. An accelerated method results in relatively large amounts of depreciation in earlier years and reduced amounts in later years. It is based on the assumption that plant assets provide greater economic benefit in their earlier years than in later years. The most common accelerated method is the declining-balance method.

5. **Account for the disposal of depreciable assets not involving exchanges.** Long-term depreciable assets may be disposed of by being discarded, sold, or exchanged. When long-term assets are disposed of, it is necessary to record the depreciation up to the date of disposal and to remove the carrying value from the accounts by removing the cost from the asset account and the depreciation to date from the accumulated depreciation account. If a long-term asset is sold at a price that differs from its carrying value, there is a gain or loss that should be recorded and reported on the income statement.

6. **Account for the disposal of depreciable assets involving exchanges.** In recording exchanges of similar plant assets, a gain or loss may arise. According to the Accounting Principles Board, losses, but not gains, should be recognized at the time of the exchange. When a gain is not recognized, the new asset is recorded at the carrying value of the old asset plus any cash paid. For income tax purposes, neither gains nor losses are recognized in the exchange of similar assets. When dissimilar assets are exchanged, gains and losses are recognized under both accounting and income tax rules.

7. **Identify the issues related to accounting for natural resources and compute depletion.** Natural resources are wasting assets that are converted to inventory by cutting, pumping, mining, or other forms of extraction. Natural resources are recorded at cost as long-term assets. They are allocated as expenses through depletion charges as the resources are sold. The depletion charge is based on the ratio of the resource extracted to the total estimated resource. A major issue related to this subject is accounting for oil and gas reserves.

8. **Apply the matching rule to intangible assets, including research and development costs and goodwill.** The purchase of an intangible asset should be treated as a capital expenditure and recorded at acquisition cost, which in turn should be amortized over the useful life of the asset. The FASB requires that research and development costs be treated as revenue expenditures and charged as expenses in the periods of expenditure. Software costs are treated as research and development costs and expensed until a feasible working program is developed, after which time the costs may be capitalized and amortized over a reasonable estimated life. Goodwill is the excess of the amount paid for the purchase of a business over the fair market value of the net

assets and is usually related to the superior earning potential of the business. It should be recorded only if paid for in connection with the purchase of a business, and it should be amortized over a period not to exceed 40 years.

SUPPLEMENTAL OBJECTIVE

9. **Apply depreciation methods to problems of partial years, revised rates, groups of similar items, special types of capital expenditures, and cost recovery.** In actual business practice, many factors affect depreciation calculations. It may be necessary to calculate depreciation for partial years because assets are bought and sold throughout the year, or to revise depreciation rates because of changed conditions. Because it is often difficult to estimate the useful life of a single item, and because it is more convenient, many large businesses group similar items for purposes of depreciation. Companies must also consider certain special capital expenditures when calculating depreciation. For example, expenditures for additions and betterments are capital expenditures. Extraordinary repairs, which increase the residual value or extend the life of an asset, are also treated as capital expenditures, but ordinary repairs are revenue expenditures. For income tax purposes, rapid write-offs of depreciable assets are allowed through the Modified Accelerated Cost Recovery System. Such rapid write-offs are not usually acceptable for financial accounting because the shortened recovery periods violate the matching rule.

REVIEW OF CONCEPTS AND TERMINOLOGY

The following concepts and terms were introduced in this chapter:

LO 4 **Accelerated method:** A method of depreciation that allocates relatively large amounts of the depreciable cost of an asset to earlier years and reduced amounts to later years.

SO 9 **Addition:** An enlargement to the physical layout or capacity of a plant asset.

LO 1 **Amortization:** The periodic allocation of the cost of an intangible asset to the periods it benefits.

LO 1 **Asset impairment:** Loss of revenue-generating potential of a long-lived asset prior to the end of its useful life. The loss is computed as the difference between the asset's carrying value and its fair value, as measured by the present value of the sum of the expected net cash inflows.

SO 9 **Betterment:** An improvement that does not add to the physical layout of a plant asset but rather increases the quality of the asset or its output.

LO 8 **Brand name:** A registered name that can be used only by its owner to identify a product or service.

LO 2 **Capital expenditure:** An expenditure for the purchase or expansion of a long-term asset, recorded in an asset account.

LO 1 **Carrying value:** The unexpired part of the cost of an asset, not its market value; also called *book value.*

LO 8 **Copyright:** An exclusive right granted by the federal government to the possessor to publish and sell literary, musical, or other artistic materials for a period of the author's life plus 50 years; includes computer programs.

LO 4 **Declining-balance method:** An accelerated method of depreciation in which depreciation is computed by applying a fixed rate to the carrying value (the declining balance) of a tangible long-lived asset.

LO 1 **Depletion:** The exhaustion of a natural resource through mining, cutting, pumping, or other extraction, and the way in which the cost is allocated.

LO 3 **Depreciable cost:** The cost of an asset less its residual value.

LO 1 **Depreciation:** The periodic allocation of the cost of a tangible long-lived asset (other than land and natural resources) over its estimated useful life.

LO 4 **Double-declining-balance method:** An accelerated method of depreciation in which a fixed rate equal to twice the straight-line percentage is applied to the carrying value (the declining balance) of a tangible long-lived asset.

LO 3 **Estimated useful life:** The total number of service units expected from a long-term asset.

LO 2 **Expenditure:** A payment or an obligation to make future payment for an asset or a service.

SO 9 **Extraordinary repairs:** Repairs that affect the estimated residual value or estimated useful life of an asset, whereby the carrying value of the asset is increased.

LO 8 **Franchise:** The right or license to an exclusive territory or market.

LO 7 **Full-costing method:** A method of accounting for the costs of exploration and development of oil and gas resources in which all costs are recorded as assets and depleted over the estimated life of the producing resources.

LO 8 **Goodwill:** The excess of the cost of a group of assets (usually a business) over the fair market value of the identifiable net assets if purchased individually.

SO 9 **Group depreciation:** The grouping of similar items to calculate depreciation.

LO 1 **Intangible assets:** Long-term assets that have no physical substance but have a value based on rights or advantages accruing to the owner.

LO 8 **Leasehold:** A right to occupy land or buildings under a long-term rental contract.

LO 8 **Leasehold improvements:** Improvements to leased property that become the property of the lessor at the end of the lease.

LO 8 **License:** The right to use a formula, technique, process, or design.

LO 1 **Long-term assets:** Assets that (1) have a useful life of more than one year, (2) are acquired for use in the operation of a business, and (3) are not intended for resale to customers; less commonly called *fixed assets.*

SO 9 **Modified Accelerated Cost Recovery System (MACRS):** A mandatory system of depreciation for income tax purposes, enacted by Congress in 1986, that requires a cost recovery allowance to be computed (1) on the unadjusted cost of property being recovered and (2) over a period of years prescribed by the law for all property of similar types.

LO 1 **Natural resources:** Long-term assets purchased for the economic value that can be taken from the land and used up rather than for the value associated with the land's location.

LO 3 **Obsolescence:** The process of becoming out of date; a contributor, with physical deterioration, to the limited useful life of tangible assets.

SO 9 **Ordinary repairs:** Expenditures, usually of a recurring nature, that are recorded as current period expenses. They are necessary to maintain an asset in good operating condition in order to attain its originally intended useful life.

LO 8 **Patent:** An exclusive right granted by the federal government to make a particular product or use a specific process for a specified period of time.

LO 3 **Physical deterioration:** Limitations on the useful life of a depreciable asset resulting from use and from exposure to the elements.

LO 4 **Production method:** A method of depreciation that assumes that depreciation is solely the result of use and that the passage of time plays no role in the depreciation process; it allocates depreciation based on the units of output or use during each period of an asset's useful life.

LO 3 **Residual value:** The estimated net scrap, salvage, or trade-in value of a tangible asset at the estimated date of disposal; also called *salvage value* or *disposal value.*

LO 2 **Revenue expenditure:** An expenditure for repairs, maintenance, or other services needed to maintain or operate a plant asset for its original useful life; recorded by a debit to an expense account.

LO 4 **Straight-line method:** A method of depreciation that assumes that depreciation depends only on the passage of time and that allocates an equal amount of depreciation to each accounting period in an asset's useful life.

LO 7 **Successful efforts method:** A method of accounting for oil and gas resources in which successful exploration is recorded as an asset and depleted over the estimated life of the resource; all unsuccessful efforts are immediately written off as losses.

LO 1 **Tangible assets:** Long-term assets that have physical substance.

LO 8 **Trademark:** A registered symbol or brand name that can be used only by its owner to identify a product or service.

REVIEW PROBLEM

Comparison of Depreciation Methods

LO 3
LO 4 Norton Construction Company purchased a cement mixer on January 1, 20x1, for $14,500. The mixer was expected to have a useful life of five years and a residual value of $1,000. The company engineers estimated that the mixer would have a useful life of 7,500 hours. It was used 1,500 hours in 20x1, 2,625 hours in 20x2, 2,250 hours in 20x3, 750 hours in 20x4, and 375 hours in 20x5. The company's year end is December 31.

REQUIRED

1. Compute the depreciation expense and carrying value for 20x1 to 20x5, using the following three methods: (a) straight-line, (b) production, and (c) double-declining-balance.
2. Prepare the adjusting entry to record the depreciation for 20x1 calculated in **1(a).**
3. Show the balance sheet presentation for the cement mixer after the entry in **2** on December 31, 20x1.
4. What conclusions can you draw from the patterns of yearly depreciation?

ANSWER TO REVIEW PROBLEM

1. Depreciation computed:

Depreciation Method	Year	Computation	Depreciation	Carrying Value
a. Straight-line	20x1	$13,500 × 1/5	$2,700	$11,800
	20x2	13,500 × 1/5	2,700	9,100
	20x3	13,500 × 1/5	2,700	6,400
	20x4	13,500 × 1/5	2,700	3,700
	20x5	13,500 × 1/5	2,700	1,000
b. Production	20x1	$\$13,500 \times \frac{1,500}{7,500}$	$2,700	$11,800
	20x2	$13,500 \times \frac{2,625}{7,500}$	4,725	7,075
	20x3	$13,500 \times \frac{2,250}{7,500}$	4,050	3,025
	20x4	$13,500 \times \frac{750}{7,500}$	1,350	1,675
	20x5	$13,500 \times \frac{375}{7,500}$	675	1,000
c. Double-declining-balance	20x1	$14,500 × .4	$5,800	$ 8,700
	20x2	8,700 × .4	3,480	5,220
	20x3	5,220 × .4	2,088	3,132
	20x4	3,132 × .4	1,253*	1,879
	20x5		879*†	1,000

*Rounded.
†Remaining depreciation to reduce carrying value to residual value ($1,879 − $1,000 = $879).

LO 8 Trademarks

SD 2. ***America Online*** (AOL), America's largest online Internet service, filed a trademark-infringement lawsuit against ***AT&T***'s WorldNet Service seeking to block its use of such terms and phrases as "You Have Mail" and "You've Got Mail." A district court judge denied AOL's request for a temporary restraining order against AT&T's using these phrases, saying it was not clear that AOL owned them. AOL claims these terms are historically associated with its service, but AT&T says they are common Internet phrases available to all.

The Internet community is watching this case and others like it closely because the Internet is a relatively new medium in which it is not clear what rules apply. Whatever the outcome, it can have significant financial effects.[21]

What is a trademark, and why is it considered an intangible asset? Why does a trademark have value? For whom does a trademark have value? Be prepared to discuss how your answers apply to the case of AOL's use of "You Have Mail" or "You've Got Mail."

Ethical Dilemma

LO 2 Ethics and Allocation of Acquisition Costs

SD 3. ***Signal Company*** has purchased land and a warehouse for $18,000,000. The warehouse is expected to last 20 years and to have a salvage value equal to 10 percent of its cost. The chief financial officer (CFO) and the controller are discussing the allocation of the purchase price. The CFO believes that the largest amount possible should be assigned to the land because this action will improve reported net income in the future. Depreciation expense will be lower because land is not depreciated. He suggests allocating one-third, or $6,000,000, of the cost to the land. This results in depreciation expense each year of $540,000 [($12,000,000 − $1,200,000) ÷ 20 years].

The company's controller disagrees with the CFO. The controller argues that the smallest amount possible, say one-fifth of the purchase price, should be allocated to the land, thereby saving income taxes, since the depreciation, which is tax deductible, will be greater. Under this plan, annual depreciation would be $648,000 [($14,400,000 − $1,440,000) ÷ 20 years]. The annual tax savings at a 30 percent tax rate is $32,400 [($648,000 − $540,000) × .30]. How will this decision affect the company's cash flows? Ethically speaking, how should the purchase cost be allocated? Who will be affected by the decision?

Group Activity: Have each group develop the position of one of the two roles for presentation and debate.

LO 2 Ethics of Aggressive
LO 8 Accounting Policies

SD 4. Is it ethical to choose aggressive accounting practices to advance a company's business? ***America Online*** (AOL), the largest online service and Internet service provider in the United States, is one of the hottest stocks on Wall Street. From its initial stock offering in 1992, its stock price was up several thousand percent. Accounting is very important to AOL because earnings enable it to sell shares of stock and raise more cash to fund its phenomenal growth.

In its early years, AOL was one of the most aggressive companies in its choice of accounting principles. AOL's strategy called for building the largest customer base in the industry. Consequently, it spent many millions of dollars each year marketing its services to new customers. Such costs are usually recognized as operating expenses in the year in which they are incurred. However, AOL treated these costs as long-term assets, called "deferred subscriber acquisition costs," and expensed them over several years, because the company said the average customer was going to stay with the company for three years or more. The company also recorded research and development costs as "product development costs" and amortized them over five years. Both of these practices are justifiable theoretically, but they are not common practice. If the standard or more conservative practice had been followed, the company would have had a net loss in every year it has been in business.[22] This result would have greatly limited AOL's ability to raise money and grow as it has.

Explain in your own words management's rationale for adopting the accounting policies that it did. What could go wrong with management's plan? How would you evaluate the ethics of AOL's actions? Who benefits from the actions? Who is harmed by the actions? Have you seen any developments about AOL in the news?

Research Activity

SD 5. LO 1 LO 2 LO 8 **Individual Field Trip**

Visit a fast-food restaurant. Make a list of all the intangible and property, plant, and equipment assets you can identify. For each one, identify one management issue that relates to that asset. In addition, identify at least one capital expenditure and one revenue expenditure that is applicable to property, plant, and equipment assets (not to each one on your list). Bring your list to class for discussion.

Decision-Making Practice

SD 6. LO 1 **Purchase Decision and Time Value of Money Application**

Morningside Machine Works has successfully obtained a subcontract to manufacture parts for a new military aircraft. The parts are to be delivered over the next five years, and Morningside will be paid as the parts are delivered. To make the parts, new equipment will have to be purchased. Two types of equipment are available. Type A is conventional equipment that can be put into service immediately, and Type B requires one year to be put into service but is more efficient. Type A requires an immediate cash investment of $1,000,000 and will produce enough parts to provide net cash receipts of $340,000 each year for the five years. Type B may be purchased by signing a two-year non-interest-bearing note for $1,346,000. It is projected that Type B will produce net cash receipts of zero in year 1, $500,000 in year 2, $600,000 in year 3, $600,000 in year 4, and $200,000 in year 5. Neither type of equipment can be used on other contracts or will have any useful life remaining at the end of the contract. Morningside currently pays an interest rate of 16 percent to borrow money.

1. What is the present value of the investment required for each type of equipment? (Use Table 3 in the appendix on future value and present value tables.)
2. Compute the net present value of each type of equipment based on your answer in **1** and the present value of the net cash receipts projected to be received. (Use Tables 3 and 4 in the appendix on future value and present value tables.)
3. Write a memorandum to the board of directors that recommends the option that appears to be best for Morningside based on your analysis (include **1** and **2** as attachments) and that explains why.

FINANCIAL REPORTING AND ANALYSIS

Interpreting Financial Reports

FRA 1. LO 3 LO 4 SO 9 **Effects of Change in Accounting Method**

Depreciation expense is a significant expense for companies in which plant assets are a high proportion of assets. The amount of depreciation expense in a given year is affected by estimates of useful life and choice of depreciation method. In 2000, ***Century Steelworks Company,*** a major integrated steel producer, changed the estimated useful lives for its major production assets. In addition, Century Steelworks changed the method of depreciation for other steel-making assets from straight-line to the production method.

The company's 2000 annual report states, "A recent study conducted by management shows that actual years-in-service figures for our major production equipment and machinery are, in most cases, higher than the estimated useful lives assigned to these assets. We have recast the depreciable lives of such assets so that equipment previously assigned a useful life of 8 to 26 years now has an extended depreciable life of 10 to 32 years."

The report goes on to explain that the new production method of depreciation "recognizes that depreciation of production equipment and machinery correlates directly to both physical wear and tear and the passage of time. The production method of depreciation, which we have now initiated, more closely allocates the cost of these assets to the periods in which products are manufactured."

The report summarized the effects of both actions on the year 2000 in the following manner:

Incremental Increase in Net Income	In Millions	Per Share
Lengthened lives	$11.0	$ .80
Production method		
Current year	7.3	.53
Prior years	2.8	.20
Total increase	$21.1	$1.53

During 2000, Century Steelworks reported a net loss of $83,156,500 ($6.03 per share). Depreciation expense for 2000 was $87,707,200.

In explaining the changes, the controller of Century Steelworks was quoted in an article in *Business Journal* as follows: "There is no reason for Century Steelworks to continue to depreciate our assets more conservatively than our competitors do." But the article quotes an industry analyst who argues that by slowing its method of depreciation, Century Steelworks could be viewed as reporting lower-quality earnings.

REQUIRED

1. Explain the accounting treatment when there is a change in the estimated lives of depreciable assets. What circumstances must exist for the production method to produce the effect it did in relation to the straight-line method? What would Century Steelworks' net income or loss have been if the changes had not been made? What may have motivated management to make the changes?
2. What does the controller of Century Steelworks mean when he says that Century had been depreciating "more conservatively than our competitors do"? Why might the changes at Century Steelworks indicate, as the analyst asserts, "lower-quality earnings"? What risks might Century face as a result of its decision to use the production method of depreciation?

International Company

FRA 2.

LO 8 Accounting for Trademarks: U.S. and British Rules

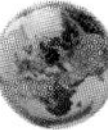

When the British company ***Grand Metropolitan*** (Grand Met) purchased ***Pillsbury,*** it adopted British accounting policies with regard to intangibles. Many analysts felt this gave British companies advantages over U.S. companies, especially in buyout situations.[23] For example, under the U.S. rules, as discussed in this chapter, intangible assets such as trademarks are recorded at their acquisition cost, which is often nominal, and the cost is amortized over a reasonable life. Under British accounting standards, on the other hand, firms are able to record the value of trademarks for the purpose of increasing the total assets on their balance sheets. Further, they do not have to amortize the value if management can show that the value can be preserved through extensive brand support. Grand Met, therefore, elected to record such famous Pillsbury trademarks as the Pillsbury Doughboy, Green Giant vegetables, Häagen Dazs ice cream, and Van de Kamp fish at an estimated value and not to amortize them. Analysts say that British rules made Pillsbury more valuable to Grand Met than to Pillsbury stockholders and thus led to Pillsbury's being bought by the British firm.

Write a one-page paper that addresses the following questions: What is the rationale behind the argument that the British company has an advantage due to the differences between U.S. and British accounting principles? Do you agree with U.S. or British accounting rules regarding trademarks? Defend your answers.

Toys "R" Us Annual Report

FRA 3.

LO 1 Long-Term Assets
LO 2
LO 3
LO 4
LO 8

1. Refer to the consolidated balance sheets and to the note on property and equipment in the notes to consolidated financial statements in the Toys "R" Us annual report to answer the following questions: What percentage of total assets in 2000 was property and equipment? What is the most significant type of property and equipment? Does Toys "R" Us have a significant investment in land? What other kinds of things are included in the property and equipment category? (Ignore leased property under capital leases for now.)

2. Refer to the summary of significant accounting policies and to the note on property and equipment in the Toys "R" Us annual report. What method of depreciation does Toys "R" Us use? How long does management estimate its buildings to last as compared to furniture and equipment? What does this say about Toys "R" Us's need to remodel its stores?
3. Refer to the statement of cash flows in the Toys "R" Us annual report. How much did Toys "R" Us spend on property and equipment (capital expenditures, net) during 2000? Is this an increase or a decrease from prior years?
4. Refer again to the income statement and note on property and equipment. What are leaseholds and leasehold improvements? How significant are these items? How does the amount of rent expense (see note on leases) and appreciation and amortization compare with the net earnings in 2000?

Fingraph® Financial Analyst™

FRA 4.

LO 1 Comparison of Long-Term
LO 4 Assets
LO 7
LO 8

Choose any two companies from the same industry in the Fingraph® Financial Analyst™ CD-ROM software. The industry chosen should be one in which long-term assets are likely to be important. Choose an industry such as airlines, manufacturing, consumer products, consumer food and beverage, or computers.

1. In the annual reports for the companies you have selected, read the long-term asset section of the balance sheet and any reference to any long-term assets in the summary of significant accounting policies or notes to the financial statements. What are the most important long-term assets for each company? What depreciation methods do the companies use? Are there any long-term assets that appear to be characteristic of the industry? What intangible assets do the companies have, and how important are they?
2. Display and print in tabular and graphical form the Balance Sheet Analysis page. Prepare a table that compares the gross and net property, plant, and equipment.
3. Locate the statements of cash flows in the two companies' annual reports. Prepare another table that compares depreciation (and amortization) expense from the operating activities section with the net purchases of property, plant, and equipment (net capital expenditures) from the investing activities section for two years. Does depreciation (and amortization) expense exceed replacement of long-term assets? Are the companies expanding or reducing their property, plant, and equipment?
4. Find and read references to long-term assets and capital expenditures in management's discussion and analysis in each annual report.
5. Write a one-page executive summary that highlights the most important long-term assets and the accounting policies for long-term assets, and compares the investing activities of the two companies, including reference to management's assessment. Include the Fingraph® page and your tables as attachments to your report.

Internet Case

FRA 5.

LO 4 SEC and Forms 10-K
LO 5
LO 8

Public corporations are required not only to communicate with their stockholders by means of an annual report, but also to submit an annual report to the Securities and Exchange Commission (SEC). The annual report to the SEC is called a Form 10-K and is a source of the latest information about a company. Through the Needles Accounting Resource Center web site at http://college.hmco.com, access the SEC's EDGAR files to locate either H. J. Heinz Company's or Ford Motor Company's Form 10-K. Find the financial statements and the notes to the financial statements. Scan through the notes to the financial statements and prepare a list of information you find related to long-term assets, including intangibles. For instance, what depreciation methods does the company use? What are the useful lives of its property, plant, and equipment? What intangible assets does the company have? Does the company have goodwill? How much does the company spend on research and development? In the statement of cash flows, how much did the company spend on new property, plant, and equipment (capital expenditures)? Summarize your results and be prepared to discuss them as well as your experience in using the SEC's EDGAR database.

Group Activity: Divide students into groups according to the company researched and have each group compile a comprehensive list of information about its company.

ENDNOTES

1. H. J. Heinz Company, *Annu al Report*, 2000.
2. *Statement of Financial Accounting Standards No. 121*, "Accounting for the Impairment of Long-Lived Assets and for Long-Lived Assets to Be Disposed Of" (Norwalk, Conn.: Financial Accounting Standards Board, 1995).
3. Leslie Canley, "Pacific Telesis Plans a Charge of $3.3 Billion," *The Wall Street Journal*, September 8, 1995.
4. Ford Motor Company, *Annual Report*, 1999.
5. Ibid.
6. *Statement of Position No. 98-1*, "Accounting for the Costs of Computer Software Developed or Planned for Internal Use" (New York: American Institute of Certified Public Accountants, 1996).
7. *Statement of Financial Accounting Standards No. 34*, "Capitalization of Interest Cost" (Norwalk, Conn.: Financial Accounting Standards Board, 1979), par. 9–11.
8. Len Boselovic, "A Look at How the SEC Disposed of Chambers' Claims," *Pittsburgh Post-Gazette*, May 14, 1995.
9. *Financial Accounting Standards: Original Pronouncements as of July 1, 1977* (Norwalk, Conn.: Financial Accounting Standards Board, 1977), ARB No. 43, Ch. 9, Sec. C, par. 5.
10. Accounting Principles Board, *Opinion No. 29*, "Accounting for Nonmonetary Transactions" (New York: American Institute of Certified Public Accountants, 1973) and Emerging Issues Task Force, *EITF Issue Summary 86-29*, "Nonmonetary Transactions: Magnitude of Boot and the Exceptions to the Use of Fair Value" (Norwalk, Conn.: Financial Accounting Standards Board, 1986). The specific criteria for similar assets are the subject of more advanced courses.
11. *Statement of Financial Accounting Standards No. 25*, "Suspension of Certain Accounting Requirements for Oil and Gas Producing Companies" (Norwalk, Conn.: Financial Accounting Standards Board, 1979).
12. Adapted from Accounting Principles Board, *Opinion No. 17*, "Intangible Assets" (New York: American Institute of Certified Public Accountants, 1970), par. 2.
13. "What's in a Name?" *Time*, May 3, 1993.
14. Passed by the Financial Accounting Standards Board on May 16, 2001.
15. *Statement of Financial Accounting Standards No. 2*, "Accounting for Research and Development Costs" (Norwalk, Conn.: Financial Accounting Standards Board, 1974), par. 12.
16. General Motors, *Annual Report*, 1998.
17. Abbott Laboratories, *Annual Report*, 1998; and Roche Group, *Annual Report*, 1998.
18. *Statement of Financial Accounting Standards No. 86*, "Accounting for the Costs of Computer Software to be Sold, Leased, or Otherwise Marketed" (Norwalk, Conn.: Financial Accounting Standards Board, 1985).
19. Edward P. McTague, "Accounting for Trade-Ins of Operational Assets," *National Public Accountant* (January 1986), p. 39.
20. Polaroid Corporation, *Annual Report*, 1997.
21. "AOL Loses Round in AT&T Suit," Times Mirror Company web site <www.TimesMirror.com>, January 5, 1999.
22. "Stock Gives Case the Funds He Needs to Buy New Technology," *Business Week*, April 15, 1996.
23. Joanne Lipman, "British Value Brand Names—Literally," *The Wall Street Journal*, February 9, 1989, p. B4; and "Brand Name Policy Boosts Assets," *Accountancy*, October 1988, pp. 38–39.

12

Current Liabilities

LEARNING OBJECTIVES

1 Identify the management issues related to recognition, valuation, classification, and disclosure of current liabilities.

2 Identify, compute, and record definitely determinable and estimated current liabilities.

3 Define *contingent liability.*

SUPPLEMENTAL OBJECTIVE

4 Compute and record the liabilities associated with payroll accounting.

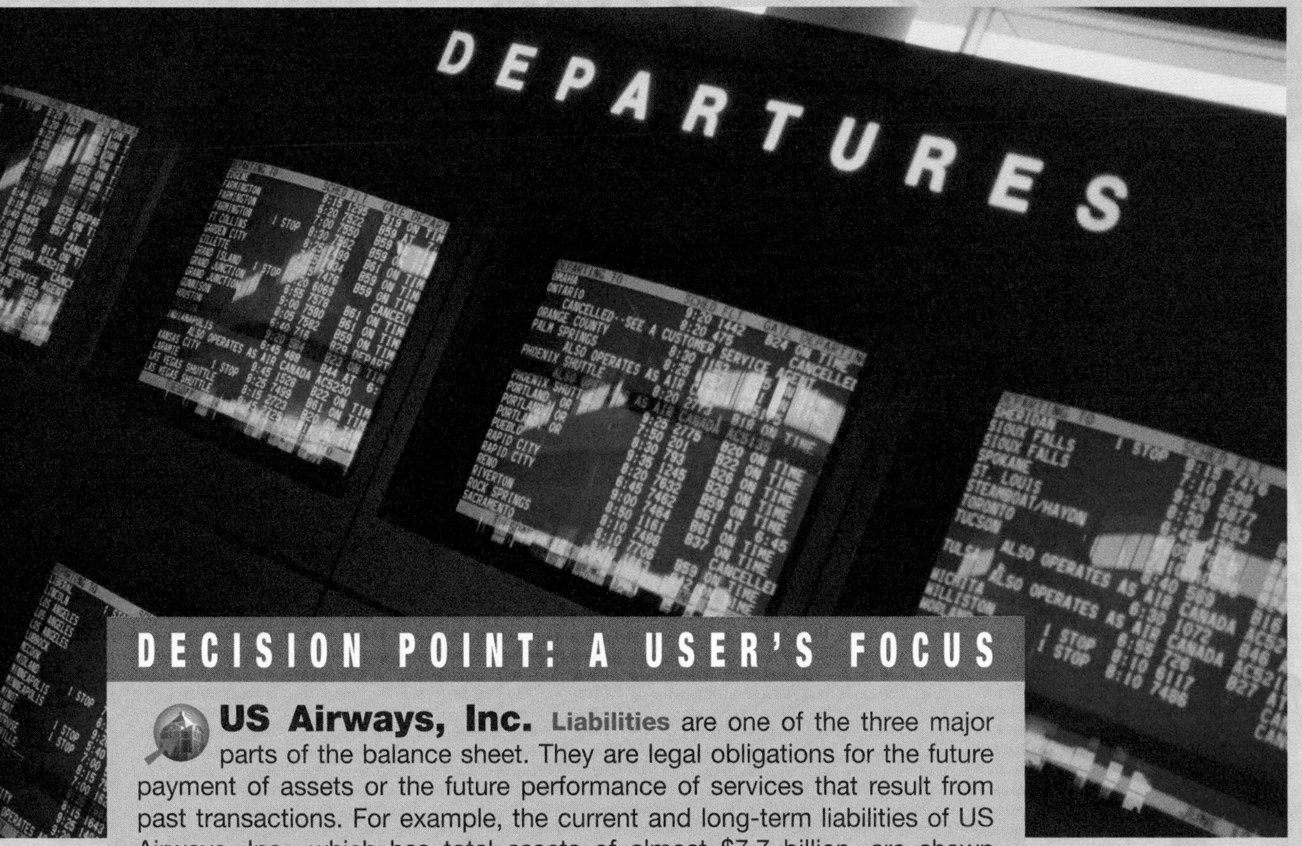

DECISION POINT: A USER'S FOCUS

US Airways, Inc. **Liabilities** are one of the three major parts of the balance sheet. They are legal obligations for the future payment of assets or the future performance of services that result from past transactions. For example, the current and long-term liabilities of US Airways, Inc., which has total assets of almost $7.7 billion, are shown here.[1] Current Maturities of Long-Term Debt; Accounts Payable; Accrued Aircraft Rent; Accrued Salaries, Wages, and Vacation; and Other Accrued Expenses for the most part will require an outlay of cash in the next year. Traffic Balances Payable will require payments to other airlines, but those may be partially offset by amounts owed from other airlines. Unused Tickets are tickets already paid for by passengers and represent services that must be performed. Long-Term Debt will require cash outlays in future years. Altogether these liabilities represent 60 percent of total assets. How does the decision of US Airways' management to incur so much debt relate to the goals of the business?

Terminology Note: US Airways uses "Accrued Expenses" to group liability accounts such as Salaries Payable and Interest Payable.

Critical Thinking Question: What accounting concept underlies the recognition of the current liabilities called accrued expenses? **Answer:** The matching rule.

Liabilities are important because they are closely related to the goals of profitability and liquidity. Liabilities are sources of cash for operating and financing activities when they are incurred, but they are also obligations that use cash when they are paid as required. Achieving the appropriate level of liabilities is critical to business success. A company that has too few liabilities may not be earning up to its potential. A company that has too many liabilities, however, may be incurring excessive risks. This chapter focuses on the management and accounting issues involving current liabilities, including payroll liabilities and contingent liabilities.

Financial Highlights

(In millions)

Current Liabilities	**1999**	1998	1997
Current Maturities of Long-Term Debt	**$ 116**	$ 71	$ 186
Accounts Payable	**474**	430	323
Traffic Balances Payable and Unused Tickets	**635**	752	707
Accrued Aircraft Rent	**236**	166	187
Accrued Salaries, Wages and Vacation	**341**	329	311
Other Accrued Expenses	**699**	521	492
Total Current Liabilities	**$2,501**	$2,269	$2,206
Long-Term Debt, Net of Current Maturities	**$2,113**	$1,955	$2,426

Management Issues Related to Accounting for Current Liabilities

OBJECTIVE

1 Identify the management issues related to recognition, valuation, classification, and disclosure of current liabilities

The primary reason for incurring current liabilities is to meet needs for cash during the operating cycle. The proper identification and management of current liabilities also requires an understanding of how they are recognized, valued, classified, and disclosed.

Related Text Assignments:
Q: 1, 2, 3, 4, 5
SE: 1, 2
E: 1, 2
P: 1
SD: 5
FRA: 1, 2, 3, 4

Managing Liquidity and Cash Flows

The operating cycle is the process of converting cash to purchases, to sales, to accounts receivable, and back to cash. Most current liabilities arise in support of this cycle, as when accounts payable arise from purchases of inventory, accrued expenses arise from operating costs, and unearned revenues arise from customers' advance payments. Short-term debt is used to raise cash during periods of inventory buildup or while waiting for collection of receivables. Cash is used to pay current maturities of long-term debt and to pay off liabilities arising from operations.

Failure to manage the cash flows related to current liabilities can have serious consequences for a business. For instance, if suppliers are not paid on time, they may withhold shipments that are vital to a company's operations. Continued failure to pay current liabilities can lead to bankruptcy. To evaluate a company's ability to pay its current liabilities, three measures of liquidity—working capital, the current ratio, and the quick ratio—are often used. Current liabilities are a key component of each of these measures. They typically equal from 25 to 50 percent of total assets.

US Airways' short-term liquidity as measured by working capital deteriorated from 1997 to 1999 (in millions):

	Current Assets	−	Current Liabilities	=	Working Capital
1999	$2,096	−	$2,501	=	($405)
1998	$2,364	−	$2,269	=	$ 95
1997	$2,777	−	$2,206	=	$571

Enrichment Note: Unused tickets are often a significant liability for airlines. Like all service providers, airlines earn revenue by providing a service. The receipt of cash is usually incidental to revenue recognition.

This measure highlights the need for US Airways' management to focus on the management of short-term liquidity because it has deteriorated significantly over the three-year period. It is common for airlines to have low or negative working capital because unearned ticket revenue is a current liability, but the cash from these ticket sales is quickly consumed in operations. On the assumption that only a small portion of unearned ticket revenues will be repaid to customers, unearned ticket revenue might be excluded from current liabilities for purposes of analysis. The healthiest airlines have positive working capital when unearned ticket revenue is excluded.

Another consideration with managing a company's liquidity position and cash flows is the amount of time its creditors are willing to give it to pay its accounts payable. Common measures of this time are the **payables turnover** and the **average days' payable**. The payables turnover is the number of times on average that accounts payable are paid in an accounting period and shows the relative size of a company's accounts payable. The average days' payable measures how long, on average, a company takes to pay its accounts payables.

For example, Radio Shack Corporation, which operates more than 7,000 electronics retail locations, must carefully plan its purchases and payables. It had accounts payable of $234.8 million in 1999 and $206.4 million in 1998. Its purchases are determined by cost of goods sold adjusted for the change in inventory. An increase in inventory means purchases were more than cost of goods sold, and a

Figure 1
Payables Turnover for Selected Industries

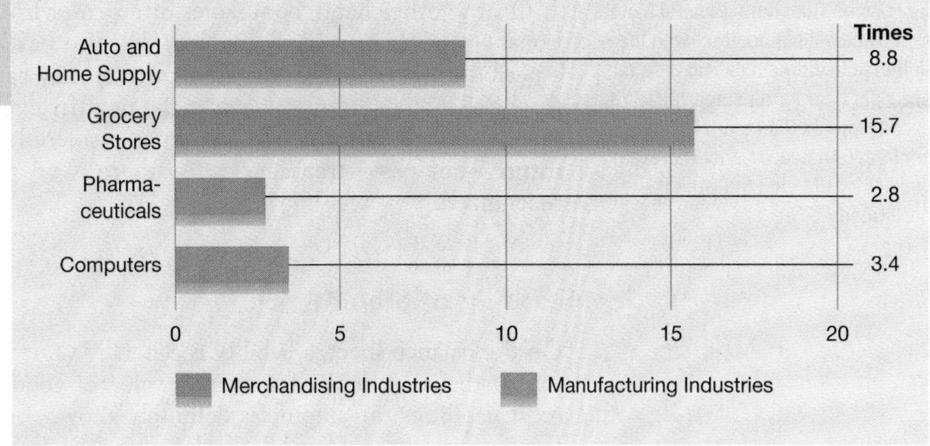

Source: Data from Dun & Bradstreet, *Industry Norms and Key Business Ratios*, 1999–2000.

decrease in inventory means that purchases were less than cost of goods sold. Radio Shack's cost of goods sold was \$2,042.7 million and its inventory decreased by \$50.7 million.[2] Its payables turnover is computed as follows:

K/R

$$\text{Payables Turnover} = \frac{\text{Cost of Goods Sold} \pm \text{Change in Merchandise Inventory}}{\text{Average Accounts Payable}}$$

$$= \frac{\$2{,}042.7 - \$50.7}{(\$234.8 + \$206.4) \div 2}$$

$$= \frac{\$1{,}992.0}{\$220.6} = 9.0 \text{ times}$$

To find the average days' payable, the number of days in a year is divided by the payables turnover:

K/R

$$\text{Average Days' Payable} = \frac{365 \text{ days}}{\text{Payables Turnover}} = \frac{365 \text{ days}}{9.0} = 40.6 \text{ days}$$

The payables turnover of 9.0 times and the resulting average days' payable of 40.6 days are consistent with customary 30-day credit terms, with some purchases having longer terms.

The chart in Figure 1 shows the payables turnover for various other industries. The payables turnover should be considered in relation to the inventory turnover and the receivables turnover to get a full picture of a company's operating cycle and liquidity position.

Recognition of Liabilities

Timing is important in the recognition of liabilities. Failure to record a liability in an accounting period very often goes along with failure to record an expense. The two errors lead to an understatement of expense and an overstatement of income.

A liability is recorded when an obligation occurs. This rule is harder to apply than it might appear. When a transaction obligates a company to make future payments, a liability arises and is recognized, as when goods are bought on credit. However, current liabilities often are not represented by direct transactions. One of the key reasons for making adjusting entries at the end of an accounting period is to recognize unrecorded liabilities. Among these accrued liabilities are salaries payable and interest payable. Other liabilities that can only be estimated, such as taxes payable, must also be recognized through adjusting entries.

Discussion Question: General Motors signs a new labor contract with the United Auto Workers calling for a raise of $1 per hour for all employees. What liability should GM record for the new contract? **Answer:** None. There is no liability for GM until the work is performed.

On the other hand, companies often enter into agreements for future transactions. For instance, a company may agree to pay an executive $50,000 a year for a period of three years, or a public utility may agree to buy an unspecified quantity of coal at a certain price over the next five years. Such contracts, though they are definite commitments, are not considered liabilities because they are for future—not past—transactions. As there is no current obligation, no liability is recognized.

Valuation of Liabilities

On the balance sheet, a liability is generally valued at the amount of money needed to pay the debt or the fair market value of goods or services to be delivered. For most liabilities the amount is definitely known, but for some it must be estimated. For example, an automobile dealer who sells a car with a one-year warranty must provide parts and service during the year. The obligation is definite because the sale of the car has occurred, but the amount of the obligation can only be estimated. Such estimates are usually based on past experience and anticipated changes in the business environment. Additional disclosures of the fair value of liabilities may be required in the notes to the financial statements, as explained below.

Classification of Liabilities

The classification of liabilities directly matches the classification of assets. **Current liabilities** are debts and obligations expected to be satisfied within one year or within the normal operating cycle, whichever is longer. Such liabilities are normally paid out of current assets or with cash generated from operations. **Long-term liabilities**, which are liabilities due beyond one year or beyond the normal operating cycle, have a different purpose. They are used to finance long-term assets, such as aircraft in the case of US Airways. The distinction between current and long-term liabilities is important because it affects the evaluation of a company's liquidity.

Disclosure of Liabilities

To explain some accounts, supplemental disclosure in the notes to the financial statements may be required. For example, if a company has a large amount of notes payable, an explanatory note may disclose the balances, maturities, interest rates, and other features of the debts. Any special credit arrangements, such as issues of commercial paper and lines of credit, should also be disclosed. For example, The Goodyear Tire & Rubber Company, which manufactures and sells tires, vehicle components, industrial rubber products, and rubber-related chemicals, disclosed its credit arrangements in the notes to the financial statements. Excerpts from that note follow:

Enrichment Note: Financial liabilities, such as loans, notes, and other borrowings, are considered financial instruments. The market value of financial instruments is reported in the notes to the financial statements.

Note 10. Short-Term Debt and Financing Arrangements

At December 31, 1999, the Company had short-term uncommitted credit arrangements totaling $2.0 billion, of which $.83 billion were unused. These arrangements are available to the Company or certain of its international subsidiaries through various international banks at quoted market interest rates. There are no commitment fees or compensating balances associated with these arrangements.

The company had outstanding debt obligations which are due within one year amounting to $2.32 billion at December 31, 1999. Commercial paper

> and domestic short-term bank debt represented $1.46 billion of this total with a weighted average interest rate of 6.29% at December 31, 1999. . . . The remaining $.86 billion was international subsidiary short-term debt with a weighted average interest rate of 4.79% at December 31, 1999.[3]

This type of disclosure is helpful in assessing whether a company has additional borrowing power, because unused lines of credit allow a company to borrow on short notice, up to the agreed credit limit, with little or no negotiations.

Common Categories of Current Liabilities

Current liabilities fall into two major groups: (1) definitely determinable liabilities and (2) estimated liabilities.

Definitely Determinable Liabilities

OBJECTIVE

2 Identify, compute, and record definitely determinable and estimated current liabilities

Related Text Assignments:
Q: 6, 7, 8, 9, 10, 11, 12, 13, 14, 15, 16
SE: 3, 4, 5, 6, 7, 8
E: 3, 4, 5, 6, 7, 8, 9
P: 1, 2, 3, 4, 6, 7, 8
SD: 1, 2, 3, 4, 5
FRA: 2, 4

Current liabilities that are set by contract or by statute and can be measured exactly are called **definitely determinable liabilities**. The related accounting problems are to determine the existence and amount of each such liability and to see that it is recorded properly. Definitely determinable liabilities include accounts payable, bank loans and commercial paper, notes payable, accrued liabilities, dividends payable, sales and excise taxes payable, current portions of long-term debt, payroll liabilities, and unearned or deferred revenues.

ACCOUNTS PAYABLE Accounts payable, sometimes called trade accounts payable, are short-term obligations to suppliers for goods and services. The amount in the Accounts Payable account is generally supported by an accounts payable subsidiary ledger, which contains an individual account for each person or company to which money is owed.

Point to Emphasize: On the balance sheet, the order of presentation for current liabilities is not as strict as for current assets. Generally, Accounts Payable or Notes Payable appears first, and the rest follow.

BANK LOANS AND COMMERCIAL PAPER Management will often establish a **line of credit** from a bank; this arrangement allows the company to borrow funds when they are needed to finance current operations. For example, Lowe's Companies, Inc., a large home improvement center and consumer durables company, reported in its 1999 annual report that "the company had a $300 million revolving credit facility with a syndicate of 11 banks, expiring lines of credit of $218 million . . . and $50 million available, on an unsecured basis, for the purposes of short-term borrowing."[4]

A promissory note for the full amount of the line of credit is signed when the credit is granted, but the company has great flexibility in using the available funds. The company can increase its borrowing up to the limit when it needs cash and reduce the amount borrowed when it generates enough cash of its own. Both the amount borrowed and the interest rate charged by the bank may change daily. The bank may require the company to meet certain financial goals (such as maintaining specific profit margins, current ratios, or debt to equity ratios) in order to retain the line of credit.

Figure 2
Two Promissory Notes: One with Interest Stated Separately; One with Interest in Face Amount

CASE 1: INTEREST STATED SEPARATELY

Chicago, Illinois   August 31, 20xx

Sixty days after date I promise to pay First Federal Bank the sum of $5,000 with interest at the rate of 12% per annum.

Sandra Caron
Caron Corporation

CASE 2: INTEREST IN FACE AMOUNT

Chicago, Illinois   August 31, 20xx

Sixty days after date I promise to pay First Federal Bank the sum of $5,000.

Sandra Caron
Caron Corporation

Clarification Note: Only the used portion of the line of credit is recognized as a liability in the financial statements.

Companies with excellent credit ratings may borrow short-term funds by issuing **commercial paper**, unsecured loans that are sold to the public, usually through professionally managed investment firms. The portion of a line of credit currently borrowed and the amount of commercial paper issued are usually combined with notes payable in the current liabilities section of the balance sheet. Details are disclosed in a note to the financial statements.

NOTES PAYABLE Short-term notes payable, which also arise out of the ordinary course of business, are obligations represented by promissory notes. These notes may be used to secure bank loans, to pay suppliers for goods and services, and to secure credit from other sources.

The interest may be stated separately on the face of the note (Case 1 in Figure 2), or it may be deducted in advance by discounting it from the face value of the note (Case 2 in Figure 2). The entries to record the note in each case follow.

Case 1
A = L + OE
\+ \+

Case 2
A = L + OE
\+ −
    \+

Case 1—Interest Stated Separately

Aug. 31	Cash	5,000	
	Notes Payable		5,000
	Issued 60-day, 12 percent promissory note with interest stated separately		

Case 2—Interest in Face Amount

Aug. 31	Cash	4,900	
	Discount on Notes Payable	100	
	Notes Payable		5,000
	Issued 60-day promissory note with $100 interest included in face amount		

Point to Emphasize: The effective interest rate on the loan in Case 2 is 12.24% ($100/$4,900 × 360/60). Note: For ease of computation, 360 days are used to compute interest on notes.

Note that in Case 1 the money received equaled the face value of the note, whereas in Case 2 the money received ($4,900) was less than the face value ($5,000) of the note. The discount of $100 ($5,000 × .12 × 60/360) equals the amount of the interest for 60 days. Although the dollar amount of interest on each of these notes is the same, the effective interest rate is slightly higher in Case 2 because the amount received is slightly less ($4,900 in Case 2 versus $5,000 in

Case 1). Discount on Notes Payable is a contra account to Notes Payable and is deducted from Notes Payable on the balance sheet.

On October 30, when the note is paid, each alternative is recorded as follows:

Case 1
A = L + OE
− − −

Case 2
A = L + OE
− −
A = L + OE
+ −

Case 1—Interest Stated Separately

Date	Account	Debit	Credit
Oct. 30	Notes Payable	5,000	
	Interest Expense	100	
	Cash		5,100
	Payment of note with interest stated separately		
	$\$5{,}000 \times \frac{60}{360} \times .12 = \$100$		

Case 2—Interest in Face Amount

Date	Account	Debit	Credit
Oct. 30	Notes Payable	5,000	
	Cash		5,000
	Payment of note with interest included in face amount		
30	Interest Expense	100	
	Discount on Notes Payable		100
	Interest expense on note payable		

Accrued Liabilities A key reason for making adjusting entries at the end of an accounting period is to recognize and record liabilities that are not already in the accounting records. This practice applies to any type of liability. As you will see, accrued liabilities can include estimated liabilities.

Here the focus is on interest payable, a definitely determinable liability. Interest accrues daily on interest-bearing notes. At the end of the accounting period, an adjusting entry should be made in accordance with the matching rule to record the interest obligation up to that point in time. Let us again use the example of the two notes presented above. If we assume that the accounting period ends on September 30, or 30 days after the issuance of the 60-day notes, the adjusting entries for each case would be as follows:

Case 1
A = L + OE
+ −

Case 2
A = L + OE
+ −

Case 1—Interest Stated Separately

Date	Account	Debit	Credit
Sept. 30	Interest Expense	50	
	Interest Payable		50
	To record interest expense for 30 days on note with interest stated separately		
	$\$5{,}000 \times \frac{30}{360} \times .12 = \$50$		

Case 2—Interest in Face Amount

Date	Account	Debit	Credit
Sept. 30	Interest Expense	50	
	Discount on Notes Payable		50
	To record interest expense for 30 days on note with interest included in face amount		
	$\$100 \times \frac{30}{60} = \$50$		

Point to Emphasize: Both of the above entries have exactly the same impact on the financial statements.

In Case 2, Discount on Notes Payable will now have a debit balance of $50, which will become interest expense during the next 30 days.

Dividends Payable Cash dividends are a distribution of earnings by a corporation. The payment of dividends is solely the decision of the corporation's board of directors. A liability does not exist until the board declares the dividends. There is usually a short time between the date of declaration and the date of payment of dividends. During that short time, the dividends declared are considered current liabilities of the corporation.

Common Student Error: Students often try to compute sales tax on the basis of total cash collections rather than sales. Emphasize the difference between cash receipts and sales.

Sales and Excise Taxes Payable Most states and many cities levy a sales tax on retail transactions. There is a federal excise tax on some products, such as automobile tires. A merchant who sells goods subject to these taxes must collect the taxes and forward them periodically to the appropriate government agency. The amount of tax collected represents a current liability until it is remitted to the government. For example, assume that a merchant makes a $100 sale that is subject to a 5 percent sales tax and a 10 percent excise tax. Assuming that the sale takes place on June 1, the entry to record the sale is as follows:

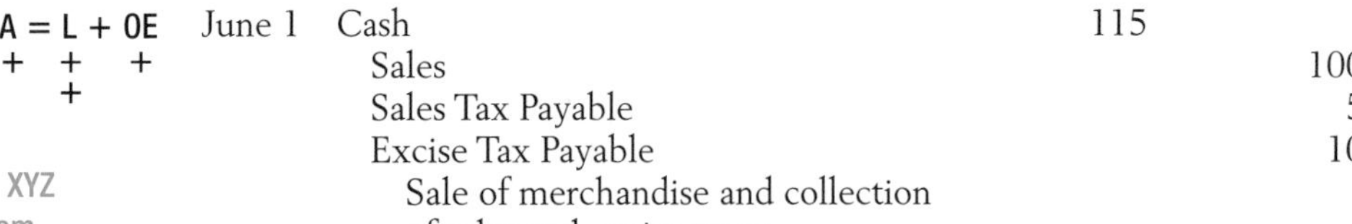

A = L + OE
\+ + +
\+

June 1	Cash	115	
	Sales		100
	Sales Tax Payable		5
	Excise Tax Payable		10
	Sale of merchandise and collection of sales and excise taxes		

Reinforcement Exercise: XYZ Company collects $171 from customers, which includes a 6% sales tax and an 8% excise tax. How much were sales? **Answer:** $150; $171 = sales + 6% sales tax + 8% excise tax = $171 ÷ 1.14 = $150.

The sale is properly recorded at $100, and the taxes collected are recorded as liabilities to be remitted at the proper times to the appropriate government agencies.

Enrichment Note: Liabilities such as bank loans, notes payable, and current portions of long-term debt are considered financial instruments.

CURRENT PORTIONS OF LONG-TERM DEBT If a portion of long-term debt is due within the next year and is to be paid from current assets, then that current portion is properly classified as a current liability. For example, suppose that a $500,000 debt is to be paid in installments of $100,000 per year for the next five years. The $100,000 installment due in the current year should be classified as a current liability. The remaining $400,000 should be classified as a long-term liability. Note that no journal entry is necessary. The total debt of $500,000 is simply reclassified when the financial statements are prepared, as follows:

Current Liabilities	
Current Portion of Long-Term Debt	$100,000
Long-Term Liabilities	
Long-Term Debt	400,000

PAYROLL LIABILITIES For most organizations, the cost of labor and related payroll taxes is a major expense. In some industries, such as banking and airlines, payroll costs represent more than half of all operating costs. Payroll accounting is important because complex laws and significant liabilities are involved. The employer is liable to employees for wages and salaries and to various agencies for amounts withheld from wages and salaries and for related taxes. The term **wages** refers to payment for the services of employees at an hourly rate. The term **salaries** refers to the compensation of employees who are paid at a monthly or yearly rate.

Because payroll accounting applies only to the employees of an organization, it is therefore important to distinguish between employees and independent contractors. Employees are paid a wage or salary by the organization and are under its direct supervision and control. Independent contractors are not employees of the organization, so they are not accounted for under the payroll system. They offer services to the organization for a fee, but they are not under its direct control or supervision. Some examples of independent contractors are certified public accountants, advertising agencies, and lawyers.

Figure 3 provides an illustration of payroll liabilities and their relationship to employee earnings and employer taxes and other costs. Two important observations may be made. First, the amount payable to employees is less than the amount of earnings. This occurs because employers are required by law or are requested by employees to withhold certain amounts from wages and send them directly to government agencies or other organizations. Second, the total employer liabilities exceed employee earnings because the employer must pay additional taxes and make other contributions, such as for pensions and medical care, that increase the cost and liabilities. The most common withholdings, taxes, and other payroll costs are described on page 524.

Figure 3
Illustration of Payroll Liabilities

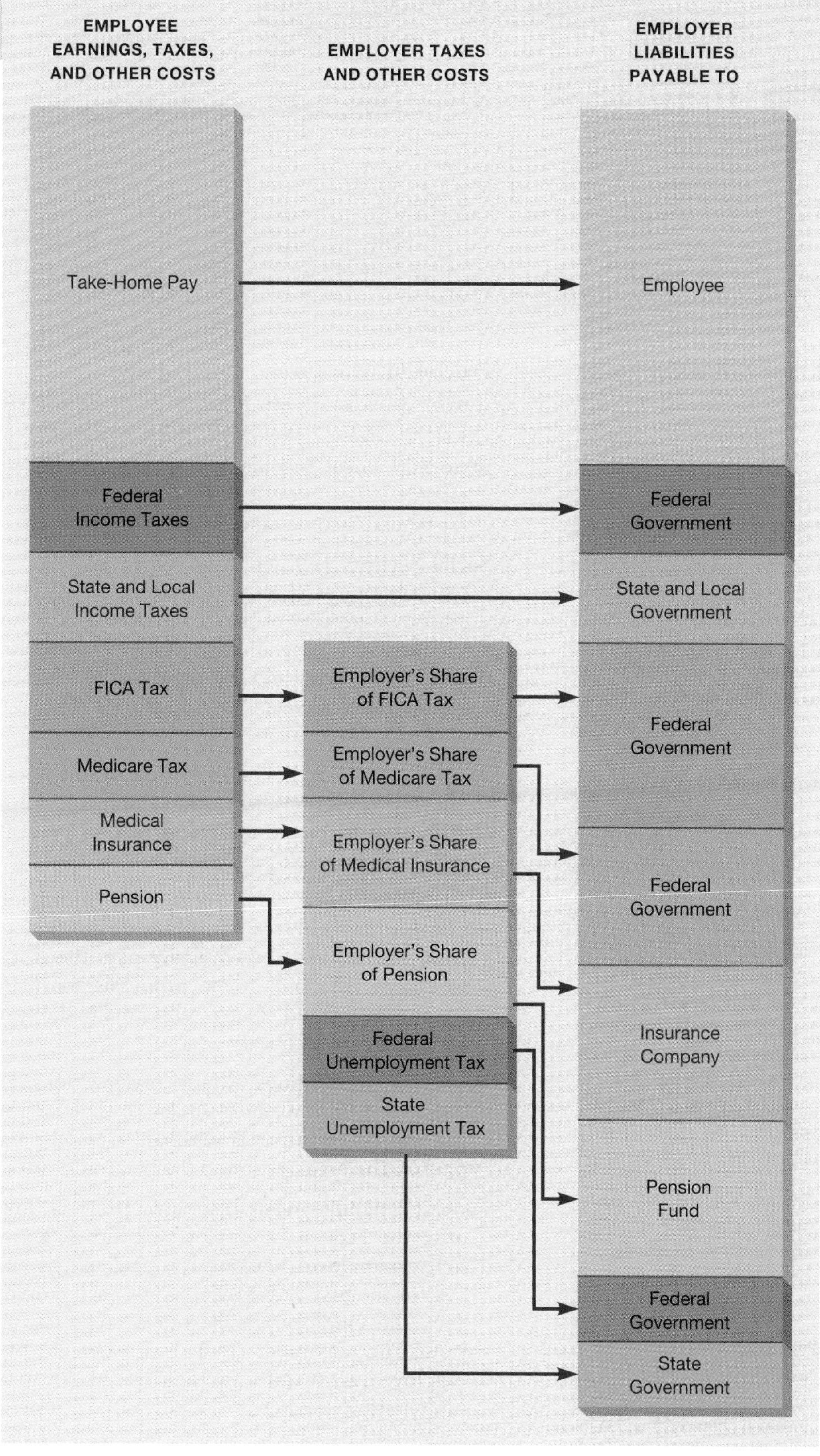

FOCUS ON BUSINESS TECHNOLOGY

The processing of payroll is an ideal application for computers because it is a very routine and complex procedure that must be done with absolute accuracy: Employees want to be paid exactly what they are owed, and failure to pay the taxes and other costs as required can result in severe penalties and high interest charges. Consequently, many companies purchase carefully designed and tested computer software for use in preparing the payroll. Other companies do not process their own payroll but rely on outside businesses that specialize in providing such services. Many of these service suppliers, such as Automatic Data Processing, Inc., are successful and fast growing.

Instructional Strategy: Assign discussion of SD 3 to small groups in class. Ask one person from each group to present one alternative (not necessarily the group's choice as the best solution) and explain why that alternative would be ethical or unethical.

Point to Emphasize: In most of the end-of-chapter problems, students will not be required to compute income tax withholdings—those amounts will be given. They might be asked, however, to compute social security and Medicare withholdings and unemployment taxes.

Federal Income Taxes Federal income taxes are collected on a "pay as you go" basis. Employers are required to withhold appropriate taxes from employees' paychecks and pay them to the United States Treasury.

State and Local Income Taxes Most states and some local governments have income taxes. In most cases, the procedures for withholding are similar to those for federal income taxes.

Social Security (FICA) Tax The social security program (the Federal Insurance Contribution Act) offers retirement and disability benefits and survivor's benefits. About 90 percent of the people working in the United States fall under the provisions of this program. The 2001 social security tax rate of 6.2 percent was paid by *both* employee and employer on the first $80,400 earned by an employee during the calendar year. Both the rate and the base to which it applies are subject to change in future years.

Medicare Tax A major extension of the social security program is Medicare, which provides hospitalization and medical insurance for persons over age 65. In 1999, the Medicare tax rate was 1.45 percent of gross income, with no limit, paid by *both* employee and employer.

Enrichment Note: For many organizations, a large portion of the cost of labor is not reflected in employees' regular paychecks. Vacation pay, sick pay, personal days, health insurance, life insurance, and pensions are some of the additional costs that may be negotiated between employers and employees.

Medical Insurance Many organizations provide medical benefits to employees. Often, the employee contributes a portion of the cost through withholdings from income and the employer pays the rest, usually a greater amount, to the insurance company. Some proposals for national health-care reform, if they become law, could change substantially the way medical insurance is funded and provided in this country.

Pension Contributions Many organizations also provide pension benefits to employees. In a manner similar to that for medical insurance, a portion of the pension contribution is withheld from the employee's income and the rest is paid by the organization to the pension fund.

Common Student Confusion: Students often have difficulty understanding the difference between employee-related and employer-related payroll liabilities.

Point to Emphasize: The employee bears all the tax for federal, state, and local income taxes. The employer and employee share FICA and Medicare taxes. The employer bears FUTA and state unemployment taxes.

Federal Unemployment Insurance (FUTA) Tax This tax, referred to as FUTA after the Federal Unemployment Tax Act, is intended to pay for programs to help unemployed workers. It is paid *only* by employers and recently was 6.2 percent of the first $7,000* earned by each employee. Against this federal tax, however, the employer is allowed a credit for unemployment taxes paid to the state. The maximum credit is 5.4 percent of the first $7,000 earned by each employee. Most states set their rate at this maximum. Thus, the FUTA tax most often paid is .8 percent (6.2 percent − 5.4 percent) of the taxable wages.

State Unemployment Insurance Tax All state unemployment programs provide for unemployment compensation to be paid to eligible unemployed workers.

* This amount may vary from state to state.

This compensation is paid out of the fund provided by the 5.4 percent of the first $7,000 (varies in some states) earned by each employee. In some states, employers with favorable employment records may be entitled to pay less than 5.4 percent.

To illustrate the recording of the payroll, assume that on February 15 total employee wages are $32,500, with withholdings of $5,400 for federal income taxes, $1,200 for state income taxes, $2,015 for social security tax, $471 for Medicare tax, $900 for medical insurance, and $1,300 for pension contributions. The entry to record this payroll follows:

A = L + OE	Date	Account	Debit	Credit
+ −	Feb. 15	Wages Expense	32,500	
+		Employees' Federal Income Taxes Payable		5,400
+		Employees' State Income Taxes Payable		1,200
+		Social Security Tax Payable		2,015
+		Medicare Tax Payable		471
+		Medical Insurance Payable		900
+		Pension Contributions Payable		1,300
+		Wages Payable		21,214
		To record payroll		

Note that the employees' take-home pay is only $21,214, although $32,500 was earned.

Using the same data, the additional employer taxes and other benefits costs would be recorded as follows, assuming that the payroll taxes correspond to the discussion above and that the employer pays 80 percent of the medical insurance premiums and half of the pension contributions:

A = L + OE	Date	Account	Debit	Credit
+ −	Feb. 15	Payroll Taxes and Benefits Expense	9,401	
+		Social Security Tax Payable		2,015
+		Medicare Tax Payable		471
+		Medical Insurance Payable		3,600
+		Pension Contributions Payable		1,300
+		Federal Unemployment Tax Payable		260
+		State Unemployment Tax Payable		1,755
		To record payroll taxes and other costs		

Note that the payroll taxes and benefits increase the total cost of the payroll to $41,901 ($9,401 + $32,500), which exceeds by almost 29 percent the amount earned by employees. This is a typical situation.

Business-World Example: See the Decision Point about US Airways at the beginning of this chapter for an example of an unearned revenue account with a substantial balance.

UNEARNED REVENUES **Unearned revenues** represent obligations for goods or services that the company must provide or deliver in a future accounting period in return for an advance payment from a customer. For example, a publisher of a monthly magazine who receives annual subscriptions totaling $240 would make the following entry:

A = L + OE	Account	Debit	Credit
+ +	Cash	240	
	Unearned Subscriptions		240
	Receipt of annual subscriptions in advance		

The publisher now has a liability of $240 that will be reduced gradually as monthly issues of the magazine are mailed.

A = L + OE	Account	Debit	Credit
− +	Unearned Subscriptions	20	
	Subscription Revenues		20
	Delivery of monthly magazine issues		

FOCUS ON BUSINESS PRACTICE

Many companies promote their products by issuing coupons that offer "cents off" or other enticements for purchasers. Since four out of five shoppers use coupons, companies are forced by competition to distribute them. The total value of unredeemed coupons, each of which represents a potential liability for the issuing company, is truly staggering. NCH Promotional Services, a company owned by Dun & Bradstreet, estimates that almost 300 billion coupons are issued annually. Of course, the liability depends on how many of the coupons will actually be redeemed. NCH estimates that number at approximately 6 billion, or about 2 percent. That is not a large percentage, but the value of the redeemed coupons is estimated to be more than $4 billion.[5]

Many businesses, such as repair companies, construction companies, and special-order firms, ask for a deposit or advance from a customer before they will begin work. Such advances are also current liabilities until the goods or services are actually delivered.

Estimated Liabilities

Point to Emphasize: Estimated liabilities are recorded and presented on the financial statements in the same way as definitely determinable liabilities. The only difference is that estimated liabilities involve some uncertainty in their computation.

Estimated liabilities are definite debts or obligations of which the exact dollar amount cannot be known until a later date. Since there is no doubt about the existence of the legal obligation, the primary accounting problem is to estimate and record the amount of the liability. Examples of estimated liabilities are income taxes, property taxes, product warranties, and vacation pay.

INCOME TAXES The income of a corporation is taxed by the federal government, most state governments, and some cities and towns. The amount of income taxes liability depends on the results of operations. Often the results are not known until after the end of the year. However, because income taxes are an expense in the year in which income is earned, an adjusting entry is necessary to record the estimated tax liability. The entry is as follows:

A = L + OE				
+ −	Dec. 31	Income Taxes Expense	53,000	
		Estimated Income Taxes Payable		53,000
		To record estimated federal income taxes		

Sole proprietorships and partnerships do *not* pay income taxes. Their owners must report their share of the firm's income on their individual tax returns.

Enrichment Note: The process of accruing property tax each month could be applied to income taxes if a company desires monthly financial statements.

PROPERTY TAX PAYABLE Property taxes are levied on real property, such as land and buildings, and on personal property, such as inventory and equipment. Property taxes are a main source of revenue for local governments. They are usually assessed annually against the property involved. Because the fiscal years of local governments and their assessment dates rarely correspond to a firm's fiscal year, it is necessary to estimate the amount of property tax that applies to each month of the year. Assume, for instance, that a local government has a fiscal year of July 1 to June 30, that its assessment date is November 1 for the current fiscal year, and that its payment date is December 15. Assume also that on July 1, Janis Corporation estimates that its property tax assessment for the coming year will be $24,000. The adjusting entry to be made on July 31, which would be repeated on August 31, September 30, and October 31, would be as follows:

A = L + OE			
+ −	July 31	Property Tax Expense	2,000	
		Estimated Property Tax Payable		2,000
		To record estimated property tax expense for the month		
		$24,000 ÷ 12 months = $2,000		

On November 1, the firm receives a property tax bill for $24,720. The estimate that was made in July was too low. The charge should have been $2,060 per month. Because the difference between the actual assessment and the estimate is small, the company decides to absorb in November the amount undercharged in the previous four months. Therefore, the property tax expense for November is $2,300 [$2,060 + 4($60)] and is recorded as follows:

A = L + OE				
+ −	Nov. 30	Property Tax Expense	2,300	
		Estimated Property Tax Payable		2,300
		To record estimated property tax		

The Estimated Property Tax Payable account now has a balance of $10,300. The entry to record payment on December 15 would be as follows:

A = L + OE				
+ −	Dec. 15	Estimated Property Tax Payable	10,300	
−		Prepaid Property Tax	14,420	
		Cash		24,720
		Payment of property tax		

Discussion Question: Where does the account Prepaid Property Tax appear in the financial statements? Answer: In the current asset section.

Beginning December 31 and each month afterward until June 30, property tax expense is recorded by a debit to Property Tax Expense and a credit to Prepaid Property Tax in the amount of $2,060. The total of these seven entries will reduce the Prepaid Property Tax account to zero on June 30.

Discussion Question: Recording product warranty expense in the year of the sale follows which accounting rule? Answer: The matching rule.

Instructional Strategy: Assign E 7 to small groups in class. The exercise works well as a substitute for a lecture on warranties or can be used to check students' comprehension and application skills.

PRODUCT WARRANTY LIABILITY When a firm places a warranty or guarantee on its product at the time of sale, a liability exists for the length of the warranty. The cost of the warranty is properly debited to an expense account in the period of sale because it is a feature of the product or service sold and thus is included in the price paid by the customer for the product. On the basis of experience, it should be possible to estimate the amount the warranty will cost in the future. Some products or services will require little warranty service; others may require much. Thus, there will be an average cost per product or service.

For example, assume that a muffler company guarantees that it will replace free of charge any muffler it sells that fails during the time the buyer owns the car. The company charges a small service fee for replacing the muffler. This guarantee is an important selling feature for the firm's mufflers. In the past, 6 percent of the mufflers sold have been returned for replacement under the guarantee. The average cost of a muffler is $25. Assume that during July, 350 mufflers were sold. The accrued liability would be recorded as an adjustment at the end of July as shown below:

A = L + OE				
+ −	July 31	Product Warranty Expense	525	
		Estimated Product Warranty Liability		525
		To record estimated product warranty expense:		
		Number of units sold	350	
		Rate of replacement under warranty	× .06	
		Estimated units to be replaced	21	
		Estimated cost per unit	×$ 25	
		Estimated liability for product warranty	$525	

Point to Emphasize: The date of the December 5 entry is not important. It would be the same if it happened during January or July. Note that the debit is to the liability account and not to the warranty expense account.

When a muffler is returned for replacement under the warranty, the cost of the muffler is charged against the Estimated Product Warranty Liability account. For example, assume that on December 5 a customer returns with a defective muffler and pays a $10 service fee to have the muffler replaced. Assume that this particular muffler cost $20. The entry is as follows:

A = L + OE
\+ − +
−

Dec. 5	Cash	10	
	Estimated Product Warranty Liability	20	
	Service Revenue		10
	Merchandise Inventory		20
	Replacement of muffler under warranty		

VACATION PAY LIABILITY In most companies, employees earn the right to paid vacation days or weeks as they work during the year. For example, an employee may earn two weeks of paid vacation for each 50 weeks of work. Therefore, the person is paid 52 weeks' salary for 50 weeks' work. Theoretically, the cost of the two weeks' vacation should be allocated as an expense over the whole year so that month-to-month costs will not be distorted. The vacation pay represents 4 percent (two weeks' vacation divided by 50 weeks) of a worker's pay. Every week worked earns the employee a small fraction (4 percent) for vacation pay.

Vacation pay liability can amount to a substantial amount of money. For example, in its annual report Delta Air Lines, Inc., reported at its 1999 year end a vacation pay liability of $470 million.[6]

Reinforcement Exercise: Durling Corporation offers four weeks of paid vacation per year to all employees. Because of this, no employees leave. What is the vacation pay expense for the month of April if the combined salary expense is $18,000? **Answer:** $1,500 (4/48 × $18,000).

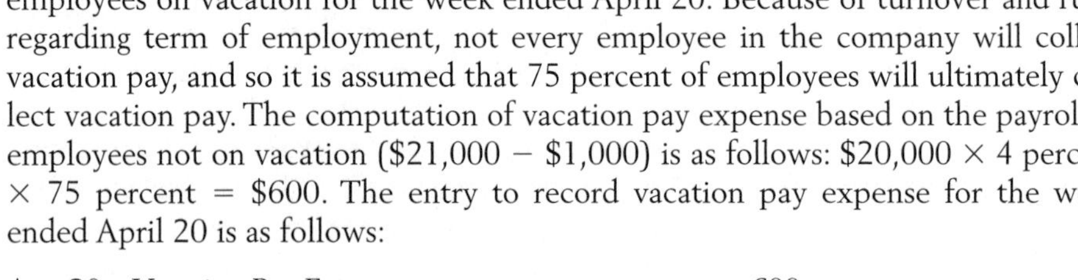

Suppose that a company with a vacation policy of two weeks of paid vacation for each 50 weeks of work has a payroll of $21,000, of which $1,000 was paid to employees on vacation for the week ended April 20. Because of turnover and rules regarding term of employment, not every employee in the company will collect vacation pay, and so it is assumed that 75 percent of employees will ultimately collect vacation pay. The computation of vacation pay expense based on the payroll of employees not on vacation ($21,000 − $1,000) is as follows: $20,000 × 4 percent × 75 percent = $600. The entry to record vacation pay expense for the week ended April 20 is as follows:

A = L + OE
\+ −

Apr. 20	Vacation Pay Expense	600	
	Estimated Liability for Vacation Pay		600
	Estimated vacation pay expense		

At the time employees receive their vacation pay, an entry is made debiting Estimated Liability for Vacation Pay and crediting Cash or Wages Payable. For

FOCUS ON BUSINESS PRACTICE

In the early 1980s, American Airlines, Inc., developed a frequent-flier program that gave free trips and other awards to customers based on the number of miles they flew on the airline. Since then, the number of similar programs by other airlines has mushroomed, and it is estimated that 38 million people now belong to airlines' frequent-flier programs. Today, U.S. airlines have more than 3 trillion miles outstanding. Seven to eight percent of all passengers are traveling on free tickets. Estimated liabilities for these tickets have become an important consideration in evaluating an airline's financial position. Complicating the estimate is that almost half the "miles" have been earned on purchases from hotel, car rental, and telephone companies and from the use of credit cards. In the latter cases, the companies giving the miles must pay the airlines at the rate of $.02 per mile. Thus, a free ticket obtained with 25,000 miles provides revenue to the airline of $500.[7]

example, the entry to record the $1,000 paid to employees on vacation during August is as follows:

A* = L + OE
− −
*Assumes cash paid.

Aug. 31	Estimated Liability for Vacation Pay	1,000	
	Cash (or Wages Payable)		1,000
	Wages of employees on vacation		

The treatment of vacation pay presented in this example may also be applied to other payroll costs, such as bonus plans and contributions to pension plans.

Contingent Liabilities

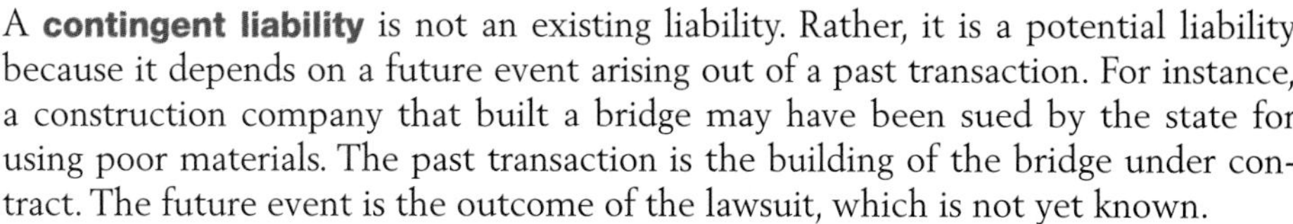

OBJECTIVE
3 Define *contingent liability*

Related Text Assignments:
Q: 17, 18
SE: 3
SD: 1, 2, 4
FRA: 2, 4, 5

Point to Emphasize: Contingencies are recorded when they are probable and can be reasonably estimated.

A **contingent liability** is not an existing liability. Rather, it is a potential liability because it depends on a future event arising out of a past transaction. For instance, a construction company that built a bridge may have been sued by the state for using poor materials. The past transaction is the building of the bridge under contract. The future event is the outcome of the lawsuit, which is not yet known.

Two conditions have been established by the FASB for determining when a contingency should be entered in the accounting records: (1) the liability must be probable and (2) it must be reasonably estimated.[8] Estimated liabilities such as the estimated income taxes liability, warranty liability, and vacation pay liability that were described earlier meet those conditions. Therefore, they are accrued in the accounting records. Potential liabilities that do not meet both conditions (probable and reasonably estimated) are reported in the notes to the financial statements. Losses from such potential liabilities are recorded when the conditions set by the FASB are met.

According to a survey of 600 large companies, the most common types of contingencies reported were litigation, which can involve many different issues, and environmental concerns.[9] The following example of contingent liabilities comes from the notes in the annual report of General Motors Corp., the world's largest automobile manufacturer:

> GM is subject to potential liability under government regulations and various claims and legal actions which are pending or may be asserted against them. Some of the pending actions purport to be class actions. The aggregate ultimate liability of GM under these government regulations and under these claims and actions, was not determinable at December 31, 1999. After discussion with counsel, it is the opinion of management that such liability is not expected to have a material adverse effect on the Corporation's consolidated financial statements.[10]

Payroll Accounting Illustrated

SUPPLEMENTAL OBJECTIVE
4 Compute and record the liabilities associated with payroll accounting

Earlier in this chapter, the liabilities associated with payroll accounting were identified and discussed. This section will focus on the calculations, records, and control requirements of payroll accounting. To demonstrate the concepts, the illustrations are shown in manual format, but, in actual practice, most businesses (including small businesses) use a computer to process payroll.

Related Text Assignments:
Q: 19, 20, 21
SE: 9, 10
E: 10, 11, 12
P: 5
SD: 5

Computation of an Employee's Take-Home Pay

Besides setting minimum wage levels, the federal Fair Labor Standards Act (also called the Wages and Hours Law) regulates overtime pay. Employers who take part in interstate commerce must pay overtime to employees who work beyond 40 hours a week or more than eight hours a day. This pay must be at least one and one-half times the regular rate. Work on Saturdays, Sundays, or holidays may also call for overtime pay or some sort of premium pay under separate wage agreements. Overtime pay under union or other employment contracts may exceed these minimums.

Discussion Question: What would change if Mr. Jones had worked 6 hours on Wednesday and 11 hours on Thursday? **Answer:** His pay would go up by $8 because of the two extra hours of overtime.

For example, suppose that the employment contract of Robert Jones calls for a regular wage of $8 an hour, one and one-half times the regular rate for work over eight hours in any weekday, and twice the regular rate for work on Saturdays, Sundays, or holidays. He works the following days and hours during the week of January 18, 20xx:

Day	Total Hours Worked	Regular Time	Overtime
Monday	10	8	2
Tuesday	8	8	0
Wednesday	8	8	0
Thursday	9	8	1
Friday	10	8	2
Saturday	2	0	2
	47	40	7

Jones's wages would be calculated as follows:

Regular time	40 hours × $8	$320
Overtime, weekdays	5 hours × $8 × 1.5	60
Overtime, weekend	2 hours × $8 × 2	32
Total wages		$412

Once Jones's wages are known, his take-home pay can be calculated. Since his total earnings for the week of January 18 are $412.00, his social security tax is 6.2 percent, or $25.54 (he has not earned over $80,400), and his Medicare tax is 1.45 percent, or $5.97. The amount to be withheld for federal income taxes depends in part on Jones's earnings and in part on the number of his exemptions. All employees are required by law to indicate exemptions by filing a Form W-4 (Employee's Withholding Exemption Certificate). Every employee is entitled to one exemption for himself or herself and one for each dependent.

Based on the information in the Form W-4, the amount of withholding is determined by referring to a withholding table provided by the Internal Revenue Service. For example, the withholding table in Figure 4 shows that for Jones, a married employee who has a total of four exemptions and is paid weekly, the withholding on total wages of $412 is $31. Actual withholding tables change periodically to reflect changes in tax rates and tax laws. Assume also that Jones's union dues are $2.00, his medical insurance premiums are $7.60, his life insurance premium is $6.00, he places $15.00 per week in savings bonds, and he contributes $1.00 per week to United Charities.

Jones's net (take-home) pay can now be computed as follows:

WEEKLY PAYROLL PERIOD—EMPLOYEE MARRIED												
And the wages are—		And the number of withholding allowances claimed is—										
		0	1	2	3	4	5	6	7	8	9	10 or more
At least	*But less than*	The amount of income tax to be withheld will be—										
$300	$310	$37	$31	$26	$20	$14	$ 9	$ 3	$ 0	$ 0	$0	$0
310	320	38	33	27	22	16	10	5	0	0	0	0
320	330	40	34	29	23	17	12	6	1	0	0	0
330	340	41	36	30	25	19	13	8	2	0	0	0
340	350	43	37	32	26	20	15	9	4	0	0	0
350	360	44	39	33	28	22	16	11	5	0	0	0
360	370	46	40	35	29	23	18	12	7	1	0	0
370	380	47	42	36	31	25	19	14	8	2	0	0
380	390	49	43	38	32	26	21	15	10	4	0	0
390	400	50	45	39	34	28	22	17	11	5	0	0
400	410	52	46	41	35	29	24	18	13	7	1	0
410	420	53	48	42	37	31	25	20	14	8	3	0
420	430	55	49	44	38	32	27	21	16	10	4	0

Figure 4
Sample Withholding Table

Point to Emphasize: The expense to the company is the gross earnings, not the net take-home pay.

Total earnings		$412.00
Deductions		
Federal income taxes withheld	$31.00	
Social security tax	25.54	
Medicare tax	5.97	
Union dues	2.00	
Medical insurance	7.60	
Life insurance	6.00	
Savings bonds	15.00	
United Charities contribution	1.00	
Total deductions		94.11
Net (take-home) pay		$317.89

Payroll Register

The **payroll register**, which is prepared each pay period, is a detailed listing of the firm's total payroll. A payroll register is presented in Exhibit 1. Note that the name, hours, earnings, deductions, and net pay of each employee are listed. Compare the entry for Robert Jones in the payroll register with the January 18 entry in the employee earnings record of Robert Jones presented in Exhibit 2. Except for the first column, which lists the employee names, and the last two columns, which show the wage or salary as either sales or office expense, the columns are the same. The columns help employers record the payroll in the accounting records and meet legal reporting requirements. The last two columns in Exhibit 1 are needed to divide the expenses in the accounting records into selling and administrative categories.

Exhibit 1
Payroll Register

Payroll Register — Pay Period: Week ended January 18

		Earnings			Deductions								Payment		Distribution	
Employee	Total Hours	Regular	Overtime	Gross	Federal Income Taxes	Social Security Tax	Medicare Tax	Union Dues	Medical Insurance	Life Insurance	Savings Bonds	Other: A—United Charities	Net Earnings	Check No.	Sales Wages Expense	Office Wages Expense
Linda Duval	40	160.00		160.00	11.00	9.92	2.32		5.80				130.96	923		160.00
John Franks	44	160.00	24.00	184.00	14.00	11.41	2.67	2.00	7.60			A 10.00	136.32	924	184.00	
Samuel Goetz	40	400.00		400.00	53.00	24.80	5.80		10.40	14.00		A 3.00	289.00	925	400.00	
Robert Jones	47	320.00	92.00	412.00	31.00	25.54	5.97	2.00	7.60	6.00	15.00	A 1.00	317.89	926	412.00	
Billie Matthews	40	160.00		160.00	14.00	9.92	2.32		5.80				127.96	927		160.00
Rosaire O'Brien	42	200.00	20.00	220.00	22.00	13.64	3.19	2.00	5.80				173.37	928	220.00	
James Van Dyke	40	200.00		200.00	20.00	12.40	2.90		5.80				158.90	929		200.00
		1,600.00	136.00	1,736.00	165.00	107.63	25.17	6.00	48.80	20.00	15.00	14.00	1,334.40		1,216.00	520.00

Exhibit 2
Employee Earnings Record

Employee Earnings Record

Employee's Name Robert Jones — Social Security Number 444-66-9999
Address 777 20th Street — Sex Male — Employee No. 705
Marshall, Michigan 52603 — Single ____ Married X — Weekly Pay Rate ____
Date of Birth September 20, 1962 — Exemptions (W-4) 4 — Hourly Rate $8
Position Sales Assistant — Date of Employment July 15, 1988 — Date Employment Ended ____

20xx		Earnings			Deductions								Payment		
Period Ended	Total Hours	Regular	Overtime	Gross	Federal Income Taxes	Social Security Tax	Medicare Tax	Union Dues	Medical Insurance	Life Insurance	Savings Bonds	Other: A—United Charities	Net Earnings	Check No.	Cumulative Gross Earnings
Jan 4	40	320.00	0	320.00	17.00	19.84	4.64	2.00	7.60	6.00	15.00	A 1.00	246.92	717	320.00
11	44	320.00	48.00	368.00	23.00	22.82	5.34	2.00	7.60	6.00	15.00	A 1.00	285.24	822	688.00
18	47	320.00	92.00	412.00	31.00	25.54	5.97	2.00	7.60	6.00	15.00	A 1.00	317.89	926	1,100.00

Recording the Payroll

The journal entry for recording the payroll is based on the column totals from the payroll register. The journal entry to record the January 18 payroll follows. Note that each account debited or credited is a total from the payroll register. If the payroll register is considered a special-purpose journal, the column totals can be posted directly to the ledger accounts, with the correct account numbers shown at the bottom of each column.

Toys "R" Us. How does this ratio compare to that in other industries, as represented by Figure 1? Toys "R" Us is a seasonal business. Would you expect short-term borrowings and accounts payable to be unusually high or unusually low at the balance sheet date of January 29, 2000? How does management use short-term financing to meet its needs for cash during the year?

Fingraph® Financial Analyst™

FRA 4.
LO 1 Comparison of
LO 2 Current Liabilities and
LO 3 Working Capital

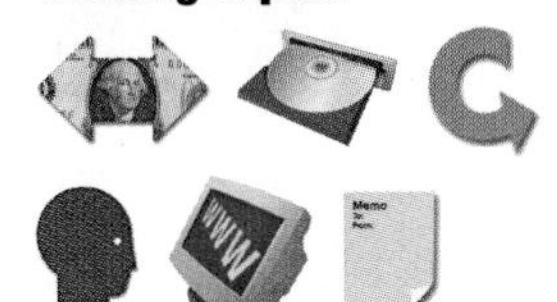

Choose any two companies from the same industry in the Fingraph® Financial Analyst™ CD-ROM software. The industry chosen should be one in which current liabilities are likely to be important. Choose an industry such as airlines, manufacturing, consumer products, consumer food and beverage, or computers.

1. In the annual reports for the companies you have selected, read the current liability section of the balance sheet and any reference to any current liabilities in the summary of significant accounting policies or notes to the financial statements. What are the most important current liabilities for each company? Are there any current liabilities that appear to be characteristic of the industry? Which current liabilities are definitely determinable and which appear to be accrued liabilities?
2. Display and print in tabular and graphical form the Current Assets and Current Liabilities Analysis page. Prepare a table that compares the current ratio and working capital for both companies for two years.
3. Find and read references to current liabilities in the liquidity analysis section of management's discussion and analysis in each annual report.
4. Write a one-page executive summary that highlights the most important types of current liabilities for this industry and compares the current ratio and working capital trends of the two companies, including reference to management's assessment. Include the Fingraph® page and your table as an attachment to your report.

Internet Case

FRA 5.
LO 3 Investigation of Status of Famous Contingencies

Some of the most famous contingent liabilities in history include the suits against tobacco companies such as ***RJR Nabisco, Inc.,*** and ***Philip Morris Incorporated*** and the *Valdez* oil spill case against ***Exxon Corporation.*** Investigate the current status of any one of these cases, including Texaco, by first going to the Needles Accounting Resource Center web site at http://college.hmco.com and clicking on one of these companies' web links. Then find the company's latest annual report and look in the notes to the financial statements under Contingencies. Report what you find about the case, including the possibility that the case has been settled or is no longer reported.

ENDNOTES

1. US Airways, Inc., *Annual Report*, 1999.
2. Radio Shack Corporation, *Annual Report*, 1999.
3. The Goodyear Tire & Rubber Company, *Annual Report*, 1999.
4. Lowe's Companies, Inc., *Annual Report*, 1999.
5. Raju Narisetti, "P&G Ad Chief Plots Demise of the Coupon," *The Wall Street Journal*, April 17, 1996.
6. Delta Air Lines, Inc., *Annual Report*, 1999.
7. Scott McCartney, "Free Airline Miles Become a Potent Tool for Selling Everything," *The Wall Street Journal*, April 16, 1996.
8. *Statement of Financial Accounting Standards No. 5*, "Accounting for Contingencies" (Norwalk, Conn.: Financial Accounting Standards Board, 1975).
9. American Institute of Certified Public Accountants, *Accounting Trends & Techniques*, 1999.
10. General Motors Corp., *Annual Report*, 1999.
11. Ibid.
12. Sun Microsystems Inc., *Annual Report*, 1999; Cisco Systems, *Annual Report*, 1999.
13. Man Nutzfahrzeuge Aktiengesellschaft, *Annual Report*, 1997.

13 Partnerships

LEARNING OBJECTIVES

1. Identify the principal characteristics, advantages, and disadvantages of the partnership form of business.
2. Record partners' investments of cash and other assets when a partnership is formed.
3. Compute and record the income or losses that partners share, based on stated ratios, capital balance ratios, and partners' salaries and interest.
4. Record a person's admission to a partnership.
5. Record a person's withdrawal from a partnership.
6. Compute the distribution of assets to partners when they liquidate their partnership.

DECISION POINT: A USER'S FOCUS

KPMG International Many people think of partnerships as relatively small business organizations, and usually they are right. However, some partnerships, among them law firms, investment companies, real estate companies, and accounting firms, are very large. An example is KPMG International, an integrated professional services firm with 800 offices in 150 countries. The firm provides accounting and auditing services, tax services, and management consulting services. With over 100,000 employees, it is one of the largest partnerships in the world. In 1999, the firm was growing rapidly with revenues of over $12 billion, $5.7 billion of which came from the United States. How does a partnership this large organize to accomplish its objectives?[1]

KPMG International is organized as a limited liability partnership. In a normal partnership, the personal financial resources of all partners are subject to risk of loss if the partnership suffers a loss it cannot bear. Accounting firms are at risk of suffering large losses as a result of lawsuits from investors who lose money investing in a company audited by the accounting firm. Because KPMG is organized as a limited liability partnership, partners are liable to the extent of their partnership interest in the firm but do not subject their other personal assets to risk.

Financial Highlights

(In millions of dollars)

	1999	1998	1997
Annual revenue	$12,200	$10,400	$9,000

Business-World Example: Because of mergers, the former "Big Eight" has been reduced to the "Big Five." They are Arthur Andersen & Co., Deloitte & Touche, Ernst & Young, KPMG International, and Pricewaterhouse Coopers.

Critical Thinking Question: How does a partnership located only in the United States differ from one with offices around the world? **Answer:** While technology permits worldwide communication, accommodations, such as the translation of monetary amounts from international operations into U.S. dollars, would be required to summarize total partnership performance.

Partnership Characteristics

OBJECTIVE

1 Identify the principal characteristics, advantages, and disadvantages of the partnership form of business

Related Text Assignments:
Q: 1, 2, 3, 4, 5
SE: 1
SD: 1, 3, 4
FRA: 1, 2, 3

The Uniform Partnership Act, which has been adopted by most states, defines a **partnership** as "an association of two or more persons to carry on as co-owners of a business for profit." Partnerships are treated as separate entities in accounting. They differ in many ways from the other forms of business. The next few paragraphs describe some of the important characteristics of a partnership.

Voluntary Association

Point to Emphasize: Partnerships and sole proprietorships are not legal entities; corporations are. All three, however, are considered accounting entities.

A partnership is a voluntary association of individuals rather than a legal entity in itself. Therefore, a partner is responsible under the law for his or her partners' business actions within the scope of the partnership. A partner also has unlimited liability for the debts of the partnership. Because of these potential liabilities, an individual must be allowed to choose the people who join the partnership. A person should select as partners individuals who share his or her business objectives.

PARTNERSHIP AGREEMENT A partnership is easy to form. Two or more competent people simply agree to be partners in a common business purpose. Their agreement is known as a **partnership agreement**. The partnership agreement does not have to be in writing; however, good business practice calls for a written document that clearly states the details of the arrangement. The contract should specify the name, location, and purpose of the business; the partners and their respective duties; the investments of each partner; the methods for distributing income and losses; and the procedures for the admission and withdrawal of partners, the withdrawal of assets allowed each partner, and the liquidation (termination) of the business.

Enrichment Note: Many types of organizations have been created by law. They include S corporations and limited partnerships. Each provides legal (especially tax) advantages and disadvantages.

LIMITED LIFE Because a partnership is formed by a contract between partners, it has a **limited life**: Anything that ends the contract dissolves the partnership. A partnership is dissolved when (1) a new partner is admitted, (2) a partner withdraws, (3) a partner goes bankrupt, (4) a partner is incapacitated (to the point where he or she cannot perform as obligated), (5) a partner retires, (6) a partner dies, or (7) the partnership ends according to the partnership agreement (for example, when a large project is completed). However, if the partners want the partnership to continue legally, the partnership agreement can be written to cover each of these situations. For example, the partnership agreement can state that if a partner dies, the remaining partner or partners must purchase the deceased partner's capital at book value from the heirs.

FOCUS ON INTERNATIONAL BUSINESS

American businesses are expanding into emerging markets throughout the world. Many of these markets, such as those of Hungary, Poland, the Czech Republic, India, and China, are in the process of privatizing public entities. This means that operations such as steel mills, cement factories, and utilities that were previously run by the government are being converted into private enterprises. Many countries require that local investors own a substantial proportion of the newly formed businesses. One way of accomplishing this is to form joint ventures, which match a country's need for outside capital and operational know-how with investors' interest in business expansion and profitability. Joint ventures often take the form of partnerships among two or more corporations and other investors. Any income or losses from operations will be divided among the participants according to a predetermined agreement.

Mutual Agency Each partner is an agent of the partnership within the scope of the business. Because of this **mutual agency**, any partner can bind the partnership to a business agreement as long as he or she acts within the scope of the company's normal operations. For example, a partner in a used-car business can bind the partnership through the purchase or sale of used cars. But this partner cannot bind the partnership to a contract to buy men's clothing or any other goods that are not related to the used-car business. Because of mutual agency, it is very important for an individual to choose business partners who have integrity and who share his or her business objectives.

Unlimited Liability All partners have **unlimited liability** for their company's debt, which means that each partner is personally liable for all the debts of the partnership. If a partnership is in poor financial condition and cannot pay its debts, the creditors must first satisfy their claims from the assets of the partnership. If the assets are not enough to pay all debts, the creditors can seek payment from the personal assets of each partner. If one partner's personal assets are used up before the debts are paid, the creditors can claim additional assets from the remaining partners who are able to pay. Each partner, then, could be required by law to pay all the debts of the partnership.

Point to Emphasize: Unlimited liability means that potential responsibility for debts is not limited by one's investment, as it is in a corporation. Each person is personally liable for all debts of the partnership, including those arising from contingent liabilities such as lawsuits. Liability can be avoided only by filing for personal bankruptcy.

Co-ownership of Partnership Property When individuals invest property in a partnership, they give up the right to their separate use of the property. The property has become an asset of the partnership and is now owned jointly by all the partners.

Participation in Partnership Income Each partner has the right to share in the company's income and the responsibility to share in its losses. The partnership agreement should state the method of distributing income and losses to each partner. If the agreement describes how income should be shared but does not mention losses, losses are distributed in the same way as income. If the partners fail to describe the method of income and loss distribution in the partnership agreement, the law states that income and losses must be shared equally.

Advantages and Disadvantages of Partnerships Partnerships have both advantages and disadvantages. One advantage is that a partnership is easy to form, change, and dissolve. Also, a partnership facilitates the pooling of capital resources and individual talents; it has no corporate tax burden (because a partnership is not a legal entity for tax purposes, it does not have to pay a federal income tax, as do corporations, but must file an informational return); and it gives the partners a certain amount of freedom and flexibility.

On the other hand, there are the following disadvantages: the life of a partnership is limited; one partner can bind the partnership to a contract (mutual agency); the partners have unlimited personal liability; and it is more difficult for a partnership to raise large amounts of capital and to transfer ownership interests than it is for a corporation.

Point to Emphasize: There is no federal income tax on partnerships. However, an informational return must be filed, and partners are taxed at their personal rates. There may be state or local business taxes assessed on a partnership, however. One example of this is the Michigan Single Business Tax.

Critical Thinking Question: What makes limited partnerships attractive to investors? **Answer:** Limited risk and price per unit of ownership. If price per unit is low enough, demand for ownership units may increase.

Other Forms of Association

Two other common forms of association that are a type of partnership or similar to a partnership are limited partnerships and joint ventures.

Enrichment Note: Several legal formats bridge the gap between general partnership and corporation; a limited partnership is just one of them. Each type of organization can have both legal and tax advantages.

Limited Partnerships A **limited partnership** is a special type of partnership that, like corporations, confines the limited partner's potential loss to the amount of his or her investment. Under this type of partnership the unlimited liability disadvantage of a partnership can be overcome. Usually, the limited partner-

FOCUS ON BUSINESS PRACTICE

Limited partnerships are sometimes used in place of the corporate form to raise funds from the public. Because possible investor losses are normally restricted to the amount of the investment, the limited partnership has some characteristics of the corporate form. Limited partnerships are used to obtain financing for many projects, such as locating and drilling oil and gas wells, manufacturing airplanes, and developing real estate (including shopping centers, office buildings, and apartment complexes). For example, Alliance Capital Management Limited Partnership is one of the largest investment advisors, managing more than $90 billion in assets for corporate and individual investors. The company's partnership units, or shares of ownership, sell on the New York Stock Exchange and can be purchased by the individual investor. In 2000, the units were selling at about $48 each and paid an annual dividend of $3.16 per share.[2]

ship has a general partner who has unlimited liability but allows other partners to limit their potential loss. The potential loss of all partners in an ordinary partnership is limited only by personal bankruptcy laws.

JOINT VENTURES In today's global environment, more companies are looking to form alliances similar to partnerships, called *joint ventures*, with other companies rather than to venture out on their own. A **joint venture** is an association of two or more entities for the purpose of achieving a specific goal, such as the manufacture of a product in a new market. Many joint ventures have an agreed-upon limited life. The entities forming joint ventures usually involve companies but can sometimes involve governments, especially in emerging economies. A joint venture brings together the resources, technical skills, political ties, and other assets of each of the parties for a common goal. Profits and losses are shared on an agreed-upon basis.

Accounting for Partners' Equity

OBJECTIVE

2 Record partners' investments of cash and other assets when a partnership is formed

Related Text Assignments:
Q: 6, 7, 8
SE: 2
E: 1
P: 1, 5
SD: 3

Although accounting for a partnership is very similar to accounting for a sole proprietorship, there are differences. One is that the owner's equity in a partnership is called **partners' equity**. In accounting for partners' equity, it is necessary to maintain separate Capital and Withdrawals accounts for each partner and to divide the income and losses of the company among the partners. The differences in the Capital accounts of a sole proprietorship and a partnership are shown below:

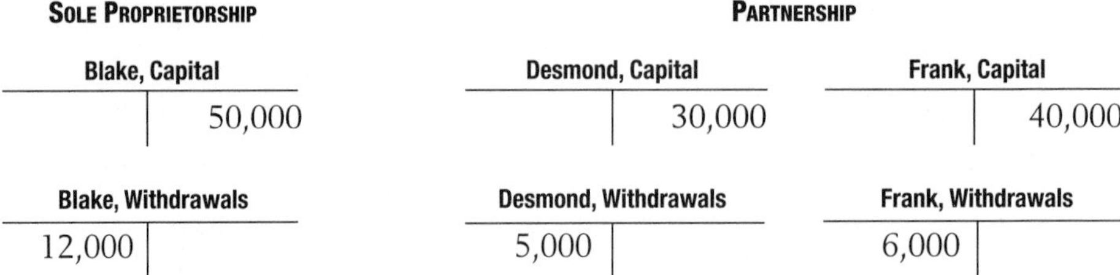

SOLE PROPRIETORSHIP		PARTNERSHIP			
Blake, Capital		**Desmond, Capital**		**Frank, Capital**	
	50,000		30,000		40,000
Blake, Withdrawals		**Desmond, Withdrawals**		**Frank, Withdrawals**	
12,000		5,000		6,000	

In the partners' equity section of the balance sheet, the balance of each partner's Capital account is listed separately:

Liabilities and Partners' Equity

Total Liabilities		$28,000
Partners' Equity		
Desmond, Capital	$25,000	
Frank, Capital	34,000	
Total Partners' Equity		59,000
Total Liabilities and Partners' Equity		$87,000

Each partner invests cash or other assets or a combination of the two in the partnership according to the partnership agreement. Noncash assets should be valued at their fair market value on the date they are transferred to the partnership. The assets invested by a partner are debited to the proper account, and the total amount is credited to the partner's Capital account.

Teaching Note: When accounts receivable are among the assets invested, they are recorded at the gross amounts. An allowance for uncollectible accounts is also recorded. The net result is the realizable value of the accounts receivable.

To show how partners' investments are recorded, let's assume that Jerry Adcock and Rose Villa have agreed to combine their capital and equipment in a partnership to operate a jewelry store. According to their partnership agreement, Adcock will invest $28,000 in cash and $37,000 worth of furniture and displays, and Villa will invest $40,000 in cash and $30,000 worth of equipment. Related to the equipment is a note payable for $10,000, which the partnership assumes. The journal entries to record the partners' initial investments are as follows:

A = L + OE	20x1			
+ +	July 1	Cash	28,000	
+		Furniture and Displays	37,000	
		Jerry Adcock, Capital		65,000
		Initial investment of Jerry Adcock in Adcock and Villa		
A = L + OE	1	Cash	40,000	
+ + +		Equipment	30,000	
+		Note Payable		10,000
		Rose Villa, Capital		60,000
		Initial investment of Rose Villa in Adcock and Villa		

Focus on Business Technology

The Internet is fostering the formation of many joint ventures by companies that are normally competitors. Among recent developments of this type are the following:

- Eight metals companies, including Allegheny Technologies Inc. and Alcoa Inc., have formed a joint venture to establish online service to provide products to businesses in the metals industries.
- Accor, Europe's largest hotel chain; Hilton International; and Forte Hotels have launched an Internet joint venture enabling customers to make online bookings at their hotels. This counters a similar effort involving seven other hotel chains including Marriott, Hyatt, and Holiday Inn.
- General Motors Corporation and other companies have formed an Internet joint venture to consolidate and coordinate the purchase of parts and supplies in the manufacture of automobiles.

Point to Emphasize: Old book values from previous entities are irrelevant to the new entity.

Point to Emphasize: Villa's noncash contribution is equal to the fair market value of the equipment less the amount owed on the equipment.

The values assigned to the assets would be included in the partnership agreement. These values can differ from those carried on the partners' personal books. For example, the equipment that Rose Villa contributed had a value of only $22,000 on her books, but its market value had increased considerably after she purchased it. The book value of Villa's equipment is not important. The fair market value of the equipment at the time of transfer *is* important, however, because that value represents the amount of money Villa has invested in the partnership. Later investments are recorded the same way.

Distribution of Partnership Income and Losses

OBJECTIVE

3 Compute and record the income or losses that partners share, based on stated ratios, capital balance ratios, and partners' salaries and interest

Related Text Assignments:
Q: 9, 10, 11
SE: 3, 4, 5
E: 2, 3, 4
P: 1, 2, 5, 6
SD: 2
FRA: 1

Point to Emphasize: The division of income is one area in which a partnership differs from a corporation. In corporations each common share receives an equal dividend. Partners can use any method they agree on to divide partnership income.

Point to Emphasize: The computations of each partner's share of net income are relevant to the closing entries in which the Income Summary account is closed to the partners' Capital accounts.

Common Student Confusion: Students often change the entry to close out Income Summary when the method of distributing partnership income changes. Regardless of how partnership income is divided, the accounts used in the entry to close out Income Summary never change. When there are losses to a partner or the partnership, the debits and credits switch, but the accounts are always the same.

Income and losses can be distributed according to whatever method the partners specify in the partnership agreement. To avoid later disputes, the agreement should be specific and clear. If a partnership agreement does not mention the distribution of income and losses, the law requires that they be shared equally by all partners. Also, if a partnership agreement mentions only the distribution of income, the law requires that losses be distributed in the same ratio as income.

The income of a partnership normally has three components: (1) return to the partners for the use of their capital (called *interest on partners' capital*), (2) compensation for direct services the partners have rendered (partners' salaries), and (3) other income for any special characteristics or risks individual partners may bring to the partnership. The breakdown of total income into its three components helps clarify how much each partner has contributed to the firm.

If all partners contribute equal capital, have similar talents, and spend the same amount of time in the business, then an equal distribution of income and losses would be fair. However, if one partner works full time in the firm and another devotes only a fourth of his or her time, then the distribution of income or losses should reflect the difference. (This concept would apply to any situation in which the partners contribute unequally to the business.)

Several ways for partners to share income are (1) by stated ratios, (2) by capital balance ratios, and (3) by salaries to the partners and interest on partners' capital, with the remaining income shared according to stated ratios. *Salaries* and *interest* here are not the same as *salaries expense* and *interest expense* in the ordinary sense of the terms. They do not affect the amount of reported net income. Instead, they refer to ways of determining each partner's share of net income or loss on the basis of time spent and money invested in the partnership.

Stated Ratios

One method of distributing income and losses is to give each partner a stated ratio of the total income or loss. If each partner is making an equal contribution to the firm, each can assume the same share of income and losses. It is important to understand that an equal contribution to the firm does not necessarily mean an equal capital investment in the firm. One partner may devote more time and talent to the firm, whereas the second partner may make a larger capital investment. And, if the partners contribute unequally to the firm, unequal stated ratios—60 percent and 40 percent, perhaps—can be appropriate.

Let's assume that Adcock and Villa had a net income last year of $30,000. Their partnership agreement states that the percentages of income and losses distributed to Jerry Adcock and Rose Villa should be 60 percent and 40 percent, respectively.

The computation of each partner's share of the income and the journal entry to show the distribution are as follows:

Adcock ($30,000 × .60)	$ 18,000
Villa ($30,000 × .40)	12,000
Net Income	$30,000

A = L + OE	Date	Account	Debit	Credit
	20x2			
−	June 30	Income Summary	30,000	
+		Jerry Adcock, Capital		18,000
+		Rose Villa, Capital		12,000
		Distribution of income for the year to the partners' Capital accounts		

Capital Balance Ratios

If invested capital produces the most income for the partnership, then income and losses may be distributed according to capital balances. The ratio used to distribute income and losses here may be based on each partner's capital balance at the beginning of the year or on the average capital balance of each partner during the year. The partnership agreement must describe the method to be used.

Ratios Based on Beginning Capital Balances To show how the first method works, let's look at the beginning capital balances of the partners in Adcock and Villa. At the start of the fiscal year, July 1, 20x1, Jerry Adcock, Capital showed a $65,000 balance, and Rose Villa, Capital showed a $60,000 balance. (Actually, these balances reflect the partners' initial investment; the partnership was formed on July 1, 20x1.) The total partners' equity in the firm, then, was $125,000 ($65,000 + $60,000). Each partner's capital balance at the beginning of the year divided by the total partners' equity at the beginning of the year is that partner's beginning capital balance ratio:

	Beginning Capital Balance	Beginning Capital Balance Ratio
Jerry Adcock	$ 65,000	65,000 ÷ 125,000 = .52 = 52%
Rose Villa	60,000	60,000 ÷ 125,000 = .48 = 48%
	$125,000	

The income that each partner should receive when distribution is based on beginning capital balance ratios is determined by multiplying the total income by each partner's capital ratio. If we assume that income for the year was $140,000, Jerry Adcock's share of that income was $72,800, and Rose Villa's share was $67,200.

Jerry Adcock	$140,000 × .52 =	$ 72,800
Rose Villa	140,000 × .48 =	67,200
		$140,000

Ratios Based on Average Capital Balances If Adcock and Villa use beginning capital balance ratios to determine the distribution of income, they do not consider any investments or withdrawals made during the year. But investments and withdrawals usually change the partners' capital ratios. If the partners believe that their capital balances are going to change dramatically during the year, they can choose average capital balance ratios as a fairer means of distributing income and losses.

The following T accounts show the activity over the year in Adcock and Villa's partners' Capital and Withdrawals accounts:

Jerry Adcock, Capital			Jerry Adcock, Withdrawals	
	7/1/x1	65,000	1/1/x2	10,000

Rose Villa, Capital			Rose Villa, Withdrawals	
	7/1/x1	60,000	11/1/x1	10,000
	2/1/x2	8,000		

Jerry Adcock withdrew $10,000 on January 1, 20x2, and Rose Villa withdrew $10,000 on November 1, 20x1, and invested an additional $8,000 of equipment on February 1, 20x2. Again, the income for the year's operation (July 1, 20x1, to June 30, 20x2) was $140,000. The calculations for the average capital balances and the distribution of income are as follows:

Average Capital Balances

Partner	Date	Capital Balance ×	Months Unchanged	=	Total		Average Capital Balance
Adcock	July–Dec.	$65,000 ×	6	=	$390,000		
	Jan.–June	55,000 ×	6	=	330,000		
			12		$720,000	÷ 12 =	$ 60,000
Villa	July–Oct.	$60,000 ×	4	=	$240,000		
	Nov.–Jan.	50,000 ×	3	=	150,000		
	Feb.–June	58,000 ×	5	=	290,000		
			12		$680,000	÷ 12 =	56,667
					Total average capital		$116,667

Average Capital Balance Ratios

$$\text{Adcock} = \frac{\text{Adcock's Average Capital Balance}}{\text{Total Average Capital}} = \frac{\$60{,}000}{\$116{,}667} = .514 = 51.4\%$$

$$\text{Villa} = \frac{\text{Villa's Average Capital Balance}}{\text{Total Average Capital}} = \frac{\$56{,}667}{\$116{,}667} = .486 = 48.6\%$$

Distribution of Income

Partner	Income	×	Ratio	=	Share of Income
Adcock	$140,000	×	.514	=	$ 71,960
Villa	140,000	×	.486	=	68,040
				Total income	$140,000

Instructional Strategy: To check students' ability to apply LO 3, divide the class into small groups and ask each group to complete two items from P 1, part 2 (such as 2a and 2f). Vary the assignments, but try to assign each item to at least two groups. Allow time for completion. Then have a representative of each group present the answer to one item, using the chalkboard, overheads, or flip charts. If the presenter has difficulty, a member of the backup group may help.

Notice that to determine the distribution of income (or loss), you have to determine (1) the average capital balances, (2) the average capital balance ratios, and (3) each partner's share of income or loss. To compute each partner's average capital balance, you have to examine the changes that have taken place during the year in each partner's capital balance, changes that are the product of further investments and withdrawals. The partner's beginning capital is multiplied by the number of months the balance remains unchanged. After the balance changes, the new balance is multiplied by the number of months it remains unchanged. The process continues until the end of the year. The totals of these computations are added, and then they are divided by 12 to determine the average capital balances. Once the average capital balances are determined, the method of figuring capital balance ratios for sharing income and losses is the same as the method used for beginning capital balances.

Salaries, Interest, and Stated Ratios

Point to Emphasize: Partnership income or loss cannot be divided solely on the basis of salaries or interest. An additional component, such as stated ratios, is needed.

Teaching Note: Students often enter salaries and interest as expenses. Remind them that using salaries and interest to divide income or loss among partners has no effect on the income statement. Partners' salaries and interest are used only to allow the equitable division of the partnership's net income.

Partners generally do not contribute equally to a firm. To make up for unequal contributions, a partnership agreement can allow for partners' salaries, interest on partners' capital balances, or a combination of both in the distribution of income. Again, salaries and interest of this kind are not deducted as expenses before the partnership income is determined. They represent a method of arriving at an equitable distribution of income or loss.

To illustrate an allowance for partners' salaries, we assume that Adcock and Villa have agreed that they will receive salaries—$8,000 for Adcock and $7,000 for Villa—and that any remaining income will be divided equally between them. Each salary is charged to the appropriate partner's Withdrawals account when paid. Assuming the same $140,000 income for the first year, the calculations for Adcock and Villa are as follows:

	Income of Partner		Income
	Adcock	Villa	Distributed
Total Income for Distribution			$140,000
Distribution of Salaries			
Adcock	$ 8,000		
Villa		$ 7,000	(15,000)
Remaining Income After Salaries			$125,000
Equal Distribution of Remaining Income			
Adcock ($125,000 × .50)	62,500		
Villa ($125,000 × .50)		62,500	(125,000)
Remaining Income			—
Income of Partners	$70,500	$69,500	$140,000

Reinforcement Exercise: What is the entry for Adcock and Villa on June 30 if net income is $14,000? **Answer:** $7,500 for Adcock and $6,500 for Villa. The salaries ($15,000 total) are distributed first, which leaves a $1,000 negative balance to be distributed equally.

Salaries allow for differences in the services that partners provide the business. However, they do not take into account differences in invested capital. To allow for capital differences, each partner can receive a stated interest on his or her invested capital in addition to salary. Suppose that Jerry Adcock and Rose Villa agree to pay annual salaries of $8,000 for Adcock and $7,000 for Villa, to receive 10 percent interest on their beginning capital balances, and to share any remaining income equally. If we assume income of $140,000, the calculations for Adcock and Villa are as follows:

	Income of Partner		Income
	Adcock	Villa	Distributed
Total Income for Distribution			$140,000
Distribution of Salaries			
Adcock	$ 8,000		
Villa		$ 7,000	(15,000)
Remaining Income After Salaries			$125,000
Distribution of Interest			
Adcock ($65,000 × .10)	6,500		
Villa ($60,000 × .10)		6,000	(12,500)
Remaining Income After Salaries and Interest			$112,500
Equal Distribution of Remaining Income			
Adcock ($112,500 × .50)	56,250		
Villa ($112,500 × .50)		56,250	(112,500)
Remaining Income			—
Income of Partners	$70,750	$69,250	$140,000

Clarification Note: If there is a negative balance after salaries or salaries and interest have been distributed, the terms *Remaining Income After Salaries* and *Remaining Income After Salaries and Interest* become *Negative Balance After Salaries* and *Negative Balance After Salaries and Interest.* The computation proceeds in exactly the same way, regardless of whether the balance is positive or negative.

Enrichment Note: When negotiating a partnership agreement, be sure to look at (and negotiate) the impact of both profits (net income) and losses.

If the partnership agreement allows for the distribution of salaries or interest or both, the amounts must be allocated to the partners even if profits are not enough to cover the salaries and interest. In fact, even if the company has a loss, these allocations must still be made. The negative balance or loss after the allocation of salaries and interest must be distributed according to the stated ratio in the partnership agreement, or equally if the agreement does not mention a ratio.

For example, let's assume that Adcock and Villa agreed to the following conditions for the distribution of income and losses:

	Salaries	Interest	Beginning Capital Balance
Adcock	$70,000	10 percent of beginning	$65,000
Villa	60,000	capital balances	60,000

FOCUS ON BUSINESS PRACTICE

Partners in professional accounting firms are often held in high esteem and envied for the high incomes that some of them make. Partners in large accounting firms can make over $250,000 per year, with top partners drawing over $800,000. However, consideration of those incomes should take into account the risks that partners take and the fact that the incomes of partners in small accounting firms are often much lower. Partners are not compensated in the same way as managers in corporations. Partners' income is not guaranteed, but rather is based on the performance of the partnership. Also, each partner is required to make a substantial investment of capital in the partnership. This capital remains at risk for as long as the partner chooses to stay in the partnership. For instance, in one notable instance, when many savings and loan institutions were failing, the partners in a major accounting firm lost their total investments as well as their income when their firm was subjected to lawsuits and other losses. The firm was eventually liquidated.

The income for the first year of operation was $140,000. The computation for the distribution of the income and loss is as follows:

	Income of Partner		Income
	Adcock	Villa	Distributed
Total Income for Distribution			$140,000
Distribution of Salaries			
Adcock	$70,000		
Villa		$60,000	(130,000)
Remaining Income After Salaries			$ 10,000
Distribution of Interest			
Adcock ($65,000 × .10)	6,500		
Villa ($60,000 × .10)		6,000	(12,500)
Negative Balance After Salaries and Interest			($ 2,500)
Equal Distribution of Negative Balance*			
Adcock ($2,500 × .50)	(1,250)		
Villa ($2,500 × .50)		(1,250)	2,500
Remaining Income			—
Income of Partners	$75,250	$64,750	$140,000

*Notice that the negative balance is distributed equally because the agreement does not indicate how income and losses should be distributed after salaries and interest are paid.

On the income statement for the partnership, the distribution of income or losses is shown below the net income figure. Exhibit 1 shows how this is done.

Exhibit 1
Partial Income Statement for Adcock and Villa

Adcock and Villa
Partial Income Statement
For the Year Ended June 30, 20x2

Net Income		$140,000
Distribution to the Partners		
Adcock		
Salary Distribution	$70,000	
Interest on Beginning Capital Balance	6,500	
Total	$76,500	
One-Half of Remaining Negative Amount	(1,250)	
Share of Net Income		$ 75,250
Villa		
Salary Distribution	$60,000	
Interest on Beginning Capital Balance	6,000	
Total	$66,000	
One-Half of Remaining Negative Amount	(1,250)	
Share of Net Income		64,750
Net Income Distributed		$140,000

Dissolution of a Partnership

OBJECTIVE

4 Record a person's admission to a partnership

Related Text Assignments:
Q: 12, 13
SE: 6, 7, 8
E: 5
P: 3, 5, 7
SD: 5

Dissolution of a partnership occurs whenever there is a change in the original association of partners. When a partnership is dissolved, the partners lose their authority to continue the business as a going concern. That the partners lose this authority does not necessarily mean that the business operation is ended or interrupted. However, it does mean—from a legal standpoint as well as an accounting one—that the separate entity ceases to exist. The remaining partners can act for the partnership in finishing the affairs of the business or form a new partnership that will be a new accounting entity. The dissolution of a partnership takes place through the admission of a new partner, the withdrawal of a partner, or the death of a partner.

Admission of a New Partner

Business-World Example: Dissolution of a partnership is a legal issue. Consider Ernst & Young, which admits over one hundred partners each year. The entity continues to operate despite the legal changes it must make.

Point to Emphasize: Admission of a new partner never has an impact on net income. Regardless of the price a new partner pays, there are never any income statement accounts in the entry to admit a new partner.

The admission of a new partner dissolves the old partnership because a new association has been formed. Dissolving the old partnership and creating a new one require the consent of all the old partners and the ratification of a new partnership agreement. When a new partner is admitted, a new partnership agreement should be in place.

An individual can be admitted into a partnership in one of two ways: (1) by purchasing an interest in the partnership from one or more of the original partners or (2) by investing assets in the partnership.

PURCHASING AN INTEREST FROM A PARTNER When an individual is admitted to a firm by purchasing an interest from an old partner, each partner must agree to the change. The transaction is a personal one between the old and new partners, but the interest purchased must be transferred from the Capital account of the selling partner to the Capital account of the new partner.

Suppose that Jerry Adcock decides to sell his interest, assumed to be $70,000, in Adcock and Villa to Richard Davis for $100,000 on August 31, 20x3, and that Rose Villa agrees to the sale. The entry to record the sale on the partnership books looks like this:

A = L + OE	20x3			
	Aug. 31	Jerry Adcock, Capital	70,000	
−		Richard Davis, Capital		70,000
+		Transfer of Jerry Adcock's equity to Richard Davis		

Point to Emphasize: When a partner sells his or her interest directly to a new partner, the partner, not the partnership, realizes the gain or loss. In this case, Adcock has a gain of $30,000, but the assets, liabilities, and total equity of the partnership do not change.

Notice that the entry records the book value of the equity, not the amount Davis pays. The amount Davis pays is a personal matter between him and Adcock. Because the amount paid does not affect the assets or liabilities of the firm, it is not entered in the records.

Here's another example of a purchase: Assume that Richard Davis purchases half of Jerry Adcock's $70,000 interest in the partnership and half of Rose Villa's interest, assumed to be $80,000, by paying a total of $100,000 to the two partners on August 31, 20x3. The entry to record this transaction on the partnership books would be as follows:

A = L + OE	20x3			
−	Aug. 31	Jerry Adcock, Capital	35,000	
−		Rose Villa, Capital	40,000	
+		Richard Davis, Capital		75,000
		Transfer of half of Jerry Adcock's and Rose Villa's equity to Richard Davis		

Clarification Note: If the account did not reflect the current value of the assets, the asset accounts (and Capital accounts) would need to be adjusted before admitting the new partner.

INVESTING ASSETS IN A PARTNERSHIP When a new partner is admitted through an investment in the partnership, both the assets and the partners' equity in the firm increase. The increase occurs because the assets the new partner invests become partnership assets, and as partnership assets increase, partners' equity increases as well. For example, assume that Jerry Adcock and Rose Villa have agreed to allow Richard Davis to invest $75,000 in return for a one-third interest in their partnership. The Capital accounts of Jerry Adcock and Rose Villa are assumed to be $70,000 and $80,000, respectively. Davis's $75,000 investment equals a one-third interest in the firm after the investment is added to the previously existing capital of the partnership:

Jerry Adcock, Capital	$ 70,000
Rose Villa, Capital	80,000
Davis's investment	75,000
Total capital after Davis's investment	$225,000
One-third interest ($225,000 ÷ 3)	$ 75,000

The journal entry to record Davis's investment is as follows:

A = L + OE	20x3			
+ +	Aug. 31	Cash	75,000	
		Richard Davis, Capital		75,000
		Admission of Richard Davis to a one-third interest in the company		

Point to Emphasize: The original partners receive a bonus because the entity is worth more as a going concern than the fair value of the net assets would otherwise indicate. That is, the new partner is paying for unrecorded partnership value.

BONUS TO THE OLD PARTNERS Sometimes a partnership may be so profitable or otherwise advantageous that a new investor is willing to pay more than the actual dollar interest he or she receives in the partnership. For instance, suppose an individual pays $100,000 for an $80,000 interest in a partnership. The $20,000 excess of the payment over the interest purchased is a **bonus** to the original partners. The bonus must be distributed to the original partners according to the partnership agreement. When the agreement does not cover the distribution of bonuses, a bonus should be distributed to the original partners in accordance with the method for distributing income and losses.

Assume that Adcock and Villa has operated for several years and that the partners' capital balances and the stated ratios for distribution of income and loss are as follows:

Partners	Capital Balances	Stated Ratios
Adcock	$160,000	55%
Villa	140,000	45
	$300,000	100%

Richard Davis wants to join the firm. He offers to invest $100,000 on December 1 in return for a one-fifth interest in the business and income. The original partners agree to the offer. The computation of the bonus to the original partners follows:

Partners' equity in the original partnership		$300,000
Cash investment by Richard Davis		100,000
Partners' equity in the new partnership		$400,000
Partners' equity assigned to Richard Davis ($400,000 × ⅕)		$ 80,000
Bonus to the original partners		
Investment by Richard Davis	$100,000	
Less equity assigned to Richard Davis	80,000	$ 20,000
Distribution of bonus to original partners		
Jerry Adcock ($20,000 × .55)	$ 11,000	
Rose Villa ($20,000 × .45)	9,000	$ 20,000

Reinforcement Exercise: What would the entry be if Davis pays $700,000 for a 40 percent ownership in the partnership? **Answer:**

Cash	700,000	
Jerry Adcock, Capital		165,000
Rose Villa, Capital		135,000
Richard Davis, Capital		400,000

The journal entry that records Davis's admission to the partnership is as follows:

A = L + OE				
+ +	20x3 Dec. 1	Cash	100,000	
+		Jerry Adcock, Capital		11,000
+		Rose Villa, Capital		9,000
		Richard Davis, Capital		80,000
		Investment by Richard Davis for a one-fifth interest in the firm, and the bonus paid to the original partners		

Enrichment Note: Human capital plays a large part in the profitability of entities traditionally organized as partnerships (for example, accounting firms, legal firms, and medical practices). When a new partner is admitted, this human capital is recognized in the Capital account of the new partner who receives a bonus.

BONUS TO THE NEW PARTNER There are several reasons for a partnership to want a new partner. A firm in financial trouble might need additional cash. Or the original partners, wanting to expand the firm's markets, might need more capital than they themselves can provide. Also, the partners might know a person who would bring a unique talent to the firm. Under such conditions, a new partner could be admitted to the partnership with the understanding that part of the original partners' capital will be transferred (credited) to the new partner's Capital account as a bonus.

For example, suppose that Jerry Adcock and Rose Villa have invited Richard Davis to join the firm. Davis is going to invest $60,000 on December 1 for a one-fourth interest in the company. The stated ratios for distribution of income or loss for Adcock and Villa are 55 percent and 45 percent, respectively. If Davis is to receive a one-fourth interest in the firm, the interest of the original partners represents a three-fourths interest in the business. The computation of Davis's bonus is as follows:

Total equity in partnership		
Jerry Adcock, Capital		$160,000
Rose Villa, Capital		140,000
Investment by Richard Davis		60,000
Partners' equity in the new partnership		$360,000
Partners' equity assigned to Richard Davis ($360,000 × ¼)		$ 90,000
Bonus to new partner		
Equity assigned to Richard Davis	$90,000	
Less cash investment by Richard Davis	60,000	$ 30,000
Distribution of bonus from original partners		
Jerry Adcock ($30,000 × .55)	$16,500	
Rose Villa ($30,000 × .45)	13,500	$ 30,000

Exhibit 2
Statement of Liquidation Showing Gain on Sale of Assets

Adcock, Villa, Davis & Company
Statement of Liquidation
February 2–20, 20x4

Explanation	Cash	Other Assets	Accounts Payable	Adcock, Capital (30%)	Villa, Capital (30%)	Davis, Capital (40%)	Gain (or Loss) from Realization
Balance 2/2/x4	$ 60,000	$340,000	$120,000	$85,000	$95,000	$100,000	
1. Collection of Accounts Receivable	35,000	(40,000)					($ 5,000)
	$ 95,000	$300,000	$120,000	$85,000	$95,000	$100,000	($ 5,000)
2. Sale of Inventory	110,000	(100,000)					10,000
	$205,000	$200,000	$120,000	$85,000	$95,000	$100,000	$ 5,000
3. Sale of Plant Assets	200,000	(200,000)					
	$405,000	—	$120,000	$85,000	$95,000	$100,000	$ 5,000
4. Payment of Liabilities	(120,000)		(120,000)				
	$285,000		—	$85,000	$95,000	$100,000	$ 5,000
5. Distribution of Gain (or Loss) from Realization				1,500	1,500	2,000	(5,000)
	$285,000			$86,500	$96,500	$102,000	—
6. Distribution to Partners	(285,000)			(86,500)	(96,500)	(102,000)	
	—			—	—	—	

Notice that the cash distributed to the partners is the balance in their respective Capital accounts. Cash is not distributed according to the partners' stated ratios.

Loss on Sale of Assets

Point to Emphasize: The case here is almost the same as the previous one because losses are allocated on the same basis as gains. The only difference is that entry 3 in this case and entry 5 in the first case switch the debits and credits.

We discuss two cases involving losses on the sale of a company's assets. In the first, the losses are small enough to be absorbed by the partners' capital balances. In the second, one partner's share of the losses is too large for his capital balance to absorb.

When a firm's assets are sold at a loss, the partners share the loss on liquidation according to their stated ratios. For example, assume that during the liquidation of Adcock, Villa, Davis & Company, the total cash received from the collection of accounts receivable and the sale of inventory and plant assets was $140,000. The statement of liquidation appears in Exhibit 3, and the journal entries for the liquidation are as follows:

Point to Emphasize: This example uses a compound entry for what was included in entries 1, 2, and 3 in the first example. If students have difficulty with the concept, here is an opportunity to break the entry down into its three component parts.

A = L + OE	Date	Account	Debit	Credit	Explanation on Statement of Liquidation
	20x4				
+ −	Feb. 15	Cash	140,000		1
−		Gain or Loss from Realization	200,000		
−		Accounts Receivable		40,000	
−		Merchandise Inventory		100,000	
		Plant Assets		200,000	
		Collection of accounts receivable and the sale of inventory and plant assets			
− −	16	Accounts Payable	120,000		2
		Cash		120,000	
		Payment of accounts payable			
−	20	Jerry Adcock, Capital	60,000		3
−		Rose Villa, Capital	60,000		
−		Richard Davis, Capital	80,000		
+		Gain or Loss from Realization		200,000	
		Distribution of the loss on assets to the partners			
− −	20	Jerry Adcock, Capital	25,000		4
−		Rose Villa, Capital	35,000		
−		Richard Davis, Capital	20,000		
		Cash		80,000	
		Distribution of cash to the partners			

In some liquidations, a partner's share of the loss is greater than his or her capital balance. In such a situation, because partners are subject to unlimited liability, the partner must make up the deficit in his or her Capital account from personal assets. For example, suppose that after the sale of assets and the payment of liabilities, the remaining assets and partners' equity of Adcock, Villa, Davis & Company look like this:

Assets		
Cash		$ 30,000
Partners' Equity		
Adcock, Capital	$25,000	
Villa, Capital	20,000	
Davis, Capital	(15,000)	$ 30,000

Richard Davis must pay $15,000 into the partnership from personal funds to cover his deficit. If he pays cash to the partnership, the following entry would record the cash contribution:

A = L + OE	Date	Account	Debit	Credit
	20x4			
+ +	Feb. 20	Cash	15,000	
		Richard Davis, Capital		15,000
		Additional investment of Richard Davis to cover the negative balance in his Capital account		

Discussion Question: What is the balance in Richard Davis, Capital after the February 20 entry? **Answer:** Zero.

1. Income was $272,600.
2. Income was $77,800.
3. The loss was $28,400.

P 3. **LO 4 LO 5 Admission and Withdrawal of a Partner**

Alicia, Roberta, and Joanne are partners in the Image Gallery. The balances in the Capital accounts of Alicia, Roberta, and Joanne as of November 30, 20xx, are $50,000, $60,000, and $90,000, respectively. The partners share income and losses in a ratio of 2:3:5.

REQUIRED

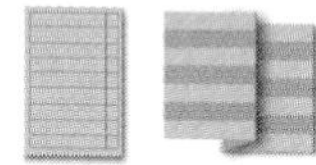

Prepare journal entries for each of the following independent conditions: (a) Luke pays Joanne $100,000 for four-fifths of Joanne's interest. (b) Luke is to be admitted to the partnership with a one-third interest for a $100,000 cash investment. (c) Luke is to be admitted to the partnership with a one-third interest for a $160,000 cash investment. A bonus, based on the partners' ratio for income and losses, is to be distributed to the original partners when Luke is admitted. (d) Luke is to be admitted to the partnership with a one-third interest for an $82,000 cash investment. A bonus is to be given to Luke on admission. (e) Alicia withdraws from the partnership, taking $66,000 in cash. (f) Alicia withdraws from the partnership by selling her interest directly to Luke for $70,000.

P 4. **LO 6 Partnership Liquidation**

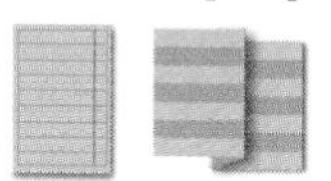

The balance sheet of the GDL Partnership as of August 31, 20xx, is as follows:

GDL Partnership
Balance Sheet
August 31, 20xx

Assets		Liabilities	
Cash	$ 12,000	Accounts Payable	$ 960,000
Accounts Receivable	240,000	**Partners' Equity**	
Inventory	528,000		
Equipment (net)	924,000	Gary, Capital	144,000
Total Assets	$1,704,000	Dawn, Capital	360,000
		Leslie, Capital	240,000
		Total Liabilities and Partners' Equity	$1,704,000

The partners—Gary, Dawn, and Leslie—share income and losses in the ratio of 5:3:2. Because of a mutual disagreement, the partners have decided to liquidate the business.

Assume that Gary cannot contribute any additional personal assets to the company during liquidation and that the following transactions occurred during liquidation: (a) Accounts receivable were sold for 60 percent of their book value. (b) Inventory was sold for $552,000. (c) Equipment was sold for $600,000. (d) Accounts payable were paid in full. (e) Gain or loss from realization was distributed to the partners' Capital accounts. (f) Gary's deficit was transferred to the remaining partners in their new income and loss ratio. (g) The remaining cash was distributed to Dawn and Leslie.

REQUIRED

1. Prepare a statement of liquidation.
2. Prepare journal entries to liquidate the partnership and distribute any remaining cash.

P 5.
LO 2 LO 3 LO 4 LO 6 Comprehensive Partnership Transactions

Sam Flippo and Henry McCovey formed a partnership on January 1, 20x1, to operate a computer software store. To begin the partnership, Flippo transferred cash totaling $116,000 and office equipment valued at $84,000 to the partnership. McCovey transferred cash of $56,000, land valued at $36,000, and a building valued at $300,000. In addition, the partnership assumed the mortgage of $232,000 on the building.

On December 31, the partnership reported a loss of $16,000 for its first year. In the partnership agreement, the owners had specified the distribution of income and losses by allowing salaries of $20,000 to Flippo and $48,000 to McCovey, interest of 10 percent on beginning capital, and the remaining amount to be divided in the ratio of 3:2.

On January 1, 20x2, the partners brought Mel Stanford, who was experienced in the software business, into the partnership. Stanford invested $56,000 in the partnership for a 20 percent interest. The bonus to Stanford was transferred from the original partners' accounts in the ratio of 3:2.

During 20x2, the partnership earned an income of $108,000. The new partnership agreement required that income and losses be divided by allowing salaries of $20,000, $48,000, and $60,000 for Flippo, McCovey, and Stanford, and by paying interest of 10 percent on capital balances at the beginning of the year. Remaining amounts were to be divided equally.

Unhappy with the level of income, the partners decided to liquidate the partnership on January 1, 20x3. On that date, the assets and liabilities of the partnership were as follows: Cash, $244,000; Accounts Receivable, $152,000; Land, $36,000; Building (net), $280,000; Office Equipment (net), $108,000; Accounts Payable, $108,000; and Mortgage Payable, $204,000.

The office equipment was sold for $72,000, and the accounts receivable were valued at $128,000. The accounts payable were paid. The losses were distributed equally to the partners' Capital accounts. Flippo agreed to accept the accounts receivable plus cash in payment for his partnership interest. McCovey accepted the land, building, and mortgage payable at book value plus cash for his share in the liquidation. Stanford was paid in cash.

REQUIRED

Prepare entries in journal form to record all the facts above. Support your computations with schedules, and prepare a statement of liquidation in connection with the January 1, 20x3, entries.

ALTERNATE PROBLEMS

P 6.
LO 3 Distribution of Income: Salary and Interest

Gloria and Dennis are partners in a tennis shop. They have agreed that Gloria will operate the store and receive a salary of $52,000 per year. Dennis will receive 10 percent interest on his average capital balance during the year of $250,000. The remaining income or losses are to be shared by Gloria and Dennis in a 2:3 ratio.

REQUIRED

Determine each partner's share of income and losses under each of the following conditions. In each case, the income or loss is stated before the distribution of salary and interest.

1. Income was $84,000.
2. Income was $44,000.
3. The loss was $12,800.

P 7.
LO 4 LO 5 Admission and Withdrawal of a Partner

Renee, Esther, and Jane are partners in Seabury Woodwork Company. Their capital balances as of July 31, 20x4, are as follows:

Renee, Capital		Esther, Capital		Jane, Capital	
	90,000		30,000		60,000

Each partner has agreed to admit Maureen to the partnership.

REQUIRED

Prepare the journal entries to record Maureen's admission to or Renee's withdrawal from the partnership under each of the following independent conditions: (a) Maureen pays Renee $25,000 for 20 percent of Renee's interest in the partnership. (b) Maureen invests $40,000 cash in the partnership and receives an interest equal to her investment. (c) Maureen invests $60,000 cash in the partnership for a 20 percent interest in the business. A bonus is to be recorded for the original partners on the basis of their capital balances. (d) Maureen invests $60,000 cash in the partnership for a 40 percent interest in the business. The original partners give Maureen a bonus according to the ratio of their capital balances on July 31, 20x4. (e) Renee withdraws from the partnership, taking $105,000. The excess of assets over the partnership interest is distributed according to the balances of the Capital accounts. (f) Renee withdraws by selling her interest directly to Maureen for $120,000.

P 8. **LO 6 Partnership Liquidation**

Nguyen, Waters, and Leach are partners in a retail lighting store. They share income and losses in the ratio of 2:2:1, respectively. The partners have agreed to liquidate the partnership. Here is the partnership balance sheet before the liquidation.

Nguyen, Waters, and Leach Partnership
Balance Sheet
May 31, 20x3

Assets		Liabilities	
Cash	$140,000	Accounts Payable	$180,000
Other Assets	440,000	**Partners' Equity**	
Total Assets	$580,000		
		Nguyen, Capital	200,000
		Waters, Capital	120,000
		Leach, Capital	80,000
		Total Liabilities and Partners' Equity	$580,000

The other assets were sold on June 1, 20x3, for $360,000. Accounts payable were paid on June 4, 20x3. The remaining cash was distributed to the partners on June 11, 20x3.

REQUIRED

1. Prepare a statement of liquidation.
2. Prepare the following journal entries: (a) the sale of the other assets, (b) payment of the accounts payable, (c) the distribution of the partners' gain or loss on liquidation, and (d) the distribution to the partners of the remaining cash.

EXPANDING YOUR CRITICAL THINKING, COMMUNICATION, AND INTERPERSONAL SKILLS

SKILLS DEVELOPMENT

Conceptual Analysis

SD 1. LO 1 **Partnership Agreement**

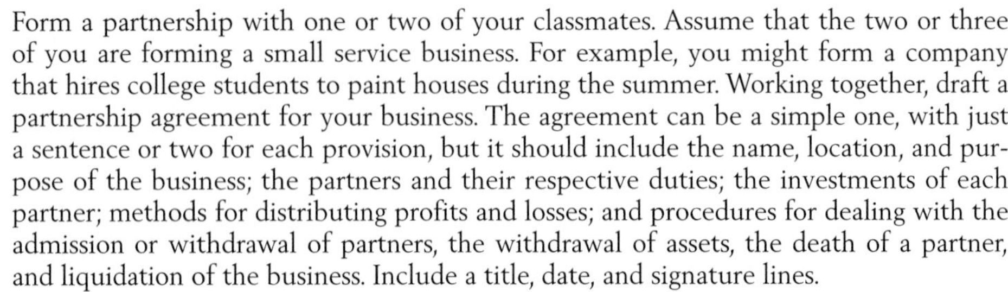

Form a partnership with one or two of your classmates. Assume that the two or three of you are forming a small service business. For example, you might form a company that hires college students to paint houses during the summer. Working together, draft a partnership agreement for your business. The agreement can be a simple one, with just a sentence or two for each provision, but it should include the name, location, and purpose of the business; the partners and their respective duties; the investments of each partner; methods for distributing profits and losses; and procedures for dealing with the admission or withdrawal of partners, the withdrawal of assets, the death of a partner, and liquidation of the business. Include a title, date, and signature lines.

Group Activity: Assign groups to prepare partnership agreements.

SD 2. LO 3 **Distribution of Partnership Income and Losses**

List, Donohue, and Han, who are forming a partnership to operate an antiques gallery, are discussing how income and losses should be distributed. Among the facts they are considering are the following:

a. List will contribute cash for operations of $100,000, Donohue will contribute a collection of antiques valued at $300,000, and Han will not contribute any assets.
b. List and Han will handle day-to-day business operations. Han will work full time, and List will devote about half-time to the partnership. Donohue will not devote time to day-to-day operations. A full-time clerk in a retail store would make about $20,000 in a year, and a full-time manager would receive about $30,000.
c. The current interest rate on long-term bonds is 8 percent.

You have just been hired as the partnership's accountant. Write a memorandum describing an equitable plan for distributing income and losses. State your reasons why this plan is equitable. According to your plan, which partner will gain the most if the partnership is very profitable, and which will lose the most if the partnership has large losses?

Ethical Dilemma

SD 3. LO 1, LO 2, LO 5 **Death of Partner**

South Shore Realty was started 20 years ago when J. B. Taylor, C. L. Sklar, and L. A. Hodges established a partnership to sell real estate near Galveston, Texas. The partnership has been extremely successful. In 20xx, Taylor, the senior partner, who in recent years had not been very active in the partnership, died. Unfortunately, the partnership agreement is vague about how the partnership interest of a partner who dies should be valued. It simply states that "the estate of a deceased partner shall receive compensation for his or her interest in the partnership in a reasonable time after death." The attorney for Taylor's family believes that the estate should receive one-third of the assets of the partnership based on the fair market value of the net assets (total assets less total liabilities). The total assets of the partnership are $10 million in the accounting records, but the assets are worth at least $20 million. Because the firm's total liabilities are $4 million, the attorney is asking for $5.3 million (one-third of $16 million).

								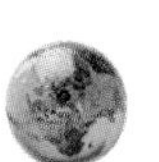				
Cash Flow	CD-ROM	Communication	Critical Thinking	Ethics	General Ledger	Group Activity	Hot Links to Real Companies	International	Internet	Key Ratio	Memo	Spreadsheet

Sklar and Hodges do not agree, but all parties want to avoid a protracted, expensive lawsuit. They have decided to put the question to an arbitrator, who will make a determination of the settlement.

Here are some other facts that may or may not be relevant. The current balances in the partners' Capital accounts are $1.5 million for Taylor, $2.5 million for Sklar, and $2.0 million for Hodges. Net income in 20xx is to be distributed to the Capital accounts in the ratio of 1:4:3. Before Taylor's semiretirement, the distribution ratio was 3:3:2. Assume you or your group is the arbitrator and develop what you would consider a fair distribution of assets to Taylor's estate. Defend your solution.

Research Activity

LO 1 Basic Research Skills

SD 4. The limited partnership is a form of business that was particularly important to the U.S. economy in the 1980s. To find the latest developments or to study the practical applications of a particular subject, such as limited partnerships, it is helpful to use periodical indexes in the library to find articles relating to that subject. Three periodical indexes relevant to accounting and business are *The Accountant's Index*, the *Business Periodicals Index*, and *The Wall Street Journal Index*. Use one or more of those periodical indexes in your school library to find three articles about limited partnerships. Sometimes the articles are not listed under the heading "Limited Partnerships"; instead, they appear under the uses of limited partnerships. Some examples are real estate, investments, research and development, and cattle or livestock. Write a short summary of each article, relating the content of the article to the content of this chapter or explaining why the limited partnership form of business was important in the situation described in the article.

Decision-Making Practice

LO 4 Potential Partnership Purchase

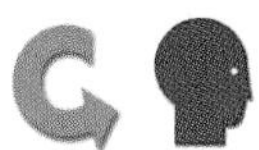

SD 5. The ***A-One Fitness Center,*** owned by John Kiel and Sunjat Patel, has been very successful since its inception five years ago. Kiel and Patel work 10 to 11 hours a day at the business. They have decided to expand by opening up another fitness center in the north part of town. Kiel has approached you about becoming a partner in the business. He and Patel are interested in you because of your experience in operating a small gym. Also, they need additional funds to expand their business. Projected income after the expansion but before partners' salaries for the next five years is as follows:

20x1	20x2	20x3	20x4	20x5
$100,000	$120,000	$130,000	$140,000	$150,000

Currently, Kiel and Patel each draw a $25,000 salary and share remaining profits equally. They are willing to give you an equal share of the business for $142,000. You will receive a $25,000 salary and one-third of the remaining profits. You would work the same hours as Kiel and Patel. Your salary for the next five years where you currently work is expected to be as follows:

20x1	20x2	20x3	20x4	20x5
$34,000	$38,000	$42,000	$45,000	$50,000

Here is financial information for the A-One Fitness Center:

Current Assets	$ 45,000	Long-Term Liabilities	$100,000
Plant and Equipment, net	365,000	John Kiel, Capital	140,000
Current Liabilities	50,000	Sunjat Patel, Capital	120,000

1. Compute your capital balance if you decide to join Kiel and Patel in the fitness center partnership.
2. Analyze your expected income for the next five years.
3. Should you invest in the A-One Fitness Center?
4. Assume that you do not consider Kiel and Patel's offer of partnership to be a good one. Develop a counteroffer that you would be willing to accept (be realistic).

FINANCIAL REPORTING AND ANALYSIS

Interpreting Financial Reports

FRA 1. **LO 1 LO 3 Effects of Lawsuit on Partnership**

The ***Springfield Clinic*** is owned and operated by ten local doctors as a partnership. Recently, a paralyzed patient sued the clinic for malpractice, for a total of $20 million. The clinic carries malpractice liability insurance in the amount of $10 million. There is no provision for the possible loss from this type of lawsuit in the partnership's financial statements. The condensed balance sheet for 20xx is as follows:

Springfield Clinic Condensed Balance Sheet December 31, 20xx		
Assets		
Current Assets	$246,000	
Property, Plant, and Equipment (net)	750,000	
Total Assets		$996,000
Liabilities and Partners' Equity		
Current Liabilities	$180,000	
Long-Term Debt	675,000	
Total Liabilities		$855,000
Partners' Equity		141,000
Total Liabilities and Partners' Equity		$996,000

1. How should information about the lawsuit be disclosed in the December 31, 20xx, financial statements of the partnership?
2. Assume that the clinic and its insurance company settle out of court by agreeing to pay a total of $10.1 million, of which $100,000 must be paid by the partnership. What effect will the payment have on the clinic's December 31, 20xx, financial statements? Discuss the effect of the settlement on the Springfield Clinic doctors' personal financial situations.

International Company

FRA 2. **LO 1 International Joint Ventures**

Nokia, the Finnish telecommunications company, has formed an equally owned joint venture with ***Capital Corporation,*** a state-owned Chinese company, to develop a center for the manufacture and development of telecommunications equipment in China, the world's fastest-growing market for this kind of equipment. The main aim of the development is to persuade Nokia's suppliers to move close to the company's main plant. The Chinese government looks favorably on companies that involve local suppliers.[4] What advantages does a joint venture have over a single company in entering a new market in another country? What are the potential disadvantages?

Toys "R" Us Annual Report

The partnership chapter is not applicable to Toys "R" Us.

Fingraph® Financial Analysis™

The partnership chapter is not applicable to this case.

Internet Case

FRA 3. **LO 1 Comparison of Career Opportunities in Partnerships and Corporations**

Accounting firms are among the world's largest partnerships and provide a wide range of attractive careers for business and accounting majors. Through the Needles Accounting Resource Center at http://college.hmco.com, you can explore careers in public accounting by linking to the web site of one of the big five accounting firms. The firms are Arthur Andersen, Deloitte & Touche, Ernst & Young, KPMG International, and PricewaterhouseCoopers. Each firm's home page has a career opportunity section. For the firm you choose, compile a list of facts about the firm—size, locations, services, and career opportunities. Do you have the interest and background for a career in public accounting? Why or why not? How do you think working for a large partnership would differ from or be the same as working for a large corporation? Be prepared to discuss your findings in class.

ENDNOTES

1. KPMG International, Internet site, May 16, 2000. KPMG has announced plans to separate its consulting practice as a corporation.
2. Information excerpted from the 1990 and 2000 annual reports of Alliance Capital Management Limited Partnership; wsj.com, November 17, 2000.
3. Anita Raghavan, "Goldman Scrambles to Find $250 Million in Equity Capital from Private Investors," *The Wall Street Journal*, September 15, 1994.
4. "Nokia Unveils Plans for Chinese Centre," *Financial Times London*, May 9, 2000.

14 Contributed Capital

LEARNING OBJECTIVES

1 Identify and explain the management issues related to contributed capital.

2 Define *start-up and organization costs* and state their effects on financial reporting.

3 Identify the components of stockholders' equity.

4 Account for cash dividends.

5 Identify the characteristics of preferred stock, including the effect on distribution of dividends.

6 Account for the issuance of stock for cash and other assets.

7 Account for treasury stock.

8 Account for the exercise of stock options.

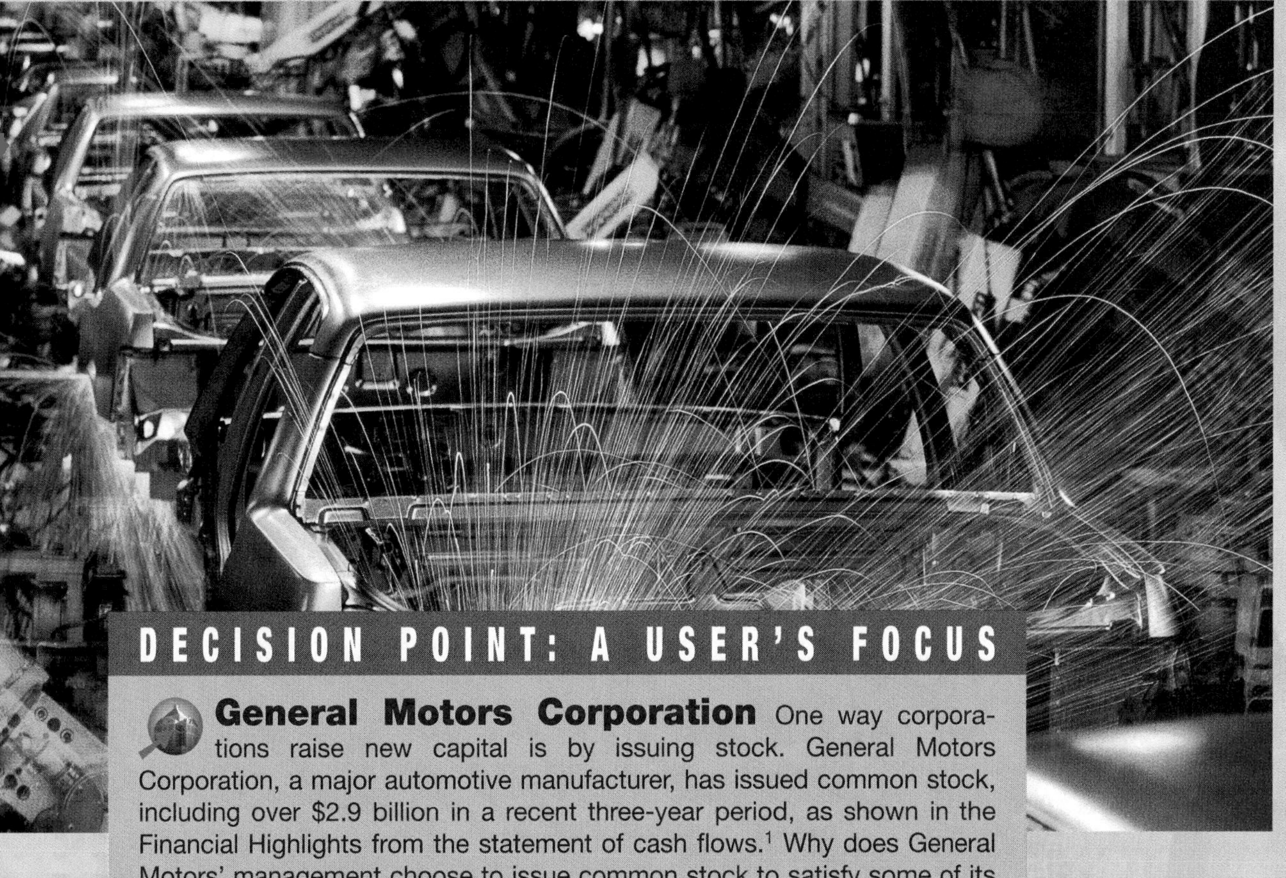

DECISION POINT: A USER'S FOCUS

General Motors Corporation One way corporations raise new capital is by issuing stock. General Motors Corporation, a major automotive manufacturer, has issued common stock, including over $2.9 billion in a recent three-year period, as shown in the Financial Highlights from the statement of cash flows.[1] Why does General Motors' management choose to issue common stock to satisfy some of its needs for new capital? What are some disadvantages of this approach?

There are advantages to financing with common stock. First, financing with common stock is less risky than financing with bonds, because dividends on common stock are not paid unless the board of directors decides to pay them. In contrast, if the interest on bonds is not paid, a company can be forced into bankruptcy. Second, when a company does not pay a cash dividend, the cash generated by profitable operations can be invested in the company's operations. Third, and most important for General Motors, a company may need the proceeds of a common stock issue to improve the balance between liabilities and stockholders' equity. The company lost more than $23.5 billion in 1992, drastically reducing its stockholders' equity. However, by issuing common stock over the next several years, General Motors improved its debt to equity ratio and its credit rating.

Financial Highlights
(In millions of dollars)

	1999	1998	1997
Proceeds from issuing common stock	$2,005	$343	$614

On the other hand, issuing common stock has certain disadvantages. Unlike the interest on bonds, dividends paid on stock are not tax deductible. Furthermore, when it issues more stock, the corporation dilutes its ownership. This means that the current stockholders must yield some control to the new stockholders. It is important for accountants to understand the nature and characteristics of corporations as well as the process of accounting for a stock issue and other types of stock transactions.

Critical Thinking Question: On the balance sheet, is contributed capital reported at current market value or at the market value on the date of issue? **Answer:** Market value at the date of issue. Contributed capital does not fluctuate with market value changes.

Management Issues Related to Contributed Capital

OBJECTIVE

1 Identify and explain the management issues related to contributed capital

A **corporation** is defined as "a body of persons granted a charter recognizing them as a separate legal entity having its own rights, privileges, and liabilities distinct from those of its members."[2] In other words, a corporation is a legal entity separate and distinct from its owners.

VIDEO CASE

Lotus Development Corporation

Objectives

- To become familiar with the advantages of a corporation, especially in equity financing.
- To identify the ways investors obtain return on investment in a corporation.
- To show how stock buybacks affect return on equity as a measure of profitability.

Background for the Case

The story of software giant Lotus Development Corporation is a prototype of the recent history of high-technology companies. When Lotus was founded in the early 1980s, its landmark spreadsheet program Lotus 1-2-3 was an overnight sensation at corporations because of its ability to make rapid calculations based on mathematical relationships in large databases. Lotus 1-2-3 went far beyond the rudimentary spreadsheets that preceded it by incorporating a database module and graphics capability. In October 1983, investors stampeded for the company's initial public offering of 2.6 million shares at $18 per share for a total of $46.8 million. For several years the company had no real competition. By 1992, more than 11 million units of Lotus 1-2-3 had been sold, but the company was unable to solidify its position by developing any new blockbuster products. Microsoft gained on Lotus and eventually passed it with its spreadsheet program Excel. Finally, Lotus developed a hit "groupware" product called Lotus Notes, which boosts productivity by enabling co-workers to share information and work together electronically on complex tasks. The large audit firm Coopers & Lybrand (now PricewaterhouseCoopers), for example, networks more than 2,000 auditors all over the world and the knowledge of experts in various parts of the firm via Lotus Notes. Many other big companies such as Ford, Unilever, and Citicorp (now Citigroup) are also using Lotus Notes successfully. The success of Lotus Notes attracted the notice of IBM, which had failed to develop its own groupware product. In 1995, IBM made a hostile takeover bid for Lotus and bought out the company. In fewer than 15 years, Lotus had gone from an intriguing startup to a mature company with sales of more than $1 billion and, finally, to a takeover candidate for a giant competitor.

For more information about Lotus, which is now a division of IBM, visit the company's or IBM's web site through the Needles Accounting Resource Center at:
http://college.hmco.com

Required

View the video on Lotus Development Corporation that accompanies this book. As you are watching the video, take notes related to the following questions:

1. All corporations must raise equity capital in the form of common stock. In your own words, what is common stock? What is the relationship of par value to market value of the common stock? What is an initial public offering (IPO)? Why was this IPO important in Lotus's early history?
2. Investors in corporations desire to receive an adequate return on their investment. What are the ways investors can receive a return? In what way did Lotus's shareholders receive a return?
3. From 1991 to 1993, the Lotus board of directors authorized the repurchase of 7,700,000 shares of the company's approximately 44,000,000 shares. What impact will the repurchase of these shares have on the investors' return? What role did the takeover by IBM play in achieving an adequate return to Lotus shareholders?
4. Return on equity is a common measure of management's ability to meet the company's profitability goal. What role do common stock buybacks (purchases of treasury stock) play in the company's increasing return on equity?

Related Text Assignments:
Q: 1, 2, 3, 4, 5, 8
SE: 1, 2
E: 1
P: 2, 7
SD: 1, 4, 5, 6
FRA: 1, 3, 4, 5

The management of contributed capital is a critical component in the financing of a corporation. Important issues faced by management in the area of contributed capital are managing under the corporate form of business, using equity financing, determining dividend policies, and evaluating performance using return on equity.

Forming a Corporation

To form a corporation, most states require individuals, called incorporators, to sign an application and file it with the proper state official. This application contains the **articles of incorporation**. If approved by the state, these articles become, in effect, a contract, called the company charter, between the state and the incorporators. The company is then authorized to do business.

The authority to manage the corporation is delegated by the stockholders to the board of directors and by the board of directors to the corporate officers (see Figure 1). That is, the stockholders elect the board of directors, which sets company policies and chooses the corporate officers, who in turn carry out the corporate policies by managing the business.

STOCKHOLDERS A unit of ownership in a corporation is called a **share of stock**. The articles of incorporation state the maximum number of shares of stock that the corporation will be allowed, or authorized, to issue. The number of shares held by stockholders is the outstanding capital stock; this is generally less than the number authorized in the articles of incorporation. To invest in a corporation, a stockholder transfers cash or other resources to the corporation. In return, the stockholder receives shares of stock representing a proportionate share of ownership in the corporation. The stockholder may then transfer the shares at will. Corporations may have more than one kind of capital stock, but we will refer only to common stock.

BOARD OF DIRECTORS As noted, the stockholders elect the board of directors, which in turn decides on the major business policies of the corporation. Among the specific duties of the board are authorizing contracts, setting executive salaries, and arranging major loans with banks. The declaration of dividends is also an important function. Only the board has the authority to declare dividends. **Dividends** are distributions of resources, generally in the form of cash, to the stockholders. Paying dividends is one way of rewarding stockholders for their investment when the corporation has been successful in earning a profit. (The other way is through a rise in the market value of the stock.) There is usually a delay of two or three weeks between the time the board declares a dividend and the date of the actual payment.

The board of directors varies in composition from company to company, but it usually contains several corporate officers and several outsiders. Today, the formation of an **audit committee** with several outside directors is encouraged to make sure that the board will be objective in evaluating management's performance. One function of the audit committee is to engage the company's independent auditors and review their work. Another is to ensure that proper systems safeguard the company's resources and that reliable accounting records are kept.

Figure 1
The Corporate Form of Business

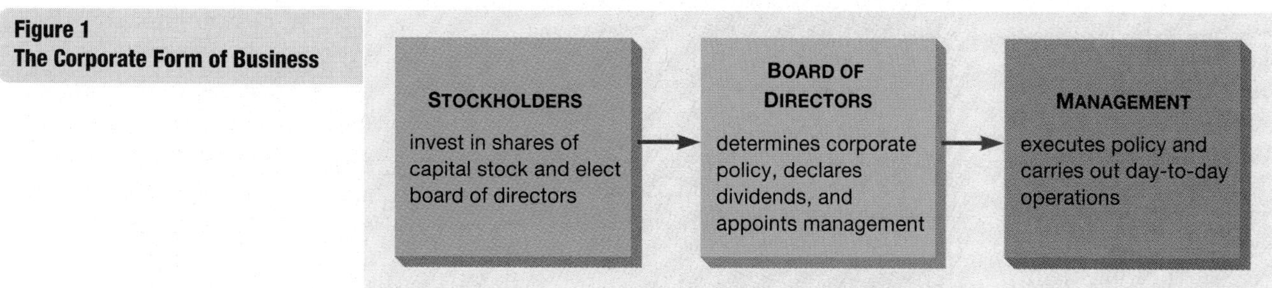

MANAGEMENT The board of directors appoints managers to carry out the corporation's policies and run day-to-day operations. The management consists of the operating officers, who are generally the president, vice presidents, controller, treasurer, and secretary. Besides being responsible for running the business, management has the duty of reporting the financial results of its administration to the board of directors and the stockholders. Though management must, at a minimum, make a comprehensive annual report, it may and generally does report more often. The annual reports of large public corporations are available to the public. Excerpts from many of them are used throughout this book.

Managing Under the Corporate Form of Business

Although sole proprietorships and partnerships outnumber corporations in the United States, corporations dominate the economy in total dollars of assets and output of goods and services. Corporations are well suited to today's trends toward large organizations, international trade, and professional management. Figure 2 shows the amount and sources of new funds raised by corporations in recent years. The amount raised increased dramatically after 1990. In 1998, the amount of new corporate capital was $1,802 billion, of which $1,650 billion, or 92 percent, came

Figure 2
Sources of Capital Raised by Corporations in the United States

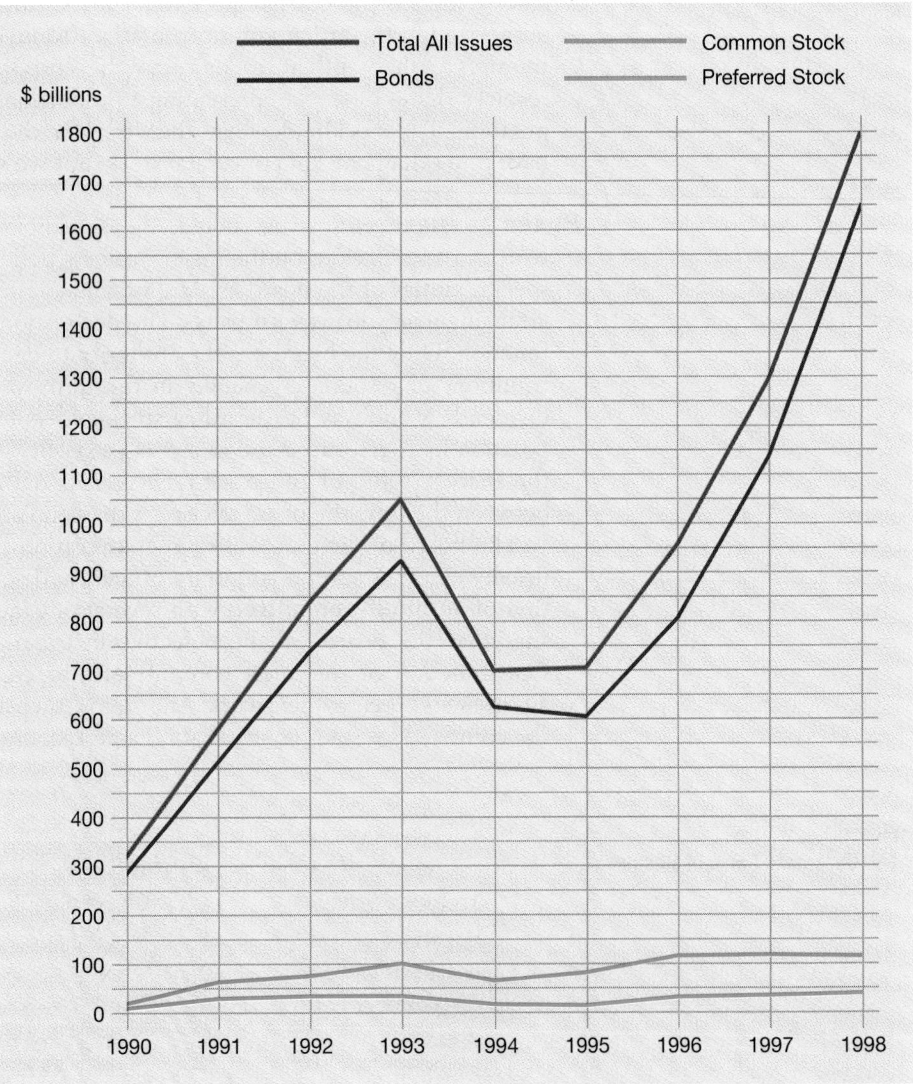

Source: Data from *Securities Industry Yearbook 1999–2000* (New York: Securities Industry Association, 1999), p. 1001.

convertible stocks, or PERCs, which are automatically convertible into common stock after three years if the company does not redeem or call them first and retire them. What reasons can you give for the popularity of preferred stock, and of PERCs in particular, when the tax-deductible interest on bonds is less costly? Discuss both the company's and the investor's standpoints.

SD 3. **LO 7 Purposes of Treasury Stock**

Many companies in recent years have bought back their common stock. For example, *IBM,* with large cash holdings, has spent almost $27 billion over five years buying back its stock. What are the reasons that companies buy back their own shares? What is the effect of common stock share buybacks on earnings per share, return on equity, return on assets, debt to equity, and the current ratio?

Ethical Dilemma

SD 4. **LO 1 Ethics of Incorporating an Accounting Firm**

Traditionally, accounting firms have organized as partnerships or as professional corporations, a form of corporation that in many ways resembles a partnership. In recent years, some accounting firms have had large judgments imposed upon them as a result of lawsuits by investors who lost money when they invested in companies the firms have audited that went bankrupt. Because of the increased risk of large losses from malpractice suits, accounting firms are allowed to incorporate as long as they maintain a minimum level of partners' capital and carry malpractice insurance. Some accounting practitioners feel that incorporating would be a violation of their responsibility to the public. What features of the corporate form of business would be most advantageous to the partners of an accounting firm? Do you think it is a violation of the public trust for an accounting firm to incorporate?

Research Activity

SD 5. **LO 1, LO 3, LO 4, LO 5, LO 6, LO 8 Comparison of Stockholders' Equity Characteristics**

Select the annual reports of three corporations using either your library or the Fingraph® Financial Analyst™ CD-ROM software that accompanies this text. You can choose them from the same industry or at random, at the direction of your instructor. (**Note:** You may be asked to use these companies again in the Research Activities in later chapters.) Prepare a table with a column for each corporation. Then answer the following questions for each corporation: Does the corporation have preferred stock? If so, what are the par value and the indicated dividend, and is the preferred stock cumulative or convertible? Is the common stock par value or no-par? What is the par value or stated value? What cash dividends, if any, were paid in the past year? What is the dividends yield? From the notes to the financial statements, determine whether the company has an employee stock option plan. What are some of its provisions? What is the return on equity? Be prepared to discuss the characteristics of the stocks and dividends for your selected companies in class.

Decision-Making Practice

SD 6. **LO 1, LO 3 Analysis of Alternative Financing Methods**

Companies offering services to the computer technology industry are growing quickly. Participating in this growth, ***Northeast Servotech Corporation*** has expanded rapidly in recent years. Because of its profitability, the company has been able to grow without obtaining external financing. This fact is reflected in its current balance sheet, which contains no long-term debt. The liability and stockholders' equity sections of the balance sheet on March 31, 20xx, are shown at the top of the next page.

The company now has the opportunity to double its size by purchasing the operations of a rival company for $4,000,000. If the purchase goes through, Northeast Servotech will become the top company in its specialized industry in the northeastern part of the country. The problem for management is how to finance the purchase. After much study and discussion with bankers and underwriters, management has prepared three financing alternatives to present to the board of directors, which must authorize the purchase and the financing.

Alternative A: The company could issue $4,000,000 of long-term debt. Given the company's financial rating and the current market rates, management believes the company will have to pay an interest rate of 12 percent on the debt.

Northeast Servotech Corporation Balance Sheet March 31, 20xx		
Liabilities		
Current Liabilities		$ 500,000
Stockholders' Equity		
Common Stock, $10 par value, 500,000 shares authorized, 100,000 shares issued and outstanding	$1,000,000	
Paid-in Capital in Excess of Par Value, Common	1,800,000	
Retained Earnings	1,700,000	
Total Stockholders' Equity		4,500,000
Total Liabilities and Stockholders' Equity		$5,000,000

Alternative B: The company could issue 40,000 shares of 8 percent, $100 par value preferred stock.

Alternative C: The company could issue 100,000 additional shares of $10 par value common stock at $40 per share.

Management explains to the board that the interest on the long-term debt is tax-deductible and that the applicable income tax rate is 40 percent. The board members know that a dividend of $.80 per share of common stock was paid last year, up from $.60 and $.40 per share in the two years before that. The board has had a policy of regular increases in dividends of $.20 per share. The board feels that each of the three financing alternatives is feasible and now wants to study the financial effects of each alternative.

1. Prepare a schedule to show how the liabilities and stockholders' equity sections of Northeast Servotech's balance sheet would look under each alternative, and compute the debt to equity ratio (total liabilities ÷ total stockholders' equity) for each.
2. Compute and compare the cash needed to pay the interest or dividends for each kind of new financing net of income taxes in the first year.
3. How might the cash needed to pay for the financing change in future years under each alternative?
4. Prepare a memorandum to the board of directors that evaluates the alternatives in order of preference based on cash flow effects, giving arguments for and against each one.

Group Activity: Assign the alternatives to different groups to analyze and present to the class as the "board of directors."

FINANCIAL REPORTING AND ANALYSIS

Interpreting Financial Reports

LO 1 Effect of Stock Issue
LO 3
LO 6

FRA 1. ***Netscape Communications Corporation,*** now a part of AOL–Time Warner, is a leading provider of software, applications, and tools that link people and information over networks, the Internet, and the World Wide Web. It is one of the great success stories of the Internet age. Netscape went public with an IPO in June 1995 and issued shares at a price of $14 per share. On November 14, 1996, Netscape announced a common stock issue in an ad in *The Wall Street Journal:*

6,440,000 Shares
NETSCAPE
Common Stock
Price $53¾ a share

If Netscape sold all these shares at the offering price of $53.75, the net proceeds before issue costs would be $346.15 million.

A portion of the stockholders' equity section of the balance sheet adapted from Netscape's 1995 annual report is shown below.

	1995	1994
	(In thousands)	
Common Stock, $.0001 par value, 200,000,000 shares authorized, 12,003,594 shares in 1994 and 81,063,158 shares in 1995 issued and outstanding	$ 8	$ 1
Additional Paid-in Capital	196,749	18,215
Accumulated Deficit	(16,314)	(12,873)

REQUIRED

1. Assume the net proceeds from the sale of 6,440,000 shares at $53.75 were $342.6 million after issue costs. Record the stock issuance on Netscape's accounting records in journal form.
2. Prepare the portion of the stockholders' equity section of the balance sheet shown above after the issue of the common stock, based on the information given. Round all answers to the nearest thousand.
3. Based on your answer in **2,** did Netscape have to increase its authorized shares to undertake this stock issue?
4. What amount per share did Netscape receive and how much did Netscape's underwriters receive to help in issuing the stock if investors paid $53.75 per share? What do the underwriters do to earn their fee?

International Company

LO 3 LO 4 Stockholders' Equity and Dividends

FRA 2. *Roche Group* is a giant Swiss pharmaceutical company. Its stockholders' equity shows how little importance common stock, called *share capital,* typically plays in the financing of Swiss companies:[16]

	1999	1998
Shareholders' Equity (in millions of Swiss francs)		
Share Capital	160	160
Retained Earnings	26,669	21,655
Total Shareholders' Equity	26,829	21,815

When Swiss companies need financing, they often rely on debt financing from large Swiss banks and from other debt markets. With only 160 million Swiss francs (1.6 million shares) in share capital, Roche has had few stock issues in its history. This amount compares to over 43 billion Swiss francs in liabilities. Also, Roche has been enormously profitable, having built up retained earnings of more than 26 billion Swiss francs over the years. The company also pays a substantial dividend that totaled 750 million Swiss francs in 1999. Calculate the dividends per share and dividends yield assuming a share price of 18,100 Swiss francs. Also, assuming that dividends and net income were the only factors that affected retained earnings during 1999, how much did Roche earn in 1999 in U.S. dollars (use an exchange rate of 1.7 Swiss francs to the dollar)? What was Roche's return on equity?

Toys "R" Us Annual Report

LO 1 LO 3 LO 7 LO 8 Stockholders' Equity

FRA 3. Refer to the Toys "R" Us annual report to answer the following questions:

1. What type of capital stock does Toys "R" Us have? What is the par value? How many shares are authorized, issued, and outstanding at the end of 2000?

2. What is the dividends yield for Toys "R" Us and its relationship to the investors' total return? Does the company rely mostly on stock or on earnings for its stockholders' equity?
3. From the statement of stockholders' equity, how has management's policy with regard to treasury stock changed over the past three years? What favorable effects did the stock buybacks have?
4. Does the company have a stock option plan? To whom do the stock options apply? Do employees have significant stock options? Given the market price of the stock shown in the report, do these options represent significant value to the employees?
5. Calculate and discuss the price/earnings ratio and return on equity for 1999 and 2000. The average share price for the fourth quarter was $18 and $15 for 1999 and 2000, respectively.

Fingraph® Financial Analyst™

FRA 4.

LO 1 LO 3 LO 7 LO 8 Comparative Analysis of Stockholders' Equity

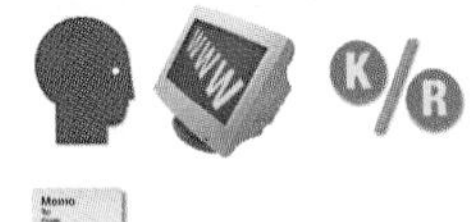

Select any two companies from the same industry in the Fingraph® Financial Analyst™ CD-ROM software.

1. In the annual reports for the companies you have selected, identify the stockholders' equity section of the balance sheet and reference to any stockholders' equity accounts in the summary of significant accounting policies or notes to the financial statements. Do the companies have more than one kind of capital stock? What are the characteristics of each type of capital stock? Do the companies have treasury stock? Do the companies have an employee stock option plan?
2. Find the earnings per share and dividends per share in the annual reports for both companies. Also, find in the financial section of your local paper the current market prices of the companies' common stock. Prepare a table that summarizes this information and that shows the price/earnings ratio and the dividends yield.
3. Locate the statements of cash flows in the two companies' annual reports. Has the company issued capital stock or repurchased its stock in the last three years?
4. Find and read references to capital stock in management's discussion and analysis in each annual report.
5. Write a one-page executive summary that highlights the types of capital stock for these companies, the significance of treasury stock, and any employee stock option plan; also compare the price/earnings ratio and the dividends yield trends of the two companies, including reference to management's assessment. Include your table as an attachment to your report.

Internet Case

FRA 5.

LO 1 LO 4 LO 5 LO 6 LO 7 LO 8 Comparison of Financing of Internet Companies

Many Internet start-up companies have gone public in recent years. These companies are generally unprofitable and require a great deal of cash to finance expansion. They also reward their employees with stock options. Choose any two of the following Internet companies: ***Amazon.com, Yahoo, eBay Inc.,*** and ***AOL–Time Warner***. Through the Needles Accounting Resource Center at http://college.hmco.com, find companies under web links and go to the web sites for the two companies you have selected. In the latest annual report for each of the companies, look at the financing activities section of the statement of cash flows for the last three years. How have your two companies financed their businesses? Have they issued stock or long-term debt? Have they purchased treasury stock, paid dividends, or issued stock under stock option plans? Are the companies profitable (see net income or earnings at the top of the statement)? Are your findings in line with your expectations about these young Internet companies? Find each company's stock price, either on the Web (many companies have it on their homepage) or in the newspaper, and compare it to the average issue price of that company's past stock issues. Summarize your findings and conclusions.

Endnotes

1. General Motors Corporation, *Annual Report,* 1999.
2. Copyright © 2000 by Houghton Mifflin Company. Adapted and reproduced by permission from *The American Heritage Dictionary of the English Language,* Fourth Edition.
3. Abbott Laboratories, *Annual Report,* 1999.
4. *Statement of Position No. 98-5,* "Report on the Costs of Start up Activities" (New York: American Institute of Certified Public Accountants, 1998).
5. Suzanne McGee, "Europe's New Markets for IPOs of Growth Start-Ups Fly High," *The Wall Street Journal,* February 22, 1999.
6. Microsoft Corporation, Inc., *Annual Report,* 1997.
7. G. Christian Hill, "Microsoft Plans Preferred Issue of $750 Million," *The Wall Street Journal,* December 3, 1996.
8. American Institute of Certified Public Accountants, *Accounting Trends & Techniques* (New York: AICPA, 1999).
9. The Coca-Cola Company, *Annual Report,* 1999, and IBM Corporation, *Annual Report,* 1999.
10. Fred P. Bleakley, "Management Problem: Reinvest High Profits or Please Institutions?" *The Wall Street Journal,* October 16, 1995.
11. American Institute of Certified Public Accountants, *Accounting Trends & Techniques* (New York: AICPA, 1999).
12. *Statement of Accounting Standards No. 123,* "Accounting for Stock-Based Compensation" (Norwalk, Conn.: Financial Accounting Standards Board, 1995).
13. Elizabeth MacDonald, "Options' Effect on Earnings Sparks Debate," *The Wall Street Journal,* May 13, 1999.
14. Announcement, *The Wall Street Journal,* February 19, 1999, p. C19.
15. Tom Herman, "Preferreds' Rich Yields Blind Some Investors to Risks," *The Wall Street Journal,* March 24, 1992.
16. Roche Group, *Annual Report,* 1999.

15 The Corporate Income Statement and the Statement of Stockholders' Equity

LEARNING OBJECTIVES

1. Identify the issues related to evaluating the quality of a company's earnings.
2. Prepare a corporate income statement.
3. Show the relationships among income taxes expense, deferred income taxes, and net of taxes.
4. Describe the disclosure on the income statement of discontinued operations, extraordinary items, and accounting changes.
5. Compute earnings per share.
6. Prepare a statement of stockholders' equity.
7. Account for stock dividends and stock splits.
8. Calculate book value per share.

DECISION POINT: A USER'S FOCUS

DaimlerChrysler AG DaimlerChrysler AG is one of the largest automobile companies in the world. Interpreting the operating results of such a company is not always easy. For instance, consider DaimlerChrysler's performance for the three-year period from 1997 to 1999, as measured by earnings per share.[1] The company's statements are presented in Euros, the new European currency. Net income per share declined from e6.90 to e5.03 in 1998 but rebounded to e5.73 in 1999. However, income before extraordinary items declined from e6.90 in 1997 to e5.09 in 1999. Someone not familiar with the structure and use of corporate income statements might be confused by this apparent contradiction. Which is the best measure of DaimlerChrysler's performance?

Financial Highlights

	1999	1998	1997
Earnings per share (in Euros):			
Basic earnings per share			
Income before extraordinary items	5.09	5.16	6.90
Extraordinary items	.64	(.13)	—
Net income	5.73	5.03	6.90

Earnings or net income per share is the "bottom line" that many investors look at to judge the success or failure of a company. Just looking at the bottom line, however, can be misleading. The corporate income statement contains a number of infrequent increases and decreases made more or less at the discretion of management that will result in variations in results. In 1998, DaimlerChrysler had a loss on early extinguishment of debt that reduced its earnings per share by e.13. In 1999, the company had a gain on the disposal of a business that increased earnings per share by e.64. These latter items are called *extraordinary items,* or rare items that occur because management has made the decision to engage in these transactions. Because of these items, net income per share is not the best gauge of DaimlerChrysler's ongoing performance in its normal operations. Net income before extraordinary items is a better measure. Knowledge of issues involving quality of earnings and the components of corporate income statements is essential to understanding and analyzing the operations of companies like DaimlerChrysler.

Critical Thinking Question: Why is it important to know which items included in earnings are recurring and which are one-time items? **Answer:** Earnings from continuing operations before nonrecurring items give a good signal about future results. In assessing the company's future earnings potential, nonrecurring items are excluded because they are not expected to continue.

Performance Measurement: Quality of Earnings Issues

OBJECTIVE

1 Identify the issues related to evaluating the quality of a company's earnings

Related Text Assignments:
Q: 1, 2, 4
SE: 1
E: 1
P: 1
SD: 1, 3
FRA: 5

Current and expected earnings are important factors to consider in evaluating a company's performance and analyzing its prospects. In fact, a survey of 2,000 members of the Association for Investment Management and Research indicated that the two most important economic indicators in evaluating common stocks were expected changes in earnings per share and expected return on equity.[2] Net income is a key component of both measures.

Because of the importance of net income, or the "bottom line," in measuring a company's prospects, there is significant interest in evaluating the quality of the net income figure, or the **quality of earnings**. The quality of a company's earnings refers to the substance of earnings and their sustainability into future accounting periods. The quality of earnings may be affected by (1) the accounting methods and estimates the company's management chooses and (2) the nature of nonoperating items on the income statement.

Choice of Accounting Methods and Estimates

Point to Emphasize: Two companies in the same industry could have comparable earnings quantity but not comparable earnings quality. In order to assess the quality of reported earnings, one must know the methods and estimates used to compute income. GAAP allows several choices of methods and estimates, all yielding different results.

Choices of accounting methods and estimates affect a firm's operating income. To assure proper matching of revenues and expenses, accounting requires cost allocations and estimates of data that will not be known with certainty until some future date. For example, accountants estimate the useful life of assets when they are acquired. However, technological obsolescence could shorten the expected useful life, or excellent maintenance and repairs could lengthen it. The actual useful life will not be known with certainty until some future date. The choice of estimate affects both current and future operating income.

Because there is considerable latitude in the choice of estimates, management and other financial statement users must be aware of the impact of accounting estimates on reported operating income. Estimates include percentage of uncollectible accounts receivable, sales returns, useful life, residual or salvage value, total units of production, total recoverable units of natural resource, amortization period, expected warranty claims, and expected environmental cleanup costs.

These estimates are not all equally important to every firm. The relative importance of each estimate depends on the industry in which the firm operates. For example, the estimate of uncollectible receivables for a credit card firm, such as

American Express, or a financial services firm, such as Bank of America, can have a

FOCUS ON BUSINESS PRACTICE

Quality of earnings is an important issue for investors. For example, analysts for Twentieth Century Mutual Funds, a major investment company, make adjustments to a company's reported financial performance to create a more accurate picture of the company's ongoing operations. Assume a paper company reports earnings of $1.30 per share, which makes year-to-year comparisons unusually strong. Upon further investigation, however, it is found that the per share number includes a one-time gain on the sale of assets of $.25 per share. Twentieth Century would list the company in its data base as earning only $1.05 per share. "These kinds of adjustments help assure long-term decisions aren't based on one-time events."[3]

material impact on earnings, but the choice of useful life may be less important because depreciable assets represent only a small percentage of total assets. Toys "R" Us has very few receivables, but it has substantial investment in depreciable assets; thus choice of useful life and residual value are much more important than uncollectible accounts receivable.

Business-World Example: The problems in the savings and loan industry are a good example of the importance of estimating uncollectible accounts, which have an impact on both earnings and assets.

Ethical Consideration: Ask your students what ethical considerations exist when making accounting estimates.

The choice of methods also affects a firm's operating income. Generally accepted accounting methods include uncollectible receivable methods (net sales or aging of accounts receivable), inventory methods (last-in, first-out [LIFO], first-in, first-out [FIFO], or average cost), depreciation methods (accelerated, production, or straight-line), and revenue recognition methods. These methods are designed to match revenues and expenses. Costs are allocated based on a determination of the benefits to the current period (expenses) versus the benefits to future periods (assets). The expenses are estimates, and the period or periods benefited cannot be demonstrated conclusively. The estimates are also subjective, because in practice it is hard to justify one method of estimation over another.

For these reasons, management, the accountant, and the financial statement user need to understand the possible effects of different accounting procedures on net income and financial position. Some methods and estimates are more conservative than others because they tend to produce a lower net income in the current period. For example, suppose that two companies have similar operations, but one uses FIFO for inventory costing and straight-line (SL) for computing depreciation, whereas the other uses LIFO for inventory costing and double-declining-balance (DDB) for computing depreciation. The income statements of the two companies might appear as follows:

	FIFO and SL	LIFO and DDB
Net Sales	$500,000	$500,000
Goods Available for Sale	$300,000	$300,000
Less Ending Inventory	60,000	50,000
Cost of Goods Sold	$240,000	$250,000
Gross Margin	$260,000	$250,000
Less: Depreciation Expense	$ 40,000	$ 80,000
Other Expenses	170,000	170,000
Total Operating Expenses	$210,000	$250,000
Operating Income	$ 50,000	$ —

Discussion Questions: 1. Who is responsible for the content of financial statements? 2. Which group's performance is being reported on in financial statements?
Answer: 1. Management is responsible for the content of financial statements. 2. Financial statements report on the performance of management. *Note:* Students should be aware that when a group is responsible for reporting on its own activity, usually the best or most favorable position will be reported. Ethical considerations may also be mentioned here.

The operating income for the firm using LIFO and DDB is lower because, in periods of rising prices, the LIFO inventory costing method produces a higher cost of goods sold, and, in the early years of an asset's useful life, accelerated depreciation yields a higher depreciation expense. The result is lower operating income. However, future operating income is expected to be higher.

The $50,000 difference in operating income stems only from the differences in accounting methods. Differences in the estimated lives and residual values of the plant assets could lead to an even greater variation. In practice, of course, differences in net income occur for many reasons, but the user must be aware of the discrepancies that can occur as a result of the accounting methods chosen by management. In general, an accounting method or estimate that results in lower current earnings is considered to produce a better quality of operating income.

The existence of such alternatives could cause problems in the interpretation of financial statements were it not for the conventions of full disclosure and consistency. Full disclosure requires that management explain the significant accounting policies used in preparing the financial statements in a note to the statements.

Consistency requires that the same accounting procedures be followed from year to year. If a change in procedure is made, the nature of the change and its monetary effect must be explained in a note.

Nature of Nonoperating Items

The corporate income statement consists of several components, as shown in Exhibit 1. The top of the statement presents income from current ongoing operations, called *income from continuing operations.* The lower part of the statement can contain such nonoperating items as discontinued operations, extraordinary gains and losses, and effects of accounting changes. Those items may drastically affect the bottom line, or net income, of the company. In fact, in Exhibit 1, earnings per common share associated with continuing operations were $2.81, but net income per share was $3.35, or 19.2 percent higher.

For practical reasons, the calculations of trends and ratios are based on the assumption that net income and other components are comparable from year to year and from company to company. However, in making interpretations, the astute analyst will always look beyond the ratios to the quality of the components. For example, restructuring charges, if they are large enough, can make a company's

Point to Emphasize: These examples also stress that a single year's information is not adequate without a trend for use as a reference.

Exhibit 1
A Corporate Income Statement

Junction Corporation
Income Statement
For the Year Ended December 31, 20x1

Revenues		$925,000
Less Costs and Expenses		500,000
Income from Continuing Operations Before Income Taxes		$425,000
Income Taxes Expense		144,500
Income from Continuing Operations		$280,500
Discontinued Operations		
Income from Operations of Discontinued Segment (net of taxes, $35,000)	$90,000	
Loss on Disposal of Segment (net of taxes, $42,000)	(73,000)	17,000
Income Before Extraordinary Items and Cumulative Effect of Accounting Change		$297,500
Extraordinary Gain (net of taxes, $17,000)		43,000
Subtotal		$340,500
Cumulative Effect of a Change in Accounting Principle (net of taxes, $5,000)		(6,000)
Net Income		$334,500
Earnings per Common Share:		
Income from Continuing Operations		$ 2.81
Discontinued Operations (net of taxes)		.17
Income Before Extraordinary Items and Cumulative Effect of Accounting Change		$ 2.98
Extraordinary Gain (net of taxes)		.43
Cumulative Effect of Accounting Change (net of taxes)		(.06)
Net Income		$ 3.35

Business-World Example: Discontinued operations, extraordinary items, and cumulative effects of a change in accounting principle are more likely to occur in large, public corporations. A knowledge of these items is important when analyzing the financial results of such companies. These items do not occur as frequently in small, private business corporations.

Point to Emphasize: Discontinued operations, extraordinary gains and losses, and the cumulative effect of a change in accounting principle must appear as separate items below income from continuing operations. They are all shown net of taxes.

Point to Emphasize: Income from continuing operations is different from net income; it is a better indicator of future performance than net income is.

External users of financial statements depend on management's honesty and openness in disclosing factual information about a company. In the vast majority of cases, management's reports are reliable, but on occasion, employees (called *whistle-blowers*) may publicly disclose wrongdoing on the part of their company. For example, after the internal audit chief of W. R. Grace, a chemical company, was fired, he made known to the SEC his concerns of deliberate deferral of reporting of income by W. R. Grace. The goal was to show growth in earnings within the targeted range of 20–24 percent, which analysts were expecting. Later the company reversed the deferral of income to offset poor operating results. The SEC is currently investigating W. R. Grace for fraudulently manipulated earnings.[4]

return on equity look better. In a recent year, Boeing Company, an aircraft manufacturer, took charges of $4 billion resulting in a loss of $178 million. The effect of this charge reduced equity by almost 20 percent. Return on equity should increase in next period.[5] Although such write-offs reduce a company's net worth, they usually do not affect current cash flows or operations and in most cases are ignored by analysts assessing current performance.

Instructional Strategy: Quality of earnings issues, in many cases, call attention to ethical considerations. To explore those issues, ask students to complete SD 3 as a one-page written assignment to be graded and discussed in class. Use a straw poll to assess students' agreement with the viewpoints expressed.

In some cases, a company may boost income by including one-time gains. For example, Sears, Roebuck and Co., a multiline retailer providing a wide array of merchandise and services, used a gain from the change of an accounting principle to bolster its net income by $136 million, or $.35 per share, in 1997. Without the gain, earnings per share (EPS) actually decreased from $3.12 to $2.92, not increased as Sears originally reported.[6] The quality of Sears's earnings is in fact lower than it might appear on the surface. Unless analysts are prepared to go beyond the "bottom line" in analyzing and interpreting financial reports, they can come to the wrong conclusions.

The Corporate Income Statement

OBJECTIVE

2 Prepare a corporate income statement

Related Text Assignments:
Q: 3
SE: 2
E: 2, 3
P: 2, 3, 7
SD: 4
FRA: 4, 5, 6

Parenthetical Note: Both single-step and multistep income statements are commonly used in corporate annual reports. Whichever format is used, the income statement must be all-inclusive.

Accounting organizations have not specified the format of the income statement because they have considered flexibility more important than a standard format. Either the single-step or the multistep form can be used. However, the accounting profession has taken the position that income for a period should be all-inclusive, **comprehensive income**, which is different from net income.[7] Comprehensive income is the change in a company's equity during a period from sources other than owners and includes net income, change in unrealized investment gains and losses, and other items affecting equity. Companies are reporting comprehensive income and its components as a separate financial statement, or as part of another financial statement.

In the first year of this requirement, 347 of 600 large companies reported comprehensive income. Of these, 78 percent reported comprehensive income on the statement of stockholders' equity, 10 percent reported it on a separate statement, and only 2 percent reported it on the income statement.[8]

Net income or loss for a period includes all revenues, expenses, gains, and losses over the period, except for prior period adjustments. As a result, several items must be added to the income statement, among them discontinued operations, extraordinary items, and accounting changes. The Financial Accounting Standards Board has proposed adding goodwill amortization to this list, moving it down from income from operations. In addition, earnings per share figures must be disclosed. Exhibit 1 illustrated a corporate income statement and the required disclosures. The following sections discuss the components of the corporate income statement, beginning with income taxes expense.

Income Taxes Expense

OBJECTIVE

3 Show the relationships among income taxes expense, deferred income taxes, and net of taxes

Related Text Assignments:
Q: 5, 6
SE: 3
E: 3, 4, 5
P: 2, 3, 7
SD: 4
FRA: 2

Corporations determine their taxable income (the amount on which taxes are paid) by subtracting allowable business deductions from includable gross income. The federal tax laws determine which business expenses may be deducted and which cannot be deducted from taxable gross income.*

The tax rates that apply to a corporation's taxable income are shown in Table 1. A corporation with taxable income of $70,000 would have a federal income tax liability of $12,500: $7,500 (the tax on the first $50,000 of taxable income) plus $5,000 (25 percent of the $20,000 earned in excess of $50,000).

Income taxes expense is the expense recognized in the accounting records on an accrual basis that applies to income from continuing operations. This expense may or may not equal the amount of taxes actually paid by the corporation and recorded as income taxes payable in the current period. The amount payable is determined from taxable income, which is measured according to the rules and regulations of the income tax code.

Common Student Confusion: Most people think it is illegal to keep accounting records on a basis different from income tax records. They don't realize that it is normal because the Internal Revenue Code and GAAP often do not agree. To work with two conflicting sets of guidelines, the accountant must keep two sets of records.

For the sake of convenience, most small businesses keep their accounting records on the same basis as their tax records, so that the income taxes expense on the income statement equals the income taxes liability to be paid to the Internal Revenue Service (IRS). This practice is acceptable when there is no material difference between the income on an accounting basis and the income on an income tax basis. However, the purpose of accounting is to determine net income in accordance with generally accepted accounting principles, not to determine taxable income and tax liability.

Management has an incentive to use methods that minimize the firm's tax liability, but accountants, who are bound by accrual accounting and the materiality concept, cannot let tax procedures dictate their method of preparing financial statements if the result would be misleading. As a consequence, there can be a material difference between accounting and taxable incomes, especially in larger businesses. This discrepancy can result from differences in the timing of the recognition of revenues and expenses under the two accounting methods. Some possible variations are shown below.

	Accounting Method	Tax Method
Expense recognition	Accrual or deferral	At time of expenditure
Accounts receivable	Allowance	Direct charge-off
Inventories	Average cost	FIFO
Depreciation	Straight-line	Modified Accelerated Cost Recovery System

Deferred Income Taxes

Point to Emphasize: The discrepancy between GAAP-based tax expense and Internal Revenue Code–based tax liability produces the need for the Deferred Income Taxes account.

The accounting method used to accrue income taxes expense on the basis of accounting income whenever there are differences between accounting and taxable income is called **income tax allocation**. The account used to record the difference between the income taxes expense and income taxes payable is called **Deferred Income Taxes**. For example, Junction Corporation shows income taxes expense of $144,500 on its income statement but has actual income taxes payable

*Rules for calculating and reporting taxable income in specialized industries such as banking, insurance, mutual funds, and cooperatives are highly technical and may vary significantly from those discussed in this chapter.

Table 1. Tax Rate Schedule for Corporations, 2000

Taxable Income		Tax Liability	
Over	But Not Over		Of the Amount Over
—	$ 50,000	0 + 15%	—
$ 50,000	75,000	$ 7,500 + 25%	$ 50,000
75,000	100,000	13,750 + 34%	75,000
100,000	335,000	22,250 + 39%	100,000
335,000	10,000,000	113,900 + 34%	335,000
10,000,000	15,000,000	3,400,000 + 35%	10,000,000
15,000,000	18,333,333	5,150,000 + 38%	15,000,000
18,333,333	—	6,416,667 + 35%	18,333,333

Note: Tax rates are subject to change by Congress.

Enrichment Note: The federal income tax is progressive. That is, the rate increases as taxable income increases.

to the IRS of $92,000. The entry that follows is to record the estimated income taxes expense applicable to income from continuing operations using the income tax allocation procedure.

A = L + OE				
+ −	Dec. 31	Income Taxes Expense	144,500	
+		Income Taxes Payable		92,000
		Deferred Income Taxes		52,500
		To record estimated current and deferred income taxes		

In other years, it is possible for Income Taxes Payable to exceed Income Taxes Expense, in which case the same entry is made except that Deferred Income Taxes is debited.

The Financial Accounting Standards Board has issued specific rules for recording, measuring, and classifying deferred income taxes.[9] Deferred income taxes are recognized for the estimated future tax effects resulting from temporary differences in the valuation of assets, liabilities, equity, revenues, expenses, gains, and losses for tax and financial reporting purposes. Temporary differences include revenues and expenses or gains and losses that are included in taxable income before or after they are included in financial income. In other words, the recognition point for revenues, expenses, gains, and losses is not the same for tax and financial reporting. For example, advance payments for goods and services, such as magazine subscriptions, are not recognized in financial income until the product is shipped, but for tax purposes they are usually recognized as revenue when cash is received. The result is that taxes paid exceed tax expense, which creates a deferred income tax asset (or prepaid taxes).

Clarification Note: Deferred Income Taxes is classified as a liability when it has a credit balance and as an asset when it has a debit balance. It is further classified as either current or long-term depending on when it is expected to reverse.

Classification of deferred income taxes as current or noncurrent depends on the classification of the related asset or liability that created the temporary difference. For example, the deferred income tax asset mentioned above would be classified as current if unearned subscription revenue is classified as a current liability. On the other hand, the temporary difference arising from depreciation is related to a long-term depreciable asset. Therefore, the resulting deferred income tax would be classified as long-term. However, if a temporary difference is not related to an asset or liability, then it is classified as current or noncurrent based on its expected date of reversal. Temporary differences and the classification of deferred income taxes that results are covered in depth in more advanced courses.

Each year, the balance of the Deferred Income Taxes account is evaluated to determine whether it still accurately represents the expected asset or liability in light of legislated changes in income tax laws and regulations. If changes have occurred, an adjusting entry to bring the account balance into line with current laws is required. For example, a decrease in corporate income tax rates, like the one that occurred in 1987, means that a company with deferred income tax liabilities will pay less in taxes in future years than the amount indicated by the credit balance of its Deferred Income Taxes account. As a result, the company would debit Deferred Income Taxes to reduce the liability and credit Gain from Reduction in Income Tax Rates. This credit increases the reported income on the income statement. If the tax rate increases in future years, a loss would be recorded and the deferred income tax liability would be increased.

In any given year, the amount a company pays in income taxes is determined by subtracting (or adding, as the case may be) the deferred income taxes for that year, as reported in the notes to the financial statements, from (or to) income taxes expense, which is reported in the financial statements. In subsequent years, the amount of deferred income taxes can vary based on changes in tax laws and rates.

Some understanding of the importance of deferred income taxes to financial reporting can be gained from studying a survey of the financial statements of 600 large companies. About 67 percent reported deferred income taxes with a credit balance in the long-term liability section of the balance sheet.[10]

Net of Taxes

Teaching Note: To present a conceptual overview of intraperiod tax allocation, draw a box and label it *total income taxes expense.* Then divide the box into five sections and label them *continuing operations, discontinued operations, extraordinary items, cumulative effect,* and *prior period adjustments.* Finally, explain that if the income tax is not divided among the appropriate sections of the income statement or statement of retained earnings, the figures in those statements will be distorted. The idea is to let the tax follow the item.

The phrase **net of taxes**, as used in Exhibit 1, means that the effect of applicable taxes (usually income taxes) has been considered in determining the overall effect of an item on the financial statements. The phrase is used on the corporate income statement when a company has items that must be disclosed in a separate section. Each such item should be reported net of the applicable income taxes to avoid distorting the income taxes expense associated with ongoing operations and the resulting net operating income. For example, assume that a corporation with operating income before taxes of $120,000 has a total tax expense of $66,000 and that the total income includes a gain of $100,000 on which a tax of $30,000 is due. Also assume that the gain is not part of normal operations and must be disclosed separately on the income statement as an extraordinary item (explained later). This is how the tax expense would be reported on the income statement:

Operating Income Before Taxes	$120,000
Income Taxes Expense	36,000
Income Before Extraordinary Item	$ 84,000
Extraordinary Gain (net of taxes, $30,000)	70,000
Net Income	$154,000

If all the tax expense were deducted from operating income before taxes, both the income before extraordinary item and the extraordinary gain would be distorted.

A company follows the same procedure in the case of an extraordinary loss. For example, assume the same facts as before except that the total tax expense is only $6,000 because of a $100,000 extraordinary loss. The result is a $30,000 tax savings, shown as follows:

Operating Income Before Taxes	$120,000
Income Taxes Expense	36,000
Income Before Extraordinary Item	$ 84,000
Extraordinary Loss (net of taxes, $30,000)	(70,000)
Net Income	$ 14,000

In Exhibit 1, the total of the income tax items is $149,500. That amount is allocated among five statement components, as follows:

Income taxes expense on income from continuing operations	$144,500
Income tax on income from a discontinued segment	35,000
Income tax savings on the loss on the disposal of the segment	(42,000)
Income tax on the extraordinary gain	17,000
Income tax savings on the cumulative effect of a change in accounting principle	(5,000)
Total income taxes expense	$149,500

Discontinued Operations

OBJECTIVE

4 Describe the disclosure on the income statement of discontinued operations, extraordinary items, and accounting changes

Related Text Assignments:
Q: 7, 8, 9
E: 3
P: 2, 3, 7
SD: 1, 4
FRA: 4, 5

Enrichment Note: A segment is a separate line of business or class of customer; it must be distinguishable physically and operationally for financial reporting purposes. Discontinuing *part* of a segment does not qualify for separate disclosure in this section.

Large companies in the United States usually have many **segments**. A segment may be a separate major line of business or serve a separate class of customer. For example, a company that makes heavy drilling equipment may also have another line of business, such as the manufacture of mobile homes. A large company may discontinue or otherwise dispose of certain segments of its business that do not fit its future plans or are not profitable. **Discontinued operations** are segments of a business that are no longer part of its ongoing operations. Generally accepted accounting principles require that gains and losses from discontinued operations be reported separately on the income statement. Such separation makes it easier to evaluate the ongoing activities of the business.

In Exhibit 1, the disclosure of discontinued operations has two parts. One part shows that after the date of the decision to discontinue, the income from operations of the segment that has been disposed of was $90,000 (net of $35,000 taxes). The other part shows that the loss from the disposal of the segment was $73,000 (net of $42,000 tax savings). Computation of the gains or losses is covered in more advanced accounting courses. The disclosure has been described, however, to give a complete view of the corporate income statement.

Extraordinary Items

Point to Emphasize: To qualify as extraordinary, an event must be unusual (not in the ordinary course of business) and must not be expected to occur again in the foreseeable future. Occasionally, judgment must be exercised when it is not clear whether an event meets these two criteria.

The Accounting Principles Board, in its *Opinion No. 30*, defines **extraordinary items** as "events or transactions that are distinguished by their unusual nature *and* by the infrequency of their occurrence."[11] Unusual and infrequent occurrences are explained in the opinion as follows:

> Unusual Nature—the underlying event or transaction should possess a high degree of abnormality and be of a type clearly unrelated to, or only incidentally related to, the ordinary and typical activities of the entity, taking into account the environment in which the entity operates.
>
> Infrequency of Occurrence—the underlying event or transaction should be of a type that would not reasonably be expected to recur in the foreseeable future, taking into account the environment in which the entity operates.[12]

If an item is both unusual and infrequent (and material in amount), it should be reported separately from continuing operations on the income statement. The disclosure allows readers to identify gains or losses in income that would not be expected to happen again soon. Items usually treated as extraordinary include (1) an uninsured loss from flood, earthquake, fire, or theft; (2) a gain or loss resulting from the passage of a new law; (3) the expropriation (taking) of property by a foreign government; and (4) a gain or loss from the early retirement of debt. Gains or losses from extraordinary items should be reported on the income statement after discontinued operations. And they should be shown net of applicable taxes. In a recent year, 74 (12 percent) of 600 large companies reported extraordinary items on their income statements.[13] In Exhibit 1, the extraordinary gain was $43,000 after applicable taxes of $17,000.

Accounting Changes

Enrichment Note: A change in accounting method (principle) violates the convention of consistency. Such a change is allowed, however, when it can be demonstrated that the new method will produce more useful financial statements. The effect of the change is disclosed just above net income on the income statement.

Consistency, which is one of the basic conventions of accounting, means that companies must apply the same accounting principles from year to year. However, a company is allowed to make accounting changes if current procedures are incorrect or inappropriate. For example, a change from the FIFO to the LIFO inventory method can be made if there is adequate justification for the change. Adequate justification usually means that if the change occurs, the financial statements will better show the financial activities of the company. A company's desire to lower the amount of income taxes it pays is not considered adequate justification for an accounting change. If justification does exist and an accounting change is made, generally accepted accounting principles require the disclosure of the change in the financial statements.

Ethical Consideration: Some accounting changes can produce a significant increase in net income without an accompanying improvement in performance. The user of financial statements should be aware that some businesses implement an accounting change solely for the increase in net income that results.

The **cumulative effect of an accounting change** is the effect that the new accounting principle would have had on net income in prior periods if it had been applied instead of the old principle. This effect is shown on the income statement immediately after extraordinary items.[14] For example, assume that in the five years prior to 20xx, Junction Corporation had used the straight-line method to depreciate its machinery. This year, the company retroactively changed to the double-declining-balance method of depreciation. The controller computed the cumulative effect of the change in depreciation charges (net of taxes) as $6,000, as follows:

Cumulative, five-year double-declining-balance depreciation	$29,000
Less cumulative, five-year straight-line depreciation	18,000
Before tax effect	$11,000
Income tax savings	5,000
Cumulative effect of accounting change	$ 6,000

Relevant information about the accounting change is shown in the notes to the financial statements. The change results in $11,000 of depreciation expense for prior years being deducted in the current year, in addition to the current year's depreciation costs included in the $500,000 costs and expenses section of the income statement. This expense must be shown in the current year's income statement as a reduction in income (see Exhibit 1). In 1997, 62, or 10 percent, of 600 large companies reported changes in accounting procedures.[15] Further study of accounting changes is left to more advanced accounting courses.

Earnings per Share

OBJECTIVE

5 Compute earnings per share

Related Text Assignments:
Q: 10, 11, 12
SE: 4
E: 3, 6
P: 2, 3, 7
SD: 3
FRA: 5, 6

Readers of financial statements use earnings per share information to judge a company's performance and to compare it with the performance of other companies. Because such information is so important, the Accounting Principles Board concluded that earnings per share of common stock should be presented on the face of the income statement.[16] As shown in Exhibit 1, the information is usually disclosed just below the net income.

An earnings per share amount is always shown for (1) income from continuing operations, (2) income before extraordinary items and the cumulative effect of accounting changes, (3) the cumulative effect of accounting changes, and (4) net income. If the statement shows a gain or loss from discontinued operations or a gain or loss on extraordinary items, earnings per share amounts can also be presented for them. The following per share data from the income statement of Minnesota Mining and Manufacturing Company (3M) show why it is a good idea to study the components of earnings per share.[17]

Financial Highlights

	Years Ended December 31		
	1999	1998	1997
Earnings per share—Basic:			
Continuing operations	$4.39	$3.01	$5.14
Extraordinary loss	—	(.10)	—
Net income	$4.39	$2.91	$5.14

Enrichment Note: Earnings per share is a measure of a corporation's profitability. It is one of the most closely watched financial statement ratios in the business world. Its disclosure, within or below the income statement, is required.

Note that net income was influenced by a special item in 1998: An extraordinary loss decreased income from continuing operations by $.10 per share to a basic net income of $2.91 per share. In 1999, the company had no special items; thus, 100 percent of 3M's basic earnings per share were attributable to continuing operations.

Basic earnings per share is net income applicable to common stock divided by the weighted-average number of common shares outstanding. To compute this figure, one must determine if during the year the number of common shares outstanding changed, and if the company paid preferred stock dividends.

When a company has only common stock and has the same number of shares outstanding throughout the year, the earnings per share computation is simple. From Exhibit 1, we know that Junction Corporation reported net income of $334,500. Assume that the company had 100,000 shares of common stock outstanding for the entire year. The earnings per share of common stock is computed as follows:

$$\text{Earnings per Share} = \frac{\$334{,}500}{100{,}000 \text{ shares}} = \$3.35 \text{ per share}$$

If the number of shares outstanding changes during the year, it is necessary to figure the weighted-average number of shares outstanding for the year. Suppose that Junction Corporation had the following amounts of common shares outstanding during various periods of the year: January–March, 100,000 shares; April–September, 120,000 shares; and October–December, 130,000 shares. The weighted-average number of common shares outstanding and basic earnings per share would be found this way:

100,000 shares × $^3/_{12}$ year	25,000
120,000 shares × $^6/_{12}$ year	60,000
130,000 shares × $^3/_{12}$ year	32,500
Weighted-average common shares outstanding	117,500

Point to Emphasize: The earnings per share calculation is based on the weighted-average number of shares outstanding during the year, much like the calculation of interest on a bank account.

$$\text{Basic Earnings per Share} = \frac{\text{Net Income}}{\text{Weighted-Average Common Shares Outstanding}}$$

$$= \frac{\$334{,}500}{117{,}500 \text{ shares}} = \$2.85 \text{ per share}$$

If a company has nonconvertible preferred stock outstanding, the dividend for that stock must be subtracted from net income before earnings per share for common stock are computed. Suppose that Junction Corporation has preferred stock on which the annual dividend is $23,500. Earnings per share on common stock would be $2.65 [($334,500 − $23,500) ÷ 117,500 shares].

Companies with a capital structure in which there are no bonds, stocks, or stock options that could be converted into common stock are said to have a **simple**

capital structure. The earnings per share for these companies is computed as shown on the previous page. Some companies, however, have a **complex capital structure**, which includes exercisable stock options or convertible stocks and bonds. Those convertible securities have the potential of diluting the earnings per share of common stock. *Potential dilution* means that a stockholder's proportionate share of ownership in a company could be reduced through the conversion of stocks or bonds or the exercise of stock options, which would increase the total shares outstanding.

For example, suppose that a person owns 10,000 shares of a company, which equals 2 percent of the outstanding shares of 500,000. Now suppose that holders of convertible bonds convert the bonds into 100,000 shares of stock. The person's 10,000 shares would then equal only 1.67 percent (10,000 ÷ 600,000) of the outstanding shares. In addition, the added shares outstanding would lower earnings per share and would most likely lower market price per share.

Point to Emphasize: A company with potentially dilutive securities (such as convertible preferred stock or bonds) has a complex capital structure and must present two earnings per share figures—basic and diluted. The latter figure is the more conservative of the two.

Because stock options and convertible preferred stocks or bonds have the potential to dilute earnings per share, they are referred to as **potentially dilutive securities**. When a company has a complex capital structure, it must report two earnings per share figures: basic earnings per share and diluted earnings per share.[18] **Diluted earnings per share** are calculated by adding all potentially dilutive securities to the denominator of the basic earnings per share calculation. This figure shows stockholders the maximum potential effect of dilution of their ownership position in the company.

The difference between basic and diluted earnings per share can be significant. For example, consider the results reported by Dollar General Corporation, a successful retail discount chain:

Financial Highlights

	Years Ended December 31		
	1999	1998	1997
Basic earnings per share	$.89	$.81	$.64
Diluted earnings per share	.81	.68	.54

Note that while both measures of earnings per share are increasing, the pattern of increase is different and basic earnings per share are greater by at least 10 percent in every year.[19]

The computation of diluted earnings per share is a complex process and is reserved for more advanced courses.

The Statement of Stockholders' Equity

OBJECTIVE

6 Prepare a statement of stockholders' equity

Related Text Assignments:
Q: 13, 14, 15
SE: 5, 6, 7
E: 7, 8
P: 4, 5, 6, 8, 9
SD: 4, 5
FRA: 1, 3, 4, 5, 6

The **statement of stockholders' equity**, also called the *statement of changes in stockholders' equity*, summarizes the changes in the components of the stockholders' equity section of the balance sheet. More and more companies are using this statement in place of the statement of retained earnings because it reveals much more about the year's stockholders' equity transactions. In the statement of stockholders' equity in Exhibit 2, for example, the first line shows the beginning balance of each account in the stockholders' equity section. Each subsequent line discloses the effects of transactions on those accounts. It is possible to determine from the statement that during 20x1 Tri-State Corporation issued 5,000 shares of common stock for $250,000, had a conversion of $100,000 of preferred stock into

Contributed Capital	
Common Stock, $5 par value, 100,000 shares authorized, 30,000 shares issued and outstanding	$ 150,000
Common Stock Distributable, 3,000 shares	15,000
Paid-in Capital in Excess of Par Value, Common	75,000
Total Contributed Capital	$ 240,000
Retained Earnings	840,000
Total Stockholders' Equity	$1,080,000

Reinforcement Exercise: A corporation with 6,000 shares of $100 par value common stock outstanding declares a 15 percent stock dividend on a day when the stock's market price is $120 per share. Make the journal entry on the declaration date.
Answer:

Stock Dividends Declared	108,000	
Common Stock Distributable		90,000
Paid-in Capital in Excess of Par Value, Common		18,000

Three points can be made from this example. First, the total stockholders' equity is the same before and after the stock dividend. Second, the assets of the corporation are not reduced as in the case of a cash dividend. Third, the proportionate ownership in the corporation of any individual stockholder is the same before and after the stock dividend. To illustrate these points, assume that a stockholder owns 1,000 shares before the stock dividend. After the 10 percent stock dividend is distributed, this stockholder would own 1,100 shares, as illustrated below.

Stockholders' Equity	Before Dividend	After Dividend
Common Stock	$ 150,000	$ 165,000
Paid-in Capital in Excess of Par Value, Common	30,000	75,000
Total Contributed Capital	$ 180,000	$ 240,000
Retained Earnings	900,000	840,000
Total Stockholders' Equity	$1,080,000	$1,080,000
Shares Outstanding	30,000	33,000
Stockholders' Equity per Share	$ 36.00	$ 32.73

Stockholders' Investment		
Shares owned	1,000	1,100
Shares outstanding	30,000	33,000
Percentage of ownership	3⅓%	3⅓%
Proportionate investment ($1,080,000 × .03⅓)	$36,000	$36,000

Point to Emphasize:
$36.00 × 1,000 = $36,000
$32.73* × 1,100 = $36,003
*Rounded

Both before and after the stock dividend, the stockholders' equity totals $1,080,000 and the stockholder owns 3⅓ percent of the company. The proportionate investment (stockholders' equity times percentage ownership) remains at $36,000.

Point to Emphasize: When a large (greater than 20 to 25 percent) stock dividend is declared, the transfer from retained earnings is based on the stock's par or stated value, not on its market value.

All stock dividends have an effect on the market price of a company's stock. But some stock dividends are so large that they have a material effect. For example, a 50 percent stock dividend would cause the market price of the stock to drop about 33 percent because the increase is now one-third of shares outstanding. The AICPA has decided that large stock dividends, those greater than 20 to 25 percent, should be accounted for by transferring the par or stated value of the stock on the date of declaration from retained earnings to contributed capital.[22]

Stock Splits

Point to Emphasize: Earnings per share are reduced by stock splits and stock dividends because the number of shares has increased. Cash dividends have no effect on earnings per share.

A **stock split** occurs when a corporation increases the number of issued shares of stock and reduces the par or stated value proportionally. A company may plan a stock split when it wants to lower the stock's market value per share and increase the demand for the stock at this lower price. This action may be necessary if the market value per share has become so high that it hinders the trading of the stock

or if the company wants to signal to the market its success in achieving its operating goals. For example, the action of The Gillette Company in a recent year in declaring a 2-for-1 stock split and raising its cash dividend achieved these strategic objectives. These actions were viewed positively by the market by pushing the share price to $106 from an earlier share price of $77. After the stock split, the number of shares outstanding doubled, thereby cutting the share price in half and also the dividend per share. Most important, each stockholder's total wealth is unchanged as a result of the stock split.

Business-World Example: Stock splits greater than 2 for 1 are unusual. Splits such as 3 for 2 or 4 for 3 are far more common. On occasion, companies whose stock sells for a very low price will perform a reverse stock split, which reduces the number of shares and increases the market price.

To illustrate a stock split, suppose that Caprock Corporation has 30,000 shares of $5.00 par value stock outstanding. The market value is $70.00 per share. The corporation plans a 2-for-1 split. This split will lower the par value to $2.50 and increase the number of shares outstanding to 60,000. A stockholder who previously owned 400 shares of the $5.00 par stock would own 800 shares of the $2.50 par stock after the split. When a stock split occurs, the market value tends to fall in proportion to the increase in outstanding shares of stock. For example, a 2-for-1 stock split would cause the price of the stock to drop by approximately 50 percent, to about $35.00. It would also halve earnings per share and cash dividends per share (if the board does not increase the dividend). The lower price and the increase in shares tend to promote the buying and selling of shares.

A stock split does not increase the number of shares authorized. Nor does it change the balances in the stockholders' equity section of the balance sheet. It simply changes the par value and the number of shares issued, both shares outstanding and shares held as treasury stock. Therefore, an entry is not necessary. However, it is appropriate to document the change by making a memorandum entry in the general journal.

July 15 The 30,000 shares of $5 par value common stock that are issued and outstanding were split 2 for 1, resulting in 60,000 shares of $2.50 par value common stock issued and outstanding.

The change for the Caprock Corporation is as follows:

Before Stock Split (from page 642)

Contributed Capital	
Common Stock, $5 par value, 100,000 shares authorized, 30,000 shares issued and outstanding	$ 150,000
Paid-in Capital in Excess of Par Value, Common	30,000
Total Contributed Capital	$ 180,000
Retained Earnings	900,000
Total Stockholders' Equity	$1,080,000

After Stock Split

Point to Emphasize: A stock split affects only the common stock calculation. In this case, there are twice as many shares after the split, but par value is now half of what it was.

Contributed Capital	
Common Stock, $2.50 par value, 100,000 shares authorized, 60,000 shares issued and outstanding	$ 150,000
Paid-in Capital in Excess of Par Value, Common	30,000
Total Contributed Capital	$ 180,000
Retained Earnings	900,000
Total Stockholders' Equity	$1,080,000

Point to Emphasize: As long as the newly outstanding shares do not exceed the previously authorized shares, permission from the state is not needed for a stock split.

Although the amount of stockholders' equity per share would be half as much, each stockholder's proportionate interest in the company would remain the same.

If the number of split shares will exceed the number of authorized shares, the board of directors must secure state and stockholders' approval before it can issue additional shares.

Book Value

OBJECTIVE

8 Calculate book value per share

Related Text Assignments:
Q: 18
SE: 10
E: 12
P: 6
SD: 4, 5
FRA: 4, 5

Discussion Question: What is the significance of book value per share of stock? Answer: Book value per share represents the equity of one share of stock in the net assets (assets minus liabilities) of a corporation. It can apply to both common and preferred stock.

K/R

Point to Emphasize: To determine the equity applicable to common shareholders, subtract the total call value of preferred stock plus any dividends in arrears (if the preferred stock is cumulative) from total stockholders' equity. To determine the book value per share, simply divide the equity applicable to each type of stock by the number of shares.

The word *value* is associated with shares of stock in several ways. Par value or stated value is set when the stock is authorized and establishes the legal capital of a company. Neither par value nor stated value has any relationship to a stock's book value or market value. The **book value** of a company's stock represents the total assets of the company less its liabilities. It is simply the stockholders' equity of the company or, to look at it another way, the company's net assets. The **book value per share**, therefore, represents the equity of the owner of one share of stock in the net assets of the corporation. That value, of course, does not necessarily equal the amount the shareholder would receive if the company were sold or liquidated. It differs in most cases because assets are usually recorded at historical cost, not at the current value at which they could be sold.

To determine the book value per share when a company has only common stock outstanding, divide the total stockholders' equity by the total common shares outstanding. In computing the shares outstanding, common stock distributable is included. Treasury stock (shares previously issued and now held by the company), however, is not included. For example, suppose that Caprock Corporation has total stockholders' equity of $1,030,000 and 29,000 shares outstanding after recording the purchase of treasury shares. The book value per share of Caprock's common stock is $35.52 ($1,030,000 ÷ 29,000 shares).

If a company has both preferred and common stock, the determination of book value per share is not so simple. The general rule is that the call value (or par value, if a call value is not specified) of the preferred stock plus any dividends in arrears is subtracted from total stockholders' equity to determine the equity pertaining to common stock. As an illustration, refer to the stockholders' equity section of Tri-State Corporation's balance sheet in Exhibit 3. Assuming that there are no dividends in arrears and that the preferred stock is callable at $105, the equity pertaining to common stock is calculated as follows:

Total stockholders' equity	$2,014,400
Less equity allocated to preferred shareholders (3,000 shares × $105)	315,000
Equity pertaining to common shareholders	$1,699,400

There are 41,300 shares of common stock outstanding (41,800 shares issued less 500 shares of treasury stock). The book values per share are computed as follows:

Preferred Stock: $315,000 ÷ 3,000 shares = $105 per share
Common Stock: $1,699,400 ÷ 41,300 shares = $41.15 per share

If we assume the same facts except that the preferred stock is 8 percent cumulative and that one year of dividends is in arrears, the stockholders' equity would be allocated as follows:

Total stockholders' equity		$2,014,400
Less: Call value of outstanding preferred shares	$315,000	
Dividends in arrears ($300,000 × .08)	24,000	
Equity allocated to preferred shareholders		339,000
Equity pertaining to common shareholders		$1,675,400

The book values per share are then as follows:

Preferred Stock: $339,000 ÷ 3,000 shares = $113 per share
Common Stock: $1,675,400 ÷ 41,300 shares = $40.57 per share

Undeclared preferred dividends fall into arrears on the last day of the fiscal year (the date shown on the financial statements). Also, dividends in arrears do not apply to unissued preferred stock.

Chapter Review

REVIEW OF LEARNING OBJECTIVES

Check out ACE, a self-quizzing program on chapter content, at http://college.hmco.com.

1. **Identify the issues related to evaluating the quality of a company's earnings.** Current and prospective net income is an important component in many ratios used to evaluate a company. The user should recognize that the quality of reported net income can be influenced by certain choices made by management. First, management exercises judgment in choosing the accounting methods and estimates that are used in computing net income. Second, discontinued operations, extraordinary gains or losses, and changes in accounting methods may affect net income positively or negatively.

2. **Prepare a corporate income statement.** The corporate income statement shows comprehensive income—all revenues, expenses, gains, and losses for the accounting period, except for prior period adjustments. The top part of the corporate income statement includes all revenues, costs and expenses, and income taxes that pertain to continuing operations. The bottom part of the statement contains any or all of the following: discontinued operations, extraordinary items, and accounting changes. Earnings per share data should be shown at the bottom of the statement, below net income.

3. **Show the relationships among income taxes expense, deferred income taxes, and net of taxes.** Income taxes expense is the taxes applicable to income from operations on an accrual basis. Income tax allocation is necessary when differences between accrual-based accounting income and taxable income cause a material difference between income taxes expense as shown on the income statement and actual income tax liability. The difference between income taxes expense and income taxes payable is debited or credited to an account called Deferred Income Taxes. *Net of taxes* is a phrase used to indicate that the effect of taxes has been considered when showing an item on the income statement.

4. **Describe the disclosure on the income statement of discontinued operations, extraordinary items, and accounting changes.** Because of their unusual nature, a gain or loss on discontinued operations and on extraordinary items, and the cumulative effect of accounting changes must be disclosed on the income statement separately from continuing operations and net of income taxes. Relevant information about any accounting change is shown in the notes to the financial statements.

5. **Compute earnings per share.** Stockholders and other readers of financial statements use earnings per share data to evaluate a company's performance and to compare it with the performance of other companies. Therefore, earnings per share data are presented on the face of the income statement. The amounts are computed by dividing the income applicable to common stock by the number of common shares outstanding for the year. If the number of shares outstanding has varied during the year, then the weighted-average number of common shares outstanding should be used in the computation. When the company has a complex capital structure, both basic and diluted earnings per share must be disclosed on the face of the income statement.

Amortizing a Bond Premium

In our example on pages 674–675, Vason Corporation issued $100,000 of five-year bonds at a premium because the market interest rate of 8 percent was less than the face interest rate of 9 percent. The bonds were sold for $104,100, which resulted in an unamortized premium of $4,100. Like a discount, a premium must be amortized over the life of the bonds so that it can be matched to its effects on interest expense during that period. In the following sections, the total interest cost is calculated and the bond premium is amortized using the straight-line and the effective interest methods.

Calculation of Total Interest Cost

Because the bondholders paid more than face value for the bonds, the premium of $4,100 ($104,100 − $100,000) represents an amount that the bondholders will not receive at maturity. The premium is in effect a reduction, in advance, of the total interest paid on the bonds over the life of the bond issue.

The total interest cost over the issue's life can be computed as follows:

Cash to be paid to bondholders	
Face value at maturity	$100,000
Interest payments ($100,000 × .09 × 5 years)	45,000
Total cash paid to bondholders	$145,000
Less cash received from bondholders	104,100
Total interest cost	$ 40,900

Discussion Question: Why is a bond premium deducted from interest payments in calculating total interest cost? **Answer:** Because a bond premium represents a bonus paid for a bond that the corporation never has to return to the bondholders. In effect, it counters the higher-than-market interest the corporation is paying on the bond.

Or, alternatively:

Interest payments ($100,000 × .09 × 5 years)	$ 45,000
Less bond premium	4,100
Total interest cost	$ 40,900

Notice that the total interest payments of $45,000 exceed the total interest cost of $40,900 by $4,100, the amount of the bond premium.

Methods of Amortizing a Bond Premium

The two methods of amortizing a bond premium are the straight-line method and the effective interest method.

STRAIGHT-LINE METHOD Under the straight-line method, the bond premium is spread evenly over the life of the bond issue. As with bond discounts, the amount of the bond premium amortized and the interest cost for each semiannual period are computed in four steps.

1. Total Interest Payments = Interest Payments per Year × Life of Bonds

$$= 2 \times 5 = 10$$

Point to Emphasize: The bond interest expense recorded is less than the amount of the interest paid because of the amortization of the bond premium. The matching rule dictates that the premium be amortized over the life of the bond.

2. Amortization of Bond Premium per Interest Period $= \dfrac{\text{Bond Premium}}{\text{Total Interest Payments}}$

$$= \frac{\$4,100}{10} = \$410$$

3. Cash Interest Payment = Face Value × Face Interest Rate × Time

$$= \$100,000 \times .09 \times \frac{6}{12} = \$4,500$$

4. Interest Cost per Interest Period = Interest Payment − Amortization of Bond Premium
= $4,500 − $410 = $4,090

On July 1, 20x0, the first semiannual interest date, the entry would be:

A* = L + OE
− − −
*Assumes cash paid.

20x0			
July 1	Bond Interest Expense	4,090	
	Unamortized Bond Premium	410	
	Cash (or Interest Payable)		4,500
	Paid (or accrued) semiannual interest to bondholders and amortized the premium on 9 percent, five-year bonds		

Point to Emphasize: Whether a bond is originally sold at a discount or a premium, on the maturity date its carrying value will equal its face value.

Notice that the bond interest expense is $4,090, but the amount received by the bondholders is the $4,500 face interest payment. The difference of $410 is the debit to Unamortized Bond Premium. This lowers the credit balance of the Unamortized Bond Premium account and the carrying value of the bonds payable by $410 each interest period. Assuming that the bond issue remains unchanged, the same entry will be made on every semiannual interest date over the life of the bond issue. When the bond issue matures, there will be no balance in the Unamortized Bond Premium account, and the carrying value of the bonds payable will be $100,000, exactly equal to the amount due the bondholders.

As noted earlier in this chapter, the straight-line method should be used only when it does not lead to a material difference from the effective interest method.

EFFECTIVE INTEREST METHOD Under the straight-line method, the effective interest rate changes constantly, even though the interest expense is fixed, because the effective interest rate is determined by comparing the fixed interest expense with a carrying value that changes as a result of amortizing the discount or premium. To apply a fixed interest rate over the life of the bonds based on the actual market rate at the time of the bond issue requires the use of the effective interest method. Under this method, the interest expense decreases slightly each period (see Table 2, Column B) because the amount of the bond premium amortized increases slightly (Column D). This occurs because a fixed rate is applied each period to the gradually decreasing carrying value (Column A).

Teaching Note: To test understanding, ask students why the amounts in each column increase, decrease, or remain the same. For example, the amounts in Column B decrease because the carrying value (the principal on which interest is calculated) decreases each period.

The first interest payment is recorded as follows:

A* = L + OE
− − −
*Assumes cash paid.

20x0			
July 1	Bond Interest Expense	4,164	
	Unamortized Bond Premium	336	
	Cash (or Interest Payable)		4,500
	Paid (or accrued) semiannual interest to bondholders and amortized the premium on 9 percent, five-year bonds		

Notice that the unamortized bond premium (Column E) decreases gradually to zero as the carrying value decreases to the face value (Column F). To find the amount of premium amortized in any one interest payment period, subtract the effective interest expense (the carrying value times the effective interest rate, Column B) from the interest payment (Column C). In semiannual interest period 5, for example, the amortization of premium is $393, calculated as follows: $4,500 − ($102,674 × .04).

VISUAL SUMMARY OF THE EFFECTIVE INTEREST METHOD The effect of the amortization of a bond premium using the effective interest method on carrying value and interest expense can be seen in Figure 3 (based on data from Table 2).

Table 2. Interest and Amortization of a Bond Premium: Effective Interest Method

	A	B	C	D	E	F
Semiannual Interest Period	Carrying Value at Beginning of Period	Semiannual Interest Expense at 8% to Be Recorded* (4% × A)	Semiannual Interest to Be Paid to Bondholders (4½% × $100,000)	Amortization of Bond Premium (C − B)	Unamortized Bond Premium at End of Period (E − D)	Carrying Value at End of Period (A − D)
0					$4,100	$104,100
1	$104,100	$4,164	$4,500	$336	3,764	103,764
2	103,764	4,151	4,500	349	3,415	103,415
3	103,415	4,137	4,500	363	3,052	103,052
4	103,052	4,122	4,500	378	2,674	102,674
5	102,674	4,107	4,500	393	2,281	102,281
6	102,281	4,091	4,500	409	1,872	101,872
7	101,872	4,075	4,500	425	1,447	101,447
8	101,447	4,058	4,500	442	1,005	101,005
9	101,005	4,040	4,500	460	545	100,545
10	100,545	3,955†	4,500	545	—	100,000

*Rounded to the nearest dollar.
†Last period's interest expense equals $3,955 ($4,500 − $545); it does not equal $4,022 ($100,545 × .04) because of the cumulative effect of rounding.

Point to Emphasize: Over the life of a bond, the premium or discount amortized increases each period.

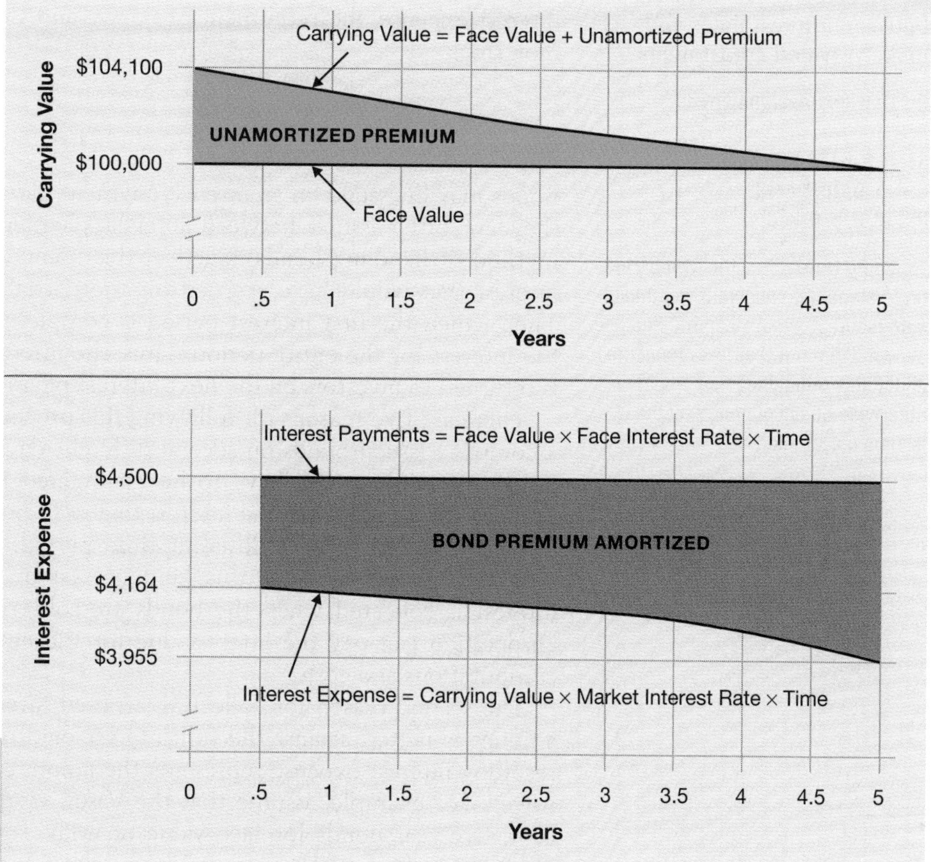

Figure 3
Carrying Value and Interest Expense—Bonds Issued at a Premium

FOCUS ON BUSINESS TECHNOLOGY

Interest and amortization tables like those in Tables 1 and 2 are ideal applications for computer spreadsheet software such as Lotus and Microsoft Excel. Once the tables have been constructed with the proper formula in each cell, only five variables must be entered to produce the entire table. The five variables are the face value of the bonds, the selling price, the life of the bonds, the face interest rate, and the effective interest rate.

Notice that initially the carrying value (issue price) is greater than the face value, but that it gradually decreases toward the face value over the life of the bond issue. Notice also that interest payments exceed interest expense by the amount of the premium amortized and that interest expense decreases gradually over the life of the bond because it is based on the gradually decreasing carrying value (multiplied by the market interest rate).

Other Bonds Payable Issues

OBJECTIVE

6 Account for bonds issued between interest dates and make year-end adjustments

Related Text Assignments:
Q: 8
SE: 3, 5, 6, 7
E: 4, 5, 9, 10, 11, 12
P: 1, 2, 3, 5, 6, 7, 8

Teaching Note: Students will better understand the concept if you duplicate Figure 4 and explain the timeline shown. Point out that this procedure eliminates difficulties that would otherwise be encountered by the issuing corporation.

Several other issues arise in accounting for bonds payable. Among these issues are the sale of bonds between interest payment dates, the year-end accrual of bond interest expense, the retirement of bonds, and the conversion of bonds into common stock.

Sale of Bonds Between Interest Dates

Bonds may be issued on an interest payment date, as in the previous examples, but they are often issued between interest payment dates. The generally accepted method of handling bonds issued in this manner is to collect from investors the interest that would have accrued for the partial period preceding the issue date. Then, when the first interest period is completed, the corporation pays investors the interest for the entire period. Thus, the interest collected when bonds are sold is returned to investors on the next interest payment date.

There are two reasons for following this procedure. The first is a practical one. If a company issued bonds on several different days and did not collect the accrued interest, records would have to be maintained for each bondholder and date of purchase. In such a case, the interest due each bondholder would have to be computed on the basis of a different time period. Clearly, large bookkeeping costs would be incurred under this kind of system. On the other hand, if accrued interest is collected when the bonds are sold, on the interest payment date the corporation can pay the interest due for the entire period, eliminating the extra computations and costs.

The second reason for collecting accrued interest in advance is that when that amount is netted against the full interest paid on the interest payment date, the resulting interest expense represents the amount for the time the money was borrowed. For example, assume that the Vason Corporation sold $100,000 of 9 percent, five-year bonds for face value on May 1, 20x0, rather than on January 1, 20x0, the issue date. The entry to record the sale of the bonds is as follows:

Point to Emphasize: This schedule is based on the same principle as the schedule in Table 2 (amortization of a bond premium).

Teaching Note: Draw three rectangles of equal size to represent the monthly fixed mortgage payment. Divide each rectangle into two parts, principal and interest, and reduce the interest section with each successive rectangle. Point out that interest is always calculated first, and that principal reduction equals whatever remains of the mortgage payment.

Table 3. Monthly Payment Schedule on a $50,000, 12 Percent Mortgage

	A	B	C	D	E
Payment Date	Unpaid Balance at Beginning of Period	Monthly Payment	Interest for 1 Month at 1% on Unpaid Balance* (1% × A)	Reduction in Debt (B − C)	Unpaid Balance at End of Period (A − D)
June 1					$50,000
July 1	$50,000	$800	$500	$300	49,700
Aug. 1	49,700	800	497	303	49,397
Sept. 1	49,397	800	494	306	49,091

*Rounded to the nearest dollar.

Installment Notes Payable

Point to Emphasize: Although both mortgages payable and installment notes payable involve a series of payments, mortgages are used to finance real estate, whereas installment notes are used to finance other types of assets.

A long-term note can be paid at its maturity date by making a lump-sum payment that includes the amount borrowed plus the interest. Often, however, the terms of a note will call for a series of periodic payments. Such a note is called an **installment note payable** because each payment includes the interest to date plus a repayment of part of the amount that was borrowed.

For example, let's assume that on December 31, 20x1, $100,000 is borrowed on a 15 percent installment note, to be paid annually over five years. The entry to record the note is as follows:

A = L + OE
\+ \+

20x1			
Dec. 31	Cash	100,000	
	Notes Payable		100,000
	Borrowed $100,000 at 15 percent on a five-year installment note		

Payments of Accrued Interest Plus Equal Amounts of Principal Installment notes most often call for payments consisting of accrued interest plus equal amounts of principal repayment. The amount of each installment decreases because the amount of principal on which the accrued interest is owed decreases by the amount of the previous principal payment. Banks use installment notes to finance equipment purchases by businesses; such notes are also common for other kinds of purchases when payment is spread over several years. They can be set up on a revolving basis whereby the borrower can borrow additional funds as the installments are paid. Moreover, the interest rate charged on installment notes may be adjusted periodically as market interest rates change.

Point to Emphasize: The only way to set up equal principal payments each period is to vary the total payment made. That is, the total payment equals the uniform principal payment plus a decreasing interest payment.

On our sample installment note for $100,000, the principal declines by an equal amount each year for five years, or by $20,000 per year ($100,000 ÷ 5 years). The interest is calculated on the balance of the note that remains each year. Because the balance of the note declines each year, the amount of interest declines as well. For example, the entries for the first two payments of the installment note would be as follows:

A = L + OE
− − −

20x2			
Dec. 31	Notes Payable	20,000	
	Interest Expense	15,000	
	Cash		35,000
	Made first installment payment on note $100,000 × .15 = $15,000		

A = L + OE	20x3			
– – –	Dec. 31	Notes Payable	20,000	
		Interest Expense	12,000	
		Cash		32,000
		Made second installment payment on note $80,000 × .15 = $12,000		

Notice that the amount of the payment decreases from $35,000 to $32,000 because the amount of interest accrued on the note has decreased from $15,000 to $12,000. The difference of $3,000 is the interest on the $20,000 that was repaid in 20x2. Each subsequent payment decreases by $3,000, as the note itself decreases by $20,000 each year until it is fully paid. This example assumes that the repayment of principal and the interest rate remain the same from year to year.

PAYMENTS OF ACCRUED INTEREST PLUS INCREASING AMOUNTS OF PRINCIPAL Less commonly, the terms of an installment note, like those used for leasing equipment, may call for equal periodic (monthly or yearly) payments. Under this method, the interest is deducted from the equal payments to determine the amount by which the principal will be reduced each year.

Point to Emphasize: This situation, unlike the previous one, is exactly the same as a typical mortgage payment plan.

This procedure, presented in Table 4, is similar to that for mortgages, shown in Table 3. Each equal payment of $29,833 is allocated between interest and principal reduction. Each year the interest is calculated on the remaining principal. As the principal decreases, the annual interest also decreases, and because the payment remains the same, the amount by which the principal decreases becomes larger each year. The entries for the first two years, with data taken from Table 4, follow:

A = L + OE	20x2			
– – –	Dec. 31	Notes Payable	14,833	
		Interest Expense	15,000	
		Cash		29,833
		Made first installment payment on note		
A = L + OE	20x3			
– – –	Dec. 31	Notes Payable	17,058	
		Interest Expense	12,775	
		Cash		29,833
		Made second installment payment on note		

Similar entries will be made for the next three years.

Table 4. Payment Schedule on a $100,000, 15 Percent Installment Note

	A	B	C	D	E
Payment Date	Unpaid Principal at Beginning of Period	Equal Annual Payment	Interest for 1 Year at 15% on Unpaid Principal* (15% × A)	Reduction in Principal (B – C)	Unpaid Principal at End of Period (A – D)
					$100,000
20x2	$100,000	$29,833	$15,000	$14,833	85,167
20x3	85,167	29,833	12,775	17,058	68,109
20x4	68,109	29,833	10,216	19,617	48,492
20x5	48,492	29,833	7,274	22,559	25,933
20x6	25,933	29,833	3,900†	25,933	—

*Rounded to the nearest dollar.
†The last year's interest equals $3,900 ($29,833 – $25,933); it does not exactly equal $3,890 ($25,933 × .15) because of the cumulative effect of rounding.

How is the equal annual payment calculated? Because the $100,000 borrowed is the present value of the five equal annual payments at 15 percent interest, it is possible to use present value tables to calculate the annual payments. Using Table 4 from the appendix on future value and present value tables, here is the calculation:

Periodic Payment × Factor (Table 4 in the appendix on future value and present value tables: 15%, 5 periods) = Present Value

Periodic Payment × 3.352 = $100,000

Periodic Payment = $100,000 ÷ 3.352

= $29,833

Table 4 shows that five equal annual payments of $29,833 at 15 percent will reduce the principal balance to zero (except for the discrepancy due to rounding).

Long-Term Leases

Instructional Strategy: Assign SD 5 in class to small groups. Restate the expected response so that students stay focused. Collect the memos. One way to debrief is to ask two students to enact a role-play, with one as the CFO and the other as a staff member. A second approach to debriefing is to solicit one issue from each group until the list is complete. Grade memos as class participation or written assignment. Award bonus points for role playing.

Terminology Note: From the lessee's point of view, a lease is treated as either an operating lease or a capital lease. An operating lease is a true rental and is treated as such. A capital rental, however, is in substance an installment purchase, and the leased asset and related liability must be recognized at their present value.

There are several ways for a company to obtain new operating assets. One way is to borrow money and buy the asset. Another is to rent the equipment on a short-term lease. A third way is to obtain the equipment on a long-term lease. The first two methods do not create accounting problems. In the first case, the asset and liability are recorded at the amount paid, and the asset is subject to periodic depreciation. In the second case, the lease is short term in relation to the useful life of the asset, and the risks of ownership remain with the owner, called the **lessor**. This type of agreement is called an **operating lease**. It is proper accounting procedure for the renter, called the **lessee**, to treat operating lease payments as an expense and to debit the amount of each monthly payment to Rent Expense.

The third alternative, a long-term lease, is one of the fastest-growing ways of financing operating equipment in the United States today. It has several advantages. For instance, a long-term lease requires no immediate cash payment, and it costs less than a short-term lease. Acquiring the use of plant assets under long-term leases does cause several accounting challenges, however. Often, such leases cannot be canceled. Also, their duration may be about the same as the useful life of the asset. Finally, they may provide for the lessee to buy the asset at a nominal price at the end of the lease. The lease is much like an installment purchase because the risks of ownership are transferred to the lessee. Both the lessee's available assets and its legal obligations (liabilities) increase because the lessee must make a number of payments over the life of the asset.

The Financial Accounting Standards Board has described this kind of long-term lease as a **capital lease**. The term reflects the provisions of such a lease, which make the transaction more like a purchase or sale on installment. The FASB has ruled that in the case of a capital lease, the lessee must record an asset and a long-term liability equal to the present value of the total lease payments during the lease term. In doing so, the lessee must use the present value at the beginning of the lease.[7] Much like a mortgage payment, each lease payment consists partly of interest expense and partly of repayment of debt. Further, depreciation expense is figured on the asset and entered on the records of the lessee.

Point to Emphasize: Under a capital lease, depreciation must be recorded by the lessee, using any allowable method. Depreciation is *not* recorded under an operating lease, however, because the leased asset is not recognized on the lessee's books.

Suppose, for example, that Isaacs Company enters into a long-term lease for a machine used in its manufacturing operations. The lease terms call for an annual payment of $4,000 for six years, which approximates the useful life of the machine (see Table 5). At the end of the lease period, the title to the machine passes to Isaacs. This lease is clearly a capital lease and should be recorded as an asset and a liability according to FASB *Statement No. 13*.

A lease is a periodic payment for the right to use an asset or assets. Present value techniques can be used to place a value on the asset and on the corresponding liability associated with a capital lease. If Isaac's interest cost is 16 percent, the present value of the lease payments can be computed as follows:

Table 5. Payment Schedule on a 16 Percent Capital Lease

	A	B	C	D
Year	Lease Payment	Interest (16%) on Unpaid Obligation* (D × 16%)	Reduction of Lease Obligation (A − B)	Balance of Lease Obligation (D − C)
Beginning				$14,740
1	$ 4,000	$2,358	$ 1,642	13,098
2	4,000	2,096	1,904	11,194
3	4,000	1,791	2,209	8,985
4	4,000	1,438	2,562	6,423
5	4,000	1,028	2,972	3,451
6	4,000	549†	3,451	—
	$24,000	$9,260	$14,740	

*Computations are rounded to the nearest dollar.
†The last year's interest equals $549 ($4,000 − $3,451); it does not exactly equal $552 ($3,451 × .16) because of the cumulative effect of rounding.

Periodic Payment × Factor (Table 4 in the appendix on future value and present value tables: 16%, 6 periods) = Present Value

$4,000 × 3.685= $14,740

The entry to record the lease contract is as follows:

A = L + OE
+ +
	Equipment Under Capital Lease
	  Obligations Under Capital Lease
	    To record capital lease on machinery
		14,740	
			14,740

Equipment Under Capital Lease is classified as a long-term asset; Obligations Under Capital Lease is classified as a long-term liability. Each year, Isaacs must record depreciation on the leased asset. Using straight-line depreciation, a six-year life, and no salvage value, the following entry would record the depreciation:

A = L + OE
− −
	Depreciation Expense, Equipment
	Under Capital Lease
	  Accumulated Depreciation, Equipment
	  Under Capital Lease
	    To record depreciation expense on capital lease
		
		2,457
			
			2,457

The interest expense for each year is computed by multiplying the interest rate (16 percent) by the amount of the remaining lease obligation. Table 5 shows these calculations. Using the data in the table, the first lease payment would be recorded as follows:

A = L + OE
− − −
	Interest Expense (Column B)
	Obligations Under Capital Lease (Column C)
	  Cash
	    Made payment on capital lease
		2,358
		1,642
			
			4,000

Pensions

Most employees who work for medium- and large-sized companies are covered by some sort of pension plan. A **pension plan** is a contract between a company and its employees in which the company agrees to pay benefits to the employees after they retire. Many companies contribute the full cost of the pension, but frequently the employees also pay part of their salary or wages toward their pension. The contributions from both parties are typically paid into a **pension fund**, from which benefits are paid to retirees. In most cases, pension benefits consist of monthly payments to retired employees and other payments upon disability or death.

Teaching Note: Students often have difficulty understanding the difference between a defined contribution plan and a defined benefit plan. An example or two of actual pension situations, such as your own, would make the distinction clear.

There are two kinds of pension plans. Under a *defined contribution plan*, the employer is required to contribute an annual amount specified by an agreement between the company and its employees or by a resolution of the board of directors. Retirement payments depend on the amount of pension payments the accumulated contributions can support. Under a *defined benefit plan*, the employer's annual contribution is the amount required to fund pension liabilities arising from employment in the current year, but the exact amount will not be determined until the retirement and death of the current employees. Under a defined benefit plan, the amount of future benefits is fixed, but the annual contributions vary depending on assumptions about how much the pension fund will earn. Under a defined contribution plan, each year's contribution is fixed, but the benefits vary depending on how much the pension fund earns.

Point to Emphasize: Accounting for a defined benefit plan is far more complex than accounting for a defined contribution plan. Fortunately, accountants can rely on the calculations of professional actuaries, whose expertise includes the mathematics of pension plans.

Accounting for annual pension expense under a defined contribution plan is simple. After the required contribution is determined, Pension Expense is debited and a liability (or Cash) is credited.

Accounting for annual expense under a defined benefit plan is one of the most complex topics in accounting; thus, the intricacies are reserved for advanced courses. In concept, however, the procedure is simple. First, the amount of pension expense is determined. Then, if the amount of cash contributed to the fund is less than the pension expense, a liability results, which is reported on the balance sheet. If the amount of cash paid to the pension plan exceeds the pension expense, a prepaid expense arises and appears on the asset side of the balance sheet. For example, the annual report for Philip Morris Companies, Inc., includes among assets on the balance sheet a prepaid pension of $1,367 million.[8]

In accordance with the FASB's *Statement No. 87*, all companies should use the same actuarial method to compute pension expense.[9] However, because of the need to estimate many factors, such as the average remaining service life of active employees, the expected long-run return on pension plan assets, and expected future salary increases, the computation of pension expense is not simple. In addition, actuarial terminology further complicates pension accounting. In nontechnical terms, the pension expense for the year includes not only the cost of the benefits earned by people working during the year but interest costs on the total pension obligation (which are calculated on the present value of future benefits to be paid) and other adjustments. Those costs are reduced by the expected return on the pension fund assets.

All employers whose pension plans do not have sufficient assets to cover the present value of their pension benefit obligations (on a termination basis) must record the amount of the shortfall as a liability on their balance sheets. The investor no longer has to read the notes to the financial statements to learn whether or not the pension plan is fully funded. However, if a pension plan does have sufficient assets to cover its obligations, then no balance sheet reporting is required or permitted.

Other Postretirement Benefits

Point to Emphasize: Other postretirement benefits should be expensed when earned by the employee, not when received after retirement. This practice conforms to the matching rule.

In addition to pensions, many companies provide health care and other benefits to employees after retirement. In the past, these **other postretirement benefits** were accounted for on a cash basis; that is, they were expensed when the benefits were paid, after an employee had retired. The FASB has concluded, however, that those benefits are earned by the employee, and that, in accordance with the matching rule, they should be estimated and accrued during the period of time the employee is working.[10]

The estimates must take into account assumptions about retirement age, mortality, and, most significantly, future trends in health care benefits. Like pension benefits, such future benefits should be discounted to the current period. In a field test conducted by the Financial Executives Research Foundation, it was determined that the change to accrual accounting increased postretirement benefits by two to seven times the amount recognized on a cash basis.

Chapter Review

REVIEW OF LEARNING OBJECTIVES

Check out ACE, a self-quizzing program on chapter content, at http://college.hmco.com.

1. **Identify the management issues related to issuing long-term debt.** Long-term debt is used to finance long-term assets and business activities that have long-term earnings potential, such as property, plant, and equipment and research and development. In issuing long-term debt, management must decide (1) whether or not to have long-term debt, (2) how much long-term debt to have, and (3) what types of long-term debt to have. Among the advantages of long-term debt financing are that (1) common stockholders do not relinquish any control, (2) interest on debt is tax deductible, and (3) financial leverage may increase earnings. Disadvantages of long-term financing are that (1) interest and principal must be repaid on schedule, and (2) financial leverage can work against a company if a project is not successful.

2. **Identify and contrast the major characteristics of bonds.** A bond is a security that represents money borrowed from the investing public. When a corporation issues bonds, it enters into a contract, called a *bond indenture*, with the bondholders. The bond indenture identifies the major conditions of the bonds. A corporation can issue several types of bonds, each having different characteristics. For example, a bond issue may or may not require security (secured versus unsecured bonds). It may be payable at a single time (term bonds) or at several times (serial bonds).

3. **Record the issuance of bonds at face value and at a discount or premium.** When bonds are issued, the bondholders pay an amount equal to, less than, or greater than the bonds' face value. Bondholders pay face value for bonds when the interest rate on the bonds approximates the market rate for similar investments. The issuing corporation records the bond issue at face value as a long-term liability in the Bonds Payable account.

   Bonds are issued at an amount less than face value when their face interest rate is lower than the market rate for similar investments. The difference between the face value and the issue price is called a *discount* and is debited to Unamortized Bond Discount.

   When the face interest rate on bonds is greater than the market interest rate on similar investments, investors are willing to pay more than face value for the bonds. The difference between the issue price and the face value is called a *premium* and is credited to Unamortized Bond Premium.

4. **Use present values to determine the value of bonds.** The value of a bond is determined by summing the present values of (a) the series of fixed interest payments of the bond issue and (b) the single payment of the face value at maturity. Tables 3 and 4 in the appendix on future value and present value tables should be used in making these computations.

DECISION POINT: A USER'S FOCUS

Marriott International, Inc. Marriott International, Inc., is a world leader in lodging and contract services. The balance sheet, income statement, and statement of stockholders' equity presented in the company's annual report give an excellent picture of management's philosophy and performance.

Those three financial statements are essential to the evaluation of a company, but they do not tell the entire story. Some information that they do not contain is presented in a fourth statement, the statement of cash flows, as shown in the Financial Highlights on the next page.[1] This statement shows how much cash was generated by the company's operations during the past three years and how much was used in or came from investing and financing activities. Marriott feels that maintaining adequate cash flows is important to the future of the company. In fact, Marriott's emphasis on cash flows is reflected in its executive compensation plan for its chief executive officer and senior executive officers. A review of the plan indicates that a measure of cash flows, at the firm or business group level, is the financial measure given the highest weight in determining compensation. Why would Marriott emphasize cash flows to such an extent?

Strong cash flows are essential to management's key goal of liquidity. If cash flows exceed the amount needed for operations and expansion, the company will not have to borrow additional funds. The excess cash flows will be available to reduce the company's debt and improve its financial position by lowering its debt to equity ratio. Another reason for the emphasis on cash flows may be the belief that strong cash flows from operations create shareholder value or increase the market value of the company's stock.

The statement of cash flows demonstrates management's commitments for the company in ways that are not readily apparent in the other financial statements. For example, the statement of cash flows can show whether management's focus is on the short term or the long term. This statement is required by the FASB[2] and satisfies the FASB's long-held position that a primary objective of financial statements is to provide investors and creditors with information about a company's cash flows.[3]

Critical Thinking Question: How does Marriott's shift from earnings to cash flows as a means of evaluating managers benefit the company's profitability? **Answer:** The shift motivates managers to improve cash flows from operations. If underlying that improvement is better collection of receivables and lower levels of inventory, then earnings will benefit from lower asset financing costs.

Point to Emphasize: It is common practice to combine the change in cash for the period with the beginning cash to produce the ending cash balance.

Point to Emphasize: The statement of cash flows helps financial statement users answer many questions that cannot be answered readily by referring to the other three financial statements. It fills the gaps by disclosing a business's inflows and outflows of cash, categorized by activity, during the period.

Financial Highlights: Consolidated Statement of Cash Flows

Marriott International, Inc., and Subsidiaries

	1999	1998	1997
		(In millions)	
Operating Activities			
Net income	**$400**	$ 390	$ 324
Adjustments to reconcile to cash provided by operations:			
Depreciation and amortization	**162**	140	126
Income taxes	**87**	76	64
Timeshare activity, net	**(102)**	28	(118)
Other	**19**	(22)	88
Working capital changes:			
Accounts receivable	**(126)**	(104)	(190)
Inventories	**(17)**	15	(3)
Other current assets	**(38)**	(16)	(15)
Accounts payable and accruals	**326**	98	266
Cash provided by operations	**711**	605	542
Investing Activities			
Capital expenditures	**(929)**	(937)	(520)
Acquisitions	**(61)**	(48)	(859)
Dispositions of property and equipment	**436**	332	571
Loan advances	**(144)**	(48)	(95)
Loan collections and sales	**54**	169	47
Other	**(143)**	(192)	(190
Cash used in investing activities	**(787)**	(724)	(1,046)
Financing Activities			
Issuance of long-term debt	**831**	1,294	16
Repayment of long-term debt	**(173)**	(473)	(15)
Redemption of convertible subordinated debt	**(120)**	—	—
Issuance of common stock	**43**	15	—
Dividends paid	**(52)**	(37)	—
Purchase of treasury stock	**(354)**	(398)	—
Advances (to) from Old Marriott	—	(100)	576
Cash provided by (used in) financing activities	**175**	301	577
Increase/(Decrease) in Cash and Equivalents	**99**	182	73
Cash and Equivalents, beginning of year	**390**	208	135
Cash and Equivalents, end of year	**$489**	$ 390	$ 208

Instructional Strategy: Using information in P 1 and P 7, create a *Jeopardy* game. State a transaction and have students provide the cash flow classification. Use each item again, asking, "What is the effect on cash?" Spread difficult transactions as evenly as possible. Award prizes, which could include class participation points of varying levels, to top teams.

Overview of the Statement of Cash Flows

OBJECTIVE

1 Describe the statement of cash flows, and define *cash* and *cash equivalents*

Related Text Assignments:
Q: 1, 2
E: 1
P: 1, 7

The **statement of cash flows** shows how a company's operating, investing, and financing activities have affected cash during an accounting period. It explains the net increase (or decrease) in cash during the accounting period. For purposes of preparing this statement, **cash** is defined to include both cash and cash equivalents. **Cash equivalents** are defined by the FASB as short-term, highly liquid investments, including money market accounts, commercial paper, and U.S. Treasury bills. A company maintains cash equivalents to earn interest on cash that would otherwise remain unused temporarily. Suppose, for example, that a company has $1,000,000 that it will not need for 30 days. To earn a return on this amount, the company may place the cash in an account that earns interest (such as a money market account), it may loan the cash to another corporation by purchasing that corporation's short-term notes (commercial paper), or it may purchase a short-term obligation of the U.S. government (Treasury bills). In this context, short-term refers to original maturities of 90 days or less. Since cash and cash

VIDEO CASE

Goodyear Tire & Rubber Company

Objectives

- To state the purposes of the statement of cash flows.
- To identify the three components of the statement of cash flows.
- To identify the reasons why cash flows from operating activities usually differs from net income.
- To understand the importance of cash flows from investing and financing activities.

Background for the Case

Goodyear was founded in 1898 by Frank Seiberling, who borrowed $3,500 to start a bicycle tire factory and subsequently began making tires for horseless carriages. Today Goodyear is the world's largest tire and rubber company, with factories in 28 countries and more than 100,000 employees. In a recent year, sales exceeded $14 billion.

In addition to Goodyear brand tires, the company makes Dunlop, Kelly, Fulda, Lee, Sava, and Debica tires and rubber products for the automotive and industrial markets.

Goodyear's vision is to be ranked by all measures as the best tire and rubber company in the world. It intends to accomplish this vision by achieving

- fast and profitable growth in all core businesses.
- a number 1 or 2 market position.
- strategic acquisitions and expansions.
- lowest cost producer.

To achieve these objectives, especially "fast and profitable growth" and "strategic acquisitions and expansions," Goodyear will need adequate funding. Management expects the funding to come from strong cash flows, divestiture of underperforming, nonstrategic assets, and debit issues. Within this framework, management must maintain the company's financial health and a strong balance sheet, with a debt to debt plus equity ratio of 25 to 30 percent.

Goodyear's performance in meeting the challenge of achieving adequate funding requires an ability to read and understand the statement of cash flows.

For more information about Goodyear Tire & Rubber Company, visit the company's web site through the Needles Accounting Resource Center at:
http://college.hmco.com

Required

1. What are the purposes and three main components of the statement of cash flows?
2. What is the most important amount in the statement of cash flows and why?
3. What is the relationship of cash flows from operating activities to net income for Goodyear, and how do you account for the difference?
4. What are the principal investing and financing activities for Goodyear?

Discussion Question: Why are money market accounts, commercial paper (short-term notes), and U.S. Treasury bills considered cash equivalents? **Answer:** Because they are highly liquid, temporary (90 days or less) holding places for cash that is not currently needed to operate the business. They can be converted quickly into cash if needed.

equivalents are considered the same, transfers between the Cash account and cash equivalents are not treated as cash receipts or cash payments. In effect, cash equivalents are combined with the Cash account on the statement of cash flows.

Cash equivalents should not be confused with short-term investments or marketable securities, which are not combined with the Cash account on the statement of cash flows. Purchases of marketable securities are treated as cash outflows and sales of marketable securities as cash inflows on the statement of cash flows. In this chapter, cash will be assumed to include cash and cash equivalents.

Purposes of the Statement of Cash Flows

OBJECTIVE

2 State the principal purposes and uses of the statement of cash flows

Related Text Assignments:
Q: 3, 4

The primary purpose of the statement of cash flows is to provide information about a company's cash receipts and cash payments during an accounting period. A secondary purpose of the statement is to provide information about a company's operating, investing, and financing activities during the accounting period. Some information about those activities may be inferred by examining other financial statements, but it is on the statement of cash flows that all the transactions affecting cash are summarized.

Internal and External Uses of the Statement of Cash Flows

Point to Emphasize: Management uses the statement of cash flows to make various investing and financing decisions. Investors and creditors, on the other hand, use the statement primarily to assess cash flow prospects, as outlined in *Statement of Financial Accounting Concepts No. 1* of the FASB.

The statement of cash flows is useful internally to management and externally to investors and creditors. Management uses the statement to assess liquidity, to determine dividend policy, and to evaluate the effects of major policy decisions involving investments and financing. In other words, management may use the statement to determine if short-term financing is needed to pay current liabilities, to decide whether to raise or lower dividends, and to plan for investing and financing needs.

Investors and creditors will find the statement useful in assessing the company's ability to manage cash flows, to generate positive future cash flows, to pay its liabilities, to pay dividends and interest, and to anticipate its need for additional financing. Also, they may use the statement to explain the differences between net income on the income statement and the net cash flows generated from operations. In addition, the statement shows both the cash and the noncash effects of investing and financing activities during the accounting period.

Classification of Cash Flows

OBJECTIVE

3 Identify the principal components of the classifications of cash flows, and state the significance of noncash investing and financing transactions

Related Text Assignments:
Q: 5, 6
SE: 1
E: 1
P: 1, 7
SD: 2, 3
FRA: 4

The statement of cash flows classifies cash receipts and cash payments into the categories of operating, investing, and financing activities. The components of these activities are illustrated in Figure 1 and summarized below.

1. **Operating activities** include the cash effects of transactions and other events that enter into the determination of net income. Included in this category as cash inflows are cash receipts from customers for goods and services, interest and dividends received on loans and investments, and sales of trading securities. Included as cash outflows are cash payments for wages, goods and services, expenses, interest, taxes, and purchases of trading securities. In effect, the income statement is changed from an accrual to a cash basis.

2. **Investing activities** include the acquiring and selling of long-term assets, the acquiring and selling of marketable securities other than trading securities or cash equivalents, and the making and collecting of loans. Cash inflows include the cash received from selling long-term assets and marketable securities and from collecting loans. Cash outflows include the cash expended for purchases of long-term assets and marketable securities and the cash loaned to borrowers.

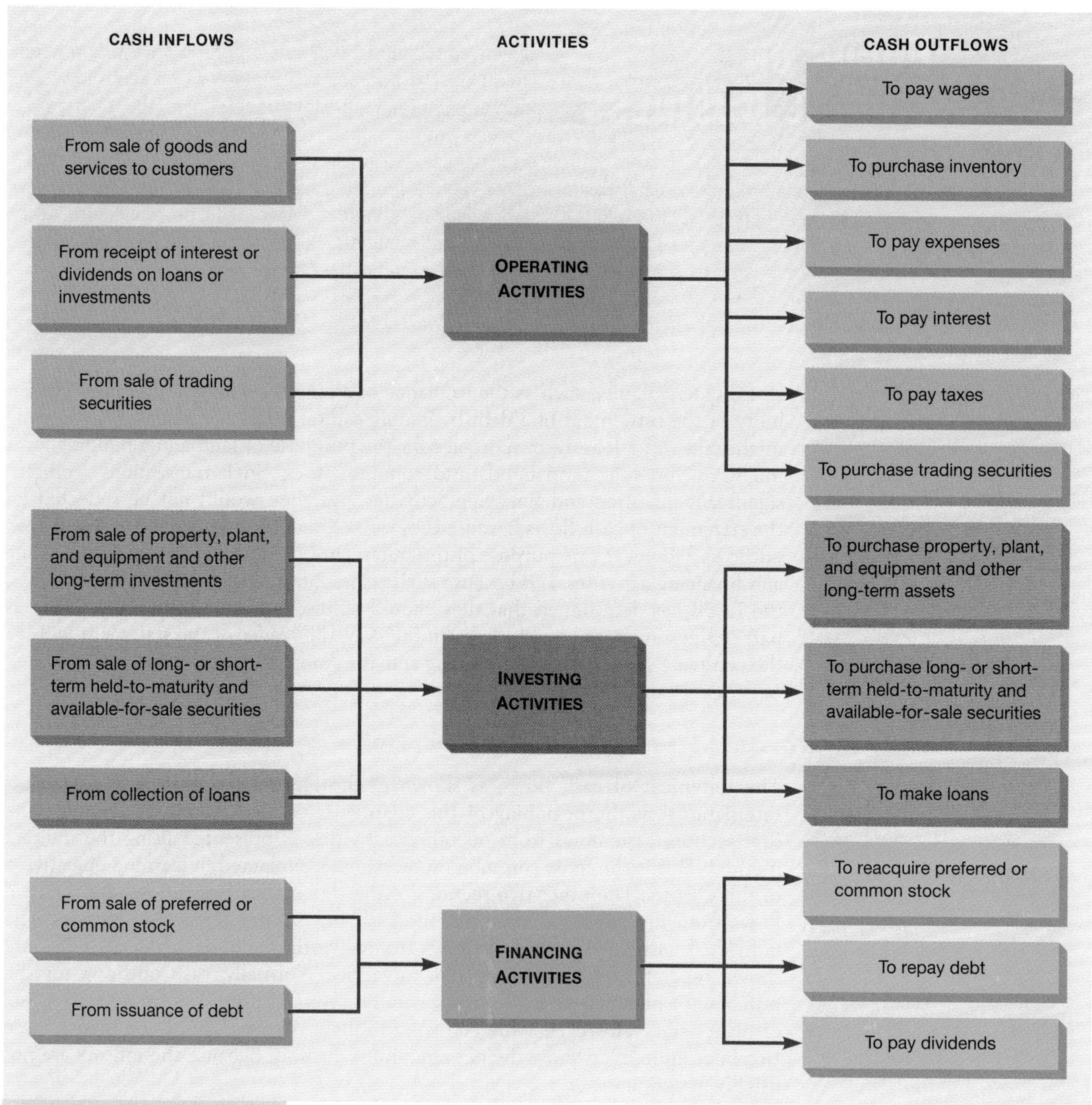

Figure 1
Classification of Cash Inflows and Cash Outflows

Teaching Note: Refer to a completed statement of cash flows, like the ones in Exhibits 4 and 7, so students can become aware of their goal. Then distinguish among the three types of activities. Operating activities arise from the day-to-day sale of goods and services, investing activities involve long-term assets and investments, and financing activities deal with stockholders' equity accounts and debt (borrowing).

3. **Financing activities** include obtaining resources from or returning resources to owners and providing them with a return on their investment, and obtaining resources from creditors and repaying the amounts borrowed or otherwise settling the obligations. Cash inflows include the proceeds from issues of stocks and from short-term and long-term borrowing. Cash outflows include the repayments of loans (excluding interest) and payments to owners, including cash dividends. Treasury stock transactions are also considered financing activities. Repayments of accounts payable or accrued liabilities are not considered repayments of loans under financing activities, but are classified as cash outflows under operating activities.

A company will occasionally engage in significant **noncash investing and financing transactions** involving only long-term assets, long-term liabilities, or

FOCUS ON INTERNATIONAL BUSINESS

Despite the importance of the statement of cash flows in assessing the liquidity of companies in the United States, considerable variation in its use and format has existed in other countries. For example, the principal directives related to financial reporting for the European Union do not address the statement of cash flows. In many countries, the statement shows the change in working capital instead of the change in cash and cash equivalents. However, international accounting standards require the statement of cash flows, and international financial markets expect it to be presented. As a result, most multinational companies include the statement in their financial reports.

Discussion Question: If noncash investing and financing transactions do not produce cash flows, why must they be disclosed? **Answer:** Because they involve activities that might be considered important to the reader. Also, many noncash transactions involve a simultaneous inflow and outflow of cash and will require cash flows in the future.

stockholders' equity, such as the exchange of a long-term asset for a long-term liability or the settlement of a debt by issuing capital stock. For instance, a company might take out a long-term mortgage for the purchase of land and a building, or it might convert long-term bonds into common stock. Such transactions represent significant investing and financing activities, but they would not be reflected on the statement of cash flows because they do not involve either cash inflows or cash outflows. However, one purpose of the statement of cash flows is to show investing and financing activities, and because such transactions will affect future cash flows, the FASB has determined that they should be disclosed in a separate schedule as part of the statement of cash flows. In this way, the reader of the statement will see the company's investing and financing activities more clearly.

Format of the Statement of Cash Flows

The statement of cash flows, as shown in the Financial Highlights for Marriott International at the beginning of this chapter, is divided into three sections. The first section, cash flows from operating activities, is presented using the indirect method. This is the most common method and is explained in learning objective 5 of this chapter. The other two sections of the statement of cash flows are the cash flows from investing activities and the cash flows from financing activities. The individual cash inflows and outflows from investing and financing activities are shown separately in their respective categories. Normally, cash outflows for the purchase of plant assets are shown separately from cash inflows from the disposal of plant assets. However, some companies follow the practice of combining these two lines in order to show the net amount of outflow, because the inflows are not usually material.

A reconciliation of the beginning and ending balances of cash is shown near the bottom of the statement. It shows that Marriott International had a net increase in cash of $99 million in 1999, which together with the beginning balance of $390 million results in $489 million of cash and cash equivalents on hand at the end of the year.

Analyzing the Statement of Cash Flows

OBJECTIVE

4 Analyze the statement of cash flows

Like the other financial statements, the statement of cash flows can be analyzed to reveal significant relationships. Two areas analysts examine when studying a company are cash-generating efficiency and free cash flow.

Related Text Assignments:
Q: 7, 8
SE: 2, 3
E: 2
P: 2, 3, 4, 6, 8, 9
SD: 3, 4
FRA: 1, 2, 3, 4, 5

Cash-Generating Efficiency

Cash-generating efficiency is the ability of a company to generate cash from its current or continuing operations. Three ratios are helpful in measuring cash-generating efficiency: cash flow yield, cash flows to sales, and cash flows to assets. These ratios are computed and discussed below for Marriott International for 1999.[4] Data for the computations are obtained from the Financial Highlights for Marriott International at the beginning of this chapter and below; all dollar amounts used to compute the ratios are stated in millions.

Enrichment Note: The cash flow yield enables users to assess whether sufficient cash flows underlie earnings. Serious questions would be raised if cash flow yield was less than 1.0. For example, receivables and inventories could be growing too fast, perhaps signaling a slowdown in sales growth or a problem managing receivables collection or inventory levels.

Point to Emphasize: The change in cash shown in the comparative balance sheets provides a check figure for the statement of cash flows.

Cash flow yield is the ratio of net cash flows from operating activities to net income, as follows:

$$\text{Cash Flow Yield} = \frac{\text{Net Cash Flows from Operating Activities}}{\text{Net Income}}$$

$$= \frac{\$711}{\$400}$$

$$= 1.8 \text{ times}$$

Marriott International provides a good cash flow yield of 1.8 times; that is, operating activities are generating about 80 percent more cash flow than net income. If special items, such as discontinued operations, appear on the income statement and are material, income from continuing operations should be used as the denominator.

Financial Highlights for Marriott International
(In millions of dollars)

	1999	1998	1997
Net Sales	$8,739	$7,968	$7,236
Total Assets	7,324	6,233	5,161

Cash flows to sales is the ratio of net cash flows from operating activities to sales.

$$\text{Cash Flows to Sales} = \frac{\text{Net Cash Flows from Operating Activities}}{\text{Net Sales}}$$

$$= \frac{\$711}{\$8{,}739}$$

$$= 8.1\%$$

Marriott generates cash flows to sales of 8.1 percent. The company generated a positive but relatively small percentage of net cash from sales.

Cash flows to assets is the ratio of net cash flows from operating activities to average total assets, as follows:

$$\text{Cash Flows to Assets} = \frac{\text{Net Cash Flows from Operating Activities}}{\text{Average Total Assets}}$$

$$= \frac{\$711}{(\$7{,}324 + \$6{,}233) \div 2}$$

$$= 10.5\%$$

The cash flows to assets is higher than cash flows to sales because Marriott has a good asset turnover ratio (sales ÷ average total assets) of approximately 1.3 times (10.5% ÷ 8.1%). Cash flows to sales and cash flows to assets are closely related to the profitability measures profit margin and return on assets. They exceed those measures by the amount of the cash flow yield ratio because cash flow yield is the ratio of net cash flows from operating activities to net income.

Instructional Strategy: Ask students to compute the cash flow measures called for in FRA 1 as homework. Then, in class, form small groups and have them complete the required analysis. Remind students that in evaluating any measure, it's important to look in detail at all components. Discuss the groups' results, and, on the chalkboard, list all causes of the decline in cash flow performance.

Although Marriott's cash flow yield and cash flows to assets are relatively good, its efficiency at generating cash flows from operating activities, as measured by cash flows to sales, could be improved.

Free Cash Flow

It would seem logical for the analysis to move along to investing and financing activities. For example, in 1999 Marriott has a net cash outflow of $787 million in the investing activities section, which could indicate that the company is expanding. However, that figure mixes capital expenditures for plant assets, which reflect management's expansion of operations, with the acquisition of hotel chains and loans and repayments. Also, cash flows from financing activities provided $175 million, but that figure combines financing activities associated with long-term debt and stocks with dividends paid to stockholders. While something can be learned by looking at those broad categories, many analysts find it more informative to go beyond them and focus on a computation called free cash flow.

Point to Emphasize: Free cash flow should be interpreted in light of the company's overall need for cash. For instance, the purchase of treasury stock will also reduce the amount of cash that is free for operating uses.

Free cash flow is the amount of cash that remains after deducting the funds the company must commit to continue operating at its planned level. The commitments must cover current or continuing operations, interest, income taxes, dividends, and net capital expenditures. Cash requirements for current or continuing operations, interest, and income taxes must be paid or the company's creditors and the government can take legal action. Although the payment of dividends is not strictly required, dividends normally represent a commitment to stockholders. If these payments are reduced or eliminated, stockholders will be unhappy and the price of the company's stock will fall. Net capital expenditures represent management's plans for the future.

If free cash flow is positive, it means that the company has met all of its planned cash commitments and has cash available to reduce debt or expand. A negative free cash flow means that the company will have to sell investments, borrow money, or issue stock in the short term to continue at its planned levels. If free cash flow remains negative for several years, a company may not be able to raise cash by issuing stock or bonds.

Since cash commitments for current or continuing operations, interest, and income taxes are incorporated in cash flows from current operations, free cash flow for Marriott is computed as follows (in millions):

$$\begin{aligned}\text{Free Cash Flow} &= \text{Net Cash Flows from Operating Activities} - \text{Dividends} \\ &\quad - \text{Purchases of Plant Assets} + \text{Sales of Plant Assets} \\ &= \$711 - \$52 - \$929 + \$436 \\ &= \$166\end{aligned}$$

Enrichment Note: Dividends should be a distribution of the operating success of the firm. If a company has negative net cash flows from operating activities or an amount of net cash flows inadequate to cover payment of dividends, it will have to borrow money, issue stock, or sell assets to pay a dividend.

Purchases and sales of plant assets appear in the investing activities section of the statement of cash flows. Marriott reports both capital expenditures and dispositions of property and equipment. Dividends are found in the financing activities section. Marriott has positive free cash flow of $166 million due primarily to its strong operating cash flow of $711 million and $436 million cash received on disposal of property and equipment. The cash provided by financing activities was the lowest in three years, only $175 million, and possible because of increasing cash provided by operations. The company repaid long-term debt of $293 million ($173 + $120) while issuing new debt of $831 million. Marriott also issued common stock in the amount of $43 million and purchased treasury stock for $354 million. The result is that financing activities were a positive $175 million.

FOCUS ON BUSINESS PRACTICE

Because the statement of cash flows has been around for only a decade, no generally accepted analyses have yet been developed. For example, the term *free cash flow* is commonly used in the business press, but there is no agreement on its definition. An article in *Forbes* defines *free cash flow* as "cash available after paying out capital expenditures and dividends, *but before taxes and interest*"[5] [emphasis added]. In *The Wall Street Journal,* free cash flow was defined as "operating income less maintenance-level capital expenditures."[6] The definition with which we are most in agreement is the one used in *Business Week,* which is net cash flows from operating activities less net capital expenditures and dividends. This "measures truly discretionary funds—company money that an owner could pocket without harming the business."[7]

Cash flows can vary from year to year, so it is best to look at trends in cash flow measures over several years when analyzing a company's cash flows. Marriott's cash flow yield has shown little variation over the past three years. Management sums up in the annual report:

> **Cash from Operations**
> The company's operating cash flow is stable, and typically does not fluctuate widely within an economic cycle.[8]

The Indirect Method of Preparing the Statement of Cash Flows

OBJECTIVE

5 **Use the indirect method to determine cash flows from operating activities**

Related Text Assignments:
Q: 9, 10, 11
SE: 4, 5
E: 3, 4, 5
SD: 1

To demonstrate the preparation of the statement of cash flows, we will work through an example step by step. The data for this example are presented in Exhibits 1 and 2. Those two exhibits present Ryan Corporation's balance sheets for December 31, 20x1 and 20x0, and its 20x1 income statement. Since the changes in the balance sheet accounts will be used for analysis, those changes are shown in Exhibit 1. Whether the change in each account is an increase or a decrease is also shown. In addition, Exhibit 2 contains data about transactions that affected noncurrent accounts. Those transactions would be identified by the company's accountants from the records.

There are four steps in preparing the statement of cash flows:

1. Determine cash flows from operating activities.
2. Determine cash flows from investing activities.
3. Determine cash flows from financing activities.
4. Use the information obtained in the first three steps to compile the statement of cash flows.

Common Student Confusion: Because so much of financial accounting focuses on accrual accounting, students may have difficulty converting to a cash accounting basis. Explain that net income doesn't necessarily represent the cash generated from operating activities because it is based primarily on revenue earned (not received) and expenses incurred (not paid).

Determining Cash Flows from Operating Activities

The first step in preparing the statement of cash flows is to determine cash flows from operating activities. The income statement indicates a business's success or failure in earning an income from its operating activities, but it does not reflect the inflow and outflow of cash from those activities. The reason is that the income statement is prepared on an accrual basis. Revenues are recorded even though the

Ryan Corporation
Comparative Balance Sheets
December 31, 20x1 and 20x0

	20x1	20x0	Change	Increase or Decrease
Assets				
Current Assets				
Cash	$ 46,000	$ 15,000	$ 31,000	Increase
Accounts Receivable (net)	47,000	55,000	(8,000)	Decrease
Inventory	144,000	110,000	34,000	Increase
Prepaid Expenses	1,000	5,000	(4,000)	Decrease
Total Current Assets	$238,000	$185,000	$ 53,000	
Investments Available for Sale	$115,000	$127,000	($ 12,000)	Decrease
Plant Assets				
Plant Assets	$715,000	$505,000	$210,000	Increase
Accumulated Depreciation	(103,000)	(68,000)	(35,000)	Increase
Total Plant Assets	$612,000	$437,000	$175,000	
Total Assets	$965,000	$749,000	$216,000	
Liabilities				
Current Liabilities				
Accounts Payable	$ 50,000	$ 43,000	$ 7,000	Increase
Accrued Liabilities	12,000	9,000	3,000	Increase
Income Taxes Payable	3,000	5,000	(2,000)	Decrease
Total Current Liabilities	$ 65,000	$ 57,000	$ 8,000	
Long-Term Liabilities				
Bonds Payable	295,000	245,000	50,000	Increase
Total Liabilities	$360,000	$302,000	$ 58,000	
Stockholders' Equity				
Common Stock, $5 par value	$276,000	$200,000	$ 76,000	Increase
Paid-in Capital in Excess of Par Value, Common	189,000	115,000	74,000	Increase
Retained Earnings	140,000	132,000	8,000	Increase
Total Stockholders' Equity	$605,000	$447,000	$158,000	
Total Liabilities and Stockholders' Equity	$965,000	$749,000	$216,000	

Exhibit 1
Comparative Balance Sheets with Changes in Accounts Indicated for Ryan Corporation

Point to Emphasize: The direct and indirect methods relate only to the operating activities section of the statement of cash flows. They are both acceptable for financial reporting purposes.

cash for them may not have been received, and expenses are recorded even though the cash for them may not have been expended. As a result, to arrive at cash flows from operations, the figures on the income statement must be converted from an accrual basis to a cash basis.

There are two methods of converting the income statement from an accrual basis to a cash basis: the direct method and the indirect method. Under the **direct method**, each item on the income statement is adjusted from the accrual basis to the cash basis. The result is a statement that begins with cash receipts from sales

Exhibit 2
Income Statement and Other Information on Noncurrent Accounts for Ryan Corporation

Ryan Corporation Income Statement For the Year Ended December 31, 20x1		
Net Sales		$698,000
Cost of Goods Sold		520,000
Gross Margin		$178,000
Operating Expenses (including Depreciation Expense of $37,000)		147,000
Operating Income		$ 31,000
Other Income (Expenses)		
Interest Expense	($23,000)	
Interest Income	6,000	
Gain on Sale of Investments	12,000	
Loss on Sale of Plant Assets	(3,000)	(8,000)
Income Before Income Taxes		$ 23,000
Income Taxes		7,000
Net Income		$ 16,000

Other transactions affecting noncurrent accounts during 20x1:

1. Purchased investments in the amount of $78,000.
2. Sold investments for $102,000 that cost $90,000.
3. Purchased plant assets in the amount of $120,000.
4. Sold plant assets that cost $10,000 with accumulated depreciation of $2,000 for $5,000.
5. Issued $100,000 of bonds at face value in a noncash exchange for plant assets.
6. Repaid $50,000 of bonds at face value at maturity.
7. Issued 15,200 shares of $5 par value common stock for $150,000.
8. Paid cash dividends in the amount of $8,000.

Point to Emphasize: The direct and indirect methods will always produce the same net figure. The direct method, however, is more easily understood by the average reader because it results in a more straightforward presentation of operating cash flows than does the indirect method.

and interest and deducts cash payments for purchases, operating expenses, interest payments, and income taxes to arrive at net cash flows from operating activities. The **indirect method**, on the other hand, does not require the individual adjustment of each item on the income statement, but lists only those adjustments necessary to convert net income to cash flows from operations. Because the indirect method is more common, it will be used to illustrate the conversion of the income statement to a cash basis in the sections that follow. The direct method is presented in a supplemental objective at the end of the chapter.

FOCUS ON BUSINESS PRACTICE

The direct method and the indirect method of determining cash flows from operating activities produce the same results. If the direct method is used, a reconciliation of net income to net cash flows from operating activities must be provided in a separate schedule. The FASB recommends, but does not require, the direct method, but a survey of large companies showed that an overwhelming majority, 98 percent, chose to use the indirect method.[9] The reasons for choosing the indirect method vary, but chief financial officers tend to prefer it because it is easier and less expensive to implement. Also, with the required reconciliation under the direct method, the same information is provided as under the indirect method.

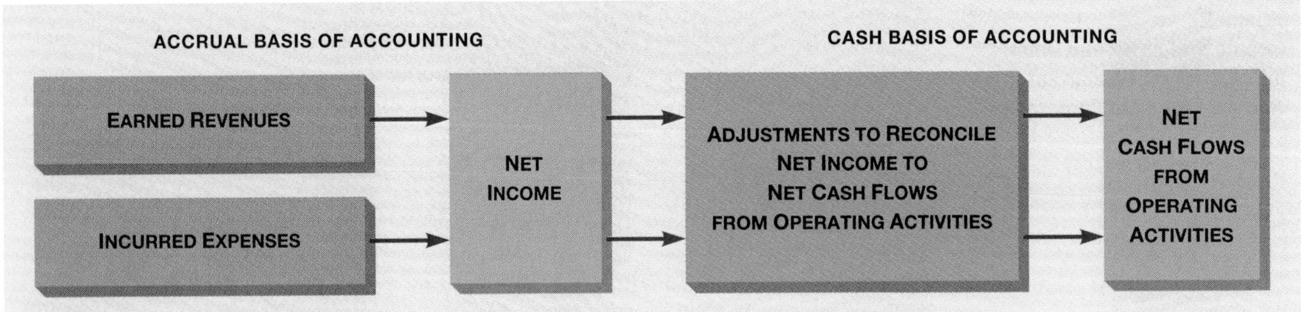

Figure 2
Indirect Method of Determining Net Cash Flows from Operating Activities

The indirect method, as illustrated in Figure 2, focuses on items from the income statement that must be adjusted to reconcile net income to net cash flows from operating activities. The items that require attention are those that affect net income but not net cash flows from operating activities, such as depreciation and amortization, gains and losses, and changes in the balances of current asset and current liability accounts. The reconciliation of Ryan Corporation's net income to net cash flows from operating activities is shown in Exhibit 3. Each adjustment is discussed in the following sections.

Point to Emphasize: The indirect method begins with net income and adjusts up or down to produce net cash flows from operating activities.

Common Student Error: Students often have the mistaken notion that items such as depreciation expense represent cash inflows because they are added back to net income under the indirect method. These items, however, represent no cash flow and are added back to cancel the deductions taken when arriving at accrual-based net income.

DEPRECIATION Cash payments for plant assets, intangibles, and natural resources occur when the assets are purchased and are reflected as investing activities on the statement of cash flows at that time. When depreciation expense, amortization expense, and depletion expense appear on the income statement, they simply indicate allocations of the costs of the original purchases to the current accounting period; they do not affect net cash flows in the current period. The amount of such expenses can usually be found by referring to the income statement or a note to the financial statements. For Ryan Corporation, the income statement reveals depreciation expense of $37,000, which would have been recorded as follows:

A = L + OE			
− −			

	Debit	Credit
Depreciation Expense	37,000	
Accumulated Depreciation		37,000
To record annual depreciation on plant assets		

Point to Emphasize: Operating expenses on the income statement include depreciation expense, which does not require a cash outlay.

The recording of depreciation involved no outlay of cash even though depreciation expense appears on the income statement. Thus, to derive cash flows from operations, an adjustment for depreciation is needed to increase net income by the amount of depreciation recorded.

GAINS AND LOSSES Gains and losses that appear on the income statement also do not affect cash flows from operating activities and need to be removed from this section of the statement of cash flows. The cash receipts generated from the disposal of the assets that resulted in the gains or losses are shown in the investing section of the statement of cash flows. Thus, gains and losses are removed from net income (preventing double counting) to reconcile net income to cash flows from operating activities. For example, on the income statement, Ryan Corporation showed a $12,000 gain on the sale of investments, and this is subtracted from net income to reconcile net income to net cash flows from operating activities. The reason for this is that the $12,000 is already included (added) in the investing activities section as part of the $102,000 cash from the sale of the investment. Because the gain is included in the calculation of net income, the $12,000 gain needs to be subtracted to prevent double counting. Also, Ryan Corporation showed a $3,000 loss on the sale of plant assets. Following the same logic, the $3,000 loss is already reflected in the $5,000 sale of plant assets in the investing activities section. Thus, the $3,000 is added to net income to reconcile net income to net cash flows from operating activities.

Parenthetical Note: It is possible to earn a profit yet realize a negative cash flow from operating activities. Similarly, it is possible to suffer a net loss yet realize a positive cash flow from operating activities.

Clarification Note: Gains and losses by themselves do not represent cash flows; they are merely bookkeeping adjustments. For example, when a long-term asset is sold, it is the *proceeds* (cash received), not the gain or loss, that constitute cash flow.

Flanders Corporation Income Statement For the Year Ended June 30, 20x2		
Sales		$2,081,800
Cost of Goods Sold		1,312,600
Gross Margin		$ 769,200
Operating Expenses (including Depreciation Expense of $120,000)		378,400
Income from Operations		$ 390,800
Other Income (Expenses)		
Loss on Disposal of Equipment	($ 8,000)	
Interest Expense	(75,200)	(83,200)
Income Before Income Taxes		$ 307,600
Income Taxes		68,400
Net Income		$ 239,200

Flanders Corporation Comparative Balance Sheets June 30, 20x2 and 20x1	20x2	20x1
Assets		
Cash	$ 334,000	$ 40,000
Accounts Receivable (net)	200,000	240,000
Inventory	360,000	440,000
Prepaid Expenses	1,200	2,000
Property, Plant, and Equipment	1,256,000	1,104,000
Accumulated Depreciation, Property, Plant, and Equipment	(366,000)	(280,000)
Total Assets	$1,785,200	$1,546,000
Liabilities and Stockholders' Equity		
Accounts Payable	$ 128,000	$ 84,000
Notes Payable (due in 90 days)	60,000	160,000
Income Taxes Payable	52,000	36,000
Mortgage Payable	720,000	560,000
Common Stock, $5 par value	400,000	400,000
Retained Earnings	425,200	306,000
Total Liabilities and Stockholders' Equity	$1,785,200	$1,546,000

LO 4 The Work Sheet and the
LO 7 Statement of Cash Flows:
LO 8 Indirect Method

P 9. Use the information for O'Brien Corporation given in **P 6** to answer the following requirements.

REQUIRED

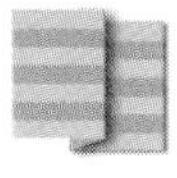

1. Prepare a work sheet to gather information for the preparation of the statement of cash flows.
2. Answer requirements **1, 2,** and **3** in **P 6** if that problem was not assigned.

Expanding Your Critical Thinking, Communication, and Interpersonal Skills

Skills Development

Conceptual Analysis

SD 1. **LO 5 SO 9 Direct Versus Indirect Method**

Collins Industries, Inc., a manufacturing company, uses the direct method of presenting cash flows from operating activities in its statement of cash flows. As noted in the text, most companies use the indirect method.[10]

Explain the difference between the direct and indirect methods of presenting cash flows from operating activities. Then choose either the direct or the indirect method and tell why it is the best way of presenting cash flows from operations. Be prepared to discuss your opinion in class.

Group Activity. Assign in-class groups. Have each group develop a position for either the direct or indirect method of presentation and defend that position in a debate.

Ethical Dilemma

SD 2. **LO 3 Ethics and Cash Flow Classifications**

Chemical Waste Treatment, Inc., is a fast-growing company that disposes of chemical wastes. The company has an $800,000 line of credit at its bank. One section in the loan agreement says that the ratio of cash flows from operations to interest expense must exceed 3.0. If this ratio falls below 3.0, the company must reduce the balance outstanding on its line of credit to one-half the total line if the funds borrowed against the line of credit exceed that amount.

After the end of the fiscal year, the controller informs the president: "We will not meet the ratio requirements on our line of credit in 20x2 because interest expense was $1.2 million and cash flows from operations were $3.2 million. Also, we have borrowed 100 percent of our line of credit. We do not have the cash to reduce the credit line by $400,000." The president says, "This is a serious situation. To pay our ongoing bills, we need our bank to increase our line of credit, not decrease it. What can we do?" "Do you recall the $500,000 two-year note payable for equipment?" replied the controller. "It is now classified as 'Proceeds from Notes Payable' in cash flows provided from financing activities in the statement of cash flows. If we move it to cash flows from operations and call it 'Increase in Payables,' it would increase cash flows from operations to $3.7 million and put us over the limit." "Well, do it," ordered the president. "It surely doesn't make any difference where it is on the statement. It is an increase in both places. It would be much worse for our company in the long term if we failed to meet this ratio requirement."

What is your opinion of the president's reasoning? Is the president's order ethical? Who benefits and who is harmed if the controller follows the president's order? What are management's alternatives? What would you do?

Research Activity

SD 3. **LO 3 LO 4 Basic Research Skills**

Select the annual reports of three corporations, using one or more of the following sources: your library or the Fingraph® Financial Analyst™ CD-ROM software that

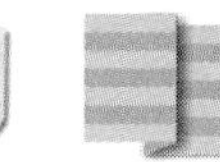

Cash Flow | CD-ROM | Communication | Critical Thinking | Ethics | General Ledger | Group Activity | Hot Links to Real Companies | International | Internet | Key Ratio | Memo | Spreadsheet

accompanies this text. You may choose them from the same industry or at random, at the direction of your instructor. (If you did a related exercise in a previous chapter, use the same three companies.) Prepare a table with a column for each corporation. Then, for any year covered by the statement of cash flows, answer the following questions: Does the company use the direct or the indirect approach? Is net income more or less than net cash flows from operating activities? What are the major causes of differences between net income and net cash flows from operating activities? Compute cash flow efficiency ratios and free cash flow. Does the dividend appear secure? Did the company make significant capital expenditures during the year? How were the expenditures financed? Do you notice anything unusual about the investing and financing activities of your companies? Do the investing and financing activities provide any insights into management's plan for each company? If so, what are they? Be prepared to discuss your findings in class.

Decision-Making Practice

SD 4. May Hashimi, president of ***Hashimi Print Gallery, Inc.,*** is examining the following income statement, which has just been handed to her by her accountant, Lou Klein, CPA.

LO 4 Analysis of Cash Flow
LO 7 Difficulty

Hashimi Print Gallery, Inc. Income Statement For the Year Ended December 31, 20x2	
Net Sales	$884,000
Cost of Goods Sold	508,000
Gross Margin	$376,000
Operating Expenses (including Depreciation Expense of $20,000)	204,000
Operating Income	$172,000
Interest Expense	24,000
Income Before Income Taxes	$148,000
Income Taxes	28,000
Net Income	$120,000

After looking at the statement, Hashimi said to Klein, "Lou, the statement seems to be well done, but what I need to know is why I don't have enough cash to pay my bills this month. You show that I earned $120,000 in 20x2, but I have only $24,000 in the bank. I know I bought a building on a mortgage and paid a cash dividend of $48,000, but what else is going on?" Klein replied, "To answer your question, we have to look at comparative balance sheets and prepare another type of statement. Take a look at these balance sheets." The statement handed to Hashimi is on the next page.

1. To what statement is Klein referring? From the information given, prepare the additional statement using the indirect method.
2. Hashimi Print Gallery, Inc., has a cash problem despite profitable operations. Why?

Hashimi Print Gallery, Inc. Comparative Balance Sheets December 31, 20x2 and 20x1		
	20x2	20x1
Assets		
Cash	$ 24,000	$ 40,000
Accounts Receivable (net)	178,000	146,000
Inventory	240,000	180,000
Prepaid Expenses	10,000	14,000
Building	400,000	—
Accumulated Depreciation	(20,000)	—
Total Assets	$832,000	$380,000
Liabilities and Stockholders' Equity		
Accounts Payable	$ 74,000	$ 96,000
Income Taxes Payable	6,000	4,000
Mortgage Payable	400,000	—
Common Stock	200,000	200,000
Retained Earnings	152,000	80,000
Total Liabilities and Stockholders' Equity	$832,000	$380,000

FINANCIAL REPORTING AND ANALYSIS

Interpreting Financial Reports

FRA 1.
LO 4 Cash-Generating Efficiency and Free Cash Flow

The statement of cash flows for ***Tandy Corporation,*** the owner of Radio Shack and other retail store chains, appears on the next page. For the two years shown, compute the cash-generating efficiency ratios of cash flow yield, cash flows to sales, and cash flows to assets. Also compute free cash flow for the two years. Assume that you report to an investment analyst who has asked you to analyze Tandy's statement of cash flows for 1998 and 1999. Prepare a memorandum to the investment analyst that assesses Tandy's cash-generating efficiency and evaluates its available free cash flow in light of its financing activities. Are there any special operating circumstances that should be taken into consideration? Refer to your computations and to Tandy's Statement of Cash Flows as attachments. The following data come from Tandy's annual report (in thousands):[11]

	1999	1998	1997
Net Sales	$4,126.2	$4,787.9	$5,372.2
Total Assets	2,142.0	1,993.6	2,317.5

Tandy Corporation
Statement of Cash Flows
For the Years Ended December 31, 1999 and 1998

(In millions)	1999	1998
Cash flows from operating activities:		
Net income (loss)	$297.9	$ 61.3
Adjustments to reconcile net income (loss) to net cash provided by operating activities:		
Restricted stock awards	9.6	82.6
Provision for loss on sale of Computer City	—	108.2
Depreciation and amortization	90.2	99.0
Deferred income taxes and other items	49.0	(4.0)
Provision for credit losses and bad debts	9.9	12.5
Changes in operating assets and liabilities:		
Receivables	(38.3)	(36.7)
Inventories	52.6	85.6
Other current assets	15.1	17.7
Accounts payable, accrued expenses and income taxes	75.6	(11.4)
Net cash provided by operating activities	561.6	414.8
Investing activities:		
Additions to property, plant and equipment	(102.4)	(131.5)
Proceeds from sale of property, plant and equipment	5.6	6.7
Proceeds from sale of Computer City	—	36.5
Investment in North Point Communication	(20.0)	—
Other investing activities	(4.2)	(4.7)
Net cash used by investing activities	(121.0)	(93.0)
Financing activities:		
Purchases of treasury stock	(422.2)	(337.4)
Proceeds from sale of common stock put options	4.4	0.3
Sale of treasury stock to employee stock plans	39.5	35.4
Proceeds from exercise of stock options	42.0	22.4
Dividends paid	(42.5)	(44.8)
Changes in short-term borrowings, net	(42.3)	(44.9)
Additions to long-term borrowings	100.6	45.7
Repayments of long-term borrowings	(20.0)	(39.9)
Net cash used by financing activities	(340.5)	(363.2)
Increase (decrease) in cash and cash equivalents	100.1	(41.4)
Cash and cash equivalents, beginning of period	64.5	105.9
Cash and cash equivalents, end of period	$164.6	$ 64.5

International Company

FRA 2.
LO 4 Comparison of Cash Flow Generation Ratios

The following data pertain to two of Japan's most well-known and successful companies[12] (numbers are in billions of yen):

	Sony Corporation		Canon, Inc.	
	1999	1998	1999	1998
Net sales	¥6,415	¥6,425	¥2,622	¥2,826
Net income	179	222	70	110
Average total assets	6,351	6,041	2,658	2,792
Net cash flows from operating activities	663	612	309	247
Dividends	25	22	15	16
Net capital expenditures	340	356	202	194

Calculate the cash flow yield, cash flows to sales, cash flows to assets, and free cash flow for the two years for each company. Which company is most efficient in generating cash flow? Which company has the best year-to-year trend? Which company most likely will need external financing?

Toys "R" Us Annual Report

FRA 3.
LO 4 Analysis of the Statement of Cash Flows

Refer to the statement of cash flows in the Toys "R" Us annual report to answer the following questions:

1. Does Toys "R" Us use the direct or the indirect method of reporting cash flows from operating activities? Other than net earnings, what are the most important factors affecting cash flows from operating activities? Explain the trend of each.
2. Based on the cash flows from investing activities, would you say that Toys "R" Us is a contracting or an expanding company?
3. Calculate the cash flow yield, cash flows to sales, cash flows to assets, and free cash flow for the last three years for Toys "R" Us. How would you evaluate the company's cash-generating efficiency? Does Toys "R" Us need external financing? If so, where has it come from?

Fingraph® Financial Analyst™

FRA 4.
LO 3 Cash Flow Analysis
LO 4

Choose any two companies from the same industry in the Fingraph® Financial Analyst™ CD-ROM software.

1. In the annual reports for the companies you have selected, identify the statement of cash flows. Do the companies use the direct or indirect form of the statement?
2. Display and print in tabular and graphical form the Statement of Cash Flows: Operating Activities Analysis page. Prepare a table that compares the cash flow yield, cash flows to sales, and cash flows to assets for both companies for two years. Are the ratios moving in the same or opposite directions? Study the operating activities sections of the statements to determine the main causes of differences between the net income and cash flows from operations. How do the companies compare?
3. Display and print in tabular and graphical form the Statement of Cash Flows: Investing and Financing Activities Analysis page. Prepare a table that compares the free cash flow for both companies for two years. How do the companies compare? Are the companies growing or contracting? Study the investing and financing activities sections of the statements to determine the main causes of differences between the companies.
4. Find and read references to cash flows in the liquidity analysis section of management's discussion and analysis in each annual report.
5. Write a one-page executive summary that reports your findings from parts **1–4,** including your assessment of the companies' comparative liquidity. Include the Fingraph® pages and your tables as attachments to your report.

Internet Case

FRA 5.
LO 4 Follow-up Analysis of Cash Flows

Through the Needles Accounting Resource Center at http://college.hmco.com, go to the annual report on the web site for ***Marriott International, Inc.*** Find the financial statements including the statement of cash flows. Compare Marriott's cash flow performance for the most recent year with the 1999 statement at the beginning of this chapter by (1) identifying major changes in operating, investing, and financing activities, (2) reading management's financial review of cash flows, and (3) calculating the cash flow ratios (cash flow yield, cash flows to sales, cash flows to assets, and free cash flow) for the most recent year. Be prepared to discuss your conclusions in class.

ENDNOTES

1. Marriott International, Inc., *Annual Report*, 1999.
2. *Statement of Financial Accounting Standards No. 95*, "Statement of Cash Flows" (Norwalk, Conn.: Financial Accounting Standards Board, 1987).
3. *Statement of Financial Accounting Concepts No. 1*, "Objectives of Financial Reporting for Business Enterprises" (Norwalk, Conn.: Financial Accounting Standards Board, 1978), par. 37–39.
4. Marriott International, Inc., *Annual Report*, 1999.
5. Gary Slutsker, "Look at the Birdie and Say: 'Cash Flow,' " *Forbes*, October 25, 1993.
6. Jonathan Clements, "Yacktman Fund Is Bloodied but Unbowed," *The Wall Street Journal*, November 8, 1993.
7. Jeffrey Laderman, "Earnings, Schmearnings—Look at the Cash," *Business Week*, July 24, 1989.
8. Marriott International, Inc., *Annual Report*, 1999.
9. American Institute of Certified Public Accountants, *Accounting Trends & Techniques* (New York: AICPA, 1999).
10. Ibid.
11. Tandy Corporation, *Annual Report*, 1999.
12. Sony Corporation, *Annual Report*, 1999; and Canon, Inc., *Annual Report*, 1999.

18 Financial Performance Evaluation

LEARNING OBJECTIVES

1. Describe and discuss financial performance evaluation by internal and external users.
2. Describe and discuss the standards for financial performance evaluation.
3. State the sources of information for financial performance evaluation.
4. Apply horizontal analysis, trend analysis, and vertical analysis to financial statements.
5. Apply ratio analysis to financial statements in a comprehensive evaluation of a company's financial performance.

Exhibit 4
Comparative Income Statements with Horizontal Analysis

Sun Microsystems, Inc.
Consolidated Income Statements
For the Years Ended June 30, 2000 and 1999

			Increase (Decrease)	
(In millions, except per share amounts)	2000	1999	Amount	Percentage
Net Revenues	$15,721	$11,806	$3,915	33.2
Costs of Sales	7,549	5,670	1,879	33.1
Gross Margin	$ 8,172	$ 6,136	$2,036	33.2
Operating Expenses:				
Research and Development	1,630	1,280	350	27.3
Selling, General and Administrative	4,137	3,215	922	28.7
Purchased In-Process Research and Development	12	121	(109)	(90.1)
Total Operating Expenses	$ 5,779	$ 4,616	$1,163	25.2
Operating Income	$ 2,393	$ 1,520	$ 873	57.4
Gain on Sale of Investment, Net	208	0	208	*
Interest Income, Net	170	85	85	100.0
Income Before Income Taxes	$ 2,771	$ 1,605	$1,166	72.6
Provision for Income Taxes	917	575	342	59.5
Net Income	$ 1,854	$ 1,030	$ 824	80.0
Net Income per Common Share—Basic	$ 1.18	$ 0.67	$ 0.51	76.1
Net Income per Common Share—Diluted	$ 1.10	$ 0.63	$ 0.47	74.6
Shares Used in the Calculation of the Net Income per Common Share—Basic	1,576	1,544	32	2.1
Shares Used in the Calculation of the Net Income per Common Share—Diluted	1,689	1,641	48	2.9

* Not meaningful.
Source: Sun Microsystems, Inc., *Annual Report*, 2000.

Trend Analysis

A variation of horizontal analysis is **trend analysis**, in which percentage changes are calculated for several successive years instead of for two years. Trend analysis, with its long-run view, is important because it may point to basic changes in the nature of a business. In addition to providing comparative financial statements, most companies present a summary of operations and data about other key indicators for five or more years. Net revenues and operating income from Sun Microsystems' summary of operations, together with a trend analysis, are presented in Exhibit 5.

Trend analysis uses an **index number** to show changes in related items over a period of time. For index numbers, the base year is equal to 100 percent. Other years are measured in relation to that amount. For example, the 2000 index for Sun Microsystems' net revenues was figured as follows (dollar amounts in millions):

$$\text{Index} = 100 \times \left(\frac{\text{Index Year Amount}}{\text{Base Year Amount}}\right) = 100 \times \left(\frac{\$15{,}721}{\$7{,}095}\right) = 221.6$$

Exhibit 5
Trend Analysis

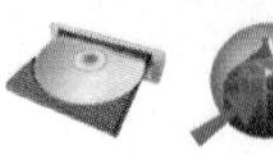

Sun Microsystems, Inc.
Net Revenues and Operating Income
Trend Analysis

	2000	1999	1998	1997	1996
Dollar Values (in millions)					
Net Revenues	15,721	11,806	9,862	8,661	7,095
Operating Income	2,393	1,520	1,114	1,099	675
Trend Analysis (in percentages)					
Net Revenues	221.6	166.4	139.0	122.1	100.0
Operating Income	354.5	225.2	165.0	162.8	100.0

Source: Sun Microsystems, Inc., *Annual Report*, 2000.

Enrichment Note: Trend analysis is usually done for a five-year period to reflect the general five-year economic cycle that affects the U.S. economy. Cycles of other lengths exist and are tracked by the National Bureau of Economic Research. Trend analysis needs to use the appropriate cycle time to cover the complete cycle's impact on the business being studied.

The trend analysis presented in Exhibit 5 clearly shows that operating income has grown faster than net revenues at Sun Microsystems. However, both net revenues and operating income have increased every year. Figure 1 presents these trends in graphic form.

Vertical Analysis

In **vertical analysis**, percentages are used to show the relationship of the different parts to a total in a single statement. The analyst sets a total figure in the statement equal to 100 percent and computes each component's percentage of that total. (The total figure would be total assets or total liabilities and stockholders' equity on the balance sheet, and net revenues or net sales on the income statement.) The resulting statement of percentages is called a **common-size statement**. Common-size balance sheets and common-size income statements for Sun Microsystems are shown in financial statement form in Exhibits 6 and 7 and in pie-chart form in Figures 2 and 3.

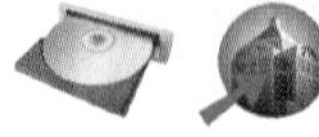

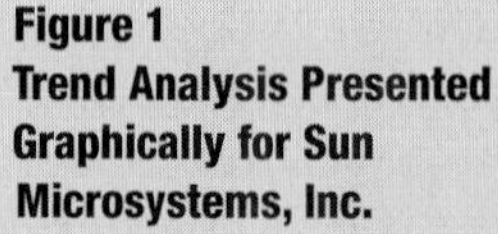

Figure 1
Trend Analysis Presented Graphically for Sun Microsystems, Inc.

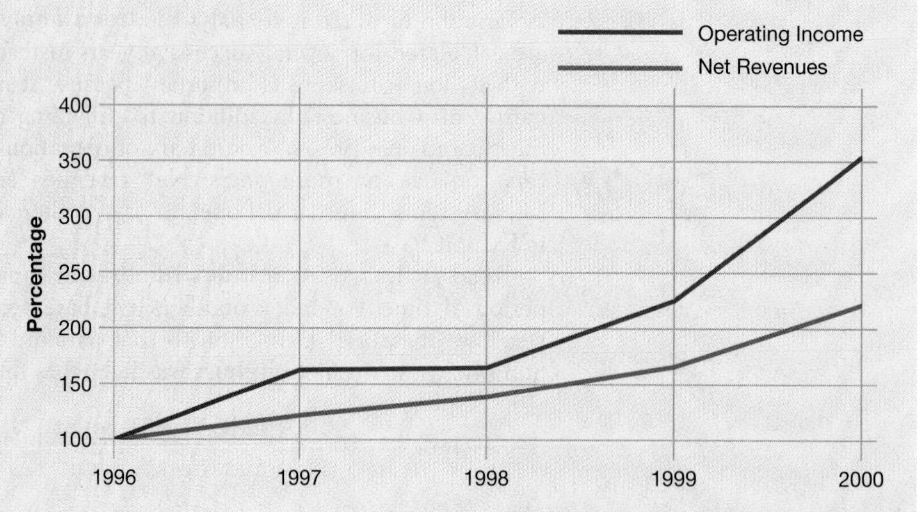

Exhibit 6
Common-Size Balance Sheets

Sun Microsystems, Inc. Common-Size Balance Sheets June 30, 2000 and 1999	2000	1999
Assets		
Current Assets	48.6%	72.8%
Net Property, Plant and Equipment	14.8	19.0
Long-Term Investments	31.8	
Other Assets, Net	4.8	8.2
Total Assets	100.0%	100.0%
Liabilities and Stockholders' Equity		
Current Liabilities	33.6%	38.2%
Deferred Income Taxes	2.6	2.3
Long-Term Debt and Other Obligations	12.2	2.3
Total Liabilities	48.4%	42.7%
Total Stockholders' Equity	51.6	57.3
Total Liabilities and Stockholders' Equity	100.0%	100.0%

Note: Amounts do not precisely total 100 percent in all cases due to rounding.
Source: Sun Microsystems, Inc., *Annual Report,* 2000.

Figure 2
Common-Size Balance Sheets Presented Graphically for Sun Microsystems, Inc.

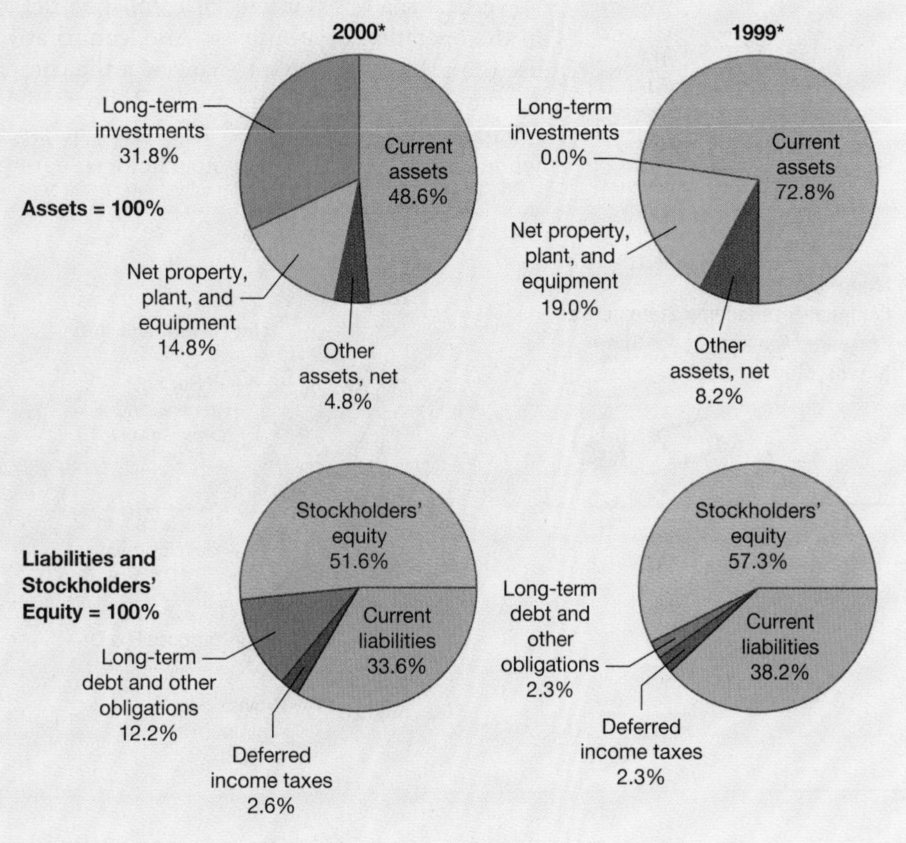

* Rounding causes some additions not to total precisely.

Exhibit 7
Common-Size Income Statements

Sun Microsystems, Inc. Common-Size Income Statements For the Years Ended June 30, 2000 and 1999	2000	1999
Net Revenues	100.0%	100.0%
Cost of Sales	48.0	48.0
Gross Margin	52.0%	52.0%
Operating Expenses:		
Research and Development	10.4%	10.8%
Selling, General and Administrative	26.3	27.2
Purchased In-Process R&D	0.1	1.0
Total Operating Expenses	36.8%	39.1%
Operating Income	15.2%	12.9%
Gain on Sale of Investment, Net	1.3	0.0
Interest, Net	1.1	0.7
Income Before Income Taxes	17.6%	13.6%
Provision for Income Taxes	5.8	4.9
Net Income	11.8%	8.7%

Note: Rounding causes some additions and subtractions not to total precisely.
Source: Sun Microsystems, Inc., *Annual Report*, 2000.

Vertical analysis is useful for comparing the importance of specific components in the operation of a business. Also, comparative common-size statements can be used to identify important changes in the components from one year to the next. As shown in Exhibit 6 and Figure 2, from 1999 to 2000 the composition of Sun Microsystems' assets shifted from current assets toward long-term investments, while current liabilities and stockholders' equity decreased due to new long-term

Figure 3
Common-Size Income Statements Presented Graphically for Sun Microsystems, Inc.

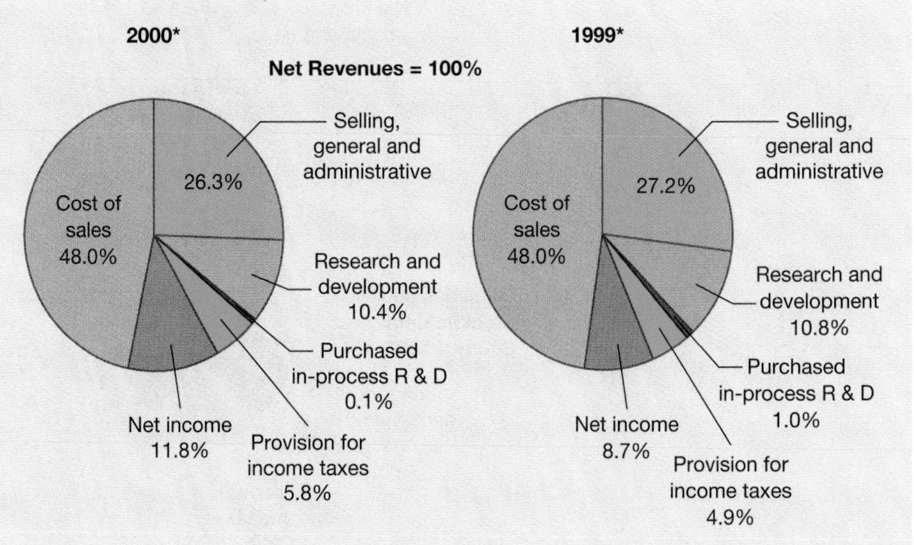

*Rounding causes some additions not to total precisely.
Note: Interest and gains are not presented.

Common Student Error: Because percentages look identical in their presentation, students must be warned to discern what base amount is used when a percentage describes an item. For example, inventory may be 50 percent of *total current assets* but only 10 percent of *total assets.*

Parenthetical Note: Common-size statements can be used in some situations to compare characteristics of firms reporting in different currencies.

debt. The main conclusions to be drawn from this analysis are that current assets and current liabilities make up a large portion of Sun Microsystems' financial structure and that until 2000 the company had few long-term liabilities.

The common-size income statements in Exhibit 7, illustrated in Figure 3, show that from 1999 to 2000 Sun Microsystems reduced its operating expenses by 2.3 percent of revenues (39.1% − 36.8%). This reduction contributed to an increase in operating income as a percentage of net revenues of 2.3 percent (15.2% − 12.9%).

Common-size statements are often used to make comparisons between companies. They allow an analyst to compare the operating and financing characteristics of two companies of different size in the same industry. For example, the analyst might want to compare Sun Microsystems with other companies in terms of percentage of total assets financed by debt or in terms of selling, general, and administrative expenses as a percentage of net revenues. Common-size statements would show those and other relationships.

Ratio Analysis

Ratio analysis is a technique of financial performance evaluation that identifies meaningful relationships between the components of the financial statements. To be most meaningful, the interpretation of ratios must include a study of the underlying data. Ratios are useful in evaluating a company's financial position and operations and in comparing financial data for several years or for several companies. The primary purpose of ratios is to point out areas needing further investigation. To interpret ratios correctly, an analyst must have a general understanding of the company and its environment. Ratios may be expressed in several ways. For example, a ratio of net income of $100,000 to sales of $1,000,000 may be stated as (1) net income is 1/10 or 10 percent of sales; (2) the ratio of sales to net income is 10 to 1 (10:1), or sales are 10 times net income; or (3) for every dollar of sales, the company has an average net income of 10 cents.

Comprehensive Illustration of Ratio Analysis

OBJECTIVE

5 Apply ratio analysis to financial statements in a comprehensive evaluation of a company's financial performance

Related Text Assignments:
Q: 9, 10, 11, 12, 13, 14, 15, 16
SE: 6, 7, 8, 9, 10
E: 5, 6, 7, 8, 9
P: 2, 3, 4, 5, 6
SD: 1, 6
FRA: 2, 3, 4

The financial condition and operating results of any company can be evaluated through the use of comprehensive ratio analysis. Sun Microsystems' performance as reported in its annual report can be compared for the years 1999 and 2000 with regard to the following objectives: (1) liquidity, (2) profitability, (3) long-term solvency, (4) cash flow adequacy, and (5) market strength. Most data for the analyses come from the financial statements presented in Exhibits 3 and 4. Other data are presented as needed.

Evaluating Liquidity

Liquidity is a company's ability to pay bills when they are due and to meet unexpected needs for cash. All the ratios that relate to liquidity involve working capital or some part of it, because debts are paid out of working capital. Liquidity is also closely related to the cash flow ratios.

The liquidity ratios from 1999 to 2000 for Sun Microsystems are presented in Exhibit 8. The **current ratio** and the **quick ratio** are measures of short-term debt-paying ability. The principal difference between the two is that the numerator of the current ratio includes inventories and prepaid expenses. Inventories take longer to convert to cash than do the assets included in the numerator of the quick ratio.

Exhibit 8
Liquidity Ratios of Sun Microsystems, Inc.

(Dollar amounts in millions)	2000	1999

Current ratio: Measure of short-term debt-paying ability

$$\frac{\text{Current Assets}}{\text{Current Liabilities}} \qquad 2000: \frac{\$6{,}877}{\$4{,}759} = 1.4 \text{ times} \qquad 1999: \frac{\$6{,}188}{\$3{,}248} = 1.9 \text{ times}$$

Quick ratio: Measure of short-term debt-paying ability

$$\frac{\text{Cash} + \text{Marketable Securities} + \text{Receivables}}{\text{Current Liabilities}}$$

$$2000: \frac{\$1{,}849 + \$626 + \$2{,}690}{\$4{,}759} = \frac{\$5{,}165}{\$4{,}759} = 1.1 \text{ times}$$

$$1999: \frac{\$1{,}101 + \$1{,}591 + \$2{,}310}{\$3{,}248} = \frac{\$5{,}002}{\$3{,}248} = 1.5 \text{ times}$$

Receivable turnover: Measure of relative size of accounts receivable and effectiveness of credit policies

$$\frac{\text{Net Sales}}{\text{Average Accounts Receivable*}}$$

$$2000: \frac{\$15{,}721}{(\$2{,}690 + \$2{,}310) \div 2} = \frac{\$15{,}721}{\$2{,}500} = 6.3 \text{ times}$$

$$1999: \frac{\$11{,}806}{(\$2{,}310 + \$1{,}846) \div 2} = \frac{\$11{,}806}{\$2{,}078} = 5.7 \text{ times}$$

Average days' sales uncollected: Measure of average days taken to collect receivables

$$\frac{\text{Days in Year}}{\text{Receivable Turnover}} \qquad 2000: \frac{365 \text{ days}}{6.3 \text{ times}} = 57.9 \text{ days} \qquad 1999: \frac{365 \text{ days}}{5.7 \text{ times}} = 64.0 \text{ days}$$

Inventory turnover: Measure of relative size of inventory

$$\frac{\text{Cost of Goods Sold}}{\text{Average Inventory*}}$$

$$2000: \frac{\$7{,}549}{(\$557 + \$308) \div 2} = \frac{\$7{,}549}{\$433} = 17.4 \text{ times}$$

$$1999: \frac{\$5{,}670}{(\$308 + \$346) \div 2} = \frac{\$5{,}670}{\$327} = 17.3 \text{ times}$$

Average days' inventory on hand: Measure of average days taken to sell inventory

$$\frac{\text{Days in Year}}{\text{Inventory Turnover}} \qquad 2000: \frac{365 \text{ days}}{17.4 \text{ times}} = 21.0 \text{ days} \qquad 1999: \frac{365 \text{ days}}{17.3 \text{ times}} = 21.1 \text{ days}$$

Payables turnover: Measure of relative size of accounts payable

$$\frac{\text{Cost of Goods Sold} +/- \text{Change in Inventory*}}{\text{Average Accounts Payable*}}$$

$$2000: \frac{\$7{,}549 + \$249}{(\$924 + \$756) \div 2} = \frac{7{,}798}{840} = 9.3 \text{ times}$$

$$1999: \frac{\$5{,}670 - \$38}{(\$756 + \$496) \div 2} = \frac{5{,}632}{626} = 9.0 \text{ times}$$

Average days' payable: Measure of average days taken to pay accounts payable

$$\frac{\text{Days in Year}}{\text{Payables Turnover}} \qquad 2000: = \frac{365 \text{ days}}{9.3 \text{ times}} = 39.3 \text{ days} \qquad 1999: = \frac{365 \text{ days}}{9.0 \text{ times}} = 40.6 \text{ days}$$

*1998 figures are from Sun Microsystems' 1999 annual report.
Source: Sun Microsystems, Inc., *Annual Report*, 2000.

Point to Emphasize: When comparing company ratios to published ratios, be aware that publishers often redefine the contents of the ratios. While the general content is similar, variations occur. Be sure to evaluate exactly what information a published source says it uses to calculate its ratios.

Teaching Note: To reinforce the different presentations of ratios, avoid the use of only one format in class discussion. Present one format and ask a student to express the relationship in a different format.

Enrichment Note: Other classifications of ratios may be presented. Some of these include productivity ratios and efficiency ratios.

Teaching Note: Review the concept of balance sheet classification according to liquidity.

At Sun Microsystems, both ratios decreased from 1999 to 2000. The current ratio was 1.9 times in 1999 and 1.4 times in 2000, and the quick ratio was 1.5 times in 1999 and 1.1 in 2000. The primary reason for the decreasing results is that current liabilities grew at a faster rate than current assets.

Analysis of two major components of current assets, receivables and inventory, shows improving trends. The major change in this category of ratios is in the receivable turnover. The relative size of accounts receivable and the effectiveness of credit policies are measured by the **receivable turnover**, which rose from 5.7 times in 1999 to 6.3 times in 2000. The related ratio of **average days' sales uncollected** decreased by about six days, from 64.0 days in 1999 to 57.9 days in 2000. The **inventory turnover**, which measures the relative size of inventories, remained stable. Inventory turnover increased from 17.3 times in 1999 to 17.4 times in 2000. This results in a stable **average days' inventory on hand** of 21.1 days in 1999 and 21 days in 2000.

Average days' sales uncollected is added to average days' inventory on hand to determine the **operating cycle**, the time it takes to sell products and collect for them. At Sun Microsystems, the operating cycle decreased from 85.1 days in 1999 (64.0 days + 21.1 days) to 78.9 days in 2000 (57.9 days + 21.0 days). Related to the operating cycle is the number of days the company takes to pay its accounts payable. The **payables turnover** increased from 9.0 times in 1999 to 9.3 times in 2000. This results in average days' payable of 40.6 days in 1999 and 39.3 days in 2000. Thus, if the **average days' payable** is subtracted from the operating cycle, the days of financing required fall from 44.5 days in 1999 to 39.6 days in 2000, a significant improvement. Overall, Sun Microsystems' liquidity remains strong.

Evaluating Profitability

Point to Emphasize: Profit often is expressed in many different ways in accounting literature. Examples are income before income taxes, income after income taxes, and net operating income. If students are aware of the content of net income data in profitability ratios, they will draw appropriate conclusions about the results of ratio computation.

Profitability reflects a company's ability to earn a satisfactory income so that investors and stockholders will continue to provide capital to the company. Profitability is also closely linked to liquidity because earnings ultimately produce cash flow. For this reason, evaluating profitability is important to both investors and creditors. The profitability ratios of Sun Microsystems, Inc., are shown in Exhibit 9.

From 1999 to 2000, **profit margin**, which measures the net income produced by each dollar of sales, increased from 8.7 to 11.8 percent, and **asset turnover**, which measures how efficiently assets are used to produce sales, decreased from 1.7 to 1.4 times. The result is an increase in overall earning power of the company, or **return on assets**, from 14.5 percent in 1999 to 16.4 percent in 2000. These relationships are illustrated in the computations that follow.

Focus on Business Practice

Efforts to link managers' compensation to the company's performance measures and to the creation of shareholder wealth are increasing. One such measure compares the return on assets to the company's cost of debt and equity capital. If the return on assets exceeds the cost of financing the assets with debt and equity, then management is indeed creating value for the shareholders. Coca-Cola calls this excess *economic profit.* In 1998 Coca-Cola reported economic profits of $2.48 billion, with its stock price tracking the growth and decline of these economic profits.

Exhibit 9
Profitability Ratios of Sun Microsystems, Inc.

(Dollar amounts in millions)	2000	1999
Profit margin: Measure of net income produced by each dollar of sales		
$\frac{\text{Net Income*}}{\text{Net Sales}}$	$\frac{\$1,854}{\$15,721} = 11.8\%$	$\frac{\$1,030}{\$11,806} = 8.7\%$
Asset turnover: Measure of how efficiently assets are used to produce sales		
$\frac{\text{Net Sales}}{\text{Average Total Assets}^{\dagger}}$	$\frac{\$15,721}{(\$14,152 + \$8,499) \div 2}$	$\frac{\$11,806}{(\$8,499 + \$5,711) \div 2}$
	$= \frac{\$15,721}{\$11,326} = 1.4 \text{ times}$	$= \frac{\$11,806}{\$7,105} = 1.7 \text{ times}$
Return on assets: Measure of overall earning power, or profitability		
$\frac{\text{Net Income}}{\text{Average Total Assets}^{\dagger}}$	$\frac{\$1,854}{\$11,326} = 16.4\%$	$\frac{\$1,030}{\$7,105} = 14.5\%$
Return on equity: Measure of the profitability of stockholders' investments		
$\frac{\text{Net Income}}{\text{Average Stockholders' Equity}^{\dagger}}$	$\frac{\$1,854}{(\$7,309 + \$4,867) \div 2}$	$\frac{\$1,030}{(\$4,867 + \$3,514) \div 2}$
	$= \frac{\$1,854}{\$6,088} = 30.5\%$	$= \frac{\$1,030}{\$4,191} = 24.6\%$

*In comparing companies in an industry, some analysts use income before income taxes as the numerator to eliminate the effect of differing tax rates among firms.
†1998 figures are from Sun Microsystems' 1999 annual report.
Source: Sun Microsystems, Inc., *Annual Report*, 2000.

Enrichment Note: In both asset turnover and return on assets, the analysis is improved if only productive assets are used in the calculations. For example, unfinished new plant construction or investments in obsolete or nonoperating plants could be removed from the asset base to give a better picture of the productivity of assets.

	Profit Margin		Asset Turnover		Return on Assets
	$\frac{\text{Net Income}}{\text{Net Sales}}$	×	$\frac{\text{Net Sales}}{\text{Average Total Assets}}$	=	$\frac{\text{Net Income}}{\text{Average Total Assets}}$
2000	11.8%	×	1.4	=	16.5%
1999	8.7%	×	1.7	=	14.8%

The small difference in the two sets of return on assets figures results from the rounding of the ratios used in the above computation. Finally, the profitability of stockholders' investments, or **return on equity**, was also higher at 24.6 percent in 1999 and 30.5 percent in 2000.

Instructional Strategy: Divide the class into small groups and ask them to discuss SD 1. After about ten minutes, debrief the case. This exercise highlights the links between profit margin, return on equity, and market value. To summarize, review Profit Margin × Asset Turnover = Return on Assets. The difference between return on assets and return on equity is a function of leverage.

Evaluating Long-Term Solvency

Long-term solvency has to do with a company's ability to survive for many years. Investors and creditors evaluate long-term solvency ratios to detect early signs that a company is headed for financial difficulty. Studies have indicated that accounting ratios can show as much as five years in advance that a company may fail.[3] Declining profitability and liquidity ratios are key indicators of possible business failure. Two other ratios that analysts often consider when assessing long-term solvency are debt to equity and interest coverage. Long-term solvency ratios are shown in Exhibit 10.

Exhibit 10
Long-Term Solvency Ratios of Sun Microsystems, Inc.

(Dollar amounts in millions)	2000	1999
Debt to equity ratio: Measure of capital structure and leverage		
$\frac{\text{Total Liabilities}}{\text{Stockholders' Equity}}$	$\frac{\$6,843}{\$7,309}$ = .9 times	$\frac{\$3,632}{\$4,867}$ = .7 times
Interest coverage ratio: Measure of creditors' protection from default on interest payments		
$\frac{\text{Income Before Income Taxes + Interest Expense}}{\text{Interest Expense}}$	$\frac{\$2,771 + \$84}{\$84}$ = 34.0 times	$\frac{\$1,605 + \$1}{\$1}$ = 1,606.0 times

Source: Sun Microsystems, Inc., *Annual Report*, 2000.

Discussion Question: What is the difference between liquidity and solvency? **Answer:** Liquidity is a firm's ability to meet its current obligations, whereas solvency is a firm's ability to meet its maturing obligations as they become due, without losing the ability to continue operations.

Increasing amounts of debt in a company's capital structure mean that the company is becoming more heavily leveraged. Increasing debts negatively affect long-term solvency because they represent increasing legal obligations to pay interest periodically and the principal at maturity. Failure to make those payments can result in bankruptcy. The **debt to equity ratio** measures capital structure and leverage by showing the amount of a company's assets provided by creditors in relation to the amount provided by stockholders. Sun Microsystems' debt to equity ratio was only .7 times in 1999 and .9 times in 2000. Recall from Exhibit 3 that the company has little short-term debt and increasing long-term debt, and that it has ample current assets as reflected by its current ratio and quick ratio. All of these factors contribute to long-term solvency. As to the future, "The Company believes the level of financial resources is a significant competitive factor in its industry, and it may choose at any time to raise additional capital through debt or equity financing to strengthen its financial position, facilitate growth, and provide the Company with additional flexibility to take advantage of business opportunities that may arise."[4]

If debt is risky, why have any? The answer is that the level of debt is a matter of balance. Despite its riskiness, debt is a flexible means of financing business operations. Sun Microsystems is using debt to help finance an increase in long-term investments. The interest paid on that debt is deductible for income tax purposes, whereas dividends paid on stock are not. Because debt usually carries a fixed interest charge, the cost of financing can be limited and leverage can be used to advantage. If the company is able to earn a return on assets greater than the cost of interest, it can make an overall profit.* However, the company runs the risk of not earning a return on assets equal to the cost of financing those assets, thereby incurring a loss.

Business-World Example: Because of innovative financing plans and other means of acquiring assets, a beneficial modern-day ratio is the fixed charges ratio. This ratio includes interest, lease payments, and all other fixed obligations that must be met through earnings.

The **interest coverage ratio** measures the degree of protection creditors have from a default on interest payments. Because of its increasing amount of long-term debt, Sun Microsystems' interest coverage ratio declined from 1,606.0 times in 1999 to 34.0 times in 2000. Interest coverage is not a problem for the company despite this decline because interest coverage of 34 is more than adequate.

Evaluating Cash Flow Adequacy

Because cash flows are needed to pay debts when they are due, cash flow measures are closely related to liquidity and long-term solvency. Sun Microsystems' cash

*In addition, there are advantages to being a debtor in periods of inflation because the debt, which is a fixed dollar amount, may be repaid in cheaper dollars.

Exhibit 11
Cash Flow Adequacy Ratios of Sun Microsystems, Inc.

(Dollar amounts in millions)	2000	1999
Cash flow yield: Measure of the ability to generate operating cash flows in relation to net income		
Net Cash Flows from Operating Activities / Net Income	$\frac{\$3,754}{\$1,854}$ = 2.0 times	$\frac{\$2,511}{\$1,030}$ = 2.4 times
Cash flows to sales: Measure of the ability of sales to generate operating cash flows		
Net Cash Flows from Operating Activities / Net Sales	$\frac{\$3,754}{\$15,721}$ = 23.9%	$\frac{\$2,511}{\$11,806}$ = 21.3%
Cash flows to assets: Measure of the ability of assets to generate operating cash flows		
Net Cash Flows from Operating Activities / Average Total Assets*	$\frac{\$3,754}{(\$14,152 + \$8,499) \div 2}$ = $\frac{\$3,754}{\$11,326}$ = 33.1%	$\frac{\$2,511}{(\$8,499 + \$5,711) \div 2}$ = $\frac{\$2,511}{\$7,105}$ = 35.3%
Free cash flow: Measure of cash generated or cash deficiency after providing for commitments		
Net Cash Flows from Operating Activities − Dividends − Net Capital Expenditures	$3,754 − $0 − $982 = $2,772	$2,511 − $0 − $740 = $1,771

*The 1998 figure is from Sun Microsystems' 1999 annual report.
Source: Sun Microsystems, Inc., *Annual Report,* 2000.

flow adequacy ratios are presented in Exhibit 11. By most measures, the company's ability to generate positive operating cash flows showed improvement from 1999 to 2000. Key to the improvement was that net cash flows from operating activities had a large increase, from $2,511 million in 1999 to $3,754 million in 2000, while net income, net sales, and average total assets increased by lesser amounts. **Cash flow yield**, or the relationship of cash flows from operating activities to net income, decreased from 2.4 to 2.0 times. **Cash flows to sales**, or the ability of sales to generate operating cash flows, increased from 21.3 percent to 23.9 percent. **Cash flows to assets**, or the ability of assets to generate operating cash flows, decreased from 35.3 percent to 33.1 percent.

Free cash flow, the cash generated or the cash deficiency after providing for commitments, also increased and remains very positive, primarily because the increase in capital expenditures was smaller than the increase in net cash flows from operating activities and because the company pays no dividends. Management's comment with regard to cash flows in the future is, "The Company believes that the liquidity provided by existing cash, cash equivalents, and investments along with the borrowing arrangements . . . will provide sufficient capital to meet the Company's capital requirements through fiscal 2001."[5]

Evaluating Market Strength

The market price of a company's stock is of interest to the analyst because it represents what investors as a whole think of the company at a point in time. Market price is the price at which the stock is bought and sold. It provides information about how investors view the potential return and risk of owning the company's

	Lewis Corporation	Ramsey Corporation
Assets		
Cash	$ 160,000	$ 384,800
Marketable Securities	406,800	169,200
Accounts Receivable (net)	1,105,600	1,970,800
Inventories	1,259,600	2,506,800
Prepaid Expenses	108,800	228,000
Property, Plant, and Equipment (net)	5,827,200	13,104,000
Intangibles and Other Assets	1,106,400	289,600
Total Assets	$9,974,400	$18,653,200
Liabilities and Stockholders' Equity		
Accounts Payable	$ 688,000	$ 1,145,200
Notes Payable	300,000	800,000
Income Taxes Payable	100,400	146,800
Bonds Payable	4,000,000	4,000,000
Common Stock, $20 par value	2,000,000	1,200,000
Paid-in Capital in Excess of Par Value, Common	1,219,600	7,137,200
Retained Earnings	1,666,400	4,224,000
Total Liabilities and Stockholders' Equity	$9,974,400	$18,653,200

	Lewis Corporation	Ramsey Corporation
Net Sales	$25,120,000	$50,420,000
Costs and Expenses		
Cost of Goods Sold	$12,284,000	$29,668,000
Selling Expenses	9,645,200	14,216,400
Administrative Expenses	1,972,000	4,868,000
Total Costs and Expenses	$23,901,200	$48,752,400
Income from Operations	$ 1,218,800	$ 1,667,600
Interest Expense	388,000	456,000
Income Before Income Taxes	$ 830,800	$ 1,211,600
Income Taxes	400,000	600,000
Net Income	$ 430,800	$ 611,600
Earnings per share	$ 4.31	$ 10.19

5. Prepare an analysis of market strength by calculating for each company the (a) price/earnings ratio and (b) dividends yield.
6. Indicate in the right-hand column which company had the more favorable ratio in each case.
7. How could the analysis be improved if information from prior years were available?

ALTERNATE PROBLEMS

LO 5 Analyzing the Effects of Transactions on Ratios

P 5. Benson Corporation, a clothing retailer, engaged in the transactions listed in the first column of the table below. Opposite each transaction is a ratio and space to mark the effect of each transaction on the ratio.

Transaction	Ratio	Effect		
		Increase	Decrease	None
a. Issued common stock for cash.	Asset turnover			
b. Declared cash dividend.	Current ratio			
c. Sold treasury stock.	Return on equity			
d. Borrowed cash by issuing note payable.	Debt to equity ratio			
e. Paid salaries expense.	Inventory turnover			
f. Purchased merchandise for cash.	Current ratio			
g. Sold equipment for cash.	Receivable turnover			
h. Sold merchandise on account.	Quick ratio			
i. Paid current portion of long-term debt.	Return on assets			
j. Gave sales discount.	Profit margin			
k. Purchased marketable securities for cash.	Quick ratio			
l. Declared 5 percent stock dividend.	Current ratio			
m. Purchased a building.	Free cash flow			

REQUIRED

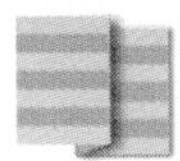

Place an X in the appropriate column to show whether the transaction increased, decreased, or had no effect on the indicated ratio.

LO 5 Ratio Analysis

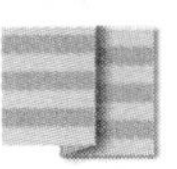

P 6. The condensed comparative income statements and balance sheets of Basie Corporation appear below and on the next page. All figures are given in thousands of dollars, except earnings per share.

Basie Corporation
Comparative Income Statements
For the Years Ended December 31, 20x2 and 20x1

	20x2	20x1
Net Sales	$800,400	$742,600
Cost of Goods Sold	454,100	396,200
Gross Margin	$346,300	$346,400
Operating Expenses		
Selling Expenses	$130,100	$104,600
Administrative Expenses	140,300	115,500
Total Operating Expenses	$270,400	$220,100
Income from Operations	$ 75,900	$126,300
Interest Expense	25,000	20,000
Income Before Income Taxes	$ 50,900	$106,300
Income Taxes	14,000	35,000
Net Income	$ 36,900	$ 71,300
Earnings per share	$ 1.23	$ 2.38

Basie Corporation
Comparative Balance Sheets
December 31, 20x2 and 20x1

	20x2	20x1
Assets		
Cash	$ 31,100	$ 27,200
Accounts Receivable (net)	72,500	42,700
Inventory	122,600	107,800
Property, Plant, and Equipment (net)	577,700	507,500
Total Assets	$803,900	$685,200
Liabilities and Stockholders' Equity		
Accounts Payable	$104,700	$ 72,300
Notes Payable (due in less than one year)	50,000	50,000
Bonds Payable	200,000	110,000
Common Stock, $10 par value	300,000	300,000
Retained Earnings	149,200	152,900
Total Liabilities and Stockholders' Equity	$803,900	$685,200

Additional data for Basie Corporation in 20x2 and 20x1 are as follows:

	20x2	20x1
Net cash flows from operating activities	$64,000	$99,000
Net capital expenditures	$119,000	$38,000
Dividends paid	$31,400	$35,000
Number of common shares	30,000	30,000
Market price per share	$40	$60

Balances of selected accounts at the end of 20x0 were Accounts Receivable (net), $52,700; Inventory, $99,400; Accounts Payable, $64,800; Total Assets, $647,800; and Stockholders' Equity, $376,600. All of the bonds payable were long-term liabilities.

REQUIRED

Perform the following analyses. Round percentages and ratios to one decimal place, and consider changes of .1 or less to be neutral. After making the calculations, indicate whether each ratio had a favorable (*F*) or unfavorable (*U*) change from 20x1 to 20x2.

1. Conduct a liquidity analysis by calculating for each year the (a) current ratio, (b) quick ratio, (c) receivable turnover, (d) average days' sales uncollected, (e) inventory turnover, (f) average days' inventory on hand, (g) payables turnover, and (h) average days' payable.
2. Conduct a profitability analysis by calculating for each year the (a) profit margin, (b) asset turnover, (c) return on assets, and (d) return on equity.
3. Conduct a long-term solvency analysis by calculating for each year the (a) debt to equity ratio and (b) interest coverage ratio.
4. Conduct a cash flow adequacy analysis by calculating for each year the (a) cash flow yield, (b) cash flows to sales, (c) cash flows to assets, and (d) free cash flow.
5. Conduct a market strength analysis by calculating for each year the (a) price/earnings ratio and (b) dividends yield.

EXPANDING YOUR CRITICAL THINKING, COMMUNICATION, AND INTERPERSONAL SKILLS

SKILLS DEVELOPMENT

Conceptual Analysis

SD 1.
LO 2 Standards for Financial
LO 5 Performance Evaluation

Helene Curtis, a well-known, publicly owned corporation, became a takeover candidate and sold out in the 1990s after years of poor profit performance. "By almost any standard, Chicago-based Helene Curtis rates as one of America's worst-managed personal care companies. In recent years its return on equity has hovered between 10% and 13%, well below the industry average of 18% to 19%. Net profit margins of 2% to 3% are half that of competitors. . . . As a result, while leading names like Revlon and Avon are trading at three and four times book value, Curtis trades at less than two-thirds book value."[6] Considering that many companies in other industries are happy with a return on equity of 10 percent to 13 percent, why is this analysis so critical of Curtis's performance? Assuming that Curtis could double its profit margin, what other information would be necessary to project the resulting return on stockholders' investment? Why are Revlon's and Avon's stocks trading for more than Curtis's? Be prepared to discuss your answers to these questions in class.

SD 2.
LO 3 Using Segment Information

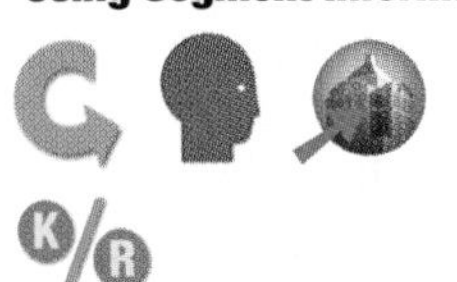

Refer to Exhibit 1, which shows the segment information of ***Goodyear Tire & Rubber Company.*** In what business segments does Goodyear operate? What is the relative size of the business segments in terms of sales and total segment income in the most recent year? Which segment is most profitable in terms of the performance measure return on assets? In the tires segment, which region of the world is largest and which is most profitable in terms of return on assets?

SD 3.
LO 3 Use of Published Reports

Refer to Exhibit 2, which contains the ***PepsiCo, Inc.,*** listing from Mergent's *Handbook of Dividend Achievers.* Assume that an investor has asked you to assess PepsiCo's recent history and prospects. Write a memorandum to the investor that addresses the following points:

1. PepsiCo's earnings history. (What generally has been the relationship between PepsiCo's return on assets and its return on equity over the years 1993 to 1999? What does this tell you about the way the company is financed? What figures back up your conclusion?)
2. The trend of PepsiCo's stock price and price/earnings ratio for the seven years shown.
3. PepsiCo's prospects, including developments that are likely to affect the future of the company.

Ethical Dilemma

SD 4.
LO 3 Management of Earnings

Managers of most companies are very sensitive to the fact that analysts watch key performance measures, such as whether the firm is meeting earnings targets. A slight weakening of analysts' confidence can severely affect the price of a company's stock. The Securities and Exchange Commission (SEC) has been cracking down on the management of earnings to achieve financial goals by targeting companies for review. For instance, the SEC filed a complaint against ***W. R. Grace & Co.*** for releasing $1.5 mil-

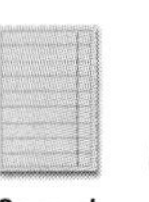

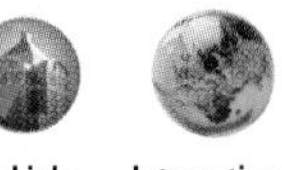

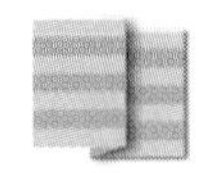

Cash Flow | CD-ROM | Communication | Critical Thinking | Ethics | General Ledger | Group Activity | Hot Links to Real Companies | International | Internet | Key Ratio | Memo | Spreadsheet

lion from reserves into earnings in order to meet earnings targets. Grace officials say that the amount is immaterial and that it is in accord with accounting rules to book an immaterial item. (It was about 1.5 percent of net income.) The SEC, on the other hand, argues that it is a matter of principle: "Does anyone think that it's acceptable to intentionally book an error for the purpose of making earnings targets?" Some think such action on the part of the SEC will harm confidence in the companies.[7] Do you think it is unethical for a company's management to increase earnings periodically through the use of one-time transactions, such as adjustments of reserves or sale of assets, on which it has a profit?

Research Activity

SD 5.

LO 3 Use of Investors' Services

Find *Moody's Investors Service* or *Standard & Poor's Industry Guide* in your library. Locate reports on three corporations. You may choose the corporations at random or choose them from the same industry, if directed to do so by your instructor. (If you did a related exercise in a previous chapter, use the same three companies.) Write a summary of what you learned about each company's financial performance, including what measures of performance were mentioned in the write-ups and the company's prospects for the future, and be prepared to discuss your findings in class.

Decision-Making Practice

SD 6.

LO 4 Effect of One-Time Item
LO 5 on Loan Decision

Apple a Day, Inc., and ***Unforgettable Edibles, Inc.,*** both operate food catering businesses in the metropolitan area. Their customers include *Fortune* 500 companies, regional firms, and individuals. The two firms reported similar profit margins for the current year, and both determine bonuses for managers based on reaching a target profit margin and return on equity. Each firm has submitted a loan request to you, a loan officer for City National Bank, with the following information:

	Apple a Day	Unforgettable Edibles
Net Sales	$625,348	$717,900
Cost of Goods Sold	225,125	287,080
Gross Margin	$400,223	$430,820
Operating Expenses	281,300	371,565
Operating Income	$118,923	$ 59,255
Gain on Sale of Real Estate		81,923
Interest Expense	(9,333)	(15,338)
Income Before Income Taxes	$109,590	$125,840
Income Taxes	25,990	29,525
Net Income	$ 83,600	$ 96,315
Average Stockholders' Equity	$312,700	$390,560

1. Perform a vertical analysis and prepare a common-size income statement for each firm. Compute profit margin and return on equity.
2. Discuss your results, the bonus plan for management, and loan considerations. Make a recommendation about which company is a better risk for receiving the loan.

Financial Reporting and Analysis

Interpreting Financial Reports

FRA 1.

LO 4 Trend Analysis

H. J. Heinz Company is a global company engaged in several lines of business, including food service, infant foods, condiments, pet foods, tuna, and weight control food products. A five-year summary of operations and other related data for Heinz appears at the top of the next page.[8]

Five-Year Summary of Operations and Other Related Data H. J. Heinz Company and Subsidiaries					
	1999	1998	1997	1996	1995
	(Dollars in thousands, except per share data)				
Summary of Operations					
Sales	$9,299,610	$9,209,284	$9,397,007	$9,112,265	$8,086,794
Cost of products sold	5,944,867	5,711,213	6,385,091	5,775,357	5,119,597
Interest expense	258,815	258,616	274,746	277,411	210,585
Provision for income taxes	360,790	453,415	177,193	364,342	346,982
Net income	474,341	801,566	301,871	659,319	591,025
Other Related Data					
Dividends paid: Common	484,817	452,966	416,923	381,871	345,358
Total assets	8,053,634	8,023,421	8,437,787	8,623,691	8,247,188
Total debt	3,376,413	5,806,905	5,997,366	3,363,828	3,401,076
Shareholders' equity	1,803,004	2,216,516	2,440,921	2,706,757	2,472,869

REQUIRED

Prepare a trend analysis for Heinz with 1995 as the base year and discuss the results. Identify important trends and tell whether the trends are favorable or unfavorable. Discuss significant relationships among the trends.

International Company

FRA 2.
LO 5 Comparison of International Company Operating Cycles

Ratio analysis enables one to compare the performance of companies whose financial statements are presented in different currencies. For instance, selected 1999 data for two large pharmaceutical companies—one American, ***Pfizer, Inc.,*** and one Swiss, ***Roche***—are presented below (in millions):[9]

	Pfizer, Inc. (U.S.)	Roche (Swiss)
Net Sales	$14,133	SFr.27,567
Cost of Goods Sold	2,528	8,734
Accounts Receivable	3,864	6,178
Inventories	1,654	6,546
Accounts Payable	951	2,378

Accounts receivable in 1998 were $2,914 for Pfizer and SFr.4,535 for Roche. Inventories in 1998 were $1,828 for Pfizer and SFr.5,389 for Roche. Accounts payable in 1998 were $971 for Pfizer and SFr.2,088 for Roche.

For each company calculate the receivable, inventory, and payables turnovers and the respective days associated with each. Then determine the operating cycle for each company and the days of financing required for current operations. Compare the results.

Group Activity: Divide the class into groups to make the calculations. Ask half of the groups to analyze Pfizer and the other half to analyze Roche. Have the entire class compare and discuss results.

Toys "R" Us Annual Report

FRA 3.
LO 5 Comprehensive Ratio Analysis

Refer to the Toys "R" Us annual report, and conduct a comprehensive ratio analysis that compares data from 2000 and 1999. If you have been computing ratios for Toys "R" Us in previous chapters, you may prepare a table that summarizes the ratios for 2000 and 1999 and show calculations only for the ratios not previously calculated. If this is the first time you are doing a ratio analysis for Toys "R" Us, show all your computations. In

either case, after each group of ratios, comment on the performance of Toys "R" Us. Round your calculations to one decimal place. Prepare and comment on the following categories of ratios:

Liquidity analysis: Current ratio, quick ratio, receivable turnover, average days' sales uncollected, inventory turnover, average days' inventory on hand, payables turnover, and average days' payable (Accounts Receivable, Inventory, and Accounts Payable were [in millions] $175, $2,464, and $1,280, respectively, in 1998.)

Profitability analysis: Profit margin, asset turnover, return on assets, and return on equity (Comment on the effect of the restructuring in 1999 on the company's profitability.)

Long-term solvency analysis: Debt to equity ratio and interest coverage ratio

Cash flow adequacy analysis: Cash flow yield, cash flows to sales, cash flows to assets, and free cash flow

Market strength analysis: Price/earnings ratio and dividends yield

Fingraph® Financial Analyst™

FRA 4.
LO 5 Comprehensive Financial Performance Evaluation

Choose any company in the Fingraph® Financial Analyst™ CD-ROM software database.

1. Display and print for the company you have selected the following pages:
   a. Balance Sheet Analysis
   b. Current Assets and Current Liabilities Analysis
   c. Liquidity and Asset Utilization Analysis
   d. Income from Operations Analysis
   e. Statement of Cash Flows: Operating Activities Analysis
   f. Statement of Cash Flows: Investing and Financing Activities Analysis
   g. Market Strength Analysis
2. Prepare an executive summary that describes the financial condition and performance of your company for the past two years. Attach the pages you printed above in support of your analysis.

Internet Case

FRA 5.
LO 2 Use of Investors' Services
LO 3

Through the Needles Accounting Resource Center at http://college.hmco.com, go to the web site for ***Moody's Investors Service.*** Click on Ratings, which will show revisions of debt ratings issued by Moody's in the past few days. Choose a rating that has been upgraded or downgraded and read the short press announcement related to it. What reasons does Moody's give for the change in rating? What is Moody's assessment of the future of the company or institution? What financial performance measures are mentioned in the article? Write a summary of your findings and be prepared to share it in class.

ENDNOTES

1. Adapted from Material Sciences Corporation, *Annual Report*, 1998.
2. *Statement of Financial Accounting Standards No. 131*, "Segment Disclosures" (Norwalk, Conn.: Financial Accounting Standards Board, 1997).
3. William H. Beaver, "Alternative Accounting Measures as Indicators of Failure," *Accounting Review*, January 1968; and Edward Altman, "Financial Ratios, Discriminant Analysis and the Prediction of Corporate Bankruptcy," *Journal of Finance*, September 1968.
4. Sun Microsystems, Inc., "Management's Discussion and Analysis," *Annual Report*, 2000.
5. Ibid.
6. *Forbes*, November 13, 1978, p. 154.
7. Elizabeth MacDonald, "Firms Say SEC Earnings Scrutiny Goes Too Far," *The Wall Street Journal*, February 1, 1999.
8. H. J. Heinz Company, *Annual Report*, 1999.
9. Pfizer, Inc., *Annual Report*, 1999; and Roche Group, *Annual Report*, 1999.

19 A Manager's Perspective: The Changing Business Environment

LEARNING OBJECTIVES

1. Define *management accounting* and distinguish between management accounting and financial accounting.
2. Explain the management cycle and its connection to management accounting.
3. Identify the management philosophies of continuous improvement and discuss the role of management accounting in implementing those philosophies.
4. Define *performance measures*, recognize the uses of those measures in the management cycle, and prepare an analysis of nonfinancial data.
5. Identify the important questions a manager must consider before requesting or preparing a management report.
6. Compare accounting for inventories and cost of goods sold in service, merchandising, and manufacturing organizations.
7. Identify the standards of ethical conduct for management accountants.

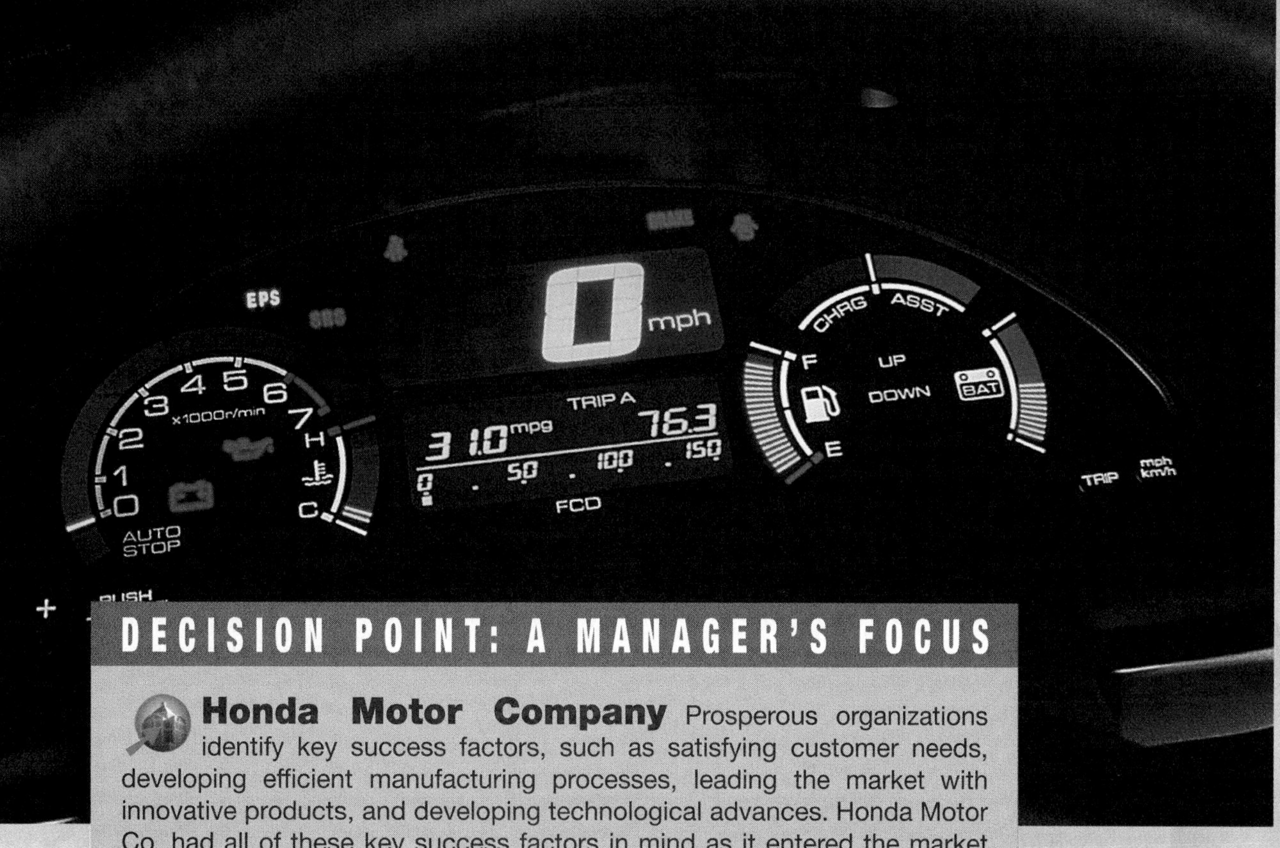

DECISION POINT: A MANAGER'S FOCUS

Honda Motor Company Prosperous organizations identify key success factors, such as satisfying customer needs, developing efficient manufacturing processes, leading the market with innovative products, and developing technological advances. Honda Motor Co. had all of these key success factors in mind as it entered the market with the introduction of Insight, its next-generation "green car," to be sold in the United States. This vehicle is a hybrid, running on both a gas engine and an electric motor. Priced at less than $20,000, the Insight gets more than 70 miles to the gallon. One of several second-generation green cars, it meets both the regulators' demand for zero-emission vehicles and consumers' demand for inexpensive, practical transportation.[1]

Satisfying consumers' needs and meeting regulators' demands through the introduction of new technologies and innovative vehicle designs are just part of Honda's strategy to stay agile, flexible, and ahead of its competitors. Equally important for Honda is the development of efficient manufacturing operations. Over the next few years, by experimenting with new manufacturing methods, Honda "should become capable of halving the time and cost for a new-model introduction," says Masaki Iwai, Honda's senior managing director.[2] The way Honda plans to achieve those savings on new models runs counter to traditional wisdom among big auto producers: that an auto maker must sell four million vehicles a year to recoup the cost of developing new technologies and models. In contrast, Honda's president, Hiroyuki Yoshino, states, "If you spend small, then you don't have to sell a lot to be profitable." So Honda is standardizing manufacturing tools and eliminating the need to modify its assembly lines. Model-specific sub-assembly lines will feed their products to a new, shorter vehicle assembly line. Subassemblies are also Honda's answer to containing costs, maintaining quality, and staying independent. Honda executives question the current industry practice of outsourcing so much work to parts suppliers that control over quality and product integration may be sacrificed.

All of these innovations demonstrate Honda's desire to maintain its reputation as an industry leader. Honda needs objective, quantifiable performance standards to measure its ability to attain the key success factors mentioned above. What is management accounting's role in the design and production of a vehicle like the Insight? What performance measures would you suggest for developing efficient manufacturing processes and satisfying customer needs related to the Insight?

Management accounting has provided and will continue to provide Honda with relevant, useful information for making decisions about the selling and leasing prices for the car and the cost of new materials and new production processes. Management accounting uses tools such as budgets and performance measures to help Honda managers develop, manufacture, sell, and distribute the Insight using limited resources. Budgets influence daily operating goals for the workers and provide targets for evaluating the workers' performance. Performance measures for the production process may include the time to complete one cycle of the production process, the number of setups, and the time to rework errors in the production process. Number of customer complaints, number of service change notices, and number of customer referrals are potential performance measures of customer satisfaction. As Honda continues to improve the Insight through time and cost savings, management accounting will provide quantifiable information to support Honda's achievement of its strategic key success factors.

VIDEO CASE

UPS

Objectives

- To define management accounting.
- To describe the management cycle and its connection to management accounting.
- To recognize performance measures.

Background for the Case

UPS, one of the largest package distribution companies in the world, transports more than three billion parcels and documents annually. UPS supports its commitment to serving the needs of customers throughout the world with more than 500 airplanes, 147,000 vehicles, and 2,400 facilities in over 200 countries.

Like many other companies, UPS relies on management accounting information to plan, execute, review, and report its business activities. Management accounting helps managers at UPS make better decisions about embracing new technology, managing environmental issues, and improving fuel efficiency.

For more information about UPS, visit the company's web site through the Needles Accounting Resource Center web site at:

http://college.hmco.com

Required

View the video on UPS that accompanies this book. As you are watching the video, take notes related to the following questions:

1. In your own words, how would you define management accounting?
2. Describe the management cycle and explain how management accounting information helps managers at UPS move through each stage of the management cycle.
3. Define the term *performance measures* and give examples of some performance measures used by UPS.

What Is Management Accounting?

OBJECTIVE

1 Define *management accounting* and distinguish between management accounting and financial accounting

Related Text Assignments:
Q: 1, 2, 3, 4
SE: 1
E: 1
MRA: 1

Management accounting consists of accounting techniques and procedures for gathering and reporting financial, production, and distribution data to meet management's information needs. The management accountant is expected to provide timely, accurate information—including budgets, standard costs, variance analyses, support for day-to-day operating decisions, and analyses of capital expenditures. The Institute of Management Accountants defines **management accounting** as

> the process of identification, measurement, accumulation, analysis, preparation, interpretation, and communication of financial [and nonfinancial] information used by management to plan, evaluate, and control within the organization and to assure appropriate use and accountability for its resources.[3]

The information that management accountants gather and analyze is used to support the actions of management. All business managers need accurate and timely information to support pricing, planning, operating, and many other types of decisions. Managers of manufacturing, merchandising, government, and service organizations all depend on management accounting information. Multidivisional corporations need larger amounts of information and more complex accounting and reporting systems than do small businesses. But small and medium-sized businesses make use of certain types of financial and operating information as well. The types of data needed to ensure efficient operating conditions do not depend entirely on an organization's size.

Common Student Error: Students often think that management accounting is a subordinate activity to financial accounting. Management accounting is a process that includes financial accounting, tax accounting, information analysis, and other accounting activities.

Point to Emphasize: Financial accounting requires consistency and comparability to ensure the usefulness of information to those outside the firm. Management accounting can use innovative analyses and presentation techniques to enhance information's usefulness to management within the firm.

Management accounting information helps organizations make better decisions. Such decisions make all organizations become more cost-effective and help manufacturing, retail, and service organizations become more profitable. Financial accounting takes the results of management decisions about the actual operating, investing, and financing activities and prepares reports for external parties (investors, creditors, and governmental agencies).

Both management accounting and financial accounting (1) provide an information system crucial to reporting and analysis, (2) provide reports used by individuals to analyze and make decisions, and (3) develop relevant, objective product cost information for valuing inventories included on the balance sheet.

Table 1 compares management accounting to financial accounting. Management accounting data are essential for management planning, control, performance measurement, and decision making. Employees and managers need accounting information to handle daily operations efficiently and effectively, so as to achieve the organization's goals. Management reports are very flexible. Either historical or future information may be reported without any formal guidelines or restrictions. The information may communicate dollar amounts or physical measures of time or objects, such as number of hours worked or number of inspections. The information may be relevant and objective for decision-making purposes or may be more subjective for estimating future activities. Management accounting reports can be prepared monthly, quarterly, or annually. Management may also request reports daily or for special purposes.

In contrast, financial accounting communicates economic information to external parties. In profit-generating organizations, such as manufacturing, retail, and service organizations, owners and creditors contribute money to assist managers in investing in resources and generating profits from operating activities. Government agencies, such as the Internal Revenue Service and the Securities and Exchange Commission, also require reports. Managers must distribute financial reports to those parties to show the organization's actual performance. The reports are histor-

Table 1. Comparison of Management and Financial Accounting

Areas of Comparison	Management Accounting	Financial Accounting
Report format	Flexible format, driven by user's needs	Based on generally accepted accounting principles
Purpose of reports	Provide information for planning, control, performance measurement, and decision making	Report on past performance
Primary users	Employees, managers, suppliers	Owners, lenders, customers, government agencies
Units of measure	Historical or future dollar; physical measure in time or number of objects	Historical dollar
Nature of information	Future-oriented; objective for decision making, more subjective for planning; relies on estimates	Historical, objective
Frequency of reports	Prepared as needed; may or may not be on a regular basis	Prepared on a regular basis (minimum of once a year)

ical and measured in dollars. Generally accepted accounting principles require that specific standards and procedures be followed in the preparation of these reports. Financial reports include objective information that is prepared and distributed regularly, usually on an annual basis.

Management Accounting and the Management Cycle

OBJECTIVE

2 Explain the management cycle and its connection to management accounting

Related Text Assignments:
Q: 5, 6
SE: 2
E: 2

To better understand the relationship between management and management accounting, let's take a look at the management cycle and the connections between it and management accounting.

The Management Cycle

Management is expected to use resources wisely, operate profitably, pay debts, and abide by laws and regulations. These expectations motivate managers to establish the objectives, goals, and strategic plans of the organization and to guide and control

Figure 1
The Management Cycle

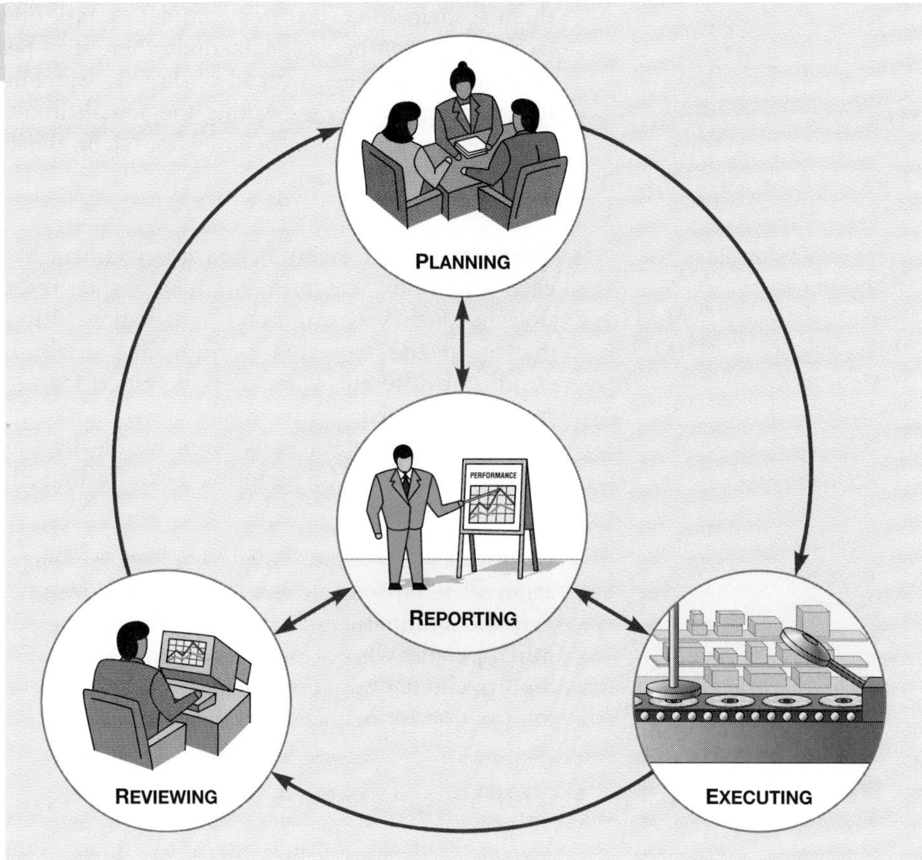

Teaching Note: Ask a student to apply the management cycle to a personal activity, such as taking a vacation, applying for a job, obtaining a college degree, or raising funds for a campus organization.

operating, investing, and financing activities to reach those goals. The management process differs from organization to organization, but traditionally management operates in four stages: (1) planning, (2) executing, (3) reviewing, and (4) reporting. Figure 1 illustrates these stages as an overall management cycle. Each stage of the cycle is discussed below.

Planning Management needs to plan the future operating, investing, and financing activities of the organization. Appropriate objectives and goals must be established and organizational policies enacted. Strategic planning represents the formulation of long-term tactics, objectives, and organizational policies. Management strives to complement the organization's strategic plans with annual operating plans. The development of strategic and operating plans requires managers to make decisions concerning various alternatives. These plans often include expectations about the performance of individuals, working teams, products, or services.

Executing Planning alone does not guarantee satisfactory operating results. Management must implement the strategic and operating plans by executing activities, or tasks, in ways that maximize the use of available resources. Smooth operations require one or more of the following: (1) hiring and training of personnel, (2) properly matching human and technical resources to the work that must be done, (3) purchasing or leasing facilities, (4) maintaining an inventory of products for sale, and (5) identifying operating activities, or tasks, that minimize waste and improve the quality of the products or services.

Management performs, or executes the plan, by overseeing the daily operations of the organization. In small organizations, managers often have frequent direct contact with their employees. They supervise their employees and interact with them to help them learn or complete a task or to improve their performance. In larger, more complex organizations, there may be less direct contact between managers and employees. Instead of directly watching employees, management monitors performance by measuring the actual time taken to complete an activity (for example, number of inspection hours) or the frequency of an activity (such as number of inspections).

Point to Emphasize: Revenues and expenses accumulated in accounting systems for financial reporting purposes are also used in management accounting to support budgeting of next year's business activities.

REVIEWING In many organizations, financial rewards are given to those managers who follow the plan and manage their resources well. Thus, control of operations becomes very important to managers. Often managers compare actual performance to the expected performance established at the planning stage. Any significant differences are then identified for further analysis. Problems that arise may be corrected, or the original plans may be revised as a result of changes in the organization's operating environment. Ideally, the adjustments made in this review stage will improve the performance of future activities.

REPORTING Because managers have an obligation to use resources wisely, management is responsible for reporting the results of operations to external parties. Periodic summaries of past performance are sent to stockholders, creditors, and other people who are interested in the organization's operations. Also, internal reports about evaluations of past performance compared to plans provide useful information for management decision making.

How Management Accounting Supports the Management Cycle

Management accounting serves the many information needs of managers by (1) developing plans and analyzing alternatives; (2) communicating plans to key personnel; (3) evaluating performance; (4) reporting the results of activities; and (5) accumulating, maintaining, and processing an organization's financial and nonfinancial information. These management accounting activities complement the management cycle.

For example, let's suppose that Abbie Awani is about to open her own retail business, Sweet Treasures Candy Store. She plans to purchase candy and other confections from various candy manufacturers and to sell them after some repackaging. What types of information does Awani need before she opens the doors of her new store? Her first need is for a business plan so that she can apply for a start-up loan from a local bank. This plan includes a full description of the business as well as a complete budget for the first two years of operations. The budget includes a forecasted income statement, a forecasted statement of cash flows, and a forecasted balance sheet for both years.

Since Awani does not have a financial background, she will consult a local accounting firm to help her with this project. But she can provide relevant input into the business plan. She needs to decide (1) the types of candy she wants to sell; (2) the volume of sales she anticipates; (3) the selling price for each product; (4) the monthly costs of leasing or purchasing facilities, employing personnel, and maintaining the facilities; and (5) the number of display counters, storage units, and cash registers that she will need.

Once she obtains the loan and opens the business, Awani's information needs continue. She must now

FOCUS ON BUSINESS TECHNOLOGY

When Toys "R" Us formed an independent e-commerce unit, toysrus.com, its managers developed a business plan. They analyzed alternative ways in which the online unit could function within Toys "R" Us. What advantages would toysrus.com have over its online competition? The majority-owned Internet unit has its parent's international buying power, its customers can pick up and return purchases through the worldwide network of Toys "R" Us retail stores, and its name is already known.[4]

based management seeks continuous improvement by emphasizing the ongoing reduction or elimination of nonvalue-adding activities. The theory of constraints helps managers focus resources on the efforts that will produce the most effective improvements.

Each of these management tools can be used as an individual system, or parts of them can be combined to create a new operating environment. Some aspects of them can be employed in service industries, such as banking, as well as in manufacturing. By continuously trying to improve and fine-tune operations, these management tools contribute to the same basic results for any organization: Product or service costs and delivery time are reduced, and the quality of the product or service and customer satisfaction are increased.

Performance Measures and the Analysis of Nonfinancial Data

OBJECTIVE

4 Define *performance measures*, recognize the uses of those measures in the management cycle, and prepare an analysis of nonfinancial data

Related Text Assignments:
Q: 13, 14, 15, 16
SE: 5, 6
E: 5, 6, 7
P: 1, 2, 6
SD: 1, 2, 5
MRA: 3, 4, 5

Performance measures are quantitative tools that gauge an organization's performance in relation to a specific goal or an expected outcome. Performance measures may be financial or nonfinancial. Financial performance measures include return on investment, net income as a percentage of sales, and the costs of poor quality as a percentage of sales. All of these examples use monetary information to measure the performance of a profit-generating organization or its segments, such as divisions, departments, product lines, sales territories, or operating activities.

Nonfinancial performance measures can include the number of times an object (product, service, or activity) occurs or the time taken to perform a task. Examples include number of customer complaints, number of orders shipped the same day, hours of inspection, and time to fill an order. Such performance measures are useful in reducing or eliminating waste and inefficiencies in operating activities.

Use of Performance Measures in the Management Cycle

Teaching Strategy: In class, ask students to work in teams to identify other examples of financial and nonfinancial performance measures. Emphasize that each measure should tie to a specific object.

Discussion Question: What measures could be used to express poor quality? **Answers:** Dollar measures (cost of rework, cost of spoilage) and nondollar measures (number of rejected units, rework labor hours, or percentage of good units to total production).

Management uses performance measures in all stages of the management cycle. In the planning stage, management establishes performance measures, or benchmarks, to motivate performance that will support the goals and objectives of the strategic plan. For example, many organizations want employees to increase quality, reduce costs, increase customer satisfaction, and increase efficiency and timeliness. As you will recall from earlier in the chapter, Abbie Awani selected the number of customer complaints as a performance measure to monitor service quality.

During the executing stage, performance measures guide and motivate the performance of employees and assist in assigning costs to products, departments, or operating activities. Awani will record the number of customer complaints during the year. She can group the information by type of complaint or the employee involved in the service.

In the reviewing stage, management uses performance measures to improve future performance by analyzing significant differences between actual and planned performance. By comparing the actual and planned number of customer complaints, Awani can identify problem areas and consider solutions.

In the reporting stage, performance measurement information is useful in communicating performance evaluations and developing new budgets. If Awani needed a formal report, she could have her accountant prepare a performance evaluation analysis based on this information.

The Balanced Scorecard

Instructional Strategy: Divide the class into groups and ask them to discuss SD1. Each group will report its results to the class. Emphasize that the activities they discussed are used to continuously improve the skills and knowledge required to be an expert. Suggest that continuous improvement applies to every activity we perform—as individuals or as members of an organization.

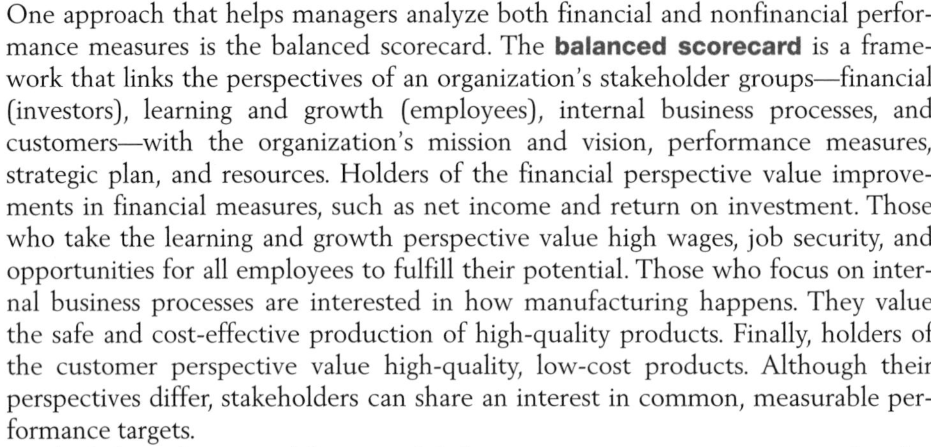

One approach that helps managers analyze both financial and nonfinancial performance measures is the balanced scorecard. The **balanced scorecard** is a framework that links the perspectives of an organization's stakeholder groups—financial (investors), learning and growth (employees), internal business processes, and customers—with the organization's mission and vision, performance measures, strategic plan, and resources. Holders of the financial perspective value improvements in financial measures, such as net income and return on investment. Those who take the learning and growth perspective value high wages, job security, and opportunities for all employees to fulfill their potential. Those who focus on internal business processes are interested in how manufacturing happens. They value the safe and cost-effective production of high-quality products. Finally, holders of the customer perspective value high-quality, low-cost products. Although their perspectives differ, stakeholders can share an interest in common, measurable performance targets.

The balanced scorecard framework helps an organization to measure and evaluate itself from a variety of viewpoints. Organizations that use a balanced scorecard can continuously improve because they have clear, measurable performance targets that acknowledge the interdependence and differing perspectives of their stakeholder groups. For example, in its balanced scorecard, Whirlpool measures financial performance, customer satisfaction, total quality, people commitment, and growth and innovation. Such performance measures, which lead to satisfied customers, investors, and employees and which continuously improve internal business processes, create value for all of an organization's stakeholder groups.

Analysis of Nonfinancial Data

Managers often face situations that require the analysis of nonfinancial data. For instance, managers can use nonfinancial measures to monitor changes in internal business processes and determine whether performance targets are being met. The following example illustrates how a manager uses nonfinancial data to analyze changes in a service organization.

Teaching Note: Explain how using nonfinancial measures in an international business environment often eliminates the problems associated with different currencies and different accounting standards.

Lynda Babb supervises tellers at Kings Beach National Bank. The bank has three drive-up windows, each with a full-time teller. Historically, each teller served an average of 30 customers per hour. However, on November 1, 20x5, management implemented a new check-scanning procedure that has cut back the number of customers served per hour.

Data on the number of customers served for the three-month period ended December 31, 20x5, are shown in Part A of Exhibit 1. Each teller works an average of 170 hours per month. Window 1 is always the busiest; Windows 2 and 3 receive progressively less business. The October figure of 30 customers per hour is derived from the averages for all three windows.

Ms. Babb is preparing a report for management on the effects of the new procedure. Part B of Exhibit 1 shows her analysis of the number of customers served over the three months by each teller window. She computed the number of customers served per hour by dividing the number of customers served by the monthly average hours worked per teller (170). By averaging the customer service rates for the three tellers, she got 28.43 customers per hour per window for November and 28.83 customers for December. As you can see, the service rate has decreased since October. But December's average is higher than November's, which means the tellers, as a group, are becoming more accustomed to the new procedure. Part C of Exhibit 1 is a graphic comparison of the number of customers served per hour.

Exhibit 1
Analysis of Nonfinancial Data—Bank

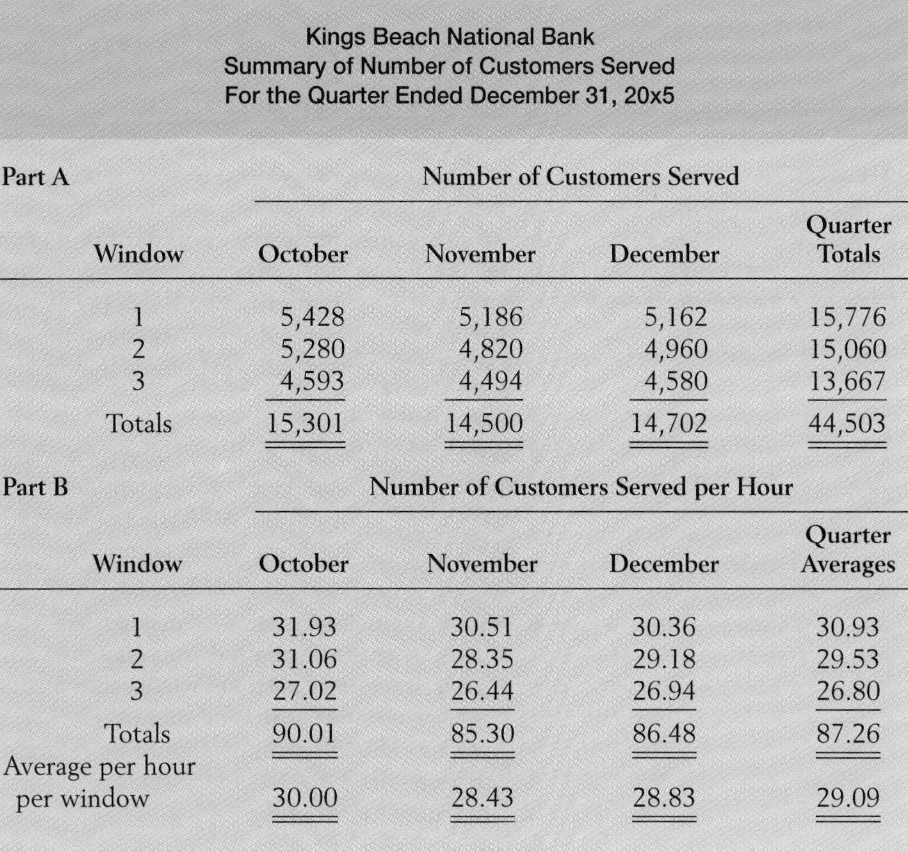

Kings Beach National Bank
Summary of Number of Customers Served
For the Quarter Ended December 31, 20x5

Part A

Window	October	November	December	Quarter Totals
	Number of Customers Served			
1	5,428	5,186	5,162	15,776
2	5,280	4,820	4,960	15,060
3	4,593	4,494	4,580	13,667
Totals	15,301	14,500	14,702	44,503

Part B

Window	October	November	December	Quarter Averages
	Number of Customers Served per Hour			
1	31.93	30.51	30.36	30.93
2	31.06	28.35	29.18	29.53
3	27.02	26.44	26.94	26.80
Totals	90.01	85.30	86.48	87.26
Average per hour per window	30.00	28.43	28.83	29.09

Part C: Graphic Comparison of the Number of Customers Served per Hour

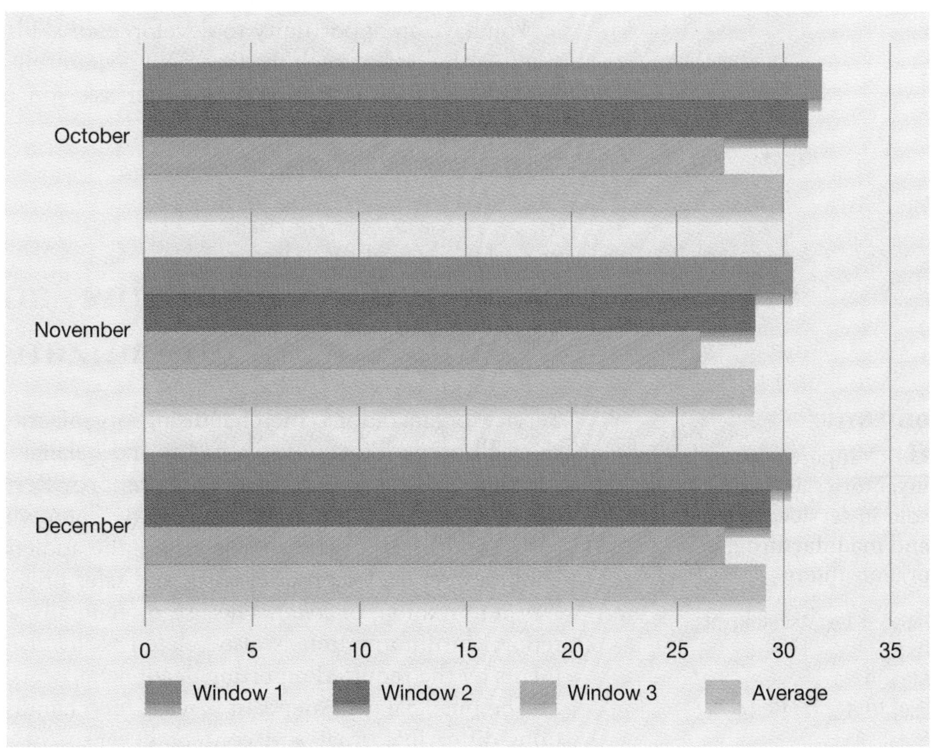

Management Accounting Reports and Analyses

OBJECTIVE

5 Identify the important questions a manager must consider before requesting or preparing a management report

Related Text Assignments:
Q: 17
SE: 7
E: 8
P: 3, 7
SD: 4
MRA: 2, 3

Point to Emphasize: Stress the concepts of generating useful information and reducing information overload.

As a manager, you may need to recommend the purchase of a particular machine, request money to develop a new form of packaging, or present a marketing plan for your organization's most popular product or service. Regardless of the assignment, you will have to prepare some type of report. Often the report will require relevant accounting information to support your position.

The keys to successful report preparation are the four *W*s: Why? Who? What? and When? Keep the following points in mind as you prepare your report.

- **Why?** Know the purpose of the report. Focus on it as you write.
- **Who?** Identify the audience for your report. Communicate at a level that matches your audience's understanding of the issue and their familiarity with accounting information. A detailed, informal report may be appropriate for your manager, but a more concise summary may be necessary for other audiences, such as the president or board of directors of your organization.
- **What?** What information is needed? *Select the relevant information.* Know the sources of that information. You may draw information from specific documents or from interviews with knowledgeable managers and employees.

  What method of presentation is best? *Develop the most effective method of presentation.* The information should be relevant and easy to read and understand. You may need to include visuals, such as bar charts or graphs, to present accounting information.
- **When?** Know the due date for the report. Strive to prepare an accurate report on a timely basis. Remember that you may have to balance accuracy and timeliness. Some accuracy may be lost if the report is urgent.

You have an opportunity to develop your skills in reporting accounting information. At the end of each management accounting chapter, you will find Managerial Reporting and Analysis problems that ask you to formulate reports that include accounting information.

Service, Merchandising, and Manufacturing Organizations

OBJECTIVE

6 Compare accounting for inventories and cost of goods sold in service, merchandising, and manufacturing organizations

Related Text Assignments:
Q: 18
SE: 8, 9
E: 9, 10, 11, 12, 13, 14
P: 4, 5, 8

Service organizations, merchandising organizations, and manufacturing organizations all prepare income statements and balance sheets. Their financial statements illustrate the four *W*s of successful reports. Reporting on the financial health of the organization is the purpose, or *why*. The owners, creditors, and outside parties for whom the reports are prepared are the audience, or *who*. The facts about assets, liabilities, service or product costs, and sales presented in the reports are the necessary information, or *what*. The use of generally accepted presentation methods to report the information is also related to *what*. Completing and filing the statements by the required reporting deadline answers the question of *when*.

The financial statements of service, merchandising, and manufacturing organizations differ in format and content because the operations of the three kinds of organizations differ. Let's look at how these organizations' operations, income statements, and balance sheets differ.

Service organizations

- sell services, not products,
- maintain no inventory accounts on the balance sheet, and
- determine the cost of services sold instead of calculating the cost of goods sold.

Merchandising organizations

- purchase products that are ready for resale,
- maintain only one inventory account on the balance sheet, and
- include the cost of purchases in the calculation of cost of goods sold.

Manufacturing organizations

- design and manufacture products for sale,
- maintain three inventory accounts on the balance sheet, and
- include the cost of goods manufactured in the calculation of cost of goods sold.

Instructional Strategy: Ask students to complete E 10 individually. Then have pairs of students compare their answers and discuss any differences. Debrief the exercise by asking various pairs to share their answers with the class.

Service organizations, such as UPS, Enterprise Rent-a-Car, and Accenture (formerly Andersen Consulting), provide services such as package delivery, rental cars, and consulting expertise. Service organizations maintain no inventories for resale. To calculate the cost of sales for a service organization, the following equation is used:

$$\text{Cost of Sales} = \text{Net Cost of Services Sold}$$

For example, Sweet Treasures Candy Store contracts with UPS to deliver 50 boxes of candy. The cost of sales for UPS would include the wages and salaries of personnel plus the expenses of trucks, planes, supplies, and anything consumed by UPS to deliver the packages for Sweet Treasures.

Discussion Question: Is a fast-food restaurant a merchandising, service, or manufacturing operation? **Answer:** Students may decide that it is a merchandising or service operation, a manufacturer, or all three. Use this example to stress that manufacturing operations are also in the business of selling products and services.

Merchandising organizations, such as Wal-Mart, Toys "R" Us, and Home Depot, purchase products that are ready for resale. These organizations maintain one inventory account, called Merchandise Inventory, that reflects the costs of products held for resale. To calculate the cost of goods sold for a merchandising organization, the following equation is used:

$$\text{Cost of Goods Sold} = \begin{array}{c}\text{Beginning}\\ \text{Merchandise}\\ \text{Inventory}\end{array} + \begin{array}{c}\textbf{Net Cost of}\\ \textbf{Purchases}\end{array} - \begin{array}{c}\text{Ending}\\ \text{Merchandise}\\ \text{Inventory}\end{array}$$

For example, Sweet Treasures Candy Store had a balance of \$3,000 in the Merchandise Inventory account on December 31, 20x2. During the next year, the company purchased candy products totaling \$23,000 (adjusted for purchase discounts, purchases returns and allowances, and freight-in). At December 31, 20x3, the Merchandise Inventory balance was \$4,500. The cost of goods sold is thus \$21,500 for the period 20x3.

$$\text{Cost of Goods Sold} = \$3{,}000 + \$23{,}000 - \$4{,}500 = \$21{,}500$$

Teaching Note: Demonstrate to students that the work in process inventory is the source of goods for the finished goods inventory in a manufacturing organization, just as purchases are the source of goods for the merchandise inventory in a merchandising organization.

Manufacturing organizations, such as Motorola, Sony, and IBM, use materials, labor, and manufacturing overhead to manufacture products for sale. Materials are purchased and used in the production process. The Materials Inventory account shows the balance of the cost of unused materials. During the production process, the costs of manufacturing the product are accumulated in the Work in Process Inventory account. The balance of the Work in Process Inventory account represents the costs of unfinished product. Once the product is complete and ready for sale, the cost of the goods manufactured is transferred to and reflected in the Finished Goods Inventory account. The balance in the Finished Goods Inventory account is the cost of unsold completed product. When the product is sold,

Figure 3
Comparison of Financial Statements for Service, Merchandising, and Manufacturing Organizations

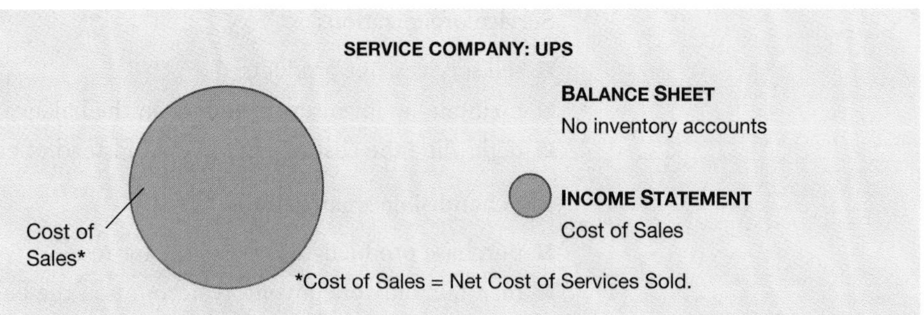

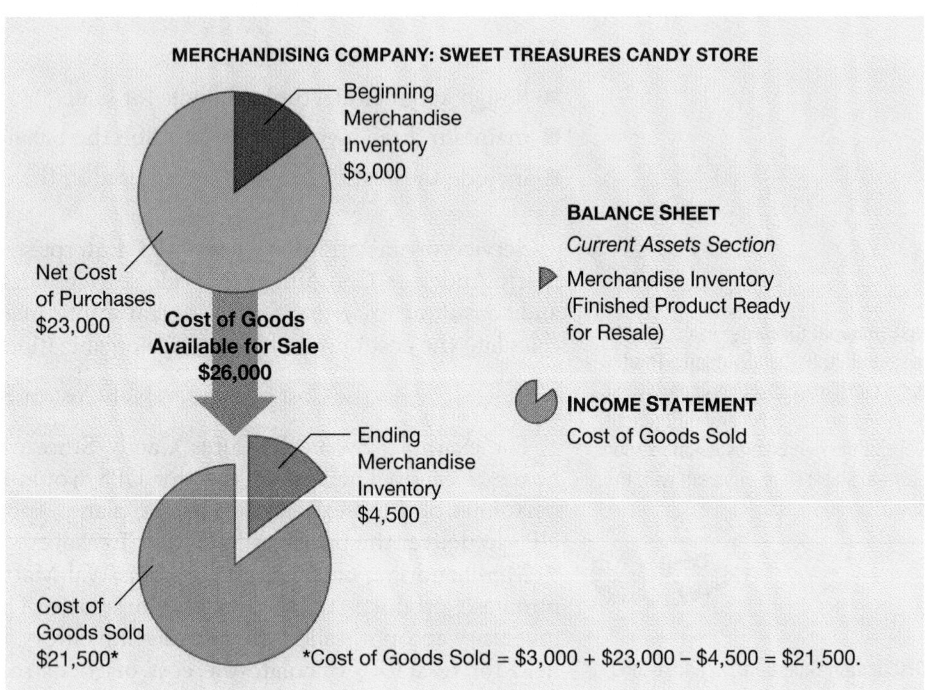

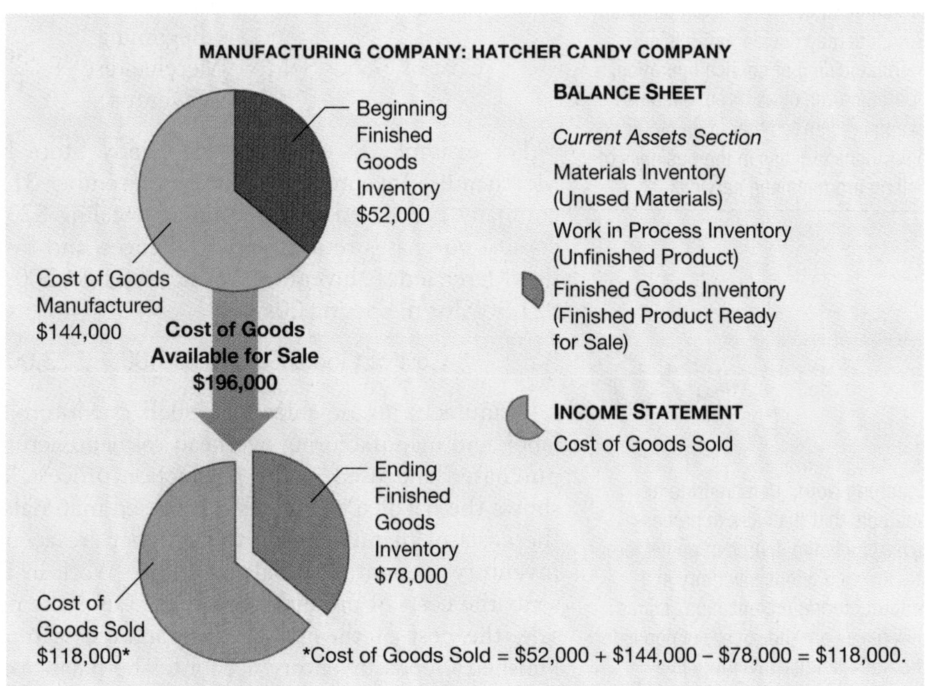

the manufacturing organization calculates the cost of goods sold using the following equation:

$$\text{Cost of Goods Sold} = \begin{matrix}\text{Beginning}\\ \text{Finished Goods}\\ \text{Inventory}\end{matrix} + \begin{matrix}\textbf{Cost of}\\ \textbf{Goods}\\ \textbf{Manufactured}\end{matrix} - \begin{matrix}\text{Ending}\\ \text{Finished Goods}\\ \text{Inventory}\end{matrix}$$

For example, Hatcher Candy Company, a supplier to Sweet Treasures Candy Store, had a balance of \$52,000 in the Finished Goods Inventory account on December 31, 20x2. During the next year, Hatcher manufactured candy products totaling \$144,000. At December 31, 20x3, the Finished Goods Inventory balance was \$78,000. The cost of goods sold is \$118,000 for the period 20x3.

$$\text{Cost of Goods Sold} = \$52{,}000 + \$144{,}000 - \$78{,}000 = \$118{,}000$$

All of these organizations use the following income statement format:

$$\text{Sales} - \begin{pmatrix}\text{Cost of Sales}\\ \text{or}\\ \text{Cost of Goods Sold}\end{pmatrix} = \begin{matrix}\text{Gross}\\ \text{Margin}\end{matrix} - \begin{matrix}\text{Operating}\\ \text{Expenses}\end{matrix} = \text{Net Income}$$

Figure 3 compares the financial statements for service, merchandising, and manufacturing organizations. Note in particular the differences in the inventories and cost of goods sold sections for merchandising and manufacturing organizations. By combining the beginning Merchandise Inventory balance with the net cost of purchases for Sweet Treasures Candy Store, we calculate a "pie" called *cost of goods available for sale*. By counting and valuing unsold merchandise in the Merchandise Inventory account, we slice from the pie the ending Merchandise Inventory balance for the balance sheet, leaving the cost of goods sold for the income statement. Similarly, if we combine the beginning Finished Goods Inventory balance with the cost of goods manufactured for Hatcher Candy Company, we calculate a "pie" called *cost of goods available for sale*. By counting and valuing the unsold products in Finished Goods Inventory, we can slice from the pie the ending Finished Goods Inventory balance for the balance sheet, leaving the cost of goods sold for the income statement. Notice that for service organizations, such as UPS, the "pie" is called *cost of sales*. The cost of sales appears only in the income statement. No portion of it appears on the balance sheet because a service organization has no inventory accounts.

Standards of Ethical Conduct

OBJECTIVE

7 Identify the standards of ethical conduct for management accountants

Related Text Assignments:
Q: 19, 20
SE: 10
E: 15
SD: 3

Point to Emphasize: It is crucial for business students to recognize situations that give rise to ethical conflicts and to be prepared to address these issues.

Managers are responsible to external parties (for example, owners, creditors, governmental agencies, and the local community) for the proper use of organizational resources and the financial reporting of their actions. Conflicts may arise that require managers to balance the interests of all external parties. For example, the community wants a safe living environment, while owners seek to maximize profits. If management decides to purchase an expensive device to extract pollutants from the production process, it will protect the community, but profits will decline. The benefit will be greater for the community than for the owners. On the other hand, management could achieve higher profits for the owners by purchasing a less expensive, less effective pollution device that would protect the community less well. Such potential conflicts between external parties can create ethical dilemmas for management and for accountants.

Management accountants and financial managers have a responsibility to help management balance the needs of the various external parties. Thus the accounting

Exhibit 2
Standards of Ethical Conduct for Practitioners of Management Accounting and Financial Management

Practitioners of management accounting and financial management have an obligation to the public, their profession, the organization they serve, and themselves, to maintain the highest standards of ethical conduct. In recognition of this obligation, the Institute of Management Accountants has promulgated the following standards of ethical conduct for practitioners of management accounting and financial management. Adherence to these standards, both domestically and internationally, is integral to achieving the Objectives of Management Accounting. Practitioners of management accounting and financial management shall not commit acts contrary to these standards nor shall they condone the commission of such acts by others within their organizations.

Competence. Practitioners of management accounting and financial management have a responsibility to:

- Maintain an appropriate level of professional competence by ongoing development of their knowledge and skills.
- Perform their professional duties in accordance with relevant laws, regulations, and technical standards.
- Prepare complete and clear reports and recommendations after appropriate analysis of relevant and reliable information.

Confidentiality. Practitioners of management accounting and financial management have a responsibility to:

- Refrain from disclosing confidential information acquired in the course of their work except when authorized, unless legally obligated to do so.
- Inform subordinates as appropriate regarding the confidentiality of information acquired in the course of their work and monitor their activities to assure the maintenance of that confidentiality.
- Refrain from using or appearing to use confidential information acquired in the course of their work for unethical or illegal advantage either personally or through third parties.

Integrity. Practitioners of management accounting and financial management have a responsibility to:

- Avoid actual or apparent conflicts of interest and advise all appropriate parties of any potential conflict.
- Refrain from engaging in any activity that would prejudice their ability to carry out their duties ethically.
- Refuse any gift, favor, or hospitality that would influence or would appear to influence their actions.
- Refrain from either actively or passively subverting the attainment of the organization's legitimate and ethical objectives.
- Recognize and communicate professional limitations or other constraints that would preclude responsible judgment or successful performance of an activity.

(continued)

Ethical Consideration: Ask students to identify the dollar-value limits on gifts, lunches, or favors that would not violate the integrity standard. To stimulate discussion, then ask them what dollar value would influence their behavior?

profession must operate with the highest standards of performance. To provide guidance, the Institute of Management Accountants has formally adopted standards of ethical conduct for practitioners of management accounting and financial management. Those standards emphasize that management accountants have responsibilities in the areas of competence, confidentiality, integrity, and objectivity. The full statement is presented in Exhibit 2.

The International Organization for Standardization (ISO) is a worldwide federation of national standards bodies from over 130 countries. It was formed in 1947 to improve the international exchange of goods and services and to promote worldwide cooperation in intellectual, scientific, technological, and economic activities. ISO standards are international agreements that guide business. Without the more than 12,000 standards developed by the ISO, businesses would lack guidelines for communicating, measuring, and even producing uniform goods and services. For example, one series of standards, ISO 14000, provides a framework for managing environmental issues.[6]

2. Assuming that the following information reflects the results of operations for 20x5, calculate the (a) gross margin, (b) cost of goods sold, (c) cost of goods available for sale, and (d) cost of goods manufactured.

Net Income	$133,200
Operating Expenses	48,000
Sales	450,000
Finished Goods Inventory 12/31/x4	68,000

Expanding Your Critical Thinking, Communication, and Interpersonal Skills

Skills Development

Conceptual Analysis

SD 1. **LO 3 LO 4 Continuous Improvement**

Achieving high quality requires high standards of performance. To maintain high standards of quality, individuals and organizations must continuously improve their performance. To illustrate this, select your favorite sport or hobby.

1. Answer the following questions:
   a. What standards would you establish to assess your actual performance?
   b. What process would you design to achieve high quality in your performance?
   c. When do you know you have achieved high quality in your performance?
   d. Once you know you perform well, how easy would it be for you to maintain that level of expertise?
   e. What can you do to continuously improve your performance?
2. If you owned a business, which of the questions in **1** would be important to answer?
3. Answer the questions in **1**, assuming you own a business.

SD 2. **LO 4 Performance Measures**

According to *The Wall Street Journal*, ***General Motors Corp.*** apparently retreated from its plan to revamp the way it makes small cars. Called Project Yellowstone, the plan called for GM to build two U.S. plants that would use modular assembly systems. GM's suppliers would develop and supply large chunks of cars, like dashboards, to those plants for final assembly. The amount of GM's investment and the number of employees needed to assemble the cars would be greatly reduced. The United Auto Workers union blasted the new approach as an attempt to eliminate union jobs.[7]

1. What financial performance measures mentioned in the chapter would have prompted GM's desire to try a new approach?
2. The balanced scorecard uses performance measures that link to the perspectives of all stakeholder groups. Who are GM's stakeholders, and what performance measures do they value?
3. Refer to the discussion of Honda Motor Co. in the Decision Point at the beginning of this chapter. How does GM's modular assembly plan differ from Honda's?
4. In your opinion, what options does GM have if it wishes to pursue the use of modular assembly systems?

Communication

Critical Thinking

Ethics

Group Activity

Hot Links to Real Companies

International

Internet

Memo

Spreadsheet

Ethical Dilemma

SD 3. **LO 7 Professional Ethics**

Grace Albems is the controller for the ***Atlanta Corporation.*** Albems has been with the company for 17 years and is being considered for the job of chief financial officer (CFO). Her boss, the current CFO and former company controller, will be Atlanta Corporation's new president. Albems has just discussed the year-end closing with her boss, who made the following statement during the conversation:

> Grace, why are you so inflexible? I'm only asking you to postpone the write-off of the $2,500,000 obsolete inventory for ten days so that it won't appear on this year's financial statements. Ten days! Do it. Your promotion is coming up, you know. Make sure you keep all the possible outcomes in mind as you complete your year-end work. Oh, and keep this conversation confidential—just between you and me. OK?

Identify the ethical issue or issues involved and state the appropriate solution to the problem. Be prepared to defend your answer.

Research Activity

SD 4. **LO 5 Management Reports**

The registrar's office of ***Swink County College*** is responsible for maintaining a record of each student's grades and credits for use by students, instructors, and administrators.

1. Assume that you are a manager in the registrar's office and that you recently joined a team of managers to review the grade-reporting process. State how you would prepare a grade report for students and a grade report for instructors by answering the following questions.
   a. Who will read the grade report?
   b. Why must the registrar's office prepare the grade report?
   c. What information should the grade report contain?
   d. When is the grade report due?
2. Why do differences exist between the information in a grade report for students and the information in a grade report for instructors?
3. Visit the registrar's office of your school in person, or access it through your school's home page. Obtain a copy of your grade report and a copy of the forms the registrar's office uses to report grades to instructors at your school. Compare the information on the actual grade report forms to the information you listed in **1** above. Explain any differences.
4. What can the registrar's office do to make sure that grade reports present all necessary information in a manner that communicates effectively to users?

Decision-Making Practice

SD 5. **LO 4 Nonfinancial Data Analysis**

As a subcontractor in the jet aircraft industry, ***Air Gears Manufacturing Company*** specializes in the production of housings for landing gears on jet airplanes. Production begins on Machine 1, which bends pieces of metal into cylinder-shaped housings and trims off the rough edges. Machine 2 welds the seam of the cylinder and pushes the entire piece into a large die to mold the housing into its final shape.

Joe Mee, the production supervisor, believes that too much scrap (wasted metal) is created in the current process. To help him, James Kincaid began preparing an analysis by comparing the amounts of actual scrap generated with the amounts of expected scrap for production in the last four weeks. His incomplete report appears at the top of the next page. Because of a death in his family, Kincaid cannot complete the analysis. Mee asks you to complete the following tasks and submit a recommendation to him.

1. Present the information in two ways.
   a. Prepare a table that shows the difference between the actual and the expected scrap in pounds per machine per week. Calculate the difference in pounds and as a percentage (divide the difference in pounds by the expected pounds of scrap

Air Gears Manufacturing Company Comparison of Actual Scrap and Expected Scrap Four-Week Period				
	Scrap in Pounds		Difference	
	Actual	Expected	Pounds	Percentage
Machine 1				
Week 1	36,720	36,720		
Week 2	54,288	36,288		
Week 3	71,856	35,856		
Week 4	82,440	35,640		
Machine 2				
Week 1	43,200	18,180		
Week 2	39,600	18,054		
Week 3	7,200	18,162		
Week 4	18,000	18,108		

for each week). If the actual poundage of scrap is less than the expected poundage, record the difference as a negative. (This means there is less scrap than expected.)

b. Prepare a line graph for each machine showing the weeks on the *X* axis and the pounds of scrap on the *Y* axis.

2. Examine the differences for the four weeks for each machine and determine which machine operation is creating excessive scrap.
3. What could be causing this problem?
4. What could Mee do to identify the specific cause of such problems sooner?
5. Write a memo summarizing your findings in **1** through **4** above.

Managerial Reporting and Analysis

Interpreting Management Reports

MRA 1. **LO 1** **Management Information**

Obtain a copy of a recent annual report for a publicly held organization in which you have a particular interest. (Copies of annual reports are available at your campus library, at a local public library, on the Internet, or by direct request to an organization.) Assume that you have just been appointed to a middle-management position in a division of the organization you have chosen. You are interested in obtaining information that will help you better manage the activities of your division and have decided to thoroughly review the contents of the annual report in an attempt to learn as much as possible. You particularly want to know about:

1. Size of inventory maintained
2. Ability to earn income
3. Reliance on debt financing
4. Types, volume, and prices of products or services sold
5. Type of production process used
6. Management's long-range strategies
7. Success (profitability) of the division's various product lines
8. Efficiency of operations
9. Operating details of your division

REQUIRED

1. Write a brief description of the organization and its products, services, or activities.
2. From a review of the financial statements and the accompanying disclosure notes, prepare a written summary of the information you found that pertained to items 1 through 9 above.
3. Is any of the information you seek in other sections of the annual report? If so, which information, and where is it found?
4. The annual report also includes other types of information you may find helpful in your new position. In outline form, summarize the additional information you think will help you.

Formulating Management Reports

MRA 2.

LO 5 Management Information Needs

In MRA 1, you examined your new employer's annual report and noted some useful information. You still wish to find out if your new division's products are competitive, but you cannot find the necessary information in the annual report.

REQUIRED

1. What kinds of information do you want to know about your competition?
2. Why is this information relevant? (Link your response to a particular decision about your organization's products or services. For example, you might seek information to help you determine a new selling price.)
3. From what sources could you obtain the information you need?
4. When would you want to obtain this information?
5. Create a report that will communicate your findings to your superior.

International Company

MRA 3.

LO 4 Management
LO 5 Information Needs

McDonald's is the leading competitor in the fast-food restaurant business. More than 40 percent of McDonald's restaurants are located outside the United States. One component of McDonald's marketing strategy is to increase sales by expanding its foreign markets. The company uses quantitative and qualitative financial and nonfinancial information in making decisions about new restaurant locations in foreign markets. For example, the following types of information would be important to such a decision: the cost of a new building (financial quantitative information), the estimated number of hamburgers to be sold in the first year (nonfinancial quantitative information), and site desirability (qualitative information).

REQUIRED

You are a member of a management team that must decide whether or not to open a new restaurant in England. Identify at least two examples each of the (a) financial quantitative, (b) nonfinancial quantitative, and (c) qualitative information you will need before you can make a decision.

Group Activity: Divide the class into groups and ask them to discuss this MRA. Then debrief the entire class by asking one person from each group to summarize his or her group's discussion.

Excel Spreadsheet Analysis

MRA 4.

LO 4 Nonfinancial Data

Refer to assignment **P 6** in this chapter. Lindy Raymond needs to analyze the work performed by each shift in each department during Weeks 1 through 4.

REQUIRED

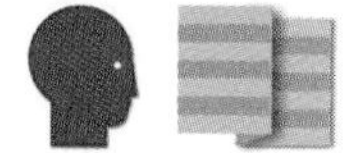

1. For each department, calculate the average labor hours worked per board for each shift during Weeks 1 through 4. Carry your solution to two decimal places. (*Note*: Hours worked per board = hours worked each week ÷ boards produced each week.)
2. Using the ChartWizard and the information from **1**, prepare a line graph for each department that compares the hours per board worked by the first and second shifts

and the estimate for that department during Weeks 1 through 4. Below is the suggested format to use for the information table necessary to complete the line graph for the Molding Department.

	Molding Department			
	Week 1	Week 2	Week 3	Week 4
First shift	3.50	3.20	3.40	3.80
Second shift	3.60	3.40	3.80	4.20
Estimated	3.40	3.40	3.40	3.40

3. Examine the four graphs that you prepared in **2.** Which shift is more efficient in all four departments? List some reasons for the differences between the shifts.

Internet Case

MRA 5.
LO 4 Comparison of Performance Measures

Refer to the Decision Point for this chapter on Honda Motor Company's new green car, the Insight. Toyota Motor Company also has introduced a green car called the Prius. Search Toyota's web site at http://www.toyota.com for data concerning the Prius's success. Compare those data with Honda Motor Company's data on the Insight at http://www.honda.com. (**Hint:** Review annual reports, press releases, and model sites, or use the company's search engine.)

REQUIRED

1. List the financial and nonfinancial measures used by Toyota. List the measures used by Honda.
2. Use the data you found to prepare a brief comparison of the two cars. Do the two companies use comparable performance measures? If so, evaluate the performance of the Prius and the Insight. If the measures are not comparable, how does their focus differ?

ENDNOTES

1. Frederic M. Biddle, "A Little Gas Fuels Hope for a New Type of Electric Car," *The Wall Street Journal*, July 9, 1999.
2. Northiko Shirouzu, "Honda Bucks Industry Wisdom, Aiming to Be Small and Efficient," *The Wall Street Journal*, July 9, 1999.
3. Institute of Management Accountants, *Statement No. 1A* (New York, 1982). Since this definition was prepared, the importance of nonfinancial information has increased significantly. Words in brackets were added by the authors.
4. William M. Bulkeley, "Toys 'R' Us Names Hasbro's Barbour for Online Unit," *The Wall Street Journal*, August 3, 1999.
5. AICPA web site, www.aicpa.org, "The New Finance."
6. ISO web site, www.iso.ch/infoe, "ISO 14000."
7. Gregory L. White, "GM Appears to Step Back from Proposal," *The Wall Street Journal*, March 30, 1999.

20 Cost Concepts and Cost Allocation

LEARNING OBJECTIVES

1. State how managers use information about costs in the management cycle.
2. Identify various approaches managers use to classify costs.
3. Define and give examples of the three elements of product cost and compute a product unit cost for a manufacturing organization.
4. Describe the flow of product-related activities, documents, and costs through the Materials Inventory, Work in Process Inventory, and Finished Goods Inventory accounts.
5. Prepare a statement of cost of goods manufactured and an income statement for a manufacturing organization.
6. Define *cost allocation* and explain how cost objects, cost pools, and cost drivers are used to apply manufacturing overhead.
7. Calculate product unit cost using the traditional allocation of manufacturing overhead costs.
8. Calculate product unit cost using activity-based costing to assign manufacturing overhead costs.
9. Apply costing concepts to a service organization.

DECISION POINT: A MANAGER'S FOCUS

Caterpillar Caterpillar, the world's leading manufacturer of construction and mining equipment, diesel and natural gas engines, and industrial gas turbines, makes some of the world's most complex and expensive vehicles. For instance, the Caterpillar 797 is the biggest mining truck ever made. Think of it as a two-story house, going down the road at 40 miles per hour on six 13-foot-high tires, carrying a load weighing 360 tons. The truck and its load are twice the weight of a fully loaded Boeing 747 aircraft. Each truck takes 11 days to build and costs about $2.5 million. The accuracy of this cost figure is important to management because it is used in many ways, including to set the price of $3.5 million for the Caterpillar 797.[1] Determining the cost of the truck requires complex analyses of many factors. What are some of those factors, and how do they bear on management decisions?

The cost of the Caterpillar 797 includes not only the costs of the materials and labor used in making the truck, but also a large component for overhead, such as the factory, electricity, supervision, maintenance, and other costs that cannot be directly traced to the truck. Operating costs for selling and administration must also be considered. To help management make decisions that will enable Caterpillar to sell these trucks for a profit, all related costs must be analyzed in terms of their traceability and behavior, whether or not they add value, and how they will affect the financial statements. Because many of the costs will not be directly traceable to the Caterpillar 797 or to specific departments, management must use a method of allocation to assign them. Possibilities include traditional allocation methods and newer methods such as activity-based costing. This chapter provides an introduction to cost classification, reporting, and allocation and will serve as the foundation for the techniques that will be presented in subsequent chapters.

Critical Thinking Question: Why are many of Caterpillar's costs not directly traceable to the equipment it makes? Answer: Many of Caterpillar's costs, such as the costs of its factories, factory maintenance, insurance, and utilities, benefit all products manufactured by Caterpillar in its factories. Thus, such costs are not traceable to a specific product and must be allocated, or divided, among all the products.

Cost Information and the Management Cycle

OBJECTIVE

1 State how managers use information about costs in the management cycle

Related Text Assignments:
Q: 1
E: 1
SD: 1

One of the primary goals of a company is to be profitable. Because owners expect to earn profits, managers have a responsibility to use resources wisely and generate revenues that will exceed the costs of the organization's operating, investing, and financing activities. In this chapter, we will focus on costs related to production activities in a manufacturing organization and to service activities in a service organization. First, let's look at information about costs and the management cycle for manufacturing, retail, and service companies.

Use of Cost Information in the Management Cycle

In the management cycle, managers use operating cost information to plan, execute, review, and report the results of operating activities. Figure 1 provides an overview of operating costs and the management cycle.

PLANNING In the planning stage, managers of manufacturing organizations, such as John Deere, Motorola, or General Motors, use estimated product cost information to develop budgets for production, direct materials, direct labor, and manufacturing overhead, and to determine the selling prices or sales levels required to cover all costs. In retail organizations, such as Sears, PepBoys, or Macy's, managers work with estimates of the cost of merchandise purchases to develop budgets for purchases and net income and to determine the selling prices or sales units required to cover all costs. In service organizations, like Citibank, Humana, or Accenture (formerly Andersen Consulting), managers utilize the estimated costs of rendering services to develop budgets, estimate fee revenues, and plan human resource needs.

EXECUTING In the executing stage, managers of manufacturing organizations use estimated product unit costs to estimate the gross margin and operating income on products sold and to make decisions about such matters as dropping a product line, outsourcing the manufacture of a part or subassembly to another manufacturer, bidding on a special order, or negotiating a selling price. In retail organizations, managers work with the estimated cost of merchandise purchases to estimate gross margin, operating income, and value of merchandise sold and to make decisions about such matters as reducing selling prices for clearance sales, offering lower selling prices for bulk sales orders, or dropping a product line. In service organizations, managers find the estimated cost of services helpful in estimating profitability and making decisions about such matters as bidding on future service assignments or projects, lowering the fee to charge a customer, dropping a service provided, or negotiating a fee.

Teaching Note: To help students see the complete management cycle for each type of organization, move through the cycle for manufacturing, retail, and service organizations separately, adding your own illustrations.

REVIEWING In the reviewing stage, managers want to know about significant differences between estimated costs and actual costs. The identification of variances between estimated and actual product costs (for manufacturing organizations), estimated and actual costs of merchandise purchased (for retail organizations), and estimated and actual costs of services rendered (for service organizations) helps managers to determine the causes of cost overruns and enables them to adjust future actions to reduce potential problems.

Figure 1
Operating Costs and the Management Cycle

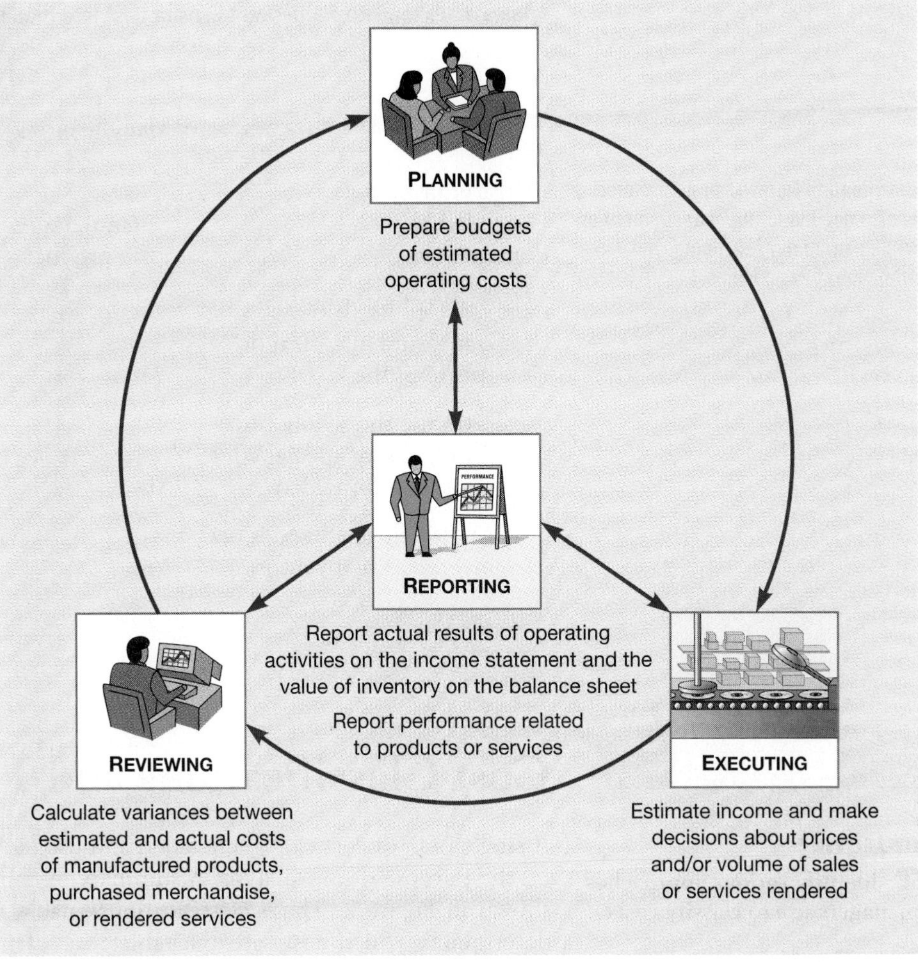

Reporting In the reporting stage, managers expect to see financial statements that include the actual costs associated with operating activities in the executing stage of the management cycle and also performance evaluation reports that summarize the variance analyses calculated in the reviewing stage. This is true for manufacturing, retail, and service organizations.

Cost Information and Organizations

Table 1 lists examples of the types and uses of cost information for different types of organizations. For a manufacturing organization, the product costs include the costs of direct materials, direct labor, and manufacturing overhead. For a retail organization, the costs of a purchased product include adjustments for freight-in costs, purchase returns and allowances, and purchase discounts. For a service organization, the costs to provide a service include the costs of labor and related overhead. Ultimately, a company is profitable only when revenues from sales or services rendered exceed all its costs, including both the costs of products and services and operating costs. Among such costs are the cost to manufacture or purchase a product or to render a service, plus the costs of marketing, distributing, installing, and repairing a product or the costs of marketing and supporting the delivery of services.

Table 1. Examples of Types and Uses of Cost Information for Different Types of Organizations

	Type of Organization		
	Manufacturing	Retail	Service
Cost information needed by management	Cost to manufacture the product	Cost to purchase the product	Cost to provide the service
Uses of cost information:			
To measure historical or future profits	Yes	Yes	Yes
To decide the selling price for regular or special sales or services provided	Yes	Yes	Yes
To value finished goods or merchandise inventories	Yes	Yes	Not applicable

Clarification Note: Cost information is also needed for the management of selling, promoting, shipping, and administrative activities.

Cost Classifications and Their Uses

OBJECTIVE

2 Identify various approaches managers use to classify costs

Related Text Assignments
Q: 2, 3, 4, 5
SE: 1
E: 2
SD: 1, 4
MRA: 5

A single item of cost can be classified and used in several different ways, depending on the purpose of the analysis. A summary of commonly used cost classifications is shown in Figure 2. These classifications enable managers to (1) control costs by determining which costs are traceable to a particular destination, or cost object, such as a service or product; (2) calculate the number of units that must be sold to obtain a certain level of profit (cost behavior); (3) identify the costs of activities that add value to a product or service and activities that do not; and (4) classify costs for the preparation of financial statements. An understanding of these cost classifications will help managers select and use relevant information to operate efficiently, provide quality products or services, and satisfy customer needs.

Cost Traceability

Managers rely on management accountants to trace costs to cost objects, such as products or services, sales territories, departments, or operating activities. By tracing costs as directly as possible to cost objects, managers can develop a fairly accurate measurement of costs. Managers use these direct and indirect measures of costs to support pricing decisions or decisions to reallocate resources to other cost objects.

Direct costs are costs that can be conveniently or economically traced to a cost object. For example, the wages of production line workers can be conveniently traced to the product, because the time worked and the related hourly wages can be easily found by looking at time cards and payroll records. Similarly, the costs of an engine can be easily traced to an automobile's cost.

In some cases, however, even though a material becomes part of a finished product, the expense of tracing its cost is too great. Some examples include nails in furniture, bolts in automobiles, and rivets in airplanes. Such costs are considered indirect costs of the product. **Indirect costs** are costs that cannot be conveniently or economically traced to a cost object. Even though indirect costs may be difficult to trace, they must be included in the cost of a product. Therefore, management

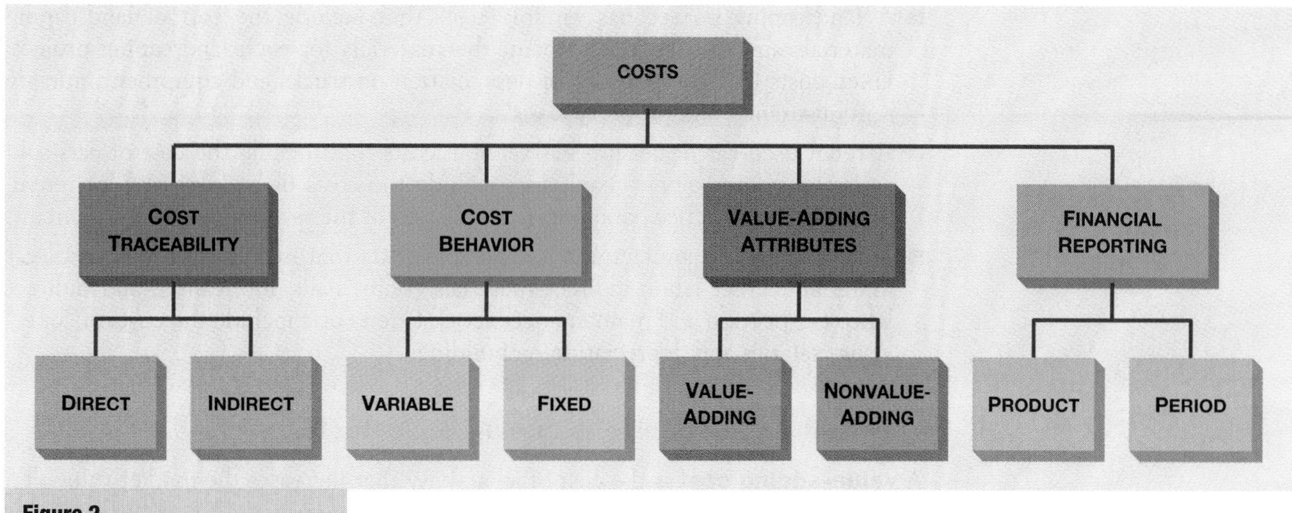

Figure 2
Overview of Cost Classifications

accountants use a formula to assign indirect costs to products. For example, insurance costs for the factory cannot be conveniently traced to individual products, but, for the sake of accuracy, they must be included in each product's cost. Management accountants solve the problem by assigning a portion of the factory insurance costs to each product manufactured.

Regardless of the type of organization—service, retail, or manufacturing—classifying costs is important. The following examples illustrate a cost object and its related direct and indirect costs for three kinds of organizations.

- In a service organization, such as an accounting firm, costs can be traced to a specific service, such as tax return preparation. Direct costs for tax return preparation services include the costs of paper, computer usage, and labor to prepare the return. Indirect costs include the costs of supplies, office rental, utilities, secretarial labor, telephone usage, and depreciation of office furniture.
- In a retail organization, such as a department store, costs can be traced to a department. For example, the direct costs of the shoe department include the costs of shoes and the wages of employees working in that department. Indirect costs include the costs of utilities, insurance, property taxes, storage, and handling.
- In a manufacturing organization, costs can be traced to the product. Direct costs of the product include the costs of direct materials and direct labor. Indirect costs include the costs of utilities, depreciation of equipment, insurance, property taxes, inspection, maintenance of machinery, storage, handling, and cleaning.

Cost Behavior

Instructional Strategy: Divide the class into small groups. Ask groups to identify three fixed and three variable costs found in all fast-food restaurants and discuss why it is important for managers to identify those costs. Groups may present their findings to the class and take questions from other students.

Managers are also interested in the way costs respond to changes in volume or activity. By analyzing those patterns of behavior, managers gain information about how changes in selling prices or operating costs affect the net income of the organization. Costs can be separated into variable costs and fixed costs. A **variable cost** is a cost that changes in direct proportion to a change in productive output (or any other measure of volume). A **fixed cost** is a cost that remains constant within a defined range of activity or time period.

Viewing costs as variable or fixed is important to managers of any type of organization. The following examples illustrate variable and fixed costs for service, retail, and manufacturing organizations:

- A landscaping service has variable costs that include the cost of landscaping materials and direct labor to plant the materials for each landscaping project. Fixed costs include the costs of depreciation on trucks and equipment, nursery rent, insurance, and property taxes.
- A retail used-car dealership has variable costs that include the cost of cars sold and sales commissions. Fixed costs include the costs of building and lot rental, depreciation on office equipment, and salaries of the receptionist and accountant.
- A lawn mower manufacturer has variable costs that include the costs of direct materials, direct labor, indirect materials (bolts, nails, lubricants), and indirect labor (inspection and maintenance labor). Fixed costs include the costs of supervisory salaries and depreciation on buildings.

Value-Adding Versus Nonvalue-Adding Costs

A **value-adding cost** is the cost of an activity that increases the market value of a product or service. A **nonvalue-adding cost** is the cost of an activity that adds cost to a product or service but does not increase its market value. In the spirit of continuous improvement, managers examine the value-adding attributes of the activities and processes in their organization. Their goal is to reduce or eliminate activities that do not add value to the products or services. The organization identifies the characteristics of the product or service that customers value and would be willing to pay for. This information influences the design of future products or the delivery of future services. The organization's management also identifies the operating activities that provide the value. Activities that do not add value are reduced or eliminated. For example, the depreciation of a machine that shapes a part assembled into the final product is a value-adding cost; the depreciation of a sales department automobile is a nonvalue-adding cost.

Costs incurred to improve the quality of a product are value-adding costs if the customer is willing to pay more for the higher-quality product; otherwise, they are nonvalue-adding costs because they do not increase the product's market value. The costs of administrative activities such as accounting and human resources are nonvalue-adding costs; they are necessary for the operation of the business, but they do not add value to the product.

Point to Emphasize: Product costs remain assets until they are expensed and transferred from the Finished Goods Inventory account to Cost of Goods Sold.

Business-World Example: To demonstrate that the length of time costs remain in inventory is not a consideration in determining product costs, ask the class to identify the product costs and period costs of a local fast-food operation. Such operations maintain a direct materials inventory, have a rapid turnover in work in process inventory, and have virtually no finished goods inventory at any given time.

Costs for Financial Reporting

Managers must prepare financial statements for external parties using a required format based on generally accepted accounting principles. For purposes of financial reporting, costs are divided into product costs and period costs. **Product costs**, or *inventoriable costs*, are costs assigned to inventory; they include direct materials, direct labor, and manufacturing overhead. Product costs appear on the income

United Parcel Service (UPS) has taken a proactive role in its commitment to efficient and responsible management of resources. UPS recycles computer paper, letter envelopes, and delivery notices, and it also records delivery information electronically, which saves an estimated 30,000 trees annually. UPS also helps customers protect the environment by (1) devising the best packaging methods to prevent product damage and minimize waste and (2) developing national package-retrieval services to collect a customer's packaging. For example, Ethan Allen, Inc., a furniture maker and retailer, uses UPS's services to retrieve foam-sheet shipping material, which makes money for Ethan Allen in addition to reducing its disposal costs.[2]

Table 2. Examples of Cost Classifications for a Candy Manufacturer

Cost Examples	Traceability to Product	Cost Behavior	Value Attribute	Financial Reporting
Sugar for candy	Direct	Variable	Value-adding	Product (direct materials)
Labor for mixing	Direct	Variable	Value-adding	Product (direct labor)
Labor for supervision	Indirect	Fixed	Nonvalue-adding	Product (manufacturing overhead)
Depreciation on mixing machine	Indirect	Fixed	Value-adding	Product (manufacturing overhead)
Sales commission	—*	Variable	Value-adding†	Period
Accountant's salary	—*	Fixed	Nonvalue-adding	Period

* Sales commission and accountant's salary are not product costs. Therefore, these costs are not directly or indirectly traceable in traditional business operations.

† Sales commission can be value-adding because customers' perceptions of the salesperson and the selling experience can strongly affect their perceptions of the product's or service's market value.

Teaching Note: The concepts of product costs and period costs can also be explained using the matching rule: Product costs must be charged to the period in which the product generates revenue, and period costs are charged against the revenue of the current period.

statement as cost of goods sold or on the balance sheet as finished goods inventory. **Period costs**, or *noninventoriable costs*, are costs of resources consumed during the accounting period and not assigned to products. They appear as operating expenses on the income statement. For example, selling and administrative expenses are period costs.

Table 2 shows how some sample costs of a candy manufacturer can be classified in terms of traceability, behavior, value attribute, and financial reporting.

Elements of Product Costs

OBJECTIVE

3 Define and give examples of the three elements of product cost and compute a product unit cost for a manufacturing organization

Related Text Assignments:
Q: 6,7,8,9
SE: 2,3
E: 3
P: 1
MRA: 5

Product costs include all costs related to the manufacturing process. The three elements of product cost are (1) direct materials costs, (2) direct labor costs, and (3) manufacturing overhead costs, which are indirect manufacturing costs.

Direct Materials Costs

All manufactured products are made from basic direct materials. **Direct materials costs** are the costs of materials that can be conveniently and economically traced to specific units of product. Some examples of direct materials are iron ore for steel, sheet steel for automobiles, and sugar for candy.

Discussion Question: When would materials such as paint or small parts be accounted for as direct materials? Answer: When their relative costs are high and have a material effect on product cost.

Discussion Question: Is the paint on a toy (or other object) a direct or an indirect material? Answer: The paint is physically a direct material because it is attached to the product. However, because it is inexpensive, it is often accounted for as an indirect cost.

Direct Labor Costs

The manufacturing process includes all activities required to make a product, including maintenance, handling, inspecting, moving, and storing. **Direct labor costs** are the costs of labor to complete production activities that can be conveniently and economically traced to specific units of product. The wages of machine operators and other workers involved in actually shaping the product are direct labor costs.

Manufacturing Overhead Costs

The third element of product cost includes all manufacturing costs that cannot be classified as direct materials or direct labor costs. **Manufacturing overhead costs** are production-related costs that cannot be practically or conveniently traced directly to an end product. This assortment of costs is also called *factory overhead*,

FOCUS ON BUSINESS TECHNOLOGY

Technology and new manufacturing processes have produced entirely new patterns of product costs. The three elements of product cost are still direct materials, direct labor, and manufacturing overhead. However, the percentage that each element contributes to the total cost of a product has changed. During the 1950s, 1960s, and 1970s, direct labor was the dominant cost element, making up over 40 percent of total product cost. Direct materials contributed 35 percent and manufacturing overhead around 25 percent of total cost. Seventy-five percent of total product cost was a direct cost, traceable to the product. Improved production technology caused a dramatic shift in the three product cost elements. People were replaced by machines, and direct labor was reduced significantly. Today, only 50 percent of the cost of a product is directly traceable to the product; the other 50 percent is manufacturing overhead, an indirect cost.

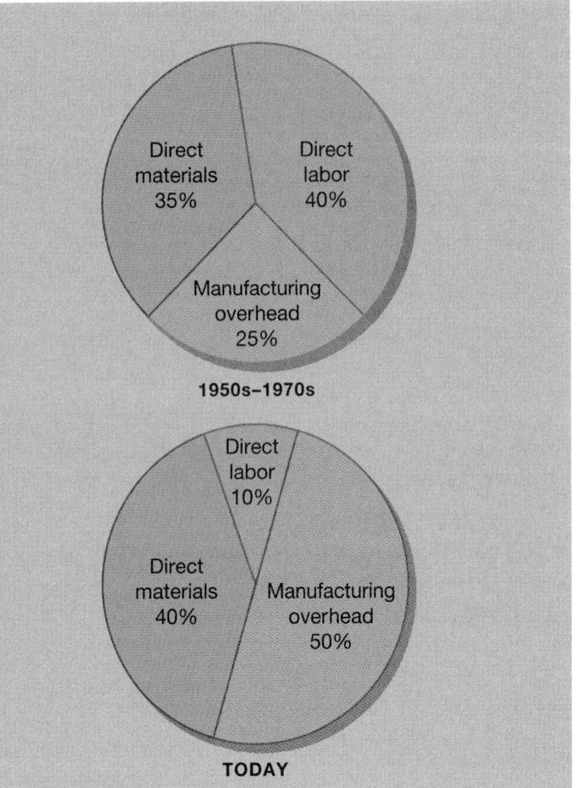

Point to Emphasize: Direct materials and direct labor are costs that can be conveniently and economically traced to the product. This is an application of cost-benefit analysis.

factory burden, or *indirect manufacturing costs*. Two common components of manufacturing overhead costs are indirect materials costs and indirect labor costs. **Indirect materials costs** are the costs of materials that cannot be conveniently or economically traced to a unit of product. Labor costs for production-related activities that cannot be conveniently or economically traced to a unit of product are **indirect labor costs**. Examples of the major components of manufacturing overhead costs are as follows:

- **Indirect materials costs:** costs of nails, rivets, lubricants, and small tools
- **Indirect labor costs:** costs of labor for maintenance, inspection, engineering design, supervision, materials handling, and machine handling
- **Other indirect manufacturing costs:** costs of building maintenance, machinery and tool maintenance, property taxes, property insurance, depreciation on plant and equipment, rent, and utilities

As indirect costs, manufacturing overhead costs are allocated to a product's cost using traditional or activity-based costing methods, which will be explained later in this chapter.

To illustrate product costs and the manufacturing process, we will learn how Angelo Sanchez, the owner of Angelo's Rolling Suitcases, Inc., operates part of his business. In the 1990s, Sanchez began building rolling suitcases, versions of the flight crew bag used for years by airline pilots and flight attendants. The suitcases are made of ballistic nylon fabric wrapped around a rigid frame. They have a retractable pull handle at one end and wheels at the other end. Stair skids protect the fabric from abrasion, and carrying handles on the side and top of the bag improve handling.

Sanchez identified the following elements of the product cost of one rolling suitcase:

- **Direct material costs:** costs of the frame, ballistic nylon fabric, retractable pull handle, and wheels
- **Direct labor costs:** costs of labor used to build the rolling suitcase
- **Manufacturing overhead costs:** indirect materials costs, such as the costs of zippers, interior mesh storage pockets, garment straps, carrying handles, stair skids, and wheel lubricants; indirect labor costs, such as the costs of labor associated with moving the materials to the production area and inspecting the rolling suitcase during its construction; other overhead costs, such as depreciation on the building and equipment used to make the rolling suitcases plus the utilities, property taxes, and insurance expenses related to the manufacturing plant

Computing Product Unit Cost in a Manufacturing Company

Product unit cost is the manufacturing cost of a single unit of product. It is computed by either (1) dividing the total cost of direct materials, direct labor, and manufacturing overhead by the total number of units produced or (2) determining the cost per unit for each element of the product cost and summing those per-unit costs.

Point to Emphasize: Many management decisions require estimates of future costs. Managers often use actual cost as a basis for estimating future cost.

Unit cost information helps managers price products and calculate gross margin and net income. Managers or accountants can calculate the product unit cost using actual costing, normal costing, or standard costing methods. Table 3 summarizes the use of actual or estimated costs for the three cost-measurement methods.

The **actual costing** method uses the *actual* costs of direct materials, direct labor, and manufacturing overhead to calculate the actual product unit cost at the *end* of the accounting period, when actual costs are known. The actual product unit cost is assigned to the finished goods inventory on the balance sheet and to the cost of goods sold on the income statement. For example, assume that Angelo's Rolling Suitcases, Inc., produced 30 rolling suitcases on December 28, 20x4, for a corporate customer in Salt Lake City. Jamie Estrada, the company's accountant, calculated that the actual costs for the Salt Lake City order were direct materials, \$540; direct labor, \$420; and manufacturing overhead, \$240. The actual product unit cost for the order was \$40.

Direct materials (\$540 ÷ 30 rolling suitcases)	\$18
Direct labor (\$420 ÷ 30 rolling suitcases)	14
Manufacturing overhead (\$240 ÷ 30 rolling suitcases)	8
Product cost per rolling suitcase (\$1,200 ÷ 30 rolling suitcases)	\$40

In this case, the product unit cost was computed after the job was completed and all cost information was known. However, sometimes a company needs to know product unit cost while production is under way, when the actual direct materials costs and direct labor costs are known, but the actual manufacturing

Table 3. Summary of the Use of Actual or Estimated Costs in Three Cost-Measurement Methods

Product Cost Elements	Actual Costing	Normal Costing	Standard Costing
Direct materials	Actual costs	Actual costs	Estimated costs
Direct labor	Actual costs	Actual costs	Estimated costs
Manufacturing overhead	Actual costs	Estimated costs	Estimated costs

Clarification Note: Estimated costs are also called *projected, standard, predetermined,* or *budgeted costs.*

overhead costs are uncertain. Then the product unit cost will include an estimate of the manufacturing overhead applied to the product.

The **normal costing** method combines *actual* direct materials and direct labor costs with *estimated* manufacturing overhead costs to determine a normal product unit cost. Manufacturing overhead costs must be estimated because the actual amount of such indirect costs for each product is difficult to determine. The normal costing method is simple and allows a smoother, more even assignment of manufacturing overhead costs to production *during* the year. It also contributes to better pricing decisions and profitability estimates. However, at the end of the year, any difference between the estimated and the actual costs must be identified and removed so that the financial statements show only the actual product costs.

Assume that normal costing was used to price the Salt Lake City order for rolling suitcases. Manufacturing overhead was applied to the product's cost using an estimated, or predetermined, overhead rate of 60 percent of direct labor costs. Based on that method, the costs for the order included the actual direct materials cost of $540.00, the actual direct labor cost of $420.00, and the estimated manufacturing overhead cost of $252.00 ($420.00 × .6). The normalized product unit cost was $40.40.

Direct materials ($540.00 ÷ 30 rolling suitcases)	$18.00
Direct labor ($420.00 ÷ 30 rolling suitcases)	14.00
Manufacturing overhead ($252.00 ÷ 30 rolling suitcases)	8.40
Product cost per rolling suitcase ($1,212 ÷ 30 rolling suitcases)	$40.40

In this case, the product unit cost was computed using actual and estimated cost information. Later in this chapter, we will discuss various methods of assigning manufacturing overhead costs to finished products.

Sometimes managers need product costing information before the accounting period begins, so that they can control operating activities. Or sometimes an organization needs to price a proposed product for a customer. In such situations, product unit costs must be estimated, and the **standard costing** method can be helpful. This method uses *estimated* (or standard) costs of direct materials, direct labor, and manufacturing overhead to calculate the standard product unit cost. This estimated product unit cost is useful as a benchmark for pricing decisions during the year and for controlling product costs.

Assume Angelo's must place a bid to manufacture 20 rolling suitcases for a new Italian customer. Using standard cost information, Estrada has *estimated* the following costs: $20 per unit for direct materials, $15 per unit for direct labor, and $9 for manufacturing overhead (assuming a standard, or predetermined, overhead rate of 60 percent of direct labor cost). The standard cost per unit would be $44.

Direct materials	$20
Direct labor	15
Manufacturing overhead ($15 × .6)	9
Product cost per rolling suitcase	$44

The $44 product unit cost is useful for estimating the gross margin for the job and deciding the price to bid for the Italian company's business. Standard costing is discussed in more detail in another chapter.

Prime Costs and Conversion Costs

The three elements of manufacturing costs may be grouped into prime costs and conversion costs. **Prime costs** are the primary costs of production and are the sum of the direct materials costs and direct labor costs. **Conversion costs** are the costs

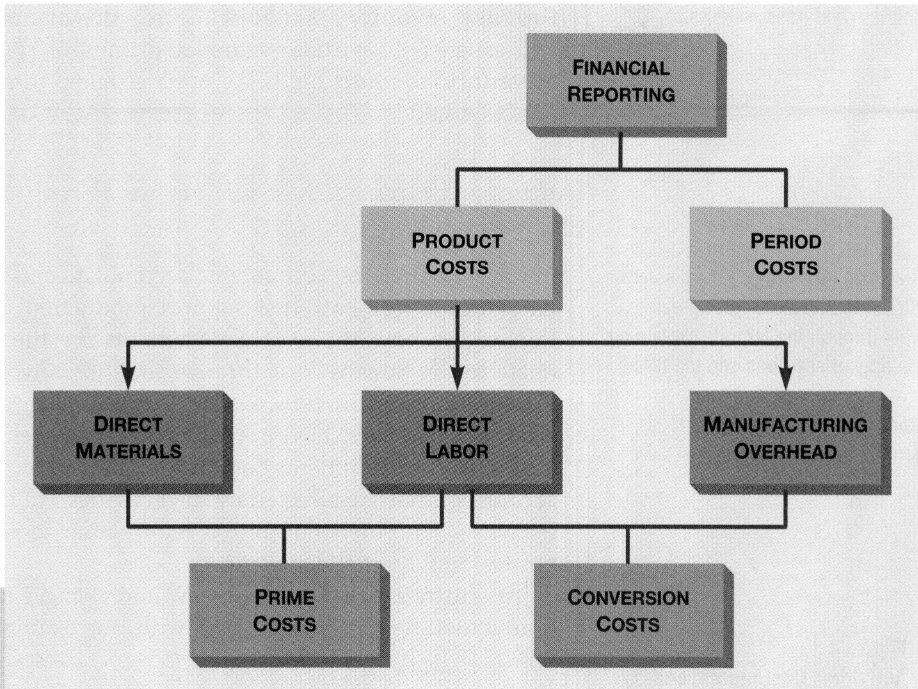

Figure 3
Relationships Among Product Costs

of converting direct materials into finished product and are the sum of direct labor costs and manufacturing overhead costs. Using the figures for the actual unit cost of Angelos's rolling suitcases, the prime costs and conversion costs per unit are as follows:

	Prime Costs	Conversion Costs
Direct materials	$18	NA
Direct labor	14	$14
Manufacturing overhead	NA	8
Totals	$32	$22

These classifications are important for understanding the costing methods discussed in later chapters. Figure 3 summarizes the relationships among the product cost classifications presented so far.

Manufacturing Inventory Accounts

OBJECTIVE

4 Describe the flow of product-related activities, documents, and costs through the Materials Inventory, Work in Process Inventory, and Finished Goods Inventory accounts

Manufacturing organizations use a number of production and production-related activities to transform materials into finished products. Materials are brought into the organization through purchasing, receiving, inspecting, moving, and storing activities. Production activities convert the materials into a finished product using labor, equipment, and other resources. Moving and storing activities transfer the completed product to the finished goods storage area. The accounting system tracks these activities as product costs flowing through the Materials Inventory, Work in Process Inventory, and Finished Goods Inventory accounts. The **Materials Inventory account** holds the balance of the cost of unused materials, the **Work In**

Related Text Assignments:
Q: 10, 11, 12
SE: 4, 5
E: 4, 5

Process Inventory account records the manufacturing costs that are incurred and assigned to partially completed units of product, and the **Finished Goods Inventory account** holds the costs assigned to all completed products that have not been sold.

Document Flows and Cost Flows Through the Inventory Accounts

Teaching Note: Turn the classroom into a factory. Starting at the door, walk through the factory, explaining the flow of activities and the three inventory accounts. Use construction blocks or a simple product to demonstrate.

In many companies, accountants accumulate and report manufacturing costs based on source documents that support production and production-related activities. Looking at how the source documents for the three elements of product cost relate to the flow of costs through the three inventory accounts for a manufacturing organization provides insight into when an activity must be recorded in the accounting records. Figure 4 summarizes the relationships among the production activities, the documents for each of the three cost elements, and the inventory account(s) that are affected by the activities. An organization may use paper documents or computer-transmitted information to communicate with suppliers, customers, and internal departments.

To illustrate the document flow and changes in inventory balances for production activities, we will continue with our example of Angelo's Rolling Suitcases, Inc.

Figure 4
Activities, Documents, and Cost Flows Through the Inventory Accounts of a Manufacturing Organization

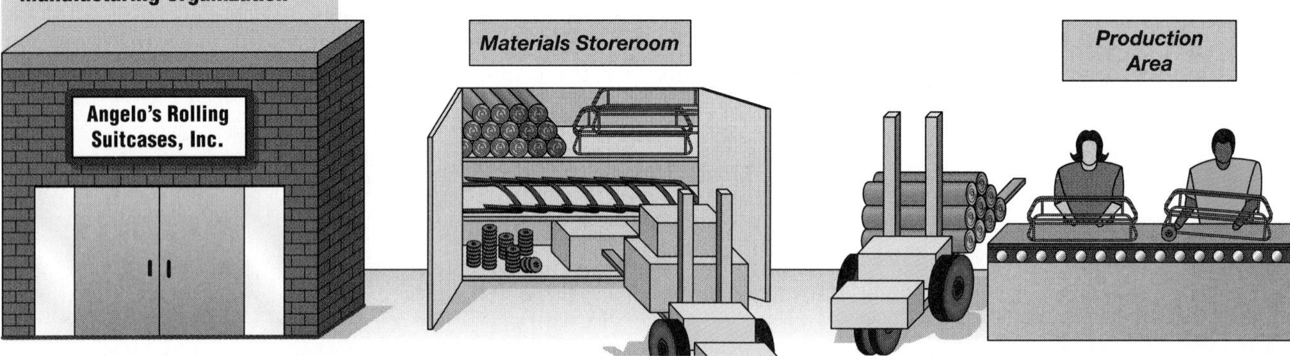

	ACTIVITY	Purchase, receive, inspect, move, and store materials in materials storeroom	Move materials to production area
	DOCUMENT	Purchase request Purchase order Receiving report Vendor's invoice	Materials request
INVENTORY ACCOUNT AFFECTED/ CHANGE IN BALANCE	MATERIALS INVENTORY	Increases for cost of materials purchased	Decreases for cost of materials used in the production process, whether direct or indirect
	WORK IN PROCESS INVENTORY		Increases for cost of direct materials used in the production process
	FINISHED GOODS INVENTORY		

Teaching Note: Some companies use sophisticated computer programs to match receiving reports to purchase orders.

Purchasing Materials The same process is used for purchasing both direct and indirect materials. The purchasing process starts with a *purchase request* for specific quantities of materials needed in the manufacturing process but not currently available in the materials storeroom. A qualified manager approves the request. Based on the information in the purchase request, the Purchasing Department sends *purchase orders* to its suppliers. When the materials arrive, an employee on the receiving dock counts and examines them and prepares a *receiving report*. Later, an accounting clerk matches the information on the receiving report with the descriptions and quantities listed on the purchase order. A material handler moves the newly arrived materials from the receiving area to the materials storeroom. Soon, Angelo's receives a *vendor's invoice* requesting payment for the purchased materials. The cost of those materials increases the balance of the Materials Inventory account.

Materials Requisition and Conversion When the rolling suitcases are scheduled for production, the storeroom clerk receives a *materials request form*. The materials request form is essential for controlling materials. Besides providing the supervisor's approval signature, it describes the types and quantities of materials the storeroom clerk must pick and send to the production area, and it authorizes the release of those materials into production. If the materials request form has been approved by the appropriate manager, the storeroom clerk has the

Convert materials into finished product using direct labor and manufacturing overhead Package some types of products	Move completed units of product to finished goods storage area	Sell units of product to customer; pack and ship product
Time card Job order cost card Vendors' invoices for manufacturing overhead items	Job order cost card	Sales invoice Shipping document
Increases for costs of direct labor and manufacturing overhead	Decreases for cost of completed units of product	
	Increases for cost of completed units of product	Decreases for cost of goods sold

material handler move the materials to the production floor. The cost of the direct materials transferred will increase the balance of the Work in Process Inventory account and decrease the balance of the Materials Inventory account. The cost of the indirect materials transferred will increase the balance of the Manufacturing Overhead account and decrease the balance of the Materials Inventory account.

The production employees assemble the rolling suitcases. Each production employee prepares a *time card* to record the number of hours he or she has worked on this and other orders each day. The costs of the direct labor and manufacturing overhead used to manufacture the rolling suitcases increase the balance of the Work in Process Inventory account. A *job order cost card* is used to record all costs incurred as the products move through production.

PRODUCT COMPLETION AND SALE Employees place completed rolling suitcases in individual boxes, then move the boxes to the finished goods storeroom and store them there until the scheduled shipment date. The balance of the Finished Goods Inventory account increases and the balance of the Work in Process Inventory account decreases for the cost of the completed rolling suitcases.

When suitcases are sold, a clerk prepares a *sales invoice* while another employee fills the order by removing the rolling suitcases from the storeroom, packaging them, and shipping them to the customer. A *shipping document* shows the quantity and description of the products that were shipped. The cost of the rolling suitcases sold increases the Cost of Goods Sold account and decreases the balance of the Finished Goods Inventory account.

The Manufacturing Cost Flow

Manufacturing cost flow is the flow of manufacturing costs (direct materials, direct labor, and manufacturing overhead) from their incurrence through the Materials Inventory, Work in Process Inventory, and Finished Goods Inventory accounts into the Cost of Goods Sold account. A defined, structured manufacturing cost flow is the foundation for product costing, inventory valuation, and financial reporting. The manufacturing cost flow as it relates to the accounts in the general ledger and the production activity at Angelo's Rolling Suitcases, Inc., for the year ended December 31, 20x4, is summarized in Figure 5. To show the basic flows in this example, we assume that all materials can be traced directly to the rolling suitcases. This means there are no indirect materials in the Materials Inventory account. We also work with the actual amount of manufacturing overhead, not an applied amount.

Because there are no indirect materials in this case, the Materials Inventory account shows the balance of unused direct materials. The cost of direct materials purchased increases the Materials Inventory account, and the cost of direct materials requested and used by the Production Department decreases the balance. The following formula may be used to summarize the activity of the Materials Inventory account for the year:

Materials Inventory, Ending Balance		Materials Inventory, Beginning Balance		Cost of Direct Materials Purchased		Cost of Direct Materials Used
$5,000	=	$10,000	+	$20,000	−	$25,000

The Work in Process Inventory account records the balance of partially completed units of product. As direct materials and direct labor are used, their costs are added to the Work in Process Inventory account. The cost of manufacturing overhead for the current period is also added. The total costs of direct materials,

Figure 5
Manufacturing Cost Flow: An Example

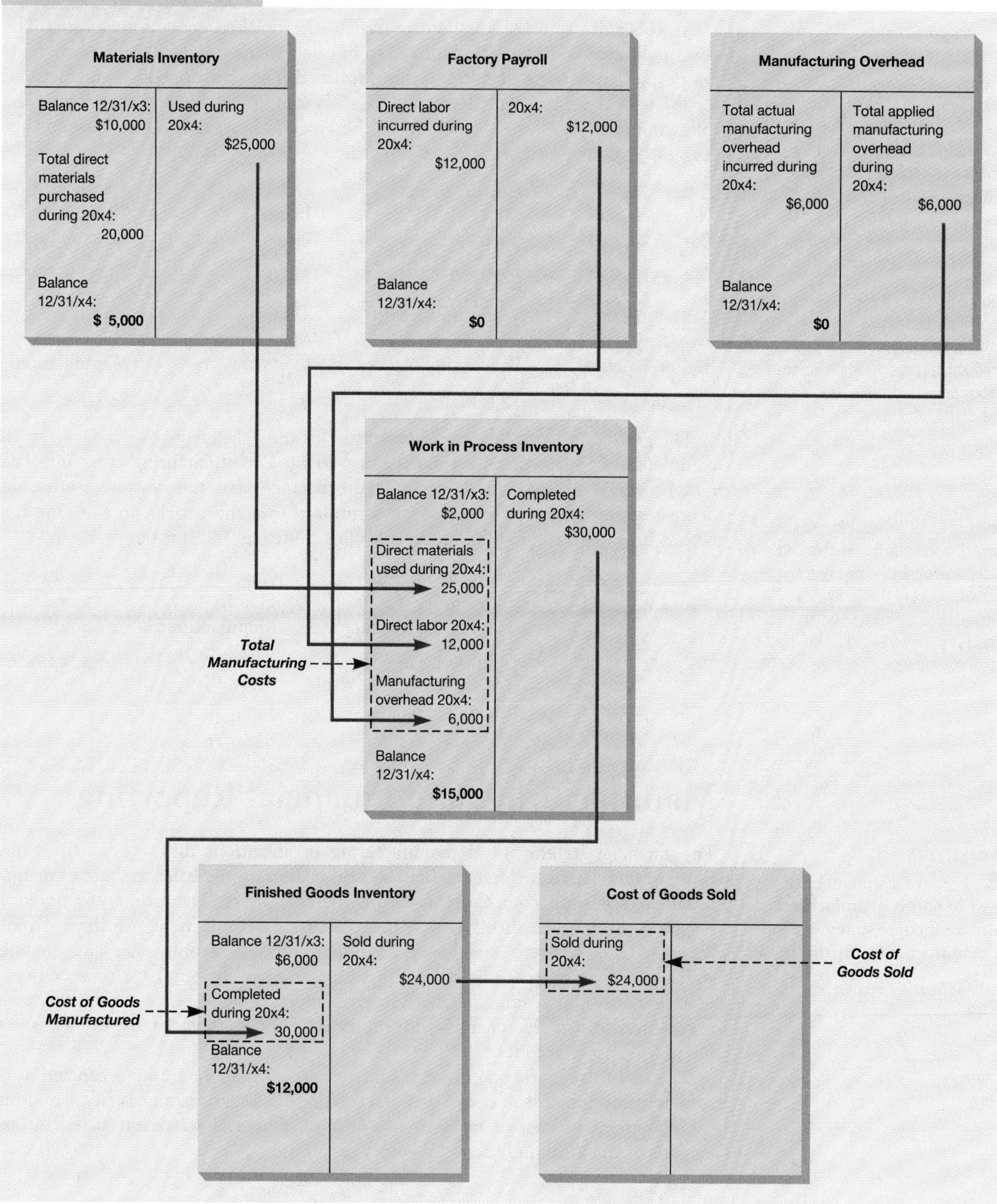

direct labor, and manufacturing overhead incurred and transferred to work in process inventory during an accounting period are called **total manufacturing costs**. Total manufacturing costs increase the balance of the Work in Process Inventory account.

As goods are finished, they are moved to the finished goods storage area. The cost of all units completed and moved to finished goods storage during an accounting period is the **cost of goods manufactured**. The cost of goods manufactured for the period decreases the balance of the Work in Process Inventory account. The following formulas show the activity in the Work in Process Inventory account for Angelo's Rolling Suitcases, Inc., for the year:

Point to Emphasize: When costs are transferred from one inventory account to another in a manufacturing company, they remain assets. They are inventoriable product costs and are not expensed until the finished goods are sold.

Teaching Note: It is often helpful to show that Materials Inventory and Work in Process Inventory support the production process, while Finished Goods Inventory supports the sales and distribution functions.

Total Manufacturing Costs	=	Cost of Direct Materials Used	+	Direct Labor Costs	+	Manufacturing Overhead Costs
$43,000	=	$25,000	+	$12,000	+	$6,000

Work in Process Inventory, Ending Balance	=	Work in Process Inventory, Beginning Balance	+	Total Manufacturing Costs	−	Cost of Goods Manufactured
$15,000	=	$2,000	+	$43,000	−	$30,000

The Finished Goods Inventory account holds the balance of costs assigned to all completed products that have not been sold by a manufacturing company. The cost of goods manufactured increases the balance, and the cost of goods sold decreases the balance. The following formula shows the activity in the Finished Goods Inventory account for Angelo's Rolling Suitcases, Inc., for the year:

Point to Emphasize: When a sale occurs, Accounts Receivable and Sales are increased by the *revenue* amount. Cost of Goods Sold is increased and Finished Goods Inventory is decreased by the *cost* amount, or inventory carrying value.

Finished Goods Inventory, Ending Balance	=	Finished Goods Inventory, Beginning Balance	+	Cost of Goods Manufactured	−	Cost of Goods Sold
$12,000	=	$6,000	+	$30,000	−	$24,000

Manufacturing and Financial Reporting

OBJECTIVE

5 Prepare a statement of cost of goods manufactured and an income statement for a manufacturing organization

Related Text Assignments:
Q: 13
SE: 6
E: 6
P: 2, 3
MRA: 1, 3

The financial statements of manufacturing organizations differ very little from those of merchandising organizations. Account titles on the balance sheet of manufacturers are similar to those used by merchandisers. The primary difference between the balance sheets is that manufacturing organizations use three inventory accounts whereas merchandising organizations use only one. The income statements for a merchandiser and a manufacturer are also similar. However, manufacturers use the heading Cost of Goods Manufactured in place of the Purchases account. Also, the Merchandise Inventory account is replaced by the Finished Goods Inventory account.

The key to preparing an income statement for a manufacturing organization is to determine the cost of goods manufactured. This dollar amount is calculated on the statement of cost of goods manufactured, a special statement based on an analysis of the Work in Process Inventory account.

Statement of Cost of Goods Manufactured

At the end of the period, the flow of all manufacturing costs incurred during the period is summarized in the **statement of cost of goods manufactured.** The

Exhibit 1
Statement of Cost of Goods Manufactured and Income Statement for a Manufacturing Organization

Angelo's Rolling Suitcases, Inc.
Statement of Cost of Goods Manufactured
For the Year Ended December 31, 20x4

Step			
Step 1	Direct Materials Used		
	Materials Inventory, December 31, 20x3	$10,000	
	Direct Materials Purchased	20,000	
	Cost of Direct Materials Available for Use	$30,000	
	Less Materials Inventory, December 31, 20x4	5,000	
	Cost of Direct Materials Used		$25,000
Step 2	Direct Labor		12,000
	Manufacturing Overhead		6,000
	Total Manufacturing Costs		$43,000
Step 3	Add Work in Process Inventory, December 31, 20x3		2,000
	Total Cost of Work in Process During the Year		$45,000
	Less Work in Process Inventory, December 31, 20x4		15,000
	Cost of Goods Manufactured		$30,000

Angelo's Rolling Suitcases, Inc.
Income Statement
For the Year Ended December 31, 20x4

Sales		$50,000
Cost of Goods Sold		
Finished Goods Inventory, December 31, 20x3	$ 6,000	
Cost of Goods Manufactured	30,000	
Total Cost of Finished Goods Available for Sale	$36,000	
Less Finished Goods Inventory, December 31, 20x4	12,000	
Cost of Goods Sold		24,000
Gross Margin		$26,000
Selling and Administrative Expenses		16,000
Net Income		$10,000

flow of manufacturing costs incurred at Angelo's Rolling Suitcases, Inc., for the year ended December 31, 20x4, is shown in Figure 5, and the period's statement of cost of goods manufactured is shown in Exhibit 1. It is helpful to think of the statement of cost of goods manufactured as being developed in three steps.

STEP 1 Compute the cost of direct materials used. To do so, add the beginning balance in the Materials Inventory account to the direct materials purchased

($10,000 + $20,000). The subtotal represents the cost of direct materials available for use during the period ($30,000). Then, subtract the ending balance of Materials Inventory from the cost of direct materials available for use. The difference is the cost of direct materials used during the period ($30,000 − $5,000 = $25,000).

STEP 2 Calculate total manufacturing costs for the period ($43,000). As shown in Exhibit 1, the costs of direct materials used ($25,000) and direct labor ($12,000) are added to total manufacturing overhead costs incurred ($6,000) during the period.

STEP 3 Determine the total cost of goods manufactured for the period. Add the beginning balance in Work in Process Inventory to total manufacturing costs for the period to arrive at the total cost of work in process during the period. From this amount, subtract the ending balance in Work in Process Inventory to get the cost of goods manufactured ($45,000 − $15,000 = $30,000).

The term *total manufacturing costs* should not be confused with the cost of goods manufactured. To understand the difference between these two dollar amounts, look again at the computations in Exhibit 1. Total manufacturing costs of $43,000 incurred during the period are added to the beginning balance in Work in Process Inventory. Costs of $2,000 in the beginning balance are, by definition, costs from an earlier period. The costs of two accounting periods are now being mixed to arrive at the total cost of work in process during the period ($43,000 + $2,000 = $45,000). The costs of products still in process ($15,000) are then subtracted from the total cost of work in process during the year. The remainder, $30,000, is the cost of goods manufactured (completed) during the current year. It is assumed that the items in beginning inventory were completed first. The costs attached to the ending balance of Work in Process Inventory are part of the current period's total manufacturing costs. However, they will not become part of the cost of goods manufactured until the next period, when the products are completed.

Common Student Error: It is important that students do not confuse the cost of goods manufactured with the cost of goods sold.

Cost of Goods Sold and the Income Statement

Exhibit 1 demonstrates the relationship between the income statement and the statement of cost of goods manufactured. The total amount of the cost of goods manufactured during the period is carried over to the income statement. There, it is used to compute the cost of goods sold. The beginning balance of Finished Goods Inventory is added to the cost of goods manufactured to get the total cost of finished goods available for sale during the period ($6,000 + $30,000 = $36,000). The cost of goods sold is then computed by subtracting the ending balance in Finished Goods Inventory (the cost of goods completed but not sold) from the total cost of finished goods available for sale ($36,000 − $12,000 = $24,000). The cost of goods sold is considered an expense in the period in which the related products are sold.

Teaching Note: An alternative to the cost of goods manufactured calculation uses the cost flow concept. Current manufacturing costs (direct materials, direct labor, and manufacturing overhead) become the cost of goods manufactured if the Work in Process Inventory balance remains unchanged in the accounting period. Similarly, the cost of goods manufactured becomes the cost of goods sold if the Finished Goods Inventory remains unchanged in the period.

Cost Allocation

OBJECTIVE

6 **Define** *cost allocation* and explain how cost objects, cost pools, and cost drivers are used to apply manufacturing overhead

The product cost elements of direct materials and direct labor can be easily traced to a product, but manufacturing overhead costs are indirect costs that must be collected and allocated in some manner. **Cost allocation** is the process of assigning or applying collected indirect costs to specific cost objects using an allocation base that represents a major function of the business. A **cost object** is the destination

Related Text Assignments:
Q: 14, 15, 16, 17
SE: 7, 8, 9
E: 7, 8, 9
P: 4, 6, 8
SD: 2
MRA: 4

of an assigned, or allocated, cost. For example, a cost may be assigned to a particular product, service, or department. For purposes of product costing, cost allocation is the assignment of manufacturing overhead costs to the product (cost object) during the accounting period.

To understand cost allocation, you also need to understand the terms *cost pool* and *cost driver*. For purposes of product costing, a **cost pool** is a collection of overhead costs related to a cost object (a production-related activity). A **cost driver** is an activity that causes the cost pool to increase in amount as the cost driver increases in volume. Cost allocation requires (1) the pooling of manufacturing overhead costs that are affected by a common activity and (2) the selection of a cost driver whose activity level causes a change in the cost pool.

The Manufacturing Overhead Allocation Process

Teaching Note: Allocation, by its very nature, is a relatively arbitrary process. It is important to stress that a rational allocation scheme is best. Rational allocation approaches help avoid behavioral problems for management.

The process of applying or assigning manufacturing overhead costs is part of the management cycle presented in Figure 1. In the planning stage, manufacturing overhead costs are estimated and an application rate is calculated. In the executing stage, manufacturing overhead costs are applied to products during the production process as manufacturing overhead costs are incurred and recorded. In the reviewing stage, the difference between the actual and applied manufacturing overhead costs is calculated and analyzed. The difference is then disclosed in the reporting stage.

There are four steps in the process of applying manufacturing overhead. Figure 6 shows the relationship of the four steps over a time period that includes the planning process and the manufacturing process for one year. Figure 6 also describes each step and its timing, procedure, and journal entry, if needed.

STEP 1 In Step 1, the planning step, a predetermined overhead rate is calculated in traditional settings and an activity pool rate is calculated in activity-based costing settings. If a rate is calculated before an accounting period begins, managers can better estimate the product costs by applying manufacturing overhead costs in the same way to all units of production during the year. For example, using a single, plantwide overhead rate requires the grouping of all estimated manufacturing overhead costs into one cost pool with direct labor hours or machine hours as the cost driver. No journal entry is required because no business activity has taken place.

STEP 2 In Step 2, the application step, the estimated manufacturing overhead costs are assigned to the product's costs as units are manufactured. The actual cost driver level (for example, the actual number of direct labor hours used to complete the product) is multiplied by the predetermined manufacturing overhead rate or activity pool rate for that cost driver. The purpose of this calculation is to assign a fairly consistent manufacturing overhead cost to each unit produced during the accounting period. The allocation, or application, of overhead to the product is recorded by increasing the Work in Process Inventory account and reducing the Manufacturing Overhead account.

STEP 3 Step 3, the recording step, occurs during the accounting period when the actual manufacturing overhead costs are recorded as they are incurred. These costs will be part of the actual product cost and include the costs of indirect materials, indirect labor, depreciation, property taxes, and other production costs. Recording the actual manufacturing overhead costs requires an increase in the Manufacturing Overhead account and a decrease in asset accounts or an increase in contra-asset or liability accounts.

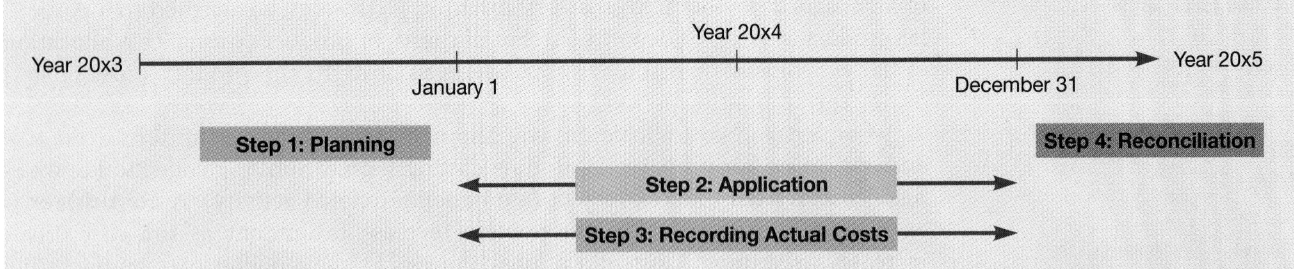

	Step 1: Planning	Step 2: Application	Step 3: Recording Actual Costs	Step 4: Reconciliation
Description	Calculate a predetermined manufacturing overhead rate	Apply manufacturing overhead costs to production	Record actual manufacturing overhead costs	Calculate the difference between applied and actual manufacturing overhead costs
When	Before accounting period	During accounting period as units are produced	During accounting period as costs are incurred	At the end of the accounting period
Procedure	Divide the cost pool of total estimated overhead costs by the total estimated cost driver level	Multiply the predetermined overhead rate for each cost pool by the actual cost driver level	Record actual manufacturing overhead costs when incurred	Calculate and record the difference between the actual and applied manufacturing overhead costs
Journal entry?	No	Yes Increase Work in Process Inventory account Decrease Manufacturing Overhead account	Yes Increase Manufacturing Overhead account Decrease asset accounts Increase contra-asset or liability accounts	Yes If applied > actual, then increase Manufacturing Overhead account Decrease Cost of Goods Sold account If applied < actual, then increase Cost of Goods Sold account Decrease Manufacturing Overhead account

Figure 6
The Manufacturing Overhead Allocation Process

STEP 4 At the end of the accounting period, during Step 4, the reconciliation step, the difference between the applied manufacturing overhead costs and the actual manufacturing overhead costs is calculated. If the manufacturing overhead costs applied to production during the accounting period are greater than (over) the actual manufacturing overhead costs, the difference in the amounts represents overapplied overhead costs. The Manufacturing Overhead account is increased and the Cost of Goods Sold account is decreased by this difference, assuming the difference is not material. If the difference is material, adjustments are made to the Work in Process Inventory, Finished Goods Inventory, and Cost of Goods Sold accounts. If the manufacturing overhead costs applied to production during the accounting period are less than (under) the actual manufacturing overhead costs, the difference in the amounts represents underapplied overhead costs. The Cost of Goods Sold account is increased and the Manufacturing Overhead account is decreased by this difference, assuming the difference is not material. The adjustment for overapplied or underapplied overhead costs, whether it is immaterial or material, is necessary to reflect the actual manufacturing overhead costs on the income statement.

Instructional Strategy: Divide the class into small groups and assign SD 2. Groups may present their results to the class and take questions from other students. Emphasize that knowing product costs can help in designing a quality product despite cost constraints.

MANAGERIAL REPORTING AND ANALYSIS

Interpreting Management Reports

MRA 1. **LO 5 Financial Performance Measures**

Rico Manufacturing Company makes sheet metal products for heating and air conditioning installations. For the past several years, the income of the company has been declining, and this past year, 20x1, was particularly poor. The company's statements of cost of goods manufactured and income statements for 20x0 and 20x1 are shown at the bottom of the preceding page and below.

You have been asked to comment on why the company's profitability has deteriorated.

REQUIRED

1. In preparing your comments on the decline in income, compute the following ratios for each year:
   a. Ratios of cost of direct materials used to total manufacturing costs, direct labor to total manufacturing costs, and total manufacturing overhead to total manufacturing costs. Round to one decimal place.
   b. Ratios of sales salaries and commission expense, advertising expense, other selling expenses, administrative expenses, and total selling and administrative expenses to sales. Round to one decimal place.
   c. Ratios of gross margin to sales and net income to sales. Round to one decimal place.

Rico Manufacturing Company
Income Statements
For the Years Ended December 31, 20x1 and 20x0

	20x1		20x0	
Sales		$2,942,960		$3,096,220
Cost of Goods Sold				
Finished Goods Inventory, Beginning	$ 142,640		$ 184,820	
Cost of Goods Manufactured	2,040,275		1,997,490	
Total Cost of Finished Goods Available for Sale	$2,182,915		$2,182,310	
Less Finished Goods Inventory, Ending	186,630		142,640	
Cost of Goods Sold		1,996,285		2,039,670
Gross Margin		$ 946,675		$1,056,550
Selling and Administrative Expenses				
Sales Salaries and Commission Expense	$ 394,840		$ 329,480	
Advertising Expense	116,110		194,290	
Other Selling Expenses	82,680		72,930	
Administrative Expenses	242,600		195,530	
Total Selling and Administrative Expenses		836,230		792,230
Income from Operations		$ 110,445		$ 264,320
Other Revenues and Expenses				
Interest Expense		54,160		56,815
Income Before Income Taxes		$ 56,285		$ 207,505
Less Income Taxes Expense		19,137		87,586
Net Income		$ 37,148		$ 119,919

2. From your evaluation of the ratios computed in 1, state the probable causes of the decline in net income.
3. What other factors or ratios do you believe should be considered in determining the cause of the company's decreased income?

Formulating Management Reports

MRA 2.
LO 9 Management Decision for a Supporting Service Function

As the manager of grounds maintenance for ***INNET***, a large insurance company in California, you are responsible for maintaining the grounds surrounding the three buildings, the six entrances to the property, and the recreational facilities, which include a golf course, a soccer field, jogging and bike paths, and tennis, basketball, and volleyball courts. Maintenance activities include gardening (watering, mowing, trimming, sweeping, and removing debris) and upkeep of land improvements (repairing concrete and gravel areas and replacing damaged or worn recreational equipment).

Early in January 20x2, you received a memo from the president requesting information about the cost of operating your department for the last twelve months. She has received a bid from Fantastic Landscapes, Inc., to perform the gardening activities you now perform. You are to prepare a cost report that will help the president in deciding whether to continue gardening activities within the company or to outsource the work to another company.

REQUIRED

1. Before preparing your report, answer the following questions.
   a. What kinds of information do you need about your department?
   b. Why is this information relevant?
   c. Where would you go to obtain this information (sources)?
   d. When would you want to obtain this information?
2. Prepare a draft of the cost report that would best communicate the costs of your department. Show only headings and line items. How would you change your report if the president asked you to reduce the costs of operating your department?
3. One of your department's costs is Maintenance Expense, Garden Equipment.
   a. Is it a direct or indirect cost for the Grounds Maintenance Department?
   b. Is it a product or a period cost?
   c. Is it a variable or a fixed cost?
   d. Does the activity add value to the provision of insurance services?
   e. Is it a budgeted or an actual cost in your report?

International Company

MRA 3.
LO 5 Management Information Needs

The ***Muntok Pharmaceuticals Corporation*** manufactures the majority of its three pharmaceutical products in Indonesia. Inventory information for April 20x1 was as follows:

Account	April 30	March 31
Materials Inventory	$228,100	$258,400
Work in Process Inventory	127,200	138,800
Finished Goods Inventory	114,100	111,700

Purchases of direct materials for April were $612,600, which included natural materials, basic organic compounds, catalysts, and suspension agents. Direct labor costs were $160,000, and actual manufacturing overhead costs were $303,500. Sales for the company's three pharmaceutical products for April were $2,188,400. General and administrative expenses were $362,000.

REQUIRED

1. Prepare a statement of cost of goods manufactured and an income statement for the month ended April 30.
2. Why don't the total manufacturing costs equal the cost of goods manufactured?
3. What additional information would you need to determine the profitability of each pharmaceutical product line?
4. Tell whether each of the following is a product cost or a period cost:
   a. Import duties for suspension agent materials
   b. Shipping expenses to deliver manufactured products to the United States

c. Rent on manufacturing facilities in Jakarta
d. Salary of the American production line manager working at the Indonesian manufacturing facilities
e. Training costs for an Indonesian accountant

Excel Spreadsheet Analysis

MRA 4.
LO 6 LO 7 LO 8 Application of Manufacturing Overhead: Traditional and Activity-Based Costing Approaches

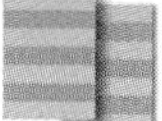

Refer to assignment P 8 in this chapter. Assume that Woo So, the controller of Sea Scout, Inc., has received some additional information from the production manager, Leif Sonder. Sonder reported that robotic equipment has been installed on the factory floor to increase productivity. As a result, direct labor hours per unit will decrease by 20 percent. Depreciation and other machine costs for the robots will increase total manufacturing overhead from $220,000 to $320,000 for the year, which will increase the assembly activity cost pool from $80,000 to $180,000. The cost driver level for the assembly cost pool will change from 5,000 machine hours to 2,000 machine hours for the Rigger II and from 5,000 machine hours to 8,000 machine hours for the BioScout. The cost driver levels and cost pool amounts for setup, inspection, and engineering activities will remain the same.

REQUIRED

1. Using the traditional method of applying overhead:
   a. Calculate the predetermined overhead rate.
   b. Compute the amount of the total manufacturing overhead costs applied to each product line.
   c. Calculate the product unit cost for each product line.
2. Using the activity-based costing method:
   a. Calculate the manufacturing overhead activity cost rate for each activity pool.
   b. Compute the manufacturing overhead costs applied to each product line by activity pool and in total.
   c. Calculate the product unit cost for each product line.
3. Complete the following table and discuss the differences in the costs assigned to the two product lines resulting from the additional information in this assignment.

Product unit cost	Rigger II	BioScout
Traditional		
Activity-based costing	______	______
Difference: decrease (increase)	======	======

Internet Case

MRA 5.
LO 2 LO 3 Identification of Costs for a Manufacturing Company

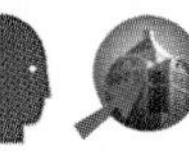

Through the Needles Accounting Resource Center web site at http://college.hmco.com, assess the web site for either Gateway Inc. or Dell Computer Corporation. Both companies manufacture and sell computers over the telephone or the Internet. To manufacture their products, both companies buy component parts from other companies and assemble the final product. Become familiar with the product line sold by the company you have chosen. For one of those products, such as a desktop or laptop computer, give examples of a direct and an indirect cost, a variable and a fixed cost, a value-adding and a nonvalue-adding cost, and a product and a period cost. Also, give examples of the three elements of product cost: direct materials, direct labor, and manufacturing overhead.

ENDNOTES

1. Bruce Upbin, "Sharpening the Claws," *Forbes*, July 26, 1999.
2. www.ups.com/about/inits.html.
3. Neal R. Pemberton, Logan Arumugam, and Nabil Hassan, "From Obstacles to Opportunities," *Management Accounting*, Institute of Management Accountants, March 1996.
4. Kathy Williams and James Hart, "Walker: Deploying a Mainframe Solution," *Management Accounting*, Institute of Management Accountants, June 1997.

21 Costing Systems: Job Order and Process Costing

LEARNING OBJECTIVES

1. Discuss the role information about costs plays in the management cycle and explain why product unit cost is important.
2. Distinguish between the different types of product costing systems and identify the information each provides.
3. Explain the cost flow in a job order costing system for a manufacturing company.
4. Prepare a job order cost card and compute a job order's product unit cost.
5. Explain the product flow and the cost flow in a process costing system.
6. Prepare a process cost report.
7. Evaluate operating performance using information about product cost.

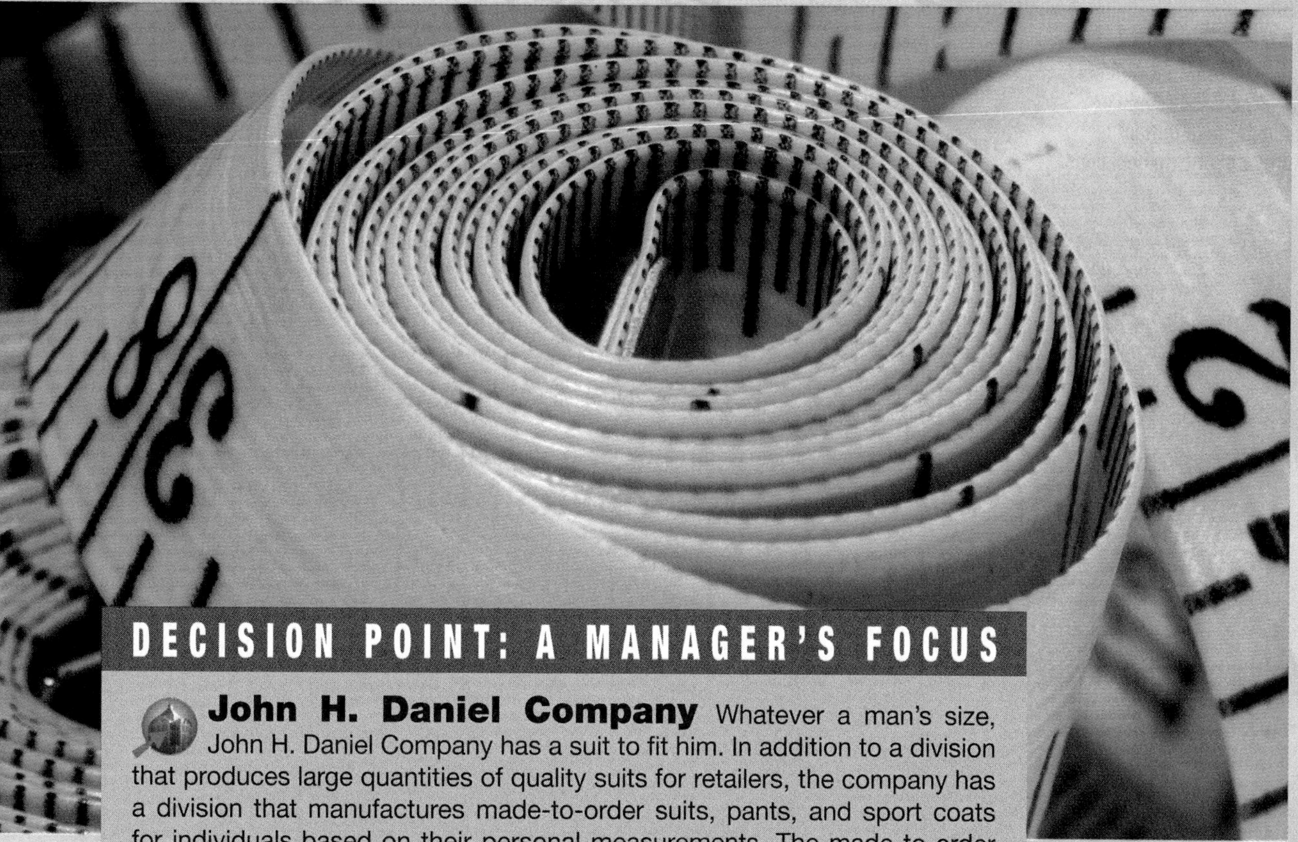

DECISION POINT: A MANAGER'S FOCUS

John H. Daniel Company Whatever a man's size, John H. Daniel Company has a suit to fit him. In addition to a division that produces large quantities of quality suits for retailers, the company has a division that manufactures made-to-order suits, pants, and sport coats for individuals based on their personal measurements. The made-to-order process begins when one of over 300 custom tailors from around the United States visits an individual customer at his home or office to show him the latest fabrics and styles for suits. When the customer has made his selections, the tailor takes various measurements to guarantee the fit. The tailor then transmits the customer's measurements to John H. Daniel Company's manufacturing plant in Knoxville, Tennessee, along with the customer's choices of fabric, suit model, leg finish, and pocket type. At the factory, state-of-the-art technology is used to cut the fabric to the order's specifications. A skilled, specialized team sews the pieces together and presses the finished suit. The suit is shipped to the custom tailor, who delivers it for final fitting and approval at a time convenient for the customer. The whole process generally takes less than five weeks to complete.

Is the product costing system used when making ready-made suits appropriate for the production of made-to-order suits? Why would John H. Daniel Company consider implementing a different product costing system for each division? What performance measures would be most useful in evaluating the results of each division? The nature of production usually determines the product costing system that should be used. The custom suit approach involves producing unique, made-to-order suits according to the specific requirements given in an individual's order. John H. Daniel Company's other division produces a continuous flow of predetermined styles of suits. Because the production processes differ, each division will probably need its own costing system to determine the cost of a suit.

How the cost of a suit is computed will differ because the approach to manufacturing custom orders differs from the approach to manufacturing large quantities of similar products. When a product is custom-made, it is possible to collect the costs of each order. When a product is mass-produced, however, the costs of a specific unit cannot be collected

Critical Thinking Question: Why is it important for a company to design a product costing system that reflects its production processes? **Answer:** To help managers make better product costing and pricing decisions.

because there is a continuous flow of similar products. Instead, costs are collected by process, department, work cell, or activity.

Performance measures will also differ for John H. Daniel Company's two types of suit businesses. For the custom suit business, management can measure the profitability of each order by comparing the order's cost and price. For the mass-produced suit business, management will measure performance by comparing the budgeted and actual costs for a process, department, work cell, or activity.

Product Cost Information and the Management Cycle

OBJECTIVE

1 Discuss the role information about costs plays in the management cycle and explain why product unit cost is important

Related Text Assignments:
Q: 1, 2, 3
SE: 1
SD: 1, 2
MRA: 1, 2, 3, 5

Managers depend on relevant and reliable information about costs in managing their organizations. The role of the management accountant is to develop a management information system that provides managers with the cost information they need. Although companies vary in their approaches to gathering, analyzing, and reporting information about costs, managers share the same basic concerns as they move through the management cycle. Figure 1 summarizes the management cycle and the concerns managers address with relevant and timely information about costs.

Planning

During the planning stage, managers use information about costs to set performance expectations and estimate unit costs. In manufacturing companies, such as Toyota, Harley-Davidson, and Levi Strauss and Co., managers use information about costs to develop budgets, establish product prices, and plan production volumes. In service organizations, such as Century 21, H & R Block, and Orkin Exterminating Company, Inc., managers use cost information to develop budgets, establish prices, set sales goals, and determine human resource needs. Notice that during the planning stage, knowledge of unit costs helps both manufacturing and service company managers set reasonable selling prices and determine how much the products or services should cost to deliver.

Executing

During the executing stage, managers make decisions about controlling costs, managing the company's activity volume, assuring quality, and negotiating prices. They use timely cost and volume information and actual unit costs to support their decision-making. In manufacturing companies, managers use information about costs to decide whether to drop a product line, add a production shift, outsource the manufacture of a subassembly to another manufacturer, bid on a special order, or negotiate a selling price. In service organizations, managers use cost information to make decisions about bidding on future service proposals, dropping a current service, outsourcing a task to an independent contractor, adding staff, or negotiating a price. All of these decisions can have far-reaching effects, including possible changes in unit cost or quality.

Figure 1
Uses of Information About Costs in the Management Cycle

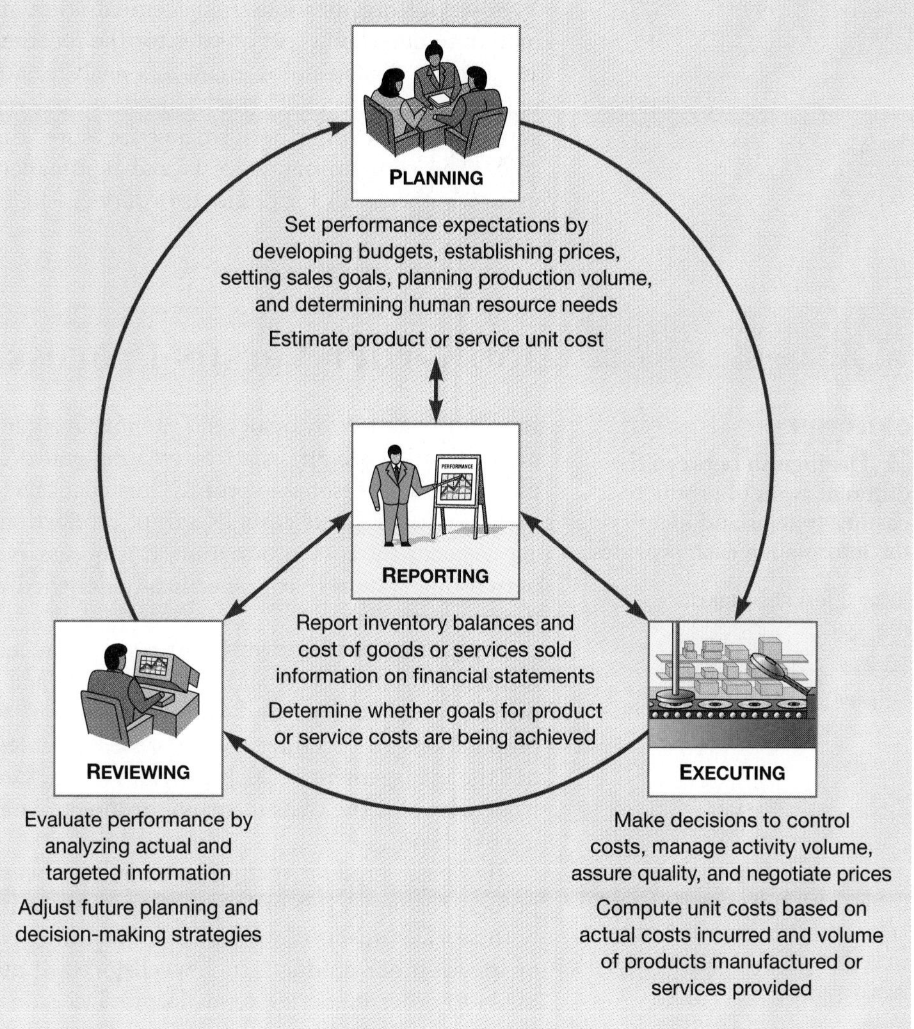

Reviewing

Managers watch for changes in cost or quality during the reviewing stage. They compare actual and targeted total costs and unit costs. They also monitor relevant price and volume information. Managers analyze this information to evaluate their performance and adjust future planning and decision-making strategies. For example, if a product's quality is suffering, managers can study the design, material purchasing, and manufacturing processes to determine the source of the problem. Then they can make changes that will assure the product's quality. In a service business, if operating costs have risen too high, managers can break down the unit cost of service into its many components. Then they can analyze where costs can be cut or how the service can be performed more efficiently.

Reporting

Finally, during the reporting stage of the management cycle, financial statements and internal performance evaluation reports are prepared. In manufacturing companies, management accountants use product unit costs to determine both inventory balances for the organization's balance sheet and the cost of goods sold for its income statement.

In service organizations, management accountants use unit cost of service information to determine cost of sales for the income statement. In both manufacturing and service organizations, managers analyze internal reports that compare actual unit costs and targeted costs. Those internal reports also contain actual and targeted values for other performance measures that the organization has chosen for goals. The comparisons of costs and nonfinancial measures help managers determine whether goals for products or services are being achieved.

Job Order Versus Process Costing

OBJECTIVE

2 Distinguish between the different types of product costing systems and identify the information each provides

Related Text Assignments:
Q: 4, 5, 6, 7
SE: 2
E: 1, 2, 3
MRA: 2, 3

If an organization is to succeed, its managers must sell its products or services at prices that exceed the costs of creating and delivering those products or services plus provide a reasonable profit. Thus, managers need extensive information about such product-related costs as setup, production, and distribution. To meet managers' needs for cost information, it is necessary to develop a highly reliable product costing system that is specifically designed to record and report the organization's operations.

A **product costing system** is a set of procedures used to account for an organization's product costs and provide timely and accurate unit cost information for pricing, cost planning and control, inventory valuation, and financial statement preparation. The product costing system enables managers to track costs throughout the management cycle. It provides a structure for recording the revenue earned from sales plus the costs incurred for direct materials, direct labor, and manufacturing overhead.

Point to Emphasize: In a job order costing system, the specific job or batch of product, not a department or work center, is the focus of cost accumulation.

Two basic product costing systems have been developed: job order costing and process costing. A **job order costing system** is a product costing system used by both service organizations and manufacturing companies that make large, unique, or special-order products, such as customized publications, specially built cabinets, made-to-order draperies, or, as in our Decision Point, custom suits. Under such a system, the costs of direct materials, direct labor, and manufacturing overhead are traced to a specific job order or batch of products. A **job order** is a customer order for a specific number of specially designed, made-to-order products. Job order costing measures the cost of each complete unit. It uses one Work in Process Inventory account to summarize the costs of all jobs. This account is supported by job order cost cards or a subsidiary ledger of accounts for each job.

Point to Emphasize: The product cost arrived at by both job order and process costing systems is an average cost. Process costing usually averages cost over a greater volume of product.

A **process costing system** is a product costing system used by companies that produce large amounts of similar products or liquids, or that have a continuous production flow. Makers of paint, soft drinks, bricks, milk, or paper would use a process costing system, as would the John H. Daniel Company's retail suit division. Under such a system, the costs of direct materials, direct labor, and manufacturing overhead are first traced to processes, departments, or work cells and then assigned to the products manufactured by those processes, departments, or work cells. A process costing system uses several Work in Process Inventory accounts, one for each process, department, or work cell. Table 1 summarizes the characteristics of job order and process costing systems.

In reality, few actual production processes perfectly match either a job order costing system or a process costing system. Thus, the typical product costing system combines parts of both job order costing and process costing to create a hybrid system designed specifically for an organization's particular production process. For example, an automobile maker may use process costing to track the costs of manufacturing a basic car and then use job order costing to track the costs of customized features, such as a convertible or hardtop, or an automatic transmis-

Figure 2
Job Order Cost Card—Manufacturing Company

Job Order: CC

JOB ORDER COST CARD
Augusta, Inc.
Spring Hill, Florida

Customer: Stock Batch: X Custom: ______
Specifications: Two general-purpose golf carts
Date of Order: 2/26/x7
Date of Completion: 3/6/x7

Costs Charged to Job	Previous Months	Current Month	Cost Summary
Direct Materials	$165	$1,038	$1,203
Direct Labor	127	1,320	1,447
Manufacturing Overhead (85% of direct labor cost)	108	1,122	1,230
Totals	$400	$3,480	$3,880
Units Completed			2
Product Unit Cost			$1,940

Point to Emphasize: Product unit cost in a job order costing system is the total cost of the job or batch divided by the number of items in the job or batch. This is an average cost for the good units manufactured for that job or batch.

a job order cost card as a job progresses toward completion. When a job is finished, the costs on its job order cost card are totaled. The product unit cost is computed by dividing the total costs for the job by the number of good units produced.

The costs for completed Job CC are shown on the job order cost card in Figure 2. Two golf carts were produced at a total cost of $3,880, and so the product unit cost was $1,940. One of the golf carts was sold, and the other remained in finished goods inventory. Recall that at year end, it was discovered that manufacturing overhead amounting to $3 had been overapplied. Because the amount was small, the entire $3 was subtracted from the cost of the cart that was sold. That adjustment is shown in Exhibit 1 as a $3 deduction from the Cost of Goods Sold account (Transaction 11), so that the ending balance of that account is $1,937. The cost of the other golf cart remains in the Finished Goods Inventory account at the full product unit cost of $1,940.

FOCUS ON BUSINESS PRACTICE

BrightHouse, a 17-person Atlanta-based company, is known as the slowest company its clients will ever meet, and one of the most expensive. To generate breakthrough ideas for its clients, BrightHouse will work with only one client at a time. The price tag for this exclusive ten-week relationship is high, at least $500,000. Clients such as Coca-Cola, Holiday Inn, Home Depot, and Coty, Inc., have willingly engaged the firm to reap the benefits of its deliberate four-step process—investigation, incubation, illumination, and illustration—to develop great ideas. As Joey Reiman, CEO of BrightHouse, tells his clients, "You only have to see us once."[3]

Job Order Cost Card for a Service Organization

Many service organizations, like BrightHouse in the preceding Focus on Business Practice, use job order costing to compute the cost of providing their services. The only significant difference between service and manufacturing organizations is that in service organizations, costs are not associated with a physical product that can be assembled, stored, and valued. Services are rendered and cannot be held in inventory. Examples of services include auto repair, swimming pool maintenance, income tax return preparation, Red Cross disaster relief, and medical care. Because service organizations do not manufacture products, they have little or no cost for materials. The most important cost in a service organization is labor, which is carefully accounted for through the use of time cards.

The cost flow for services is similar to the cost flow for manufactured products. Job order cost cards are used to keep track of the costs incurred for each job. Job costs include labor, materials and supplies, and service overhead. For many service organizations, each job is based on a contract that requires the customer to pay for all costs incurred plus a predetermined amount of profit. Such contracts are called **cost-plus contracts**, and the "plus" provides a profit based on the amount of costs incurred. When the job is complete, the costs on the completed job order cost card become the cost of services. The cost of services is adjusted at the end of the accounting period for the difference between the applied service overhead costs and the actual service overhead costs.

For example, Gartner Landscaping Services employs 15 people and serves the San Francisco Bay area. The company earns its revenue from designing and installing landscapes for homes and offices. The job order cost card for the Rico Corporation's landscaping job is shown in Figure 3. Costs have been categorized into three separate activities: Landscape Design, Landscape Installation, and Job-Site Cleanup. Costs have been tracked to the Rico Corporation job for its duration, and now that the job is finished, it is time to complete the job order cost card. The service overhead charge for Landscape Design is 40 percent of design labor cost, and the service overhead cost for Landscape Installation is 50 percent of installation labor cost. Total costs incurred for this job were $5,400. The cost-plus contract has a 15 percent profit guarantee; therefore, $810 of profit margin is added to the total cost to arrive at the total contract revenue of $6,210, which is the amount billed to Rico.

The Process Costing System

OBJECTIVE

5 Explain the product flow and the cost flow in a process costing system

Related Text Assignments:
E: 9
P: 5
SD: 4
MRA: 3

As discussed earlier, a process costing system is used by businesses that produce large amounts of similar products or liquids, or that have a continuous production flow. In such production processes, it is difficult to determine when one batch ends and another begins.

Production Flows in a Process Costing System

In companies that use process costing, the steps in the production process can be combined in hundreds of ways. Two basic production flows are illustrated in Figure 4. Example 1 shows a series of three processing steps, or departments. The completed product from one department becomes the direct materials for the next

Exhibit 2
Process Costing Approach: FIFO Method

Kernan Computer Products Company
Process Cost Report—Computer Mice
For the Month Ended February 28, 20x3

A. Schedule of Equivalent Production*		Equivalent Units	
Units—Stage of Completion	Units to Be Accounted For	Direct Materials Costs	Conversion Costs
Beginning inventory—units started last period but completed in this period	6,200		
Direct materials costs—100% complete		—	
Conversion costs—60% complete (40% × 6,200)			2,480
Units started and completed in this period	52,500	52,500	52,500
Ending inventory—units started but not completed in this period	5,000		
Direct materials costs—100% complete		5,000	
Conversion costs—45% complete (45% × 5,000)			2,250
Totals	63,700	57,500	57,230

B. Unit Cost Analysis Schedule Total Cost Analysis	Costs from Beginning Inventory		Current Period Costs		Total Costs to Be Accounted For
Direct materials costs	$20,150		$189,750		$209,900
Conversion costs	21,390		320,488		341,878
Totals	$41,540		$510,238		$551,778
Computation of Equivalent Unit Costs	**Current Period Costs**	÷	**Equivalent Units**	=	**Cost per Equivalent Unit**
Direct materials costs	$189,750		57,500		$3.30
Conversion costs	320,488		57,230		5.60
Totals	$510,238				$8.90

C. Cost Summary Schedule	Cost of Goods Transferred to Finished Goods Inventory		Cost of Ending Work in Process Inventory		Total Costs to Be Accounted For
Beginning inventory					
Costs from preceding period	$ 41,540				
Costs to complete this period					
Direct materials costs: none	—				
Conversion costs: 2,480 units × $5.60	13,888				
Subtotal	$ 55,428				
Units started and completed 52,500 units × $8.90	467,250				
Ending inventory*					
Direct materials costs: 5,000 units × $3.30			$16,500		
Conversion costs: 2,250 units × $5.60			12,600		
Totals	$522,678	+	$29,100	=	$551,778

*If there is no beginning inventory, the computations are the same, except that there are no units for beginning inventory.

Part A of Exhibit 2 assumes the following facts for February 20x3:

- 6,200 units in beginning work in process inventory, 60 percent complete
- 52,500 units started and completed during the period, 100 percent complete
- 5,000 units in ending work in process inventory, 45 percent complete

Being careful to account for only the work that was done in February, Kernan completes its schedule of equivalent production for February 20x3 as follows.

Common Student Error: Because many sample situations simplify the solution by stating that direct materials are added at the beginning of the process, students often think that direct materials are always placed into production then. Explain situations in which direct materials are added at different stages of production (e.g., for paint, cans for packaging are added at the end).

Point to Emphasize: Units in beginning work in process inventory represent work accomplished in the previous accounting period that has already been assigned a certain portion of its total cost. Those units must be completed in the current period, incurring additional costs.

Common Student Error: The number of units started and completed is not the same as the total number of units completed during the period. Total units completed includes two categories—units in beginning work in process inventory and units started and completed.

BEGINNING INVENTORY All direct materials are added at the beginning of the production process. Thus, the 6,200 partially completed units that began February as work in process were already 100 percent complete with regard to direct materials, and no further direct materials were added. Unlike direct materials costs, conversion costs are incurred uniformly throughout the production process. The 6,200 partial units were 60 percent complete with regard to conversion costs at February 1. To complete those units, the remaining 40 percent of conversion costs were incurred during February. Thus, the equivalent production for conversion costs in February for these units is 2,480 units (40% × 6,200). That amount is entered in the far right column.

UNITS STARTED AND COMPLETED IN THIS PERIOD The costs of the 52,500 units started and completed during February were all incurred during this accounting period. Thus, the full amount of 52,500 is entered as the equivalent units for both direct materials costs and conversion costs.

ENDING INVENTORY Because all direct materials are added at the beginning of the production process, the 5,000 mice in process at the end of February are 100 percent complete in regard to direct materials. The full amount of 5,000 is thus entered as the equivalent units for direct materials costs. However, conversion costs are incurred uniformly throughout the production process. The 5,000 mice in ending inventory are only 45 percent complete in terms of conversion costs. As a result, the amount of 2,250 equivalent units (45% × 5,000) is entered in the far right column.

TOTALS The schedule of equivalent production is completed by summing all units to be accounted for, all equivalent units for direct materials costs, and all equivalent units for conversion costs. Part A of Exhibit 2 shows that for the month of February, Kernan needed to account for a total of 63,700 units. Equivalent units for direct materials costs totaled 57,500, and equivalent units for conversion costs totaled 57,230. Once Kernan knows February's equivalent unit amounts, it can complete the other two parts of the process cost report and compute the month's unit costs.

The Unit Cost Analysis Schedule

Thus far we have focused on accounting for *units* of productive output—in our example, computer mice. We now turn to cost information. The **unit cost analysis schedule**, which is Part B in Exhibit 2, is used to accumulate all costs charged to the Work in Process Inventory account of each production process, department, or work cell, and to compute the cost per equivalent unit for direct materials costs and conversion costs. A unit cost analysis schedule has two sections: the total cost analysis and the computation of equivalent unit costs.

The following additional information about the manufacture of computer mice is available for February 20x3:

Costs from beginning inventory	
Direct materials costs	$ 20,150
Conversion costs	21,390
Current period costs	
Direct materials costs	189,750
Conversion costs	320,488

Point to Emphasize: In the unit cost analysis schedule, all costs must be accounted for, including both costs from beginning inventory and costs incurred during the current period.

Teaching Note: Computing the cost per equivalent unit is the basis for assigning production costs to units so that those costs will logically follow units as they move to subsequent processes, departments, or work cells and eventually to finished goods inventory.

Common Student Error: Students often round product unit costs to even dollars. Rounding may lead to a significant difference in total costs, giving the impression that the costs have been miscalculated. Suggest that students carry product unit costs to two decimal places where appropriate.

This information enables us to complete the unit cost analysis schedule. As shown in Exhibit 2, all costs for the period are accumulated in the section of the schedule called "Total Cost Analysis." Included are the direct materials costs and conversion costs from beginning inventory and the direct materials costs and conversion costs incurred during the current period. All direct materials costs and conversion costs for the period are summed in the Total Costs to Be Accounted For column. Total mouse-related costs to be accounted for equal $551,778, which is the sum of $209,900 in direct materials costs and $341,878 in conversion costs.

In the second section of the unit cost analysis schedule, the section called "Computation of Equivalent Unit Costs," the costs of making the products during the current period are computed. Thus, *only costs incurred in the current period* are used. The direct materials costs and conversion costs for the period are divided by their respective units of equivalent production for the period to arrive at the cost per equivalent unit. The second section of Part B shows that the total cost of $8.90 per equivalent unit consists of $3.30 per equivalent unit for direct materials costs ($189,750 ÷ 57,500 equivalent units) plus $5.60 per equivalent unit for conversion costs ($320,488 ÷ 57,230 equivalent units). Note that the equivalent units were taken from the schedule of equivalent production in Part A of Exhibit 2.

Costs attached to units in beginning inventory are *not* included in the computation of equivalent unit costs. Under the FIFO cost flow assumption, separate costing analyses are used for each accounting period. Therefore, costs attached to beginning inventory are treated separately, in the cost summary schedule.

The Cost Summary Schedule

The final phase of the process costing analysis is to prepare the **cost summary schedule**, shown as Part C in Exhibit 2. This schedule is used to determine the costs to be transferred to the Finished Goods Inventory account of a production process, department, or work cell and the ending balance in the Work in Process Inventory account. The information in this schedule comes from the schedule of equivalent production and the unit cost analysis schedule.

Continuing the example of computer mice, Part C of Exhibit 2 shows that the costs transferred to the Finished Goods Inventory account included $41,540 attached to the 6,200 units in beginning inventory, the costs of completing the units in beginning inventory, and the costs of producing the 52,500 units started and completed during February. Part A of Exhibit 2 shows that 2,480 equivalent units of conversion costs were required to complete the 6,200 units in the beginning work in process inventory. Because the equivalent unit conversion cost for February is $5.60, the cost to complete the units carried over from January was $13,888 (2,480 units × $5.60). The 52,500 units started and completed in February each cost $8.90 to produce. Their combined cost of $467,250 is added to the $55,428 required to produce the 6,200 units from beginning inventory to arrive at the total of $522,678 transferred to the Finished Goods Inventory account.

All costs remaining in the Work in Process Inventory account for computer mice after the costs of completed units have been transferred out represent the costs of the mice still in production at the end of February. As shown in Part C of Exhibit 2, the ending Work in Process Inventory balance of $29,100 is made up of $16,500 of direct materials costs (5,000 units × $3.30 per unit) and $12,600 of conversion costs (5,000 units × 45 percent × $5.60 per unit). Note that the unit figures come from the schedule of equivalent production (Part A of Exhibit 2).

Point to Emphasize: The cost summary schedule and its supporting calculations are developed for the purpose of assigning a value to *one* transaction—the transfer of goods from one department to another or to finished goods inventory. The ending balance in the Work in Process Inventory account represents the costs that remain after this transfer.

When the cost summary schedule is completed, a computational check is performed, as shown in the last line of Exhibit 2. The total cost of completed units transferred to the Finished Goods Inventory account is added to the costs of unfinished units in the Work in Process Inventory account to arrive at the total costs to be accounted for. This figure is compared with the total costs to be accounted for in the unit cost analysis schedule (Part B). The two totals should be equal, except possibly for a minor difference due to rounding. In Exhibit 2, the two figures are the same, so we know that all costs of the computer mice have been accounted for and that no calculation errors were made in the February cost analysis.

Using Information About Product Cost to Evaluate Performance

OBJECTIVE

7 Evaluate operating performance using information about product cost

Related Text Assignments:
Q: 20
SE: 10
E: 15
MRA: 4

The job order and process costing systems provide valuable information to managers. Both systems provide unit costs that can be used in determining a product's price. In addition, the information supplied by the two systems is used to compute the balances in the Materials Inventory, Work in Process Inventory, and Finished Goods Inventory accounts on the balance sheet and the cost of goods sold on the income statement.

Both the job order and the process costing systems supply managers with much more information that is useful in tracking and evaluating operating performance. The following measurements help managers analyze operating efficiency:

- Cost trends of a product or product line
- Units produced per time period
- Materials usage per unit produced
- Labor cost per unit produced
- Special order needs of customers
- Comparisons of the cost-effectiveness of changing to a more advanced production process

Teaching Note: Remind students that performance measures are quantitative tools that help managers assess the performance of a specific process or expected outcome.

Instructional Strategy: To reinforce the use of cost information to evaluate performance, ask students to complete E 15 individually. Then have students form groups of four to discuss their responses. Debrief the entire class by asking one student from each group to summarize his or her group's conclusions.

Cost trends can be developed from product cost data over several time periods. Such trends can help managers identify areas of rising costs or areas where cost-effectiveness has improved. Tracking units produced per time period, a figure that is easily pulled from a product cost analysis, can help managers evaluate operating efficiency.

Direct materials and labor costs are significant parts of a product's cost and should be monitored constantly. Trends in direct materials usage and labor costs per unit produced can help managers determine optimal resource usage.

Anticipating customers' needs is very important to managers. Job order cost cards summarize the amount, costs, and type of product a specific customer has ordered. By tracking such information, managers can see which customers are increasing their orders and which are reducing them and can take action to improve customer relations.

Finally, decisions to purchase new, automated machinery and equipment are often based on the savings that the change is expected to produce. Managers can estimate product unit costs for the new equipment and compare them with cost trends for the existing equipment to decide whether to make a purchase.

B. Unit Cost Analysis Schedule Total Cost Analysis	Costs from Beginning Inventory		Current Period Costs		Total Costs to Be Accounted For
Direct materials costs	$ 8,100		$202,500		$210,600
Conversion costs	11,800		583,200*		595,000
Totals	$19,900		$785,700		$805,600
Computation of Equivalent Unit Costs	**Current Period Costs**	÷	**Equivalent Units**	=	**Cost per Equivalent Unit**
Direct materials costs	$202,500		405,000		$ .50
Conversion costs	583,200		393,600		1.48
Totals	$785,700				$1.98

* $299,200 + $284,000 = $583,200

C. Cost Summary Schedule	Cost of Goods Transferred to Packing Department	Cost of Ending Work in Process Inventory	Total Costs to Be Accounted For
Beginning inventory			
Costs from preceding period	$ 19,900		
Costs to complete this period			
Direct materials costs	—		
Conversion costs: 4,800 units × $1.48	7,104		
Subtotal	$ 27,004		
Units started and completed			
383,400 units × $1.98	759,132		
Ending inventory			
Direct materials costs:			
21,600 units × $.50		$10,800	
Conversion costs:			
5,400 units × $1.48		7,992	
Totals	$786,136	$18,792	$804,928*

*Difference due to rounding.

2. The amount of $786,136 should be transferred to the Work in Process Inventory account of the Packing Department.

Chapter Assignments

BUILDING YOUR KNOWLEDGE FOUNDATION

QUESTIONS

1. How do manufacturing and service organizations use information about costs during the planning stage of the management cycle?
2. List some kinds of decisions managers make using cost information during the executing stage of the management cycle.
3. How do managers use cost information during the reviewing stage of the management cycle?
4. What is a product costing system?
5. What is a job order costing system? What kinds of companies use such a system?
6. What is a job order?
7. What are the main similarities and differences between a job order costing system and a process costing system? (Focus on the characteristics of each system.)
8. Why is the Manufacturing Overhead account reconciled at year end?
9. What is the purpose of a job order cost card? Identify the kinds of information recorded on that document.
10. Explain how to compute product unit cost in a job order costing system. How are the necessary data accumulated?
11. What is the main difference between a service organization and a manufacturing organization? How does that affect the costing system of a service organization?
12. What three schedules are included in a process cost report?
13. Define the term *equivalent production* (or *equivalent units*).
14. Why must actual unit data be changed to equivalent unit data to cost products in a process costing system?
15. Define the term *conversion costs*. Why are conversion costs used in process costing computations?
16. Why do you think it would be easier to compute equivalent units without units in beginning inventory than with units in beginning inventory?
17. What are the purposes of the unit cost analysis schedule?
18. What two important dollar amounts come from the cost summary schedule? How do they relate to the year-end financial statements?
19. Describe how to check the accuracy of the results in the cost summary schedule.
20. What type of operating performance can be evaluated by (a) units produced per time period, (b) labor cost per unit produced, and (c) special order needs of customers?

SHORT EXERCISES

SE 1. **LO 1 Uses of Product Cost Information**

Kerri's Kennel provides boarding for dogs and cats. Kerri must make several decisions soon. Write *yes* or *no* to indicate whether knowing the cost to board one animal per day (that is, the product unit cost) can help Kerri answer the following questions.

1. Is the boarding fee high enough to cover my costs?
2. How much profit will I make if I board an average of ten dogs per day for fifty weeks?
3. What costs can I reduce so I can compete with the boarding fee charged by my competitor?

SE 2. **LO 2 Job Order Versus Process Costing**

Indicate whether each of the following is a characteristic of job order costing or of process costing.

1. Several Work in Process Inventory accounts are used, one for each process, department, or work cell in the process.
2. Costs are grouped by process, department, or work cell.

Expanding Your Critical Thinking, Communication, and Interpersonal Skills

Skills Development

Conceptual Analysis

SD 1.

LO 1 Business Plans

In the past 20 years, *Fortune* 500 companies have eliminated over 5 million jobs, yet the overall U.S. economy has grown by almost 30 million jobs. Most of the new jobs have been created by new businesses. A key step in starting a new company is a realistic analysis of the people, opportunities, context, risks, and rewards of the venture and the formulation of a business plan. Notice the similarities between the questions managers answer in the management cycle and the nine questions every great business plan should answer:[4]

- Who is the new venture's customer?
- How does the customer make decisions about buying this product or service?
- To what degree is the product or service a compelling purchase for the customer?
- How will the product or service be priced?
- How will the venture reach all the identified customer segments?
- How much does it cost (in time and resources) to acquire a customer?
- How much does it cost to produce and deliver the product or service?
- How much does it cost to support a customer?
- How easy is it to retain a customer?

Assume you are a consultant who has been hired for your knowledge of the management cycle. Write a memo that discusses how the nine questions fit into the management cycle.

SD 2.

LO 1 Role of Cost Information in Software Development

Michael Cassidy, the CEO of ***Direct Hit Technologies, Inc.,*** has a problem: when is "good enough" good enough? As the creator of search technology that makes finding relevant information on the Internet both quick and easy, Cassidy worries about how many developer hours should be devoted to a new product. His industry's rule of thumb is that developing and shipping new software generally takes six to nine months. Direct Hit Technologies, Inc., attempts to develop and ship product much more quickly, so from the industry's viewpoint, the company is successful in meeting the industry's measure of performance.

Another performance measure Cassidy uses to answer his question is a "good enough" calculation based on the economic value (not cost) of what his company's developers create. Taking the estimated current market valuation of his firm and dividing it by the number of product developers in the firm, he arrives at the market value created per developer. Given that his firm has been in existence one year, it is also the value created per developer for a year. By dividing this annual creation value per developer by the number of workdays in the year, Cassidy arrives at an added value a developer creates in one workday of approximately $10,000. Thus, the company's "good enough" measure focuses on whether a new product's potential justifies an investment of time by someone who is worth $10,000 per day. The salary cost of the company's developers is not used in the "good enough" calculation. Why is that cost not relevant?[5]

Communication

Critical Thinking

Ethics

Group Activity

Hot Links to Real Companies

International

Internet

Memo

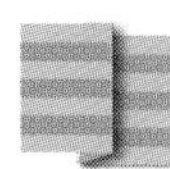
Spreadsheet

Ethical Dilemma

SD 3.
LO 3 Ethical Job Order Costs

Kevin Rogers, the production manager for ***Stitts Metal Products Company***, entered the office of controller Ed Harris and asked, "Ed, what gives here? I was charged for 330 direct labor hours on Job AD22 and my records show that we only spent 290 hours on that job. That 40-hour difference caused the total cost of direct labor and manufacturing overhead for the job to increase by over $5,500. Are my records wrong, or was there an error in the direct labor assigned to the job?" Harris responded, "Don't worry about it, Kevin. This job won't be used in your quarterly performance evaluation. Job AD22 was a federal government job, a cost-plus contract, so the more costs we assign to it, the more profit we make. We decided to add a few hours to the job in case there is some follow-up work to do. You know how fussy the feds are."

What should Kevin Rogers do? Discuss Ed Harris's costing procedure.

Research Activity

SD 4.
LO 5 Process Costing Systems

Locate an article about a company that you believe would use a process costing system. Conduct your search using the business section of your local newspaper, *The Wall Street Journal*, or other business periodicals.

Prepare a short report that describes the product(s) the company makes and its production process, and explains why it probably uses a process costing system. Bring this information to class to share with your classmates. Be sure to include the company's name and identify the article's title, author(s), and publication date.

Group Activity: Group students according to type of production process and ask them to discuss their findings. If time allows, pair students with different production processes and ask them to explain their company to their partner.

Decision-Making Practice

SD 5.
LO 3 Analysis of Job Order
LO 4 Costing Systems

Zavala Manufacturing Company is a small family-owned business that makes specialty plastic products. Since it was started three years ago, the company has grown quickly and now employs ten production people. Because of the nature of its products, the company uses a job order costing system. The company's manual accounting system is falling behind in processing transactions.

Two months ago, in May, the company's accountant quit. You have been called in to help management. The following information has been given to you.

Beginning inventory balances (December 31):	
Materials Inventory	$50,420
Work in Process Inventory (Job K-2)	59,100
Finished Goods Inventory (Job K-1)	76,480
Direct materials requested for production during the year:	
Job K-2	$33,850
Job K-4	53,380
Job K-5	82,400
Direct labor for the year:	
Job K-2	$25,300
Job K-4	33,480
Job K-5	45,600

The company purchased materials only once (in February), for $126,500. All jobs use the same materials. For the current year, the company has been using a manufacturing overhead application rate of 150 percent of direct labor costs. So far, two jobs, K-2 and K-4, have been completed, and Jobs K-1 and K-2 have been shipped to customers. Job K-1 contained 3,200 units; Job K-2, 5,500 units; and Job K-4, 4,600 units. The beginning Work in Process Inventory balance for Job K-2 consisted of $16,975 of direct materials, $16,850 of direct labor, and $25,275 of manufacturing overhead.

1. Calculate the product unit costs for Jobs K-1, K-2, and K-4, and the costs so far for Job K-5.

2. From the information given, prepare job order cost cards for Jobs K-2, K-4, and K-5, and compute the current balances in the Materials Inventory, Work in Process Inventory, Finished Goods Inventory, and Cost of Goods Sold accounts.
3. The president has asked you to analyze the current job order costing system. Do you think the system should be changed? How? Why? Prepare an outline of your response to the president.

MANAGERIAL REPORTING AND ANALYSIS

Interpreting Management Reports

MRA 1.
LO 1 Interpreting Nonfinancial Data

Eagle Manufacturing supplies engine parts to ***Cherokee Cycle Company***, a major U.S. manufacturer of motorcycles. Eagle, like all parts suppliers for Cherokee, has always added a healthy profit margin to its cost when calculating its selling price to Cherokee. Recently, however, several new suppliers have offered to provide parts to Cherokee for lower prices than Eagle has been charging.

Because Eagle wants to keep Cherokee's business, a team of managers analyzed the company's product costs and decided to make minor changes in the company's manufacturing process. No new equipment was purchased, and no additional labor was required. Instead, the machines were rearranged and some of the work was reassigned.

To monitor the effectiveness of the changes, Eagle introduced three new performance measures to its information system: inventory levels, lead time (total time required for a part to move through the production process), and productivity (number of parts manufactured per person per day). Eagle's goal was to reduce the quantities of the first two performance measures and to increase the quantity of the third.

A section of a recent management report, shown below, summarizes the quantities for each performance measure before and after the changes in the manufacturing process were made.

Measure	Before	After	Improvement
Inventory in dollars	$21,444	$10,772	50%
Lead time in minutes	17	11	35%
Productivity (parts per person per day)	515	1,152	124%

REQUIRED

1. Do you believe Eagle improved the quality of its manufacturing process and the quality of its engine parts? Explain your answer.
2. Can Eagle lower its selling price to Cherokee? Explain your answer.
3. Was the design of the product costing system affected by the introduction of the new measures? Explain your answer.
4. Do you believe that the new measures caused a change in Eagle's cost per engine part? In what way?

Formulating Management Reports

MRA 2.
LO 1 Product Costing Systems
LO 2 and Nonfinancial Data

Refer to the information in MRA 1. Jordan Smith, the president of ***Eagle Manufacturing***, wants to improve the quality of the company's operations and products. She believes waste exists in the design and manufacture of standard engine parts. To begin the improvement process, she has asked you (1) to identify sources of waste, (2) to develop performance measures to account for the waste, and (3) to estimate the current costs associated with such waste. She has asked you to write a memo presenting your findings within two weeks so that she can begin strategic planning to revise the selling price for engine parts to Cherokee.

You have identified two sources of costly waste. The Production Department is redoing work that was not done correctly the first time, and the Engineering Design Department is redesigning products that were not designed according to customer specifications the first time. Having improper designs has caused the company to buy parts that are not used in production. You have also obtained the following information from the product costing system:

Direct labor costs	$673,402
Engineering design costs	124,709
Indirect labor costs	67,200
Depreciation on production equipment	84,300
Supervisors' salaries	98,340
Direct materials costs	432,223
Indirect materials costs	44,332

REQUIRED

1. In preparation for writing your memo, answer the following questions.
   a. For whom are you preparing the memo? What is the appropriate length of the memo?
   b. Why are you preparing the memo?
   c. What information is needed for the memo? Where can you get such information? What performance measure would you suggest for each activity? Is the accounting information sufficient for your memo?
   d. When is the memo due? What can be done in order to provide accurate and timely information?
2. Prepare an outline of the sections you would want in your memo.

International Company

MRA 3.

LO 1 Design of a Product
LO 2 Costing System
LO 5

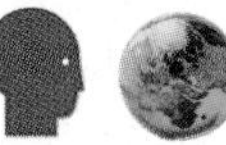

The ***Al Khali Corporation***'s copper mines hold 63 percent of the 23.2 million tons of copper in Saudi Arabia. The owners of the mining operation are willing to invest millions of dollars in the latest pyrometallurgical copper extraction processes. The production managers are currently examining both batch and continuous methods of applying the new copper extraction process. The method they choose will replace the hydrometallurgical process now in use.

What effect will the method selected by the production managers have on the design of the product costing system? What effect would changing from hydrometallurgical to pyrometallurgical processing have on the design of the product costing system if both processes use continuous methods of extraction?

Excel Spreadsheet Analysis

MRA 4.

LO 6 FIFO Process Costing:
LO 7 One Process—Two Time Periods

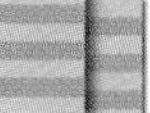

Seader Corporation produces a line of home products in its Fargo, North Dakota, plant. The Shaping Department has been making two-gallon chili pots for the past three months. The production process has been automated, so the product can now be produced in one operation rather than in the three operations that were needed before the automated machinery was purchased. All direct materials are added at the beginning of the process, and conversion costs are incurred uniformly throughout the process. Operating data for May and June 20x5 were as follows:

	May	June
Beginning Work in Process Inventory		
Units (May: 40% complete)	220	?
Direct materials costs	$ 400	$ 360
Conversion costs	$ 125	$ 134
Production during the month		
Units started	24,000	31,000
Direct materials costs	$35,000	$74,400
Conversion costs	$26,000	$29,695
Ending Work in Process Inventory		
Units (May: 70% complete; June: 60% complete)	200	320
Unit costs		
Direct materials costs	$ 1.80	$?
Conversion costs	.96	?
Product unit cost	$ 2.76	$?

REQUIRED

1. Prepare a process cost report for June 20x5, including (a) a schedule of equivalent units, (b) a unit cost analysis schedule, and (c) a cost summary schedule. (Round unit costs to two decimal places: round all other dollar amounts to the nearest dollar.)

2. From the information in the cost summary schedule, identify the amount that should be transferred out of the Work in Process Inventory account, and state where those dollars should be transferred.
3. Compare the product costing results of the Shaping Department for the current month with those for the previous month. What is the most significant change? What are some possible causes of this change?

Internet Case

MRA 5.
LO 1 Interpreting Web Sites

Refer to the opening Decision Point in this chapter about the custom suit manufacturer John H. Daniel Company. Do a key word search for other clothing manufacturers. Select two companies that make similar clothes and access their web sites. Conduct an Internet shopping audit similar to the one P. Kelly Mooney does as the intelligence director for Resource Marketing, Inc., a technology marketing and communications company based in Columbus, Ohio.

Mooney uses five principles to evaluate Internet shopping sites on aspects such as prepurchase customer service, gift giving, special promotions, and postpurchase follow-through. Mooney describes the five principles as follows:[6]

- **Don't just do it:** The web site is more than the company's catalogue loaded online.
- **Don't let your seams show:** Shopping is designed to seamlessly guide customers according to their needs in every retail environment, both online and in person (if applicable).
- **Own the customer experience:** The web site is easy, intuitive, and accessible because the company is good at asking customers about the types of information they want. As a result, the site becomes personalized to the customer and the kind of service he or she desires.
- **Avoid barriers to entry:** The web site should center on the customer. It should have clear connection paths, quick-loading graphics, well-organized pages, crisp self-help features, and personal e-mail responses that state all details of the shopping transaction in plain language.
- **Trust is a must:** The web site does not follow a one-size-fits-all information-gathering approach. Shortcuts allow customers to browse and learn to trust the company as a valued adviser.

Use Mooney's five principles to answer the following questions about the two companies you chose.

1. Identify the companies, their product lines, and their URLs. Taking a customer's perspective, describe your impressions of their web sites and their custom offerings.
2. Compare the companies' order forms. Do the companies request the same measurements and other information? Are their prices comparable for like items? How do the order forms differ?
3. Assume you are the manager of each company you chose. Did your product unit cost influence your pricing decisions? What other factors had a significant effect on the prices you set?
4. If the companies' financial statements are available on their web sites, review the figures for cost of goods sold and inventories. Describe your findings. Do the financial results agree with your previous impressions?

ENDNOTES

1. Robert L. Simison, "Toyota Finds Way to Make Custom Car in 5 Days," *The Wall Street Journal*, August 6, 1999.
2. Associated Press, "$75 Screws? The Pentagon Pays It." *The Gainesville Sun*, March 19, 1998.
3. Curtis Sittenfeld, "This Old House Is a Home for New Ideas," *Fast Company*, July–August 1999.
4. William A. Sahlman, "How to Write a Great Business Plan," *Harvard Business Review*, July–August 1997.
5. Gina Imperato, "When Is 'Good Enough' Good Enough?" *Fast Company*, July–August 1999.
6. P. Kelly Mooney, "The Experienced Customer," *Net Company*, Fall 1999.

22 Activity-Based Systems: Activity-Based Management and Just-in-Time

LEARNING OBJECTIVES

1. Explain the role of activity-based systems in the management cycle.
2. Define *activity-based management (ABM)* and discuss its relationship with the supply network and the value chain.
3. Distinguish between value-adding and nonvalue-adding activities, and describe process value analysis.
4. Define *activity-based costing*, and explain how a cost hierarchy and a bill of activities are used.
5. Define the *just-in-time (JIT) operating philosophy* and identify the elements of a JIT operating environment.
6. Identify the changes in product costing that result when a firm adopts a JIT operating environment.
7. Define and apply *backflush costing*, and compare the cost flows in traditional and backflush costing.
8. Compare ABM and JIT as activity-based systems.

DECISION POINT: A MANAGER'S FOCUS

United Parcel Service and eLogistics.net

United Parcel Service knows that a critical part of its future success will come from taking advantage of the Internet to provide a variety of distribution and logistics services. As the largest package distributor in the world in both volume and revenue, UPS wants to move from the low-margin business of delivering boxes into the more lucrative business of purveying information over the Web. As part of this repositioning effort for ecommerce, UPS established a separate company, eLogistics.net, to create efficient supply networks for its customers by centralizing their online information and logistics needs. eLogistics.net seeks to become the premier global nerve center where vendors, manufacturers, dealers, and other customers can track product progress at every stage of production and distribution. For example, not only could a manufacturer waiting for a shipment of materials for a particular project check where the materials were and when they would arrive, but so could other affected vendors, dealers, and customers.[1] How can activity-based systems help eLogistics.net managers compete globally?

The managers at eLogistics.net can use activity-based systems to better determine the costs of their company's services and to identify and reduce or eliminate business activities that do not add value for the company's customers. eLogistics.net will also provide quantitative activity-based information to its customers so that their managers can use activity-based systems to determine the costs of their products or services. Activity-based management (ABM) and the just-in-time (JIT) operating philosophy rely on the examination of activities to minimize waste, reduce costs, and improve the allocation of resources. eLogistics.net and its customers can use ABM plus its tool, activity-based costing (ABC), to improve product and service costing. These systems will help managers make better decisions about pricing, adding or dropping product or service lines, changing production or distribution processes, and contracting with other companies to provide products or services. The information provided by eLogistics.net will help customers using JIT to improve their production processes, manage their inventory levels, and schedule timely production.

Critical Thinking Question: How can activity-based systems help an organization compete? **Answer:** By helping managers determine the costs of products or services, eliminate nonvalue-adding activities, improve resource allocation, and make better decisions about pricing, products or services, processes, inventories, scheduling, and outsourcing.

UPS and eLogistics.net realize business is changing rapidly. To meet the varied needs of their users, supply networks must provide universal access to information in real time. ABM and JIT allow the managers of eLogistics.net to define new, customizable ways to process and view business.

Activity-Based Systems and Management

OBJECTIVE

1 Explain the role of activity-based systems in the management cycle

Related Text Assignments:
Q: 1, 2, 3, 4, 5
SE: 1
E: 1

Teaching Note: Ask students to visit Dell's web site and answer the following questions: How many market segments is Dell currently targeting? What are they? How do Dell's computer packages differ for each market segment? www.dell.com

Many companies operate in volatile business environments that are strongly influenced by customer demands. Company managers know that customers buy value, usually in the form of quality products or services that are delivered on a timely basis for a reasonable price. Companies generate revenue when customers see value and buy their product or service. Thus, companies measure value as the revenue generated by the company (customer value = revenue generated).

Value exists when some characteristic of a product or service satisfies customers' wants or needs. For example, Dell Computer Corporation knows that one market segment is customers who appreciate convenience. In response to their needs, Dell creates value and increases revenue by selling computer systems called Dell Dimension Systems. They include the latest microprocessor, monitor, graphics card, CD-ROM or DVD drive, sound card, modem, speakers, and preinstalled Microsoft software products. Microsoft creates value and increases revenue by offering its customers "free" upgrades of selected software on the Internet.

To create value and to satisfy customer needs for quality, reasonable price, and timely delivery, managers must

- Work with suppliers and customers
- View the organization as a collection of value-adding activities
- Use resources for value-adding activities
- Reduce or eliminate nonvalue-adding activities
- Know the total cost of creating value for a customer

If an organization's strategic plan focuses on providing products or services that customers esteem, then managers will work with suppliers and customers to find ways to collectively improve quality, reduce costs, and improve delivery time. Managers will also focus their attention internally to find the best ways of using resources to create or maintain value in their products or services. This requires matching the resources to operating activities that add value to a product or service. Managers will examine all business activities, including research and development, purchasing, production, storing, selling, shipping, and customer service, so that they can successfully allocate resources. In addition, managers need to know the **full product cost**, which includes not only the costs of direct materials and direct labor, but also the costs of all production and nonproduction activities required to satisfy the customer. For example, the full product cost of a Dell Dimension System includes not only the cost of the computer components and software, but also the costs of taking the sales order, processing the order, packaging and shipping the system, and providing subsequent customer service for warranty work and software upgrades. If the activities are executed well and in agreement with the strategic plan, and if costs are assigned fairly, the company can improve product pricing and product quality, increase productivity, and generate revenues (value) and profits.

Harley-Davidson's value chain is incorporated into its organizational chart. The chart consists of three overlapping circles—a Create Demand Circle, a Produce Products Circle, and a Support Circle; in the center, where the three circles overlap, is the Leadership and Strategy Council. The three circles represent self-directed work teams of eight or nine senior managers. The Create Demand Circle focuses on sales and marketing issues. The Produce Products Circle is responsible for engineering and manufacturing. The Support Circle handles legal, financial, human resource, and communication concerns. The Leadership and Strategy Council coordinates issues that involve all the circles—strategic plans, operating budgets, and policies affecting all employees. The council consists of the chief operating officer and six managers elected by their circle peers. Because it is made up of interconnected circles, Harley's organizational chart emphasizes the interdependence and collaboration necessary for value chain success. It also reinforces the company's ethical code of valuing both individuals and teamwork.[3]

Teaching Note: It is helpful to briefly illustrate how the value chain is part of a supply network by using a local business as an example.

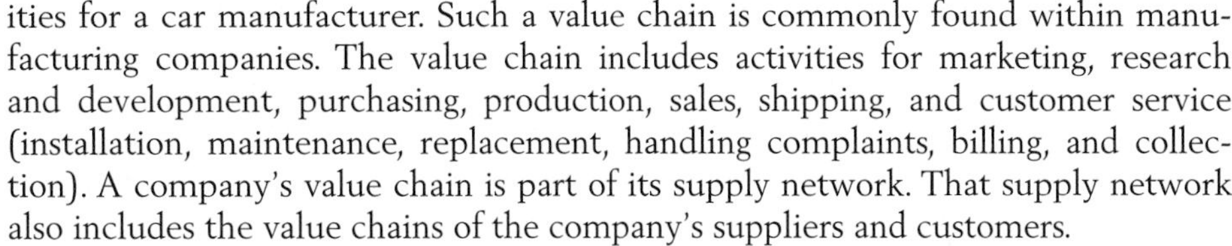

ities for a car manufacturer. Such a value chain is commonly found within manufacturing companies. The value chain includes activities for marketing, research and development, purchasing, production, sales, shipping, and customer service (installation, maintenance, replacement, handling complaints, billing, and collection). A company's value chain is part of its supply network. That supply network also includes the value chains of the company's suppliers and customers.

A company can enhance its profitability by understanding not only its own value chain, but also how its value-adding activities fit into its suppliers' and customers' value chains. Working with suppliers and customers across the entire supply network provides opportunities to reduce the total cost of making a product, even though costs for one activity may be increased. For example, assume that Ford Motor Co. decided to place order entry computers in its car dealerships. The new computers would streamline the entry and processing of orders, plus make the orders more accurate. In this case, even though Ford would incur the cost of the computers, the total cost of making and delivering a car would decrease because the cost of placing and processing an order would decrease. When organizations work cooperatively with others in their supply network, new processes can be introduced that will reduce the total costs of products or services.

ABM in a Service Organization

Let's look at how ABM can be implemented in a service organization. Western Data Services, Inc. (WDSI) offers strategic data-base marketing to help organizations increase sales. WDSI's basic package of services includes the design of a mail piece (either a Classic Letter with or without inserts or a Self-Mailer), creation and maintenance of marketing data bases containing information about the client's target group, and a production process that prints a promotional piece and prepares it for mailing. WDSI's primary customers tend to be financial institutions throughout the western states, but the company also serves small businesses and nonprofit organizations.

Carl Marcus, the owner and manager of WDSI, reviewed his company's supply network as part of his strategic plan. As shown in Figure 3, WDSI's supply network includes one supplier, WDSI as a service provider, one customer group (financial institutions), and the customer group's customers. In reality, WDSI has a number of suppliers, including office supply companies, printers, and computer stores. However, Marcus chose to include only WDSI's most significant supplier, Pitney Bowes, because of the significant expense involved in using Pitney Bowes's

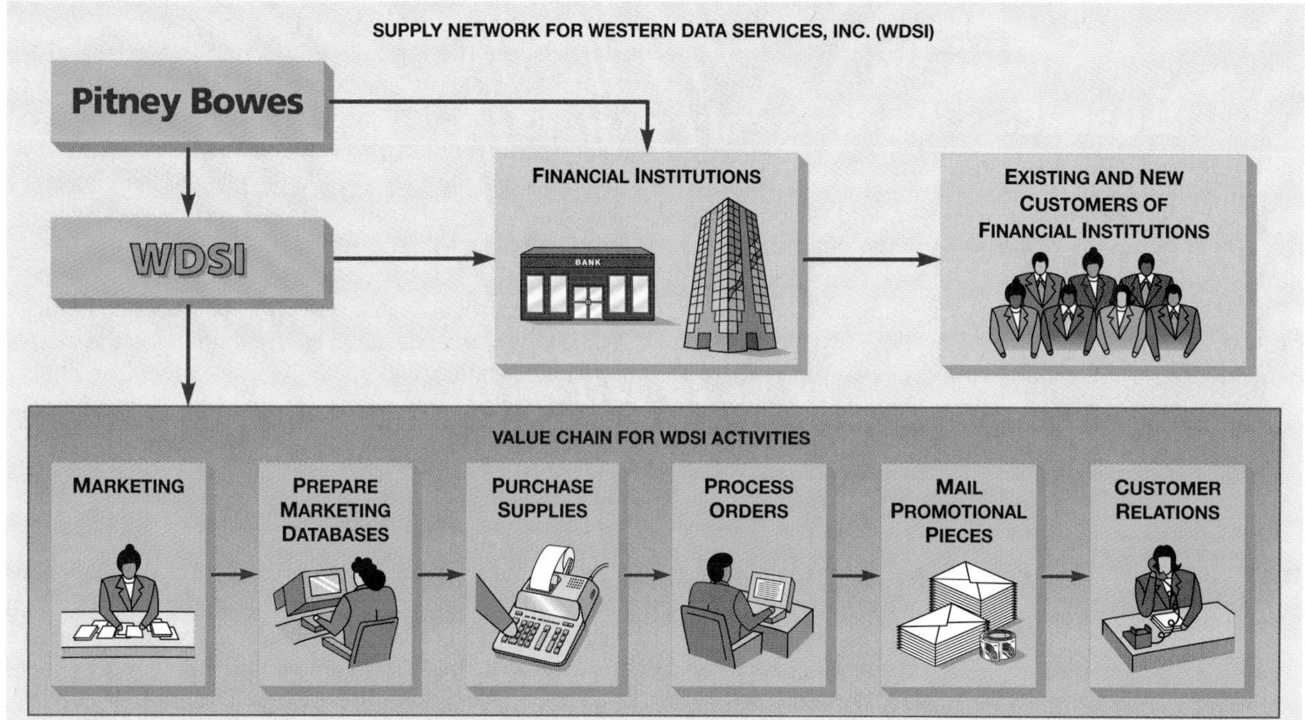

Figure 3
Supply Network and Value Chain for a Service Organization

equipment to fold, insert, address, seal, and meter mail pieces. Marcus chose financial institutions as the primary customer group in the supply network because they represented 75 percent of his revenues. The customers of the financial institutions are included in the supply network because those individuals and businesses receive the mail pieces prepared by WDSI. Based on his understanding of the supply network, Marcus has changed WDSI's strategy to work with Pitney Bowes and the financial institutions to improve WDSI's services.

Another part of Carl Marcus's strategy is to manage processes and activities using ABM and ABC. Marcus developed a value chain of activities for the company so that he could identify all major operating activities, the resources each activity consumes, and the cause for the resource usage. As shown in Figure 3, WDSI's value chain includes marketing, preparing marketing data bases, purchasing supplies, processing orders, mailing promotional pieces, and customer relations.

Value-Adding and Nonvalue-Adding Activities and Process Value Analysis

OBJECTIVE

3 Distinguish between value-adding and nonvalue-adding activities, and describe process value analysis

Related Text Assignments:
Q: 8, 9
SE: 4
E: 4, 5
P: 1
SD: 2, 5
MRA: 1, 4, 5

An important element of activity-based management is the identification of value-adding and nonvalue-adding activities. A **value-adding activity** is an activity that adds value to a product or service as perceived by the customer. Examples include preparing the engineering design of a new car, assembling the car, painting the car, and installing seats and airbags. A **nonvalue-adding activity** is an activity that adds cost to a product or service but does not increase its market value. Examples include the repair of machines, shop floor clean-up, moving materials, and building maintenance. All of those activities require time and use resources but add no value for the customer. The costs of both types of activities are accumulated to measure performance and to determine if the goal of reducing nonvalue-adding activities has been achieved.

Teaching Note: To reinforce the concepts of value-adding and nonvalue-adding activities, ask students who have jobs to identify the aspects of their jobs that add value and do not add value.

Common Student Error: It is important for students to understand that the customer's perspective governs whether an activity adds value to a product or service.

Process value analysis (PVA) is an analytical method of identifying all activities and relating them to the events that cause or drive the need for the activities and the resources consumed. It helps companies using ABM to manage activities. PVA forces managers to look critically at all existing phases of their operations. When nonvalue-adding activities and costs are reduced and cost traceability is improved, product costs become significantly more accurate. This in turn improves management decisions and increases profitability.

Customers value a quality product delivered on a timely basis for a reasonable price. To mimimize costs, company managers continuously seek to improve processes and activities. To manage the cost of an activity, a manager can reduce the activity's frequency or eliminate it. For example, inspection costs can be reduced if an inspector samples one of every three engines received from a supplier rather than inspecting every engine. If the supplier is a reliable source of high-quality engines, such a reduction in inspection activity is appropriate. Another way to reduce cost is to contract to have an activity performed by an external party, also called *outsourcing*. Companies are outsourcing purchasing, accounting, and information systems maintenance to companies that either have more expertise or can perform the work at a lower cost.

Other activities can be eliminated completely if business processes are changed. For example, some accounting recordkeeping activities can be eliminated if a company purchases materials just in time for production and makes the product just in time for customer delivery. This change to a just-in-time operating philosophy eliminates the need to accumulate costs as the product is made.

By identifying nonvalue-adding activities, companies can reduce costs and redirect resources to value-adding activities. For example, PVA has enabled companies such as Westinghouse Electric, Pepsi-Cola North America, and Land O'Lakes, Inc., to significantly reduce the costs of managing small-dollar purchases. Managers reviewed and analyzed the activities of purchasing supplies, recording and paying small bills, setting up accounts, and establishing credit with seldom-used suppliers. Once managers identified the nonvalue-adding activities, they were able to determine their costs. Management's response was to stop performing those activities internally. Instead, they chose the less expensive alternative of using a special credit card known as a procurement card (or purchasing card) with Visa, MasterCard, or American Express to handle large volumes of small-dollar purchases.

Value-Adding and Nonvalue-Adding Activities in a Service Organization

Let's look at the value-adding and nonvalue-adding activities in a service organization by continuing with our illustration. Carl Marcus, the owner and manager of WDSI, a strategic data-base marketing company, has examined the activities related to the design, processing, and mailing of Classic Letters. Table 1 shows the value-adding activities for Classic Letters and how those activities add value. When Marcus's customers ask for data-base marketing services, these are the activities they pay for. Marcus also identified a number of nonvalue-adding activities, which include the following:

- Prepare a job order form and schedule the job
- Order, receive, inspect, and store paper, envelopes, and supplies
- Set up machines to process a specific letter size
- Log the total number of items processed in a batch
- Bill the client, plus record and deposit payments from the client

After reviewing the list of nonvalue-adding activities, Marcus arranged with his suppliers to have paper, envelopes, and other supplies delivered the day a job was

Table 1. Value-Adding Activities for a Service Organization

Western Data Services, Inc.
Value-Adding Activities for the Classic Letter

Value-Adding Activities	How the Activity Adds Value
Design the letter	Enhances the effectiveness of the communication
Create a data base of customer names and addresses sorted in ZIP code order	Increases the probability that the client will efficiently and effectively reach the targeted customer group
Verify the conformity of mailing information with USPS requirements	Ensures that the client's mailing will receive the best postal rate
Process the job: A computer prints a personalized letter. A machine folds the letter, inserts it and other information into an envelope, prints the address on the envelope, and seals and meters the envelope.	Creates the client mailing
Deliver the letters to the post office	Begins the delivery process

performed. This helped reduce WDSI's storage costs. Marcus was also able to reduce the costs of some value-adding activities. The cost of verifying the conformity of mailing information with United States Postal Service (USPS) requirements was reduced by purchasing computer software that verifies addresses, determines postage, and helps WDSI's employees select a sorting scheme that eliminates sorting by hand. Now Marcus is ready to determine the unit costs for the Classic Letter service and the Self-Mailer service.

Implementing Activity-Based Costing

OBJECTIVE

4 Define *activity-based costing*, and explain how a cost hierarchy and a bill of activities are used

Related Text Assignments:
Q: 10, 11, 12, 13
SE: 5, 6
E: 6, 7, 8
P: 2, 3, 6, 7
MRA: 1, 3, 4

Point to Emphasize: Indirect costs are assigned to cost objects using an appropriate allocation scheme.

The issue of how to assign costs fairly to products or services to determine their unit cost has been refined by management accountants as ready access to value chain data has improved. For example, in an earlier chapter you learned about manufacturing overhead rates and the more recent refinement of those rates into activity cost rates. You may recall that traditional overhead allocation methods used cost drivers such as direct labor hours, direct labor costs, or machine hours to assign manufacturing overhead costs to products. However, in the mid-1980s, organizations realized that their product costing systems did not accurately assign manufacturing overhead costs to the product lines. This leads to inaccurate product unit costs and poor pricing decisions. In response, organizations began to critically evaluate their operating processes. They overhauled their product costing systems to more accurately identify the costs of their products or services.

In the search for more accurate product costing, many organizations embraced activity-based costing (ABC). **Activity-based costing** is a method of assigning costs that calculates a more accurate product cost by identifying all of an organiza-

Focus on Business Technology

Digital postage has become a reality. The digital stamp, a blotchy encrypted image, is produced by a customer—using his or her own computer and printer—who has set up an online account with an authorized U.S. Postal Service vendor. Each digital stamp is unique because it is encoded with information about the sender and the recipient. Postal officials, after years of testing for fraud and counterfeiting, now believe the necessary security systems are in place. They are authorizing companies to sell digital postage nationally.[4]

tion's major operating activities. It traces the indirect costs to those activities and assigns activity costs to products using a cost driver that is related to the cause of the cost. Since its introduction as a viable cost allocation technique, organizations in the United States and throughout the world have adopted ABC.

Activity-based costing is important to activity-based management because it improves the allocation of activity-driven costs to cost objects. To implement activity-based costing, managers

1. Identify and classify each activity
2. Estimate the cost of resources for each activity
3. Identify a cost driver for each activity and estimate the quantity of each cost driver
4. Calculate an activity cost rate
5. Assign costs to cost objects based on the level of activity required to make the product or provide the service

Two tools help in the implementation of ABC—a cost hierarchy and a bill of activities.

Teaching Note: Ask students to identify sample activities in a cost hierarchy for a clothing manufacturer. Unit level: sew a garment. Batch level: process a client's order for products. Product level: design a dress style. Facility level: provide management, maintenance, and space for the manufacturing operation.

The Cost Hierarchy A **cost hierarchy** is a framework for classifying activities according to the level at which their costs are incurred. Many companies use this framework to manage the allocation of activity-based costs to products or services. In a manufacturing company, the cost hierarchy typically has four levels: the unit level, the batch level, the product level, and the facility level.

- **Unit-level activities** are performed each time a unit is produced. For example, in the engine-installation process for a car manufacturer, unit-level activities include assembling engine subassemblies and connecting engines to car frames. These activities vary with the number of cars produced.
- **Batch-level activities** are performed each time a batch of goods is produced. These activities vary with the number of batches prepared. Examples of batch-level activities in an engine-installation process include setup, inspection, scheduling, and materials handling.
- **Product-level activities** are performed to support the diversity of products in a manufacturing plant. Examples of product-level activities include implementing engineering change notices and redesigning the installation process.
- **Facility-level activities** are performed to support a facility's general manufacturing process. Examples for a car manufacturer include managing, maintaining, lighting, securing, and insuring the manufacturing plant.

Note that the frequency of activities varies across levels and that both value-adding and nonvalue-adding activities are included in the cost hierarchy. Service organizations can also use a cost hierarchy to group activities. The four levels typically are the unit level, the batch level, the service level, and the operations level. Table 2 lists examples of activities in the cost hierarchies for a manufacturing company and a service organization.

The Bill of Activities Once the cost hierarchy is created, the managers group the activities into the specified levels and prepare a summary of the activity costs assigned to the selected cost objects. A **bill of activities** is a list of activities and related costs that is used to compute the costs assigned to activities and the

Table 2. Sample Activities in Cost Hierarchies

Activity Level	Car Manufacturer: Engine Installation	Direct Mail Service: Preparing a Mailing to Bank Customers
Unit level	Install engine Test engine	Print and fold letter Insert letter and other information into envelope Seal and meter envelope
Batch level	Set up installation process Move engines Inspect engines	Retool machines Verify correct postage Bill client
Product or service level	Redesign installation process	Train employees Develop and maintain computer systems and data bases
Facility or operations level	Provide facility management, maintenance, lighting, security, and space	Provide facility management, maintenance, lighting, security, and space

product unit cost. More complex bills of activities group activities into activity pools and include activity cost rates and cost driver levels used to assign costs to cost objects. A bill of activities may be used as the primary document, or as a supporting schedule, to calculate the product unit cost in job order or process costing. It may also be used in a service organization.

Exhibit 1 illustrates a bill of activities for WDSI. In this example, Carl Marcus uses the bill of activities to see how activity costs contributed to unit costs. WDSI provides two types of services:

- The Classic Letter service involves the printing, folding, collating, and inserting of letters and other materials into a printed, addressed envelope that is then metered and sealed. The cost of the Classic Letter service includes the cost of direct materials (envelopes, letters, other materials), postage, and service overhead.
- The Self-Mailer is a one-page solicitation that can be refolded and returned to the client's address. The cost of the Self-Mailer service includes the costs of direct materials (a single page of paper for each mailer), postage, and service overhead.

The volume of mailings for a customer could vary from 150 to 20,000 addresses in a single mailing. The sizes of the data bases that were prepared and the number of machine setups and inspection hours varied from job to job. The service overhead costs for the activities identified in the cost hierarchy are assigned to the two services using ABC. The activity costs are calculated for the service overhead related to each service. These are then added to the costs of direct materials and postage to calculate a unit cost.

Carl Marcus chose to group activities by unit level, batch level, service level, and operations level.

- At the unit level, Marcus included the costs of all activities needed to process each Classic Letter and Self-Mailer; he used machine hours as the cost driver.
- At the batch level, for each job, Marcus included the costs of all activities required to prepare the data base of names and addresses for mailing, set up the machines, and inspect the letters for compliance with the postal regulations. He selected as the cost drivers the number of names in the data base, direct labor hours, and inspection hours.

Exhibit 1
Bill of Activities for a Service Organization

Western Data Services, Inc.
Bill of Activities for Classic Letter and Self-Mailer
For the Month Ended May 31, 20x1

		Classic Letter (110,000 letters)		Self-Mailer (48,000 self-mailers)	
Activity	Activity Cost Rate	Cost Driver Level	Activity Cost	Cost Driver Level	Activity Cost
Unit level					
Process letters	$20 per machine hour	300 machine hours	$ 6,000	120 machine hours	$ 2,400
Batch level					
Prepare data bases	$85 per 1,000 names	50,000 names	4,250	20,000 names	1,700
Set up machines	$10 per direct labor hour	220 direct labor hours	2,200	100 direct labor hours	1,000
Inspect for USPS compliance	$12 per inspection hour	100 inspection hours	1,200	80 inspection hours	960
Service level					
Develop data bases	$25 per design hour	118 design hours	2,950	81 design hours	2,025
Solicit new customers	$3 per solicitation	300 solicitations	900	95 solicitations	285
Operations level					
Provide utilities and space	$15 per machine hour	300 machine hours	4,500	50 machine hours	750
Total activity costs assigned to services			$ 22,000		$ 9,120
Total volume			110,000		48,000
Activity costs per unit (total activity costs ÷ total volume)			$ 0.20		$ 0.19
Cost summary					
Direct materials cost			$ 7,700		$ 5,280
Postage costs			17,600		7,680
Activity costs (includes labor and overhead)			22,000		9,120
Total costs for month			$ 47,300		$22,080
Unit cost (total costs for month ÷ total volume)			$ .43		$ .46

- At the service level, Marcus included the costs of all activities required to develop data bases for new clients and to solicit new business for WDSI, and he used design hours and number of solicitations as the cost drivers.
- Finally, at the operations level, Marcus included the costs of all activities related to providing utilities and space. He used machine hours as the cost driver.

Marcus prepared a bill of activities for one month ending May 31, 20x1. He supported each activity's cost with information about the activity cost rate and the cost driver level. He also calculated the total activity costs and activity cost per unit assigned to each type of service. At the bottom of the bill of activities for the month, Marcus prepared a summary of the total costs of the services and calculated the unit cost for each service (the total costs divided by the number of units mailed).

Point to Emphasize: A bill of activities summarizes costs relating to a product or service and supports the calculation of the product or service unit cost.

The cost information gathered in the bill of activities helped Carl Marcus estimate the company's profits by allowing him to compare his costs with his revenues. To be competitive, he is currently offering the Classic Letter service for $.50 per letter and the Self-Mailer service for $.45 per mailer. The Classic Letter service is generating a positive gross margin of $.07 ($.50 − $.43) per letter, but the Self-Mailer service shows a negative gross margin of $.01 ($.45 − $.46) per mailer. Marcus must find ways to increase fee revenue, reduce costs, or increase service volume for the Self-Mailer service. ABC can help him reduce costs, because the activity costs, including labor and overhead, are categorized by activities and grouped into activity levels. Marcus can examine those activities to identify and reduce or eliminate some of the company's nonvalue-adding activities.

Activity-Based Costing for Selling and Administrative Activities

Activity-based costing may also be used for nonmanufacturing costs. For example, selling and administrative expenses may be pooled by activity and applied to products, services, customer groups, or sales territories. Because customer groups and sales territories differ in their complexity and diversity, each should support its related costs. Customers who buy the most products or services often place larger or more frequent orders. Thus, a larger portion of the costs of selling and administrative activities can be traced to those customers than to customers who buy smaller amounts or order less frequently. Sales territories can differ in size and number of customers served. As a result, some sales territories may require more support services than other sales territories.

Point to Emphasize: Activity-based costing reflects the cause-and-effect relationships between costs and individual processes, products, services, or customers.

ABC can be used to group selling and administrative activities and assign the costs of those activities to cost objects, such as customer groups and sales territories. For many companies, similar customers, such as distributors or retailers, are often treated as a single group because it is difficult to assign costs to individual customers. The costs of selling and administrative activities include salaries, benefits, depreciation on buildings and equipment, sales commissions, and utilities. Such costs are grouped into activity pools and assigned to cost objects, such as customer groups or sales territories, using cost drivers, such as the number of sales calls, sales orders, invoices, or billings.

Exhibit 2 presents a customer-related income statement for WDSI. A similar format can be used to create an income statement for any cost object. Service organizations typically group clients according to significant characteristics, such as length of time required to perform the service or frequency of service. In our example, Carl Marcus can use the ABC information to review the profitability of each customer or customer group. He can also use the information to compare selling and administrative costs across customer groups or to plan profits based on changes in those activities.

Star Bakery
Income Statement for State Prisons Customer Group
For the Year Ending December 31, 20x1

Sales ($5 per case × 50,000 cases)				$250,000
Cost of goods sold ($3.50 per case × 50,000 cases)				175,000
Gross margin				$ 75,000
Less: Selling and administrative activities costs				
Activity	**Activity Cost Rate**	**Cost Driver Level**	**Activity Cost**	
Make sales calls	$60 per sales call	60 sales calls	$ 3,600	
Prepare sales orders	$10 per sales order	900 sales orders	9,000	
Handle inquiries	$5 per minute	1,000 minutes	5,000	
Ship products	$1 per case sold	50,000 cases	50,000	
Process invoices	$20 per invoice	950 invoices	19,000	
Process credit	$20 per notice	40 notices	800	
Process billings and collections	$7 per billing	1,050 billings	7,350	
Total selling and administrative activity costs				94,750
Net income (loss) contributed by state prisons				$(19,750)

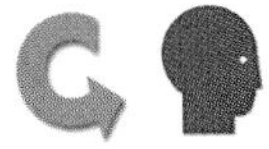

selling doughnuts and snack foods to ten state prisons in three states. The controller has prepared the income statement shown above for the State Prisons customer group. The controller has also provided information about selling and administrative activities for customer groups that have similar characteristics. For 20x1, the planned activity cost rates and the annual cost driver levels for each selling and administrative activity are as follows:

Activity	Activity Cost Rate	Planned Annual Cost Driver Level
Make sales calls	$60 per sales call	59 sales calls
Prepare sales orders	$10 per sales order	850 sales orders
Handle inquiries	$5.10 per minute	1,000 minutes
Ship products	$.60 per case sold	50,000 cases
Process invoices	$1 per invoice	500 invoices
Process credit	$10 per notice	5 notices
Process billings and collections	$4 per billing	600 billings

You have been called in as a consultant on the State Prisons customer group.

REQUIRED

1. Calculate the planned activity cost for each activity.
2. Calculate the differences between the planned activity cost and the State Prisons customer group's activity costs for 20x1.
3. From your evaluation of the differences calculated in **2** and your review of the income statement, identify the nonvalue-adding activities and state which selling and administrative activities should be examined.
4. What actions might the company take to reduce the costs of nonvalue-adding selling and administrative activities?

Group Activity: Provide data for **1** and **2** to groups and ask them to discuss and answer **3** and **4**.

Formulating Management Reports

MRA 2.
LO 5 Manufacturing Processes

Classic Clubs, Inc., manufactures professional golf clubs. Demand has been so great that the company built a special plant that makes only custom-crafted clubs. The clubs are shaped by machines but vary according to the customer's sex, height, weight, and arm length. Ten basic sets of clubs are produced, five for females and five for males. Slight variations in machine setup produce the differences in the club weights and lengths. In the past six months, several problems have developed. Even though one computer numerically controlled machine is used in the manufacturing process, the company's backlog is growing rapidly. Customers are complaining that delivery is too slow. Quality is declining because clubs are being pushed through production without proper inspection. Working capital is tied up in excessive amounts of inventory and storage space. Workers are complaining about the pressure to produce the backlogged orders. Machine breakdowns are increasing. Production control reports are not useful because they are not timely and contain irrelevant information. The company's profitability and cash flow are suffering.

Classic Clubs, Inc., has hired you as a consultant to define the problem and suggest a possible solution to the current dilemma. Denise Rodemeyer, the president, asks that you complete your work within a month so that she can prepare an action plan to present to the board of directors at the mid-year board meeting.

REQUIRED

1. In memo form, prepare a response to Rodemeyer. Recommend specific changes in the manufacturing processes.
2. To help you prepare this report, answer the following questions.
   a. What kinds of information do you need to prepare this report?
   b. Why is this information relevant?
   c. Where would you go to obtain this information (sources)?
   d. When would you want to obtain this information?

International Company

MRA 3.
LO 4 ABM and ABC in a Service Business

Kendle and Watson, a CPA firm, has provided audit, tax, and management advisory services to businesses in the London area for over 50 years. Recently, the firm decided to use ABM and activity-based costing to assign its overhead costs to those service functions. Bellamy Kendle is interested in seeing the difference in the average cost per audit job between the traditional and the activity-based costing approaches. The following information has been provided to assist in the comparison.

Total direct labor costs	£400,000
Other direct costs	120,000
Total direct costs	£520,000

Overhead costs are as follows:

Traditional costing data:

Overhead costs were assigned at a rate of 120 percent of direct labor costs.

Activity-based costing data:

Activity	Cost Driver	Activity Cost Rate	Activity Usage for Audit Function
Professional development	Number of employees	£2,000 per employee	50 employees
Administration	Number of jobs	£1,000 per job	50 jobs
Client development	Number of new clients	£5,000 per new client	29 new clients

REQUIRED

1. Using direct labor cost as the cost driver, calculate the total costs for the audit function. What is the average cost per job?
2. Using activity-based costing to assign overhead, calculate the total costs for the audit function. What is the average cost per job?

3. Calculate the difference in total costs between the two approaches. Why would activity-based costing be the better approach to assigning overhead to the audit function?

Excel Spreadsheet Analysis

MRA 4.

LO 3 ABC in Planning and
LO 4 Control

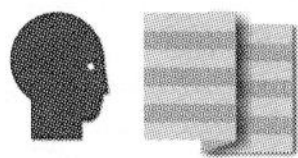

Refer to the income statement for the State Prisons customer group for the year ending December 31, 20x1, in **MRA 1**. Sally Star, the owner of ***Star Bakery***, is in the process of budgeting net income for 20x2. She has asked the controller to prepare a budgeted income statement for the State Prisons customer group. Sally estimates that the selling price per case, the number of cases sold, the cost of goods sold per case, and the activity costs for making sales calls, preparing sales orders, and handling inquiries will remain the same for 20x2. She has contracted with a new freight company to ship the 50,000 cases at $.60 per case sold. She has also analyzed the processes for invoicing, reviewing credit, billing, and collecting and has decided it would be less expensive for a customer service agency to do the work. The agency will charge the bakery 1.5 percent of the total sales revenue.

REQUIRED

Using an Excel spreadsheet:

1. Prepare a budgeted income statement for the State Prisons customer group for the year ending December 31, 20x2.
2. Refer to the information in **MRA 1**. Assuming the planned activity cost rate and planned annual cost driver level for each selling and administrative activity remain the same in 20x2, calculate the planned activity cost for each activity.
3. Calculate the differences between the planned activity costs and the State Prisons customer group's activity costs for 20x2.
4. Evaluate the results of changing freight companies and outsourcing the customer service activities.

Internet Case

MRA 5.

LO 2 Zero Time and
LO 3 the Value Chain

New words enter our vocabulary on a daily basis. Business conversations now commonly include such terms as *e-mail, sync, 24/7, JIT,* and *ABC*. One term introduced in this chapter was *zero time*. Zero time, as first discussed in **SD 2,** is the ability to react instantaneously to customers to provide customer value whenever and wherever possible. Do a quick search on the Web using *zero time*. What products, services, or organizations do you find? List three of your findings and do a brief summary of them to share in class.[7]

ENDNOTES

1. Scott Kirsner, "Venture Vérité, United Parcel Service," *Wired*, September 1999.
2. Gary Cokins, "Learning to Love ABC," *Journal of Accountancy*, August 1999.
3. Gina Imperato, "Harley Shifts Gears," *Fast Company*, June–July 1997.
4. George Anders, "Postal Service Soon to Let Two Firms Nationally Sell Computer-Made Stamps," *The Wall Street Journal*, July 19, 1999.
5. Alexander Kogan, Ephraim F. Sudit, and Miklos A. Visarhelyi, "Management Accounting in the Era of Electronic Commerce," *Management Accounting*, Institute of Management Accountants, September 1997.
6. Gina Imperato, "Time for Zero Time," *Net Company*, Fall 1999.
7. Gina Imperato, "first.site," *Net Company*, Fall 1999.

23 Cost Behavior Analysis

LEARNING OBJECTIVES

1. Define *cost behavior* and explain how managers use this concept in the management cycle.
2. Identify specific types of variable and fixed cost behavior, and discuss how operating capacity and relevant range relate to cost behavior.
3. Define *mixed cost*, and use the high-low method to separate the variable and fixed components of a mixed cost.
4. Define *cost-volume-profit analysis* and discuss how managers use this analysis.
5. Compute a breakeven point in units of output and in sales dollars, and prepare a breakeven graph.
6. Define *contribution margin* and use the concept to determine a company's breakeven point for a single product and for multiple products.
7. Apply cost-volume-profit analysis to estimated levels of future sales and to changes in costs and selling prices.
8. Apply cost-volume-profit analysis to a service business.

DECISION POINT: A MANAGER'S FOCUS

Cummins Engine Company, Inc. Cummins Engine Company, Inc., is a manufacturing company whose main office is located in Columbus, Indiana.[1] Cummins facilities in the United States, Mexico, and China manufacture diesel engines and other parts for large trucks. The trucking industry, in which Cummins operates, is a very cyclical industry. This means that the number of engines that are made and sold varies greatly from year to year depending on whether the economy is strong or weak. How does the variability in the demand for Cummins's engines affect management's planning for profitability?

Cummins's management must carefully consider the behavior of the many costs of making engines and determine a selling price that will take into account the variability of demand. For example, the total cost of direct materials, such as steel, and direct labor will vary based on the number of engines produced in any one year. The costs of direct materials and direct labor are roughly the same for each engine the company makes. In contrast, the total cost of operating the factories and manufacturing equipment used in making the engines will not change significantly from year to year in response to the number of engines produced. However, the amount of those costs applied to each engine will vary depending on the number of engines produced. To project the profitability of a particular year, management must take into account both the selling price and the estimated production and sales of engines and the effects those estimates have on the unit cost of the engines. This chapter focuses on the analysis of cost behavior and its role in achieving profitability.

Critical Thinking Question: What factors affect the replacement of manufacturing equipment? **Answer:** Usage, obsolescence, and maintenance needs of the equipment; volume of business; and planned net income.

Cost Behavior Patterns and the Management Cycle

OBJECTIVE

1 Define *cost behavior* and explain how managers use this concept in the management cycle

Related Text Assignments:
Q: 1, 2
SE: 1
SD: 1

Teaching Note: Cost behavior is closely linked to the concept of cost controllability. Generally, variable costs can be controlled more easily in the short run than can fixed costs.

The expectation that an organization's management will generate income for its owners and maintain liquidity for its creditors requires managers to find ways to make good decisions. One common way of making good decisions is to use cost behavior to analyze alternative courses of action. **Cost behavior** is the way costs respond to changes in volume or activity. Some costs vary with volume or operating activity; others remain fixed as volume changes. Between those two extremes are costs that exhibit characteristics of each type.

Uses of Cost Behavior in the Management Cycle

An understanding of cost behavior is extremely helpful as managers move through the planning, executing, reviewing, and reporting stages of the management cycle, as shown in Figure 1.

PLANNING In the planning stage, managers want to know how many units must be sold to cover all costs or to generate a targeted amount of profit, or operating income. Managers want to know how changes in planned operating, investing, or financing activities will affect operating income. As German sports shoe manufacturer Adidas completed the acquisition of Salomon SA, a French ski and sporting goods maker, its management began to estimate income from future operations. They used cost behavior to estimate how the addition of new lines of sporting equipment, such as Salomon skis and snowboards, Taylor Made golf clubs, and Mavic cycling equipment, would contribute to the organization's operating income.

Car manufacturers, such as Chrysler, also use cost behavior in the planning stage to decide how to change the output of trucks and cars to meet changing sales demand. If increased demand for trucks suggests the need to increase truck production and decrease car production, management can use cost behavior analysis to estimate the changes in operating income for those product lines. Because the truck segment is more profitable for Chrysler, the company's net income should increase if truck production is increased.

EXECUTING Managers use information about cost behavior in almost every decision they make. For example, managers at Cummins Engine must understand the changes in income that can result from a decision to buy new, more productive manufacturing equipment or to launch an advertising campaign to promote a new series of engines. Throughout the executing stage of the management cycle, managers must understand cost behavior to determine the impact of their decisions on operating income.

REVIEWING AND REPORTING Managers at Adidas, Chrysler, and Cummins Engine also need to understand cost behavior when reviewing operations and preparing reports. Variable costing income statements are commonly used to analyze how changes in cost and sales affect the profitability of product lines, sales territories, customers, departments, or other segments. Other reports based on cost behavior are used when deciding whether to eliminate a product line, accept a special order, or contract with another company to provide services previously performed internally.

Figure 1
The Use of Cost Behavior in the Management Cycle

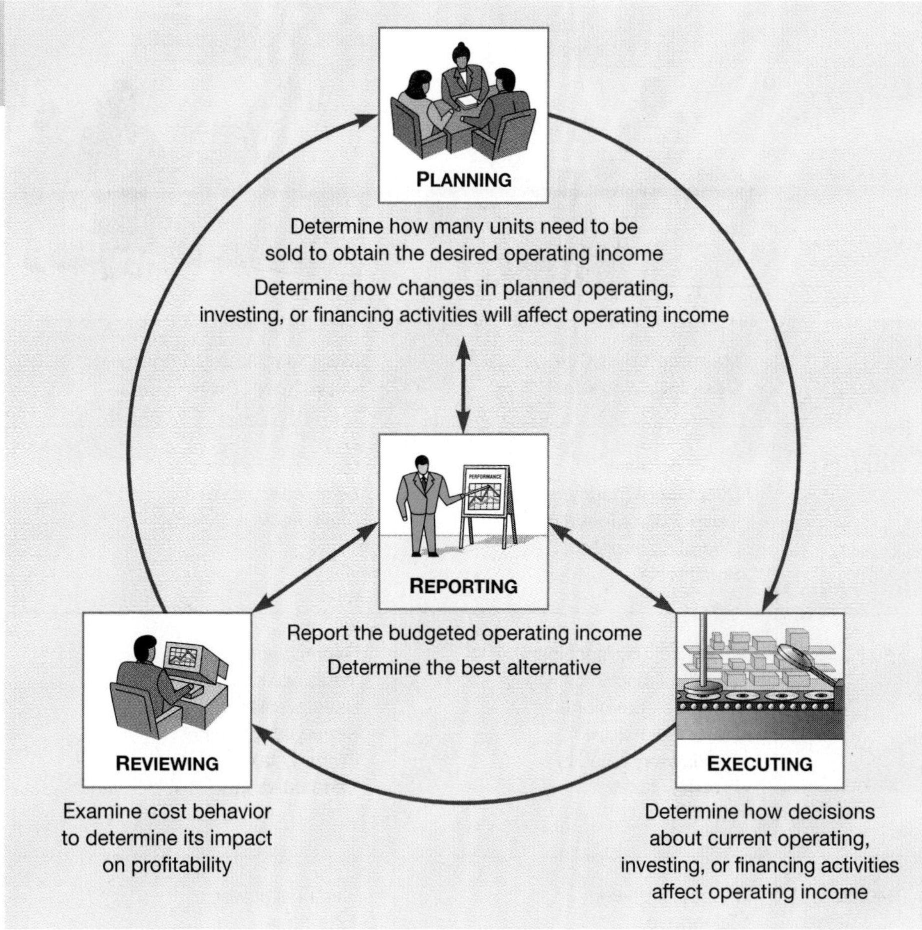

Our discussion in this chapter will focus primarily on cost behavior as it relates to production. But cost behavior can also be observed in other activities. For example, increases in the number of shipments affect shipping costs; the number of units sold or total sales revenue affects the cost of sales commissions; and the number of customers billed or the number of hours to bill affects total billing costs. Costs behave in much the same way in service organizations as they do in manufacturing organizations. We look specifically at the costs of service organizations later in the chapter.

The Behavior of Variable Costs

OBJECTIVE

2 **Identify specific types of variable and fixed cost behavior, and discuss how operating capacity and relevant range relate to cost behavior**

Related Text Assignments:
Q: 3, 4, 5, 6, 7, 8, 9
SE: 2
E: 1, 2
P: 1, 8
SD: 1, 4, 5

Total costs that change in direct proportion to changes in productive output (or any other measure of volume) are called **variable costs**. To explore how variable costs work, consider tire costs for Land Rover, a maker of off-road vehicles. Each new vehicle has four tires, and each tire costs $48. The total cost of tires, then, is $192 for one vehicle, $384 for two, $576 for three, $768 for four, $960 for five, $1,920 for ten, and $19,200 for one hundred. In the production of off-road vehicles, the total cost of tires is a variable cost. On a per-unit basis, however, a variable cost remains constant. In this case, the cost of tires per vehicle is $192 whether the auto maker produces one vehicle or one hundred vehicles. True, the cost of tires varies depending on the number purchased and whether discounts are available for purchases of large quantities. But once the purchase has been made, the cost per tire is established. Figure 2 illustrates other examples of variable costs. All of those

Costs	Manufacturing Company—Desk Manufacturer	Merchandising Company—Department Store	Service Company—Bank
VARIABLE	Direct materials Direct labor (hourly) Indirect labor (hourly) Operating supplies Small tools	Merchandise to sell Sales commissions Shelf stockers (hourly)	Computer equipment leasing (based on usage) Computer operators (hourly) Operating supplies Data storage disks
FIXED	Depreciation, machinery and building Insurance premiums Labor (salaried) Supervisory salaries Property taxes	Depreciation, building Insurance premiums Buyers (salaried) Supervisory salaries Property taxes (on equipment and building)	Depreciation, furniture and fixtures Insurance premiums Salaries: Programmers Systems designers Bank administrators Rent, buildings
MIXED	Electrical power Telephone Heat	Electrical power Telephone Heat	Electrical power Telephone Heat

Figure 2
Examples of Variable, Fixed, and Mixed Costs

costs—whether incurred by a manufacturer, a service business, or a merchandiser—are variable based on either productive output or total sales.

Terminology Note: By definition, there are no variable costs at the level of zero production, which is why variable costs are sometimes described as the direct costs of production, sales, and administration.

Point to Emphasize: Variable costs change in *direct proportion* to changes in activity. That is, they increase *in total* with an increase in volume and decrease *in total* with a decrease in volume, but they remain the same on a *per-unit* basis.

Point to Emphasize: Variable costs are incurred in all functional areas, not just in manufacturing.

OPERATING CAPACITY Because variable costs increase or decrease in direct proportion to volume or output, it is important to know an organization's operating capacity. **Operating capacity** is the upper limit of an organization's productive output capability, given its existing resources. It describes just what an organization can accomplish in a given time period. Operating capacity can be expressed in several ways, including total labor hours, total machine hours, and total units of output. Any increase in volume or activity over operating capacity requires additional expenditures for buildings, machinery, personnel, and operations. In our discussion of cost behavior patterns, we assume that operating capacity is constant and that all activity occurs within the limits of current operating capacity. Cost behavior patterns can change when additional operating capacity is added.

There are three common measures, or types, of operating capacity: theoretical, or ideal, capacity; practical capacity; and normal capacity. **Theoretical (ideal) capacity** is the maximum productive output for a given period, assuming that all machinery and equipment is operating at optimum speed, without interruption. Theoretical capacity is useful in estimating maximum production levels, but an organization never operates at ideal capacity. In fact, the concept had little relation to actual operations until the advent of the just-in-time operating environment.

Enrichment Note: In the theory that underlies the just-in-time operating environment, theoretical capacity acts as a benchmark, a relatively constant reference point until a total capacity adjustment is made (such as adding more plant or equipment).

Terminology Note: Practical capacity is sometimes called *engineering capacity.*

Business-World Example: A time period of five years is often used to calculate average activity for normal capacity. This common time frame corresponds to the economic cycle of many businesses. However, some businesses use different time periods to correspond to specific cycles in their industries.

The concept that drives the just-in-time environment is the continuous improvement of operations, with the long-term goal of approaching ideal capacity.

Practical capacity is theoretical capacity reduced by normal and expected work stoppages. Production is interrupted by machine breakdowns and downtime for retooling, repairs and maintenance, and employees' work breaks. Such normal interruptions and the resulting reductions in output are considered when measuring practical capacity.

Most organizations do not operate at either theoretical or practical capacity. Both measures include **excess capacity**, machinery and equipment kept on standby. This extra equipment is used when regular equipment is being repaired. Also, during a slow season, a company may use only part of its equipment, or it may work just one or two shifts instead of around the clock. Because it is necessary to consider so many different circumstances, managers often use a measure called normal capacity, rather than practical capacity, when planning operations. **Normal capacity** is the average annual level of operating capacity needed to meet expected sales demand. The sales demand figure is adjusted for seasonal changes and industry and economic cycles. Therefore, normal capacity is a realistic measure of what an organization is likely to produce, not what it can produce.

Each variable cost should be related to an appropriate measure of capacity, but in many cases, more than one measure of capacity applies. Operating costs can be related to machine hours used or total units produced. Sales commissions, on the other hand, usually vary in direct proportion to total sales dollars.

There are two reasons for carefully selecting the basis for measuring the activity of variable costs. First, an appropriate activity base simplifies cost planning and control. Second, the management accountant must combine (aggregate) many variable costs with the same activity base so that the costs can be analyzed in a reasonable way. Such aggregation also provides information that allows management to predict future costs.

Terminology Note: An activity base is often called *denominator activity;* it is the activity for which relationships are established. The basic relationships should not change greatly if activity fluctuates around the level of denominator activity.

The general guide for selecting an activity base is to relate costs to their most logical or causal factor. For example, machinery setup costs should be considered variable in relation to the number of setups needed for a particular job. This will allow machinery setup costs to be budgeted and controlled more effectively.

LINEAR RELATIONSHIPS AND THE RELEVANT RANGE The traditional definition of a variable cost assumes that there is a linear relationship between cost and volume, that costs go up or down as volume increases or decreases. You saw that relationship in our tire example earlier. Figure 3 shows another linear relationship.

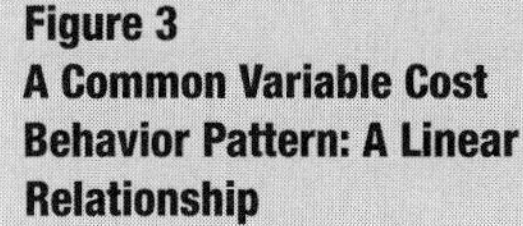

Figure 3
A Common Variable Cost Behavior Pattern: A Linear Relationship

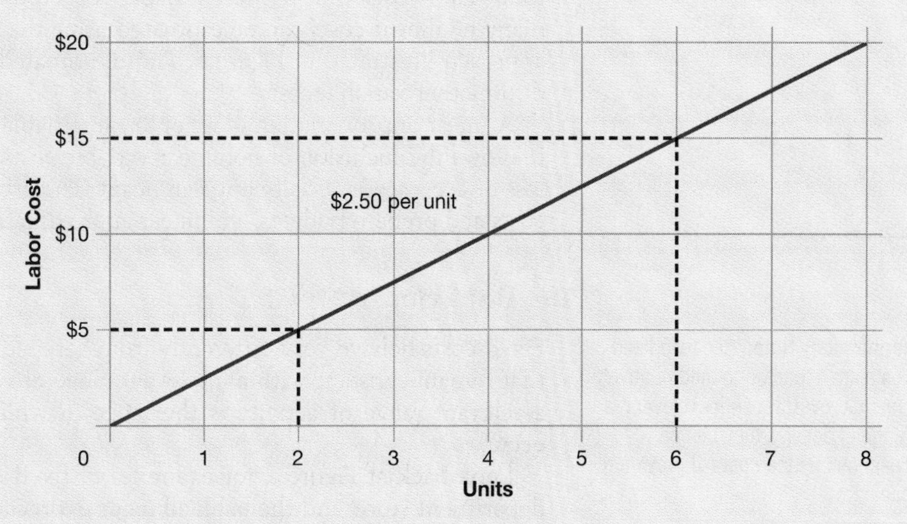

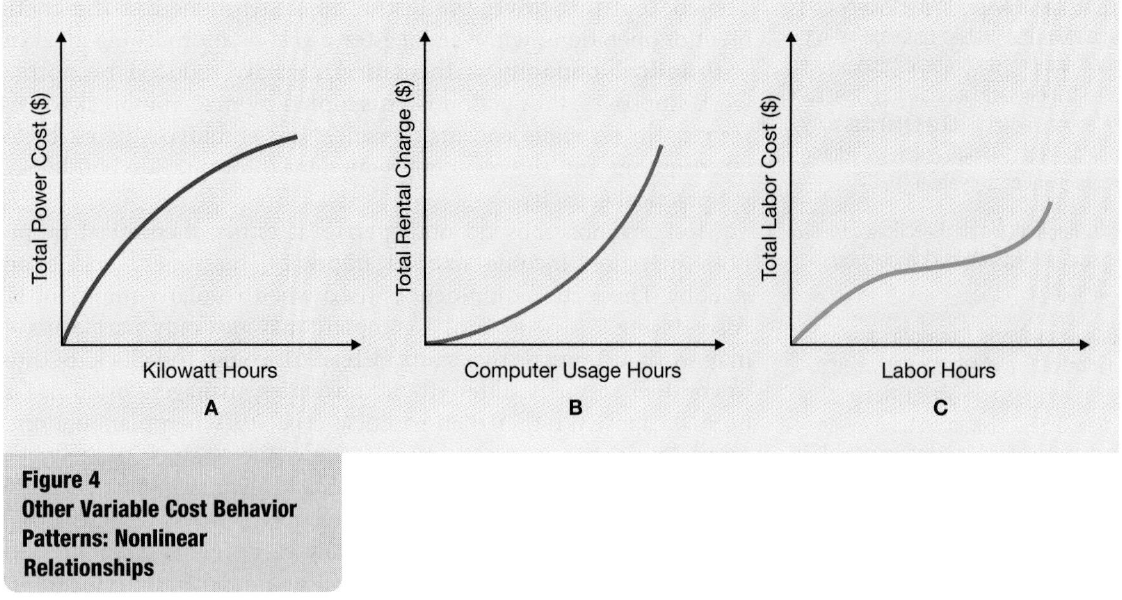

Figure 4
Other Variable Cost Behavior Patterns: Nonlinear Relationships

There, each unit of output requires $2.50 of labor cost. Total labor costs grow in direct proportion to the increase in units of output: For two units, total labor costs are $5.00; for six units, the organization incurs $15.00 in labor costs.

Many costs, however, vary with operating activity in a nonlinear fashion. In Figure 4, graph A shows the behavior of power costs as usage increases and the unit cost of power consumption falls. Graph B shows the behavior of rental costs when each additional hour of computer usage costs more than the previous hour. And graph C shows how labor costs vary as efficiency increases and decreases. These three nonlinear cost patterns are variable in nature, but they differ from the straight-line variable cost pattern shown in Figure 3.

Variable costs with linear relationships to a volume measure are easy to analyze and project for cost planning and control. Nonlinear variable costs are not easy to use. But all costs must be included in an analysis if the results are to be useful to management. To simplify cost analysis procedures and make variable costs easier to use, accountants have developed a method of converting nonlinear variable costs into linear variable costs. This method is called *linear approximation* and relies upon the concept of relevant range. **Relevant range** is the span of activity in which a company expects to operate. Within that range, it is assumed that both total fixed costs and per-unit variable costs are constant. Under that assumption, many nonlinear costs can be estimated using the straight-line linear approximation approach illustrated in Figure 5. Those estimated costs can then be treated as part of the other variable costs.

Terminology Note: Relevant range is that range of activity in which costs are expected to behave as predicted.

A linear approximation of a nonlinear variable cost is not a precise measure, but it allows the inclusion of nonlinear variable costs in cost behavior analysis, and the loss of accuracy is usually not significant. The goal is to help management estimate costs and prepare budgets, and linear approximation helps accomplish that goal.

The Behavior of Fixed Costs

Terminology Note: Because fixed costs are expected to hold relatively constant over the entire relevant range of activity, they can be described as the costs of providing capacity.

Fixed costs behave very differently from variable costs. **Fixed costs** are total costs that remain constant within a relevant range of volume or activity. Remember that a relevant range of activity is the range in which actual operations are likely to occur.

Look back at Figure 2 for examples of fixed costs. The desk manufacturer, the department store, and the bank all incur depreciation costs and fixed annual insur-

Figure 5
The Relevant Range and Linear Approximation

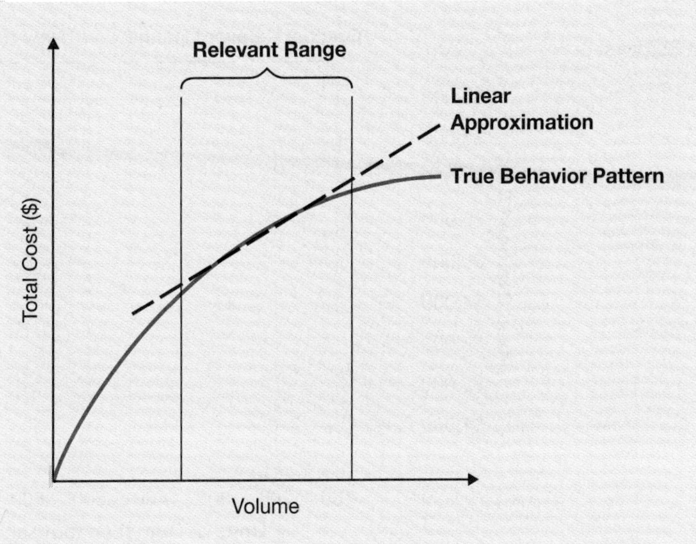

Clarification Note: Nonlinear costs can be roughly estimated by treating them as if they were linear (variable) costs within set limits of volume.

ance premiums. In addition, all salaried personnel have fixed earnings for a particular period. The desk manufacturer and the department store own their buildings and must pay annual property taxes. The bank, on the other hand, pays an annual fixed rental charge for the use of its building.

As the examples in Figure 2 suggest, a particular time period is identified when discussing fixed costs because, according to economic theory, all costs tend to be variable in the long run. A change in plant capacity, machinery, labor requirements, or other production factors causes fixed costs to increase or decrease. Thus, a cost is fixed only within a limited time period. For planning purposes, management usually considers a one-year time period, and fixed costs are expected to be constant within that period.

Of course, fixed costs change when activity exceeds the relevant range. For example, assume that a local manufacturing organization needs one supervisor for an eight-hour work shift. Production can range from zero to 500,000 units per month per shift; the relevant range, then, is from zero to 500,000 units. The supervisor's salary is $4,000 per month. The cost behavior analysis is as follows:

Units of Output per Month	Total Supervisory Salaries per Month
0–500,000	$4,000
Over 500,000–1,000,000	**$8,000**

If a maximum of 500,000 units can be produced per month per shift, any output above 500,000 units would require another work shift and another supervisor. Like all fixed costs, the new fixed cost remains constant in total within the new relevant range.

What about unit costs? Fixed costs per unit change as volume increases or decreases. *Unit fixed costs vary inversely with activity or volume.* On a per-unit basis, fixed costs go down as volume goes up. That pattern holds true as long as the firm is operating within the relevant range of activity. Look at how supervisory costs per unit fall as the volume of activity increases within the relevant range.

Volume of Activity	Cost per Unit
100,000 units	$4,000 ÷ 100,000 = $.0400
300,000 units	$4,000 ÷ 300,000 = $.0133
500,000 units	$4,000 ÷ 500,000 = $.0080
600,000 units	**$8,000** ÷ 600,000 = $.0133

Figure 6
A Common Fixed Cost Behavior Pattern

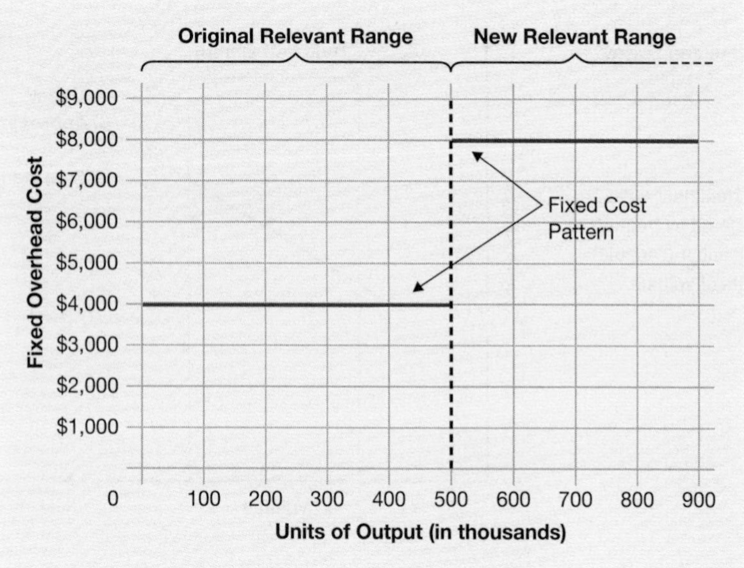

The per-unit cost increases to $.0133 at the 600,000-unit level because that activity level is above the relevant range, which means another shift must be added and another supervisor must be hired.

Figure 6 shows this behavior pattern. The fixed supervisory costs for the first 500,000 units of production are $4,000. Those costs hold steady at $4,000 for any level of output within the relevant range. But if output goes above 500,000 units, another supervisor must be hired, pushing fixed supervisory costs to $8,000.

Mixed Costs

OBJECTIVE

3 **Define *mixed cost,* and use the high-low method to separate the variable and fixed components of a mixed cost**

Related Text Assignments:
Q: 10, 11, 12
SE: 2, 3
E: 3
P: 1, 8
SD: 4, 5

Some costs cannot be classified as either variable or fixed. A **mixed cost** has both variable and fixed cost components. Part of the cost changes with volume or usage, and part of the cost is fixed over the period. Telephone cost is an example. Monthly telephone cost includes charges for long-distance calls plus a service charge and charges for extra telephones. The long-distance charges are variable because they depend on the amount of use; the service charge and the cost of the additional telephones are fixed costs.

EXAMPLES OF MIXED COSTS Many costs have both variable and fixed components. Utilities costs often fall into this category. Like telephone costs, the costs of

FOCUS ON BUSINESS TECHNOLOGY

Airline companies, such as United, American, and Delta, use their unique cost structure to make pricing decisions that will increase profitability. Airlines have a high proportion of fixed costs relative to the variable costs associated with an additional passenger. In other words, it does not cost much extra to include an additional passenger on a flight as long as a seat is available. In principle, the objective is simple: Keep the prices high on seats that will sell anyway and reduce prices on seats that are less likely to sell, with the goal of filling as many seats as possible on every flight. In practice, this is a very complex process; it is made possible by very sophisticated software that often results in minute-to-minute price changes. After years of development, the airlines have refined the system so that they can increase their profitability by increasing the revenue from each flight.

Figure 7
Behavior Patterns of Mixed Costs

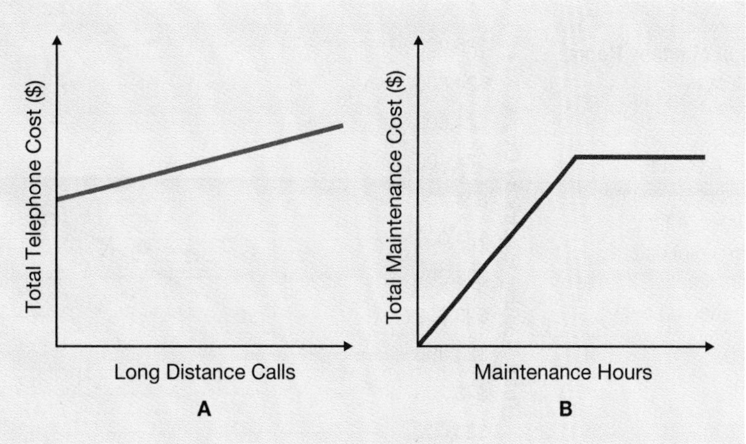

Point to Emphasize: Many cost accounts in a business fall into the mixed-cost category.

Reinforcement Exercise: Ask your students to consider their personal expenses and to classify each of the following as variable, fixed, or mixed:

Rent (fixed)
Water (mixed)
Electricity (mixed)
Gasoline (variable)
Postage (variable)

Point to Emphasize: A scatter diagram is a useful tool for cost analysis. A scatter diagram can be posted with original data and then updated as new information becomes available. As time passes, the diagram presents a visual display of cost behavior and any changes that have occurred. In addition, such a diagram is easy to create and maintain.

electricity and gas heat normally consist of a fixed base amount and additional charges related to usage. Figure 7 shows just two of the many behavior patterns of mixed costs. Graph A depicts the total telephone cost for an organization. The monthly bill begins with a fixed charge for the service and increases as long-distance calls are made. Graph B illustrates a special contractual arrangement. In Graph B, the annual cost of equipment maintenance that is provided by an outside company increases for each maintenance hour worked, up to a maximum amount per period. After the maximum is reached, additional maintenance is done at no cost.

THE HIGH-LOW METHOD OF SEPARATING COSTS For cost planning and control, mixed costs must be divided into their respective variable and fixed components. The separate components can then be grouped with other variable and fixed costs for analysis. When there is doubt about the behavior pattern of a particular cost, especially a mixed cost, it helps to plot past costs and related measures of volume in a scatter diagram. A **scatter diagram** is a chart of plotted points that helps determine if there is a linear relationship between a cost item and its related activity measure. It is a form of linear approximation. If the diagram suggests that a linear relationship exists, a cost line can be imposed on the data by either visual means or statistical analysis.

For example, last year, the Evelio Corporation's Winter Park Division incurred the following machine hours and electricity costs.

Month	Machine Hours	Electricity Costs
January	6,250	$ 24,000
February	6,300	24,200
March	6,350	24,350
April	6,400	24,600
May	6,300	24,400
June	6,200	24,300
July	6,100	23,900
August	6,050	23,600
September	6,150	23,950
October	6,250	24,100
November	6,350	24,400
December	6,450	24,700
Totals	75,150	$290,500

Figure 8
Scatter Diagram of Machine Hours and Electricity Costs

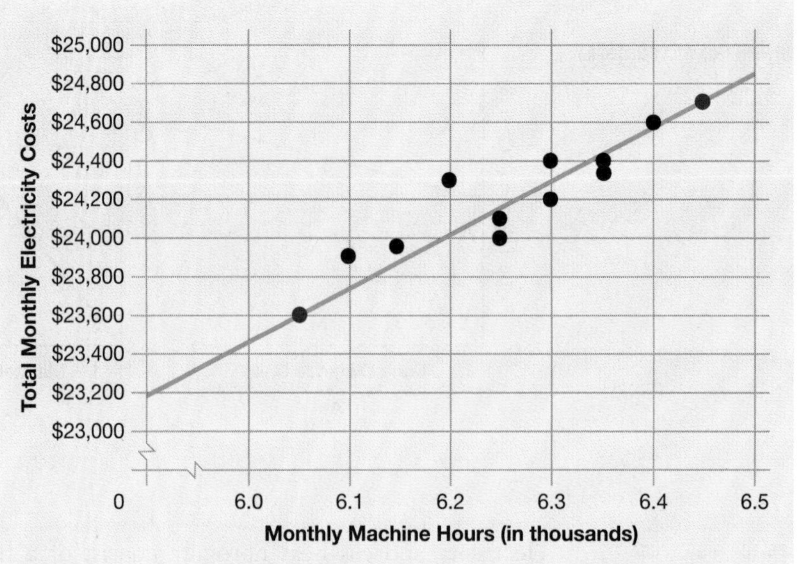

Point to Emphasize: A scatter diagram shows how closely volume and costs are correlated. A tight, closely associated group of data is better for linear approximation than a random or circular pattern of data points.

Enrichment Note: The high-low method is based on the premise that only two points are necessary to define a linear cost-volume relationship.

Point to Emphasize: The disadvantage of using the high-low method is that it is based on only two data observations. If one or both data points are not representative of the remaining data set, the estimate of variable and fixed costs may not be accurate. The advantage is that the method can be used when limited data are available.

Clarification Note: If the highest or lowest level of activity occurs more than once in the data set and each occurrence has a different cost value, the *average* of all the values for that level of activity should be used.

Figure 8 shows a scatter diagram of those data. The diagram suggests a linear relationship between machine hours and the cost of electricity. To determine the variable and fixed components of this mixed cost, we apply the **high-low method**, a common, three-step approach to separating variable and fixed costs.

Step 1: Calculate the variable cost per activity base.
Select the periods of highest and lowest activity within the accounting period. In our example, the Winter Park Division experienced its highest machine-hour activity in December and its lowest machine-hour activity in August. Find the difference between the highest and lowest amounts for both the machine hours and their related electricity costs.

Volume	Month	Activity Level	Cost
Highest	December	6,450 machine hours	$24,700
Lowest	August	6,050 machine hours	23,600
Difference		400 machine hours	$ 1,100

To determine the variable cost per machine hour, divide the difference in cost by the difference in machine hours.

Variable Cost per Machine Hour = $1,100 ÷ 400 Machine Hours
= $2.75 per Machine Hour

Step 2: Calculate the total fixed costs.
Compute total fixed costs for a month by selecting the information from the month with either the highest or the lowest volume. Let's select the month with the highest volume.

Total Fixed Costs = Total Costs − Total Variable Costs

Total Fixed Costs for December = $24,700.00 − (6,450 × $2.75) = $6,962.50

You can check your answer by recalculating total fixed costs using the month with the lowest activity. Total fixed costs will be the same.

Total Fixed Costs for August = $23,600.00 − (6,050 × $2.75) = $6,962.50

Instructional Strategy: To check students' comprehension of the high-low method, assign E 3. Students can work in self-selected teams of two or three. Groups that answer correctly may be rewarded with a bonus of 2 quiz points. State ground rules, such as whether notes or text may be used, before activity begins.

Step 3: Calculate the formula to estimate the total costs within the relevant range.

Total Cost per Month = \$6,962.50 + \$2.75 per Machine Hour

Remember that the cost formula will work only within the relevant range. In this example, the formula would work for amounts between 6,050 machine hours and 6,450 machine hours. To estimate the electricity costs for machine hours outside the relevant range (in this case, below 6,050 machine hours or above 6,450 machine hours), a new cost formula must be calculated.

Cost-Volume-Profit Analysis

OBJECTIVE

4 Define *cost-volume-profit analysis* and discuss how managers use this analysis

Related Text Assignments:
Q: 13, 14
SE: 4
MRA: 1, 3

One business of Sony Records is the production and distribution of popular compact disks (CDs). Producing CDs is a complex process that requires the hiring and organizing of hundreds of people, including the musicians, and the maintenance of studios and offices. The company hopes, of course, that all its CDs will be hits, but the reality is that only some will be. At the least, the company wants to break even—that is, not lose any money—on each CD. Cost-volume-profit analysis is an important tool that enables the company's managers to understand how many CDs they must sell to avoid losing money and what their profit potential is if they have a hit. It is also an important tool in setting sales targets.

Cost-volume-profit (C-V-P) analysis is an examination of the cost behavior patterns that underlie the relationships among cost, volume of output, and profit. C-V-P analysis usually applies to a single product, product line, or division of a company. The word *profit* is used in the C-V-P equation because that figure is only a part of the entire company's operating income. In cases involving the income statement of an entire company, the term *operating income* is more appropriate than *profit*. In the context of C-V-P analysis, *profit* and *operating income* mean the same thing. C-V-P analysis is a tool for both planning and control. The process involves a number of techniques and problem-solving procedures based on the cost behavior patterns in an organization. The techniques express relationships among revenue, sales mix, cost, volume, and profit. Those relationships provide a general model of financial activity that managers can use for short-range planning, evaluating performance, and analyzing alternatives.

For planning, managers can use C-V-P analysis to calculate net income when sales volume is known. Or, through C-V-P analysis, managers can decide the level of sales needed to reach a target amount of net income. C-V-P analysis is also used extensively in budgeting.

The C-V-P relationship is expressed in a simple equation.

Sales Revenue = Variable Costs + Fixed Costs + Profit

Or

$$S = VC + FC + P$$

Point to Emphasize: Because C-V-P analysis involves grouping costs by behavior, it helps managers identify relevant costs for decision-making. Often, variable costs are relevant to a decision, but many fixed costs are not.

Cost-volume-profit analysis is a way of measuring how well the departments in an organization are performing. At the end of a period, sales volume and related actual costs are analyzed to find actual net income. A department's performance is measured by comparing actual costs with expected costs, costs that have been computed by applying C-V-P analysis to actual sales volume. The result is a performance report on which managers can base the control of operations.

Basic C-V-P analysis can also be applied to measure the effects of alternative choices: changes in variable and fixed costs, expansion or contraction of sales volume, increases or decreases in selling prices, or other changes in operating methods

Focus on International Business

How does C-V-P analysis in Japan, Germany, Great Britain, or Canada differ from the same analysis in the United States? The only difference is in the measures used. The procedures and formulas remain the same. Instead of expressing volume in pounds or gallons, those countries use metric measures, such as grams and liters. Whereas our cost and profit amounts are expressed in dollars, Japan's amounts would be in yen, Germany's in euros, Great Britain's in British pounds, and Canada's in Canadian dollars. Most management accounting procedures and analyses are appropriate for use by companies in any free economy. All that changes are the units of measurement.

Instructional Strategy: Assign MRA 3. Divide the class into groups, and ask the students to discuss the MRA. Then debrief the entire class by asking one student from each group to summarize his or her group's findings for one or more of the requirements.

or policies. Cost-volume-profit analysis is useful for making decisions about product pricing, product mix analysis (when an organization produces more than one product or offers more than one service), adding or dropping a product line, and accepting special orders. There are many applications of C-V-P analysis, and all are used by managers to plan and control operations effectively.

Breakeven Analysis

OBJECTIVE

5 Compute a breakeven point in units of output and in sales dollars, and prepare a breakeven graph

Related Text Assignments:
Q: 15
SE: 5
E: 4, 5, 6
P: 2, 6
SD: 3
MRA: 1

Common Student Error: When asked to identify the breakeven point, students often name the intersection of the total revenue and total cost lines in the breakeven graph. Explain that this point is just the product of a set of coordinates. The breakeven point must be described in terms of units or sales dollars.

Teaching Note: Display a breakeven graph. Then, ask students to describe the effect of several individual adjustments to the model, such as an increase in selling price, a decrease in variable cost per unit, or an increase in fixed costs. Ask them to describe the movement of the breakeven point along either the revenue line or the cost line as each adjustment is made. Demonstrate the effect with a straightedge.

Breakeven analysis uses the basic elements of cost-volume-profit relationships. The **breakeven point** is the point at which total revenues equal total costs. Breakeven, then, is the point at which an organization begins to earn a profit. When a new venture or product line is being planned, the likelihood of the project's success can be quickly measured by finding its breakeven point. If, for instance, breakeven is 50,000 units and the total market is only 25,000 units, the idea should be abandoned promptly.

Sales (S), variable costs (VC), and fixed costs (FC) are used to compute the breakeven point, which can be stated in terms of sales units or sales dollars. The general equation for finding the breakeven point is:

$$S = VC + FC$$

For example, Dakota Products, Inc., makes special wooden stands for portable compact disk players that include a protective storage compartment for the disks. Variable costs are \$50 per unit, and fixed costs average \$20,000 per year. Each wooden stand sells for \$90. Given this information, we can compute the breakeven point for this product in sales units (x equals sales units):

$$\begin{aligned} S &= VC + FC \\ \$90x &= \$50x + \$20{,}000 \\ \$40x &= \$20{,}000 \\ x &= 500 \text{ Units} \end{aligned}$$

and in sales dollars:

$$\$90 \times 500 \text{ Units} = \$45{,}000$$

We can also make a rough estimate of the breakeven point using a graph. This method is less exact, but it does yield meaningful data. Figure 9 shows a breakeven graph for Dakota Products, Inc. The graph has five parts.

1. A horizontal axis in volume or units of output
2. A vertical axis in dollars of revenue
3. A line running horizontally from the vertical axis at the level of fixed costs

Figure 9
Graphic Breakeven Analysis: Dakota Products, Inc.

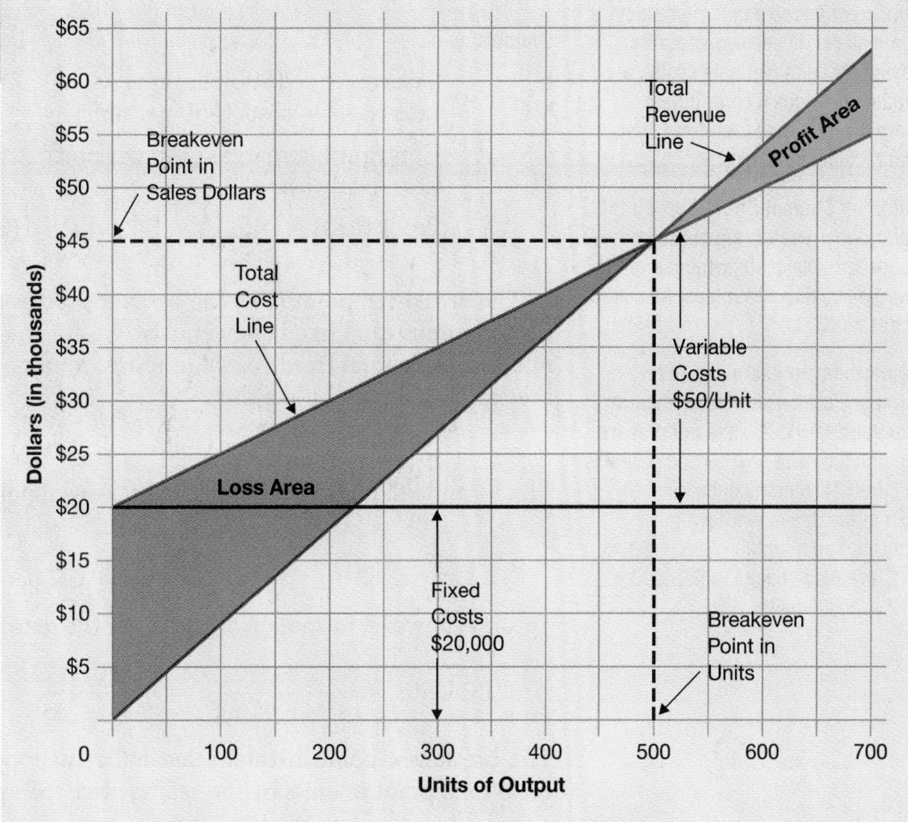

Point to Emphasize: Graphs can be very powerful management tools because they visually depict relationships between revenues and expenses that otherwise might not be evident.

Point to Emphasize: Sensitivity analysis is one of the important benefits of using C-V-P analysis. Different variables can be adjusted and the resulting impact on profit can be evaluated.

Business-World Example: The C-V-P model shown in Figure 9 is a static model. The modern business environment is dynamic—prices, advertising, and wages all fluctuate. Those variables can be expressed in computer simulation languages to produce a dynamic model.

4. A total cost line that begins at the point where the fixed cost line crosses the vertical axis and slopes upward to the right (The slope of the line depends on the variable cost per unit.)
5. A total revenue line that begins at the origin of the vertical and horizontal axes and slopes upward to the right (The slope depends on the selling price per unit.)

Discussion Question: Why does the total revenue line start at the origin (zero units, zero dollars) of the graph while the total cost line usually starts higher on the vertical axis? **Answer:** At zero sales, there is zero revenue; at zero sales and production, there is no variable cost, yet fixed costs still exist.

At the point where the total revenue line crosses the total cost line, revenues equal total costs. The breakeven point, stated in either units or dollars of sales, is found by extending broken lines from this point to the axes. As Figure 9 shows, Dakota Products, Inc., will break even when 500 wooden stands have been made and sold for $45,000.

Contribution Margin

OBJECTIVE

6 **Define *contribution margin* and use the concept to determine a company's breakeven point for a single product and for multiple products**

Related Text Assignments:
Q: 16
SE: 6, 7, 8
E: 5, 6, 7, 8, 9
P: 2, 3, 4, 6, 7
SD: 4
MRA: 1, 5

A simpler method of determining the breakeven point uses contribution margin. **Contribution margin** is the amount that remains after total variable costs are subtracted from sales. A product line's contribution margin represents its net contribution to paying off fixed costs and earning a profit.

$$S - VC = CM$$

Profit is what remains after fixed costs are paid and subtracted from the contribution margin.

$$CM - FC = P$$

The example that follows uses contribution margin to determine the profitability of Dakota Products, Inc.

Point to Emphasize: The maximum *total contribution* a unit of product can make is its selling price. After paying for itself (variable costs), a product provides a contribution margin to help pay total fixed costs and then earn a profit.

Common Student Error: Explain that *contribution margin* equals sales minus variable costs, whereas *gross margin* equals sales minus the cost of goods sold.

Reinforcement Exercise: ABC Company sells its single product at $20 each. Variable costs per unit are $8, and the fixed cost for the period is $96,000. How many units must be sold to break even? **Answer:** Contribution margin = $20 − $8 = $12. Breakeven units = $96,000 ÷ $12 = 8,000 units.

		Units Produced and Sold		
Symbols		**250**	**500**	**750**
S	Sales revenue ($90 per unit)	$22,500	$45,000	$67,500
VC	Less variable costs ($50 per unit)	12,500	25,000	37,500
CM	Contribution margin ($40 per unit)	$10,000	$20,000	$30,000
FC	Less fixed costs	20,000	20,000	20,000
P	Profit (loss)	($10,000)	—	$10,000

The breakeven point (BE) can be expressed as the point at which contribution margin minus total fixed costs equals zero (or the point at which contribution margin equals total fixed costs). In terms of units of product, the equation for the breakeven point looks like this:

$$(\text{CM per Unit} \times \text{BE Units}) - \text{FC} = 0$$

The formula that also generates the breakeven point in units is

$$\text{BE Units} = \frac{\text{FC}}{\text{CM per Unit}}$$

To show how the formula works, we use the data for Dakota Products, Inc.

$$\text{BE Units} = \frac{\text{FC}}{\text{CM per Unit}} = \frac{\$20{,}000}{\$90 - \$50} = \frac{\$20{,}000}{\$40} = 500 \text{ Units}$$

The breakeven point in total sales dollars may be determined by multiplying the breakeven point in units by the selling price (SP) per unit.

$$\text{BE Dollars} = \text{SP} \times \text{BE Units} = \$90 \times 500 \text{ Units} = \$45{,}000$$

An alternative way of determining the breakeven point in total sales dollars is to divide the fixed costs by the contribution margin ratio. The contribution margin ratio is the contribution margin divided by the selling price.

$$\text{CM Ratio} = \frac{\text{CM}}{\text{SP}} = \frac{\$40}{\$90} = .444, \text{ or } 4/9$$

$$\text{BE Dollars} = \frac{\text{FC}}{\text{CM Ratio}} = \frac{\$20{,}000}{4/9} = \$45{,}000$$

FOCUS ON BUSINESS PRACTICE

Understanding their costs helps fast-food restaurants, such as McDonald's, increase their profitability in at least two ways. First, such restaurants encourage customers to buy "value meals," combinations of three products (such as sandwich, drink, and fries) at a lower total price than the three items purchased separately. Although the contribution margin of a value meal is lower than the combined contribution margins of the three products sold separately, McDonald's knows from experience that value meals lead to higher total sales. Second, McDonald's offers to "supersize" an order for the bargain price of only a few cents more. Supersizing increases the total contribution margin because the additional variable cost of the larger size is very small. Profitability is enhanced even though revenue is increased by only a small amount. Selling larger sizes is so important to a fast-food restaurant's profitability that a common performance measure is the percentage of value meals that are supersized.

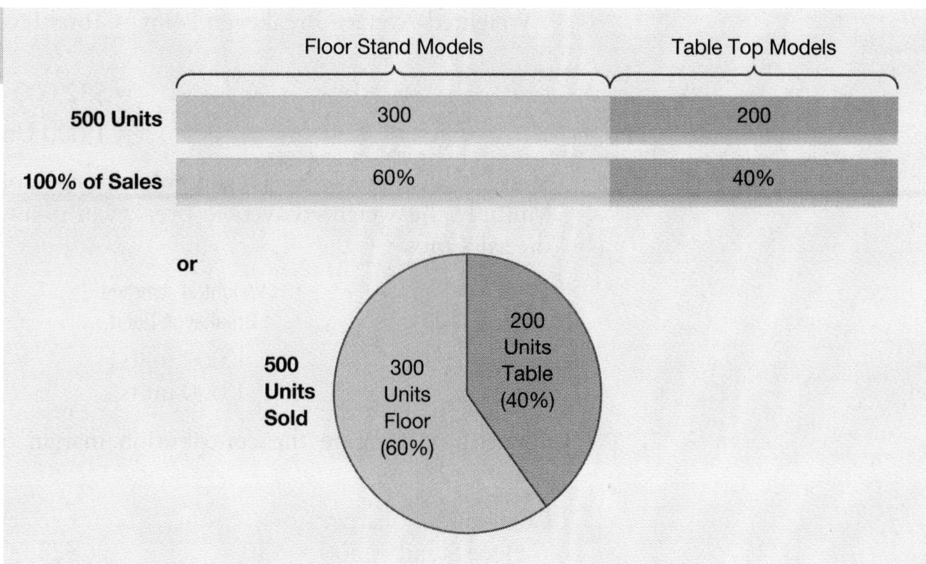

Multiple Products (Sales Mix)

Many manufacturing organizations sell a variety of products to satisfy different customer needs. These products frequently have different variable and fixed costs or different selling prices. To calculate the breakeven point for each product, the unit contribution margin for each product must be weighted by the sales mix. The **sales mix** is the proportion of each product's unit sales relative to the organization's total unit sales. Let's assume that Dakota Products, Inc., sells two types of wooden stands for portable compact disk players: the Floor Stand model, which is placed on the floor and has high storage capacity, and the Tabletop model, which is smaller and can be placed in entertainment units. If Dakota sells 500 units, of which 300 units are Floor Stands and 200 units are Tabletops, the sales mix would be 3:2. For every 3 Floor Stand models sold, 2 Tabletop models are sold. The sales mix can also be stated in percentages. Of the 500 units sold, 60 percent (300 ÷ 500) are Floor Stand sales and 40 percent (200 ÷ 500) are Tabletop sales (see Figure 10).

The breakeven point for multiple products can be computed in three steps. We will illustrate using Dakota Products, Inc.'s sales mix of 60 percent Floor Stands to 40 percent Tabletops; total fixed costs of $32,000; and the selling price, variable cost per unit, and contribution margin per unit for each product line presented in Step 1 below.

Step 1: Compute the weighted-average contribution margin.
Calculate the weighted-average contribution margin by multiplying the contribution margin for each product by its percentage of the sales mix.

	Sales		Variable Costs		Contribution Margin (CM)		Percentage of Sales Mix		Weighted-Average CM
Floor Stand	$90	−	$50	=	$40	×	.60	=	$24
Tabletop	$40	−	$20	=	$20	×	.40	=	$ 8
Weighted-average contribution margin									$32

Step 2: Calculate the weighted-average breakeven point.
Compute the weighted-average breakeven point by dividing total fixed costs by the weighted-average contribution margin.

$$\text{Weighted-Average Breakeven Point} = \text{Total Fixed Costs} \div \text{Weighted-Average Contribution Margin}$$
$$= \$32{,}000 \div \$32$$
$$= 1{,}000 \text{ Units}$$

Step 3: Calculate the breakeven point for each product.
Multiply the weighted-average breakeven point by each product's percentage of the sales mix.

		Weighted-Average Breakeven Point		Sales Mix		Breakeven Point
Floor Stand	=	1,000 units	×	.60	=	600 Units
Tabletop	=	1,000 units	×	.40	=	400 Units

To verify, determine the contribution margin of each product and subtract the total fixed costs.

Contribution margin	
Floor Stand = 600 × \$40 =	\$24,000
Tabletop = 400 × \$20 =	8,000
Total contribution margin	\$32,000
Less fixed costs	32,000
Profit	—

Planning Future Sales

OBJECTIVE

7 Apply cost-volume-profit analysis to estimated levels of future sales and to changes in costs and selling prices

Related Text Assignments:
Q: 17, 18
SE: 9
E: 6, 9, 10
P: 3, 4, 5, 6, 7
SD: 2
MRA: 2, 4, 5

Enrichment Note: The incremental approach also can be used in "what if" analysis. The firm's profit or loss is affected by the sales difference times the unit contribution margin.

The primary goal of a business venture is not to break even; it is to generate profits. C-V-P analysis adjusted for targeted profit can be used to estimate the profitability of a venture. This approach is excellent for "what if" analysis, in which managers select several scenarios and compute the anticipated profit for each. For instance, what if sales increase by 17,000 units? What effect will the increase have on anticipated profit? What if sales increase by only 6,000 units? What if fixed costs are reduced by \$14,500? What if the variable unit cost increases by \$1.40? Each scenario generates a different amount of profit or loss.

To illustrate how C-V-P analysis can be applied, assume that the president of Dakota Products, Inc., Les Tibbs, has set \$4,000 in profit as this year's goal for the compact disk stands. If all the data in our earlier example stay as they were, how many compact disk stands must Dakota Products, Inc., make and sell to reach the target profit? Again, x equals the number of units.

$$S = VC + FC + P$$
$$\$90x = \$50x + \$20{,}000 + \$4{,}000$$
$$\$40x = \$24{,}000$$
$$x = 600 \text{ Units}$$

The answer is 600 units. To check the answer, insert all known data into the equation.

$$S - VC - FC = P$$
$$(600 \text{ Units} \times \$90) - (600 \times \$50) - \$20{,}000 = \$4{,}000$$
$$\$54{,}000 - \$30{,}000 - \$20{,}000 = \$4{,}000$$

The contribution margin approach can also be used for profit planning. To do so, we simply add the target profit to the numerator of the contribution margin breakeven equation:

$$\text{Target Sales Units} = \frac{FC + P}{\text{CM per Unit}}$$

Using the data from the Dakota Products, Inc., example, the number of sales units needed to generate $4,000 in profit is computed this way:

$$\text{Target Sales Units} = \frac{\text{FC} + \text{P}}{\text{CM per Unit}} = \frac{\$20{,}000 + \$4{,}000}{\$40} = \frac{\$24{,}000}{\$40} = 600 \text{ Units}$$

Let's continue to look at the planning activities of Dakota Products, Inc. The contribution income statement below focuses on cost behavior, not cost function. All variable costs related to production, selling, and administration are subtracted from sales to determine the total contribution margin. All fixed costs related to production, selling, and administration are subtracted from the total contribution margin to determine operating income. This format is used internally by managers to help make decisions about the company's operations.

Dakota Products, Inc.
Contribution Income Statement
For the Year Ended December 31, 20x4

	Per Unit	Total for 600 Units
Sales revenue	$90	$54,000
Less variable costs	50	30,000
Contribution margin	$40	$24,000
Less fixed costs		20,000
Operating income*		$ 4,000

*Note that in an income statement it is more appropriate to refer to profit as operating income.

Les Tibbs wants the members of the planning team to consider three alternatives to the original plan shown in the contribution income statement. In the following sections, we examine each alternative and its impact on operating income. In the summary, we will review our work and analyze the different breakeven points.

Teaching Note: Before working each alternative, ask students to determine the change in the breakeven point (an increase or decrease) due to each change in variables. See Exhibit 1 for new breakeven point calculations.

ALTERNATIVE 1: DECREASE VARIABLE COSTS, INCREASE SALES VOLUME The planning team worked with production, purchasing, and sales employees to determine the operating income if the company purchased and used pine rather than oak to make the wooden compact disk stands. If pine is used, the direct materials cost per unit will decrease by $3. The company plans to stain the pine to meet the needs of a new customer group, which will increase the sales volume by 10 percent. What will be the estimated operating income for this alternative? How will this alternative affect operating income?

SOLUTION

	Per Unit	Total for 660 units
Sales revenue	$90	$59,400
Less variable costs	47	31,020
Contribution margin	$43	$28,380
Less fixed costs		20,000
Operating income		$ 8,380
Increase in operating income ($8,380 – $4,000)		$ 4,380

A different way to determine the impact of changes in selling price, cost, or sales volume on operating income is to analyze only the information that changes between the original plan and the proposed alternative. In Alternative 1, variable costs will decrease by $3 (from $50 to $47), which will increase the contribution margin per unit by $3 (from $40 to $43) for the 600 wooden stands planned to be sold. This will increase the total contribution margin and operating income by $1,800 ($3 × 600).

In addition, a sales increase of 60 units (.10 × 600) will increase the total contribution margin and operating income by $2,580 ($43 × 60). The total increase in operating income due to the decrease in variable costs and the increase in sales volume will be $4,380.

SOLUTION

Analysis of Changes Only

Increase in contribution margin from	
Planned sales [($43 – $40) × 600 units]	$1,800
Additional sales ($43 × 60 units)	2,580
Increase in operating income	$4,380

ALTERNATIVE 2: INCREASE FIXED COSTS, INCREASE SALES VOLUME Instead of changing the direct materials, the Marketing Department suggested that a $500 increase in advertising costs would increase sales volume by 5 percent. What will be the estimated operating income for this alternative? How will this alternative affect operating income?

SOLUTION

	Per Unit	Total for 630 units
Sales revenue	$90	$56,700
Less variable costs	50	31,500
Contribution margin	$40	$25,200
Less fixed costs		20,500
Operating income		$ 4,700
Increase in operating income ($4,700 – $4,000)		$ 700

Additional advertising costs will affect both sales volume and fixed costs. The sales volume will increase by 30 stands, from 600 units to 630 units (600 × 1.05), which increases the total contribution margin and operating income by $1,200 (from $24,000 to $25,200). Fixed costs will increase from $20,000 to $20,500, which decreases operating income by $500. The increase in operating income will be $700 ($1,200 – $500).

SOLUTION

Analysis of Changes Only

Increase in contribution margin from	
additional units sold [$40 × (600 × .05)]	$1,200
Less increase in fixed costs	500
Increase in operating income	$ 700

ALTERNATIVE 3: INCREASE SELLING PRICE, DECREASE SALES VOLUME Les Tibbs asked the planning team to evaluate the impact of a $10 increase in selling price on the company's operating income. The planning team believes that competitors are selling the same product at a lower price. If the selling price is increased, the team estimates that the sales volume will decrease by 15 percent. What will be the estimated operating income for this alternative? How will this alternative affect operating income?

costs include depreciation of equipment, $8,500; building rental, $14,000; promotional costs, $12,500; and other fixed costs, $8,099.

REQUIRED

1. Using the contribution margin approach, compute the number of loan applications the company must process to (a) break even and (b) earn a target profit of $14,476.
2. Continuing the same approach, compute the number of applications the company must process to earn a target profit of $20,000 if promotional costs increase by $5,662.
3. Assuming the original information and the processing of 500 applications, compute the loan application fee the company must charge if the target profit is $41,651.
4. Polly Bar believes that 750 loan applications is the maximum number her staff can handle. How much more can be spent on promotional costs if the highest fee tolerable to the customer is $280, if variable costs cannot be reduced, and if the target profit for such loan applications is $50,000?

Alternate Problems

LO 5 **Breakeven Analysis**
LO 6
LO 7
LO 8

P 6. Locke & Lobel, a law firm in downtown St. Paul, is considering the development of a legal clinic for middle- and low-income clients. Paraprofessional help would be employed, and a billing rate of $18 per hour would be used. The paraprofessionals would be law students who would work for only $9 per hour. Other variable costs are anticipated to be $5.40 per hour, and annual fixed costs are expected to total $27,000.

REQUIRED

1. Compute the breakeven point in billable hours.
2. Compute the breakeven point in total billings.
3. Find the new breakeven point in total billings if fixed costs should go up by $2,340.
4. Using the original figures, compute the breakeven point in total billings if the billing rate is decreased by $1 per hour, variable costs are decreased by $.40 per hour, and fixed costs go down by $3,600.

LO 6 **Planning Future Sales:**
LO 7 **Contribution Margin Approach**

P 7. Hans Echt is the president of the Ivers Plastics Division of Treat Industries. Management is considering a new product featuring a dashing medieval knight posed on a beautiful horse. Called Chargin' Knight, this product is expected to have global market appeal and become the mascot for many high school and university athletic teams. Expected variable unit costs are: direct materials, $18.50; direct labor, $4.25; production supplies, $1.10; selling costs, $2.80; and other, $1.95. Annual fixed costs are: depreciation, building and equipment, $36,000; advertising, $45,000; and other, $11,400. Treat Industries plans to sell the product for $55.00.

REQUIRED

1. Using the contribution margin approach, compute the number of products the company must sell to (a) break even and (b) earn a target profit of $70,224.
2. Using the same data, compute the number of products that must be sold to earn a target profit of $139,520 if advertising costs rise by $40,000.
3. Using the original information and sales of 10,000 units, compute the new selling price the company must use to make a target profit of $131,600. (**Hint:** Calculate contribution margin per unit first.)
4. According to the vice president of marketing, Stanley Mendoza, the most optimistic annual sales estimate for the product would be 15,000 units, and the highest competitive selling price the company can charge is $52.00 per unit. How much more can be spent on fixed advertising costs if the selling price is $52.00, if the variable costs cannot be reduced, and if the target profit for 15,000 unit sales is $251,000?

LO 2 **Cost Behavior and**
LO 3 **Projection for a**
LO 8 **Service Business**

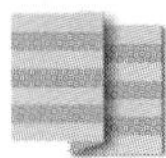

P 8. Howard Painting Company, located in Summer Haven, specializes in refurbishing exterior painted surfaces. In the humid South, exterior surfaces are hit hard with insect debris. A special refurbishing technique, called pressure cleaning, is needed before the surface can be primed and repainted. The technique involves the following steps:

1. Unskilled laborers trim trees and bushes 2 feet away from the structure.
2. Skilled laborers clean the building with a high-pressure cleaning machine, using about 6 gallons of Debris-Luse per job.

3. Unskilled laborers apply a coat of primer.
4. Skilled laborers apply oil-based exterior paint to the entire surface.

On average, skilled laborers work 12 hours per job, and unskilled laborers work 8 hours.

The special pressure-cleaning and refurbishing process generated the following operating results during 20x1:

Skilled labor	$20.00 per hour
Unskilled labor	$8.00 per hour
Gallons of Debris-Luse used	3,768 gallons at $5.50 per gallon
Paint primer	7,536 gallons at $15.50 per gallon
Paint	6,280 gallons at $16.00 per gallon
Paint spraying equipment	$600.00 per month depreciation
Two leased vans	$800.00 per month total
Rent for storage building	$450.00 per month

The utilities costs for the year were as follows:

Month	Number of Jobs	Cost	Hours Worked
January	42	$3,950	840
February	37	3,550	740
March	44	4,090	880
April	49	4,410	980
May	54	4,720	1,080
June	62	5,240	1,240
July	71	5,820	1,420
August	73	5,890	1,460
September	63	5,370	1,260
October	48	4,340	960
November	45	4,210	900
December	40	3,830	800
Totals	628	$55,420	12,560

REQUIRED

1. Classify the costs as variable, fixed, or mixed.
2. Using the high-low method, separate mixed costs into their variable and fixed components. Use total hours worked as the basis.
3. Compute the average cost per job for 20x1. (**Hint:** Divide the total of all costs for 20x1 by the number of jobs completed.)

EXPANDING YOUR CRITICAL THINKING, COMMUNICATION, AND INTERPERSONAL SKILLS

SKILLS DEVELOPMENT

Conceptual Analysis

SD 1. **LO 1** **Concept of Cost Behavior** **LO 2**

Pacific Coast Shrimp Company is a very small company. It owns an ice house and shrimp preparation building, a refrigerated van, and three shrimp boats. Steven Black inherited the company from his father three months ago. The company employs three boat crews of four people each and five processing workers. Willman and Yang, a local accounting firm, has kept the company's financial records for many years.

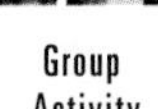

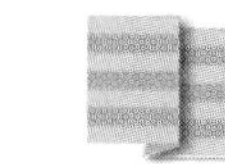

Communication | Critical Thinking | Ethics | Group Activity | Hot Links to Real Companies | International | Internet | Memo | Spreadsheet

In her last analysis of operations, Su Yang stated that the company's fixed cost base of $100,000 is satisfactory for this type and size of business. However, variable costs have averaged 70 percent of sales over the last two years, a percentage that is too high for the volume of business. For example, last year only 30 percent of the company's sales revenue of $300,000 contributed toward covering the fixed costs. As a result, the company reported a $10,000 operating loss.

Black wants to improve the company's net income, but he is confused by Yang's explanation of the fixed and variable costs. Prepare a response to Black from Yang in which you explain the concept of cost behavior as it relates to Pacific Coast's operations. Include ideas for improving the company's net income based on changes in fixed and variable costs.

SD 2.
LO 7 Comparison of Service
LO 8 Business Approaches to Sales Mix, Breakeven Concepts, and Performance Measures

Allstate Insurance Co. and ***GEICO*** are two well-known insurers of motorists. Allstate has agents and offices all over the country. GEICO sells only through the mail and over the Internet. In addition to collision and liability coverage for automobiles, each company offers life insurance and homeowners' insurance. When a motorist buys auto insurance from Allstate, the agent will usually offer life insurance and homeowners' insurance as well. This strategy usually leads to increased profitability for the company. Identify and discuss the role that fixed costs and sales mix contribution margin can play in increasing profitability. Suggest a performance measure that could be used to evaluate agents who sell auto insurance. What is the role of variable costs? Although GEICO usually sells its policies at lower prices than Allstate does, it is a very profitable company. What is it about the relationship of GEICO's fixed and variable costs that allows it to do this?

Group Activity: Divide the class into groups and have them discuss this SD. Ask one student from each group to summarize his or her group's discussion, and use the presentations as a lead-in to the coverage of Learning Objectives 7 and 8.

Ethical Dilemma

SD 3.
LO 5 Breaking Even and Ethics

Cindy Ginsberg is the supervisor of the New Product Division of ***Fricker Corp.***, located in Jackson, Wyoming. Ginsberg's annual bonus is based on the success of new products and is computed on the amount of sales over and above each product's projected breakeven point. In reviewing the computations supporting her most recent bonus, she found that a large order for 7,500 units of product WR4, which had been refused by a customer and returned to the company, had been included in the calculations. She later found out that the company's accountant had labeled the return an overhead expense and had charged the entire cost of the returned order to the plantwide Manufacturing Overhead account. The result was that product WR4 exceeded breakeven by more than 5,000 units and Ginsberg's bonus from that product amounted to over $800. What actions should Ginsberg take? Be prepared to discuss your response.

Research Activity

SD 4.
LO 2 Cost Behavior and
LO 3 Contribution Margin in a
LO 6 Fast-Food Restaurant

Make a trip to a local fast-food restaurant. Observe all aspects of the operation and take notes on the entire process. Describe the procedures used to take, process, and fill an order and deliver the food to the customer. Based on your observations, make a list of the costs incurred by the owner. Then identify at least three variable costs and three fixed costs. Can you identify any potential mixed costs? Why is the restaurant willing to sell a large drink for only a few cents more than a medium drink? How is the restaurant able to offer a "value meal" (for example, sandwich, large drink, and fries) for considerably less than those items would cost if they were bought separately? Bring your notes to class and be prepared to discuss your findings.

Decision-Making Practice

SD 5.
LO 2 Mixed Costs
LO 3

Officials of the ***Minnetonka Golf and Tennis Club*** are putting together a budget for the year ending December 31, 20x6. A problem has caused the budget to be delayed by more than four weeks. Ray Lobo, the club treasurer, indicated that two expense items were creating the problem. The items were difficult to account for because they were called "mixed costs," and he did not know how to break them down into their variable and fixed components. An accountant friend and golfing partner told him to use the high-low method to divide the costs into their variable and fixed parts.

The two cost categories are Electricity Expense and Repairs and Maintenance Expense. Information about last year's spending patterns and the activity measures related to each cost is shown below.

	Electricity Expense		Repairs and Maintenance	
Month	Amount	Kilowatt-Hours	Amount	Labor Hours
January	$ 7,500	210,000	$ 7,578	220
February	8,255	240,200	7,852	230
March	8,165	236,600	7,304	210
April	8,960	268,400	7,030	200
May	7,520	210,800	7,852	230
June	7,025	191,000	8,126	240
July	6,970	188,800	8,400	250
August	6,990	189,600	8,674	260
September	7,055	192,200	8,948	270
October	7,135	195,400	8,674	260
November	8,560	252,400	8,126	240
December	8,415	246,600	7,852	230
Totals	$92,550	2,622,000	$96,416	2,840

1. Using the high-low method, compute the variable cost rates that were used last year for each expense. What was the monthly fixed cost for electricity and for repairs and maintenance?
2. Compute the total variable cost and total fixed cost for each expense category for last year.
3. Lobo believes that for the coming year the electricity rate will increase by $.005 and the repairs rate will rise by $1.20. Usage of all items and their fixed cost amounts will remain constant. Compute the projected total cost for each category. How will those increases in costs affect the club's profits and cash flow?

MANAGERIAL REPORTING AND ANALYSIS

Interpreting Management Reports

LO 4 **Cost-Volume-Profit**
LO 5 **Analysis**
LO 6

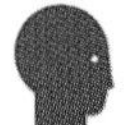

MRA 1. *Nambe-Casa, Ltd.*, is an international importer-exporter of fine china. The company was formed in 1963 in Albuquerque, New Mexico. The company has distribution centers in the United States, Europe, and Australia. Although the company was very successful in its early years, its profitability has steadily declined. As a member of a management team selected to gather information for the next strategic planning meeting, you are asked to review the most recent income statement for the company. The income statement is at the top of the next page. Sales in 20x1 were 15,000 sets of fine china.

REQUIRED

1. For each set of fine china, calculate the (a) selling price, (b) variable purchases cost, (c) variable distribution cost, (d) variable sales commission, and (e) contribution margin.
2. Calculate the breakeven point in units and in sales dollars.

Nambe-Casa, Ltd. Contribution Income Statement For the Year Ended December 31, 20x1		
Sales revenue		$13,500,000
Less variable costs		
Purchases	$6,000,000	
Distribution	2,115,000	
Sales commissions	1,410,000	
Total variable costs		9,525,000
Contribution margin		$ 3,975,000
Less fixed costs		
Distribution	$ 985,000	
Selling	1,184,000	
General and administrative	871,875	
Total fixed costs		3,040,875
Operating income		$ 934,125

3. Historically, variable costs should be about 60 percent of sales. What was the ratio of variable costs to sales for 20x1? List three actions Nambe-Casa could take to correct the difference.
4. How would fixed costs have been affected if Nambe-Casa had sold only 14,000 sets of fine china?

Formulating Management Reports

MRA 2.
LO 7 Cost-Volume-Profit Analysis

Refer to the information in **MRA 1**. In January 20x2, Laura Casa, the president and chief executive officer of Nambe-Casa, Ltd., conducted a strategic planning meeting with her officers. Below is a summary of the information provided by two of the officers.

> Rita O'Toole, vice president of sales: A review of the competitors indicates that the selling price of a set of china should be lowered to $890. We plan to sell 15,000 sets of fine china again in 20x2. To encourage increased sales, we should raise sales commissions to 12 percent of the selling price.
>
> Maurice Moonitz, vice president of distribution: We have signed a contract with a new shipping line for foreign shipments. We will be able to reduce the fixed distribution costs by 10 percent and reduce variable distribution costs by 4 percent.

Laura Casa needs your help. She is concerned that the changes may not improve operating income sufficiently in 20x2. If operating income does not increase by at least 10 percent, she will want to find other ways to reduce the company's costs. Because the new year has already started and changes need to be made quickly, she requests your report within five days.

REQUIRED

1. Prepare an estimated contribution income statement for 20x2. Your report should show the budgeted (estimated) operating income based on the information provided above and in **MRA 1**. Will the changes improve operating income sufficiently? Explain.
2. In preparation for writing your report, answer the following questions:
   a. Why are you preparing the report?
   b. Who needs the report?
   c. What were the sources of information for your report?
   d. When is the report due?

International Company

MRA 3.
LO 4 C-V-P Analysis and Decision Making

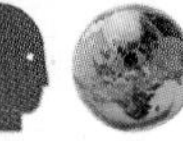

The ***Goslar Corporation*** cuts stones used in the construction and restoration of cathedrals throughout Europe. Granite, marble, and sandstone are cut into a variety of dimensions for walls, ceilings, and floors. The German-based company has operations in Italy and Switzerland. Otto Schrock, the controller, recently determined that the breakeven point was $325,000 in sales. In preparation for a quarterly planning meeting, Schrock must provide information for the following six proposals, which will be discussed individually by the planning team.

a. Increase the selling price of marble slabs by 10 percent.
b. Change the sales mix to respond to the increased sales demand for marble slabs. As a result, the company would increase production of marble slabs and decrease the production and sales of sandstone, the least profitable product.
c. Increase fixed production costs by $40,000 annually for the depreciation of new stone-cutting equipment.
d. Increase the variable costs by 1 percent for increased export duties on foreign sales.
e. Decrease the sales volume of the sandstone slabs because of political upheavals in eastern Europe.
f. Decrease the number of days that a customer can wait before paying without being charged interest.

REQUIRED

1. For each proposal, determine if cost-volume-profit (C-V-P) analysis would provide useful financial information.
2. Indicate whether each proposal that lends itself to C-V-P analysis would show an increase, decrease, or no impact on profit. Consider each decision separately and assume sales volume is not affected.

Excel Spreadsheet Analysis

MRA 4.
LO 7 Planning Future Sales

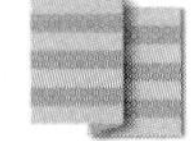

Refer to the information in **MRA 2**. In January 20x2, Laura Casa gathered information about a decrease in the selling price of a set of china to $890, an increase in sales commissions to 12 percent of the selling price, a decrease in fixed distribution costs of 10 percent, a decrease in variable distribution costs of 4 percent, and planned sales of 15,000 sets. Based on an analysis of this information, she found that Nambe-Casa would not increase its 20x2 operating income by at least 10 percent over the previous year's income.

Rita O'Toole reported that a new salesperson had just obtained a sales contract with an Australian distributor for 4,500 sets of china. The selling price, variable purchases cost per unit, 12 percent sales commission, and total fixed costs will be the same, but the variable distribution costs will be $160 per unit.

REQUIRED

Using an Excel spreadsheet, complete the following:

1. Calculate the target operating income for 20x2.
2. Prepare a contribution income statement for 20x2 based on the information presented in **MRA 1** and the adjustments presented in **MRA 2**. Do you agree with Laura Casa that Nambe-Casa's projected operating income for 20x2 will be less than the operating income for 20x1? Explain.
3. Calculate the total contribution margin from the Australian sales.
4. Prepare a revised contribution income statement for 20x2 by combining the information from **2** and **3** above.
5. Does Nambe-Casa need the Australian sales to achieve its target operating income for 20x2?

Internet Case

MRA 5.
LO 6 LO 7 Projecting Revenues and Costs

Select a company on the Internet or refer to the Needles Accounting Resource Center web site at http://college.hmco.com for links to selected companies. Study the Letter to the Stockholders in the most recent annual report for the company you have chosen. Many initiatives or actions discussed in that section were part of the company's strategic plan and were included in planning activities for the year. Identify at least three initiatives or actions that you believe were part of the company's planning activities for the year that affected sales or costs. Also identify one initiative or action that the company is planning for the coming year that you would expect to affect revenue or expenses for next year.

ENDNOTE

1. Linda Hall and Jane Lambert, "Cummins Engine Changes Its Depreciation," *Management Accounting*, Institute of Management Accountants, July 1996.

24 The Budgeting Process

LEARNING OBJECTIVES

1 Define *budgeting* and explain its role in the management cycle.

2 Describe the master budget process for different types of organizations, and list the guidelines for preparing budgets.

3 Prepare a budgeted income statement and supporting operating budgets.

4 Prepare a cash budget.

5 Prepare a budgeted balance sheet.

DECISION POINT: A MANAGER'S FOCUS

The HON Company The HON Company, the largest manufacturer of mid-priced office furniture in the United States and Canada, wants to improve productivity and customer service while developing new products and services. However, balancing gradual improvements with innovation is difficult. The HON Company, one of nine subsidiaries of HON Industries, operates as a profit center. The managers of HON Company are responsible for generating profits and managing resources in accordance with its parent company's strategic plan. The company feels tremendous pressure to compete in an industry that has a few major customers who want good quality, low prices, and on-time delivery. To manage costs and make full use of production capacity, managers at the HON Company use a process called continuous quarterly budgeting to implement their budgets. At the beginning of each quarter, teams work to create a four-quarter budget. Through this budgeting process, top management expects to motivate the various departments to continuously improve productivity and reduce delivery time while planning the introduction of new products and variations of existing products.[1]

How does the quarterly budget process work? First, a team from sales and marketing develops a sales budget by product, geographic territory, and distribution channel. The president and senior staff review the sales budget to see that it meets the goals of the strategic plan. Second, the scheduling team prepares a production and shipping schedule to coordinate those activities at the different manufacturing plants. Third, the managers responsible for each of the five functional areas (research and development; production; distribution; customer service; and selling, general, and administrative) prepare cost/expense budgets. Fourth, the company accounting group reviews the budgets and analyzes the contents to ensure that the budgets reflect the strategic plan. Fifth, the HON Company controller prepares a complete set of budgeted financial statements and additional information, including productivity measures, budgeted sales attributable to new product introductions, and major equipment expenditures.

Critical Thinking Question: How do you think management minimizes the time required to prepare continuous quarterly budgets? **Answer:** A computerized budgeting system allows managers to change only specific items as needed and to transfer information more quickly to higher-level managers.

The process of preparing quarterly budgets has proved to be very valuable for HON Company. The continuous budgeting process informs employees about new products and procedures and permits improvements to occur more quickly. Continuous quarterly budgeting successfully connects strategic planning to operations by helping the workers see the corporate vision, target their actions to support the vision, and monitor the results of their actions. Continuous quarterly budgeting helps the managers and employees of the HON Company to continuously improve productivity and customer service while integrating innovation through the development of new products.

VIDEO CASE

Enterprise Rent-A-Car

Objectives

- To become familiar with the budgeting process and budgets
- To understand the relationship between strategic plans and operating budgets
- To describe the role of budgeting in the management cycle

Background for the Case

Because its core business is not the airport market, Enterprise Rent-A-Car does not have the high profile most of its competitors enjoy; however, with over $5.6 billion in annual revenues (revenue growth of about 20 percent per year for the last 11 years) and more than 4,400 locations, it is the largest car rental company in North America and one of the top 50 privately owned companies.

The 44-year old company focuses on the home-city market, which is divided into two segments. The first segment serves people who need replacement vehicles when their own cars are not available—for instance, when they are scheduled for lengthy repair work. The second segment serves people with discretionary needs for another or different type of car for a short period, such as for a weekend trip or vacations.

Enterprise prides itself on providing excellent customer service, including free pickup from a customer's home, office, or repair shop. The company accomplishes its goals by providing incentives to motivate employees, coupled with a decentralized organization that allows great latitude in decision making. Enterprise's managers prepare budgets to integrate, coordinate, and communicate the operating plans necessary to achieve these strategic objectives. The budgeting system must allow measurement of performance for each location and each employee. Good systems and budgeting also facilitate the company's objective of expanding into global markets in Canada, the United Kingdom, and Germany.

For more information about Enterprise Rent-A-Car, visit the company's web site through the Needles Accounting Resource Center at

http://college.hmco.com

Required

View the video on Enterprise Rent-A-Car that accompanies this book. As you are watching the video, take notes related to the following questions:

1. As part of the planning process, many large, successful companies prepare budgets. In your own words, explain what a budget is and list all the reasons you believe a company like Enterprise would prepare a set of budgets.
2. Companies that prepare strategic plans also prepare budgets. What is the relation between Enterprise's strategic plans and its operating budgets?
3. What is the role of budgeting in the management cycle?

The Budgeting Process

OBJECTIVE

1 Define *budgeting* and explain its role in the management cycle

Related Text Assignments:
Q: 1, 2, 3, 4, 5, 6, 7, 8
SE: 1, 2, 3, 4
E: 1, 2, 3, 4
SD: 1, 3
MRA: 1, 2, 5

Point to Emphasize: A budget is a management tool. The quality of the tool, when used in the proper manner, influences the quality of the results achieved.

Point to Emphasize: The preparation stage is the planning part of the budgeting process. Budgeting also helps in controlling operations.

Point to Emphasize: Cost control is not the same as cost reduction. The concept of control recognizes that costs must be incurred but that their amounts should be no greater than necessary to achieve an organization's desired goals.

Enrichment Note: Any budget, even a poorly prepared one, is probably better than no budget at all. As the budgeting process is refined, the benefits to the organization will increase.

Planning is an important ongoing process for organizations. A review of the current use of available resources for financing, investing, and operating activities is necessary to plan for the efficient use of future resources. **Budgeting** is the process of identifying, gathering, summarizing, and communicating financial and nonfinancial information about an organization's future activities. The budgeting process provides managers with the opportunity to carefully match the goals of the organization with the resources necessary to accomplish those goals.

A **budget** is a plan of action that forecasts future transactions, activities, and events in financial or nonfinancial terms. Budgets are synonymous with managing an organization. The term *organization* is important because budgets are used in government and not-for-profit organizations (such as hospitals, universities, professional organizations, and charities) as well as in profit-oriented businesses. All types of organizations rely on plans to help them accomplish their objectives. All types of organizations have managers whose responsibilities are determined by top management or a board of directors; budgets are used to plan for and assess those areas of responsibility and to measure managers' performance.

All organizations need cash to purchase resources in order to accomplish their goals. Whenever cash needs to be managed and accounted for, budgets are used. Budgets establish (1) minimum desired, or target, levels of cash receipts and (2) limits on the spending of cash for particular purposes. The primary difference between not-for-profit organizations and profit-oriented organizations is that a profit-oriented organization sells a product or service for the purpose of making a profit. Profit-oriented organizations often use the term *profit planning* rather than *budgeting*.

Budgets can be used to communicate information, coordinate activities and resource usage, motivate employees, and evaluate performance. Budgets come in many forms. Some budgets present financial information based on the availability of resources. Such budgets should reflect a fair assignment of resources to the different organizational activities over a future period. For example, a cash budget shows the planned use of cash resources for operating, investing, and financing activities. Other budgets show planned activities to meet certain requirements or standards established in the planning stage. For example, a production budget shows planned production in units.

The budgeting process is as important in today's globally competitive operating environment as it is in more traditional settings. In fact, budgeting becomes even more important when just-in-time (JIT) or total quality management (TQM) concepts are applied and when computers and other electronic operating and data-gathering devices are used. In such cases, actual operating data are made available quickly, and budgets are updated continuously to accommodate management's need for performance evaluation.

Discussion Question: Describe some additional benefits of budgeting.
Answer: (1) There will be improved communication between the organization's segments, (2) managers will become better general managers and acquire a better understanding of the organization's environment, and (3) managers will better understand the impact of their actions on other operations within the organization.

Budgeting and Goals

LONG-TERM GOALS Annual operating plans cannot be made unless the people preparing the budget know the direction that top management expects the organization to take. Long-term goals, which are projections covering a five- to ten-year period, must be set by top management. Those goals should take into consideration economic and industry forecasts, employee-management relations, and the structure and role of management in leading the organization. They should include statements about the expected quality of products or services, growth rates, and desired market share.

Managers need to develop a strong ethical culture within their organizations so that they can minimize unethical or illegal activities. Unethical behavior in organizations hurts business. As employee productivity and loyalty decrease, employee turnover and absenteeism increase. Employees may also become lax in their compliance with organizational policies and procedures and, for example, fail to adhere to budgets and use them properly. As a result, the organization may project a poor image to customers, suppliers, and the community. Organizations can spend as much as $5,000 per employee on efforts to control unethical behavior. To avoid such costly problems and foster an ethical culture in their organizations, managers can:

- Develop a code of ethics that communicates the organization's ethical values.
- Increase employee awareness of ethical behavior through training programs.
- Provide a process to guide employees when they are facing an ethical dilemma.
- Develop a process to promote, monitor, and positively influence the ethical behavior of the organization's employees.
- Personally demonstrate ethical behavior.[2]

Point to Emphasize: Because long-term plans are developed by top management, communication is necessary to inform lower levels of management of those goals.

Enrichment Note: Long-term plans are often expressed in more subjective terms, such as increasing market share, becoming the industry leader, or having the best quality in the market.

Vague aims are not sufficient. The long-term goals should set specific targets and expected timetables and name the people responsible for achieving the goals. For example, assume that a company currently holds only 4 percent of its product's market share. The company's long-term goals may state that the vice president of marketing is to develop plans and strategies to ensure that the company controls 10 percent of the market in five years and increases its share to 15 percent by the end of ten years.

Once all goals have been developed, they should be compiled into a total long-term strategic plan. That plan should include a range of targets and goals and give direction to the company's efforts to achieve those goals. It should include future profit projections and describe new products and services in general terms.

Point to Emphasize: As plans are formulated for time periods closer to the current date, they become more specific and quantified. The annual budget is a very specific plan of action.

SHORT-TERM GOALS The long-term goals must be carefully developed because they are used to prepare yearly operating plans and targets. The short-term plan involves every part of the enterprise and is much more detailed than the long-term goals. To arrive at the short-term plan, the long-term goals must be restated in terms of what should be accomplished during the next year. Decisions must be made about sales and profit targets by product or service, human resource needs and expected changes, and plans for introducing new products or services. The resulting short-term targets and goals form the basis for the organization's operating budget for the year.

Once management has set the short-term goals, the controller or budget director takes charge of preparing the budget. This person designs a complete set of budget-development plans and a timetable with deadlines for all parts of the year's operating plan. Specific people must be named to carry out each part of the budget's development, and their responsibilities, targets, and deadlines must be clearly described.

THE IMPORTANCE OF PARTICIPATION The success of a budget strongly depends on how well the organization handles the human aspects of the budgeting process. All appropriate people, from top managers to first-line supervisors, must participate actively and honestly in preparing the budget. Such cooperation will occur only if each person realizes that he or she is important to the process.

The budget director plays a crucial role in the development of an effective budgeting system. This person must be able to communicate with people at all levels of the organization. Top management presents the budget targets and organizational goals to the budget director. The budget director then communicates those targets and goals to relevant managers throughout the organization. If the managers detect potential problems, they notify the budget director, who analyzes the information and passes it along to top management. In light of the new data, top management reassesses and restructures the targets and goals. It then gives the revised targets and goals to the budget director, and the process begins again. The budget director is at the center of the budgeting process, collecting and distributing information and coordinating all the budgeting activities.

The budget director depends on the cooperation of the other participants in the budgeting process. Those people must be carefully identified and informed of their responsibilities. The identification process begins with the senior managers. They choose the people who, under their supervision, will actually prepare the data. Because an organization's main activities—such as engineering, production, sales, and employee training—take place at its lower levels, information must flow from the supervisors of those activities through middle managers to senior executives. Each person in the chain of communication plays a part in both developing and implementing the budget. Thus, the key to success is **participative budgeting**, a process in which personnel at all levels of an organization meaningfully and actively take part in the creation of budgets. If every manager has a voice in setting the goals for his or her unit, every manager will feel personally motivated to ensure the success of the budgeting process.

Top management must be sensitive to its role in the budgeting process. Senior executives who dictate goals and expect employees at lower levels of the organization to implement them are not practicing participative budgeting. Such dictated targets are often difficult to attain, and managers at operational levels may not be motivated to achieve such goals if they had no input in preparing the goals. Problems may also arise if top management allows the budget director to develop the budget without consulting other managers. In that case, managers may feel that budgeting is not a top priority and that budgets need not be taken seriously. Such difficulties can be avoided if top management recognizes the importance of communicating its support for the budgeting process and of allowing managers at all levels to play meaningful roles in the development of their budgets.

Budgeting and the Management Cycle

To achieve the goals of profitability and liquidity, managers of many organizations use the budgeting process throughout the management cycle to help them plan, execute, review, and report the organization's financing, investing, and operating activities. Figure 1 illustrates the relationships between budgeting and the management cycle. Budgets originate in the planning stage, which is the stage emphasized in this chapter. Budgeting activities at Hi-Flyer Company, a manufacturer of flying disks used for recreation and tournament play, illustrate the relationship between budgeting and the management cycle. The owner, Skye King, believes that the future growth of Hi-Flyer Company depends on a good budgeting process.

PLANNING The planning process includes the development of long-term and short-term plans to achieve important success factors, such as high-quality products, reasonable cost, and timely delivery. Skye King believes that budgets help his organization's managers match long-term goals with short-term business activities by carefully distributing workloads and resources throughout the organization, such as to specific products, departments, sales territories, and activities. Because he recognizes the importance of participative budgeting, King includes managers from all levels of the organization in the budgeting process. Budget teams use budget

Figure 1
Budgeting and the Management Cycle

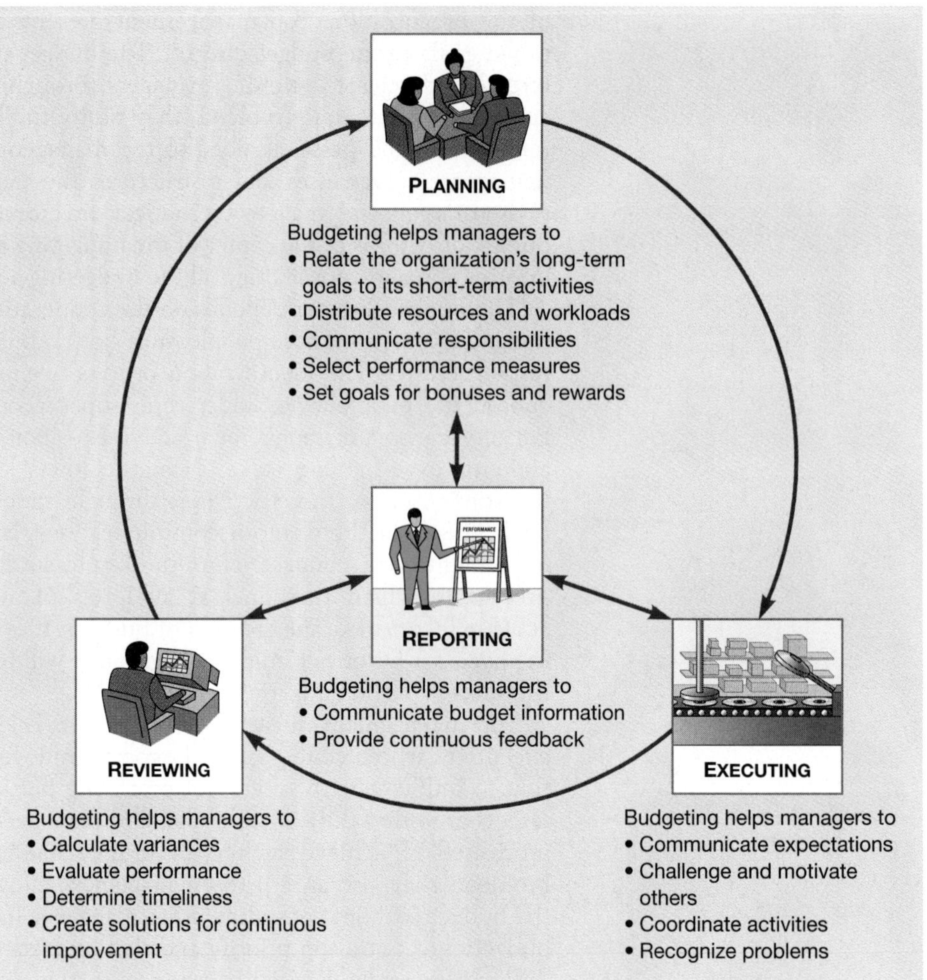

information to communicate responsibilities to the individuals who are accountable for a particular segment of the organization. Careful selection and introduction of performance measures can challenge and motivate individuals or teams to achieve goals and earn bonuses and rewards for their efforts. Senior management recently selected profits, number of units sold, and cycle time (the time to take, manufacture, and ship a sales order) as measures of performance for granting bonuses to individuals and teams at Hi-Flyer Company.

EXECUTING During the executing stage, managers use budget information for communication, benchmarking, and problem recognition. The managers of Hi-Flyer Company use budget information daily, weekly, and monthly to communicate expectations about the performance of activities and the availability of resources for segments of the organization. For example, Abe Dillon, the production manager, uses the planned units of production as an operating target for the production employees. He has also established the number of defective flying disks as a performance measure to motivate workers to manufacture quality products. In addition, Skye King uses standard product costs, generated during the budget process, to submit bids for sales orders, estimate profits, and calculate the expected profitability of a product during the operating period.

REVIEWING In the reviewing stage, managers calculate variances, evaluate performance, review the timeliness of activities performed, and create solutions for

Focus on Business Technology

When an organization decides to market its products or services on the Internet's World Wide Web, it must create a web site and build the site's costs into its budget. Developing a web site includes making decisions about access to the Internet, content on the site (online brochures or product news), graphic design, and functionality. In addition to basic development costs, the organization will incur costs for faster connections, data-base applications that update information easily, and animations and three-dimensional logos. After the web site has been developed, additional costs include monthly site maintenance fees, data-base development, and network integration. In addition, U.S. organizations that choose to use a custom domain server pay a yearly licensing fee to Internic, a government agency that oversees Internet activity.

Point to Emphasize: Although we present the four stages of the management cycle linearly, organizations are dynamic and managers may move through one stage, such as the executing stage, more often than another stage, such as the planning stage. For example, as part of the reviewing stage, a manager may evaluate performance reports on a weekly basis. On the other hand, as part of the planning stage, a manager may prepare a capital expenditures budget for new equipment only once a year.

continuous improvement. As mentioned earlier, Hi-Flyer's managers use the performance measures developed during the planning stage as targets for actual performance during the executing stage. By comparing the budget and actual information, they can identify variances between planned and actual activity. They review the variances to identify both waste and savings in production, sales, purchasing, packing, shipping, accounting, and other business activities. If problems are identified, the managers can work together to find solutions that will enable the organization to continuously improve its products and processes. Hi-Flyer's managers perform budget analyses on a regular basis because doing so helps them chart the course of future operations and evaluate past performance. If Hi-Flyer Company establishes realistic goals, then comparing the actual results with budgeted targets can help management assess how well the organization performed.

Reporting The reporting stage occurs throughout the year because managers need to continuously report on budget information and provide feedback about the organization's operating, investing, and financing activities. Budgets are reports showing plans for future actions. As such, they serve as a reference point for many other reports. For example, performance reports based on budget information support bonuses and promotions. Other budget-based reports support operating decisions. In this chapter, we will focus on how budgets are prepared during the planning stage.

The Master Budget

OBJECTIVE

2 Describe the master budget process for different types of organizations, and list the guidelines for preparing budgets

Related Text Assignments:
Q: 9, 10, 11, 12
SE: 5
E: 5
SD: 1, 3, 5
MRA: 2, 4

Suppose you want to start a new business, but first you must obtain a bank loan to supply some of the cash you need to begin operations. Before the bank will agree to loan you money, you must demonstrate that you can repay the principal and interest with cash generated by profitable operations. To do so, you will prepare a set of budgeted, or pro forma, financial statements for the bank to review. Now assume that you receive the bank loan and that, over ten years, your company becomes successful. Every year you will continue to prepare a set of budgeted financial statements so that you can match long-term goals to short-term activities and plan for the resources necessary to operate, finance, and invest in your business.

A **master budget** is a set of budgets that consolidates an organization's financial information into budgeted financial statements for a future period of time. A

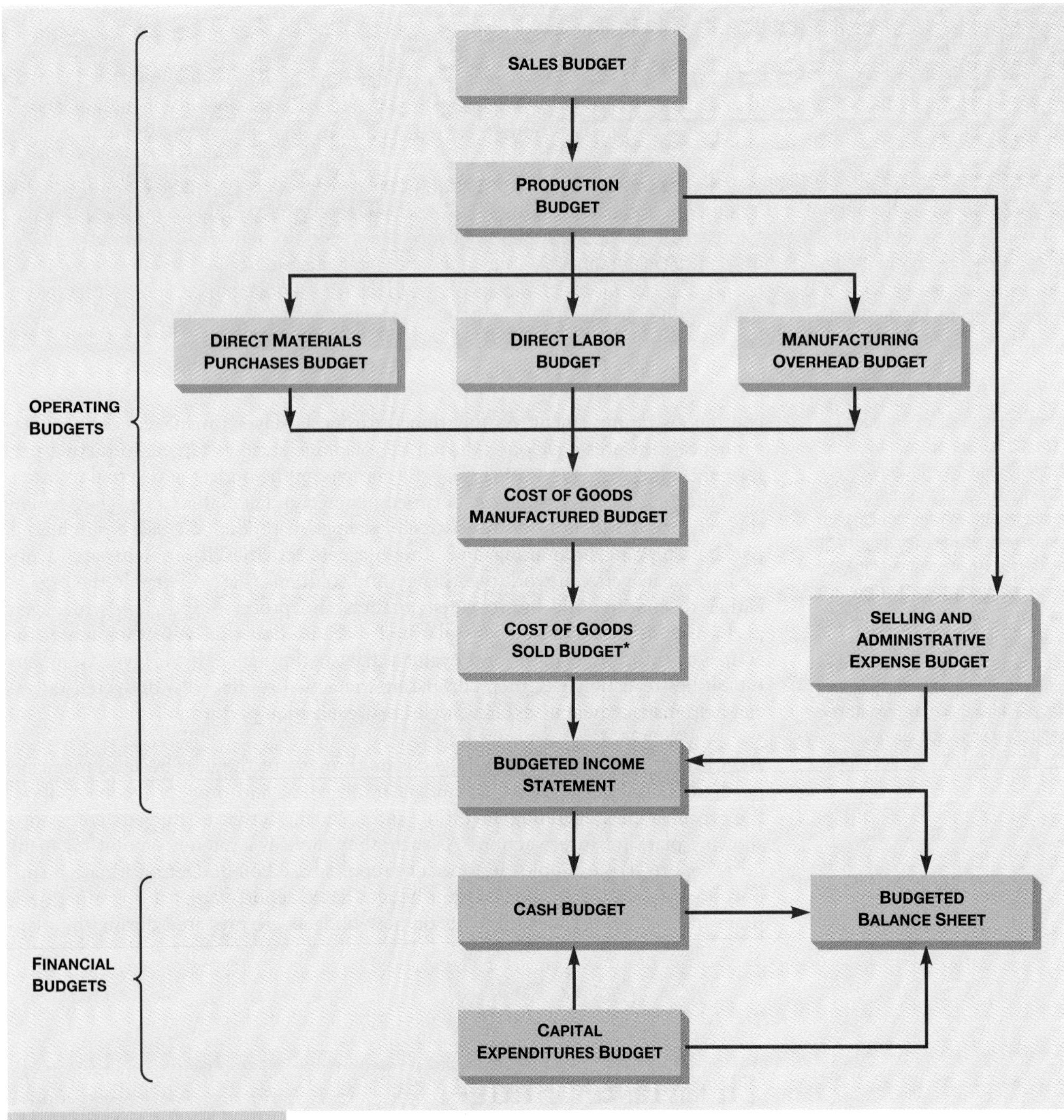

Figure 2
Preparation of a Master Budget for a Manufacturing Organization

*Some organizations choose to include the cost of goods sold budget in the budgeted income statement.

Teaching Note: At this point, discuss spreadsheet applications in budgeting, as well as the linking of spreadsheets.

master budget includes a set of operating budgets that supports a budgeted income statement. In addition, a master budget presents a set of financial budgets that includes a budgeted balance sheet, a cash budget, and a capital expenditures budget. Regardless of the type of organization, the master budget provides helpful information for planning, executing, reviewing, and reporting organizational activities. Figures 2, 3, and 4 display the preparation of a master budget for a manufacturing organization, a retail organization, and a service organization, respectively.

Figure 3
Preparation of a Master Budget for a Retail Organization

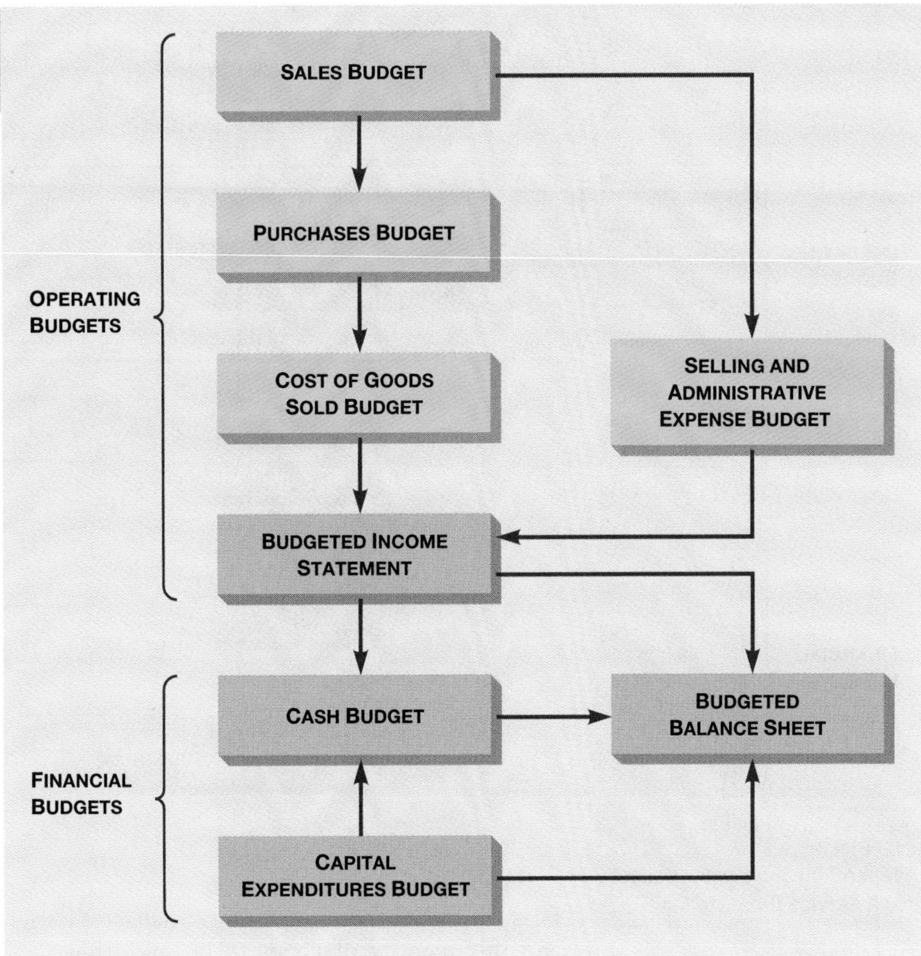

The master budget process has some similarities in all three types of organizations. All three types of organizations need a set of operating budgets to support the budgeted income statement. The information from the operating budgets and the capital expenditures budget affects the cash budget and the budgeted balance sheet. The cash budget also provides information for the budgeted balance sheet.

The main difference in the master budget process for the three types of organizations involves the preparation of operating budgets for the budgeted income statement. The operating budgets for manufacturing organizations like Intel or John Deere include budgets for sales, production, direct materials purchases, direct labor, manufacturing overhead, cost of goods manufactured, and selling and administrative expenses. The preparation of those budgets for a manufacturing organization will be explained under the next learning objective.

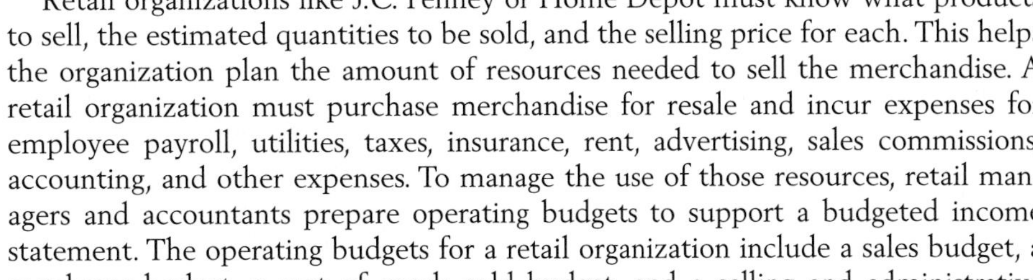

Retail organizations like J.C. Penney or Home Depot must know what products to sell, the estimated quantities to be sold, and the selling price for each. This helps the organization plan the amount of resources needed to sell the merchandise. A retail organization must purchase merchandise for resale and incur expenses for employee payroll, utilities, taxes, insurance, rent, advertising, sales commissions, accounting, and other expenses. To manage the use of those resources, retail managers and accountants prepare operating budgets to support a budgeted income statement. The operating budgets for a retail organization include a sales budget, a purchases budget, a cost of goods sold budget, and a selling and administrative expense budget. The sales budget is prepared first because it is used to estimate

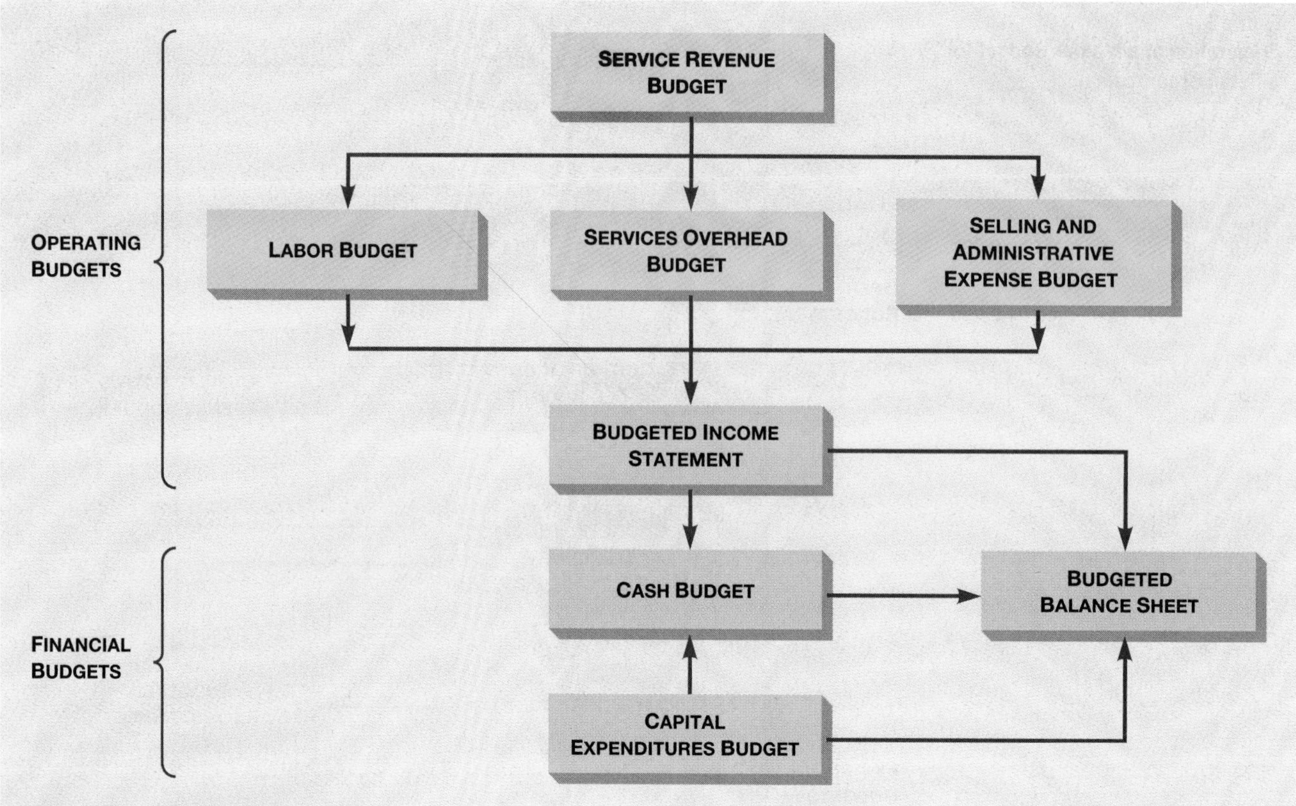

Figure 4
Preparation of a Master Budget for a Service Organization

sales volume and revenues. Once managers know how many sales dollars to expect and the quantity of goods to be sold, they can develop other budgets that will enable them to manage the organization's resources so that they can generate profits on those sales. The purchases budget determines the quantity of merchandise needed to meet the sales demand and maintain a minimum level of inventory.

Rather than manufacture and sell products, service organizations such as Union Pacific Railroad or Columbia Healthcare invest money in human resources to provide services. Managers of service organizations must know the types and amounts of services to perform. Managers must also know the labor hours needed to complete those services, the level of expertise of their employees, and the labor rates for the planned services. In addition, service organizations must incur costs for utilities, taxes, insurance, rent, advertising, accounting, and other expenses.

A service organization also prepares a set of operating budgets to support the budgeted income statement. The operating budgets include budgets for service revenue, labor, services overhead, and selling and administrative expenses. The labor budget reflects the estimated labor hours and labor rates to provide the services. The managers use that information to estimate the amount of human and technical resources needed for the accounting period and to set prices for services.

Guidelines for Budget Preparation

Attention to the suggestions presented in Table 1 will help managers improve the quality of the budgets they prepare. Managers need to know why the budget is being prepared, who will read and use it, how the information will be presented, and where the information can be found. Meaningful, accurate information is gathered from appropriate documents or interviews with the employees, suppliers, or

Exhibit 3
Direct Materials Purchases Budget

Hi-Flyer Company
Direct Materials Purchases Budget
For the Year Ended December 31, 20x1

	Quarter				
	1	2	3	4	Year
Total Production Units (Exhibit 2)	12,000	28,000	13,000	37,500	90,500
× 10 Ounces per Unit	10	10	10	10	10
Total Production Needs in Ounces	120,000	280,000	130,000	375,000	905,000
Add Desired Ounces of Ending Direct Materials Inventory	56,000	26,000	75,000	30,000	30,000
	176,000	306,000	205,000	405,000	935,000
Less Desired Ounces of Beginning Direct Materials Inventory	24,000	56,000	26,000	75,000	24,000
Total Ounces of Direct Materials to Be Purchased	152,000	250,000	179,000	330,000	911,000
× Cost per Ounce	$ .05	$ .05	$ .05	$ .05	$ .05
Total Cost of Direct Materials Purchases	$ 7,600	$12,500	$ 8,950	$ 16,500	$45,550

Note 1: Desired ounces of ending direct materials inventory = 20% of *next* quarter's budgeted production needs in ounces.
Note 2: Desired ounces of beginning direct materials inventory = 20% of *current* quarter's budgeted production needs in ounces.
Note 3: Assume that budgeted production needs in ounces for the first quarter of 20x2 = 150,000 ounces.
Note 4: The desired direct materials inventory balance at December 31, 20x0 = 24,000 ounces × $.05 per ounce = $1,200 and at December 31, 20x1 = 30,000 ounces × $.05 per ounce = $1,500.

The first step in preparing a direct labor budget is to estimate the total direct labor hours by multiplying the estimated direct labor hours per unit by the anticipated units of production (see Exhibit 2). The second step in preparing such a budget is to calculate the total budgeted direct labor cost by multiplying the estimated total direct labor hours by the estimated direct labor cost per hour. The Human Resources Department provides an estimate of the hourly labor wages for the workers.

Total Budgeted Direct Labor Cost	=	Estimated Total Direct Labor Hours	×	Estimated Direct Labor Cost per Hour

Exhibit 4 illustrates the direct labor budget for Hi-Flyer Company, using these formulas to estimate the total budgeted direct labor cost. The Production Department needs an estimated .10 direct labor hour to complete one Hi-Flyer. The Human Resources Department estimates a direct labor cost of $6 per direct labor hour. In this example, Hi-Flyer Company needs only one production department. Organizations that require varying production processes and varying levels of expertise may prepare either separate schedules for each type of labor or one comprehensive direct labor budget.

Hi-Flyer Company
Direct Labor Budget
For the Year Ended December 31, 20x1

	Quarter 1	Quarter 2	Quarter 3	Quarter 4	Year
Total Production Units (Exhibit 2)	12,000	28,000	13,000	37,500	90,500
× Direct Labor Hours per Unit	.1	.1	.1	.1	.1
Total Direct Labor Hours	1,200	2,800	1,300	3,750	9,050
× Direct Labor Cost per Hour	$ 6	$ 6	$ 6	$ 6	$ 6
Total Direct Labor Cost	$7,200	$16,800	$7,800	$22,500	$54,300

Exhibit 4
Direct Labor Budget

THE MANUFACTURING OVERHEAD BUDGET The **manufacturing overhead budget** is a detailed schedule of anticipated manufacturing costs, other than direct materials and direct labor costs, that must be incurred to meet the production expectations of a future period. The manufacturing overhead budget has two purposes: (1) to integrate the overhead cost budgets developed by the managers of production and production-related service departments and (2) to group information for the calculation of manufacturing overhead rates for the forthcoming accounting period.

Exhibit 5
Manufacturing Overhead Budget

Hi-Flyer Company
Manufacturing Overhead Budget
For the Year Ended December 31, 20x1

	Quarter 1	Quarter 2	Quarter 3	Quarter 4	Year
Variable Overhead Costs					
Factory Supplies	$ 2,160	$ 5,040	$ 2,340	$ 6,750	$ 16,290
Employee Benefits	2,880	6,720	3,120	9,000	21,720
Inspection	1,080	2,520	1,170	3,375	8,145
Maintenance and Repair	1,920	4,480	2,080	6,000	14,480
Utilities	3,600	8,400	3,900	11,250	27,150
Total Variable Overhead	$11,640	$27,160	$12,610	$36,375	$ 87,785
Fixed Overhead Costs					
Depreciation, Machinery	$ 2,810	$ 2,810	$ 2,810	$ 2,810	$ 11,240
Depreciation, Building	3,225	3,225	3,225	3,225	12,900
Supervision	9,000	9,000	9,000	9,000	36,000
Maintenance and Repair	2,150	2,150	2,150	2,150	8,600
Other Overhead Expenses	3,175	3,175	3,175	3,175	12,700
Total Fixed Overhead	$20,360	$20,360	$20,360	$20,360	$81,440
Total Manufacturing Overhead Costs	$32,000	$47,520	$32,970	$56,735	$169,225

Teaching Note: Estimates of variable manufacturing overhead may be based on units produced or other consumption measures, such as direct labor hours, number of employees, or machine hours.

The presentation of information in the manufacturing overhead budget is flexible. Grouping information by activities is useful for organizations using activity-based costing. This approach helps the accountant to more easily determine the application rates for each cost pool.

The Hi-Flyer Company prefers to group information into variable and fixed costs for cost-volume-profit analysis during the executing stage of the management cycle (see Exhibit 5). The manufacturing overhead rate for Hi-Flyer Company is the estimated total manufacturing costs divided by the estimated total direct labor hours. The predetermined manufacturing overhead rate for 20x1 is $18.70 per direct labor hour ($169,225 ÷ 9,050 direct labor hours), or $1.87 per unit ($18.70 per direct labor hour × .10 direct labor hour per unit). The variable portion of the manufacturing overhead rate is $9.70 per direct labor hour ($87,785 ÷ 9,050 direct labor hours), which includes factory supplies, $1.80; employee benefits, $2.40; inspection, $.90; maintenance and repair, $1.60; and utilities, $3.00.

Point to Emphasize: Remember that selling and administrative expenses are period costs, not product costs.

THE SELLING AND ADMINISTRATIVE EXPENSE BUDGET A **selling and administrative expense budget** is a detailed plan of operating expenses, other than those of the production function, needed to support the sales and overall operations of the organization for a future period. The accountant uses the estimated selling and administrative expense budget to estimate cash payments for products or services used in nonproduction-related activities. Exhibit 6 illustrates the selling and

Exhibit 6
Selling and Administrative Expense Budget

Hi-Flyer Company
Selling and Administrative Expense Budget
For the Year Ended December 31, 20x1

	Quarter				
	1	2	3	4	Year
Variable Selling and Administrative Expenses					
Delivery Expenses	$ 800	$ 2,400	$ 800	$ 3,200	$ 7,200
Sales Commissions	1,000	3,000	1,000	4,000	9,000
Accounting	700	2,100	700	2,800	6,300
Other Administrative Expenses	400	1,200	400	1,600	3,600
Total Variable Selling and Administrative Expenses	$ 2,900	$ 8,700	$ 2,900	$11,600	$ 26,100
Fixed Selling and Administrative Expenses					
Sales Salaries	$ 4,500	$ 4,500	$ 4,500	$ 4,500	$ 18,000
Executive Salaries	12,750	12,750	12,750	12,750	51,000
Depreciation, Office Equipment	925	925	925	925	3,700
Taxes and Insurance	1,700	1,700	1,700	1,700	6,800
Total Fixed Selling and Administrative Expenses	$19,875	$19,875	$19,875	$19,875	$ 79,500
Total Selling and Administrative Expenses	$22,775	$28,575	$22,775	$31,475	$105,600

Exhibit 7
Cost of Goods Manufactured Budget

Hi-Flyer Company Cost of Goods Manufactured Budget For the Year Ended December 31, 20x1			Sources of Data
Direct Materials Used			
Direct Materials Inventory, December 31, 20x0	$ 1,200		Exhibit 3, Note 4
Purchases for 20x1	45,550		Exhibit 3
Cost of Direct Materials Available for Use	$46,750		
Less Direct Materials Inventory, December 31, 20x1	1,500		Exhibit 3, Note 4
Cost of Direct Materials Used		$ 45,250	
Direct Labor Costs		54,300	Exhibit 4
Manufacturing Overhead Costs		169,225	Exhibit 5
Total Manufacturing Costs		$268,775	
Work in Process Inventory, December 31, 20x0*		—	
Less Work in Process Inventory, December 31, 20x1*		—	
Cost of Goods Manufactured		$268,775	

*It is a company policy to have no units in process at the beginning or end of the year.

administrative expense budget for Hi-Flyer Company, which groups expenses into variable and fixed components for purposes of cost behavior analysis, cost-volume-profit analysis, and profit planning.

THE COST OF GOODS MANUFACTURED BUDGET The **cost of goods manufactured budget** is a detailed schedule that summarizes the costs of production for a future period. The sources of budget information for the total manufacturing costs are the budgets for direct materials, direct labor, and manufacturing overhead (Exhibits 3, 4, and 5). Most manufacturing organizations anticipate some work in process at the beginning or end of the future period. However, we assume that the Hi-Flyer Company has a policy of no work in process on December 31 of any year. Exhibit 7 summarizes the costs of production for Hi-Flyer Company. The budgeted, or standard, product unit cost for one Hi-Flyer is rounded to $2.97 ($268,775 ÷ 90,500 units).

The Budgeted Income Statement

Teaching Note: Time spent explaining the interrelationships of each of the operating budgets and the projected financial statements will help eliminate some student questions later.

After the operating budgets have been prepared, the budget director or the controller can prepare the budgeted income statement for the period. A **budgeted income statement** projects an organization's net income based on the estimated revenues and expenses for a future period. Information about projected sales and costs comes from several operating budgets. Hi-Flyer Company's budgeted income statement for 20x1 is shown in Exhibit 8. Note that the right side of both Exhibits 7 and 8 identifies the sources of key elements, which makes it possible to trace the statement's development. At this point, you can review the overall preparation of the operating budgets by comparing the preparation flow in Figure 2 to the schedules in Exhibits 1 through 8. You will notice that the budgeted cost of goods sold was included in the budgeted income statement instead of being shown as a separate schedule.

Exhibit 8
Budgeted Income Statement

Hi-Flyer Company Budgeted Income Statement For the Year Ended December 31, 20x1			Sources of Data
Sales		$450,000	Exhibit 1
Cost of Goods Sold			
Finished Goods Inventory, December 31, 20x0*	$ 2,970		
Cost of Goods Manufactured	268,775		Exhibit 7
Total Cost of Goods Available for Sale	$271,745		
Less Finished Goods Inventory, December 31, 20x1*	4,455		
Cost of Goods Sold		267,290	
Gross Margin		$182,710	
Selling and Administrative Expenses		105,600	Exhibit 6
Income from Operations		$ 77,110	
Interest Expense (8% × $70,000)		5,600	
Income Before Income Taxes		$ 71,510	
Income Taxes Expense (30%)		21,453	
Net Income		$ 50,057	

*Finished goods inventory balances assume that product unit costs were the same in 20x0 and 20x1.

December 31, 20x0	December 31, 20x1	
1,000 units	1,500 units	(Exhibit 2)
× $ 2.97	× $ 2.97	(Exhibit 7)
$2,970	$4,455	

The Capital Expenditures Budget

A **capital expenditures budget** is a detailed plan outlining the amount and timing of anticipated capital expenditures for a future period. Buying equipment, building a new store outlet, purchasing and installing a materials handling system, and acquiring another business are examples of capital expenditure decisions that require a capital expenditures budget. Budgeting for capital expenditures decisions is discussed in another chapter. In our illustration, Hi-Flyer Company plans to purchase a new extrusion machine for $30,000. The company will pay $15,000 in the first quarter of 20x1, when the order is placed, and $15,000 in the second quarter of 20x1, when the equipment is received.

Cash Budgeting

OBJECTIVE
4 Prepare a cash budget

A **cash budget** is a projection of the cash receipts and cash payments for a future period. It summarizes the cash flow forecasts of planned transactions in all phases of a master budget. This information helps managers plan for short-term loans when the cash balance is low and for short-term investments when the cash balance is high. The elements of a cash budget can relate to operating, investing, or financing activities, as shown by the examples in Table 2.

Table 2. Elements of a Cash Budget

Activities	Cash Receipts From*	Cash Payments For*
Operating	Cash sales Cash collections on credit sales Interest income from investments Cash dividends from investments	Purchases of direct materials Purchases of indirect materials Direct labor Manufacturing overhead expenses Selling expenses Administrative expenses Interest expense
Investing	Sale of investments Sale of long-term assets	Purchase of investments Purchase of long-term assets
Financing	Loan proceeds Proceeds from issue of stock Proceeds from issue of bonds	Loan repayment Cash dividends to stockholders

*Classifications correspond to the statement of cash flows.

Related Text Assignments:
Q: 17
SE: 8, 9
E: 11
P: 3, 5, 7
SD: 2
MRA: 3

Point to Emphasize: The cash budget depends heavily on information from the operating budgets. Therefore, errors in those budgets could be compounded in the cash budget.

The cash budget excludes some planned noncash transactions, such as depreciation expense, amortization expense, issuance and receipt of stock dividends, uncollectible accounts expense, and gains and losses on sales of assets. Some organizations also exclude deferred taxes and accrued interest.

Information about cash receipts comes from several sources, including the sales budget, cash collection records and trends, the budgeted income statement, the cash budgets from previous periods, and financial records of notes, stocks, and bonds. Information about cash payments comes from operating budgets, capital expenditures budgets, the previous year's financial statements, loan records, and the budgeted income statement. The accountant will convert credit sales to cash inflows and materials purchases on credit to cash outflows and disclose those conversions on supporting schedules for the cash budget.

Teaching Note: Students will not understand how certain amounts in the cash budget are determined. Be sure to identify which figures are given and which ones must be obtained mathematically.

PREPARING A CASH BUDGET In our illustration, the cash budget summarizes cash inflows and cash outflows for the four quarters of 20x1 and for the entire year. A useful format for the preparation of a cash budget is:

Estimated Ending Cash Balance	=	Total Estimated Cash Receipts	−	Total Estimated Cash Payments	+	Estimated Beginning Cash Balance

Many organizations also need to prepare supporting schedules for cash inflows or cash outflows that fluctuate over time. For example, the Hi-Flyer Company expects to receive cash from cash sales and credit sales in 20x1. The projected collection of that cash is shown in Exhibit 9, the schedule of expected cash collections from customers. Cash sales will represent 20 percent of the current quarter's sales, and the remaining 80 percent of sales will be credit sales. Experience has shown that 60 percent of all credit sales are collected in the quarter of sale, 30 percent are collected in the quarter following sale, and 10 percent are collected in the second quarter following sale.

Exhibit 9 shows that in the first quarter of 20x1, Hi-Flyer Company will collect \$38,000 of the \$48,000 balance of accounts receivable at December 31, 20x0. The company will collect the remaining portion of the \$48,000 balance (\$10,000) in the second quarter of 20x1. The estimated ending balance of Accounts Receivable

Exhibit 9
Schedule of Expected Cash Collections from Customers

Hi-Flyer Company
Schedule of Expected Cash Collections from Customers
For the Year Ended December 31, 20x1

	Quarter				
	1	2	3	4	Year
Accounts Receivable, Dec. 31, 20x0	$38,000	$ 10,000	—	—	$ 48,000
Cash Sales	10,000	30,000	$10,000	$ 40,000	90,000
Collections of Credit Sales					
First Quarter ($40,000)	24,000	12,000	4,000		40,000
Second Quarter ($120,000)		72,000	36,000	12,000	120,000
Third Quarter ($40,000)			24,000	12,000	36,000
Fourth Quarter ($160,000)				96,000	96,000
Total Cash to Be Collected from Customers	$72,000	$124,000	$74,000	$160,000	$430,000

Note 1: 20% of sales are cash sales, 80% are credit sales. Credit sales are collected as follows: 60% of all credit sales are collected in the quarter of sale, 30% are collected in the quarter following sale, and 10% are collected in the second quarter following sale.
Note 2: The Accounts Receivable balance at December 31, 20x0, is $48,000, which is $8,000 from 20x0 third quarter sales [($100,000 × .80) × .10] and $40,000 from 20x0 fourth quarter sales [($125,000 × .80) × .40].
Note 3: The Accounts Receivable balance at December 31, 20x1, is $68,000, which is $4,000 from the third quarter's sales [($50,000 × .80) × .10] and $64,000 from the fourth quarter's sales [($200,000 × .80) × .40].

at December 31, 20x1, is $68,000, which is $4,000 from the third quarter's credit sales [($50,000 × .80) × .10] plus $64,000 from the fourth quarter's sales [($200,000 × .80) × .40]. The expected cash collections from this exhibit flow to the total cash receipts section of the cash budget.

Our illustration continues with the preparation of a schedule of expected cash payments for direct materials. To simplify the illustration, Hi-Flyer Company will pay 50 percent of the invoices it receives in the quarter of purchase and the remaining 50 percent in the following quarter. The estimated ending balance of Accounts Payable at December 31, 20x1, is $8,250 (50 percent of the fourth-quarter direct materials purchases of $16,500). Exhibit 10 shows the schedule for 20x1, which supports the first line of the cash payments section of the cash budget.

The cash budget in Exhibit 11 lists the cash receipts and cash payments, as well as the cash increase or decrease for the period. The cash increase or decrease plus the period's beginning cash balance equals the ending cash balance for the period. In the example in Exhibit 11, you can see that the beginning cash balance for the first quarter was $20,000. This amount also represents the beginning cash balance for the year 20x1. In addition, notice that each quarter's budgeted ending cash balance becomes the next quarter's beginning cash balance. To assist you in following the development of this budget, the sources for all information are listed on the right side of the exhibit.

Many organizations maintain a minimum cash balance to cover unusual expenditures. If the ending cash balance on the cash budget falls below the minimum required cash level, short-term borrowing may be necessary during the year to cover planned cash payments. If the ending cash balance is significantly larger than

Exhibit 10
Schedule of Expected Cash Payments for Direct Materials

Hi-Flyer Company
Schedule of Expected Cash Payments for Direct Materials
For the Year Ended December 31, 20x1

	Quarter				
	1	2	3	4	Year
Accounts Payable, Dec. 31, 20x0	$4,200	—	—	—	$ 4,200
First Quarter ($7,600)	3,800	$ 3,800			7,600
Second Quarter ($12,500)		6,250	$ 6,250		12,500
Third Quarter ($8,950)			4,475	$ 4,475	8,950
Fourth Quarter ($16,500)				8,250	8,250
Total Cash Payments for Direct Materials	$8,000	$10,050	$10,725	$12,725	$41,500

Note 1: 50% of the direct materials purchases are paid in the quarter of purchase and 50% are paid in the following quarter.
Note 2: The Accounts Payable balance at December 31, 20x0, is $4,200, or 50% of the 20x0 fourth-quarter direct materials purchases of $8,400.
Note 3: The Accounts Payable balance at December 31, 20x1 is $8,250, or 50% of the fourth-quarter direct materials purchases of $16,500.

the organization needs, the excess cash may be invested in short-term securities to generate additional income.

Let's examine the 20x1 cash budget for the Hi-Flyer Company presented in Exhibit 11. If we assume that management wants a minimum of $10,000 cash available at the end of each quarter, the balance at the end of the first quarter indicates a problem. Hi-Flyer's management has several options for managing the low cash balance for the first quarter. The organization can borrow cash to cover the first quarter's cash needs, delay purchase of the equipment until the second quarter, or reduce some of the operating expenses. On the other hand, the balance at the end of the fourth quarter may be excessively high, which could lead management to invest a portion of the idle cash in short-term securities.

FOCUS ON BUSINESS PRACTICE

Hexacomb Corporation and other companies use budgets in their "open-book management" system to motivate employees to achieve company goals. Hexacomb's "beat the budget" bonus system offers employees bonuses based on their plant's performance. Management consults with employees at each of the company's seven plants to develop an annual budget. Scorecards, which include an income statement, a balance sheet, and relevant nonfinancial measures, are distributed throughout the plants to track actual performance compared to the budget. Managers and employees review the financial information each month and adjust operating activities, if necessary. If profits exceed the budgeted amount for the seven plants, half of the excess amount is placed into a bonus pool. Employees collect the bonus if their plant beats its budget.[4]

Exhibit 11
Cash Budget

Hi-Flyer Company
Cash Budget
For the Year Ended December 31, 20x1

	Quarter 1	Quarter 2	Quarter 3	Quarter 4	Year	Sources of Data
Cash Receipts						
Expected Cash Collections from Customers	$ 72,000	$124,000	$74,000	$160,000	$430,000	Exhibit 9
Total Cash Receipts	$ 72,000	$124,000	$74,000	$160,000	$430,000	
Cash Payments						
Direct Materials	$ 8,000	$ 10,050	$10,725	$ 12,725	$ 41,500	Exhibit 10
Direct Labor	7,200	16,800	7,800	22,500	54,300	Exhibit 4
Factory Supplies	2,160	5,040	2,340	6,750	16,290	Exhibit 5
Employee Benefits	2,880	6,720	3,120	9,000	21,720	Exhibit 5
Inspection	1,080	2,520	1,170	3,375	8,145	Exhibit 5
Maintenance and Repair	1,920	4,480	2,080	6,000	14,480	Exhibit 5
Utilities	3,600	8,400	3,900	11,250	27,150	Exhibit 5
Supervision	9,000	9,000	9,000	9,000	36,000	Exhibit 5
Maintenance and Repair	2,150	2,150	2,150	2,150	8,600	Exhibit 5
Other Overhead Expenses	3,175	3,175	3,175	3,175	12,700	Exhibit 5
Delivery Expenses	800	2,400	800	3,200	7,200	Exhibit 6
Sales Commissions	1,000	3,000	1,000	4,000	9,000	Exhibit 6
Accounting	700	2,100	700	2,800	6,300	Exhibit 6
Other Administrative Expenses	400	1,200	400	1,600	3,600	Exhibit 6
Sales Salaries	4,500	4,500	4,500	4,500	18,000	Exhibit 6
Executive Salaries	12,750	12,750	12,750	12,750	51,000	Exhibit 6
Taxes and Insurance	1,700	1,700	1,700	1,700	6,800	Exhibit 6
Capital Expenditures	15,000	15,000	—	—	30,000	Note
Interest Expense	1,400	1,400	1,400	1,400	5,600	Exhibit 8
Income Taxes	5,363	5,363	5,363	5,364	21,453	Exhibit 8
Total Cash Payments	$ 84,778	$117,748	$74,073	$123,239	$399,838	
Cash Increase (Decrease)	$(12,778)	$ 6,252	$ (73)	$ 36,761	$ 30,162	
Beginning Cash Balance	20,000	7,222	13,474	13,401	20,000	
Ending Cash Balance	$ 7,222	$ 13,474	$13,401	$ 50,162	$ 50,162	

Note: A new extrusion machine costing $30,000 will be paid for in two quarterly installments of $15,000 each in the first and second quarters of 20x1.

The Budgeted Balance Sheet

OBJECTIVE

5 Prepare a budgeted balance sheet

The final step in developing the master budget is to prepare a budgeted balance sheet. A **budgeted balance sheet** projects the financial position of an organization for a future period. As shown in Figure 2, all budgeted information is used in this process. The budgeted balance sheet at December 31, 20x1, for the Hi-Flyer Company is illustrated in Exhibit 12. To assist you in following the development of

Exhibit 12
Budgeted Balance Sheet

Hi-Flyer Company
Budgeted Balance Sheet
For the Year Ended December 31, 20x1

				Sources of Data
Assets				
Current Assets				
Cash		$ 50,162		Exhibit 11
Accounts Receivable		68,000		Exhibit 9, Note 3
Direct Materials Inventory		1,500		Exhibit 7
Work in Process Inventory		—		Exhibit 7, Note
Finished Goods Inventory		4,455		Exhibit 8, Note
Total Current Assets			$124,117	
Property, Plant, and Equipment				
Land		$ 50,000		
Plant and Equipment	$200,000			Note 1
Less Accumulated Depreciation	45,000	155,000		Note 2
Total Property, Plant, and Equipment			205,000	
Total Assets			$329,117	
Liabilities				
Current Liabilities				
Accounts Payable			$ 8,250	Exhibit 10, Note 3
Total Current Liabilities			$ 8,250	
Long-Term Liabilities				
Notes Payable			70,000	Note 3
Total Liabilities			$ 78,250	
Stockholders' Equity				
Contributed Capital				
Common Stock		$150,000		Note 4
Retained Earnings		100,867		Note 5
Total Stockholders' Equity			250,867	
Total Liabilities and Stockholders' Equity			$329,117	

Note 1: The Plant and Equipment balance includes the $30,000 equipment purchase.
Note 2: The Accumulated Depreciation balance includes the 20x1 depreciation expense totaling $27,840 for Machinery, Building, and Equipment ($11,240, $12,900, and $3,700, respectively).
Note 3: Management plans no change in the Notes Payable balance.
Note 4: Management plans no change in the Common Stock balance.
Note 5: The Retained Earnings balance at December 31 equals the beginning Retained Earnings balance plus the 20x1 projected net income ($50,810 and $50,057, respectively).

Related Text Assignments:
Q: 18, 19
SE: 10
P: 4, 8

this statement, the sources of all information are listed on the right side of the exhibit and notes are included at the bottom.

Budget Implementation

Terminology Note: Budgeted financial statements often are referred to as forecasted financial statements or pro forma statements.

Point to Emphasize: Proper communication cannot be overemphasized because good communication can eliminate many of the problems that typically arise in the budget process.

When the master budget is completed, management must decide whether to accept the proposed master budget and the planned operating results it presents, or to change the plans and revise the budget. Once the master budget has been accepted, it must be implemented.

Budget implementation is the responsibility of the budget director. Two elements discussed earlier—communication and support—determine the success of this process. Proper communication of expectations and targets to all key people in the organization is essential. All involved employees must know what is expected of them and must receive directions on how to achieve their goals. Equally important, top management must support the budgeting process and encourage implementation of the budget. The process will succeed only if middle- and lower-level managers can see that top management is truly interested in the outcome and is willing to reward people for meeting the budget goals.

Chapter Review

Review of Learning Objectives

Check out ACE, a self-quizzing program on chapter content, at http://college.hmco.com.

1. **Define *budgeting* and explain its role in the management cycle.** Budgeting is the process of identifying, gathering, summarizing, and communicating financial and nonfinancial information about future activities in an organization. Budgeting helps managers (1) relate the organization's long-term goals to short-term goals and activities and distribute resources during the planning stage; (2) communicate expectations, motivate others, and coordinate activities during the executing stage; (3) evaluate performance and solve problems during the reviewing stage; and (4) communicate budget information, report the organization's financing, investing, and operating activities, and provide continuous feedback during the reporting stage of the management cycle.

2. **Describe the master budget process for different types of organizations, and list the guidelines for preparing budgets.** A master budget is a set of budgets that consolidates an organization's financial information into budgeted financial statements for a future period of time. A master budget includes a budgeted income statement supported by a set of operating budgets, a budgeted balance sheet, and a cash budget. The operating budgets (1) for a manufacturing organization include budgets for sales, production, direct materials purchases, direct labor, manufacturing overhead, and selling and administrative expenses; (2) for a retail organization include budgets for sales, merchandise purchases, and selling and administrative expenses; and (3) for a service organization include budgets for service revenue, labor, services overhead, and selling and administrative expenses. Preliminary planning involves knowing the purpose of the budget, the user group and their information needs, the sources of budget information, and the budget components.

3. **Prepare a budgeted income statement and supporting operating budgets.** The initial step in preparing a budgeted income statement is to prepare a sales budget. After preparing the sales budget, managers or accountants at a manufacturing organization prepare a production budget followed by budgets for direct materials purchases, direct labor, manufacturing overhead, selling and administrative expenses, cost of goods manufactured, and cost of goods sold. The information from those operating budgets supports the information on the budgeted income statement.

4. **Prepare a cash budget.** A cash budget is a projection of the cash receipts and cash payments for a future period. A cash budget summarizes the cash flows expected to result from planned transactions for a future period. A cash budget identifies the organization's projected ending cash balance and shows a manager when short-term borrowing or investing may be appropriate.

   The preparation of a cash budget begins with the projection of all expected sources of cash. Next, all expected cash payments are found by analyzing all other operating budgets and the capital expenditures budget within the master budget. The difference between the two totals is the cash increase or decrease anticipated for the period. That total, combined with the period's beginning cash balance, yields the ending cash balance.

5. **Prepare a budgeted balance sheet.** The final step in the master budget process is to prepare a budgeted balance sheet for the company. All budgeted data are used in this process.

REVIEW OF CONCEPTS AND TERMINOLOGY

The following concepts and terms were introduced in this chapter:

LO 1 **Budget:** A plan of action that forecasts future transactions, activities, and events in financial or nonfinancial terms.

LO 5 **Budgeted balance sheet:** A statement that projects the financial position of an organization at the end of a future period.

LO 3 **Budgeted income statement:** A statement that projects an organization's net income based on the estimated revenues and expenses for a future period.

LO 1 **Budgeting:** The process of identifying, gathering, summarizing, and communicating financial and nonfinancial information about an organization's future activities.

LO 3 **Capital expenditures budget:** A detailed plan outlining the amount and timing of anticipated payments for long-term assets for a future period.

LO 4 **Cash budget:** A projection of the cash receipts and cash payments for a future period.

LO 3 **Cost of goods manufactured budget:** A detailed schedule that summarizes the costs of production for a future period.

LO 3 **Direct labor budget:** A detailed schedule that identifies the quantity of direct labor needs for a future period and the labor costs associated with those needs.

LO 3 **Direct materials purchases budget:** A detailed schedule that identifies the quantity of purchases required for budgeted production and inventory needs and the costs associated with those purchases.

LO 3 **Manufacturing overhead budget:** A detailed schedule of anticipated manufacturing costs, other than direct materials and direct labor costs, that must be incurred to meet the production expectations of a future period.

LO 2 **Master budget:** A set of budgets that consolidates an organization's financial information into budgeted financial statements for a future period of time.

2. Production Budget

Dov's Bath Oils Production Budget For the Year Ended December 31, 20x2					
	Quarter				
	1	2	3	4	Year
Sales in Units (Budget 1)	4,000	?	?	?	?
Add Desired Units of Ending Finished Goods Inventory	300	?	?	600	600
Desired Total Units	4,300				
Less Desired Units of Beginning Finished Goods Inventory	400	?	?	?	400
Total Production Units	3,900	?	?	?	?

Note 1: Desired units of ending finished goods inventory = 10% of *next* quarter's budgeted sales.
Note 2: Desired units of beginning finished goods inventory = 10% of *current* quarter's budgeted sales.

3. Direct Materials Purchases Budget

Dov's Bath Oils Direct Materials Purchases Budget For the Year Ended December 31, 20x2					
	Quarter				
	1	2	3	4	Year
Total Production Units (Budget 2)	3,900	3,200	5,000	5,100	17,200
× 3 Ounces per Unit	3	?	?	?	?
Total Production Needs in Ounces	11,700	?	?	?	?
Add Desired Ounces of Ending Direct Materials Inventory	1,920	?	?	3,600	3,600
	13,620				
Less Desired Ounces of Beginning Direct Materials Inventory	2,340	?	?	?	2,340
Total Ounces of Direct Materials to be Purchased	11,280	?	?	?	
× Cost per Ounce	$ .10	?	?	?	?
Total Cost of Direct Materials Purchases	$ 1,128	?	?	?	?

Note 1: Desired ounces of ending direct materials inventory = 20% of *next* quarter's budgeted production needs in ounces.
Note 2: Desired ounces of beginning direct materials inventory = 20% of *current* quarter's budgeted production needs in ounces.
Note 3: Assume that budgeted production needs in ounces for the first quarter of 20x3 = 18,000 ounces.

4. Direct Labor Budget

Dov's Bath Oils Direct Labor Budget For the Year Ended December 31, 20x2					
	Quarter				
	1	2	3	4	Year
Total Production Units (Budget 2)	3,900	?	?	?	?
× Direct Labor Hours per Unit	.1	?	?	?	?
Total Direct Labor Hours	390	?	?	?	?
× Direct Labor Cost per Hour	$ 7	?	?	?	?
Total Direct Labor Cost	$2,730	?	?	?	?

5. Manufacturing Overhead Budget

Dov's Bath Oils Manufacturing Overhead Budget For the Year Ended December 31, 20x2					
	Quarter				
	1	2	3	4	Year
Variable Overhead Costs					
Factory Supplies ($.05)	$ 195	?	?	?	?
Employee Benefits ($.25)	975	?	?	?	?
Inspection ($.10)	390	?	?	?	?
Maintenance and Repair ($.15)	585	?	?	?	?
Utilities ($.05)	195	?	?	?	?
Total Variable Overhead	$2,340	?	?	?	?
Fixed Overhead Costs					
Depreciation, Machinery	$ 500	?	?	?	?
Depreciation, Building	700	?	?	?	?
Supervision	1,800	?	?	?	?
Maintenance and Repair	400	?	?	?	?
Other Overhead Expenses	600	?	?	?	?
Total Fixed Overhead	$4,000	?	?	?	?
Total Manufacturing Overhead Costs	$6,340	?	?	?	?

	Amount	Percent of Sales
Net Sales		
Radios	$ 780,000	43.94%
Appliances	640,000	36.06
Telephones	280,000	15.77
Miscellaneous	75,000	4.23
Net Sales	$1,775,000	100.00%
Less Cost of Goods Sold	763,425	43.01
Gross Margin	$1,011,575	56.99%

On the basis of this information and your analysis in **1**, what should the budget director say to the managers of the Motor Division? Mention specific areas of the budget that may need to be revised and give your reasons.

Managerial Reporting and Analysis

Interpreting Management Reports

MRA 1. **LO 1 Interpreting Budget Formulation Policies**

Husin Corporation is a manufacturing company with annual sales of $25,000,000. The controller, Victor Subroto, appointed Yolanda Alvillar as budget director. She created the following budget formulation policy based on a calendar-year accounting period.

May 20x2	Meeting of corporate officers and budget director to discuss corporate plans for 20x3.
June 20x2	Meeting(s) of division managers, department heads, and budget director to communicate 20x3 corporate objectives. At this time, relevant background data are distributed to all managers and a time schedule is established for development of 20x3 budget data.
July 20x2	Managers and department heads continue to develop budget data. Complete 20x3 monthly sales forecasts by product line and receive final sales estimates from sales vice president.
Aug. 20x2	Complete 20x3 plans for monthly production activity and anticipated inventory levels. Division managers and department heads should communicate preliminary budget figures to budget director for coordination and distribution to other operating areas.
Sept. 20x2	Development of preliminary 20x3 master budget. Revised budget data from all functional areas to be received. Budget director will coordinate staff activities, including the integration of labor requirements, direct materials and supplies requirements, unit cost estimates, cash requirements, and profit estimates, and prepare preliminary 20x3 master budget.
Oct. 20x2	Meeting with corporate officers to discuss preliminary 20x3 master budget. Corporate officers should communicate any corrections, additions, or deletions to budget director. All authorized changes to be incorporated into the 20x3 master budget.
Nov. 20x2	Submit final draft of 20x3 master budget to corporate officers for approval. Publish approved budget and distribute to all corporate officers, division managers, and department heads.

REQUIRED

1. Comment on the proposed budget formulation policy.
2. What changes in the policy would you recommend?

Formulating Management Reports

MRA 2. **LO 1 LO 2 LO 3 Budgeted Financial Statement Preparation**

Assume that you have just signed a partnership agreement with your cousin Eddie to open a bookstore near the college campus. You believe that you will be able to provide excellent service at prices lower than your local competition. To begin operations, you and Eddie have decided to apply for a loan from the Small Business Administration (SBA). Part of the application requires you to submit financial statements forecasting the bookstore's first two years of operating activity and its financial position at the end of the second year. The application is due within six weeks. Because of your expertise in accounting and business, Eddie has asked you to develop the budgeted financial statements.

REQUIRED

1. List the budgeted financial statements and supporting schedules you believe you must prepare.
2. Who needs the budgeted financial statements?
3. Why are you preparing budgeted financial statements?
4. What information do you need to develop on the budgeted financial statements? How will you obtain the information?
5. When must you have the budgeted financial statements prepared?
6. In what ways can you and Eddie use the budgeted financial statements that you have prepared?

International Company

MRA 3.
LO 4 Goals and the Budgeting Process

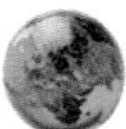

3M manufactures a variety of products ranging from office supplies to household sponges and laser imagers for CAT scanners to reflective materials for roads. Because of the company's aggressive research and development activities, many of its products have been redesigned to satisfy the needs of Asian customers. Business has been so successful that sales in the Asia-Pacific division of 3M have doubled in the past five years. Facilities are in Malaysia, South Korea, India, Thailand, and Taiwan.[5]

Based on 3M's strategic plan for next year, two goals for the Asia-Pacific division have been developed. They include a 25 percent growth in sales volume and the construction of a $14 million manufacturing plant in Shanghai that will begin operations in the third quarter of the year.

REQUIRED

The manager for the Asia-Pacific Division is preparing the cash budget for next year's operations. How would the budgeted cash receipts and cash payments on the cash budget be affected by the two goals?

Excel Spreadsheet Analysis

MRA 4.
LO 2 The Budgeting Process
LO 3

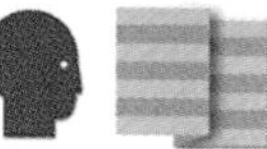

Refer to the Hi-Flyer Company's master budget presented in this chapter for the year ending December 31, 20x1. Skye King has decided to increase the budgeted sales in the first quarter by 5,000 units to reflect sales to a new customer in Canada. The expenses for this sale will include direct materials, direct labor, variable manufacturing overhead, and variable selling and administrative expenses. The delivery expense for the Canadian customer will be $.18 per unit rather than the regular $.08 per unit. The desired units of beginning finished goods inventory will remain at 1,000 units.

REQUIRED

Use the Excel Templates software and the changes stated above to complete the following:

1. Prepare a revised budgeted income statement and supporting operating budgets.
2. What was the change in income from operations? Would you recommend accepting the order? Why?

Internet Case

MRA 5.
LO 1 The Budgeting Process

Managers of the HON Company and HON Industries use relevant operational information to prepare quarterly budgets for the next year. HON's web site presents the actual results of some of the long-term and short-term plans that were originally included in company budgets. Prepare a short report that includes a list of the historical or planned events, activities, or factors that would influence the information in the next period's budget for HON Industries. Conduct your research by reviewing the Decision Point in this chapter, the *Management Accounting* article on which the Decision Point is based, and the most recent operations review in the Investor Relations section of the HON Industries web site (see the Needles Accounting Resource Center web site at http://college.hmco.com for access to these materials).

ENDNOTES

1. Ralph Drtina, Steve Hoeger, and John Schaub, "Continuous Budgeting at the HON Company," *Management Accounting*, Institute of Management Accountants, January 1996.
2. Adapted from Larry Ponemon, "Building an Effective Business Ethics Process," *Management Accounting*, Institute of Management Accountants, June 1996.
3. From "Budgeting for an International Business," by Paul V. Mannino and Ken Milani. *Management Accounting*, February 1992, p. 39. Reprinted courtesy of the Institute of Management Accountants.
4. John Case, "Opening the Books," *Harvard Business Review*, March–April 1997.
5. "3M: Business Booms in Asia," *Asian Business*, Vol. 29, No. 22, February 1993.

25 Performance Measurement Using Standard Costing

LEARNING OBJECTIVES

1. Define *standard costs* and describe how managers use standard costs in the management cycle.
2. Identify the six elements of, and compute, a standard unit cost.
3. Describe how to control costs through variance analysis.
4. Compute and analyze direct materials variances.
5. Compute and analyze direct labor variances.
6. Define and prepare a flexible budget.
7. Compute and analyze manufacturing overhead variances.
8. Explain how variances are used to evaluate managers' performance.

During October, the number of good units produced was used to compute the 2,100 standard machine hours allowed. Your analysis of these data should include the steps outlined below.

REQUIRED

1. Prepare a monthly flexible budget for the company for operating activity at 2,000 machine hours, 2,200 machine hours, and 2,500 machine hours.
2. Formulate a flexible budget formula for the company.
3. The company's normal operating capacity is 2,200 machine hours per month. Compute the fixed manufacturing overhead rate at this level of activity. Then break the rate down into individual rates for each element of fixed manufacturing overhead.
4. Prepare a detailed comparative cost analysis for October. All variable and fixed manufacturing overhead costs should be included. Your report form should include the following five columns: (a) cost category, (b) cost per machine hour, (c) costs applied, (d) actual costs incurred, and (e) variance.
5. Develop a manufacturing overhead variance analysis for October that identifies the controllable manufacturing overhead variance and the manufacturing overhead volume variance.
6. Prepare an analysis of the variances. Are some of the fixed costs controllable by the manager? Defend your answer.

Internet Case

MRA 5.

LO 1 Resources for Development of Standards

Assume that you have recently taken a job at a company that manufactures components for automobiles. You have been assigned the task of establishing manufacturing standards. You want to gather as much background information as you can about the development of manufacturing standards and hope to find organizations that can give you helpful information.

Use a standard search engine, such as Yahoo, to search for sites about standards, manufacturing, and automobile manufacturers that may be of help. Visit the sites that look most interesting. Make a list of the five sites you think will be most useful. Bring your list to class and compare your findings with those of your classmates.

ENDNOTES

1. http://www.rubgrp.com/main.html. Other sources include brochures and practice manual pages received from The Rubicon Group and a personal telephone interview with Dennis Evans, of the Rubicon Group, January 30, 1998.
2. "Up to Speed: United Parcel Service Gets Deliveries Done by Driving Its Workers," *The Wall Street Journal*, April 22, 1986.
3. Carole Cheatham, "Updating Standard Cost Systems," *Journal of Accountancy*, The American Institute of Certified Public Accountants, December 1990.
4. http://www.euro.net/innovation/Management_Base_/Man_Guide_Rel_1.081/controland-monitoring.html, July 14, 1997.

26 Performance Management and Evaluation

LEARNING OBJECTIVES

1. Describe how the balanced scorecard aligns performance with organizational goals and explain the balanced scorecard's role in the management cycle.
2. Discuss performance measurement and state the issues that affect management's ability to measure performance.
3. Define *responsibility accounting* and describe the role responsibility centers play in performance management and evaluation.
4. Prepare performance reports for the various types of responsibility centers, including reports based on flexible budgets for cost centers and variable costing for profit centers.
5. Use the traditional performance measures of return on investment and residual income to evaluate investment centers.
6. Use economic value added to evaluate investment centers.
7. Explain how properly linked performance incentives and measures add value for all stakeholders in performance management and evaluation.

DECISION POINT: A MANAGER'S FOCUS

Vail Resorts PEAKS at Vail Resorts is an all-in-one card for guests of four Colorado vacation spots. The PEAKS card can be used at Vail, Breckenridge, Keystone, and Beaver Creek resorts to pay for lift tickets, skiing or snowboarding lessons, equipment rentals, dining, and more. Guests like its convenience and its program for earning points toward free or reduced-rate lift tickets, dining, and lodging. Guests enroll in the PEAKS system by filling out a one-page form that asks for their name, street address, e-mail address, phone number, date of birth, credit card number, and a signed charge privilege authorization. Data for up to eight family members may be linked into one membership account. Each family member receives a bar-coded picture identification card that is scanned each time he or she rides the ski lifts, attends ski school, or charges purchases, dining, or lodging. The card is usually worn on a souvenir cord around the guest's neck and can be used whenever the guest visits one of the four resorts.[1] How can the managers of the Vail Resorts Management Company use the PEAKS card and its integrated data base to better manage and evaluate the performance of their resorts?

Managers like PEAKS because it enables them to collect huge amounts of information in a very simple way and because the data have so many uses. Guests enter new data each time they scan their cards. Those data become part of an integrated management information system that allows managers to measure and control costs, quality, and performance at all four resorts. The system's ability to store both financial and nonfinancial data about all aspects of the resorts enables the managers to learn about and balance the interests of all the company's stakeholders: financial (investors), learning and growth (employees), internal business processes, and customers. The system allows managers to answer traditional financial questions about measuring cost of sales and valuing inventory (such as food ingredients in its restaurants and merchandise in its shops) and to obtain performance information about the resorts' activities, products, services, and customers. In addition, managers and employees receive timely feedback about their performance measures so that they can continuously improve.

Critical Thinking Question: How do managers use an integrated data base to evaluate performance?
Answer: The data base gives managers real-time access to information about cost, quality, and performance.

Organizational Goals and the Balanced Scorecard

OBJECTIVE

1 Describe how the balanced scorecard aligns performance with organizational goals and explain the balanced scorecard's role in the management cycle

Related Text Assignments:
Q: 1, 2, 3, 4
SE: 1
E: 1, 2
SD: 1
MRA: 1

The **balanced scorecard**, developed by Robert S. Kaplan and David P. Norton, is a framework that links the perspectives of an organization's four basic stakeholder groups—financial (investors), learning and growth (employees), internal business processes, and customers—with the organization's mission and vision, performance measures, strategic plan, and resources. To succeed, an organization must add value for all groups in both the short and the long term. Thus, an organization will determine each group's objectives and translate them into performance measures that have specific, quantifiable performance targets. Ideally, managers should be able to see how their actions contribute to the achievement of organizational goals and understand how their compensation is related to their actions. The balanced scorecard assumes that an organization will get only what it measures.

VIDEO CASE

Harley-Davidson, Inc.

Objectives

- To describe the role a performance measurement and evaluation system plays in business today.
- To become familiar with how the balanced scorecard provides a framework for performance management and accountability.
- To show how responsibility accounting is useful in performance evaluation.
- To understand the value of linking organizational goals, objectives, measures, targets, and performance-based pay.

Background for the Case

Harley-Davidson continues to excel at providing motorcyclists and the general public an expanding line of motorcycles and branded products and services. Strong sales of motorcycles, apparel, parts, insurance, product licensing, and financial services have enabled the company to sustain and improve upon its success. Harley's journey to success can be charted through its performance management and evaluation system. Performance measures like market share, units shipped, revenue, operating profit, and number of employees illustrate its remarkable turnaround. In the 1980s, Harley overcame near bankruptcy to emerge today as the internationally recognized company that "fulfills dreams through the experience of motorcycling." Like many other companies, Harley-Davidson uses a performance management and evaluation system to identify how well it is doing, where it is going, and what improvements will make it more profitable.

For more information about Harley-Davidson, Inc., visit the company's web site through the Needles Accounting Resource Center at

http://college.hmco.com

Required

View the video on Harley-Davidson that accompanies this book. As you are watching the video, take notes related to the following questions

1. What role does performance measurement and evaluation play in business today?
2. In your own words, describe the balanced scorecard. Who are its stakeholders?
3. Define responsibility accounting. Why is it useful in performance evaluation?
4. Explain how Harley uses PEP to link performance goals, objectives, measures, and targets. Why does this linking process improve the effectiveness of its performance management and evaluation system?

The Balanced Scorecard and the Management Cycle

We will use the Decision Point about the PEAKS card to illustrate the use of the balanced scorecard in the management cycle.

Discussion Question: Whose interests must a manager consider? **Answer:** The interests of the four basic stakeholder groups—financial (investors), learning and growth (employees), internal business processes, and customers. Some businesses, such as Harley-Davidson, also include the interests of government and their community (see Focus on Business Practice, p. 1115).

PLANNING During the planning stage, the balanced scorecard provides a framework that enables managers to translate their organization's vision and strategy into operational terms. Managers evaluate the company vision from the perspective of each stakeholder group and seek to answer one key question for each group:

- **Financial (investors):** To achieve our organization's vision, how should we appear to our shareholders?
- **Learning and growth (employees):** To achieve our organization's vision, how should we sustain our ability to improve and change?
- **Internal business processes:** To succeed, at what business processes must our organization excel?
- **Customers:** To achieve our organization's vision, how should we appear to our customers?

Point to Emphasize: The alignment of an organization's strategy with all the perspectives of the balanced scorecard results in performance objectives that benefit all stakeholders.

These key questions align the organization's strategy from all perspectives and result in performance objectives that are mutually beneficial to all stakeholders. Once the organization's objectives are set, managers can select performance measures and set performance targets to translate objectives into an action plan.

For example, if Vail Resorts' collective vision and strategy is customer satisfaction, the following overall objectives might be established:

Perspective	Objective
Financial (investors)	Customer satisfaction means revenue growth.
Learning and growth (employees)	Customer satisfaction means cross-trained, customer-service-oriented employees.
Internal business processes	Customer satisfaction means reliable products and short delivery cycles.
Customers	Customer satisfaction means keeping customer loyalty through repeat visits and redeemed PEAKS points.

These overall objectives would be translated into specific performance objectives and measures for managers. For example, a ski lift manager's performance objective for customer satisfaction might be measured in terms of the following:

- **Financial (investors):** hourly lift cost, lift ticket sales in dollars and in units
- **Learning and growth (employees):** number of cross-trained tasks per employee, employee turnover
- **Internal business processes:** number of accident-free days, number and cost of mechanical breakdowns, average lift cycle time (that is, the time between getting in line to ride the ski lift and completing the ski run)
- **Customers:** average number of ski runs per daily lift ticket, number of repeat customers, number of PEAKS points redeemed

Figure 1 summarizes the planning stage of the management cycle, during which Vail Resorts' managers first link their organization's vision and strategy to objectives, then link the objectives to logical performance measures, and, finally, set performance targets. As a result, a ski lift manager will have a mix of performance measures that balances the perspectives and needs of all stakeholders.

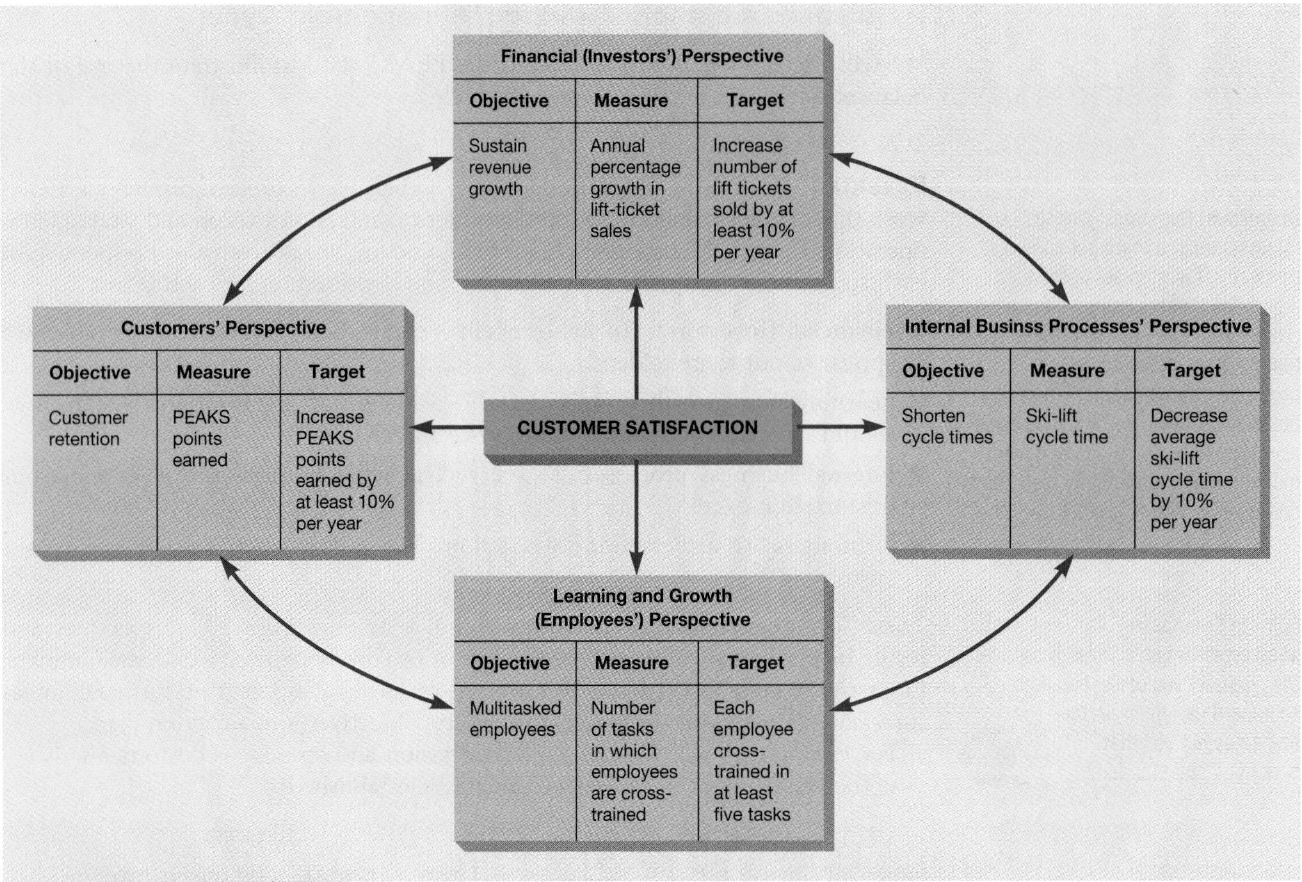

Financial (Investors') Perspective

Objective	Measure	Target
Sustain revenue growth	Annual percentage growth in lift-ticket sales	Increase number of lift tickets sold by at least 10% per year

Customers' Perspective

Objective	Measure	Target
Customer retention	PEAKS points earned	Increase PEAKS points earned by at least 10% per year

CUSTOMER SATISFACTION

Internal Businss Processes' Perspective

Objective	Measure	Target
Shorten cycle times	Ski-lift cycle time	Decrease average ski-lift cycle time by 10% per year

Learning and Growth (Employees') Perspective

Objective	Measure	Target
Multitasked employees	Number of tasks in which employees are cross-trained	Each employee cross-trained in at least five tasks

Figure 1
Sample Balanced Scorecard of Linked Objectives, Measures, and Targets

Source: Adapted from Robert S. Kaplan and David P. Norton, "Using the Balanced Scorecard as a Strategic Management System," *Harvard Business Review*, January–February 1996.

EXECUTING Managers use the mutually agreed-upon strategic objectives for the entire organization as the basis for decision making within their individual areas of responsibility. This practice ensures that they consider the needs of all stakeholder groups. For example, when making decisions about available ski lift capacity, the ski lift manager at Vail Resorts will balance such factors as lift-ticket sales, snow conditions, equipment reliability, trained staff availability, and length of wait for ski lifts.

Teaching Note: Emphasize that if managers want results, they must understand the causal relationship between their actions and the organization's overall performance. If the relationship can be measured and tracked, it can be improved.

When managers understand the causal relationship between their actions and their company's overall performance, they can see new ways to be more effective. For example, a ski lift manager may hypothesize that short waiting lines for the ski lifts would improve customer satisfaction and lead to more visits to the ski lift. The ski lift manager could test this possible cause-and-effect relationship by measuring and tracking the length of ski lift waiting lines and the number of visits to the ski lift. If a causal relationship exists, the manager can improve the performance of the ski lift operation by doing everything possible to ensure that waiting lines are short.

REVIEWING Managers will review financial and nonfinancial results frequently during the year, at year end, and over longer periods to evaluate their strategies in meeting the objectives and performance targets set during the planning stage. They will compare performance objectives and targets with actual results to determine if the targets were met, what measures need to be changed, and what strategies or

Figure 2
The Balanced Scorecard and the Management Cycle

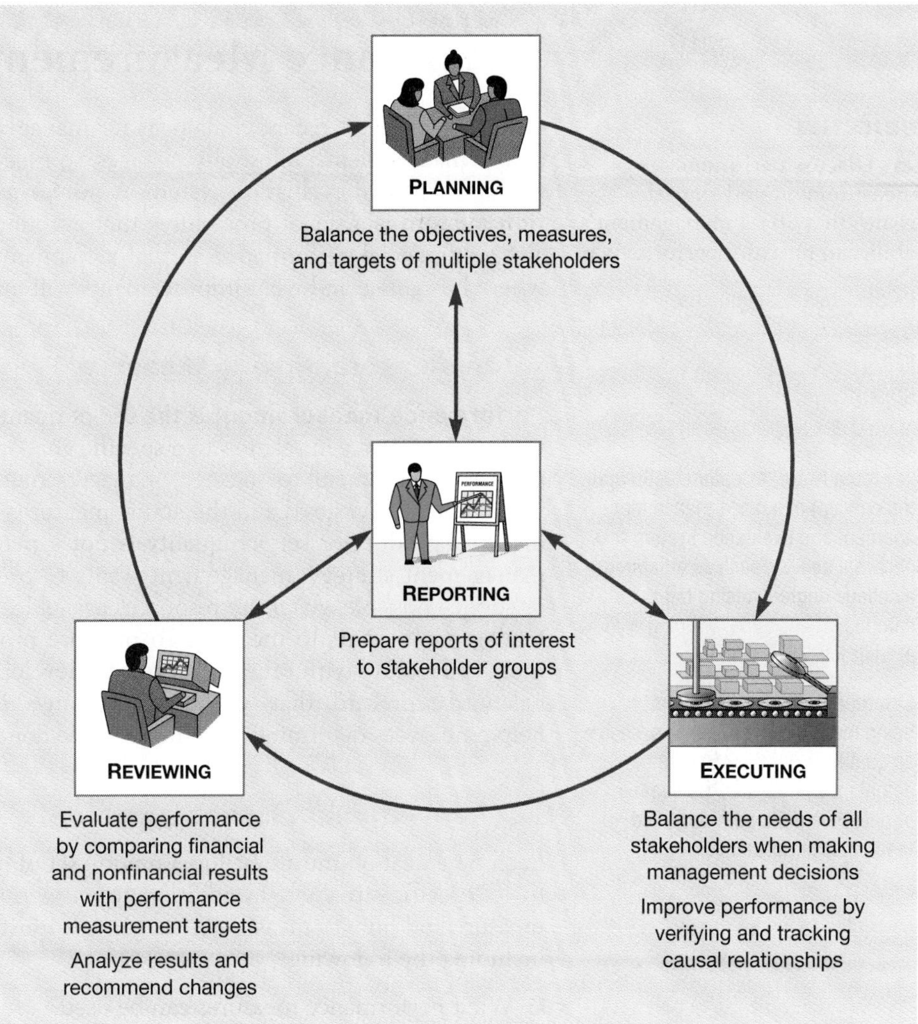

objectives need revision. For example, the ski lift manager at Vail Resorts would analyze the reasons for performance gaps and make recommendations to improve the performance for the ski lift area.

REPORTING Finally, during the reporting stage of the management cycle, a variety of reports are prepared. For example, the data base makes it possible to prepare financial performance reports, customer PEAKS statements, internal business process reports for targeted performance measures and results, and performance appraisals of individual employees. Such reports enable managers to monitor and evaluate performance measures that add value for stakeholder groups.

As you can see in Figure 2, the balanced scorecard adds dimension to the management cycle. Managers plan, execute, review, and report on the organization's performance from multiple perspectives. By balancing all stakeholders' needs, managers are more likely to achieve their objectives in both the short and the long term.

FOCUS ON BUSINESS PRACTICE

Harley-Davidson, Inc., has identified not four but six stakeholder groups. In addition to balancing the needs of investors, employees, business processes, and customers, Harley managers also consider the interests of government and the community at large. Taking a broader perspective enables the company to sustain its competitive advantage and implement effective employee reward programs.[2]

Performance Measurement

OBJECTIVE

2 Discuss performance measurement and state the issues that affect management's ability to measure performance

Related Text Assignments:
Q: 5
E: 3, 4
SD: 1, 4, 5
MRA: 2, 3

Teaching Note: Ask students to apply the concept of a performance management and evaluation system to a personal activity, such as obtaining a college degree, raising funds for a campus organization, or doing well at their job.

Common Student Error: What is being measured by managers, such as quality, is not the same as the actual measures, such as number of defective units per hour, used to monitor performance.

One of the biggest recent challenges for managers is the realization that as a company's management philosophy changes, so must the measures in its performance management and evaluation system. A **performance management and evaluation system** is a set of procedures that account for and report on both financial and nonfinancial performance, so that a company can identify how well it is doing, where it is going, and what improvements will make it more profitable.

What to Measure, How to Measure

Performance measurement is the use of quantitative tools to gauge an organization's performance in relation to a specific goal or an expected outcome. For performance measurement to succeed, managers must be able to distinguish between what is being measured and the actual measures used to monitor performance. For instance, product or service quality is not a performance measure. It is part of a management strategy: management wants to produce the highest-quality product or service possible, given the resources available. Product or service quality is what management wants to measure. To measure product or service quality, managers must collaborate with other managers to develop a group of measures, such as the balanced scorecard, that will identify changes in product or service quality and help employees determine what needs to be done to improve quality.

Other Measurement Issues

Each organization must develop a unique set of performance measures appropriate to its specific situation. In addition to answering the basic questions of what to measure and how to measure, management must consider a variety of other issues, including the following:

- What performance measures can be used?
- How can managers monitor the level of product or service quality?
- How can managers monitor production and other business processes to identify areas that need improvement?
- How can managers measure customer satisfaction?
- How can managers monitor financial performance?
- Are there other stakeholders to whom a manager is accountable?
- What performance measures do government entities impose on the company?
- How can a manager measure the company's effect on the environment?

Focus on International Business

The *tableau de bord*, or "dashboard," was developed by French process engineers around 1900 as a concise performance measurement system that helped managers understand the cause-and-effect relationships between business actions and performance. The indicators, both financial and nonfinancial, allowed managers at any level to monitor their progress in terms of the mission and objectives of their unit and their company overall. Like a set of nested Russian dolls, each unit's key success factors and key performance indicators were integrated with those of other units with which it was interdependent and needed to collaborate. The dashboard continues to encourage a performance measurement system that focuses on and supports an organization's strategic plan.[3]

Responsibility Accounting

OBJECTIVE

3 Define ***responsibility accounting*** and describe the role responsibility centers play in performance management and evaluation

Related Text Assignments:
Q: 6, 7, 8, 9, 10, 11, 12
SE: 2, 3
E: 5, 6, 7
P: 1, 3, 7
SD: 2, 5
MRA: 2

As part of their performance management systems, many organizations assign resources to specific areas of responsibility and track how the managers of those areas use those resources. For example, DaimlerChrysler Corp. assigns resources to its Jeep, Eagle, and Mercedes automotive divisions and holds the managers of those divisions responsible for generating revenue and managing costs. In addition, the company may give the managers resources to invest in assets that will support the growth of their divisions. Within each division, other managers are assigned responsibility for such tasks as manufacturing subassemblies or assembling automobiles. All managers at all levels are then evaluated in terms of their ability to manage their areas of responsibility in keeping with organizational goals.

To assist in performance management and evaluation, many organizations use responsibility accounting. **Responsibility accounting** is an information system that classifies data according to areas of responsibility and reports each area's activities by including only the revenue, cost, and resource categories that the assigned manager can control. A **responsibility center** is an organizational unit whose manager has been assigned the responsibility of managing a portion of the organization's resources. The activity of a responsibility center dictates the extent of a manager's responsibility.

Types of Responsibility Centers

Teaching Note: Ask students to identify at least one example of each type of responsibility center.

There are five types of responsibility centers: (1) cost centers, (2) discretionary cost centers, (3) revenue centers, (4) profit centers, and (5) investment centers.

COST CENTERS A responsibility center whose manager is accountable only for controllable costs that have well-defined relationships between the center's resources and products or services is called a **cost center**. Manufacturing companies such as DaimlerChrysler, Apple Computer, and Kraft use cost centers to manage assembly plants, where the relationship between the costs of resources (direct material, direct labor) and the resulting products is well defined.

Nonmanufacturing organizations use cost centers to manage activities in which resources are clearly linked with a service provided at no additional charge. For example, in nursing homes and hospitals, there is a clear relationship between the costs of food and direct labor and the number of inpatient meals served.

The performance of a cost center is usually evaluated by comparing an activity's actual cost with its budgeted cost and analyzing the resulting variances. You may recall this performance evaluation process from the chapter on standard costing.

DISCRETIONARY COST CENTERS A responsibility center whose manager is accountable for costs only and in which the relationship between resources and products or services produced is not well defined is called a **discretionary cost center**. Units that perform administrative activities, such as accounting, human resources, and legal services, are typical examples of discretionary cost centers. These centers, like cost centers, have approved budgets that set spending limits.

Because the spending and use of resources in discretionary cost centers are not clearly linked to the production of a product or service, cost-based measures cannot usually be used to evaluate performance (although such centers are penalized if they exceed their approved budgets). For example, among the performance measures used to evaluate the research and development activities at manufacturing companies such as DaimlerChrysler, Monsanto, and Intel are the number of patents obtained and the number of cost-saving innovations developed. At service organizations, such as the United Way, a common measure of administrative activities is how low their costs are as a percentage of total contributions.

REVENUE CENTERS A responsibility center whose manager is accountable primarily for revenue and whose success is based on its ability to generate revenue is called a **revenue center**. Examples of revenue centers are Hertz's national car reservation center and the clothing retailer Nordstrom's e-commerce order department. A revenue center's performance is usually evaluated by comparing its actual revenue with its budgeted revenue and analyzing the resulting variances. Performance measures at both manufacturing and service organizations may include sales dollars, number of customer sales, or sales revenue per minute.

PROFIT CENTERS A responsibility center whose manager is accountable for both revenue and costs and for the resulting operating income is called a **profit center**. A good example is the local store of a national chain such as Wal-Mart, Kinko's, or Jiffy Lube. The performance of a profit center is usually evaluated by comparing the figures in its actual income statement with the figures in its master or flexible budget income statement. You may recall this type of comparison from previous chapters.

INVESTMENT CENTERS A responsibility center whose manager is accountable for profit generation and can also make significant decisions about the resources the center uses is called an **investment center**. For example, the president of DaimlerChrysler's Jeep Division, the president of Harley-Davidson's Buell subsidiary, and the president of Brinker International's Chili's Grill and Bar Concept can control revenues, costs, and the investment of assets to achieve organizational goals. The performance of these centers is evaluated using such measures as return on investment, residual income, and economic value added. These measures are used in all types of organizations, both manufacturing and nonmanufacturing, and are discussed later in this chapter.

The key characteristics of the five types of responsibility centers are summarized in Table 1.

Organizational Structure and Performance Management

Teaching Strategy: Obtain the organization chart for your college, your city government, or a local business and use it to discuss the types of responsibility centers.

Much can be learned about an organization by examining how its managers organize activities and resources. A company's organizational structure formalizes its lines of managerial authority and control. An **organization chart** is a visual representation of an organization's hierarchy of responsibility for the purposes of management control. Within an organization chart, the five types of responsibility centers are arranged by level of management authority and control.

A responsibility accounting system establishes a communications network within an organization that is ideal for gathering and reporting information about the operations of each area of responsibility. The system is used to prepare budgets

FOCUS ON BUSINESS TECHNOLOGY

There is a new profession—information architect. An information architect develops meaningful ways to report information in print and on the web. In *Understanding USA*, Richard Saul Wurman and a team of 12 information architects have created a graph-rich book (downloadable at http://www.understandingusa.com or for sale in bookstores) that is the result of a $1 million project backed by many blue-chip organizations. The team's message to managers: Keep it simple. If you define what is important and what you can omit, and if you stay honest, reporting information becomes simple.[4]

Table 1. Types of Responsibility Centers

Responsibility Center	Manager Accountable For	How Performance Is Measured	Examples
Cost center	Only controllable costs; there are well-defined links between the costs of resources and the resulting products or services	Compare actual costs with flexible and master budget costs Analyze resulting variances	Product: Manufacturing assembly plants Service: Food service for hospital inpatients
Discretionary cost center	Only controllable costs; the links between the costs of resources and the resulting products or services are *not* well defined	Compare actual non-cost-based measures with targets Determine compliance with preapproved budgeted spending limits	Product or service: Administrative activities such as accounting, human resources, and research and development
Revenue center	Revenue generation	Compare actual revenue with budgeted revenue Analyze resulting variances	Product: Phone or e-commerce sales for pizza delivery Service: National car-rental reservation center
Profit center	Operating income resulting from controllable revenues and costs	Compare actual variable costing income statement with the budgeted income statement	Product or service: Local store of a national chain such as Wal-Mart, Kinko's, or Jiffy Lube
Investment center	Controllable revenues, costs, and the investment of resources to achieve organizational goals	Return on investment Residual income Economic value added	Product: Jeep Division of DaimlerChrysler Service: Chili's Grill and Bar Concept of Brinker International, Inc.

by responsibility area and to report the actual results of each responsibility center. The report for a responsibility center should include only the costs, revenues, and resources the manager of that center can control. Such costs and revenues are called **controllable costs and revenues** because they result from a manager's actions, influence, or decisions. A responsibility accounting system ensures that managers will not be held responsible for items they cannot change.

By examining a typical corporate organization chart, you can see how a responsibility accounting system works. Figure 3 shows part of the management structure for Café Cubano, a multiconcept restaurant chain like Brinker International, Inc., or Vicorp Restaurants. Typically, several vice presidents report to the president of a restaurant division like Chili's or Village Inn. Notice that the figure shows examples of all five types of responsibility centers. The office of Consuelo Jorges, the division president, is an investment center because capital investment decisions are made at the division level. The Vice President—Restaurants, Ruben Lopez, manages both profit and revenue centers. The Vice President—Administration, Manuel Segundo, supervises three discretionary cost centers, and the Vice President—Food Products, Orlena Torres, is responsible for the operation of the central kitchen, a cost center.

In a responsibility accounting system, the performance reports for each level of management are tailored to each manager's individual needs for information. Because the system provides a report for every manager and because lower-level managers report to higher-level managers, the same information may appear in varying formats in several different reports. When information about lower-level operations appears in upper-level managers' reports, it is usually summarized and

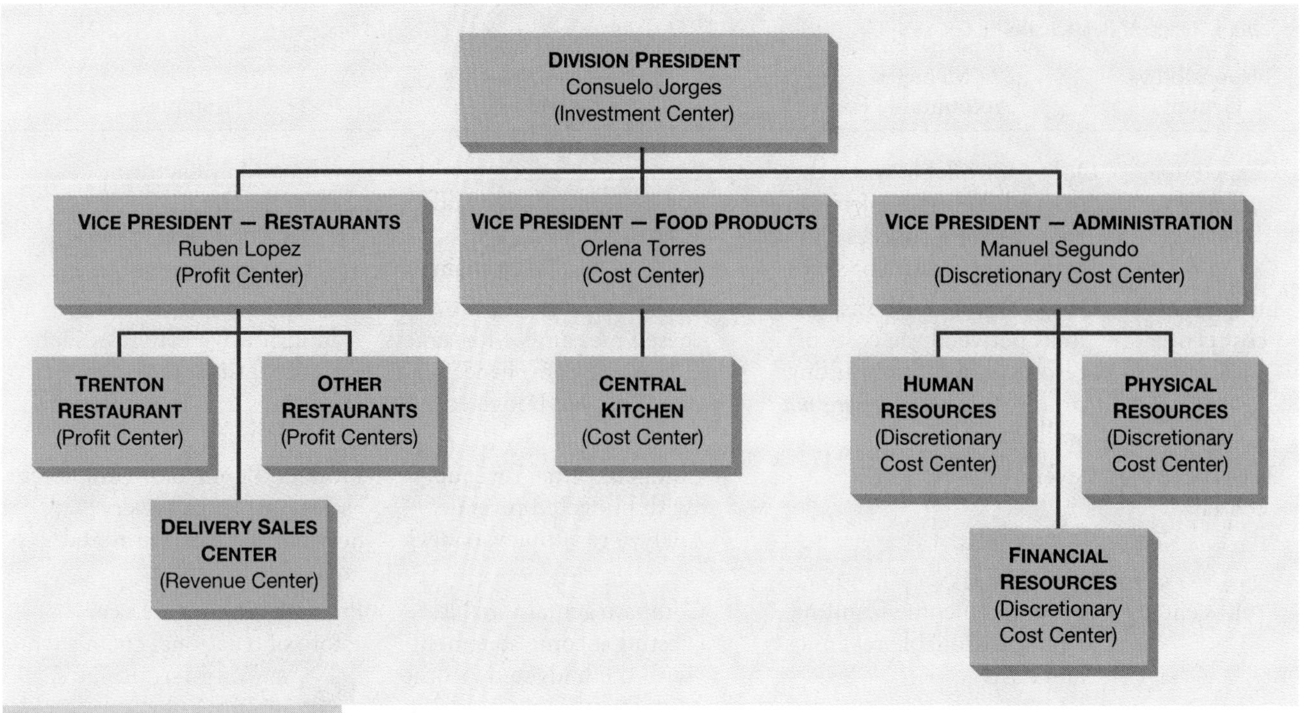

Figure 3
Partial Organization Chart of Café Cubano, a Restaurant Chain

condensed. Performance reporting by responsibility level enables an organization to trace the source of a cost, revenue, or resource to the manager who controls it and to evaluate that manager's performance accordingly.

Performance Evaluation

OBJECTIVE
4 Prepare performance reports for the various types of responsibility centers, including reports based on flexible budgets for cost centers and variable costing for profit centers

Related Text Assignments:
Q: 13, 14, 15, 16
SE: 4, 5
E: 8, 9, 10, 11
P: 1, 2, 3, 6, 7
SD: 4, 5

Because performance reports contain information about costs, revenues, and resources that are controllable by individual managers, they allow comparisons between actual performance and budget expectations. Such comparisons allow management to evaluate an individual's performance with respect to responsibility center objectives and companywide objectives and to recommend changes. It is important to emphasize that performance reports should contain only costs, revenues, and resources controllable by the manager. If a performance report includes items that the manager cannot control, the credibility of the entire responsibility accounting system can be called into question. It is up to management to structure and interpret the performance results fairly.

The content and format of a performance report depend on the nature of the responsibility center. Let us now take a closer look at the performance reports for cost centers and profit centers.

Evaluating Cost Center Performance

Point to Emphasize: Only controllable items should be included on a manager's performance report.

Teaching Note: Use SE 4 to introduce the performance report format for a cost center.

Orlena Torres, the Vice President—Food Products at Café Cubano, is responsible for the central kitchen, where basic preparation is done on the various food products the restaurants sell. Because the costs in the central kitchen have well-defined relationships with the resulting products, it is a cost center. To ensure that the central kitchen is meeting its performance goals, Torres has decided to evaluate the performance of each food item produced. To do so, she will prepare a separate

Exhibit 1
Central Kitchen's Performance Report on Café Cubano's House Dressing

	Actual Results	Variance	Flexible Budget	Variance	Master Budget
Gallons produced	1,200	0	1,200	200 (U)	1,000
Center costs					
Direct materials ($.25 per gallon)	$312	$12 (U)	$300	$50 (U)	$250
Direct labor ($.05 per gallon)	72	12 (U)	60	10 (U)	50
Variable overhead ($.03 per gallon)	33	3 (F)	36	6 (U)	30
Fixed overhead	2	3 (F)	5	0	5
Total cost	$419	$18 (U)	$401	$66 (U)	$335
Performance measures					
Defect-free gallons to total produced	.98	.01 (U)	N/A		.99
Average throughput time per gallon	11 minutes	1 minute (F)	N/A		12 minutes

Note: (F) = favorable comparison; (U) = unfavorable comparison.

report for each product that compares its actual costs with the corresponding amounts from the flexible and master budgets. The performance report for Café Cubano's House Dressing, one of the chain's signature menu items, is presented in Exhibit 1.

Instructional Strategy: Divide the class into groups and ask them to prepare the performance report for E 11. Emphasize the value of flexible budgeting. Have each group assess each of the other reports by taking a quick look at it and assigning a letter grade. Debrief the class by asking for the important features of a cost center's performance report.

FLEXIBLE BUDGETING You will recall that favorable (positive, or F) and unfavorable (negative, or U) variances between actual costs and the flexible budget can be further examined by using standard costing to compute specific variances for direct materials, direct labor, and manufacturing overhead. Also, you will remember that the flexible budget is a cost control tool used to evaluate performance and is derived by multiplying actual unit output by the standard unit costs. Refer to the chapter on standard costing for further information on performance evaluation using variances or the flexible budget.

Evaluating Profit Center Performance

Ruben Lopez, the Vice President—Restaurants, oversees many restaurants. Because the restaurants are profit centers, each is accountable for its own revenues and costs, and for the resulting operating income. A profit center's performance is usually evaluated by comparing its actual income statement results to its budgeted income statement.

VARIABLE COSTING **Variable costing** is a method of preparing profit center performance reports that classifies a manager's controllable costs as either variable or fixed. Variable costing produces a variable costing income statement instead of a traditional income statement. A variable costing income statement is the same as a contribution income statement, the format of which you may recall from its use in cost-volume-profit analysis. Such an income statement is useful in performance management and evaluation because it focuses on cost variability and the profit center's contribution to operating income.

Teaching Strategy: In class, have students work in teams to prepare the performance report for E 9. Emphasize the variable costing income statement approach.

When variable costing is used to evaluate profit center performance, the variable cost of goods sold and the variable selling and administrative expenses are subtracted from sales to arrive at the contribution margin for the center. All controllable fixed costs of a profit center, including those from manufacturing, selling, or

Exhibit 2
Variable Costing Income Statement Versus Traditional Income Statement for Trenton Restaurant

Variable Costing Income Statement		Traditional Income Statement	
Sales	$2,500	Sales	$2,500
Variable cost of goods sold	1,575	Cost of goods sold	1,745
Variable selling expenses	325	($1,575 + $170 = $1,745)	
Contribution margin	$ 600	Gross margin	$ 755
Fixed manufacturing costs	170	Variable selling expenses	325
Fixed selling expenses	230	Fixed selling expenses	230
Profit center income	$ 200	Profit center income	$ 200

administrative activities, are subtracted from the contribution margin to determine the operating income.

The variable costing income statement differs from the traditional income statement prepared for financial reporting, as illustrated by the two versions of income statements in Exhibit 2 for Trenton Restaurant, part of the Café Cubano restaurant chain. In the traditional income statement, all manufacturing costs are assigned to cost of goods sold, but in the variable costing income statement, only the variable manufacturing costs are included. Under variable costing, direct materials costs, direct labor costs, and variable manufacturing overhead costs are the only cost elements used to compute variable cost of goods sold. Fixed manufacturing costs are considered costs of the current accounting period. Notice that fixed manufacturing costs are listed with fixed selling expenses after the contribution margin has been computed.

The manager of a profit center may also want to measure and evaluate nonfinancial information. For example, Ruben Lopez of Café Cubano may want to track the number of food orders processed and the average amount of a sales order at Trenton Restaurant. The resulting report, based on variable costing and flexible budgeting, is shown in Exhibit 3.

Exhibit 3.
Performance Report Based on Variable Costing and Flexible Budgeting for Trenton Restaurant

	Actual Results	Variance	Flexible Budget	Variance	Master Budget
Meals served	750		750	250 (U)	1,000
Sales (average meal $2.85)	$2,500.00	$362.50 (F)	$2,137.50	$712.50 (U)	$2,850.00
Controllable variable costs					
Variable cost of goods sold ($1.50)	1,575.00	450.00 (U)	1,125.00	375.00 (F)	1,500.00
Variable selling expenses ($.40)	325.00	25.00 (U)	300.00	100.00 (F)	400.00
Contribution margin	$ 600.00	$112.50 (U)	$ 712.50	$237.50 (U)	$ 950.00
Controllable fixed costs					
Fixed manufacturing	170.00	30.00 (F)	200.00	0.00	200.00
Fixed selling	230.00	20.00 (F)	250.00	0.00	250.00
Profit center income	$ 200.00	$ 62.50 (U)	$ 262.50	$237.50 (U)	$ 500.00
Other nonfinancial performance measures					
Number of orders processed	300	50 (F)	N/A		250
Average sales order	$8.34	$3.06 (U)	N/A		$11.40

Note: (F) = favorable comparison; (U) = unfavorable comparison.

In Saarlouis, Germany, old blue jeans have found a new use as sound-deadening material in Ford Motor Company cars. Because of Ford's ethical recycling practices, old jeans are shredded, treated, and bonded before they are packed under the hood of every Ford Focus car produced in Ford's German manufacturing facility. What inventive recycling![5]

Although performance reports will vary in format depending on the type of responsibility center, they share some common themes. For example, all responsibility center reports compare a center's actual results to its budgeted figures and focus on the differences. Frequently, comparisons are made to a flexible budget as well as to the master budget. Only the items controllable by the manager are included in the performance report. Nonfinancial measures are also examined to achieve a more balanced view of the manager's responsibilities.

Evaluating Investment Center Performance

OBJECTIVE

5 Use the traditional performance measures of return on investment and residual income to evaluate investment centers

Related Text Assignments:
Q: 17, 18
SE: 6, 7, 8
E: 12
P: 3, 4, 5, 7, 8
SD: 3
MRA: 4

The performance evaluation of an investment center must do more than compare controllable revenues and costs with budgeted amounts. Because the managers of investment centers also control resources and invest in assets, other performance measures must be used to hold them accountable for revenues, costs, and the capital investments they specifically control. In this section we will focus on how to compute the traditional performance evaluation measures of return on investment and residual income. Later in the chapter we will discuss the relatively new performance measure of economic value added.

Return on Investment Traditionally the most common performance measure that takes into account both operating income and the assets invested to earn that income is **return on investment (ROI)**. Return on investment is computed as follows:

$$\text{Return on Investment (ROI)} = \frac{\text{Operating Income}}{\text{Assets Invested}}$$

In this formula, assets invested is the average of the beginning and ending asset balances for the period.

Of course, properly measuring the income and the assets specifically controlled by a manager is critical to the quality of this performance measure. Using ROI, it is possible to evaluate the manager of any investment center, whether it is an entire company or a unit within a company, such as a subsidiary, division, or other business segment. For example, assume that the Café Cubano Restaurant Division had actual operating income of \$610 and that the average assets invested were \$800. The master budget called for \$890 in operating income and \$1,000 in invested assets. As shown in Exhibit 4, the budgeted ROI for Consuelo Jorges, the president of the division, would be 89 percent, and the actual ROI would be 76 percent. The actual ROI was lower than the budgeted ROI because the division's actual operating income was lower than expected relative to the actual assets invested.

Common Student Error: Students often ignore profit margin and asset turnover and just remember the basic ROI formula. Emphasize that profit margin focuses on the income statement and asset turnover focuses on the balance sheet aspects of ROI.

For investment centers, the ROI computation is really the aggregate measure of many interrelationships. The basic ROI equation of Operating Income ÷ Assets Invested can be rewritten to show the many elements a manager can influence within the aggregate ROI number. Two important indicators of performance are profit margin and asset turnover. **Profit margin** is the ratio of operating income to sales; it represents the percentage of each sales dollar that results in profit. **Asset turnover** is the ratio of sales to average assets invested; it indicates the productivity

Exhibit 4
Performance Report Based on Return on Investment for the Café Cubano Restaurant Division

	Master Budget	Actual Results	Variance
Operating income	$ 890	$610	$280 (U)
Assets invested	$1,000	$800	$200 (F)
Performance measure			
ROI	89%	76%	13% (U)

ROI = Operating Income ÷ Assets Invested
$890 ÷ $1,000 = .89 = 89%
$610 ÷ $800 = .76 = 76%

of assets, or the number of sales dollars generated by each dollar invested in assets. Return on investment is equal to profit margin multiplied by asset turnover:

$$\text{ROI} = \text{Profit Margin} \times \text{Asset Turnover}$$

or

$$\text{ROI} = \frac{\text{Operating Income}}{\text{Sales}} \times \frac{\text{Sales}}{\text{Assets Invested}} = \frac{\text{Operating Income}}{\text{Assets Invested}}$$

Profit margin and asset turnover help to explain changes in ROI for a single investment center or differences of ROI among investment centers. Therefore, the formula ROI = Profit Margin × Asset Turnover is useful for analyzing and interpreting the elements that make up a business's overall return on investment.

Teaching Note: Use SD 3 to discuss how a manager's decisions affect ROI.

DuPont, one of the first organizations to recognize the many interrelationships that affect ROI, designed a formula similar to the one diagrammed in Figure 4. You can see that ROI is affected by a manager's decisions about pricing, product sales mix, capital budgeting for new facilities, product sales volume, and other financial matters. In essence, a single ROI number is a composite index of many cause-and-effect relationships and interdependent financial elements. A manager can improve ROI by increasing sales, decreasing costs, or decreasing assets.

Because of the many factors that affect return on investment, management should use this measure cautiously in evaluating performance. If ROI is overemphasized, investment center managers may react with business decisions that favor their personal ROI performance at the expense of companywide profits or the long-term success of other investment centers. To avoid such problems, other performance measures should always be used in conjunction with ROI. Possibilities include comparisons of revenues, costs, and operating income with budget amounts or past trends; sales growth percentages; market share percentages; or other key variables in the organization's activity. ROI should also be compared with budgeted goals and with past ROI trends because changes in this ratio over time can be more revealing than any single number.

Point to Emphasize: ROI is expressed as a percentage, and residual income is expressed in dollars.

RESIDUAL INCOME Because of the pitfalls of using ROI as a performance measure, other approaches to evaluating investment centers have evolved. For example, companies such as General Motors, General Electric, Coca-Cola, and UPS now use residual income to measure performance. **Residual income (RI)** is the operating income that an investment center earns above a minimum desired return on invested assets. Residual income is not a ratio, but a dollar amount. It is the amount of profit left after subtracting a predetermined desired income target for an investment center. The formula for computing the residual income of an investment center is as follows:

$$\text{Residual Income} = \text{Operating Income} - (\text{Desired ROI} \times \text{Assets Invested})$$

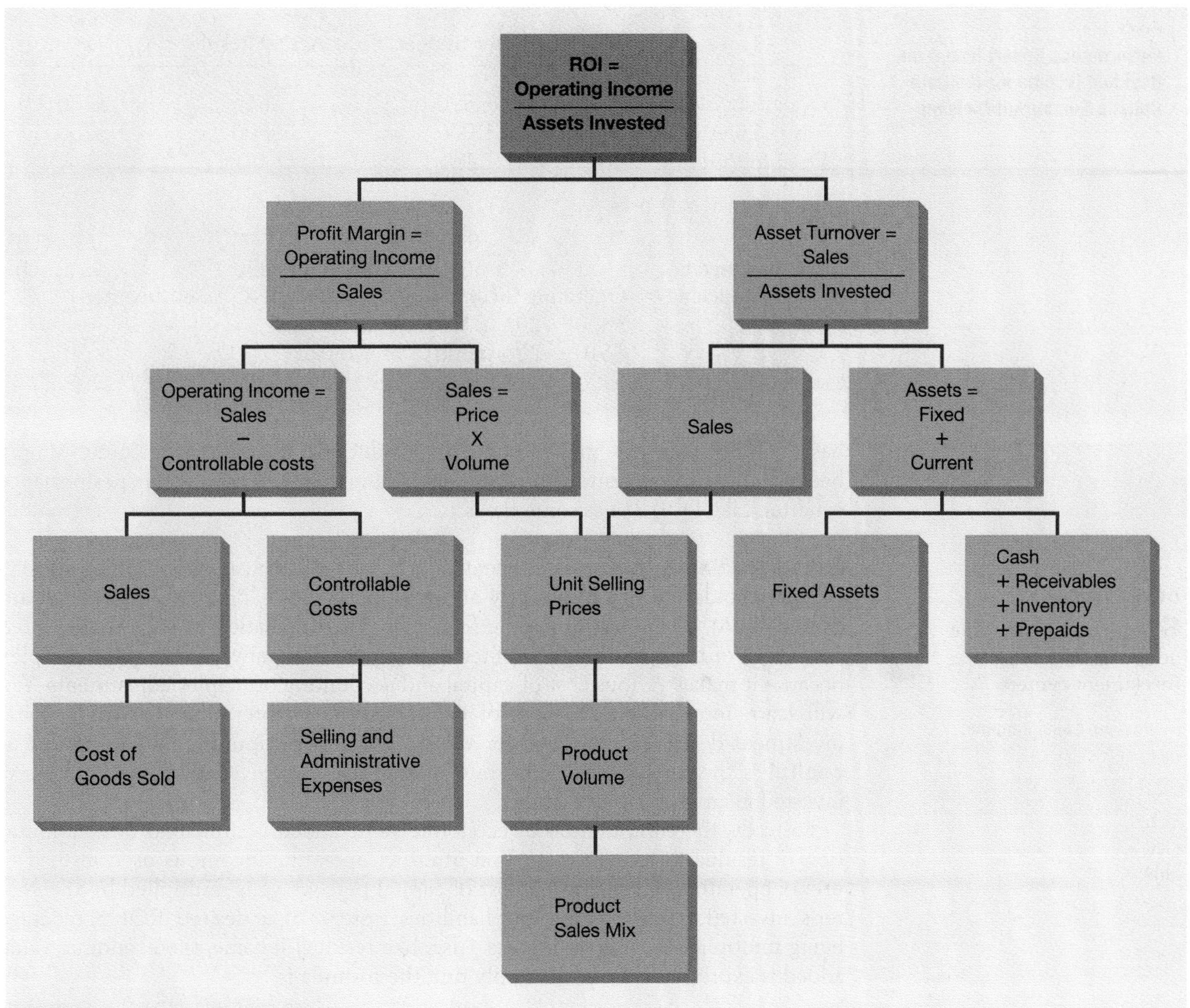

Figure 4
Factors That Affect the Return on Investment Calculation

As in the computation of ROI, assets invested is the average of the center's beginning and ending asset balances for the period.

The desired RI will vary from investment center to investment center depending on the type of business and the level of risk assumed. The performance report based on residual income for Consuelo Jorges, the president of the Café Cubano Restaurant Division, is shown in Exhibit 5. Assume that the president's residual income performance target is to exceed a 20 percent return on assets invested in the division. Note that the division's residual income is $450, which was lower than the $690 projected in the master budget.

Comparisons with other residual income figures will strengthen the analysis. To add context to the analysis of the division and its manager, questions such as the following need to be answered: How did the division's residual income for this year compare to those of previous years? Did the actual residual income exceed the budgeted residual income? How did this division's residual income compare with amounts generated by other investment centers of the company?

Caution is called for when using residual income to compare investment centers within a company. For their residual income figures to be comparable, all investment centers must have equal access to resources and similar asset investment

Exhibit 5
Performance Report Based on Residual Income for the Café Cubano Restaurant Division

	Master Budget	Actual Results	Variance
Operating income	\$ 890	\$610	\$280 (U)
Assets invested	\$1,000	\$800	\$200 (F)
Desired ROI	20%		
Performance measures			
ROI	89%	76%	13% (U)
Residual income	\$ 690	\$450	\$240 (U)

Residual Income = Operating Income − (Desired ROI × Assets Invested)

\$890 − 20%(\$1,000) = \$690

\$610 − 20%(\$800) = \$450

bases. Some managers may be able to produce larger residual incomes simply because their investment centers are larger rather than because their performance is better. Like ROI, RI has some flaws.

OBJECTIVE

6 Use economic value added to evaluate investment centers

Related Text Assignments:
Q: 19
SE: 9
E: 13
P: 4, 5, 8
MRA: 3

ECONOMIC VALUE ADDED Recently, more and more businesses have been using the shareholder wealth created by an investment center, or the **economic value added (EVA)**, as an indicator of performance. The calculation of EVA, a registered trademark of the consulting firm Stern Stewart & Company, can be quite complex because it makes various cost of capital and accounting principles adjustments. You will learn more about the cost of capital in the chapter that discusses capital investment decisions. However, for the purposes of computing EVA, the **cost of capital** is the minimum desired rate of return on an investment, such as assets invested in an investment center.

Basically, the computation of economic value added is similar to the computation of residual income, except that after-tax operating income is used instead of pretax operating income, and a cost of capital percentage is multiplied by the center's invested assets less current liabilities instead of a desired ROI percentage being multiplied by invested assets. Also, like residual income, the economic value added is expressed in dollars. Simply put, the formula is

Economic Value Added = After-Tax Operating Income − Cost of Capital in Dollars

or

Economic Value Added = After-Tax Operating Income − [Cost of Capital × (Total Assets − Current Liabilities)]

A very basic computation of economic value added for Consuelo Jorges, the president of the Café Cubano Restaurant Division, is shown in Exhibit 6. The

Exhibit 6
Performance Report Based on Economic Value Added for the Café Cubano Restaurant Division

	Master Budget	Actual Results	Variance
Performance measures			
ROI	89%	76%	13% (U)
Residual income	\$690	\$450	\$240 (U)
Economic value added		\$334	

Economic Value Added = After-Tax Operating Income − [Cost of Capital × (Total Assets − Current Liabilities)]

\$400 − 12%(\$800 − \$250) = \$334

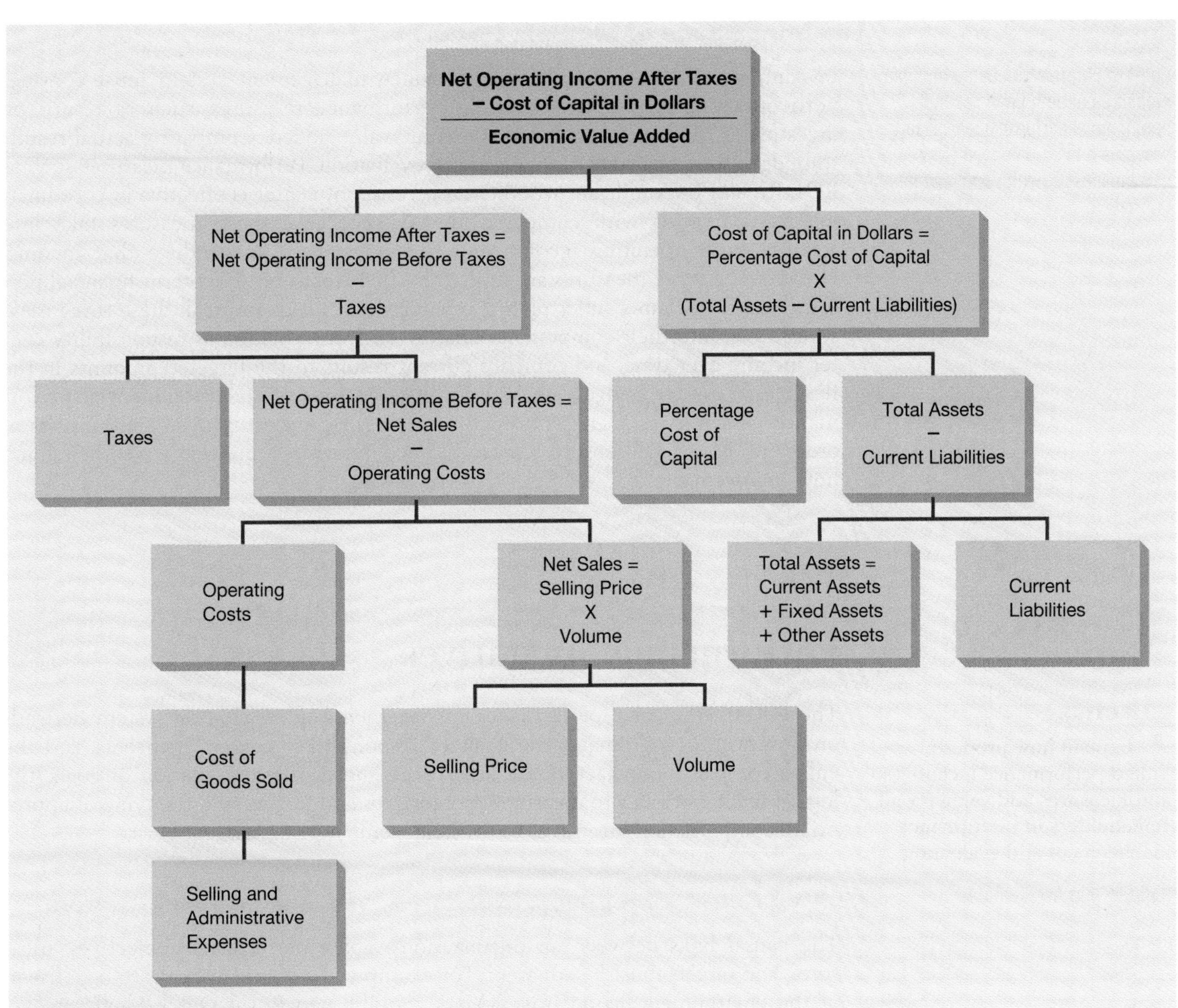

Figure 5
Factors Affecting the Computation of Economic Value Added

report assumes that the division's after-tax operating income is $400, its total assets are $800, its current liabilities are $250, and the cost of capital is 12 percent.

The report shows that the division has added $334 to its economic value after taxes and cost of capital. In other words, the division produced after-tax profits of $334 in excess of the cost of capital required to generate those profits.

Because many factors affect the economic value of an investment center, management should be cautious when drawing conclusions about performance. The evaluation will be more meaningful if the current EVA is compared to EVAs from previous periods, target EVAs, and EVAs from other investment centers.

The factors that affect the computation of economic value added are illustrated in Figure 5. An investment center's economic value is affected by managers' decisions on pricing, product sales volume, taxes, cost of capital, capital investments, and other financial decisions. In essence, the economic value added number is a composite index drawn from many cause-and-effect relationships and interdependent financial elements. A manager can improve the economic value of an investment center by increasing sales, decreasing costs, decreasing assets, or lowering the cost of capital.

Instructional Strategy: Divide the class into three groups. Assign each group an office of the international consulting company in MRA 3. Have each group discuss how their office would answer the questions posed in MRA 3 and determine their office's economic value added. Emphasize each office's position by having two members from each group form a panel to present an in-class discussion.

The Importance of Multiple Performance Measures

Point to Emphasize: Using multiple measures of both financial and nonfinancial performance over time presents a more balanced view of a business's health and how to improve it.

In summary, to be effective, a performance management system must consider both operating results and multiple performance measures, such as return on investment, residual income, and economic value added. Comparing actual results to budgeted figures adds meaning to the evaluation. Performance measures such as ROI, RI, and EVA indicate whether an investment center is effective in coordinating its own goals with companywide goals because those measures take into account both operating income and the assets used to produce that income. However, all three measures are limited by their focus on short-term financial performance. To obtain a fuller picture, management needs to break these three measures down into their components, analyze such information as responsibility center income over time, and compare current results to the targeted amounts in the flexible or master budgets. In addition, the analysis of such nonfinancial performance indicators as average throughput time, employee turnover, and number of orders processed will ensure a more balanced view of a business's well-being and how to improve it.

Performance Incentives

OBJECTIVE

7 Explain how properly linked performance incentives and measures add value for all stakeholders in performance management and evaluation

Related Text Assignments:
Q: 20
SE: 10
E: 14, 15
SD: 4, 5
MRA: 3, 5

The effectiveness of a performance management and evaluation system depends on how well it coordinates the goals of responsibility centers, managers, and the entire company. Two factors are key to the successful coordination of goals: the logical linking of goals to measurable objectives and targets, and the tying of appropriate compensation incentives to the achievement of the targets.

Linking Goals, Objectives, Measures, and Performance Targets

The causal links between an organization's goals, performance objectives, measures, and targets must be apparent. For example, if a company seeks to be a friend of the environment, as do Bristol-Myers Squibb and Royal Dutch/Shell,[6] it may choose the following linked goal, objective, measure, and performance target:

Goal	Objective	Measure	Performance Target
To be a friend of the environment	To reduce the company's environmental risk	Number of products recycled	To recycle at least 10 percent of products sold

Instructional Strategy: Use SE 10 to demonstrate the linking of performance objectives to measures and targets.

You may recall that the balanced scorecard also links objectives, measures, and targets, as shown in Figure 1 earlier in this chapter.

Performance-Based Pay

The tying of appropriate compensation incentives to performance targets increases the likelihood that the goals of responsibility centers, managers, and the entire organization will be well coordinated. Unfortunately, this linkage does not always happen. A 1999 survey done by AnswerThink reported that only 58 percent of companies link bonuses, merit pay increases, and profit sharing to the measurable performance of strategic and tactical plans.[7] Responsibility center managers are more likely to achieve their performance targets if their compensation depends on it. **Performance-based pay** is the linking of employee compensation to the achievement of measurable business targets. For example, at DaimlerChrysler all

132,000 German factory employees are eligible for some type of performance-based pay, such as cash bonuses, profit sharing, or stock options.[8]

Common Student Error: Students may assume all businesses have comparable approaches to performance-based pay. Emphasize that each business will design a compensation program specific to the achievement of its organizational goals.

Cash bonuses, awards, profit-sharing plans, and stock option programs are common types of incentive compensation. Cash bonuses are usually given to reward an individual's short-term performance. A bonus may be stated as a fixed dollar amount or as a percentage of a target figure, such as 5 percent of operating income or 10 percent of the dollar increase in operating income. An award may be a trip or some other form of recognition for desirable individual or group performance. For example, many companies sponsor a trip for all managers who have met their performance targets during a specified period. Other companies award incentive points that may be redeemed for goods or services. (Notice that awards can be used to encourage both short-term and long-term performance.) Profit-sharing plans reward employees with a share of the company's profits. Employees often receive company stock as recognition of their contribution to a profitable period. Using stock as a reward encourages employees to think and act as investors as well as employees and encourages a stable work force. In other words, in terms of the balanced scorecard, they assume two stakeholder perspectives and take both a short- and a long-term viewpoint. Stock options give individual employees the right to purchase a certain number of shares at a specific price within a certain period. Companies use stock options to motivate employees to achieve financial targets that increase the company's stock price. Managers like stock options because the options enable them to realize a profit if the actual stock price rises above their granted option price. Stock options usually have specific performance requirements attached to them. Because many of the variables that affect stock price are beyond a manager's control, stock options may not be the best way to promote the coordination of goals.

The Coordination of Goals

Point to Emphasize: The causal links between an organization's goals, objectives, measures, performance targets, and compensation incentives must be easy to understand.

What performance incentives and measures should a company use to manage and evaluate performance? What actions and behaviors should an organization reward? Which incentive compensation plans work best? The answers to such questions depend on the facts and circumstances of each organization. What promotes the coordination of goals for one organization may not do so for another. To be effective, incentive plans must be developed with input from all employees. All must understand the causal links between goals, objectives, measures, and performance targets. To determine the right performance incentives for their organization, employees and managers must answer several questions:

- When should the reward occur? Will we give the reward now or sometime in the future?
- Whose performance should be rewarded? Will we reward the performance of responsibility centers, of individual managers, or of the entire company?
- How should the reward be computed?
- On what should the reward be based?
- What performance criteria should be used?
- Does our performance incentive plan address the interests of all our stakeholders?

The effectiveness of a performance management and evaluation system relies on the coordination of responsibility center, managerial, and company goals. Performance can be optimized by linking goals to measurable objectives and targets and by tying appropriate compensation incentives to the achievement of the targets. Common types of incentive compensation include cash bonuses, awards, profit-sharing plans, and stock option programs. Each organization's unique circumstances will determine its correct mix of measures and compensation incentives. If management values the perspectives of all of its stakeholder groups, its performance management and evaluation system will balance and benefit all interests.

Chapter Review

REVIEW OF LEARNING OBJECTIVES

Check out ACE, a self-quizzing program on chapter content, at http://college.hmco.com.

1. **Describe how the balanced scorecard aligns performance with organizational goals and explain the balanced scorecard's role in the management cycle.** The balanced scorecard is a framework that links the perspectives of an organization's four basic stakeholder groups—financial (investors), learning and growth (employees), internal business processes, and customers—with the organization's mission and vision, performance measures, strategic plan, and resources. Ideally, managers should be able to see how their actions contribute to the achievement of organizational goals and understand how their compensation is linked to their actions. The balanced scorecard assumes that an organization will get what it measures.

2. **Discuss performance measurement and state the issues that affect management's ability to measure performance.** An effective performance measurement system accounts for and reports on both financial and nonfinancial performance so that an organization can ascertain how well it is doing, where it is going, and what improvements will make it more profitable. Each organization must develop a unique set of performance measures appropriate to its specific situation. In addition to answering basic questions about what to measure and how to measure, management must consider a variety of other issues. Managers must collaborate with other managers to develop a group of measures, such as the balanced scorecard, that will help managers determine what needs to be done to improve performance.

3. **Define *responsibility accounting* and describe the role responsibility centers play in performance management and evaluation.** Responsibility accounting is an information system that classifies data according to areas of responsibility and reports each area's activities by including only the revenue, cost, and resource categories that the assigned manager can control. There are five types of responsibility centers: cost centers, discretionary cost centers, revenue centers, profit centers, and investment centers. Performance reporting by responsibility center allows the source of a cost, revenue, or resource to be traced to the manager who controls it and thus makes it easier to evaluate a manager's performance.

4. **Prepare performance reports for the various types of responsibility centers, including reports based on flexible budgets for cost centers and variable costing for profit centers.** Performance reports contain information about costs, revenues, and resources that are controllable by individual managers. The content and format of a performance report depend on the nature of the responsibility center. The performance of a cost center may be evaluated by comparing its actual costs with the corresponding amounts in the

flexible and master budgets. A flexible budget is derived by multiplying actual unit output by predetermined standard unit costs for each cost item in the report. The resulting variances between actual costs and the flexible budget can be examined further by using standard costing to compute specific variances for direct materials, direct labor, and manufacturing overhead. A profit center's performance is usually evaluated by comparing its actual income statement results to its budgeted income statement. When variable costing is used, the profit center manager's controllable costs are classified as either variable or fixed. The resulting performance report takes the form of a contribution income statement instead of a traditional income statement. The variable costing income statement is useful because it focuses on cost variability and the profit center's contribution to operating income.

5. **Use the traditional performance measures of return on investment and residual income to evaluate investment centers.** Traditionally, the most common measure of performance is return on investment (ROI). The basic formula for this performance measure is ROI = Operating Income ÷ Assets Invested. Return on investment may also be examined in terms of profit margin and asset turnover. In that case, ROI = Profit Margin × Asset Turnover, where Profit Margin = Operating Income ÷ Sales and Asset Turnover = Sales ÷ Assets Invested. Residual income (RI) is the operating income that an investment center earns above a minimum desired return on invested assets. Residual income is expressed as a dollar amount: Residual Income = Operating Income − (Desired ROI × Assets Invested). It is the amount of profit left after subtracting a predetermined desired income target for an investment center.

6. **Use economic value added to evaluate investment centers.** Economic value added (EVA) measures the shareholder wealth created by an investment center. The calculation of economic value added can be quite complex because it is a composite of many cause-and-effect relationships and interdependent financial elements. Basically, the concept of economic value added is similar to residual income. Economic Value Added = After-Tax Operating Income − Cost of Capital (expressed in dollars). A manager can improve the economic value of an investment center by increasing sales, decreasing costs, decreasing assets, or lowering the cost of capital.

7. **Explain how properly linked performance incentives and measures add value for all stakeholders in performance management and evaluation.** The effectiveness of a performance management and evaluation system depends on how well it coordinates the goals of responsibility centers, managers, and the entire company. Performance can be optimized by linking goals to measurable objectives and targets and by tying appropriate compensation incentives to the achievement of those targets. Common types of incentive compensation include cash bonuses, awards, profit-sharing plans, and stock option programs. Each organization's unique circumstances will determine its correct mix of measures and compensation incentives. If management values the perspectives of all of its stakeholder groups, its performance management and evaluation system will balance and benefit all interests.

Review of Concepts and Terminology

The following concepts and terms were introduced in this chapter:

LO 5 **Asset turnover:** The productivity of assets, or the number of sales dollars generated by each dollar invested in assets; Sales ÷ Assets Invested.

LO 1 **Balanced scorecard:** A framework that links the perspectives of an organization's four basic stakeholder groups—financial (investors), learning and growth (employees), internal business processes, and customers—with the organization's mission and vision, performance measures, strategic plan, and resources.

LO 3 **Controllable costs and revenues:** Costs and revenues that result from a manager's actions, influence, or decisions.

LO 3 **Cost center:** A responsibility center whose manager is accountable for only controllable costs that have well-defined relationships between the center's resources and products or services.

LO 6 **Cost of capital:** The minimum desired rate of return on an investment, such as assets invested in an investment center.

LO 3 **Discretionary cost center:** A responsibility center whose manager is accountable for costs only and in which the relationship between resources and products or services produced is not well defined.

LO 6 **Economic value added (EVA):** The shareholder wealth created by an investment center; Economic Value Added = After-Tax Operating Income − Cost of Capital in Dollars.

LO 3 **Investment center:** A responsibility center whose manager is accountable for profit generation and can also make significant decisions about the resources the center uses.

LO 3 **Organization chart:** A visual representation of an organization's hierarchy of responsibility for the purposes of management control.

LO 7 **Performance-based pay:** The linking of employee compensation to the achievement of measurable business targets.

LO 2 **Performance management and evaluation system:** A set of procedures that account for and report on both financial and nonfinancial performance, so that a company can identify how well it is doing, where it is going, and what improvements will make it more profitable.

LO 2 **Performance measurement:** The use of quantitative tools to gauge an organization's performance in relation to a specific goal or an expected outcome.

LO 3 **Profit center:** A responsibility center whose manager is accountable for both revenue and costs and for the resulting operating income.

LO 5 **Profit margin:** The percentage of each sales dollar that results in profit; Operating Income ÷ Sales.

LO 5 **Residual income (RI):** The operating income that an investment center earns above a minimum desired return on invested assets; Residual Income = Investment Center's Operating Income − (Desired ROI × Assets Invested).

LO 3 **Responsibility accounting:** An information system that classifies data according to areas of responsibility and reports each area's activities by including only the revenue, cost, and resource categories that the assigned manager can control.

LO 3 **Responsibility center:** An organizational unit whose manager has been assigned the responsibility of managing a portion of the organization's resources. The five most common forms of responsibility center are cost centers, discretionary cost centers, revenue centers, profit centers, and investment centers.

LO 5 **Return on investment (ROI):** A traditional performance measure that takes into account both operating income and the assets invested to produce that income; ROI = Operating Income ÷ Assets Invested. ROI can also be expressed as Profit Margin × Asset Turnover.

LO 3 **Revenue center:** A responsibility center whose manager is accountable primarily for revenue and whose success is based on its ability to generate revenue.

LO 4 **Variable costing:** A method of preparing profit center performance reports that classifies a manager's controllable costs as either fixed or variable and produces a contribution income statement.

REVIEW PROBLEM

Evaluating Profit Center and Investment Center Performance

LO 3
LO 4
LO 5

Winter Wonderland is a full-service resort and spa. Mary Fortenberry, the resort's general manager, is responsible for guest activities, administration, and food and lodging. In addition, she is solely responsible for the resort's capital investments. The organization chart below shows the resort's various activities and the levels of authority Fortenberry has established.

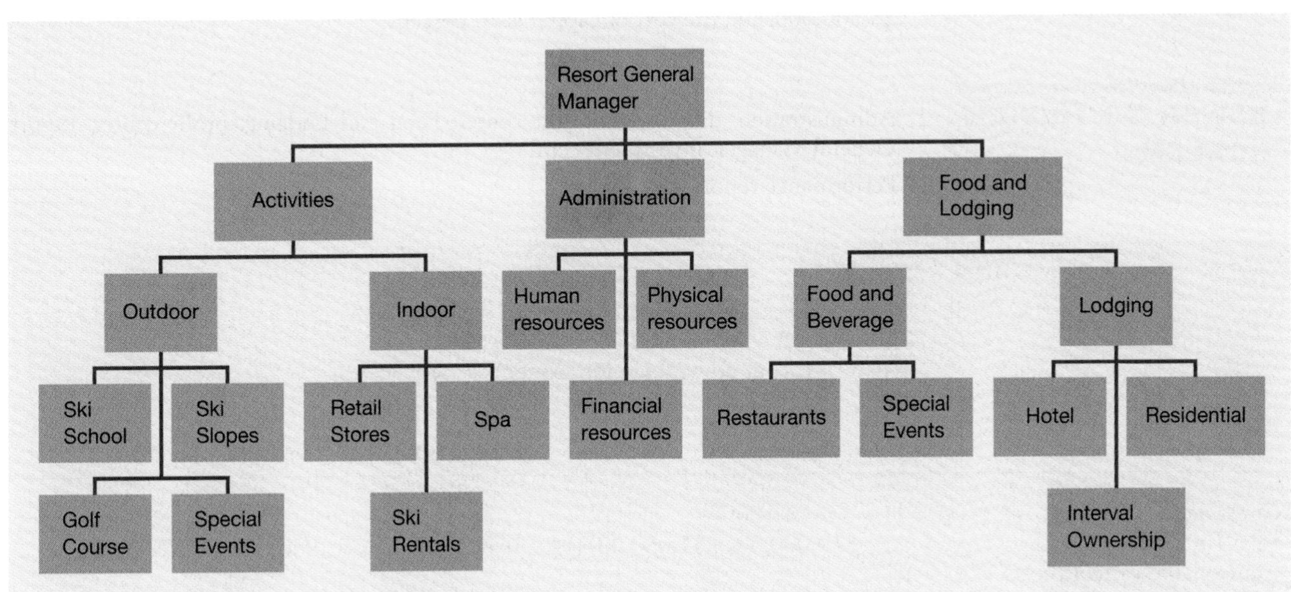

Three divisional managers receive compensation based on their division's performance and have authority to make employee compensation decisions for their division. Alexandra Patel manages the Food and Lodging Division, which had the following master budget and actual results for the year ended June 30, 20x4.

Winter Wonderland
Food and Lodging Division
For the Year Ended June 30, 20x4

	Master Budget	Actual Results
Guest days	4,000	4,100
Sales (in thousands)	$38,000	$40,000
Variable cost of sales	24,000	25,000
Variable selling and administrative expenses	4,000	4,250
Fixed selling and administrative expenses	2,500	2,500
Fixed cost of sales	2,000	1,800

REQUIRED

1. What types of responsibility centers are Administration, Food and Lodging, and Resort General Manager?
2. Assume that Food and Lodging is a profit center. Prepare a performance report using variable costing and flexible budgeting. Determine the variances between actual results and the corresponding figures in the flexible budget and the master budget.
3. Assume that the divisional managers have been assigned responsibility for capital expenditures and that their divisions are thus investment centers. Food and Lodging

is expected to generate a desired ROI of at least 30 percent on average assets invested of $10,000,000.

a. Compute the division's return on investment and residual income using the average assets invested in both the actual and the budget calculations.
b. Using the ROI and residual income, evaluate Alexandra Patel's performance as divisional manager.

4. Compute the division's actual economic value added if the division's assets are $12,000,000, current liabilities are $3,000,000, after-tax operating income is $4,500,000, and the cost of capital is 20 percent.

ANSWER TO REVIEW PROBLEM

1. Administration: discretionary cost center; Food and Lodging: profit center; Resort General Manager: investment center.
2. Performance report:

Winter Wonderland
Food and Lodging Division
For the Year Ended June 30, 20x4
(Dollar amounts in thousands)

	Actual Results	Variance	Flexible Budget	Variance	Master Budget
Guest days	4,100	0	4,100	100 (F)	4,000
Sales (in thousands)	$40,000.00	$1,050.00 (F)	$38,950.00	$ 950.00 (F)	$38,000.00
Controllable variable costs					
Variable cost of sales	25,000.00	400.00 (U)	24,600.00	600.00 (U)	24,000.00
Variable selling and administrative expenses	4,250.00	150.00 (U)	4,100.00	100.00 (U)	4,000.00
Contribution margin	$10,750.00	$ 500.00 (F)	$10,250.00	$ 250.00 (F)	$10,000.00
Controllable fixed costs					
Fixed selling and administrative expenses	2,500.00	0	2,500.00	0	2,500.00
Fixed cost of sales	1,800.00	200.00 (F)	2,000.00	0	2,000.00
Division operating income	$ 6,450.00	$ 700.00 (F)	$ 5,750.00	$250.00 (F)	$ 5,500.00

3. a. **Return on investment**
Actual results: $6,450,000 ÷ $10,000,000 = 64.50%
Flexible budget: $5,750,000 ÷ $10,000,000 = 57.50%
Master budget: $5,500,000 ÷ $10,000,000 = 55.00%

Residual income
Actual results: $6,450,000 – 30%($10,000,000) = $3,450,000
Flexible budget: $5,750,000 – 30%($10,000,000) = $2,750,000
Master budget: $5,500,000 – 30%($10,000,000) = $2,500,000

b. Alexandra Patel's performance as the divisional manager of Food and Lodging exceeds company performance expectations. Actual ROI was 64.5 percent, whereas the company expected an ROI of 30 percent and the flexible budget and the master budget showed projections of 57.50 percent and 55 percent, respectively. Residual income also exceeded expectations. The Food and Lodging Division generated $3,450,000 in residual income when the flexible budget and master budget had projected RIs of $2,750,000 and $2,500,000. The performance report for the division shows 100 more guest days than had been anticipated and a favorable controllable fixed cost variance. As a manager, Patel will investigate the unfavorable variances associated with her controllable variable costs.

4. Economic value added:

$4,500,000 – 20%($12,000,000 – $3,000,000) = $2,700,000

Chapter Assignments

Building Your Knowledge Foundation

Questions

1. What four basic stakeholder groups are included in the balanced scorecard?
2. In the planning stage of the management cycle, once performance objectives are set, what do managers do?
3. Why is it important for managers to see the causal relationships between their actions and the company's overall performance?
4. How does the balanced scorecard add dimension to the management cycle?
5. What is a performance management and evaluation system?
6. Define responsibility accounting.
7. Describe a responsibility center.
8. What is the difference between a cost center and a discretionary cost center?
9. What is a revenue center?
10. Compare and contrast a cost center, a profit center, and an investment center.
11. What is the role of a responsibility accounting system in an organization?
12. How does a company's organizational structure affect its responsibility accounting system?
13. What types of information are contained in performance reports?
14. What types of comparisons are contained in a performance report for a cost center?
15. Why is a contribution income statement useful in performance management and evaluation?
16. What are some similarities between the performance reports for the various kinds of responsibility centers?
17. Why is return on investment more than a ratio of two numbers?
18. How does residual income differ from return on investment?
19. What are the similarities and differences between residual income and economic value added?
20. Why do incentive plans use performance-based pay?

Short Exercises

LO 1 Balanced Scorecard

SE 1. One of your college's overall goals is customer satisfaction. In light of that goal, match each of these stakeholders' perspectives with the appropriate objective:

Perspective	Objective
1. Financial (investors)	a. Customer satisfaction means that the faculty engages in cutting-edge research.
2. Learning and growth (employees)	b. Customer satisfaction means that students receive their degrees in four years.
3. Internal business processes	c. Customer satisfaction means that the college has a winning athletics program.
4. Customers	d. Customer satisfaction means that fund-raising campaigns are successful.

LO 3 Responsibility Centers

SE 2. Identify each of the following as a cost center, a discretionary cost center, a revenue center, a profit center, or an investment center.

1. The manager of center A is responsible for generating cash inflows and incurring costs with the goal of making money for the company. The manager has no responsibility for assets.
2. Center B produces a product that is not sold to an external party.
3. The manager of center C is responsible for the telephone order operations of a large retailer.

4. Center D designs, produces, and sells products to external parties. The manager makes both long-term and short-term decisions.
5. Center E provides human resource support for the other centers in the company.

SE 3. **LO 3 Controllable Costs**

Sam Rittorno is the manager of the Paper Cutting Department in the Northwest Division of Williams Paper Products. Identify each of the following costs as either controllable or not controllable by Rittorno.

1. Salaries of cutting machine workers
2. Cost of cutting machine parts
3. Cost of electricity for the Northwest Division
4. Lumber Department hauling costs
5. Vice president's salary

SE 4. **LO 4 Cost Center Performance Report**

Complete the following performance report for cost center C for the month ended December 31, 20x4.

	Actual Results	Variance	Flexible Budget	Variance	Master Budget
Units produced	80	0	?	20 (U)	100
Center costs					
Direct materials	$ 84	$?	$ 80	$?	$100
Direct labor	150	?	?	40 (F)	200
Variable overhead	?	20 (U)	240	?	300
Fixed overhead	280	?	250	?	250
Total cost	$?	$44 (U)	$?	$120 (F)	$850
Performance measures					
Defect-free units to total produced	75%	?	N/A		90%
Average throughput time per unit	12 minutes	?	N/A		10 minutes

SE 5. **LO 4 Profit Center Performance Report**

Complete the following performance report for profit center P for the month ended December 31, 20x4.

	Master Budget	Actual Costs	Variance
Sales	$120	?	$ 20 (F)
Controllable variable costs			
Variable cost of goods sold	?	25	10 (U)
Variable selling and administrative expenses	5	15	?
Contribution margin	$100	$100	$?
Controllable fixed costs	60	?	10 (F)
Profit center income	?	$ 50	$ 10 (F)
Performance measures			
Number of orders processed	?	50	20 (F)
Average daily sales	$4.00	?	.66 (F)
Number of units sold	?	100	40 (F)

SE 6. **LO 5 Return on Investment**

Complete the return on investment, gross margin, and asset turnover calculations for investment centers D and V:

	Subsidiary D	Subsidiary V
Total sales	$1,650	$2,840
Operating income	$ 180	$ 210
Average assets invested	$ 940	$1,250
Profit margin	?	7.39%
Asset turnover	1.76 times	?
ROI	?	?

LO 5 Return on Investment

SE 7. Complete the return on investment, profit margin, asset turnover, and average assets invested calcuations for investment centers J and K:

	Subsidiary J	Subsidiary K
Total sales	$2,000	$2,000
Operating income	$ 500	$ 800
Beginning assets invested	$4,000	$ 500
Ending assets invested	$6,000	$1,500
Average assets invested	?	?
Profit margin	25%	?
Asset turnover	?	2 times
ROI	?	?

LO 5 Residual Income

SE 8. Complete the residual income and average assets invested calculations for investment centers H and F:

	Subsidiary H	Subsidiary F
Total sales	$20,000	$25,000
Operating income	$ 1,500	?
Beginning assets invested	$ 4,000	$ 500
Ending assets invested	$ 6,000	?
Average assets invested	?	$ 1,000
Desired ROI	20%	20%
Residual income		$ 600

LO 6 Economic Value Added

SE 9. Complete the economic value added calculations for investment centers M and N:

	Subsidiary M	Subsidiary N
Total sales	$15,000	$18,000
After-tax operating income	$ 1,000	$ 1,100
Total assets	$ 4,000	$ 5,000
Current liabilities	$ 1,000	?
Total assets − current liabilities	?	$ 3,500
Cost of capital	15%	15%
Economic value added	?	?

LO 7 Coordination of Goals

SE 10. One of your college's goals is customer satisfaction. In view of that goal, identify each of the following as a linked objective, measure, or performance target.

To have successful fund-raising campaigns
Number of publications per year per tenure-track faculty
To increase the average donation by 10 percent
Average number of dollars raised per donor
To have faculty engage in cutting-edge research
To increase the number of publications per faculty member by at least one per year

Exercises

LO 1 Balanced Scorecard

E 1. Volker Industries is considering adopting the balanced scorecard and has compiled the list of possible performance measures shown on the next page. Select the balanced scorecard perspective that best matches each performance measure.

Performance Measure	Balanced Scorecard Perspective
1. Residual income	a. Financial (investors)
2. Customer satisfaction rating	b. Learning and growth (employees)
3. Employee absentee rate	c. Internal business processes
4. Growth in profits	d. Customers
5. On-time deliveries	
6. Manufacturing process time	

LO 1 Balanced Scorecard

E 2. B2B Online Products is considering adopting the balanced scorecard and has compiled the following list of possible performance measures. Select the balanced scorecard perspective that best matches each performance measure.

Performance Measure	Balanced Scorecard Perspective
1. Economic value added	a. Financial (investors)
2. Employee turnover	b. Learning and growth (employees)
3. Average daily sales	c. Internal business processes
4. Defect-free units	d. Customers
5. Number of repeat customer visits	
6. Employee training hours	

LO 2 Performance Measures

E 3. Alex Thurmon wants to measure his division's product quality. Link an appropriate performance measure with each balanced scorecard perspective:

Product Quality	Possible Performance Measures
1. Financial (investors)	a. Number of defective products returned
2. Learning and growth (employees)	b. Number of products failing inspection
3. Internal business processes	c. Increased market share
4. Customers	d. Savings from employee suggestions

LO 2 Performance Measures

E 4. Thea Montana wants to measure customer satisfaction within her region. Link an appropriate performance measure with each balanced scorecard perspective:

Customer Satisfaction	Possible Performance Measures
1. Financial (investors)	a. Number of cross-trained staff
2. Learning and growth (employees)	b. Customer satisfaction rating
3. Internal business processes	c. Time lapse from order to delivery
4. Customers	d. Dollar sales to repeat customers

LO 3 Responsibility Centers

E 5. Identify the most appropriate type of responsibility center for each of the following organizational units.

1. A pizza store in a pizza chain
2. The ticket sales center of a major airline
3. The South American segment of a multinational company
4. A subsidiary of a business conglomerate
5. The information technology area of a company
6. A manufacturing department of a large corporation
7. An eye clinic in a community hospital
8. The food-service function at a nursing home
9. The food-preparation plant of a large restaurant chain
10. The catalog order department of a retailer

LO 3 Controllable Costs

E 6. Sweet Delights produces pies. The company has the following three-tiered manufacturing structure:

Vice President—Production
↑
Plant Manager
↑
Production Supervisors

Identify the manager responsible for each of the following costs.

1. Repair and maintenance costs
2. Materials handling costs
3. Direct labor
4. Supervisors' salaries
5. Maintenance of plant grounds
6. Depreciation, equipment
7. Plant manager's salary
8. Cost of materials used
9. Storage of finished goods
10. Property taxes, plant
11. Depreciation, plant

LO 3 Organization Chart

E 7. Hooper Industries wants to formalize its management structure by designing an organization chart. The company has a president, a board of directors, and two vice presidents. Four discretionary cost centers—Financial Resources, Human Resources, Information Resources, and Physical Resources—report to one of the vice presidents. The other vice president has one manufacturing plant with three subassembly areas reporting to her. Draw the company's organization chart.

LO 4 Performance Reports

E 8. Jackie Huang, a new employee at Welborne, Inc., is learning about the various types of performance reports. Describe the typical contents of a performance report for each type of responsibility center.

LO 4 Variable Costing Income Statement

E 9. Garden, LLC, owns a chain of gourmet vegetarian take-out markets. Last month, Store P generated the following information: sales, $890,000; direct materials, $220,000; direct labor, $97,000; variable overhead, $150,000; fixed overhead, $130,000; variable selling and administrative expenses, $44,500; and fixed selling expenses, $82,300. There were no beginning or ending inventories. Average daily sales (25 business days) were $35,600. Customer orders processed totaled 15,000. Garden had budgeted monthly sales of $900,000; direct materials, $210,000; direct labor, $100,000; variable overhead, $140,000; fixed overhead, $140,000; variable selling and administrative expenses, $45,000; and fixed selling expenses, $85,000. The store had been projected to do $36,000 in daily sales and process 16,000 customer orders. Using this information, prepare a performance report for Store P.

LO 4 Variable Costing Income Statement

E 10. The income statement in the traditional reporting format for Bonsai Products, Inc., for the year ended December 31, 20x3, is as follows.

Bonsai Products, Inc.
Income Statement
For the Year Ended December 31, 20x3

Sales	$296,400
Less Cost of Goods Sold	112,750
Gross Margin	$183,650
Less Operating Expenses	
Selling Expenses	
Variable	$ 69,820
Fixed	36,980
Administrative Expenses	27,410
Operating Income	$ 49,440

Total fixed manufacturing costs for 20x3 were $16,750. All administrative expenses are considered to be fixed.

Using this information, prepare an income statement for Bonsai Products, Inc., for the year ended December 31, 20x3, using the variable costing format.

LO 4 Performance Report for a Cost Center

E 11. Newberry, LLC, owns a blueberry processing plant. Last month, the plant generated the following information: blueberries processed, $50,000; direct labor, $10,000; variable overhead, $12,000; and fixed overhead, $13,000. There were no beginning or ending inventories. Average daily pounds processed (25 business days) were 2,000. Average rate of processing was 250 pounds per hour. At the beginning of the month, Newberry had budgeted costs of blueberries, $45,000; direct labor, $10,000; variable overhead,

$14,000; and fixed overhead, $14,000. The plant had been projected to process 2,000 pounds daily at the rate of 240 pounds per hour. Using this information, prepare a performance report for the month for the blueberry processing plant. Include a flexible budget and a computation of variances in your report. Indicate whether the variances are favorable (F) or unfavorable (U) to the performance of the plant.

LO 5 Investment Center Performance

E 12. Ocala Associates is evaluating the performance of three divisions: Glenn, Oaks, and Springs. Using the following data, compute the return on investment and residual income for each division, compare the divisions' performance, and comment on the factors that influenced performance.

	Glenn	Oaks	Springs
Sales	$100,000	$100,000	$100,000
Operating income	$ 10,000	$ 10,000	$ 20,000
Assets invested	$ 25,000	$ 12,500	$ 25,000
Desired ROI	40%	40%	40%

LO 6 Economic Value Added

E 13. Leesburg, LLP, is evaluating the performance of three divisions: Lake, Sumpter, and Poe. Using the following data, compute the economic value added by each division and comment on each division's performance.

	Lake	Sumpter	Poe
Sales	$100,000	$100,000	$100,000
After-tax operating income	$ 10,000	$ 10,000	$ 20,000
Total assets	$ 25,000	$ 12,500	$ 25,000
Current liabilities	$ 5,000	$ 5,000	$ 5,000
Cost of capital	15%	15%	15%

LO 7 Performance Incentives

E 14. Palatka Consulting is advising Graham Industries on the short-term and long-term effectiveness of cash bonuses, awards, profit sharing, and stock options as performance incentives. Prepare a chart identifying each incentive as either long-term or short-term or both.

LO 7 Goal Congruence

E 15. Necessary Novelties, Inc., has adopted the balanced scorecard to motivate its managers toward the companywide goal of leading its industry in innovation. Identify the four stakeholder perspectives that would link to the following objectives, measures, and targets.

Perspective	Objective	Measure	Target
	Profitable new products	New product ROI	New product ROI of at least 75%
	Work force with cutting-edge skills	Percentage of employees cross-trained on work-group tasks	100% of work group cross-trained on new tasks within 30 days
	Agile product design and production processes	Time to market (the time between a product idea and its first sales)	Time to market less than one year for 80% of product introductions
	Successful product introductions	New product market share	Capture 80% of new product market within one year

PROBLEMS

LO 3 Evaluating Cost
LO 4 Center Performance

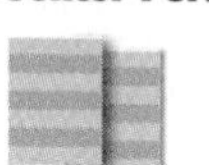

P 1. Metal Products, LLC, manufactures metal beverage containers for a variety of drinks. One division manufactures soft drink beverage cans for the North American market. The division has two plants that operate 24 hours a day, 365 days a year. The plants are evaluated as cost centers. Small tools and plant supplies are considered variable overhead. Depreciation and rent are considered fixed overhead. The master budget for a plant and the operating results of the two North American plants, East Coast and West Coast, are as follows:

	Master Budget	East Coast	West Coast
Center costs			
Rolled aluminum ($.01)	$4,000,000	$3,492,000	$5,040,000
Lids ($.005)	2,000,000	1,980,000	2,016,000
Direct labor ($.0025)	1,000,000	864,000	1,260,000
Small tools and supplies ($.0013)	520,000	432,000	588,000
Depreciation and rent	480,000	480,000	480,000
Total cost	$8,000,000	$7,248,000	$9,384,000
Performance measures			
Cans processed per hour	45,662	41,096	47,945
Average daily pounds of scrap metal	5	6	7
Cans processed (in millions)	400	360	420

REQUIRED

1. Prepare a performance report for the East Coast plant. Include a flexible budget and variance analysis.
2. Prepare a performance report for the West Coast plant. Include a flexible budget and variance analysis.
3. Compare the two plants and comment on their performance.

P 2.

LO 4 Traditional and Variable Costing Income Statements

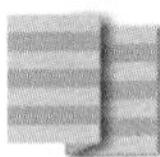

Roofing tile is the major product of the Zygo Corporation. The company had a particularly good year in 20x4, as shown by its operating data. It sold 88,400 cases of tile. Variable cost of goods sold was $848,640; variable selling expenses were $132,600; fixed manufacturing overhead was $166,680; fixed selling expenses were $152,048; and fixed administrative expenses were $96,450. Selling price was $18 per case. There were no partially completed jobs in process at the beginning or at the end of the year. Finished goods inventory had been used up at the end of the previous year.

REQUIRED

1. Prepare the year-end income statement for the Zygo Corporation using the traditional reporting format.
2. Prepare the year-end income statement for the Zygo Corporation using the variable costing format.

P 3.

LO 3 Evaluating Profit and
LO 4 Investment Center
LO 5 Performance

Janeece Olin, the managing partner of the law firm Olin, Comfort, and Clark, LLP, makes asset acquisition and disposal decisions for the firm. As managing partner, she supervises the partners in charge of the firm's three branch offices. Those partners have authority to make employee compensation decisions. The partners' compensation depends on the profitability of their branch office. Victoria Luna manages the Seminole Branch, which has the following master budget and actual results for 20x4.

	Master Budget	Actual Results
Billed hours	5,000	4,900
Revenue	$250,000	$254,800
Controllable variable costs		
Direct labor	120,000	137,200
Variable overhead	40,000	34,300
Contribution margin	$ 90,000	$ 83,300
Controllable fixed costs		
Rent	30,000	30,000
Other administrative expenses	45,000	42,000
Branch operating income	$ 15,000	$ 11,300

REQUIRED

1. Assume that the Seminole Branch is a profit center. Prepare a performance report that includes a flexible budget. Determine the variances between actual results, the flexible budget, and the master budget.
2. Evaluate Victoria Luna's performance as manager of the Seminole Branch.
3. Assume that the branch managers are assigned responsibility for capital expenditures and that the branches are thus investment centers. Seminole Branch is

expected to generate a desired ROI of at least 30 percent on average invested assets of $40,000.

a. Compute the branch's return on investment and residual income.
b. Using the ROI and residual income, evaluate Victoria Luna's performance as branch manager.

LO 5 Return on Investment
LO 6 and Residual Income

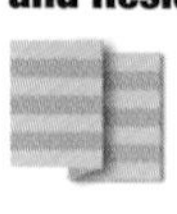

P 4. The financial results for the past two years for Ornamental Iron, a division of the Iron Foundry Company, follow.

Iron Foundry Company
Ornamental Iron Division
Balance Sheet
For the Years Ended December 31, 20x3 and 20x4

	20x4	20x3
Assets		
Cash	$ 5,000	$ 3,000
Accounts Receivable	10,000	8,000
Inventory	30,000	32,000
Other Current Assets	600	600
Fixed Assets	128,300	120,300
Total Operating Assets	$173,900	$163,900
Liabilities and Stockholders' Equity		
Current Liabilities	$ 13,900	$ 10,000
Long-Term Liabilities	90,000	93,900
Stockholders' Equity	70,000	60,000
Total Liabilities and Stockholders' Equity	$173,900	$163,900

Iron Foundry Company
Ornamental Iron Division
Income Statement
For the Years Ended December 31, 20x3 and 20x4

	20x4	20x3
Sales	$180,000	$160,000
Cost of Goods Sold	100,000	90,000
Selling and Administrative Expenses	27,500	26,500
Operating Income	$ 52,500	$ 43,500
Taxes	17,850	14,790
After-Tax Operating Income	$ 34,650	$ 28,710

REQUIRED

1. Compute the division's profit margin, asset turnover, and return on investment for 20x4 and 20x3. Beginning total assets for 20x3 were $157,900. Round to two decimal places.
2. The desired return on investment for the division has been set at 12 percent. Compute Ornamental Iron's residual income for 20x4 and 20x3.
3. The cost of capital for the division is 8 percent. Compute the division's economic value added for 20x4 and 20x3.

P 5. **LO 5 LO 6 Return on Investment and Economic Value Added**

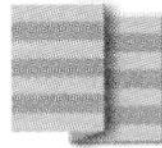

The balance sheet for the New Products Division of NuBone Corporation showed invested assets of $200,000 at the beginning of the year and $300,000 at the end of the year. During the year, the New Products Division's operating income was $12,500 on sales of $500,000.

REQUIRED

1. Compute the division's residual income if the desired ROI is 6 percent.
2. Compute the following performance measures for the division:
   a. Profit margin
   b. Asset turnover
   c. Return on investment
3. Recompute the division's return on investment under each of the following independent assumptions:
   a. Sales increase from $500,000 to $600,000, causing operating income to rise from $12,500 to $30,000.
   b. Invested assets at the beginning of the year are reduced from $200,000 to $100,000.
   c. Operating expenses are reduced, causing operating income to rise from $12,500 to $20,000.
4. Compute NuBone's economic value added if total corporate assets are $500,000, current liabilities are $80,000, after-tax operating income is $50,000, and the cost of capital is 8 percent.

Alternate Problems

P 6. **LO 4 Traditional and Variable Costing Income Statements**

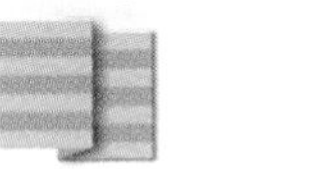

Interior designers often use the deluxe carpet products of Sierra Mills, Inc. The Maricopa blend is the company's top product line. In March 20x5, Sierra produced and sold 174,900 square yards of Maricopa blend. Factory operating data for the month included variable cost of goods sold of $2,623,500 and fixed manufacturing overhead of $346,875. Other expenses included variable selling expenses, $166,155; fixed selling expenses, $148,665; and fixed general and administrative expenses, $231,500. Total sales revenue equaled $3,935,250. All production took place in March, and there was no work in process at month end. Goods are usually shipped when completed.

REQUIRED

1. Prepare the March 20x5 income statement for Sierra Mills, Inc., using the traditional reporting format.
2. Prepare the month-end income statement for Sierra Mills, Inc., using the variable costing format.

P 7. **LO 3 LO 4 LO 5 Return on Investment and Residual Income**

Portia Landau is the president of a company that owns six multiplex movie theaters. Portia has delegated decision-making authority to the theater managers for all decisions except those relating to capital expenditures and film selection. The theater managers' compensation depends on the profitability of their theaters. Anne Burgman, the manager of the Highlands Theater, had the following master budget and actual results for the month:

	Master Budget	Actual Results
Tickets sold	120,000	110,000
Revenue—tickets	$840,000	$880,000
Revenue—concessions	480,000	330,000
Controllable variable costs		
Concessions	120,000	99,000
Direct labor	420,000	330,000
Variable overhead	540,000	550,000
Contribution margin	$240,000	$231,000
Controllable fixed costs		
Rent	55,000	55,000
Other administrative expenses	45,000	50,000
Theater operating income	$140,000	$126,000

REQUIRED

1. Assuming that the theaters are profit centers, prepare a performance report for the Highlands Theater. Include a flexible budget. Determine the variances between actual results, the flexible budget, and the master budget.
2. Evaluate Anne Burgman's performance as manager of the Highlands Theater.
3. Assume that the managers are assigned responsibility for capital expenditures and that the theaters are thus investment centers. Highlands Theater is expected to generate a desired ROI of at least 6 percent on average invested assets of $2,000,000.
   a. Compute the theater's return on investment and residual income.
   b. Using the ROI and residual income, evaluate Anne Burgman's performance as manager.

P 8. **LO 5 Return on Investment**
LO 6 and Economic Value Added

Micanopy Company makes replicas of Indian artifacts. The balance sheet for the Arrowhead Division showed that the company had invested assets of $300,000 at the beginning of the year and $500,000 at the end of the year. During the year, the Arrowhead Division's operating income was $80,000 on sales of $1,200,000.

REQUIRED

1. Compute the Arrowhead Division's residual income if the desired ROI is 20 percent.
2. Compute the following performance measures for the division:
   a. Profit margin
   b. Asset turnover
   c. Return on investment
3. Compute Micanopy Company's economic value added if total corporate assets are $6,000,000, current liabilities are $800,000, after-tax operating income is $750,000, and the cost of capital is 12 percent.

EXPANDING YOUR CRITICAL THINKING, COMMUNICATION, AND INTERPERSONAL SKILLS

SKILLS DEVELOPMENT

Conceptual Analysis

SD 1. **LO 1 Performance Measures**
LO 2 and the Balanced Scorecard

Identify several performance measures for a business located near you and link each measure with a specific stakeholder's perspective from the balanced scorecard. Be sure to select at least one performance measure for each perspective. If you were the manager of the business, how would you set performance targets for each measure? Prepare an e-mail-style report stating the business's name, location, and activities and your linked performance measures and perspectives. Be prepared to discuss your business and performance measures in class.

Group Activity: Have students complete the above assignment by working in groups of four to six, with each group member assuming a different stakeholder perspective (add government and community if you want more than four perspectives). The group

Communication

Critical Thinking

Ethics

Group Activity

Hot Links to Real Companies

International

Internet

Memo
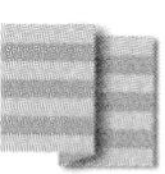
Spreadsheet

should become familiar with the background of the business and interview the business's manager or accountant. Ask the group to discuss all perspectives and to prepare a report summarizing their findings.

SD 2.

LO 3 Comparison of Business Types Using Responsibility Accounting

The structure of an organization will affect its responsibility accounting system. ***Accenture***, a major management consulting firm, organizes its consultants by industry and location. ***Target***, formerly Dayton-Hudson Corporation, has a division for each major retail department store chain it owns: Target, Mervyn's, Marshall Field's, Dayton's, and Hudson's. ***Monsanto***, a manufacturer, structures its organization by products: agricultural, pharmaceutical, and nutritional (the latter includes NutraSweet).

What is a responsibility accounting system, what is it based on, and what is the criterion for including an item in a manager's operating report? Discuss the general effects that organizational structure has on the creation of a responsibility reporting system and give an example of a cost center, a profit center, and an investment center at Accenture, Dayton-Hudson Corporation, and Monsanto.

Ethical Dilemma

SD 3.

LO 5 Effects of Manager's Decisions on ROI

Craig Cooper is the manager of the upstate store of a large farm products retailer. His company is a stable, consistently profitable member of the farming industry. The upstate store is doing fine despite severe drought conditions. At the beginning of the year, corporate headquarters set a targeted return on investment for the store of 20 percent. The upstate store currently averages $140,000 in invested assets (beginning invested assets, $130,000; ending invested assets, $150,000) and is projected to have an operating income of $30,800. Cooper is considering whether to take one or both of the following actions before year end:

- Retain $5,000 in bills owed by the store in a desk drawer until the start of the next fiscal year.
- Write down $3,000 in store inventory (nonperishable emergency flood supplies) to zero value because Cooper was unable to sell the items all year.

Currently Cooper's bonus is based on store profits. Next year, corporate headquarters is changing its performance incentive program so that bonuses will be based on a store's actual return on investment.

1. What effect would each of Cooper's possible actions have on the store's operating income this year? (**Hint**: Use Figure 4 to trace the effects.) In your opinion, is either action unethical?
2. Independent of part **1**, if corporate headquarters changes its performance incentive plan for store managers, how will the inventory writedown affect next year's income and return on investment if the items are sold for $4,000 next year? In your opinion, does Cooper have an ethical dilemma?

Research Activity

SD 4.

LO 2 Earnings Management
LO 4
LO 7

Many large multinational companies have recently taken large one-time write-offs or applied other downsizing or reengineering accounting practices that have affected the measurement of the company's performance in only one year. Conduct a search for the financial statements of a company that has recently taken a sizable reduction in income in just one year. Conduct your search using the Needles Accounting Resource Center web site at http:/college.hmco.com or do a keyword search using an Internet search engine. Prepare a one-page description of your findings. Include the name of the company, the reason for the large decrease in income, and the probable effect on the company's ROI. Be prepared to present your findings to your classmates.

Decision-Making Practice

SD 5. *Aldo's Tortillas* was acquired by ***Mesa Foods*** several years ago. Aldo's has continued to operate as an independent company, except that Mesa Foods has exclusive authority over capital investments, production quantity, and pricing decisions because Mesa has become Aldo's only customer since the acquisition. Mesa uses return on investment to evaluate the performance of Aldo's manager. The most recent performance report is as follows:

LO 2 Types of Performance
LO 3 Centers
LO 4
LO 7

Mesa Foods Performance Report for Aldo's Tortillas For the Year Ended June 30, 20x4	
Sales	$6,000
Variable cost of goods sold	$3,000
Variable administrative expenses	1,000
Variable corporate expenses (% of sales)	600
Contribution margin	$1,400
Fixed overhead (includes depreciation of $100)	$ 400
Fixed administrative expenses	500
Operating income	$ 500
Average assets invested	$5,500
Return on investment	9.09%

1. Analyze the items listed in the performance report and identify the items Aldo controls and those Mesa controls. In your opinion, what type of responsibility center is Aldo's Tortillas? Explain your response.
2. Prepare a revised performance report for Aldo's Tortillas and an accompanying memo to the president of Mesa Foods that explains why it is important to change the content of the report. Cite some basic principles of responsibility accounting to support your recommendation.

MANAGERIAL REPORTING AND ANALYSIS

Interpreting Management Reports

MRA 1. *IT, Inc.*, has adopted the balanced scorecard approach to motivate the managers of its product divisions toward the companywide goal of leading its industry in innovation. The company's selected performance measures and scorecard results were as follows:

LO 1 Balanced Scorecard Results

Measure	Division A	Division B	Division C	Performance Target
New product ROI	80%	75%	70%	75%
Employees cross-trained in new tasks within 30 days	95	96	94	100
New product's time to market less than one year	85	90	86	80
New product's market share one year after introduction	50	100	80	80

Can you effectively compare the performance of three divisions against the targets? What other measures mentioned in this chapter are needed to effectively evaluate performance?

Formulating Management Reports

MRA 2.
LO 2 Responsibility Centers
LO 3

Wood4Fun makes wooden playground equipment for the institutional and consumer markets. The company strives for low-cost, high-quality production because it operates in a highly competitive market in which product price is set by the marketplace and is not based on production costs. The company is organized into responsibility centers. The vice president of manufacturing is responsible for three manufacturing plants. The vice president of sales is responsible for four sales regions. Recently, these two vice presidents began to disagree about whether the manufacturing plants are cost centers or profit centers. The vice president of manufacturing views the plants as cost centers because the managers of the plants control only product-related costs. The vice president of sales believes the plants are profit centers because product quality and product cost strongly affect company profits.

1. Identify the controllable performance Wood4Fun values and wants to measure. Give at least three examples of performance measures Wood4Fun could use to monitor such performance.
2. For the manufacturing plants, what type of responsibility center is most consistent with the controllable performance Wood4Fun wants to measure?
3. For the sales regions, what type of responsibility center is most appropriate?

International Company

MRA 3.
LO 2 Economic Value Added
LO 6 and Performance
LO 7

Barcelona Consulting offers environmental consulting services worldwide. The managers of branch offices are rewarded for superior performance with bonuses based on the economic value the office adds to the company. Here are last year's operating results for the entire company and for its three offices, expressed in millions of U.S. dollars.

	Worldwide	Europe	Americas	Asia
Cost of capital	9%	10%	8%	12%
Total assets	$210	$70	$70	$70
Current liabilities	80	10	40	30
After-tax operating income	15	5	5	5

1. Compute economic value added for each office and worldwide. What factors affect each office's economic value added? How can an office improve its EVA?
2. If managers' bonuses are based on economic value added to office performance, what specific actions will managers be motivated to take?
3. Is economic value added the only performance measure needed to adequately evaluate investment centers? Explain your response.

Excel Spreadsheet Analysis

MRA 4.
LO 5 Return on Investment and Residual Income

Alexandra Patel, the manager of the Food and Lodging Division at Winter Wonderland, has hired you as a consultant to help her examine her division's performance under several different circumstances.

1. Type the following format into a spreadsheet to compute the Food and Lodging Division's actual return on investment and residual income. Match your data entry to the rows and columns shown below. Data are from parts **3** and **4** of this chapter's

Review Problem. (**Hint:** When entering the formulas, type = in front of the formula in the cell. Then the spreadsheet will know to compute the answer. Remember to format each cell for the type of numbers it holds, such as percentage, currency, or general.)

A	B	C	D	E
1				
2	**Investment Center**		Food and Lodging Division	
3			**Actual Results**	
4	**Sales**		$40,000,000	
5	**Operating income**		$ 6,450,000	
6	**Average assets invested**		$10,000,000	
7	**Desired ROI**		30%	
8				
9	**Return on Investment**		D5/D6	
10				
11	**Profit Margin**		D5/D4	
12				
13	**Asset Turnover**		D4/D6	
14				
15	**Residual Income**		D5-(D7*D6)	
16				

2. Patel would like to know how the figures would change if Food and Lodging had a desired ROI of 40 percent and average assets invested of $10,000,000. Revise your spreadsheet from **1** to compute the division's return on investment and residual income under those conditions.
3. Patel also wants to know how the figures would change if Food and Lodging had a desired ROI of 30 percent and average assets invested of $12,000,000. Revise your spreadsheet from **1** to compute the division's return on investment and residual income under those conditions.
4. Does the use of formatted spreadsheets simplify the computation of ROI and residual income? Do such spreadsheets make it easier to do "what-if" analyses?

Internet Case

MRA 5.
LO 7 Top Executive Compensation

Are top executives paid too much? Do the companies run by the most highly paid executives perform better than other companies? Do U.S. executives make more than their foreign counterparts? These are some of the questions asked annually in articles and surveys about executive compensation. Use the Internet to locate the top executive salary rankings compiled annually by business publications and other sources. Study the rankings and select several U.S. and foreign companies in the same industry for comparison.

Hint: There are several ways to access this type of information on the Internet. One approach is to do key word searches using search terms like *executive compensation* or *executive salary survey*. Another approach is to access a business publication web site such as www.forbes.com and do key word searches of their articles. It is also possible to access corporate web sites to view their annual reports. Some corporate sites are even searchable by key word.

1. In your review of top executive compensation, what types of incentives did you find included in annual compensation?
2. Are the companies with the highest-paid executives the best performers in their industry?
3. Do U.S. executives receive higher pay than their foreign counterparts? If so, do the U.S. companies perform better than their foreign counterparts?

ENDNOTES

1. PEAKS Resorts, http://www.peakscard.com or 1-800-842-8062.
2. Rich Teerlink, "Harley's Leadership U-Turn," *Harvard Business Review*, July–August 2000.
3. Marc J. Epstein and Jean-François Manzoni, "The Balanced Scorecard and Tableau de Bord: Translating Strategy into Action," *Management Accounting*, August 1997.
4. Jill Rosenfeld, "Information as if Understanding Mattered," *Fast Company*, March 2000.
5. "Blue Jeans to Help Keep Cars Quiet, Who Thinks This Stuff Up?" *Fast Company*, May 2000.
6. Ans Kolk, "Green Reporting," *Harvard Business Review*, January–February 2000.
7. Russ Banham, "Better Budgets," *Journal of Accountancy*, February 2000.
8. Julia Flynn, "Use of Performance-Based Pay Spreads Across Continental Europe, Survey Says," *The Wall Street Journal*, November 17, 1999.

27 Analysis for Decision Making

LEARNING OBJECTIVES

1 Explain how managers make short-run decisions during the management cycle, and identify the steps in the management decision cycle.

2 Define and explain incremental analysis and its related concepts.

3 Prepare evaluations of alternatives for make-or-buy decisions, special order decisions, product mix decisions, and sell or process-further decisions.

4 Identify the types of projected costs and revenues used to evaluate alternatives for capital investment.

5 Apply the concept of the time value of money.

6 Analyze capital investment proposals using the net present value method.

7 Analyze capital investment proposals using the accounting rate-of-return method and the payback period method.

Incremental Analysis Illustrated

Related Text Assignments:
Q: 4, 5
SE: 2
E: 2
SD: 2
MRA: 3

Teaching Note: Incremental analysis is a technique used not only by businesses, but also by individuals to solve daily problems. You might reinforce this concept by asking your students to perform an incremental analysis to decide which of two vehicles, a Saturn coupe or a Lincoln Town Car, to purchase, given different operating costs and gas mileage.

The method of comparing alternatives by focusing on the differences in their projected revenues and costs is called **incremental analysis**. Incremental analysis is also called *differential analysis*. Incremental analysis ignores revenues or costs that stay the same or that do not differ among the alternatives.

For example, assume that a management accountant is preparing a report to help the managers of Lennox Company decide which of two mill blade grinders—C or W—to buy. The grinders have the same purchase price but have different revenue and cost characteristics. The company currently owns Grinder B, which it bought three years ago for $15,000 and which now has accumulated depreciation of $9,000 and a carrying value of $6,000. Grinder B is now obsolete because of advances in technology and cannot be sold or traded in.

The accountant has collected the following annual revenue and operating cost estimates for the two new machines:

	Grinder C	Grinder W
Increase in revenue	$16,200	$19,800
Increase in annual operating costs		
Direct materials	4,800	4,800
Direct labor	2,200	4,100
Variable manufacturing overhead	2,100	3,050
Fixed manufacturing overhead (depreciation included)	5,000	5,000

The first step in the incremental analysis is to eliminate any irrelevant revenues and costs. Revenues are irrelevant if they will not differ between the alternatives. Irrelevant costs include sunk costs and costs that will not differ between the alternatives. A **sunk cost** is a cost that was incurred because of a previous decision and that cannot be recovered through the current decision. An example of a sunk cost is the carrying value of Grinder B. A manager might be tempted to say that the grinder cannot be junked because the company still has $6,000 invested in it. However, the manager would be incorrect because the book value of the old grinder represents money that was spent in the past and so does not affect the decision about whether to replace the old grinder with a new one. The old grinder would be of interest only if it could be sold or traded in, and the amount received for it would be different, depending on which new grinder was chosen. In that case, the amount of the sale or trade-in value would be relevant to the decision because it would affect the future cash flows of the alternatives.

Another look at the figures for Grinders C and W reveals two other irrelevant costs. The costs of direct materials and fixed manufacturing overhead (depreciation included) can also be eliminated from the analysis because they are the same for both alternatives.

Once the irrelevant revenues and costs have been identified, the incremental analysis can be prepared, using only the projected revenues and expenses that will differ between the alternative grinders, as shown in Exhibit 1. The analysis shows that Grinder W would produce $750 more in operating income than Grinder C. Given that the costs of buying the two grinders are the same, this report would favor the purchase of Grinder W.

Because incremental analysis focuses on only the quantitative differences among the alternatives, it simplifies management's evaluation of a decision and reduces the time needed to choose the best course of action. However, incremental analysis is only one input to the final decision. Management needs to consider other issues. For instance, the manufacturer of Grinder C might have a reputation for providing better quality or service than the manufacturer of Grinder W.

Exhibit 1
Incremental Analysis

Lennox Company
Incremental Analysis

	Grinder C	Grinder W	Difference in Favor of Grinder W
Increase in revenues	$16,200	$19,800	$3,600
Increased operating costs that differ between alternatives			
Direct labor	2,200	4,100	(1,900)
Variable manufacturing overhead	2,100	3,050	(950)
Total revelant operating costs	$ 4,300	$ 7,150	($2,850)
Resulting change in operating income	$11,900	$12,650	$ 750

Point to Emphasize: Both revenues and costs come into play in an incremental analysis. In the Difference column, positive numbers indicate increases in revenues or savings, and negative numbers (numbers in parentheses) indicate increases in costs.

Question: Should the company purchase Grinder C or Grinder W?
Decision: Purchase Grinder W.

Special Considerations in Short-Run Decision Analysis

When analyzing short-run decisions, managers must consider the effects of opportunity costs and the need to prepare special decision reports.

Point to Emphasize: Opportunity costs arise when the choice of one course of action eliminates the possibility of another course of action.

OPPORTUNITY COSTS **Opportunity costs** are the revenues forfeited or lost when one alternative is chosen over another. For example, consider a plant nursery that has been in business for many years at the intersection of two highways. Suburbs have grown up around the nursery, and the developer of a shopping mall has offered the nursery owner a high price for the land. The interest that could be earned from investing the proceeds of the sale is an opportunity cost for the nursery owner. It is revenue that the nursery owner has chosen to forgo to continue operating the nursery in that location.

A bank teller who is deciding whether to go back to school full-time to earn a degree in finance also needs to consider opportunity cost. In this case, the opportunity cost is the salary the teller would lose by returning to school. The total cost of the degree includes not only tuition, books, supplies, and living expenses, but also the amount of salary forgone while the teller is a full-time student. This opportunity cost is one reason many people choose to work full-time and attend college part-time.

Opportunity costs often come into play when a company is operating at or near capacity and must choose what product to manufacture. For example, assume that Lennox Company, which currently produces 20,000 units of Product A, has the option of producing 15,000 units of Product B, a higher-priced product, but it cannot produce both. The amount of income from the 20,000 units of Product A is an opportunity cost of manufacturing Product B.

TRADITIONAL VERSUS SPECIAL DECISION REPORTS The contribution margin format of income reporting, as discussed in the chapter on cost-volume-profit analysis, is often used in decision analysis. Contribution margin is commonly used to make decisions about selling special orders and to select the appropriate product mix when a resource is constrained.

Income statements in the contribution margin format and incremental analyses work best when quantitative information is being compared. In some cases, however, managers may be considering many alternatives, each of which would be best

Exhibit 4
Contribution Margin Analysis: Product Mix Decision

Point to Emphasize: Although Ghost Master yields the lowest contribution margin per unit, only one machine hour (the scarce resource) is required. In this unique situation, Ghost Master is the best of the three alternative products to market; Rising Star is the worst.

Question: In what order should the products be manufactured?
Decision: Manufacture games in the following order: Ghost Master, Road Warrior, and Rising Star.

Bradley Enterprises
Product Mix Decision
Contribution Margin Analysis

	Rising Star	Ghost Master	Road Warrior
Selling price per unit	$24.00	$18.00	$32.00
Less variable costs			
Manufacturing	$12.50	$10.00	$18.75
Selling	6.50	5.00	6.25
Total unit variable costs	$19.00	$15.00	$25.00
Contribution margin per unit (A)	$ 5.00	$ 3.00	$ 7.00
Machine hours per unit (B)	2	1	2.5
Contribution margin per machine hour (A ÷ B)	$ 2.50	$ 3.00	$ 2.80

Master, and Road Warrior—using the same production equipment. The total productive capacity is being used. Following are the product line statistics.

	Rising Star	Ghost Master	Road Warrior
Current production and sales (units)	20,000	30,000	18,000
Machine hours per unit	2	1	2.5
Selling price per unit	$24.00	$18.00	$32.00
Unit variable manufacturing costs	$12.50	$10.00	$18.75
Unit variable selling costs	$6.50	$5.00	$6.25

Should the company try to sell more of one product and less of another? If so, which computer game should be produced first? Second? Last?

Because total productive capacity is being used, the only way to expand the production of one product is to reduce the production of another. The product mix analysis of Bradley Enterprises is shown in Exhibit 4. Though contribution reporting is used here, contribution margin per product is not the important figure for a decision about shifts in product mix. In the analysis, Road Warrior has the highest contribution margin per unit. However, all products use the same machinery and all machine hours are filled. So machine hours are the scarce resource.

The analysis in Exhibit 4 goes one step beyond the computation of contribution margin per unit. A product mix decision such as this one should use two decision variables: contribution margin per unit and machine hours required per unit. For instance, Rising Star requires two machine hours to generate $5 of contribution margin. But Ghost Master would generate $6 of contribution margin using the same two machine hours. For this reason, we have calculated contribution margin per machine hours. Based on this information, management can readily see that Bradley Enterprises should produce and sell as much of Ghost Master as possible. Next, it should push Road Warrior. If any productive capacity remains, it should manufacture Rising Star.

Sell or Process-Further Decisions

Sometimes two or more products or services are created simultaneously from a common direct material or input. Such products, called **joint products**, cannot be identified as separate products during some or all of the production process. Only

at a specific point, called the **split-off point**, do joint products become separate and identifiable. Petroleum manufacturing often results in joint products. For example, when Exxon Corporation refines crude oil, it is only after the split-off point that gasoline, motor oil, and kerosene become identifiable as separate products.

Some products may be sold at the split-off point and others may be processed further. Extra processing adds value to a product and increases its selling price, but it also adds costs. Thus, manufacturers must often decide which approach will be more profitable. **Sell or process-further analysis** helps managers determine whether to sell a joint product at the split-off point or process it further. This technique enables managers to analyze the incremental costs and revenues of the two possible courses of action to see whether the increase in total revenue will exceed the additional costs of processing. *Joint costs incurred before split-off do not affect the decision.* Those costs are irrelevant to the decision because they are incurred regardless of the point at which the products are sold. Only future costs that will differ between alternatives are relevant to the decision.

The goal of a sell or process-further decision is to maximize operating income. For example, assume that Hilbrich Gardening Supplies, Inc., manufactures products that enhance plant growth. In one process, three products—Gro-Pow, Gro-Pow II, and Gro-Supreme—emerge from the joint or common initial phase. For each 20,000-pound batch of materials converted into products, $120,000 in joint production costs are incurred. At split-off, 50 percent of the output becomes Gro-Pow, 30 percent becomes Gro-Pow II, and 20 percent becomes Gro-Supreme. Each product must be processed beyond split-off, and the following additional variable costs are incurred.

Product	Pounds	Additional Processing Costs
Gro-Pow	10,000	$24,000
Gro-Pow II	6,000	38,000
Gro-Supreme	4,000	33,500
Totals	20,000	$95,500

Linda & Parks Landscapers has offered to purchase any or all of the joint product at split-off for the following prices per pound: Gro-Pow, $8; Gro-Pow II, $24; and Gro-Supreme, $40. To help decide whether to sell at split-off or process the product further, Hilbrich management performed the analysis shown in Exhibit 5. The first part of the exhibit lists the unit selling prices of the three products at split-off. The second part is an incremental analysis that compares the increases in revenue and processing costs for each alternative. The analysis shows that further processing of Gro-Pow increases operating income by $16,000 and further processing of Gro-Supreme increases operating income by $6,500. Hilbrich should therefore consider further processing those two products. However, the company loses $2,000 by further processing Gro-Pow II. Thus, it will save money if Linda & Parks buys Gro-Pow II at the split-off point. Note that the joint processing costs of $120,000 are irrelevant to the decision because they will be incurred with either alternative.

Measuring incremental costs for additional processing beyond split-off can create problems. Additional costs of direct materials, direct labor, and variable manufacturing overhead are incremental because they are caused by additional processing. However, supervisors' salaries, property taxes, insurance, and other fixed costs incurred regardless of the production decision are not incremental costs. Incremental processing costs should include only production costs incurred if a product is processed beyond split-off. Fixed manufacturing overhead costs common to other production activity must be excluded from a sell or process-further incremental analysis.

Exhibit 5
Incremental Analysis: Sell or Process-Further Decision

Question: Should joint products be processed further? **Decision:** Sell Gro-Pow II at the split-off point and further process Gro-Pow and Gro-Supreme.

Hilbrich Gardening Supplies, Inc.
Sell or Process-Further Decision
Incremental Analysis

Unit selling prices

Product	If Sold at Split-Off	If Sold After Processing Further
Gro-Pow	$ 8	$12
Gro-Pow II	24	30
Gro-Supreme	40	50

Incremental analysis per 20,000-pound batch

Product	(1) Pounds	(2) Total Revenue if Sold at Split-Off	(3) Total Revenue if Sold After Processing Further	(4) Incremental Revenue (3) − (2)	(5) Incremental Costs	(6) Effect on Operating Income (4) − (5)
Gro-Pow	10,000	$ 80,000	$120,000	$40,000	$24,000	$16,000
Gro-Pow II	6,000	144,000	180,000	36,000	38,000	(2,000)
Gro-Supreme	4,000	160,000	200,000	40,000	33,500	6,500

Capital Investment Decisions

OBJECTIVE

4 Identify the types of projected costs and revenues used to evaluate alternatives for capital investment

Related Text Assignments:
Q: 11, 12, 13, 14
SE: 6
MRA: 2, 3

Among the most significant decisions facing management are **capital investment decisions**, which are decisions about when and how much to spend on capital facilities and other long-term projects. Capital facilities and projects may include machinery, systems, or processes; building additions, renovations, or new structures; entire new divisions or product lines; or distribution and software systems. Thus, decisions about installing new equipment, replacing old equipment, expanding the production area by adding to a building, buying or building a new factory, or acquiring another company are all examples of capital investment decisions. Spending on capital assets is expensive. A new factory or production system may cost millions of dollars and require several years to complete. When making capital investment decisions, managers must be careful to select the alternatives that contribute the most to profits.

Capital Investment Analysis: A Cooperative Venture

The process of making decisions about capital investments is called **capital investment analysis**, or *capital budgeting*. This analysis is an important tool both for large corporations, such as Microsoft, and for smaller companies, such as Standard Locknut & Lockwasher, Inc., in Westfield, Indiana. Capital investment

Discussion Question: What is capital investment analysis? **Answer:** Capital investment analysis is a decision process for the purchase of capital facilities such as buildings and equipment.

analysis consists of identifying the need for a capital investment, analyzing courses of action to meet that need, preparing reports for managers, choosing the best alternative, and dividing funds among competing needs. People in every part of the organization participate in capital investment analysis. Financial analysts supply a target cost of capital or desired rate of return and an estimate of how much money can be spent annually on capital facilities. Marketing specialists predict sales trends and new product demands, which help in determining which operations need expansion or new equipment. Managers at all levels help identify facility needs and often prepare preliminary cost estimates of the desired capital investments. Then all work together to implement the projects selected and to keep results within revenue and cost estimates.

Measures Used in Capital Investment Analysis

When evaluating a proposed capital investment, managers must predict how the new asset will perform and how it will benefit the company. Various measures are used to estimate the benefits to be derived from a capital investment.

NET INCOME AND NET CASH INFLOWS Each capital investment analysis must include a measure of the expected benefit from the investment project. The measure of expected benefit depends on the method of analyzing capital investment alternatives. One possible measure is net income, calculated in the usual way. Increases in net income resulting from the capital investment must be determined for each alternative. A more widely used measure of expected benefit is projected cash flows. **Net cash inflows** are the balance of increases in projected cash receipts over increases in projected cash payments resulting from a capital investment. In some cases, equipment replacement decisions involve alternatives that do not increase current revenue. In such cases, **cost savings** are the benefits, such as reduced costs, from proposed capital investments.

Either net cash inflows or cost savings can be used as the basis for an evaluation, but one measure should not be confused with the other. If the analysis involves cash receipts, net cash inflows are used. If the analysis involves only cash outlays, cost savings are used. All the investment alternatives must be measured and evaluated consistently.

EQUAL VERSUS UNEQUAL CASH FLOWS Projected cash flows may be the same for each year of an asset's life, or they may vary from year to year. Unequal cash flows are common and must be analyzed for each year of an asset's life. Proposed projects with equal annual cash flows require less detailed analysis. Both a project with equal cash flows and one with unequal cash flows are illustrated and the analysis of cash flows is explained later in this chapter.

CARRYING VALUE OF ASSETS **Carrying value** is the undepreciated portion of the original cost of a fixed asset. When evaluating a decision to replace an asset, the carrying value of the old asset is irrelevant because it is a past, or historical, cost and will not be altered by the decision. Net proceeds from the asset's sale or disposal are relevant, however, because the proceeds affect cash flows and may differ for each alternative.

DEPRECIATION EXPENSE AND INCOME TAXES Depreciation expense affects the determination of net income but does not require a current outlay of cash. It can, however, affect cash flows because of its effects on income taxes. In this chapter it is assumed that those effects have been taken into consideration in computing net

A significant advantage of the net present value method is that it incorporates the time value of money into the analysis of proposed capital investments. A capital investment's future cash inflows and outflows are discounted using the company's minimum rate of return to determine their present values. The minimum rate of return, or lowest acceptable rate, should at least equal the company's average cost of debt and equity capital.

Tables 3 and 4 in the appendix on future value and present value tables are used to discount each future cash inflow and cash outflow over the life of the asset to the present. If the net present value is positive (if the total of the discounted net cash inflows exceeds the cash investment at the beginning), the rate of return on the investment will exceed the company's minimum rate of return, or hurdle rate, and the project can be accepted. Conversely, if the net present value is negative (if the cash investment at the beginning exceeds discounted net cash inflows), the return on the investment is less than the minimum rate of return, and the project should be rejected. If the net present value is zero (if discounted cash inflows equal discounted cash outflows), the project meets the minimum rate of return and can be accepted.

THE NET PRESENT VALUE METHOD ILLUSTRATED Assume that Sophia Company is considering the purchase of a laser imaging machine that will improve efficiency in its Imaging Department. Management must choose between two models of the machine.

Model M will cost $17,500 and will have an estimated residual value of $2,000 after five years. It is projected to produce cash inflows of $6,000, $5,500, $5,000, $4,500, and $4,000 during its five-year life.

Model N will cost $21,000 and will have an estimated residual value of $2,000. It is projected to produce cash inflows of $6,000 per year for five years.

The company's minimum rate of return is 16 percent.

Point to Emphasizes: If the net present value is zero, the investment would earn the minimum rate of return.

Because Model M is expected to produce unequal cash inflows, Table 3 in the appendix on future value and present value tables is used to determine the present value of the cash inflows from each year of the machine's life. The net present value of Model M is determined as follows:

Model M

Year	Net Cash Inflows	16% Factor	Present Value
1	$6,000	.862	$ 5,172.00
2	5,500	.743	4,086.50
3	5,000	.641	3,205.00
4	4,500	.552	2,484.00
5	4,000	.476	1,904.00
Residual value	2,000	.476	952.00
Total present value of cash inflows			$17,803.50
Less purchase price of Model M			17,500.00
Net present value			$ 303.50

All the factors for this analysis can be found in the column for 16 percent in Table 3 of the appendix on future value and present value tables. The factors discount the individual cash flows, including the expected residual value, to the present. The amount of the investment in Model M is deducted from the total present value of the cash inflows to arrive at the net present value of $303.50. Because the net

FOCUS ON INTERNATIONAL BUSINESS

Because capital investments are long-term projects that require commitments of large amounts of money to be spent in anticipation of profitable future returns, many things, in addition to costs, can influence their evaluation. International trade and national economies can also be part of the capital investment decision. A case in point is Thai Tech Steel Co., located in Samut Prakan, Thailand. Company managers were planning to purchase a new computer system. However, because they were uneasy about the economies of Thailand and other Southeast Asian nations, they decided to postpone the purchase. They wanted to observe economic trends, such as currency depreciations, stock market gyrations, and interest rate changes, for a time before deciding to purchase the computer system. In uncertain economies, a short payback period becomes an important consideration in capital investment decisions.[4]

present value is positive, the proposed investment in Model M will achieve at least the minimum rate of return.

Because Model N is expected to produce equal cash receipts in each year of its useful life, Table 4 in the appendix on future value and present value tables is used to determine the combined present value of those future cash inflows. However, Table 3 is used to determine the present value of the machine's residual value. The net present value of Model N is calculated as follows:

Model N

Year	Net Cash Inflows	16% Factor	Present Value
1–5	$6,000	3.274	$19,644.00
Residual value	2,000	.476	952.00
Total present value of cash inflows			$20,596.00
Less purchase price of Model N			21,000.00
Net present value			($ 404.00)

Table 4 is used to determine the factor of 3.274, which is found in the column for 16 percent and the row for five periods. Because the residual value is a single inflow in the fifth year, the factor of .476 must be taken from Table 3 (the column for 16 percent and the row for five periods). The result is a net present value of ($404). Because the net present value is negative, the proposed investment in Model N will not achieve the minimum rate of return.

The two analyses show that Model M should be chosen because it has a positive net present value and would achieve at least the company's minimum rate of return. Model N should be rejected because it does not achieve the minimum rate of return.

The Accounting Rate-of-Return Method

OBJECTIVE

7 Analyze capital investment proposals using the accounting rate-of-return method and the payback period method

The **accounting rate-of-return method** is an imprecise but easy way to measure the estimated performance of a capital investment. This method measures expected performance using two variables: (1) estimated annual net income from the project and (2) average investment cost. The basic equation is

$$\text{Accounting Rate of Return} = \frac{\text{Project's Average Annual Net Income}}{\text{Average Investment Cost}}$$

Related Text Assignments:
Q: 19, 20
SE: 9, 10
E: 11, 12
P: 5, 8
SD: 4
MRA: 2, 3, 5

To compute average annual net income, use the cost and revenue data prepared for evaluating the project. Average investment in a proposed capital facility is calculated as follows:

$$\text{Average Investment} = \left(\frac{\text{Total Investment} - \text{Residual Value}}{2}\right) + \text{Residual Value}$$

To see how this equation is used in evaluating a proposed capital investment decision, assume the Gordon Company is interested in purchasing a new bottling machine. The company's management will consider only projects that promise to yield more than a 16 percent return. Estimates for the proposal include revenue increases of \$17,900 a year and operating cost increases of \$11,696 a year (including depreciation and taxes). The cost of the machine is \$51,000. Its residual value is \$3,000. To determine if the company should invest in the machine, compute the accounting rate of return as follows:

$$\text{Accounting Rate of Return} = \frac{\$17{,}900 - \$11{,}696}{\left(\frac{\$51{,}000 - \$3{,}000}{2}\right) + \$3{,}000}$$

$$= \frac{\$6{,}204}{\$27{,}000}$$

$$= 23.0\%$$

Point to Emphasize: The accounting rate-of-return method is appealing because it is easy to understand. It has flaws, however, such as the failure to consider the time value of money.

The projected rate of return is higher than the 16 percent minimum, so management should think seriously about making the investment.

The accounting rate-of-return method is widely used because it is easy to understand and apply. It does have several disadvantages, however. First, net income is used instead of cash flows. Second, the method is unreliable if estimated annual net incomes differ from year to year. Third, the time value of money is not considered in the analysis. Thus, future and present dollars are treated as equal.

The Payback Period Method

Discussion Question: What does the payback period method measure?
Answer: It measures the estimated length of time necessary to recover in cash the cost of an investment.

Instead of measuring a capital investment's rate of return, many managers estimate the cash flow the investment will generate. Their goal is to determine the minimum time it will take to recover the initial investment. If two or more investment alternatives are being studied, management should choose the investment that pays back its initial cost in the shortest time. That period of time is known as the payback period, and the method of evaluation is called the **payback period method**. The payback period is computed as follows:

$$\text{Payback Period} = \frac{\text{Cost of Investment}}{\text{Annual Net Cash Inflows}}$$

Focus on Business Practice

Organizations often use activity-based costing (ABC) in the preparation of annual operating budgets. In such cases, data must be broken down by the various activities of the organization. The same approach can be taken to creating information for capital investment analysis. Using ABC, managers identify the operating activities that will be affected by the decision and forecast cash flows for each activity. This approach provides a more detailed look at future cash flows and increases the accuracy of the forecasts supporting the decision.[5]

To apply the payback period method to the proposed capital investment of the Gordon Company, begin by determining the net cash inflows. To do so, first find and eliminate the effects of all noncash revenue and expense items included in the analysis of net income. In this case, the only noncash expense or revenue is machine depreciation. To calculate this amount, you must know the asset's life and the depreciation method. Suppose the Gordon Company uses the straight-line method of depreciation, and the new bottling machine will have a ten-year service life. Using this information and the facts given earlier, the payback period is computed as follows:

Teaching Note: Your students may wonder why the estimated residual value is ignored in this calculation. Explain that the payback period logically must be the same, regardless of the expected residual value. In addition, they may be confused by the $4,800 deduction for depreciation. Explain that depreciation is merely being "backed out" because it is a noncash expense.

$$\text{Annual Depreciation} = \frac{\text{Cost} - \text{Residual Value}}{10 \text{ (years)}}$$

$$= \frac{\$51{,}000 - \$3{,}000}{10}$$

$$= \$4{,}800 \text{ per year}$$

$$\text{Payback Period} = \frac{\text{Cost of Machine}}{\text{Cash Revenue} - \text{Cash Expenses}}$$

$$= \frac{\$51{,}000}{\$17{,}900 - (\$11{,}696 - \$4{,}800)}$$

$$= \frac{\$51{,}000}{\$11{,}004}$$

$$= 4.6 \text{ years}$$

If the company's desired payback period is five years or less, this proposal would be approved.

If a proposed capital investment has unequal annual net cash inflows, the payback period is determined by subtracting each annual amount (in chronological order) from the cost of the capital investment. When a zero balance is reached, the payback period has been determined. This will often occur in the middle of a year. The portion of the final year is computed by dividing the amount needed to reach zero (the unrecovered portion of the investment) by the entire year's estimated cash inflow. The Review Problem at the end of the chapter illustrates this process.

Like the accounting rate-of-return method, the payback period method is widely used because it is easy to compute and understand. It is especially useful where there is rapid technological change, such as in Internet companies, and when risk is high, such as when investing in countries with emerging economies. However, the disadvantages of this approach far outweigh its advantages. First, the payback period method does not measure profitability. Second, it ignores differences in the present values of cash flows from different periods; thus it does not adjust cash flows for the time value of money. Finally, the payback period method emphasizes the time it takes to recover the investment rather than the long-term return on the investment. It ignores all future cash flows after the payback period is reached.

Chapter Review

Review of Learning Objectives

Check out ACE, a self-quizzing program on chapter content, at http://college.hmco.com.

1. **Explain how managers make short-run decisions during the management cycle, and identify the steps in the management decision cycle.** Both quantitative information and qualitative information are important for short-run decision analysis. Such information should be relevant, timely, and presented in a format that is easy to use in decision making. In the planning stage of the management cycle, managers estimate the cost and revenue information that will be useful for short-run decisions. Managers use this information during the executing stage to make decisions to make or buy a part, accept a special order, select the appropriate product mix given a resource constraint, or sell a product as is or process it further. In the reviewing stage, each decision is evaluated to determine if the forecasted results were obtained. Reporting occurs throughout the cycle to evaluate the information selected, the decision made, and the effect of that decision on the organization.

   The management decision cycle begins with discovery of a problem or need. Then alternative courses of action to solve the problem or meet the need are identified. Next, a complete analysis to determine the effects of each alternative on business operations is prepared. With those supporting data, the decision maker chooses the best alternative. After the decision has been carried out, the managers conduct a postdecision review to see if the decision was correct or if other needs have arisen.

2. **Define and explain incremental analysis and its related concepts.** Incremental analysis helps managers compare alternatives by focusing on the differences in their projected revenues and costs. Any data that relate to future costs, revenues, or uses of resources and that will differ among alternative courses of action are considered relevant decision information. Projected sales or estimated costs, such as direct materials or direct labor, that differ for each decision alternative are examples of relevant information. The managers organize relevant information to determine which alternative contributes the most to profits or incurs the lowest costs. Only data that differ for each alternative appear in the report. Sunk costs are past costs that are irrelevant to the decision process. Opportunity costs are revenues or income that is forgone as a result of choosing one alternative over another.

3. **Prepare evaluations of alternatives for make-or-buy decisions, special order decisions, product mix decisions, and sell or process-further decisions.** Make-or-buy analysis helps managers decide whether to make or buy a part used in product assembly by identifying the costs of each alternative and their effects on revenues and existing costs. An incremental analysis of the expected costs and revenues for each alternative identifies the best alternative. To analyze special orders, managers must determine if there is unused capacity and find the lowest acceptable selling price for a product. Generally, fixed costs are irrelevant to the decision because those costs are covered by regular operations. Contribution margin analysis shows whether the special order increases income. Product mix analysis is used to find the most profitable combination of products when a company uses a common scarce resource to make more than one product. (A similar approach may be used for decisions involving the profitability of sales territories, service lines, or corporate segments.) The analysis uses the contribution margin format but goes one step further by examining the contribution margin per unit of scarce resource. Sell or process-further analysis

is based on comparisons of incremental costs and revenues of processing a product further. Any previous costs, including joint costs, are irrelevant to this decision because they are identical for both alternatives.

4. **Identify the types of projected costs and revenues used to evaluate alternatives for capital investment.** Methods of evaluating capital investments evaluate net cash inflows or cost savings. The analysis process must take into consideration whether each period's cash flows will be equal or unequal. Except when considering their after-income-tax effect on cash flows, the carrying values and depreciation expense of assets awaiting replacement are irrelevant because they do not affect current or future cash flows. Net proceeds from the sale of an old asset and estimated residual value of a new facility represent future cash flows and must be part of the estimated benefit of a project. Depreciation expense on replacement equipment is relevant to evaluations based on after-tax cash flows.

5. **Apply the concept of the time value of money.** Cash flows of equal dollar amounts at different times have different values because of the effect of compound interest. This phenomenon is known as the time value of money. Of the evaluation methods discussed in this chapter, only the net present value method takes into account the time value of money.

6. **Analyze capital investment proposals using the net present value method.** The net present value method incorporates the time value of money into the analysis of a proposed capital investment. A minimum required rate of return, usually the average cost of capital, is used to discount an investment's expected future cash flows to their present values. The present values are added together, and the amount of the initial investment is subtracted from their total. If the resulting amount, called the net present value, is positive, the rate of return on the investment will exceed the required rate of return and the investment should be accepted. If the net present value is negative, the return on the investment will be less than the minimum rate of return and the investment should be rejected.

7. **Analyze capital investment proposals using the accounting rate-of-return method and the payback period method.** When managers use the accounting rate-of-return method to evaluate two or more capital investment proposals, they select the alternative that yields the highest ratio of average annual net income to average cost of investment. The payback period method of evaluating a capital investment focuses on the minimum length of time needed to get back in cash the amount of the initial investment. Both methods are easy to use, but they are very rough measures and they do not consider the time value of money. As a result, the net present value method is preferred.

Review of Concepts and Terminology

The following concepts and terms were introduced in this chapter:

LO 7 **Accounting rate-of-return method:** A capital investment evaluation method designed to measure the estimated performance of a potential capital project. It is calculated by dividing the project's average annual net income by the average cost of the investment.

LO 4 **Capital investment analysis:** The process of making decisions about capital investments. It includes identifying the need for a capital investment, analyzing different courses of action to meet that need, preparing reports for managers, choosing the best alternative, and dividing funds among competing needs; also called *capital budgeting*.

LO 4 **Capital investment decisions:** Management decisions about when, where, and how much to spend on capital facilities and other long-term projects.

LO 4 **Carrying value:** The undepreciated portion of the original cost of a fixed asset.

LO 5 **Compound interest:** The interest cost for two or more periods when the amount on which interest is computed changes in each period to include all interest paid in previous periods.

LO 4 **Cost savings:** Benefits, such as reduced costs, from a proposed capital investment.

LO 5 **Future value:** The amount an investment will be worth at a future date if invested at compound interest.

LO 2 **Incremental analysis:** A technique used in decision analysis that compares alternatives by focusing on the differences in their projected revenues and costs; also called *differential analysis*.

LO 5 **Interest:** The cost associated with the use of money for a specific period of time.

LO 3 **Joint products:** Two or more products or services that are created simultaneously from a common direct material or input and cannot be identified as separate products until the split-off point in the process.

LO 3 **Make-or-buy analysis:** A decision analysis that helps management choose whether to make or buy some or all parts used in product assembly by identifying the costs of each alternative and their effects on existing revenues and costs.

LO 1 **Management decision cycle:** The five steps managers take in making decisions and following up on them.

LO 4 **Net cash inflows:** The balance of increases in projected cash receipts over increases in projected cash payments resulting from a proposed capital investment.

LO 6 **Net present value method:** A technique for evaluating capital investments in which all future cash flows for a proposed project are discounted to their present value, and the amount of the initial investment is subtracted from their sum. All capital investments are evaluated in the same way, and the projects with the highest net present value—the amount that exceeds the initial investment—can be selected for implementation.

LO 2 **Opportunity costs:** The revenues forfeited or lost when one alternative is chosen over another.

LO 5 **Ordinary annuity:** A series of equal payments or receipts that will begin one time period from the current date.

LO 7 **Payback period method:** A capital investment evaluation method that bases the decision to invest in a capital project on the minimum length of time it will take to get back in cash the amount of the initial investment.

LO 5 **Present value:** The amount that must be invested today at a given rate of compound interest to produce a given future value.

LO 3 **Product mix analysis:** A decision analysis designed to determine the most profitable combination of products or services when a company produces more than one product or offers more than one service and resources are constrained.

LO 3 **Sell or process-further analysis:** A decision analysis designed to help management determine whether to sell a product or process it further to increase its market price and profits.

LO 1 **Short-run decision analysis:** The systematic examination of any decision whose effects will be most felt over the next year or less.

LO 5 **Simple interest:** The interest cost for one or more periods when the amount on which the interest is computed (the principal) stays the same from period to period.

LO 3 **Special order analysis:** A decision analysis designed to help managers decide whether to accept or reject a special order for products at a price below the normal selling price.

LO 3 **Split-off point:** A specific point in the production or development process at which two or more joint products or services become separate and identifiable.

LO 2 **Sunk cost:** A cost that was incurred because of a previous decision and that cannot be recovered through the current decision.

LO 5 **Time value of money:** The concept that cash flows of equal dollar amounts separated by a time interval have different present values because of the effects of compound interest.

REVIEW PROBLEM

Capital Investment Analysis

LO 4 LO 5 LO 6 LO 7

The Roland Construction Company specializes in developing large shopping centers. The company is considering the purchase of a new earth-moving machine and has gathered the following information:

Purchase price	$600,000
Residual value	$100,000
Desired payback period	3 years
Minimum rate of return	15%

The cash flow estimates are as follows:

Year	Cash Inflows	Cash Outflows	Net Cash Inflows	Projected Net Income
1	$ 500,000	$260,000	$240,000	$115,000
2	450,000	240,000	210,000	85,000
3	400,000	220,000	180,000	55,000
4	350,000	200,000	150,000	25,000
Totals	$1,700,000	$920,000	$780,000	$280,000

REQUIRED

1. Analyze the Roland Construction Company's investment in the new earth-moving machine. In your analysis use (a) the net present value method, (b) the accounting rate-of-return method, and (c) the payback period method.
2. Summarize your findings from **1** and recommend a course of action.

ANSWER TO REVIEW PROBLEM

1a. Net present value method (Factors are from Table 3 in the appendix on future value and present value tables.)

Year	Net Cash Inflows	Present-Value Factor	Present Value
1	$240,000	.870	$208,800
2	210,000	.756	158,760
3	180,000	.658	118,440
4	150,000	.572	85,800
4	100,000 (residual value)	.572	57,200
Total present value			$629,000
Less cost of original investment			600,000
Net present value			$ 29,000

1b. Accounting rate-of-return method

$$\text{Accounting Rate of Return} = \frac{\text{Average Annual Net Income}}{\text{Average Investment Cost}}$$

$$= \frac{\$280{,}000 \div 4}{\left(\dfrac{\$600{,}000 - \$100{,}000}{2}\right) + \$100{,}000}$$

$$= \frac{\$70{,}000}{\$350{,}000} = \underline{\underline{20\%}}$$

5. The following five years of cash inflows, discounted at 10%:

Year 1	$35,000
Year 2	20,000
Year 3	30,000
Year 4	40,000
Year 5	50,000

6. The amount of $70,000 to be received at the beginning of year 7, discounted at 14%

E 8.
LO 5 Present Value Computations

Two machines—Machine N and Machine O—are being considered in a replacement decision. Both machines have about the same purchase price and an estimated ten-year life. The company uses a 12 percent minimum rate of return as its acceptance-rejection standard. Following are the estimated net cash inflows for each machine.

Year	Machine N	Machine O
1	$12,000	$17,500
2	12,000	17,500
3	14,000	17,500
4	19,000	17,500
5	20,000	17,500
6	22,000	17,500
7	23,000	17,500
8	24,000	17,500
9	25,000	17,500
10	20,000	17,500
Residual value	14,000	12,000

1. Compute the present value of future cash flows for each machine, using Tables 3 and 4 in the appendix on future value and present value tables.
2. Which machine should the company purchase, assuming that both involve the same capital investment?

E 9.
LO 6 Capital Investment Decision: Net Present Value Method

Petrol Service Station is planning to invest in car wash equipment valued at $250,000. The owner estimates that the equipment will increase annual net cash inflows by $46,000. The equipment is expected to have a ten-year useful life with an estimated residual value of $50,000. The company requires a 14 percent minimum rate of return.

Using the net present value method, prepare an analysis to determine whether the company should purchase the equipment. How important is the estimate of residual value to this decision? Use Tables 3 and 4 in the appendix on future value and present value tables.

E 10.
LO 6 Capital Investment Decision: Net Present Value Method

Jefferson and Associates wants to buy an automatic extruding machine. The equipment would have a useful life of six years, cost $220,000, and increase annual net cash inflows by $57,500. Assume there is no residual value at the end of six years. The company's minimum rate of return is 14 percent.

Using the net present value method, prepare an analysis to determine whether the company should purchase the machine. Use Tables 3 and 4 in the appendix on future value and present value tables.

E 11.
LO 7 Capital Investment Decision: Accounting Rate-of-Return Method

Heber Corporation manufactures metal hard hats for construction workers. Recently, management has tried to raise productivity to meet the growing demand from the real estate industry. The company is now thinking about buying a new stamping machine. Management has decided that only capital investments that yield at least a 14 percent return will be accepted. The new machine would cost $325,000, revenue would increase by $98,400 per year, the residual value of the new machine would be $32,500, and operating cost increases (including depreciation) would be $74,600 per year.

Using the accounting rate-of-return method, decide whether the company should invest in the machine. (Show all computations to support your decision.)

E 12.
LO 7 Capital Investment Decision: Payback Period Method

Super Sounds, Inc., a manufacturer of stereo speakers, is thinking about adding a new injection molding machine. The machine could produce speaker parts that the company now buys from outsiders. The machine has an estimated life of 14 years and will cost $425,000. Gross cash revenue from the machine will be about $400,000 per year, and related cash expenses should total $310,050. The payback period should be five years or less. Use the payback period method to determine whether the company should invest in the new machine. Show computations to support your answer.

PROBLEMS

LO 3 Make-or-Buy Decision

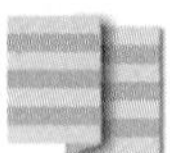

P 1. The Iron Refrigerator Company purchases and installs defrost clocks in its products. The clocks cost $144 per case, and each case contains twelve clocks. The supplier recently gave advance notice that, effective in 30 days, the price will rise by 50 percent. The company has idle equipment that, with only a few minor changes, could be used to produce similar defrost clocks.

Cost estimates have been prepared under the assumption that the company could make the product itself. Direct materials would cost $9.00 per clock. Direct labor would be 10 minutes per clock at a labor rate of $12.00 per hour. Variable manufacturing overhead would be $6.50 per clock. Fixed manufacturing overhead, which would be incurred under either alternative, would be $32,420 a year for depreciation and $234,000 a year for other costs. Production and usage are estimated at 75,000 clocks a year. (Assume that idle equipment cannot be used for any other purpose.)

REQUIRED

1. Prepare an incremental analysis to determine whether the defrost clocks should be made within the company or purchased from the outside supplier at the higher price.
2. Compute the total unit cost to make one clock and to buy one clock after the price hike.

LO 3 Special Order Decision

P 2. On March 26, Barca Industries received a special order request for 150 ten-foot aluminum fishing boats. Operating on a fiscal year ending May 31, the division already has orders that will allow it to produce at budget levels for the period. However, extra capacity exists that could be used to produce the additional 150 boats.

The terms of the special order call for a selling price of $625 per boat, and the customer will pay all shipping costs. No sales personnel were involved in soliciting the order.

The ten-foot fishing boat has the following cost estimates: direct materials, aluminum, two 4′ × 8′ sheets at $145 per sheet; direct labor, 14 hours at $14.50 per hour; variable manufacturing overhead, $5.75 per direct labor hour; fixed manufacturing overhead, $4.50 per direct labor hour; variable selling expenses, $46.50 per boat; and variable shipping expenses, $57.50 per boat.

REQUIRED

Prepare an incremental analysis for management to use in deciding whether to accept or reject the special order. What decision should be made?

LO 3 Sell or Process-Further Decision

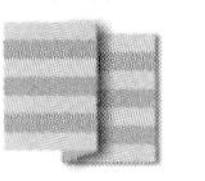

P 3. All-Bagels, Inc., produces and sells 20 types of bagels by the dozen. Bagels are priced at $6.00 per dozen and cost $.20 per unit to produce. The company is considering further processing the bagels into two products: bagels with cream cheese and bagel sandwiches. It would cost an additional $.50 per unit to produce bagels with cream cheese, but the new selling price would be $2.50 each. It would cost an additional $1.00 per sandwich to produce bagel sandwiches, but the new selling price would be $3.50 each.

REQUIRED

1. Identify the relevant per-unit costs and revenues for the alternatives.
2. Based on the information in **1**, should All-Bagels, Inc., expand its product offerings?
3. Suppose that All-Bagels, Inc., did expand its product line to include bagels with cream cheese and bagel sandwiches. Based on customer feedback, the company determined that it could further process those two products into bagels with fruit and cream cheese and bagel sandwiches with cheese. The company's accountant compiled the following information:

Product (per unit)	Sales Revenue if Sold with No Further Processing	Sales Revenue if Processed Further	Additional Processing Costs
Bagels with cream cheese	$2.50	$3.50	Fruit: $1.00
Bagel sandwiches	$3.50	$4.50	Cheese: $ .50

Perform an incremental analysis to determine if All-Bagels, Inc., should process its products further. Explain your findings.

P 4.
LO 6 Capital Investment Decision: Net Present Value Method

The management of Toughware Plastics has been looking at a proposal to purchase a new plastic injection-style molding machine. With the new machine, the company would not have to buy small plastic parts to use in production. The estimated useful life of the machine is 15 years, and the purchase price, including all setup charges, is $400,000. Residual value is estimated to be $40,000. The net addition to the company's cash inflows due to the savings from making the parts is estimated to be $70,000 a year. Toughware Plastic's management has decided on a minimum rate of return of 14 percent. Use Tables 3 and 4 in the appendix on future value and present value tables.

REQUIRED

1. Using the net present value method, determine if the company should purchase the machine. Support your answer.
2. If management had decided on a minimum rate of return of 16 percent, should the machine be purchased? Show all computations to support your answer.

P 5.
LO 7 Accounting Rate-of-Return and Payback Period Methods

The Quoque Company is expanding its production facilities to include a new product line, a sporty automotive tire rim. Using new computerized machinery, tire rims can now be produced with little labor cost. The controller has advised management about two such machines. The details about each machine follow.

	Cal Machine	Hawk Machine
Cost of machine	$500,000	$550,000
Residual value	50,000	55,000
Net income	34,965	40,670
Annual net cash inflows	91,215	90,170

The minimum rate of return is 12 percent. The maximum payback period is six years. (Where necessary, round calculations to the nearest dollar.)

REQUIRED

1. For each machine, compute the projected accounting rate of return.
2. Compute the payback period for each machine.
3. From the information generated in **1** and **2**, which machine should be purchased? Why?

ALTERNATE PROBLEMS

P 6.
LO 3 Make-or-Buy Decision

The Shoshone Furniture Company is famous for its dining room furniture. One full department is engaged in the production of the Cottonwood line, an elegant but affordable dining room set. To date, the company has been manufacturing all pieces of the set, including the six chairs.

Management has just received word that a company in Durango, Colorado, is willing to produce the chairs for Shoshone at a total purchase price of $3,000,000 for the annual demand. Company records show that the following costs have been incurred in the production of the chairs: wood materials, $22.50 per chair; cloth materials, $8.50 per chair; direct labor, 1.2 hours per chair at $12.00 per hour; variable manufacturing overhead, $5.00 per direct labor hour; fixed manufacturing overhead, depreciation, $135,000; and fixed manufacturing overhead, other, $109,400. Fixed manufacturing overhead would continue whether or not the chairs are produced. Assume that idle facilities cannot be used for any other purpose and that annual usage is 60,000 chairs.

REQUIRED

1. Prepare an incremental analysis to determine whether the chairs should be made by the company or purchased from the outside supplier in Durango.
2. Compute the variable unit cost to make one chair and to buy one chair.

P 7.
LO 6 Capital Investment Decision: Net Present Value Method

Le Filet is a famous restaurant in the French Quarter of New Orleans. "Bouillabaisse Nadia" is the house specialty. Management is currently considering the purchase of a machine that would prepare all the ingredients, automatically mix them, and cook the dish to the restaurant's specifications. The machine will function for an estimated 12 years, and the purchase price, including installation, is $250,000. Estimated residual

value is $25,000. This labor-saving device is expected to increase cash flows by an average of $42,000 per year during its estimated useful life. For capital investment decisions, the restaurant uses a 12 percent minimum rate of return.

Use Tables 3 and 4 in the appendix on future value and present value tables.

REQUIRED

1. Using the net present value method, determine if the company should purchase the machine. Support your answer.
2. If management had decided on a minimum rate of return of 14 percent, should the machine be purchased? Show all computations to support your answer.

P 8. **LO 6 LO 7 Comprehensive Capital Investment Decision**

Gonzalez Corporation wants to buy a new rubber-stamping machine. The machine will provide the company with a new product line: pressed rubber food trays for kitchens. Two machines are being considered; the data for each machine follow.

	Exalt Machine	Landis Machine
Cost of machine	$350,000	$370,000
Net income	39,204	48,642
Annual net cash inflows	64,404	75,642
Residual value	28,000	40,000
Estimated useful life in years	10	10

The company's minimum rate of return is 16 percent, and the maximum allowable payback period is 5.0 years.

REQUIRED

1. Compute the net present value for each machine.
2. Compute the projected accounting rate of return for each machine.
3. Compute the payback period for each machine.
4. Based on the information in **1, 2,** and **3,** which machine should be purchased? Why?

EXPANDING YOUR CRITICAL THINKING, COMMUNICATION, AND INTERPERSONAL SKILLS

SKILLS DEVELOPMENT

Conceptual Analysis

SD 1. **LO 1 Management Decision Cycle**

Two weeks ago your cousin Jonathan moved from New York City to Houston. He has found that he needs a car to drive to work and to run errands. He has no experience in selecting a car, so he has asked for your help.

Using the management decision cycle presented in this chapter, write him a letter explaining how he can approach making this decision.

How would your response change if the president of your company asked you to help make a decision about acquiring a fleet of cars for use by sales personnel?

SD 2. **LO 2 Identification of Sunk Costs and Opportunity Costs**

Motorola Inc. originated a $5 billion project, called Iridium, that launched 66 low earth orbiting satellites for global communication using pagers and mobile phones. From the beginning, the Iridium project had technical and marketing problems. Instead of the 600,000 subscribers it was expected to have, it had only 55,000. A basic problem with the system was that a subscriber had to buy a mobile phone that cost $3,000

Communication

Critical Thinking

Ethics

Group Activity

Hot Links to Real Companies

International

Internet

Memo

Spreadsheet

and weighed more than one pound. Few potential users wanted to do this. As a result, Iridium had to file for bankruptcy. Motorola, which had an 18 percent ownership of Iridium, had invested $1.6 billion, and had to decide if it was willing to invest more in an effort to save the project. Some investors wanted to see Motorola cut its losses and move on. Others were concerned about recouping the enormous expenditure that had already been made. What are sunk costs and how do they differ from opportunity costs? How do these concepts apply to the decision by Motorola's management to continue or discontinue support for the Iridium Project?[6]

Ethical Dilemma

SD 3.
LO 3 Ethics of a Make-or-Buy Decision

Karen Gore is the assistant controller for ***Railing Corp.,*** a leading producer of home appliances. Her friend Ed Jason is the supervisor of the Cookware Department. Jason has the authority to decide whether parts are purchased from outside vendors or manufactured in his department. Gore recently conducted an internal audit of the parts being manufactured in the Cookware Department, including a check of the prices currently charged by vendors for similar parts. She found over a dozen parts that could be purchased for less than they cost the company to produce. When she approached Jason about the situation, he replied that if those parts were purchased from outside vendors, two automated machines would be idled for several hours a week. Increased machine idle time would have a negative effect on his performance evaluation and could reduce his yearly bonus. He reminded Gore that he was in charge of the decision to make or purchase those parts and asked her not to pursue the matter any further.

What should Gore do in this situation? Discuss her options.

Research Activity

SD 4.
LO 6 Capital Investment Decision
LO 7

Computers are important in today's business world. Every business can benefit from computers' capabilities, which include rapid data processing, timely report generation, automated accounting systems, and the use of specialized software packages for such areas as payroll, accounts receivable, accounts payable, and tax return preparation. Make a trip to a local computer retailer. Inquire about the various types of computers available and identify one that would be useful to a local nursery selling landscape plants and gardening supplies and equipment. Find out the cost of this computer. Make notes of the model name, its special features and capabilities, and its cost. After gathering those data, identify the benefits that the nursery's controller would include in an analysis to justify the purchase of the computer. Describe the effect of each benefit on cash flows and profitability. Be prepared to discuss your findings in class.

Decision-Making Practice

SD 5.
LO 5 Using Net Present Value
LO 6

The ***McCall Hotel Syndicate*** owns four resort hotels in Europe. Because the Paris operation has been booming over the past five years, management has decided to build an addition. The proposed wing, which will increase the hotel's capacity by 20 percent, can be built at a cost of $30,000,000. The new structure will have an increased residual value of $3,000,000.

Erin McVan, the controller, has started an analysis of the net present value for the project. She has calculated the annual net cash inflows by subtracting the increase in cash operating expenses from the increase in cash inflows from room rentals.

Year	Net Cash Inflows
1–20 (each year)	$3,900,000

Capital investment projects must generate a 12 percent minimum rate of return to qualify for consideration.

Using net present value analysis, evaluate the proposal and make a recommendation to management. Explain how your recommendation would change if management were willing to accept a 10 percent minimum rate of return. Use Tables 3 and 4 in the appendix on future value and present value tables.

Group Activity: Have students work in groups to complete SD 5. Select one person from each group to report the group's findings to the class.

MANAGERIAL REPORTING AND ANALYSIS

Interpreting Management Reports

MRA 1. **LO 3 Special Order Decision**

Roscoe Can Opener Company is a subsidiary of ***Boedigheimer Appliances, Inc.*** The can opener Roscoe produces is in strong demand. Sales during the present year, 20x2, are expected to hit 1,000,000 units. Full plant capacity is 1,150,000 units, but 1,000,000 units is considered normal capacity for the current year. The following unit price and cost breakdown is applicable in 20x2:

	Per Unit
Sales price	$22.50
Less manufacturing costs	
Direct materials	$6.00
Direct labor	2.50
Overhead: Variable	3.50
Fixed	1.50
Total manufacturing costs	$13.50
Gross margin	$ 9.00
Less selling and administrative expenses	
Selling: Variable	$ 1.50
Fixed	1.00
Administrative, fixed	1.25
Packaging, variable*	.75
Total selling and administrative expenses	$ 4.50
Operating income	$ 4.50

*Three types of packaging are available: deluxe, $.75/unit; plain, $.50/unit; and bulk pack, $.25/unit.

During November, the company received three requests for special orders from large chain-store companies. Those orders are not part of the budgeted 1,000,000-unit sales for 20x2, but company officials think that sufficient capacity exists for one order to be accepted. The orders received and their terms are:

Order 1: 75,000 can openers @ $20.00 per unit, deluxe packaging

Order 2: 90,000 can openers @ $18.00 per unit, plain packaging

Order 3: 125,000 can openers @ $15.75 per unit, bulk packaging

Because the orders were placed directly with company officials, no variable selling costs will be incurred.

REQUIRED

1. Analyze the profitability of each of the three special orders.
2. Which special order should be accepted?

Formulating Management Reports

MRA 2. **LO 4 LO 5 LO 6 LO 7 Evaluating a Capital Investment Proposal**

Quality work and timely output are the distinguishing characteristics of ***Rock Photo, Inc.*** Rock Photo is a nationally franchised company with over 50 outlets located in the southern states. Part of the franchise agreement promises a centralized photo developing process with overnight delivery to the outlets.

Because of the tremendous increase in demand for its photo processing, Emma Dubois, the corporation's president, is considering the purchase of a new, deluxe processing machine by the end of this month. Dubois wants you to formulate a memo showing your evaluation. Your memo will be presented to the board of directors' meeting next week.

According to your research, the new machine will cost $320,000. The machine will function for an estimated five years and should have a $32,000 residual value. All capital investments are expected to produce a 20 percent minimum rate of return, and the investment should be recovered in three years or less. All fixed assets are depreciated using the straight-line method. The forecasted increases in operating results for the new machine are as follows:

	Cash Flow Estimates	
Year	Cash Inflows	Cash Outflows
1	$310,000	$210,000
2	325,000	220,000
3	340,000	230,000
4	300,000	210,000
5	260,000	180,000

REQUIRED

1. In preparation for writing your memo, answer the following questions.
   a. What kinds of information do you need to prepare this memo?
   b. Why is the information relevant?
   c. Where would you find the information?
   d. When would you want to obtain the information?
2. Analyze the purchase of the machine and decide if the company should purchase it. Use (a) the net present value method, (b) the accounting rate-of-return method, and (c) the payback period method.

International Company

MRA 3.

LO 1 LO 2 LO 4 LO 6 LO 7 Using Qualitative Information in Capital Investment Decisions

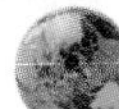

The board of directors of the ***Tanashi Corporation*** met to review a number of proposed capital investments that would improve the quality of company products. One production line manager requested the purchase of new computer-integrated machines to replace the older machines in one of the ten production departments at the Tokyo plant.

Although the production line manager had presented quantitative information to support the purchase of the new machines, the board members asked the following important questions:

1. Why do we want to replace the old machines? Have they deteriorated? Are they obsolete?
2. Will the new machines require less cycle time?
3. Can we reduce inventory levels or save floor space by replacing the old machines?
4. How expensive is the software used with the new machines?
5. Will we be able to find highly skilled employees to maintain the new machines? Or can we find workers who are trainable? What would it cost to train those workers? Would the training disrupt the staff by causing relocations?
6. Would the implementation of the machines be delayed because of the time required to recruit new workers?
7. How would the new machines affect other parts of the manufacturing systems? Would the company lose some of the flexibility in its manufacturing systems if it introduced the new machines?

The board members believe that the qualitative information needed to answer their questions could lead to the rejection of the project, even though it would have been accepted based on the quantitative information.

REQUIRED

1. Identify the questions that can be answered with quantitative information. Give examples of the quantitative information that could be used.
2. Identify the questions that can be answered with qualitative information. Explain why such information could negatively influence the capital investment decision even though the quantitative information suggests a positive outcome.

Excel Spreadsheet Analysis

MRA 4.

LO 3 Sell or Process-Further Decision in a Service Organization

  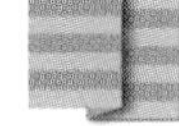

Maya Marketeers, Inc., has developed a promotional program for a large shopping center in Tempe, Arizona. After investing $360,000 in developing the original promotion campaign, the firm has received an offer from its client for an add-on contract that includes the original promotion areas of (1) TV advertising program, (2) series of brochures for mass mailing, and (3) special rotating BIG SALE schedule for 10 of the 28 tenants in the shopping center. Following are the revenue terms from the original contract with the shopping center and the offer for an add-on contract, which extends the original contract terms.

	Contract Terms	
	Original Contract Terms	Extended Contract Including Add-On Terms
TV advertising campaign	$520,000	$ 580,000
Brochure package	210,000	230,000
Rotating BIG SALE schedule	170,000	190,000
Totals	$900,000	$1,000,000

Maya estimates that the following additional costs will be incurred by extending the contract:

	TV Campaign	Brochures	BIG SALE Schedule
Direct labor	$30,000	$ 9,000	$7,000
Variable overhead	22,000	14,000	6,000
Fixed overhead*	12,000	4,000	2,000

*80 percent are fixed costs applied to this contract.

REQUIRED

1. Using an Excel spreadsheet, compute the costs that will be incurred for each part of the add-on portion of the contract.
2. Should Maya Marketeers, Inc., accept the add-on contract, or should it ask for a final settlement check based on the original contract only? Defend your answer.
3. Assuming Maya wants to continue working with the client, how should it counter-offer for the add-on contract?

Internet Case

MRA 5.

LO 6 Comparison of Capital
LO 7 Investment Disclosures by Two Large Companies

Companies vary in the amount of information they disclose about their criteria for selecting capital investments. Through the Needles Accounting Resource Center web site at http://college.hmco.com, access the web sites for International Paper Company and The Coca-Cola Company. Find management's discussion and analysis also called (financial review), which precedes the presentation of the financial statements. In that section, find the discussion of investments. Which company provides the more in-depth discussion? Do either or both disclose their criteria for making capital investment decisions? Also, look at the investing activities listed in the statement of cash flows for each company. What is the extent of capital expenditures for each company? Compare each company's capital investments with the amount of total assets on the balance sheet. Which company is more of a growth company? Explain.

ENDNOTES

1. Data Warehousing Institute, *Data Warehousing: What Works?* Volume 4. Gaithersburg, Md.: Data Warehousing Institute, 1997.
2. From Roger B. Smith, "Ethics in Business: An Essential Element of Success," *Management Accounting,* June 1990. Reprinted by permission of the Institute of Management Accountants.
3. From a speech by Jim Croft, vice president of finance and administration of the Field Museum, Chicago, November 14, 2000.
4. Wayne Arnold, "High-Tech Hopes in Asia May Be Laid Low," *The Wall Street Journal,* November 5, 1997.
5. Steve Coburn, Hugh Grove, and Tom Cook, "How ABC Was Used in Capital Budgeting," *Management Accounting,* Institute of Management Accountants, May 1997.
6. "The Ball and Chain," *Wireless Week,* June 21, 1999; and "Iridium to Be Reborn Relatively Debt-Free?" *Newsbytes New Network,* August 19, 1999.

E 14. Investment of Idle Cash

Scientific Publishing Company, a publisher of college books, has just completed a successful fall selling season and has $5,000,000 in cash to invest for nine months, beginning on January 1. The company placed the cash in a money market account that is expected to pay 12 percent annual interest compounded monthly. Interest is credited to the company's account each month. How much cash will the company have at the end of nine months, and what entries are made to record the investment and the first two monthly (February 1 and March 1) interest amounts?

E 15. Accumulation of a Fund

Laferia Corporation borrowed $3,000,000 from an insurance company on a five-year note. Management agreed to set aside enough cash at the end of each year to accumulate the amount needed to pay off the note at maturity. Since the first contribution to the fund will be made in one year, four annual contributions are needed. Assuming that the fund will earn 10 percent compounded annually, how much will the annual contribution to the fund be (round to nearest dollar), and what will be the journal entry for the first contribution?

E 16. Negotiating the Sale of a Business

Horace Raftson is attempting to sell his business to Ernando Ruiz. The company has assets of $900,000, liabilities of $800,000, and owner's equity of $100,000. Both parties agree that the proper rate of return to expect is 12 percent; however, they differ on other assumptions. Raftson believes that the business will generate at least $100,000 per year of cash flows for twenty years. Ruiz thinks that $80,000 in cash flows per year is more reasonable and that only ten years in the future should be considered. Using Table 4 in the appendix on future value and present value tables, determine the range for negotiation by computing the present value of Raftson's offer to sell and of Ruiz's offer to buy.

ENDNOTE

1. Accounting Principles Board, *Opinion No. 21*, "Interest on Receivables and Payables" (New York: American Institute of Certified Public Accountants, 1971), par. 13.

Appendix D

Future Value and Present Value Tables

Table 1 provides the multipliers necessary to compute the future value of a *single* cash deposit made at the *beginning* of year 1. Three factors must be known before the future value can be computed: (1) the time period in years, (2) the stated annual rate of interest to be earned, and (3) the dollar amount invested or deposited.

Example—Table 1 Determine the future value of $5,000 deposited now that will earn 9 percent interest compounded annually for five years. From Table 1, the necessary multiplier for five years at 9 percent is 1.539, and the answer is

$$\$5{,}000 \times 1.539 = \$7{,}695$$

Where r is the interest rate and n is the number of periods, the factor values for Table 1 are

$$\text{FV Factor} = (1 + r)^n$$

Situations requiring the use of Table 2 are similar to those requiring Table 1 except that Table 2 is used to compute the future value of a *series* of *equal* annual deposits at the end of each period.

Table 1. Future Value of $1 After a Given Number of Time Periods

Periods	1%	2%	3%	4%	5%	6%	7%	8%	9%	10%	12%	14%	15%
1	1.010	1.020	1.030	1.040	1.050	1.060	1.070	1.080	1.090	1.100	1.120	1.140	1.150
2	1.020	1.040	1.061	1.082	1.103	1.124	1.145	1.166	1.188	1.210	1.254	1.300	1.323
3	1.030	1.061	1.093	1.125	1.158	1.191	1.225	1.260	1.295	1.331	1.405	1.482	1.521
4	1.041	1.082	1.126	1.170	1.216	1.262	1.311	1.360	1.412	1.464	1.574	1.689	1.749
5	1.051	1.104	1.159	1.217	1.276	1.338	1.403	1.469	1.539	1.611	1.762	1.925	2.011
6	1.062	1.126	1.194	1.265	1.340	1.419	1.501	1.587	1.677	1.772	1.974	2.195	2.313
7	1.072	1.149	1.230	1.316	1.407	1.504	1.606	1.714	1.828	1.949	2.211	2.502	2.660
8	1.083	1.172	1.267	1.369	1.477	1.594	1.718	1.851	1.993	2.144	2.476	2.853	3.059
9	1.094	1.195	1.305	1.423	1.551	1.689	1.838	1.999	2.172	2.358	2.773	3.252	3.518
10	1.105	1.219	1.344	1.480	1.629	1.791	1.967	2.159	2.367	2.594	3.106	3.707	4.046
11	1.116	1.243	1.384	1.539	1.710	1.898	2.105	2.332	2.580	2.853	3.479	4.226	4.652
12	1.127	1.268	1.426	1.601	1.796	2.012	2.252	2.518	2.813	3.138	3.896	4.818	5.350
13	1.138	1.294	1.469	1.665	1.886	2.133	2.410	2.720	3.066	3.452	4.363	5.492	6.153
14	1.149	1.319	1.513	1.732	1.980	2.261	2.579	2.937	3.342	3.798	4.887	6.261	7.076
15	1.161	1.346	1.558	1.801	2.079	2.397	2.759	3.172	3.642	4.177	5.474	7.138	8.137
16	1.173	1.373	1.605	1.873	2.183	2.540	2.952	3.426	3.970	4.595	6.130	8.137	9.358
17	1.184	1.400	1.653	1.948	2.292	2.693	3.159	3.700	4.328	5.054	6.866	9.276	10.760
18	1.196	1.428	1.702	2.026	2.407	2.854	3.380	3.996	4.717	5.560	7.690	10.580	12.380
19	1.208	1.457	1.754	2.107	2.527	3.026	3.617	4.316	5.142	6.116	8.613	12.060	14.230
20	1.220	1.486	1.806	2.191	2.653	3.207	3.870	4.661	5.604	6.728	9.646	13.740	16.370
21	1.232	1.516	1.860	2.279	2.786	3.400	4.141	5.034	6.109	7.400	10.800	15.670	18.820
22	1.245	1.546	1.916	2.370	2.925	3.604	4.430	5.437	6.659	8.140	12.100	17.860	21.640
23	1.257	1.577	1.974	2.465	3.072	3.820	4.741	5.871	7.258	8.954	13.550	20.360	24.890
24	1.270	1.608	2.033	2.563	3.225	4.049	5.072	6.341	7.911	9.850	15.180	23.210	28.630
25	1.282	1.641	2.094	2.666	3.386	4.292	5.427	6.848	8.623	10.830	17.000	26.460	32.920
26	1.295	1.673	2.157	2.772	3.556	4.549	5.807	7.396	9.399	11.920	19.040	30.170	37.860
27	1.308	1.707	2.221	2.883	3.733	4.822	6.214	7.988	10.250	13.110	21.320	34.390	43.540
28	1.321	1.741	2.288	2.999	3.920	5.112	6.649	8.627	11.170	14.420	23.880	39.200	50.070
29	1.335	1.776	2.357	3.119	4.116	5.418	7.114	9.317	12.170	15.860	26.750	44.690	57.580
30	1.348	1.811	2.427	3.243	4.322	5.743	7.612	10.060	13.270	17.450	29.960	50.950	66.210
40	1.489	2.208	3.262	4.801	7.040	10.290	14.970	21.720	31.410	45.260	93.050	188.900	267.900
50	1.645	2.692	4.384	7.107	11.470	18.420	29.460	46.900	74.360	117.400	289.000	700.200	1,084.000

Table 2. Future Value of $1 Paid in Each Period for a Given Number of Time Periods

Periods	1%	2%	3%	4%	5%	6%	7%	8%	9%	10%	12%	14%	15%
1	1.000	1.000	1.000	1.000	1.000	1.000	1.000	1.000	1.000	1.000	1.000	1.000	1.000
2	2.010	2.020	2.030	2.040	2.050	2.060	2.070	2.080	2.090	2.100	2.120	2.140	2.150
3	3.030	3.060	3.091	3.122	3.153	3.184	3.215	3.246	3.278	3.310	3.374	3.440	3.473
4	4.060	4.122	4.184	4.246	4.310	4.375	4.440	4.506	4.573	4.641	4.779	4.921	4.993
5	5.101	5.204	5.309	5.416	5.526	5.637	5.751	5.867	5.985	6.105	6.353	6.610	6.742
6	6.152	6.308	6.468	6.633	6.802	6.975	7.153	7.336	7.523	7.716	8.115	8.536	8.754
7	7.214	7.434	7.662	7.898	8.142	8.394	8.654	8.923	9.200	9.487	10.090	10.730	11.070
8	8.286	8.583	8.892	9.214	9.549	9.897	10.260	10.640	11.030	11.440	12.300	13.230	13.730
9	9.369	9.755	10.160	10.580	11.030	11.490	11.980	12.490	13.020	13.580	14.780	16.090	16.790
10	10.460	10.950	11.460	12.010	12.580	13.180	13.820	14.490	15.190	15.940	17.550	19.340	20.300
11	11.570	12.170	12.810	13.490	14.210	14.970	15.780	16.650	17.560	18.530	20.650	23.040	24.350
12	12.680	13.410	14.190	15.030	15.920	16.870	17.890	18.980	20.140	21.380	24.130	27.270	29.000
13	13.810	14.680	15.620	16.630	17.710	18.880	20.140	21.500	22.950	24.520	28.030	32.090	34.350
14	14.950	15.970	17.090	18.290	19.600	21.020	22.550	24.210	26.020	27.980	32.390	37.580	40.500
15	16.100	17.290	18.600	20.020	21.580	23.280	25.130	27.150	29.360	31.770	37.280	43.840	47.580
16	17.260	18.640	20.160	21.820	23.660	25.670	27.890	30.320	33.000	35.950	42.750	50.980	55.720
17	18.430	20.010	21.760	23.700	25.840	28.210	30.840	33.750	36.970	40.540	48.880	59.120	65.080
18	19.610	21.410	23.410	25.650	28.130	30.910	34.000	37.450	41.300	45.600	55.750	68.390	75.840
19	20.810	22.840	25.120	27.670	30.540	33.760	37.380	41.450	46.020	51.160	63.440	78.970	88.210
20	22.020	24.300	26.870	29.780	33.070	36.790	41.000	45.760	51.160	57.280	72.050	91.020	102.400
21	23.240	25.780	28.680	31.970	35.720	39.990	44.870	50.420	56.760	64.000	81.700	104.800	118.800
22	24.470	27.300	30.540	34.250	38.510	43.390	49.010	55.460	62.870	71.400	92.500	120.400	137.600
23	25.720	28.850	32.450	36.620	41.430	47.000	53.440	60.890	69.530	79.540	104.600	138.300	159.300
24	26.970	30.420	34.430	39.080	44.500	50.820	58.180	66.760	76.790	88.500	118.200	158.700	184.200
25	28.240	32.030	36.460	41.650	47.730	54.860	63.250	73.110	84.700	98.350	133.300	181.900	212.800
26	29.530	33.670	38.550	44.310	51.110	59.160	68.680	79.950	93.320	109.200	150.300	208.300	245.700
27	30.820	35.340	40.710	47.080	54.670	63.710	74.480	87.350	102.700	121.100	169.400	238.500	283.600
28	32.130	37.050	42.930	49.970	58.400	68.530	80.700	95.340	113.000	134.200	190.700	272.900	327.100
29	33.450	38.790	45.220	52.970	62.320	73.640	87.350	104.000	124.100	148.600	214.600	312.100	377.200
30	34.780	40.570	47.580	56.080	66.440	79.060	94.460	113.300	136.300	164.500	241.300	356.800	434.700
40	48.890	60.400	75.400	95.030	120.800	154.800	199.600	259.100	337.900	442.600	767.100	1,342.000	1,779.000
50	64.460	84.580	112.800	152.700	209.300	290.300	406.500	573.800	815.100	1,164.000	2,400.000	4,995.000	7,218.000

EXAMPLE—TABLE 2 What will be the future value at the end of 30 years if $1,000 is deposited each year on January 1, beginning in one year, assuming 12 percent interest compounded annually? The required multiplier from Table 2 is 241.3, and the answer is

$$\$1{,}000 \times 241.3 = \$241{,}300$$

The factor values for Table 2 are

$$\text{FVa Factor} = \frac{(1 + r)^n - 1}{r}$$

Table 3. Present Value of $1 to Be Received at the End of a Given Number of Time Periods

Periods	1%	2%	3%	4%	5%	6%	7%	8%	9%	10%	12%
1	0.990	0.980	0.971	0.962	0.952	0.943	0.935	0.926	0.917	0.909	0.893
2	0.980	0.961	0.943	0.925	0.907	0.890	0.873	0.857	0.842	0.826	0.797
3	0.971	0.942	0.915	0.889	0.864	0.840	0.816	0.794	0.772	0.751	0.712
4	0.961	0.924	0.888	0.855	0.823	0.792	0.763	0.735	0.708	0.683	0.636
5	0.951	0.906	0.883	0.822	0.784	0.747	0.713	0.681	0.650	0.621	0.567
6	0.942	0.888	0.837	0.790	0.746	0.705	0.666	0.630	0.596	0.564	0.507
7	0.933	0.871	0.813	0.760	0.711	0.665	0.623	0.583	0.547	0.513	0.452
8	0.923	0.853	0.789	0.731	0.677	0.627	0.582	0.540	0.502	0.467	0.404
9	0.914	0.837	0.766	0.703	0.645	0.592	0.544	0.500	0.460	0.424	0.361
10	0.905	0.820	0.744	0.676	0.614	0.558	0.508	0.463	0.422	0.386	0.322
11	0.896	0.804	0.722	0.650	0.585	0.527	0.475	0.429	0.388	0.350	0.287
12	0.887	0.788	0.701	0.625	0.557	0.497	0.444	0.397	0.356	0.319	0.257
13	0.879	0.773	0.681	0.601	0.530	0.469	0.415	0.368	0.326	0.290	0.229
14	0.870	0.758	0.661	0.577	0.505	0.442	0.388	0.340	0.299	0.263	0.205
15	0.861	0.743	0.642	0.555	0.481	0.417	0.362	0.315	0.275	0.239	0.183
16	0.853	0.728	0.623	0.534	0.458	0.394	0.339	0.292	0.252	0.218	0.163
17	0.844	0.714	0.605	0.513	0.436	0.371	0.317	0.270	0.231	0.198	0.146
18	0.836	0.700	0.587	0.494	0.416	0.350	0.296	0.250	0.212	0.180	0.130
19	0.828	0.686	0.570	0.475	0.396	0.331	0.277	0.232	0.194	0.164	0.116
20	0.820	0.673	0.554	0.456	0.377	0.312	0.258	0.215	0.178	0.149	0.104
21	0.811	0.660	0.538	0.439	0.359	0.294	0.242	0.199	0.164	0.135	0.093
22	0.803	0.647	0.522	0.422	0.342	0.278	0.226	0.184	0.150	0.123	0.083
23	0.795	0.634	0.507	0.406	0.326	0.262	0.211	0.170	0.138	0.112	0.074
24	0.788	0.622	0.492	0.390	0.310	0.247	0.197	0.158	0.126	0.102	0.066
25	0.780	0.610	0.478	0.375	0.295	0.233	0.184	0.146	0.116	0.092	0.059
26	0.772	0.598	0.464	0.361	0.281	0.220	0.172	0.135	0.106	0.084	0.053
27	0.764	0.586	0.450	0.347	0.268	0.207	0.161	0.125	0.098	0.076	0.047
28	0.757	0.574	0.437	0.333	0.255	0.196	0.150	0.116	0.090	0.069	0.042
29	0.749	0.563	0.424	0.321	0.243	0.185	0.141	0.107	0.082	0.063	0.037
30	0.742	0.552	0.412	0.308	0.231	0.174	0.131	0.099	0.075	0.057	0.033
40	0.672	0.453	0.307	0.208	0.142	0.097	0.067	0.046	0.032	0.022	0.011
50	0.608	0.372	0.228	0.141	0.087	0.054	0.034	0.021	0.013	0.009	0.003

Table 3 is used to compute the value today of a single amount of cash to be received sometime in the future. To use Table 3, you must first know: (1) the time period in years until funds will be received, (2) the stated annual rate of interest, and (3) the dollar amount to be received at the end of the time period.

EXAMPLE—TABLE 3 What is the present value of $30,000 to be received 25 years from now, assuming a 14 percent interest rate? From Table 3, the required multiplier is .038, and the answer is

$$\$30{,}000 \times .038 = \$1{,}140$$

14%	15%	16%	18%	20%	25%	30%	35%	40%	45%	50%	Periods
0.877	0.870	0.862	0.847	0.833	0.800	0.769	0.741	0.714	0.690	0.667	1
0.769	0.756	0.743	0.718	0.694	0.640	0.592	0.549	0.510	0.476	0.444	2
0.675	0.658	0.641	0.609	0.579	0.512	0.455	0.406	0.364	0.328	0.296	3
0.592	0.572	0.552	0.516	0.482	0.410	0.350	0.301	0.260	0.226	0.198	4
0.519	0.497	0.476	0.437	0.402	0.328	0.269	0.223	0.186	0.156	0.132	5
0.456	0.432	0.410	0.370	0.335	0.262	0.207	0.165	0.133	0.108	0.088	6
0.400	0.376	0.354	0.314	0.279	0.210	0.159	0.122	0.095	0.074	0.059	7
0.351	0.327	0.305	0.266	0.233	0.168	0.123	0.091	0.068	0.051	0.039	8
0.308	0.284	0.263	0.225	0.194	0.134	0.094	0.067	0.048	0.035	0.026	9
0.270	0.247	0.227	0.191	0.162	0.107	0.073	0.050	0.035	0.024	0.017	10
0.237	0.215	0.195	0.162	0.135	0.086	0.056	0.037	0.025	0.017	0.012	11
0.208	0.187	0.168	0.137	0.112	0.069	0.043	0.027	0.018	0.012	0.008	12
0.182	0.163	0.145	0.116	0.093	0.055	0.033	0.020	0.013	0.008	0.005	13
0.160	0.141	0.125	0.099	0.078	0.044	0.025	0.015	0.009	0.006	0.003	14
0.140	0.123	0.108	0.084	0.065	0.035	0.020	0.011	0.006	0.004	0.002	15
0.123	0.107	0.093	0.071	0.054	0.028	0.015	0.008	0.005	0.003	0.002	16
0.108	0.093	0.080	0.060	0.045	0.023	0.012	0.006	0.003	0.002	0.001	17
0.095	0.081	0.069	0.051	0.038	0.018	0.009	0.005	0.002	0.001	0.001	18
0.083	0.070	0.060	0.043	0.031	0.014	0.007	0.003	0.002	0.001		19
0.073	0.061	0.051	0.037	0.026	0.012	0.005	0.002	0.001	0.001		20
0.064	0.053	0.044	0.031	0.022	0.009	0.004	0.002	0.001			21
0.056	0.046	0.038	0.026	0.018	0.007	0.003	0.001	0.001			22
0.049	0.040	0.033	0.022	0.015	0.006	0.002	0.001				23
0.043	0.035	0.028	0.019	0.013	0.005	0.002	0.001				24
0.038	0.030	0.024	0.016	0.010	0.004	0.001	0.001				25
0.033	0.026	0.021	0.014	0.009	0.003	0.001					26
0.029	0.023	0.018	0.011	0.007	0.002	0.001					27
0.026	0.020	0.016	0.010	0.006	0.002	0.001					28
0.022	0.017	0.014	0.008	0.005	0.002						29
0.020	0.015	0.012	0.007	0.004	0.001						30
0.005	0.004	0.003	0.001	0.001							40
0.001	0.001	0.001									50

The factor values for Table 3 are

$$\text{PV Factor} = (1 + r)^{-n}$$

Table 3 is the reciprocal of Table 1.

Table 4 is used to compute the present value of a *series* of *equal* annual cash flows.

EXAMPLE—TABLE 4 Arthur Howard won a contest on January 1, 2002, in which the prize was $30,000, the money was payable in 15 annual installments of $2,000 every December 31, beginning in 2002. Assuming a 9 percent interest rate, what is

Table 4. Present Value of $1 Received Each Period for a Given Number of Time Periods

Periods	1%	2%	3%	4%	5%	6%	7%	8%	9%	10%	12%
1	0.990	0.980	0.971	0.962	0.952	0.943	0.935	0.926	0.917	0.909	0.893
2	1.970	1.942	1.913	1.886	1.859	1.833	1.808	1.783	1.759	1.736	1.690
3	2.941	2.884	2.829	2.775	2.723	2.673	2.624	2.577	2.531	2.487	2.402
4	3.902	3.808	3.717	3.630	3.546	3.465	3.387	3.312	3.240	3.170	3.037
5	4.853	4.713	4.580	4.452	4.329	4.212	4.100	3.993	3.890	3.791	3.605
6	5.795	5.601	5.417	5.242	5.076	4.917	4.767	4.623	4.486	4.355	4.111
7	6.728	6.472	6.230	6.002	5.786	5.582	5.389	5.206	5.033	4.868	4.564
8	7.652	7.325	7.020	6.733	6.463	6.210	5.971	5.747	5.535	5.335	4.968
9	8.566	8.162	7.786	7.435	7.108	6.802	6.515	6.247	5.995	5.759	5.328
10	9.471	8.983	8.530	8.111	7.722	7.360	7.024	6.710	6.418	6.145	5.650
11	10.368	9.787	9.253	8.760	8.306	7.887	7.499	7.139	6.805	6.495	5.938
12	11.255	10.575	9.954	9.385	8.863	8.384	7.943	7.536	7.161	6.814	6.194
13	12.134	11.348	10.635	9.986	9.394	8.853	8.358	7.904	7.487	7.103	6.424
14	13.004	12.106	11.296	10.563	9.899	9.295	8.745	8.244	7.786	7.367	6.628
15	13.865	12.849	11.938	11.118	10.380	9.712	9.108	8.559	8.061	7.606	6.811
16	14.718	13.578	12.561	11.652	10.838	10.106	9.447	8.851	8.313	7.824	6.974
17	15.562	14.292	13.166	12.166	11.274	10.477	9.763	9.122	8.544	8.022	7.120
18	16.398	14.992	13.754	12.659	11.690	10.828	10.059	9.372	8.756	8.201	7.250
19	17.226	15.678	14.324	13.134	12.085	11.158	10.336	9.604	8.950	8.365	7.366
20	18.046	16.351	14.878	13.590	12.462	11.470	10.594	9.818	9.129	8.514	7.469
21	18.857	17.011	15.415	14.029	12.821	11.764	10.836	10.017	9.292	8.649	7.562
22	19.660	17.658	15.937	14.451	13.163	12.042	11.061	10.201	9.442	8.772	7.645
23	20.456	18.292	16.444	14.857	13.489	12.303	11.272	10.371	9.580	8.883	7.718
24	21.243	18.914	16.936	15.247	13.799	12.550	11.469	10.529	9.707	8.985	7.784
25	22.023	19.523	17.413	15.622	14.094	12.783	11.654	10.675	9.823	9.077	7.843
26	22.795	20.121	17.877	15.983	14.375	13.003	11.826	10.810	9.929	9.161	7.896
27	23.560	20.707	18.327	16.330	14.643	13.211	11.987	10.935	10.027	9.237	7.943
28	24.316	21.281	18.764	16.663	14.898	13.406	12.137	11.051	10.116	9.307	7.984
29	25.066	21.844	19.189	16.984	15.141	13.591	12.278	11.158	10.198	9.370	8.022
30	25.808	22.396	19.600	17.292	15.373	13.765	12.409	11.258	10.274	9.427	8.055
40	32.835	27.355	23.115	19.793	17.159	15.046	13.332	11.925	10.757	9.779	8.244
50	39.196	31.424	25.730	21.482	18.256	15.762	13.801	12.234	10.962	9.915	8.305

the present value of Mr. Howard's prize on January 1, 2002? From Table 4, the required multiplier is 8.061, and the answer is:

$$\$2{,}000 \times 8.061 = \$16{,}122$$

The factor values for Table 4 are

$$\text{PVa Factor} = \frac{1 - (1 + r)^{-n}}{r}$$

Table 4 is the columnar sum of Table 3. Table 4 applies to *ordinary annuities,* in which the first cash flow occurs one time period beyond the date for which the present value is to be computed.

14%	15%	16%	18%	20%	25%	30%	35%	40%	45%	50%	Periods
0.877	0.870	0.862	0.847	0.833	0.800	0.769	0.741	0.714	0.690	0.667	1
1.647	1.626	1.605	1.566	1.528	1.440	1.361	1.289	1.224	1.165	1.111	2
2.322	2.283	2.246	2.174	2.106	1.952	1.816	1.696	1.589	1.493	1.407	3
2.914	2.855	2.798	2.690	2.589	2.362	2.166	1.997	1.849	1.720	1.605	4
3.433	3.352	3.274	3.127	2.991	2.689	2.436	2.220	2.035	1.876	1.737	5
3.889	3.784	3.685	3.498	3.326	2.951	2.643	2.385	2.168	1.983	1.824	6
4.288	4.160	4.039	3.812	3.605	3.161	2.802	2.508	2.263	2.057	1.883	7
4.639	4.487	4.344	4.078	3.837	3.329	2.925	2.598	2.331	2.109	1.922	8
4.946	4.772	4.607	4.303	4.031	3.463	3.019	2.665	2.379	2.144	1.948	9
5.216	5.019	4.833	4.494	4.192	3.571	3.092	2.715	2.414	2.168	1.965	10
5.453	5.234	5.029	4.656	4.327	3.656	3.147	2.752	2.438	2.185	1.977	11
5.660	5.421	5.197	4.793	4.439	3.725	3.190	2.779	2.456	2.197	1.985	12
5.842	5.583	5.342	4.910	4.533	3.780	3.223	2.799	2.469	2.204	1.990	13
6.002	5.724	5.468	5.008	4.611	3.824	3.249	2.814	2.478	2.210	1.993	14
6.142	5.847	5.575	5.092	4.675	3.859	3.268	2.825	2.484	2.214	1.995	15
6.265	5.954	5.669	5.162	4.730	3.887	3.283	2.834	2.489	2.216	1.997	16
6.373	6.047	5.749	5.222	4.775	3.910	3.295	2.840	2.492	2.218	1.998	17
6.467	6.128	5.818	5.273	4.812	3.928	3.304	2.844	2.494	2.219	1.999	18
6.550	6.198	5.877	5.316	4.844	3.942	3.311	2.848	2.496	2.220	1.999	19
6.623	6.259	5.929	5.353	4.870	3.954	3.316	2.850	2.497	2.221	1.999	20
6.687	6.312	5.973	5.384	4.891	3.963	3.320	2.852	2.498	2.221	2.000	21
6.743	6.359	6.011	5.410	4.909	3.970	3.323	2.853	2.498	2.222	2.000	22
6.792	6.399	6.044	5.432	4.925	3.976	3.325	2.854	2.499	2.222	2.000	23
6.835	6.434	6.073	5.451	4.937	3.981	3.327	2.855	2.499	2.222	2.000	24
6.873	6.464	6.097	5.467	4.948	3.985	3.329	2.856	2.499	2.222	2.000	25
6.906	6.491	6.118	5.480	4.956	3.988	3.330	2.856	2.500	2.222	2.000	26
6.935	6.514	6.136	5.492	4.964	3.990	3.331	2.856	2.500	2.222	2.000	27
6.961	6.534	6.152	5.502	4.970	3.992	3.331	2.857	2.500	2.222	2.000	28
6.983	6.551	6.166	5.510	4.975	3.994	3.332	2.857	2.500	2.222	2.000	29
7.003	6.566	6.177	5.517	4.979	3.995	3.332	2.857	2.500	2.222	2.000	30
7.105	6.642	6.234	5.548	4.997	3.999	3.333	2.857	2.500	2.222	2.000	40
7.133	6.661	6.246	5.554	4.999	4.000	3.333	2.857	2.500	2.222	2.000	50

An *annuity due* is a series of equal cash flows for N time periods, but the first payment occurs immediately. The present value of the first payment equals the face value of the cash flow; Table 4 then is used to measure the present value of $N - 1$ remaining cash flows.

EXAMPLE—TABLE 4 Determine the present value on January 1, 2002, of 20 lease payments; each payment of $10,000 is due on January 1, beginning in 2002. Assume an interest rate of 8 percent.

$$\text{Present Value} = \text{Immediate Payment} + \begin{cases}\text{Present Value of 19 Subsequent}\\ \text{Payments at 8\%}\end{cases}$$

$$= \$10{,}000 + (\$10{,}000 \times 9.604) = \$106{,}040$$

Company Name Index

Subject Index

Note **Boldface** type indicates key terms.